230.5809 MACC
McClymond, Mi
1958-
The theology
 Edwards

The Theology of Jonathan Edwards

The Theology of Jonathan Edwards

MICHAEL J. McCLYMOND AND
GERALD R. McDERMOTT

OXFORD
UNIVERSITY PRESS

OXFORD
UNIVERSITY PRESS

Oxford University Press, Inc., publishes works that further
Oxford University's objective of excellence
in research, scholarship, and education.

Oxford   New York
Auckland   Cape Town   Dar es Salaam   Hong Kong   Karachi
Kuala Lumpur   Madrid   Melbourne   Mexico City   Nairobi
New Delhi   Shanghai   Taipei   Toronto

With offices in
Argentina   Austria   Brazil   Chile   Czech Republic   France   Greece
Guatemala   Hungary   Italy   Japan   Poland   Portugal   Singapore
South Korea   Switzerland   Thailand   Turkey   Ukraine   Vietnam

Copyright © 2012 by Oxford University Press, Inc.

Published by Oxford University Press, Inc.
198 Madison Avenue, New York, New York 10016

www.oup.com

Oxford is a registered trademark of Oxford University Press

All rights reserved. No part of this publication may be reproduced,
stored in a retrieval system, or transmitted, in any form or by any means,
electronic, mechanical, photocopying, recording, or otherwise,
without the prior permission of Oxford University Press.

Library of Congress Cataloging-in-Publication Data
McClymond, Michael James,
The Theology of Jonathan Edwards / Michael J. McClymond
and Gerald R. McDermott.
p. cm.
ISBN 978-0-19-979160-6
1. Edwards, Jonathan, 1703–1758. I. McDermott, Gerald R. (Gerald Robert) II. Title.
BX7260.E3M34 2011
230'.58092—dc22   2011003597

1 3 5 7 9 8 6 4 2

Printed in the United States of America
on acid-free paper

*For Sarah Frances McClymond, poet
and bibliophile,*

*and for Sean Edwards McDermott, enthusiast
and Edwards-phile*

Contents

Acknowledgments — xi

PART ONE: *Historical, Cultural, and Social Contexts*

1. Overture to a Symphony — 3
2. Edwards: A Theological Life — 23
3. Edwards's Intellectual Context — 40
4. Edwards's Spirituality — 60
5. The Question of Development: Did Edwards Change? — 77

PART TWO: *Topics in Edwards's Theology*

Section 1: *Methods and Strategies*

6. Beauty and Aesthetics — 93
7. Metaphysics — 102
8. Typology: Scripture, Nature, and All of Reality — 116
9. Revelation: Scripture, Reason, and Tradition — 130
10. Apologetics — 149
11. Biblical Exegesis — 167
12. The Concept of a History of Redemption — 181

Section 2: *The Triune God, the Angels, and Heaven*

13. God as Trinity: Father, Son, and Holy Spirit	193
14. The End of God in Creation	207
15. Providence and History	224
16. The Person and Work of Jesus Christ	244
17. The Holy Spirit	262
18. The Angels in the Plan of Salvation	273
19. Heaven is a World of Love	295

Section 3: *Theological Anthropology and Divine Grace*

20. The Affections and the Human Person	311
21. Edwards's Calvinism and Theology of the Covenants	321
22. Free Will and Original Sin	339
23. Salvation, Grace, and Faith: An Overview	357
24. Conversion: A Divine and Supernatural Light	373
25. Justification and Sanctification	389
26. The Theme of Divinization	410
27. Theology of Revival	424

Section 4: *Church, Ethics, Eschatology, and Society*

28. The Church	451
29. Edwards on (and in) the Ministry	465
30. The Sacraments: Baptism and the Lord's Supper	482
31. The Voice of the Great God: A Theology of Preaching	494
32. Public Theology, Society, and America	513
33. True Virtue, Christian Love, and Ethical Theory	528
34. Edwards on (and in) Mission	549

35. Eschatology ... 566

36. Christianity and Other Religions ... 580

PART THREE: *Legacies and Affinities: Edwards's Disciples and Interpreters*

37. Selective Readings: Edwards and the New Divinity ... 601

38. Mixed Reactions: Princeton and Andover Seminaries and Nineteenth-Century American Culture ... 625

39. New Beginnings: The Twentieth-Century Recovery of Jonathan Edwards ... 637

40. Interpretations I: Edwards and Modern Philosophy ... 649

41. Interpretations II: Jonathan Edwards and the Reformed Tradition ... 663

42. Interpretations III: Edwards and the Revival Tradition ... 675

43. Interpretations IV: Edwards and the Catholic and Orthodox Traditions ... 695

44. Interpretations V: Edwards and Contemporary Theology ... 709

45. Conclusion: Edwards as a Theological Bridge ... 718

Index ... 729

Acknowledgments

We wish here to express our appreciation and gratitude to a host of scholars, most notably Kenneth Minkema of Yale University and Douglas Sweeney of Trinity Evangelical Divinity School. Ken is Executive Editor of *The Works of Jonathan Edwards* and Executive Director of the Jonathan Edwards Center. Moreover, he is an encyclopedia of all things Edwardsean and was unfailingly helpful at every stage of our writing, commenting on every one of the forty-five chapters that appear here—and even on one that we later found it necessary to omit. Our second major reader and commentator was Doug, another accomplished Edwardsean, author of many books and articles, and director of a newly established center for Edwards studies at his home institution. Like Ken, Doug commented on chapters too numerous to list separately.

We are also indebted to many other Edwards experts who made suggestions on various chapters: David Bebbington, Robert Caldwell, Ava Chamberlain, Conrad Cherry, Joseph Conforti, Oliver Crisp, Stephen Crocco, William Danaher, Allen Guelzo, Philip Gura, W. Ross Hastings, E. Brooks Holifield, Wilson Kimnach, David Kling, Sang Lee, M. X. Lesser, George Marsden, Adriaan C. Neele, Mark Noll, Amy Plantinga Pauw, Stuart Piggin, Rick Pointer, Phil Sinitiere, F. Allan Story, Jr., Kyle Strobel, Steven Studebaker, Peter Thuesen, Miklos Vetö, Helen Westra, Rachel Wheeler, and Avihu Zakai. Andrew Russell—a PhD student at Saint Louis University—labored long and hard on our behalf to organize an extensive bibliography of primary and secondary sources on Edwards. He undertook the daunting task of securing printed copies, photocopies, or electronic scans of a mountain of materials, and worked on the index. Zachary Kostopoulos supplied further assistance with the index. Participants in Michael's PhD seminar—Elissa McCormack, Scott McDermott (unrelated to Gerald), Robert Rexroat, Luke Ritter, Andrew Russell, and Benjamin Wayman—read through and commented on the entire manuscript. Thanks are due to Forbes Library in Northampton, Massachusetts, for permission to use images found in these pages, and to their gracious staff, especially Julie Bartlett and Elise Bernier-Feeley.

Gerald gives credit where credit is due—to his wife Jean, whose love and support were invaluable in these months of research and writing. He also thanks other scholars whose suggestions made this a better book—Robert Benne, Paul Hinlicky, and the pastors in the Edwards Reading Group in Salem, Virginia. Judy Pinckney was a terrific clerical help at many stages of this project, as were Jeffrey Martin and Rebecca Heller at the Fintel Library of Roanoke College. Wendy Andree's careful eyes in proofreading and index-preparing were much appreciated. T. D. Bozeman's zeal for precision and elegance was an early model, never duplicated. Gerald is especially appreciative for the financial and intellectual support given this project by Byron Johnson and the Baylor Institute for Studies of Religion. Michael is grateful to his friends in the St. Louis area and further afield for their interest, support, and prayer while he was writing with Gerald. He thanks his colleagues in the Department of Theological Studies at Saint Louis University for listening to him expound his half-formed hunches in hallways, elevators, and other unlikely locations. He also thanks Kathryn for the Christmas gift of the two-volume fine-print edition of the *Works*; David Kelsey at Yale, who first stirred his interest in Edwards; Thomas Schafer for granting him access to transcriptions of Edwards's *Miscellanies* while he was teaching in California; Wilson Kimnach and Harry Stout for their hospitality on visits to Yale; W. Clark Gilpin, who supervised his University of Chicago dissertation; and Mark Noll who asked some twenty years ago—and then again four years ago—whether he was continuing his research on Edwards. We both thank George Marsden for the inspiration he has given to us and to many other students of Edwards's life, writings, and thought.

The authors are responsible for all errors of fact or interpretation that our book may contain, and we encourage all friendly efforts toward a correction of our errors. We hope that the book will serve as a starting point for many new lines of inquiry and investigation.

Abbreviations for Frequently Cited Sources

Aquinas, *Summa Theologica* = Thomas Aquinas, Saint. *Summa Theologica*. 5 vols. Westminster, MD: Christian Classics, 1981 [1947]. This work is cited by part, question, and article numbers.

AV = Authorized Version, or King James Version, of the Bible. All scripture quotations are from this version unless otherwise noted.

BW = Edwards Jonathan. *The Salvation of Souls: Nine Previously Unpublished Sermons on the Call of Ministry and the Gospel by Jonathan Edwards*. Edited by Richard A. Bailey and Gregory A. Wills. Wheaton, IL: Crossway Books, 2002.

Calvin, *Institutes* = Calvin, Jean. *Institutes of the Christian Religion*. 2 vols. Edited by John T. McNeil; translated by Ford Lewis Battles. The Library of Christian Classics, 20–21. Philadelphia, PA: Westminster Press, 1960. This work is cited by book, chapter, and section numbers.

WH = Edwards, Jonathan. *The Works of President Edwards*. 2 vols. Edited by Edward Hickman; with a memoir by Sereno E. Dwight. Edinburgh: Banner of Truth Trust, 1984 [1834].

WJE = Edwards, Jonathan. *The Works of Jonathan Edwards*. 26 vols. New Haven, CT: Yale University Press, 1957–2008.

WJEO = Edwards, Jonathan. *The Works of Jonathan Edwards Online*. The online edition of Edwards's *Works* is located at http://edwards.yale.edu. It is maintained by the Jonathan Edwards Center at Yale University and is available free of charge. It offers access not only to the 26-volume printed edition of Edwards's *Works*, along with the "Editor's Introduction" to each volume, but an additional 47 volumes of material online. All references to volumes 27–73 are cited here as WJEO.

The Theology of Jonathan Edwards

PART ONE

Introduction

Historical, Cultural, and Social Contexts

I
Overture to a Symphony

LET US BEGIN with a musical parable. Imagine that you have the opportunity to attend a concert at the local symphony hall. Through the good graces of a friend—connected with the orchestra—you obtain some free tickets to the concert and proceed to invite half a dozen of your friends to come with you. On the way to the concert, you examine the tickets and discover that the seats are not adjacent. In fact they are widely scattered through the hall, with one in the front left, another in the front right, one in the back right corner, and two others in the first and second balconies. Arriving at the hall just before the concert, you and your friends scatter to your respective seats, agreeing to meet outside the hall at the end of the concert.

The music is everything that you had hoped it would be. There are guest soloists from Europe and from New York City. The conductor leads brilliantly. The instrumentalists play with polish and passion. A single violin commences the performance, lifting a melodious yet lonely air. Soon this violin carries a second along with it, and then a cello, a viola, and the entire string section then swells into the opening theme. Beginning as if from a great distance, the percussion section slowly enters in, followed by the horns and the woodwinds. As the first movement comes to a close, and as the second begins, you notice that the melody has shifted. It is no longer the strings but the woodwinds that dominate. The center of gravity has moved from stage left to stage right. Oboes and clarinets—sometimes together, sometimes separately—pick up and gradually unfold a new theme. Violins, along with violas, cellos, and basses, follow the woodwinds' lead. The horns interject, punctuating the atmosphere and setting the woodwinds, though briefly, into the musical background. Listening attentively, you notice that a few of the violins have never ceased to play the original theme from the first movement. The composer has coordinated and harmonized the two themes to play simultaneously. As the woodwinds unfold their theme, the violins continue theirs. The woodwind theme reemerges during the third movement, when the violins once again seize the foreground.

As you meet up after the performance, the discussion begins. "What was your favorite part?" "That percussion section was amazing." "Yes, I was following the tympani player all the way through the performance." "Really?" says your other friend, a bit surprised. "But didn't you like the violin part?" "Well, yes, but I thought that the percussion part made the performance." Silence falls. The rest obviously disagree. After a moment's pause, another pipes in: "Well, the opening movement was good, but it was nothing like the second movement." Another moment of silence follows.

As you and your friends compare impressions on the performance, you notice that your placement within the symphony hall seems to have affected the way that each one has heard the symphony. The one who focused on the percussion section was seated up in the second balcony where, apparently, the acoustics of the concert hall caused the sound of the percussion instruments to be more audible. The person who most enjoyed the woodwinds in the second movement also happened to be sitting in the front right—very close to the woodwind section. The friend in the front left—near the strings—had a different impression of the flow and structure of the composition. By the time that the conversation has ended, and you have arrived back at home, you realize how one musical performance can be heard in multiple ways. Not least of all, you feel yourself fortunate for having ended up with the ticket that put you front and center in the concert hall, so that you could readily hear all the instruments in the concert and more fully appreciate their intricate interplay in the course of the symphony.

This parable may help us understand something about Jonathan Edwards. His theology has been construed in many different ways during the two and a half centuries since his death. One factor that helps account for this diversity of impressions is the sheer bulk of his writings—which run to an astounding seventy-three large volumes of text in the online edition of *The Works of Jonathan Edwards*. Scholars today are just beginning to reckon with the *magnitude* of Edwards's thought. Those who have different impressions may simply be reading different parts of the collected writings.

To construe Edwards's theology as a whole, one might distinguish the imaginary orchestra into five parts—violins, the other strings (violas, cellos, and basses), woodwinds, brass, and percussion. To appreciate the music requires that one pay attention to all five constituents in the orchestra. Our description of five parts may seem a bit abstract, coming at the beginning of this lengthy volume. The chapters that succeed will offer a fuller elaboration. Yet what follows here is a brief summation of these multiple parts or aspects in Edwards's theology.

A first constituent—let us say the violins—is Edwards's notion of *Trinitarian communication*, reflected most clearly in such writings as the *Discourse on the Trinity* and *End of Creation*. It was shaped by his reading of the Johannine writings of the New Testament, and might be compared to the patristic or early Christian thinkers. It is important to recognize this side of Edwards's theology, since it undergirds all that he had to say regarding salvation. God, as Edwards often said, is a "communicating being." God's self-communication or overflow transpired from all eternity among the three persons of the Trinity, and then occurred once again in the creation of the world. A key aspect of this divine communication consists in Edwards's notion of divine beauty. God's beauty is the divinity of divinity, that which distinguishes God from everything else.[1] Beauty is the first principle of being, the first of God's perfections, the key to his doctrine of the Trinity. It is also what most distinguished Edwards from other thinkers in the history of Christian thought.

The second constituent—let us say the violas, cellos, and basses—may be described as *creaturely participation*. This aspect appears in *End of Creation* and *Treatise on Grace*, and is a corollary of the first. God communicates, and the creature participates. Edwards's God is not self-enclosed. Rather, God is the sort of God in whom creatures can participate. Indeed, there is no salvation apart from participation. The God who first overflowed in the creation of the world, acted once again in the economy of salvation to transmit divine knowledge (through the Son) and divine love and happiness (through the Spirit) to all elect creatures. Participation in God, for Edwards, is a voluntary, joyful participation in God's beauty. Beauty is basic to conversion and to the Christian life. God's beauty is beautifying. God not only possesses spiritual beauty but confers it on others. Beauty links God, self, and world. Creatures exhibit a beautiful and beautifying benevolence to God's beauty and to God's reflected beauty in the cosmos.

The third constituent—corresponding to the horn section—is *necessitarian dispositionalism*. Edwards held that the essence of all being—even that of God—consisted in disposition or habit. Disposition is not a quality possessed by a thing but is the *essence* of the thing. Reality is thus inherently dynamic. Edwards's dispositionalism suggests that human beings are guided and shaped above all by their affections—the sum of which constitutes their temperament or character. Our loves or affections are the truest indicators of who we are. It is disposition that renders a person either pleasing or displeasing to God. God chiefly looks not to outward actions but to inward dispositions. Moreover, dispositions precede actions. God changes people by changing their dispositions. This may be termed the Augustinian aspect of Edwards's anthropology and soteriology. *Religious Affections* represents the most extended treatment of

---

1. WJE 2:298.

dispositionalism in Edwards's writings. Edwards's dispositionalism includes a *necessitarian* aspect. As shown in *Freedom of the Will* and *Original Sin*, human beings invariably follow their own tastes or inclinations, so that, as Edwards argues in *Freedom of the Will*, "the will always *is* as the greatest apparent good."[2] *Original Sin* traces the root of evil inclination to its origins.

The fourth constituent—the woodwinds—consists in Edwards's conviction of *theocentric voluntarism*, affirming the divine priority in all of reality. This could be called the Calvinistic or theocentric aspect of Edwards's theology. From the time that Edwards first embraced the notion of divine sovereignty, he delighted in the affirmation that salvation came from God "immediately" and that all honor and glory for salvation goes to God alone. God's grace is prevenient—that is, it comes prior to human responses to God and enables them to occur. Edwards's vision of divine priority applied not only to redemption but also to creation. As he argued in *Original Sin* and throughout his *Miscellanies*, God continually recreates the world every second, and God himself is the reality sustaining all of creation. Nothing exists apart from God's continual recreation of it, and the substance of every existent thing is God's knowing and willing of that thing. God is the substance even of heaven and of hell.

The fifth and final constituent of the symphony—the percussion section—is what we will call Edwards's *harmonious constitutionalism*. The basic conception is set forth in certain notebook entries (see Miscellany 29 and 1263) and in *Justification by Faith Alone*. This could be described as Edwards's Thomistic aspect. In Edwards's thinking, salvation is less like a chain of beads than like a net in which each part of the net holds the rest in place. All aspects of salvation are interrelated because all are willed together in God's eternity and according to God's decree (Miscellany 29). God decrees rain because God decrees the prayers of his people. Equally, one can say that God decrees prayers because God decrees rain.[3] Both rest on the eternal, gracious will of God. In light of this reasoning, he can say that faith is not the only "condition" of justification. Obedience is also a condition.[4] Yet faith, obedience, and all other dispositions and actions of the regenerate soul are rooted in God's gracious will. Edwards's account here is similar to that of Thomas Aquinas.[5] In Miscellany 1263 Edwards

---

2. WJE 1:144.

3. WJE 13:216–17.

4. WJE 19:152–54, 201–10.

5. "The will of God is reasonable," writes Thomas Aquinas, "not because anything is to God a cause of willing, but in so far as He wills one thing to be on account of another." *Summa Theologica*, 1a, q.19, a.5.

applies a notion of God's "arbitrary operations" to the whole course of redemptive history, which exists as a network in which every element is willed by God in relation to, and because of, every other element. God's "arbitrary operations" are thus applied both to the lives of individual saints and to the entire course of redemptive history.[6] Edwards found harmony where other theologians found disharmony, antinomy, or paradox: between faith and reason, matter and spirit, nature and grace, God and creature.

To enjoy the symphony most fully, one must listen to all instruments at once. One also needs to discern which instruments are carrying the melody at any given point. In auditory terms, there is an acoustical foreground and background. If the strings carry the melody, then one would not want to give all of one's attention to the horns. Someone who plays the drums, for personal reasons, might want to focus attention on the tympani. That would be one way of listening to the symphony, though most other listeners would likely regard this as an idiosyncratic approach and not recommended for the ordinary concertgoer.

What the authors of this volume "hear" in Edwards's writings is a symphony in which the melody begins in the string section, among the violins, often accompanied by the violas, cellos, and basses. In the course of the symphony, the melody periodically shifts into the woodwind section, then back and forth between the strings and woodwinds, and finally concludes with all of the strings together—violins, cellos, and basses—playing in ravishing harmony. Trinitarian communication and creaturely participation—that is, the violins and the other strings—play in sweet unison in the conclusion to *End of Creation* and in the famous sermon "Heaven is a World of Love" at the end of *Charity and Its Fruits*. At various points in the symphony, the horns punctuate the performance and thus offer a welcome relief from a constant focus on the strings and the woodwinds. Finally, the percussion section—Edwards's conception of cosmic harmony—underlies the entire performance of the strings, woodwinds, and brass. Trinitarian communication and creaturely participation carry the tune throughout most of the symphony. They are the Alpha and Omega, the prologue and the epilogue.

Sang Lee supports such a conclusion: "For Edwards what God does in history and what God is in his being are absolutely consistent. The immanent Trinity...is not a speculative theory far removed from the story of God's salvation here on earth, but rather the very ground and pattern for that story."[7] Along similar lines, Robert Jenson writes that "in Edwards...the roles of Jesus and his

---

6. WJE 23:201–10.

7. Sang Lee, "Jonathan Edwards's Dispositional Conception of the Trinity: A Resource for Contemporary Reformed Theology," in David Willis and Michael Welker, eds., *Toward the Future of Reformed Theology: Tasks, Topics, Traditions* (Grand Rapids, MI: Eerdmans, 1999), 445–46.

Father and their Spirit in our history, and the roles of those three 'persons' in God's own reality, intersect with each other to make but one divine history. Of a metaphysical break between God's triune history with us and God's 'own' 'immanent' being, Edwards knows nothing."[8] Not only God's disposition to create, but the creature's dispositional participation in God, is integral to the larger pattern. The force that animates and directs the music throughout is God's sovereign and loving will, which does not discover beauty in creatures but rather creates this beauty. Roland Delattre adds that "the beauty Edwards finds in God does not consist in being beautiful but in creating or bestowing beauty" and "the Christian life is a life made new by participation in the life of God."[9]

A caveat regarding many existing interpretations of Edwards's theology is that they capture one or another part of the symphony, yet fail to construe the sound and flow of the whole. Some listeners seem to be sitting so close to the woodwind section (i.e., the Calvinistic or theocentric aspect) that they cannot hear the violins and other strings (i.e., divine communication and creaturely participation), and so they miss out on some of loveliest melodies and most refined harmonies of Edwards's music. Moreover, the violins and other strings frame the structure of the symphony, setting out the major musical themes at the outset and resolving them at the conclusion. Inattentiveness to the strings results in a one-sided listening experience. On the other hand, it should be clear that the woodwinds carry the melody for at least a part of the performance, and so it is possible to overemphasize the strings and so to neglect the woodwinds—or, for that matter, the horns or the percussion instruments. A full appreciation of Edwards's theology requires that one attend to the whole range of musical instruments that play simultaneously to create the total performance that we call the symphony.

In the second half of the twentieth century, many Jonathan Edwardses have appeared. Perry Miller's Edwards was a naturalist masquerading as a theologian and moving beyond the Calvinist tradition. Conrad Cherry replaced this portrait with an Edwards who subordinated natural theology to a redemptive theology based on the Calvinistic covenants. Later scholars found Edwards to be an innovator who broke with classical substance metaphysics, while others insisted that he remained within the confines of the *Westminster Confession of Faith* and traditional substance metaphysics. Students of Ed-

---

8. Robert W. Jenson, *America's Theologian: A Recommendation of Jonathan Edwards* (New York: Oxford University Press, 1988), 93.

9. Roland Delattre, "Jonathan Edwards, H. Richard Niebuhr, and Beyond," in Sang Lee and Allen C. Guelzo, eds., *Edwards in Our Time: Jonathan Edwards and the Shaping of American Religion* (Grand Rapids, MI: Eerdmans, 1999), 74-75.

wards divided over what they took to be the fulcrum of Edwards's theological vision: one argued for faith, another for aesthetics, another for divine glory, another for the divine Trinity, and still others for spiritual perception and apologetics. One found Edwards's genius in his use of an Enlightenment-style critique to supersede the Enlightenment's limitations. Other debates raged over whether he was medieval, modern, or even postmodern.

Why so many different views of Edwards? How could he have inspired depictions that appear to be mutually exclusive? The answer may lie in the method that Edwards used in developing his theology.

The Ethos and Method of Edwards's Theology

Edwards's intellectual style was venturesome, unfettered, self-critical, and developmental. By developmental we mean something akin to what Whitney Oates, in his introduction to *The Basic Writings of St. Augustine*, referred to as an "open system" approach.[10] The open system thinker approaches most intellectual issues as works-in-progress and hence returns again and again to the same perennial themes. If this sort of thinker lives longer, then the chances are that his or her thinking will change. Growth is a sign of life—and not necessarily a sign of intellectual weakness or vacillation. As John Henry Newman wrote: "In a higher world it is otherwise, but here below to live is to change, and to be perfect is to have changed often."[11] This does not mean that the open system thinker is chaotic or undirected, but that there are broad patterns that emerge over time and are continually refined and developed. New insights come along, and when they do, they force a reshaping of familiar patterns. The result is a continual unfolding of thought. In principle the process is unending.

In contrast, a closed system thinker lays stress on systematicity. Once a given intellectual issue is discussed and resolved, the closed system thinker moves on to another topic. Closed system thinkers attract commentators, who may embellish the system or fill in a gap here or there but will rarely suggest any new departures. Oates considered Plato and Augustine to be open system thinkers, and Aristotle a closed system thinker. The advantage of the open system is its prospect for new insight and development, while the risk is that later followers will imitate only the experimental method and leave behind the foundational principles. This seems to have happened among Edwards's followers by the late

---

10. Whitney Oates, Introduction to *Basic Writings of Saint Augustine*, 2 vols. (New York: Random House, 1948), 1: ix–xii.

11. John Henry Newman, *An Essay on the Development of Doctrine* (London: Longmans, Green, 1920), 445.

nineteenth century, when Andover Seminary's "progressive orthodoxy" lost its vital connection with Edwards's key ideas and guiding vision (ch. 38).

To a greater extent than previously recognized, Edwards's theology was the product of a distinctive approach to study namely, *a method of investigation and discovery by writing*. Edwards spent the bulk of his study time composing closely reasoned pieces that evaluated the strong and weak points of a given proposition, argued its pros and cons, and responded to objections. Every new assertion had to make its way through a jungle-like thicket of counter-assertions. Dialectical reasoning was Edwards's forte—the machete he used to cut through the jungle. In 1757 he wrote to the trustees at Princeton College that his method of study "has been very much by writing.' He would "improve every important hint; pursuing the clue to the utmost, when anything in reading, meditation or conversation, has been suggested" to his mind that might "promise light in any weighty point." This method became "habitual" and he found as time went on that "the further I traveled in this way, the more and wider the field opened."[12]

Though the *Miscellanies* were not by any means the only notebooks that Edwards kept over the years, Edwards's thought process is best seen through an examination of this numbered, sequential, and internally cross-referenced set of thematic essays. The *Miscellanies* show us that Edwards did not merely gather opinions from others but used books and conversation and his own ruminations to develop his thinking on "weighty point[s]." On many days up to twelve hours a day, and for more than thirty-five years, he wrote out his "best" thoughts "on innumerable subjects." When Edwards's treatises were finally written and published, they were often based on reflections gathered from five, ten, or even twenty or more years. Instead of generating new material—like most authors—when he was beginning to compose a new treatise, Edwards was habitually engaged in *considering multiple topics at the same time*. He kept many balls in the air throughout his life. In any given six-month period he was adding new reflections to his private notebooks on a dozen or more different subjects—returning often to traditional themes but invariably adding a new twist. Above all, Edwards was writing—constantly writing. It comes as no surprise to learn that he regularly ran short of paper, since paper was not available to him in limitless quantities. Wanting to keep his ideas flowing freely, and lacking sources of new paper, Edwards sometimes scrawled his reflections in tiny print into the corners of

---

12. WJE 16:726–27. A parallel to Edwards is found in William Ellery Channing, the Unitarian who in his early years had come under the influence of Edwards's disciple, Samuel Hopkins. An observer wrote of Channing what might equally have been written of Edwards: "His time was more occupied in writing than in reading...following out a train of thought pen in hand. Writing was with him, as he often said, the one great means of making clear to himself his own thoughts." (William Henry Channing, *The Life of William Ellery Channing*; Boston: American Unitarian Association, 1904 [1880], 86–87).

his own manuscripts, onto scraps of discarded paper, and onto the margins of unused books (including those in French that he could not read).[13]

Though Edwards often ran short of paper, he seems never to have run short on ideas. His challenge lay in organizing and disciplining the sprawling set of reflections that he was constantly generating. Two of his chief intellectual strategies might be described as *concatenation* and *subsumption*. The former refers to Edwards's search for connections among ideas that might ordinarily be thought of as disconnected. In general Edwards's thought might be described as a quest for unity amid plurality, and so he regularly sought to find associations of ideas that few had seen before him. This concatenation of ideas can be seen in the *Miscellanies*, where headings for entries linked seemingly disparate subjects. Consider, for instance, the imposing caption for Miscellany 664b: "THE WISDOM OF GOD IN THE WORK OF REDEMPTION; FALL OF THE ANGELS; FALL OF MAN; CONFIRMATION OF THE ANGELS; CHRIST'S RIGHTEOUSNESS OR OBEDIENCE; DEATH AND SUFFERINGS OF CHRIST; DAY OF JUDGMENT; CONSUMMATION OF ALL THINGS; SEPARATE SPIRITS." In this entry Edwards proceeded from the original design of God in eternity for the work of redemption, through the fall of both angels and human beings, to the redemptive act of Christ's suffering and death, to consummation in judgment and beyond. Eternity, creation, eschatology, redemption, Christology, soteriology, and ontology were all linked through multiple levels of association and in ways that would not have been apparent to other thinkers.[14]

Subsumption refers to the ways in which Edwards's insights were absorbed into ever-expanding and more general categories. For example, the *Miscellanies* reveal three stages in Edwards's thinking on God's "end." In the initial stage (Miscellany 3), Edwards maintained the position—surprising in the light of the final argument of *End of Creation*—that human happiness per se was God's end in creating the world. He reasoned that a perfect Creator does not need anything, such as happiness, as a consequence of creating a world. Later Edwards noticed the biblical teaching that God created the world for his own "name," "glory," or "praise." During an intermediate phase (Miscellany 243), he held that human happiness and divine glory were both "ultimate ends" in God's creating, and yet that they stood independent of one another. For a thinker such as Edwards, an ultimate duality in God's cosmic purpose was unsatisfying. So, in his final phase (Miscellany 332), he merged human happiness with divine glory under the rubric of God's "communication."

---

13. WJE 16:726–27. Researchers for *The Works of Jonathan Edwards* learned over time to decipher these indistinct scribblings. See the discussion in Thomas A. Schafer, "Manuscript Problems in the Yale Edition of Jonathan Edwards," *Early American Literature* 3 (1968), 159–71.

14. WJE 18:202–11.

Communication was the conceptual category that allowed him to subsume the two earlier ideas that had originated independently in his reflections.[15]

Another example of subsumption was his evolution of thinking on the covenants. The first phase can be seen in several *Miscellanies* entries in 1723, in which he argued that there is no real distinction between the covenants of grace and works, and that the covenant of redemption was simply the Trinity's way of fulfilling the covenant of works. The conditions were fulfilled by Christ. Ten years later, in 1733, when Edwards was disturbed by a perceived laxity in the church, he spoke of a marriage covenant between Christ and the church that included attendant conditions for believers. By 1746 he further developed this line of thinking, arguing that of the covenant of grace "introduces Persons to a right to" the covenant of redemption. The covenant of redemption was a fulfillment of the covenant of works, and all other covenants were simply "expressions" of the covenant of redemption. Christ "never does anything, more or less, than is contained in that eternal covenant [of redemption]."[16] By his last decade, Edwards had subsumed the covenant of grace under the covenant of redemption—itself subsumed under a covenant of works—yet now in more sophisticated fashion than at the beginning of his thinking thirty years before.

The result of Edwards's openness to new ideas, his method of research by writing, and intellectual strategies such as concatenation and subsumption, was an unusual combination of traditionality and originality. His basic themes were deeply indebted to his theological tradition, but he spent thousands of hours reexamining these themes from new angles. He came up with novel, original arguments for orthodox doctrines, and over the course of time his entire theology acquired a distinctive character. He showed a surprising reliance on human reasoning to support doctrines that most others had chosen to leave within the realm of mystery. This is one reason why Charles Hodge and other Princetonians referred to his theology as excessively "metaphysical." He exhibited a kind of dialectical fearlessness as he explored the logic of such age-old conundrums as the relation between divine sovereignty and human freedom, the meaning of secular history, the imputation of Adam's sin to humanity, and the inner life of the Holy Trinity. Edwards's orthodox conclusions have always appealed to theological conservatives, while his openness to fresh ways of thinking have made him attractive to theological liberals. This is why Edwards is one of the few modern theologians whose writings are of interest to thinkers from all sides of the theological spectrum.

---

15. WJE 13:199–200, 358–59, 410.

16. WJE 20.445, 167, 475; Sermon on Isaiah 55:3, ms at Jonathan Edwards Center, 8; Sermon on Hebrews 13:8, WH2:950.

Overture to a Symphony

FIGURE 1.1 Cerebral, saintly, impassive, or aloof—these portraits illustrate the diversity of ways in which Edwards has been interpreted (Courtesy of the Forbes Library, Northampton, Massachusetts).

Themes in Edwards's Theology

A preliminary explanation is in order regarding the structure of our book on Edwards's theology. It should be readily apparent to readers that the chapters do not follow the traditional theological loci (i.e., topics) commonly used by Protestant systematic theologians. The standard set of topics begins with God and the Trinity, and then moves on to the creation of the world, humanity and human nature, Jesus Christ, the Christian church, the sacraments, and the "last things" or eschatology. Such a sequence, broadly speaking, is apparent in Peter Lombard's *Sentences* (1150s)—the foundational work for theological instruction in Western Europe during the high middle ages—and in Philipp Melanchthon's *Loci Communes Theologici* (1521)—the first Protestant work of *systematic* theology. This framework is even more conspicuous in the major theological surveys by so-called Protestant scholastics—both Lutheran and Reformed—from the late sixteenth century until the early eighteenth century.[17] Yet it should be noted that many of the greatest Christian thinkers did not strictly follow this sequence or confine themselves to it. A scrutiny of Thomas Aquinas's *Summa Theologica* (1265–74), John Calvin's *Institutes of the Christian Religion* (1559), and Karl Barth's *Church Dogmatics* (1932–68) shows that these influential theologians adapted the standard pattern to suit their own purposes, to highlight the themes they wished to emphasize, and to deemphasize ideas and doctrines they wished to ignore. For this reason, the traditional loci are not necessarily a helpful format for expounding the writings of Christian theologians, except perhaps for those theologians who evidently relied on this framework for their thinking and writing.

Jonathan Edwards—along with Augustine and Martin Luther—was a Christian thinker who did not leave behind a comprehensive, systematic survey of his own theology. As we will see later (chs. 5, 12), Edwards toward the end of his life developed a plan to write a major work that summarized his thought, under the title *A History of the Work of Redemption*. In his letter to the college trustees in New Jersey, he described his projected work as covering the same ground as a traditional Protestant systematic theology but as being "a body of divinity in an entire new method, being thrown into the form of an history."[18]

---

17. On Peter Lombard and his *Sentences*, see Philipp W. Rosemann, *The Story of a Great Medieval Book*, Rethinking the Middle Ages Series (Toronto: University of Toronto Press, 2007); and "Peter Lombard's Sentences," at http://www.wordtrade.com/religion/christianity/lombardsentences.htm (accessed 20 May 2011). A translation of Melanchthon's *Loci Communes* appeared in Wilhelm Pauck, *Melanchthon and Bucer*, Library of Christian Classics (Philadelphia, PA: Westminster Press, 1969).

18. WJE 16:727.

While there is much that we do not know about Edwards's intentions, we do know that he intended to use an historical sequence and not the topical sequence of the traditional loci. He sought to unfold the content of Christian theology in temporal succession. Our book takes seriously this methodological innovation of Edwards's later years and employs it in the organization of our own work (see esp. chs. 13–19).

The first major section of our book, Part I—"Historical, Cultural, and Social Contexts" (chs. 2–5)—establishes a biographical, intellectual, and spiritual milieu for our analysis of Edwards's writings. The historical contextualization that we offer in this book does not end, however, with the fifth chapter. In fact, nearly all of the chapters in our book situate Edwards's thought in some kind of historical context, and many chapters touch at least briefly on the influence later exerted by Edwards's thought. Thus the opening chapters on historical context (chs. 2–5) and the closing chapters on Edwards's legacies (chs. 37–45), are not wholly unlike the chapters in between. Following chapters 2–5, there is another section that also has a foundational character. Part II, Section 1—referred to as "Methods and Strategies" (chs. 6–12)— recounts the metaphysical and methodological principles that undergird the whole of Edwards's thought and that need to be grasped before any examination of his theological reasoning. The themes of these methodological chapters intertwine in complex ways. Being and beauty are interrelated for Edwards, while typology links to beauty, to biblical exegesis, and to Edwards's understanding of redemptive history. Much of what he has to say about being, beauty, exegesis, typology, and redemptive history relate back to his apologetic interests and his concern to defend Christian claims of divine revelation against attacks from the deists.

At this point in our book, we turn to the large-scale structure of Edwards's theology. Part II, Section 2 (chs. 13–19)—"The Triune God, the Angels, and Heaven"—unfolds Edwards's thought in its redemptive-historical dimension. As just noted, *A History of the Work of Redemption* was to be the title of Edwards's unwritten masterwork. It should be apparent, though, that such major works as *Religious Affections* (1746), *Freedom of the Will* (1754), and *Original Sin* (1758) offered an extended analysis of the human self in its created, fallen, and redeemed conditions. Edwards had not only a redemptive-historical but an anthropological dimension to his theology. Part II, Section 3 of the book—"Theological Anthropology and Divine Grace" (chs. 20–27)— treats Edwards's analysis of the human situation. The final section that treats topics in Edwards's theology—Part II, Section 4, "Church, Ethics, Eschatology, and Society" (chs. 28–36)—looks at the ecclesial, social, and ethical dimensions of Edwards's theology. While this section may not be as tightly integrated as the redemptive-historical or anthropological sections, Edwards's ecclesial and social thought is one of his major achievements and an essential part of his corpus. In *Nature of True Virtue* (written in 1755, published in 1765), for example, Edwards presented an ethical philosophy without ever quoting scripture. He plainly intended for this work to contribute to Enlightenment-era discussions of morality. Our book's final section, Part III—"Legacies and Affinities" (chs. 37–45), examines the variety of ways in which Edwards has influenced theology in America, American culture, modern philosophy, religious revivals and revivalism, and contemporary theology. It also shows how his thought may be viewed against the backdrop of historic Calvinism as well as the Roman Catholic and Orthodox traditions.

Despite the length of this book, it is only an introduction to Edwards's theology. An analogy may help to explain this. In some parts of the western United States, the traveler will find a roadside location labeled as a "scenic view" or "vista point," where one may pull off and take a moment to appreciate the landscape. The greatest sight of all—Arizona's Grand Canyon—offers multiple vista points. Each point allows one to see most of the canyon, though each shows a better view of some parts than of others. Similarly, the various chapters in our book are like vista points encircling an immense terrain. Here one gets glimpses into Edwards's theology that are biographical (ch. 2), contextual (ch. 3), spiritual (ch. 4), developmental (ch. 5), aesthetic (ch. 6), metaphysical (ch. 7), typological (ch. 8), apologetic (ch. 10), exegetical (ch. 11), redemptive-historical (ch. 12), Trinitarian (ch. 13), providentialist (ch. 15), christological (ch. 16), pneumatological (ch. 17), angelic (ch. 18), heavenly (ch. 19), affective (ch. 20), Calvinistic (ch. 21), and so forth. Nearly every chapter offers a distinct angle of vision on Edwards's entire intellectual project. No single chapter shows everything, however, and all the chapters taken together do not provide an exhaustive picture. Those who want to know the terrain well should not only view the vistas but hike the canyon for themselves.

Forty-four chapters follow this one, outlining Edwards's intellectual background, his principal theological concerns, and the legacies that followed. In this last part of our introduction we will provide a snapshot of the themes that run throughout our analysis of Edwards's corpus. Many of these themes (in italics) correspond to chapter titles, but nearly every one of them reappears in numerous chapters because of Edwards's concatenations and associations of ideas.

We turn now to a brief synopsis of the chapters that follow, with Edwards's key themes highlighted in italicized letters. Edwards's *spirituality* laid emphasis on seeking after God. Contemplative, ascetic, self-abnegating, and solitary, his spiritual and intellectual existence was characterized by a continual questing after greater grace and greater understanding. *Beauty* was one of Edwards's architectonic principles, flowing from consent within the Trinity (primary beauty) and reflected in its typological representations in the natural and human worlds (secondary beauty). It was the distinguishing characteristic of God and also of being itself. Edwards's new view of reality was embodied in a complex and many-sided *metaphysics* that centered on dispositional ontology and ontic enlargement, first within God (i.e., the Trinity) and then external to God (i.e., creation). Edwards developed an idealist or immaterialist viewpoint, in which God alone is "substance" and all other things exist as ideas in God's mind. God is "Being in general"—an all-inclusive Being who continuously recreates the world. In Edwards's *typology*, the world itself and all of human experience are simply teeming with "images and shadows" of God's reality. Nature, history, and the Bible are sown with symbols of spiritual reality, and these interconnect with one another so that all reality teaches us something of God and God's nature. Typology was less a method than a worldview for Edwards. The types were not creations of human fancy but were built into the world by God the great Typologist.

God communicates to humanity through objective *revelation* in scripture and subjective illumination by the Spirit who makes real to the saints that objective revelation. Knowledge of historical-redemptive tradition is necessary to interpret scripture properly. Edwards's *apologetics* had two major aspects. Alongside the explicit apology (miracles, fulfilled prophecy, proofs for God), there was an "implicit apology" that offered a root-and-branch reinterpretation of major western intellectual traditions (e.g., metaphysics, natural philosophy, moral philosophy, and historical narrative). Edwards's *biblical exegesis* showed a catholic tendency insofar as he embraced the medieval tradition of seeing multiple senses in scripture—the literal-historical plus various spiritual senses of scripture (typological, allegorical, moral, and anagogical). The Bible's semantic plenitude did not overturn the literal sense for Edwards, but neither was it limited to the literal sense. The *history of redemption* was Edwards's new organizing principle for theology, in contrast to the classical model of the theological loci (i.e., God, humanity, Christ, salvation, etc.). Edwards sought to render the content of Christian theology as a successive unfolding through the biblical era, church history, and into the future, by means of an eschatological forecasting of the future. Such an approach to theology fit with Edwards's new understanding of reality as unfolding, expanding, and thus essentially temporal and historical.

Almost alone among Christian thinkers of his era, Edwards made the *Trinity* a vital center of theological reflection. His dispositional accent became clear in his account of the Trinity that combined the psychological and the social models in an innovative way. Unlike others in the western tradition, Edwards stressed the ontological priority of the Father among the three persons of the Trinity, so that his thinking could play something of a mediating role in the *filioque* debate between East and West. What is more, he strongly emphasized the role of the Holy Spirit, as the "sum of good" that comes to believers in Christ. Like certain Catholic thinkers, and unlike almost all Protestants, Edwards devoted great attention to the theme of *the end of creation*—the purpose of God in creating the world. He insisted that God creates both for his own glory and for the happiness of creatures, using the category of "emanation" or "communication" to hold together these seemingly disparate aims. God communicates, and creatures participate in, God's own love for himself, knowledge of himself, and joy in himself. Edwards's interpretation of *providence and history* stressed the conflict between good and evil and the progressive march toward an eschatological telos, but not without cyclical elements. All events lie within God's plan, though only God can see the "river" of providence and its total pattern. Scripture offers a key to interpreting the meaning of history. Edwards highlighted the role of suffering in God's plan, particularly the sufferings of Christ and his church.

Edwards's view of *Jesus Christ* was thoroughly Trinitarian. He upheld the satisfaction theory of the atonement, and yet also emphasized the aesthetic, rational, and personal aspects of Christ's passion. Edwards combined an "Alexandrian" stress on Jesus' divinity and his divine epiphany with an "Antiochene" stress on the sufferings and progressive development of Jesus' humanity. As Christ creates and draws more souls into his body, he undergoes ontic enlargement. For Edwards, the *Holy Spirit* does not merely "apply" the benefits purchased by Christ in his sufferings, but the Spirit is the very "purchase" itself—the very good that the saints enjoy. As a "vital principle" indwelling and acting in believers, the Holy Spirit's presence results in love, joy, peace, and the flourishing of all other Christian virtues. Edwards's notebooks reflected an original and unique view of *the angels* that was intertwined with Edwards's Christology and his teaching that Jesus became "King of angels" at the time of his exaltation and ascension—when the unfallen angels were also "confirmed" in grace. Christ occupies the place once held by Lucifer and is exalted above him. The angels have been in some sense "reconciled" to God through Christ's incarnation, and constitute "one family" with elect humans. Edwards presented a pervasively social view of *heaven* as a state in which the saints not only have a transformed relationship with God but also with one another. Envy ceases and each saint delights in the goodness and beauty of the others. Heaven is a "progressive state" of unending, increasing grace and glory.

Edwards's anthropology and soteriology were based on his conception of the human person as a cluster of *affections* that determines nearly everything that a person feels, thinks, and does. The affections are not equivalent to emotions, but represent the "heart" that drives mind, will, and emotions. Godly affections are rooted in love and a sense of the divine beauty. In his teaching on *original sin and the unfree will*, Edwards originated the idea that Adam's union with his posterity is due to an "arbitrary constitution" of God. He argued that the fallen will is unfree because it is determined by sinful "motives," and that the Arminian view of a spontaneous will is logically incoherent and self-refuting. His distinction between "natural ability" and "moral ability" sought to show how an unfree will can be held responsible for its choices. Yet Edwards also reworked Reformed categories regarding *salvation* (e.g., common vs. special grace, faith, regeneration, justification) in novel ways. *Grace* is free and not dependent on human worthiness or sincerity. It is the presence of the Holy Spirit in action, and at the same time a new disposition. It has a "physical" effect on the soul, and is efficacious rather than irresistible (which would imply human passivity). Edwards also taught that love is an aspect of true *faith*, akin to Aquinas's notion of love as a form of faith.

For Edwards, no salvation or true apprehension of God exists apart from *conversion* and regeneration. In part because of his pastoral experiences amid revival, Edwards rejected the older Puritan "morphology of conversion," and used a Lockean notion of sensation as a model for his understanding of a "divine and supernatural light" producing "the sense of the heart." Conversion involved both illumination and infusion. Yet Edward also taught continuing conversion—that regeneration was in some sense a lifelong series of experiences that replicated in form the pattern set in the original conversion. Edwards maintained his continuity with his Reformed tradition by emphasizing that grace is unmerited and that believers are saved by Christ's righteousness rather than their own. Yet he insisted that the legal, forensic idea of *justification* is based on an actual union of believers with Christ through faith. Faith itself has a "natural fitness," therefore, to bring the blessing of union with Christ. Moreover, faith is not the only "condition" of justification or salvation, but "perseverance" and "obedience" are as well. Edwards also made room for "reward" as a key aspect in his soteriology. He tied his teaching on *sanctification* to the notion of the Holy Spirit as a vital, active principle at work in believers. Edwards's theology emphasized not only sanctification (God's work in us) but also *divinization or deification* (our participation in God). Salvation means progressive participation in the very life of the Triune God, and in this process human life is increasingly transfigured into God's likeness. At this point Edwards drew near to Eastern Christian and Orthodox conceptions of salvation.

Edwards's *theology of revival* combined openness and caution in roughly equal measures. He insisted that no one could say in advance how God might choose to act in the midst of a revival, and yet that discernment was needed to sift the wheat from the chaff. Edwards's position was thus intermediate between that of the "Old Lights" (e.g., Charles Chauncy) and that of the radical "New Lights" (e.g., Andrew Croswell) who reveled in the novel and anti-authoritarian aspects of revival. Edwards held to a Puritan "gathered church" ecclesiology that stressed the sufferings and afflictions of the *church* in this present world. His ideal was a church free from pride, envy, and self-will, where ministers faithfully performed their duties and congregants gratefully appreciated their pastor and one another. Edwards's ordination sermons revealed his *pastoral theology* and his vision of the minister as a "burning and a shining light"—that is, preeminently a preacher and teacher. The minister was to be a shepherd, guide, and fisher of souls, and was called to sacrifice his own well-being for the sake of others—just as Christ did. Edwards had a robust theology of the *sacraments* that eclipsed that of his seventeenth-century Puritan forbears. While for them the primary value of the sacraments was to provide seals of the covenant, Edwards stressed communion with God and viewed the Eucharist as an occasion at which Christ was uniquely present to his people. Edwards's notion of *preaching* rested on a "rhetoric of sensation" (Perry Miller) that presumed that spiritual things did not seem real to most people. The preacher was not only to inform the understanding but to awaken hearers' hearts and imaginations in an encounter with spiritual realities.

Despite the contention of many scholars that Edwards was happy to let those outside the church go to hell (in a worldly and otherworldly sense), Edwards demonstrated a deep concern for civil and *public life*, and developed an elaborate conception of life in the public square for both citizens and magistrates. He believed that the American colonies had entered into a national covenant with God, but was pessimistic about New England's spiritual status. Yet if Edwards kept a critical distance from narrow nationalisms, he shared the prejudices of his day regarding African-Americans and slavery. Edwards conceived of *true virtue* as participation in the divine life, love as the source and sum of all virtue, and the natural virtues as God-ordained images of divine virtues. He rejected Aristotelian notions of habituation, by which one acquires true virtue through repetitive performance. He was distinctive among post-Enlightenment Christian ethicists because he focused on character rather than law. Many ethicists reduced all morality to an undifferentiated love or benevolence, but Edwards delineated a range of virtues that all related back to love. For Edwards, the virtue and practice of Christian love comprehended all other virtues and practices. *Love* was the "sum" of all. Edwards's theology was more centered on love than on either faith or hope, though it included these other elements. Love was God's means of coming into unity with us, our means of uniting with God, and our means of uniting with one another. Love was thus essential to the fulfillment of God's purposes on earth and in heaven. The Holy Spirit was the Spirit of love—love's principle, source, and energy.

Missions for Edwards were a chapter in the larger story of the history of revival, which was the main story line in what he called the history of redemption. In his estimation, Christian mission was the principal means used by God to gather together one body of believers joined to Christ, to effect the triumph of good over evil, to perfect the beauty of the elect, and to glorify the Trinity. Edwards's *eschatology* involved an optimistic vision of a gradual, stepwise progression of God's purposes through the overthrow of "Antichrist" (Roman Catholicism, Islam, etc.) and the "glorious times" of the church. Christ came not twice but four times—with each "coming" an advancement over what went before. Heaven and hell were both defined in terms of God's presence (as either edifying or afflictive), and the new heavens and new earth were to be a newly refurbished realm above an old earth that was to be turned into a lake of fire. Employing the best sources available in his day, Edwards studied *non-Christian religions* more than any other colonial American, and he identified certain teachings in them as confirmations of his own theology. He believed that divine "inspiration" occurred in various degrees and was not limited to the biblical authors. Edwards pondered—but did not ultimately resolve—the question of the possibility of salvation for "the heathen."

Following Edwards's death, the thinkers of the so-called *New Divinity* pursued a number of themes from Edwards's thought—including the freedom of the will, the use of "means" of grace prior to conversion, the nature of the atonement, the life of disinterested benevolence, and the coming of Christ's kingdom. Stung into action by the fashionable skepticism of their day, Samuel Hopkins, Joseph Bellamy, and Nathanael Emmons developed a sophisticated defense of Christianity—relying in part on a selective republication of Edwards's notebook entries—and they promoted New Light Calvinism through several lean decades before they were rewarded with revivals just prior to and after 1800. Edwardsean Calvinism then emerged as a driving cultural force that propelled American churches into revivals, global missions, abolitionism, and other causes in the decades prior to the Civil War. Yet cultural mavens like Harriet Beecher Stowe and Oliver Wendell Holmes disavowed Edwards's Calvinism and reflected the *mixed reactions* to Edwards during the 1800s. Andover Seminary began by embracing Edwardseanism in the early 1800s and more or less jettisoning it by the century's end. Conservative Presbyterians were tepid toward Edwards, appreciating his stout defense of Calvinism but uncomfortable with his innovations. The American *revival tradition* was deeply indebted to and engaged with Edwards's ideas. This was true of Congregationalists, Presbyterians, Baptists, Methodists, and Holiness Christians in the 1800s, as well as Pentecostals, Fundamentalists, Evangelicals, and Charismatics in the 1900s.

By the start of the 1900s, Edwards was a distant memory for most educated Americans—like a figure from the age of Homer. Yet the economic, political, and military woes of the 1930s and 1940s propelled a *twentieth-century recovery* of Edwards, led by Perry Miller and others, and eventuating in the publication project of *The Works of Jonathan Edwards* (1957–2008). Neo-Orthodox theology in Europe and America, and a resurgence of scholarship on the American Puritans, added to the growing interest in Edwards. Most representatives of *modern philosophy* were not interested in Edwards, though there was a debate in the late 1800s regarding the sources of Edwards's idealism, and throughout the 1900s there were philosophers (William Harder Squires, Mikos Vetö, Stephen Daniel, and Oliver Crisp) who showed that it was possible to engage and appropriate Edwards's thought from widely differing points of view. In *contemporary theology* such disparate authors as H. Richard Niebuhr, Paul Ramsey, John Piper, Amy Plantinga Pauw, Gerald McDermott, and Belden Lane drew from and developed Edwards's ideas on the history of redemption, narrative theology, theocentric ethics, the enjoyment of God, Trinitarian thought, public theology, and the beauties of God and the natural world. This volume's *conclusion* treats Edwards as a *bridge figure* between diverse and sometimes conflicting parties in the Christian world—Western (Latin) and Eastern (Orthodox) Christianity, Catholicism and Protestantism, conservatism and liberalism, and charismatic and non-charismatic Christianity. In each case, Edwards's thought connects to both sides of an apparent polarity, and this feature could make him a thinker of exceptional importance for the global Christian community in its twenty-first century.

2

Edwards: A Theological Life

A THEOLOGICAL LIFE

JONATHAN EDWARDS WAS an activist, preacher, contemplative, missionary, philosopher, and theologian. He will be remembered for all these and more, but his most enduring legacy will be the theological vision that in profundity and influence has led many to regard him as the greatest religious thinker in the history of the Americas.

Early Years

The fifth of eleven children and the only boy, Edwards was born on October 5, 1703, into a ministerial family in East Windsor, Connecticut.[1] His father, the Rev. Timothy Edwards, had earned the terminal theological degree (MA) from Harvard College, and over his sixty years of ministry was known as one of Connecticut's most learned pastors. Esther Stoddard Edwards, Jonathan's mother, directed women in the Bible and theology. Her father, the Rev. Solomon Stoddard, was the famous "Pope" of the Connecticut River Valley, a theologian in his own right and a powerful preacher.[2] Both Timothy and Solomon had led revivals in their churches, and both were concerned about theologies of conversion and church membership.

These were matters of debate ever since the Puritans first founded the Massachusetts Bay Colony. They insisted that full church membership (and therefore voting and office-holding rights) would be given only to those who could relate a story of the Spirit's work within them. But then when many of their baptized children failed to experience a work of grace, most ministers—including Timothy Edwards—approved the Half-Way Covenant (1662), whereby

---

1. His father referred to his "sixty feet of daughters," since each grew to be at least six feet tall. George M. Marsden, *Jonathan Edwards: A Life* (New Haven: Yale University Press, 2003), 18.

2. Ibid., 19.

these "half-way" citizens (baptized by water but not the Spirit, as far as they knew) could have their own children baptized and thus enter the covenant. After Massachusetts lost its charter in 1684 and New Englanders learned they had to tolerate other Protestants, standards for church membership and receiving the Lord's Supper were further relaxed. Toward the end of the seventeenth century, Stoddard accepted as members those who professed belief and avoided scandal, and admitted the unconverted to the Lord's Supper because he believed it a "converting ordinance." Timothy Edwards continued to require a "relation" or story of one's experience of grace for church membership, and opposed Stoddard's policy of open communion. Perhaps it is not surprising that the only male scion of this theological clan directed much of his own thinking to the question of how one can recognize a work of grace.

Timothy and Esther home-schooled (as most educated parents did) their only son in the Bible, Reformed theology, the Greco-Roman classics, and ancient languages. They started him in Latin at age six; by the age of twelve he was reading Latin, Greek, and a smattering of Hebrew. He started college (the Connecticut Collegiate School, which later became Yale) at one month shy of his thirteenth birthday (the usual age), and graduated in 1720 (age 16) after studying grammar, rhetoric, logic, ancient history, arithmetic, geometry, astronomy, metaphysics, ethics, and natural science. This was supplemented by theological studies in Calvin, Owen, and Ames (whose *Marrow of Theology* he was required to memorize).

Graduate Study and an Early Pastorate

After graduating as valedictorian of his class, Edwards proceeded to two years of graduate study at Yale. It was during this period, in his seventeenth year, that he experienced what seems to have been his conversion. In his *Personal Narrative*, written perhaps twenty years later, Edwards recalled that while he had built a prayer booth in a swamp as a child and often felt "much affected," it was only in this spring of 1721, while meditating on 1 Timothy 1:17, that he came to see the beauty of God's holiness and no longer felt God's sovereignty was a "horrible" doctrine.[3] He explained the difference between pre-conversion spiritual experiences and saving grace in his 1734 sermon "Divine and Supernatural Light": "There is a difference between having an opinion that God is holy and gracious, and having a *sense* of the loveliness and beauty of that holiness and grace."[4]

---

3. *Personal Narrative* is now lost and was never dated, but is thought to have been written in 1740.

4. WJE 17:408–26, citing 414. Emph. added.

In New Haven, Edwards began to think in fresh ways about natural philosophy or science, being and the mind, writing about them in a series of notebooks he started there. In "Of Atoms," he concluded that mechanistic portrayals of reality that ignore God's immediate exercise of power are flawed, for without God there is nothing. "So that the substance of bodies at last becomes either nothing, or nothing but the Deity acting in that particular manner in those parts of space where he thinks fit. So that, speaking most strictly, there is no proper substance but God himself."[5] These were the seed thoughts he later developed into an idealist metaphysics in which physical objects are the means God uses to communicate with other minds. This was a synthesis of immaterialism (material objects are really there but produced moment-to-moment by the divine mind) and empiricism that Edwards used to refute Hobbes' materialism and Descartes' dualism.

After completing graduate studies, Edwards preached at an English Presbyterian congregation in New York City for eight months (August 1722–April 1723). New York City then had about 7,000 inhabitants, and Edwards's little church was near what we now call Ground Zero, toward the bottom of Manhattan Island. Here he started his spiritual "Diary" and "Resolutions," whose ardent yearnings still excite young readers but weary their seniors. For example, Edwards wrote, "Resolved, never to do any manner of thing, whether in soul or body, less or more, but what tends to the glory of God; nor be, nor suffer it, if I can avoid it.... Resolved, to strive to my utmost every week to be brought higher in religion, and to a higher exercise of grace, than I was the week before."[6]

It was in this New York pastorate that Edwards also started his *Miscellanies*, theological notebooks that eventually grew to more than one million words. Here Edwards began his emphasis on beauty that evolved into the most developed aesthetic theology in the history of western Christian thought. His very first entry in these massive notebooks, at about age twenty, proposed, "Holiness is a most beautiful and lovely thing.... 'Tis the highest beauty and amiableness, vastly above all other beauties."[7] Edwards went on here and in his published works to argue that "God is God, and distinguished from all other beings, and exalted above 'em, chiefly by his divine beauty, which is infinitely diverse from all other beauty." God's nature is the true beauty, the criterion of all beauty, and the source or fountain of all beauty.[8]

---

5. WJE 6:215.

6. WJE 16:753, 755 (Resolutions 4 and 30).

7. WJE 13:163.

8. WJE 2:298; WJE 8:550–60.

Here he also began his recasting of Calvinism in response to Arminianism and deism and other challenges to Reformed orthodoxy. He used the work of John Locke and Isaac Newton as tools, but did so critically. Edwards was inspired by Newton's vision of the universe as in relationship and constantly changing, but the New England theologian was less inductive and far more deductive as a thinker. Edwards borrowed Lockean psychology—the notions that an idea is the object of the mind and that all ideas come from sensation or reflection. But unlike Locke, he held that some ideas such as causality are innate, and that some knowledge (such as God's giving us a simple idea) is immediate. Overall, Edwards learned from Locke a "total experiential orientation of thought," but went further than Locke in linking sense and intellectual understanding.[9]

In September 1723, when Edwards was one month shy of his twentieth birthday, he delivered the valedictory address at Yale College for his master's degree. One year before, the rector of Yale had closed commencement with words from the Book of Common Prayer, signaling that the leadership of Yale had passed to what Edwards and Reformed orthodoxy believed was crypto-Catholic Arminian heresy. Edwards's *Quaestio* (academic disputation) on justification by faith was intended to move Yale back toward Reformation truths. During these months, he began a careful commentary on the biblical book of Revelation. He also wrote his famous letter on spiders that not only provided unprecedented detail on the activities of these creatures but celebrated "the exuberant goodness of the Creator, who hath not only provided for all the necessities, but also for the pleasure and recreation of all sorts of creatures, even the insects."[10]

After a brief tenure as pastor in Bolton, Connecticut, Edwards accepted Yale's invitation to be its senior tutor—in effect, president—in May 1724, and spent the next two years there. This was a difficult time for the young professor because of unruly students and frequent sickness. His "Diary" and letters reveal that saintliness did not come easily. He was sometimes "violently beset with temptation," and would figure "some sum in Arithmetic or Geometry" for relief.[11] During this period and throughout his life, there were periods of depression interspersed with occasional experiences of spiritual ecstasy. By

---

9. John E. Smith, *Jonathan Edwards: Puritan, Preacher, Philosopher* (Notre Dame, IN: University of Notre Dame Press, 1992), 26.

10. John E. Smith, Harry S. Stout, Kenneth P. Minkema, eds., *A Jonathan Edwards Reader* (New Haven: Yale University Press, 1995), 5.

11. The intensity that Edwards ascribed to the temptation has led some to suggest it might have been sexual in nature; Marsden, *Edwards*, 106–107.

the end of his Yale tenure he was world weary: he felt "fears, perplexities, multitudes of cares and distraction of mind."[12] He seemed glad to accept his grandfather Stoddard's invitation in 1726 to join him in Northampton as junior pastor.

Northampton Pastor

He was twenty-three when he arrived, and spent his next twenty-three years in what was the largest and most influential church outside Boston, preaching two sermons every Sabbath in an academic gown and powdered periwig, and delivering a lecture on most Wednesdays. In 1729, two years after Edwards had been ordained at Northampton, Stoddard died and Edwards took over as senior pastor.

Northampton's new shepherd was quite tall (6'1") for his time and very thin, had a clear but not strong voice, and spoke with fervid solemnity. His sermons "might be compared to Bach's fugues, exploring every variation of a theme."[13] Contemporaries marveled at their logic, remarking that accepting a sermon's premise would lead inexorably to agreement with its conclusion.

Less than a year after arriving at Northampton, Edwards married Sarah Pierpont, whose minister father was a founder of Yale. Some years before, Jonathan had been smitten by Sarah's "wonderful sweetness, calmness and universal benevolence of mind."[14] Their marriage, which George Whitefield thought "sweeter" than any he had seen, produced eleven children.[15]

Edwards was not a people person. He declined the tradition of regular calls on his parishioners, inviting them instead to let him know when they wanted a visit. Part of his motivation no doubt was to protect his time in his study, where he regularly worked twelve to fourteen hours each day when he was not away preaching or in town attending meetings.[16] He rose at 4 a.m. in the summer and 5 a.m. in the winter, chopping wood for exercise in cold months and riding a horse or walking in the woods otherwise. Family tradition tells us

---

12. WJE 16:786.

13. Marsden, Edwards, 129.

14. WJE 16:790.

15. George Whitefield's Journals, ed. Iain Murray (Edinburgh: Banner of Truth Trust, 1960), entry for October 19, 1740, 476.

16. As Kenneth Minkema has noted, he was often called away from his study for meetings, councils, traveling, guest preaching, visiting, and conducting personal business. So he did not study and write for this many hours every day.

that on warm days he carried a pen and paper to jot down thoughts that would strike him; if it was too cold, he took colored pieces of cloth, mentally attached each new idea to a distinct color, and used the color to remember and record the thoughts when he got home.

Three of his most famous addresses in the 1730s sounded recurring themes in his theology. The first was a lecture invited in 1731 by the Boston clergy. This was a prestigious opportunity that was also intimidating, since Edwards did not share the Harvard credentials of the leading clergy. Once again Edwards challenged Arminian presumptions with his *God Glorified in the Work of Redemption By the Greatness of Man's Dependence on Him*, which became his first published work.[17] Edwards emphasized two themes that were developed through the rest of his career—God's sovereignty and the Trinity.

> [In 1 Cor. 1.29–31 we are] shown our dependence on each person in the Trinity for all our good. We are dependent on Christ the Son of God, as he is our wisdom, righteousness, sanctification, and redemption. We are dependent on the Father, who has given us Christ, and made him to be these things to us. We are dependent on the Holy Ghost, for 'tis of him that we are in Christ Jesus; 'tis the Spirit of God that gives us faith in him, whereby we receive him, and close with him.[18]

In *A Divine and Supernatural Light* (1734), Edwards outlined the source and nature of true religion. He argued that it does not come from natural convictions such as conscience or mere impressions on the imagination, but is instead a taste or vision of the beauty of God in Christ. God uses means such as Scripture and preaching to convey this sense, but the true cause is the immediate work of the Holy Spirit. Edwards's text was Matthew 16:17, where Jesus told Peter that it was not "flesh and blood" that had "revealed" to him that he was the messiah, but revelation from "my Father which is in heaven." He compared this revelation to the taste of honey: "There is a difference between having a rational judgment that honey is sweet, and having a sense of its sweetness. A man may have the former, that knows not how honey tastes; but a man can't have the latter, unless he has an idea of the taste of honey in his mind." So too for seeing the "divine excellency": "He that is spiritually enlightened...don't

---

17. "Arminian" has been a fluid term in history and was in Edwards's day, as well. Its use in this volume is for a rationalistic Calvinism that increasingly rejected the idea of human incapacity to respond to God, and instead thought of salvation as a cooperative process in which human beings turn toward God by their natural ability and so gain God's favor (ch. 3).

18. WJE 17:201.

merely rationally believe that God is glorious, but he has a sense of the gloriousness of God in his heart."[19]

The Little Awakening

Later that same year Edwards revisited the theme of his master's degree *Quaestio* for a lecture that became his first published treatise, *Justification by Faith Alone*. His main purpose was to teach that people should not "trust in their own righteousness for justification, which is a thing fatal to the soul." But Edwards went further than Reformation platitudes when he warned that "a man is not justified by faith only, but also by works" when works are understood as the proper "acts or expressions of faith." So he declaimed against, on the one hand, thinking that our works save us, and on the other, thinking that "good works [are] not necessary to salvation." In other words, he opposed Pelagians (who say unaided free will can keep God's commandments) and Arminians (who believe God waits for us to take the initiative in salvation and sanctification) on the one hand, and antinomians (literally, "against the law") on the other.[20]

This lecture on justification, which Edwards turned into two sermons, made a deep impression on the Northampton congregation, especially its young people. Before too long, the "Little Awakening" broke out, eventually culminating in a spiritual earthquake that rocked not only Edwards's congregation but spread to other towns up and down the Connecticut River Valley. Unlike previous revivals under Stoddard and other Puritans, this awakening reached as many men as women, and many older people. Within three months, three hundred (half the adults) in Edwards's church said they were converted. Most of the rest were seeking or moved. The whole town, Edwards reported in his *Faithful Narrative* (1738), "seemed to be full of the presence of God; it never was so full of love, nor so full of joy."[21] Church services were packed, often marked by tears of sorrow for sin and the unconverted, and tears of joy and love.

Just two days after Edwards finished his glowing account of the revival, his uncle Joseph Hawley slit his own throat. Hawley had had a history of depression; Edwards said he was not surprised that Satan would respond so dramatically to a work of the Spirit. The awakening collapsed like a pin-pricked balloon. When his converts cooled in their affections for Christ and discipleship, Edwards's

---

19. WJE 17:414, 413.
20. WJE 19:241, 236, 234.
21. WJE 4:151.

sermons and notebooks moved away from an emphasis on affections alone to stress on perseverance in faith and the kind of behavior that true faith displays.

In 1739 Edwards moved, homiletically and theologically, to a survey of the vast history of redemption, from before the creation to after the millennium at the end of the world. In a series of thirty sermons, Edwards chronicled in both sacred and secular history the coordination of history and Scripture, attempting to show both how the sacred and secular interpenetrate under God's direction, and also how history is a massive demonstration of the truths of Reformed theology. Once again, in apologetic response to deists and Arminians, Edwards's purpose was to highlight God's sovereignty and the work of the Trinity: "The Work of Redemption.... 'Tis but one design that is done to which all the offices of Christ do directly tend, and in which all the persons of the Trinity do conspire and all the various dispensations that belong to it are united, as the several wheels in one machine, to answer one end and produce one effect."[22] Against the deists, Edwards insisted that history and Scripture are not conflicting but in "harmony," and against Arminians Edwards argued that God is truly sovereign and not dependent on human volition to accomplish his ends.

The History of the Work of Redemption series was the beginning of Edwards's reconsideration of theological method. Until this point he had been planning to write a "Rational Account of the Main Doctrines of the Christian Religion Attempted," in the standard manner of systematic theologies organized according to traditional *loci*.[23] But the *Work of Redemption* was the outline for "an entire new method" that substituted history for theology as queen of the sciences. Theology was still Edwards's obsession, but his vision of God would be unfolded through story, which he considered "a method which appears to me the most beautiful and entertaining, wherein every doctrine, will appear to greatest advantage in the brightest light."[24] It was to have woven together doctrine, apologetics, philosophy, ethics and even the world religions under the control of a grand narrative. When his life was cut short at Princeton in 1758, he was about to commence this mammoth project.

Downpours and Discernment

A year after he delivered his *History of Redemption* series, the dam burst. Historians have referred to the resulting flood as the Great Awakening. The

---

22. WE 9:118.
23. WE 6:396–97.
24. WE 16:727–28.

downpours of the Spirit were triggered by George Whitefield's preaching tour of the colonies in 1739, and fed by Edwards's famous sermon, "Sinners in the Hands of an Angry God." When Whitefield came to Northampton on Edwards's invitation in October 1740, the church was entranced by the 26-year-old celebrity from England: Sarah wrote that all one could hear was muffled sobs. In the following July, Edwards was asked by the Rev. Peter Reynolds at Enfield, Connecticut, to help prepare his congregation for awakening. Edwards delivered a sermon that he had previously preached at Northampton, but with no visible effect. This "Sinners" sermon emphasized God's holding back his wrath from deserving sinners. Edwards's images (an arrow pointed at one's heart, a spider held over a fire) were so effective this time that his Enfield listeners cried out and Edwards had to stop several times. As far as we can tell, he was never able to finish.

In the next decade, Edwards rose to become the foremost theologian of awakening and revival. His first opportunity was an invitation to speak at another Yale commencement, this time on September 10, 1741. His *Distinguishing Marks of a Work of the Spirit of God* (published November 1741) listed nine characteristics of a revival that should *not* be used for deciding whether a movement is of the Spirit, such as "effects on the bodies of men...a great deal of noise about religion...great imprudences and irregularities...many errors in judgment, and some delusions of Satan intermixed with the work...[some] fall[ing] away into gross errors or scandalous practices...[and] ministers insisting very much on the terrors of God's holy law." All these things are to be expected, both because of Satan's opposition and human error. Then Edwards proposed five marks of a work of the Spirit of God among people: It would "raise their esteem of that Jesus that was born of the Virgin" and is God in the flesh; turn people away from "Satan's kingdom" of sin and "worldly lusts"; produce "a greater regard to the Holy Scriptures"; lead "persons to truth" such as the "sin-hating God," and their own sin and helplessness; and "a spirit of love to God and man" joined to humility—the "two things most contrary to the spirit of the Devil." Edwards closed by warning that in awakenings study should not be neglected, that we cannot "discern the state of the souls of others," and that to oppose this awakening was to oppose God.[25]

This address, and the behavior of deluded revivalists like James Davenport, only added fuel to the fires of contention. So in 1742 Edwards wrote another long defense of the awakening, *Some Thoughts Concerning the Revival*, which highlighted, as a method of promoting the revival, the religious raptures of his

---

25. WJE 4:228–83.

wife Sarah, but without mentioning her name. This "soul...did as it were swim in the rays of Christ's love, like a little mote swimming in the beams of the sun.... [and]seemed almost to leave the body; dwelling in a pure delight that fed and satisfied the soul...from time to time, for years together."[26]

After this awakening subsided, and as many of its converts returned to worldly ways, Edwards became more circumspect in judging whether religious experience produces regeneration. His *Religious Affections* (1746) was a careful exploration of the nature of true religion and good and bad ways of discerning its presence. The book argues first that religious experience is centered in what he called the "affections." These lie at a deeper level of the human person than either thoughts or feelings, and in fact are the source and motivating power of thoughts and feelings. Indeed, he claimed they are at the root of all spiritual experience, both true and false. Holy affections are the source of all true religion, and other kinds of affections are at the root of false religion. By "affections" Edwards meant strong inclinations of the soul that are manifested in thinking, feeling, and choosing. So the affections are not emotions but give rise to emotion; they are strong inclinations and so not simply preferences; and they involve mind, will and feeling at the same time. In fact, the thoughts of the mind are directed by the affections. Holy inclinations will lead one to love God (feelings), think rightly about God (thought), and try to obey his commandments (acts of the will). Unholy affections will cause a person to feel distaste for faith and Christians (feelings), believe there are excellent reasons for rejecting faith (thought), and refuse to pray or attend church or promote the influence of religion in society (actions).

The rest of the *Religious Affections* is divided between twelve "negative" or unreliable signs of true religion (criteria Christians typically use to determine the presence of true faith) and twelve "positive" or reliable signs of grace (criteria that Edwards says Christians *ought* to use). For example, one of the negative signs is frequent and passionate praise for God. Edwards said that true believers would praise God often, but that the Israelites praised God just before worshiping the Golden Calf, and people praised Jesus as he rode into Jerusalem on his donkey but a few days later cried out, "Crucify him! Crucify him." So the mere fact of enthusiastic praise is not a reliable sign of true grace. Far more telling is whether our faith is founded in "the loveliness of the moral excellency of divine things" rather than "any conceived relation they bear to self, or self-interest."[27] The regenerate person will of course be grateful for

---

26. WJE 4:332.

27. WJE 2:253, 240.

what God has done in Christ for her, but her principal motivation for Christian life will be the beauty of the holiness she sees in Jesus Christ. Seeing that beauty is the very center of Edwards's vision of God:

> This is the beauty of the Godhead, and the divinity of Divinity (if I may so speak), the good of the infinite Fountain of Good; without which God himself (if that were possible to be) would be an infinite evil: without which, we ourselves had better never have been; and without which there had better have been no being. He therefore in effect knows nothing, that knows not this: his knowledge is but the shadow of knowledge, or the form of knowledge, as the Apostle calls it.[28]

"Christian practice" (behavior) is Edwards's twelfth and most important sign of regeneration, "the chief of all the signs of grace, both as an evidence of the sincerity of professors unto others, and also to their own consciences."[29] This does not mean perfection, but commitment over time to the lordship of Christ. What someone does in her life is finally more illustrative of grace than what she says.

Last Things

If the 1740s were a decade in which Edwards developed a sophisticated theology of awakening and spiritual discernment, it also saw the culmination of his lifelong passion for eschatology. When he wrote his *Personal Narrative* in his thirties, he recalled being dazzled by the millennial future in his twentieth year: "Sometimes Mr. Smith and I walked there [in New York] together, to converse of the things of God; and our conversation used much to turn on the advancement of Christ's kingdom in the world, and the glorious things that God would accomplish for his church in the latter days."[30] We know this recollection was not inaccurate because in a diary entry from the same year we find him lamenting the insufficiency of his prayers for the millennium.[31] In 1747, when 29-year-old missionary David Brainerd was dying in Edwards's home, the two often discussed the coming glorious days of the church, and the young

---

28. WJE 2:274.

29. WJE 2:406.

30. WJE 16:797. The "Mr. Smith" mentioned here was an ardent Calvinist and recent immigrant from England, whose son was a student at Yale with Edwards (Marsden, *Edwards*, 47).

31. WJE 16:784.

man's "vehement thirsting" for the millennial age only sharpened the pastor's own eschatological hopes.³²

In that same year Edwards published *An Humble Attempt to Promote Explicit Agreement and Visible Union of God's People in Extraordinary Prayer for the Revival of Religion and the Advancement of Christ's Kingdom on Earth*. Its purpose was to bring about "that *last* and greatest enlargement and most glorious advancement of the church of God on earth"—a long period of revival that would eventuate in a literal millennium—by means of a "concert of prayer" in which churches in the British Isles and the colonies would meet monthly to pray for this end-time "abundant effusion of his Holy Spirit on all the churches."³³

In *Some Thoughts* Edwards had speculated that the New England awakenings might "prove to be the dawning of a general revival."³⁴ By this he seems to have meant not the millennium per se, but a worldwide series of revivals that would precede the millennium.³⁵ In *Humble Attempt* he deplored the "lamentable moral and religious state of these American colonies" and "New England in particular," and emphasized the universality of "those great effusions of God's Spirit."³⁶ Neither before *Some Thoughts* (1743) nor after did Edwards give America or New England a special role to play in end-time revivals or the millennium.

The 1740s were also a time in which Edwards refined his skill as biblical exegete. In 1730 he had begun his single-volume commentary on the Bible—the "Blank Bible"—a tiny Bible disbounded and interleaved between 900 pages of blank, ruled quarto foolscap (each page sixteen inches by thirteen inches). He filled another single-volume notebook on the Bible (*Notes on Scripture*), worked on a commentary on the book of Revelation, and produced numerous comments on the Bible in his enormous private notebooks (the *Miscellanies*), not to mention churning out over the course of his career twenty-five years' worth of weekly sermons, of which 1,200 are still extant. They develop scores of themes, but among the most prominent are these three: (1) that the Old Testament is a massive typological system pointing not only to New Testament truths and events, but also to church history and eschatology;

---

32. WJE 7:532.

33. WJE 5:313; orig. emph.

34. WJE 4:466.

35. McDermott, *One Holy and Happy Society: The Public Theology of Jonathan Edwards* (University Park: Penn State Press, 1992), 37–92.

36. WJE 5:357, 333.

(2) that all of reality is an expression of the Trinity's desire to communicate its beauty and being to others; and (3) history is a massive story of redemption controlled by Christ and encompassing every atom and moment.

Exile

In 1750 New England was shocked when an overwhelming majority of voting members of the Northampton church—all male—voted to dismiss Edwards from the pastorate. Tensions had been rising ever since 1744, when Edwards called out publicly several young single men in the church for harassing single women with knowledge gained from a midwife's illustrated manual—that day's version of pornography. Others were offended by his beliefs, expressed in *Religious Affections*, that qualifications for full church membership should be tightened—beliefs that he made explicit in 1748 and 1749. When Edwards formally proposed in 1749 to change qualifications for communion—thus rejecting Stoddard's open communion policy—by restricting it to those who could tell him they hoped they were regenerate, Edwards faced open revolt. Many felt their own membership status was threatened, as well as their chances of having their children baptized.

There were other factors. Edwards had contended with the congregation for years over his salary, and his attempts to rewrite a church covenant with new behavioral standards persuaded many that his standards were "virtually monastic."[37] His refusal to make regular house calls and his repeated sermonic chidings of their beliefs and behavior over the years, especially those of the movers and shakers in town, contributed to the growing resentment. After preaching a sobering and plaintive farewell sermon that reminded his listeners they would all meet again before God, Edwards and his family endured a humiliating year of preaching to these same people in order to pay his bills. Finally, in the summer of 1751, Edwards moved into exile as a missionary to a small English congregation and 150 Mahican and Mohawk families in Stockbridge (western Massachusetts).

The Stockbridge years (August 1751–January 1758) were no retreat from conflict. The village was crowded with refugees (from the colonial wars with the French and their Indian allies) and soldiers, some of whom took shelter in the Edwards home. One Sunday morning in 1754, Canadian Indians, whom Edwards believed had been instigated by the French, attacked and killed three white worshipers. The mission was wracked by recurrent party strife between

---

37. Marsden, *Edwards*, 160, 6.

Edwards and the same Williams clan (see ch. 34) that had helped drive him out of Northampton.

But troubles within and without did not prevent Edwards from applying himself assiduously to his missionary tasks. For the seven years until he departed for Princeton in January 1758, Edwards held four services most Sundays: two for his Indian charges and two for the white congregation. During the week, while pursuing his theological projects, he expended considerable time and effort defending Indians against greedy whites who were manipulating the Stockbridge mission for their own aggrandizement. Despite recurrent physical distress and public vilification of his efforts, Edwards wrote numerous letters to Boston and London pleading his Indian parishioners' rights to education and justice. He obtained land and had it plowed for Indian families, for example, and made sure that five Indian boys found lodging in white homes so they could receive an education. Edwards took at least one of the boys into his own home.[38]

The Great Works

In the midst of this turmoil, Edwards wrote four of his greatest works. *Freedom of the Will* (1754), his most important treatise in philosophical theology, took up the question of how to reconcile divine sovereignty with human freedom. His first move was to attack the notion of a will separate from the whole person. The will, he averred, is that by which the self chooses. So the question is not whether the will is free but whether the person is free; it is not a question of what but who. Acts of the will are expressions of the affections of a person. These are the strong and deep inclinations that drive a person's feeling, thinking, and choosing. Hence the acts of the will are determined by the affections.

But if choices of the will are determined, how can they be free? Edwards answered this question by distinguishing between moral and natural freedom. Moral freedom is the freedom to act according to one's affections, whether they be morally good or morally bad. A generous man is morally free to give away what he has, but a stingy man is not. Natural freedom, on the other hand, is freedom to act according to the laws of nature. I can continue typing this page since nothing in physical nature is preventing me. But I cannot walk through a brick wall, since the laws of nature stop me. The unregenerate whose affections disincline them from submitting to God's law

---

38. WJE 16:634, 638.

therefore are morally unfree to change their hearts and surrender to him. But there is nothing in nature that would prevent them from doing so, which would involve going to church, reading the Bible, giving money to God's work and the poor, helping their enemies, and taking time to pray. They are morally unfree to do these things but are naturally free. Besides, they have voluntarily decided *not* to do these things. Edwards's final move was to show this same dynamic in God. God too is bound to act according to his affections, but since he acts voluntarily, he too is free. Thus it is no contradiction to say that God is sovereign over all—even over human choices—by determining their wills, and also that human beings are free in their choices of the will.[39]

At Stockbridge Edwards also labored to respond to the Enlightenment view of human nature, which had been recently unfolded in John Taylor's *Scripture-Doctrine of Original Sin Proposed to Free and Candid Examination* (1740). Taylor had written that human nature is essentially good, that it is not nature but free will that leads to human corruption, and that the imputation of Adam's sin to us is unjust. In his own *Original Sin* (1758), Edwards pointed to the universality of sin and evil throughout history to challenge Taylor's first contention. On the question of whether nature or free will causes corruption, he asked,

> How comes it to pass, that the free will of mankind has been determined to evil, in like manner before the flood, and after the flood; under the law, and under the gospel; among both Jews and Gentiles, under the Old Testament; and since that, among Christians, Jews and Mahometans; among Papists and Protestants; in those nations where civility, politeness, arts and learning most prevail, and among the Negroes and Hottentots in Africa, the Tartars in Asia, and Indians in America, towards both the poles, and on every side of the globe; in greatest cities, and obscurest villages; in palaces, and in huts, wigwams and cells underground?[40]

On our connection with Adam's sin, Edwards argued that God originally planted two kinds of principles in humanity—an inferior principle of self-love and a superior principle of love for God and righteousness. In the beginning the superior principle dominated. But when the first man fell, the superior

---

39. This is known as compatibilism, the view that God's sovereignty over the human will is compatible with freedom of the human will.

40. WJE 3:194.

principle departed because God had departed, and the inferior principle took control. Therefore Adam's sin came from his own nature when God withdrew his own nature from his first human creatures.

But Adam's sin was continuous with ours for two reasons. First, we are from him and in him, just as the branches of a tree are from and in the tree and an acorn is derived from the oak. Edwards proposed that the universe is recreated every nanosecond by God, and that his decision to make us one identity with that which had our names as babies is no different from considering us joined to Adam. Second, we consent to his sin when we sin today. Adam's posterity shares his punishment "by virtue of the full consent of the hearts of Adam's posterity to that first apostacy [sic]. And therefore the sin of the apostasy is not theirs, merely because God *imputes* it to them; but it is *truly* and *properly* theirs, and on that ground, God imputes it to them."[41]

Edwards's last two treatises were meant to be read together, *The End for Which God Created the World* and *Nature of True Virtue* (published in tandem in 1765). Both were responses to deist attacks on orthodoxy. Matthew Tindal, Thomas Chubb, and John Toland alleged that the God of orthodoxy is an egotistical being obsessed with applause. One of Edwards's answers to this criticism uses the concept of "true value." We think egotism is wrong, he begins, because it conflicts with the nature of things—that which indeed is of the greatest value. An egotist has a "disposition to prefer self as if it were more than all." We recognize this as vicious because we know that no individual can possibly be of greater worth than the whole system of beings. But God is so great that all other beings are as nothing to him, and all other excellence is as nothing, even less than nothing, in comparison. And God knows that he is infinitely the most valuable being. So it is fitting that other beings should recognize this with praise, because it conforms to the "true nature and proportion of things."[42]

Another answer hangs on the notion of the public good. "In created beings, self-interest can be opposed to the public welfare. But this cannot be so with respect to the supreme being, who is the fountain of being and goodness to the whole. He alone is good for the whole system, so it is appropriate that worship should be given him."[43] So yes, Edwards wrote, God created the worlds for his own glory, but it so happens that God is glorified when humans find their joy in him. Their greatest happiness comes from devoting their lives to God and his praise. Therefore God's glory and human flourishing are one and the same.

---

41. WJE 3:408. Orig. emph.

42. WJE 8:451.

43. WJE 8:451–52.

True Virtue's first chapter singles out "the more considerable Deists" as the ultimate proof of universal agreement among religious thinkers "that virtue most essentially consists in love." This treatise is essentially an attack on "schemes of religion or philosophy" that are concerned with ethics but "have not a supreme regard to God, and love to him." In all such schemes, Edwards pronounced peremptorily, "there is nothing of the nature of true virtue or religion in them." In other words, *True Virtue* exposes the vacuity of all theological or philosophical proposals that separate morality from its integral dependence on religion. In contrast, true virtue is "consent and union with being in general." This alone is "the primary and most essential beauty."[44]

College Presidency and Sudden Departure

At the end of 1757, the trustees of the College of New Jersey (at Princeton) invited Edwards to become the new president. When he wrote to accept their offer, he said he was planning to write his full version of the *History of the Work of Redemption*, a *Harmony of the Old and New Testament* (which would include messianic prophecies, types in the Old Testament, and the doctrinal harmony between the Testaments), and "many other things." At the beginning of 1758, he moved to Princeton and assumed office on February 16. But shortly thereafter smallpox broke out in a nearby town, the College trustees recommended vaccinations, and Edwards set an example by getting inoculated on February 23. Tragically, the serum was corrupted, and Edwards's throat became so swollen that he could not swallow the antidote he needed. On his deathbed, he asked his physician to tell his wife that their "uncommon union...as been of such a nature, as I trust is spiritual, and therefore will continue forever." He instructed that "as to my funeral...any additional sum of money that might be expected to be laid out that way, I would have it disposed of to charitable uses."[45]

Edwards died on March 22, 1758.

---

44. WJE 8:541, 560, 548.

45. Marsden, *Jonathan Edwards*, 494.

3
Edwards's Intellectual Context

NINETEENTH-CENTURY AND EARLY twentieth-century interpreters often viewed Edwards as a lonely thinker, islanded in the American colonies and cut off from the mainland of intellectual life in Great Britain and Continental Europe. Leslie Stephen colorfully compared Edwards to a German university professor who had been plopped down in the New England wilderness.[1] Yet during the last generation, a different picture emerged. Scholars today speak of a "Transatlantic Republic of Letters" during the early 1700s that brought the well-educated on both sides of the ocean into increasingly close contact and served as a signal and vanguard of the emerging Enlightenment movement. Norman Fiering's *Jonathan Edwards's Moral Thought and Its British Context* (1981) demonstrated the breadth and depth of Edwards's reading and knowledge of contemporary British and European authors. William Morris's *The Young Jonathan Edwards* (1991) traced the roots of Edwards's metaphysical ideas to such largely forgotten figures as Francis Burgersdijk and Adrian Heereboord—described as Dutch Calvinist Suaresian Aristotelian late scholastic logicians. Capping off decades of scholarship, Peter Thuesen's 2008 introduction to the final volume in the printed *Works of Jonathan Edwards* documented the hundreds of books that Edwards read, summarized, excerpted, expounded, and debated in his own writings.

Edwards's reading, as attested by Thuesen, included not only theological works by Puritan, Anglican, and Dissenting ministers, but also logical and metaphysical books, deistic and skeptical authors, works in history and geography, political writings, exegetical and biblical studies, scientific works, novels and other literary writings, books of poetry, works on comparative religions and cultures, and a few Jewish and Islamic sources as well. Thomas Johnson in a 1931 essay declared that Edwards's intellectual world was "tightly bound

---

1. Cited in David W. Bebbington, "Remembered Around the World: The International Scope of Edwards's Legacy," in David W. Kling and Douglas A. Sweeney, eds., *Jonathan Edwards at Home and Abroad: Historical Memories, Cultural Movements, Global Horizons* (Columbia, SC: University of South Carolina Press, 2003), 191.

by theological dogma." Yet Thuesen showed this judgment to have been mistaken. In an era when many books were theological in character, Edwards read widely in the non-theological works available to him. Moreover, he expanded and developed his own thinking on a range of topics through interacting with a wide spectrum of divergent theological and non-theological authors. To be sure, Edwards was well versed in Reformed scholasticism (i.e., Latin theological authors from the late 1500s through the early 1700s) as well as English authors from the 1600s representing what Cotton Mather called the "Good old Puritan Divinity." Yet Edwards was also conversant with a new style of literature, variously termed "polite," "catholick," or "latitudinarian," that was rapidly coming into vogue during his formative years. Peter Thuesen writes that "the fruitful tension between Enlightenment 'latitude' and Reformed traditionalism animated Edwards's entire career."[2]

An understanding of Edwards's ideas requires an understanding of his historical context. Conventional wisdom on the eighteenth century has involved a number of false dichotomies. One of these pits enlightenment (reason or science) against religion (faith or tradition). Edwin Gaustad some decades ago described the debates of Edwards's day as part of the age-old contest "between enlightenment and piety, between reason and faith.... On the one hand the forces of reason, clarity, humanism, logic, liberalism, naturalism are deployed. Against these time-honored stalwarts stand the ranks of revelation, mystery, theism, emotion, conservatism, supernaturalism, medievalism."[3] Yet it is important to note that many Enlightenment intellectuals were religious rather than anti-religious. Isaac Newton's manuscripts contained about as much biblical interpretation as natural philosophy. Early modern philosophy had few materialists—like Thomas Hobbes—and many more devout thinkers like Nicholas Malebranche, Ralph Cudworth, and Bishop George Berkeley, who all viewed philosophy as subservient to theology. Among biblical scholars, there were not only critical scholars like Baruch Spinoza but more orthodox authors

---

2. William Sparkes Morris, "The Genius of Jonathan Edwards," in Jerald C. Brauer, ed., *Reinterpretation in American Church History* (Chicago: University of Chicago, 1968), 29–65, citing 30. Peter J. Thuesen, "Editor's Introduction," in WJE 26:1–113 (citing 3). Prior to Thuesen, the only attempt to sound the range of Edwards's reading was Thomas H. Johnson, "Jonathan Edwards's Background of Reading," *Publications of the Colonial Society of Massachusetts* 28 (1931) 193–222 (citing 222). On Edwards's personal library as compared with others', see Thuesen in WJE 26:46. See also Norman Fiering, *Jonathan Edwards's Moral Thought and Its British Context* (Chapel Hill, NC: University of North Carolina, 1981); and William Sparkes Morris, *The Young Jonathan Edwards: A Reconstruction* (Brooklyn, NY: Carlson, 1991).

3. Edwin Scott Gaustad, *The Great Awakening in New England* (New York: Harper, 1957), 81.

such as Jean LeClerc, Matthew Poole, and Augustin Calmet.[4] Pious scholars hoped that their labors would promote an intellectual and spiritual purification of church, of politics, and of the academy. Reversing the usual stereotype, the devout Enlightenment often appealed to *reason* while the secular Enlightenment appealed to *tradition*. For example, the deist John Toland combined searching criticisms of traditional Christian beliefs with an interest in reviving Druidism—the religion of the pre-Christian Britons—and in Freemasonry—claiming roots among the ancient Egyptians.[5]

Another unhelpful dichotomy sets Roman Catholic scholasticism against Protestant biblicism. According to the stereotype, the early Protestants rejected the use of philosophy in theological reasoning and followed the letter of the Bible's teaching, while Catholics avidly embraced philosophy and fell into a rigid, deadening scholasticism that obscured the meaning of the Bible. Yet recent research shows this view to be deficient. Stephen A. Wilson writes: "An ever-increasing stream of new research in the Reformed tradition has sought to depict scholasticism as a common method of discourse categorically present in all continental theology curricula from the twelfth century to the eighteenth—whether Catholic, Lutheran, Reformed, Anglican or Dissenting—and thus presupposing no particular doctrinal content." Some now speak of "Calvinist Thomists" who used Aristotle's logic and Aquinas's moral teaching in Reformed theology, leading to a "subtle and mostly unacknowledged rapprochement between Protestants and Catholics on...Christian ethics."[6] Adriaan Neele has shown that Reformed scholastics like Petrus van Mastricht understood theology in affective and practical terms, as an art or science of "living to God through Christ."[7] Within their volumes of Latin prose, scholastic authors showed a keen interest in practical and experiential applications of their theological ideas.

---

4. For historical background to early modern biblical scholarship, see the excellent work by Robert E. Brown, *Jonathan Edwards and the Bible* (Bloomington, IN: Indiana University Press, 2002).

5. Gerald R. McDermott, *Jonathan Edwards Confronts the Gods: Christian Theology, Enlightenment Religion, and Non-Christian Faiths* (New York: Oxford University Press, 2000), 26.

6. Stephen A. Wilson, *Virtue Reformed: Rereading Jonathan Edwards's Ethics* (Leiden; Brill, 2005) 17–18, citing John Patrick Donnelly, S.J., "Calvinist Thomism," *Viator* 7 (1976): 441. Especially important for Reformed scholasticism has been the indefatigable work of Richard A. Muller, including *After Calvin: Studies in the Development of a Theological Tradition* (New York: Oxford University Press, 2003) and *Post-Reformation Reformed Dogmatics: The Rise and Development of Reformed Orthodoxy*, ca. 1520–1725, 4 vols. (Grand Rapids, MI: Baker Academic, 2003). See also Willem J. Asselt and Eer Dekker, eds., *Reformation and Scholasticism: An Ecumenical Enterprise* (Grand Rapids, MI: Baker Academic, 2001) and Adriaan C. Neele, *Petrus van Mastricht (1630–1706); Reformed Orthodoxy: Method and Piety* (Leiden: Brill, 2009).

7. Neele, *Petrus van Mastricht*, 95–96.

A third dichotomy places British empiricism against Continental rationalism. The perception of two opposing philosophical traditions goes back to Francis Bacon, who wrote of a "Rational School of philosophers" that "corrupted natural philosophy by... logic: fashioning the world out of categories."[8] Bacon compared the empirical method of learning through observation to the bumblebee that gathers honey from flower to flower, and the rational method to the spider that spins a web from its own belly. While Continental and British philosophers have differed—and still do differ—in intellectual temper, one can only maintain a complete dichotomy between the two by isolating some British thinkers (Francis Bacon, John Locke, and David Hume) from other British thinkers who showed resemblances to their Continental peers (the Cambridge Platonists and George Berkeley). The late 1600s witnessed not only an advancement of empirical science in Britain but also a major resurgence in Platonic and Neoplatonic philosophy at Cambridge University—the very institution that produced such natural philosophers as Isaac Newton. A strict dichotomy between British empiricism and Continental rationalism does not hold up.

In summary, then, the formative period of Jonathan Edwards's life was an era of rapidly changing cultures, competing philosophical systems, international exchanges of ideas, and vehement debates between traditionalists and innovators in the fields of literature, politics, and religion. It was a complex, variegated age, not reducible to easy dichotomies or simplistic contrasts—an era more like our own than we might at first recognize.

The Seventeenth-Century Puritan and Scholastic Background

The Puritans might be described as the marching wing of the Church of England.[9] They had rejected the fixed forms and practices of traditional Catholicism in favor of a freer, less structured form of faith and worship, and a set of beliefs and practices that they believed were based on the Bible rather than human traditions. John Calvin had referred to the fallen human mind as a

---

8. Francis Bacon, *New Organon*, Book I, Aphorisms 52–53.

9. The following paragraphs are indebted to David D. Hall, "The New England Background," in Stephen J. Stein, ed., *The Cambridge Companion to Jonathan Edwards* (Cambridge, UK: Cambridge University Press, 2007), 61–79; Harry S. Stout, "The Puritans and Edwards," in Nathan O. Hatch and Harry S. Stout, eds., *Jonathan Edwards and the American Experience* (New York: Oxford University Press, 1988), 142–59; and Miklos Vetö, *Le pensée de Jonathan Edwards* (Paris: Cerf, 1987), 1–8.

"factory of idols" and of "lying imaginations."[10] Taking this to heart, the Puritans of the late 1500s and 1600s sought to purify the English church and their own lives of sin and corruption through a strict adherence to God's Word. Some contemporary observers, on encountering the anti-traditionalism of the Puritans, believed that they were a lawless and dangerous sect that threatened the political and religious order. While the Puritans challenged the religious status quo in England, the majority were hardly undisciplined or antinomian. If anything, they tended in the opposite direction. In their zeal to glorify God, they used severe discipline within their communities to enforce strict conformity to all of God's "ordinances." Thomas Cartwright went so far as to say that submission to the church's ecclesial discipline was a condition of salvation.[11] Speaking broadly, there was a two-fold focus in Puritanism—an inward stress on the cultivation of a God-pleasing spiritual life, and an outward stress on the reform of church structures and of society itself to conform to God's purposes. With their sense of a religious purpose and destiny, the Puritans viewed themselves as a "chosen people"—like the ancient Israelites. They sought to achieve in New England something that they believed had not been accomplished in the rest of Christendom since the time of the Protestant Reformation.

The Puritans understood the church as "a company of People combined together by holy Covenant with God, and one with another."[12] The implication was that being a Christian involved far more than being baptized or casually attending worship. All of one's life was to be submitted to God's will and to a community of people who followed God together. The word "covenant" captured multiple aspects of the Puritan vision—God's eternal purpose to save humanity from sin ("the covenant of redemption"), the special bond that God maintained with the New England colonies that committed themselves to God's work ("the national covenant"), the mutual agreement among a local gathering of believers to walk in God's ways ("the church covenant"), and finally the individual choice and decision to commit oneself to God ("owning the covenant"). From the Puritan standpoint, the false teachings, hypocritical practices, and empty ceremonies of the Catholic and Anglican churches had

---

10. John Calvin, *Institutes of the Christian Religion*, I.11.8, I.5.11.

11. In an early *Miscellanies* entry (from 1722–23), Edwards argues that "excommunication has great influence on the favor of God thus, because it is a great and dreadful sin to be justly excommunicated" (WJE 13:171).

12. Perry Miller, *The New England Mind: The Seventeenth Century* (Cambridge, MA: Harvard University Press, 1982 [1939]), 435.

forced them to establish new and distinctive communities. The struggles and sufferings of the 1630s and 1640s imprinted themselves on Puritan memories for generations. Any attempt to establish governance by bishops in the American churches revived the odious memory of King Charles I and Archbishop Laud. "Let all mankind know," wrote Cotton Mather in 1702, "that we came into the Wilderness, because we would worship God without that Episcopacy, that Common Prayer, and those unwarrantable Ceremonies, with which the Land of our Fore Fathers' Sepulchres has been defiled; we came hither because we would have our Posterity settled under the pure and full Dispensations of the Gospel; defended by Rulers, that should be of our selves."[13]

The New England Congregationalists defined the visible church solely in terms of local assemblies, and therefore they refused to recognize any binding authority in ecclesial structures of a larger, trans-local character (e.g., synods, councils, bishops, archbishops, popes). On their view, it was the local assemblies that had received directly from Christ the full power to exercise authority in all matters of church life, sacraments, and jurisdiction.[14] The Anglicans had erred in founding the local assembly or congregation not as a fellowship of common belief and confession but on the basis of geographical criteria (i.e., the local parish church) and on historical grounds (i.e., a succession of episcopal leadership). Early New England's defining document—*The Cambridge Platform* (1648)—defined the members of the Congregational churches as "saints by calling" who "walk in blameles [sic] obedience to the word" and are "Visible, in respect of the profession of their faith."[15]

This stress on churches composed of "visible saints" raised many questions as to how, when, and where each person was to demonstrate the genuineness of his or her profession of faith, and who exactly was to make this determination. From the mid-1600s into the mid-1700s, the Congregational churches struggled with issues of church membership. During the 1630s,

---

13. Cotton Mather, *Magnalia Christi Americana* (London: Thomas Parkhurst, 1702), Bk. 3, p. 6; cited in Edward M. Griffin, *Old Brick: Charles Chauncy of Boston, 1705–1787* (Minneapolis, MN: University of Minnesota Press, 1980), 127 (partially italicized in the original).

14. By the late 1600s and early 1700s—and especially in Connecticut, under *The Saybrook Platform* (1708)—ministers' associations and synods took on some measure of authority. Some have called this "Presbygationalism" (i.e., a cross between the Congregational and the Presbyterian systems of church governance), which modified the pure system of local and Congregational governance.

15. *The Cambridge Platform* (1648), chs. 2–3; in Williston Walker, *The Creeds and Platforms of Congregationalism* (New York: Pilgrim Press, 1991 [1893]), 204–205.

FIGURE 3.1 The eighteenth-century New England population was concentrated in the coastal region and in the Connecticut River Valley, where Edwards spent most of his lifetime (Thomas Jefferys, *A map of the most inhabited part of New England; containing the provinces of Massachusets Bay and New Hampshire, with the colonies of Konektikut and Rhode Island, divided into counties and townships: The whole composed from actual surveys and its situation adjusted by astronomical observations* [London: 1755]. Library of Congress, Geography and Map Division).

churches in New England began to require members to give not merely a generalized profession of faith but a specific recounting (known as a "relation") regarding their personal experiences of God's work in their soul.[16] This

---

16. *The Cambridge Platform*, ch. 12, stated that "a personall & publick confession, & declaring of Gods manner of working upon the soul, is both lawfull, expedient, & usefull" (Walker, *Creeds*, 223).

was a higher standard for membership than was customary at the time in England or in Europe—even among stricter Protestants. Only full adult members, moreover, had the right to bring their children for baptism. Yet the New England leaders who set these stringent membership requirements also insisted that it was only God who certainly knew whom he had predestined for salvation. Churches had to exercise a "judgment of charity" with regard to people's profession of faith. *The Cambridge Platform* recognized that a church seeking to restrict itself to "visible saints" would inevitably contain some who were "unsound & hypocrites inwardly." For only God knew the heart.[17] Yet, so far as possible, these churches sought to exclude from membership those who did not meet the test as "visible saints."

When many New Englanders shrank from making a public "relation" of faith—and their numbers swelled over the decades—the Congregational churches came to a crisis. Would they maintain their membership standards in their original strictness or would they relax them? And what if the number of professing church members shrank to an ever smaller segment of the population? Clearly the religious mission of New England was at stake. The so-called Half-Way Covenant (1662) extended infant baptism so that it was available not only to the children of parents who were baptized and *professing* but also to the children of parents who were baptized yet *unprofessing*. This decision made baptism a kind of hereditary birthright in families with early New England roots. Despite controversy, most congregations eventually made their peace with the "half-way" approach, which required a double-booking system to take account of full members and half members in each congregation. Further controversy erupted after the publication of Solomon Stoddard's *The Doctrine of Instituted Churches Explained* (1700), which affirmed the notion of national churches, denied the necessity of church covenants, and allowed the admission of unconverted persons to the Lord's Supper. For Stoddard, the Lord's Supper could function as a "converting ordinance."[18] These early debates over church membership and admission to the sacraments were part of the background to the later communion controversy in Northampton and to

---

17. *The Cambridge Platform* (ch. 3), in Walker, *Creeds*, 206. See Edmund Morgan, *Visible Saints* (Ithaca, NY: Cornell University Press, 1974), 57ff. On early seventeenth-century Puritanism, see Theodore Dwight Bozeman, *The Precisianist Strain: Disciplinary Religion and Antinomian Backlash in Puritanism to 1638* (Chapel Hill, NC: University of North Carolina Press, 2004).

18. On the Half-Way Covenant and the controversy over "Stoddardeanism," see Walker, *Creeds*, 238–87, and Philip F. Gura, "Solomon Stoddard's Irreverent Way," *Early American Literature* 21 (1986): 29–43.

Edwards's eventual dismissal from his pastorate there in 1750. It is noteworthy that Edwards's father, Timothy Edwards, contended with his congregation during the 1730s over his stringency in admission to baptism and the Lord's Supper.[19]

For the first generations of colonists, New England was "the marvel of modern times" and its inhabitants were pioneers in the army of Jesus Christ. God was closely following all the vicissitudes of his people, and was sending them signs and warnings from day to day and year to year. No other people on earth, said Increase Mather, had God speaking to them in such a way.[20] The Reforming Synod (1679) asked where in the world there had been any people raised to such a level of importance in so brief a time. God had a "special relation" with New England and "his name ... is written upon us with large letters from the beginning." This special relationship also meant that God expected more of New England than of other lands.

This self-identification as God's chosen people also allowed the New Englanders to identify their enemies as enemies of God. Prior to their arrival, the American desert had been a realm of darkness. Their enemies were the king of France, the Pope, and the Devil. The victory of the British forces over the French at Cape Breton in 1745 showed the harmony between prayer and military success. Thomas Prince stated that this victory foreshadowed the spread of the kingdom of God from the Atlantic to the Pacific Oceans, and from the rivers of Canada southward. During this period an eschatological vision of the American Continent began to take shape. America would have not only a brilliant secular future but would function as a mission base for the evangelization of the world. Some said that America might become the seat of God's earthly kingdom. Yet from the early 1600s to the later 1700s, most regarded

---

19. On the complex topic of Edwards's dismissal, one may sample a variety of views in David D. Hall, WJE 12:17–85; Patricia Tracy, *Jonathan Edwards, Pastor: Religion and Society in Eighteenth-Century Northampton* (New York: Hill and Wang, 1980), 147–94; Iain H. Murray, *Jonathan Edwards: A New Biography* (Edinburgh: Banner of Truth Trust, 1987), 313–49 and George Marsden, *Jonathan Edwards: A Life* (New Haven, CT: Yale University Press, 2003), 341–74. In Timothy Edwards's case, the dispute in part centered on the minister's powers vis-à-vis those of the congregation members—an ambiguous point in the New England system of church governance. See Kenneth P. Minkema, "The Edwardses: A Ministerial Family in Eighteenth-Century New England" (PhD diss., University of Connecticut, 1988), 108–47.

20. On the American Puritans' providentialist worldview, see the excellent work by David D. Hall, *Worlds of Wonder, Days of Judgment: Popular Religious Belief in Early New England* (New York: Knopf, 1989).

secular prosperity as secondary to fulfillment of the nation's spiritual mission.[21]

The Changing Climate of the Late 1600s and Early 1700s

Toward the end of the 1600s and the beginning of the 1700s, the New England colonies underwent a complex cultural shift that Henry F. May described as "the Moderate Enlightenment" and Harry S. Stout referred to as "anglicization."[22] A growing liberalism muted the shriller notes of the older Calvinism. The new attitude toward religion was characterized by moderation and the avoidance of extremes—a "reasonable religion." In large part this change occurred as American colonials began to take their cultural cues from the other side of the Atlantic, and especially the "polite" literature coming out of post-Restoration Britain. During this era, the writings of Samuel Clarke, Lord Shaftesbury, and Francis Hutcheson were supplanting the older Puritan theology at Harvard and Yale Colleges. The early eighteenth century was the age of Isaac Newton in natural science, John Locke in philosophy, Joseph Addison in literature, and Archbishop John Tillotson in ecclesiastical life. These luminaries stirred excitement among educated New Englanders, who could not "resist English influence in dress, speech, literary style, or architecture." Stout concluded that "for New England elites, England supplied standards of urbanity, sophistication, and broad-mindedness to be emulated." There were multiple reasons for anglicization. Among these were the presence of ruling officials from abroad, the English laws of toleration, increased transatlantic trade, heightened military cooperation between the mother country and the colonies, and the growing dissemination of English literature in America. The English influence was especially strong among the educated and mercantile elites in

---

21. Edward Johnson, *Johnson's Wonder-Working Providence* (New York: Scribner's 1910), 71, 60; Increase Mather, *The Times of Men* (Boston: Printed by John Foster, 1675); cited in Sacvan Bercovitch, *The Puritan Origins of the American Self* (New Haven, CT: Yale University Press, 1975), 51; Walker, *Creeds*, 424; Perry Miller and Thomas H. Johnson, *The Puritans*, 2 vols. (New York: Harper & Row, 1963), 1:245; Alan Heimert, *Religion and the American Mind* (Cambridge, MA: Harvard University Press, 1966), 86, 84, 82, 395; James Davidson, *The Logic of Millennial Thought* (New Haven, CT: Yale University Press), 127, 67; all cited in Vetö, *Le pensée*, 7–8.

22. Henry F. May, *The Enlightenment in America* (New York: Oxford University Press, 1976), 3–101; Harry S. Stout, *The New England Soul: Preaching and Religious Culture in Colonial New England* (New York: Oxford University Press, 1986), 127–47, 222–28. Stout drew on the earlier work of John M. Murrin, "Anglicizing an American Colony: The Transformation of Provincial Massachusetts," PhD diss., Yale University, 1966.

coastal cities, and it reshaped the institutions of law and government to conform to English standards.²³

On the other hand, the older New Englanders' sense of being a "covenant people" did not disappear. The doctrine of the covenant had given to New Englanders a sense of common purpose and corporate identity, and thus set them apart from other nations. Congregational liberals in Boston sought to enjoy the best of both worlds—the glittering fashions of London and the religious mission given them by God. The first two generations had grown up believing that their Congregationalism was a sacred trust—an idea memorialized in Cotton Mathers's massive *Magnalia Christi Americana* (1702). Yet by the early eighteenth century, a softening had occurred. Most had adopted a more ecumenical attitude and no longer viewed Congregationalism as the only valid pattern for the church. This does not mean that the New Englanders had become secular or had rejected what Cotton Mather famously called the "errand into the wilderness." Instead it meant that they sought to retain and hold onto a sense of religious mission in a rapidly shifting cultural and political context. Their stress was less on particular forms of church government than on personal devotion and morality. Terms like "piety," "virtue," and "union" were more widely used and were applied to non-Congregational Protestants. Cotton Mather called for a united Protestant front that was defined in terms of a zeal for good deeds or well-doing: "Let no man pretend unto the name of a Christian, who does not approve the proposal of a perpetual endeavor to do good in the world."²⁴

Yet others went further than Mather did in changing with the times. Chief among the innovators were the anti-Mather Boston ministers led by Harvard tutor (and later president) John Leverett, Cambridge pastor William Brattle, and his merchant brother, Thomas Brattle. They adhered to Calvinism in broad terms and yet showed a "catholick spirit" that drew deeply from Anglicanism as well as Presbyterianism. In 1699, they installed Benjamin Colman as their pastor, who abandoned the traditional tests for saving grace for full membership and opened communion to all. The worship services were anglicized by including scripture readings without commentary and recitations of the Lord's Prayer. While most other churches did not adopt its practices, the Brattle Street Church exerted widespread influence in Boston.²⁵

---

23. Stout, *New England Soul*, 127–28.

24. Stout, *New England Soul*, 127–29; citing Cotton Mather, *Bonifacius: An Essay Upon the Good*; ed. David Levin (Cambridge, MA: Belknap Press, 1966) 18–19.

25. See John Corrigan, *The Prism of Piety: Catholick Congregational Clergy at the Beginning of the Enlightenment* (New York: Oxford University Press, 1991).

Changes came to Harvard College as well. Leverett was the first and only non-minister president of the college before the nineteenth century. The ministerial students, though numerous, were no longer the hub of the school, but studied alongside future judges, merchants, magistrates, and royal officers, who came to Harvard not to be trained as ministers but to made into gentlemen. Harvard students began absorbing what later historians called the Whig view of history—a narrative focused on the struggle for individual liberties, often in opposition to kings and aristocrats. Bequests of books by Thomas Hollis to Harvard's library and Jeremiah Dummer to Yale brought contemporary English writers to the attention of the students. Literary works such as Joseph Addison's *Pleasures of the Imagination* (1707) encouraged students to venture into the realm of *belles letters*. Even Cotton Mather wrote a set of *Political Fables*—on the rival political factions in Boston—that strove for "wit and urbanity" and "deliberately sought...to bring the manners of London to solid Boston." A new generation of tolerant Anglican authors were read and appreciated for their style as much as their substance. None was more widely read and admired than Archbishop Tillotson. Almost every surviving student library inventory included his works. To express a sense of the vastness and order of the cosmos, preachers like Tillotson adopted a new rhetoric and aesthetic, stressing such terms as "stupendous," "sublime," and "unlimited." Epithets for God only rarely used before began to be more common, such as "Almighty Being," "Great Governor," and "Supreme Architect." This cosmic deity was said to "smile" or "frown" upon his creation, overseeing its operations according to a flawless design that conformed to natural law.[26]

The Spectrum of Heterodoxy—Socinianism, Arianism, Deism, and Arminianism

The theological opinions of the 1700s should not be reduced to a simple dyad of Benjamin Franklin's deism and Jonathan Edwards's evangelicalism. Instead there was a spectrum of views. The forms of heterodoxy

---

26. Stout, *New England Soul*, 130–33, 345 n.14, 345 n.16; citing Miller, *The New England Mind: From Colony to Province* (Boston: Beacon Press, 1961), 170. See Norman Fiering, "Transatlantic Republic of Letters: A Note on the Circulation of Learned Periodicals to Early Eighteenth-Century America," *William and Mary Quarterly* 33 (1976): 642–60; and Fiering, "The First American Enlightenment: Tillotson, Leverett, and Philosophical Anglicanism," *New England Quarterly* 44 (1981): 307–44.

were manifold—Socinian (from the late 1500s), Arminian (from the early 1600s), Latitudinarian (from the mid-1600s), deist (from the late 1600s), and Arian (an ancient term, revived in the early 1700s). From the standpoint of orthodox Calvinism, each of these terms referred to a particular departure from biblical and theological truth. Yet the terms—in times past and more recently—have been used in conflicting ways and often with overlapping meanings.

The Socinians were named after the Italian jurist Faustus Socinus (Sozzini), who subjected Christian teachings to a searching rational critique. Rejecting the doctrine of Jesus' atoning death, the Socinians by the early 1600s had already moved away from belief in Jesus' divinity and the doctrine of the Trinity. The Socinians thus were forerunners of the Unitarians in Britain, America, and elsewhere. In the eyes of their critics, the Socinians had made Jesus into a mere man. By the early 1700s, a group of leading English intellectuals—including Samuel Clarke, William Whiston, and Isaac Newton—affirmed a Son of God who had exalted and god-like status and yet neither existed eternally nor shared full ontological equality with God the Father. Their position was close to that of the fourth-century Arians. Technically, these Arians were not Socinians, and yet they, like the Socinians, were non-Trinitarian. Some Anglican leaders of the era—e.g., Bishop Benjamin Hoadly—may have held Arian views of Christ.[27]

The term "deist" had a wide application, and scholars have frequently disputed the definition of the term.[28] Perhaps it would be best to speak of "deisms," since John Toland's deism was not that of Anthony Collins, Benjamin Franklin, Voltaire, Thomas Paine, or Thomas Jefferson. Despite family resemblances, their views diverged significantly.[29] Some deists—like Toland, Thomas Chubb, and the Earl of Shaftesbury—doubted the immortality of

---

27. See Maurice Wiles, "The Rise and Fall of British Arianism," in *Archetypal Heresy: Arianism Through the Centuries* (Oxford, UK: Clarendon Press, 1996), 62–164; and Thomas C. Pfizenmaier, *The Trinitarian Theology of Dr. Samuel Clarke (1675–1729): Context, Sources, and Controversy* (Leiden: Brill, 1997). On Socinianism, see Klaus Scholder, *The Birth of Modern Critical Theology* (London: SCM Press, 1990), 26–45; and H. John McLachlan, *Socinianism in Seventeenth-Century New England* (London: Oxford University Press, 1951).

28. The following paragraphs summarize Gerald R. McDermott, *Jonathan Edwards Confronts the Gods: Christian Theology, Enlightenment Religion, and Non-Christian Faiths* (New York: Oxford University Press, 2000), 17–33.

29. Paul Hazard writes: "There was not one deism, but several, all different, all mutually opposed, and even at daggers drawn with one another" (*European Thought in the Eighteenth Century: From Montesquieu to Lessing*; New Haven, CT: Yale University Press, 1954), 393. See also "The Definition of Deism," in Roland N. Stromberg, *Religious Liberalism in Eighteenth-Century England* (Oxford, UK: Oxford University Press, 1954), 52–69.

the soul, but others, like Charles Blount and William Wollaston, considered this essential. Matthew Tindal thought that rewards and punishments in a future life were fundamental to faith, while Lord Bolingbroke regarded them as dubious. Most deists believed that moral principles could be derived from abstract reasoning, but Shaftesbury and Bolingbroke scoffed at this notion. Shaftesbury and Tindal held that people were innately benevolent, while Bolingbroke was just as convinced that they were controlled by self-interest. Toland was a materialist while Tindal and most other deists believed in a soul. Most deists believed in human free will, though Collins denied it. It is not surprising then that some refer to the "elusiveness of deism" and regarded the word as a label of convenience rather than a precise term of analysis.[30] According to one interpretation, the decline of the deists' influence was due to this very diversity and the conspicuous failure to arrive at a consensus in identifying the "rational" or "self-evident" principles of religion.[31]

Beginning in the 1690s, the deists began by defending the pre-eminence of Christianity on the grounds that it alone was "reasonable" and so corresponded to the true nature of religion. Yet soon the deists became aware that their views were diverging from historic, traditional Christian beliefs, and so the deists transformed themselves into the champions of a natural rather than revealed religion.[32] As Christian insiders who gradually became outsiders, the deists shared many of the same principles and presuppositions as their orthodox colleagues, and this made it difficult for the latter to differentiate themselves from the deists and to oppose them.

The deists reflected a broad tendency—shared by orthodox writers of the era—toward a moralizing or ethicizing of Christianity. Many intellectuals presumed that religion existed to promote good behavior. The Earl of Shaftesbury wrote that "the end of religion is to render us more perfect and more accomplished in all moral duties and performances." Ben Franklin commented that the problem with doctrinal sermons is that they made their hearers good Presbyterians rather than good citizens. Some deists held that Christian teachings had value in enforcing morality even if the teachings, taken literally, were false. When Anthony Collins was asked why he sent his household servants to church, when he did not attend himself, he replied: "I do it that they may

---

30. Robert E. Sullivan, *John Toland and the Deist Controversy* (Cambridge, MA: Harvard University Press, 1982), 205–34.

31. Paul Ramsey, "Editor's Introduction," in WJE 1:67–68.

32. J. K. S. Reid, *Christian Apologetics* (Grand Rapids, MI: Eerdmans, 1969), 147.

neither rob nor murder me."³³ A Massachusetts sermon—Lemuel Briant's *The Absurdity and Blasphemy of Depreciating Moral Virtue* (1749)—stirred controversy by asserting that the "true Sense of Revelation" and "perfect Religion of Jesus" was nothing other than a "refined System of Morality." For Briant, human happiness depended on "good Behaviour."³⁴ Contributing to the ethicizing of Christianity was a new humanitarian philosophy that asserted that human nature was marked by an essential benevolence or good will. Francis Hutcheson replaced the egoistic reading of human nature in Thomas Hobbes and Bernard Mandeville with an altruistic interpretation.³⁵ This theory of intrinsic benevolence contradicted Calvinistic notions of depravity, and Edwards challenged Hutcheson's theory in *The Nature of True Virtue*.

Most deists believed that it was possible to start with abstract reasoning and on this basis to draw inferences regarding what doctrines were or were not compatible with the goodness or justice of God. All deists rejected the doctrine of original sin and held that God would be unjust if he allowed the transgression of one man—Adam—to bring condemnation on his posterity. They had no place for a mediator or sin-bearer, and thus they rejected the notion of atonement. Thomas Chubb and others held that God granted forgiveness on the basis of repentance and good deeds. Miracles were another Christian tenet that deists rejected, as Matthew Tindal remarked: "Miracles [are] for fools and reasons for wise men." The deists were even more hostile to traditional Judaism than to traditional Christianity. Anthony Collins called the Jews an "illiterate, Barbarous and Ridiculous People."³⁶ Underlying the deists' negative attitude toward both Judaism and Christianity was the so-called scandal of particularity—the notion that God revealed himself to particular peoples at particular times and not to all human beings and from the very beginning of history.³⁷ It was unreasonable,

---

33. Anthony Ashley Cooper [Third Earl of Shaftesbury], *Characteristic of Men, Manners, Opinions, Times*, ed. Lawrence E. Klein, Cambridge Texts in the History of Philosophy (Cambridge, UK: Cambridge University Press, 1999), 196; Benjamin Franklin, *Autobiography and Selections from Other Writings* (New Haven, CT: Yale University Press, 1964), 147; and Anthony Collins, as quoted in Mark Pattison, "Tendencies of Religious Thought in England, 1688–1750," in *Essays and Reviews*, 8th ed. (London: Longman, Green, 1861), 274.

34. Alan Heimert and Perry Miller, eds., *The Great Awakening: Documents Illustrating the Crisis and Its Consequences* (Indianapolis, IN: Bobbs-Merrill, 1967), 542.

35. See Norman Fiering, "Irresistible Compassion," *Journal of the History of Ideas* 37 (1976): 195–218.

36. Matthew Tindal, *Christianity as Old as the Creation* (London, 1730), 192; Anthony Collins, *A Discourse on Freethinking* (London, 1713), 121, cited in McDermott, *Jonathan Edwards Confront the Gods*, 27.

37. Historical responses to the scandal of particularity are recounted in Bruce Marshall, *Christology in Conflict: The Identity of a Savior in Rahner and Barth* (Oxford, UK: Blackwell, 1987), 1–14.

deists held, for God to act in arbitrary fashion by playing favorites with one group of people over another. The purported arbitrariness of special revelation drove deists away from traditional views regarding the Old and New Testaments, the person of Jesus Christ, and salvation through faith in Christ.

Closer to the viewpoint of the Calvinists was the position known as Arminianism, named after Jacob Arminius, the Dutch theologian who led the Remonstrants (i.e., protesters) in opposing the strict form of Calvinism embodied in the so-called Five Points of the Synod of Dordt (1618–19).[38] Arminianism was not deism. While deists denied the reality of miracles, Arminians affirmed the miracles and saw them as confirming the truth of Christianity. Yet Arminians did not see eye to eye with Calvinists. In the eighteenth-century American context, "Arminianism" was not used strictly to denote Arminius's followers but became a catch-all designation for a variety of departures from strict, five-point Calvinism.

In effect, the Arminians softened the sharp antitheses of Calvinist thought. Where the Calvinists set forth a stark, unqualified assertion—e.g., human beings apart from grace can do *nothing* to turn themselves toward salvation— the Arminians offered a qualified position that human beings can do *very little* to prepare themselves for salvation. Arminians held that Christ died for all humanity, that divine predestination hinged on God's foreknowledge of human faith or obedience, that human beings were not entirely depraved, and that it was possible for those once saved to fall away permanently and thus lose their eternal salvation. From the time that John Wesley preached his controversial sermon, "Free Grace" (1740), Arminianism—which had earlier been associated with a milder sort of theological rationalism—now became associated with New Light and pro-revival sentiments and thus "evangelical Arminianism" took its birth among the Wesleyans. Some argue that Arminianism—at least its eighteenth-century version—was not so much a form of anti-Calvinism as it was a variant of Calvinism. Yet from a strict or "five-point" Calvinist position, any affirmation of a natural human ability to believe, obey, or turn toward God, apart from special grace, weakened the foundation and threatened the entire edifice of Calvinist theology.[39] What is more, strict Calvinists thought of Arminianism as a halfway house on the way to deism.

---

38. The five points were: (1) total depravity, (2) unconditional election, (3) limited atonement, (4) irresistible (or efficacious) grace, and (5) perseverance in grace. Edwards touches on all five in *Freedom of the Will* (WJE 1:430–39).

39. See Roger Olsen, *Arminian Theology; Myths and Realities* (Downers Grove, IL: InterVarsity Press, 2006). Wesley's Arminianism differed from the characteristic versions of Arminianism in the seventeenth-century Netherlands and eighteenth-century New England by not,

Students of Edwards generally consider Arminianism to have been his principal nemesis, and not without reason. Prior to the time of the American Revolution, there were far more Arminians than deists in New England, and such works as *Freedom of the Will* (1754) and *Original Sin* (1758) were explicitly directed against Arminianism.[40] Yet Edwards followed with keen interest the various forms of heterodoxy in England. No less than one quarter of the roughly 1,400 entries in the *Miscellanies* dealt with deism. While Edwards evidently wanted to refute both Arminianism and deism, his arguments against deism were largely confined to the unpublished *Miscellanies*, and the arguments against Arminianism were conspicuous in such published works as *Freedom of the Will* and *Original Sin*.

Did Arminianism Exist in Eighteenth-Century New England?

Scholars have debated the extent of Arminianism and deism among the clergy and laity of New England during the 1700s. In general, one can say that overt deistic views did not appear in North American publications until almost a century later than they did in England—that is, during the 1790s rather than the 1690s.[41] Regarding Arminianism, one author referred to its supposed existence in eighteenth-century New England as a "myth."[42] Others have seen the use of

---

strictly speaking, affirming a "natural ability" to turn to God but only what Wesley called a "gracious ability." The human will could not choose good apart from grace, said Wesley, and yet there was a "prevenient grace" that came to all people universally (and not only to some, as Calvinists said) and gave them freedom to choose good.

40. Not all of Edwards's intellectual antagonists in *Freedom of the Will* and *Original Sin* were Arminian, but the *views* he sought there to refute were Arminian. Among the authors whom Edwards refuted in *Freedom of the Will* was Thomas Chubb—properly classified as a deist rather than an Arminian. Yet Edwards's argument there engages Chubb's theory of the human will, not his specifically deist teachings. Likewise, John Taylor, whose *Scripture Doctrine of Original Sin* (1740) was a key factor in provoking Edwards's *Original Sin*, has been classified as a Socinian or early Unitarian and not as an Arminian (Clyde Holbrook, "Editor's Introduction," in WJE 3:69–70). With regard to the doctrine of original sin, John Wesley concurred with Edwards in opposing Taylor and even in writing his own extensive treatise against Taylor see *The Works of John Wesley*, 14 vols. [London: Wesleyan Book Room, 1872], 9:191–465).

41. Anti-Calvinist and Arminian views appeared among Cambridge Platonists and Latitudinarians in the mid-1600s, while American "Arminianism" did not appear until the early to mid-1700s. British anti-Trinitarianism became conspicuous soon after 1700, while in New England it appeared in the debates over the election of Henry Ware to the Harvard College faculty in 1805. And as noted, overt deism was not expressed in the American context until the time of Ethan Allen and Thomas Paine—about a century after such views were publicly aired in England. In several respects, then, there was a century-long time lag in doctrinal developments.

42. Gerald J. Goodwin, "The Myth of 'Arminian-Calvinism' in Eighteenth-Century New England," *New England Quarterly* 41 (1968): 213–37.

the term "Arminian" as an overreaction. Strict Calvinists, it is said, responded to tiny departures from orthodoxy with the slur word "Arminian." Nonetheless, there are good reasons to think that internal theological shifts were already taking place in Congregational Calvinist circles during the early 1700s.

A first consideration is the so-called Great Apostasy at Yale College in 1723, in which the college rector or president—Timothy Cutler—shocked the community by leaving Congregationalism for Anglicanism. While the theological issues in dispute related principally to church governance, the move into Anglicanism for Cutler and others involved an embrace of Arminian teachings on salvation as well.[43] Some years after this, Edwards's first publication, "God Glorified in Man's Dependence" (1731), offered a strong anti-Arminian argument. Reading between the lines of the sermon—as Perry Miller did—one may see it as a manifesto for a renewal of Calvinism.[44] By 1737, Edwards wrote of the "great noise that was in this part of the country about Arminianism, which seemed to appear with a very threatening aspect upon the interest of religion here. The friends of vital piety trembled for fear of the issue."[45] These words had reference to the Robert Breck affair of 1733–34, involving a young man who was blocked from a Boston-area pulpit and later ordained by a congregation in Springfield, Massachusetts, over the objections of a ministers' association that included Edwards. Up to ten different witnesses—by Edwards's accounting—attested to Breck's having made unorthodox statements to the effect that God would not condemn those who had not heard of Christ, that people could be saved by virtue alone and without faith, that some passages in the Bible were corrupt, and that the teaching of predestination discouraged people from doing their duty.[46]

In the aftermath of the Great Awakening of 1740–41, Old Light opposition to evangelical revivals solidified, as did a self-conscious Arminian perspective among many in the same Old Light party. The revivals had thus the unintended effect of bringing permanent polarization between evangelical and

---

43. See Marsden, *Jonathan Edwards*, 83–84. Cutler's shocking act at the Yale College commencement was to utter the phrase, "and let all the people say, amen." Yet for Puritans who had long struggled against Anglican dominance, it was as though—in Marsden's phrase—a commencement speaker at a Baptist university had concluded with a prayer to the Blessed Virgin.

44. "God Glorified" in WJE 17:196–216; analyzed in Perry Miller, *Jonathan Edwards* (New York: William Sloane, 1949), 3–34.

45. WJE 4:148.

46. See David Hall in WJE 12:6; Marsden, *Jonathan Edwards*, 176–77, 543 n.15; and Edwards in WJE 12:157–59.

liberal clergy. Liberal views were especially strong in eastern Massachusetts, where within a few decades the Unitarian movement would find its stronghold.[47] An early expression of the emerging religious liberalism—Lemuel Briant's *The Absurdity and Blasphemy of Depreciating Moral Virtue* (1749)—stirred a storm of protest. Briant was not removed from office, and yet he resigned his pastorate under harsh criticism and died only a year later, a martyr to the Arminian cause. The Old Light Calvinist Samuel Niles—who prior to Briant's sermon had denied the existence of Arminianism in New England—issued a rebuttal to Briant that sought to "reject all Pretenses of Justification in God's sight by our Moral virtues." Another of the liberal clergy, Ebenezer Gay, argued in *Natural Religion as Distinguished From Revealed* (1759) that human beings were "naturally disposed toward Religion," just as the planets are attracted to one another by gravitation. "Revealed religion is an *Additional* to Natural," said Gay, thereby reversing the traditional notion that special revelation had priority over natural revelation.[48]

Church controversies—like those surrounding Breck and Briant—likely had a chilling effect. Liberal clergy were indisposed to speak their minds and air their theological views. A clear-cut case is that of Charles Chauncy. Correspondence indicates that Chauncy was already convinced of the doctrine of universal salvation in the 1750s, or about thirty years before he published *Salvation for All Men* (1784). During these years Chauncy quietly made converts to his views by giving portions of his unpublished manuscript to selected disciples. They spoke in code language about the manuscript they had read, asking one another at ministers' gatherings whether they had "tasted the pudding."[49] Throughout the 1700s, the New England clergy were still formally bound to traditional doctrinal formulae like the *Westminster Confession* and the *Savoy Declaration*, so liberals had little incentive to publicize their opinions.

Juxtaposing these bits of evidence, it seems clear that liberalizing or Arminian views were emerging among some in the New England clergy from the 1730s through the 1750s, and that it was just this development that elicited some of Edwards's weightiest writings, such as *Freedom of the Will*, *Original*

---

47. On the rise of religious liberalism in New England, see Bruce Kuklick, *Churchmen and Philosophers: From Jonathan Edwards to John Dewey* (New Haven, CT: Yale University Press, 1985), 81–85.

48. Stout, *New England Soul*, 224–25.

49. Edward M. Griffin, *Old Brick: Charles Chauncy of Boston, 1705–1787* (Minneapolis, MN: University of Minnesota Press, 1980), 126–27, 170. One of Chauncy's disciples, Jeremy Belknap, wrote in 1782 that "the doctrine of universal restitution has long been kept as a secret among learned men" (170).

Sin, End of Creation, and *True Virtue.* Norman Fiering summarized his achievement in engaging the ideas of his day: "Moral philosophers had begun the process of converting into secular and naturalistic terms crucial parts of the Christian heritage. Edwards in a sense reversed the ongoing process by assimilating the moral philosophy of his time and converting it back into the language of religious thought and experience.... His purpose, contrary to that of the *philosophe,* was to turn the best thought of his time to the advantage of God."[50]

---

50. Fiering, *Jonathan Edwards's Moral Thought,* 60–61.

4

Edwards's Spirituality

IN BOTH POPULAR and academic usage, the term "spirituality" is not sharply defined. It may refer to an experience, exposition, or example of the religious or devotional life.[1] Yet in all of these senses, spirituality is a key theme in the writings of Jonathan Edwards. He was a man of intense spiritual experience, who devoted immense effort to giving spiritual instruction to others, and who has been regarded as a model and paragon of Christian piety for some two hundred and fifty years. George S. Claghorn writes that "personal communion with the Almighty...was to be a hallmark of his theology."[2] Joseph Haroutunian notes that Calvinism, in Edwards, became a "living affair" because "he 'felt' the sweet majesty and glory of the Creator."[3] John E. Smith comments that "Edwards painted a complex and subtle picture of what genuine religion should be."[4] This chapter will explore the complexity of Edwards's spiritual teaching, which often incorporated both sides of what are imagined to be polar oppositions—affective versus intellectual, mystical versus rational, active versus receptive, interior versus exterior, introspective versus outward-looking, and solitary versus communal. George Marsden judges that "piety preceded intellect" in Edwards, so that one might well begin an analysis of his theology by considering his spirituality—as we do in this chapter.[5]

Edwards's wide background of reading in spirituality was based, in the first instance, on books available in the libraries of his father and grandfa-

---

[1]. William C. Spohn defines "spirituality" as "the conviction that reality transcends the empirical realm and that human alienation and fragmentation can be healed by connection with that transcendent realm" ("Spirituality and Its Discontents: Practices in Jonathan Edwards's *Charity and Its Fruits*," *Journal of Religious Ethics* 31 [2003]: 255).

2. WJE 16:745.

3. Joseph G. Haroutunian, "Jonathan Edwards: A Study in Godliness," *Journal of Religion* 11 (1931): 405.

4. John E. Smith, "Piety and Practice in the American Character," *Journal of Religion* 54 (1974): 174.

5. George Marsden, *Jonathan Edwards: A Life* (New Haven, CT: Yale University Press, 2003), 330.

ther—Timothy Edwards and Solomon Stoddard. Timothy Edwards's owned many standard Puritan works, by such authors as Richard Baxter, John Flavel, John Goodwin, Thomas Hooker, Cotton Mather, Increase Mather, John Norton, John Owen, Ebenezer Pemberton Sr., Joseph Sewall, William Twisse, Samuel Willard, and William Williams. Stoddard possessed some of the more technical works by Thomas Aquinas, John Calvin, René Descartes, and Francisco Suarez.[6] Edwards's reading in the area of spirituality featured numerous works in the genre of what Peter Thuesen calls the "affectionate practical English writers"—e.g. Richard Baxter, John Flavel, John Owen—who all stressed the practical disciplines needed to increase one's desire for and love of God.

Among the key texts that describe Edwards's spiritual experiences and encapsulate his spiritual teachings are the early "Diary" and "Resolutions," the brief but revealing "Personal Narrative," an important letter of spiritual advice in 1741 to Deborah Hatheway—an eighteen-year-old convert who lacked a pastor—and the treatises *Religious Affections, Life of Brainerd, Some Thoughts Concerning the Revival,* and *Humble Attempt,* as well as many of the sermons. The discussion in this chapter falls into three sections that highlight the themes of *discipline, enjoyment,* and *consummation*—each of which is exemplified in the "Personal Narrative." Edwards's spiritual life involved vigorous, disciplined exertion: "It was my continual strife day and night, and constant inquiry, how I should be more holy, and live more holily... I sought an increase of grace and holiness... with vastly more earnestness, than ever I sought grace, before I had it.... The heaven I desired was a heaven of holiness." Almost immediately following this passage is another that presents the Christian life not as a struggle but as a matter of quiet restfulness and tranquil enjoyment: "The soul of a true Christian... appeared like such a little white flower, as we see in the spring of the year; low and humble on the ground, opening its bosom, to receive the pleasant beams of the sun's glory... diffusing around a sweet fragrancy... in the midst of other flowers... all in like manner opening their bosoms, to drink in the light of the sun."[7] The juxtaposition is striking. To a high degree, Edwards's spirituality exemplified activity and receptivity, struggle and enjoyment. A third theme was consummation. Edwards's spirituality pressed toward eschatological fulfillment: "It was my comfort to think of that state, where there is fullness of joy; where reigns

---

6. Peter Thuesen, "Editor's Introduction," in WJE 26:5–6. On seventeenth-century New England spirituality, see the excellent work by Charles Hambricke-Stowe, *The Practice of Piety: Puritan Devotional Disciplines in Seventeenth-Century New England* (Chapel Hill, NC: University of North Carolina Press, 1982).

7. WJE 16:795–96.

heavenly, sweet, calm and delightful love, without alloy; where there are continually the dearest expressions of this love; where is the enjoyment of the persons loved, without ever parting.... And how sweetly will the mutual lovers join together to sing the praises of God and the Lamb...to all eternity!"[8] Because earthly experiences of God were inherently partial and incomplete, so was the language used to describe them. Especially in his "Personal Narrative" Edwards signaled that words could not adequately capture the meaning that he intended. His experiences of God were ineffable.

Discipline

Linked to Edwards's stress on discipline are a cluster of related ideas—his concern for his own and others' *awakening* from spiritual slumber, the need for *mortification* of sinful desires, the call to *rigor, self-examination*, and *practice*, the need for a continual *seeking* after greater grace, and a *Platonic* and *otherworldly* aspect, expressed in *solitude* with God and detachment from mundane concerns. Edwards believed that those who continued in sin and disobedience against God were in objective danger of divine judgment. A number of his sermons—and not only the famous "Sinners in the Hands of an Angry God"—sought to alert and awaken the unregenerate to the danger of their condition.[9] While it would be a mistake to view these sermons as the sum of Edwards's spirituality, it would also be one-sided to neglect them. He writes that "without true repentance for sin, there is no escaping eternal ruin."[10] Edwards's applied to himself, first and foremost, the exhortations he directed toward others in his awakening sermons. He himself seems to have been ever watchful lest he too should sink into complacency. The maintenance of spiritual awakening required that one undergo a process of mortification, in putting one's sin to death: "By repentance sin receives his deadly wound, such a wound as is never cured, but increases until it has quite deprived the body of sin of all its life."[11] Mortification was

---

8. WJE 16:798.

9. Among the published awakening sermons are "Sinners in the Hands of an Angry God" (WJE 22:404–18), "Unreasonableness of Indetermination in Religion" (WJE 19:93–105), "The Folly of Looking Back in Fleeing out of Sodom" (WJE 19:323–35), "The Torments of Hell are Exceeding Great" (WJE 14:301–28), "The Warnings of Scripture" (WH 2:68–71), "Men Naturally God's Enemies" (WH 2:130–41), "A Warning to Professors" (WH 2:185–90), "The Final Judgment" (WH: 2:190–201), "Sinners in Zion Tenderly Warned" (WH 2:201–206), "Self-Flatteries" (WH 2:217–20), and "Natural Men in a Dreadful Condition" (WH 2:817–29).

10. WJE 10:511.

11. WJE 10:568, cf. 16:764, 775.

necessary for each of us because of our inborn sinfulness, for "if it weren't for our natural enmity to God and aversion to holiness, all the laws of God would be performed as easily as the sun shines or as a river glides down between its banks."[12]

Breaking from sin was a lifelong process, for true saints always continued in a "godly sorrow and mourning for sin."[13] Repentance and sorrow for sin had the effect of weaning the believer away from the charms and seductions of earthly life, which might otherwise captivate the soul: "Such is the folly of the world. They pursue violently after the world, slave and tire themselves for a little of it, are exceedingly anxious and careful about it." The "wise man," said Edwards, is no "self-tormentor," for "he neglects and despises the world; cares little for it."[14] The lack of mortification among believers, he ruefully noted, is a key reason that "many Christians do not sensibly increase in grace."[15] One means of directing the heart toward God was through "earnest and constant prayer to God...by which God carries on a conviction of sin and makes men sensible what they are, whereby he humbles and abases them before him."[16] At the same time, Edwards recognized certain limits to the process of mortification and self-denial. Even in his youthful "Diary" he wrote that "too constant a mortification and too vigorous an application to religion may be prejudicial to health."[17] Edward's ambivalence regarding David Brainerd hinged on this point. Brainerd's self-denial and mortification was so extreme that it ruined his health and likely contributed to his premature death. David Weddle refers to him as a "flagellant on horseback."[18] Yet it is clear that Edwards's own self-mortification struck his contemporaries as extreme. His critic, Timothy Cutler,

---

12. WJE 10:636.

13. WJE 2:366–67. This point was the first of Martin Luther's *Ninety-Five Theses*: "Our Lord and Master Jesus Christ,...willed that the whole life of believers should be repentance" ("Disputation of Doctor Martin Luther on the Power and Efficacy of Indulgences," in *The Works of Martin Luther, With Introductions and Notes*, ed. Henry Eyster Jacobs, et al.; Philadelphia, PA: A. J. Holman, 1915; 1:29).

14. WJE 10:410.

15. WJE 16:764.

16. Michael D. McMullen, ed., *The Glory and Honor of God: Volume 2 of the Previously Unpublished Sermons of Jonathan Edwards* (Nashville, TN: Broadman & Holman, 2004), 94.

17. WJE 16:763.

18. Weddle took this memorable phrase from Richard Ellsworth Day, *Flagellant on Horseback: The Life Story of David Brainerd* (Philadelphia, PA: Judson Press, 1950). See David A. Weddle, "The Melancholy Saint: Jonathan Edwards's Interpretation of David Brainerd as a Model of Evangelical Spirituality," *Harvard Theological Review* 81 (1988) 297–318, citing 308. Weddle judged that Brainerd was problematic for Edwards because "the very passion that drove him" seems also to have undone him (300).

referred to Edwards's "emaciated" appearance from too much study and too little food.[19]

In his rigorous approach to the spiritual life, Edwards was very much a product of the Puritan tradition. The youthful "Resolutions" were perhaps the clearest expression of spiritual strenuousness: "Resolved, to live with all my might, while I do live.... Resolved, never to do anything, which I should be afraid to do, if it were the last hour of my life.... Resolved, to think much on all occasions of my own dying, and of the common circumstances which attend death.... Resolved, to maintain the strictest temperance in eating and drinking.... Resolved, never to speak anything that is ridiculous, or matter of laughter on the Lord's day."[20] These "Resolutions" show an austere young man who lived his life with a kind of monastic or military discipline. (The ban on Sunday humor would hardly fit with today's pulpit, where preachers feel obligated to regale their congregations with lighthearted remarks!) Edwards seems at this stage to have kept a graded, numerical score of his own performance in keeping his duties, commenting that "the weekly account rose higher than ordinary" and then lamenting that "I fell exceedingly low in the weekly account."[21] Yet his experience with a rule-governed life was an unhappy one, and in the "Personal Narrative" he later noted that he early on had acted "with too great dependence on my own strength; which afterwards proved a great damage to me."[22]

Like so many Puritans before him, Edwards stressed throughout his life and ministry the benefit and even necessity of self-examination. Even though he did not assign the same role to self-examination in attaining assurance of salvation as did some earlier writers, it continued to play a role for him.[23] Throughout his life, Edwards was preoccupied with distinguishing true from false religion, and some measure of self-examination was essential to drawing this distinction. Thus in his early "Diary" he spoke of "searching and tracing back all the real reasons why I do them not [i.e., his duties], and narrowly searching out all the subtle subterfuges of my thoughts...that I may know what are the very first originals of my defect."[24] In the opening to the "Personal Narrative" he noted that

---

19. Timothy Cutler wrote that he was "very much emaciated, and impaired in his health, and it is doubtful whether he will attain the age of forty" (cited in Marsden, *Jonathan Edwards*, 193).

20. WJE 16:753–56.

21. WJE 16:763, 765.

22. WJE 16:795, cf. 16:803.

23. Haroutunian asserted that "the kind of unhealthy introspection which is supposed to be characteristic of Puritan religion made Edwards genuinely miserable" ("Godliness," 402).

24. WJE 16:777.

had "a variety of concerns and exercises about my soul from my childhood," commented on the "self-righteous pleasure" he found in pursuing religious exercises, and said that he was "ready to think, many are deceived with such affections, and such a kind of delight, as I then had in religion, and mistake it for grace."[25] An early sermon on "The Duty of Self-Examination" spoke of self-examination as a duty that was "miserably neglected...although it be what above all others most directly respects our own safety."[26] The letter to Deborah Hatheway stressed the need to remember one's sins as an aspect of self-abasement before God: "Though God has forgiven and forgotten your past sins, yet don't forget 'em yourself: often remember what a wretched bond slave you was in the land of Egypt."[27]

Like his Puritan predecessors, Edwards believed that human beings often fooled themselves. As Ava Chamberlain has noted, the word "hypocrite" in contemporary usage suggests a person who deceives others (with a display of religiosity) but is not himself or herself deceived. Yet for Edwards the "hypocrite" was often self-deceived. It was quite possible then to make a profession of faith that was sincere and and yet erroneous.[28] *Religious Affections* addressed this issue of hypocrisy and implicitly relied on self-examination as the means of applying its teachings. Once someone had read the treatise, he or she would introspect to determine whether these affections were gracious or natural. The advice to Deborah Hatheway nonetheless contained an interesting qualification regarding self-examination. He says that if she were to "fall into doubts about the state of your soul," then she should not "consume too much of your time...in poring and puzzling thoughts about old experiences," but engage in "an earnest pursuit after renewed experiences, new light, and new, lively acts of faith and love."[29] Edwards thought that assurance of salvation derived more from the immediacy of present experience than from an analysis of past experience.

Edwards's spirituality was *practical*. In *Religious Affections*, he asserted that the "holy affections have their exercise and fruit in Christian practice" and

---

25. WJE 16:790–91.

26. WJE 10:489. See also the sermons "Self-Examination and the Lord's Supper" (WJE 17:264–72), "True Grace Distinguished from the Experience of Devils" (WJE 25:608–40), and "Christian Cautions" (WH 2:173–85).

27. WJE 16:92.

28. Ava Chamberlain, "Self-Deception as a Theological Problem in Jonathan Edwards's 'Treatise Concerning Religious Affections,'" *Church History* 63 (1994): 541–56, esp. 543. "Counterfeit affections were those that, while having a gracious appearance, were the effects of natural causes" (550).

29. WJE 16:93.

went even further to claim that "Christian practice is the *principal sign* by which Christians are to judge, both of their own and others' sincerity of godliness."[30] Edwards commended David Brainerd by noting that "all his inward illuminations, affections, and comforts, seemed to have a direct tendency to practice, and to issue in it."[31] His approach to the spiritual life was poles apart from that sort of spiritual romanticism that made motives, intentions, and pious feelings paramount, and actions optional. Those who had pious desires and transports of soul were fooling themselves if they imagined that this was sufficient in and of itself. At the same time, this practical, external thrust in Edwards's spirituality was balanced by his affirmation of the centrality of the "affections" (ch. 20) and the need to cultivate the interior life.

Edwards stressed *seeking* after God. The remarkable letter to Deborah Hatheway in 1741 offered spiritual advice free of theological complexities. Here Edwards's spirituality of seeking came through clearly: "Don't leave off seeking, striving and praying for the very same things that we exhort unconverted persons to strive for, and a degree of which you have had in conversion." He added that "there are very few requests that are proper for a natural person, but that in some sense are proper for the godly."[32] Edwards was advising Hatheway to follow his own example, since Edwards's conversion was not the conclusion but merely the beginning of an intense pursuit of God: "I had vehement longings of soul after God and Christ, and after more holiness; wherewith my heart seemed to be full, and ready to break." [33] In the human journey toward God, there was—quite literally—no limit as to how far one might progress. Heaven itself was to be a "progressive state," and in some sense one might say that the seeking after God never ends, not even in the life beyond. *End of Creation* concludes with a vision of elect creatures continually drawing nearer and yet never attaining perfect union with God.[34] Everlasting progress was the purpose and calling of all the saints.

Edwards's quest for God reflected a kind of *otherworldiness*. Describing his early days as a new convert, he writes that "my mind was greatly fixed on divine things; I was almost perpetually in the contemplation of them." In the same context, he describes his "calm, sweet abstraction of soul from all the concerns of this world; and a kind of vision, or fixed ideas and imaginations,

---

30. WJE 2:383, 406–407.

31. WJE 7:510.

32. WJE 16:91–92.

33. WJE 16:794–95.

34. WJE 8:530–36.

of being alone in the mountains, or some solitary wilderness, far from all mankind."[35] The contemplation of God, for Edwards, went hand in hand with a detachment from earthly preoccupations. Edwards associated "temporal concerns"—specifically, his tutorship at Yale College—with a time of spiritual declension: "After I went to New Haven, I sunk in religion...greatly diverted in my mind, with some temporal concerns, that exceedingly took up my thoughts, greatly to the wounding of my soul."[36] The numerous stories regarding Edwards's absentmindedness, and his detachment from the affairs of his own household, point in the same direction. He seems to have been a man most at home in reflection, meditation, prayer, and study. Moreover, Edwards early on recognized in Sarah Pierpont an otherworldliness that marked her as his true soul mate: "She hardly cares for anything, except to meditate on him [i.e., God]" and "she expects after a while to be received up to where he is, to be raised out of the world and caught up into heaven; being assured that he loves her too well to let her remain at a distance from him always." In Edwards's eyes, Sarah had no worldly aspirations: "If you present all the world before her, with the richest of its treasures, she disregards it and cares not of it."[37] Edwards's later, disguised account of his wife's spiritual experience in *Some Thoughts Concerning the Revival* (1743) stressed Sarah's "views of the glory of the divine perfections," so that her "soul remained in a kind of heavenly Elysium, and did as it were swim in the rays of Christ's love, like a little mote swimming in the beams of the sun." After describing this experience, he expressed his unqualified approval: "If such things are enthusiasm, and the fruits of a distempered brain, let my brain be evermore possessed of that happy distemper!"[38]

Edwards's spirituality emphasized the need for *solitude*. Near the beginning of the "Personal Narrative" he wrote that with his "schoolmates" he "built a booth in a swamp, in a very secret and retired place, for a place of prayer. And besides I had particular secret places of my own in the woods." Later in the same text, following his conversion experience, Edwards commented that "I very frequently used to retire into a solitary place, on the banks of Hudson's River, at some distance from the city, for contemplation on divine things...and had many sweet hours there." Edwards also commended Sarah Pierpont for her solitary devotion to God: "She loves to be alone, and to wander in the fields

---

35. WJE 16:793–94.
36. WJE 16:798–99.
37. WJE 16:789–90.
38. WJE 4:332, 341.

and on the mountains, and seems to have someone invisible always conversing with her."[39] One might draw a contrast between Edwards's "Personal Narrative" and Augustine's *Confessions*. In the latter work, every major development in Augustine's spiritual life is linked with a fellow human being—his mother, his mistress, his teaching in Milan, his affiliation with the Manichees, his friendship with Alypius, and so on. Yet in Edwards's case there is almost a complete absence of other people from the narrative. Outside of a small circle of admirers that Edwards acquired in his adult life (e.g., Samuel Hopkins, Joseph Bellamy) it is hard to identify Edwards's friends. With perhaps one exception, no enduring friendships seem to have dated from his youth.[40] This is not to say that Edwards was not a dutiful, and even exemplary, husband, father, and citizen. Yet when he described his spiritual life, he spoke principally of his solitary experiences. For W. Clark Gilpin, Edwards's solitude was an integral element in his quest for personal transformation—the place where he discovered himself and discerned his vocation.[41]

Enjoyment

Alongside of Edwards's stress on discipline was his description of *enjoyment* in the spiritual life—a theme highlighted in recent years in the reflections on "Christian hedonism" by pastor-scholar John Piper.[42] Edwards's writings shifted effortlessly back and forth from describing the process of spiritual seeking to picturesque, poignant, and sometimes lyrical evocations of his experiences of utter delight and absorption in God. The foundation of Edwards's teaching on spiritual enjoyment was his belief in and experience of God's goodness. Believers, he insisted, must realize that "nothing that they need, nothing that they ask of God, nothing that their desires can extend themselves to, nothing that their capacity can contain, no good that can be enjoyed by them, is so great, so excellent that God begrutches it to them."[43]

---

39. WJE 16:791, 797, 790.

40. The possible exception is the man whom Edwards called "my dear friend, Mr. John Smith" (WJE 16:770), with whom Edwards resided during his eight-month pastorate in New York City (1722–23), and who with his family is mentioned in the "Personal Narrative" (WJE 16:797).

41. W. Clark Gilpin, "'Inward, Sweet Delight in God': Solitude in the Career of Jonathan Edwards," *Journal of Religion* 82 (2002): 523–38, esp. 525–26, 532, 538.

42. John Piper, *Desiring God: Meditations of a Christian Hedonist* (Downer's Grove, IL: InterVarsity Press, 2004).

43. WJE 19:781.

Under the broad theme of enjoyment, there is a complex of ideas that frequently recurs in Edwards's writings and that interlock with one another—humility, happiness, holiness, heaven, beauty, affection, and participation. The happy life is necessarily a humble life. Pride, by contrast, leads ultimately to misery. The happy life is also a holy life. Holiness largely consists in humility. Holiness in the saints is a beautiful thing and is an expression of God's own beauty in them. Holiness is a foretaste of the heavenly life. Holiness means a participation in God's own life and character.[44] The experience of holiness will be perfectly fulfilled in heaven. The heavenly life also affords a perfect experience of God's beauty, so that beauty and heaven go hand in hand. The experience of God's beauty provokes the human affection for God. Affection for God leads human beings to desire to please God, and thus affection leads in a way of pure, humble, heavenly devotion. Heaven is a place of perfect humility, since human beings in that state will properly understand themselves in relation to God. Heaven is also a place where human beings will participate in God's own happiness and joy. In seeing God's beauty, we can participate in God's happiness, which is God's own happiness in himself.

The Christian life, as Edwards understood it, was a "happy" life. For only in the Christian life could people fulfill the purpose for which they were created—the knowledge and enjoyment of God. In *End of Creation*, Edwards went so far as to affirm that God's glory and the creature's happiness are not "properly and entirely distinct" from one another.[45] The creature's happiness *is* God's glory and God's glory *is* the creature's happiness. Edwards was in continuity with a wide stream of Christian eudaemonism—including Augustine, Thomas Aquinas, such Puritans as Richard Baxter, and such Anglicans such as Jeremy Taylor and C. S. Lewis—in holding that true religion was the satisfaction of the deepest needs and longings of the human heart.[46]

---

44. On the theme of participation in God, see Fred W. Youngs, "The Place of Spiritual Union in the Thought of Jonathan Edwards," PhD dissertation, Drew University, 1986; and Michael J. McClymond, "Salvation as Divinization: Jonathan Edwards, Gregory Palamas and the Theological Uses of Neoplatonism," in Paul Helm and Oliver D. Crisp, eds., *Jonathan Edwards: Philosophical Theologian* (Aldershot, UK: Ashgate, 2003), 139–60.

45. WJE 8:458.

46. A countervailing view has its roots in the writings of Martin Luther, and finds its secular correlate in the ethics of Immanuel Kant and its theological expression in Anders Nygren's *Agape and Eros* (London: SPCK, 1953). This view sets natural human instincts and desires ("eros") in opposition to divine love ("agape"). On Edwards's understanding of love, see Paul Ramsey's "Editor's Introduction" (WJE 8:1–104).

Puritan writers had long held that the pleasures of true religion transcended worldly pleasures. Godly pleasures were enduring and soul-refreshing rather than transient and guilt-laden.

For Edwards, the happiness of true religion consisted in the saints' "holy affections." *Religious Affections* had for its main thesis the proposition that "true religion, in great part, consists in holy affections." Affections, for Edwards, were the driving, motivating factor that stirred human beings to act. Affections were "very much the spring of men's actions."[47] Yet Edwards did not separate affections from intellect or understanding. Affections did not correspond to what commonly today are referred to as feelings. Instead they represent the fundamental disposition and inclination of the human self—a complex synthesis of emotion, volition, and intellect (ch. 20).[48] Despite his stress on the affections, Edwards did not accept all religious affections—even when intense—as signs of grace. Bodily effects proved nothing one way or another. Talking about spiritual things was no test of genuine spirituality, and neither was an engagement in external religious duties, or having confidence in being in God's favor.[49] Instead, gracious affections had an outward, God-ward focus: "The first objective ground of gracious affections, is the transcendently excellent and amiable nature of divine things, as they are in themselves; and not any conceived relation they bear to self or self-interest." Gracious affections were attended with a "spiritual conviction...of the reality and certainty of divine things," "with evangelical humiliation," with "the lamb-like, dovelike spirit and temper of Jesus Christ," and with "beautiful symmetry and proportion."[50] A "very distinguishing" quality of gracious affections was "that gracious affections, the higher they are raised, the more is a spiritual appetite and longing of soul after spiritual attainments, increased. On the contrary, false affections rest satisfied in themselves."[51] This is where Edwards's spirituality of seeking coincided with his spirituality of enjoyment. True enjoyment of God never brought the believer into satiety or complacency, but led toward deeper desires for more of God's presence and grace.

---

47. WJE 2:95, 100.

48. See Michael J. McClymond, "Jonathan Edwards," in John Corrigan, ed., *The Oxford Handbook to Religion and Emotion* (New York: Oxford University Press, 2008), esp. 404–409.

49. WJE 2:127, 131, 135, 163, 167.

50. WJE 2:240, 291, 311, 344, 365.

51. WJE 2:376.

A striking thing in Edwards's approach to the spiritual life was his constant emphasis on *beauty*. Some have claimed that Edwards had more to say about beauty than any other major Christian thinker since the time of Augustine (ch. 6). The first sentence in the very first entry of Edwards's *Miscellanies* reads—"holiness is a most beautiful and lovely thing."[52] An experience of the beauty of holiness was Edwards's starting point. For Edwards, there was no such thing as beauty at second hand. Beauty was something that could not be seen without being appreciated. The stress in Edwards's writings lay on what he called "primary beauty"—the beauty that consisted in the wonderful harmony and "consent" of spiritual things—and not the "secondary beauty" that resided in the symmetry and shapeliness of material things.[53] Edwards's own sense of the beauty of God began with his conversion experience and the phenomenon of the "new sense" as recounted in the *Personal Narrative*—"a sense of the glory of the divine being; a new sense, quite different from anything I ever experienced before."[54] He claimed that the perception of spiritual beauty was foundational to conversion: "This sense of divine beauty, is the first thing in the actual change made in the soul, in true conversion, and is the foundation of everything else belonging to that change." A view of God's beauty does not puff up but rather humbles the believing soul: "That sense of the supreme, holy beauty and glory of God and Christ...mortifies pride, and truly humbles the soul."[55]

Edwards highlighted dependence on God and the necessity of humility. His first publication was the sermon "God Glorified in Man's Dependence."[56] Yet rather than conceiving of humility as a duty imposed on him, Edwards seemed to enjoy placing himself in the posture of supplicant before God. He relished the thought of lying low before God, and wrote of his "ardency of soul to be, what I know not otherwise how to express, than to be emptied and annihilated; to lie in the dust, and to be full of Christ alone."[57] Humility was thus not a grim or desolate experience but an aspect of enjoying God. In accordance with his teaching in *Religious Affections*, Edwards did not rest content in that level of humility that he had attained to but longed to increase in humility before God: "I have greatly longed of late, for a broken heart, and to lie low

---

52. WJE 13:163.
53. WJE 8:561–74.
54. WJE 16:792.
55. WJE 25:636–37.
56. WJE 17:196–216.
57. WJE 16:801.

before God. And when I ask for humility of God, I can't bear the thoughts of being no more humble, than other Christians."[58] Just as humility was beneficial and necessary, so pride was destructive and dangerous. The "best defense" against falling into many kinds of spiritual error is "humility and self-diffidence." In his writings on revival, Edwards insisted that pride—and especially spiritual pride—is the most dangerous of sins: "Pride is the worst viper that is in the heart...the most secret, deceitful and unsearchable in its ways of working."[59] Those who fall into spiritual pride may become completely unresponsive to correction from other people. Indeed, the proud person may interpret criticisms from others as marks of persecution and signs of his own superiority.

Edwards's spirituality rested on a sense of the interrelatedness of reality. George Marsden wrote that "the key to Edwards's thought is that everything is related because everything is related to God."[60] It comes as no surprise then that the physical, natural universe played a key role. This becomes evident in one striking passage in the "Personal Narrative," where, following his experience of conversion and the "new sense" of God's glory, Edwards says that he began to perceive the divine glory in nature: "The appearance of everything was altered: there seemed to be, as it were, a calm, sweet cast, or appearance of divine glory, in almost everything...in the sun, moon and stars; in the clouds, and blue sky; in the grass, flowers, trees; in the water, and all nature."[61] Perry Miller suggested a line of intellectual development that led from Edwards's meditations on nature to the Transcendentalist ruminations of Ralph Waldo Emerson a century later (ch. 40). Some have viewed Edwards as a full-blown nature mystic—a sort of colonial John Muir. Yet several important qualifications are in order. First, Edwards clearly stated in his writings that an appreciation of nature's "secondary beauty" did not necessarily lead to an appreciation of God's "primary beauty." Nature was not a stairway to heaven. Second, Edwards taught that only regenerate persons were able to discern the images and shadows of God's beauty in the natural world. Not all had eyes to see. Conversion was foundational in Edwards's spirituality. This feature distinguished him from Ralph Waldo Emerson and from Friedrich Schleiermacher, who both viewed the natural world as a vehicle for

---

58. WJE 16:803.

59. WJE 4:277.

60. Marsden, *Jonathan Edwards*, 460.

61. WJE 16:793–94. See the discussion of nature in Edwards's writings in Paul David Johnson, "Jonathan Edwards's 'Sweet Conjunction,'" *Early American Literature* 16 (1981–82) 270–81.

transcendent experiences and yet did not limit such experiences to the converted. Third, the sequence of experiences in the "Personal Narrative" is crucial. Edwards's new God concept did not derive from his experiences of nature, but rather the reverse. His "new sense" of God's glory transformed his perception of the natural world. This is not to say that the natural world played no role in Edwards's spirituality, but rather that its role was subordinate to his overriding concern for the reality, presence, power, and beauty of God.

Some authors have wondered where sexuality fit into Edwards's spirituality and theology. In his revival writings, he noted the hidden dangers posed by sexual desires, when "the mutual embraces and kisses of persons of different sexes, under the notion of Christian love and holy kisses" could have "the most direct tendency quickly to turn Christian love into unclean and brutish lust, which won't be the better, but ten times the worse, for being christened by the name of Christian love."[62] Yet in suggesting that sexual lust could prove to be an enemy of the soul, Edwards was not saying anything novel. George Marsden proposed that Edwards, in his earlier years, may have struggled with lust, and that this might be linked with a spiritual letdown during the early 1720s that Edwards only vaguely alluded to in his autobiographical writings. The matter is obscure because the references are few and indefinite.[63]

The "Personal Narrative" showed a repeated and striking use of the language of rapture—being "wrapt up to God," "wrapt and swallowed up in God," or "totally wrapt up in...Christ." Edwards also cited the biblical Song of Songs that—with its complex and interlocking erotic and spiritual meanings—had long been a favorite among Christian mystics: "The whole book of Canticles used to be pleasant to me; and I used to be much in reading it, about that time."[64] Edwards's quest for solitude and seclusion with God, noted above, could be a sign that he indeed regarded God as his "lover." Paula Cooey concluded that Edwards's concept of virtuous love was "unabashedly sensual" and was thus a refreshing alternative to the bloodless abstractions of most ethical theorists.[65] Dennis Barbour found a sublimated sexuality in Edwards's writings

---

62. WJE 4:468.

63. Sometime around 1724—at about the age of twenty-one—Edwards read the widely reprinted eighteenth-century anti-masturbation manual, *Onania; or, The Heinous Sin of Self-Pollution*. The title is included and crossed off in his "Catalogue" of reading (WJE 26:111, 173). This is an indication of Edwards's interest in the topic, but is not in itself an evidence of sexual struggle.

64. WJE 16:792–93, 801.

65. Paul M. Cooey, "Eros and Intimacy in Edwards," *Journal of Religion* 69 (1989): 484–501.

and held that he had "more affinity with the Catholic mystics than with the Transcendentalists."[66] Yet Barbour linked his interpretation of the "Personal Narrative" to the questionable theories of James Leuba, who viewed religious mysticism as a manifestation of frustrated or sublimated sexual desire.[67] The sublimation theory is too simplistic to function as a catch-all explanation for the eroticized language of the mystics. On the other hand, the general assertion that Edwards's spirituality included an erotic aspect would seem to be unassailable, however one might interpret his language.

Consummation

A third and final aspect of Edwards's spirituality to be treated here is the stress on *consummation*, with the subthemes of *unity, community, eschatology,* and *heaven*. The basic point is that Edwards's experience of and teaching on the spiritual life pressed toward a fulfillment beyond this present life. One major aspect of fulfillment was unity. Heaven will be "one holy and happy society" that included not only the Father, Son, and Spirit but a "vast assembly of saints and angels."[68] Edwards wrote that "union is one of the most amiable things that pertains to human society; yea, 'tis one of the most beautiful and happy things on earth, which indeed makes earth most like heaven."[69] Throughout his pastoral writings, Edwards lauded the virtues of unity, concord, and agreement in civil society and within the local congregation (ch. 28).[70] He regretted deeply the manifestations of strife and division in the town of Northampton both before and after the revivals there in 1734–35 and in 1740–41. It is intriguing that someone who valued his solitude as much as Edwards did, and who spent so many hours alone, should so highly prize and praise the benefits of community.

The idea of community tied into some of Edwards's most abstract notions. In "The Mind" he wrote that "one alone, without any reference to any more, cannot be excellent; for in such a case there can be no manner of rela-

---

66. Dennis H. Barbour, "The Metaphor of Sexuality in Jonathan Edwards's 'Personal Narrative,'" *Christianity and Literature* 47 (1998): 285–94, citing 286.

67. James H. Leuba, *The Psychology of Religious Mysticism* (New York: Harcourt, Brace, 1926). References to sexual love in mystical literature can in fact be interpreted in various ways—as substitutions or sublimations, as analogies or metaphors, or as vehicles or expressions of a non-physical, divine form of love.

68. WJE 5:446.

69. WJE 5:364–65.

70. See the sermons "Living Peaceably With One Another" (WJE 14:118–33) and "Peaceable and Faithful Amid Division and Strife" (WJE 19:658–79).

tion no way, and therefore, no such thing as consent."⁷¹ If one applies this insight to the theme of spirituality, one might conclude that solitary existence must be incomplete. A secluded hermit is deficient—both because of what he fails to receive from others and what they fail to receive from him. In heaven, the happiness of each one is linked to the happiness of all others (ch. 19). Far from feeling any jealousy, they are delighted at the thought that others are happy, and perhaps more happy in heaven than they are themselves. The happiness of each individual saint is increased by the happiness that he or she sees in all the others.⁷² To be sure, a solitary person can "consent" to God. Yet Edwards in his descriptions of the ideal community on earth and in heaven offered a rich, textured, and expansive vista of mutual consents among the glorified saints.

Throughout his writings, Edwards showed a focus on *eschatology*. From his earliest years, Edwards said that he "had great longings for the advancement of Christ's kingdom in the world. My secret prayer used to be in great part taken up in praying for it."⁷³ This theme of "latter-day glory" came up in *Some Thoughts Concerning the Revival*, and then again in the *Humble Attempt*, where he spoke of this "glory" on earth as "not yet accomplished" and yet also as "unspeakably great." Edwards anticipated "an abundant outpouring of the Spirit of God, far greater and more extensive than ever yet has been." He cited biblical language (Rom. 8:22) concerning the "groaning" of the creation to come into its consummation: "The 'whole creation' is, as it were, earnestly waiting for that day, and constantly groaning and travailing in pain to bring forth the felicity and glory of it." He concluded that that "certainly it is fit, that the church of God should be in travail for that, which...the whole creation travails in pain for."⁷⁴ The plan for concerted prayer in the *Humble Attempt* brought together several of Edwards's preoccupations—prayer as dependence on God, visible unity among believers, the outpouring of the Holy Spirit, and hope for the "latter-day glory."⁷⁵

Edwards's spirituality and his reflections on heaven were intertwined. True saints according to the scriptures were "strangers and pilgrims on earth." For

---

71. WJE 6:337.

72. WJE 8:375–78.

73. WJE 16:797.

74. WJE 5:329, 344, 351.

75. In addition to *Humble Attempt* (WJE 5:309–436), see also the sermons "Importunate Prayer for Millennial Glory" (WJE 22:368–77) and "The Suitableness of Union in Extraordinary Prayer for the Advancement of God's Church" (WJE 25:200–206).

this reason life was to be pursued as "only a journey toward heaven." "The way to heaven is an heavenly life," wrote Edwards, and "we must be traveling towards heaven in a way of imitation of those that are in heaven." This is to be a sole aim and "all other concerns of life ought to be entirely subordinated to this." For "in heaven alone is [the] attainment of our highest good. God is the highest good of the reasonable creature. The enjoyment of him is our proper happiness."[76] In the *Personal Narrative*, Edwards described heaven as a place where there was full and unhindered enjoyment of God. He wrote of the "clogs" and hindrances that prevented the full expression of desire for God at the present time: "It used...to appear a great part of the happiness of heaven, that there the saints could express their love to Christ. It appeared to me a great clog and hindrance and burden to me, that what I felt within, I could not express.... The inward ardor of my soul, seemed to be hindered and pent up, and could not freely flame out as it would."[77] Edwards's fullest depiction of heaven appeared in a number of his sermons.[78] There he depicts heaven as an active and progressive state in which the saints will forever advance into closer relationship with God and with one another. In his notebooks, Edwards discusses the possibility that heaven will facilitate something analogous to musical performance and harmony among the saints, yet on a vastly higher level than we experience at the present time (ch. 19). This celestial state is beyond our present powers of understanding and description, according to Edwards. It is simply ineffable, since "nothing on earth can represent the glories of heaven."[79] Nonetheless, Edwards's reflections on heaven had pertinence for the present time, since they embodied the aim toward which all spiritual striving in the present time ought to be directed.

---

76. WJE 16:429–30, 433, 435, 437.

77. WJE 16:795.

78. See "Heaven is a World of Love" (WJE 8:366–97), "Degrees of Glory" (WJE 19:612–27), "Serving God in Heaven" (WJE 17:253–61), "The True Christian's Life a Journey Toward Heaven" (WJE 17:429–46), and "Praise, One of the Chief Employments of Heaven" (WH 2:913–17).

79. WJE 14:134–60.

5

The Question of Development: Did Edwards Change?

PERRY MILLER ARGUED that Edwards's thinking did not change over time but only "deepened." In his characteristically evocative way, Miller mused:

> Edwards was not the sort who undergoes a long development or whose work can be divided into "periods." His whole insight was given him at once, preternaturally early, and he did not change: he only deepened.... His works are statement and restatement of an essentially static conception, worked over and over, as upon a photographic plate, to bring out more detail or force from it clearer prints.[1]

In certain respects Miller was right. Edwards arrived at many crucial concepts—beauty, being, consent, holiness, etc.—during his post-adolescent years, and these concepts remained central throughout the course of his lifetime. The first line of the first entry into the million-word *Miscellanies* announced a theme that Edwards long continued to expound: "Holiness is a most beautiful and lovely thing."[2] Yet it is necessary to challenge Miller's claim regarding Edwards's thought as "essentially static." In fact, his thinking shifted repeatedly in response to changing circumstances in the Northampton church, the American colonies, and the transatlantic social and intellectual contexts.

When Miller published his book in 1949, he could not have been aware of the particulars of Edwards's life later to be revealed through the publication of *The Works of Jonathan Edwards (1957–2008)*. The indefatigable efforts of George Claghorn in assembling all of Edwards's extant letters (WJE 16), the publication of the full transcription of the *Miscellanies* with expert introductions (WJE 13, 18, 20, 23), George Marsden's definitive biography, and the continual advance of secondary literature have all contributed to an image of

---

1. Perry Miller, *Jonathan Edwards* (New York: William Sloane, 1949), 44–45.
2. WJE 13:163.

Edwards as a thinker continually in process and continually reviewing and rethinking his own positions (ch. 1). Today the links between his life, his social and cultural context, and his ideas are clearer than ever.

In Edwards's theologizing, there were a number of distinct phases that merit discussion, each of which will be referred to in this chapter as a new "turn" in his thinking.

The Experiential-Empirical Turn (Mid- to Late 1730s)

The earliest specimen of writing we have from Edwards is a boyhood letter from 1716 that refers to an outpouring of the Holy Spirit that occurred in his father's congregation: "Through the wonderful mercy and goodness of God there hath been in this place a very remarkable stirring and pouring out of the Spirit of God, and likewise now is, but I think I have reason to think it is in some measure diminished, but I hope not much. About thirteen have been joined to the church in an estate of full communion."[3] This letter—sounding the themes of spiritual awakening, spiritual decline, and admission to church membership—is a foreshadowing of much of Edwards's later writing. From his youth, Edwards had been an observer of revivals. His eminent grandfather Solomon Stoddard was renowned for the periodic "harvests" that occurred five times in the course of his decades-long ministry. So Edwards grew up in the context of periodic religious awakenings. What is more, Edwards also manifested a bent toward empirical science in his youth, as reflected in the famous "Spider Letter" and other early scientific papers.[4] He showed a gift for intricate and exhaustive description of natural phenomena—a talent later transferred from the realm of nature to that of the spirit.

Despite an earlier acquaintance with New England revivals, the events of the 1734–35 Northampton Awakening changed Edwards and his thinking in decisive ways. In short, one might say that the 1730s revival turned Edwards into a psychologist of religion. George Claghorn notes that "revivalistic concerns remained central" in Edwards' personal correspondence from the 1730s through the 1740s.[5] As the faithful shepherd of a large congregation (the largest west of Boston) while it was undergoing a spiritual awakening of historic proportions, Edwards was compelled to scrutinize the stirrings of grace in the lives of hundreds. As pastor, he had a vocational duty to discern. The conversations and interviews conducted with parishioners—followed by his writing of the groundbreaking

---

3. WJE 16:29.

4. See the "Spider Letter," in WJE 6:163–69, which is published there with other scientific writings.

5. George Claghorn, in "Editor's Introduction," WJE 16:9.

Faithful Narrative (1737)—were pivotal in his development as an empirical observer of spiritual experiences. The text itself was something new, in fact a new genre of writing—the first full-scale revival narrative ever written. The combination of detailed empirical scrutiny with incisive theological analysis was unprecedented. Some have argued that there is a line of intellectual development that connects Edwards with William James and the later discipline of the psychology of religion—an empirical science of religious experiences.[6] Most secular thinkers of the 1700s conceived of human beings in a way that sharply distinguished "reason" from "the passions" and privileged the former over the later. Yet Edwards offered a unified anthropology in which "affections" (not to be identified with "emotions") were signifiers of the self at its deepest level. By taking affections seriously, and as objects worthy of detailed scrutiny, Edwards's theology bequeathed a rich legacy to later investigators of the religious life—whether religious or secular in stance (ch. 20).

Edwards was willing to consider first-hand accounts of spiritual experience that had not first passed through a filter of theological correctness. As a result of this decidedly empiricist and a posteriori approach to religious life, he made a decisive departure from the older Puritan "morphology of conversion" that he had already been questioning in his late teen years—as shown in his "Diary."[7] In Edwards's empirical approach to revivals, the doctrine of conversion had to be congruent with the actual experiences of conversion as reported to him. Edwards interpreted scripture and doctrine in light of new experiences, and this continued to be the case in his later reflections during the Great Awakening of the 1740s. When the prevailing theory conflicted with the evidence of actual experiences, Edwards was willing to abandon the theory and propound a new one.[8] This attentiveness to experience

---

6. Wayne Proudfoot, "From Theology to a Science of Religions: Jonathan Edwards and William James on Religious Affections," *Harvard Theological Review* 82 (1989): 149–68.

7. Regarding his own conversion, Edwards wrote: "The reason why I, in the least, question my interest in God's love and favor, is, 1. Because I cannot speak so fully to my experience of that preparatory work, of which divines speak; 2. I do not remember that I experienced regeneration, exactly in those steps, in which divines say it is generally wrought" (WJE 16:759). On the conventional "steps," see ch. 24.

8. This is not to say—methodologically speaking—that Edwards regarded experience as the final source or authority for theological assertions. Nor does it mean that Edwards held to what George Lindbeck called the "experiential-expressivist" view of theology, as attributed to Friedrich Schleiermacher (Lindbeck, *The Nature of Doctrine: Religion and Theology in a Postliberal Age*; Philadelphia, PA: Westminster Press, 1984). On the other hand, Edwards's teaching in certain areas—e.g., his doctrine of conversion, theology of revival—could be described as a biblically-guided interpretation of spiritual experience.

and openness to novelty has given Edwards a hearing with twentieth-century Pentecostalisms and Charismatics (ch. 42)—even though he did not acknowledge any operation of the charismatic gifts of the Spirit during his own day. What Pentecostalisms have appreciated is Edwards's willingness to judge by "fruits" or outcomes and not in terms of preconceived ideas about what sorts of experience should or should not occur. Whether in the reflections of the Harvard psychologist William James or in the spiritual ruminations of contemporary Pentecostalisms, Edwards's experiential-empirical approach has won admirers.

The Ethical-Rigorist Turn (Early to Mid-1740s)

Edwards's theological development during the 1740s has to be seen in the context of the post-revival spiritual letdowns. The process occurred in two stages, first in the later 1730s (after the 1734–35 awakening) and then throughout the 1740s (following the Great Awakening of 1740–41). Edwards was deeply affected by the changes he witnessed. As early as the 1730s, his letters "reveal a vein of circumspection and wariness that may have resulted from his disappointment after the revival of 1734–35." Then again in 1742 he wrote of the "abatement of the liveliness" of his congregation's "affections in religion."[9] What we are here calling the ethical-rigorist turn—as well as the ecclesial-sacramental turn—were both responses to the situation in Northampton. The 1734–35 revival ended abruptly with the suicide of Joseph Hawley, Edwards's uncle by marriage.[10] Following this melancholy episode, there was a larger issue in what Edwards perceived to be a widespread falling away from the intense, exuberant spirituality of the awakening. He could not escape the conclusion, in George Marsden's words, that "he had overestimated the extent of genuine awakening."[11]

One mark of spiritual decline was the return of the "frolicking" that was common among young people up through the early 1730s, when the revival brought a change in their behavior. Edwards's words in *Faithful Narrative* (1737) regarding "mirth and company-keeping" were code language for youthful sexual promiscuity in the town. Patricia Tracy and George Marsden have noted that premarital sex was fairly common in Northampton, and that it was

---

9. George Claghorn, "Editor's Introduction," in WJE 16:10, 13.

10. For references see, WJE 4:46, 109, 206.

11. George Marsden, *Jonathan Edwards: A Life* (New Haven, CT: Yale University Press, 2003), 189.

tolerated by many in the older generation so long as marriage took place in case of pregnancy. A scandal ensued only if young men got women pregnant and then refused to marry them. Edwards pressed for marriage in a case of fornication involving Elisha Hawley and a pregnant Martha Root, and yet the two families settled out of court without any marriage taking place.[12] These events revealed both an implicit sexual double standard—whereby young men often got away with their sexual escapades—and Edwards's declining authority. While he did not treat sexual transgressions as greater than other forms of wrongdoing, he regarded them as overt expressions of sinful self-love. In his own post-adolescent years, Edwards had practiced a "sparingness" in diet. This was an ascetic self-discipline that he undertook—as his "Diary" shows—to combat his own unruly desires.[13] In the midst of the revivals, Edwards seemed at one with his people. Yet during each of the post-revival letdowns, the contrast between the self-denying, saintly pastor and his Northampton congregation became increasingly apparent (see ch. 29).

One theme that emerged in Edwards's writing in response to the pastoral situation was a stress on "perseverance" and "obedience"—sometimes combined in the phrase "universal persevering obedience"—as the mark of the genuine convert. As early as 1729–30, several *Miscellanies* entries discussed "perseverance," and yet the number of such entries mushroomed from 1736 to 1739. So also with the entries related to "obedience."[14] It is clear that the post-revival situation of the later 1730s brought Edwards to reflect on these themes. Previously he had stressed an immediate experience of the "divine and supernatural light" as a key element in attaining assurance of salvation. Yet now he emphasized that perseverance was a condition of justification and a means of assurance: "Not only the first act of faith, but after-acts of faith, and perseverance in faith, do justify the sinner."[15] In the

---

12. See Patricia J. Tracy, *Jonathan Edwards, Pastor: Religion and Society in Eighteenth-Century Northampton* (New York: Hill and Wang, 1980), 90–91, 106–11, 130–1, 160–66; Marsden, *Jonathan Edwards*, 189, 131; and George Claghorn, in "Editor's Introduction," in WJE 16:14–15.

13. Marsden, *Jonathan Edwards*, 107.

14. Thomas Schafer's index (WJE 13:142) shows that there were entries on "perseverance" (nos. 415, 428, 467) during the years 1729–30; see WJE 13:474–75, 480, 508. The entries on "perseverance" appeared in increasing numbers in 1736–39 (nos. 711, 726, 729, 744-corol 1., 750, 755, 773, 774, 795, 799, 823); see WJE 18:340–41, 352–57, 387–88, 398, 403–404, 422–25, 496–97, 498–500, 534–35. On "obedience," see the entries from 1736–39 (nos. 790, 819, 876); see WJE 18:474–88, 530–31, and WJE 20:119.

15. WJE 18:355.

winter of 1737–38, Edwards preached a lengthy sermon series on the parable of the wise and foolish virgins (Matthew 25:1–13) to show that Christian practice was an essential sign of grace. Notebook entries from the late 1730s—"Signs of Godliness" and "Directions for Judging of Persons' Experiences"—exhibited Edwards's stress on holiness and his reluctance to accept reports of spiritual experience at face value unless they were corroborated by Christian practice.[16] Edwards's sermon series, *Charity and Its Fruits* (1738), was yet another reflection of his deep concern over his new converts in the years after the Northampton awakening. If Christian love was the test of faith, then it was difficult to escape the conclusion that the Northamptonites were failing.[17]

The years following the Great Awakening may have involved an even greater spiritual drop-off than during the late 1730s. Edwards sought to provoke his parishioners to spiritual rededication with a public covenant renewal ceremony in 1742. Yet the older generation continued to quarrel among themselves, while the younger people tended to "lasciviousness." The "Bad Book" episode showed that some of those who had once renounced the ways of sin were still living in them. Young men from prominent families defied Edwards, as epitomized in Timothy Root's declaration that "I won't worship a wig."[18]

As the 1740s wore on, Edwards began increasingly to depict the Christian life in terms of self-denial and self-sacrifice. This theme can be viewed autobiographically—as an expression of Edwards's experience of pouring out his life and energy on behalf of ungrateful parishioners. Yet this was also Edwards's prescription for others who wished, as he did, to be a faithful Christian. As Wilson Kimnach points out, Edwards's ordination sermons during the 1740s show a "focused and insistent" stress on "the heroism of the professional ministry."[19] At the center of his evocations of the Christ-like minister was the figure of David Brainerd, immortalized in *The Life of David Brainerd* (1749). It was Brainerd, above all others, who exemplified Edwards's emerging themes

---

16. Kenneth P. Minkema, "Edwards, Jonathan," in Michael J. McClymond, ed., *Encyclopedia of Religious Revivals in America*, 2 vols. (Westport, CT: Greenwood Press, 2007), 1:153, citing "Signs of Godliness" and "Directions for Judging of Persons' Experiences" in WJE 21:469–510, 22–24.

17. Marsden, *Jonathan Edwards*, 190.

18. George Claghorn, in "Editor's Introduction," in WJE 16:14; Marsden, *Jonathan Edwards*, 298–99.

19. Wilson Kimnach, "Editor's Introduction," in WJE 25:15. On the theme of self-sacrifice, see Michael J. McClymond, "Agape, Mutuality, and Self-Sacrifice: An Exploration into the Theology of Jonathan Edwards and the Concept of Godly Love," in Matthew T. Lee and Amos Yong, eds., *The Science and Theology of Godly Love* (Dekalb, IL: Northern Illinois University Press, forthcoming).

of perseverance, obedience, separation from the world, solitariness (if need be), self-denial, asceticism, and self-sacrifice. Marsden went so far as to suggest that "Edwards was much more interested in the sacrifice involved in Brainerd's mission than in its success."[20]

Certain passages in the "Personal Narrative" suggest that Edwards may have had affinities with mystical notions of a pure or disinterested love for God. His intellectual resignation to God was shown when he wrote that "absolute sovereignty is what I love to ascribe to God...showing mercy on whom he will show mercy, and hardening and eternally damning whom he will." At the moment of conversion, Edwards sought to be "wrapt and swallowed up in God." His own conversion, he claimed, did not coincide with thoughts regarding his own salvation: "It never came into my thought, that there was anything spiritual, or of a saving nature in this." Later in the "Personal Narrative" he expressed a longing for self-annihilation: "My heart as it were panted after this, to lie low before GOD, and in the dust; that I might be nothing, and that God might be all." He recalled an experience of 1737: "I felt withal, an ardency of soul to be, what I know not otherwise how to express, than to be emptied and annihilated; to lie in the dust, and to be full of Christ alone; to love him with a holy and pure love."[21] The language of "annihilation" and "pure love" in this passage is reminiscent of such Catholic mystics as François Fénelon and Madame Guyon. In the fragmentary texts that are extant, Sarah Edwards displayed—even more obviously than Jonathan—a kinship to the Catholic "pure love" tradition and its negations of the self.[22] In sum, then, the 1730s and 1740s show Edwards gravitating toward a conception of the Christian life that highlighted ethical practice, perseverance through difficulties, self-sacrifice on behalf of others, and, at times, a quasi-mystical impetus toward self-abnegation and the annihilation of the self within what Edwards called "a holy and pure love" of God.

---

20. Marsden, *Jonathan Edwards*, 332.

21. WJE 16:792–93, 796, 801.

22. In her journal, Sarah recorded that "I should be willing to die in darkness and horror, if it was most for the glory of God." No less was she "willing to die on the rack, or at the stake, or any other tormenting death." She was ready to "be kept out of heaven" for "a thousand years, if it be God's will, and for his honour and glory." She spoke of her "absolute indifference as to any external circumstances" and her "entire emptiness of self-love." Quoted from Sereno Dwight, "Memoirs of Jonathan Edwards," in Edward Hickman, ed., *The Works of Jonathan Edwards*, 2 vols. (Edinburgh: The Banner of Truth Trust, 1984 [1834]), 1:lxvi, lxviii, lxv. See Julie Ellison, "The Sociology of 'Holy Indifference': Sarah Edwards's Narrative," *American Literature* 56 (1984): 479–95. On the significance and influence of French "pure love" mysticism, see Patricia A. Ward, *Experimental Theology in America: Madame Guyon, Fénelon, and Their Readers* (Waco, TX: Baylor University Press, 2009), and Michael J. McClymond, "Christian Mysticism—Help or Hindrance to Godly Love? A Case Study of Madame Guyon (1648–1717)," in Matthew T. Lee and Amos Yong, eds., *Godly Love: Impediments and Possibilities* (Lanham, MD: Lexington Books, forthcoming).

The Ecclesial-Sacramental Turn (Late 1740s)

Edwards's change of policy regarding admission to the Lord's Supper is better known than some of his other changes, and so may be treated more concisely here (see further, ch. 30). *Humble Inquiry* (1749), "Narrative of Communion Controversy" (1750), and *Misrepresentations Corrected* (1752) are the literary landmarks of this conspicuous and momentous shift in Edwards's personal, pastoral, and theological life. Edwards's ejection from his church in June 1750 is the biographical milestone.

Yet two points are crucial in understanding this alteration. First, the change regarding communion needs to be viewed against the backdrop—just discussed—of what Edwards perceived to be the progressive spiritual declension of Northampton during the 1740s. Stoddard's long-established policy of open communion to all baptized persons was failing to bring the spiritual benefit that Stoddard had attributed to it. Indeed, the open communion policy was part and parcel of the laxness, deadness, and moral compromise that Edwards was witnessing all around him. Second, the change regarding communion is misunderstood if regarded as merely a "communion controversy." At every stage there were deeper ecclesiological issues that went beyond the question of access to communion. In the late 1740s, Edwards was beginning to inquire into the spiritual status of those seeking baptism for their children, and this led some parishioners to fear that he had abandoned the Half-Way Covenant with its clear differentiation of a low standard for baptismal qualification and a high standard for eucharistic participation. The "communion controversy" was thus a "sacramental controversy" that involved the issue of baptism as well as communion. Better yet, one might dub it an "ecclesial controversy," since the nature of the church community and church membership were the underlying issues.

Edwards's break with Stoddard's sacramental policy was a shift in ecclesiology—in the direction of a purer church, based on common confession and strict discipline, and away from the national, territorial, and civil conception of the church that Stoddard had championed. To be sure, there is debate as to *when* Edwards changed his views on admission to the Eucharist, and even *whether* Edwards had ever fully embraced Stoddard's position, or was simply willing to put up with a practice that he may—even in the 1720s—have deemed less than ideal. Yet the sacramental and ecclesial issues took on a new meaning in the context of the spiritual letdown of the later 1740s because Edwards became convinced that a business-as-usual approach to his pastoral ministry would only magnify the spiritual damage and loss that he saw taking place within his congregation. Hence Edwards underwent what we might call an ecclesial-sacramental turn at this stage in his development.

The Calvinistic-Controversial Turn (Late 1740s to Early 1750s)

In speaking of a Calvinistic-controversial turn, our point is not that Edwards's views changed in midlife but rather than he came to a point when he felt compelled to speak out, and to engage in public controversy, regarding the "doctrines of grace" as defined and affirmed by Calvinists. So the stress lies on the word "controversial" in describing this turn in Edwards's thinking. If we accept the "Personal Narrative" (around 1739) as a reliable record of Edwards's early development, then it seems that Edwards during his teen years and indeed "from childhood up" had questioned "the doctrine of God's sovereignty, in choosing whom he would to eternal life, and rejecting whom he pleased." Undoubtedly Edwards here refers to the historic Reformed doctrine of unconditional predestination, and he writes that "it used to appear like a horrible doctrine to me." Yet around the time of Edwards's conversion and "new sense" of divine glory (about 1721), he came to accept the sovereignty of God with a sense of "delightful conviction." "Absolute sovereignty is what I love to ascribe to God. But my first conviction was not with this."[23]

Throughout his voluminous writings, Edwards left no evidence that he ever shifted from—or seriously questioned—the Calvinistic stance that he adopted when he was converted. His first publication, "God Glorified in Man's Dependence" (1731), was noticeably Calvinistic. Both Perry Miller and George Marsden interpreted the sermon as a manifesto for Calvinist renewal.[24] During the 1730s, Edwards perceived a growth of "Arminianism"—a moralistic, mitigated version of Calvinism, affirming that human beings had at least some capacity to turn themselves toward God through their natural powers (ch. 3). In 1735, a Springfield, Massachusetts, congregation's offer of a pastorate to Robert Breck—a young Harvard graduate with outspoken anti-Calvinist views—brought the theological issues out into the open. The swirl of issues surrounding Breck convinced Edwards that the "Arminian" threat was far more pressing and dangerous to the cause of orthodoxy and vital religion that he had earlier imagined. The forces of rationalism had gone far toward undermining sound doctrine and so Edwards sought to address the challenge, most notably in *Freedom of the Will* (1754) and *Original Sin* (1758).

---

23. WJE 16:792.

24. "God Glorified in Man's Dependence" is found in WJE 17:200–16. On the preaching of his sermon, see Perry Miller, *Jonathan Edwards*, 3–34, and George Marsden, *Jonathan Edwards*, 137–42.

The "Controversies Notebooks" and other writings on grace show the extent to which Edwards had become preoccupied with the "doctrines of grace" during the 1740s and 1750s. A late letter speaks of the "almost inconceivably pernicious" doctrines of Arminianism.[25] The presumption of the human will's "self-determining" power underlay all manner of theological error, and therefore needed to be utterly refuted. "Most alarming was how popular the deceptive doctrines had suddenly become in New England," writes Marsden.[26] Clergy and laity were ignoring or abandoning the old theological landmarks.

Edwards's earliest literary ambition—as revealed in "The Mind" and the outline for a "Rational Account"—was to write a book that was a general apologetic for Christianity and not for Calvinism as such. Yet as Edwards saw the growth of Arminianism the plan to write on behalf of Calvinism took center stage for him in the 1750s. By the mid- to late 1750s, Edwards had returned to a revised version of his original plan for a "Rational Account," no longer as a philosophical project but as *A History of the Work of Redemption*.[27] It was only after Edwards had completed his polemical works *Freedom of the Will* (1754) and *Original Sin* (1758) that he felt free to resume his work on redemptive history. Thus one may speak of a Calvinistic-controversial turn not because of a change of views on Edwards's part, but because of a perceived change in the theological climate.

The Cultural-Historical Turn (Mid- to Late 1750s)

Perhaps Edwards's most surprising intellectual turn occurred in the 1750s as he pondered the magnum opus he intended to write. Gerald McDermott's monograph, *Jonathan Edwards Confronts the Gods* (2000), demonstrated the extent of Edwards's engagement with non-Christian religions and cultures in his later years. McDermott concluded that Edwards had done more study of non-Christian religions than any other colonial American. There were early signs of this interest. While still a student at Yale, Edwards's "Catalogue" of books indicated that he was interested in finding "a book Comparing all Religions with the Xtian [i.e., Christian]."[28] The *Miscellanies* from the

---

25. WJE 16:719.

26. Marsden, *Jonathan Edwards*, 433.

27. See Ava Chamberlain's "Editor's Introduction," in WJE 18:24–34.

28. Peter Thuesen, "Editor's Introduction," in WJE 26:13.

1750s—and especially those from 1757–58—show an accelerating pace of research into non-Christian faiths. Edwards transcribed a wealth of information on this topic from all information sources available to him.

So what was going on? Toward the end of his life, Edwards was in the process of reconceptualizing the history of redemption as a history of religions. The story he wanted to tell was to include various non-Christian religions in addition to Christianity. What we are calling a cultural-historical turn denotes Edwards's late-life preoccupation with "other" cultures—i.e., other than Anglo-American, English-language, and Protestant. Moreover, he was not only interested in identifying God's work within non-Christian cultures and religions but also in the secular aspects of Western civilization. This was an arena where few—if any—of Edwards's theological contemporaries would have looked to describe and depict a redemptive history.

To grasp Edwards's cultural-historical turn, one must consider multiple sources—including the unpublished "Redemption Notebooks," the 1757 letter to the trustees of the College of New Jersey, and the late *Miscellanies*.[29] Read together, these pieces of evidence show that Edwards's uncompleted summa was to be novel in several ways. This work was to be an account of Christian theology in an "entire new method" and "thrown into the form of a history." Given Edwards's wide acquaintance with earlier theological works, it is striking to find him mentioning the novelty of his own emerging work and doing it in such a high-profile way—in a formal letter to his possible future employers. This indicates that Edwards's concept for the project was well advanced by 1757 and that his chosen method was innovative indeed. John Wilson's analysis of the "Redemption Notebooks" shows that Edwards began concentrated work on this project no earlier than 1755, that his "intellectual energies were becoming centered on this project, and that accepting the trustees' invitation would require him to turn aside from that project in a far more immediate sense than has usually been thought to be the case."[30] Striking by its absence from the letter to the college trustees is any overt mention of the study of non-Christian religions. Perhaps the non-Christian aspect of the massive project was simply too unconventional for Edwards to mention in a brief letter, where it might easily be misconstrued (ch. 12).

---

29. The letter to the college trustees is given in WJE 16:725–30; see also John F. Wilson, "Appendix B: Jonathan Edwards's Notebooks for *A History of the Work of Redemption*, in WJE 9:543–56.

30. John F. Wilson, "Appendix B," in WJE 9:555.

Yet the later *Miscellanies* remove all doubt. Edwards's was setting out to write a comprehensive account of redemptive history that was to include ancient Greece and Rome, China, India, and other "heathen" or non-Christian traditions. Continuing the so-called *prisca theologia* of the ancient church fathers and Renaissance humanists, Edwards held that beyond the written revelation of scripture there were also oral and unwritten traditions among the various peoples of earth (chs. 9, 36). "Immediate instructions" came to the patriarchs and ancients in visions, miracles and inspiration of his Spirit—to men such as Noah, Abraham, Isaac, Jacob, Job, and Melchizedek. These messages were passed on to later generations by oral tradition. This primeval revelation—though later distorted by human sin and pressed into the service of idolatry—contained genuine anticipations of later Christian teachings. Those in China and India held to something like the doctrine of the Trinity, while notions of propitiatory sacrifice, indwelling by spirits (or the Spirit), and other doctrines were widely diffused. Pagan religions were thus a preparation for—and foreshadowing of—the Christian gospel.

Just as with the other four "turns" noted in this chapter, the cultural-historical turn was shaped by Edwards's social milieu. During the 1750s in Stockbridge, he was engaged in ministry among adherents of a non-Western culture and non-Christian religion (i.e., Native Americans). Believing that whites might learn from Native Americans, as well as Native Americans from whites, and that they might both play some role in shaping a multicultural and multilingual future for the church, he sent his son, Jonathan Edwards Jr., to learn the Indians' language.[31] American blacks, Africans, Native Americans, whites, and those from far-off nations were all equals in the sight of God. Edwards's final intensive study of non-Christian religions and cultures was molded by his daily encounters with Native Americans. This missionary endeavor in a North American context launched his thinking in a global direction.

From the preceding, it should be clear that Edwards's theology was by no means a finished product when he began his pastorate in the 1720s. Nor was he islanded and isolated in his reflections—a man shut up in his study, thinking solitary thoughts. Instead every development noted above had something to do with Edwards's context. The introduction to this volume (ch. 1) noted that Edwards was an open rather than closed-system thinker. This meant that he was not seeking to create a system of timeless truths. Instead he engaged in prolonged reflection on a set of central issues, and as he did so he advanced further in his ideas and insights.

---

31. George Claghorn, "Editor's Introduction," in WJE 16:22.

PART TWO

Topics in Edwards's Theology

SECTION I
Methods and Strategies

6

Beauty and Aesthetics

EDWARDS CAME TO the theme of beauty at the commencement of his theological development. The very first entry into the *Miscellanies* began with the words: "Holiness is a most beautiful and lovely thing."[1] Edwards regarded beauty as fundamental to his understanding of God, as the first of God's perfections, as key to the doctrine of the Trinity, as a defining aspect of the natural world, as basic to the phenomenon of conversion, as visible in the lives of saints, and as marking the difference between the regenerate and the unregenerate mind. Edwards's interpreters have underscored the centrality of beauty to his thought. Roland Delattre wrote, "Beauty is fundamental to Edwards's understanding of being. It is the first principle of being, the inner, structural principle of being-itself."[2] Louis Mitchell remarked that "the language of beauty provided Edwards with a framework to express his understanding of genuine religious experience."[3] Alan Heimert noted the way that Edwards understood beauty as an attractive and motivating power: "It was not ratiocination, but an aesthetic perception of the good, that according to Edwards determined human action."[4] This stress on beauty set Edwards apart from other Protestant authors, as Douglas Elwood said: "His stress on the primacy of the aesthetic over the moral and legal in our experience of God places the old Calvinism on a very different footing."[5] The Hungarian scholar Katalin Kallay commented that other Puritan writers were "centered around ethical norms," while Edwards's "focus on divine beauty and aesthetics" makes him interesting, accessible, and relevant today.[6] One might

---

1. WJE 13:163.

2. Roland Delattre, *Beauty and Sensibility in the Thought of Jonathan Edwards; An Essay in Aesthetics and Theological Ethics* (New Haven and London: Yale University Press, 1968), 1.

3. Louis Mitchell, *Jonathan Edwards on the Experience of Beauty*, Studies in Reformed Theology and History (Princeton, NJ: Princeton Theological Seminary, 2003), ix.

4. Alan Heimert, *Religion and the American Mind: From the Great Awakening to the Revolution* (Cambridge, MA: Harvard University Press, 1966), 194.

5. Douglas Elwood, *The Philosophical Theology of Jonathan Edwards* (New York: Columbia University Press, 1960), 3.

6. Katalin G. Kallay, "Alternative Viewpoint: Edwards and Beauty," in Gerald R. McDermott, ed., *Understanding Jonathan Edwards: An Introduction to America's Theologian* (New York: Oxford University Press, 2009), 127.

interpret the whole of Edwards's theology as the gradual, complex outworking of a primal vision of God's beauty that came to him in the wake of his conversion experience.

Yet if Edwards's treatment of beauty is distinctive, it is also unexpected. No earlier Calvinistic author had assigned such a pivotal role to beauty. Friedrich Schleiermacher—as a Plato scholar and theological liberal—might have been expected to give a large place to beauty in his theology, and yet he did not assign it the constitutive role that Edwards did. Continental Protestantism had to wait two centuries longer than American Protestantism, until Karl Barth in the 1930s and 1940s began to reflect on the importance of beauty for theology. When Barth ventured into this field, he expressed trepidation: "Owing to its connexion with the ideas of pleasure, desire and enjoyment (quite apart from its historical connexion with Greek thought), the concept of the beautiful seems to be a particularly secular one, not at all adapted for introduction into the language of theology, and indeed extremely dangerous."[7] There are many reasons to regard Edwards as an original and venturesome thinker. Yet his placement of beauty at the heart of his theology may have been the boldest stroke of all.

Primary and Secondary, Divine and Creaturely Beauty

In approaching beauty, Edwards's outlook was Platonic. He was not an aesthetician in the sense that he was preoccupied with physical beauty for its own sake. Still less was he an advocate of *l'art pour l'art*—"art for art's sake." He had almost nothing to say regarding manmade beauties. Edwards's Platonism led him to distinguish physical from spiritual beauties. Throughout his writings he lauded spiritual beauty as a thing immeasurably greater and higher than any earthly or physical beauties. The former he described as "primary beauty" and the latter as "secondary beauty."[8] As spirit was truly real and bodies were "shadows" of spirit (ch. 7), so spiritual beauties were genuine, permanent, and real, while bodily beauties were "shadows" of spiritual beauties. To the extent that Edwards wrote on physical beauties, he referred them back to the Creator as "images" or "shadows of divine things."[9] Natural beauties were types (ch. 8). "The beauty of the world," he wrote, "consists wholly of sweet mutual consents, either within itself or with the supreme being. As to the corporeal world,

---

7. Karl Barth, *Church Dogmatics*, II/1 (Edinburgh: T. & T. Clark, 1957), 651–52.

8. WJE 8:561–74 contains an extended discussion of primary and secondary beauty.

9. WJE 11:50–130 contains Edwards's notebook entries describing the types of spiritual things in nature.

though there are many other sorts of consents, yet the sweetest and most charming beauty of it is its resemblance of spiritual beauties." This "beauty...peculiar to natural things" is "surpassing the art of man."[10] Beauties deriving from the artifice of human beings could be deceitful and misleading, but not so the beauties of nature when properly perceived in relation to the Creator.

Yet the Creator's handiwork in the natural world was really only an antechamber to the sanctuary of beauty. It was in the realm of spirit that one found true beauty. As Norman Fiering noted, "For Edwards all that is ordinarily meant by 'beauty' was to be understood only as a symbolic counterpoint to a higher kind of correspondence, that of wills."[11] Only intelligent and volitional beings could exhibit and express spiritual beauty by giving "consent"—a term that implied volition, affection, and love—to God's being and to one another. A stone might "consent" to the law of gravity but not to the law of love. "The highest excellency...must be the consent of spirits one to another."[12] The natural world had beauty, and yet its beauty consisted in its systemic analogy to the "mutual love" between intelligent beings: "The sweet harmony between the various parts of the universe is only an image of mutual love."[13]

In one of Edwards's most striking statements, he asserted that beauty constituted the "divinity" of God: "This is the beauty of the Godhead, and the divinity of the Divinity (if I may so speak), the good of the infinite Fountain of Good; without which God himself (if that were possible to be) would be an infinite evil." Stated in other words, "God is God, and distinguished from all other beings, and exalted above 'em, chiefly by his divine beauty, which is infinitely diverse from all other beauty." Divine beauty is "that...wherein the truest idea of divinity does consist." Beauty and holiness were almost interchangeable terms, for "the beauty of the divine nature does primarily consist in God's holiness."[14] God's beauty was the source of all created beauty: "All the beauty to be found throughout the whole creation, is but the reflection of the diffused beams of the Being who hath an infinite fullness of brightness and glory."[15] God created the world to manifest God's beauty, or rather, Christ's beauty:

---

10. WJE 6:305.

11. Norman Fiering, *Jonathan Edwards's Moral Thought and Its British Context* (Chapel Hill: University of North Carolina Press, 1981), 82.

12. WJE 6:337.

13. WJE 6:337–38.

14. WJE 2:274, 298, 258.

15. WJE 8:550–51.

> The Son of God created the world for this very end, to communicate himself in an image of his own excellency. He communicates himself properly only to spirits; and they only are capable of being proper images of his excellency, for they only are properly beings.... Yet he communicates a sort of shadow or glimpse of his excellencies to bodies, which as we have seen, are but the shadows of being, and not real beings.[16]

In another context, he wrote that "all the beauties of the universe do as immediately result from the efficiency of Christ as a cast of an eye or smile of the countenance depends on the efficiency of the human soul."[17] It follows that "when we are delighted with flowery meadows and gentle breezes of wind, we may consider that we only see the emanations of the sweet benevolence of Jesus Christ." The differing aspects of the natural world express differing aspects of Christ's beauty: "There are also many things wherein we may behold his awful majesty: in the sun in his strength, in comets, in thunder, in the towering thunder clouds, in ragged rocks and the brows of mountains."[18] God's beauty overflows, for, as Delattre wrote, "beauty is not self-contained."[19]

Even in Edwards's early writing in "The Mind," beauty had a Trinitarian dimension. He linked beauty to his distinctive concept of "proportion," and this meant that beauty involved internal complexity or diversity. As Edwards expressed it, "one alone, without reference to any more, cannot be excellent."[20] So it is also with God, for God's "infinite beauty is his infinite mutual love of himself." Edwards explained: "God's excellence consists in the love of himself.... But he exerts himself towards himself no other way than in infinitely loving and delighting in himself, in the mutual love of the Father and the Son. This makes the third, the personal Holy Spirit or the holiness of God, which is his infinite beauty, and this is God's infinite consent to being in general." While all beauty in creatures was a beauty by participation in God's beauty, so all beauty in God derived from God's inmost nature and not from any source outside of God. He writes: "'Tis peculiar to God that he has beauty within himself, consisting in being's consenting with his own being, or the love of himself in his own Holy Spirit; whereas the excellence of others is in loving others, in loving God, and in the

---

16. WJE 13:279.

17. WJE 13:330.

18. WJE 13:279.

19. Delattre, *Beauty and Sensibility*, 24, orig. emph.

20. WJE 6:337.

communications of his Spirit."[21] Delattre observed that "the model of beauty is the beautifying rather than the beautiful."[22] Beauty was never something static, but was instead a dynamic and creative principle operating within the Trinity and the created World. In his *Discourse on the Trinity*, Edwards asserted that "God is infinitely happy in the enjoyment of himself" and that "[the] Holy Ghost is divine beauty, love and joy."[23] Because the Holy Spirit is God's gift to human beings, and this gift of God is indeed God himself, the spiritual beauty that exists in the saints is nothing other than an extension of God's own beauty as it is "emanated" or "communicated" to them. As Sang Lee has noted, there is a "repetition" of the being and beauty of God among the saints and in the holy community that they constitute: "To know and love God, therefore, is to know and love the beauty of God, and to know the ultimate nature of the world is to know and love the world as an image of God's beauty."[24] In *End of Creation*, Edwards further developed the logic of God's love for himself. While the saints in a special sense are bearers of divine beauty, the same is true to some degree of every existing thing, so the world as a whole is an overflow and expression of God's beauty.

But what exactly *is* beauty? Edwards's early text, "The Mind," noted: "There is nothing [that has] been more without a definition than excellency, although it be what we are more concerned with than anything else whatsoever." As the discussion unfolds, the term "excellency" is understood as a synonym for beauty. He goes on to explain that "proportion is pleasant to the mind and disproportion unpleasant" and that "proportion" itself is "an equality, or likeness of ratios."[25] "All beauty," says Edwards, "consists in similarity or identity of relations." He illustrated this visually in his notebook by drawing arrangements of dots on the page in patterns that are mirror images of one another. The mirrored patterns, he comments, are more beautiful than any patterns of dots that exhibit no correspondences or symmetries. Not some but all forms of beauty, says Edwards, involve patterned relationships of part to whole and whole to part: "In every case, what is called correspondence, symmetry, regularity and the like, may be resolved into equalities; though the equalities in a beauty in any

---

21. WJE 6:363–65.

22. Delattre, *Beauty and Sensibility*, 25 [italicized in the original], 108.

23. WJE 21:113, 144.

24. Sang Hyun Lee, "Edwards and Beauty," in Gerald R. McDermott, ed., *Understanding Jonathan Edwards: An Introduction to America's Theologian* (New York: Oxford University Press, 2009), 113–25, citing 113.

25. WJE 6:332.

degree complicated are so numerous that it would be a most tedious piece of work to enumerate them." The natural response of the human mind on encountering these patterns of symmetry and correspondence is delight or pleasure: "The pleasures of the senses... are the result of equality."[26]

In "The Mind," Edwards presented a classical or neoclassical ideal of beauty. For the Romantics of the early 1800s, beauty did not need to be proportioned. One might consider, for instance, the landscape painters who composed their scenes asymmetrically, sometimes featuring a tiny human figure in the corner of the painting overshadowed by a cliff or a range of mountain peaks.[27] Appealing to notions of the sublime, the Romantics welcomed disproportion and sometimes reveled in wildness or disorder. In contrast to such aesthetic ideals, Edwards's theory of beauty reminds one of the sculptured and geometric precision of the gardens of the Palace of Versailles. His aesthetic ideal fit with eighteenth-century neoclassicism. On the other hand, Edwards did not limit himself to the idea of beauty as a straightforward or uncomplicated proportion among a set of elements. He embraced the idea that beauty—whether physical or spiritual—could and would include disproportion as well as proportion. The point arose in Edwards's discussion of "confined beauty" in contrast to "extended beauty," where the context or framing of the object determines whether an object appears as beautiful. The basic principle is "that [which] is beautiful with respect to the universality of things has a generally extended excellence and a true beauty."[28] Beauty in the highest and truest sense was beauty that appeared when a thing was considered in the broadest context, that is, "with respect to the generality of things." What seems to be disproportionate in a narrow context might appear proportionate in a broader context. In this case, disproportion would be part of a higher proportion—like a jazz chord that jangles when played by itself but harmonizes within a progression of chords.

An opposite situation occurs when something appears to be beautiful when taken in a narrow context, and yet appears disproportionate—or even hideous—when considered in a larger context. Though Edwards does not elaborate this point, it might be helpful to consider what Katalin Kallay refers to as the case of "undeniably decadent or diabolic beauty."[29] One might ask why

---

26. WJE 6:334–35.

27. An example of Romantic disproportion in a landscape is John Turner's *Hadleigh Castle* (1829).

28. WJE 6:344.

29. Kallay, "Alternative Viewpoint," 129.

the character of Satan in Milton's *Paradise Lost* may be captivating and aesthetically pleasing to a reader? Or why the great villains of literature and film—Count Dracula, Lady Macbeth, Hannibal Lecter—often draw more interest than the heroes? The attractiveness of the diabolic figure in a drama could be a paradigm case of Edwards's "confined beauty": "That which is beautiful...only with respect to itself and a few other things, and not as a part of that which contains all things—the universe—is false beauty, and a confined beauty."[30] The villain is not merely disproportioned but—so to speak—perfectly disproportioned. Because the wicked character is eminently adapted for evil aims rather than good, he or she might have a semblance of beauty in his or her adaptedness for evil, though Edwards, as indicated, would certainly regard this as a form of "false" or "confined beauty." Viewed in the context of universal Being, Satan is "odious" and not at all "amiable."

Any discussion of Edwards's idea of beauty would be incomplete if it did not take into account the subjective response to beauty. As Delattre observed, Edwards's teaching on beauty and aesthetics moved back and forth from an objective to a subjective pole. "Taken together," he wrote, "beauty and sensibility may be said to be the objective and subjective components of the moral or spiritual life."[31] For Edwards, beauty was both objective and subjective. Beauty had an effect, and the effect was an affect (i.e., feeling). Yet Edwards balanced the objective and subjective aspects of beauty so that neither eclipsed the other. But how was it possible for human beings to perceive beauties of a spiritual sort? This question leads into Edwards's entire theory of spiritual sensibility and the "sense of the heart"—a topic of considerable intricacy, and treated elsewhere in this volume (chs. 10, 20, 24).[32]

A key point for Edwards was that spiritual beauty was not apparent to all. Only a mind reborn and renewed through the Holy Spirit could appreciate the spiritual beauties exhibited in God himself, the truths of the gospel, the virtues of the saint, and the community of faith. "When the true beauty...is discovered to the soul, it as it were opens a new world to its view." The converse is also true, since "he who sees the beauty of holiness, must necessarily see the hatefulness of sin, its contrary." This spiritual sense is "infinitely more noble" than any other sense, since "the object of this sense [is] infinitely greater and more

---

30. WJE 6:344.

31. Delattre, *Beauty and Sensibility*, 3.

32. For a fuller account of spiritual sensibility, see Michael J. McClymond, *Encounters With God: An Approach to the Theology of Jonathan Edwards* (New York: Oxford University Press, 1998), 9–26.

important."[33] The taste and relish for divine beauty flows from divine grace, as indicated in the *Treatise on Grace*: "The first effect of the power of God in the heart in regeneration, is to give the heart a divine taste or sense, to cause it to have relish of the loveliness and sweetness of the supreme excellency of the divine nature." Edwards added that "this is all the Spirit of God needs to do, in order to a production of all good effects in the soul."[34] The perception of divine beauty was spiritually efficacious. With the conferral of this spiritual taste, all good consequences would follow. Without this spiritual taste, no moral goodness or true virtue would be possible. "If the moral beauty of God be hid, the enmity of the heart will remain in its full strength, no love will be enkindled... whereas the first glimpse of the moral and spiritual glory of God shining into the heart, produces all these effects."[35]

As the saints perceive and respond to God's beauty, they themselves acquire a beauty that is "the moral image of God in them."[36] The beauty of the saints consists in a comprehensive and well-ordered moral and spiritual character, free from disproportion and deformity, so that they become "proportioned Christians."[37] As Edwards noted in *Religious Affections*: "Another thing wherein those affections that are truly gracious and holy, differ from those that are false, is beautiful symmetry and proportion."[38] Similarly, in *Charity and Its Fruits*, Edwards spoke of the concomitant development of various virtues or of "Christian graces concatenated together."[39] Faith, love, hope, humility, repentance, thankfulness, reverence, submission, patience, contentment, meekness—these and all other graces of the Christian life grow together and not in isolation. The spiritual beauty of the saints consists in a complex of discrete though interrelated virtues.

As each saint responds to the beauty of God, so each responds to the beauty of other saints. For one person's consent to being is not isolated from that of another person, and "it is naturally agreeable to perceiving being that being should consent to being."[40] As a result, there is a multiplying effect of consent

---

33. WJE 2:273–75.

34. WJE 21:174.

35. WJE 2:264–65.

36. WJE 2:258.

37. WJE 8:338.

38. WJE 2:365.

39. WJE 8:326–38.

40. WJE 6:365. "Being's consent to being must needs be agreeable to perceiving being" (WJE 6:362).

and beauty within the community of the saints. Each saint not only consents to God but to the consent of other saints to God—a process that comes to consummation in heaven (ch. 19). The holy community, joined together in unity, is a community of consent that possesses its own special beauty. For "union is spoken of in Scripture as the peculiar beauty of the church of Christ," and "'tis one of the most beautiful and happy things on earth, which indeed makes earth most like heaven."[41] Krister Sairsingh writes: "The church is the community which re-presents the divine community of consent. And in this human community of co-consenters to being in general, the divine glory becomes visible."[42] Conrad Cherry comments that, Edwards's "theory of virtue brought into symbiotic relation the beauty of the cosmos, the beauty of human morality, and the beauty of divine benevolence."[43]

---

41. WJE 5:365.

42. Krister Sairsingh, "Jonathan Edwards and the Idea of Divine Glory: His Foundational Trinitarianism and its Ecclesial Import," PhD diss., Harvard University, 1986, 287; cited in Mitchell, *Jonathan Edwards on the Experience of Beauty*, 15.

43. Conrad Cherry, *Nature and Religious Imagination: From Edwards to Bushnell* (Philadelphia, PA: Fortress Press, 1980), 62.

7
Metaphysics

PERRY MILLER, WHEN introducing the first volume in the Yale University Press edition of Edwards's *Works* in 1957, referred to Edwards as "the greatest philosopher-theologian yet to grace the American scene."[1] Intellectual historian Bruce Kuklick commented that "the foundation stone in the history of American philosophy is Jonathan Edwards."[2] For more than two centuries, there has been a general recognition of Edwards's high stature as metaphysician or philosophical thinker. Yet opinions on Edwards's "philosophy" have varied widely. Twentieth-century philosophers interpreted it in strikingly different ways (ch. 40). Even Miller's lavish praise for Edwards involved an ambiguity. Which term—"philosopher" or "theologian"—better typified Edwards? Was he a philosopher who engaged in theology or a theologian who dabbled in philosophy? Or was he an innovator who somehow combined the two? Moreover, which of Edwards's many philosophical ideas or arguments were most fundamental to his thinking? Was there some root idea in Edwards's thought—being, beauty, empiricism, idealism, theocentrism, divine causality, etc.—that served to explain everything else? A rich literature has sprung up to address such questions.[3]

---

1. WJE 1:viii.

2. Bruce Kuklick, "Jonathan Edwards and American Philosophy," in Nathan O. Hatch and Harry S. Stout, eds., *Jonathan Edwards and the American Experience* (New York: Oxford University Press, 1986), 246.

3. Among the recent contributors on Edwards's philosophy are Wallace E. Anderson, "Editor's Introduction," in WJE 6:1–143; Jonathan Chai, *Jonathan Edwards and the Limits of Enlightenment Philosophy* (New York: Oxford University Press, 1998); Oliver Crisp, "Jonathan Edwards on the Divine Nature," *Journal of Reformed Theology* 3 (2009): 175–201; Stephen H. Daniel, "Edwards as Philosopher," in Stephen Stein, ed., *The Cambridge Companion to Jonathan Edwards* (Cambridge, UK: Cambridge University Press, 2007), 162–79, and *The Philosophy of Jonathan Edwards: A Study in Divine Semiotics* (Bloomington, IN: Indiana University Press, 1994); Roland Delattre, *Beauty and Sensibility in the Thought of Jonathan Edwards* (New Haven: Yale University Press, 1968); Douglas Elwood, *The Philosophical Theology of Jonathan Edwards* (New York: Columbia University Press, 1960); Paul Helm and Oliver D. Crisp, eds., *Jonathan Edwards: Philosophical Theologian* (Aldershot, UK: Ashgate, 2003); Sang Hyun Lee, *The Philosophical Theology of Jonathan Edwards* (Princeton, NJ: Princeton University Press, 1988); Michael J. McClymond, *Encounters With God: An Approach to the Theology of Jonathan Edwards* (New York: Oxford University Press, 1998), 27–36; Richard R. Niebuhr, "Being and Consent," in Sang Hyun Lee, ed., *The Princeton Companion to Jonathan Edwards* (Princeton,

A century ago, the dominant question among scholars regarding Edwards's philosophy was what intellectual sources he may have drawn upon in developing his idealism or immaterialism. A consensus emerged that Edwards was not dependent on the writings of the well-known British idealist, George Berkeley, but independently arrived at similar conclusions. This conclusion was propounded by H. N. Gardiner in a 1900 essay and later confirmed in Wallace Anderson's analysis in the "Editor's Introduction" to Edwards's *Scientific and Philosophical Writings* (1980). The outcome of this discussion was an accent on Edwards's independence and originality. Neither Edwards's idealism nor the other major aspects of his philosophical thought were simply borrowed from elsewhere. The same conclusion emerged from Norman Fiering's patient work on Edwards's intellectual sources.[4] Edwards drew eclectically from the Puritan authors, Cambridge Platonists, Continental metaphysicians, and Locke's empiricism, and yet he actively transmuted and refashioned nearly all of the ideas that he appropriated from the sources he read. So it would be misleading to pigeonhole Edwards an adherent of one or another early modern school of thought. Edwards's originality may help to explain the interest he has stirred in philosophers of widely differing types (ch. 40).

Characterizing Edwards as a Metaphysical Thinker

Outside of the consensus regarding Edwards's idealism, there has been much debate regarding basic issues in Edwards's philosophy. An A-to-Z listing of terms applied to Edwards would include: aesthetic, atomistic, Calvinist, determinist, dispositional, dynamic, empiricist, idealist, immaterialist, Lockean, modern, medieval, monistic, mystical, Neoplatonic, Newtonian, occasionalist, panentheist, pantheistic, rationalist, relational, sensationalist, symbolic, theocentric, typological, and unitary. A case could be made for nearly all of these

---

NJ: Princeton University Press, 2005), 34–43; Miklos Vetö, "Edwards and Philosophy," in Gerald R. McDermott, ed., *Understanding Jonathan Edwards: An Introduction to America's Theologian* (New York: Oxford University Press, 2009), 151–70, and *La pensée de Jonathan Edwards* (Paris: Les Éditions du Cerf, 1987), esp. 42–65 (2nd. Ed., Paris: L'Harmattan, 2007); and Avihu Zakai, "The Age of Enlightenment," in Stephen Stein, ed., *The Cambridge Companion to Jonathan Edwards* (Cambridge, UK: Cambridge University Press, 2007), 80–99. An English translation of the expanded, second edition (2007) of Vetö's major work on Edwards will soon be appearing as: *The Thought of Jonathan Edwards*, translated by Philip Choniere-Shields (Eugene, OR: Wipf & Stock, forthcoming).

4. See Norman Fiering, *Jonathan Edwards' Moral Thought and Its British Context* (Chapel Hill, NC: University of North Carolina Press, 1981); and Fiering, "The Rationalist Foundations of Jonathan Edwards' Metaphysics," in Nathan O. Hatch and Harry S. Stout, eds., *Jonathan Edwards and the American Experience* (New York: Oxford University Press, 1988), 73–101.

terms. Perry Miller highlighted the empiricist aspect and Edwards's indebtedness to John Locke, commenting that "the simplest, and most precise, definition of Edwards's thought is that it was Puritanism recast into the idiom of empirical psychology."[5] Norman Fiering challenged this reading of Edwards by noting his affinities with the Cambridge Platonists and with Continental thinkers, especially those dubbed as the "theocentric metaphysicians"—Norris, More, Cudworth, Malebranche, and Leibniz.[6]

During the late twentieth century, a number of interpreters sought to identify a fundamental motif that integrates the whole of Edwards's metaphysical and philosophical reflection.[7] Thus Perry Miller stressed Edwards's empiricism, while Douglas Elwood spoke of God's "immediacy" to all creatures, Roland Delattre accented "beauty and sensibility," Sang Lee wrote of Edwards's "dispositional ontology," and Stephen Daniel centered on "semiotics." In the end, none succeeded in convincing the others. Sang Lee's emphasis on "disposition" or "dispositional ontology" had perhaps the widest influence in shaping recent readings of Edwards's philosophy or philosophical theology. Yet during the first decade of the new millennium, Oliver Crisp, Stephen Holmes, and Steven Studebaker expressed strong reservations about Lee's "dispositional" interpretation of Edwards.[8] The diversity of views regarding Edwards's philosophy should warn against an overreliance on any single line of interpretations. One of the best recent studies—Miklos Vetö's *Le pensée de Jonathan Edwards* (1987; 2007, 2nd ed.)—offers an intensive examination of Edwards's philosophical thought and yet does not trace it back to a single root principle.

From the time of Martin Luther onward, Protestant theologians were often dubious about the value of philosophical reflection in the sphere of Christian theology. Luther himself rejected the dominant Aristotelian philosophy of his day, declaring at the beginning of his theological career that "the whole of Aristotle is to theology as darkness is to light."[9] Nearer to our own time, Karl Barth,

---

5. Miller, *Jonathan Edwards*, 62.

6. Fiering, "Rationalist Foundations of Jonathan Edwards' Metaphysics," 73–101.

7. The term "fundamental motif" comes from Anders Nygren, who describes is as "the basic idea or the driving power of the religion concerned, or what it is that gives it its character as a whole" (*Agape and Eros*, rev. ed; Philadelphia, PA: Westminster, 1953; 35).

8. For a detailed account of this complex debate, see Michael J. McClymond, "Hearing the Symphony: A Critique of Some Critics of Sang Lee's and Amy Pauw's Accounts of Jonathan Edwards' God," in Don Schweitzer, ed., *Jonathan Edwards as Contemporary: Essays in Honor of Sang Hyun Lee* (New York: Peter Lang, 2010), 67–92.

9. H. T. Lehmann and J. Grimm, eds., *Luther's Works*, 55 volumes (Philadelphia, PA: Fortress Press, 1957), 31:112–13.

in his early *Epistle to the Romans*, spoke of God as "wholly Other," and hence as inexplicable in terms of ordinary metaphysical categories. In his *Church Dogmatics*, Barth castigated the characteristic Roman Catholic teaching on *analogia entis*—the idea that all existing things bear some analogy to God's being—as "the invention of Antichrist."[10] To be sure, the Protestant scholastics, as noted earlier (ch. 3), were ready to adopt philosophical principles in theological reasoning, and one can even speak of "Calvinist Thomists" during the 1600s. Yet Edwards's embrace of metaphysics and metaphysical argumentation distinguished him from Reformation thought (Luther, Calvin) as well as twentieth-century Neo-Orthodoxy or Neo-Reformational theology (Karl Barth). It placed him nearer to such patristic and medieval thinkers as Augustine, Anselm, Aquinas, and Bonaventure. The entire structure of Edwards's reasoning implied an *analogia entis*—a cosmos in which God and creatures are both alike and unlike in important ways (ch. 43). This feature has led readers to refer to him as "medieval" though also recognizably "modern."

Inasmuch as every existing thing reflects its Creator, the universe is filled with signs and vestiges of God's presence. The whole body of Edwards's metaphysical and typological reflections rested on a notion of continuity between Creator and creation. At the same time, Edwards never compromised his assertion of the radical transcendence of God. As Miklos Vetö suggests, it was the very presence and immediacy of God to all existing things that established Edwards's God as transcendent. Yet the converse was also true. Because God was completely transcendent, God did not exist only here or there, and could be immediately present to all creatures without qualification. Paradoxically, God was immanent by virtue of his transcendence, and transcendent by virtue of his immanence.[11]

There has been debate as to whether Edwards's metaphysical writings, and especially the youthful reflections of the "The Mind" (1723–26), are relevant for the interpretation of the later published works. According to one line of interpretation, "The Mind" and the other philosophical writings of the early years offered a fleeting glimpse of what might have been, had Edwards chosen to be a philosopher rather than a pastor. On this view, Edwards was a metaphysician

---

10. Karl Barth, *Church Dogmatics*, Vol. 1, Part 1, trans. G. T. Thomson (Edinburgh: T. & T. Clark, 1936), x.

11. Vetö elaborates on the paradoxical continuity and discontinuity between Edwards's God and the world: "Edwards paraît professer une continuité d'être entre Dieu et la création mais cette continuité résulte paradoxalement d'une différence extrême. C'est précisément parce que la créature est néant et vanité en elle-même, qu'elle apparaît comme effacée devant Dieu et en continuité ininterrompue avec Lui" (*Le pensée de Jonathan Edwards*, 49).

manqué or failed philosopher. While this judgment has some initial plausibility, it fails to account for the ways in which metaphysical reflection entered into the works of Edwards's maturity. *Religious Affections*, for instance, developed the idea that divine grace in the soul of the converted was equivalent to Locke's "new simple idea." *Original Sin*, in affirming the doctrine of God's continuous creation of the world, reasserted a position defined in Edwards's early metaphysical writings. *End of Creation*—written near the end of Edwards's life—argued that the glory of God could just as well not exist as not be perceived by intelligent creatures. Edwards derived this conclusion from the idealistic premises first set forth in "The Mind."[12] So it does not seem that Edwards ever abandoned metaphysics. Some later writings—especially *End of Creation* and *The Nature of True Virtue*—were among the most resolutely philosophical pieces that he ever wrote. What is more, the failed philosopher idea rests on a mistaken reading of the early as well as the later texts. There was a driving theological interest in Edwards's youthful philosophical texts and even in his technical, scientific writings. He often added one or more "corollaries" in these early essays that addressed the issue of God's relation to the natural world. It appears then that Edwards was a budding theologian even in his earliest period, and that the gap between the youthful and the mature thinker should not be overemphasized.

If there is a single theme that draws together the many disparate lines of thought in Edwards's metaphysical and scientific writings, it may well be theocentrism. For Edwards, God was the measure of all things. He wrote that "God is the prime and original being, the first and last, and the pattern of all, and has the sum of all perfection."[13] In another passage Edwards wrote that "God is, and there is none else."[14] Douglas Elwood commented that "he was a man of one idea, and that one idea was God."[15] Because God's existence was the only fully realized existence, everything else seemed shadowy in comparison. Edwards's theocentrism put him at odds with the intellectual currents of his day. Throughout the 1700s, Enlightenment thinkers reveled in their growing understanding of the material universe but showed far less interest in God and spiritual realities. Edwards turned the tables on any earthbound

---

12. WJE 2:205; WJE 3:402; WJE 8:430–33.

13. WJE 6:363.

14. WJE 6:345. It should be noted that Edwards's phrasing—that has sounded pantheistic to some readers comes directly from scripture, and especially the Book of Isaiah, e.g., "I am the Lord...there is none beside me" (Is. 45:5–6; cf. 45:14, 18, 21, 22; Authorized Version).

15. Elwood, *Philosophical Theology*, 11.

philosophy. For him the existence of God was axiomatic while that of creatures was problematic.

Intertwined with Edwards's insistence on God's metaphysical priority was his rejection of materialism. Edwards regarded as pernicious the theory of Thomas Hobbes that all substance was material. Materialism undermined Christian teaching by casting doubt on the reality of the soul, angels and demons, heaven and hell, and, of course, God himself. Edwards likely learned about Hobbes's views through seeing them discussed in the writings of Henry More. A possible response to Hobbes's materialism would have been for Edwards to admit that matter was substance indeed yet not the only substance. Along these lines, Descartes's philosophy had divided the world into the realm of matter or the "extended thing" (*res extensa*) in distinction from the soul or "thinking thing" (*res cogitans*). Yet this dualistic viewpoint was little better than materialism since it vastly extended the scope of the mechanistic system and sought to explain all animal behavior and all but a few forms of human activity in terms of naturalistic principles.[16] Edwards responded to materialism in a more radical way. He offered a vigorous antithesis to materialism: no matter was properly substance, spiritual realities were more substantial than bodies, and God was the only true substance or self-subsisting being.

As Vetö has noted, Edwards offered three paths to God in his metaphysical and scientific reflections. One was the physical way, reducing all material bodies to resistance, and resistance itself to an immediate exercise of God's power throughout the so-called material universe. A second route was logical, and it argued from the impossibility of any disjunction between being and nothing to the reality of being as necessarily existent. A third approach began with the idealist assumption that all existing things must be known as existing, and that the ground of all existence is the ideas of things as they exist in the mind of God.[17] The following discussion will trace these three lines of thought in Edwards and then offer some concluding reflections on Edwards's concept of God.

The Physical Way to God—Atomism and Natural Philosophy

In his early years, Jonathan Edwards was an enthusiastic exponent of the new physics of Isaac Newton, just beginning to make its impact in New England

---

16. Anderson, "Editor's Introduction," WJE 6:54, 56, 59.
17. Vetö, *Le pensée de Jonathan Edwards*, 48.

during the early 1700s. According to the atomist viewpoint, all phenomena of nature might be explained in terms of the sizes, shapes, and motions of elementary particles and the laws that governed them. The natural philosophy of atomism was law-governed and even deterministic since it suggested that all the atoms of the universe behaved according to fixed rules. Even a small change in the movements and combinations of the atoms might result in a major change in the future development of the universe. On its face, the atomic philosophy seemed inimical to belief in God. It appeared to carry the implication that human beings live in a closed universe of materialistic and mechanical cause and effect. What is remarkable about Edwards is that his commitment to atomism went hand in hand with an affirmation of God's moment-by-moment role in the universe. As Avihu Zakai noted, he "appropriated the atomic doctrine... but Christianized it" by linking it explicitly to the existence and activity of God.[18]

Edwards's early essay "Of Atoms" (ca. 1721) interpreted physical bodies in terms of their solidity, and solidity as a resistance to division or displacement.[19] The existence of any body implied a determinate resistance in a particular time and place. Yet, as Edwards noted, one could not simply assert that matter is self-subsistent—as Hobbes seemed to do—for matter's power or way of resisting had to lie in some cause beyond itself. Edwards concluded that "no matter, is, in the proper sense, matter," and that solidity or resistance was "from the immediate exercise of God's power." This led to the further conclusion that solidity was "nothing but the Deity acting in that particular manner in those parts of space where he thinks fit." Thus the "very substance of the body itself" must be "nothing but the divine power, or the constant exertion of it."[20] This line of argument overturned John Locke's claim that there is an unknown substance or substratum that supports solidity and the other qualities perceived in physical entities. Locke distinguished between "primary qualities" that resided within bodies themselves (e.g., extension in space) and "secondary qualities" (e.g., colors) that were a function of perception rather than of bodies themselves. Yet Edwards rejected this view. Because the essence of bodies—solidity or resistance—was a mode of God's activity, the same was true of all so-called primary and secondary qualities. He concluded that "if solidity is not so [i.e., an inherent property of bodies], neither are the other properties of body, which depend upon it.... So that there is neither real

---

18. Zakai, "The Age of Enlightement," 87.

19. "Of Atoms," in WJE 6:208–18.

20. WJE 6:235, 215, 350–51.

substance nor property belonging to bodies; but all that is real, it is immediately in the first being [i.e. God]."[21]

Throughout his writings, Edwards maintained that God constantly upholds the physical universe. Sometimes he asserted this in unusual ways, as when he stated, "The mere exertion of a new thought is a certain proof of God. For certainly there is something that immediately produces and upholds that thought; here is a new thing, and there is a necessity of a cause."[22] In various passages, Edwards showed a tendency toward occasionalism or the idea that all events are effects of God's agency and that creatures are not properly capable of producing effects on one another. According to Edwards's biblical interpretation, "it [is] most agreeable to the Scripture, to suppose creation to be performed new every moment."[23] Edwards's presentation of God's creative power in *Original Sin* suggested that no created thing could be a cause of its own existence from moment to moment: "God's upholding created existence, or causing its existence, is altogether equivalent to an *immediate production out of nothing*, at each moment, because its existence at this moment is not merely in part from God, but wholly from him; and not in any part or degree from its antecedent existence."[24]

In Miscellany 629, Edwards showed the double-sidedness of his understanding of divine causality. On the one hand, he stated that "natural things... in metaphysical strictness, are not proper causes of the effects, but only occasions." Yet he at once qualified this point when he added that "God produces all effects; but yet he ties natural events... to fixed, determinate and unchangeable rules, which are called laws of nature."[25] It becomes clear that Edwards did not repudiate the so-called secondary causality in favor of primary causality or divine action. It was not as though God had swallowed up the realm of creaturely causes and left nothing behind but God. In that case, it might be appropriate to apply the epithet "pantheistic" to Edwards—a claim made by the conservative Calvinistic critic Charles Hodge.[26] Yet Edwards upheld the

---

21. WJE 6:238. See Daniel, "Edwards as Philosopher," 166–67.

22. WJE 13:373.

23. WJE 13:418.

24. WJE 3:402, emph. orig. See also WJE 13:210, 288.

25. WJE 18:157.

26. After analyzing Edwards's understanding of divine causality and his denial that creatures are "substances," Charles Hodge wrote: "This doctrine, therefore, in its consequences, is essentially pantheistic" (*Systematic Theology*, 3 vols; Grand Rapids, MI: Eerdmans, 1986 reprint; 2:220).

integrity of the natural, creaturely order by stating that God has regular ways of acting or "fixed, determinate...rules" and that these are fittingly referred to as laws of nature. Miscellany. 1263 depicted miracles as God's extraordinary mode of acting and the everyday events of the natural world as God's ordinary mode of acting. The falling of a leaf from a tree and the resurrection of Jesus from the dead were both part of a single, unbroken continuum of divine action.[27] Yet they differed. Daily life included countless events describable by general laws—e.g., Newtonian gravitation to describe a falling object. The extraordinary events of redemptive history were singular, unparalleled, and unprecedented occurrences that followed from God's immediate volition and hence they followed no general laws that the human mind might discover or comprehend.[28]

One issue left unresolved in Edwards's early scientific writings pertained to the status of Spirit (i.e., God's Spirit) as compared with spirit (i.e., human or angelic spirit) and both of these in contrast and comparison with material bodies. If the essence of *matter* consisted in inertial resistance to being moved, then what was the essence of *spirit*? As we will see below in the discussion of idealism, Edwards assigned a measure of independence to human souls or spirits. They were more akin to God's Mind, containing the ideas of all created things, than they were to brute, inert, unthinking matter. Yet human spirits, no less than bodies, depended on God for their continuing existence.

The Logical Way to God—Being as Necessary

Following an ancient tradition in Christian philosophy, Edward understood God as the great "I AM" or as "Being in general." Though earlier Puritans would not have disagreed with Edwards on this point, they generally did not build much of their theological reflection on this equation of God with being. Yet from the time that Edwards composed his early essay "Of Being," he was preoccupied with God as a necessary, infinite, pervasive, encompassing, and all-inclusive Being. He spoke of God as *ens entium* ("the Being of beings") and declared that "in metaphysical strictness and propriety, he is, and there is none else." Or, again, "God and real existence are the same."[29] In this aspect of this thought, Edwards departed from the philosophy of John Locke, who

---

27. WJE 23:201–12.

28. For further commentary on the significance of Miscellany 1263, see McClymond, *Encounters With God*, 109–11.

29. WJE 6:238, 364, 345. On God as Being in general, see also WJE 6:345, 363; WJE 8:461, 621; WJE 13:213.

stated that it was vain to "let loose our thoughts into the vast Ocean of Being."[30] This speculative element in Edwards set him apart from the down-to-earth attitude of Locke and other British empiricists and aligned him with Continental thinkers like Malebranche and Leibniz as well as with the Cambridge Platonists.

Edwards began his reflection on being with the observation that the human mind cannot conceive of total non-existence—a state of complete nothingness: "That there should absolutely be nothing at all is utterly impossible.... Indeed, we can mean nothing else by 'nothing' but a state of absolute contradiction."[31] What is inconceivable in principle to the human mind, he reasoned, must be impossible in actuality. The attempt to conceive of nothing was like an effort in drawing a square circle. An attempt to think the unthinkable showed the inherent contradiction involved. Hence Edwards concluded that being necessarily must exist. Edwards's ontological argument—if one wishes to term it as such—was an indirect proof that seeks sought to establish the necessity of being from the impossibility of conceiving nothingness or nonbeing. Being, he argued, is in effect the highest of all categories and thus can not properly be set in distinction and in contradiction to anything else. Being is a necessary category.

In "Of Being," Edwards shifted from asserting that *some being necessarily must exist* to stating that *being as such must exist necessarily*—admittedly a different claim. The youthful writings show us a mind brimming with a sense of its own newly discovered capabilities, and perhaps for this reason the arguments sometimes leapfrog without supplying the intermediate steps. If Edwards had written "Of Being" in his later years, he might have offered a tighter argument. Yet the early essay, despite its flaws, bears witness to Edwards's fundamental intuition that all reality is grounded in the reality of a necessary being: "God is a necessary being, because it's a contradiction to suppose him not to be. No being is a necessary being but he whose nonentity is a contradiction."[32] In one surprising passage, Edwards invokes "space" as a necessary being. He stated that "space is this necessary, eternal, infinite and omnipresent being."[33] At this juncture Edwards followed the lead of Henry More, whom Edwards had read and who previously proposed this line of reasoning. He later backed off from this early identification of space with God or God with space.

---

30. John Locke, *An Essay Concerning Human Understanding*, Book 1, Chapter 1, Section 7.
31. WJE 6:202.
32. WJE 13:213.
33. WJE 6:203.

In Miscellany 135, Edwards claimed that the only difference between God and created spirits is their magnitude: "Many have wrong conceptions of the difference between the nature of the Deity and created spirits. The difference is no contrariety, but what naturally results from his greatness and nothing else.... So that if we should suppose the faculties of a created spirit to be enlarged infinitely, there would be the Deity to all intents and purposes."[34] Edwards associated God's greatness with the expansiveness of space, and with God's being as "inclusive" of all other existences. Though God's being was infinite and unlimited, every creature might be ranged alongside of all others as part of a chain of being. "An *Archangel*," he tells us, "must be supposed to have more existence...than a *worm* or a *flea*."[35] In his treatises on *End of Creation* and *True Virtue*, Edwards wrote of every created thing as possessing a "degree of existence," depending on the sort of thing that it is, and a "degree of excellence," according to which it is ranked against all other entities in its class. What resulted from this line of reasoning was a calculus of value according to which God and indeed all moral beings were bound to give to every creature the respect and regard due to it according to its respective level of "existence" and "excellence." *End of Creation* developed its argument for God's supremacy by appealing to this notion of degrees of "existence" and "excellence" (ch. 14).

The Epistemological Way to God—Idealism or Immaterialism

A third way that Edwards argued from the reality of the world to the existence of God lay in the realm of mind and ideas. Not only the concept of matter, and the concept of being, but a proper understanding of the functioning of minds intimated that there was some kind of an ultimate Mind that comprehended all things. Edwards's title, "The Mind," showed the importance he assigned to his reflections on ideas and minds. The essay "Of Being" contained the statement: "How doth it grate upon the mind, to think that something should be from all eternity, and nothing all the while be conscious of it."[36] This did not mean that the world was "confined within his [i.e., man's] skull." But it meant that the material world only existed to the extent that it was known and perceived. At this stage Edwards drew a distinction between

---

34. WJE 13:295.
35. WJE 8:546, n. 6.
36. WJE 6:203.

created bodies and created spirits. The "material universe," he wrote, is "absolutely dependent on the conception of the mind for its existence, and does not exist as spirits do, whose existence does not consist in, nor in dependence on, the conception of other minds."[37] Created spirits, while still dependent on God, were more God-like than mere bodies because spirits were capable in some measure of knowing God, the physical universe, themselves, and one another.

When Edwards sought to find the ultimate ground of all reality, he invoked an all-pervasive and all-inclusive Mind that he identified with God—the cause of solidity and resistance in physical bodies, and the necessary being implied by all existing things. In Edwards's argumentation, the three lines of reasoning—from bodies, from being, and from mind—all converged toward his concept of God. The "substance" or underlying substratum of all reality was God, or rather God's knowledge of all things: "God is as it were the only substance, or rather, the perfection and steadfastness of his knowledge, wisdom, power, and will."[38] In speaking of God as the sole substance, Edwards did not have in mind some kind of static divine substance of which finite realities were modifications—a philosophy like that of Baruch Spinoza. Instead he conceived of God as an incessantly active though inherently stable source of finite reality. He elaborated this point in a striking run-on sentence from "The Mind": "And indeed, the secret lies here: that which truly is the substance of all bodies is the infinitely exact and precise and perfectly stable idea in God's mind, together with his stable will that the same shall gradually be communicated to us, and to other minds, according to certain fixed and exact established methods and laws: or in somewhat different language, the infinitely exact and precise divine idea, together with an answerable, perfectly exact, precise and stable will with respect to correspondent communications to created minds, and effects on their minds."[39] Only Edwards would attempt to say so much in a single sentence!

This theocentric idealism differed strikingly from the anthropocentric idealism of German thinkers such as Immanuel Kant, Johann Gottlieb Fichte, and Georg Wilhelm Friedrich Hegel. Without a robust conception of God, the battle between materialism and idealism is like a tug of war between two sets of antagonists. The materialists seek to drag the mind into the realm of the body while idealists try to pull the body into the sphere of mind. The outcome is likely to be inconclusive. Yet Edwards's theocentric

---

37. WJE 6:368.
38. WJE 6:398.
39. WJE 6:344.

philosophy managed to avoid this choice between two antitheses. He did not unfold his reasoning from the side of the human mind nor from that of the human body. Instead, his starting point was the prior actuality of God. Using such an approach, consciousness did not need to be reduced to the level of material entities. Nor, on the other hand, was the material world dissolved into a haze of mere appearances. The human mind, Edwards realized, was not ontologically sufficient to sustain the cosmos. There had to be a firmer foundation. The divine mind in its infinity knew all things at all times and in all in their specificity and depth. From a theocentric standpoint, one might ask: What firmer foundation for reality could there be than the ideas of all things within the mind of God? In this aspect of his philosophy Edwards unwittingly followed the precedent of patristic and medieval thinkers. Long before, Augustine had modified Plato's theory of ideas by proposing that the divine Mind contained the ideas of all things, while Thomas Aquinas later assigned efficacy to God's knowledge: "The knowledge of God is the cause of things."[40]

Once one grasps the centrality of God to Edwards's reasoning, it is possible to understand how he was able to combine empiricism with idealism. In a nutshell, his stress on the priority of the divine Mind allowed him to maintain the empiricist principle that there is nothing in the mind that was not first in the senses with the idealist principle that the objects of sense experience are ideal objects. Edwards expressed his agreement with Lockean empiricism as follows: "All acts of the mind are from sensation; all ideas begin from thence, and there can never be any idea, thought or act of the mind unless the mind first received some ideas from sensation."[41] Sense experience thus has a self-evidential character. What we know by our senses—as in Edwards's famous example that honey is sweet—we know immediately and not as the result of deductive or inductive reasoning. "Things that we know by immediate sensation, we know intuitively, and they are properly self-evident truths: as, grass is green, the sun shines, honey is sweet."[42]

Wallace Anderson suggested that Edwards's thought is better termed immaterialist than idealist. His point was not to prioritize human minds over physical bodies—the major thrust in most idealist theories. Rather his intention was to establish that human minds and physical bodies were both completely dependent on God for their existence at each moment. The divine

---

40. Thomas Aquinas, *Summa Theologica*, 1a, q.14 a. 8.

41. WJE 6:390.

42. WJE 6:346; cf. WJE 6:369.

Mind undergirded all reality and there was no "matter" at all if that term referred to a self-subsistent reality that stood on its own apart from God. Edwards's immaterialism had theological roots. For him even the glory of God was as good as nonexistent if it had no manifestation in consciousness: "For goodness has no existence but with relation to perception."[43] Anderson explained that Edwards early in his life "was convinced that the primary and essential element in religion consists in cognition—a unique consciousness and knowledge of God," and that "he became convinced that religion, taken in this sense, is the very purpose of the entire creation."[44] The knowledge of God was the most "worthy" element of the creation—the bull's-eye, as it were, that directed God's intention in fashioning a world (ch. 14).[45] Idealism was simply an extension of Edwards's theological conviction that God's glory, to be truly glorious, must reverberate in the hearts and mind of his creatures. He generalized this point into the sweeping principle that "nothing has any existence anywhere else but in consciousness."[46]

In conclusion, we should note that Edwards's metaphysical reasoning was never detached from his theological concepts and convictions. His God was never abstract, but was the mighty "I AM" who spoke in thunder and performed mighty acts. Robert Jenson noted that "Edwards's free metaphysical speculation is precisely his way of 'viewing' God beauty."[47] Philosophical reasoning, for Edwards, was a means of affirming God's transcendent greatness and glory.

---

43. WJE 18:395.

44. Anderson, "Editor's Introduction," in WJE 6:78–79.

45. WJE 8:432.

46. WJE 6:204.

47. Robert W. Jenson, *America's Theologian: A Recommendation of Jonathan Edwards* (New York: Oxford University Press, 1988), 22.

8

Typology: Scripture, Nature, and All of Reality

JONATHAN EDWARDS MADE extensive use of the age-old Christian tradition of typology to interpret the Old Testament foreshadowings ("types") of New Testament fulfillments ("antitypes"). But he expanded that traditional use to view the entire "system of nature" as the "voice of God to intelligent creatures," proclaiming the glories of Christ and his redemption.[1] No part of the natural world was exempt: "I believe that the whole universe, heaven and earth, air and seas, and the divine constitution and history of the holy Scriptures, be full of images of divine things, as full as a language is of words."[2] In a manner of thinking going back to Plato, Edwards considered everything in nature a pointer to something in a world beyond nature, and the second world as more real than the first: "The whole outward creation, which is but the shadow of beings, is so made as to represent spiritual things."[3]

But for Edwards it was not only Scripture and the natural world that pointed to the history of redemption. All of history—not only what is called biblical history—is also "signification, marking the presence of something else." Each thing in nature and history can be understood only as the sign of the other to which it points. Philosophically, then, all being is communicative. As Stephen H. Daniel puts it, for Edwards communication is the condition for the possibility of (created) being rather than its consequence. That is, things are words, and creation is a book waiting to be read. Theologically, this means that beings give glory to God because they express God. Grace is therefore the understanding of being as essentially communicative, and sin the denial of

---

1. WJE 23:359–76; WJE 9:218, 289; Miscellany 702 in WJE 18:283–309.

2. Edwards used three words to denote things or persons in nature, history, or scripture that signify spiritual truths or realities: "types," "images," and "shadows." The latter two were subsets of the first, and he considered images to be more revealing than shadows; Edwards referred to images as "pictures" but said shadows were "dark resemblances." Images reveal more of the referent ("substance") than do shadows. WJE 11:54, 62–63, 81.

3. WJE 11:152; WJE 13:434. This concept of nature as a shadow of the world of divine ideas may have been influenced by Edwards's reading in the Cambridge Platonists.

meaning by attempting to affirm one's significance apart from the system of divine semiotics. In the jargon of postmoderns, things are "always already" defined in terms of their intentionality.[4]

Typology therefore was not only a major theme in Edwards's theology but also an integral part of the way he viewed reality. His literary corpus is evidence of this. *Types* is one of three notebooks which he devoted exclusively to elaboration of his typological scheme. The other two were *Images of Divine Things* and *Types of the Messiah*. Other notebooks, such as the *Notes on Scripture*, the *Blank Bible*, and the "Book of Controversies" contain numerous references to typology.[5]

Edwards's Place in the Tradition

Historically, typology has been contrasted with allegory, which stems from the Greek words *allos* (other) and *agoria* (speaking) and means, literally, speaking otherwise than one seems to speak. Customarily, allegory has meant a figurative representation of some generalization about human existence.[6] It goes back to Homeric scholars who allegorized certain passages in Homer which they felt to be unworthy of the bard. Philo (c. 20 BC-40 AD) and other Alexandrian Jews adopted this allegorical technique in order to render the Hebrew Bible less offensive to Greek culture. Often it has been said that Philo downplayed the historical context of Scripture—arguing that the abstracted meaning of a text was more real than its historical referent—and Christian typology followed his lead. But Henri DeLubac argued persuasively that for most of the first 1,500 years of Christian thought typology took seriously the historical reality of Old Testament events and saw them as God-given pointers to New Testament realities, especially Christ and salvation. According to DeLubac and Beryl Smalley, there were some who disconnected the meaning of a text from any relation to its historical

---

4. Stephen H. Daniel, *The Philosophy of Jonathan Edwards: A Study in Divine Semiotics* (Bloomington: Indiana University Press, 1994), 34, 131–34, 83. On the notion of "always already," see Paul Ricoeur *Time and Narrative*, 3 vols., translated by Kathleen McLaughlin and David Pellauer (Chicago: University of Chicago Press, 1984), 1:57.

5. See WJE vols. II, 15, 21, 24.

6. On the history of Christian typology, see Sacvan Bercovitch, ed., *Typology and Early American Literature* (Amherst, MA.: University of Massachusetts Press, 1972), especially Thomas M. Davis, "The Traditions of Puritan Typology," in Bercovitch, ed., 11–46; Mason I. Lowance, Jr., *The Language of Canaan: Metaphor and Symbol in New England from the Puritans to the Transcendentalists* (Cambridge: Harvard University Press, 1980); Ursula Brumm, *American Thought and Religious Typology*, trans. John Hoaglund (New Brunswick: Rutgers University Press, 1970); Barbara Kiefer Lewalski, *Protestant Poetics and the Seventeenth-Century Religious Lyric* (Princeton: Princeton University Press, 1979).

referent, but most medievals agreed that all non-literal meanings must build upon the historical or literal sense. Origen and Cassian were key figures in the development of what came to be known as the fourfold sense of Scripture (although Origen often used only three senses): each text was believed to have a literal (historical) meaning, a tropological (moral) meaning, the allegorical (doctrinal) meaning, and the anagogical (eschatological) meaning.[7]

In the sixteenth century, William Tyndale emphasized the preeminence of the historical or literal sense. He insisted that all interpretations, including the typological and allegorical, must arise from the literal sense and be proved by it. Luther, Calvin, and the Puritans argued that the Bible uses similitudes and allegories only to clarify the literal, historical sense. But the Reformers still used typology to interpret the Bible. Luther condemned only "Alexandrian allegory" and used what he called the "literal" and "spiritual" senses to claim that "every bit" of the Old Testament applied to Christ. Calvin said that the ritual practices of the Old Testament law would be ridiculous unless understood typologically. He taught that the angel of the Lord in the Old Testament was in fact Christ, and that typology is the key to understanding the Old Testament.[8]

By the seventeenth century, a clear demarcation had been drawn between allegory and type. Allegory was Greek (Platonic) and dealt with abstract essences; types were Jewish and concerned with historical existence. In allegory, the physical world was a symbol of the spiritual universe discovered by a human mind, while a type was an historically true symbol instituted by God to perform a specific function. The difference between the two could be seen by the concept of linear time. The allegory was simply the Platonic representation of one thing by another; time was irrelevant. But the type by definition preceded the antitype in time, one instituted by the divine author to foreshadow the other. According to Erich Auerbach, the type (which he called a "figural interpretation") "deals with concrete events whether past, present, or future, and not with concepts or abstractions."[9]

---

7. See esp. Henri DeLubac, *Medieval Exegesis*, Vol 1: *The Four Senses of Scripture*, trans. Mark Sebanc (Grand Rapids and Edinburgh: Eerdmans and T. and T. Clark, 1998); Beryl Smalley, *The Study of the Bible in the Middle Ages* (Notre Dame: University of Notre Dame Press, 1978), 83–195.

8. Calvin, *Institutes*, 2.10.20. Paul Althaus, *The Theology of Martin Luther* (Philadelphia: Fortress, 1966), 90–96.

9. Eric Auerbach, "Figura," in *Scenes from the Drama of European Literature*, Theory and History of Literature 9, ed. Wlad Godzich and Jochen Schulte-Sasse (Minneapolis: University of Minnesota Press, 1984), 53. William G. Madsen helpfully adds that the "type looks forward in time, not upward through the scale of being"; "From Shadowy Types to Truth," in *The Lyric and Dramatic Milton*, ed. Joseph Summers (New York: Columbia University Press, 1965), 99–100.

Edwards felt free to incorporate allegory within typology, but only while subordinating them to the historical events of redemption. He also warned of the danger of letting allegory go too far. He portrayed himself as walking a middle road between the rationalists and deists on the left, who "cry down all types," and the Catholic and Anglican exegetes who were "for turning all into nothing but allegory and not having it be true history."[10] Edwards was devoted to the primacy of historical reference, yet for him the antitypes were not just New Testament persons and events but the entire drama of redemption, from eternity through time and back into eternity.

He therefore made extensive use of the typological tradition, building on but going beyond the historical sense toward what he considered the more important referents in the history of redemption.[11] This was especially true in his interpretation of the Old Testament. Like Augustine (who had confessed the literal sense of certain sections of the Torah "killed" him spiritually) and Calvin (who had called the Pentateuch's ceremonial law "ridiculous" without the help of typology), Edwards said much in the Old Testament is "wholly insignificant and so wholly impertinent and vain" unless it is understood typologically. Typology gave him the tool he needed to unify the biblical testaments, particularly at those junctures where the literal sense by itself could not fulfill the theological vision which he believed united the Scriptures.[12]

Defending the System

Edwards knew this way of reading Scripture and reality was not self-evident, even to the regenerate. Nevertheless, he believed the world was nearly as full of evidence for this system of correspondences as it was of the types themselves. For at one level, one regenerate seeing of the types is enough to show the validity of the entire system. Seeing is believing. But there were also rational reasons for believing there was such a system.[13]

Edwards found his first rationale for the system in scripture, which he thought by itself validated the tradition's practice of seeing a divinely purposed

---

10. WJE 11:151; Wallace E. Anderson, "Editor's Introduction," in WJE 11: 11–24.

11. Stein, "The Spirit and the Word," in *Jonathan Edwards and the American Experience*, eds. Harry S. Stout and Nathan O. Hatch (New York: Yale University Press, 1988), 123, 124. See also his "The Quest for the Spiritual Sense: The Biblical Hermeneutics of Jonathan Edwards," *Harvard Theological Review* 70 (1977): 99–113.

12. Augustine, *Confessions*, 5.14; Calvin, *Institutes*, 2.7.1; WJE 11:306, 305, 219.

13. William Wainwright, "Jonathan Edwards and the Language of God," *Journal of the American Academy of Religion* 48 (1980): 519–30.

relationship between Old Testament types and New Testament antitypes. The Old Testament itself often uses "types and figures" to typify future things: the bowing down of the sheaves of Joseph's brothers towards Joseph's sheaf foreshadowed their literal bowing to him in Egypt, Pharaoh's dream of fat and gaunt cows truly predicted fat and lean years, Daniel's four beasts accurately forecast the rise of four pagan empires, and all the Hebrew prophets' prophecies were fulfilled. The Epistle to the Hebrews showed that even the Bible's silence about Melchizedek's birth and death had typological significance. Edwards took as an inspired indicator of a biblical system of typology: "If so small things in Scripture are typical, it is rational to suppose that Scripture abounds with types."[14] The Apostle Paul wrote in 1 Corinthians that the Old Testament's admonition not to muzzle an ox was "for our sake, no doubt," and that the stories of the Israelites' idolatry in the wilderness "were [for] our examples [tupoi]."[15] Paul referred to Abraham's two sons in Galatians 4:21–23 as an "allegory" for the two covenants. This Galatians passage, said Edwards, was a "great confirmation" that "the history of the Old Testament in general is intended to be typical of spiritual things."

In a move that departed in style if not substance from the Puritan typological tradition, Edwards also argued that Scripture endorses a system of types in nature. When Jesus proclaimed that he was the true light and true vine and true bread, he implied that all lights and vines and breads in this world are pointers to their antitypes in Jesus. Paul did the same for seed and sowing in springtime when he used them in 1 Corinthians 15 to argue for the resurrection of bodies. Unless God intended seed and planting to be types of spiritual realities, Paul's argument would not have made sense: "If the sowing of seed and its springing were not designedly ordered to have an agreeableness to the resurrection, there could be no sort of argument in that which the Apostle alleges; either to argue the resurrection itself or the manner of it, either its certainty, or probability or possibility."[16]

Edwards called on the heathen world as another warrant for his system. If even the heathen, he suggested, recognized God's signature in nature, surely we should as well. "The very wiser heathens seemed to be sensible that the divine Being, in the formation of the natural world, designed to teach us moral lessons: so Ovid, concerning the correct posture of man."[17]

---

14. WJE 11:192, 151.

15. WJE 11:146, 192; 1 Cor. 9:9–10; 10:1–4, 6, 11; WJE 11:146.

16. WJE 11:62–63, 53.

17. WJE 11:98; Ovid, *Metamorphosis*, bk. I, ll. 84–86: "And, though all other animals are prone, and fix their gaze upon the earth, he gave to man an uplifted face and bade him stand erect and turn his eyes to heaven" (trans. F.J. Miller [Cambridge: Loeb Library, 1966]).

Edwards's second rationale came from the natural world itself. Its structure points to its meaning. The world is full of natural and moral analogies that by themselves suggest intelligent ordering by a Being outside the structure, and an order of being above and beyond the structure. There is a great analogy, for example, between "works of creation and providence." The less perfect seems to be made in imitation of the more perfect, as an image reflects its substance. Animals appear to be an image of humans in many respects, plants similarly of animals, and minerals of plants.[18]

If there is analogy between humans and those beings lower on the great chain of being, there is analogy between humans and beings above them as well. Angels are like humans in many respects, while retaining important differences. But those differences are related analogically to corresponding aspects in human beings. Even the saints manifest analogy in differences among them. Inferior and superior saints, both on earth and in heaven, are arranged hierarchically based on the degree of their holiness. Some are higher and others are lower, and while there will be no envy or pride in heaven because the higher saints will be more loving and therefore more beloved by those below them, nevertheless there will be differences between levels based on analogy.[19]

There is also an analogy to be observed in the use of language. Edwards quoted George Turnbull, a disciple of Newton, Locke, and Shaftesbury, and author of *The Principles of Moral Philosophy* (1740), to demonstrate an analogy between the natural and moral worlds based on the correspondence between moral language and things in nature: "No words can express moral ideas, but so far as there is such an analogy betwixt the natural and moral world, that objects in the latter may be shadowed forth, pictured or imaged to us by some resemblances to them in the former." Edwards reasoned that if moral philosophy needs to use language from nature to express moral concepts, and if such a use seems to be successful, there must actually be an ontological analogy between the two worlds. One must have been created with the purpose of representing the other.[20]

A third rationale was teleological. Edwards reasoned from the end or purpose of creation to the character of the natural world. The fact that the purpose of mortal and natural life is spiritual made it seem reasonable that the

---

18. WJE 18:192; WJE 11:53, 69–70, 55–56.

19. WJE 8:374–78; WJE 18:239–42.

20. George Turnbull, *An Enquiry into the Wise and Good Government of the Moral World*, 2 vols. (London: J. Noon, 1740), 54–55; WJE 11:125–26.

natural world would represent spiritual truths. "Spiritual things are the crown and glory, the head and soul, the very end, the alpha and omega of all other works. So what therefore can be more agreeable to wisdom than that they should be so made as to shadow them forth[?]"[21]

Finally, there was aesthetic evidence—or more accurately, a warrant drawn from the structure of beauty. Edwards argued in the *Nature of True Virtue* that earthly ("secondary") beauty is based on agreement between or union of different things, and that this kind of beauty—which we observe in things like plants and architecture and music—is an image of or analogous to the spiritual consent of different minds in a heavenly society of intelligent beings united in a benevolent agreement of heart. This in itself did not prove the typological nature of secondary beauty, but it provided further evidence that such a system may exist. Edwards argued that it would be reasonable for such a system to exist if indeed the source, pattern, and fountain of all secondary beauty is also beauty itself.[22]

Since the world seems so full of analogies at so many different levels, and since Scripture corroborates what reason infers, Edwards concluded that "the inferior and shadowy parts" of the world indeed represent the "more real and excellent, spiritual and divine." In fact, it seemed to be God's principle "to make inferior things shadows of the supernatural and most excellent, outward things shadows of spiritual, and all other things shadows of those things that are the end of all things and the crown of all things."[23]

Why God Uses Types

It seems appropriate and "fitting," to use one of Edwards's favorite words, for God to use types. For Edwards, God is "a communicative being" whose most overwhelming disposition is to communicate his perfections. As Edwards argued in *The End for Which God Created the World*, this is the reason for the creation: apart from the creation and God's continuing exercise of his attributes toward the creation, many of God's attributes would lie dormant.[24]

But there was a problem. God is infinite, and his creation is finite. How could the sublime things of infinite divinity be communicated to finite minds?

---

21. WJE 13:434–45.

22. WJE 8:564–65; WJE 8:550–51, 556.

23. WJE 13:434–35; see also WJE 11:191.

24. WJE 13:410; WJE 8:434–35, 438–39; see Janice Knight, "Learning the Language of God," Jonathan Edwards and the Typology of Nature," *William and Mary Quarterly* 3rd ser., 48 (1991): 543–51; WJE 8:429.

Edwards's answer was a paraphrase of Calvin's notion of accommodation. God accommodates his truth to our finite understandings just as human adults change their manner of presentation when teaching children. Ordinary discourse only distorts heavenly things because of the incommensurable gap between infinite, non-material realities and human concepts expressed with words grounded in finite, material things.[25]

Therefore God uses types, which, though also employing material images to express immaterial realities, nevertheless by the power of imagery suggest to the human mind what lies beyond the visible world. So types are employed by God first because of their pedagogical value. Many types are pictures of sorts, and a picture is worth a thousand words—or at least a hundred. For example, Edwards wrote, "temple of the Holy Ghost" expresses in three words what would otherwise take one hundred. "By such similitudes a vast volume is represented to our minds in three words, and things that we are not able to behold directly are represented before us in lively pictures."[26] These pictures so cohere with human sensibilities—or, to put it in Edwards's terms, there is such an analogy or harmony between them—that the human mind is naturally led to see the substance that the types represent. "The affairs of the Jewish church are so much of a shadow, that a mind so prepared and exercised would naturally be led to the substance" if it is "of a poetical and gracious disposition."[27] As this last quotation indicates, the types do not have power in and of themselves to portray the spiritual world. The typological system is not transparent to all. There is no salvation by the imagination. Salvation is only by Christ and the power of his Spirit, who alone can provide the sense of the heart, which alone can read the types.

But the types also have affective value. Because they are drawn from the sensory world and commonly employ material objects as images, fallen human beings, who are more familiar with the material than the immaterial world, can more easily understand them. They are more affected "by those things [they] see with [their] eyes and hear with [their] ears and have experience of."[28] If types are more accessible because they are grounded in sensory experience, they are also more enjoyable. Types provide "pleasure" and "delight." We know this, Edwards argued, from the great enjoyment people derive from "the imitative arts, in painting, poetry, fables, metaphorical language [and] dramatic performances. This disposition appears early in children." Perhaps because it is enjoyable, subjects

---

25. WJE 18:583; Calvin, *Institutes*, 2.11.13; 1.17.13; WJE 20:188; WJE 10:418.
26. WJE 13:181.
27. WJE 13:363–64.
28. WJE 14:140.

taught by types are more easily remembered, and moral lessons taught are received with deeper impression and greater conviction.[29] God therefore adapts his teaching method to human nature. He instructs the human race in a way that is best suited to the creature. Types are an aid to memory, they reinforce their lesson with extra strength and conviction, and they bring pleasure and delight. Finally, Edwards connected types to the arts. Both, he explained, appeal to the same aesthetic and erotic capacities. Each uses the principle of *mimesis* and fulfills human desires for the dramatic and the beautiful. Types, then, are a part of the divine aesthetic, the way in which God unites pedagogy and aesthetics.

Reading the Types

Obviously, if types are divine pedagogy, human beings must be able to comprehend them. If the typological system is "a certain sort of language, as it were, in which God is wont to speak to us," we must be able to understand that language.[30] Edwards was convinced that we are—if we possess a (regenerate) sense of the heart.

He was also convinced that the entire cosmos is *"full of images of divine things,* as full as a language is of words." Hence life is a school for learning the types, so that one can ever be receiving communication from the Creator: "The multitude of those things that I have mentioned are but a very small part of what is really intended to be signified and typified by these things: but that there is room for persons to be learning more and more of this language and seeing more of that which is declared in it to the end of the world without discovering all."[31]

How do we learn the language? Edwards left a somewhat cryptic answer to this question. He said that while God has not explained all the types in Scripture, those that have been explained are enough to show us how to interpret the rest. In other words, biblical precedent is to be the primary guide. So if Paul has already explained that Hagar and Sarah represent the two covenants, we should learn several lessons, chief among them being that the antitype is always related to the work of redemption by Christ.[32]

---

29. WJE 11:191.

30. WJE 11:150. The portions of this notebook that I quote in this section were composed in Northampton during the mid-1740s; "Notes on the Manuscript of 'Types,'" WJE 11:145.

31. WJE 11:152; emph. added. Therefore there is no indication that Edwards "decided to cease attempting identification of particular divine images" (WJE 10:236).

32. WJE 11:151.

Edwards added that there are several methods for learning any language. Sometimes one is "naturally trained up in it, learning it by education," which might mean in this case being taught the divine idiom by God himself, as in Adam's case before the fall. Edwards hastened to explain that "that is not the way in which corrupt mankind learned divine language." They received the divine language in the forms of hieroglyphics and dark symbols without interpretation, which explains in part why human history was dominated by idolatry.[33]

The best way to learn the divine idiom is "by much use and acquaintance together with good taste or judgment, by comparing one thing with another and having our senses as it were exercised to discern it." Here Edwards was both alluding to his descriptions of regeneration as a "taste" and "sense of the heart"[34] (ch. 24) and invoking Hebrews 5:14, which describes mature Christians as "those who by reason of use have their senses exercised to discern both good and evil.[35] His point seemed to be that a person with the sense of the heart is to use the biblical precedents and her own sense of what is harmonious with the work of redemption to discover and then interpret a type.

Edwards warned that this is a tricky business that must be conducted with special care. Without such care, the divine idiom will not be learned, and one's interpretation of the types will miss their "proper beauty." So there is an aesthetic test: if one's interpretation of a type does not display the divine beauty, one has missed its meaning. The interpretation then will sound "very harsh in the ears of those that are well versed in the language."[36]

Typological Media—Scripture, Nature and History

Like his predecessors in the typological tradition, Edwards believed that the prototypical and archetypal standard for the entire system was to be found in the Bible. Not only were the sharpest and clearest images found here—that is, the antitypes of Christ and his redemption, and the most pointed Old Testament types, as well—but the Scriptures also remained the hermeneutical standard against which all the other types in nature and history were to be measured.[37]

---

33. WJE 11:151, 193; WJE 15:400–10.

34. See WJE 2:282–83, and WJE 18:452–66.

35. WJE 11:151.

36. WJE 11:151.

37. Thus it is not true that Edwards exalted nature "to a level of authority co-equal with revelation." Perry Miller, ed., *Images or Shadows of Divine Things* (Westport, CT: Greenwood Press, 1948), 28.

If anything, Edwards saw even more typological import in the Old Testament than did many of his predecessors. The Hebrew Bible did not contain types just here and there; nearly every stroke of the pen made by the biblical authors was typical in some way of "Christ and his redemption."

> Thus almost everything that was said or done that we have recorded in Scripture from Adam to Christ, was typical of Gospel things: persons were typical persons, their actions were typical actions, the cities were typical cities, the nation of the Jews and other nations were typical nations, the land was a typical land, God's providences towards them were typical providences, their worship was typical worship, their houses were typical houses, their magistrates typical magistrates, their clothes typical clothes, and indeed the world was a typical world.[38]

Like Luther and other Christian theologians in the tradition, Edwards found the Christian gospel in the Hebrew Bible. Early in his career, he said that God's providences to the Jews, David's history, the temple, and the prophets were all "full of gospel." Later in his career, in his sermons on the work of redemption, he detailed some of what he meant by this early claim. The redemption by Christ was typified by the exodus of the Jews from Egypt and their miraculous return from Babylon. The waters of the Noahic flood were typical of the blood of Christ that washes away the sins of the world. The cultus of the law that included "all the precepts that relate to building the tabernacle that was set up in the wilderness and all the forms, and circumstances, and utensils of it" were directed by God "to show forth something of Christ." The following entry from his "Notes on the Bible" is an example of the hundreds of entries Edwards made in his notebooks to document the ways in which the law prefigured the gospel.

> EXODUS 25:23–40. Concerning the SHOWBREAD TABLE, and the golden CANDLESTICK. These both were to stand continually in the holy place before the veil of the holy of holies, one on the north side and the other on the south. Each of these seems to represent both a divine person and also the church. Each represents a divine person. The showbread represents Christ, and was set on [the] south side at God's right hand, as Christ is often represented as being set at God's right hand in heaven, being next to God the Father in his office, and above the Holy

---

38. WJE 9:289; WJE 13:435; see also WJE 13:325, 363–64, 431–33, 434–35; WJE 18: 335; WJE 23: 500–501.

Spirit in the economy of the persons of the Trinity. The candlestick, or at least the oil and lamps of it, represent the Holy Spirit, and is set at the left hand of God's throne. Christ is as it were "the bread of God." This bread is called the showbread, in the Hebrew, *Lechem Panim*, "the bread of God's face," or "presence." So Christ, in Isa. 63:9, is called *Malak Panim*, "the angel of God's face," or "presence." This bread had pure frankincense set on it, which undoubtedly signifies the merits of Christ, and so proves the bread that had this pure frankincense on it to be a type of Christ.[39]

These figures in the ceremonial aspects of the law represent only one of three kinds of types. These are institutional types; but there are also providential and personal types. The greatest institutional type is the practice of sacrifice; the greatest providential type is the Exodus, and the greatest personal type is David.[40]

David is a type of Christ both in his humiliation (typified by David's suffering and exile from Jerusalem) and his militant state, at war with his enemies (typified by David's wars against his opponents). Solomon typified Christ in his triumphal state, reigning in peace. The altar that Noah built to the Lord after the floodwaters had receded typified Christ's sacrifice. Moses' burning bush represents both the sufferings of Christ in the fire of God's wrath and Israel's sufferings in Egypt, just as the bush burning without being destroyed signifies both Israel and Christ suffering without perishing. The building of the temple represents not only the human nature of Christ but also Christ's church and heaven.[41]

Edwards did not limit typology to the Bible but looked to "the whole outward creation" for "shadows of beings...made to represent divine things." Thus "the pattern of the cosmos" is one of "infinite representation." Every last part of the creation is emblematic of the divine, an effulgent crystal with supernatural meaning: even the tiniest leaf in a flower is a word from God, the sun shows forth God's glory, the clouds and mountains bespeak God's majesty, and the green fields and pleasant flowers testify to "his grace and mercy."[42]

The great markers of the days and seasons burst with meaning. The sun, for example, which makes plants flourish when it shines after rain, is a type

---

39. WJE 13:432; WJE 9:175, 263, 151, 182; WJE 15: 571–72.
40. WJE 9:204.
41. WJE 9:227, 152–53, 175; WJE 11:197; WJE 9:224.
42. WJE 13:434. Miller, ed., *Images and Shadows*, 27; WJE 17:52–56; WJE 18:429–30.

of the Sun of Righteousness who heals the soul's afflictions; the stars are types of the saints in glory, and the moon is an image of earthly glory and all the good of earthly life, which like the moon ever changes, rising and falling, waxing and waning. Birds flying in the sky are also types of the saints in heaven, but "to a fainter degree" than the stars. Another image for the saint is a tree, which grows so large from such tiny beginnings in a little twig. "Hence it may be argued," Edwards noted cryptically, "that infants do belong to the church."[43]

Not all of Edwards's images were so pleasant. The snake that slithers on its belly is a type of the curse God put on the devil (it would be at enmity with the woman, whose holy seed would bruise its head; Gen. 3:15). And human excrement represents the "corruption and filthiness that the heart of man is naturally full of," just as "the many foldings and turnings in the bowels...[denote] the great and manifold intricacies, secret windings and turnings, shifts, wiles and deceits that are in [human] hearts."[44]

If types are in nature, they can also be found in non-biblical history. Edwards wrote in his enormous *Types of the Messiah*[45] miscellany that "many things in the state of the ancient Greeks and Romans" were typical of gospel things. For example, his *Images* notebook contains a long entry comparing the celebration of a military triumph in the Roman Empire to Christ's ascension. Just as the Roman emperor's triumphal chariot was followed by senators and ransomed citizens, Christ was accompanied on his return to glory by principalities and powers and ransomed citizens of heaven. The Roman procession was closed by the sacrifice of a great white ox; so too Christ at the ascension entered the holly of holies with his own blood. The Roman emperor treated the people in the capital with gifts, and Christ did the same for his church.[46]

The experience of the saints in history is also typical. For instance, all the saints' enjoyment of family and friends is but a shadow of the joy they will experience in God, who is the substance. Their delight is but a scattered beam from the sun of Infinite Delight—a stream or drop taken from the fountain and ocean called God.[47] Some of Edwards's most important Puritan predecessors made similar, if not as extensive, use of nature. John Flavel used natural metaphors and allegorized a few of his biblical types in his *Husbandry*

---

43. WJE 11:85, 85–86, 99, 85, 85–86, 99.
44. WJE 11:92, 94.
45. WJE 11:191–324.
46. WJE 11:191, 82–84.
47. WJE 17:437–38.

Spiritualized: Or, the Heavenly Use of Earthly Things (1654). While Cotton Mather emphasized historical correspondences, he nevertheless showed occasional interest in spiritualized symbols from nature and history in his *Magnalia Christi Americana* (1702) and "Biblia Americana."[48] Both he and his uncle Samuel Mather endowed Old Testament types with moral value outside the Bible.[49]

But Edwards expanded the boundaries of scriptural typology. Far more freely than his predecessors, he used its nomenclature to identify types in nature and history. Others had dabbled, but Edwards pressed this new application with enthusiasm and creative vigor. He never developed in treatise form a systematic rationale for his system. But his notes to himself over the course of his career represent careful reflection on the implications of his proposition that all the world is typical.

Edwards pressed those implications even further by proposing that God has planted types of true religion even in religious systems that are finally false. We will see in chapter 36 that Edwards believed the near-universal practice of human sacrifice in world religions was divinely intended as a type of the perfect sacrifice of God's Son. Even the ghastly practice of human sacrifice, inspired by the devil, was used by God to prepare peoples for the sacrifice made by the God-man. Edwards also taught that pagan idolatry—in which deities were believed to inhabit material forms—was a type of the true Incarnation. Pagan sacrifices showed the heathen that sin "must be suffered for," and thus displayed the need for God's mercy.[50]

For Edwards, then, Scripture overflows with a surplus of meaning. It points from Old Testament to New Testament realities, and is the guidebook to a world full of divine signs. Amidst what others would call the discordances of life, Edwards found persistent symmetry. Scripture and nature were finally harmonious in his system, as were secular and sacred history, even the history of religions. The key to seeing this intricate system of signs displaying cosmic harmony was typology.

---

48. Lowance, *Language of Canaan*, 177. See also Lowance, "Typology and the New England Way: Cotton Mather and the Exegesis of Biblical Types," *Early American Literature* 4 (1969): 15–37.

49. Lowance, *Language of Canaan*, 87. On Puritans who taught that God communicates through nature, see James F. Maclear, "'The Heart of New England Rent': The Mystical Element in Early Puritan History," *Mississippi Valley Historical Review* 42 (1956): 621–52; Geoffrey Nuttall, *The Holy Spirit in Puritan Faith and Experience* (Oxford: Oxford University Press, 1946); Janice Knight, "Learning the Language of God," 535, 544n.

50. WJE 13:405–406.

9

Revelation: Scripture, Reason, and Tradition

AT THE BEGINNING of his career, Jonathan Edwards declared that "God is a communicating being." Near the end of his life he reiterated that theme, saying that "the thing which God aimed at in the creation of the world...was that communication of himself." More specifically, God's intent was to communicate "his own happiness." Even if his human creatures knew everything they needed to know about the divine nature, God would still "converse" because "God made spirits to have communion." Therefore the whole universe was an ongoing revelation of the divine being, a "gradual" communication of the Son of God. God's purpose is "an increasing communication of himself throughout eternity" because he desires "friendship" with his creatures, and friendship "requires conversation." The result is "increasing knowledge of God, love to him and joy in him" by these creatures.[1]

The Nature of Revelation

Revelation is not simply the impartation of knowledge or even happiness. It is participation in divine being itself. This is why Edwards preferred to speak of God's "communication" of himself. It owes to the very nature of the Trinity, in which each person gives unreservedly of himself to the other. The Father has an "eternal inclination to communicate himself," which is expressed perfectly in the Son, who is the "transcript of the divine perfections." The Son also has a "natural inclination to communicate himself" because of "his love and goodness," which are then poured out on "the church, or the saints." The result is

---

1. WJE 13:410; WJE 8:443; WJE 13:272, 339; WJE 18:98; WJE 8:443; WJE 23:350; WJE 8:443. Edwards's theology of revelation was more pointed and developed than that of the Reformers because he was addressing his era's greatest challenge to orthodox faith—the deists' claim that God was silent beyond what could be gleaned from nature and reason. Gerald R. McDermott, *Jonathan Edwards Confronts the Gods* (New York: Oxford University Press, 2000), 17–70. On this theme of divine communication, we are indebted to William M. Schweitzer, "Interpreting the Harmony of Reality: Jonathan Edwards's Theology of Revelation," PhD diss., University of Edinburgh, 2008.

a new "trinity, and image of the eternal Trinity" in which "Christ is the everlasting father, and believers are his seed, and the Holy Spirit, the Comforter, is the third person in Christ, being his delight and love flowing out towards the church." Hence the content of revelation is God himself: God communicates his Son, "an emanation of his own perfect fullness," to believers, who then participate in "increasing knowledge of God, love to him, and joy in him." This is participation in the Spirit, who returns this love and delight back "toward the Lord Jesus Christ."[2]

Revelation was one part of the "two-fold light" that God gives his human creatures for the sake of their "true happiness." The other part was the "light of nature," which comes through "those works of creation and God's common providence, that all mankind behold." Revelation was "above" the light of nature and itself consists of two parts. First were "immediate instructions" given in visions, miracles and inspiration of his Spirit—to men such as Noah, Abraham, Isaac, Jacob, Job, and Melchizedek. These messages were passed on to others by oral tradition. The second part of revelation consisted of "written revelation" from Moses (author of the first books of the Bible) all the way to the apostle John, the author of the last portions of the New Testament.[3]

Edwards refused to separate the cognitive component of revelation from the communication of God's own being and frequently spoke of revelation as a vision of God that illuminates all of reality:

> [Revelation is that which] reveals God to the soul, enables it to apprehend him as he is, and to have a right apprehension of the perfections and glory of that being who is the being of beings, the first and the last. And proportionately, as it discovers him, it gives a right understanding of all other things.[4]

Edwards argued that it is "agreeable to reason" that a God who "created us to serve him and enjoy him" would "some way reveal himself" so that his creatures would know "how they obtain peace with him and enjoy his favor." It is "most reasonable to suppose" that God would show them "what manner of being he is," his works of creation and providence, and how they are to "regulate themselves." For if he did not reveal himself and his intentions, they would be "left wholly and entirely in the dark." But it was not only for human well-being

---

2. WJE 13:273, 259, 273; WJE 8:435, 433; WJE 13:274.
3. WJE 19:710.
4. WJE 19:725.

that there was revelation. It also was critical to God's own pleasure. Because God "loves himself, loves his own end" and would not be frustrated, he made sure to provide "necessary means for the clear, evident and distinct knowledge" for his creatures, so that they would serve his ends for the creation. Therefore, Edwards told the Stockbridge Indians in 1753, "'Tis unreasonable to think that God would always keep silence and never say anything to mankind."[5]

Revelation in History

Edwards believed that "the church in all ages...has enjoyed a revelation one way or other." Revelation did not start with the Jewish people but has existed "from the beginning." Against the deists who argued that God has not spoken except through reason, which is available to all, Edwards insisted that nearly all humans in history had received or had access to revelation, and therefore all knowledge of true religion among "the heathen" (those outside of Judaism and Christianity) was from revelation rather than the light of natural reason.[6]

In the "first ages" of the world human beings received revelation of the great religious truths, directly or indirectly, from God himself. These truths were then passed down by tradition from one generation to the next. Adam, for example, was alive for two-thirds of the time before the Flood, so that "a very great part" of those still alive before the Flood heard from his own mouth "the things which passed between him and his Creator in paradise." Noah was commissioned by God to preach to the world for 120 years.[7]

God placed Abraham's family "as it were in the midst of the earth, between Asia, Europe and Africa, in the midst of those nations which were most considerable and famous for power, knowledge and the arts." Through that family and their descendants, whom he intended to be a "city on an hill...a light to the world," he conferred "visible tokens of His presence...manifesting himself there, and from thence, to the world." As a result, Abraham's family was known in all the principal nations of the world. His acquaintance with Melchizedek proved that the great works of God for his family were sufficient to have awakened "the attention and consideration of all the nations in that part of the world, and to have led them to the knowledge and worship of the only true God."[8]

---

5. WJE 14:232; WJE 18:402; WJE 23:255, 257; sermon on 2 Tim. 3.16, in John H. Gerstner, *The Rational Biblical Theology of Jonathan Edwards* (Orlando: Ligonier, 1991), 1:240.

6. WJE 19:710.

7. WJE 3:170.

8. WJE 3:171–72.

Similar things took place in Jacob's and Joseph's time. God's wonders on their behalf "were done in the sight of the nations of the world, tending to awaken them and lead them to the knowledge and obedience of the true God." In Moses' and Joshua's time, God manifested himself in miracles quite publicly—"in view as it were of the whole world." The world was shaken, "the whole frame of the visible creation, earth, seas, and rivers, the atmosphere, the clouds, sun, moon and stars, were affected; miracles greatly tending to convince the nations of the world of the vanity of their false gods."[9]

Unfortunately, human finitude and sinful corruption caused the revelation to be distorted, resulting in superstition and idolatry.[10] The breakdown was caused in part by a problem of language. All original peoples shared hieroglyphs with the Egyptians to represent divine things taught by Noah and his sons, who founded the nations after the flood. Over the course of time, pagans dissociated the symbol from its referent. "Men attached themselves to the letter and the signs without understanding the spirit and the thing signified." This accounted for idols and "vile superstitions." It also explained the similarity between the stories of Christ's sufferings and the legends of pagan heroes: the heathen took the symbols of Christ's sufferings and applied them to their own champions. By this mechanism and others, the original purity of divine revelation was continually breaking down, corrupted by profane and demonic admixtures. God used the Jews to retard the process of degeneration by periodically acting on their behalf with miracles, which reminded the heathen of the traditions they had once learned from their fathers but subsequently forgot.[11]

Edwards recounted this drama in his private commentary on selected biblical passages: "The knowledge of true religion was for some time kept up in the world by tradition. And there were soon great corruptions and apostasies crept in, and much darkness overwhelmed [a] great part of the world." By the time of Moses, most of the truth that had previously been taught by tradition was lost. So "God took care that there might be something new, [which] should be very public, and of great fame, and much taken notice of abroad, in the world heard, that might be sufficient to lead sincere inquirers to the true God." Hence the heathen nations in the Ancient Near East heard about the exodus of the Jews from Egypt, the miracles God performed for them in the wilderness, Joshua's conquests of the Canaanites, and the sun standing still. The defeated Canaanites fled to Africa, Asia, Europe and the isles of the sea "to

---

9. WJE 3:173.

10. WJE 20:222–26, 303–11.

11. WJE 23:190–91; WJE 13:421–26.

carry the tidings of those things.... so that, in a manner, the whole world heard of these great things."¹²

After these wondrous acts of God, knowledge of true religion was maintained for several generations. But by the time of David, much had been forgotten and distorted. So God acted once more, this time for David and Solomon, "to make his people Israel, who had the true religion, [be] taken notice of among the heathens." The diaspora after the Babylonian captivity spread knowledge of the true God even further abroad, so that "the nations of the world, if their heart had been well disposed to seek after the truth, might have had some means to have led 'em in their sincere and diligent inquiries to the knowledge of the true God and his ways."¹³

According to Edwards, God saw to it that heathen philosophers came looking for news. Heathen "wise men" and "philosophers" obtained "scraps of light and truth ... by travelling from one country to another," especially Judea, Greece, and Phoenicia. Edwards noted that Plato, for instance, had come to Egypt to learn what he could of the Jewish religion.¹⁴

Revelation of Jesus Christ and in Scripture

If revelation has gone out from the beginning of history, and not only to the Jews but around the world and to various cultures, its principal subject since the beginning has been Jesus Christ. "Jesus Christ is the sum and substance of the gospel," wrote Edwards, "the main subject of revelation since the Fall." Even the heathen heard of "restoration by a divine Redeemer," who would be a "Middle God ... [who] was not to expiate and put an end to crimes but by his own great sufferings." Jesus Christ was not only divine author of all revelation but also the content of all that revelation. He was both Revealer and Revealed. But "the principal thing that is revealed" was not simply redemption through his person and work, but "the excellency [beauty] and sufficiency of Christ." The "natural man" who does not have the Spirit may hear the Word in church and read the Bible, but "understands nothing of" that beauty and sufficiency without the divine and supernatural light (ch. 24). Yet "true Christians do understand this: they have seen the King in his beauty." It was the King in all his beauty who was the heart and sum of all revelation from God to humanity.¹⁵

---

12. WJE 15:369–72.

13. WJE 15:369–72.

14. WJE 19:713.

15. WJE 13:148; WJE 23:479; WJE 19:731; WJE 14:250.

The surest and clearest way to find the beauty of Jesus Christ, the heart of revelation, was in the only written revelation God gave to the church, its Bible. Edwards often called it the "Word of God." At times he referred to it as "the word of Christ," at other times "the word of life." Throughout his life, he mixed and matched the words of his *Personal Narrative*—"a sweet, excellent, life-giving word"—to depict the Bible. He taught that God "indited" (composed or inspired) the Bible through its human authors, so that in it we find "perfection" that requires an "infinite understanding" to see its fullness. Edwards was not unaware of critical problems in the Bible. For example, he contended with developing biblical criticism that suggested Moses was not the author of the Pentateuch, struggled to reconcile apparently conflicting resurrection accounts, and made nineteen arguments against the notion that the apostles taught the return of Christ in their generation. But he remained convinced that the Scriptures should be "our guide in all things, in our thoughts of religion, and of ourselves."[16]

In 1753, Edwards preached a sermon to the Stockbridge Indians trying to prove that the Bible is the Word of God by reason alone. He gave multiple lines of evidence to support his claim: there is no comparable Word among the heathen, the Bible provides right notions of God (the way of forgiveness and salvation, God's rules and commandments, a Savior, the end of the world and judgment), miracles and prophecies confirm it, the Bible has enlightened so many nations, the devil opposes it, it has prevailed against great opposition, no man could have written such a book, no book so reaches the hearts of people, and good people all love it. The more wicked they are, the more they are against it.[17]

Elsewhere Edwards gave other "rational proofs" of the Bible's unique inspiration. In the *Miscellanies* he cited the Jews' survival as a people across millennia, and in *Freedom of the Will* he proposed that the scriptures were divine because they taught doctrines that wise and great men rejected because of the blindness of their minds and the prejudices of their hearts, yet they were doctrines "exactly agreeable to the most demonstrable, certain and natural dictates of reason."[18]

Finally, however, for Edwards as for Calvin, the rational proofs paled in importance beside the testimony of the Holy Spirit that is found by those

---

16. WJE 16:801; WJE 17:180; WJE 13:203; WJE 15:423–69, 154–56; WJE 20:57–64; WJE 2:438.

17. Sermon on 2 Tim. 3:16, in Alexander Grosart, ed., *Selections from the Unpublished Writings of Jonathan Edwards* (Ligonier, PA: Soli Deo Gloria, 1992), 191–96.

18. WJE 23:72; WJE 1:439.

with a rightly disposed mind in the pages of scripture itself. Although we just saw a Stockbridge sermon in which Edwards argued from reason, Edwards's most vigorous arguments from reason for the Bible's inspiration are found closer to the beginning of his career. Even at Stockbridge, Edwards argued for the self-validating character of the Bible as much as for its attestation by reason. As he gained pastoral experience, Edwards devoted less energy to rational proofs and concluded that the ultimate proof is the simple proclamation of the gospel. Already in 1727 the young pastor told his congregation that there are three ways to see that the Scriptures are the Word of God, and two of them circumvented reason. One was to see the "excellency" in the Bible, and the other was to receive true light into their minds from God's Word. After enumerating many "evidences" for the Bible's inspiration, he added, "[There are] the stamps and characters of divinity everywhere appearing in the Bible, that are self-evident proofs of its coming from God." Even in 1728– 29 he was conceding that the saints' faith in the Bible as the Word of God is based on "the intrinsic signatures of divinity which they see in it ... signatures of divine majesty ... divine wisdom and of divine holiness.... They do as it were hear God speak, and they are assured of the divinity of his speech, for he speaks like a God. His speech is not like the speech of men, but like the speech of God: divinely excellent, holy, wise, awful and gracious." In a 1740 sermon on the uses of reason, the maturing pastor preached that "divine revelation in these things don't go a begging for credit and validity by approbation and applause of our understandings." Several years later, in *Religious Affections*, he once again proclaimed that the gospel "don't go abroad a begging for its evidence, so much as some think; it has its highest and most proper evidence in itself."[19]

In a series of sermons titled "The Wisdom of God Displayed in the Way of Salvation," Edwards explained the self-attestation of scripture in terms reminiscent of Calvin. The gospel has no need of external evidences and arguments, he declared, for there is enough evidence within it for those who have been spiritually enlightened to distinguish it from "the effects of human invention." An enlightened mind will see "evident appearances of the divine perfections" and "the stamp of divine glory" in it.[20]

---

19. WJE 14:233, 251–52; BW, 127; WJE 2:307.

20. "The Wisdom of God Displayed in the Way of Salvation," in WH 2:153–54. See also Miscellany 333: "The Scriptures themselves are an evidence of their own divine authority" (WJE 13:410).

Because revelation is from God, it is not without mystery. Against deist screeds such as John Toland's *Christianity Not Mysterious* (1696) that revelation cannot contain anything above human understanding, Edwards argued that "it would be very strange indeed, if there should not be some great mysteries, quite beyond our comprehension, and attended with difficulties which it is impossible for us fully to solve and explain." After all, he suggested, mystery is to be expected because religion is concerned with things that are not the objects of our senses. We can easily imagine that a revelation about the invisible God, and a future state when we are separated from the body, would contain mystery. Things of that world would be very different from things of this world, things of sense, and all that earthly language is meant to express.[21]

Revelation is also progressive. God did not give it all at once because God's glory would have been too overwhelming for human beings. This is why the Kingdom of Christ, and revelation of it, proceeded slowly and gradually, lest the sight of it blind and obliterate finite creation. Only the gradual unfolding of revelation over the course of history could begin to show the fullness of God's glory in anything approaching its completeness. The purpose of revelation is the glory of God, which involves the display of God's attributes, which can be displayed fully only by seeing their gradual unfolding through the history of redemption. This history, which proceeds in progressive fashion in Scripture, gives God the opportunity to both "exercise his goodness" and display that goodness, which is his joy. God rejoices in his own acts, which means that the progressive unfolding of revelation is God's chosen method to maximize his joy and glory.[22]

In what could be called his psychology of revelation, Edwards described how revelation comes to a saint. So while there is the history of revelation, there is also the inner world of revelation to the heart: "Divine revelation is in the hearts of those that do truly entertain it, as a light that shines in a dark place." This is not the immediate revelation that we saw at the beginning of this chapter, but "spiritual illumination" in which persons become "inwardly sensible of the divine excellency, giving a new spiritual sense, [or] a new sense of [the] heart, a new spiritual relish."[23]

Edwards's famous sermon "A Divine and Supernatural Light" distinguished this light from conviction of sin, an "impression made upon the imagination,"

---

21. WJE 23:359–76
22. WJE 9:355–56; WJE 18:238–39; WJE 8:447.
23. WJE 19:724; WJE 25:303–304.

and religious feelings that have been caused by "mere principles of nature." The Word of God "is no proper cause of this effect," for while "the mind can't see the excellency of any doctrine, unless that doctrine be first in the mind," seeing the excellency must be "immediately from the Spirit of God." The Spirit conveys "a true sense of the divine excellency of the things revealed in the Word of God, and a conviction of the truth and reality of them." This divine light reveals the "superlative glory" in "the ways and works of God revealed in the gospel." The person who is thus enlightened "don't [sic] merely rationally believe that God is glorious, but he has a real sense of the gloriousness of God in his heart." Edwards compared this new sense to tasting honey or seeing a beautiful woman.[24]

> There is a difference between having a rational judgment that honey is sweet, and having a sense of its sweetness. A man may have the former, that knows not how honey tastes; but a man can't have the latter, unless he has an idea of the taste of honey in his mind. So there is a difference between believing that a person is beautiful, and having a sense of his beauty. The former may be obtained by hearsay, but the latter only by seeing the countenance.[25]

Therefore we can say that, while Edwards taught an *objective* history of revelation that was given to the world whether human beings received it or not, there was also for him a process of *subjective* revelation that is given by the Spirit to make that objective revelation visible and real to the saints.

At the same time, Edwards was wary of some claims to revelation. He rejected the continuing validity of tongues, prophecy, and ecstatic knowledge. These were "extraordinary gifts of the Spirit" given for temporary use while the church was in its "infancy or childhood." Their purpose was to establish the chief means of grace, which is the Word of God, especially the New Testament canon. These gifts helped confirm the word of Christ and the apostles. Once the church had come to a state of "manhood" when the canon of Scripture was completed, these "extraordinary influences of the Spirit of God withdrew and vanished away." These special gifts were by "immediate revelation" to the mind, without going through the ordinary media of "sense or reason" or "any former revelation." Edwards preached in 1748 that there had been claims by

---

24. WJE 17: 410–12, 413.

25. WJE 17: 414. Edwards's use of the pronoun "his" in "his beauty" was probably an eighteenth-century convention. Writers in that century typically did not refer to the beauty of a man's "face," but would speak of his "countenance" or "features." Per Kenneth Minkema.

"wild people of late" that they had received revelation "by some voice or in some dream or vision, or by words or ideas immediately and miraculously excited." God spoke in this way to the patriarchs, Moses, the prophets, and the apostles, but since the closure of the canon God has been speaking only in "ordinary" ways. These are "when things are known by sense and experience" through the outward senses, or by "intuitively seeing...sentiments and affections," or through reason and the testimony of our fellow creatures. Learning through Scripture is another ordinary means of knowledge.

Those who claimed extraordinary revelation failed to accept the word of the apostles as the rule of the church of Christ in all succeeding times, and "take upon themselves to be an additional foundation." "Many deceivers" had made wild predictions, but none had come to pass. Edwards thought some wanted to add to biblical revelation, and he appealed to church tradition to refute them: "No writings that have been written since that time [of the apostles] have ever steadily been acknowledged by any part of the Christian church." He accepted "spiritual illumination," which he said always conveys a sense of the divine excellency by a new sense of the heart, but seemed to associate "special, personal revelations from God" with claiming a new truth "not declared in the Bible before this." In other words, he seemed not to consider the possibility of prophecy or direct inspiration that reinforces rather than augments or contradicts the message of Scripture.[26]

Reason: Its Promise and Limits

Toward the end of his life, Edwards defined reason as the faculty that judges the truth of a proposition either immediately by self-evidence or by inference from an intuitively self-evident proposition—"that power or faculty an intelligent being has to judge of the truth of propositions, either immediately, by only looking on the propositions, which is judging by intuition and self-evidence; or by putting together several propositions, which are already evident by intuition, or at least whose evidence is originally derived from intuition."[27]

This definition is not remarkable, but the lofty terms with which Edwards viewed reason are striking. Considered apart from its fallen condition, reason was "a participation of the divine essence," "the rational image of God in man," and the "highest" faculty "designed by our maker to ever rule and exalt sense, imagination, and passion." It distinguished humans from beasts. The soul,

---

26. WJE 25:280–87, 282, 294, 282, 289–90, 300, 292, 303–304.

27. WJE 23:359.

on his account, was essentially rational—"that thinking being that is contained in the body of every living man."[28]

Edwards had considerable faith in the power of reason to discover religious truth. First and foremost, it could prove God's existence. In fact, this task was "short and easy and what we naturally fall into," for God implanted within the human mind a principle of causation that pointed to the existence of God.[29] His unshakeable conviction that "whatever begins to be must have a cause" was the "foundation of all reasoning about the existence of things." Without it we could not establish the existence of God or of anything else. Edwards offered his own versions of the ontological, cosmological, and teleological arguments of God's existence (chs. 7 & 10).[30] Remarkably, Edwards held that reason—when considered apart from its sinful corruption—was capable of perceiving what is most important about God to know: his excellency and glory. This is noteworthy because, for Edwards, the vision of God's beauty or excellency distinguishes the saved from the damned. Eventually even the damned and the demons in hell will see God's holiness, yet only the saints will see the *beauty* of God's holiness. Yet Edwards preached in 1740 that reason—without any special illumination by the Holy Spirit—was as capable of knowing God's glory and excellency "as of any other knowledge whatsoever—and which is as plainly and abundantly manifested as anything whatsoever, innumerable ways, both in the word and works of God."[31]

For Edwards, the knowledge about God acquired by the unregenerate reason in reflecting on the natural world and on scripture was a means of grace. It gave the unregenerate "the greatest advantage for the obtaining grace" as "outward means that do most exhibit the truth to our minds." Conversely, false notions about God were barriers to grace. "A false notion gives no opportunity for grace to act, but on the contrary, will hinder its acting." Insofar as knowledge—illuminated by grace—could be a means of grace for the unregenerate, rational arguments could prepare the way for grace: "Rational arguments may savingly convince the soul of the truth of the things of religion."[32]

---

28. WJE 13:342; WJE 10:195; WJE 17:67; WJE 10:3-7, 195; WJE 3:168; WJE 10:309.

29. WJE 13:373. This, of course, is what later philosophers called "the principle of sufficient reason."

30. WJE 1:181, 183. On proofs, see McDermott, *Jonathan Edwards Confronts the Gods*, 57–59.

31. WH 2:252. This would seem to contradict Edwards's notion that only the regenerate can see God's beauty (as opposed to earthly beauty). But in this sermon, Edwards meant unprejudiced and regenerate reason when he said that reason could behold God's excellency. There he made clear that although the unregenerate mind is "as capable of it, as of any other knowledge whatsoever... it] can see nothing at all of it."

32. WJE 13:86; WJE 18:162.

If reason could be a means of grace, it could also bring condemnation. A true knowledge of God destroyed the excuses that the unregenerate might otherwise make on the day of judgment. In comparison with his Reformed predecessors, Edwards had less to say about an accusatory or condemning knowledge of God. One *Miscellanies* entry treats God's revelation to the heathen at some length and yet never mentions the idea of condemnation.[33]

After regeneration by the Holy Spirit, reason functions as a "great friend." Assisted by divine revelation and the Spirit's influence, reason helps the soul grow in the knowledge of divine things. In the process of regeneration, the Spirit becomes united to the human mind, which then manifests a new inclination toward the truth. The Spirit, so to speak, casts a light on "divine objects" so that they become alluring. Their "beauty and sweetness...draw forth" the exercises of the mind, and thereby stimulate the mind to act as it should. Upon seeing the beauty of divine things, reason moves toward trust in Christ and henceforth is regulated by the love of Christ.[34]

Despite the promise and possibilities of reason, human beings were not able to find God or the fullness of spiritual truth through unaided reason. This was not the fault of reason as originally given from God, but a reflection of reason's corruption by sin. For Edwards, history proved that there had been no major moral reformation of the world before Christ. Even the Greek and Roman philosophers, despite flashes of brilliance, had all missed the mark: "All the endeavors of philosophers had proved in vain, for many ages, to reform the world," either morally or spiritually before Christ.[35]

The religions of the heathen nation were further proof of reason's failure. Even in their most flourishing state, the Greeks and Romans worshipped a multitude of gods "with innumerable ridiculous and monstrous rites and ceremonies." Some would even offer their children "to be cruelly tormented to death in the fire to [an] idol, burning them to death in burning brass."[36] There were exceptions to the rule. Socrates and Plato, for example, were heathen philosophers who based their morality on religious foundations. Yet even Plato failed to condemn publicly the idolatries of his day. In sum, the whole world lay in religious darkness until the coming of Christ. Despite the truths taught by the "wisest heathen," the Greek and Roman worlds embraced "the absurdest opinions and practices that all civilized nations now acknowledge to

---

33. WJE 23:84–85; WJE 23:355.
34. WJE 25:547; WJE 17:411, 415; WJE 8:178, 185.
35. WJE 2:140.
36. WJE 19:712.

be crazy foolishness." This universal "darkness in religious things" proved that there was no remedy before Christ. No nation ever freed itself from this state by its own wisdom. Indeed, no one could do so.[37]

Most important of all, reason could not demonstrate how sinful humans might be reconciled to their Creator. Locke and the deists may have been right to say that reason could show the necessity of repentance after sin, but they were wrong to believe that reason could show sinners how to achieve true repentance. Assurance of salvation was also impossible to attain by reason alone. Since God is just as well as merciful, reason itself could not assure us that God is ready to forgive. Reason could never prove that God would forgive all sins without exception. Nor could it prove to what extent repentance was necessary. The light of nature might show us the general shape of true religion but not its specific beliefs and practices. Human beings have thus not come to know the true God through reason. Even if people had gained such knowledge, they still would not know if God wanted to save them or to damn them.[38]

For Edwards, then, reason could arrive at some religious truths, but they would not be properly known unless seen in their relationship to Christ and his redemption. So reason could provide a "notional" knowledge of Christ through the text of scripture but not a saving knowledge of God. At this point, the radical nature of Edwards's rejoinder to deism can be seen: he rejected not only the sufficiency of reason in knowing God but the sufficiency of (unilluminated) scripture as well. Scripture was the rational means by which spiritual knowledge comes, yet spiritual knowledge came only by revelation of the beauty of God in Christ.

The Role of Tradition

Edwards professed repeatedly that our only authority in religion is the written text of scripture. But in practice he seemed to operate with the tacit recognition that the Bible can be read only through and with tradition. What is more, the ultimate religious authority of scripture was mediated through a story of divine redemption known by reflection and transmitted through tradition. Though Edwards downplayed tradition in his explicit statements, it proved to be significant in his actual practice of theological reflection.

In his narrative of the communion controversy, penned sometime after 1750, Edwards cited his grandfather Solomon Stoddard's words approvingly: "He, who believes principles because our forefathers affirm them, makes

---

37. WJE 20:291; WJE 9:399.

38. WJE 23:261–64, 175, 263–64.

idols of them."[39] In other words, one should never accept anything as religiously binding simply because Christians in previous times believed them. Edwards went so far as to raise this precept to the status of "Protestant principle" later in his narrative: "[It is] easily resolved...[w]hether, on Protestant principles, the determination of ancestors as to matters of religion and the worship of God, binds future generations without their consent, either express or implied."[40] Edwards here implied, in good Enlightenment fashion, that no one should be bound to earlier traditions without first giving consent to them. Edwards's words did not suggest however that he regarded tradition as useless. Arguments from "the fathers" and from the early church could be helpful in two ways. They could confirm the truth of a doctrine or practice by showing that one's interpretation of the Bible was "more probable." They could also serve a heuristic function by prodding one to look into the scriptures for things one had not seen before.

Yet Edwards was convinced that no matter how "very rational [and] probable" traditional arguments might be, God "never designed that the dependence of his church should be *at all* upon them [the Fathers or other traditional authorities]." Edwards argued on democratic, fallibilistic, and fiduciary grounds. If traditional authorities functioned as the primary sources of authority, then ordinary Christians would be at a disadvantage. Only "learned men" would have the training and time to master such authorities. Yet the scriptures are "not so large, but that *all* may be well acquainted with them." It is "God's mercy" that His "rule" is "contained within so small a compass...that 'tis not beyond the capacity of ordinary Christians to manage it, and become well acquainted with it." With the help of their ministers, humble farmers could see what they needed to see for "themselves."[41] Second, the inherent fallibility of theologians and church leaders makes it unsafe to rely on them. We have no reason to expect that God has protected them from "unavoidable mistakes." They may have corrupted the truth, and we cannot expect that "providence" would have always prevented such corruption. Even if they had no intention of changing what they had received, their historical conditions might have caused loss or distortion. Christians in the earliest generations were few and scattered, and they could have misunderstood or forgotten what the apostles had told them—"either through a mistake of meaning or through defect of memory." Besides, there were few who heard all of what the apostles

---

39. WJE 12:565.

40. WJE 12:587

41. WJE 18:79. Emph. add.

taught and fewer still who understood it properly.[42] Third, Edwards reasoned that dependence on tradition would detract from dependence on scripture and God. "The more absolute and entire our dependence on the Word of God is, the greater the respect we shall have to that Word, the more we shall esteem and honor and prize it; and this respect to the Word of God will lead us to have the greater respect to God himself."[43] The temptation, Edwards suggested, would be to pay the Fathers just as much respect as the Bible, which would mean that the Fathers' wisdom would rival that of God's.

Dependence on tradition, for Edwards, was a form of dependence on divine providence. Hence the proper use of tradition hinged on the human capacity to discern God's hand in historical events. Yet this led to a problem: "The conduct of divine providence, with its reasons, is too little understood by us, to be improved as our rule. 'God has his way in the sea, his path in the mighty waters, and his footsteps are not known'" (Ps. 77.19).[44] Edwards did not believe that human beings could know with certainty why God permitted particular historical events to take place, including new developments in theology and biblical interpretation. In conclusion, then, God gave us the Word of God as our only sure rule for faith and practice.

Edwards's pessimism about our ability to interpret providence may be surprising, coming from someone who scanned the newspapers for signs of progress in the history of redemption. This was the same man who declared that local events such as drought or pestilence were signs of God's providential judgment.[45] Yet Edwards's objection to using providence as a rule was as part of his response to his opponents during the communion controversy of the late 1740s, who contended that their (and his grandfather Solomon Stoddard's) open communion policy had been blessed with conversions. Edwards's response was that God blesses those features of pastoral practice "which are very right and excellent" while overlooking and pardoning "their mistakes in opinion or practice."[46] The same could be said for the opinions of the early Church Fathers. They may have blessed multitudes with their ancient doctrines and practices, but those doctrines and practices may nevertheless have been riddled with errors. Tradition is no guarantee of truth.

---

42. WJE 13:241.

43. WJE 18:80.

44. WJE 12:319.

45. Gerald R. McDermott, *One Holy and Happy Society: The Public Theology of Jonathan Edwards* (University Park: Penn State Press, 1992), 43–48, 11–13.

46. WJE 12:319–20.

Yet Edwards was inconsistent. Or, to put it another way, his thinking on tradition was nuanced. *Sola scriptura* was his rallying cry, especially when plotting the course of Protestant progress against Catholic persecution, but he also showed in a number of ways that theology and practice must look outside the Bible to know what the Bible means.[47] Because redemption proceeded for all those ages *before* Scripture began, God's church had been founded not on Scripture per se but on *revelation*, which had used both oral tradition and the written word.[48] Therefore God's church had not always used the Bible for religious authority; for significant periods it used oral tradition, preserved through human teachers invested with authority. Edwards also observed that the history of theology was driven partly by the "gradual" illumination of the meaning of the scriptures. God chose not to unfold the sum total of his revelation at once. Just as the Bible was written by degrees and over time, so too God's Spirit imparted understanding of the Bible by degrees and over time. The most important parts of revelation have been plain from the very beginning, but God purposely made other parts "obscure and mysterious" or "difficult." This was because human beings prize something more after they have labored for it. They also find the search and discovery more "delightful."[49]

Edwards considered progressive revelation, and the progressive understanding of that revelation, to be evident from the plain text of scripture:

> There are a multitude of things in the Old Testament which the church then did not understand, but were reserved to be unfolded to the Christian church, such as most of their types and shadows and prophecies, which make up the greatest part of the Old Testament; so I believe *there are many now thus veiled, that remain to [be] discovered* by the church in the coming glorious times.[50]

Therefore Edwards expected more things to be illuminated by the Spirit during and after his lifetime. While he would affirm that scripture was the only reliable religious authority, Edwards acknowledged that one could not

---

47. See, for example, WJE 9:414, 421–22.

48. WJE 9:443: "So that the church of God has always been built on the foundation of divine revelation, and always on those revelations that were essentially the same, and which are summarily comprehended in the holy Scriptures, and ever since about Moses' time have been built on the Scriptures themselves." Edwards's emphasis is on the rule of scripture, but in the process he notes that revelation is even more foundational than scripture.

49. WJE 13:426–27; WJE 23:375.

50. WJE 13:426–27.

understand that authority without also attending to the history of theological rumination on scripture—which, at its best, was directed by the Spirit's gradual unfolding of the meaning of the written Word. This attention to, and following of, the Spirit's hermeneutical leading was, in effect, an orthodox *tradition* of theological reflection on scripture.

Edwards was himself influenced by this tradition. He acknowledged during the controversy with his congregation that he changed his mind about the issue of qualifications for communion, some years after he arrived at Northampton, only after becoming "more studied in divinity" and as he "improved in experience." Theological reading and pastoral experience led him to read the Bible differently, which in turn led him to the change in sacramental practice that eventually got him expelled. This was not unlike Edwards's own description of Martin Luther, whose new views of church and salvation came only after studying the Bible "and the writings of the ancient fathers of the church."[51] Another implicit endorsement of tradition appears in Edwards's *Religious Affections*, which drew explicitly upon sixteen earlier authors, most of them seventeenth-century English Puritans and dissenting clergy. Although most are well known to students of Puritanism, John E. Smith notes that "their contribution to the formation of Edwards's thought has been underestimated."[52]

Scholars have recently described the way in which, for Edwards after 1739, the real authority for his theological work was not the biblical text per se but his own imaginative construal of the story inscribed there, which he called the "work of redemption."[53] This was a master narrative (ch. 12) beginning in eternity with the Trinity's plan, proceeding through the "fall of man," the history of Israel, the Incarnation, and history of the church and world all the way until "the end of the world." It was centered in the work of Christ but orchestrated by all the members of the Trinity.[54] This "grand design" could not be read off the face of the biblical text, for the plot required that Christ was the real actor in all of Israel's communication with God—speaking at the burning bush, for example, and camouflaged by every appearance of "the angel of the

---

51. WJE 12:169; WJE 9:421.

52. WJE 2:52.

53. See, for example, WJE 22:4–14; and Robert E. Brown, *Jonathan Edwards and the Bible* (Bloomington: Indiana University Press, 2002) 164–96. Many have remarked on Edwards's turn from a rational approach to theology to a historical one, which would require a synthetic narrative; see, for example, Harry S. Stout and Nathan O. Hatch, Editor's Introduction, WJE 22:7.

54. WJE 9:116, 118.

Lord" in the Old Testament.[55] Only through this story, as told by Edwards and informed by traditional Protestant historiography (ch. 28), could the true meaning of the biblical text be seen. Hence the water of the Flood was a type of the blood of Christ, and the cultus of the Law that included "all the precepts that relate to building the tabernacle that was set up in the wilderness and all the forms, and circumstances, and utensils of it" were directed by God "to show forth something of Christ."[56]

Edwards's own narrative theology was informed not only by the biblical story as conceived within the canon, but also by its continuation in post-biblical history. The first two-thirds of Edwards's chapters of this history tell the biblical story, but the last third, a full ten chapters, traces the work of redemption in later "secular" history and beyond. Edwards described these sixteen-plus centuries as fulfillment of biblical prophecies, yet at the same time used the whole history—biblical and later—as the master template through which to read the meaning of the Bible itself. All of "the various dispensations of God" related in the Bible were to be understood as simply "successive motions" in this "one work," which proceeded inexorably as "one machine" to its predetermined purpose—which again could be seen only through the lens of Edwards's construal of the master narrative, "the history of the work of redemption."[57]

Finally, Edwards also remarked on how church practice was not strictly limited by biblical directives. To be sure, he could sound like a traditional Puritan in ruling out anything in Sunday worship that was not explicitly mandated in the biblical text, citing, for example, Nadab and Abihu's executions for instituting service "which was not appointed."[58] But at the same time, he argued that there were things in worship that were not part of worship per se and therefore could be acceptable even if they were neither forbidden nor anticipated by Scripture.[59] For example, when there was controversy over newly introduced musical notation and rhythmic meter in congregational singing, Edwards supported the latter when neither side could point to a decisive biblical text.[60] He introduced into the discussion an aesthetic criterion that was extra-biblical: ceremonies should be abolished, he suggested, if they

---

55. WJE 9:131, 196–98.

56. WJE 9:151, 182.

57. WJE 9:119 and *passim*.

58. WJE 20:468.

59. WJE 13:243–44.

60. George Marsden, *Jonathan Edwards: A Life* (New Haven, CT: Yale University Press, 2003), 144–45.

"have no intrinsic direct *loveliness*, nor agreeableness to the *lovely* God, or tendency to happiness."[61]

In sum, for Edwards not only the Bible but also regenerate reason and orthodox tradition were aspects of God's revelation to humanity. Such revelation was not merely an impartation of cognitive concepts but an infusion of spiritual vision and, indeed, of God's own being. By oral tradition and the written Word, by Spirit-guided reflection on the Word and the opening of human hearts to God's beauty in Christ, God communicated his own knowledge of himself, which was inextricably tied to his love for and enjoyment of his own being.

---

61. WJE 13:246–67; emph. added.

10

Apologetics

THE EIGHTEENTH CENTURY was an era of apologetics. For the first time since late antiquity, the basic truthfulness of the Christian religion was no longer taken for granted among Western thinkers. Christianity was now something that needed defending. Beginning in the 1690s, the English deists cast doubt on many basic Christian beliefs, including Jesus' divinity; the Trinity; the historical accuracy of the Bible; the possibility of miracles; Jesus' fulfillment of Old Testament prophecies; Jesus' atoning death, resurrection, and second coming; and the providential origins of the Christian church. In response, the orthodox authored countless treatises arguing that the Christian faith was more "reasonable" than its deistic alternative. One commentator noted that "the title of Locke's treatise, *The Reasonableness of Christianity* [1695], may be said to have been the solitary thesis of Christian theology in England for the great part of a century."[1] Though small in number, the opponents of orthodoxy largely set the agenda for eighteenth-century theology.

Like many of his contemporaries, Jonathan Edwards argued against deism and for the credibility of the Christian faith. Yet Edwards has been more widely recognized as a defender of particular—especially Calvinistic—doctrines than as a defender of Christianity in general. There are a number of reasons for this.

First, Edwards did not publish in his own lifetime a work devoted specifically to Christian apologetics. Instead his apologetic reflections were scattered throughout his manuscripts and especially the *Miscellanies*. Edwards's son, Jonathan Edwards Jr., transcribed and published in 1793 some of the *Miscellanies* dealing with apologetic subjects in response to the rising tide of French freethinking.[2] Nonetheless, these extracts represented only a small fraction of Edwards's apologetic writing. Many important themes—such as Edwards's engagement with non-Christian religions in the later *Miscellanies* (ch. 36)—were not at all reflected in these extracts.

---

1. Mark Pattison, "Tendencies of Religious Thought in England, 1688–1750," in *Essays and Reviews*, 8th ed. (London: Longman, Green, 1861), 258.

2. This collection, known as the *Miscellaneous Observations on Important Theological Subjects*, was included in nineteenth-century editions of Edwards'ss writings. See WH 2:460–510.

Second, Edwards is not known as an apologist because he died before he composed the great works of synthesis he had intended to write. In his letter to the trustees of the College of New Jersey, Edwards mentioned two works, *The Harmony of the Old and New Testaments*, and *History of the Work of Redemption*, both of which were to include an apologetic element. The *Harmony* was to treat "evidences" and the "correspondence between predictions and events" in biblical history. *History of Redemption* was to present Christian doctrines in a comprehensive way and to show "the admirable contexture and harmony of the whole."[3] Ava Chamberlain's analysis of the *Miscellanies* showed that the notebook entries on "Christian Religion" were integrally related to an early project of Edwards that carried the imposing title, *A Rational Account of Christianity, or, The Perfect Harmony between the Doctrines of the Christian Religion and Human Reason Manifested*. Yet during the 1730s Edwards developed a "growing conviction that salvation history...represented Christianity's best line of defense against the deists." It was not that he gave up the rational defense of the Christian faith, but he sought to show faith's rationality by an appeal to historical rather than solely logical or philosophical arguments. At the time that Edwards wrote to the college trustees, his early project for the *Rational Account* had been superseded by his plans for the *Harmony* and the *History*, which were to present a defense of the faith and "to confute deist claims."[4]

Third, Edwards's approach to apologetics was sometimes implicit and indirect rather than explicit and direct. He sought to demonstrate the validity of Christian beliefs by demonstrating their necessary interconnection with other accepted truths and their entailment with one another. It was the "admirable contexture and harmony" of various truths or arguments that gave added credibility to each one. Sometimes this implicit apology for the faith involved a rethinking of academic disciplines in order to show their hidden reliance upon and connection with foundational Christian principles. Truth, for Edwards, was an interconnected whole and not a matter of isolated statements.[5]

---

3. WJE 16:728–29. Edwards'ss *Miscellanies* might be compared with Blaise Pascal's *Pensées*— the rough notes he had prepared toward a full-scale apology for the Christian faith.

4. Ava Chamberlain, "Editor's Introduction," in WJE 18:24–34, citing 30.

5. On Edwards's apologetics and his concerns over deism, see Gerald McDermott's *Jonathan Edwards Confronts the Gods: Christian Theology, Enlightenment Religion, and Non-Christian Faiths* (New York: Oxford University Press, 2000) and "The Deist Connection: Jonathan Edwards and Islam," in Stephen J. Stein, ed., *Jonathan Edwards's Writings: Text, Context, Interpretation* (Bloomington, IN: Indiana University Press, 1996), 39–51; and the comments by three *Miscellanies* editors: Ava Chamberlain, "Editor's Introduction," in WJE 18:24–34; Amy Plantinga Pauw, "Editor's Introduction," in WJE 20:11–17; and Douglas A. Sweeney, WJE

George Marsden notes that Edwards's desire to write a great apology for Christianity was his earliest literary ambition. The "intensely ambitious" young man wanted to author "the definitive defense of the Christian religion in relation to all knowledge and all possible objections."[6] In some sense he never abandoned this aspiration, though the form and content of the proposed work changed as Edwards matured.

The Intellectual Context of Early Modernity

Brian A. Gerrish described the early modern period as "the retreat of God." By small degrees, God gradually receded from the thinking of European intellectuals and ended up as an unnecessary hypothesis. It would be "not so very far from the truth," wrote Gerrish, "if we said that the story begins with a God who does everything, moves on to a God who acts occasionally, and ends with a superannuated God who need not exist at all."[7] Many of the functions assigned to God were no longer tenable by the 1700s. The idea of "innate ideas," implanted into human minds by the Creator, was less credible in light of John Locke's *Essay Concerning Human Understanding* (1690). Locke's empirical philosophy affirmed that the human mind is stocked with ideas through sense experience. The idea of God, for Locke, was neither innate nor derived directly from sense experience. The very claim that human beings could possess a valid idea of God had become problematic. What is more, in the physical universe no less than the mental, God's status was in question. From the age of Aristotle to that of Sir Isaac Newton, thinkers had conceived of God as the "first mover" whose action was indispensable to the cosmos. Yet when Newton developed his celebrated laws of motion, he showed that the planets and other astronomical bodies could continue in motion without being acted upon from without. God's action was only needed at the beginning of the world, and not on a day-by-day basis.

23:10–29. See also Michael J. McClymond, *Encounters With God: An Approach to the Theology of Jonathan Edwards* (New York: Oxford University Press, 1998), 7, 25–26, 80–112; John Gerstner, "An Outline of the Apologetics of Jonathan Edwards," *Bibliotheca Sacra* 133 (1976): 3–10, 99–107, 195–201, 291–98; and Scott Oliphint, "Jonathan Edwards: Reformed Apologist," *Westminster Theological Journal* 57 (1995): 165–86. McClymond criticized Gerstner and Oliphint for interpreting Edwards in isolation from his eighteenth-century context (*Encounters*, 154, n.70).

6. George Marsden, *Jonathan Edwards: A Life* (New Haven, CT: Yale University Press, 2003), 110.

7. B. A. Gerrish, *A Prince of the Church: Schleiermacher and the Beginnings of Modern Theology* (Philadelphia, PA: Fortress Press, 1984), 54–55.

If one could not find God through ordinary cognition, or through the functioning of the physical universe, one might appeal to religious experience or mysticism. Yet, by the late 1600s, reliance on religious experience had become unacceptable to mainstream European and British intellectuals. Bloody religious conflicts, waged in the name of rival creeds, rent the heart of Western civilization for a century. These wars of religion undermined confidence in the competing orthodoxies of Catholicism and Protestantism, and, with them, belief in the claims of divine revelation that underlay them. Great Britain underwent social upheaval and dislocation in the mid-1600s because of religious rivalries. Consequently, there were few notions in the early eighteenth century more unpopular than the idea that God communicates truths to a select few. The words of the Anglican bishop, Joseph Butler, to John Wesley are emblematic

FIGURE 10.1 As William Hogarth shows in *Credulity, Superstition, and Fanaticism*, the eighteenth-century elite was skeptical of "enthusiastic" religion; the preacher's tonsure—beneath his wig—shows him to be a disguised Catholic priest.

of the era: "Sir, the pretending to extraordinary revelations and gifts of the Holy Ghost is a horrid thing—a very horrid thing!"[8]

Compounding the problem was the rise of the English deists, who had an "extraordinary effect... on the whole intellectual life of the eighteenth century." Professing their "honest desire for truth" and "moral seriousness," the deists set about thoroughly to reexamine and criticize all existing beliefs and practices in the name of "reason."[9] Whatever did not stand the test of "reason" as they understood it was to be revised or rejected. Most deists had "begun by defending the pre-eminence of Christianity on the ground that it alone corresponded with the true nature of religion." Yet "gradually becoming more conscious of their divergence from historic Christianity, they transformed themselves into the champions of natural, as opposed to revealed, religion."[10] The deists were thus insiders who became outsiders. As deism developed, there was a sharpening opposition between natural religion and revealed religion. Radical deists came to see Christian doctrines as unnecessary and the Bible as an inferior, limited expression of truths available to all persons through the light of natural reason. To the question of God's function in the world, the deists gave unambiguous answers. God was beyond the world, having created it and established its natural laws, and yet now was no longer involved in its day-to-day functioning. Trinity, Incarnation, Atonement, miracles—these were nonessential or perhaps even harmful beliefs. The Bible was valuable primarily or exclusively because of its ethical teaching.

Edwards opposed the deists with all the energy of his being. While they sought to distance God from the world, he upheld a radically God-centered perspective. He sought to refute the deists' concept of reason and reason's sufficiency, the deists' argument against the Bible's authority, and the deists'

---

8. Joseph Butler, as quoted in John Wesley, *Journal of the Rev. John Wesley*, 8 vols., edited by Nehemiah Curnock (London: Charles H. Kelly, n.d.), 2:257 [entry for August 1739].

9. Ernst Cassirer, *The Philosophy of the Enlightenment*, trans. Fritz C. A. Koelln and James P. Pettegrove (Boston, MA: Beacon Press, 1955), 174.

10. G. C. Joyce, quoted in J. K. S. Reid, *Christian Apologetics* (Grand Rapids, MI: Eerdmans 1969), 147. On deism in general, see Leslie Stephen, *History of English Thought in the Eighteenth Century*, 2 vols. (New York: G. P. Putnam, 1876), esp. 1:1–308; John Orr, *English Deism: Its Roots and Fruits* (Grand Rapids, MI: Eerdmans, 1934); Alan Richardson, *Christian Apologetics* (London: SCM, 1947); Roland N. Stromberg, *Religious Liberalism in Eighteenth-Century England* (Oxford, UK: Oxford University Press, 1954); Frank Manuel, *The Eighteenth Century Confronts the Gods* (Cambridge, MA: Harvard University Press, 1959); and Avery Dulles, *A History of Apologetics* (New York: Corpus, 1971).

denial of the miraculous. Though he did not often mention his intellectual opponents by name, one of the later *Miscellanies* names Lord Bolingbroke, Thomas Chubb, Henry Dodwell, David Hume, Thomas Hobbes, Benedict Spinoza, Matthew Tindal, and John Toland—a who's-who of the unorthodox.[11] The deists were a symptom of the time, an era, as Edwards said, "distinguished from all other ages of the Christian church for deadness in the practice of religion and for practical licentiousness and so of the absence of the Spirit of God and prevalence of the spirit of the devil." The corrupt *zeitgeist* had distorted the church's thinking, and Edwards believed that "the present fashionable divinity [i.e., theology] is wrong."[12]

Broadly speaking, the orthodox responses to the deist challenge from the early 1700s to the early 1800s could be divided into two categories—*evidentialist* and *experientialist*. The evidentialists, epitomized by William Paley's *A View of the Evidences of Christianity* (1794), made their case for Christianity by appealing to the historical evidences of fulfilled prophecy in Christ's coming, the Bible's historical accuracy, and the positive moral and cultural impact of Christianity in western history. Paley summed up a century of anti-deistic arguments. His discussion of "antecedent probability" rebutted David Hume's renowned argument against miracles, his treatment of "direct historical evidence" defended the credibility of the Bible, and his approach to "auxiliary evidences" expounded the morality of the gospel message, the uniqueness of Christ's character, and the remarkable spread of Christianity despite the many obstacles it encountered during its formative period.[13]

In distinction from the evidentialists, the experientialists were epitomized by Friedrich Schleiermacher's *On Religion* (1799), and—better known among English speakers—Samuel Taylor Coleridge's *Aids to Reflection* (1825). Coleridge declared that "the mode of defending Christianity adopted by ... Dr. Paley" had only increased the level of unbelief. This was because both the skeptics and Paley himself encouraged people to be "always looking out"—i.e., seeking to find God in the external world. What they discovered there was a "lifeless Machine whirled about by the dust of its own Grinding." Far better, said Coleridge, was for everyone to "look into

---

11. WJE 23:240–45.

12. WJE 18:546.

13. Paley's *Evidences of Christianity* is included as volume 2 in William Paley, *The Works of William Paley*, 5 vols. (Boston, MA: Joshua Belcher, 1810). For further exposition, see D. L. LeMahieu, *The Mind of William Paley: A Philosopher and His Age* (Lincoln, NE: University of Nebraska Press, 1976).

their own souls."[14] Friedrich Schleiermacher had argued similarly in his work *On Religion: Speeches to Its Cultured Despisers* (1799). Religious life did not rely on any identifiable, outward state of affairs. In fact, Schleiermacher went so far as to claim that "miracle" was not a special sort of event but a special way of looking at all events. All mundane occurrences were miracles—for those who had eyes to see. Religion did not consist in intellectual knowing (as the evidentialists imagined) nor in virtuous doing (as moralists and many deists proposed) but rather in devout "feeling" (German, *Gefühl*)—that is, a "contemplation of... all finite things, in and through the Infinite."[15] This "sense" or "taste" for the infinite was the essence of all true religion, and this, for Schleiermacher, was also an intrinsic element within the human consciousness and experience of the world. No evidence could disprove it. No logical argument could overturn it. Religion itself was thus invulnerable to intellectual assault.[16]

Against this backdrop, Edwards's apology for Christianity was remarkably comprehensive. The *Miscellanies* contain extensive presentations of Christian evidences, discussions of miracles, treatments of biblical history, and reconstruals of rational arguments for God's existence (e.g., ontological, cosmological, teleological), and yet also a full-scale, internal argument for Christian faith based on the "sense of the heart" and a claim that faith itself constitutes a form of evidence for God. Many later *Miscellanies* contain extracts from Theophilus Gale's *The Court of the Gentiles* (1669–82) and Andrew Michael [Chevalier] Ramsay's *The Travels of Cyrus* (1727), arguing that key elements in non-Christian religions and philosophies were either borrowed from the revelation given to Moses and the Israelites or else transmitted as part of

---

14. Samuel Taylor Coleridge, *The Collected Writings of Samuel Taylor Coleridge, Volume 9: "Aids to Reflection,"* ed. John Beer (Princeton, NJ: Princeton University Press, 1993), xliv, lxxxviii, 405–408. Coleridge stated that he did not "deny" miracles or regard them as "useless," though he sought to "build the miracle on the faith, and not the faith on the miracle" (xliv). Coleridge was thus closer to traditional theology than the early Schleiermacher of the *Speeches*.

15. Friedrich Schleiermacher, *On Religion: Speeches to Its Cultured Despisers*, trans. John Oman (New York: Harper and Row, 1958 [1893]), 36. For background, see Richard E. Crouter's "Introduction" to his new translation *On Religion* (Cambridge, UK: Cambridge University Press, 1988), 1–73.

16. Schleiermacher has been criticized for making belief in God invulnerable to intellectual assault and yet at too high a price—i.e., by denying the cognitive status of theological assertions. See Wayne Proudfoot, *Religious Experience* (Berkeley, CA: University of California, 1985). Edwards, by contrast, developed a teaching on the spiritual sense that combined cognitive and affective elements: "The heart cannot be set upon an object of which there is no idea in the understanding" (WJE 22:88). See also WJE 18:84–88.

ancient tradition handed down from the antediluvians (ch. 36). Edwards thus showed an affinity to the evidentialists. Yet decades before either Coleridge or Schleiermacher, Edwards anticipated Coleridge's call for people to "look into their own souls." The romantic argument for Christianity was partially paralleled in Edwards's appeal to an inner sensibility that made Christianity credible. While Edwards differed from Schleiermacher in major ways, the two thinkers had affinities as well. This may be one reason for Edwards's surprising appeal to Schleiermacher's twentieth-century progeny—i.e., liberal or modernist theologians. Edwards's approach to religious experience made him an appealing figure for theological revisionists who had little interest in his Calvinism or his defenses of traditional doctrines.

The discussion of Edwards's apologetics will be divided here into three sections—the *external argument* (based on both rational and evidential reasoning), the *internal argument* (based on the nature of religious experience), and, finally, what I will call *the implicit argument* (based on a rethinking of intellectual disciplines or schools of thought).

Edwards's Apology, I—The External Argument

Edwards's most sweeping argument against deism was his assertion of the insufficiency of natural reason in discovering God. "Were it not for divine revelation," wrote Edwards, "I am persuaded that there is no one doctrine of that we call natural religion [but] would, notwithstanding all philosophy and learning, forever be involved in darkness, doubts, endless disputes and dreadful confusion." If there had been no revelation, then "the world would be full of disputes about the very being of God." No one would know if there were one God or many, and whether God's nature was personal or impersonal. "Ten thousand schemes there would be about it."[17] Edwards pointed out that the philosophers of ancient Greece and Rome, for all their brilliance, never came to any consensus about the gods. Instead, the "infinite contradictions and uncertainties among the ancient philosophers" led in time to the rise of skepticism.[18] Not even the "ingenious Chinese"—whom Edwards regarded highly—came to any settled knowledge of God through natural reason alone.[19] What is more, deism failed to answer the perennial questions regarding God's purpose or will—i.e., what kind of worship God desired, how sin could be compensated for, whether

---

17. WJE 13:421–23.

18. WJE 23:448.

19. WJE 23:439.

forgiveness was available, and the nature of life after death. The deists themselves had formed no church or society of "public worship," and this was another indication of the insufficiency of natural human reason as a foundation for religious practice.[20]

The deists, argued Edwards, failed to distinguish between a priori deduction of religious truths and a posteriori vindication. "It is one thing to see that a truth is exceeding agreeable to reason, after we have been told it and have had it explained to us: "He wrote, "and another to find it out and prove it of ourselves."[21] In religious matters no less than secular, familiarity bred contempt: "We are ready to despise that which we are so used to... as the children of Israel despised manna."[22] All that was true and valuable in deism was borrowed—or rather stolen—from Christianity. The same was true of Islam, according to Edwards. This religion contained many truths adopted from the Bible, and yet Muhammad inconsistently rejected the biblical testimony to Jesus' divinity—much as the deists did.[23]

Confusion may arise because Edwards attacked the deists' reliance on reason and yet relied often on rational argument to establish his points. As John Gerstner notes: "He tended to explain rationally what most other Reformed theologians were inclined to leave in 'mystery.'"[24] He never displayed the fear or distrust of philosophy sometimes shown by Martin Luther, Blaise Pascal, Søren Kierkegaard, or Karl Barth. Edwards's distinction between regenerate and unregenerate reason helps to explain his disparate statements. Human reason had vast scope, but only after it had embraced the truths of Christian revelation by faith. Edwards concurred with Anselm's principle of "faith seeking understanding" (*fides quaerens intellectum*). Far from constraining reason, faith freed reason to explore the boundless mysteries of God and God's revelation. Edwards could thus assert both the insufficiency of natural

---

20. WJE 13:291.

21. WJE 13:421.

22. WJE 18:140.

23. Edwards described Islam as a "great kingdom of mighty power and vast extent that Satan set up against the kingdom of Christ" (WJE 9:415). McDermott judged that Edwards was "unusually vitriolic" against Islam because "the deists... were using Islam as a stick to shake at their orthodox opponents" ("The Deist Connection," 39, 43). Edwards drew many of his ideas on Islam from the little-known Johann Friedrich Stapfer's *Institutiones theologiae polemicae* (1743–7).

24. Gerstner, "Outline," 4. Gerstner highlights Edwards's reliance on reason in *The Rational Biblical Theology of Jonathan Edwards*, 3 vols. (Powhatan, VA: Berea Publications/Orlando, FL: Ligonier Ministries, 1991), 1:94–139.

reason and the indispensability of regenerate reason in theological reflection (ch. 9).²⁵

The classical arguments for God's existence—ontological, cosmological, teleological—all appear within the *Miscellanies*. The early essay "Of Being" presented a kind of ontological argument (ch. 7). The inconceivability and the nonexistence of nothingness demonstrated the existence of a necessary being or God. "God is a necessary being, because it's a contradiction to suppose him not to be. No being is a necessary being but he whose nonentity is a contradiction. We have shown that absolute nothing is the essence of all contradictions."²⁶ A related argument, connected with Edwards's idealism, was that God or "Being in general" must not only exist but be conscious, "for how doth one's mind refuse to believe, that there should be being from all eternity without its being conscious to itself that it was."²⁷ Edwards's cosmological argument for God derived from his strict notion of universal cause-and-effect relationships, as presupposed in *Freedom of the Will:* "'Tis acknowledged to be self-evident, that nothing can begin to be without a cause."²⁸ Edwards went so far as to claim that the world's continuance moment by moment is a proof for God. "'Tis certain with me that...the existence of things every moment ceases and is every moment renewed," he writes, and so "we see the same proof of a God as...if we had seen [him] create the world."²⁹

The presence of design or unity in the world was another demonstration of God's existence. "The world is evidently so created and governed as to answer but one design in all the different parts of it, and in all ages."³⁰ The same laws of nature held sway in all parts of the universe and at all times. Sometimes Edwards drew an analogy between the world and the self-organization of the human body: "There is just the same sort of knowledge of the existence of a universal mind in the world from the actions of the world...as there is of the existence of a particular mind in an human body

---

25. Philosopher William Wainwright observed the "apparent ambiguity" in Edwards's remarks on reason, but noted that he thought that "grace is needed to reason properly" (*Reason and the Heart: A Prolegomenon to a Critique of Passional Reason*; Itaca, NY: Cornell University Press, 1995), 7–54, citing 7,11.

26. WJE 13:213. See also WJE 6:202–207, 350–52 13:256, 436; 18:122; 18:190–91.

27. WJE 13:188.

28. WJE 13:254–55. Compare with WJE 1:180–85. Elsewhere Edwards noted that our imperfect ideas concerning God prevent us from understanding how God exists without being caused (WJE 18:190–91).

29. WJE 13:288.

30. WJE 18:191. See also WJE 18:392–98, and WJE 20:154–55, 280–86.

from the observations of the actions of that, in gesture, look and voice." If we do not discern a "universal mind," then the problem may lie in our limited and partial vantage point: "There wants nothing but a comprehensive view, to take in the various actions in the world and look on them at one glance."[31] It was not only the large-scale structure of the world that showed a divine design but also the intricate forms and functions of living creatures. "The contrivances of the organs of speech" were "peculiarly wonderful," and human souls themselves were "pieces of workmanship" more elaborate than any manmade machines.[32]

Edwards affirmed a moral argument for God when he spoke of an "inward testimony...of the being of God" implied in the awareness that "when we have done good or evil, we naturally expect from some superior being reward or punishment."[33] He even stated that "the being of God may be argued from the desirableness and need of it," since the world could scarcely be so defective as to lack a universal governor to relieve the miseries and correct the injustices of human life.[34] Some notebook entries treated "immortality" or the "future state." Like other eighteenth-century authors, Edwards held that a definite expectation of future rewards and punishments was needed to keep people from becoming "negligent, dull and careless" about religion.[35] A life beyond the present, for Edwards, allowed for the complete enjoyment of God (ch. 19). In a manner reminiscent of Thomas Aquinas and C. S. Lewis, Edwards argued that "God provides some proper good for the satisfaction of the appetites and desires of every living thing," and that the same must apply to "the desires of virtue and love to God."[36] Only in heaven could love be expressed with no limits of intensity or duration, and so it was only reasonable to think that God intended for such a state to exist.[37]

Edwards insisted on the divine inspiration and authority of the Bible. Like John Calvin, Edwards viewed the Bible as self-authenticating and asserted that its teachings and very words strike the mind as God-given. Despite its lack of "rhetorical ornaments," the Bible "shines brighter with the amiable simplicity

---

31. WJE 13:288.

32. WJE 13:334, 337–38. See also WJE 13:373–74.

33. WJE 13:375.

34. WJE 13:375.

35. WJE 13:294.

36. WJE 23:126.

37. On the happiness of heaven, see WJE 13:275, 303, 329, 331, 336–37, 369–70; WJE 20:455–56; and the extended treatment in WJE 8:366–97.

of truth."³⁸ The very phraseology of the Bible is so exceedingly expressive that human wisdom alone could not have contrived it, as in the "strange system of visions" in the Book of Revelation.³⁹ Another confirmation of the divine origin of the scriptures is that "wondrous universal harmony... in the aim and drift" of the writings.⁴⁰ Yet this self-authenticating truth could only be seen by a receptive mind.⁴¹ Edwards appealed also to external attestations of the Bible's veracity: "'Tis proof that Scripture [is true], that the geography is consistent."⁴² A long notebook entry discussed the canon of the New Testament writings and the substantial agreement of early Christian writers as to which books were inspired.⁴³

Like Paley, Edwards appealed to historical evidences to confirm the truth of Christianity. The monotheism of the Jews, and the forms of worship they used (as exhibited in the Psalms), bear witness that they worshiped the true God and worshiped him truly.⁴⁴ While the gods of the ancient pagans had long since been abandoned, the God of Abraham was still acknowledged by multitudes. The very survival of the Jewish people—despite the repeated attempts to exterminate them and the cultural pressures that could have caused them to assimilate to the idolatry around them—made them a "standing evidence" for God.⁴⁵ Another line of evidential argument in Edwards was based on miracles. There should be a strong presumption in favor of Jesus' miracles, since he performed them publicly and "if the matters of fact had been false, they would have been denied by Jesus' contemporaries."⁴⁶ Christ's miracles showed that "the whole course of nature" was "subject to his command" and thus established his divinity.⁴⁷ God would not have allowed an imposter to accomplish such mighty feats.⁴⁸ The resurrection, more than all other miracles, confirmed Jesus' teaching

---

38. WJE 13:202–203. Similarly John Calvin wrote that the Bible possesses an "uncultivated and almost rude simplicity," which nonetheless "inspires greater reverence for itself than any eloquence" (*Institutes of the Christian Religion*, Bk. 1, Ch. 8, Secs. 1–2.)

39. WJE 13:335–36. Compare with comments on the story of Joseph, WJE 13:339.

40. WJE 13:410.

41. WJE 13:289.

42. WJE 13:338. See also WJE 13:376.

43. WJE 20:396–427.

44. WJE 13:448.

45. WJE 23:334–40.

46. WJE 13:293.

47. WJE 13:352–53.

48. WJE 13:492.

and his divinity.[49] One notebook entry argued that Jesus was truly dead after his crucifixion and had not passed into a deathlike "swoon."[50] Jesus' accurate prophecies of the future—including the impending destruction of Jerusalem—were yet another confirmation that he was sent by God.[51] Because Jesus did not speak in the name of another—with an expression such as "thus saith the Lord"—his words bore witness to his own authority and uniqueness.[52] The history of the apostles and the early church corroborated the truth of Christianity. The dramatic change in the attitude of the apostles—from fear and dismay to boldness and confidence—showed the truth of Jesus' resurrection and his continuing presence among them.[53] Moreover, the spread of Christianity in the Roman Empire without the aid of human power, wealth, or learning was itself a kind of miracle. Nothing as remarkable has happened before or since.[54]

Many of the later *Miscellanies* dealt with "heathen traditions" that anticipated or paralleled the teachings of Christianity. Some of these included extracts from the writings of Hugo Grotius, Theophilus Gale, Andrew Michael [Chevalier] Ramsay, and other authors. Taken together, these notebook entries ran to hundreds of pages.[55] Here Edwards showed himself more tolerant and open-minded toward non-Christian religions that one might have expected (ch. 36).

Edwards's Apology, II—The Internal Argument

Edwards's teaching on spiritual perception or the "sense of heart" (chs. 20, 24) was integral to his apology for the truth of Christianity. He viewed the saints' spiritual sense as a kind of *evidence* for God—immediately present to the mind and more certain than any rational argumentation in favor of God's existence. Enlightenment thinkers emphasized the role of direct experience. Immanuel Kant defined "enlightenment" as "man's release from his self-incurred tutelage" and stressed that each individual must "dare to know."[56] Yet Edwards

---

49. WJE 13:394–95.

50. WJE 13:302–303.

51. WJE 20:254–74.

52. WJE 20:384–88.

53. WJE 13:507.

54. WJE 13:293.

55. WJE 20:227–31, 239–54, 275–80, 287–96, 302–309, 321–23, 343–58, 365–66, 456–58; and WJE 23:95–104, 123, 171, 176–77, 190–94, 214–15, 432–81, 543–75, 640–713.

56. Immanuel Kant, "What is Enlightenment?" quoted in James C. Livingston, *Modern Christian Thought: From the Enlightenment to Vatican II* (New York: Macmillan, 1971), 1.

turned empiricism to the advantage of God. Faith, he held, was a form of seeing for oneself, not a secondhand belief or a reliance on another's testimony. Those who had seen for themselves the divine "excellency" had as good a reason to be convinced of God's reality and beauty as any persons had to be convinced of the reality of the physical objects around them.

Edwards's idea of spiritual perception should be seen against the backdrop of Locke's philosophy. Locke denied innate ideas and insisted that all human ideas originated either through sensation or through the mind's reflection on ideas derived from sensation. The consequence, for Locke, was that no idea could ever be directly perceived as coming from God. Divine revelation could only reinforce ideas and principles already known through sense experience of the world. Locke's more radical disciples—the deists—immediately grasped the possible implications of their master's teaching, and they denied that there could be any distinctive religious experience reserved for saints alone. Locke, for his part, allowed that there could be "inspiration" that brought "original revelation" to the mind of an inspired individual. Yet this sort of inspiration was only knowledge—in the true sense—within the mind of the person who first experienced it. For everyone else, it was a tradition passed down. Locke wrote: "For whatsoever truth we come to the clear discovery of, from the knowledge and contemplation of our own ideas, will always be certainer to us than those which are conveyed to us by traditional revelation. For the knowledge we have that this revelation came at first from God can never be so sure as the knowledge we have from the clear and distinct perception of the agreement or disagreement of our own ideas."[57] A religion—like Christianity—that claimed to be based on a revelation of God transmitted through historical records—such as the Bible—was at an immediate disadvantage in Locke's philosophy. The skeptic could argue that *present* experiences would always be more reliable than any claims to *past* miracles, inspiration, or revelation. David Hume later drew out the skeptical implications of Locke's epistemology.

One of Edwards's earliest written reflections—"Miscellany aa"—showed the apologetic motivation of his teaching on spiritual perception:

> There may undoubtedly be such a thing as is called the testimony of faith, and a sort of certainty of faith that is different from reason, that is, is different from discourse by a chain of arguments, a certainty that is given by the Holy Spirit; and yet such a belief may be altogether

---

57. John Locke, *An Essay Concerning Human Understanding*, 4.18.4. See Locke's chapters "Faith and Reason" and "Enthusiasm" in *Essay* 4:18–19.

agreeable to reason, agreeable to the exactest rules of philosophy. Such ideas of religion may be in the mind, as a man may feel divinity in them, and so may know that they are from God, know that religion is of divine original... he is certain that what he sees and feels, he sees and feels; and he knows that what he then sees and feels is the same thing he used to call God.... Now no man can deny but that such an idea of religion may possibly be wrought by the Holy Spirit. 'Tis not unphilosophical to think so.[58]

Spiritual perception, as this passage suggested, carried immediate certainty because it was a first-hand experience. As the truism goes, seeing is believing, and there is no use arguing against someone who is an eyewitness: "When a person sees a thing with their own eyes, it gives them the greatest certainty they can have of it, greater than they can have by any information of others."[59] In *Religious Affections* he wrote, "The gospel of the blessed God don't go abroad a begging for its evidence, so much as some think; it has its highest and most proper evidence in itself."[60]

Edwards's sermon "Divine Light" described the illumination of the mind as both a scriptural and rational teaching: "The evidence that is this way obtained, is vastly better and more satisfying than all that can be obtained by the arguings of those that are most learned." Here Edwards stood Locke on his head, for he used Locke's empiricist principle—that everyone must see with his own eyes—to establish, against Locke, that the intellectual certitude of the believer's spiritual perception was *greater* than the certitude gained by mere human reasoning about God. For Edwards, the soul in conversion comes into immediate contact with God and gains a new knowledge that it could never previously have attained. The Bible describes conversion as the opening of the eyes of the blind, the unstopping of the ears of the deaf, and even the raising of the dead back to life.[61] God "illumines" the mind of the saint, "infuses" his grace, and "indwells" the body of the believer through the Holy Spirit.[62] Revelation does not merely "enlarge" natural reason—as Locke had claimed—but transcends it, conferring that which the human mind could not attain by its

---

58. WJE 13:177–78.

59. WJE 17:65. Compare WJE 2:305–307, where Edwards discusses Christians as "witnesses" to God.

60. WJE 2:307.

61. WJE 21:159–64.

62. WJE 2:206.

own resources. Nonetheless, the illumination of the believer's mind and heart was not an instance of "inspiration" or "enthusiasm"—as Locke's logic seemed to suggest. Edwards thus sought to vindicate a genuine religious knowledge based on a direct encounter with God that was not "enthusiastic."[63] His idea of spiritual perception was a response to the Enlightenment's challenge to provide rational justification for belief in God.

Edwards's Apology, III—The Implicit Argument

In speaking of an implicit argument, we refer to Edwards's strategy to appropriate and reinterpret various academic disciplines or genres of thought to bring them back into relationship with theological truth. Norman Fiering commented that "his purpose, contrary to that of the *philosophe*, was to turn the best thought of his day to the advantage of God."[64] Edwards sought to turn the tables on the Enlightenment by absorbing the best ideas of skeptical thinkers and then adapting them for Christian use.

One expression of Edwards's implicit apology was a short paper entitled *A Rational Account of the Main Doctrines of the Christian Religion Attempted*. These jottings occupied only one folio sheet and yet they outlined an audacious project. The watermark on the page derives from 1729–30, yet the handwriting indicates that Edwards continued to add to this outline during the late 1730s or the 1740s. Wallace Anderson judged that Edwards was preoccupied with the *Rational Account* for some fifteen years.[65] Ava Chamberlain dated Miscellany 832, entitled "Preface to Rational Account," during the winter of 1739–40.[66] Even though Edwards's plan for the Rational Account seems eventually to have been subsumed into the *History of the Work of Redemption and The Harmony of the Old and New Testaments* (ch. 12), it is clear that he devoted considerable time to thinking through the Rational Account. It seems likely then that Edwards's final works of synthesis would have incorporated

---

63. To be sure, Locke did not exclude divine inspiration: "God, I own, cannot be denied to be able to enlighten the understanding by a ray darted into the mind immediately from the fountain of light" (*Essay* 4.19.5). As David Laurence points out, Locke rejected as arrogant the notion that a "ray darted" was prerequisite to becoming a Christian. For Locke, "Christianity was of divine origin; but individual Christians were not" ("Jonathan Edwards, John Locke, and the Canon of Experience," *Early American Literature* 15 [1980]; 110).

64. Norman Fiering, *Jonathan Edwards's Moral Thought and Its British Context* (Chapel Hill, NC: University of North Carolina Press, 1981), 60–61.

65. WJE 6:396–97, with Anderson's comments at WJE 6:394.

66. WJE 18:47–48, 546.

substantial elements of what is indicated in the one-page outline. Though the outline is tantalizingly brief, Edwards states that the preface to the *Rational Account* was to "to shew how all arts and sciences, the more they are perfected, the more they issue in divinity, and coincide with it, and appear to be as parts of it." What he envisaged was nothing less than a comprehensive system of the sciences with theology as the queen. Arguably, no major thinker of the modern period attempted such a thing.[67] The plan for the *Rational Account* seems medieval in its way of relating human sciences to theology, as in Bonaventure's thirteenth-century treatise on *The Reduction of the Arts to Theology*.[68] Yet Edwards's system would assuredly have been a post-Lockean, post-Enlightenment effort built on the foundation of an empirical philosophy.

Edwards's reflections on metaphysics represented an implicit argument for God. The dominating question in *The Mind*, as Wilson Kimnach states, was the following: "How could one convince the most sophisticated audience that he had identified a functioning spiritual system as surely as Newton had identified the true physical system?"[69] In effect, Edwards used metaphysics as an instrument to establish the supremacy of God and of spiritual as compared with material reality. As noted earlier (ch. 7), he reversed the accepted notion that matter was real while spirit was ethereal. In Edwards's bold reinterpretation, matter was the mere shadow of spiritual reality. Moreover, God was ultimate reality, "the prime and original being, the first and the last, and the pattern of all."[70]

Another intellectual discipline that Edwards sought to appropriate and reinterpret for theological purposes was British moral philosophy—a field of study that was fast departing from its theological underpinnings during the 1700s. Lord Shaftesbury and Francis Hutcheson separated moral reflection from any essential linkage to God or theological notions. Their "moral sense" theories grounded ethics in human nature, not God's nature. Yet the task of

---

67. Some might argue that the philosopher G. W. F. Hegel or the theologian Paul Tillich attempted a system of sciences with theology at the center. Yet most scholars hold that Hegel subordinated religion to philosophy, and Tillich did not complete his description of a system of sciences.

68. "Since every science," wrote Bonaventure, "and particularly [though not only] the science contained in the Holy Scriptures, is concerned with the Trinity before all else, every science must necessarily present some trace of this same Trinity" (quoted in Jaroslav Pelikan, *The Christian Tradition: A History of the Development of Doctrine; Volume 3: The Growth of Medieval Theology [600–1300]*; Chicago, IL: University of Chicago Press, 1978; 282, cf. 305–307).

69. Wilson Kimnach, "Editor's Introduction," in WJE 10:189.

70. WJE 6:363.

Edwards's *Two Dissertations* was to arrest and reverse this process. The mission of *End of Creation* was the ethicizing of the divine, while that of *True Virtue* was the divinizing of ethics (chs. 14, 33). What held the two treatises together was their common assumption that God himself was the proper aim of all right actions—whether God's own actions or the actions of human beings. The argument of the *Two Dissertations* was a slap in the face for Enlightenment humanists who held that human beings should seek their own happiness and that God's great aim was to promote his creatures' well-being. Where Enlightenment thinkers sought to reduce religion to morality, *True Virtue* turned the tables. Not only was religion not reducible to morality, according to Edwards, but virtue in the proper sense could not even exist apart from love to God. Once again, we find an implicit apology for Christianity.

Yet another discipline that fell within Edwards's implicit argument was history. The general thesis of *History of Redemption*, as Perry Miller noted, was the unity of history.[71] Edwards compared God's providence to "a large and long river, having innumerable branches beginning in different regions...at length discharging themselves at one mouth into the same ocean." Yet our limited, human perspective made it difficult for us to perceive the unity of the whole: "The different streams of this river are ready to look like mere jumble and confusion to us because of the limitedness of our sight." Edwards affirmed that in the end, "not one of all the streams fail of coming hither at last."[72] Essentially, *History of Redemption* was a book about discernment and was not a mere compilation of facts. The work was organized so that the reader could trace the stepwise progress of God's redemptive plan. Edwards conceived history eschatologically—that is, backward from the end and not forward from the beginning. Properly interpreted then, the course of world affairs would become a means of "seeing" God, and an implicit apology for the reality and activity of God. While further examples from other intellectual disciplines might be supplied, those just noted—metaphysics, ethics, and history—are an indication of Edwards's subtle and wide-ranging effort at reinterpreting intellectual disciplines in light of the prior reality and centrality of God.

---

71. Perry Miller, *Jonathan Edwards* (New York: William Sloane, 1949), 313.

72. WJE 9:520.

11

Biblical Exegesis

THE SCOTTISH EVANGELICAL minister Thomas Gillespie read Edwards's *Religious Affections* (1746) shortly after its publication, and he decided in November 1746 to write the author to pose some questions regarding the treatise. In his letter he intoned, "I hope you will deal freely with me; for I can say, I would sit down and learn at your feet, dear Sir, accounting myself as a child in knowledge of the Scriptures, when compared with others."[1] If Gillespie's perusal of the *Religious Affections* made him feel like a "child" in biblical knowledge, then he would certainly have been impressed to have seen the cumulative result of Edwards's exegetical labors. These works fell into four categories. First, there were Edwards's commentaries on scripture, published in fragments within Sereno Dwight's edition of Edwards's writings in 1829–30, and full form in Stephen Stein's transcriptions of the *Notes on the Apocalypse* (1977), *Notes on Scripture* (1998), and *Blank Bible* (2006), as well as the jointly edited *Typological Writings* (1993). Taken collectively, these exclusively exegetical works fill five volumes in the Yale edition and include almost 2,500 pages of printed text. Yet there is more: Edwards's more than 1,200 extant sermon manuscripts contain a great deal of biblical exegesis. Furthermore, biblical exegesis is an integral part of such published works as *Religious Affections*, *Original Sin*, *End of Creation*, *Miscellanies*, and other writings. Finally, a number of exegetical texts were in preparation for future publication at the time of Edwards's death, notably the notebook for a "Harmony of the Old and New Testaments," running to some five hundred manuscript pages. Were one to extract the strictly exegetical elements of the sermons, and add them to the works already noted, the sum might come to 5,000 printed pages of material—a large fraction of the total word count of Yale University Press' *Works of Jonathan Edwards*.

In this light, one can understand Stephen Stein's comment regarding the "amazing paucity of serious scholarship" dealing with Edwards's biblical interpretation.[2] In addition to Stein's decades-long labors in transcription and

---

1. WJE 2:476.

2. Stephen Stein, "The Spirit and the Word: Jonathan Edwards and Scriptural Exegesis," in Nathan O. Hatch and Harry S. Stout, eds., *Jonathan Edwards and the American Experience* (New York: Oxford University Press, 1988), 123.

interpretation, Robert Brown, Kenneth Minkema, Douglas Sweeney, and others have advanced our understanding of the intellectual contexts and general outlines of Edwards's biblical exegesis. Yet more needs to be done, and Stein notes correctly that the "contemporary renaissance of interest in Edwards has hardly touched on this dimension of his work."[3] The present chapter is a brief scrutiny of the assumptions and characteristics of Edwards's exegesis. To summarize the content of Edwards's exegetical texts would require more space than is allowed here, though a few illustrative instances of Edwards's exegesis will receive comment.[4] Since typological interpretation is treated elsewhere (ch. 8), this chapter will highlight a number of other foundational issues in Edwards's approach to the Bible.

An Eighteenth-Century Exegete

As a young man, Edwards expressed his resolution "to study the Scriptures so steadily, constantly and frequently, as that I may find, and plainly perceive myself to grow in the knowledge of the same."[5] His earliest biographer, Samuel Hopkins, indicated that Edwards had fulfilled this resolution throughout his lifetime: "He studied the Bible more than all other Books, and more than

---

3. Not including the literature specifically on typology, the studies on Edwards's biblical exegesis include: Robert E. Brown, *Jonathan Edwards and the Bible* (Bloomington, IN: Indiana University Press, 2002); Conrad Cherry, "Symbols of Spiritual Truth: Jonathan Edwards as Biblical Interpreter," *Interpretation* 39 (1985): 263–71; Michael J. McClymond, Review of Robert E. Brown, *Jonathan Edwards and the Bible* (Bloomington, IN: Indiana University Press, 2002), in *Church History* 72 (2002): 416–18; Kenneth P. Minkema, "The Other Unfinished 'Great Work': Jonathan Edwards, Messianic Prophecy, and 'The Harmony of the Old and New Testaments,'" in Stephen J. Stein, ed., *Jonathan Edwards's Writings: Text, Context, Interpretation*, 52–65 (Bloomington, IN: Indiana University Press, 1996); Stephen J. Stein, "Editor's Introduction," in WJE 15:1–46 and in WJE 24:1–117, "Jonathan Edwards and the Rainbow: Biblical Exegesis and Poetic Imagination," *The New England Quarterly* 47 (1974): 440–56, "'Like Apples of Gold in Pictures of Silver': The Portrait of Wisdom in Jonathan Edwards's Commentary on the Book of Proverbs," *Church History* 54 (1985): 324–37, "The Quest for the Spiritual Sense: The Biblical Hermeneutics of Jonathan Edwards," *Harvard Theological Review* 70 (1977): 99–113, "The Spirit and the Word: Jonathan Edwards and Scriptural Exegesis," in Nathan O. Hatch and Harry S. Stout, eds;, *Jonathan Edwards and the American Experience*, 118–30 (New York: Oxford University Press, 1988); and Douglas A. Sweeney, "'Longing for More and More of It'?: The Strange Career of Jonathan Edwards's Exegetical Exertions," in Harry S. Stout, Kenneth P. Minkema, and Caleb J. D. Maskell, eds., *Jonathan Edwards at 300: Essays on the Tercentenary of His Birth* (Lathan, MD: University Press of America, 2005), 25–37, and *Jonathan Edwards and the Ministry of the Word* (Downers Grove, IL: IVP Academic, 2009).

4. Stein gives a concise and helpful summary of the content of the "Blank Bible," organized according to the major portions of the biblical canon, in WJE 24:23–59.

5. WJE 16:755.

most other Divines do." Edwards, says Sweeney, "devoted most of his waking life to meditating on Scripture, delving deeply into its contents, reading biblical commentaries and praying fervently for the Spirit's help interpreting and applying the Bible."[6] In Edwards's midlife description of his early experiences, he wrote that he had "the greatest delight in the holy Scriptures, of any book whatsoever. Oftentimes in reading it, every word seemed to touch my heart. I felt a harmony between something in my heart, and those sweet and powerful words." He "could not get along in reading" because "almost every sentence seemed to be full of wonders."[7]

Reading the scriptures for Edwards was both a personal delight and a theological imperative. Throughout his life, he held to the view that Christian theology was necessarily based on divine revelation. This idea is expressed in Edwards's earliest as well as his final writings. "Were it not for divine revelation," he wrote, "I am persuaded that there is no one doctrine of that which we call natural religion [but] would, notwithstanding all philosophy and learning, forever be involved in darkness, doubts, endless disputes and dreadful confusion."[8] Only through biblical revelation could humanity attain to "certainty, clearness and satisfaction in things that concern their welfare."[9] Christian theology in all aspects "depends on divine revelation."[10] This foundational conviction regarding revelation pressed Edwards, like other Protestant theologians, to emphasize scripture. The Bible, he wrote, is a "perfect rule" and indeed "the only rule of our faith and practice."[11] It is an "infallible guide."[12] In numerous works, Edwards sought to establish a given doctrine both by scriptural and by rational arguments. The twofold pattern is apparent, for example, in *End of Creation*, where the first portion of the treatise contains rational argument and the latter part the exegetical discussion.[13] Edwards's pivotal sermon on religious epistemology, "A Divine and Supernatural Light," seeks to show that its doctrine is "scriptural" and also

---

6. Samuel Hopkins, *The Life and Character of the Late Reverend Mr. Jonathan Edwards* (Boston, MA: S. Kneeland, 1765) 40–41, cited in Sweeney, 83.

7. WJE 16:797.

8. WJE 13:421.

9. WJE 23:240.

10. WJE 20:52.

11. WJE 8:363, "perfect rule;" compare WJEO 42:serm.42; WJEO 48:serm.297; WJEO 51:serm.384; and WJE 13:310, "only rule of our faith and practice."

12. WJE 14:265, WJEO 43:serm.84, WJEO 60:serm.693p.

13. WJE 8:419–63, 8:467–536.

"rational."¹⁴ *Religious Affections*, *Original Sin*, and even the revival writings like *Some Thoughts Concerning the Revival* and *Humble Attempt*, demonstrate Edwards's abiding concern to ground his positions and his arguments in the exegesis of biblical texts.

Edwards's writings show that he believed that biblical exegesis supported the truth of the Christian religion. That is, contrary to Enlightenment *philosophes* and to some eighteenth-century Christian apologists, he viewed the Bible itself as a convincing argument for faith. It showed its divine origin because of the fulfilled prophecies recorded within it. The manuscript that Edwards left unpublished at his death, "The Harmony of the Old and New Testament," was to be, in the words of Kenneth Minkema, "Edwards's contribution to the transatlantic debate over biblical messianic prophecy and the trustworthiness of the Bible."¹⁵ In this work he responded to a number of influential deistic works—Anthony Collins's *Discourse of the Grounds and Reasons of the Christian Religion* (1724) and Thomas Woolston's *Six Discourses on Miracles* (1727). He also interacted with such anti-deistic works as Edward Chandler's *Defense of Christianity, From the Prophecies of the Old Testament* (1725), Thomas Sherlock's *Use and Intent of Prophecy* (1725), and Arthur Ashley Sykes's *Essay Upon the Truth of the Christian Religion* (1725). The New Testament's fulfillment of Old Testament prophecies was not merely a matter for pious meditation by the faithful. It also offered rational grounds to convince skeptics of the Bible's authenticity and veracity.¹⁶

Despite the steady growth of modern historical criticism of the Bible in the late 1600s and early 1700s, Edwards was "relatively untouched by these changes," according to Stephen Stein. For the most part, says Stein, he still reflected a "precritical mindset."¹⁷ Yet Robert Brown's extensive study, *Jonathan Edwards and the Bible* (2002), called this judgment into question. Brown challenged the prevailing notion that biblical scholarship during the modern period could be neatly divided into a "precritical" and "critical" era—with the nineteenth century (as led by the Germans) marking the transition. According to Brown, Edwards and others participated in a "hybrid traditionalism...modified in significant ways by accommodation to the new learning."¹⁸ Akin to Edwards in

---

14. WJE 17:417–19, 4:20–23.

15. Minkema, "Harmony," 53.

16. A number of late *Miscellanies* entries address Jesus' miracles and the fulfillment of prophecy: WJE 23:265–68, 273–74, 287–88.

17. Stein, "The Spirit and the Word," 119.

18. Brown, *Jonathan Edwards and the Bible*, xvii.

this respect were a cluster of late-seventeenth- and eighteenth-century exegetes who are generally little known today—Jacques Basnage, Johann Bengel, Augustin Calmet, Theophilus Gale, Nathaniel Lardner, Jean LeClerc, Jeremiah Jones, Matthew Poole, Humphrey Prideaux, Jean Alphonse Turretin, and William Warburton. On the one hand, these authors sought to maintain traditional positions regarding the chronology and authorship of biblical texts. On the other hand, they did so by means of the same methods that others were using to challenge traditional positions. These "hybrid traditionalists" did not *assume* traditional views but *argued* for them. Thus they might be classified as either traditional or modern—depending on how one looks at them. For his part, Edwards argued at length that Moses wrote the Pentateuch, or first five books of the Old Testament. He was aware of the newer views regarding non-Mosaic authorship.[19] It should be noted that Edwards's opinion, in the 1700s, did not lie outside of the scholarly mainstream. Even the skeptic Voltaire rejected theories of the multiple authorship of the Pentateuch.[20]

Edwards opposed three groups in his approach to scripture. First, and perhaps foremost, were the Enlightenment thinkers and deists who rejected the divine origin, historical veracity, and religious authority of the Bible. Much of Edwards's exegesis of the Bible, not to mention his *Miscellanies*, engaged the ideas and arguments of the deists. Specifically he rejected the deist notion that human beings could attain to knowledge of God apart from the special revelation contained in scripture, that the Bible was historically inaccurate, that the biblical texts were forgeries, or—even worse—that the God represented in the Bible was cruel and hence unworthy of faith and worship. The second of Edwards's opponents was Roman Catholicism, which was not as often addressed as deism, inasmuch as he viewed the deists as a greater and more active threat in the English-speaking world. Edwards rejected the Roman Catholic Church's assertion of its own teaching authority, or Magisterium, and its reliance on church tradition as a guide for Christian faith and practice. He associated the Beast in the Book of Revelation with the claim "infallibly to know the truth."[21] The Catholic priesthood, Edwards believed, had attempted to usurp the Word of God that itself contained "all things that are necessary."[22] He argued that "too much weight is laid upon the testimony of the fathers," suggesting that he did not reject the role of tradition altogether and yet

---

19. WJE 15:423–69.
20. Brown, *Jonathan Edwards and the Bible*, 121.
21. WJE 5:112.
22. WJE 13:233.

judged that the Roman Catholic church—and, for that matter, the Church of England—laid undue emphasis on the authority of the church fathers (ch. 9).[23]

Edwards's third opponents were the radical evangelicals. In *Religious Affections,* he opposed "strange ecstasies and raptures... and immediate revelations from heaven." He clearly asserted that there is no such thing as continuing prophetic inspiration—a viewpoint he associated with "bastard religion."[24] Edwards linked the radical evangelicals of his day with seers and visionaries who had deceived the faithful in days past. God's purpose was for his people to rely on scripture for guidance: "It seems to me that God would have our whole dependence be upon the Scriptures, because the greater our dependence is on the Word of God, the more direct and immediate is our dependence on God himself."[25] Yet, in appealing to the scriptures, one had to use the right method, and the radical evangelicals' approach to the Bible was often dubious to Edwards. Some he encountered in the revivals of the 1730s and 1740s had passages of scripture suddenly come into their minds, and they drew the conclusion that God had spoken the words directly to them. Thus a person might vividly recall the words "your sins are forgiven" and apply the saying as a message from God. Such an approach to the Bible used something sound—God's written word—in an unsound way. Edwards even suggested that it could be Satan rather than God who brought the text to someone's mind at a particular moment.[26] Edwards's comments raised the question of hermeneutics, or the proper principles for the interpretation and application of the biblical texts.

Principles of Biblical Interpretation

In his *Personal Narrative,* Edwards wrote of a "harmony" he perceived between "something in my heart" and the "sweet and powerful words" of the Bible.

---

23. WJE 13:240. Compare WJE 18:78–80, which is cautious though a bit more positive on the role of the church fathers. For further discussion on Edwards's approach to church tradition, see Gerald R. McDermott, "Is *Sola Scriptura* Really *Sola*? Edwards, Newman, Bultmann, and Wright on the Bible as Religious Authority," in Robert Millett, ed., *By What Authority? The Vital Place of Religious Authority in American Christianity* (Macon, GA: Mercer University Press, 2009).

24. WJE 2:287.

25. WJE 18:80.

26. WJE 2:142–45, 268–70. Though Edwards might have approved some aspects of the twentieth-century Pentecostal-Charismatic movement, the practice he condemned in *Religious Affections* has a parallel in the contemporary Charismatic notion of the *"rhema* word" or specific text of scripture that comes vividly to mind—purportedly through the power of the Holy Spirit.

One notes that the "harmony" mentioned was not the harmony of the Old and New Testaments—as important as this was for Edwards. It was something yet more elemental—a "harmony" between heart and text. The biblical hermeneutics of Edwards was of a piece with his entire exposition of the spiritual life and his well-known conception of the "sense of the heart" (chs. 20, 24). One might say that the "sense" of the biblical text (i.e., its meaning) and the "sense of the heart" were interrelated. For the same divine illumination that caused the saint to perceive the beauty of God amid the wonders of the natural world also caused the saint to see both the surface level and the deeper meanings contained in holy writ. Stephen Stein makes the crucial observation that the "spiritual sense" in Edwards's reading of scripture is a "Spirit-given" sense. That is, the spiritual sense is "the product of the indwelling presence of the divine in the exegete."[27] The text of the Bible, says Edwards, is a "dead letter" apart from the work of the Holy Spirit.[28] Just as the "sense of the heart" or "new spiritual sense" comes directly from God, so it is with the understanding of the meaning of scripture. For God has reserved to himself the work of enlightening the mind with spiritual knowledge, and "there is none [who] teaches like God."[29] Directly related to this idea of Spirit-empowered interpretation is Edwards's notion of the Bible's abundance. In *Personal Narrative*, he speaks of the Bible as "full of wonders." The plethora—and, indeed, the inexhaustibility—of the Bible's meaning was basic to Edwards's hermeneutics. Without abandoning the foundational role of the literal sense, he showed a tilt toward the spiritual sense. The fecundity of the Bible, its wealth of hidden meaning, overflowed the literal sense.[30]

In the sermon "The Importance and Advantage of a Thorough Knowledge of Divine Truth" (1739), Edward laid out the basic principles of his approach to Bible.[31] He comments that the ones who "studied the longest,

---

27. Stein, "The Spirit and the Word," 123. Stein writes: "Edwards employed the same terms—spiritual sense and spiritual understanding—to refer to both the process and the product of God's grace... Spiritual understanding in this second sense was the goal and the focus of Edwards's exegetical efforts" (Stein, "Quest," 109).

28. WJE 13:340.

29. WJE 17:446.

30. Sweeney judges that "Edwards practiced literal *and* spiritual exegesis," yet insists that "he majored in the literal sense" (*Jonathan Edwards*, 102). Sweeney's former student, Dr. John Ayabe, did an analysis of all entries into the *Notes on Scripture* (WJE 15) and estimated that the ratio of entries using literal vs. non-literal interpretation was roughly four to one (email to McClymond, January 18, 2010).

31. WJE 22:83–102. Citations that follow in this paragraph all come from this sermon.

and have made the greatest attainments in the study of the Bible are also the ones who realize that they still "know but little of what is to be known." In that God himself is "infinite, and there is no end to the glory of his perfections," so also the Bible's "subject is inexhaustible." The depths of scripture will "employ... the saints and angels to all eternity." So we should for the present time makes the study of the Bible "a great part of the business of our lives." Edwards here offers something like a set of hermeneutical rules for reading scripture. "When you read," he says, "observe what you read. Observe how things come in. Take notice of the drift of the discourse, and compare one Scripture with another.... And use means to find out the meaning of the Scripture.... Procure, and diligently use other books which may help you to grow in this knowledge."

Edwards's *History of Redemption* also included some incisive comments on hermeneutics. It is not enough, he wrote, just to read the Bible, but one must understand "the drift of the Holy Ghost in it." The problem is that "most persons are to blame for their inattentive, unobservant way of reading the Scriptures." They read the Bible as though the stories concerning Abraham, David, Paul, and others were only matters of "private concerns" and thus they miss "the infinitely great things contained or pointed at in them."[32] Whenever one reads the Bible, one needs to grasp the shape of the entire Genesis-to-Revelation narrative. Before one can understand the individual parts of the Bible, one has to have some sense of the whole: "In order to see how a design is carried [to] an end, we must first know what the design is." If we do not know the "design" of God, then history "will all look like confusion, like a number of jumbled events coming to pass without any order or method, like the tossing of the waves of the sea."[33] In Edwards's biblical hermeneutics the whole has epistemological priority over the parts. This is one reason the spiritual sense is so crucial. The spiritual interpretation of scripture allows the interpreter to put the pieces together into a coherent whole. Without the spiritual sense, the events of the Old Testament might seem like a set of random and disconnected events, having little relationship to one another and even less connection with the New Testament. As often noted, one danger of the modern historical-critical reading of the Bible has been its tendency to divide and fragment the reader's approach to the text. Hans Frei spoke of pre-modern Christian renderings of the Bible as a "story-encompassing story"—that is, a narrative that absorbed the entire universe within itself. Edwards exhibited

---

32. WJE 9:291.

33. WJE 9:122, 519.

such an approach to the Bible and it was spiritual exegesis that allowed him to assign the biblical narrative its central place in his vision of the world.[34]

The Literal and Spiritual Senses in Edwards

If there is something that set Edwards apart from many of his Protestant exegetical peers during the 1700s, it was not his views regarding historical-critical issues but his thoroughgoing commitment to spiritual exegesis (ch. 8). Edwards set forth the general principle that "it has ever been God's manner from the beginning of the world to exhibit and reveal future things by symbolical representations, which were no other than types of the future things revealed."[35] He stated that "types are a certain sort of language, as it were, in which God is wont to speak to us." What is more, "the principles of human nature render types a fit method of instruction."[36] Admittedly, there was a danger of yielding to a "wild fancy" and thus "turning all into nothing but allegory and not having it to be true history." Yet, on the other hand, there was also a danger posed by those who "cry down all types."[37] Edwards called for a middle way between the two extremes. In general, his emphasis lay not on the possible errors of typology but on the fullness and abundance of types contained in the Old Testament:

> Almost everything that was said or done that we have recorded in Scripture from Adam to Christ, was typical of gospel things: persons were typical persons, their actions were typical actions, the cities were typical cities, the nation of the Jews and other nations were typical nations, the land was a typical land, God's providences toward them were typical providences, their worship was typical worship, their houses were typical houses, their magistrates typical magistrates, their clothes typical clothes, and indeed, the world was a typical world.[38]

---

34. The late Hans Frei (in lectures at Yale) spoke of modernity as bringing a "great reversal," so that the story of the modern world—and especially the rise of human skill and mastery—became the primary narrative for modern people, while the Bible was relegated to a secondary place. See Frei, *The Eclipse of Biblical Narrative: A Study in Eighteenth and Nineteenth Century Hermeneutics* (New Haven, CT: Yale University Press, 1974), and David C. Steinmetz, "The Superiority of Pre-Critical Exegesis," *Theology Today* 37 (1980): 27–38.

35. WJE 11:192.

36. WJE 10:229.

37. WJE 11:150, 148, 151.

38. WJE 13:435.

Edwards's biblical interpretation thus tended more toward fullness and fecundity than plainness and perspicuity. Types, though, were not the product of a "teeming imagination."[39] In finding types in the natural world and in the text of the Bible, the human mind discovered something that was really there. It was not the ingenuity of the interpreter but that of the Creator that had filled the world with types.

Yet Edwards went further in his spiritual exegesis, in fact much further than most others. Not contented merely with finding Old Testament anticipations of the New Testament, he stated that the events of Jesus' life were typological. In this way, the New Testament contained types no less than the Old Testament: "The things of the ceremonial law are not the only things, whereby God designedly shadowed forth spiritual things; but with an eye to such a representation, were all the transactions of the life of Christ ordered."[40] Edwards's types and antitypes in fact functioned in multiple ways. Sometimes there was a quasi-Platonic contrast of above/below or visible/invisible, such that the material universe "shadowed forth" the realities of the unseen realm. At other points, he set earlier and later events in a typological relationship, though it must be added, the "before" element was not always something from the Old Testament, nor was the "after" element necessarily a feature of the New Testament. Sometimes Edwards typologized events from the church age. Edwards's distinctive eschatological viewpoint—sometimes called postmillennial (chs. 15, 35)—gave a different slant to his practice of spiritual exegesis.

Especially in his *Notebook on the Apocalypse* and in *Humble Attempt*, the "latter day glory" that is yet to come is prefigured through events in the New Testament or in the course of church history. This line of interpretation was a form of spiritual exegesis and yet did not fall within the purview of typology as traditionally understood. It also did not correspond to what the medievals had called anagogical interpretation, since Edwards viewed earlier historical events as anticipating the "glorious times" of a future historical epoch, and not as anticipating heaven or the final state. To assign this a name, one might call it apocalyptic or eschatological typology. The longer one looks, the more one is struck by the fertility and diversity of Edwards's spiritual exegesis.

Unlike many Protestant thinkers of his day and more recently, Edwards did not regard the word "allegory" as pejorative. In fact, he refers in a matter-of-fact manner to "the allegories of the Bible."[41] When one examines Edwards's

---

39. WJE 11:323.

40. WJE 13:284.

41. WJE 2:278.

exegetical practice, it is clear that he himself engaged in allegory in certain cases. For example, in his interpretation of 2 Samuel 20, he writes that "it is probably the design of the Holy Ghost to represent something spiritual in this story."[42] The biblical chapter recounts that Joab—King David's general—was laying siege to the city of Abel-beth-maacah, where a man named Sheba went to hide after he had attempted to overthrow David in a coup. In his commentary, Edwards said almost nothing regarding the historical situation that lay behind this text. Instead he wrote that the city represented a person's heart. Sheba represented sin. Joab and his army represented the wrath of God. Joab demanded that the head of Sheba be thrown over the wall before he would lift the siege. So, said Edwards, God's wrath opposes someone until he or she repents of sin. The wise old woman stands as a symbol of the church. Stein notes that "here the spiritual sense of the chapter...had little if anything to do with the literal sense of the text."[43]

Debates Over Literal and Non-Literal Readings

Until recently, many scholars presented the early modern debates over proper biblical interpretation rather simplistically, as a battle between Catholic allegory and Protestant literalism. Yet when one examines the practice of biblical exegesis among early Protestants, one finds that the "plain," "natural," "grammatical," or "literal" method of interpretation was not used as universally or consistently as one might have guessed from the rhetoric directed against medieval and Roman Catholic interpretation.[44] Luther's own attitude toward spiritual exegesis was not negative so much as ambivalent. In his *Commentary on the Epistle to the Galatians* (1519), Luther said that he did not "disapprove" of what he called the "four-horse team"—i.e., the traditional theory of four senses—historical, allegorical, tropological (i.e., moral), and anagogical (i.e., anticipating heaven). Nonetheless, Luther did not think that the four-sense approach had sufficient support from the scriptures themselves or the church fathers. Spiritual and allegorical interpretations, said Luther, "should not be brought forward with a view to establishing a doctrine of faith."[45] Yet

---

42. WJE 24:371–72.

43. Stein, "Quest," 113.

44. Benjamin Jowett of Oxford University in 1859 declared that "Scripture has one meaning—the meaning which it had in the mind of the Prophet or Evangelist who first uttered or wrote, to hearers or readers who first received it" ("On the Interpretation of Scripture," *Essays and Reviews*, 7th ed.; London: Longman, 1861; 330–43; cited in Steinmetz, "Superiority," 27). Frederic Farrar's tome, *History of Interpretation* (New York: E. P. Dutton, 1886), recounted the errors of non-literal interpretation and the slow but steady progress of biblical literalism.

45. Jaroslav Pelikan and Walter A. Hansen, eds., *Lectures on Galatians; Luther's Works, Volume 27* (St. Louis, MO: Concordia, 1964), 311.

Douglas Sweeney notes that "Luther himself often interpreted the Bible allegorically."[46] More than the Lutherans, the Calvinists stressed the plain sense of the Bible. William Ames wrote: "Hence there is only one meaning for every place in Scripture. Otherwise the meaning of Scripture would not only be unclear and uncertain, but there would be no meaning at all—for anything which does not mean one thing surely means nothing."[47] The *Westminster Confession of Faith* stated that those doctrines that are "necessary to be known...for salvation" are "clearly propounded and opened" in scripture.[48] This was an assertion of the so-called doctrine of the perspicuity of scripture. It stood in tension with the idea of the fecundity of scripture—that multiple interpretations might be equally valid for one and the same text. As noted already, Edwards never abandoned the literal sense of scripture, yet he tilted toward an affirmation of scripture's fecundity rather than its perspicuity.

Why did so many medieval theologians affirm four senses? A famous rhyme states that, "the letter shows us what God and our Fathers did; the allegory shows us where our faith is hid; the moral meaning gives us rules of daily life; the anagogy shows us where we end our strife."[49] Henri de Lubac's *Medieval Exegesis* (1959) showed that the notion of four senses is itself a simplification of a complex, centuries-long history that distinguished a plain or literal sense from various kinds of non-literal interpretations. For almost a millennium, there were both threefold and fourfold notions regarding the senses of the Bible.[50] Some have traced the fourfold idea back to Clement of Alexandria, and still others to Augustine, Eucher, or Cassian—and the answer is unclear.[51] The threefold idea appears in Origen, Eucher, and Jerome.[52] In some cases the three or four senses might conceivably be regarded not as interpretations but as *applications* of the same text. Just as a

---

46. Sweeney, *Jonathan Edwards*, 101.

47. William Ames, *The Marrow of Theology*, trans. John D. Eusden (Philadelphia, PA: Pilgrim Press, 1968) 188.

48. *Westminster Confession*, 1.7.

49. Sweeney, *Jonathan Edwards*, 99.

50. Henri de Lubac, *Medieval Exegesis; Volume 1: The Four Senses of Scripture*, trans. Mark Sebanc (Grand Rapids, MI: Eerdmans; Edinburgh: T & T Clark, 1998), 75–115.

51. Henri de Lubac, *Medieval Exegesis*, 117–42.

52. DeLubac, *Medieval Exegesis*, 137, 139, 142. Origen writes that "just as man is said to consist of body, soul, and spirit, so also does Holy Scripture" (cited 143).

Protestant preacher might apply a given text to the hearer's moral life or hope of heaven, so, one might argue, medieval scholars produced their tropological and anagogical readings of the Bible with similar purposes in mind. Interpreted in this way, the distance between medieval Catholic and modern Protestant exegesis is not as great as generally supposed.

A common charge against spiritual interpretation was that it was a borrowing of allegorical methods as used by pagan Greeks. To expunge the embarrassment caused by the disreputable behavior of their gods and goddesses—e.g., Aphrodite's adulterous affair with Ares, Zeus' murder of his father Chronos—pagan intellectuals resorted to allegory to evade the literal meaning of their own myths. In response, DeLubac argued that patristic and medieval spiritual exegesis was a distinctly Christian approach—as he wrote, a "complete act" grounded on "the prodigious newness of the Christian fact."[53] Along similar lines, Thomas Aquinas wrote that "the author of Holy Writ is God, in whose power it is to signify his meaning, not by words only (as man also can do), but also by things themselves." Not only did words have meaning but "the things signified by the words have themselves a signification." Thomas laid stress on the historical or literal sense, and he asserted that "the spiritual sense...is based on the literal, and presupposes it."[54] For Thomas, as for Edwards, God was the primary giver of meaning, and this meant that God's significations could and did exceed those of the biblical authors themselves.[55] With its providentialist understanding of history, prioritization of the literal sense, and openness to further meanings based on the literal sense, Thomas's view of biblical interpretation is akin to that of Edwards.

Stephen Stein notes that Edwards "was concerned with the literal sense" and that "indifference to it would have been tantamount to abdication of the Protestant principle." Yet Stein balanced this with the assertion that Edwards "did not glory in the literal meaning of Scripture." For the investigation of grammatical intricacies produced a "speculative knowledge" of God, and this level of knowledge would not be salvific.[56] For the Bible to become "a

---

53. Henri deLubac, *Medieval Exegesis*, xix.

54. Thomas Aquinas, *Summa Theologica*, 1a, q.1, a.10, "Whether in Holy Scripture a Word May Have Several Senses?"

55. Steinmetz writes that "medieval theologians defended the proposition, so alien to modern biblical studies, that the meaning of Scripture in the mind of the prophet who first uttered it is only one of its possible meanings and may not, in certain circumstances, even be its primary or most important meaning" ("Superiority," 28).

56. Stein, "Quest," 106–108.

sweet, excellent, life-giving word"—in Edwards's phrase—there had to be God-given illumination.[57]

We may conclude that spiritual exegesis of the Bible appealed to Edwards for multiple reasons. It fit with his sense of the universe as a set of spiritual signs in which God's presence was all-pervasive. It also had a powerful unifying effect in drawing together his vision of reality—both the world in the text and the world beyond the text. Spiritually interpreted, the Bible became a pulsating, dynamic field of interacting signs. Viewed with spiritual understanding, the entire Bible was a vast harmony of mutual "consents." Edwards's manuscript of the "Harmony of the Old and New Testament" indicated that he believed the spiritual interconnectedness of scripture had apologetic value in confirming the truth of the Christian faith. Yet Edwards's distinctive approach to biblical interpretation did not become a vital part of his legacy in nineteenth-century America. His "New Divinity" successors (ch. 37) reflected a more moralistic and less symbolical view of nature and of scripture than Edwards did.[58] It was only in the twentieth century that the symbolic, signifying Edwards came into his own.[59]

---

57. Such spiritual illumination is different from a purely speculative knowledge of the content of biblical typology: "'Tis possible that a man might know how to interpret all the types, parables, enigmas, and allegories in the Bible and not have one beam of spiritual light in his mind; because he mayn't have the least degree of that spiritual sense of the holy beauty of divine things which has been spoken of" (WJE 2:278).

58. This point is a key theme in Conrad Cherry, *Nature and Religious Imagination: From Edwards to Bushnell* (Philadelphia, PA: Fortress Press, 1980).

59. On Edwards as a semiotician, see Stephen H. Daniel, *The Philosophy of Jonathan Edwards: A Study in Divine Semiotics* (Bloomington, IN: Indiana University Press, 1994), and the discussion of Daniel in ch. 40 of this book.

12

The Concept of a History of Redemption

ONE OF EDWARDS'S governing theological ideas—and the concept that dominated much of his private reflection during his final years—is captured in the phrase "history of redemption." Texts written between 1755 and 1758 supply some tantalizing glimpses into Edwards's intentions at the end of his life. The pertinent documents fall into three categories. The first is Edwards's well-known letter of October 19, 1757, to the trustees of the College of New Jersey (later Princeton University), expressing his reservations about accepting their offer of the presidency of the college, and citing as a reason his desire to press forward with work on his planned publications.[1] Here he set forth in considerable detail his plan for what he called "a great work" and entitled *A History of the Work of Redemption*. The second bit of evidence consists of three notebooks pertaining to the history of redemption project. John F. Wilson analyzed these notebooks in an appendix to volume 9 of Edwards's *Works*.[2] The third category of evidence consists of the later *Miscellanies*. In a nutshell, the evidence indicates that Edwards's projected *A History of the Work of Redemption* was to be an expression of what we earlier called a cultural-historical turn in his theology (ch. 5). This cultural turn denotes a preoccupation with "other" cultures—i.e., other than Anglo-American, English-language, and Protestant.

In making these claims, it is important not to assert more than is warranted. Yet Edwards's intellectual engagement with what he called the "arts and sciences" was lifelong, and the cultural turn of his final years was a long time in coming. An early entry in Edwards's lifelong "Catalogue" of books indicates that Edwards was interested in the "comparison of all Religions with the Xtian [i.e., Christian]" while he was still a student at Yale College.[3]

---

1. WJE 16:725–30.

2. John F. Wilson, "Appendix B: Jonathan Edwards's Notebooks for *A History of the Work of Redemption*, in WJE 9:543–56.

3. Peter Thuesen, "Editor's Introduction," in WJE 26:13.

Furthermore, it is clear that the cultural turn did not involve any diminution of Edwards's commitment to biblical exegesis and traditional forms of biblical interpretation. While the description of the projected *A History of the Work of Redemption* occupies the central place in the letter to the trustees, he refers also to "another great work," a *Harmony of the Old and New Testament* that exists in an impressive draft of five hundred manuscript pages.[4]

The notebooks to the redemption project shed light on Edwards's letter to the trustees and vice versa. The letter presents a formal statement regarding the governing principles of the "great work," while the notebooks provide further hints as to its possible content. A major benefit of the notebooks is in helping to establish a chronology as to when Edwards began preparing in earnest to write *A History of the Work of Redemption*. John F. Wilson, in his meticulous analysis of the notebooks' contents, concludes that Edwards wrote much of it very late in his life.[5] Wilson summarizes his investigation of the dating of the notebooks as follows: "The cumulative evidence, then, suggests that Edwards began serious and concerted work on the notebooks for this project no earlier than the spring of 1755. It is also clear that he was very much at work on them through the summer of 1757, perhaps even as he received and pondered the invitation from the trustees of the College of New Jersey." This also has implications for interpreting the letter to the trustees: "The notebooks...give a context for the passage in the well-known letter to the trustees of the College of New Jersey.... The letter should be read quite literally as indicating that Edwards's intellectual energies were becoming centered on this project, and that accepting the trustees' invitation would require him to turn aside from that project in a far more immediate sense than has usually been thought to be the case." Thus the passage in the letter that speaks of *A History of the Work of Redemption* "should be seen as a summary outline of the proposed work, fuller and more systematically developed than any single comparable passage in the notebooks."[6]

---

4. See Kenneth P. Minkema, "The Other Unfinished 'Great Work': Jonathan Edwards, Messianic Prophecy, and 'The Harmony of the Old and New Testaments,'" in Stephen J. Stein, ed., *Jonathan Edwards's Writings: Text, Context, Interpretation* (Bloomington and Indianapolis: Indiana University Press, 1996), 52–65.

5. Wilson, "Appendix B," in WJE 9:546–47, 550–55.

6. Wilson, "Appendix B," in WJE 9:553, 555.

If we consider the letter in Wilson's terms as a "summary outline of the proposed work," what do we see? A number of interesting points come to light if we read closely:

> I have had on my mind and heart (which I long ago began, not with any view to publication) a great work, which I call *A History of the Work of Redemption*, a body of divinity in an entire new method, being thrown into the form of an history, considering the affair of Christian theology, as the whole of it, in each part, stands in reference to the great work of redemption by Jesus Christ; which I suppose is to be the grand design of all God's designs, and the *summum* and *ultimum* of all the divine operations and degrees; particularly considering all parts of the grand scheme in their historical order. The order of their existence, or their being brought forth to view, in the course of divine dispensations, or the wonderful series of successive acts and events; beginning from eternity and descending from thence to the great work and successive dispensations of the infinitely wise God in time, considering the chief events coming to pass in the church of God, and revolutions in the world of mankind, affecting the state of the church and the affair of redemption, which we have an account of in history or prophecy; till at last we come to the general resurrection, last judgment, and consummation of all things; when it shall be said, 'It is done. I am Alpha and Omega, the Beginning and the End' [Rev. 22:13]. Concluding my work, with the consideration of that perfect state of things, which shall be finally settled, to last for eternity. This history will be carried on with regard to all three worlds, heaven, earth and hell: considering the connected, successive events and alterations, in each so far as the Scriptures give any light; introducing all parts of divinity in that order which is most scriptural and most natural: which is a method which appears to me the most beautiful and entertaining, wherein every divine doctrine, will appear to greatest advantage in the brightest light, in the most striking manner, showing the admirable contexture and harmony of the whole.[7]

The letter is rich in "Edwardsisms," i.e., terms with special meaning for him. These include such words and phrases as "history," "redemption," "*summum* and *ultimum*," "divine dispensations," and "beautiful and entertaining." Some of these serve as subject headings for entries in the *Miscellanies*. Other phrases,

---

7. Edwards, WJE 16:727–28.

such as "*summum* and *ultimum*," suggest a link with the treatise *End of Creation*, since these Latin terms seem to be functional equivalents for "chief end" and "ultimate end"—the topic of discussion in the opening paragraph of *End of Creation*.[8] Like *End of Creation*, which moves from creation to consummation, Edwards's unwritten *A History of the Work of Redemption* was to be bracketed on either side by God's eternity. In fact, one might read *End of Creation* as supplying the bookends for the historical material to be included in the great work. Furthermore, the lengthy notebook entry Miscellany 1263 seems relevant to the unwritten great work. This entry discusses the distinction between God's "natural" operations in history and God's "arbitrary" operations at the beginning and end of the world. Like *End of Creation*, it links redemptive history to creation and consummation, and so provides a conceptual scaffolding within which Edwards might have constructed his unwritten work.[9] The basic structure of *A History of the Work of Redemption* was to be an inverted parabola—like an upside-down St. Louis arch—as suggested by the phrasing of the letter, "beginning from eternity and descending from thence to the great work and successive dispensations of the infinitely wise God in time, considering the chief events coming to pass in the church of God, and revolutions in the world of mankind ... till at last we come to the general resurrection, last judgment, and consummation of all things."

Since the title of the projected work, *A History of the Work of Redemption*, is identical to the title of Edwards's published sermon series, this could be taken as an indication that the unwritten work was basically to be an expansion of the Northampton sermons, preached in the 1730s and published posthumously in 1777. Yet the reference to "a body of divinity in an entire [sic] new method" suggests something quite different from the sermons. Edwards knew very well what "body of divinity" signifies, and in theology this connotes a whole

---

8. Professor Thomas Schafer pointed out in conversation that Edwards customarily used Latinate English terms and phrases with a precise sense of their original meaning in Latin. Thus "arbitrary" for Edwards does not signify "capricious" but rather something "depending on the will" (Lat. *arbitrium*, "will"). "Gradual," in reference to redemptive history, means "occurring in steps" (Lat. *gradus*, "step"). So "*summum* and *ultimum*" denote that which is "highest" and that which is "furthest" or "last." A discussion of "chief" or "highest ends" and "ultimate ends" occurs at the beginning of *End of Creation*, and the distinction plays a role throughout the argument of the treatise (WJE 8:405). Hence it is plausible to suppose that the phrase in the letter, "*summum* and *ultimum*," provides a link between the unwritten masterwork and the published *End of Creation*.

9. Michael McClymond, *Encounters With God: An Approach to the Theology of Jonathan Edwards* (New York: Oxford University Press, 1998), 110, comments on the programmatic character of "Miscellany 1263"—a point also noted by Douglas Sweeney in his "Editor's Introduction" (WJE 23:21).

composed of interdependent parts. Just as there is no human body, properly speaking, if there is no head, heart, or stomach, there could be no "body of divinity" without a full treatment of all the major theological topics—the doctrines of God, anthropology, christology, soteriology, ecclesiology, and eschatology. So if we take seriously the phrase "body of divinity," then it becomes clear that the sermons in the published *A History of the Work of Redemption* barely begin to address the multifarious topics that Edwards intended to treat in his masterwork.

The phrase "entire new method" qualifies the words "body of divinity," and the words "being thrown into the form of an history" explain the method. Here Edwards casts aside any false modesty and plainly declares that he is going to do something unprecedented. His accent falls on the novelty of this new work. If Edwards's intention had been simply to expand and embellish the published *History of the Work of Redemption*, then it is hard to see how he could advance any claim to using an "entire new method." The published *History of the Work of Redemption* sat squarely within the well-established genre of the Christian "universal chronicle," as exemplified by such books as Augustine's *City of God* or Jacques Bossuet's *Discourse on Universal History* (1681). As C. A. Patrides noted, there were some sixty universal chronicles written in Western Europe by the year 1100, and a far greater number appeared in subsequent centuries up until the time of the Enlightenment.[10] It is therefore implausible to think a Christian universal chronicle—and even one done on a hitherto unrealized scale—would have counted for Edwards as a work written in "an entire new method." Only an ill-informed person would imagine this sort of sacred chronicle to be a methodological innovation.

When Edwards speaks of it being "thrown into the form of an history," the word "thrown" suggests a process of translation from one idiom to another. Edwards was well acquainted with the typical Protestant "body of divinity"— he told Joseph Bellamy that his favorite was Petrus Van Mastrict's *Theoretico-Practica Theologia* (1714)—and its essential structure was non-historical. The novelty of the unwritten work was its way of translating—or "throwing"—the traditional content of Protestant theology into an historical form. The timeless truths of the dogmaticians were to find expression in the form of narrative. In summary, then, the letter provides an outline of the proposed work, and from this brief summation it is clear that the "great work" was not to be simply an expansion of the sermon series preached in Northampton. Somehow Edwards intended to translate the content of traditional dogmatic theology

---

10. McClymond, *Encounters*, 66.

into historical or narrative form. Stephen Clark writes: "Edwards's insight is that Christian doctrine is not given whole, but emerges, revealing an organic nature as the history of redemption unfolds, and as the biblical revelation develops. It is not therefore to be merely rearranged in a scientific manner, but documented as it grows and develops."[11] But how exactly would Edwards have done this? An examination of the contents of the redemption notebooks, with a sidelong glance at the *Miscellanies*, provides a surprising answer: Edwards intended to bridge history and doctrine through a pioneering effort in cultural analysis.

The notebooks to the redemption project, as already shown, reflect a very late stage in Edwards's life and show him hard at work in laying a foundation for his "great work." What may be surprising is the degree to which he is concerned with cultural developments occurring beyond the bounds of Christendom. He has much to say regarding "heathen" peoples and their relationship to the redemptive plan of God. He writes also of the "arts and sciences" in Western culture, and concerns himself with topics that seem to have little bearing on theology, such as the natural philosophy of Sir Isaac Newton. Cultural developments, he seems to suggest, form an integral part of God's plan for history.[12]

In the letter to the trustees, Edwards said nothing about the place of non-Christian religions and cultures within his "great work." The emphasis lay on the "body of divinity." When one looks at the redemption notebooks, a different picture emerges. It becomes clear that the gospel's "preparation"—a key word for Edwards—occurs among the "heathen" no less than among the Israelites. So "the form of an history" that Edwards had in mind was not the traditional chronicle that followed the biblical narratives from Adam to Christ, and then recounted the history of Christianity from the apostles until the present day. Instead Edwards wished to expand this traditional Christian understanding of history with a full-scale consideration and critique of global religions and cultures in theological perspective. Of the three notebooks, the

---

11. Stephen M. Clark, "Jonathan Edwards: The History of Redemption" (PhD diss., Drew University, 1986), 406. Clark stresses the use of the word "redemption," indicating that Edwards's account of history is both Christ-centered and redemption-centered. That is, it gives preeminence to Jesus' obedient life and atoning death, and it understands the unfolding of all of God's purposes for creation from this standpoint (407–408).

12. Thanks are due to Kenneth Minkema, executive editor of *The Works of Jonathan Edwards*, for supplying transcriptions of Edwards's redemption notebooks prior to their appearance in the online WJE. They are cited below simply as "Notebook A," "Notebook B," and "Notebook C."

first and longest, "Notebook A," has most of the references to non-Christian religions and cultures. Here Edwards stresses the universal significance of the gospel. The "need" for Christ was apparent in all nations. An entry near the beginning of "Notebook A" makes this clear: "All Things ordered to shew the need of a [S]aviour from sin...among the Heathen." Again he writes, almost at the outset of the first notebook: "The Messiahs salvation was to be a general salvation of mankind of all nations...It was not to remove the misery of men in one or two Branche[s] or in one or two nations but in all [.]"[13]

A part of the preparation for the gospel among non-Christians consisted in traditions that anticipated Christ's coming. Edwards writes: "CONCERNING THE TRADITIONS among the HEATHEN & whether there was not a degree of Inspiration of some of the wise men among the Heathen. & whether those inspired Persons—were not good Men."[14] The final phrase in the quotation is surprising. The Puritan tradition was generally suspicious of supposed "good Men," so Edwards's openness to finding them outside of Christendom is remarkable. In "Notebook A," Edwards refers to cultural developments that were a part of God's plan. The invention of written language is one of these: "When speak[ing] of God then speak of the Invention of Letters as a great gift of God the special design of which was to prepare the way for the promoting the grant Designs of Redemption in the world."[15] One of the more interesting entries relates to Newtonian physics: "The true PHILOSOPHY of Sir Isaac Newton one thing to make way for the un[i]versal setting up of X [i.e., Christ's] kingdom."[16] Edwards's interest in Newtonian philosophy was nothing new, and the sixth volume of *The Works of Jonathan Edwards* provides plenty of evidence that he was engaged with natural philosophy in early life and even sought to find theological meaning through his scientific inquiries. Yet what is striking about the notebook entry is the suggestion that Newtonian physics is a part of God's historical and providential plan. Modern science not only concurs with orthodox theology but also somehow promotes the advancement of Christ's kingdom. How Edwards would have argued to this conclusion is

---

13. Edwards, "Notebook A," 1–2. The same idea crops up repeatedly in the first notebook. In "Notebook A," 107, Edwards intends to "shew also how all Things among the Heathen shewed the need of such a Saviour to save the Nations from their sins."

14. Edwards, "Notebook A," 4.

15. Edwards, "Notebook A," 4.

16. Edwards, "Notebook A," 4.

not at all clear, but one can see here the general tendency in "Notebook A" to view all aspects of human culture in relation to a divine redemptive plan. Edwards stated his underlying principle in another entry: "All Truth tends to confirm and illustrate divine Truth. How Philosophy the more & more it is brought to perfection the more & more does become a Branch of Divinity. How all the sciences... so far as they are truly understood and taught are like streams that empty themselves at least [last?] into divinity."[17] At the end of his life, Edwards had found an implicit argument for the truth of Christianity in the human arts and sciences (ch. 10).

One thought-provoking entry in "Notebook A" pertains to the rise of skepticism in the modern era. While Edwards might simply have condemned this trend, instead he finds something positive to say regarding it: "[PRE]SENT TIMES take notice of Gods End [in suf]fering such infidel Heretical sceptical [free]thinking spirit so exceedingly to prevail [in] this age.... How God hereby is preparing the way for the more abundant Manifestation of Truth."[18] Reading this entry at face value, it seems that even secularism could be a part of God's providential plan. The word "preparing" is interesting in this context, inasmuch as Edwards typically uses it when there is some continuity between a religious or cultural development and the work of redemption. Yet the question remains: What could Edwards have meant in saying that a "sceptical [free-]thinking spirit" was "preparing" for an "abundant Manifestation of Truth?" The more conventional reading would be to see modern skepticism in contrast to gospel truth—the darkness that accentuates the dawning light. Yet another interpretation is possible. Skepticism itself might be a part of God's purpose. Edwards's use of the word "preparing" suggests that this latter reading is more likely. The published *A History of the Work of Redemption*, as argued elsewhere (ch. 15), exhibits two distinct ways of construing the flow of history, a "contrast motif" and a "preparation motif," and generally this notebook entry fits into the latter category. One comes to the surprising conclusion that the future redemptive work of God is to be built on Western secularism as well as on "heathen traditions" outside of Christendom.

The last several hundred *Miscellanies* attest to the cultural turn in Edwards's later theologizing. Hundreds of pages are devoted to a discussion of non-Christian religions (ch. 36). His position on non-Christian religions

---

17. Edwards, "Notebook A," 8.

18. Edwards, "Notebook A," 19–20.

contained multiple elements. Individual "pagans" may have received direct, divine inspiration, non-Christian religions showed foreshadowings or "types" of biblical religion, and the common truths among world religions may have been due to traditions passed down by the founders of the nations, beginning with Noah's sons. Moreover, Edwards offered differing theological appraisals of the non-Christian religions. Greece and Rome, along with China, received favorable evaluation, while Islam and Native American religions came under censure.[19]

When one brings together the three elements of textual evidence considered here—the letter to the trustees, the redemption notebooks, and the later *Miscellanies*—a number of conclusions follow. One is struck by the differences between the description of the "great work" in the letter to the trustees and what may be inferred from both the redemption notebooks and the later *Miscellanies*. The letter underscores the novelty of Edwards's projected work, yet its newness is explained in terms of its methodology and not in terms of its content. It is written with an "entire new method," says Edwards, "being thrown into the form of an history." Edwards speaks of it as a "body of divinity," and this traditional designation suggests that the content of the work was to be traditional even if the method was not. Yet when one looks at the redemption notebooks and the later *Miscellanies*, it becomes apparent that Edwards's plan was to write a work that diverged significantly from traditional textbooks of theology. Perhaps Edwards judged that the brief letter to the trustees was not a suitable forum for a full disclosure of his revolutionary new approach to theology.

The letter to the trustees leaves us with the issue as to how Edwards intended to translate the content of traditional theology into historical narrative. In addressing this question, the later notebooks are invaluable. Taken with the letter, the redemption notebooks and the final *Miscellanies* indicate that Edwards was moving toward a cultural analysis that included both empirical and normative aspects. He was not interested in Chinese or Greco-Roman history per se, but instead he wanted to scrutinize and evaluate these cultures theologically and to assess the extent to which they presented an analogy to, anticipation of, or preparation for the coming of Christ. He was developing a method that incorporated fact and evaluation, description and assessment. Culture, for the later Edwards, functioned as the link between history and theology.

---

19. Gerald R. McDermott, *Jonathan Edwards Confronts the Gods*, 176–93 (Greece and Rome), 207–16 (China), Islam (166–75), and Native American religions (194–206).

Edwards was strictly orthodox in his commitment to a Calvinist conception of human sin and divine grace. Yet the tendency of the later notebooks was toward an appreciation of God's presence and activity within non-Christian and secular cultures. Edwards's twentieth-century disciple, H. Richard Niebuhr, noted that he did not himself hope to complete the task of Edwards's *A History of the Work of Redemption*, and yet hoped that he might prepare the way for someone else to do so: "Hence my greatest hope is that such a work as this may serve 'even as a stepping stone' to the work of some American Augustine who will write a *City of God* that will trace the story of the eternal city in its relations to modern civilization instead of to ancient Rome, or of Jonathan Edwards *redivivus* who will bring down to our own time the *History of the Work of Redemption*."[20] With regard to the theology of culture, the most prominent twentieth-century name is Paul Tillich. Despite the many differences between Edwards's and Tillich's approaches to culture, both sought to identify an implicit divine presence in the "arts and sciences" of Western civilization.[21] Tillich stated in a famous dictum that "religion is the substance of culture, and culture is the form of religion." Toward the end of his life, and following a visit to Japan, Tillich became increasingly interested in non-Western cultures and non-Christian religions, and so Tillich's early "theology of culture" was gradually becoming a "theology of cultures." When one considers Edwards uncompleted *A History of the Work of Redemption* alongside of these more recent thinkers, the effect is striking. Perry Miller, despite his hyperbolic claims for Edwards's modernity, may have been correct in insisting that Edwards anticipated some twentieth-century intellectual trends long before they arrived.

---

20. H. Richard Niebuhr, *The Kingdom of God in America* (New York: Harper & Brothers, 1937), xvi.

21. A key difference between Edwards and Tillich concerns the nature of divine revelation, which Tillich held as a universal feature of all human experiences and cultures, and which Edwards saw as specific to particular times, places, and persons. See Tillich's essay, "The Significance of the History of Religions for the Systematic Theologian," in Jerald C. Brauer, ed., *The Future of Religions* (New York: Harper and Row, 1966), 80–94.

SECTION 2

The Triune God, the Angels, and Heaven

13

God as Trinity

FATHER, SON, AND HOLY SPIRIT

THE TRINITY WAS central to Edwards's theology. Near the beginning of his scholarly career he wrote a long entry in his *Miscellanies* notebook on the subject, asserting against contemporary theologians who were loathe to discuss it that he was "not afraid to say twenty things about the Trinity which the Scripture never said." Toward the end of his life, he copied extensive extracts from Chevalier Ramsay, who found belief in a trinity among the "Chinese philosophers" and argued against deists and Unitarians "who deny the doctrine of the Trinity." The Trinity was fundamental to Edwards's most distinctive theological theme, the divine beauty, for "true, spiritual original beauty" consists in "a mutual propensity and affection of heart," whose prototype is the Trinity—"the supreme harmony of all." The Trinity was basic to another favorite Edwardsean motif, the work of redemption, which concerns "not only what Christ the mediator has done, but also what the Father and the Holy Ghost have done as united or confederated in this design of redeeming sinful men." Redemption was designed "for the glory of each of the persons." Even Edwards's ethics were stamped with a Trinitarian impress: "The revelation we now have of the Trinity ... [makes] a vast alteration with respect to the reason and obligations to many amiable and exalted duties, so that they are as it were new."[1]

While Edwards's conception of the Trinity was more basic than his metaphysics, he used his idealism to help depict it. He was convinced that "an

---

1. WJE 13:257; WJE 23:98, 186; WJE 8:564; WJE 13:329; WJE 9:117–18; WJE 13:416. For reflection on how Edwards used the Trinity to think of ethics, see William J. Danaher, Jr., *The Trinitarian Ethics of Jonathan Edwards* (Louisville, KY: Westminster John Knox, 2004). In the late nineteenth century rumors floated that Edwards was an Arian or Sabellian because Horace Bushnell had written that that he had been denied access to an Edwards manuscript on the Trinity that was of questionable orthodoxy. In 1880, Oliver Wendell Holmes demanded publication of this manuscript, but when Edwards Amasa Park defended Edwards's Trinitarian orthodoxy the following year and added that he had misplaced the treatise, suspicion grew. Only when George P. Fisher published the "Essay on the Trinity" in 1903 were the rumors put to rest. See WJE 21:111.

absolutely perfect idea of a thing is the very thing." Therefore "if a man could have an absolutely perfect idea of all that passed in his mind... for any particular space of time past—suppose the last hour—he would really, to all intents and purposes, be over again what he was that last hour." While a man's idea is never perfect, "God's idea is absolutely perfect." So God's perfect idea of himself is so real and substantial that it "generates" a person—the Son. The mutual delight that the Father and the Son take in each other is also perfect and therefore is another person, the Spirit. So there are only three—God, the idea of God, and delight in God. All other things said about God, even what are called his attributes, are "not distinct real things, but, just as in created spirits, only mere modes and relations" of the three divine Persons.[2]

> The Father is the Deity subsisting in the prime, unoriginated and most absolute manner, or the deity in its direct existence. The Son is the Deity generated by God's understanding, or having an idea of himself, and subsisting in that idea. The Holy Ghost is the Deity subsisting in act, or the divine essence flowing out and breathed forth, in God's infinite love to and delight in himself.... The divine idea and divine love... each of them are properly distinct persons.[3]

The Divine Persons

More than most early modern Christian thinkers, Edwards delineated distinct roles for each of the three divine Persons. The Father is "the fountain," "the Deity without distinction." He is the great "author" of the plan of redemption who provided a redeemer or purchaser. Although the Father and the Son are equal in divine nature, the Father is the "head" of the persons in the Trinity and Christ's personal head. Christ is subject to him and dependent on him.[4]

While we are "in" the image of Adam, the Son *is* the image of the Father. He reveals God to creatures, for he is God's "face." He is also God's Logos,

---

2. WJE 13:258; WJE 21:116; WJE 13:263; WJE 25:144; WJE 21:132. God's perfect ideas of things become the existence of those things, but there is only one perfect idea of himself and hence only one Son. Paul Helm thinks this line of reasoning is "implicitly tri-theistic," but acknowledges that Edwards leaves much in the Trinity to mystery. Paul Helm, Introduction to *Treatise on Grace & Other Posthumously Published Writings including Observations on the Trinity* (Greenwood, SC: Attic Press, 1971), 21.

3. WJE 21:131.

4. WJE 13:298; WJE 17:202; WJE 25:144.

reason, word, truth, and understanding. Although begotten by God's thinking of himself, he is perfectly substantial because in God there is no distinction between substance and act. The Son is "wholly substance and wholly act." His principal role in the history of redemption was to purchase our communion with God, which is the Holy Spirit.[5]

The Spirit, who is the "infinite delight God has in himself," is "nothing but act," or in other words God's "sweet energy." He is love because he is the mutual love between the Father and the Son. By having the Spirit, believers participate in the communion between the Father and the Son. Therefore believers do not have fellowship with the Spirit, for the Spirit is himself fellowship with the Father and the Son. Because he is divine love, he is "the sum of all good things"—the source and being of all love, holiness, and beauty.

Edwards distinguished three separate tasks for the Spirit—to "quicken" and "beautify all things," to sanctify created spirits (which means to "give them divine love"), and "to comfort and delight the souls of God's people." The Spirit's primary symbol is the dove, for "beyond all other irrational animals in the world [the dove] is remarkable and wonderful for its love to its mate." The "nature of things" tells us that it is proper for scripture to liken the Spirit to water, a spring, a river, a shower, flowing oil, and precious ointment, since these things are made to represent love and joy. In the same way, it "would be very unnatural" if we spoke of "understanding, wisdom or idea," the divine perfections of which are the Son, as being "poured out, shed abroad, burning, blowing, etc."[6]

Edwards believed that his idealist view of the Trinity was no different from the biblical portrayal. On the Father's generation of the Son as "the eternal, necessary, perfect, substantial and personal idea which God hath of himself," Edwards noted that Christ is said by scripture to be the image of God (2 Cor 4:4), in the form of God (Phil 2:6), the image of the invisible God (Col 1.15), and the "brightness of his glory, and the express image of his person" (Heb 1:13). The Bible gives him names such as "the face of God," "the shining forth of God's glory," "Amen" ("which is a Hebrew word that signifies truth"), and "the angel of the Lord." In John, he observed, Jesus says, "He that seeth me seeth him that sent me" and tells Philip, "He that hath seen me hath seen the Father" (John 12:45, 14:9). Scripture also teaches that Christ is the wisdom of God, which teaches "that he is the same with God's perfect and eternal idea." Jesus is

---

5. WJE 21:117; WJE 13:409; WJE 21:118, 116, 135.

6. WJE 13:261, 260; WJE 20:389; WJE 13:415; WJE 21:135, 123; WJE 13:265; WJE 20:445.

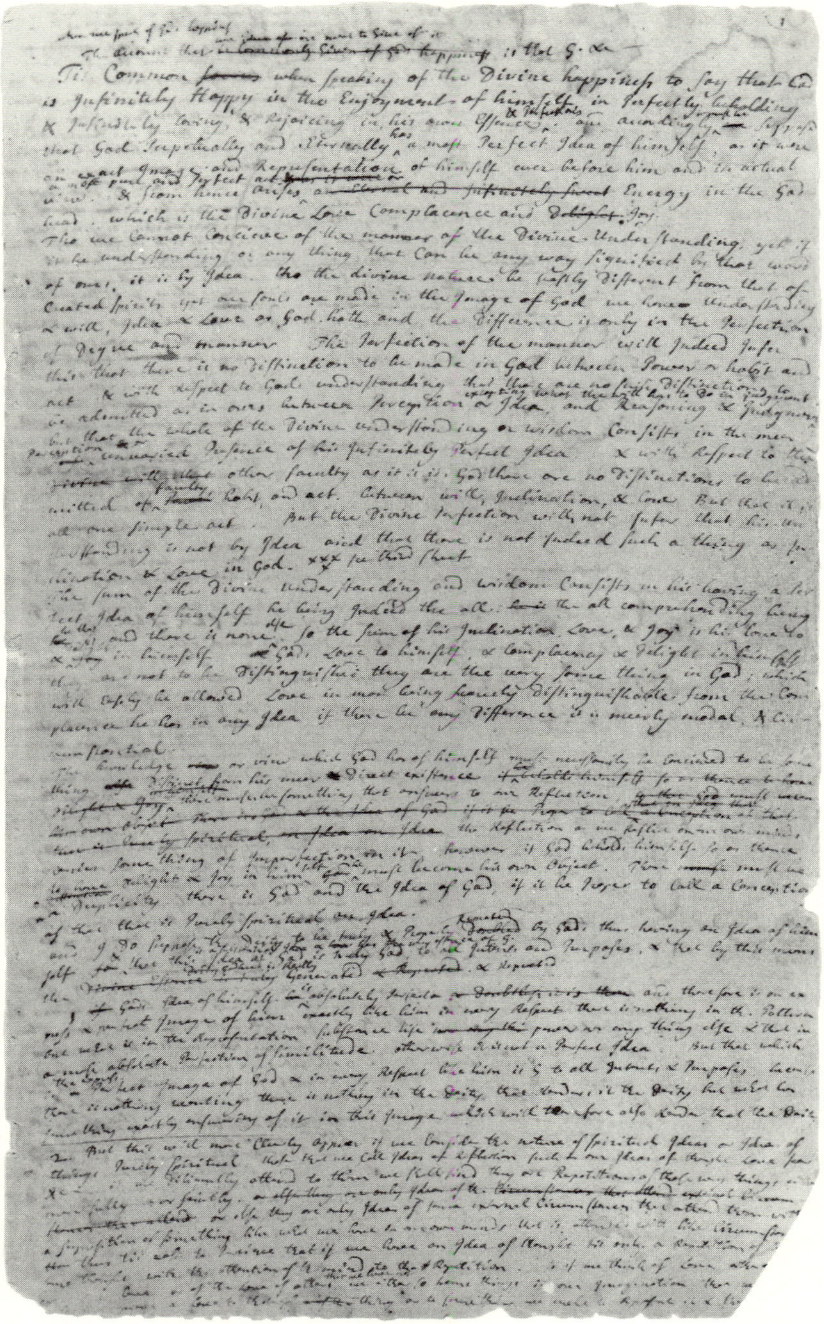

Tis Common when speaking of the Divine happiness to say that God is Infinitely Happy in the Enjoyment of himself in perfectly beholding & infinitely loving, & Rejoicing in his own Essence & perfections and accordingly it is supposed that God perpetually and Eternally has a most perfect Idea of himself, as it were an exact Image and Representation of himself ever before him and in actual view. & from hence arises a ... Energy in the God head. which is the Divine Love Complacence and Joy.

FIGURE 13.1 Edwards's manuscript on the Trinity—published posthumously—reveals the profundity of his conception of God (Beinecke Rare Book and Manuscript Library, Yale University).

called the Logos of God and light of the world, which led Edwards to ask, "Who can be so properly appointed to be [the] revealer of God to the world, as that person who is God's own perfect idea or understanding of himself?"[7]

Like Augustine, Edwards used an analysis of 1 John 4 to assert that the Spirit is love. There we are told that "God is love" (v. 8), and that if we have love in us then we have God in us (v. 12). In the next verse, Edwards points out, we are told that if we have love, it is the Spirit (v. 13). Edwards also highlighted the biblical passages about the Father's love for the Son, such as at Jesus' baptism and transfiguration ("This is my beloved Son, in whom I am well pleased") and Old Testament testimony to the Father's delight in his servant (Is 42:1). He took Proverbs 8:30 ("I was daily his delight, rejoicing always before [him]") to be the Son's declaration of love and joy between himself and the Father. This is "most pure act, and an infinitely holy and sweet energy aris[ing] between the Father and the Son: for their love and joy is [sic] mutual, in mutually loving and delighting in each other."[8]

Trinitarian Innovations

Edwards's Trinitarianism was original in a number of ways. First, Edwards departed from the Western Trinitarian tradition by rejecting its emphasis on divine simplicity, which was one of the ways in which Augustine and his successors guarded the faith against recurring Arianism. By insisting that God has no parts and all the divine attributes are common to each of the Three, they protected the notion that the second of the Three was fully equal to the First. The unfortunate result of this, however, was a risk of modalism—the idea that the Three are simply different modes of one Person. Augustine, for example, in his aversion to both Arianism and tritheism, doubted whether it is "possible for us, who are compelled to explain and to reason about the Trinity, to say three persons." In Augustine's Trinity, there are distinctions, "but in the end they do not constitute a community." Some Reformed scholastics were also reluctant to use the word "persons" for the Three, resorting instead, like Thomas Aquinas, to "modes of subsistence" to explain the relation between one essence and three hypostases. Even Karl Rahner and Karl Barth, who helped renew Trinitarian thinking in Christian theology, seemed to

---

7. WJE 21:117,119,118–21.

8. Augustine, *The Trinity* (Wash. DC: Catholic University Press, 2003) 15.5; WJE 21:121,118,121.

suggest that there is finally only one person in God. The implication of all of these ways of describing the Three is that they are merely varying modes of one divine Person.[9]

In stark contrast, Edwards started not with the divine essence, as did Augustine and the rest of the West, but with the three persons. He had no reluctance to use the word "person": in his *Treatise on Grace*, he wrote, "We have no word in the English language that does so naturally represent what the Scripture reveals of the distinction of the eternal three—Father, Son, and Holy Ghost—as to say they are one God but three persons." In Amy Plantinga-Pauw's words, Edwards "boldly affirmed plurality in God."[10]

Krister Sairsingh further underlined Edwards's insistence on the personhood of each of the Three by highlighting Edwards's declaration that each of the Three has distinctive and unique roles: the Father is the principle of happiness, the Son the principle of knowledge and understanding, and the Spirit the principle of love. Hence, as Edwards argues in his *Discourse on the Trinity*, the Father has love only because the Holy Spirit dwells in Him; the Father has understanding only because the Son dwells in Him, and so on. This is Edwards's version of *perichoresis* [lit., "dancing around"], the concept developed by John of Damascus and other Eastern Fathers for mutual indwelling and interpenetration.[11]

Edwards usually started his doctrine of God with the divine Three rather than the divine essence, perhaps because starting with God's essence suggests there is something impersonal in God before the three Persons. It also suggests, because of the dominance of the psychological model of the Trinity, that the Holy Spirit is simply the bond of love between the first two Persons, which tends to reduce the Spirit to something less than a person. But Edwards used both the psychological and social analogies for the Trinity in a synthetic way that put more weight on the latter, and at the same time restored honor to the Spirit. The psychological analogy, which goes back principally to Augustine, emphasizes the unity of the godhead by comparing it to the human mind that knows and loves itself. In like fashion, the Son and Spirit are the wisdom and love of the one God. Calvin criticized this model for being mere "speculation,"

---

9. Augustine, *The Trinity* [7.4] 232; Krister Sairsingh, "Jonathan Edwards and the Idea of Divine Glory: His Foundational Trinitarianism and Its Ecclesial Import," PhD diss., Harvard University, 1986; 72; Richard A. Muller, *Post-Reformation Reformed Dogmatics*, 4 vols. (Grand Rapids, MI: Baker Academic, 2003), 4:177–85; Amy Plantinga-Pauw, *The Supreme Harmony of All: The Trinitarian Theology of Jonathan Edwards* (Grand Rapids, MI: Eerdmans, 2002), 72.

10. WJE 21:181; Plantinga-Pauw, *Supreme Harmony*, 58.

11. WJE 21:133; Sairsingh, "Edwards," 149.

but Edwards was not troubled by this objection. The image of the Trinity, he asserted, is "in every created mind" as mind, its understanding or idea, and "the will or affection or love."[12]

The social analogy, which was articulated by the medieval thinker Richard of St. Victor, conceives of God as a society or family of persons. This analogy did not gain much traction until recent times because of the strong commitment to divine simplicity in Western or Latin theology. Each person, it was thought, was only modally distinct from the divine essence. More emphasis was placed on the concurrence of all three persons in every divine act than on distinct roles for each. As Plantinga-Pauw has shown, the Reformed tradition in particular placed divine simplicity at the head of theology and tended to "tailor the doctrine of the Trinity to fit with divine simplicity." But in a "startling departure," Edwards rejected this trend by developing "an alternative conception of divine oneness that revolved around the notions of excellency, harmony and consent." He presented God (in his words) as "three persons of the Trinity...act[ing] as a society" in the great affair of redemption. Their mutual love makes for a "fountain of happiness" that renders the Trinity an "infinitely sweet and glorious society." William Danaher suggests that even Edwards's use of the psychological model was social because he thought of God's unity as mutual participation in an identical idea. For the tradition that developed the psychological model, personhood is individuality, love is an individual's governing disposition, and the *imago dei* is found in consciousness. But for Edwards, personhood is relationality and dialogue, love is communal and interpersonal, and the *imago dei* is found in relationships.[13]

---

12. Calvin, *Institutes* 1.15.4; WJE 13:435.

13. Plantinga-Pauw, *Supreme Harmony*, 70,69; WJE 25:146, 153; William J. Danaher Jr, *The Trinitarian Ethics of Jonathan Edwards* (Louisville: Westminster John Knox, 2004), 94,108. In his otherwise fine study of the Spirit as the bond of union in Edwards's theology, Robert W. Caldwell denies a social analogy in Edwards because of the mistaken notion that "the Spirit is not strictly a consenting person alongside of the Father and the Son, but [only] the personal consent between them." Yet Edwards writes in "Miscellany 1062" on the "ECONOMY OF THE TRINITY AND THE COVENANT OF REDEMPTION" that the redemption was "determined by the perfect *consent* of *all*, and...*consultation* among the *three* persons about it...there was a joint *agreement of all*, but not properly a covenant between 'em all" [emph. added]; Caldwell, *Communion in the Spirit: The Holy Spirit as the Bond of Union in the Theology of Jonathan Edwards* (Eugene, OR: Wipf and Stock, 2006), 27–28; WJE 20:442. It is also important to note that van Mastricht, Edwards's favorite theologian, gave more attention to the social than the psychological model of the Trinity; Adriaan C. Neele, *Petrus van Mastricht (1630–1706)* (Leiden: Brill, 2009), 247. For these reasons, it is difficult to accept the thesis that Edwards used only "social language" and not a social model of the Trinity, as argued in Steve Studebaker, "Jonathan Edwards's Social Augustinian Trinitarianism: An Alternative to a Recent Trend," *Scottish Journal of Theology* 56 (2003): 268–85.

Edwards made another departure from his Reformed tradition by stressing the Holy Spirit. He thought his Puritan predecessors had diminished the Holy Spirit's role in redemption by restricting it to the application of the work of the Father and the Son. But in his essay "On the Equality of the Persons of the Trinity," Edwards asserted that that the Holy Spirit in certain respects has "superiority" among the Three, as the "principle that as it were reigns over the Godhead and governs his heart, and wholly influences both the Father and the Son in all they do." As Sang Lee has noted, this is a Spirit who is not just a bond of love but an active agent—a full-fledged Person who reigns and governs and influences. While the Father and Son have superiority in their own roles, the Spirit is "highest...though he be last, as he is the messenger sent by the other two." And because the Spirit is not only the "internal spring" and "moving cause" of the covenant of redemption but also "the great good covenanted for," his honor is all the greater.[14]

In his study of Edwards's "Trinitarian ethics," Danaher argues that Edwards made the Trinity integral to morality by recasting moral life as divinization or *theosis*. Since for Edwards God's idea is the Son, and his perfect act that loves the idea is the Holy Spirit, Christian love lifts up the believer into the triune life. When a regenerate person loves her neighbor, she not only replicates the divine pattern (which, as Danaher explains, was the Platonic and Augustinian way of construing ethics) but also *participates* in the love between the Father and the Son. To love the neighbor truly, then, is not simply to be like God but to share in God's own love for them.[15]

Patrick Sherry and others have argued that Edwards did more to relate God and beauty than anyone else in the history of Western Christian thought. But, as we saw in chapter 6, Trinity is the definition of and source of all beauty. For Edwards, "God is distinguished from all other beings and exalted above 'em, chiefly by his divine beauty." Since beauty is "consent" to being in general, the pattern of all consent is God's love among the Three Persons—each person's loving consent to the glory and will of the other two Persons, and then to the Trinity's design for the creation. This is still another, but perhaps the most significant, way in which Edwards put his mark on Christian understandings of the Trinity.[16]

---

14. Plantinga Pauw, *Supreme Harmony*, 121; WJE 21:147, 19, 147.

15. Dannaher, *Trinitarian Ethics*, 39.

16. Patrick Sherry, *Spirit and Beauty: An Introduction to Theological Aesthetics* (Birmingham, UK: SCM Press, 2002); WJE 2:298.

Trinitarian Apologetics

In an age that was allergic to what it considered "metaphysical riddles," Edwards defended the Trinity against charges that it was unbiblical and unreasonable. There had been a bitter controversy over the Trinity among Anglicans and dissenters toward the end of the seventeenth century. Then in 1712 Samuel Clarke published an Arian account entitled *Scripture-Doctrine of the Trinity*. Hubert Stogdon and Isaac Watts joined the controversy in 1719 and 1722 respectively with works criticizing any attempts to make foundational to faith doctrines not "plainly revealed" in the Bible. The implication, of course, was that the Trinity is not plainly revealed.[17]

Edwards regarded these new developments with impatience. He saw no reason to be so timid about a doctrine that for him was absolutely central to Christian faith. "There has been much cry of late," he noted at the end of 1723, "against saying one word, particularly about the Trinity, but what the scripture has said; judging it is impossible but that if we did, we should err in a thing so much above us." The young theologian thought the real error was in failing to take seriously the implications of scriptural statements—a failure that under the cloak of scholarly caution extracted the guts from true religion. A determination to take those things seriously could empower reason to discover truths like the Trinity that would stand deism and other opponents of the Trinity on their heads. "But...I am not afraid to say twenty things about the Trinity which the scripture never said. There may be deductions of reason from what has been said of the most mysterious matters, besides what has been said, and safe and certain deductions too, as well as about the most obvious and easy matters. I think that it is within the reach of naked reason to perceive certainly that there are three distinct in God."[18]

Of course, Edwards's "naked reason" was already informed by the Bible's God, as Robert Jenson has observed. Nevertheless, he thought the anti-Trinitarians of his day shared enough cultural assumptions with the orthodox to be convinced by arguments from reason. Edwards made two such arguments, one based on goodness and the other on consent. In the first, he proposed that "there must be more than a unity in infinite and eternal essence" because "otherwise the goodness of God can have no perfect exercise." God is infinitely happy and is inclined to "communicate *all* his happiness," but he cannot "communicate all his goodness to a finite being." Since God "must

---

17. Hubert Stogdon, *Seasonable Advice Relating to the Present Disputes about the Holy Trinity* (London: Bible and Crown in the Poultry, 1719); Isaac Watts, *The Christian Doctrine of the Trinity* (London: Clark, Mathews, & Ford, 1722).

18. WJE 13:256–57.

have a perfect exercise of his goodness," he therefore "must have the fellowship of a person equal with himself."[19] The procession of a third perfect person from that fellowship follows deductively.

Edwards's second argument from reason was based on consent, which he had argued previously was the basis of excellency or beauty. He proposed that "one alone, without any reference to any more, cannot be excellent; for in such a case there can be no manner of relation no way [sic], and therefore, no such thing as consent." Since "I cannot doubt but that God loves infinitely," and that there must therefore "have been an object from all eternity which God infinitely loves," Edwards concluded that "that object which God infinitely loves must be infinitely and perfectly consenting and agreeable to him." Since "one alone cannot be excellent," and we know that God is excellent, therefore "there must be a plurality in God." Based on these two notions of goodness and consent, Edwards reasoned that plurality in God is more reasonable than undifferentiated unity.[20]

For deists and others who were impressed by truth in Greco-Roman philosophy and world religions, Edwards turned to the *prisca theologia* (ch. 36) to show that "hints and shadows" of the Trinity could be found in non-Christian systems. He recorded Chevalier Ramsay's paraphrase of the "Tonchu" [*Tao Te Ching*] passage: "The source and root of all is one. This self-existent unity produces necessarily a second; the first and second by their union produce a third; in fine, these three produce all."[21] He also recorded claims that a trinity could be found in Plato, Parmenides, and the "Gods of the Malabarian trinity in *India*."[22]

Probably for the sake of reinforcing the beliefs of his orthodox readers and hearers, Edwards turned to typology, as well. In his *Discourse on the Trinity*, he reiterated his conviction that "the whole visible creation, which is but the shadow of being, is so made and ordered by God as to typify and represent spiritual things." The sun, for example, is one of nature's "two eminent images." Its "substance" represents the Father, and the "brightness and glory of the disk of the sun" stands for the Son. The Spirit can be seen in "the internal heat of the sun" and "emitted beams" of the sun. The "various sorts of rays

---

19. Robert W. Jenson, *America's Theologian: A Recommendation of Jonathan Edwards* (New York: Oxford University Press, 1988), 96; WJE 13:263–64.

20. WJE 6:337; WJE 13:283–84.

21. WJE 23:98. The passage Ramsay paraphrased is number 42 in the *Tao Te Ching*: "The Way produces one; one produces two, two produces three, three produce all beings." *Tao Te Ching*, in *The Essential Tao*, ed. Thomas Cleary (San Francisco: HarperSanFrancisco, 1991), 35.

22. WJE 23:468, 546, 567; WJE 20:227–28; WJE 23:562.

of the sun and their beautiful colors" represent the "beautiful graces and virtues of the Spirit." The second great Trinitarian image in nature is the human mind, with its understanding or idea (the Son) and its will or affection (the Spirit). Less significant but almost as memorable is Edwards's reflection on why olive oil "was the great type of the Holy Ghost." He wrote that it is because olive oil is "soft and smooth-flowing" and therefore an appropriate sign of both peace (thus olive branches as a token of peace) and love.[23]

Yet Edwards recognized that reason and typology can never "give a full explication of the Trinity, for I think it still remains an incomprehensible mystery, the greatest and the most glorious of all mysteries." After explaining how he resolved a number of problems in the doctrine, he said he knew there were "a hundred other objections" that could be made, and "puzzling doubts and questions raised, that I can't solve." And, perhaps for the sake of deists who objected to mystery in principle, he told a story of a thirteen-year-old boy in his parish who had come to his home. Edwards asked the boy if he believed that a two-inch cube was eight times as big as a one-inch cube.

When the boy replied that it seemed impossible, Edwards marched him out to his workshop and carefully cut out a two-by-two-by-two-inch block of wood. Then, to the boy's amazement, he cut the block into eight pieces, each measuring one inch on a side. But even then, the boy was not convinced. He continued to count the blocks, comparing them to another cube two inches on a side. The boy could not bring himself to believe it, and wondered if magic had been at work.

Edwards concluded with satisfaction that the puzzle in this block of wood was a greater mystery to the boy "than the Trinity ordinarily is to men." Its apparent contradiction (a two-inch cube being eight times as large as a one-inch cube) was a greater difficulty than "any mystery of religion to a Socinian or Deist"—clear evidence that if the Trinity contains mystery, so does the nature prized by anti-Trinitarians. Therefore, he suggested, they should not dismiss the Trinity on the grounds that it does not fit their idea of what is reasonable.[24]

Trinitarian Issues

In the western tradition of Trinitarian theology, the roles assigned to the divine persons had been regarded as somewhat arbitrary. According to Jenson, it was thought "appropriate" that the Son became incarnate, "but it *could* have been the Father or the Spirit." Edwards insisted the economic order of acting was not

---

23. WJE21:138–39, 127; WJE 18:239.
24. The story and comments on it are in WJE 13:192–93.

"merely arbitrary" but according to "natural decency or fitness." For the Father is first and the other two Persons "naturally originated from him and [are] dependent on him" (ch. 43, final section). The order is "fit, suitable and beautiful."[25]

For proof that the Trinitarian order is not arbitrary, Edwards argued that it existed prior to the work of redemption. In his delineation of the "economy of the Trinity" and its relation to the covenant of redemption, Edwards wrote that the Father has always been first in the order of subsistence and "head of the whole family." Therefore he is "higher in authority" than the other persons. Their offices derive from him, so that he is God "in some peculiar sense that the other persons of the Trinity are not." So if the Trinitarian order was fitting before the redemption, it was also fitting during the work of redemption—if not more so. For it was the Father's justice that had to be satisfied, not the Son's. The Son's "being and essence" had to be satisfied, but not his office. The Father was injured, and he was the one to determine who should be redeemed. The Father, not the Son, is the ultimate "Lawgiver"—the Son is Lawgiver only in the Father's name. Christ is now supreme and exercises lordship and dominion, but only as the Father's representative. "So prayer is to be directed to [the Son] secondarily as the Father's representative."[26]

After the redemption is completed, "the Redeemer...shall resign up that dominion" and the "original economical order" shall "become more visible." The Father shall be once more "the King of heaven and earth, Lawgiver and Judge of all," and the Son's "vicarious dominion" will come to an end.[27] We shall see more discussion of this in our chapters on Christology and the covenants (chs. 16, 21), but suffice it to say here that the economy of redemption illustrates both the "subordination" of the persons of the Trinity (the Son and Spirit both to the Father, and the Spirit to the Son) and also the "natural decency or fitness in that order and economy that is established." All the persons of the Trinity "consent to this order" and delight in it because it is "suitable and beautiful." For the order of subordination was "prior to the covenant of redemption," but the particular means of satisfying the Father's justice was determined by "wisdom." The covenant of redemption was a joint agreement among all three persons but a covenant only between the Father and the Son. The Spirit was the "internal spring" of what the other two persons agreed on, and the "moving cause" of their transaction.[28]

---

25. Jenson, *America's Theologian*, 95; WJE 20:431.

26. WJE 25:147, 148, 150, 151, 149; WJE 21:143.

27. WJE 20:434, 439.

28. WJE 20:430–31, 442–43.

Edwards provided resources for what could play something of a mediating role in the *filioque* debate between East and West. This controversy began when the Western church added *filioque* ("and from the Son") to the Nicene Creed (in 589 C.E. and then again in 1017 C.E.), asserting that the Spirit proceeds not only from the Father but also from the Son. The Eastern church protested not only that this was a politically imperialistic act (since the West acted unilaterally, ignoring protests from the East) but also that it subordinated the Spirit to the Son and so detracted from the harmony of the Trinity.

Edwards no doubt recognized that there are biblical grounds for *filioque*. It was Christ who poured out the Spirit upon the Church (Acts 2:33), and Christ said in John 15:26 that he would send the Spirit. But the same verse says that while Jesus would send (Greek, *pempsō*) the Spirit from the Father, the Spirit of truth proceeds (*ekporeuetai*) from the Father. Edwards tried to do justice to both statements by saying that while the Spirit "proceeds both from the Father and the Son," that procession is "from the Father originally and primarily, and from the Son as it were secondarily." Hence the Eastern Fathers' basic instinct was correct. Yet the Spirit proceeds from the Father "mediately by the Son" but from the Son "immediately." So "the Son hath this honor that the Father hath not: that that Spirit is from the Son immediately by himself." In contrast, the Father sends the Spirit only "by his beholding himself in the Son." Thus we see the appropriateness of the Western *filioque*.[29]

Finally, as Lee has observed, it is a "hallmark" of Edwards's Trinitarianism that there is no final disjunction between the immanent and economic Trinity. The inner life of God (*ad intra*) is replicated in and known through God's Trinitarian work for his creatures (*ad extra*). Early in the *Miscellanies*, Edwards wrote that just as God is glorified within himself by appearing to himself in his Son and delighting in that appearance, so too he glorifies himself "towards the creatures" by appearing to their understandings and communicating to them his own delight. Thus the reality of God's Trinitarian life *ad intra* is known through and replicated in his Trinitarian work *ad extra*. At the end of his *Discourse on the Trinity*, Edwards wrote, "What I have here supposed concerning the Trinity is exceedingly analogous to the gospel scheme, and agreeable to the whole New Testament." Lee believes that Edwards applied his vision of the Trinity to time and space "more rigorously than his predecessors in the Western church."[30]

Thus for Edwards the Trinity was anything but rarified abstraction. It was a doctrine not for mere speculation but for the enjoyment and enrichment of

---

29. WJE 21:143. See also WJE 25:150.

30. WJE 13:495; WJE 21:31, 134, 33.

God's people in the church. "Such doctrines as those of the Trinity... are glorious inlets into the knowledge and view of the spiritual world, and the contemplation of supreme things." He said he himself had "experienced how much [such a doctrine] contributes to the betterment of the heart." They showed him that we are dependent "on each person in the Trinity for all our good." We are dependent on Christ the Son of God to be our "wisdom, righteousness, sanctification, and redemption," on the Father for making Christ these things to us, and on the Spirit for giving us the faith in Christ that attaches us to Christ. That union is what brings the church into the divine family. The "persons of the Trinity" are "the natural members of the family" (of which the Father is the head and the Son is the "eldest brother of all the children"). The church is the "adopted child" in the family. This new child becomes a "partaker of the divine nature" by having the Spirit, who is the love and joy between the Father and the Son. For Edwards, then, true love and joy in the experience of ordinary believers are participation in the life of the Trinity.[31]

---

31. WJE 13:328; WJE 17:201; WJE 25:148; WJE 17:208; WJE 21:129.

14

The End of God in Creation

THE *WESTMINSTER SHORTER Catechism* opens with a question and answer: "What is the chief end of man? Man's chief end is to glorify God, and to enjoy him forever."[1] Edwards's *End of Creation* gave a complex elaboration of this simple statement regarding God's glory and human happiness. Thus it might seem to be a traditional Calvinistic treatise—and so it is, in certain respects. Yet it is also highly innovative. The philosopher I. Woodbridge Riley referred to it as "Edwards's most boldly speculative work."[2] Edwards's striking analogies in *End of Creation*—comparing God to a flowing fountain and blossoming tree—as well as his use of the word "emanation" to describe God's act in creating led to mistaken charges of pantheism against Edwards.[3] As much as any other writing, *End of Creation* illustrated Edwards's unique combination of tradition and innovation in theological reasoning.

Scholars speak of the "ultimate 'why' question," that is, the question as to why anything should exist at all. Ludwig Wittgenstein exclaimed, "How marvelous it is that anything should exist at all." Aristotle wrote that philosophy begins in wonder.[4] Edwards too shared in metaphysical amazement at the sheer fact of existence. In his early *Miscellanies*, he wrote that the world delights

---

1. Philip Schaff, *The Creeds of Christendom*. 3 vols. (New York: Harper, 1931), 3:676.

2. I. Woodbridge Riley, *American Philosophy: The Early Schools* (New York; Dodd, Mead, and Co, 1907), 179.

3. On Edwards as "pantheist," see Riley, *American Philosophy*, 126; Arthur C. McGiffert [Sr.], *Protestant Thought Before Kant* (New York: Scribners 1951), 178, n.1; and Rem B. Edwards, *A Return to Moral and Religious Philosophy in Early America* (Washington, DC: University Press of America, 1982), 65.

4. Ludwig Wittgenstein, quoted in Peter C. John, "Wittgenstein's 'Wonderful Life,'" *Journal of the History of Ideas* 49 (1988): 495–510, citing 495. Martin Heidegger, *An Introduction to Metaphysics*; New Haven: Yale University Press, 1959), 20; quoted in Paul Edwards, "Why," in Paul Edwards, ed., *The Encyclopedia of Philosophy*, 8 vols. (New York: Macmillan/London: Collier Macmillan, 1967), 8:296–302, citing 296. "For it is owing to their wonder that men both now begin and at first began to philosophize" (Aristotle, *Metaphysics*, trans. W. D. Ross; Oxford, UK: Clarendon Press, 1966; 982b).

in its own existence: "The creation had as good not be, as not rejoice in its being. For certainly it was the goodness of the Creator that moved him to create."[5] Existence itself, for Edwards, was a source of wonderment.

Yet the issue of being led to the question of goodness. When one answered the question, "what exists?" one was forced to inquire further, "what is good and what end or ends are worth choosing?" Metaphysics tied into ethics. The creation of the world, surprisingly, was an ethical issue. It was a matter of right or wrong choice—in this case, God's choice. Within Edwards's corpus, the most important text on ethics was the posthumously published *Two Dissertations* (1765), comprising *End of Creation* and *True Virtue*. Taken side by side, these two treatises argued that the love of God was the necessary context for all truly moral actions, and that morality found its proper and sole fulfillment in authentic religion. *True Virtue* approached the issue of moral choice from the standpoint of human beings, who must choose God as their supreme end if their actions are to be truly moral. *End of Creation* approached the issue of moral choice from the standpoint of God himself, who had to make himself his own supreme end in choosing and acting so that his own choices and actions might be truly moral—in sync, one might say, with the nature of reality.

Scholars have lavished praise on Edwards's *End of Creation*. A century ago, Arthur Cushman McGiffert called the essay "one of the most significant and prophetic in the whole range of modern theological literature." In the 1940s, biographer Ola Winslow commented that "the whole of his intellectual history is epitomized in these hundred pages," while Perry Miller found that it exhibited "Edwards at his very greatest." Sydney Ahlstrom spoke of a "genuine mysticism" in *End of Creation* and saw the text as typifying Edwards: "Here is the true center of Edwards's rational account of the Christian religion, around which his earliest thoughts revolved and around which all his sermons, polemics, and treatises must be grouped. It defines the lines of force according to which his other writings arrange themselves." John Piper said that "if one book captures the essence or wellspring of Edwards's theology it is this." George Marsden wrote that "this theological and Scriptural prolegomenon is essential for understanding how Edwards positioned himself in relation to the prevailing philosophies of the era."[6] Yet strangely, *End of Creation* has not

---

5. WJE 13:199.

6. Arthur Cushman McGiffert [Sr.], *Protestant Thought Before Kant* (New York: Scribner's, 1951 [1911]), 182; Ola Winslow, *Jonathan Edwards 1703–1758: A Biography* (New York: Farrar, Straus and Giroux, 1940), 310–12; Perry Miller, *Jonathan Edwards* (New York: William Sloane, 1949), 285; Sydney Ahlstrom, *A Religious History of the American People* (New Haven: Yale University Press, 1972), 309–10; John Piper, "A Personal Encounter with Jonathan Edwards," *Reformed Journal* 28 (1978) 14; and George M. Marsden, *Jonathan Edwards: A Life* (New Haven: Yale University Press, 2003), 460.

attracted much interest in the secondary literature on Edwards. Little has been published specifically on this treatise, with the exception of a few articles and a reprinted version of the text together with a popular introduction.[7] One factor that may have deterred some interpreters is the treatise's intricate and dense style. Karl Dietrich Pfisterer compared it to a "mathematical formula" so concise that it yielded "expected and unexpected deductions."[8]

This chapter will begin with a brief unpacking of the complex argument of *End of Creation*. Next we will turn to three interpretive contexts for understanding the treatise. The first is the eighteenth-century Enlightenment context and Edwards's ethicizing of God. The second lies in the medieval and modern Catholic discussions of God's end in creating the world—a little-known yet valuable backdrop. The third is what Kyoung-Chul Jang called the "logic of glorification"—Edwards's account of the saints' participatory, affective, corporate, and progressive attainment of glorification through their relationship with the triune God.

As *End of Creation* shows, God's act of creating can become more puzzling the more one ponders it. The seventeenth-century English writer John Norris—whose writings Edwards read—encapsulated the dilemma in poetry:

> In himself compendiously blest, ...
> Is one unmov'd self-center'd Point of Rest,
> Why, then, if full of bliss that ne'er could cloy,
> Would he do ought but still enjoy?
> Why not indulge his self-sufficing state,
> Live to himself at large, calm and secure,
> A wise eternal Epicure?[9]

---

7. On *End of Creation* generally, see William C. Wisner, "The End of God in Creation," *American Biblical Repository*, 3rd series 6 (1850): 430–56; George S. Hendry, "The Glory of God and the Future of Man," *Reformed World* 34 (1976): 147–57; Michael J. McClymond, "Creation in Jonathan Edwards," PhD diss., University of Chicago, 1991, 175–79, 203–99; McClymond, "Sinners in the Hands of a Virtuous God: Ethics and Divinity in Jonathan Edwards's End of Creation," *Zeitschrift für neuere Theologiegeschichte/Journal for the History of Modern Theology* 2 (1995): 1–22; McClymond, *Encounters With God: An Approach to the Theology of Jonathan Edwards* (New York: Oxford University Press, 1998), 50–64; and John Piper, *God's Passion for His Glory: Living the Vision of Jonathan Edwards, with the Complete Text of The End for Which God Created the World* (Wheaton, IL: Crossway Books, 1998).

8. Karl Dietrich Pfisterer, *The Prism of Scripture: Studies in History and Historicity in the Work of Jonathan Edwards* (Frankfurt, Germany: Peter Lang, 1975), 237.

9. John Norris, *A Divine Hymn on the Creation* (1706), quoted in Arthur O. Lovejoy, *The Great Chain of Being: A Study of the History of an Idea* (Cambridge, MA: Harvard University Press, 1933), 159–60. Lovejoy speaks of a dilemma of "Two-Gods-in-One" whereby "the concept of a Self-Sufficing Perfection, by a bold logical inversion, was ... converted into the concept of a Self-Transcending Fecundity" (43–44, 49–50).

The poem suggests various questions. If God were eternally complete and self-sufficient in himself, why would God create a world at all? On the other hand, if God were not complete and self-sufficient, would this not impugn the perfection of God? Some have called this the "full bucket paradox." If the "bucket" of divine glory was already brimful prior to God's creating the world, what—if anything—would the creation of the universe contribute to God? Yet if creating the world added nothing to God's glory, why would God have chosen to create? A further issue relates to God's freedom. Did God have a motive or reason for creating? If not, would the world be anything but a cosmic accident? On the other hand, did God have an option of not creating a world at all? If not, how could the creating of the world be a free action expressing God's grace and goodness? As we will see in this chapter, these are the sorts of questions that underlie the argument of *End of Creation*.

An Analysis of End of Creation

End of Creation appeared posthumously in 1765 along with *True Virtue* as the first of what was intended as a two-part work. The decision of Edwards's literary heirs—especially Samuel Hopkins—to publish the two treatises together suggests that Edwards himself had intended them to be read and understood together. What is more, there is internal evidence to demonstrate the connection. *True Virtue* twice refers to *End of Creation* as "the former treatise" and "the preceding discourse." Since *End of Creation* never refers explicitly to *True Virtue*, the relationship between the two is asymmetrical, or rather sequential, and Paul Ramsey explains that Edwards "intended *End of Creation* to be read first, and presupposed its argument and conclusion in all that he says in *True Virtue*."[10] One conceptual link between the two treatises lies in what might be called a principle of proportionate regard. In a number of key passages, Edwards asserts: "For 'tis fit that the regard of the Creator should be proportioned to the worthiness of objects, as well as the regard of creatures." Other passages articulate the same idea. God's "moral rectitude...consists in his having infinitely the highest regard to that which is in itself highest and best." Again Edwards writes that "his love to himself...implies a love to whatever is worthy or excellent."[11] One of the *Miscellanies* declares that "the excellency of God's nature appears in that, that he loves and seeks whatever is in itself excellent."[12]

---

10. Paul Ramsey, "Editor's Introduction," in WJE 8:7; and Ramsey in WJE 8:552 n.3.

11. WJE 8:424, 421, 460. See also WJE 8:422–23, 424, 426, 548–49, 553, 571; and WJE 6:356, 362, 381.

12. WJE 18:282.

God, no less than human beings, is under a kind of ethical constraint to take into account the inherent worth of each entity. This principle of proportionate regard is foundational for the entire argument of *End of Creation* since it gives Edwards a basis for what might otherwise seem like empty speculation concerning God's intentions in creating. Edwards's ethics are thus based on his ontology. He identifies God as "Being in general" and the highest ethical principle as "benevolence to Being in general." The recurring terms "worth," "worthy," "worthiness," "value," "fit," and "fitness" show that moral agency rests on inherent values. Like Augustine and Thomas Aquinas, Edwards believed that ethics were a matter of rightly-ordered love or charity. Right responses depend on the nature of the entities that one encounters. The principle of proportionate regard requires a calculus of values, whereby the worthiness of any object is reckoned as the mathematical product of its "degree of existence" times its "degree of excellence."[13] The principle of proportionate regard forms the backbone of *End of Creation*.[14] The general thesis—that God creates the world for his own sake—is a specific deduction or application of the principle. Because God in acting must have highest regard for what is most worthy, it follows that God created the world for his own sake. Furthermore, proportionate regard underlies *True Virtue* no less than *End of Creation*. Just as God in creating is bound to give highest regard to what is highest in "worth," so it is with creatures, who are morally bound to the principle of "benevolence to Being in general." The two treatises are like mirror images: *End of Creation* applies the principle of proportionate regard to God and God's actions, while *True Virtue* applies it to creatures and creatures' actions.

Following a brief introduction with an "explanation of terms," *End of Creation* divides into two chapters that are further subdivided. The first chapter treats "What Reason Teaches Concerning This Affair," while the second chapter considers "What is to Be Learned from Holy Scriptures." Edwards assumes that both God and human beings are goal-directed. The question is not whether God and human beings pursue an end, but rather, what end they pursue. He proceeds to differentiate various kinds of ends, classified according

---

13. What I call here a calculus of values is mentioned often, though never fully elaborated by Edwards. See WJE 8:422–23, 548–49, 571; and WJE 6:356, 362, 382.

14. Thomas Aquinas argued that "God loves all existing things" and that "the better things are more loved by God"—an anticipation of Edwards's later statements. See *Summa Theologica*, 1a, q.20, a.2, 4. Oliver O'Donovan commented that "the form of the moral life is that of an *ordered moral field* of action on the one hand, and of an *ordered moral subject* of action on the other" (*Resurrection and Moral Order*; Leicester, UK: InterVarsity Press, 1986; 183).

to two sets of paired terms—"chief ends" versus "inferior ends," and "ultimate ends" versus "subordinate ends." The first pairing establishes a *hierarchy of valuation*. Ends are more valued ("chief ends") or less valued ("inferior ends"). The second pairing sets up a *sequence of subordination* by distinguishing ends sought for their own sake ("ultimate ends") from those sought for the sake of another end ("subordinate ends"). The distinction between "subordinate" and "ultimate" ends is pivotal for the argument of *End of Creation*. For Edwards sought to show that while God made himself an "ultimate end" in creating the world, human welfare was also an "ultimate end."[15]

Edwards had inherited a Calvinist tradition that made human welfare subordinate to God's self-glorification. In the "high Calvinism" of Theodore Beza (1519–1605), the salvation of the elect in heaven and the torment of the lost in hell both contributed to the eternal manifestation God's power and glory. Beza depicted the antithetical processes of salvation and damnation in a theological flowchart, branching off into sin-hardening-judgment-damnation on one side and sin-repentance-grace-salvation on the other.[16] A striking thing about this chart was its symmetry. It was not clear that salvation had priority over damnation within God's plan. Yet Edwards opposed such a conception in *End of Creation*. He quoted biblical texts to show that "punishing men's sin.... is spoken of [in scripture] as what God proceeds to with backwardness and reluctance, the misery of the creature being not agreeable to him on its own account." Among the biblical texts Edwards cited was: "For I have no pleasure in the death of him that dieth, saith the Lord God: wherefore turn yourselves, and live ye" (Ezek. 18:32; cf. Ezek. 33:11). He also quoted verses saying that God is "slow to anger" (Neh. 9:17; cf. Ps. 103:8, 145:8, Jon. 4:2), "doth not afflict willingly" (Lam. 3:33), and is "not willing that any should perish" (2 Pet. 3:9).[17] On the basis of these passages, Edwards affirmed that salvation had priority over damnation in the grand scheme. *End of Creation* itself said virtually nothing about hell.

If Edwards rejected the high Calvinistic approach to God's purpose for humanity, he also could not go along with the emerging Enlightenment tradition that made God subordinate to human welfare. God did not exist just to make people happy. Faced with these choices, Edwards sought and found an alternative. By identifying divine glory with human happiness, Edwards made the problem of subordination—viz., of determining which end is more

---

15. WJE 8:405–8.

16. Heinrich Heppe, ed., *Reformed Dogmatics: Set Out and Illustrated from the Sources* (Grand Rapids, MI: Eerdmans, 1978), 147.

17. WJE 8:503–504. Cf. WJE 8:506–508, n.6.

"ultimate" than the other—disappear. God's glory *is* humanity's happiness, and vice versa, as he writes: "Nor ought God's glory and the creature's good to be spoken of as if they were properly and entirely distinct.... God in seeking his glory, therein seeks the good of his creatures."[18] The *Miscellanies* shed light on the development of Edwards's thought. He seems to have passed through three stages. In the initial phase, Edwards maintained the view—surprising in light of the later *End of Creation*—that human happiness per se was God's ultimate end in creating. He reasoned that a perfect Creator would not derive anything such as happiness from creatures. During an intermediate phase, he held that human happiness and divine glory were both "ultimate ends" of God in creating, but that they stood in independence of one another. Then, in the final phase, expressed in *End of Creation*, Edwards merged human happiness and divine glory under the rubric of God's "communication"—a term that referred to the flowing forth of God's glory, grace, and happiness and the creature's receiving of this glory, grace, and happiness.[19]

Edwards used bold imagery to describe the process of creation, comparing God to an overflowing "fountain" of water and to a shining "light." Perhaps the most startling image of all was the comparison of God to a tree growing outward into buds, leaves, and fruits.[20] Aware that the reader might interpret the language of fountain, light, and tree as implying a blindly necessitated or even pantheistic deity, Edwards carefully qualified his language: "Such an emanation of good is, in some sense, a multiplication of it," and "so far as the communication or external stream may be looked upon as anything besides the fountain, so far may it be looked on as an increase of good." The verbal qualifications here—"in some sense," "so far as"—glossed over the critical question of whether the "emanation" did or did not represent an increase in the divine goodness.[21]

Edwards in a sense sought to have his cake and eat it, too—that is, to have an "emanation" that did and did not increase the reservoir of divine glory and goodness. A paradox arose because Edwards placed *equal stress* on God's

---

18. WJE 8:458–59.

19. The three stages in Edwards's thinking on God's "end of creation" are marked by Miscellany 3, 243, and 332 (WJE 13:199–200, 358–59, 410). The first phase was in 1723, with phases two and three in 1727–28 (according to Schafer's system of dating, WJE 13:91–109).

20. WJE 8:433, 435.

21. WJE 8:433. Rufus Orlando Suter noted that Edwards used qualifying phrases ("as it were" was one of his most frequent) whenever he wished to downplay the appearance of monistic teaching. See Suter, "A Note on Platonism in the Philosophy of Jonathan Edwards," *Harvard Theological Review* 52 (1959): 283–84.

self-sufficiency and on God's self-diffusiveness. On the one hand, he wrote that "God is infinitely, eternally, unchangeably, and independently glorious and happy."[22] On the other hand, he asserted that "a disposition in God, as an original property of his nature, to an emanation of his own infinite fullness, was what excited him to create the world; and so that the emanation itself was aimed at by him as a last end of the creation."[23] If one emphasized the first statement, it seemed that God did not need the world and there was really no motive for God to act. Such an approach did not offer a sufficient basis for understanding God's creating. If one emphasized the second statement there was a clear motivation and reason for God to create a world. The world manifested and enlarged God's glory. Yet this increase of God's glory seemed to compromise Edwards's first statement that God is "infinitely...and independently glorious." In such a case, God's original glory was not strictly "infinite" since it could and did increase through the creating of the world. Neither was God's glory "independent" since the existence of the world enhanced God's glory. In seeking to resolve this possibly irresolvable dilemma, Edwards came close to making creation a transaction within God, so that the increase of glory was internal rather than external to God.

Edwards's Enlightened and Ethical God

In his discussion of ten "clearer statements" of theological truth from the writings of his father, Jonathan Edwards Jr. placed the argument of *End of Creation* first within his list. With respect to "the happiness of creatures' themselves" and "the declarative glory of the Creator" as rival ends of creation, the son wrote that his father was "the first, who clearly showed that they are really only one end, and that they are really one and the same thing."[24] During the late 1700s, Jonathan Edwards Jr. and other disciples of Edwards sought to maintain a Calvinistic faith against the incursions of Enlightenment humanism and anthropocentrism (ch. 37). They found the argument of *End of Creation* to be extraordinarily helpful since it affirmed God's ultimate preeminence and sovereignty and yet assigned ultimate, cosmic significance to human happiness as well. It strengthened them in believing that Calvinist theology was not a barbarous relic from a bygone age, but a theological view consistent with the best insights of an enlightened age.

---

22. WJE 8:420.

23. WJE 8:435, italicized in the original.

24. Jonathan Edwards Jr., quoted in Sereno E. Dwight, "Memoirs of Jonathan Edwards," in Edward Hickman, ed., *The Works of Jonathan Edwards*, 2 vols. (Carlisle, PA: The Banner of Truth Trust, 1984 [1834]), 1:cxcii; italicized in the original.

The backdrop to Edwards's *Two Dissertations* was the rise of British moral philosophy in the late 1600s and early 1700s as a discipline distinct from theology. Thomas Hobbes's *Leviathan* (1651) adopted an egoistic interpretation of human behavior and concluded that "right" and "wrong" were subjective terms that people applied to things that they either liked or disliked. Though Hobbes had few defenders in his day, his work raised the question as to whether morality had any necessary connection with God. Moreover, political events catalyzed a change in moral reflection. The English Civil War of the 1640s and the ensuing turbulence led many to believe that religious beliefs and doctrines were a prime cause of social unrest. Leading British intellectuals sought to establish a basis for social and ethical discussion independent of church dogmas. In political theory, the notion of the divine right of kings gave way to social contract theories.

By the late 1600s, a moralizing approach to Christianity was evident. John Locke, in *The Reasonableness of Christianity* (1695), asserted concerning Jesus and his disciples that "righteousness, or obedience to the law of God, was their great business." He added that "there is not, I think, any of the duties of morality which he [i.e., Jesus] has not...inculcated over and over again."[25] The Archbishop of Canterbury, John Tillotson, preached sermons that underscored this point—that Christianity upheld standards of good conduct.[26] According to the so-called "moral sense" hypothesis of Lord Shaftesbury and Francis Hutcheson, all persons—believer and nonbeliever alike—possessed an inherent tendency toward benevolence. For the moral sense theorists, it was appropriate to urge people to live according to their best instincts. Each person already possessed moral discernment and an innate capacity to lead an ethical life. By the early 1700s in New England, textbooks by Samuel Clarke, Lord Shaftesbury, and Francis Hutcheson were supplanting the older Puritan authors at Harvard and Yale Colleges. A complex process that John Murrin and Harry Stout termed "Anglicization" and Henry F. May called "the moderate Enlightenment," was softening the hard edges of the older Calvinism (ch. 3).

Edwards developed a complex response to the emerging moral philosophy that assimilated key elements of the new thought and yet preserved much of the

---

25. John Locke, *The Reasonableness of Christianity*, ed. I. T. Ramsey (Stanford, CA: Stanford University Press, 1958), 49.

26. See Louis Glenn Locke, Tillotson: A Study in Seventeenth Century Literature (Copenhagen: Rosenkilde and Bagger, 1954).

Puritan legacy. In his thorough analysis of British moral philosophy as a backdrop to Edwards, Norman Fiering found that Edwards's ethical thought was a reversal of the secularizing trend that was seeking gradually to transform theology into moral philosophy. Fiering explains: "Moral philosophers had begun the process of converting into secular and naturalistic terms crucial parts of the Christian heritage. Edwards in a sense reversed the ongoing process by assimilating the moral philosophy of his time and converting it back into the language of religious thought and experience."[27] Edwards rejected the optimistic moral sense theories of Shaftesbury and Hutcheson. In *Original Sin* he reaffirmed the Calvinistic doctrine of innate depravity. In *Freedom of the Will*, he argued that fallen and flawed human beings—based on "motives" arising from their character—consistently choose evil rather than good. In *True Virtue* Edwards took issue with writers who "don't wholly exclude a regard to the Deity out of their schemes of morality, but yet mention it so slightly, that they leave me room to suspect they esteem it...a subordinate part of true morality." He countered that "if true virtue consists partly in a respect to God, then doubtless it consists chiefly in it."[28] In agreement with other thinkers of his day, Edwards taught that genuine religion requires morality. This point was not controversial in Edwards's context. Yet in opposition to the tendency of his times, Edwards further insisted that genuine morality requires religion. The love of humanity was specious apart from the love of God.[29] This latter point required defense in the *Two Dissertations*.

In his analysis of *End of Creation*, Perry Miller commented on "the courageous—or, some may say, presumptuous—invasion of the Godhead by that pattern of reality Edwards has learned on earth. As far as language could go, he would say how and why God actually operates."[30] Throughout his

---

27. Norman Fiering, *Jonathan Edwards's Moral Thought and Its British Context* (Chapel Hill, NC: University of North Carolina Press, 1981), 60–61.

28. WJE 8:552–53. Francis Hutcheson, in *An Inquiry Concerning the Original of Our Ideas of Virtue or Moral Good* (1725), wrote, "Here again we might appeal to all mankind, whether there be no Benevolence but what flows from a View of Reward from the Deity? Nay, do we not see a great deal of it among those who entertain few if any Thoughts of Devotion at all?" (cited in L. A. Selby-Bigge, ed, *British Moralists, Being Selections from Writers Principally of the Eighteenth Century*, 2 vols., New York: Dover; 1:9.). In *An Essay on the Nature and Conduct of the Passions and Affections, With Illustrations on the Moral Sense* (1728), Hutcheson argued that "the bare absence of the idea of a Deity, or of affections to him, can evidence no evil" (cited in Bernard Peach, ed., *Illustrations on the Moral Sense*; Cambridge, MA: Belknap Press of Harvard University, 1971; 191).

29. On morality and religion in Edwards's thought, see William C. Spohn, "Sovereign Beauty: Jonathan Edwards and The Nature of True Virtue," *Theological Studies* 42 (1981): 394–421.

30. Miller, *Jonathan Edwards*, 301.

treatise, Edwards used human-divine analogies to understand God's actions. This feature becomes apparent in the opening, which speaks of a man who goes to get medicine or obtain honey that he wishes to eat—a down-home analogy for an elevated topic.[31] It seems that Edwards, in order to ethicize God, had to anthropomorphize God. A vindication of God as ethical required a portrayal of God as human-like or humane.

The God of *End of Creation* was not only human-like but resembled a certain kind of human being, namely, an enlightened monarch or well-bred gentleman. The wise ruler of Edwards's day was one who knew his place and his own dignity and yet cared for his people's welfare. Likewise the well-bred gentleman combined an appropriate self-regard or *amour-propre* with the principle of *noblesse oblige*—a concern for the public good. Such a gentleman exhibited both a heightened self-awareness and an awareness of others' needs—an ideal espoused by Edwards's aristocratic contemporary, Lord Shaftesbury.[32] In ancient times, Aristotle had proposed an analogous idea in his vignette of the "superior" or "great-souled man" in his *Nichomachean Ethics*.[33] In *End of Creation*, Edwards also embraced such an idea. He commented that "a truly great man"—a phrase reminiscent of Aristotle's "great-souled" man—would not be "much influenced in his conduct by a desire of popular applause." Such a person would never pander to the mob. Nonetheless it was "not beneath a man of greatest dignity and wisdom to value the wise and just esteem of others, however inferior to him." For anyone to disregard entirely the opinions of others, "instead of being an expression of greatness of mind, would show an haughty and mean spirit."[34] Here the idea of a "truly great man" served as an ethical standard, or at the least as an appropriate analogy, for God himself. The God of *End of Creation* resembled an enlightened despot of the eighteenth century in the sense that he possessed unlimited power and yet chose wisely to use it for the benefit of others.

---

31. WJE 8:405–406.

32. Lord Shaftesbury taught that good actions were engendered by good breeding: "A man of thorough good breeding, whatever else he be, is incapable of doing a rude or brutal action.... He acts from his nature, in a manner necessarily, and without reflection" (Anthony Ashley Cooper [Third Earl of Shaftesbury], *Characteristics of Men, Manners, Opinions, Times*, ed. Lawrence E. Klein, Cambridge Texts in the History of Philosophy; Cambridge, UK: Cambridge University Press, 1999; 60).

33. Aristotle, *The Ethics of Aristotle*, trans. J. A. K. Thomson (Harmondsworth, UK: Penguin, 1953), 121–22.

34. WJE 8:453, 457–58.

Roman Catholic Discussions of the End of Creation

In its genre, *End of Creation* showed stronger affinities to Roman Catholic than to Protestant discussions. Traditional Protestant theologians generally avoided discussions of the metaphysical subtleties of God's act in creating. Yet such was not the case with Roman Catholics, who from the medieval to the modern period made the "end" or "purpose" of creation a locus of theological discussion and debate.[35] Among Reformed Protestant theologians from the 1500s to the early 1700s, there seems to be no one who treated the "end of creation" in the elaborate way that Edwards did. Neither Petrus van Mastricht (Edwards's favorite) nor Francis Turretin, Johann Stapfer, William Ames, nor any of the other well-known theological writers in early New England treated this topic in depth. An analogue to *End of Creation* in the early modern period appears in the forty-page discussion of "the final end" (Latin, *De ultimo fine*) in a work by the Jesuit theologian Leonardus Lessius (1554–1623)—though there is no evidence that Edwards had encountered Lessius or any of the other Catholic authors on this theme. Among Protestant thinkers, *End of Creation* was a pioneering work and seems to have had little or no precedent as stand-alone treatise on God's end in creating the world.

Early Christian writers held that God created the world because of his goodness and for the sake of his glory. Athenagoras wrote: "It is clear that God, if the first and great reason is considered, was drawn to make man for His own sake and for the sake of the goodness and wisdom which shine forth in all of His works." Irenaeus said: "It was not therefore as if He was in need of man that God created Adam but that he might have someone on whom to bestow His benefits." Hilary of Poitiers reasoned: "God made man not because He needed his service in anything but because He is good; He made a

---

35. For Catholic discussion, see the following sources, listed chronologically: Leonardus Lessius, "*De ultimo fine*," in *De perfectionibus et moribusque divinis*, ed. P. Roh (Freiburg, Germany: Brisgoviae Sumptibus Herder, 1841 [1620], 511–50; Johann Stufler, "Die Lehre des hl. Thomas von Aquin über den Endzweck des Schöpfers und der Schöpfung," *Zeitschrift für Katholische Theologie* 41 (1917): 657–700; H. Pinard, "Creation," in *Dictionnaire de theologie catholique*, ed. A. Vacant, et al. (Paris: 1909–1950), 3:2034–201 (2163–73 on God's end in creating); Philip J. Donnelly, "Saint Thomas on the Ultimate Purpose of Creation," *Theological Studies* 2 (1941): 53–83 and "The Doctrine of the Vatican Council on the End of Creation," *Theological Studies* 4 (1943): 3–33; Johannes Brinktrine, *Die Lehre von der Schöpfung* (Paderborn: Verlag Ferdinand Schöningh, 1956), esp. 49–55, "Gott die Zweckursache aller Dinge"; Donald J. Ehr, *The Purpose of the Creator and of Creatures According to John of St. Thomas* (Techny, IL: Divine Word Publications, 1961), with a summary in Ehr's essay "Glory of God (End of Creation)," in *New Catholic Encyclopedia* (New York: Macmillan, 1967), s.v.; and Robert Butterworth, *The Theology of Creation* (Notre Dame, IN: Fides, 1969).

rational animal the sharer of His beatitude." Last but not least, Augustine wrote that "it is enough for the Christian to believe that the cause of the creation of all things was nothing but the goodness of the Creator."[36]

Medieval theologians expatiated further on the topic of God's end in creating. The treatment of creation by Thomas Aquinas in his *Summa Contra Gentiles* and *Summa Theologica* was influential and affords an instructive parallel to Edwards's discussion. Like Edwards, Thomas assumed that "every agent acts for an end."[37] Thomas further developed an idea of subordination among ends so that "in every ordered series of ends the ultimate end must be the end of all preceding ends." He applied this principle theologically by asserting that God "is more the end of everything than is any proximate end." Thomas went on to say that "God is the common good, since the good of all things taken together depends on Him."[38] Though Edwards did not use identical vocabulary, Thomas's assertion regarding God as the "common good" anticipated Edwards's assertion that God's "regard to self-interest" may not "properly be set in opposition to the public welfare" since God is "the fountain of being and good to the whole."[39] In effect, God functioned as the highest genus of good. For Thomas, as for Edwards, God's action toward creatures was grounded in God's self-regard. He stated that God "wills the multitude of things in willing and loving His own essence and perfection."[40] Thomas's adherence to the Neoplatonic axiom *omne bonum diffusivum sui* ("every good is diffusive of itself") implied that creation was an overflow of the divine goodness.

When Thomas connected the various elements of his position on God's agency in creating, the final result was a position that was much like Edwards's, as shown in the following passage:

> Every agent acts for an end.... But it does not pertain to the First Agent, Who is agent only, to act for the acquisition of some end; He purposes only to communicate His perfection, which is His goodness, while every other creature endeavors to acquire its own perfection, which is

---

36. Athenagoras, *De resurrect.*, 12; Irenaeus, *Adv. Haer*, 4.14; Hilary, In *Ps. 2; n. 15*; Augustine, *Enchr.* 9 (cf. Augustine, *De Civ. Dei*, 11.22–23); all citations are from Thomas B. Chetwood, *God and Creation* (New York: Benzinger, 1928), 123–26.

37. Thomas Aquinas, *Summa Contra Gentiles*, trans. Vernon Bourke (Notre Dame, IN: University of Notre Dame, 1975), III.2, "How Every Agent Acts for an End." Cf. Thomas Aquinas, *Summa Theologica*,, 1a2ae, q.1, a.2.

38. Thomas Aquinas, *Summa Contra Gentiles*, Bk. III, Ch. 17.

39. WJE 8:451–52.

40. Thomas Aquinas, *Summa Contra Gentiles*, Bk. I, Ch. 75.

the likeness of the divine perfection and goodness. Therefore the divine goodness is the end of all things.[41]

One notes that Thomas used the word "communicate" in a way that was reminiscent of Edwards's *End of Creation*. Thomas refused to apply the category of causality to God in the same way as the category was applied to creatures. God's "end" in acting was nothing other than himself, since there was no good outside of God that God—properly speaking—might discover in or receive from creatures. As Jacques Maritain said: "God is not subject to the causality of an end. He is Himself the end."[42] Thomas's argument that God was his own end served to safeguard God's self-sufficiency—a concern that the medieval scholastics shared with Jonathan Edwards. God communicated goodness to creatures yet did not receive goodness from them. Furthermore, this communication of goodness implied a process of assimilation on the part of the creature. Thomas wrote that "the ultimate end of [created] things is to become like God" and "all things exist in order to attain to the divine likeness."[43] Edwards echoed this idea in writing that "it was God's intention... that his works should exhibit an image of himself their author, that it might brightly appear by his works what manner of being he is, and afford a proper representation of his divine excellencies."[44]

A debate among Catholic thinkers over God's end in creating brought a division into two camps. One side stressed God's self-sufficiency, and the other God's self-communication and overflowing love. Leonardus Lessius during the early 1600s had asserted that the ultimate end of God's creative will consisted in "the extrinsic glory of God." Philip Donnelly, following Cardinal Billot and Johann Stufler, argued that Lessius's position compromised God's infinite perfection by placing the final basis for creation outside of God. In other words, Lessius had undermined the all-important affirmation that God is the "end" of his own action in creating. "The *finis operantis* [end of acting] of God's creating," wrote Donnelly "cannot possibly be finite or in any way really distinct from God." Instead it was God's "intrinsic glory" that served as the ultimate end of creation. Donnelly judged that Thomas Aquinas and

---

41. Thomas Aquinas, *Summa Theologica*, 1a, q.44, a.4. cf. Thomas Aquinas, *Summa Contra Gentiles*, Bk. III, Ch. 18, "How God is the End of All Things."

42. Jacques Maritain, *A Preface to Metaphysics: Seven Lectures on Being* (New York: Sheed and Ward, 1939), 128.

43. Thomas Aquinas, *Summa Contra Gentiles*, Bk. III, Ch. 19.

44. WJE 8:422.

Francisco Suarez both supported this view, while Lessius was guilty of "logical inconsistency" though not of "theological error."[45] The declaration of the Vatican I Council (1869–70) on God's purpose in creating seemed to support Donnelly. God created the world of his goodness to manifest his perfection, not to increase his own beatitude.[46] Of course this argument avoided one theological difficulty only to fall into another. For if God were only concerned with his own intrinsic glory, and this glory were already perfect, then why would God create at all? Earlier we referred to this as the so-called full bucket paradox.

Twentieth-century Catholic discussions of God's end in creating thus closely paralleled the pattern of *End of Creation*. Yet one cannot claim Edwards for either side in the Catholic debate. Some passages in *End of Creation* appear to make the "emanation" of goodness beyond God the basis for creation: "The emanation itself was aimed at by him as a last end of the creation." Other passages assert clearly that God's own self, or an "original property" or "disposition" toward "emanation," was the basis for creation. Generally Edwards sought to overcome the distinction between God's "intrinsic glory" and "extrinsic glory."[47] By merging these two into one, Edwards sidestepped the dilemma posed in modern Catholic discussions. Nonetheless, Edwards could be charged with blurring the Creator-creature distinction and turning creation into an event occurring *within* the Godhead. Notwithstanding Edwards's explicit assertions of God's transcendence vis-à-vis creation, some passages in *End of Creation* seemed to soften the Creator-creature distinction and so raised a question as to the consistency of Edwards's argumentation.

The Logic of Glorification

End of Creation concluded with a stunning depiction of the saints' everlasting advancement into glory. The glorification of the saints followed from God's primordial decision to glorify himself. Though *End of Creation* did not include

---

45. Donnelly, "Saint Thomas on the Ultimate Purpose," 555–56. cf. Stufler, "Lehre," 698–99.

46. The key portion of the Vatican I statement reads: "*Deus...non ad augendum suam beatitudinem nec ad acquirendam, sed ad manifestandam perfectionem suam per bona, quae creaturis impertitur...condidit creaturam*" (Henricus Denzinger, *Enchiridion Symbolorum*, 35th ed.; Freiburg, Germany: Herder, 1973; #3002).

47. Herbert W. Richardson made the following assertion foundational to his study of Edwards: "The continuity of God's internal and external glory is the principle of Edwards's theology" ("The Glory of God in the Theology of Jonathan Edwards," PhD diss., Harvard University, 1962; 3, italicized in the original).

many references to Edwards's covenantal theology, his other writings showed that he conceived all of God's purposes in history as rooted in an eternal, intra-Trinitarian pact or covenant of redemption between the Father, Son, and Spirit (ch. 21).[48] This covenant brought about an overflow of God's goodness and love into the created universe. God's purpose of displaying and manifesting his own glory included his intention to draw human beings into the divine life. Glorification implied divinization (ch. 26). In God's ultimate purpose, all good transmitted to creatures was to come through Jesus Christ: "All communicated glory to the creature must be by the Son of God who is the brightness or shining forth of his Father's glory."[49] The purpose of creation was expressed in a different way in Edwards's references to the marriage supper of the Lamb. "The end of the creation," he wrote, "was to provide a spouse for his Son Jesus Christ that might enjoy him and on whom he might pour forth his love." In this way "the last thing and issue of all things is the marriage supper of the Lamb."[50]

The saints' participation in God's own life enabled Edwards to depict eternal life as a dynamic growth and endless increase in knowledge, happiness, and love in God (ch. 19).[51] Edwards's vision of the saints' heavenly progress is akin to that of the fourth-century author Gregory of Nyssa. Gregory reasoned that heaven would be a progressive state because the capacity of the soul for blessedness would continue to increase as it received further grace from God. The effect of receiving grace was an increase of capacity for receiving grace, like "a place that always becomes larger because of what is additionally poured into it." Gregory wrote: "Such are the wonders that the participation in the Divine blessing works: it makes him into whom they come larger and more capacious...and he never stops enlarging."[52] Consequently the soul is not like a glass or pitcher

---

48. "Some things were done before the world was created, yea, from all eternity. The persons of the Trinity were as it were confederated in a design and a covenant of redemption, in which covenant the Father appointed the Son and the Son had undertaken their work, and all things to be accomplished in their work were stipulated and agreed" (WJE 9:118).

49. WJE 8:718.

50. WJE 8:708–709.

51. Kyoung-Chul Jang, "The Logic of Glorification: The Destiny of the Saints in the Eschatology of Jonathan Edwards," PhD diss., Princeton Theological Seminary, 1994, 150.

52. Gregory of Nyssa, "On the Soul and the Resurrection," in *St. Gregory of Nyssa: Ascetical Works*, trans. Virginia Woods Callahan (Washington, DC: Catholic University of America Press, 1967), 244–45; cited by Paul Ramsey, in WJE 8:728; Gregory of Nyssa, "On the Soul and the Resurrection," in Philip Schaff and Henry Wace, eds., *Nicene and Post-Nicene Fathers*, 2nd series (Grand Rapids, MI: Eerdmans, 1954 [1892]), 5:453. The Orthodox author Vladimir Lossky writes, "Desiring God more and more, the soul does not cease to grow...and its love becomes more ardent and insatiable to the extent that it is united more and more with God" (*The Vision of God*; London: The Faith Press, 1963; 74).

that becomes full and can receive no more. Instead one might compare it with a balloon that can always be further expanded. Along these lines Edwards wrote that God aims at "an infinitely perfect union of the creature with himself" even though "the particular time will never come when it can be said, that the union is now infinitely perfect."[53]

For Edwards, eternity is not the negation of time. Instead time or temporality is an inescapable aspect of creatureliness and bodiliness, and so an aspect of the life to come as well as the present life. One might say that time itself—like the saints will be glorified. Time and eternity are not opposing concepts but correlative ones. Edwards's postmillennial view of human history—involving continual development (ch. 15)—is a mirror image of Edwards's conception of an eternal heaven and its unending progress.[54] Through this process of glorification, the saints come together into corporate union as a "holy society." This happens through divine grace, as the "refulgence" of divine light "shines upon and into the creature, and is reflected back to the luminary." It also occurs, in some sense, within the Godhead. For the saints themselves are "admitted into the society of the blessed Trinity."[55]

---

53. WJE 8:536.
54. Jang, "Logic," 187, 198
55. WJE 8:736.

15

Providence and History

"HISTORY," ACCORDING TO Edward Gibbon, "is indeed, little more than the register of the crimes, follies and misfortunes of mankind." Similarly Voltaire said that "history in general is a collection of crimes" and often is "no more than accepted fiction."[1] Such cynicism regarding history, expressed here by two of the leading secular minds of the eighteenth century, followed from a sense that human affairs are too muddled and multifarious to fit into any comprehensive scheme.[2] In describing history as "accepted fiction," Voltaire intimated that past events have no inherent meaning, but only the significance that human beings read into them. An alternative to Voltaire's view of history as irrational is the notion of impersonal law in history. Thus the ancient Greeks commonly thought of history in terms of historical cycles, a theory reiterated in modern times by Oswald Spengler and others.[3] According to this hypothesis, civilizations rise and fall according to rigid laws. The development of each society through time may be charted with reference to the point it occupies on a circular path. The cyclic theory, in both its Greek and Spenglerian versions, is deeply pessimistic. It asserts that the evils of the world will ceaselessly return and denies that anything radically new or better can emerge. A different kind of impersonal law in history is the familiar modern notion of progress, which gained increasing influence in the seventeenth and eighteenth centuries and dominated the Western mind during much of the nineteenth century. The idea of linear progress—often taken to be a secularized version of Christian eschatology—leads ultimately to an optimistic vision of history, in contrast to the pessimism

---

1. Edward Gibbon, *The History of the Decline and Fall of the Roman Empire*, Vol. 1 (London: Henry Bohn, 1854), 102–103; Voltaire, *The Works of Voltaire*, 42 vols. (Paris: E. R. Dumont, 1901), 30:136; Voltaire, cited in Michael Bentley, eds., *Companion to Historiography* (New York: Routledge, 2003), 150.

2. R. G. Collingwood wrote that "Gibbon finds the motive force of history in human irrationality itself" (*The Idea of History* [Oxford: Clarendon Press, 1946; 79]).

3. On the cyclical theory of the Greeks, see Karl Löwith, *Meaning in History* (Chicago: University of Chicago Press, 1949), 4–9. See Oswald Spengler, *The Decline of the West*, trans. Charles Francis Atkinson (New York: Alfred A. Knopf, 1926–8).

of the cyclical viewpoint.⁴ It implies that the evils of the world can and will gradually disappear and affirms that history continuously advances into a newer and better state of affairs for humankind.

Defining the Genre of A History of the Work of Redemption

Edwards's sermon series, *A History of the Work of Redemption*, fell within a very different tradition of historical reflection than the cynicism of Voltaire, the cyclical pessimism of the Greeks and Spengler, or the progressive optimism of the typical late-nineteenth-century thinker.⁵ It was a Christian "universal chronicle," based on the biblical narratives yet incorporating church history as well, in the fashion of Augustine's *City of God*. Because of its universality, *History of Redemption* belongs to a different genre than Cotton Mather's *Magnalia Christi Americana* (1702). It was not national or folk history but an effort to delineate the entire story of God's dealings with humanity. *History of Redemption* showed two distinctive characteristics of the "universal chronicle," as noted by C. A. Patrides: it began with creation and treated the entire known world. By the year 1100, Western Europe possessed some sixty of these chronicles, though many were unoriginal and simply imitated forbears such as Augustine.⁶ A leading work within the genre was the *Discourse of Universal History* (1681) by the great French clergyman Bishop Jacques-Bénigne Bossuet.⁷ Yet one feature that set the *History of Redemption* apart from Bossuet's history and most other "universal chronicles" was its strong infusion of eschatology. It not only reconstructed the past and described the present but extrapolated the future.

Scholars have differed on the value and significance of *History of Redemption*.⁸ Some have seen it as the most resolutely traditional of Edwards's

---

4. Robert A. Nisbet, in *History of the Idea of Progress* (New York: Basic Books, 1980), viewed Augustine's *City of God* as the foundation for all Western philosophies of history, and the idea of progress as a secularized version of the Christian doctrine of providence. cf. J. B. Bury, *The Idea of Progress: An Inquiry into Its Origin and Growth* (London: Macmillian, 1924), and Morris Ginsberg, "Progress in the Modern Era," in Philip P. Wiener, ed., *Dictionary of the History of Ideas*, 5 vols. (New York: Scribners, 1973), 3:633–50.

5. *A History of the Work of Redemption* is found in WJE 9:113–528.

6. C.A. Patrides, *The Grand Design of God: The Literary Form of the Christian View of History* (London: Routledge and Kegan Paul, Toronto: University of Toronto Press, 1972), 29. Patrides took the main title for his book from Jonathan Edwards's letter to the Princeton trustees (xiii, 119).

7. Jacques-Bénigne Bossuet, *Discourse on Universal History* (Chicago: University of Chicago Press, 1976).

8. The most extensive study of Edwards's conception of history to date is Avihu Zakai, *Jonathan Edwards's Philosophy of History: The Reenchatnment of the World in the Age of Enlightenment* (Princeton, NJ: Princeton University Press, 2003).

major works, while others have insisted that it contains the seeds of later American progressivism and optimism. Perry Miller voiced strong yet oddly dissonant claims on behalf of the book. "If one stops with the surface narrative," wrote Miller, then the work "sounds like a story book for fundamentalists." For when it is "measured against modern scholarship...it is an absurd book, where it is not pathetic." Nonetheless, Miller asserted that Edwards "attained to the revolutionary insight...that what man sees as the truth of history is what he wills to prevail." In its summons not merely to gather data but to interpret the data of history, *History of Redemption* "becomes a pioneer work in American historiography."[9] In his extensive introduction to *History of Redemption*, John F. Wilson dismissed Miller's claim, noting that the challenge of historical interpretation is an age-old issue in Christian thought and was not new to Edwards or to the eighteenth century.[10] Subsequent to Miller, hardly anyone supported Miller's reading of *History of Redemption* as a "pioneer work" in terms of method. On the contrary, a number of writers insisted that Edwards's book does not really count as history at all. Peter Gay described *History of Redemption* as "thoroughly traditional" and commented: "In the modern sense, in the sense of Voltaire and Hume, almost none of Edwards's history is history—it is Calvinist doctrine exemplified in a distinct succession of transcendent moments." Rather than moving forward with the times and adopting the secular and nonprovidential historiography of the emergent Enlightenment, "Edwards serenely reaffirmed the faith of his fathers."[11] Without repeating Gay's polemical barbs, Wilson concurred with Gay's conclusion that *History of Redemption* is not a work of history in the modern sense of the term. Wilson wrote: "I deemphasize the importance conventionally given to the word *history* in the title, arguing instead that that work is primarily theological." Wilson referred to the text as "the Redemption Discourse" and insisted that the book "had controlling theological premises and was intended to eventuate in religious practice or conversion." Edwards understood "the human saga as the production of a play that God had authored."[12] The emphasis in Edwards's "history" was not on

---

9. Perry Miller, *Jonathan Edwards* (New York: William Sloane, 1949), 310, 312.

10. John F. Wilson, "Editor's Introduction," in WJE 9:97.

11. Peter Gay, *A Loss of Mastery: Puritan Historians in Colonial America* (Berkeley: University of California Press, 1966), 88–117, quoting 94, 97, 104, 91.

12. Wilson, "Editor's Introduction," in WJE 9:2, 27, 73. Wilson called attention to the use of a "branching structure" and explained: "The use of a branching structure...is an index of the degree to which the Discourse was governed theologically....This is the sense in which the Discourse, in spite of the title under which it was published, is profoundly unhistoriographical in any modern sense."

the free and contingent interplay of human agents but on the dominating direction given to the world by God.¹³

A longstanding issue in the interpretation of *History of Redemption* has been the role of eschatology. In *The Kingdom of God in America* (1937), H. Richard Niebuhr intimated that Edwards's interest in *History of Redemption* shifted from "the eternal kingdom" to "the kingdom coming upon earth," and that this shift linked him with the later progressivist tendencies in American thought.¹⁴ C.C. Goen's 1959 essay attributed to Edwards an original "postmillennial" viewpoint and argued that "Edwards's proposal of an imminent millennium within ordinary history was a definitive factor in the religious background of the idea of progress."¹⁵ Alan Heimert pursued an interpretation like that of Niebuhr and Goen.¹⁶ While Stephen Stein underscored the influence of Moses Lowman on Edwards's eschatology and thus cast doubt on the appropriateness of Goen's description of Edwards's view as a "radical innovation," Goen nonetheless made a convincing case for the importance of *eschatology* in *History of Redemption*.¹⁷ John F. Wilson noted that Edwards "makes the temporal process a function of a far grander whole. In crucial respects eternity is actually

---

13. Compare the judgment of Gerhard Hoffman that "die formale Periodierung der Heilsgeschichte ist durchas herrkömmlich," and "Edwards's philosophierendes Denken durchaus 'ungeschichtlicher' Struktur ist" ("Seinsharmonie und Heilsgeschichte bei Jonathan Edwards," ThD diss., Göttingen University, 1957; 148, 165).

14. H. Richard Niebuhr, *The Kingdom of God in America* (Middleton, Conn.: Wesleyan University Press, 1988 [1937]), 142–43.

15. C.C. Goen, "Jonathan Edwards: A New Departure in Eschatology," in William J. Scheick, ed., *Critical Essays on Jonathan Edwards* (Boston: G. K. Hall, 1980), 151–65, quoting 152. Goen, in his "Editor's Introduction" in WJE 4:1–95, reiterates the position taken in his earlier article. Yet see the qualifications in ch. 32 regarding Edwards's attitude toward American patriotism.

16. Describing Edwards's optimism, Alan Heimert wrote, "No longer did the tendency of history seem toward judgment, or the thoughts of the pious bent on despair.... Indeed the Edwardean Deity seemed designed as a guarantor of the millennium... in the last analysis cataclysm was inconsistent with a vision of history as the progressive enlargement of the realm of the spirit" (*Religion and the American Mind: From the Great Awakening to the Revolution*; Cambridge: Harvard University Press, 1966; 62–63, 65). Heimert called attention to Edwards's elaborate argument in his *Humble Attempt* (WJE 5:378–94) to show that the "slaying of the witnesses" in chapter 11 of the Book of Revelation had already transpired in the period prior to the Protestant Reformation, so that the darkest times of the church were already past (65).

17. See Stephen Stein, "Editor's Introduction," WJE 5:1–93, especially 54–74. Stein saw a connection between Lowman (1680–1752) and Edwards's optimism: "Lowman confirmed Edwards in his conviction that the lowest days of the church were past and the times were becoming increasingly favorable for the saints" (59).

brought within time...and time is endowed with significance by being taken up into eternity."[18]

Another pivotal issue in *History of Redemption* concerns the integration and coherence of the narrative. Perry Miller observed that "the real thesis of the *History of Redemption* is the unity of history."[19] Miller himself suggested that the basic plotline for *History of Redemption* was taken from Edwards's experience with his parish and then projected onto history at large: "The book definitely embodies Edwards's time and place; it is the history of Northampton writ large. It is a cosmic rationalization of the communal revival."[20] Gerhard Hoffman concluded that Edwards conceived of redemptive history as a "history of piety" (*Frömmigkeitsgeschichte*) mediated by the periodic "outpouring" of the Holy Spirit among God's people.[21] William Scheick, in contrast to Miller and Hoffman, viewed redemptive history as analogous to the experience of the individual believer, rather than the church at large. He expounded the ingenious hypothesis that history for Edwards "merely manifests in large the experiences of the individual soul undergoing the regenerative process."[22] In support of this assertion, Scheick cited a passage from Edwards's notebook on typology: "The gradual progress we make from childhood to manhood is a type of the gradual progress of the saints in grace."[23]

John F. Wilson presents an alternate explanation for the coherence and unity of *History of Redemption*, namely, Edwards's typological exegesis (ch. 8). "The basic terms by means of which he achieves unity," writes Wilson, are "a reliance upon, and appropriation of, the figural tradition of interpreting the Old Testament and the New."[24] From the early church onward, Christian writers used typological interpretation to establish connections between the two testaments. Christ served as the linchpin of typological exegesis, the supreme "antitype" foreshadowed by widely varied elements within the text—persons, places, stones, animals, plants, sacrifices, weather formation, agricultural phenomena, and so forth. In attempting to decode each passage in the Hebrew

---

18. Wilson, "Editor's Introduction," in WJE 9:56. On the relationship of time to eternity, see the comments at the end of ch. 14.

19. Miller, *Jonathan Edwards*, 313.

20. Miller, *Jonathan Edwards*, 315.

21. Hoffman, "Seinsharmonie und Heilsgeschichte bei Jonathan Edwards," 161–62, 167. Hoffman is one of the few authors to underscore the role of the Holy Spirit in *History of Redemption*. On the role of the Spirit, see WJE 9:143, 189, 233, 266, 300, 314, 364–65, 377, 436, 438, 441, 459–62.

22. William J. Scheick, "The Grand Design: Jonathan Edwards's *History of the Work of Redemption*," in Scheick, *Critical Essays on Jonathan Edwards*, 177–88, quoting 188.

23. Scheick, "Grand Design," 182–83, citing WJE 11:61.

24. Wilson, "Editor's Introduction," in *Works* 9:23.

Bible and refer it to the as-yet-future coming of Christ, typological interpretation showed a strong unifying tendency.[25] Edwards's key texts on typology—*Images of Divine Things*, *Types*, and *Types of the Messiah*— show his application of typology to the natural world and the centrality of Christ in his vision of nature and history alike.[26] Throughout *History of Redemption* Edwards explicitly appealed to typology, using varied terminology—"images," "types," "representing," "signifying," and "shadowing forth."[27]

This chapter builds on the existing literature on Edwards's conception of redemptive history and yet qualifies Goen's and Heimert's judgment that *History of Redemption* presents an essentially optimistic, progressivist, and rationalized vision of history. According to that interpretation, Edwards believed that he could discern the past, present, and future course of redemptive history and that this course moved consistently onward and upward. Heimert went so far as to speak of Edwards's "ultimate hubris—his assumption that in all America he alone understood the destination of history, and even the precise blueprint for its fulfillment."[28] Such a position is one-sided. Edwards's keen sense of the sufferings of the church tempered his optimism, his frequent depictions of historical decline modified his progressivism, and his recognition of the radical limitations of the human perspective on history sharply curtailed his tendency toward rationalism. Edwards's analogy of the "river" of divine providence provided a corrective to the impression of him as a smug prognosticator or glib triumphalist. The river analogy also highlights the neglected issue of *perspective* within the narrative, and the extent to which the meaning of history depended on the breadth and scope which one brought to the interpretation of individual events.

Plotting the Course of History

For Edwards, all of history cohered within a single pattern. The general thesis that he stated at the beginning of *History of Redemption* laid emphasis on the

---

25. In Edwards's biblical exposition, as Kenneth Minkema notes, "his unifying concept was Jesus Christ as the reference point of all promises." Minkema, "The Other Unfinished 'Great Work': Jonathan Edwards, Messianic Prophecy, and 'The Harmony of the Old and New Testament,'" in *Jonathan Edwards's Writings: Text, Context, Interpretation*, ed. Stephen J. Stein (Bloomington: Indiana University Press, 1996), 62.

26. Wilson writes: "His antitype, in nature as well as in apocalyptic literature, was Christ. This meant that his understanding of nature was finally determined by a Christocentric construction of the world" ("Editor's Introduction," in WJE 9:47–48).

27. See WJE 9:129, 136, 138, 144, 151–52, 163–64, 175, 177–78, 181–84, 192–93, 196, 198, 204, 213, 218, 220, 224–25, 227, 236, 253, 263, 281, 286–87, 289, 318, 331, 351, 484.

28. Heimert, *Religion and the American Mind*, 153.

continuity and comprehensiveness of God's activity in history: "The Work of Redemption is a work that God carries on from the fall of man to the end of the world."[29] Edwards explained that the work of redemption is the greatest of all God's works and that all that God does, including creation, is done for the sake of redemption. "The whole scheme of divine providence" may be regarded as "reducible to that one great Work of Redemption."[30] The salient analogies in *History of Redemption* underscored the unity, coherence, and gradual progress of God's plan. The work of redemption might be compared to the erection of "an house or temple," in which "one part after another" is set in place "till at length the topstone is laid."[31] Using a different analogy, Edwards wrote that the work of redemption in history is "very much after the same work ... in a particular soul from the time of its conversion till it is perfected and crowned in glory." There were "ups and downs," yet "in the general grace is growing."[32] Among his other analogies for the work of redemption were the elaborate preparations made before the arrival of an "extraordinary person" as one's guest,[33] a "mighty wheel" that turns away from God and returns once more, "the manifold wheels of a most curious machine,"[34] and a "large and long river" having many tributaries that join together into a single stream.[35]

To understand the development of history and to grasp its essential unity, Edwards sought to identify its underlying forces. For him, the impetus of history derived from the conflict of good and evil—Cain versus Abel, the Israelites versus the pagans, the church versus its persecutors.[36] Strife between the righteous and the wicked was the driving force of world history. He began *History of Redemption* with the theme of suffering, and he played the opening chord, so to speak, in a minor key. The text from Isaiah 51:8 is intended "to

---

29. WJE 9:116.

30. WJE 9:516; see also WJE 9:512–13.

31. WJE 9:121.

32. WJE 9:144.

33. WJE 9:292.

34. WJE 9:517–18, 525.

35. WJE 9:520.

36. Edwards uses "church" indiscriminately to refer to Israelites prior to the coming of Jesus and to Christians subsequently. Thus one encounters such odd-sounding phrases as "the Jewish Church," "the church under the Old Testament," and "the Mosaic church of Israel" (WJE 9:252, 230, 376–77). This terminology reflects Edwards's belief in the fundamental unity of God's people through space and time: "The church of God from the beginning has been one society" (WJE 9:443).

comfort the church under her sufferings and the persecutions of her enemies."[37] True religion was shown to be such by virtue of the opposition it arouses: "Contraries are well argued one from another; we may well and safely argue that a thing is good according to the degree of opposition in which it stands to evil." History showed the "baseless cruelty" suffered by the people of God.[38] Behind the various events and circumstances of religious persecution was the invisible power of Satan, animating and activating the human agencies of evil. The text of *History of Redemption* is studded with dozens of references to the devil.[39] Since one of the dominant characteristics of apocalyptic literature is the sharp demarcation of good and evil and their cataclysmic conflict with one another, one may conclude that Edwards portrayed all of history, and not merely its consummation, in apocalyptic terms.

In every age and generation, the church faced opposition, and Edwards stated sweepingly that "every true Christian has the spirit of a martyr."[40] Among the prominent persecutors of the church were the ancient pagans and "Antichrist," which Edwards generally identified with Roman Catholicism (chs. 28, 35).[41] *History of Redemption* more or less equated the triumph of Christians over their enemies with the triumph of God himself. The overthrow of paganism by Christianity moved him to celebrate: "The gospel sun...now rose and began to enlighten the heathen world, after they had continued in gross heathenish darkness for so many ages."[42] Yet the overthrow of Antichrist was to be an even more glorious event than the ancients' desertion of their pagan deities and temples. "The Kingdom of Antichrist" was "the masterpiece of all the contrivances of

---

37. WJE 9:113. Hoffman stresses the "comforting" character of *History of Redemption*: "Die Betrachtung der 'history of redemption' hat Predigtcharakter; sie soll der Kirche Trost geben in Leiden und Verfolgung." "Seinsharmonie und Heilsgeschichte bei Edwards," 166.

38. WJE 9:444.

39. See WJE 9:120–21, 123, 130–31, 148, 155, 175–76, 298, 315, 327, 345, 347–48, 356, 375, 380–82, 390–91, 393, 396–98, 403–11, 415–18, 424–32, 434, 463, 488–89, 499–500, 509, 519, 523, 525.

40. WJE 9:444, 454.

41. Based in part on his identification of Rome with "the great city" in Revelation 17:18—a passage he called "the plainest of any one passage in the whole book"—Edwards was convinced that the Roman papacy was one arm of the Antichrist. See Stein, "Editor's Introduction," in WJE 5:12. On the identification of the Roman Catholic Church with "Antichrist," see Bernard McGinn, *Antichrist: Two Thousand Years of the Human Fascination with Evil* (San Francisco: Harper, 1994), esp. 143–230. The other arm of Antichrist was Islam; see Gerald R. McDermott, *Jonathan Edwards Confronts the Gods* (New York: Oxford University Press, 2000), 166–75.

42. WJE 9:380.

the devil against the kingdom of Christ," and so its downfall signaled the end of the "the darkest and most dismal day" and the beginning of the "glorious time" of the church.⁴³ Edwards viewed Antichrist as an "apostate" rather than "heathen" power.⁴⁴ It posed an extreme danger for the saints because of its insidious imposture of true religion, as "a contrivance of the devil to turn the ministry of the Christian church into a ministry of the devil."⁴⁵ The reign of Antichrist commenced sometime subsequent to Constantine's rule in the early fourth century, and Edwards speculated that Antichrist would continue in power until 1260 years were completed.⁴⁶ Edwards did not claim to know with certainty when Antichrist would be decisively routed, yet he expected it to happen within two or three more centuries (ch. 35).⁴⁷

The prominent place of Antichrist in the narrative shows us, in the words of Stephen Stein, "Edwards's...religiously sanctioned prejudice and anti-Catholicism."⁴⁸ Edwards followed the "trail of blood" ecclesiology common to earlier Protestant historians and martyrologists. Throughout the centuries of Roman Catholic persecution, "God was pleased to maintain an uninterrupted succession of witnesses through the whole time in Germany and France, Britain and other countries," which included such groups as the Waldensians.⁴⁹ Also singled out for unfavorable mention in *History of Redemption* in addition to pagans and Catholics were Jews, Muslims, Native Americans, Anabaptists, Enthusiasts, Quakers, Socinians, Arminians, Arians, and Deists.⁵⁰ Of all the

---

43. WJE 9:409–11.

44. WJE 9:450–51.

45. WJE 9:411.

46. The number 1260 was derived from references to the Book of Daniel and Book of Revelation to a period of three and a half years, or forty-two months, traditionally interpreted so that each month included thirty days and day represented an entire year. See Stein, "Editor's Introduction," in WJE 5:13–15.

47. Edwards, WJE 9:456–57. Stephen Stein points out that Edwards was generally hesitant to make public his conjectures regarding the fulfillment of biblical prophecies: "Speculation in private, but discretion in public came to be characteristic of him" (Stein, "Editor's Introduction," in WJE 5:13, 19).

48. Stephen Stein, "Notebook on the Apocalypse by Jonathan Edwards," in Scheick, *Critical Essays on Jonathan Edwards*, 174.

49. WJE 9:419.

50. WJE 9:254, 282, 430–33, 469. The Jewish people had a somewhat paradoxical place in Edwards's conception of God's plan for history. In Edwards's conception most Jews were cut off from Christ during the present era, and yet the biblical prophecies pointed toward a future "conversion" of the people, which was to signal the arrival of the "glorious times" of the Church (Stein, "Editor's Introduction," in WJE 5:19). On Edwards's view of Judaism, see McDermott, *Jonathan Edwards Confronts the Gods*, 149–65.

religious groups mentioned by Edwards, only mainstream Protestants escaped general censure, and even they were upbraided for their spiritual coldness and defection from orthodoxy. True believers were like a tiny huddle surrounded by a hostile mob. Edwards's conception of the church in *History of Redemption* leaned in a sectarian direction—as one commonly finds in apocalyptic texts.

While history disclosed a consistent and predictable conflict between the church and the nonchurch, its pattern of development was complex and convoluted. Edwards attempted to uphold two seemingly incompatible premises, namely, that God's work of redemption moved continually in cycles of advance and decline, and that redemption edged ever closer to its completion in the "glorious times."[51] Time and again, persecution nearly destroyed the church, yet throughout history it continued to grow stronger and more influential. The path of redemptive history was cyclic and linear at the same time. Traced out in three dimensions, it resembled the movement of a corkscrew's tip, which, when viewed from the end, revolved in circles, yet, when seen from the side, progressed in a single direction. Depending on the particular passage one is reading, Edwards portrayed either an up-and-down cycle or a stepwise advance. Sometimes he dramatized the desperate plight of God's people in times past and their precarious position on the verge of utter ruin. He noted, "how often the church has been approaching the brink of ruin, and in the case seemed to [be] lost, and all hope gone."[52] Yet just as often he spoke of the steady progress of God's kingdom: "Thus we see how the light of the gospel which began to dawn immediately after the fall, and gradually grew and increased through all the ages of the Old Testament...is now come to the light of perfect day."[53] We will refer to these tendencies in *History of Redemption* as the "contrast motif" and the "preparation motif," respectively.

These two motifs showed opposing conceptions of God's activity in history and therefore they seem difficult to reconcile. The contrast motif suggested that God manifested and glorified himself through an eleventh-hour appearance

---

51. Perry Miller spoke of history as following a "zigzag course" in which "a declension...should be interpreted as a preparation for the next and greater exertion" (*Jonathan Edwards*, 315). Along similar lines Alan Heimert wrote that "Edwards adopted and announced a 'cyclical' theory of history—one not of mere repetition, but of recurrence and periodically renewed and increased momentum" (*Religion and the American Mind*, 67).

52. WJE 9:448. See also WJE 9:186.

53. WJE 9:367. The quoted statement contains a biblical allusion: "But the path of the just is as the shining light, that shineth more and more unto the perfect day" (Prov. 4:18, Authorized Version).

to save his people from certain destruction. The more hopeless the circumstance, the more glorious was the moment of deliverance. As Edwards said: "Goliath must have on all his splendid armor when the stripling David comes against him with a sling and a stone for the greater glory of David's victory."[54] In reference to the persecutions of the early Christians, Edwards wrote: "Thus was the darkest time with the Christian church just before the break of day. They were brought to the greatest extremity just before God appeared for their glorious deliverance, as the bondage of the Israelites."[55] History demonstrated that the darkest hour for God's people came just before the dawn: the oppression of the Jews under the pagan kingdoms was a prelude to the coming of the Messiah, the persecutions of the first Christians led to the conversion of the Emperor Constantine, and the slaying of God's witnesses in the Middle Ages ushered in the Protestant Reformation.

This contrast motif did not square well with notions of progress in redemptive history. It seemed to be cyclic in such a way as to exclude any advancement. If God's people were almost annihilated again and again, it would seem that every generation that survived the near-holocaust would have to rebuild from the rubble all over again—like a family forced to reconstruct its home from the foundation after a devastating storm struck it down. In one of his *Miscellanies*, Edwards used the image of rebuilding from ruins: "When he has any thing very glorious to accomplish he accomplishes it and builds it up out of [the] ruins of something that was excellent but destroyed."[56] Somewhat similar was the notion of the "wilderness" that Edwards set forth in *Some Thoughts Concerning the Revival* in support of his suggestion that the millennium might begin in America: "When God is about to turn the earth into a paradise, he don't begin his work where there is some good growth already, but in a wilderness, where nothing grows, and nothing is to be seen but dry sand and barren rocks." God does so in order "that the power of God might be the more conspicuous; that the work might appear to be entirely God's."[57]

In *History of Redemption*, Edwards uses the analogy of the sun's rising in two different and apparently incompatible ways. In keeping with the contrast motif, he speaks of the "darkest time" as coming "just before the break of day." Again and again, the people of God find themselves at the moment of deepest darkness just before sunrise. Yet in other passages he compares the course of

---

54. WJE 9:248. See WJE 9:279, 523.

55. WJE 9:394.

56. WJE 20:161–62.

57. WJE 4:356.

redemptive history to the circuit of the sun—from nighttime, to dawn, to morning, and finally to noontime brightness. We come at length to "the light of perfect day."⁵⁸

Despite the up-and-down cycles, Edwards nonetheless conceived of redemptive history as a movement from A to B, so that each successive era stood closer to the glorious consummation than the era that preceded it.⁵⁹ One of the *Miscellanies* revealed his powerful sense of advancement and novelty in history:

> God is continually causing revolutions. Providence makes a continual progress, and continually is bringing forth new things in the state of the world, and very different from whatever were before; he removes one that he may establish another. And perfection will not be obtained till the last revolution, when God's design will be fully reached.⁶⁰

All events of history were part of "God's great design" and pushed relentlessly toward "the great event," that is, the end of the world. Likewise, he wrote in *History of Redemption* that "the light of the Gospel which first began to dawn and glimmer immediately after the fall, gradually increases the nearer we come to Christ's time."⁶¹ Edwards used the term "gradual" in keeping with its Latin etymological meaning of "occurring in steps or stages." Each stage of history served as a preparation for that which came after it, and thus one might speak of a preparation motif. To return to the analogy of rebuilding, one could say that after each new storm struck the edifice, the builders erected it with stronger materials and made it larger and more impressive. Thus there was both an up-and-down cycle and a forward progress over time.

In one key passage in *History of Redemption*, Edwards distinguished "four successive great events" that were sequential phases of "Christ's coming in his kingdom." The first was the appearance of Jesus in the first century, the second was the destruction of the heathen Roman Empire in the time of Constantine, the third was the overthrow of the Antichrist, and the fourth and last was the coming of Christ to judge the world. Before each of these "comings" of Christ

---

58. WJE 5:23; WJE 9:367, 394.

59. Thomas Schafer writes: "The course of the Church in history, he believed, has been on the whole an upward one. In fact, the worst is past, Antichrist is soon to fall" ("Jonathan Edwards's Conception of the Church," *Church History* 24 [1955]: 56).

60. WJE 18:94.

61. WJE 9:189.

there was a period of spiritual degeneracy and great wickedness, and "by each of them God delivers his church ... with a glorious advancement of the state of the church."[62] The four comings of Christ stood as milestones along the road toward the eschaton. Much discussion of Edwards's eschato-logy has hinged on the distinction between "premillennialism" and "postmillennialism"—the former involving a millennium or golden age on earth inaugurated by Christ's glorious return, the latter a millennium inaugurated by the church's own efforts and culminated by Christ's return.[63] Yet Christ's "four comings" in *History of Redemption* complicate the picture to such an extent that the distinction between premillennialism and postmillennialism loses most of its pertinence. The millennium does not arrive at once in full force but *creeps in* through a process of gradual and successive inauguration. Several intermediate stages—each a semi-millennium of sorts—elapse between the church's suffering state and its final deliverance and glorification. Because of this pattern of successive inauguration, it becomes extraordinarily difficult to interpret the course of history. Each new phase of the church's revival and progress could be either the dawning of the full and final millennial glory or just a temporary upsurge to be followed by another plunge into suffering and darkness. Neither of the terms commonly applied to Edwards—premillennialism or postmillennialism—seems an accurate or apt description of his complex rendering of redemptive history.

The difficulty of tracing the course of history was shown in Edwards's ambiguous interpretation of his own era.[64] Toward the end of *History of Redemption*, Edwards concluded his summary of past redemptive history and took up the task of forecasting the near future, beyond the time of writing in the 1730s. He was especially concerned to ascertain when Antichrist would be destroyed. Edwards wrote: "We have all reason from the Scripture to conclude that just before this work of God begins [i.e., the overthrow of Antichrist] it

---

62. WJE 9:351–52.

63. Perry Miller commented: "He preached chiliasm in its starkest from. According to this ancient doctrine, there will be 'a very dark time,' which will be followed by a thousand years of the reign of Christ on earth" (*Jonathan Edwards*, 316). While Miller interpreted Edwards as a chiliast or premillennialist, Goen and Heimert viewed him as a postmillennialist.

64. The *Personal Narrative* attests to Edwards's lifelong effort to interpret current events in the light of biblical prophecies: "If I heard the least hint of any thing that happened, in any part of the world, that appeared to me, in some respect or other, to have a favorable aspect on the interests of Christ's kingdom, my soul eagerly catched at it; and it would much animate and refresh me. I used to be eager to read public news-letters, mainly for that end; to see if I could not find some news favorable to the interest of religion in the world" (WJE 16:797).

will be a very dark time with respect to the interests of religion in the world. It has been so before those glorious revivals of religion...hitherto." Almost immediately he added that "it is now a very dark time with respect to the interests of religion" and that "whether the times shall be any darker still, or how much darker before the beginning of this glorious work of God, we can't tell."[65] Here the darkness of the present time served as a basis for hope—things were so bad that they must soon get better. On the other hand, Edwards mused that the darkness might not yet have reached its limit, and deeper darkness may lie ahead. Conversely, spiritual light at the present time might mean that greater light lies just ahead. The cycles of history had unpredictable lengths and they combined with one another in complicated ways. Edwards was thus able to find hope in just about any situation and to infer an imminent millennium from either a dreary present or a splendid one.

By far the most controversial aspect in Edwards's interpretation of history was his suggestion in *Some Thoughts Concerning the Revival* (1743), in the aftermath of the Great Awakening, that the millennium might soon commence and might do so in America. The celebrated passage begins as follows:

> 'Tis not unlikely that this work of God's Spirit, that is so extraordinary and wonderful, is the dawning, or at least the prelude, of that glorious work of God, so often foretold in Scripture, which in the progress and issue of it, shall renew the world of mankind.... We can't reasonably think otherwise, than that the beginning of this great work of God must be near. And there are many things that make it probable that this work will begin in America.[66]

This brief passage became a *cause célèbre* among Edwards's detractors, including Charles Chauncy. Stephen Stein noted that "within a short time after it was printed, he became defensive about his remarks on the millennium, insisting that they had been misunderstood."[67] The quoted words contained a number of important qualifying phases—the Great Awakening is only a "dawning" or "prelude" of the "glorious work," and the whole opinion is said to be merely probable or "not unlikely." Yet there was enough in this paragraph to give grist to the mills of Edwards's critics.

---

65. WJE 9:457–58.
66. WJE 4:353.
67. Stein, "Editor's Introduction," in WJE 5:26.

In a letter to a Scottish acquaintance, Edwards bitterly complained that his true sentiments regarding the millennium had been intentionally misrepresented:

> It has been slanderously reported and printed concerning me, that I have often said that the millennium was already begun, and that it began at Northampton... but the report is very diverse from what I ever said. Indeed, I have often said, as I say now, that I looked upon the late wonderful revivals of religion as forerunners of those glorious times so often prophesied in the Scripture... but there are many that know that I have from time to time added, that there would probably be many sore conflicts and terrible conclusions, and many changes, revivings and intermissions, and returns of dark clouds, and threatening appearances, before this work shall have subdued the world, and Christ's kingdom shall be everywhere established and settled in peace.[68]

Given the complexity of the historical process, Edwards could simultaneously affirm that it was "not unlikely" that the Great Awakening was a "prelude" of the "glorious work of God" yet that it was also probably succeeded by "returns of dark clouds and threatening appearances." Since *History of Redemption* was published posthumously, Edwards's contemporaries could hardly have been expected to understand his complex conception of historical development in which alternating waves of light and darkness would lead eventually to millennial glory.

Discerning the Pattern of History

The discussion thus far has highlighted the complexity of history's course and the consequent need for discernment on the part of the would-be interpreter. Edwards himself frequently stressed this point in *History of Redemption*. He writes that "in order to see how a design is carried [to] an end, we must first know what the design is." If one does not know the "design" of God, history "will all look like confusion, like a number of jumbled events coming to pass

---

68. Letter to William McCulloch, March 5, 1743/4, in WJE 4:560. Edwards in his "Blank Bible" refers to the "late extraordinary pouring out of the Spirit here in Northampton" (WJE 24:853).

without any order or method, like the tossing of the waves of the sea."[69] In understanding God's work in history, the whole has epistemological priority over the part—that is, one cannot interpret the part without having at least an outline of the whole in one's mind. The broader patterns within history can be grasped only with the help of special guidance, and this must come to us from God. Only God is, so to speak, high enough to see the entire course of world history and far enough ahead to see how individual events contribute to history's culmination. Human beings may understand the course and direction of history insofar as they participate in God's panoramic vision of the whole.

For Edwards it was the sacred scriptures that provided the key to seeing the design of redemptive history. He wrote in *History of Redemption* that "the Scriptures are that which God designed as the proper means to bring the world to the knowledge of himself, rather than human reason or anything else."[70] Yet it was not enough merely to acknowledge the Bible, for one must understand "the drift of the Holy Ghost in it," and "most persons are to blame for their inattentive, unobservant way of reading the Scriptures." All too often, readers of the Bible approached the stories of Abraham, Isaac, Jacob, and others "as if they were only histories of the private concerns of such and such particular persons," and so "the infinitely great things contained or pointed at in them are passed over and never taken notice of."[71] Thus redemptive history involved a hermeneutical problem. It was not possible to discover the pattern apart from God's revelation in Holy Scripture, and even after receiving this revelation it was quite possible to read the biblical text yet miss the tendency and direction of God's activity in the world.[72]

Edward's image of the "river" of providence summarized all the major aspects of his historical vision touched on thus far: the ultimate unity of history, the contribution of the parts of history to the whole, God as the final goal of the historical process, the apparent reverses that ultimately contributed to

---

69. WJE 9:122, 519.

70. WJE 9:399.

71. WJE 9:291.

72. In his essay on "Historicism," C.S. Lewis applied the term to "the belief that men can, by the use of their natural powers, discover an inner meaning to the historical process" ("Historicism," in C.T. McIntire, ed., *God, History, and Historians: An Anthology of Modern Christian Views of History*; New York: Oxford University Press, 1977; 225–38, citing 225–26). Lewis judged this viewpoint to be an "illusion" and thus essentially agreed with Edwards's idea that human beings need revelation from God to understand the meaning of history.

history's advance, and, not least of all, the severe limitations of perspective that hampered the human observer. As Edwards wrote:

> God's providence may not unfitly be compared to a large and long river, having innumerable branches beginning in different regions, and at a great distance from another, and all conspiring to one common issue. After their very diverse and contrary course which they hold for a while, yet all gathering more and more together the nearer they come to their common end, and all at length discharging themselves at one mouth into the same ocean. The different streams of this river are ready to look like mere jumble and confusion to us because of the limitedness of our sight, whereby we can't see from one branch to another and can't see the whole at once, so as to see how all are united as one. A man that sees but one or two streams at a time can't tell what their course tends to. Their course seems very crooked, and the different streams seem to run for a while different and contrary ways. And if we view things at a distance, there seem to be innumerable obstacles and impediments in the way to hinder their ever uniting and coming to the ocean, as rocks and mountains and the like. But yet if we trace them they all unite at last and come to the same issue, disgorging themselves into one and the same great ocean. Not one of the streams fail of coming hither at last.[73]

This analogy was essentially *optical*, based on a panoramic or synoptic vision of history. It fit with Edwards's other references to "seeing" God or spiritual things. In this passage, however, there was a somewhat different application of the visual analogy. The postulated observer was not standing on earth looking up into heaven but lifted up into heaven glancing down toward the earth. The object of vision was not God; rather, the vantage point was God's. Human beings became aware of God's design in history and the pattern of the whole inasmuch as they were, so to speak, raised off the ground and enabled to see the world through the eyes of God. Never mind that the events of history fade away, the past is gone, the future is not yet, and only the present is visible to us. Edwards's river required a point of view that people caught in time's flow could not fully attain—a vision of the whole of history *sub specie aeternitatis*, that is, under the aspect of eternity.

The river analogy exemplified Edwards's characteristically aesthetic approach to the problem of evil. The streams of divine providence seemed

---

73. WJE 9:520. On the river of providence., see also WJE 11:77–80.

to have "very diverse and contrary courses...because of the limitedness of our sight, whereby we can't...see the whole at once." What appeared to be disharmonious when taken in isolation seemed harmonious when viewed in the perspective of the whole (ch. 6). As in *The Mind*, Edwards held an idea of "proportion" that resolved partial discords into universal concords: "Particular disproportions sometimes greatly add to the general beauty, and must necessarily be, in order to a more universal proportion."[74] In *True Virtue*, he developed the same basic notion when he distinguished "particular beauty" from "general beauty" and defined the latter as "that by which a thing appears beautiful when viewed most perfectly, comprehensively and universally, with regard to all its tendencies, and its connections with everything it stands related to."[75] The river analogy exemplified Edwards's aesthetic principle that true beauty is "general beauty" or what appears to be beautiful within the context of the whole. In substance, his position was akin to what John Hick calls "the aesthetic theme" in Augustine, namely "his affirmation of faith that, seen in its totality from the ultimate standpoint of the Creator, the universe is wholly good; for even the evil within it is made to contribute to the complex perfection of the whole."[76] Whether Edwards's view—or Augustine's—acknowledges the evilness of evil is debatable. Can that which is fully and finally contrary to God and God's order be regarded as somehow harmonious with that order? Or does such a view minimize the degree of disharmony involved? Edwards's reflections on history open the door to some profound issues.

The analogy of the river helps to explain one of the puzzling themes in Edwards's writings, namely, his near obsession with the "saints in heaven." In the later *Miscellanies*, one finds an inordinate number of entries devoted to showing that the saints are acquainted with earthly affairs and "are spectators of God's providences relating to his church here below." Edwards reasoned that the "beatifical vision" of the blessed consists not in the sight of God in isolation from the world but rather in "beholding the manifestations that he makes of himself in the work of redemption." Those in heaven have a much better view than those on earth, for "the saints in heaven will be under advantages to see

---

74. WJE 6:335.

75. WJE 8:540.

76. John Hick, *Evil and the God of Love*, rev. ed. (San Francisco: Harper and Row, 1978 [1966]), 82. According to Augustine, the existence of wicked creatures renders the world like "an exquisite poem set of with antitheses," and "as, then, these oppositions of contraries lend beauty to the language, so the beauty of the course of this world is achieved by the oppositions of contraries, as it were, by an eloquence not of words, but of things" (*City of God*, Bk. 11, Ch. 18, in *A Select Library of Nicene and Post-Nicene Fathers*, ed. Philip Schaff, 2nd series, 14 vols.; Grand Rapids, Mich.: Eerdmans, 1974–76; 2:214–15).

much more...than the saints on earth."⁷⁷ The vision of God's doings in the world leads the departed saints to a growing knowledge and appreciation of God, hence to ever greater degrees of blessedness. As Edwards argues in *End of Creation*, the knowledge of God among believers is the purpose for which the world was created, and it will go on increasing throughout all eternity (ch. 14).⁷⁸ Thus Edwards's preoccupation with the departed saints can be taken as a reflection of his concern for seeing history from God's point of view.

Several conclusions regarding *History of Redemption* are in order. Edwards considered God's perspective to be the only finally valid one for viewing history, and he saw the human perspective as radically limited, fragmented, and deficient. Even when informed and enlightened by scripture, the interpreter of history could not escape obscurity and ambiguity. Hence the project of construing history as a whole was doomed to merely partial success, even in terms of the assumptions Edwards himself set forth in *History of Redemption*. So he was neither a rationalist who presumed to know exactly what God is doing in the world nor a triumphalist who viewed every event in history as somehow contributing to the final glory.⁷⁹ The question of *perspective* is critical, for it is only from God's vantage point that the course of history is clear and unambiguous.

History of Redemption in effect projected onto history as a whole the pattern of Jesus' career—suffering and death followed by resurrection. A number of passages in the text link Edwards's historical vision with his understanding of the cross of Christ. He writes, "The glorious power of God appears in conquering his many and mighty enemies by...a poor, weak, despised man. He conquers them and triumphs over them in their own weapon, the cross of Christ." The circumstances of Jesus' coming, at a point in time where the Jewish people were "very low" and the pagan nations were "exalted to the greatest height," demonstrates that "God took a contrary method from that which human wisdom would have taken." "With a small number in their greatest weakness, he conquered his enemies in their greatest glory. Thus Christ triumphed over principalities and powers in his

---

77. WJE 18:431 and WJE 20:428. See also WJE 18:99–100, 434, 505–507; WJE 20:166, 395–96, 469–74, 493–94; and WJE 23:226–28.

78. See Paul Ramsey's Appendix 3, "Heaven is a Progressive State," in WJE 8:706–38.

79. Gerald R. McDermott, in *One Holy and Happy Society: The Public Theology of Jonathan Edwards* (University Park: Pennsylvania State University Press, 1992), notes that Edwards's position is anything but jingoistic or triumphalistic: "I was also surprised to discover that Edwards was not the provincial chauvinist he has been made out to be.... America for Edwards usually deserved condemnation, not celebration. The further he progressed in his career, the more distance he put between his country and the Kingdom of God" (viii).

cross."[80] For a biblically inspired thinker such as Edwards, the paradigm case of darkness changed into light lay in the story of Good Friday and Easter. Like his continual reliance on typological interpretation, this was but one aspect of his thoroughly Christocentric reading of history.

Although Edwards was optimistic regarding the future prospects of the church and the ultimate realization of God's kingdom on earth, he lingered over the theme of suffering. History showed no straightforward, linear advance into glory but followed a tortuous and obscure path of gains and losses, afflictions and deliverances, promised yet deferred fulfillments. God alone was able to see and to interpret the whole, together with the saints in heaven. We dwellers in the midst of history, however, suffer from our limited perspective. We cannot declare definitively whether the present darkness is a prelude to deeper darkness or the presage of a new dawn, whether the present light will shine ever brighter or be extinguished all over again.

Despite these perplexities, Edwards did not lapse into skepticism regarding the intelligibility of history. He would not have concurred with the sentiment of Voltaire that "history is just the portrayal of crimes and misfortunes." The human past was indeed filled with suffering, but this suffering was not without significance. Pains and difficulties served to prepare God's people for their ultimate glorification. Even more important for Edwards, in distinction to Gibbon and Voltaire, the outcome of history was entirely assured and known prophetically in advance. In the terms of the river analogy, God was the "ocean" into which all the streams of history finally flowed. Each tiny tributary had its ultimate destination in the ocean of divinity—an image of Edwards's that is paralleled in earlier Christian literature.[81] If one viewed events from the standpoint of the biblically revealed ending, then one gained an imperfect but nonetheless valuable insight into the course and progress of history. To use a twentieth-century analogy, history was like a mystery novel in which the conclusion explains everything that proceeds. Someone who glanced at the last few pages would have little difficulty in tracing the plotline through the earlier chapters. Seeing God's work in *History of Redemption* was a matter of viewing history from the perspective of the ending, where God and the departed saints already dwell.

---

80. WJE 9:523, 279.

81. Bernard McGinn notes the frequent use of ocean imagery by Christian writers to describe the return of souls to God. The early Christian writer Evagrius wrote, "When minds flow back into him like torrents into the sea, he changes them all completely into his nature, color, and taste. They will no longer be many but one in his unending and inseparable unity." *Epistola ad Melaniam*, epistle 6, in "Ocean and Desert as Symbols of Mystical Absorption in the Christian Tradition," *Journal of Religion* 74 (1994): 155–81, quoting 159.

16

The Person and Work of Jesus Christ

EDWARDS'S CHRISTOLOGY SEEMS to have developed from his overriding interest in the history of the work of redemption (ch. 12) and his concern to defend Christian orthodoxy against attacks from deists and other anti-Trinitarians. Deists had labeled the Trinity a fiction of priestcraft, satisfaction for sin unnecessary, and Christ an impostor for claiming to be the incarnation of God.[1] Edwards filled out his understanding of Christ as part of his defense of the Trinity, and in the midst of his deliberations on the history of redemption labored to show that "there is nothing impossible or absurd in the doctrine of the *incarnation* of Christ."[2] So while he never composed a treatise on Christology, the shape of his thinking about the nature and roles of the second person of the Trinity can be sketched from both his apologetic work and his systematic accounts of the history of redemption.[3]

Agent of Redemption and Creation

Edwards was resolutely Trinitarian in his Christology because his thinking about the Son of God developed from his vision of redemption, which started with the Trinity. In his "Blank Bible," he wrote, "The *Logos* of God is his glory, the brightness of his glory." In a sermon, he proclaimed, "God the Father is an infinite fountain of light, but Jesus Christ is the communication of this light." He said the Father can be compared to the sun, and Jesus Christ "to the light that streams forth from him by which the world is enlightened." Christ's work is to glorify God: "Jesus Christ has this honor, to be the greatest instrument of

---

1. See Gerald McDermott, *Jonathan Edwards Confronts the Gods* (New York: Oxford University Press, 2000), 17–51.

2. WJE 23:166; orig. emph.

3. Accounts of Edwardsean Christology can be found in Robert W. Caldwell, *Communion in the Spirit: The Holy Spirit as the Bond of Union in the Theology of Jonathan Edwards* (Eugene: Wipf and Stock, 2006), 74–100; Robert Jenson, "Christology," in Sang Hyun Lee, ed., *The Princeton Companion to Jonathan Edwards* (Princeton: Princeton University Press, 2005), 72–86; and Michael D. Bush, "Jonathan Edwards's Christology," unpublished ms.

glorifying God that ever was." He does this by making God known to human beings, whose participation in God's joy and love constitutes redemption. In that work of redemption, Christ is "the instrument of God's glory that drives [the] pattern of emanation and return from God's inner life into creation and back to God." The assignment of that work and the deliberations about the manner of its accomplishment began in the inner-Trinitarian "covenant of redemption."[4]

The covenant of redemption was an agreement between the Father and the Son that the Triune God would redeem fallen humanity; there was also agreement on the means of redemption (ch. 21). The Father determined "to allow a redemption, and for whom it shall be. He pitches upon a Redeemer. He proposes... precisely what he should do as the terms of man's redemption, and all the work that he should perform in this affair, and the reward he should receive." Although the Father was "the first mover" in this covenant, the Son acted "wholly in his own right, as much as the Father."[5]

Yet the redemption was planned not primarily for the sake of the redeemed but for the Son and his glory. "God's end" in the creation "was to procure a spouse, or a mystical body, for his Son...for the adequate displays of his unspeakable and transcendent goodness and grace." Each member of the elect church was chosen for the sake of being in that mystical body that would glorify the Son. Just as "God chose every particle of inanimate matter" in the "body of a man...not...as a single, separate particle, but no otherwise than in that living body," so too "particular elect persons" are chosen "singly" but only in "respect to their union in the body of Christ." For God's "special aim in all was to procure one created child" through the union of believers with his Son. Therefore, in Stephen R. Holmes's words, "the election of Christ is first; the election of His spouse, or body, next, and the election of the members of that body only third."[6]

It was because of these acts of election that the world was created, and Jesus Christ was chosen to be principal agent of creation. This was a notion

---

4. WJE 24:483; WJE 10:535; WJE 18:70; Bush, "Edwards's Christology," 65.

5. WJE 9:119; WJE 24:291; WJE 20:435–36. The covenant of redemption was a familiar topic in Puritan theology. It was developed by the German and Dutch (respectively) theologians Kaspar Olevianus (1536–87) and Johannes Cocceius (1603–69), and became the foundation for the work of redemption detailed by van Mastricht, Edwards's favorite theologian. Van Mastricht, *Theoretico-Practica Theologia* II.24; V.I.vii; Adriaan C. Neele, *Petrus van Mastricht (1630–1706)* (Leiden, The Netherlands: Brill, 2009), 262.

6. WJE 23:178–79; Stephen R. Holmes, *God of Grace and God of Glory: An Account of the Theology of Jonathan Edwards* (Grand Rapids: Eerdmans, 2000), 133.

taught by Calvin and the orthodox Reformed divines, but Edwards put more emphasis on the "aim" of the creation being the work of redemption—as shown in the conclusion to *End of Creation*.[7] Therefore, since Christ "was to be the great means of God's glory" by "that great work of Christ as mediator," it was "meet" [fitting] that he should take the principal role in creating the world. Since he was to do the "principal work" in redemption, and both the beginning and end of the world are "subordinat[ed]" to the work of redemption, it was fitting that he should be the creator at the beginning and the judge at the end. In the creation of the first human beings, his "particular and distinct" role was to "endue man with understanding and reason," while the Spirit imparted a "holy will and inclination, with original righteousness." Jesus Christ filled the earth with "emanations, or shadows" of his own excellencies.[8]

> So that when we are delighted with flowery meadows and gentle breezes of wind, we may consider that we only see the emanations of the sweet benevolence of Jesus Christ; when we behold the fragrant rose and lily, we see his love and purity.... There are also many things wherein we may behold his awful majesty: in the sun in his strength, in comets, in thunder, in the towering thunder clouds, in ragged rocks and the brows of mountains.[9]

This beautiful world, full of the emanations of Jesus Christ, was created so that he could come into it "to fulfill and answer the covenant of works." This is "what the Apostle calls 'the law of works,' Romans 3:27." It includes "all the laws of God ever given to mankind," which include "the law of nature [the Ten Commandments] and political commands," obedience to parents, and particular religious commands given to Adam, Jews, and Christ himself. The commands that Christ obeyed "may be distributed into three particular laws," namely the moral law, the ceremonial law (all the laws that pertained to him as a Jew), and the "mediatorial law," such as the commands from the Father "to work such miracles, and teach such doctrines, and so to labor in the works of his public ministry, and to yield himself to such sufferings" as the Father

---

7. Richard A. Muller, *Post-Reformation Reformed Dogmatics*, 4 vols. (Grand Rapids: Baker Academic, 1987–2003), 4:289, 314, 321–22.

8. WJE 24:1100–101; WJE 24:126.

9. WJE 13:279. Edwards called these emanations and shadows "types," which not only point to but also contain the presence of Jesus Christ. See *Images of Divine* Things and *Types* in WJE 11, and ch. 8 in this volume.

prescribed. Since the first Adam failed to fulfill the covenant of works by disobeying "that special law [not to eat from one tree in the garden] that he was subject to as a moral head and surety," Christ as the second Adam had to obey the "special law that he was subject to, in his office of mediator and surety"—the mediatorial law. This law was "infinitely more difficult" to obey than the other two, and therefore "most meritorious." The result was that Christ fulfilled "the covenant that we had broken, and that was the covenant that must be fulfilled," the covenant of works.[10]

Christ and the Covenants

Edwards rejected at least some received Reformed understandings of covenants (ch. 21). He wrote early in his theological notebooks that Reformed theologians were wrong to believe the covenant of grace was made with human beings, and that the use of the word "covenant" at this point presumed we have to do something as a condition, which make[s] "us apt to depend on our own righteousness." This is "the foundation of Arminianism." So we should "leave off distinguishing the covenant of grace and the covenant of redemption."[11] For Edwards, Arminianism had less to do with Jacob Arminius (1560–1609) than simply a confidence that we can please God by our sincere endeavors for faith and virtue, thus suggesting that we can give assistance to God in our own salvation (ch. 3). Since some in his day were using "covenant of grace" in this manner, he suggested that the term be eliminated.

But elimination of that slippery term was not enough for Edwards. Christians needed to realize there is only one basic covenant. The covenant of works "never yet was abrogated" and is the only covenant God "has ever made with man." The covenant of grace is not another covenant, properly speaking, but a faulty expression for the means used to apply to believers the fulfillment of the covenant of works. Michael Bush observes that in his sermons Edwards still referred to the covenant of grace, perhaps because the time-worn phrase seemed impossible to excise.[12] But he also adds intriguingly that Perry Miller was right after all when he claimed Edwards rejected covenant theology. Later scholars have protested, pointing to Edwards's use of not only the covenants

---

10. WJE 9:308–309; WJE 18:496; WJE 9:309; WJE 18:496: WJE 9:309.

11. WJE 13:198–99.

12. WJE 13:217. Bush adds, "Every pastor knows that some battles are not worth fighting, and Edwards was no exception." Bush, "Edwards's Christology," 85n.

of works and redemption but also the national covenant. Yet David Weir has demonstrated that classical "federal theology" presented a prelapsarian (before the Fall) covenant of works as a foil for a postlapsarian (after the Fall) covenant of grace. It was this version of federal or covenant theology that Edwards denounced.[13] Miller was mostly wrong on Edwards and covenant theology (ch. 21), but Weir's work shows that Edwards, as was his wont in many areas of theology, reconfigured what had been passed down to him.

Following a later Reformed tradition, Edwards held that the covenant of redemption established the plans for Christ's redemptive work in history, and that redemption started not with the Incarnation but immediately after the Fall. Christ then took on a new role as mediator and intercessor, assuming "the care and burden of the government of the church and world." The Father "would have no more to do with man immediately ... but only through a mediator"—his Son. So it was the second person of the Trinity who appeared to Moses at the burning bush and to the seventy elders, Joshua, Gideon, Manoah, Isaiah in chapter 6 of his prophecy, and Daniel and the three Hebrew men in the fiery furnace. All visible manifestations of God, such as the various appearances of the "angel of the Lord," were really Jesus Christ in pre-Incarnation incarnations, "in the form of that nature he was afterwards to take upon him."[14]

But Jesus did more than simply appear in Old Testament times. He communicated eternal life to the "holy men in the old world." By faith in him and "reception of Christ," Enoch was translated; Moses received eternal happiness; and Job, Samuel, and David were saved. Adam and Eve and all the holy men and women of the Old Testament were saved, in advance, as it were, by Christ's sacrifice on the Cross: "God clothed our first parents [Adam and Eve] with Christ's righteousness ... when he clothed [them] with the coats of skins," and it was Christ's death "that satisfied for Abraham's sin." The Old Testament sacrifices that God required of the Jews were worthless in themselves but were commanded because, first, they taught the Jews that sin must be satisfied by suffering, and second, they "represented every day, week, month and year" the sacrifice of Christ on Calvary. The Old Testament was also inspired by Christ, in his Spirit, especially the prophets. Finally, the Old Testament was brimming with types of Christ. The smoking furnace in Genesis 14 "signified the sufferings of Christ," Joseph's rescue of his family in Egypt was

---

13. David A. Weir, *The Origins of the Federal Theology in Sixteenth-Century Reformation Thought* (New York: Oxford University Press, 1990).

14. WJE 9:130, 131, 239, 260, 195–97. For this reason perhaps Edwards called Christ "the angel of the covenant"; WJE 23:621.

a type of salvation by Christ, the Exodus was not only directed by Christ himself but also the greatest type of salvation by Christ, all altars represent "the divine nature of Christ that sanctifies the gift and renders it satisfactory and meritorious," Samson typified Christ in that his last sufferings destroyed Satan's work, and the battle between David and Absalom's forces "represents that great battle between Christ and his true church, and Antichrist and his adherents."[15] And so on. Perhaps the most-repeated theme of the thousands of entries in the Old Testament portion of Edwards's *Blank Bible* is that this or that person or event or teaching points to Christ and his redemption.

Yet for Edwards, Christ was not only the theme and author of the Old Testament. He is the director of the world: "The universe is the chariot in which [Christ] rides, and makes progress towards the last end of all things on the wheels of his providence." At times "the under part of the wheel of a chariot seems to run backward, but it is not so." Christ is moving his work of redemption forward at all times, even when "the church of God is brought low in the world." Christ directs even "the heathen" and uses their sacrifices to point to his own Great Sacrifice. He will continue directing the world until its glorious climax, when "the world in general will... be enlightened by him: when these glorious times shall come wherein all nations shall flow to the mountain of the Lord's house" (Is. 2:2). After the final judgment, Christ will present the Church to the Father, and the Father will dress the Son "in the brightest robes of love and grace as his wedding garments." Christ will then shine with "holy, sweet ravishing beauty and delight" because of the light streaming from the Father's face, and he will communicate this same beauty and glory to the church "by his sweet shining and smiling upon her." Heaven will be transformed, Christ will "resign up" the kingdom to the Father, relinquishing his role as "supreme head," and humble himself in his adoration of the Father. This will mean "higher enjoyment" for the Son and will show the saints that the "terrible majesty" that Christ showed in the final judgment is also "transcendent humility."[16]

Christ's Satisfaction

The greatest event in all the history of redemption—and the primary focus of Edwards's Christology—was Christ's satisfaction, which comprised all of his life but reached its apex in his death. Strictly speaking, redemption is the

---

15. WJE 10:523; WJE 9:139; WJE 14:456–57; WJE 9:238, 164, 171, 175; WJE 24:336, 336, 367.
16. WJE 24:315–16; WJE 14:457; WJE 10:595, 536; WJE 20:231–34.

purchase of the elect by Christ, but satisfaction on the cross was the price paid for that purchase. Therefore "[t]hat great Christian doctrine of Christ's satisfaction... is, as it were, the centre and hinge of all doctrines of pure revelation." At its heart is the notion of infinite divine justice which "must be satisfied." God "has been dishonored and injured, and his laws have been broken." Therefore "'tis a thing really incredible that God should let sin go, without any manner of public manifestation of his abhorrence of it." For "the demerit of sin is infinite." It deserves eternal destruction and infinite suffering since the essence of sin is to desire God's murder. A hypothetical "third being of perfect wisdom," different from both the Creator and the creation, would determine that the injury to the infinite Lord of the universe should be repaired, and his majesty vindicated. To forgive such injuries without punishing infinite sin would be to neglect "the sacredness of the authority" of the Creator and obscure its majesty. Justice demands "the greatest pain and horror in the soul," and this is what Christ endured.[17]

Edwards portrayed human sin not only in terms that Anselm long before had made famous (as violating the honor of a lord) but also in mercantile terms (as incurring a debt): "The desert of our sins may be considered as a debt that we owed to divine justice." The debt was infinite because the sin was against an infinite being. Christ's sufferings were only temporal and therefore might seem finite, but they were equivalent to the eternal sufferings demanded because of the infinite dignity of [Christ's] person. "Though it was not infinite suffering, yet it was equivalent to infinite suffering, for it was [at] infinite expense." The blood that Christ spilled was an infinite price because it was God's blood. Thus Edwards endorsed a substitutionary view of the atonement similar to Calvin's: Christ "laid down his life out of love for us; he has been pleased... to put himself in our stead in the most extreme case." The "sufferings of the head may be looked upon as the suffering of the members."[18]

Edwards also spoke of Christ's satisfaction in terms of moral government. "All but Epicureans will own that all creatures that are moral agents are subjects of God's moral government, and that therefore he has given a law to his creatures." That law must have sanctions, and its threats must be fulfilled when it is violated by rebellious subjects. For the nature and being of the law requires it: if the lawgiver who threatened does not fulfill his threats, the truth of his word is thrown into question. Therefore his threats "should be fulfilled

---

17. WJE 10:525, 601; WJE 13:281; WJE 14:452; WJE 18:436, 407; WJE 23:132, 134–35; WJE 10:598.

18. WJE 14:452; Calvin, *Institutes* 2.17.4.

in every punctilio," for his authority "don't [sic] consist in the power or influence he has on another by attractives, but coercives."¹⁹

Repentance without satisfaction was not enough. "Man by sin had lost" all love for God and "there was not the least spark of it remaining." Even if a man would "shed an ocean of tears [or] blood" or "labor in the fire a thousand years to make amends," it would serve no purpose. For God had been dishonored and injured, and his laws had been broken. So God "requires something else to make amends besides the miserable service of a rebellious worm." Repentance alone is disproportionate to the greatness of the injury against God. The Israelites may have thought their Old Testament sacrifices provided satisfaction to God. Yet these offerings were animal sacrifices and so were not offerings in which God's people presented themselves. Christ, in contrast, was God's equal and he offered himself to God.²⁰

Edwards insisted throughout his sermons and treatises that Christ's sufferings did more than release believers from the penalty against sin that would have sent them to hell. These sufferings were not only to satisfy God's anger and justice. They were positive and meritorious acts that purchased happiness in heaven. The same acts of suffering and obedience served both functions—appeasing God's anger and meriting his favor. They saved believers from hell and delivered them to heaven. Christ earned merit to take himself and his elect to heaven by acting "Adam's part all over again," fulfilling the covenant of works that Adam failed. John Gerstner thinks these repeated assertions of the double use of every act by Christ showed that Edwards was dissatisfied with the traditional distinction between the active and passive obedience of Christ. Seventeenth-century Reformed divines had divided Christ's acts into two sets, the "passive" ones used for satisfaction, and the "active" ones that merited heaven. Edwards seemed to think the distinction misleading if it suggested every act of Christ was one and not the other.²¹

---

19. WJE 18.440, 442, 444, 445.

20. WJE 10:601; WJE 14:451.

21. WJE 13:173; WJE 19:514; WJE 10:525; WJE 9:304–305: John Gerstner, *The Rational Biblical Theology of Jonathan Edwards*, 3 vols. (Powhatan, VA: Berea and Ligonier, 1992), 2:414, 431. Edwards agreed that generally Christ's active obedience before the passion was active and meritorious to win heaven for the saints, and that his passive suffering during his passion was principally for satisfaction for sin. Yet he also believed that "[a]ll Christ's sufferings from his first incarnation were of a propitiatory nature, as every act of obedience from his first incarnation was meritorious...[and his] yielding himself to death...was as much his principal act of obedience, and so that by which principally he merited heaven." WJE 19:514. On the atonement theology of Edwards's successors, see ch. 37.

Beauty, Love, and the Personal

While these acts of suffering and obedience were not limited to the passion, but began with the "humiliation" of an obscure birth and continued through thirty years of poverty and reproach, the last hours of the passion were the most meritorious and beautiful. These provided the "principal" part of the propitiation. This "last act of obedience" was "that by which principally he merited heaven." It was then, in the suffering that was more than in all the rest of his life, that the saints see the "brightest effulgence" of Christ's "beauty and amiable excellency." They realize that "Jesus Christ is infinitely the most beautiful and glorious object in the world," and it is more pleasant to see him than "to look on the sun in his meridian glory." They now have the pleasure "of considering that this lovely virtue is imputed to them. 'Tis the lovely robe, and robe of love, with which they are covered. Christ gives it to them, and puts it upon them, and by the beauty of this robe recommends 'em to the favor and delight of God the Father, as well as of all heaven besides." His beauty covers our "deformity," and it is only because of his beauty that we are "accepted and loved."[22]

This return to Christ's beauty is one of several ways that Edwards's theology of the atonement differed from that of his predecessors. Holmes has noted that, while the Western theological tradition had stressed the atonement as a legal transaction, and post-Reformation Protestants had emphasized the juridical and declarative dimensions, Edwards highlighted the aesthetic, rational, and personal aspects of the passion. Edwards's mercantile metaphors—Christ "purchasing" heaven and the Holy Spirit for the elect—commonly appeared in the context of personal union with Christ through the indwelling Spirit.[23]

The personal dimension is nowhere more evident than in the enormous emphasis Edwards placed on the incarnation and atonement as expressions of love. For example, in his early notebooks he wrote that Christ's hanging on the cross "was the most wonderful act of love that ever was." In it Christ showed his infinite love for the Father. "[T]here he made an offer of his love to the world." Far from being an abstract declaration of peace, Christ taking on suffering flesh was a passionate and touching act of love—comparable to our love for the opposite sex. The same "inclination which in us is turned to the other sex, in him is turned to the church, which is his spouse." In a remarkable

---

22. WJE 18:488; WJE 10:539; WJE 18:495; WJE 13:454.

23. Holmes, *God of Grace*, 143, 148, 147.

allusion to romantic and sexual love, Edwards said that "when we feel love to anyone of the other sex, 'tis a good way to think of the love of Christ to an holy and beautiful soul."[24]

He also compared Christ's love for the church to the affections of a friend or brother. But even more, this was a love of heart-wrenching sacrifice. Christ lost on the cross infinitely more than the damned lose since "his blessedness in the love and communion with God was infinitely greater." When his passion was approaching and he could foresee the horrendous suffering he was to endure, and then when he actually felt the torments and cruelties and insults, "his love did not fail." He still yielded himself to the infinite pain. "He waded through the sea of blood and wrath." Edwards asked, "Where is there anything that can parallel this love?"[25]

The Logic of the Atonement

If Edwards seemed to prefer thinking of the satisfaction and atonement of Christ in terms of beauty and love, he also felt compelled to argue for the logic and rationality of the atonement against deist critics. Deists made at least three charges against the orthodox doctrine of the atonement—that justice could be satisfied by earnest human efforts, that God was not obligated to fulfill his threats, and that the merits of one person could not be imputed to another.[26] Against the first charge, Edwards argued that even if "all the men in the world should offer to be crucified for the sake of one man" and "if the archangel" and all the other angels "should assume human bodies" and undergo as much disgrace as Christ did and hang on crosses in pain and torment for thousands of years, divine justice still would not be satisfied. For no finite being can endure infinite wrath, the least sin deserves infinite punishment, and no finite being has the power or wisdom to fit us for heaven. "They have not the power to raze out the old image of Satan, nor skills enough to draw the image of God upon our souls."[27]

---

24. WJE 13:390, 332.

25. WJE 19:585, 588–89; WJE 13:371; WJE 18:408; WJE 19:511. Edwards details the sufferings of Jesus most vividly in his 1736 sermon on Is. 53:3(b), WJEO 51.

26. The Socinians (ch. 3) had also attacked the orthodox notion of transferral of guilt and merit, but Edwards's principal exposure to these criticisms was in deist writings. He took note of some of these in one *Miscellanies* entry devoted to Thomas Chubb (1679–1746), one of the two deists (Matthew Tindal [1657–1733] was the other) to whom Edwards referred by name. For more on deism, see McDermott, *Jonathan Edwards Confronts the Gods*, 17–51.

27. WJE 10:523–24.

Against the presumption that God does not have to fulfill his threat to Adam and his descendants that they "would surely die" (Gen. 2:17), Edwards suggested an aesthetic approach. The "fitness of things" requires that a lawgiver give regard to his own threats and their fulfillment. And if it is fitting that the divine Lawgiver pay such regard, it is apparent that the fulfillment of threats is an issue of truth. If the Lawgiver sets aside the rule he had made one time, why not twice? Or four times? And in that case, "how can the subject know but that he will *always* depart from it [the rule]?" Then God would not be trustworthy.[28]

To the belief that merit cannot be imputed to another person, Edwards replied, in the very last set of *Miscellanies* he ever wrote, with a long description of relations between a patron and a client. In such a relationship, he argued, the merit of one can become the merit of the other "in some degree." When a patron's heart is so united to that of his client "that, when the client is destroyed, he from love is willing to take his destruction on himself... then he may properly be accepted as perfectly one with regard to the interest of the client." This is true even when the client has done wrong, as long as the patron shows that he "perfectly disapproves of his offense and unworthiness." If the patron "be greater and vastly superior as to rank and degree of existence," and is willing to bear sufferings for the client, and there is "thus a mutual union between patron and client," then the patron's merit "being imputed to the client" is "in all respects proper, according to the nature of things and common sense of intelligent beings, and of no evil or improper consequence."[29] In other words, if Thomas Chubb and his fellow deists thought imputation violated common sense, then their sense was not very common.

The Person of Christ

Edwards spent comparatively little time discussing the intricacies of the doctrine of the person of Christ. His reflections on this subject were usually made in the context of, and were often framed by, his thinking about the Trinity and the work of redemption. So, for example, he said it was Christ who was chosen to suffer because in the inner- Trinitarian counsels the Father decided it would be "a glorious manifestation of the love of both natures towards man." And we shall see shortly that Edwards's understanding of the hypostatic union was modeled on Christ's union with the church in the work of redemption.[30]

---

28. WJE 23:146–47; emph. add.

29. WJE 23:487, 488, 714, 715–16.

30. WJE 18:152–53.

Because of Edwards's overwhelming interest in redemption, he returned repeatedly throughout his sermons and treatises, especially *A History of the Work of Redemption*, to Christ's three offices—prophet, priest, and king. At the fall of the first humans, Christ began to take "the care of fallen man in the execution of all his offices." From this day forward, he would "teach mankind in the exercise of his prophetic office and... intercede for fallen man in the [exercise of the] priestly [office]." Moreover "he took on him as it were the care and burden of the government of the church and of the world." As prophet, Christ was the "most eminent counselor" in the history of the world, foretelling his death and resurrection, the descent of the Holy Spirit, and the fall of Jerusalem in great detail. As priest, he made atonement for sin and procured for men the favor and blessing of God. He continues to serve as priest in heaven by pleading his own satisfaction and merits to secure believers from falling away. As king, he dispenses life as he pleases and eternal life according to his power. He defends his people as the Lord of Hosts, showing his kingly power on earth by his miracles.[31]

But if Edwards developed these familiar Reformed themes of Christ's three offices, he also felt compelled to defend orthodox Christology against new challenges coming from deism. Against the deists who said God could forgive without coming to earth as a man, Edwards insisted repeatedly on the necessity of an incarnation. Perfect human obedience and suffering were needed to fulfill the covenant of works, but "Christ merely as God was not capable" of either. The divine nature cannot suffer, "for it is impassable and infinitely above all suffering; neither is it capable of obedience to that law that was given to man." God could neither obey man's law nor suffer man's punishment. Christ had to "take upon him a created nature" because it was necessary that a man obey the law given to man, the same nature that sinned had to die, and God knew that the "same world that was the stage of man's fall and ruin should also be the stage of his redemption."[32]

Yet it was not only strict necessity that produced the incarnation; it was also the eternal Word's loving desire. Christ had always loved human nature and its shape. He had looked forward to "taking the human nature and an [*sic*] human body." That's why from time to time before the real incarnation, he "so often under the old testament appeared in human shape." These pre-incarnation incarnations were images and "earnest[s] of his future incarnation."[33]

---

31. WJE 9:130; WJE 20:254–74; sermon on Ps. 110:4, WJEO 62; sermon on Luke 22:31, WJEO 47; sermon on 1 Cor. 15:25–26, WJEO 53; sermon on John 10:37 (a), WJEO 55.

32. WJE 9:296–97.

33. WJE 24:924; WJE 13:329. At the same time, Edwards argued against Isaac Watts' view that Christ's human soul was eternal. Edwards held that it was not created until the moment of conception in Mary's womb. WJE 23:89–92; see Caldwell, *Communion in the Spirit*, 80–83.

So the Word was made flesh, and what flesh it was! Edwards marveled that "there is scarce anything that is excellent, beautiful, pleasant, or profitable but what is used in the Scripture as an emblem of Christ." He is called a lion, a lamb, the bread of life and water of life, the true vine, a rose and lily, the bright and morning star, the sun of righteousness, and the light of the world.[34]

But *how* was the Word made flesh? Early on, Edwards had determined that the only way for God to be in a creature was by the Holy Spirit acting as a bonding agent for the purpose of union, as in the union of Christ with believers. Edwards then applied this dynamic to the incarnation. When the tradition said that the Logos "assumed" human flesh, Edwards said it meant that the Spirit created Christ's human nature ex nihilo at the moment of conception in Mary's womb, and simultaneously united this human nature to the Logos. The human nature included Christ's human soul, which was originally finite, and the Spirit was acting in his customary role as a "principle of union." The result was the "sanctification" of Christ's human nature by virtue of its being joined to the Spirit of holiness. Christ's finite soul became "infinitely holy" because it was united to the infinitely holy second person in the Trinity. Edwards's famous sermon on "the excellency of Christ" is a moving depiction of the myriad paradoxes that result when the infinitely holy is joined to mere humanity: in the same person with infinite "highness" and glory are infinite humility and submission.[35]

The Hypostatic Union

Edwards explained the inner workings of this hypostatic union (from the Greek *hupostasis*, translated as "reality" or "person") by saying that the Logos speaks and acts by using the human nature of Christ, both body and soul, as an "organ." The Holy Spirit is the "means of conveyance" of the Logos' will and understanding to Christ's human will and understanding. Another way Edwards put it was to say that the Holy Spirit conveyed the Son's power and knowledge and will and acts of the divine nature to the faculties of Christ's human soul. Because Christ's human consciousness received the consciousness of the Logos, there was between them what "we call identity of consciousness." Because of this identity, there are not two persons but only one undivided person. So when "the divine person" laid down his life, "there was the act of Christ as God in it as well as man."[36]

---

34. WJE 10:535.

35. WJE 13:528; WJE 18:334; WJE 14:449; WJE 19:565–64. On the Spirit as the bond of union in the hypostatic union, see Caldwell, *Communion in the Spirit*, 80–83.

36. WJE 18:364, 412, 364; WJE 19:497.

More than one scholar has observed that this way of thinking about the hypostatic union parallels and perhaps follows Edwards's way of seeing Christ's union with his church and the inner-Trinitarian union—subjects on which Edwards wrote far more. We have seen that for Edwards the Spirit is the bond of union as the love between the Father and the Son (ch. 13), and we shall see that the "internal, spiritual harmony between Christ and the soul" is a union held in place by the Holy Spirit (ch. 17 & 23). Indeed, for Edwards, it is not the nature of Christ alone but this spiritual harmony between Christ and his church that is "the nature and genius of Christianity." The purpose of all doctrines, even the doctrine of the hypostatic union, is "to bring about this sweet harmony between the soul and Jesus Christ."[37]

If the hypostatic union was subordinated to other doctrines, it nevertheless was a "wonderful mystery." In one divine person are two natures, gloriously luminous and majestic but distinct. The human nature—not the divine—suffered and died. Yet while distinct, the two natures shared with one another. This is the doctrine of "communication of attributes" (*communicatio idiomatum*) that, as Robert Jenson has remarked, has been acknowledged by the mainstream theological tradition and yet held at arm's length. Western theology (including most of the Reformed tradition) has generally restricted its meaning to the notion that attributes from both natures can be ascribed to the person of Christ, while Lutherans have said Christ's human nature takes on the predicates of the divine nature. Edwards stepped boldly where angels feared to tread, proclaiming that the same person who made the world and fills heaven and earth is "a child in bodily clothes...sucking the breasts of a woman," both "a worm of the dust and...the King of Glory." There are many intimations in Edwards's sermons and notebooks that the humanity of this King was the same as ours. He is able to pity us because he experienced the same "difficulties," dwelt in a frail body like ours, and took upon himself "its weak, broken state." He was subject to hunger, thirst, weariness, pain, and death as other human beings are. Just as believers increase in holiness, Christ increased in the holiness of his nature. His sufferings "purged him from imputed guilt," and he was "made perfect by sufferings." When the thoughts of the Logos were communicated to his human soul by the Holy Spirit, the man Christ Jesus could grasp those thoughts only in finite ideas; he was conscious of them only "after the manner of a creature," so that he could not remember all the details of his pre-incarnate conversations with the Father "as they were in the infinite mind."[38]

---

37. WJE 13:528; WJE 19:447.

38. WJEO 54, sermon on Ps. 24:7–10, 9; WJE 23:153; Jenson, "Christology," 78; WJE 10:599; WJE 19:443; WJE 20:333. Because of this emphasis on Jesus' finite knowledge, Edwards seems to have retained the Reformed principle of *finitum non capax infiniti* and the *extra calvinisticum*. See Caldwell, *Communion in the Spirit*, 93–96.

But there are other suggestions in Edwards's writings that the divine nature so overshadowed the human nature that Christ's humanity was unlike our own. Edwards told his parishioners that Moses' burning bush was never consumed as a demonstration that Christ's human nature could never perish because of the divinity in it. He preached that Christ never had to repress lustful desires or practice mortification because of his sinless nature. Readers might wonder why Christ's sinlessness, which Edwards assumed, would require that he never had wrongful impulses. Would he not have had to deny lustful desires? If not, then it does not seem that he inherited a morally fallen human nature, as Calvin, Owen, and Barth assumed he did. Calvin believed the sinful nature was cleansed by the Holy Spirit either before or during conception, while Owen and Barth argued that the Spirit over time gradually purified Christ's fallen human nature. Edwards seems to have accepted only what W. Ross Hastings calls a metaphysically fallen nature, not a morally fallen nature. That is, Christ inherited a human nature that was subject to physical decay but was "morally impeccable." For he wrote that at birth the Holy Spirit protected the Christ child from his mother's "pollution," that because of his divine nature Christ "was not liable to fall and commit sin," and "the human soul of Jesus Christ [was] necessarily holy."[39] Did Christ, then, suffer the same temptations as we do if he did not struggle with a morally fallen nature?

Edwards would have rejected the strong kenotic theology of the nineteenth and twentieth centuries in which Christ was said to have relinquished most or all of his divine prerogatives. Edwards believed that Christ retained his divine knowledge (yet "after the manner of a creature") and omnipotence and yet chose not to exercise them: "When the Apostle says, Christ emptied himself, as Phil. 2:7, he means he *appeared* in the world without his former glory and joy." At the cross, Christ did not have the "full enjoyment of his Father," for "God hid his face and withdrew the comfortable and joyful tokens of his presence, which made him cry out, 'My God, [My God, Why hast thou forsaken me?']" But throughout that unspeakable ordeal Christ nonetheless kept his divine happiness.[40]

There are several dangers to this approach. Hastings warns that it runs the risk of blurring the persons of the Spirit and the Son, disconnecting the

---

39. WJE 19:500; WJE 9:320; W. Ross Hastings, "'Honouring the Spirit': Analysis and Evaluation of Jonathan Edwards's Pneumatological Doctrine of the Incarnation," *International Journal of Systematic Theology* 7 (2005): 297; WJE 18:414; WH 2:949; WJE 1:281.

40. WJE 13:340; WJE 18:57; WJE 15:186; WJEO 51, sermon on Rev.14:14, 6; WJE 19:500; emph. add.

God-man from fallen humanity, and making Jesus Christ appear distant and not fully human.[41] The incarnate Son could seem to be more like God acting *on* a man than *as* a man. There is also a possible impact of Edwards's christological views on his soteriology. For, as Gregory Nazianzus famously declared, what is not assumed is not redeemed. If Christ did not assume our morally fallen nature, then it is not redeemed.

Yet Edwards's privileging of the divine nature should be seen in the light of his apologetic battles against Arians and Unitarians who denied Christ's deity. Moreover, his conviction that the man Christ Jesus needed his divine nature to be holy was a call for Arminians—relying on the power of their own self-determining wills—to realize that they would fail in their ethical striving apart from union with Deity. Edwards's Christology was similar to that of John of Damascus, who described *perichoresis* as Christ's divine nature penetrating his human nature but not conversely.[42] Both the Damascene and Edwards realized that "universal truth is constituted and found precisely as some particular"—not the union of the Son of God with some abstract human "nature," but with the unique humanity created for the one person Jesus Christ. While there are difficulties in Edwards's answer to the question of how two natures could be united in one person, it is well to consider that "a fully satisfactory answer has never been given."[43]

Ontic Enlargement

One last theme in Edwards's Christology should be mentioned—ontic enlargement.[44] Or as Bush has put it, "Whatever begins in Christ, and whatever is true of Christ, soon *grows*."[45] This is true of his own manhood during the incarnation, the progressive union of the saints with the Trinity, and his own mystical body. In his treatise on the end of creation, Edwards wrote that Christ is completed and enlarged by the gradual growth of the church.

---

41. Hastings, "Honouring the Spirit," 293, 295, 297.

42. This is why some scholars have spoken of the "Alexandrian flavor" that runs through Edwards's Christology: Jenson, *America's Theologian*, 115; Caldwell, *Communion in the Spirit*, 97.

43. John of Damascus, *On the Orthodox Faith*, 3.4, and 7; Jenson, 83, 73.

44. I use this word rather than "ontological" to denote an expansion in God's relations to other beings rather than any change in God's essence.

45. Bush, "Jonathan Edwards's Christology," 197.

> God looks on the communication of himself, and the emanation of the infinite glory and good that are in himself to belong to the fullness and completeness of himself, as though he were not in his most complete and glorious state without it. Thus the church of Christ (toward whom and in whom are the emanations of his glory and communications of his fullness) is called the fullness of Christ: as though he were not in his complete state without her; as Adam was in a defective state without Eve.[46]

Edwards explained that the Trinitarian God is, in one sense, eternally complete and perfect, fully actual and self-sufficient. Yet, at the same time, God *ad extra* (God's action by the Son and Spirit in creation and history) is the external *repetition* of his own being, and therefore a kind of ontic self-enlargement, just as the beams of light from the sun are an "increase, repetition or multiplication" of its glory; God, "from his goodness, as it were enlarges himself in a more excellent and divine manner... by flowing forth, and expressing himself in [his creatures], and making them to partake of him, and rejoicing in himself expressed in them, and communicated to them."[47]

This means that Christ's work in redemption is the temporal extension of God's actuality—a repetition in time of God's internal actuality. What happens in the history of redemption does not add to God's being *ad intra* but constitutes the external extension of God's internal fullness.[48] God being is not timeless self-identity, as in some Platonic versions of the Christian deity, but the infinite sum and comprehension of the being and beauty that unfolds in the course of redemptive history. The Incarnation was something new, God's glory shown forth through the Incarnation, and Christ himself was enlarged by the growth of the church through time. This is why the church is said in scripture to be the completeness of Christ (Eph. 1:23), "as if Christ were not complete without the Church."[49]

While Edwards retained certain Reformed themes, such as Christ's limited human knowledge during his earthly life, he never felt constrained by his heritage. Unlike Calvinistic predecessors who emphasized the distinctness of the two natures in Christ in a fashion similar to that of the ancient Antiochene

---

46. WJE 8:439.

47. WJE 8:433, 461–62.

48. Sang Hyun Lee, *The Philosophical Theology of Jonathan Edwards* (Princeton: Princeton University Press, 1988), 170–242.

49. WJE 13:272.

Christology, Edwards asserted the divine nature over the human nature in a manner more like that of the Alexandrians. His teaching that the Spirit and not the Son is the agent of hypostatic union was an indication that Edwards was his own man—rarely one to follow lock-step behind his Reformed forbears.[50]

---

50. Caldwell, *Communion in the Spirit*, 96, 83–87. Caldwell points out that Edwards also differed from the Reformed mainstream by emphasizing the commonalities between the hypostatic and all other unions, such as that between Christ and his church (86–87).

17

The Holy Spirit

IT IS A truism that the Holy Spirit is the neglected or unknown member of the Trinity. The Father and the Son generally receive far more attention than the Spirit.[1] Yet the Spirit has been emphasized in times of religious resurgence—among Montanists (second century), "spiritual Franciscans" (thirteenth and fourteenth centuries), radical Protestants (sixteenth century), early modern devotional movements (Carmelite, Jansenist, Quietist, Puritan, and Pietist; seventeenth century), and Pentecostal-Charismatics (twentieth century).[2] Geoffrey Nuttall described the century prior to Edwards as "the great century of inquiry into the Spirit."[3] William Clagett, an Anglican, debated John Owen, an Independent, on the topic of the Holy Spirit. Owen's *Pneumatologia* (1674) anticipated Edwards's teaching by insisting on the immediate agency of the Spirit in regeneration, the Spirit's role in giving spiritual insight, and the Spirit's employment of the natural faculties. Clagett did not accept that the human mind must be spiritually renewed to understand divine truths and so he foreshadowed the anti-revivalists of Edwards's day.

Against this backdrop, Edwards developed an understanding of the Holy Spirit that was an expression of his personal experience, a response to the religious revivals of his day, and an original contribution to Christian theological reflection.[4] Many of Edwards's contemporaries affirmed the

---

1. Sang Lee speaks of "the Western church's typically underdeveloped doctrine of the agency of the Holy Spirit" (WJE 21:19).

2. For a survey of the early modern developments, see Ted Campbell, *The Religion of the Heart: A Study of European Religious Life in the Seventeenth and Eighteenth Centuries* (Columbia, SC: University of South Carolina Press, 1991); and Ronald A. Knox, *Enthusiasm: A Chapter in the History of Religion* (Oxford, UK: Oxford University Press, 1950).

3. Geoffrey Nuttall, *The Holy Spirit in Puritan Faith and Experience* (Oxford, UK: Blackwell, 1947), preface.

4. On Edwards's doctrine of the Holy Spirit, see Robert W. Caldwell III, "The Holy Spirit as the Bond of Union in the Theology of Jonathan Edwards," PhD diss., Trinity Evangelical Divinity School, 2003, published as *Communion in the Spirit* (Milton Keynes, UK: Paternoster, 2008),

deity and personality of the Spirit but had little more to say. Yet Edwards often wrote of the office and function of the Spirit, as in his *Personal Narrative*: "I have many times had a sense of the glory of the third person in the Trinity, in his office of Sanctifier; in his holy operations communicating divine light and life to the soul. God in the communications of his Holy Spirit, has appeared as an infinite fountain of divine glory and sweetness; being full and sufficient to fill and satisfy the soul."[5] The Spirit able "to fill and satisfy the soul" was intrinsic to Edwards's experience.

Edwards believed that Protestant theology had not given the Spirit his due. An emphasis on Christ and his atonement had inadvertently made the Spirit an afterthought. For "if we suppose no more than used to be supposed about the Holy Ghost, the concern of the Holy Ghost in the work of redemption is not equal with the Father's and the Son's, nor is there an equal part of the glory of this work [that] belongs to him." Traditional Protestantism emphasized "the paying of an infinite price by Christ's offering up himself in sacrifice." The Spirit was neither the one sacrificing himself (i.e., Christ) nor the one who received this sacrifice (i.e., the Father). Thus the Spirit became, as it were, a spectator to the great transaction of redemption, and was "merely to apply to us" the blessing purchased by Christ's death. In this way, the Spirit's function was "but a little thing" in comparison to what Christ had done. In response, Edwards proposed a different way of construing the atonement, according to which "God is himself the portion and purchased inheritance of his people" and "all our good is...in the Holy Ghost, as he is himself all our good." For the Holy Spirit is the love of God poured out into the hearts of the saints, uniting them with Father and Son. In Christ's atonement, the Holy Spirit is the "thing purchased," and, in terms of valuation, "the price, and the thing bought with that price, are equal...and therefore 'tis the same glory, and an equal glory."[6] Edwards's idea

---

and Caldwell, "The Holy Spirit as the Bond of Union in the Theology of Jonathan Edwards," in *Reformation and Revival Journal* 12 (2003): 43–58; W. Ross Hastings, "'Honouring the Spirit': Analysis and Evaluation of Jonathan Edwards's Pneumatological Doctrine of the Incarnation," *International Journal of Systematic Theology* 7 (2005): 279–99; Sang Lee, "Editor's Introduction," in WJE 21:1–106, esp. 38–62; Steven M. Studebaker, "Jonathan Edwards's Pneumatological Concept of Grace and Dispositional Soteriology," *Pro Ecclesia* 14 (2005): 324–39; and Thomas Templeton Taylor, "The Spirit of the Awakening: The Pneumatology of New England's Great Awakening in Historical and Theological Context," PhD diss., University of Illinois at Urbana-Champaign, 1988.

5. WJE 16:801.

6. WJE 21:136–38.

of spiritual exchange in the atonement made the presence and work of the Holy Spirit in the believer equal in value to the death of Jesus Christ. In this way, he emphatically asserted the preciousness of the gift of the Holy Spirit.

The Spirit, the Father, and the Son

The 1690s witnessed the beginnings of the "Trinitarian Controversy." During the same decade, the deistic debate got underway, and both developments reflected an increased emphasis on "reasonableness" in English-language theology. Anglican theologian Samuel Clarke stoked the fires of controversy with *The Scripture Doctrine of the Trinity* (1712)—a work that rejected the Athanasian Creed's affirmation of three coequal and coeternal persons in the Godhead and treated Trinitarian doctrine as nonessential. Though the debate subsided by the 1720s, Cotton Mather in 1724 was concerned that "so many of our Brethren should so openly declare, that they...can receive no CHRIST but one that is infinitely Inferiour and Posteriour to the Eternal Father."[7] Even the respected evangelical minister, hymn-writer, and British supporter of Edwards Isaac Watts fell under suspicion of being less than fully orthodox in his view of Christ.

Edwards read a number of works arising out of the Trinitarian Controversy, and the impetus he received may have stirred him, around 1730, to begin writing the *Discourse on the Trinity*. While this discourse, at first blush, was "an Augustinian explanation of the relationship between the persons of the Trinity," it also offered an account of God's external relations with human beings through the Spirit. For Edwards, in Ken Minkema's words, "the Holy Spirit was nothing less than the embodiment of God's love, and it was the Holy Spirit itself that entered into the believer's soul and became the new 'principle.'"[8] Within the Trinity, the Holy Spirit was the mutual love of the Father and the Son, as Edwards wrote: "So the Holy Spirit does in some ineffable and inconceivable manner proceed and is breathed forth both from the Father and Son, by the divine essence being wholly poured and flowing out in that infinitely intense, holy and pure love and delight that continually and unchangeably breathes forth from the Father and the Son, primarily towards each other and secondarily towards the creature."[9] With respect to the Spirit's

---

7. Kenneth Minkema, in WJE 14:43, with n.3, citing W.C. Ford, ed., *The Diary of Cotton Mather, 1681–1724*, 2 vols. (New York: Ungar, 1957), 2:296.

8. Minkema, in WJE 14:45.

9. WJE 21:185–86. Edwards spoke of the Spirit's procession in two ways. This was a procession from the Father and the Son together—known technically as "double procession"—and yet also a procession from the Father, taken singly. The idea of single procession was

work outside of the Holy Trinity, the Spirit was the source of all good: "The Holy Spirit is the sum of all good. 'Tis the fullness of God. The holiness and happiness of the Godhead consists in it; and in the communion or partaking of it consists all the true loveliness and happiness of the creature."[10]

Robert Caldwell argued that the Holy Spirit in Edwards's thought served not only as the bond of union in the Godhead, but also the model and means of all holy unions. Edwards stated the principle explicitly: "But the Spirit that proceeds from the Father and the Son is the bond of this union, as it is of all holy union between the Father and the Son, and between God and the creature, and between the creatures among themselves. All seems to be signified in Christ's prayer in...John 17:21. Therefore this Spirit of love is the 'bond of perfectness' (Col. 3:14) throughout the whole blessed society or family in heaven and earth."[11] Caldwell related the Spirit's inter-Trinitarian work to three other forms of union involving created as well as divine persons—the union of Christ's divine and human natures, the mystical union of believers with Christ, and the union of fellowship among believers.[12] The Spirit's work is to enable communion or participation in salvation: "Although Jesus Christ prepares the way for man's salvation by his righteousness and sufferings, yet 'tis the immediate work of the Holy Ghost actually to make men partakers of that salvation; 'tis he that doth the finishing stroke."[13]

The Spirit of Grace

Edwards identified God's grace with the direct, immediate presence of the Holy Spirit in the believer: "All gospel righteousness, virtue and holiness is called grace, not only because 'tis entirely the free gift of God, but because 'tis the Holy Spirit in man; which, as we have said, is grace or love.... This grace is the Holy Spirit; because it is said, we receive of Christ's fullness, and grace for his grace

---

characteristic of the early Greek Fathers, and continued into Eastern Orthodox Christianity in medieval and modern times. By contrast, the idea of double procession has been a feature of Western Christianity in both Roman Catholicism and Protestantism (chs. 13, 43).

10. WJE 21:188.

11. WJE 21:185–86.

12. Caldwell, "The Holy Spirit as the Bond of Union," iv.

13. WJE 14:377.

[John 1:16]."[14] God's Spirit, dwelling in humankind, exerts himself according to his own "proper nature": "So that true saving grace is no other than that very love of God—that is, God, in One of the Persons of the Trinity, uniting Himself to the soul of a creature, as a vital principle, dwelling there and exerting Himself by the faculties of the soul of man, in His own proper nature, after the manner of a principle of nature."[15] So intimate was the union between the Holy Spirit and the creature that the Spirit became, as it were, a "quality" of human beings: "The Spirit of God seems in Scripture to be spoken of as to become a quality of the persons in whom it resided, so that they are called spiritual persons; as when we say 'a virtuous man,' we speak of virtue as the quality of the man."[16]

The Spirit was not only present with and to human beings, but functioned as a "vital principle" in them. Yet the Holy Spirit functioned in accordance with—not in opposition to—the natural faculties. Through the conferral of the Spirit, says Edwards, "a new foundation [is] laid in the nature of the soul, for a new kind of exercises" of the saints' "ordinary faculties."[17] The sermon "A Divine and Supernatural Light" stated that the natural faculties were not rendered passive, but active, through the Spirit's agency: "'Tis not intended that the natural faculties are not made use of in it. The natural faculties are the subject of this light: and they are the subject in such a manner, that they are not merely passive, but active in it; the acts and exercises of man's understanding are concerned and made use of in it. God in letting in this light into the soul, deals with man according to his nature, or as a rational creature; and makes use of his human faculties."[18]

Sang Lee notes that Edwards's theology of grace and of the Spirit may be understood against the backdrop of medieval theology. Peter Lombard in the 1100s identified the grace of God in love or charity as the direct, unmediated presence of the Holy Spirit. Yet later theologians who followed Lombard wished to emphasize God's transformation of the self as well as God's immediate presence. This resulted in a scholastic distinction between "uncreated grace" (i.e., God's immediate presence) versus "created grace" (virtuous dispositions as effects of God's presence).[19] What became controversial, says Lee,

---

14. WJE 13:345; Sang Lee, in WJE 21:41.

15. WJE 21:194.

16. WJE 21:197.

17. WJE 2:206.

18. WJE 17:416.

19. See E.M. Burke, "Grace," in *New Catholic Encyclopedia* (New York: McGraw-Hill, 1967), 6:658–72.

was that "'created grace' for Thomas Aquinas appeared to be a kind of semi-independent or intermediary principle that could be separated from 'uncreated grace.'" For Aquinas, the virtues were intermediary principles through which grace effected human actions. Aquinas's problem with Lombard's view was that the self-moving nature of the human will might be compromised or overturned if the actions of God's grace in the self were direct or immediate. So "Aquinas rejected the Lombardian conception of grace as the direct activity of the Holy Spirit, although for him the presence of 'created grace' did not negate the Holy Spirit's continuing activity for the regenerate." The Protestant Reformers viewed "created grace" in Aquinas and others as a threat to the sovereignty and gratuitous nature of grace. In reaction against Luther, the Council of Trent went further than earlier scholasticism in describing "created grace" as an "inherent" quality in the regenerate.[20]

What about Edwards? Did he conceive of the Spirit along the lines of Aquinas or that of Lombard? Sometimes Edwards spoke of an infused disposition in a manner analogous to Thomas's intermediary habit.[21] An early miscellany referred to the "believing disposition" in a way that sounded Thomistic.[22] *Charity and Its Fruits* stated that "this blessing of the saving grace of God is a quality inherent in the nature of him who is the subject of it."[23] Yet Lee argues that references to grace as an inherent quality of the regenerate person are outnumbered by many passages that directly identify saving grace with the Holy Spirit. He wrote that "there is no other principle of grace in the soul than the very Holy Ghost dwelling in the soul and acting there as a vital principle."[24] Such a statement seems to set aside the "created grace" notion or its analogue. Lee concludes that Edwards's view was "neither simply that of Lombard nor that of Aquinas but rather a unique synthesis of the two—specifically, of Lombard's idea of grace as the Holy Spirit himself and of the Thomistic emphasis upon grace as functioning in and through the natural powers of the regenerate."[25] The Spirit worked in and through the natural faculties, and yet human beings were dependent on God's grace. For "if God should take away his Spirit out of the soul, all habits and acts of grace would of themselves cease

---

20. Sang Lee, in WJE 21:47–48.

21. Anri Morimoto, *Jonathan Edwards and the Catholic Vision of Salvation* (University Park, PA: Pennsylvania State University, 1995), 46.

22. WJE 13:214.

23. WJE 8:157.

24. WJE 21:49.

25. Sang Lee, in WJE 21:52. Lee's point regarding grace is paralleled in our discussion elsewhere of the "divine light" or "new sense" as transcending natural human abilities and yet as functioning through them (chs. 10, 20).

as immediately as light ceases in a room when a candle is carried out."[26] On a moment-by-moment basis, gracious habits and acts were a reflection of God's gracious presence through the power of the Spirit.

The Spirit of Conviction and Conversion

Seventeenth-century Puritan theology taught that the Holy Spirit, prior to a person's first exercise of faith, prepared a sinner for conversion. Edwards agreed. In reference to the biblical text of John 16:8—"and when he [i.e., the Spirit] is come, he will reprove the world of sin, and of righteousness, and of judgment"— Edwards spoke of "the threefold work of the Holy Ghost."[27] The Spirit made the world aware of the necessity of receiving Christ, the sufficiency of Christ's righteousness, and Christ's power as a judge and a deliverer.[28] Like earlier Puritans, Edwards used the term "conviction" to refer to the Spirit's work in persuading people of the gospel message. The Spirit deserved credit for this—convincing those trusting in their own righteousness to trust in Christ instead. To slight this work of the Spirit was to "rob him [the Spirit] of all the glory of convincing men of righteousness."[29] Yet how does the Spirit "convict"? The Spirit worked through sacred scripture and human reason. Neither factor could be ignored. "The Holy Ghost convinces by arguments, he enlightens the reason, and makes use of the gospel. The Word is the sword in the hand of the Spirit [Eph. 6:17]."[30] Reason and the word of God functioned in harmony with one another and with the Spirit's agency. Edwards linked the Spirit to his teaching on the "divine light." He wrote that "the Holy Spirit…lets in that divine light that discovers truth, and makes it appear as truth…by its own intrinsic evidence, which it carries with it."[31]

For Edwards, the will moved by God's special grace freely yet necessarily turned toward God. On the other hand, there were common operations of the Spirit producing convictions of sin, and such stirrings could be and often were resisted. This resistance was highly offensive to God, as Edwards explained: "There is no kind of sins so provoking to God as those committed against the inward convictions and strivings of his Holy Spirit."[32] He

---

26. WJE 21:196.
27. WJE 14:375–436.
28. WJE 14:371.
29. WJE 14:412.
30. WJE 14:393.
31. WJE 14:407.
32. WJE 19:266.

went on to say that there was "one sin against the Holy Ghost that is unpardonable" and yet many other such sins that were not unpardonable and yet "more heinous and provoking to God than other sins." The unpardonable sin—a much-debated concept based on Matthew 12:31–32—was, in effect, a limiting case of resistance to the Spirit's work. When resistance to God reached its most aggravated and terminal stage, the result was the so-called "blasphemy against the Holy Ghost" or "unpardonable sin."

How then did the human turning toward God—i.e., conversion—occur? The question leads into a "chicken and egg" issue. One might ask: Does the act of turning toward God *precede* any believing, penitent disposition in the person who converts? Or, conversely, does the act of turning toward God *follow* a believing, penitent disposition that is antecedent to any acts? Solomon Stoddard took the former view. The first acceptance of Christ was a gracious act that did not presuppose any disposition prior to the act itself.[33] In this way, Stoddard exalted the category of act over the category of disposition—a view adopted in the early 1800s by some of Edwards's disciples (known as "exercisers"; ch. 37). Yet Edwards took the latter view, according to which a righteous or holy act was only conceivable on the basis of a foregoing righteous or holy disposition. Regeneration, for Edwards, was a "new birth" whereby God imparted a "new principle of action" to human beings through the "indwelling" of the Spirit.[34] He explained the dispositional change occurring in conversion as follows: "The prime alteration that is made in conversion, that which is first and foundation of all, is the alteration of the temper and disposition and spirit of the mind." Or again, "what is done in conversion is nothing but conferring the Spirit of God, which dwells in the soul and becomes there a new principle of life and action."[35]

God's conferring of the Holy Spirit in conversion is "immediate" in both senses of the word—that is, happening without mediation and happening at once.[36] This gift of the Spirit is not limited to or governed by any fixed laws that human beings can discern. With no principle to explain why one person receives this gift and another does not, we can only say that the conferral of the Spirit occurs according to God's will. Edwards taught that regeneration by the Spirit took place by "physical infusion"—a term from the 1600s and 1700s

---

33. Thomas A. Schafer, "Solomon Stoddard and the Theology of Revival," in Stuart C. Henry, ed., *A Miscellany of American Christianity: Essays in Honor of H. Shelton Smith* (Durham, NC: Duke University Press, 1963), 353.

34. WJE 21:187.

35. WJE 14:362.

36. WJE 21:161.

that was easily misunderstood, since in this context "physical" did not refer to tangible, material realities, but rather to the change of nature (Greek, *phusis*) that came about through the agency of the Spirit. Physical infusion thus was set over and against moral suasion.[37] The change, that is, was not a mere persuasion of the will. Instead, the self's alteration commenced with a change of nature—i.e., physical infusion—that effected an alteration of dispositions and thus a change in the direction of the will.

The context for this discussion about the "infusion" of grace as "immediate," "physical," or "efficacious" was the ongoing polemic between Calvinists and Arminians. A conception of conversion as "physical" suggests—as Sang Lee notes—that "the effectiveness of God's act of grace, in other words, is not subject to the acceptance or rejection of human beings."[38] Yet it would be inaccurate to say that Edwards simply asserted Calvinistic views. The Arminians accused the Calvinists of setting aside human volition and bypassing the natural faculties—of turning people into puppets. Yet in representing the Spirit as a "vital principle" in human thought, affection, volition, and action, Edwards sought to show how it was conceivable that God worked in and through human beings without overriding their natural faculties or inclinations.[39] Like Augustine and Calvin, Edwards held that what the Spirit overcame at the time of conversion was not human nature as such but rather the disordered or corrupted nature that had imprisoned human beings in sin. In overcoming sinful inclination, God enabled each person to act in accordance with his or her own true self, and negated nothing that was proper to each person. To object to this was like arguing that drowning persons should not be rescued but should remain in their "natural state" of drowning.

According to Edwards, both God and human persons were active in the process of conversion and salvation generally. "We are not merely passive in it, nor yet does God do some and we do the rest, but God does all and we do all. God produces all and we act all."[40] Edwards's position was not a form of synergy or cooperation as ordinarily understood. The acts of faith, repentance, or obedience were not ascribed partly to God and partly to human agents, but wholly to God or wholly to the human actor—depending on the angle from which one views these acts.

The Spirit of Life and Holiness

For Edwards, the epithet "holy" was applied to the Holy Spirit as "peculiarly belonging to him, which can be no other way than that the holiness of God

---

37. WJE 21:165.

38. WJE 21:41.

39. Sang Lee, in WJE 21:43–45.

40. WJE 21:251.

does consist in him." In his biblical typology, Edwards identified the Spirit with the references to "rivers of living waters" (Jn. 7:38) and to the "oil of gladness" (Heb. 1:9). The work of the Spirit in human life was to bring about a grateful, filial obedience to God: "The more they have of this conviction, the less is their obedience from a principle of slavishness." For "they that serve God only from fear of his wrath, their service is not a service of heart or of the spirit, but only external. Fear will never make a man hearty and spiritual, though it may influence the outward actions; but he that serves God from an high esteem and supreme love and thankfulness, he serves God with the heart."[41] Since Edwards has sometimes been stigmatized for preaching terrifying sermons, this point bears emphasis. Fear was only a minor and subordinate motive for obeying God. Those who followed God's will merely because they dreaded the consequences of not doing so were not serving him from the heart. God wanted people to serve him in a sincere and unconstrained way.

Edwards found it necessary in the midst of the 1740s revivals to clarify how the Spirit did and did not direct the lives of the saints. The most general work of the Spirit was to lead believers by "inclining them to do the will of God." The Spirit's assistance was "not by immediate suggesting of words to the apprehension, which may be with a cold dead heart, but by warming the heart and filling it with a great sense of those things that are to be spoken of, and with holy affections." Like John Owen before him, Edwards understood such lofty spiritual phenomena as the gift of prophecy to be a common work of the Spirit and not necessarily a special or gracious work. "A man may have ten thousand such revelations and directions from the Spirit of God, and yet not have a jot of grace in his heart: 'tis no more than the gift of prophecy, which immediately reveals what will be, or should be hereafter; but this is but a common gift." Edwards developed this position at length in the second sermon of *Charity and Its Fruits*.[42] Edwards's position may seem counterintuitive, since there seem to be far more people who experience gracious conversion than those who manifest extraordinary gifts of the spirit, such as prophecy. Yet it was possible for someone to exercise a charismatic gift without having the Spirit indwelling as a new "vital principle." Hence Edwards wrote that prophetic gifts are "but dross and dung in comparison with the excellency of that

---

41. WJE 14:429.

42. WJE 8:149–73. Thomas Taylor notes that John Owen was wary about affirming contemporary miracles, and yet Owen commented that "God might on some occasions...put forth his power in some miraculous operations" (cited in Taylor, "The Spirit of the Awakening," 141). Edwards's position may have been close to Owen's. See chs. 35 and 42 on Edwards's view concerning the cessation of spiritual gifts.

gracious leading of the Spirit which the saints have."[43] It was not that the extraordinary gifts of the Holy Spirit were valueless for Edwards. Instead, the so-called ordinary operations of the Spirit among the regenerate were of such an exalted nature that they overshadowed all spiritual gifts that could be experienced by the regenerate and unregenerate alike.

Those who had already received the Spirit, said Edwards, needed to ask God for more abundant measures of the Spirit. Once believers in Christ came to understand the inestimable value of the Spirit, they would be stirred to ask God to pour out the Spirit afresh. For "the Holy Spirit... is the greatest blessing that can be asked." Through the Spirit comes "the sanctification of our natures, our being made partakers of the divine nature, having the love of God shed abroad in our hearts, being united to the Son of God, being the children of God, having the presence of God, the light of his countenance and communion and fellowship with him, having divine peace and joy and living a divine life, and being hereafter possessed of eternal life and glory." In a fast-day sermon from November 1740, "Praying for the Spirit," Edwards chided his congregation for being concerned about temporal well-being rather than their spiritual condition. Christians cried out when they were deprived of all of their material goods, "but when their souls pine and languish for want of spiritual blessings... how little do we hear of any cry of their necessitous, distressing circumstances." For "they can suffer months after month, if not year after year, without making any great stir about it." Previous prayers had been offered for rain, and Edwards commented that "there have been often remarkable answers of prayer given for that blessing in time of drought. But God is much more ready to bestow spiritual showers; he is more ready to shower down of his Holy Spirit than he is rain."[44] This sermon reflected Edwards's growing conviction regarding the importance of united prayer as a means of furthering revival—a conviction that culminated in the *Humble Attempt* (1747).

In summary, then, Edwards highlighted the intra-Trinitarian role of the Holy Spirit as the bond between the Father and the Son. The Spirit effected the personal union of Christ's human and divine natures, and God's spiritual union with believers. Edwards assigned dignity to the Spirit not only as conferring or applying salvation to believers, but as the very gift or blessing made possible by Christ's saving death. The Spirit was personally present to believers and was a new, vital principle of holiness that acted in and through the natural faculties. This sanctifying function of the Spirit was more important for Edwards than any extraordinary, charismatic spiritual gifts that the Spirit might confer.

---

43. WJE 4:436–37.

44. WJE 22:214, 211, 217–18, 220.

18

The Angels in the Plan of Salvation

ANGELS HAVE LONG attracted the minds of the intelligent and the inquisitive. Over the centuries a rich body of angelic lore has accumulated, much of it written by Jewish and Islamic authors as well as Christian thinkers. Among the theologians offering extensive discussions of unfallen and fallen angels were Augustine, Anselm, Aquinas, Luther, Calvin, and Karl Barth.[1] In Western literature and philosophy, angels exerted their fascination over Dante Alighieri, John Donne, John Milton, William Blake, Emily Dickinson, Carl Gustav Jung, and Rainer Maria Rilke. Depictions of angels in Western art include images of Abraham deterred from sacrificing Isaac, the annunciation of the angel Gabriel to Mary, Michael warring against Satan in heaven, and Christ with the angels at his baptism, temptation, resurrection, ascension, and second coming. Modernist theologians from the early 1800s to the mid-1900s all but banished angels from serious discussion. Friedrich Schleiermacher's theology assigned Satan to the realm of "song" and "poetry," while Rudolf Bultmann's "demythologization" program placed angels and demons within the sphere of primitive and unscientific thinking.[2] During the 1950s, Karl Barth, with his nearly 200-page discussion of angels in his *Church Dogmatics*, was nearly alone among major Christian thinkers in devoting considerable space to angels. Barth wanted to protect the angels from sentimental distortions, and he deplored paintings depicting "the infant Jesus with a veritable kindergarten of prancing babies amusing themselves in different ways and yet all contriving in some way to look pious."[3] Yet during the last generation, the angels made a comeback. Popular books on angels abound, while

---

1. See Augustine, *City of God*, Books 11–12 (passim), and *De Genesi ad litteram* (passim); Thomas Aquinas, *Summa Theologica*, 1a, qq. 50–64; Martin Luther, *Tabletalk* (passim); John Calvin, *Institutes of the Christian Religion*, 1.14.4–12; and Karl Barth, *Church Dogmatics*, III/3, *The Doctrine of Creation* (Edinburgh: T. & T. Clark, 1960), 369–531.

2. Friedrich Schleiermacher, *The Christian Faith* (Edinburgh: T. & T. Clark, 1986), 169–70 (par. 45); Rudolf Bultmann, "The New Testament and Mythology," in Hans Werner Bartsch, ed., *Kerygma and Myth* (New York: Harper and Row, 1961), 1–16.

3. Barth, *Church Dogmatics*, III/3, 492.

scholars like Mortimer Adler have argued that the angels play an essential role in philosophical discussions of mind, body, knowledge, agency, and personhood.[4]

Though Edwards has never been acknowledged as such, he is in fact one of the most important interpreters of angels and demons in the Christian tradition. Scattered throughout Edwards's writings—and especially in roughly fifty entries in his *Miscellanies*—is the equivalent of an entire book on this topic. With the exception of a single essay by Amy Plantinga Pauw, this aspect of Edwards's thought has not elicited much comment.[5] Perhaps the arcane nature of this topic, its seeming disconnection with the rest of Edwards's theology, and, above all, the lack of access to the *Miscellanies* prior to their appearance in *The Works of Jonathan Edwards*, hindered an adequate consideration of this theme.

It is an illuminating exercise to compare Edwards with Thomas Aquinas on the topic of the angels. Thomas was preoccupied with the intrinsic nature of the angels, the question of bodiless minds, and sought above all to understand the nature of the angels' knowledge. On such issues, Edwards said nothing. His greatest interest lay in the mission and function of the angels within redemptive history, and at almost every point his references to angels occur alongside references to Christ. Angelology, for Edwards, was a corollary of Christology.[6]

This focus on Christ did not mean, though, that Edwards's approach to angels was free from speculation. Within the *Miscellanies*, one finds many unexpected statements, for example, that Lucifer is a "type of Christ," that Christ replaced Lucifer as the "head of angels," that some angels rebelled when they first learned of God's plan for his Son to become incarnate as a human, that the very idea of the incarnation brought temptation to the angels, that fallen humans were elected for salvation to take the place of fallen angels, and so on. More than other theologians, Edwards highlighted Christ's

---

4. On angels in popular culture, see "Angels Among Us," *Time*, December 27, 1993, 56–65, and, for a European perspective, Uwe Wolff, "The Angels' Comeback: A Retrospect at the Turn of the Millennium," in Friedrich V. Reiterer, et al., eds., *Angels: The Concept of Celestial Beings—Origins, Development and Reception; Deuterocanonical and Cognate Literature, Yearbook 2007* (Berlin: Walter de Gruyter, 2007), 695–712. See also Mortimer Adler, *The Angels and Us* (New York: Macmillan, 1982).

5. Amy Plantinga Pauw, "Where Theologians Fear to Tread," *Modern Theology* 16 (2000): 39–59. See also the comments on Edwards's view of the angels in Harry S. Stout, "Editor's Introduction," in WJE 22:14–17; and Robert W. Caldwell III, *Communion in the Spirit: The Holy Spirit as the Bond of Union in the Theology of Jonathan Edwards* (Eugene, OR: Wipf and Stock, 2007), 171–6, 186–7.

6. Karl Rahner wrote that "angelology...can only ultimately be understood as an inner element of Christology" ("Angels," in Rahner, ed., *Encyclopedia of Theology: The Concise Sacramentum Mundi* (New York: Crossroad, 1982; 6).

ascension and his "enthronization" in heaven as a decisive event in the unfolding of redemptive history. For Edwards, Christ's ascension was the point at which Christ became the "head of angels" and the unfallen angels were for the first time "confirmed" in grace so that they would be forever removed from the danger of sinning. Edwards's angelology was traditional in its focus on the three standard medieval themes of the creation, fall, and confirmation of the angels.[7] Yet Edwards's angelology was innovative in its construal of the angels' creation, fall, and confirmation and its portrayal of the angels' place in redemptive history. Rather than situating the angels in a distant celestial realm, Edwards conceived the angels as human-like in their capacity for surprise, outrage, temptation, joy, wonder, growth, perseverance, and development. Angels and humans were two parts of "one society" in a heaven that was itself in an eternally "progressive state."

Speaking generally, Edwards's approach to angels and demons lay somewhere between that of medieval thinkers like Anselm, Aquinas, and Bonaventure—who felt free to speculate on the angels—and that of his fellow Reformer theologians John Calvin and Karl Barth—who sought to restrict their discussion to biblical statements. While Edwards launched his reflections on the angels with scriptural exegesis, he was ready to go beyond the text of the Bible. The phrases "'tis probable" and "probably" come up repeatedly in the *Miscellanies* entries on angels. The speculative or hypothetical character of his notebooks is shown by the absence of this material from the sermons and publications. Edwards's theories regarding the angels' temptation, fall, and confirmation are almost entirely missing from the works he produced for public consumption. On the other hand, Edwards returned again and again to this topic in the course of fifty-odd entries on angels and demons in his *Miscellanies*. His basic ideas on this topic were not broached in one or two entries and then dropped. Instead he presented a well-defined framework of ideas and progressively refined and embellished it over some thirty-five years. Given the bulk and the consistency of what he wrote, Edwards did not seem to regard this particular theme as secondary or tangential. Furthermore, his tantalizing comments on the unwritten "great work" on the history of redemption, described in the letter to the trustees of the College of New Jersey, give further indication of the topic's importance. The magnum opus was to be "carried on with regard to all three worlds, heaven, earth, and hell: considering the con-

---

7. David Keck, in *Angels and Angelology in the Middle Ages* (New York: Oxford University Press, 1998), writes that, for the medievals, "the three events of the creation, fall, and confirmation of the angels...constitute the essential point of departure for understanding the angels" (16).

nected, successive events and alterations, in each so far as the Scriptures give any light." This statement makes it likely that reflections on angels and demons in the *Miscellanies* were to be incorporated into the final masterwork. The angels and demons were an integral part of the "connected, successive events" of the "three worlds."[8]

Historical Background on Angels and Demons

Christian reflection and speculation on angels and demons started with a handful of biblical passages. The Old Testament Apocrypha touched on the devil's opposition to humanity: "For God created man for incorruption, and made him in the image of his own eternity, but through the devil's envy death entered the world" (Wisdom of Solomon 2:23–24; RSV). This reference to "envy" injected a new element—what a modern scholar has called the "rivalry motif," viz., that angels and humans compete for God's interest and favor. This motif makes its appearance in rabbinical literature[9] and in various non-canonical and Islamic texts.[10] As we will see, this idea has importance in Edwards's account as well.

Early Christian authors offered conjectures regarding the angels and demons. The *Shepherd of Hermas* and the writings of Athenagoras presented angels as cosmic mediators. John of Damascus wrote of national angels who "keep watch over the different parts of the earth...controlling our history giving us their aid." Irenaeus grouped angels with humans since they were endowed with freedom of choice between good and evil. Eusebius, Gregory of Nyssa, and Gregory the Great presented angels as rational creatures created to know God and to have fellowship with God's rational and spiritual nature.

---

8. WJE 16:728.

9. Georg Gäbel, "Rivals in Heaven: Angels in the Epistle to the Hebrews," in Reiterer, et al., eds., *Angels*, 357–76. In one Talmudic text, God created the angels in order to deliberate with him about the creation of humanity. They advised God not to create man and scornfully responded in the words of Psalm 8:4: "What is man?" (Gäbel, "Rivals," 363; citing bSan 38b, BerR 8:4–6 in *Midrash Rabbah*). Adam, in another rabbinical text, displayed his superior qualities by naming the animals—a feat that the angels could not equal (Bernard Bamberger, *Fallen Angels*; Philadelphia, PA: Jewish Publication Society of America, 1952; 112).

10. In the non-canonical *Life of Adam and Eve* (first century C.E.), Satan refused to acknowledge Adam by bowing to him, insisting that he had been created prior to Adam and so Adam owed the bow of respect to him. In *The Qur'an*, Iblis—or Satan—also refused to bow to Adam, and says: "I am better than he; Thou hast created me of fire, while him Thou hast created of dust" (*Qur'an* 7:11–23; cited in Bamberger, *Fallen Angels*, 112). cf. *Qur'an*, 2:30–36, 15:28–44, 17:61–65, 18:50, 20:116–23, and 38:71–78. The evil spirits or *djinn* are also said to be made of fire (*Qur'an* 15:27, 55:15).

Basil suggested that the unfallen angels received sanctification by the Holy Spirit. The fallen angels, wrote Tertullian, could not be redeemed, and this is why Christ did not become incarnate as an angel. Augustine, Fulgentius of Ruspe, and Gregory the Great asserted that the angels who resisted their initial temptation were able to continue without sin.[11]

Origen played a key role in angelology. Yet he aroused suspicions regarding his own orthodoxy by suggesting—though only as a speculation—that in future ages the fallen angels and even Lucifer himself might come to salvation. This speculation reflected Origen's emphasis on creaturely freedom. Since angels and humans possessed a will capable of choosing either good or evil, there could be no fixity of destiny—whether in heaven or in hell. Medieval discussions of the "confirmation" of the unfallen angels, and the continuing sin and impenitence of the fallen angels, addressed these issues raised by Origen's speculations. In *The City of God*, Augustine presented the idea that the election of humans to salvation was a compensation for the angels who fell: "God by his grace is gathering a people so great that from them he may fill the place of the fallen angels and restore their number. And thus that beloved Heavenly City will not be deprived of its full number of citizens."[12] Anselm later echoed this idea in *Why God Became Man*, where he discussed "the reason why the number of the angels who fell is to be made up from among men."[13]

During the High Middle Ages, Anselm, Aquinas, and Bonaventure presented a systematic account of angels and demons. Anselm's *De Casu Diaboli* pointed out that the angels as disembodied intelligences were subject to none of the passions of the flesh. Their fall could not have been due to sensual impulses. Anselm rejected the idea of an original flaw and instead proposed the idea that grace was given to some but not all angels. Thus there came to be a stress on angels as recipients of grace.[14]

Aquinas' *Summa Theologica* contains the most influential angelology of all time.[15] In this presentation, angels ranked between God and humans in terms

---

11. Irenaeus, *Adversus Haereses*. 5.24.3; Augustine, *De correptione et gratia* 10.27; Fulgentius, *De Fide ad Petrum*, 3.30; Gregory the Great, *Moralia*. 4.3.8; all cited in Barth, *Church Dogmatics*, 381–83.

12. Augustine, *City of God* (Harmondsworth, Middlesex, UK: Penguin, 1972), 22.1 (p. 1023).

13. Anselm, "Why God Became Man," I.16–18, in Eugene R. Fairweather, ed., *A Scholastic Miscellany: Anselm to Ockham* (Philadelphia, PA: Westminster Press, 1956), 125–34.

14. Bamberger, *Fallen Angels*, 202–205.

15. Thomas Aquinas, *Summa Theologica*, 1a, qq. 50–64.

of their essential dignity. Central to Aquinas' account is the idea that angels possess both intelligence and will.¹⁶ For Aquinas, the ultimate perfection of free will is not merely to do the good but to be "confirmed" in doing the good: "To be established or confirmed in the good is of the nature of beatitude." Aquinas rejected the opinion of Origen that all angels "can by reason of free-will be inclined to good and evil," since "everlasting stability is of the very nature of true beatitude." For Aquinas, the blessed angels could not advance in their degree of beatitude: "Progress belong[s] to this present condition of life. But angels are not wayfarers traveling toward beatitude, they are already in possession of beatitude. Consequently the beatified angels can neither merit more advance in beatitude." Aquinas admitted that "the joy of the angels can be increased," but he did not view this as an advance in beatitude.¹⁷

How did angels sin? Since angels have no bodies, angels could only sin through pride or envy. When did the angels sin? Aquinas rejected the view that they sinned in the first moment of their creation, yet he came close to this view. The devil sinned in the first moment *after* his creation. What is more, the confirmation of the good angels happened as soon as they resisted the temptation to fall with Satan. Aquinas maintained the view of Gregory that the Devil had been the most eminent of all the angels. Satan influenced other angels—by a kind of "exhortation"—to sin just as he had sinned, and so became the indirect cause of their fall. Ever since the first few moments after creation, when most angels remained obedient and some fell, the "beatified angels cannot sin" while the demons "remain ever obstinate in their malice."¹⁸

Setting the tone for the Reformed tradition was Calvin's *Institutes* (1559), which took a guarded stance on angels. While insisting that angels are real beings, he also held that nothing certain can be known or affirmed regarding them except what is presented in the scripture. Calvin exhorted his readers "not [to] indulge in curiosity or in the investigation of unprofitable things" such as "empty ... speculations concerning the nature, orders, and numbers of angels." The fifth- or sixth-century author Pseudo-Dionysius, though reasoning "subtly and skillfully" about the angels, wrote like "a man fallen from heaven" recounting "what he had seen with his own eyes." For Calvin, the danger was not merely that of unprofitable speculation but even of worshiping angels. Instead we must look to God as our "sole helper." The angels were called

---

16. Aquinas, *Summa Theologica*, 1a, q. 50, a. 1; 1a, q. 50, a. 3; 1a, q. 51, a. 2; 1a, q. 59, a. 3.

17. Aquinas, *Summa Theologica*, 1a, q. 62, a. 1; 1a, q. 64, a. 2; 1a, q. 62, a. 2; 1a, q. 62, a. 9.

18. Aquinas, *Summa Theologica*, 1a, q. 63, a. 2; 1a, q. 63, a. 4; 1a, q. 62, a. 5; 1a, q. 63, a. 7; 1a, q. 63, a. 8; 1a, q. 62, a. 8; 1a, q. 64, a. 2; 1a, a. 64, a. 4. See Bamberger, *Fallen Angels*, 204–205.

"hosts... because as bodyguards surround their prince, they adorn his majesty and... like soldiers... [they] carry out his commands." Calvin stressed God's sovereignty over all creatures, including the devil, and this meant that "Satan is clearly under God's power, and is so ruled by his bidding as to be compelled to render him service." "From himself and his own wickedness," says Calvin, there arises Satan's "passionate and deliberate opposition to God. By this wickedness he is urged on to attempt courses of action which he believes to be most hostile to God." Nonetheless the devil accomplishes "only those things which have been divinely permitted to him; and so he obeys his Creator."[19]

Primal History—Angelic Obedience and Rebellion

Edwards's reflections on angels and demons repeated much of the traditional wisdom. The angels were created good by God. They are bodiless or incorporeal beings. They are intelligent beings who are spectators to God's works in the universe from the moment of their creation up to the present time. They are moral beings with a capacity to choose both good and evil. They exist in vast numbers and have powers that greatly exceed those of human beings. Some angels fell through sin or disobedience, and these fallen angels are the demons. Satan was once the foremost of the unfallen angels and, after his fall, became the leader and the foremost of the demons. The angels serve as ministers of God's providence, performing many functions throughout the physical universe and in the lives of human beings. Yet there are numerous points at which Edwards's account of the angels differs from that of his predecessors. Based on his interpretations of and inferences from scripture, Edwards concluded that the angels were not confirmed in grace until long after the world's creation. In fact, the unfallen angels were unconfirmed in grace and on probation from their creation until the ascension of Christ— truly an inconceivably long period of time as compared with Aquinas's notion of an instantaneous fall from grace (for the fallen angels) and an equally instantaneous confirmation in grace (for the unfallen angels). What is more, Edwards's angels were capable of growing in grace and blessedness—a quality that makes them human-like. Unlike the heavenly figures of perfect blessedness that one finds in Aquinas's account, Edwards's angels were directly involved, invested, and interested in human affairs. They themselves— even in their unfallen state—were "reconciled" to God when the Son

---

19. Calvin, *Institutes*, I.14.3–5, I.14.17.

of God took on a creature's nature in the Incarnation. This is one reason that the angels rejoiced at Jesus' birth. In eternity, angels and humans will together make a single holy community in heaven. Edwards did not present the entire story of the angels in any single text, but he returned repeatedly to the same themes in the *Miscellanies*, and it is from there that we can piece together an interconnected narrative. The story, as Edwards tells it, sweeps from creation through all of history to consummation.

God created the angels to be "fit witnesses and spectators of God's works here below." The problem is that human beings "see but a very little... and they don't live long enough to see more than a very small part of the scheme." For this reason, "God saw fit that there should be creatures of very great discerning and comprehensive understandings" to be "spectators of the whole series of the works of God." The angels were created "in the beginning of creation" so that they could see all that transpired "from the beginning to the

FIGURE 18.1 The many compartments in Edwards's desk facilitated his simultaneous pursuit of multiple writing projects (Used with permission of the Master and Fellows of Jonathan Edwards College at Yale University and the Jonathan Edwards Trust).

consummation of all things." Edwards cites the text in Job 38:7, which speaks of the "sons of God"—taken as a reference to angels—shouting for joy when God laid the foundations of the earth.[20] Given the high stature of the angels, possessing "more excellent natural powers" than human beings, it might seem "a very improper thing that saints in some respects should be advanced above angels." Yet Edwards reasons that this is no more improper than that a "queen" of a kingdom should be advanced above "nobles and barons, of far nobler natural powers." The argument here presupposes Edwards's nuptial or bridal theology. The church, as the bride of Christ, receives its stature wholly from its relationship with Jesus Christ—the bridegroom. It is a derived rather than inherent standing. Edwards assigns momentous significance to the church's status as the Bride of Christ, for he writes that "this spouse of the Son of God, the bride...is that for which all the universe was made. Heaven and earth were created that the Son of God might be complete in a spouse."[21]

The ultimate purpose of God in creating the world, for Edwards, was linked with the Incarnation of the Son of God—the joining of the eternal Son with a human nature in the person of Jesus Christ. Despite a focus on the sufferings and the crucifixion of Christ, Edwards's reflections on God's purposes began with the Incarnation. He writes: "It seems to me very proper and suitable, that the human nature should be advanced far above the angelical nature by the incarnation of Christ." The reason for this is that "men are a more ultimate end of the creation than the angels," and "the angels...are created for this end, to minister to the creatures."[22] There is a parallel between Christ and the angels at this point. Christ's divine nature places him inherently higher than all human beings, and yet Christ humbles himself to serve humanity in his earthly life. The angels are also inherently above human beings (though not so high as Christ), yet the angels are called to serve those lower than themselves. In other passages, Edwards develops this idea further with regard to the church's ministers and eminent saints, who show their excellence by embracing a position of lowliness and servitude.

The angels, for Edwards, were limited beings with only a partial grasp of God's purposes. Based on his exegesis of certain key biblical texts (especially Eph. 3:9–11, Col. 1:26, and 1 Cor. 2:7–9), Edwards concluded that God's sweeping plan for cosmic redemption was "a secret that [God] kept within himself,

---

20. WJE 18:99.
21. WJE 13:271.
22. WJE 13:271.

was hid and sealed up in the divine understanding, and never had as yet been divulged to any other."[23] This means that the angels—though witnessing God's works in history from the beginning of creation—were not able to understand all the intricacies of God's redemptive plan. And this is where the problem began. Some angels did not—or would not—understand, accept, and embrace God's plan.

Based on his interpretation of Ezekiel 28:12–19, Edwards argues that "'tis evident that this cherub or angel [identified as Lucifer or Satan] is spoken of as the highest of all the angels."[24] As the "prince of the angels," Lucifer was above the others and "all did obeisance unto him."[25] One creature received "obeisance" from others—a picture that recalls the noncanonical texts in which Lucifer himself was supposed to bow before Adam. Because the Hebrew text of Ezekiel refers to this "cherub" as *mashiach* ("Messiah" in English), one may conclude that "Satan, before his fall, was the Messiah or Christ... exalted into his place in heaven." Yet ultimately Christ is exalted higher than Lucifer, who was "only near the throne" while Christ was allowed "to sit down forever with God on the throne." This leads to the startling statement that "Lucifer...was a type of Christ, in whom all the glory and excellency of all elect creatures is more properly summed [up]."[26]

It was the very excellence of Lucifer that became the occasion of his fall from grace. "'Twas the dignity of our nature that was greatly envied by Satan," wrote Edwards. "His haughtiness and pride, which made [him] aspire to divine honor, could not bear that, that this new, meanly born race should be made so much of and come into their room!" Nonetheless, though Satan "triumphed" and "did as it were laugh" when humans sinned, "their fall has been the occasion of their being advanced to much greater dignity than before, brought much nearer to God, far more nearly united to him, [and] are become his members, his spouse." The fall into sin ultimately brought about the advancement and exaltation of human beings—an idea known as the *felix culpa* ("happy fault")—that Edwards here embraces. Edwards goes so far as to say that Satan's tantalizing temptation of Eve,

---

23. WJE 20:485.

24. WJE 20:296–99, citing 297. On Lucifer as the highest angel, see WJE 23:212, 20:190–91.

25. WJE 20:191.

26. WJE 20:298–99. One notes that the Lucifer-Christ typology is a kind of angelic parallel to the Adam-Christ typology that appears in Paul's letter (esp. Rom. 5:12–21 and 1 Cor. 15:21–22, 45).

"ye shall be as gods" (Gen. 3:5), proved to be prophetic in a way that Satan never intended. Through the redemptive plan of the God, and the Incarnation of God's Son, human beings had indeed become "as gods." The temptation instigated by Satan thus brought about the very thing he sought to prevent—viz., the exaltation of human beings to preeminence. For Edwards, the devil undoes himself.[27] He is a self-destroyer. Edwards's presentation recalls the writings of the Greek Fathers, such as Athanasius's *On the Incarnation of the Word*. The devil may seem crafty until one considers God's plan—which is far more clever than the devil's.

Because of Lucifer's sin, a series of reversals and replacements take place. When some angels fell, "elect men are translated to supply their places, and are exalted vastly higher in heaven than they. And Jesus Christ...is translated and set in the throne that Lucifer, the chief head and prince of the angels, left, to be the head of the angels in his stead...that all the angels might do obeisance to him." Hence one might say that "God made him [i.e., Christ] his firstborn instead of Lucifer." God gave to Christ "honor, dignity and power...in an infinitely higher and more glorious manner than ever he had done to Lucifer, and appointed him to conquer, subdue and execute vengeance upon that great rebel." Yet Lucifer's fall had meaning within God's providential plan. This "sudden fall" of "the highest and most glorious of all the creatures" was intended by God "to show the emptiness and vanity of the creature."[28]

Edwards offers speculations on the particular occasion of the angels' fall into sin. It happened when the angels first learned of the "peculiar favor" that was to be given to human beings: "It seems to me probable that the temptation of the angels that occasioned their rebellion was that when God was about to create man, or had first created him, God declared his decree to the angels that one of that human nature should be his Son...and that he should be their head and king." Thus "Satan...could not bear it, thought it below him and a great debasing of him; so he conceived rebellion against the Almighty, and drew away a vast company of the heavenly hosts with him."[29] It may well be imagined that certain of the angels were leaders in this rebellion and drew the others with them into sin: "'Tis probable that of the angels that fell, some one

---

27. WJE 13:304. The Latin phrase just mentioned comes from the first part of the traditional prayer "*O felix culpa*"—"O blessed transgression that brought about such and so great a Redeemer."

28. WJE 20:191–92.

29. WJE 18:97; WJE 13:401–402.

or a few of the chief, first entertained the design of rebellion. They, being some of the highest of the angels, could not bear that which they looked upon [as] so great a degradation; and they influenced and tempted others."[30]

Edwards paints a dramatic picture of cataclysmic conflict in heaven at this moment when Lucifer turned against God and called for the rest of the angels to join him in rebellion: "When Lucifer rebelled and set up himself as a head in opposition to God...Christ the Son of God manifested himself as an opposite head, and appeared graciously to dissuade and restrain by his grace the elect angels from hearkening to Lucifer's temptation." Standing with Christ and the unfallen angels was "the glorious Michael as their captain." In support of this view, Edwards cites the "war in heaven" of Revelation 12:7–9, here interpreted not as a prediction of a final battle of good and evil at the end of days, but a depiction of a primeval struggle at the dawn of history. Even though the unfallen angels were not confirmed in goodness at this early stage, they nonetheless owed their rescue from ruin to "the free and sovereign distinguishing grace of Christ" that that "upheld and preserved" them. Edwards explained that "Christ was the Savior of the elect angels, for though he did not save them as he did elect men—from ruin they had already deserved and were condemned to...yet he saved 'em from eternal destruction they were in great danger of." The angels—no less than elect humans—relied on Christ for their spiritual well being, and they were called to "self-emptiness...and humble dependence" on Christ. Edwards also stated that the Holy Spirit is given to the angels through Christ—another analogy with the process of human salvation.[31]

It is likely that the unfallen angels experienced great consternation at the fall of Lucifer: "The elect angels probably felt great fear at the time of the revolt of Lucifer.... They were then probably the subjects of great surprise and great sense of their own danger of falling likewise." From this, Edwards concludes that the heavenly state of the angels is not the panacea commonly imagined: "'Tis a thing supposed without proof that the glorious inhabitants of heaven never felt any such thing as trouble or uneasiness of any kind. Their perfect innocency and holiness don't prove it; God may suffer an innocent creature to

---

30. WJE 18:207. Kenneth Minkema has suggested (email to McClymond, February 2010) that Edwards "obviously drew on [John Milton's] *Paradise Lost*" in his account of the angels' fall. This seems likely (though difficult to prove), and it might apply especially in the depiction of Satan as the instigator of the rebellion. Peter Thuesen noted that Edwards listed *Paradise Lost* twice in his "Catalogue" of reading and that Milton in Edwards's day had become part of a "canon of the religious sublime" ("Editor's Introduction," in WJE 26:105–106).

31. WJE 20:195.

be in a trouble for their greater happiness." It was only in the course of later redemptive history that a truly settled and peaceful state came to heaven: "The highest heavens was not a place of such happiness and rest before Christ's ascension as it was afterwards, for the angels were not till then confirmed."[32] The great difficulty for the angels was simply this—their worry that they too might fall along with Lucifer and the other angels-turned-demons. It was not until the confirmation of the unfallen angels at Christ's ascension that this particular fear was wholly and permanently removed.

If the fallen angels brought grief to those who did not fall, the fall of humanity into sin was yet another surprise and shock: "Therefore, knowing God's love to them [i.e., the humans], and election of them, before they fell, [the angels] were doubtless greatly surprised when men fell and had sinned against God: for they could no way conceive how it was possible now, consistent with the rule which God had fixed with men and with the glory of God, for God now to fulfill his own decree, and accomplish upon men those eternal designs of love, that he had given them a general intimation of."[33] Regarding Adam's fall, Edwards acknowledges the metaphysical dilemma in seeking to account for the origin of evil: "It has been a matter attended with much difficulty and perplexity, how sin came into the world." If the world was created good, then whence did sin arise? Yet there is no need of assuming that God withdrew grace from Adam—what Edwards calls "original righteousness." Instead God, from the time of Adam's creation, "had witheld [sic] his confirming grace, that grace which is given now in heaven, such grace as shall fit the soul to surmount every temptation. This was the grace Adam was to have had if he had stood, when he came to receive his reward. This grace God was not obliged to grace him." For angels and humans alike, constancy in a right relationship with God is the fruit of confirming grace, withheld by God from both until after the time of creation (ch. 22). In *History of Redemption*, Edwards argues that as soon as man fell, "Christ the eternal Son of God clothed himself with his mediatorial character and therein presented himself before the Father.... 'Tis manifest that Christ began to exercise the office of mediator between God and man as soon as man fell because mercy began to be exercised towards man immediately."[34]

The confirmation of the unfallen angels—though doubtless a gift of God's grace—was brought about by various causes. God made use of "means" to

---

32. WJE 20:197–98.

33. WJE 18:97–98.

34. WJE 13:382; WJE 9:130.

bring about this result: "The angels that stood are doubtless confirmed in holiness and their allegiance to God, so that they will never sin, and they are out of danger of it. But yet I believe God makes use of means to confirm them." They were confirmed by "the sight of the terrible destruction" of the fallen angels, by "the eternal damnation of reprobates amongst men," and by the recognition of God's "justice in the sufferings of Christ." Edwards wrote that "the fall of the angels that fell, was a great establishment and confirmation to the angels that stood. They resisted a great temptation by which the rest fell...and they resisted the enticements of the ringleaders which drew away multitudes; and the resisting and overcoming great temptation, naturally tends greatly to confirm in righteousness. And probably they had been engaged on God's side, in resisting those that fell, when there was war." The unfallen angels observed the "dreadful issue" (i.e., outcome) of the demons' revolt. Arguing by analogy, one may conclude that the saints in heaven are "made perfectly holy and impeccable by means" as well as the angels, including especially the "beatific vision."[35]

Edwards insisted that Lucifer's fall redounded to the ultimate good of the unfallen angels: "The elect angels are greatly increased, both in holiness and happiness, since the fall of those angels that fell, and are immensely more holy than ever Lucifer and his angels were." Thus "the fall of the angels laid a foundation for the greater holiness of the elect angels, as it increased their knowledge of God and themselves...and they increased in holiness by persevering in obedience." Similarly, with respect to the human race, "what the fallen angels have done for the ruin of mankind, has only proved an occasion of mankind's being exalted into their stead and to fill up that room that was left vacant in heaven by their fall."[36] This passage may be compared with Anselm's *Cur Deus Homo*, where, as noted earlier, elect humans occupy a place in heaven that was, in effect, left vacant by the fall of Lucifer and the angels who rebelled with him.

Edwards had relatively little to say regarding the nature and scope of the angels' work as ministers of divine providence. Because the angels have "limited understanding," it follows "that the different angels are appointed to different kinds of work, and that their ministry more especially respects some certain limited parts of the universality of things....some of larger and others of lesser extent." Much like Calvin, Edwards was concerned that human beings, if they could actually learn of the specific responsibilities entrusted to

---

35. WJE 13:490; WJE 18:58.
36. WJE 20:199; WJE 18:147.

the angels by God, might begin to entrust themselves to the angels and to worship the angels rather than God. For this reason, "God hath concealed the particular spheres of the angels' dominion and ministry, that we might not be tempted to idolatry...[and] worship angels, under a notion of such and such angels having a superintendency over such particular persons or affairs." Nonetheless the New Testament terms such "thrones, dominions, principalities and powers" are not merely honorific but they "properly denote rule and authority" as given to the angels. It is just that God has not revealed the details of his providential government to us.[37]

The Head of Angels—Christ and the Ministering Spirits

A number of Edwards's sermons between 1729 and 1733 focused on Christ. Beginning with a stress on the doctrine of the Incarnation and Christ's humility during his earthly life, Edwards shifted later to focus on Christ's heavenly glory as a "reward" for his earthly sufferings. He dwelt especially on the moment of Christ's "enthronization" at the time of his ascension into heaven.[38] Influenced by the Book of Revelation, Edwards reasoned that Christ at the conclusion of his earthly life and sufferings was "worthy...to receive" (Rev. 5:12) all power, glory, and blessing from the Father. During these years, Edwards developed what we might call an *enthronement theology* centering on Christ's ascension—one of his truly distinctive theological motifs. Christ at the time of his ascension became the "head of angels," for "the angels were not unconcerned in the work of redemption by Jesus Christ." As he wrote, the angels "have this benefit by the incarnation of Christ that thereby God is become a creature, and so is nearer to them." For this reason, angels and humans are "of the same family."[39] In construing Christ's cosmic story, Edwards gave more attention to

---

37. WJE 20:53–54.

38. See the following sermons—listed with text, doctrine, and approximate dates of delivery: Canticles (Song of Songs) 8:1, "The incarnation of Jesus Christ was a thing greatly longed for by the church," summer–fall 1729; Job 33:6–7, "'Tis a most desirable thing in our circumstances, to have a Mediator between God and us in our own nature, one that is flesh, that is formed out of the clay as we are," fall 1730–spring 1731; Isaiah 53:10, "That Christ should see sinners converted and saved, was part of the reward that God promised him for his sufferings," August 1731–December 1732; Revelation 5:12, "Christ was worthy of his exaltation upon the account of his being slain," August 1731–December 1732; Psalm 110:2, "Christ will rule in the midst of his enemies," May 1733. See also WJE 15:298–302 for a detailed typological interpretation of David's bringing of the ark to Jerusalem as a picture of Christ's ascension.

39. WJE 13:490; WJE 20:197; WJE 18:100.

the ascension of Christ than to the resurrection per se. Of course, Christ's story did not end with the ascension. Christ will come again to subdue his enemies and to reign in their midst. Edwards referred to this as a "second ascension"—an event even more majestic than the first ascension, when, at the end of history, Christ with his glorified saints will rise from earth into heaven to establish his reign in the new heavens and new earth.

The story of Christ's exaltation begins with humiliation. Suffering, said Edwards, had to come prior to any reward for Christ: "'Tis fit...that every creature, before he receives the eternal reward of his obedience, should have some considerable trial of his obedience." For "respect to God's authority" is only demonstrated through the overcoming of some trial. The highest creature—Christ—had to be the most greatly tested by God in respect of his obedience. "It is an honor that the holy angels have never had, to obey God in and by suffering. Herein the people of Jesus Christ, as well as Christ himself, have an higher honor in some respects than the angels." Christ himself, now the head and highest of all, had to become the lowest.[40] In terms reminiscent of the early Christian theme of *Christus Victor*, Edwards wrote that "Christ poured the greater contempt upon Satan in his victory over him, by...the contemptible means and weapons he made use of." He defeated him as "a poor, feeble, mortal man, a worm of the dust...like David who, when he went to fight with Goliath, put off the princely armor that Saul armed him with." For "the weapons that Christ made use of in fighting with the hellish giant were his poverty, afflictions, reproaches and death. His principal weapon was his own cross, the ignominious instrument of his own death."[41]

Yet the turning point in Christ's story came with the ascension, which was "the solemn day of his investiture with the glory of his kingdom...an occasion of great rejoicing to the whole church in heaven and earth." Edwards spoke of "the happy effects of Christ's enthronization." In some sense, this "enthronization" at the ascension was a renewal of what had already happened at creation: "At Christ's first enthronization after the creation, Christ was set over the angels, as he was at the second after the new creation." At Christ's exaltation, the Father declares, "let all the angels of God worship him' [Heb. 1:6]." For "it was very congruous that Christ should have this honor immediately, after such great humiliation and sufferings." If it was fitting that Christ should be publicly rewarded after his sufferings, it was no less fitting and suitable that the angels should be rewarded at

---

40. WJE 18:202–203, 206, 240.

41. WJE 18:151. Cf. WJE 18:307.

the same time. For Christ's trial and suffering were equally a trial to the angels who beheld it happening: "It was fit that the angels should be confirmed after they had seen Christ in the flesh, for this was the greatest trial of the angels' obedience that ever was." In particular, the sight of him as "a poor, obscure, despised, afflicted man" was a trial to them. Previously many angels had fallen at the mere announcement that this was to happen. Now it had occurred. This was a great trial to "those thrones, dominions, principalities, and powers." So "it was very fit that God should honor the day of the ascension and glorious exaltation of his Son, which was a day of such joy to Christ, with joining with it such an occasion of joy to the angels, as the reception of their reward of eternal life."[42] It sounds here almost as though the unfallen angels were receiving salvation because at this point they received "their reward of eternal life." Once again, Edwards sees the angelic relationship to God as analogous to the human.[43]

Edwards considered the objection that the trial of the angels' obedience "from the beginning of the world till the ascension of Christ" may have lasted too long. Yet perhaps for "those mighty spirits" it was fitting that the trial should last much longer than it did for human beings. Edwards admitted that the unfallen angels "were not absolutely certain" that they would not fall as Lucifer had until the time that they were confirmed. Yet, once Christ accomplished his work on earth, it was suitable that there should be a single community of humans and angels in a confirmed condition of beatitude: "Christ, since he appeared in the flesh, gathered together and united into one society, one family, one body, all the angels and saints in heaven and the church on earth. Now 'tis not to be supposed that part of this body are in a confirmed state, and part still in a state of probation." At the ascension, "Christ is the head of the angels, and...the angels are united to him as part of his body." This means that Christ is not only "their head of government...he is the head from whence they derive their good."

The angels receive great benefit from Christ, and the sheer fact that the Son of God took on a creaturely nature—even a human one—is of great importance to the angels as fellow creatures: "And the angels enjoy very glorious benefits by Christ's incarnation; 'tis a glorious benefit to all creatures that love God, that God is become a creature.... The angels and saints make up but

---

42. WJE 20:48; WJE 18:59.

43. See Ava Chamberlain's penetrating comments on the analogies between humans and angels in the "Editor's Introduction," in WJE 18:20–23. Amy Plantinga Pauw finds that Edwards's story of Satan and the elect angels was "a magnified version of the struggle against spiritual pride unfolding on earth" ("Where Theologians Fear to Tread," 45).

one family, though members of a different character; as in one royal house there is the queen, the children, the barons, etc. He is the head of all the rational creation; saints and angels are united in Christ, and have communion in him." In describing the heavenly assembly of the glorified saints and the unfallen angels, Edwards emphasizes that they are spectators of God's works—as becomes clear in the Book of Revelation: "When God gradually carries on the designs of grace in this world, by accomplishing glorious things in the church below, there is a new accession of joy and glory to the church in heaven. Thus the matter is represented in John's Revelations."[44]

One might even say that the angels undergo "reconciliation" to God through the person and work of Christ, and this helps to explain their joy and exuberance at Christ's birth:

> When the angels rejoiced so much at the birth of Christ, they did not merely rejoice in the happiness of another that they were no wise partakers in, but doubtless saw glorious things that accrued to them by it. They desire to look into those things, admiring at the bounty of God to them as well as to us, in coming so near to them as to become a rational creature like themselves. Yea, there is a kind of reconciliation, that is procured thereby for the angels by Christ's incarnation: for though there never was an alienation, yet there is a great distance between a God of infinite majesty and them; which would in some measure forbid that intimate enjoyment, and familiar fellowship, which so great love desires. But by God's thus coming down to the creature, everything is entirely reconciled to the natural propensity of most dear love.[45]

What Edwards describes here is a kind of metaphysical reconciliation of the unfallen angels to God—though not a moral one involving guilt and forgive-

---

44. WJE 18:59–60; WJE 13:284; WJE 18:62.

45. WJE 13:285. Cf. WJE 13:232–33; WJE 13:480–81. Edwards used a number of interesting exegetical arguments to support his idea that angels and humans are "of the same family." He pointed out that in Revelation 22:9 an angel says to John that he is "of thy brethren" (WJE 18:100). Though this is only a passing reference, it is one case in scripture where human beings and angels are spoken of together as "brethren." On this same theme, Edwards also cites Ephesians 1:10, where we read that God will "gather together in one all things in Christ," and Colossians 1:20, where we read that God will "reconcile all things unto himself...whether they be things in earth, or things in heaven." See too the sermon on 1 Timothy 2:5, "Jesus Christ is the Great Mediator and Head of Union," in Michael D. McMullen, ed., *The Glory and Honor of God: Volume 2 of the Previously Unpublished Sermons of Jonathan Edwards* (Nashville, TN: Broadman & Holman, 2004), 311–26.

ness. Because of God's drawing near to the creature in the Incarnation, both humans and angels are drawn near to God in "most dear love."

Pride, Malice, Rage, and Ruin—Satan and the Demons

For Edwards, Satan is a "restless, proud, malicious and revengeful spirit." Satan and all the demons "look upon the honor and happiness of mankind in all degrees" as "steps towards...their being set above them and over them." This explains the demons' implacable hatred for human beings: "Their pride therefore stirs them up to labor with indefatigable industry and their utmost craft...themselves to rule over them, and reign over them as god." God has a plan of salvation and Satan a plan of damnation for the human race. Edwards poses the question as to why a "devil...so cunning and subtile [sic]" would "endeavor to frustrate the designs of an omnipotent being." He comments that "although the devil be exceeding crafty and subtile, yet he is one of the greatest fools and blockheads in the world, as the subtlest of wicked men are.... Sin is of such a nature that it strangely infatuates and bewitches persons...to make them act like fools." This means that "the devil acts not according to his deliberate judgment, but is driven on to his own inexpressible torment by the fury of sin, malice, revenge and pride; is so entirely under the government of malice, that although he never attempted anything against God but he was disappointed, yet he cannot bear to lie still, and refrain from exerting himself with all his might and subtility against the interest of holiness."[46]

Satan's opposition to human salvation led him to various stratagems against God's plan of salvation. "Satan doubtless knew of the Messiah's coming into the world, and could by the prophecies guess pretty near at the time of it." Satan sought to oppose Christ and his reign by raising up the "Roman monarchy" in the time of Christ—a kingdom that would be opposed to Christ's kingdom. The cruel persecutions of the church during its first three centuries were because "Satan was very unwilling to let go his hold of so great a part of the world." After the destruction of the heathen Roman Empire, "Satan infested the church with heresies" in the form of Arianism and Pelagianism. Then there came two great works of the devil in the rise of

---

46. WJE 13:367, 306, 227. On the devil as a "fool," Aquinas wrote: "The demons much less fully understood [than the unfallen angels] the mystery of the Incarnation, when Christ was in the world... For had they fully and certainly known that he was the Son of God and the effect of His passion, they would never have procured the crucifixion of the Lord of glory" (*Summa Theologica*, 1a, q. 64, a. 1).

Antichrist—identified by Edwards with Roman Catholicism—and the birth of Islam (chs. 15, 28, 35). "The kingdom of Antichrist...seems to be the masterpiece of all the contrivances of the devil against the kingdom of Christ...to turn the ministry of the Christian church into a ministry of the devil...to make an image of ancient paganism, and more than to restore what was lost in the empire by the overthrow of paganism in Constantine's time." During the Middle Ages, "the true church" was "like the woman in the wilderness." Yet "the rise of Antichrist was gradual," with the church "growing more and more superstitious in worship." The bishop of Rome went from being the minister of a congregation to a diocesan bishop to patriarch and so on until finally usurping the place of Christ himself. The second kingdom, resembling that of Antichrist, is the "Mohammedan kingdom, which is another great kingdom of mighty power and vast extent that Satan set up against the kingdom of Christ." Edwards suggests that the locusts of Rev. 9:3–11 may refer to the armies of Islamic conquest.[47]

Yet much that Satan undertook to oppose God's purposes did not have the intended effect. The unification of the nations under the Roman emperors served to advance the propagation of the gospel, so Satan's plans were confounded. When Satan saw the gospel spreading in the early church, he decided to "lead away many people into the more remote corners of the earth." This included especially the indigenous inhabitants of America. Yet Satan's "mimicking [of] God" by leading the pagan nations into the practice of blood offerings or "satisfactory sacrifice" served to "prepared the Gentile world" for the message of Christ's sacrifice on the cross. Once again, Satan's opposition to God served ultimately to aid in the spread of the gospel message.[48] Nothing more clearly showed the wisdom of God than his capacity to "carry on his designs from age to age" by employing the acts of "a most powerful and subtle enemy...Satan." At first "the devil in heaven thought to have overcome God by strength." Yet when this failed and he was "cast down to hell," then "he thought to get the better of him by craft and subtlety. Therefore God shows by the wonderful wisdom of the gospel that he can as easily overcome him by wisdom as power." Repeatedly God turned all of the devil's efforts against himself—"God renders all Satan's incessant labors and endeavors for the overthrow of mankind...[as] a means of his own confusion and vexation." "The devil envied man, whom he esteemed so much inferior to himself...But how remarkably will he be mortified at the last day, when he shall be judged

---

47. WJE 13:305–306; WJE 9:390, 405, 410–12, 415.
48. WJE 18:525; WJE 13:391–92. Cf. WJE 9:155.

by a man, by one of the race." The saints will be judges or "assessors" with Christ of the fallen angels.[49]

While the *Miscellanies* discussed the angels more than the demons, Edwards's sermons reversed the pattern and focused more on the demons than the angels. When he preached about Satan and the demons, he stressed their hatred and malevolence for God, Christ, the church, and believers; their vigorous and untiring agency in disrupting and hindering the progress of the gospel and the conversion of sinners; and their agency within the lives of wicked people, whose thoughts and activities were, as it were, energized by Satan and by demonic power. For Edwards, wicked people were Satan's "children" in the sense that they came to take on the characteristics of their diabolic parent and to resemble the devil.[50] The result of this was a frightening picture indeed. Outside of Christ, there was no protection whatsoever from the malevolent power of Satan and his demons. The only shelter lay in the safety of Christ's embrace. Those outside of Christ were not only the target of Satan's malevolence, they were also at risk of becoming tools and instruments in the eternal ruin of others.

As to "why man has the offer of a Savior and the devils never had," Edwards said it was "probable" that the demons' sin "was attended with that malice and spite and haughty scornfulness, that was equivalent to the sin against the Holy Ghost. Their sin was a downright spiteful rebellion and a direct malicious war against God, a scorn of subjection and a proud seeking of his throne." The sin of Lucifer and the demons was a never-ending and continually renewed sin, calling for never-ending and continual punishment: "God brings the punishment of devils upon 'em for their proud rebellion in heaven this way, by making them the cause of their own torment and vexation to all eternity by their continually renewed acts of pride and spite. He gives them over forever to that same disposition which they exercised when they fell." The demons were punished for "procuring the fall of mankind: God curses the serpent for it."[51]

---

49. WJE 18:152; WJE 13:403–404, 366–67, 386.

50. On the devil's role in the lives of the unregenerate, see the following sermons: John 8:44, "Wicked men are the children of the devil," summer–fall 1729; 2 Timothy 2:26; "Wicked men are the devil's captives," October 1733; Luke 15:15–16, "The devil is a cruel master," Nov. 1742; Luke 11:21–22(b), "The devil is an enemy that is like a strong man armed," April 1754, published as "Warring With The Devil," in WJE 25:676–79; and Luke 11:24–26; "I. The devil naturally dwells in the hearts of men," July 1755.

51. WJE 13:385, 366. Like Edwards, Aquinas taught that the demons "remain ever obstinate in their malice" (*Summa Theologica*, 1a, q. 64, a. 2).

In conclusion, we may say that the angels play a quite prominent role in Edwards's theology. His discussion of the angels underscores the majesty of Christ, the dignity of the human race in God's sight, the subtlety of God's providential purposes, and the cosmic context of creaturely salvation. Through the endless ages of the world, from creation to consummation, the angels are spectators of God's works—in a way that no mere human being can ever be. Much is beautiful and uplifting in Edwards's portrayal of the elect angels and humans gathered into "one family" for all eternity. Yet not all sentient and intelligent beings will share in this blissful consummation. Satan and the demons are an inescapable part of the cosmic story, and their presence shows that evil is deep and ineradicable. The devil, as it were, spits in the face of Christ and despises the very mercy that makes God lovely and lovable to the saints. The devil will have nothing to do with this. Amy Plantinga Pauw writes: "Satan's cooperation in being a ministering spirit cannot be coerced, and his tragic refusal is not remedied, even in the eschaton."[52] The final defeat and punishment of Satan and the fallen angels demonstrates God's power—as Edwards often insisted. Yet it also bears witness to the creature's ultimate capacity for defiance of God and to the mystery of evil itself.

---

52. Plantinga Pauw, "Where Theologians Fear to Tread," 49.

19

Heaven Is a World of Love

IN HIS PERSONAL Narrative, Edwards wrote: "The heaven I desired was a heaven of holiness; to be with God, and to spend eternity in divine love, and holy communion with Christ."[1] Edwards's treatment of heaven synthesized several themes—God, love, community, eschatology, glory, and the triumph of good over evil. No less than sixty entries in the *Miscellanies* were substantially devoted to this topic.[2] Following a scriptural indication—"And now abideth faith, hope, charity, these three; but the greatest of these is charity" (1 Cor. 13:13, AV)—Edwards made love central to his account of heaven. Heaven was not a realm of faith or of hope but "a world of love."[3] In heaven the human inclinations toward the love of God and the love of fellow humans reached their fullest and most perfect expression. Some of what Edwards had to say regarding heaven was already well-established. Heaven was both God's dwelling place and a blissful state wherein God's saints received their eternal reward. Heaven was permanent rather than transitory—that is, it was not a state from which anyone might lapse. The reward of the saints in heaven was nothing other than God himself, who would himself fill the needs and desires of those who had served him in this present age.

Other points regarding heaven were distinctive to Edwards. Wilson Kimnach commented on his use of sensual language: "While Edwards's heaven...is a conventional theological conception, the imaginative specifics of his vision are more reminiscent of seventeenth-century metaphysical writers than of an eighteenth-century apostle to the Enlightenment. The concreteness of his description...is exceeded only by the sensuousness of his representation of heavenly love."[4] Heaven was also a "progressive" state in which saints and angels advanced in knowledge,

---

1. WJE 16:795.

2. WJE 13:134–35.

3. "Heaven is a World of Love" is the title of the final sermon in the series *Charity and Its Fruits* (WJE 8:366–97).

4. WJE 25:223.

holiness, and happiness.⁵ The joys of heaven did not all derive immediately from God, but came also through the mutual love and delight of glorified creatures. God's own happiness increased because of the creatures' happiness and delight in one another. Like a venerable father at a family reunion who watches over and enjoys his family's festivity, Edwards's God presided over heaven and yet did not monopolize it. To use a contemporary analogy, God is like the webmaster at a social networking website who establishes and guides online interactions and yet allows for full communication and relationship among all participants.

Edwards's heaven showed a surprising continuity with the present age. Despite the absence of sin, selfishness, death, and suffering, many aspects of heaven were carried over from the present world—bodily existence (though glorified), spatial location (though hard to define), progress over time (and thus temporality), music (or something analogous), communication among the saints (though without using spoken words), meaningful activity (of some kind), and the opportunity to meet again with people from one's earthly life (in an higher state of existence). Heaven was a place where the fragmentary, limited activities and aspirations of the present world would find their ultimate completion and fulfillment.

The History of Heaven

Experiences of persecution and suffering provoked much of the early Christian reflection on heaven. Those who had undergone afflictions in the body—torture, dismemberment, beheading, burning, or the assaults of wild beasts—would receive a restored body, a glorious crown of martyrdom, and a place near Christ's eternal throne. The second-century bishop Irenaeus taught that the martyrs would be compensated for what they had lost and suffered in the present life.⁶ Augustine proposed that the martyrs' resurrection bodies might display their scars, since their marks of suffering—like Jesus'—would add to their glory before God and fellow saints.⁷ Early Christians represented heaven in materialistic terms as a place of feasting, drinking, and bodily enjoyment. Alongside this early Christian idea of the martyrs' heaven was an ancient pagan notion of "meeting again" with earthly family and friends.

---

5. This theme of progress is so pervasive in Edwards's writings that Paul Ramsey wrote a lengthy appendix about it, "Heaven is a Progressive State" (WJE 8:706–38).

6. Colleen McDannell and Bernhard Lang, *Heaven: A History* (New Haven, CT: Yale Nota Bene, Yale University Press, 2001), 48–53.

7. Augustine, *City of God* (Harmondsworth, UK: Penguin, 1972), 1061 (XX.19).

Cicero expressed this notion in *Scipio's Dream* and *On Old Age*—works often read by learned Christians.[8]

By the fourth and fifth centuries, a turn toward asceticism began to affect the Christian view of heaven. As Colleen McDannell and Bernhard Lang wrote: "In an environment dominated by ascetic ideals, traditional images of a this-worldly millennium were too materialistic, too carnal, to be compatible with the new spirit." Over time the "anthropocentric model" of heaven as a place of reunion with loved ones and of social comforts and joys gave way to an austere "theocentric model" wherein "eternal life has little in common with everyday earthly activities." Heaven on this account was to be "eternal solitude with God alone." Mystics, ascetics, and theologians through the centuries concurred with Teresa of Avila's dictum that "God alone suffices."[9] On the theocentric model, the question of human activity in heaven dropped from view, since the blessed saints engaged in unending, uninterrupted contemplation of God. Fulfillment came only from God—in contrast to the anthropocentric model where much of the saints' joy and happiness derived from seeing and interacting with one another.

Augustine's views shifted over time. His early work, *On Faith and the Creed* (393), struggled with the notion of a "body" in heaven and deemphasized the fleshly aspects of the life beyond. In earlier works, he also suggested that heavenly consolations came from God and not from human companionship. Yet by the time of Augustine's *Retractions* (427), his perspective had softened. The blessed might eat and drink in heaven, though only for pleasure and not out of bodily necessity. Nonetheless, Augustine even in his later phase did not allow for special relationships in heaven. The individualized relationships of friendship, marriage, and household will be dissolved. There will be no strangers and yet also no special friends, for "the hearts of all will be transparent, manifest, luminous in the perfection of love." A total openness of mind and heart will unite all.[10] The later Augustine held that the bodily eyes of the glorified saints could at least indirectly see God—a point he had earlier denied. The question of seeing God was a thorny issue since the Bible at various points stated that no one can see God and yet we also read that "blessed are the pure in heart, for they shall see God" (Mt. 5:8). For Augustine, for medieval thinkers,

---

8. McDannell and Lang, *Heaven*, 60–61, 124–27, 155, 173. Cicero's idea of reunion with loved ones influenced Protestant Reformers like Melanchthon and Zwingli—and even Luther (155).

9. McDannell and Lang, *Heaven*, 54, 178–79, xxiii.

10. McDannell and Lang, *Heaven*, 58, 60–61, 64–65.

and for Edwards, too, the vision of God was one of the more complicated themes in the discussion of heaven.[11]

For Thomas Aquinas, heaven was a place of contemplation, and the active life would come to an end. Thomas thus stressed the role of the intellect in knowing God. Despite his debt to Aristotle—who stressed human sociability—Thomas held that the blessedness of heavenly saints derived essentially from God and not from fellow creatures. A solitary soul enjoying God could be perfectly happy. Yet Aquinas qualified this by stating that the saints do in fact see one another and can rejoice at one another's fellowship in God. Giles of Rome—a student of Aquinas—departed from his teacher by insisting that the heavenly saints formed a perfect community and that that community required language or communication of some sort. Since "society depends upon language, then we have to say that...language, too, is not abolished but also made perfect." For language gives "solace" even if there is no need for acquiring information. Bonaventure also stressed heaven's social dimensions. He wrote that "love will then be extended to all the saints in a way which was possible only toward one single dearest friend." Rather than saying that there are no friends in heaven, it would be truer to say that everyone is friends with everyone there.[12]

Both Martin Luther and John Calvin conceived of heaven as a place of equality. They taught that there will be no princes and no peasants in heaven. Calvin wrote that "as the world will have an end, so also will...the distinction of ranks, the different orders of dignity, and everything of that nature." This was a Reformers' heaven—a place where human hierarchies were no more. The Catholic theologian Robert Bellarmine offered a bodily and sense-based view of heaven. After discussing "eating" and "drinking" in heaven, Bellarmine analyzed the joys of heaven into those of the "understanding," "will," "memory," "eyes," "ears," "nostrils," "touch," and "taste." The most influential Puritan book on heaven—Richard Baxter's *The Saints' Everlasting Rest* (1649)—generally reflected a theocentric model. Baxter was generally more concerned with preparing for heaven than describing it. Yet Baxter anticipated Edwards by imagining heaven as a place of praise and of music: "The liveliest emblem of heaven that I know upon earth is when the people of

---

11. Augustine, in *City of God*, concluded that saints in heaven will use their bodily eyes to see how the "incorporeal God" will be "directing the whole universe" (1086–87; XXII.29). This seems to have been a mediated vision of God—less of God himself than of God's activity in the cosmos.

12. McDannell and Lang, *Heaven*, 89, 92–93; citing Thomas Aquinas, *Summa Theologica*, 2ae2a, q.181, a.4; 1a2ae, q.4, a.8.

God...join together both in heart and voice in the cheerful and melodious singing of his praises." Baxter's heaven also allowed for advancing knowledge, for God "advanceth our sense, and enlargeth our capacity...and fills up with himself all that capacity." The saints in heaven were active rather than passive and thus their "rest" was "not the rest of a stone" but "containeth a sweet and constant action." In colonial America, Increase Mather concurred with Baxter that even "Glorif'd Souls will be still attaining unto greater degrees of knowledge." Mather maintained that the glorified saints would gaze upon the glorified body of Jesus: "The Man Christ Jesus, is the most Glorious Object that Eyes can behold. It is Christ's being there, that makes Heaven to be Heaven indeed."[13]

The Theocentric Aspect—God's Place in Edwards's Heaven

For Edwards, heaven was God's place. For "heaven is a part of the creation which God has built for this end, to be the place of his glorious presence." It is the created dwelling place of the uncreated God. Jesus' glorified body occupies space and must therefore be somewhere. This implies that heaven is a spatial state: "The human nature of Christ is yet in being.... And therefore there is a certain place, a particular part of the external creation, to which Christ is gone, and where he remains." The souls of departed saints went to this place prior to the resurrection of the body for "they are not reserved in some abode distinct from the highest heaven." In this place, "God is the fountain of love, as the sun is the fountain of light...a full and overflowing and an inexhaustible fountain of love." It was God "from whom every stream of holy love, yea, every drop that is or ever was proceeds." Edwards identified the "river of life" in the Book of Revelation with the Holy Spirit, who "shall be poured forth with perfect sweetness, as a pure river of [the] water of life, clear as crystal." Moreover, "love resides and reigns in every heart there. The heart of God is the original seat or subject of it."[14]

---

13. McDannell and Lang, *Heaven*, 154, 172–75; citing John Calvin from *Corpus Reformatorum*, 77:547; and Richard Baxter from *The Saints' Everlasting Rest* (London: Printed by Robert White, 1649) 680, 28–29. Robert Bellarmine, *The Eternal Happiness of the Saints*, trans. John Dalton (London: Thomas Richardson, n.d. [1850s]), 77–82, 155–78. Increase Mather, *Meditations on the Glory of the Heavenly World* (Boston: Sold by Timothy Green, 1711), 80, 235, cited in Amy Plantinga Pauw, "'Heaven is a World of Love': Edwards on Heaven and the Trinity," *Calvin Theological Journal* 30 (1995): 393, 395.

14. WJE 8:369; WJE 25:227; WJE 8:369, 371, 373.

Heaven was a place of beauty for Edwards: "There are none but lovely objects in heaven. There is no odious or polluted person or thing to be seen." For "the whole church shall then be presented to Christ as a bride clothed in fine linen, clean and white, without spot or wrinkle." Among the saints, there will be no "false professors" or people of "hateful spirit." Yet the love and loveliness of the saints was not to be something strictly or properly their own. Love in the saints is not "as light is in the sun which shines by its own light, but as it is in the planets which shine by reflecting the light of the sun." Edwards most fully elaborated this notion of the saints as reflecting God's light in *End of Creation*. Yet the image regularly reappears. The soul of the saint is like a transparent or translucent object that becomes luminous when placed in bright sunlight.[15]

The saints' partaking in Christ means that they partake in Christ' own Sonship: "Being members of the Son, they are partakers of the Father's love to the Son.... So they are in their measure partakers of the Son's enjoyment of his Father." Here Edwards was indebted to John's Gospel, and he cited several texts from John and added: "Christ has brought it to pass, that those that the Father has given him should be brought into the household of God, that he and his Father and they should be as it were one society, one family; that his people should be in a sort admitted into that society of the three persons in the Godhead." Edwards marveled at the sheer magnitude of the blessing that God gave. For God determined that "no degree of happiness [is] too great for him to enjoy." In the present life, "when men have something in which they hope to find very great joy, there will be something to spoil it," and yet nothing will ever tarnish the joys of heaven.[16]

Heavenly vision was a basic theme in Edwards's treatment of heaven.[17] Yet there were nuances on this theme, and Edwards may have shifted over time from a more Platonic disparagement of the body toward a more body-affirming standpoint. A 1730 sermon denied that heaven involved physical vision: "'Tis not any sight with the bodily eyes." Since "God is a spirit and is not to be seen with the bodily [eyes]," he commented, we must eschew "carnal and childish notions." He stressed God's essential invisibility. Sounding like Aquinas,

---

15. WJE 8:370–71, 373–74. Edwards compares "grace" in the Christian's soul to a jewel: "The brightness that is in a diamond which the sun shines upon, is of the same nature with the brightness of the sun, but only that it is as nothing to its in degree" (WJE 2:201–202). cf. WJE 8:441–44, 531–34.

16. WJE 18:109–10, citing Jn. 17:23, 26; 16:27, 17:21–23; and WJE 18:114, 120.

17. On this theme, see Kenneth E. Kirk, *The Vision of God: The Christian Doctrine of the Summum Bonum* (London: Longmans, Green, 1932). See also Thomas Aquinas, *Summa Theologica*, Suppl., q.92, a.1–3.

Edwards wrote: "It is an intellectual view by which God is seen. God is a spiritual being, and he is beheld with the understanding." For "the eye of the soul is vastly nobler than the eye of the body." Though Edwards never surrendered the idea of an "intellectual view" of God, he joined it to an increasingly clear conception of a bodily vision of the glorified humanity of Christ in heaven. In 1747, he wrote that Christ's glorified body *was* visible, seen by the saints, and seen in its splendor: "Their beatifical vision of God is in Christ, who is that brightness or effulgence of God's glory, by which his glory shines forth in heaven." For Christ is "the sun that enlightens the heavenly Jerusalem."[18]

Edwards spoke of heavenly experience as based in the body and yet as "refined" or "subtle." While the body was still the locus of heavenly experience, both the body and its surroundings were to be transformed. Edwards linked the heavenly vision to earthly life when he described the vision of God as an extension of present-day experience: "Now the saints, while in the body, see something of Christ's glory and love; as we, in the dawning of the morning, see something of the reflected light of the sun mingled with darkness; but when separated from the body, they see their glorious and loving Redeemer, as we see the sun when risen." Since the heavenly vision of God completes and fulfills the earthly vision of God, the two experiences are not utterly unrelated.[19]

Edwards's heaven was not only a place of vision but a place of love, praise, and other forms of activity. Just as vision will be perfected in heaven, so will be the saints' expressions of love. For "they shall have nothing within themselves to clog them in the exercises and expressions of love." Presently, the saints "have a great deal of dullness and heaviness" and "carry about with them a heavy moulded body...not fitted to be an organ for a soul inflamed with high exercises of divine love." Though "love disposes them to praise...they want words to express the ardor of their souls." Yet in heaven their souls will be a "flame of fire" no longer "pent up" but "perfectly at liberty." For Edwards,

---

18. WJE 17:61, 63; WJE 25:229. In heaven "every perceptive faculty shall be an inlet of delight. Particularly then, doubtless they will have the sense of seeing, which is the noblest of all external senses; and then without doubt, the most noble sense will receive most pleasure and delight. And the external light of the heavenly world will be a perfectly different kind of light from the light of the sun" (WJE 18:350–51). One sees differences in comparing "The Pure in Heart Blessed [1730]" (WJE 17:59–86) with "True Saints, When Absent from the Body, Are Present With the Lord [1747]" (WJE 25:225–56). The contrast should not be overdrawn, though, since the earlier sermon teaches both a bodily and an intellectual vision in heaven (WJE 17:66).

19. WJE 25:230. As Mark Valeri notes (WJE 17:57), the sermon "The Pure in Heart Blessed" resembles "A Divine and Supernatural Light" (WJE 17:408–26) even though the former is talking about heavenly experiences and the latter about earthly experiences.

the liberty of heaven will not encourage indolence but will stir the saints to activity, since "the happiness of the reasonable creature don't consist in idleness but rather in action."[20]

The Anthropocentric Aspect—Humanity and Society in Edwards's Heaven

As noted earlier, the love, beauty, glory, and happiness of God are not distinct from the love, beauty, glory, and happiness of the glorified saints. The statement can also be reversed. As *End of Creation* argued, the glory of God *is* the happiness of the saints and the happiness of the saints *is* the glory of God (ch. 14). The theocentric and anthropocentric aspects of heaven were not competitive but complementary. Comparing Christ's glory with the saints', Edwards wrote that "the difference will be rather in degree of brightness than [in] kind, as the light which is reflected from a lily is the same light but less bright than the sun." Another analogy was that of a flowerbed in which the blossoms represented the saints' exuding of a portion of Christ's fragrance: "What beauteous and fragrant flowers will these be, reflecting all the sweetnesses of the Son of God!" Each saint in heaven will be an individual who delights all the others. Each will have intrinsic worth. Yet the beauty and excellence of the saints will be simply the diffused beauty and excellence of Christ himself.[21]

Heaven will be a place of mutual love: "There is undoubtedly an inconceivably pure, sweet and fervent love between the saints in glory, and their love is in proportion to the perfection and amiableness of the objects beloved." At the same time, this mutual love was compatible with hierarchy and did not require equal regard for everyone. True saints "will not desire that all should be upon a level; for they know it is best that some should be above others." The saints' love will be "mutual and answerable, though we cannot suppose that everyone will in all respects be equally beloved." Since heavenly love will be in "due proportion," it is only fitting that some are better loved than others. Edwards's heaven was hierarchical inasmuch as the love one received in heaven was based on one's inherent worth. Nonetheless, there will be no envy in heaven, since "those who are lower in glory...will be most beloved of those who are highest in glory." The overcoming of envy or rivalry is based on an ownership or "propriety" of the saints in another: "All shall have *propriety* one in another...in heaven all shall not only be related one to another, but they shall be each

---

20. WJE 8:378–79; WJE 17:254.

21. WJE 13:370, 281.

other's." Just as a parent takes delight in a child's accomplishments—feeling that these accomplishments are his or her own—so everyone in heaven will have this sort of proprietary feeling toward everyone else. In the end, there will be no dearth of love for anyone in heaven: "For all shall have as much love as they desire, and as great manifestations of love as they can bear; all shall be fully satisfied."[22]

From an early stage in his thinking, Edwards became convinced that "there are different degrees of glory in heaven" and that "this is a doctrine very fully revealed in the Scriptures." He cited the text "one star different from another star in glory" (1 Cor. 15:41).[23] Following an exegetical tradition established by Augustine and Aquinas, Edwards interpreted "in my Father's house are many mansions" (Jn. 14:2) as a reference to the heavenly saints' "different degrees of glory."[24] The differences among the saints, he reasoned, reflected differences in capacity to receive or retain God's glory. "Every vessel may be full, and yet some may hold more than others." The implication was that earthly obedience somehow prepared the saints for heavenly glory. Anticipating the objection that it would be "selfish" to seek for glory in heaven, Edwards replied that "self-love...is a good principle" insofar as it is "directed and regulated by the will and word of God." God intended for the biblical promises of reward and blessing to motivate us, and so "we may be as covetous as we will of high degrees of heavenly good." Edwards saw human self-love as inescapable (ch. 33), and this shaped his view of heaven.

Regarding the "degrees of glory," Edwards went so far as to suggest that "it seems to me probable, that there will...different offices, as it is in the church on earth." All the saints will have "their distinguishing gift," and it is likely that "saints in heaven shall be rewarded with greater exercises of the same gifts that they exercised on earth."[25] Edwards thus departed from Luther's and Calvin's conception, noted earlier, of the abolition of rank and office among heavenly saints.

---

22. WJE 8:242, 377, 376, 380, 375.

23. WJE 19:614–15.

24. WJE 19:617; cf. WJE 19:740. On "many mansions," see Augustine, *Tract. in Joan.*, 47, and Thomas Aquinas, *Summa Theologica*, Suppl., q.93, a.2.

25. WJE 19:618; cf. WJE 13:437. WJE 19:622,625; WJE 13:481. On earthly acts as developing a capacity for heavenly fulfillment, see C. S. Lewis, "The Weight of Glory," in *The Weight of Glory, and Other Addresses* (New York: Macmillan, 1949). Thomas Aquinas taught that "the diversity of beatitude" in heaven was "according to the difference of charity" (*Summa Theologica*, Supp., q.93, a.3), thus suggesting that love of God and fellowman in the present time was directly related to one's eternal reward.

Edwards's reflections included some interesting discussions of bodily function in heaven. "When the body enjoys the perfections of health and strength," he wrote, "the motion of the animal spirits are not only brisk and free, but also harmonious," which brings "delight in the soul and makes the body feel pleasantly all over." "We need not doubt, but this harmony will be in its perfection in the bodies of the saints after the resurrection... so that every part of the saints' refined bodies shall be as full of pleasure as they can hold." Seeking to clarify that the body was subordinate to the soul, he added, "And that this will not take the mind off from, but prompt and help it in spiritual delights, to which even the delights of their spiritual bodies shall be but a shadow." We should expect "pleasures of the most exquisite kind that such refined bodies are capable of." Despite his preoccupation with the saints' glorified bodies, Edwards wanted to avoid giving undue importance to bodily pleasures. So he paired his comments on bodily pleasure with qualifying assertions about the "refined" character of these pleasures and their lesser worth as compared with spiritual and mental enjoyments. Yet, in broad terms, he had a surprising amount to say about bodily pleasures in heaven.[26]

Much of the happiness of heaven will consist in the enjoyment of bodily and mental beauties in a fashion that we cannot comprehend at present. Edwards exclaimed, "How ravishing are the proportions of the reflections of rays of light, and the proportions of the vibrations of the air! And without doubt, God can contrive matter so that there shall be other sorts of proportions, that may be quite of a different kind, and may raise another sort of pleasure in the sense, and in a manner to us inconceivable, that shall be vastly more ravishing and exquisite." These unimaginable beauties "probably... will appear chiefly on the bodies of the man Christ Jesus and of the saints." Moreover, the bodies of the saints will not only be beautiful, and give delight, but will be informative and communicative in some new way. They will include a "manifestation of the excellencies of their mind; which exceeding readily will appear in their bodies, the bodies being more easily and naturally susceptive and manifestative of the affections and dispositions of the mind, than here." There will be a "bright and yet not dazzling light, which shall flow from their faces" that "shall... denote those dispositions of mind." Just as in Augustine's account, Edwards's heaven is a place of perfect, unhindered self-disclosure of

---

26. WJE 13:263; WJE 13:350–51. Edwards never developed a notion of bodily pleasure in heaven in an explicitly sexual way, as Emanuel Swedenborg and certain Romantic authors did (McDannell and Lang, *Heaven*, 210–64).

minds and hearts. It is something like earthly friendship at its best, yet raised to the utmost degree and extended universally.[27]

In heaven, communication will take place between minds without any mediation of bodily senses: "It is out of doubt with me, that there will [be] immediate intellectual views of minds, one of another and of the supreme mind, more immediate, clear and sensible than our views of bodily things with bodily eyes." At times, Edwards used quasi-scientific language, commenting that the "undulations" carrying the heavenly communications "will be infinitely finer and more adapted to a distant and exact representation." Therefore the saints in heaven will be able to "hold a delightful and most intimate conversation, at a thousand miles' distance." The saints will not only see Christ, but Christ will "intimately converse" with them.[28]

Edwards referred often to music in heaven—a theme that tied into his understanding of beauty, proportion, harmony, consent, and sociability:

> The best, most beautiful, and most perfect way that we have of expressing a sweet concord of mind to each other, is by music. When I would form in my mind an idea of a society in the highest degree happy, I think of them as expressing their love, their joy, and the inward concord and harmony and spiritual beauty of their souls by sweetly singing to each other.... But to me 'tis probable that the glorified saints, after they have again received their bodies will have ways of expressing the concord of their minds by some other emanations than sounds, of which we cannot conceive, that will be vastly more proportionate, harmonious and delightful than the nature of sounds is capable of.

The "modulations" of such heavenly music will not be in "our gross air" but in another medium altogether that will make it possible for "an infinitely more nice, exact and fine proportion." The music we now experience is only an image or analogy of a higher harmony—that of minds. Edwards's attitude toward hearing, sound, and music in heaven was more qualified than that toward vision. While the saints will in some sense see with "bodily eyes" in heaven, they seemingly will not hear with bodily ears. Yet, however they perceive it, the celestial music will be exceedingly refined. Though today it is hard "to perceive the sweetness of very complex tunes," the heavenly saints will be able to appreciate a beauty compounded from "thousands of different ratios at once."[29]

---

27. WJE 13:328, 301.
28. WJE 13:329, 369; WJE 18:107.
29. WJE 13:331, 329. cf. WJE 13:296,303.

Edwards often wrote of progress in heaven: "The glorified spirits shall grow in holiness and happiness to eternity." A starting point for this idea may have been his conjecture that the saints would not forget anything that God had done since this would diminish their heavenly bliss. This implied that "their number of ideas shall increase to eternity." For Edwards, knowledge of God and happiness in God were intertwined, and so a growth in the saints' knowledge implied an increase in happiness. He reasoned that the more that the saints see of God and of God's works, the more they will love God. It was thus mistaken to think of "the happiness of heaven" as "unchangeable." For those in heaven, "their joy is continually increased, as they see the purposes of God's grace unfolded in his wondrous providences towards his church."[30] Each new stage in redemptive history augmented the joy of the heavenly saints. For "the saints are spectators of God's providences relating to his church here below" and "a considerable part of their happiness consists in seeing the dispensations and works of God's grace towards the church on earth." While "mortal men...see but a very little," the saints in heaven see vastly more as "spectators of the whole series of the works of God." The implication was that "the church in heaven and the church on earth are more one people, one city, and one family than generally is imagined." Some thinkers had imagined heaven as an unblinking contemplation of unchanging God. Yet Edwards, at least in part, transformed the *visio Dei* into a *visio mundi*—not a vision of God in lonely splendor, but a vision of earth—or, rather, God's redemptive work on the earth. Until the final consummation, the gaze of heavenly saints was largely directed away from heaven. This was one of the more distinctive and unusual ideas in the whole of Edwards's theology.

The present condition of heavenly saints was not final or ultimate for Edwards. Like the church on earth, the church in heaven awaited the consummation of God's purposes. The heavenly church at the current time was like a woman betrothed but still anticipating her wedding day. The happiness of departed saints, as Edwards said, is "proleptical" or merely a "prelibation" of coming blessings. Yet the wedding of Christ with his church was like a marriage union whose joys never ceased to unfold, to surprise, and to delight the lovers: "How soon do earthly lovers come to an end of their discoveries of each other's beauty...how soon do they come to the most endearing expressions of love that 'tis possible to give, so that no new ways can be invented, given or received. And how happy is that love, in which there is an eternal progress in these things...and [we] shall receive, more and more endearing expressions

---

30. WJE 13:275, 444–45.

of love forever: our union will become more close, and communion more intimate." In the conclusion to *End of Creation*, God remained at an infinite height and creatures moved everlastiingly toward God, though the time will never come when it can be said it [the creature] has already arrived at this infinite height."[31]

Meeting Again in Glory

A controversy in Christian discussions of heaven related to the hope of "meeting again" with friends and loved ones in the world beyond. The Anglican bishop Joseph Hall scorned this notion: "I shall neither have need, nor use of inquiring after my kindred according to the flesh." Hall imagined that God would be all and family and friends would be as nothing to the heavenly saints. Edwards thought otherwise. As to "whether the saints, when they go to heaven, have any special comfort in there meeting with those that were their godly friends on earth," he wrote that "I think that it is evidenced that they will." The Apostle Paul, he argued, comforted the Thessalonian Christians who had lost loved ones not only with the hope of Christ's return but also with the hope of reunion with departed believers. Such an expectation of reunion was no remnant of pagan superstition but an integral part of the Christian hope. God not only resurrected individual saints. God resurrected societies of saints. God resurrected relationships. Edwards's account of heaven exhibited his irreducibly social vision of human life.[32]

Edwards went even further, noting that "the special affection that the saints have in this world to other saints that are their friends, will in some respects remain in another world." For "a former acquaintance with persons and their virtues, may occasion a particular respect in another world. They may go to heaven with a desire to see them upon that account." Far from imagining that special relationships—friendship, marriage, kinship—detracted from a pure love for God, Edwards saw them as part of the life of heaven. He rejected the hard, unrelenting attitude—reflected in some monastic and mystical traditions—that allowed no room for special relationships. "Neither do I see how it argues infirmity," he wrote, "for a saint in glory to have a special respect to another." If our earthly friendships are "duly subordinated to divine love,"

---

31. WJE 18:99–100, with n.6 (citing *Black Bible* on Heb. 6:15); WJE 13:478; WJE 18:93, 103; WJE 13:366–67; WJE 8:534.

32. Joseph Hall, *The Works of Joseph Hall* (Oxford, UK: Talboys, 1837), 8:262, from *Sursurrium Cum Deo Soliloquies* (London: Printed by William Hunt, 1651); cited in McDannell and Lang, *Heaven*, 173; WJE 18:170.

then we may expect them to "last forever," for "death don't put an end to such friendship, nor can it put an end to such friends' enjoyment of each other." A poignant expression of Edwards's own expectation appeared in the final words he dictated—through his daughter Lucy—to be delivered to his wife, Sarah, who was absent from him at the time of his death: "Give my kindest love to my dear wife, and tell her, that the uncommon union, which has so long subsisted between us, has been of such a nature as I trust is spiritual, and therefore will continue for ever."[33]

---

33. WJE 18:172–73. Sereno Dwight, "Memoirs of Jonathan Edwards," in Edward Hickman, ed., *The Works of Jonathan Edwards*, 2 vols. (Carlisle, PA: Banner of Truth, 1984 [1834]), 1:clxxvii.

SECTION 3

Theological Anthropology and Divine Grace

20

The Affections and the Human Person

YALE PHILOSOPHER JOHN E. Smith once observed that all of Jonathan Edwards's thought can be considered "one magnificent answer" to the question, "What is true religion?"[1] We would add that Edwards's answer to that question invariably involved what he called the "affections" since they lay at the heart of his theological anthropology. The human person for Edwards was a bundle of affections that determine nearly everything that person feels, thinks, and does. Therefore no treatment of his theology can escape the question of what he meant by the affections and the role that the affections play in religious experience. This chapter will explore first the importance of the affections for Edwards, then his conception of their relation to the human person and true religion, and finally his estimation of how to evaluate them.

The Importance and Nature of the Affections

Near the beginning of *Religious Affections*, Edwards portrays the affections as "springs of motion" for all forms of human activity:

> Such is man's nature, that he is very inactive, any otherwise than he is influenced by some affection, either love or hatred, desire, hope, fear or some other. These affections we see to be the springs that set men agoing, in *all* the affairs of life, and engage them in *all* their pursuits...take away all love and hatred, all hope and fear, all anger, zeal and affectionate desire, and the world would be, in a great measure, motionless and dead, there would be no such thing as activity amongst mankind, or any earnest pursuit whatsoever. 'Tis affection that engages the covetous man...'tis the affections also that actuate the voluptuous man...so in religious matters, the *spring of their actions* are very much

---

1. John E. Smith, "Editor's Introduction," WJE 2:2.

religious affections: he that has doctrinal knowledge and speculation only, without affection, never is engaged in the business of religion.²

Several things are worth noting here. Human society is a bustling affair, brimming with aspiration and endeavor. As on the floor of the New York Stock Exchange, everyone is going somewhere. Yet just below the surface are the affections that motivate these movements. Affections are both good and bad, non-religious and religious. Religious affections do not function differently from non-religious affections, but have different objects. So while everyday affections such as the desires for wealth and sensual pleasure have money and sensory gratification as their objects, religious affections seek God and spiritual things.

Furthermore, Edwards argues that genuine religion is always a matter of the affections. Mere "doctrinal knowledge and speculation" are not deep and strong enough to constitute affections and therefore genuine religion. They are "mere actings of the will and inclination of the soul." Only if they are "vigorous and lively" in their exercise do they rise to the level of "religious affections." There are "many actings of the will and inclination, that are not so commonly called affections" since they are merely weak preferences—such as preferring blueberry to strawberry jam. Such preferences raise "us little above a state of indifference." But religious affections involve "a fervent, vigorous engagement of the heart in religion" that displays itself in love for God with all the heart and soul. He compared "the business of religion," which is moved by affections, to "running, wrestling or agonizing for a great prize or crown, and fighting with strong enemies that seek our lives, and warring as those that by violence take a city or kingdom." Thus Edwards defined affections as "the more vigorous and sensible exercises of the inclination and will of the soul."³

By "soul" Edwards meant the confluence of two faculties—the "understanding" that perceives and judges, and the "inclination or will" that moves the human self toward or away from things in liking and disliking, loving and hating, approving and rejecting. This brief definition of the affections rooted in the faculties of the soul is often misunderstood in two related ways: commentators either ignore the intellectual component or reduce the affections to "emotions," thus missing Edwards's insistence on the unity of the human person. Let us treat these problems one by one.

First, note the intellectual component. For Edwards, the affections move the soul, which means they move the mind as well as the will. In the affections

---

2. WJE 2:101; emph. added.

3. WJE 2:101, 97, 99–100, 96.

of true religion, the mind is "enlightened, rightly and spiritually, to understand or apprehend divine things." True religion will always have "*knowledge* of the loveliness of divine things."[4] Holy affections, he noted, "are not heat without light,"[5] for they arise from affections that are a unity of mind and inclination in the soul. If the soul is warmed toward God, it will be drawn to certain *understandings* of God. All inclination already involves perception of the mind because of the unity of the soul and self. Edwards rejected all dichotomies that set the mind against the heart—even while such dichotomies were common during the Great Awakening debates. Opponents of the Awakening such as Charles Chauncy argued that revival preachers had merely stirred up "passions" and that true religion brought the self under the control of reason rather than emotion. Radical revivalists such as James Davenport reveled in intense emotions and derogated the intellect.[6] But Edwards's position refused the dichotomies of either side, insisting on a soul whose affections shape not only feelings and choices but also the mind. By his lights, an idea is not only intellectual but has affective content. Say the word "fire," and while for some it suggests a delightful fireside encounter with a loved one, for others it painfully recalls the loss of a home. Conversely, all affections or inclinations are united to intellectual conceptions: "The heart cannot be set upon an object of which there is no idea in the understanding."[7] This union of the intellect with the heart was missed by most in the revival debates. Many pro-revivalists assumed that religion was all about feelings and had nothing to do with the mind. "Old Lights" claimed to be in favor of reason and against emotion and revival, while "New Lights" often criticized reason while championing emotion and revival. Few grasped the subtlety of Edwards's position.

Both sides, then, and many scholars since, have wrongly assumed that Edwards's affections were the same thing as "emotions." But emotions for Edwards were only one dimension of human experience shaped by affections, along with thinking and choosing. Edwards argued that true religious affections sometimes choose *against* emotional feeling, such as when Jesus chose not to yield to his feelings of fear in the Garden of Gethsemane. When "passions" overwhelm one's better judgment, as in a fit of rage, emotions are in fact opposed to true religious affections. Furthermore, Edwards always linked affections to an object, while emotions may or may not have an object.

---

4. WJE 2:266, 271; emph. added.

5. WJE 2:266.

6. WJE 4:60. See also WJE 4:51–52, 60–65, 79–83.

7. WJE 2:266, 271; WJE 22:88.

In current English usage, the statement "I am emotional" need not imply an object of emotion. But the assertion "I am affectionate" raises the question, "Toward what or whom?"

At the center of all Edwards's thinking about affections and religious experience was his conviction of the unity of the human person. He rejected the threefold distinction of mind, will, and emotions that was common in nineteenth- and twentieth-century discussions of human psychology and went back to Plato. Edwards declared that the will and affections "are not two faculties," but different expressions of the inclination that already has intellectual judgment contained within it.[8] As we just saw, he recognized that there are times when one expression seems to conflict with the other, as when the mind must choose against the feelings. Critics then and since have proposed the will as a mediator between the two (mind and emotions). Edwards replied to his contemporaries that such a mediating will is a self-determining power that is logically incoherent and self-contradictory, as he argued in *Freedom of the Will* (ch. 22). The will, he noted, cannot determine itself. A person has a will, but one's will itself does not have a will. Ultimately all faculties cohere with one another within the unity of the human self. It must be conceded, however, that although Edwards lists the understanding as the first in the faculties of the soul, he says little concerning its nature or function. This could be because he thought its status less problematic than that of the other faculties. It is also apparent that his preoccupation with the mind, will, and affections—indeed, his authorship of volumes like *Freedom of the Will*, *Religious Affections*, and *Original Sin*—situates him in an Augustinian-voluntarist tradition that characterized the human self more in terms of its desires and choices than its thoughts and concepts.

Even the twofold distinction of understanding and inclination tends to break down in the course of Edwards's discussion in *Religious Affections*. What one calls mind or understanding is the human self in one mode of operation, while inclination is another mode. Because both understanding and inclination are expressions of the total human self, the distinction between them is more analytical than actual. They are not parts of the soul or self, as is commonly imagined. The inclination's affections include an intellectual dimension, while the mind's thoughts include an affective dimension. In this way, the two faculties are interlocking in their operations. It is therefore a basic mistake to interpret Edwards in terms of any dichotomy of intellect versus affect, or head versus heart—although some interpreters have wanted to claim him for one side or the other.

---

8. WJE 2:97.

If the human self was basically unitary for Edwards, so were the affections in one sense. That is, the godly affections were all rooted in the basic affection of love. To be sure, Edwards singled out for discussion in *Religious Affections* a variety of affections including fear, hope, love, hatred, desire, joy, sorrow, compassion, and zeal. But the affection that overshadows the rest is love, which Edwards also called charity. In *Charity and Its Fruits*, love is "the sum of all virtue," and is opposed to envy, pride, selfishness, and censoriousness. But love is not only the root of the virtues for Edwards; it is also, in some sense, the root of all godly affections and actions. One recalls Augustine's statement in *City of God* that each person's love is the "gravity" that determines whether a person rises or falls. For Edwards, the opposite of love is not hatred but indifference. A "hard heart," he wrote, is an "unaffected heart."[9] He interpreted affections in all their diversity as so many modifications of love arising from diverse circumstances in which love is expressed:

> From love arises hatred of those things which are contrary to what we love, or which oppose and thwart us in those things that we delight in: and from the various exercises of love and hatred, according to the circumstances of the objects of those affections, as present or absent, certain or uncertain, probable or improbable, arise all those other affections of desire, hope, fear, joy, grief, gratitude, anger, etc.[10]

Edwards spoke of a "counterfeit love" that produces "other false affections"—an idea reminiscent of Augustine's distinction between charity and concupiscence, two "loves" with different destinations, one driving some toward the City of Man and the other propelling others toward the City of God.[11]

Scrutinizing the Affections

Edwards did not merely delineate the affections and explain how they function in the human person. As Smith has put it, he subjected Protestantism's sacred domain—the inner life—to public tests. Edwards believed that piety needed to be rationally scrutinized. This was for the purpose of discriminating true religion from hypocrisy and self-deception. He recognized that this is a difficult task, even for a pastor obligated to make decisions regarding other persons' spiritual condition. Only God, said Edwards, can

---

9. WJE 2:102–108; WJE 8:129, 218–92; Augustine, *City of God* 11.23; WJE 2:117.
10. WJE 2:108.
11. WJE 2:150.

fathom a human soul (ch. 29). Thus he writes that "it was never God's design to give us any rules by which we may certainly know, who of our fellow professors are his, and to make a full and clear separation between sheep and goats: but that on the contrary, it was God's design to reserve this to himself, as his prerogative." A recently published text, "Directions for Judging of Persons' Experiences," shows Edwards searching for principles to evaluate members of his flock: "See to it: That the operation be much upon the will or heart, not on the imagination.... That the trouble of mind be reasonable.... That they have not only pretended convictions of sin; but a proper mourning for sin."[12] During his later years, Edwards became skeptical about definitive judgments on one's own or others' spiritual condition. Hypocrites mimicked saints, and saints resembled hypocrites. The heart was deceptive both to others and to itself.

In *Religious Affections*, the overriding sign of genuine religion is "holy practice," which lies in the realm of action rather than perception or sensibility. The only set of affections that produces the habit of holy practice is the cluster collectively titled the "new sense of the heart." This is the "disposition" or habit that the Spirit "infuses" to enable saints to see God's infinite beauty and glory. It is a "sweet idea," the "joy of joys," a sweet and ravishing "view of the moral excellency of divine things." This sight alone makes all the other divine attributes glorious and lovely. It is a taste that is diverse from all other sensations, as different as the taste of honey is from the mere intellectual idea of it. It is an "intuitive knowledge" of the supreme beauty and sweetness of the holiness and moral perfection of divine things. This beauty of holiness, Edwards proclaimed, is the most important thing in the world, the divinity of divinity, without which God would be an infinite evil, and apart from which it would be better if we had not been born and there had been no being at all. These were the extravagant claims made by Edwards for what has been called the most original idea in all of his theology.[13]

This "sense of the heart" is treated elsewhere in this volume (chs. 10, 24), but it is important here to note the scholarly debate over the relationship of this "sense" to everyday perceptions. On one side are those like Paul Helm who highlight the discontinuity between the new sense and all other human experiences.[14] Since Edwards compares the new sense to Locke's "new simple idea"—an idea, like heat or wetness, that cannot be understood without a cor-

---

12. WJE 2:43, 193; WJE 21:522–24.

13. WJE 2:242, 253, 257, 260, 206, 259, 272–73, 298; Smith, "Editor's Introduction," in WJE 2:30.

14. Paul Helm, "John Locke and Jonathan Edwards: A Reconsideration," *Journal of the History of Philosophy* 7 (1969): 51–61.

FIGURE 20.1 For Jonathan and others, Sarah Edwards offered a model of genuine spiritual experience and affections (Portrait by Joseph Badger. Used with permission of the Master and Fellows of Jonathan Edwards College at Yale University and the Jonathan Edwards Trust).

responding experience—these scholars maintain that the new sense has no connection to ordinary sense perception and implies a kind of sixth sense.[15] On the other side are those such as Perry Miller who note that Edwards denied that the new sense bypassed the natural senses. They interpret the "new sense" not as a sixth sense or vision of another world but as a deeper vision of the present world.[16] Our position is that Edwards's new sense involved an interplay of natural and gracious experience. Pace Miller, the experience of conversion is foundational to Edwards's religious epistemology. Believers are able to perceive a holy beauty in God that is invisible to nonbelievers, and in this sense believers and nonbelievers live in two different universes. Subsequent to regeneration, the believer comes to appreciate even

---

15. WJE 2:205.

16. Perry Miller, "Jonathan Edwards and the Sense of the Heart," *Harvard Theological Review* 41 (1948): 123–45.

the beauties of the natural world in new ways. While Ralph Waldo Emerson and Friedrich Schleiermacher held that a deeper vision was accessible to all human beings, Edwards made this vision dependent on a prior operation of divine grace. Pace Helm, however, the mental breakthrough of grace, or "divine and supernatural light," operates in and through the natural sense faculties, and so grace does not destroy or bypass nature but perfects it. The "new sense" is not an epistemological quirk, detached from the rest of human life. Those who undergo regeneration find that this one experience unlocks the meaning of all human experience and sheds light on all of life. Thus Edwards's "new sense" is a creative synthesis of Puritan and Enlightenment ideas, melding the discontinuities of grace with the continuities of human nature. Moreover the "new sense" became a basis for Edwards to judge between gracious and natural experiences in the midst of the eighteenth-century religious awakenings.

The argument of *Religious Affections* suggests that individuals can examine themselves to see if they delight in this divine beauty for its own sake. It may be a hard test, but for Edwards it was this vision, issuing in a disposition given to Christian practice (by which he meant things such as humility, forgiveness, mercy, fear of God, balance among the virtues, and hunger for more of God), that yields decisive evidence of grace. *Religious Affections* also outlines a set of phenomena that are unreliable as signs of grace. Some persons, for example, become convinced of God's favor because verses of scripture or other words related to Jesus Christ suddenly come to mind. Another unreliable or "no certain" sign is the presence of "very great" or "raised high" affections. Edwards points to the Israelites at the Red Sea who sang God's praises but then "tested the Lord" by forgetting his work for them and crying out to go back to Egypt.[17] Other uncertain signs are great effects on the body, fluency in talking about religious things, spiritual phenomena arising without effort, the appearance of love, many different kinds of affections, a certain order in the affections, spending much time in religious duties, mouths full of praises, assurance of salvation, and good impressions among the godly about the spiritual state of a person. All of these are common among hypocrites, who also exhibit excessive confidence in themselves, a prideful and superior spirit, censorious or judgmental attitudes toward others, and a tendency toward self-satisfaction.[18]

---

17. WJE 2:127–30.

18. WJE 2:142–45, 220, 127–90.

The Role of the Imagination

Edwards also discussed the role of the human imagination in religious experience. Early in his career, he thought God sometimes used the human imagination—for example, when people had visions and sensed God speaking to them. In *Distinguishing Marks*—a Yale commencement address in 1741—he argued that these phenomena are not antithetical to true religion: "That persons have many impressions on their imaginations, don't prove that they have nothing else." When the Holy Spirit stirs the human mind and heart, the imagination is liable to be influenced, and "such is our nature that we can't think of things invisible, without a degree of imagination." He stressed the positive functions of imagination: "It appears to me manifest in many instances I have been acquainted with, that God has really made use of this faculty [of imagination] to truly divine purposes; especially in some that are more ignorant." He concluded that the "holy frame and sense" of these people at these times were from God, but "the imaginations that attend it are but accidental" and therefore often mixed with confusion and falsehood.[19] Five years later in *Religious Affections*, Edwards was more jaded. All "imaginary sights of God and Christ and heaven, all supposed witnessing of the Spirit, and testimonies of the love of God by immediate inward suggestion; and all impressions of future events, and immediate revelations of any secret facts whatsoever…all interpretations of the mystical meaning of Scripture, by supposed immediate revelation" are simply "impressions in the head" and evidence of "false religion." These "impressions on the imagination" are symptoms of the false religion seen in heretical groups such as the Gnostics, Montanists, Antinomians, "the followers of [Anne] Hutchinson in New England" and "the late French prophets."[20] Edwards was not denouncing all uses of the imagination at this point but ruling out the validity of any that claimed "immediate revelation." This association of voices and visions with immediate revelation, which he had always rejected from his earliest writings, suggests he regarded the imagination with more wariness than before.

If Edwards was ambivalent on the role of the imagination in religious experience, he was surprisingly open to biological and psychological factors in the operation of the affections. In a state of affection, he allowed, "the motion of the blood and animal spirits begins to be sensibly altered; whence oftentimes arises some bodily sensation."[21] He said little on the metaphysical ques-

---

19. WJE 4:235–38.
20. WJE 2:285–87.
21. WJE 2:96–97.

tion of how soul and body interact—other than that it is a mystery—but implied that changes in either soul or body would affect the other.[22] When discussing temptation, he suggested that Satan cannot directly implant ideas into the human mind, as God can, but must stir up the "animal spirits" and so excite the "imagination or phantasy." This was one reason Edwards was skeptical of those claiming to have had visions of God. Diabolical influence or emotional arousal could counterfeit divine inspiration. Several years after writing *Religious Affections*, when he edited *The Life of David Brainerd*, Edwards indicated that depression or "melancholy" was a "disease" that can produce "dark thoughts" of "spiritual desertion"--the impression that God has abandoned one. He also commented that those with "a very gay and sanguine natural temper" are "much more exposed to enthusiasm" than those with different mental temperaments. Edwards thus regarded "enthusiasm"—which he defined as "imaginary sights of God and Christ" and "immediate inward impressions" of divine voices—as influenced by variations in psychological temperament.[23] Though Edwards's comments on these matters are incomplete, it is clear that he considered biological, social, and psychological factors as co-determinants of religious experience.

We may conclude with two observations. First, one of Edwards's foundational ideas was not to judge spiritual phenomena by *a priori* assumptions, but to look more deeply at underlying dynamics and more broadly at extensive connections for clues to religious validity (ch. 27). He warned that spiritual phenomena could not be taken at face value, that hypocrites deceive the righteous, and the devil counterfeits true religion. His project of spiritual discernment was among the most penetrating and subtle in Christian history.

Second, Edwards probed the affections and religious experience with an intensity unique to the eighteenth century and perhaps the centuries since. The enlightened thinkers of his century thought it beneath their dignity to philosophize concerning religious experience, especially the affections. Even less did they consider it their life's work to categorize and analyze subjective states of religious sensibility. One of Edwards's gifts to modern intellectual history was the way he made it possible, for religious and secular investigators alike, to view religious affections as phenomena worth studying.

---

22. WJE 23:166–66. He said the same about the mutual effects of body and mind: WJE 6:339.

23. WJE 2:88–89; WJE 7:91–94; WJE 2:285.

21

Edwards's Calvinism and Theology of the Covenants

EVER SINCE PERRY Miller charged that Edwards "threw over the whole covenant scheme" and "went back, not to what the first generation of New Englanders had held, but to Calvin, and who became, therefore, the first consistent and authentic Calvinist in New England," Edwards's relation to Calvin and covenants has been in question. Miller believed that Calvin's God was irrational and inscrutable, and that covenantal theology was alien to Calvin because it represented "a God chained" to "fulfilling terms" for humans who "extort salvation from God."[1] The Calvinist tradition, in Miller's view, domesticated Calvin's God for "shamelessly pragmatic" reasons: it was terrified that the decrees of election and reprobation meant human beings have no way to find salvation or know they have found it, and created the covenant for reassurance. But Edwards, according to Miller, chose Calvin and Calvin's God over Calvinism by rejecting all covenantal schemes.[2] Edwards himself contributed to this debate by the ambivalent note he penned in his preface to *Freedom of the Will*: "I utterly disclaim a dependence on Calvin, or believing the doctrines which I hold, because he believed them and taught them; and cannot justly be charged with believing in everything just as he taught."[3]

This chapter will argue that Edwards was a Calvinist but not of the sort that Miller imagined. He spent the better part of his career defending Calvinist positions, but creatively and not slavishly. Contrary to what most Edwards scholars thought in the mid-twentieth century, Edwards embraced covenantal theology, not only the covenants of works, grace, and redemption but also the church and national covenants. We shall conclude by looking at his

---

1. Perry Miller, "The Marrow of Puritan Divinity," *Errand into the Wilderness* (New York: Harper and Row, 1964), 98. This essay was first published in 1935.

2. Miller, *The New England Mind: The Seventeenth Century* (Cambridge: Belknap, 1983), 395. Peter DeJong follows Miller on this score in his *The Covenant Idea in New England Theology, 1620–1847* (Grand Rapids: Eerdmans, 1945), arguing that Edwards laid the groundwork for the final eradication of the covenant idea from New England religious life.

3. WJE 1:131.

understandings of divine decrees, perhaps the most contested of Calvinist doctrines. Here we shall find that Edwards rejected supralapsarianism but found many of these high Calvinist conceptions to be compelling and rational.

Calvinism and Edwards

Calvin, it turns out, planted the seeds of what later became covenantalism in his sermons on Deuteronomy.[4] His God was not irrational nor as arbitrary as Miller and others suggested. The reformer of Geneva said that many of God's ways, especially election and reprobation, are inscrutable, but that it was possible to know whether one is in the covenant.[5]

Edwards saw himself as an apologist for the Calvinist tradition. Carl Bogue exaggerates, but not much, when he declares, "No issue is so fundamental to the understanding of Edwards the theologian as the Calvinist-Arminian controversy."[6] A cursory review of his writings makes this plain. For example, when he was a young man, just beginning his theological notebooks, he defended the Calvinist doctrines that God decreed all that has come to pass, that the atonement was only for the elect, that saving grace was irresistible, that faith brought the imputation of a righteous state, and that perfect righteousness was won by Christ's perfect obedience.[7]

Edwards's master's thesis at Yale College on justification was directed against Arminian views of salvation, which "had less to do with Jacobus Arminius (1560–1609)...than with a rising confidence in man's ability to gain some purchase on the divine favor by human endeavor."[8] Edwards's defense of the Great Awakening, *Some Thoughts Concerning the Revival* (1742), warned that "Arminian principles" would lead one to "being a Deist." His *Life of David Brainerd* (1749) insisted that Brainerd's Christian virtues were "the effect of Calvinistical doctrines (as they are called)" and that Arminian doctrines

---

4. See George Marsden, "Perry Miller's Rehabilitation of the Puritans: A Critique," *Church History* 39 (1970), 91–105; and Paul Helm, "Calvin and Covenant: Unity and Continuity," *Evangelical Quarterly* 55 (1983), 65–81. Ola Elizabeth Winslow also perpetuated this idea that "Calvin's God had not crossed to the American continent" but instead was turned into a "reasonable rather than an arbitrary God" by the covenant: Winslow, *Jonathan Edwards, 1703–1758* (New York: Macmillan, 1941), 154–55.

5. John Calvin, *Institutes* 3.24.1–7.

6. Carl W. Bogue, *Jonathan Edwards and the Covenant of Grace* (Cherry Hill: Mack Publishing Company, 1975), 77. One could argue that Edwards's aesthetic vision (ch. 6) was just as fundamental as his defense of Calvinist doctrine.

7. WJE 13:175, 174, 170–71, 197, 188.

8. C.C. Goen, Introduction to *The Great Awakening*, WJE 4:10.

fail to produce "such a transformation of a people in point of morality." Edwards's "Book of Minutes on the Arminian Controversy" contains notes for the purpose of defending Calvinist ideas about justification, decrees of election and reprobation, free will, and original sin. He asked Scottish correspondents for "the best books that have lately been written in defense of Calvinism," and described his treatise, *Freedom of the Will*, as an attempt "to bring the late, great objections and outcries against the Calvinistic divinity, from these topics, to the test of strictest reasoning." His notebook on "Efficacious Grace" complains about Arminian replies to "the doctrines of the Calvinists," and refers to "us" Calvinists. The "Book of Controversies" defends a "Calvinistic doctrine of justification." His favorite authors were the Calvinist divines Francis Turretin and Petrus van Mastricht, and at the end of his life he told the trustees at Princeton College that, while he had just published "something on one of the main points in dispute between the Arminians and Calvinists," he hoped "to consider all the other controverted points." By that time, he had completed his great apologetic works that were defenses of Calvinist doctrines of agency (*Freedom of the Will*) and sin (*Original Sin*).[9]

Edwards's disclaimer of dependence on Calvin was simply a protest, as B. B. Warfield once put it, that he was not a "blind follower." The disclaimer was followed by a clause often ignored : "I should not take it all amiss, to be called a Calvinist, for distinction's sake." He said this even though he believed "the term 'Calvinist' is in these days, among most, a term of greater reproach than the term 'Arminian.'"[10]

Yet rather than simply reproducing the tradition he had inherited, Edwards "chose to broaden, impregnate and sometimes alter his Calvinist theology, rather than transcend it."[11] For example, his lectures on justification (published in 1738) used his vaunted "new spiritual sense" that was rooted in Calvinist concepts but developed by means of Locke's empiricism. Edwards agreed with Calvin on the nature and grounds of justification, but added an ontological foundation rooted in dispositions. Like Calvin, Edwards

---

9. WJE 4:503; WJE 7:526; WJEO 37; WJE 16:249, 491; WJE 21:273, 292, 354; WJE 16:217, 727. His preface to *Freedom of the Will* quotes almost verbatim, but without attribution, the opening statement in Calvin's *Institutes*: "Of all kinds of knowledge that we can ever obtain, the knowledge of God, and the knowledge of ourselves, are the most important." WJE 1:133. On Edwards's fondness for Turretin and Mastricht, see WJE 16:217.

10. B. B. Warfield, "Edwards and the New England Theology," in *Studies in Theology* (New York: Oxford University Press, 1932), 531; WJE 1:131.

11. Conrad Cherry, *The Theology of Jonathan Edwards: A Reappraisal* (Bloomington: Indiana University Press, 1990 [1966]), 4.

highlighted God's sovereignty but placed that doctrine within a larger vision of God's beauty. Like his Puritan predecessors, Edwards departed from Calvin's amillennialism and developed an elaborate eschatology that was distinctly postmillennial. The Book of Revelation was the only New Testament text on which Calvin did *not* write a commentary, and the only text to which Edwards devoted a full-length exposition. Edwards also put a unique spin on the Calvinist doctrines of covenants and decrees.

Covenant Theology in Edwards

John Calvin spoke primarily in terms of Old Covenant and New Covenant, corresponding roughly to the Jewish and Christian dispensations. The "classical confessional version of federal theology" (from the Latin *foedus* for covenant or pact) was first broached in a catechism by Zacharias Ursinus in 1562 and emerged among the Puritans after 1585. This federal theology contrasted a pre-Fall covenant of works to a post-Fall covenant of grace. David Weir argues that Calvinist authors introduced the covenant of works to explain God's decrees—reprobation was a punishment for violating the covenant of works. Similarly, Heinrich Heppe suggested in 1861 that covenantal theology in general was an attempt to soften the harshness of high Calvinism. Theodore Beza (1519–1605) was an influential supralapsarian who taught that God decided who would be saved and damned before consideration of the Fall. Heppe and others postulated that, for later Calvinists, the covenants were ways of viewing God as less arbitrary.[12]

Edwards inherited this classical federalism from his Puritan forbears, accepted it in principle, and used it extensively, but was not satisfied with its customary forms. In 1737, he complained that the relation of perseverance to the covenants "has not been sufficiently set forth" and often expressed his confidence that God would give the church more light on important doctrinal issues such as the covenants.[13] So it is not surprising to see Edwards recommending to his fellow Reformed divines better ways of understanding the

---

12. David A. Weir, *The Origins of the Federal Theology in Sixteenth-Century Reformation Thought* (Oxford: Clarendon Press, 1990), 1–50; Heinrich Heppe, *Dogmatik des deutschen Protestantismus im sechzehnten Jahrhundert*, I (Gotha: F.A. Perthes, 1857), 152; cited in Weir, *Origins*, 47.

13. WJE 18:353; on Edwards's expectation of more light, he wrote in a preface to Joseph Bellamy's *True Religion Delineated*, "We cannot suppose that the Church of God is already possessed of all that light...that ever God intends to give it; nor that all Satan's lurking places have already been found out." WJE 4:570.

covenants (ch. 41). Nor is it surprising to see him develop his own understanding over the course of three phases in his career.

The first phase can be seen in several *Miscellanies* entries in 1723. There he complains that when theologians distinguish the covenant of redemption (in which the three Persons of the Trinity agreed in eternity on the plan of redemption) from the covenant of grace (in which human beings receive the offer of salvation from Christ), they lay a foundation for Arminianism. For the covenant of grace then functions as a covenant between God and humanity, when in reality "God never made but one [covenant] with man, to wit, the covenant of works," wherein God promised salvation to Adam as humankind's representative on condition of Adam's perfect obedience. When God offers grace to humankind, it is customary to speak of faith as a condition. But this "tends to make us apt to depend on our own righteousness." The proper alternative, Edwards urges, is to realize "there have never been two covenants, in strictness of speech, but only two ways constituted of performing of this [one] covenant[i.e., the covenant of works]." This covenant of works "never yet was abrogated, but is a covenant stands [sic] in full force to all eternity without the failing of one tittle." The only other covenant enacted by God was the covenant of redemption, which was the Trinity's plan for the Son to fulfill the condition of the covenant of works (i.e., perfect obedience) for the sake of redeemed humanity or Christ's mystical body. So the only true covenantal condition is perfect obedience, as it was performed by Christ. All talk of "conditions" fulfilled by believers reinforces Arminian presumptions of moral worthiness. And the covenant of grace is not really a covenant—for there was no agreement between believers and the Father—but simply a "free offer of life." Faith is not the condition for receiving the offer, "for it is the receiving itself." People may talk of this free offer as a covenant but that makes it "much the more hard to think right." For "by Christ's performing the condition of the covenant [of works], the condition is as it were performed by [the members of his mystical body]." Therefore "the second" covenant (of redemption) "is as much a covenant of works as the first" (covenant with Adam).[14]

Ten years later, in 1733, Edwards seemed disturbed not so much by Arminian self-confidence as by antinomian laxity. Now he was willing to talk about a covenant distinct from the covenant of works that we are parties to—"the covenant between Christ and us as being one of the parties contracting." And at this point he was willing to talk about conditions that believers must fulfill— "first closing with Christ and a perseverance in faith and holiness." This is a

---

14. WJE 13:217, 199, 219, 217, 199, 197.

marriage covenant between Christ and his church. Just as a bride's "consenting to be the wife" and the groom's expectation of her lifelong faithfulness are conditions for his taking her, so too there are two conditions for our joining the covenant of grace—our closing with Christ and our perseverance. Closing with Christ and perseverance are both gifts from Christ that come from participation in him, but they are human conditions nonetheless.[15]

In 1739 and after, there was a third tack in Edwards's course of developing his theology of covenants. This time Edwards appeared to be responding to those like Thomas Boston, who claimed that the covenants of redemption and grace were not two distinct covenants but one and the same. Boston went on to say that Christ is the condition of the covenant of grace. To Edwards, this made no sense. Since Edwards had defined the covenant of grace as that existing between Christ and believers, it was incoherent to say Christ is the condition of that covenant. So he declared that he now had a way to "perhaps reconcile the difference between those divines that think [the covenant of redemption] and the covenant of grace the same, and those that think 'em different." The covenant that God the Father makes with believers "is the same with the covenant of redemption made with Christ before the foundation of the world, or at least is entirely included in it." This covenant had a mediator. But the covenant between Christ and believers is different and does not have a mediator: "There is a mediator between sinners and the Father to bring about a covenant union between them, but there is no mediator between Christ and sinners to bring about a marriage union between Christ and their souls."[16]

By the 1740s, then, Edwards had distinguished four different covenants having to do with salvation—the covenant of works, the covenant of redemption, the covenant of grace (with Christ as mediator between the Father and believers), and the marriage covenant between Christ and believers. He affirmed that the Bible presents a covenant of grace and treats the church as a party to it. This covenant of grace was a "renewal" of the covenant of redemption, much as the Mosaic covenant was a renewal of the Abrahamic covenant. The covenant of grace was different but not distinct from the covenant of redemption, since the promises of the latter "were properly made to Christ mystical...to Christ as a public person, as virtually containing the whole future church that he had taken as it were into himself, having taken their names on his heart, and having undertaken to stand as representing them all."

---

15. WJE 18:150–51, 149.

16. Thomas Boston, *A View of the Covenant of Grace* (Philadelphia: Towar & Hogan, 1827), 32, 84; WJE 20:477–78. On Edwards's use of Boston, see WJE 26:223–24, 423, 432–33.

In 1746, he had further developed this line of thinking. The covenant of grace, he wrote, "introduces Persons to a right to" the covenant of redemption. Yet Edwards never varied from his insistence that all the covenants were "expressions" of the covenant of redemption. Christ "never does anything, more or less, than is contained in that eternal covenant [of redemption]."[17]

Two Testaments but One Covenant

Calvin and his successors departed from a Lutheran dichotomy of law and gospel that often divorced the Old Testament from the New. Calvinists proposed instead that the two testaments were simply two "modes of dispensation" of "one and the same" covenant.[18] Edwards's development of this concept was not remarkably different from those of his predecessors among the Puritans and Reformed, but his approach was more nuanced.

Edwards used an anatomical image to represent the relationship between the two. Drawing on the distinction between the "cortex" (shell or husk) of an organ and its "medulla" (central parts or nucleus), he played on the contrasts between outer and inner, and letter and spirit. The Jewish testament was the cortex, or shell, that "envelops" the medulla of the gospel or covenant of grace. The first is comparable to the letter of the law, whose true meaning is communicated obscurely and indirectly, while the second may be likened to the spirit of the law, delivered more simply and directly.

The cortex actually consisted of two covenants, the covenant of works (that God established with Adam and his posterity) and the national covenant (that God "made and established with Israel according to the flesh"). The national covenant is "an appendage" to the covenant of works that typifies the covenant of grace and is therefore "subservient" and "subordinate" to the covenant of grace. All of its institutions were external and pointed to the internal spirit of the covenant of grace. Hence it consisted of an "external temporal society...an external earthly country...an external carnal priesthood...a worldly sanctuary...carnal sacrifices; an external altar; an external holy of holies, and an external mercy seat...external conformity to the law of God; an outward conformity to the moral law, and a conformity to an external and carnal law." Even pardon from sin and sanctification from sin were external matters under the

---

17. WJE 20.445, 167, 475; sermon on Isaiah 55:3, WJE 64; sermon on Hebrews 13:8, in Edward Hickman, ed., *The Works of Jonathan Edwards*, 2 vols. (Edinburgh: Banner of Truth Trust, 1986), 2:950.

18. John Calvin, *Institutes*, 2.10.2.

national covenant—"freedom from guilt as it excluded from external privileges, and a sanctification that consisted in the purifying of the flesh, delivering from carnal pollutions, and qualifying for carnal privileges."[19]

If Israel's national covenant was the outer shell containing an inner core of grace, it was also a means of grace in earlier times. Edwards saw the same pattern working in his own day: just as the covenant of works was "proposed" to Israel in the wilderness, "the same is now proposed in the course of a sinner's convictions in these days." Sinners are first confronted with God's demands in the covenant of works, and only by trying to meet those demands do they discover their inability and need for grace. Hence the history of God's covenants in the work of redemption is recapitulated in the religious psychology of the person coming to faith. Yet it was God's method to veil gospel truths so that the reprobate did not misuse them. The covenant of works was at once God's means of leading the elect into his inner mystery and his manner of hiding this mystery from careless, carnal people who did not deserve to see it. God used the cortex to blind the proud and provoke them to self-righteousness.[20] This helped to explain why the gospel message was imperfectly revealed in the Old Testament but manifested fully in the New Testament. God's people under the old dispensation "could not bear" a clear revelation of the covenant of grace because they were not convinced of their inability to establish their own righteousness, just as sinners of Edwards's day did not know their own sin and so could not appreciate God's covenant of grace.

The Ten Commandments thus had the appearance of a covenant of works in order to show the Israelites their own inability to follow God's commandments. Yet the Commandments also cryptically revealed the covenant of grace, since their true intent was to establish that covenant. This is evident from internal clues, according to Edwards. First, the Ten Commandments were written on "tables of the covenant," which suggested God's initiative in choosing Israel. In fact, he chose to be "married" to Israel and so founded a covenant to establish the relationship. Furthermore, Edwards laid stress on the prologue to the Ten Commandments: "I am the Lord thy God, which have brought thee out of the land of Egypt, out of the house of bondage" (Exod. 20:2). These words indicated that God had become Israel's God and redeemer before the people had shown whether or not they would obey him. So the commandments

---

19. WJE 23:500–501, 499. Edwards's use of medulla may have come from William Ames's *Medulla Theologiae* (*The Marrow of Theology*, 1629), which he had been required to memorize at Yale.

20. WJE 23:492–506.

were instructions on how to cleave to and trust a heavenly Spouse, and not terms that had to be fulfilled before a marriage began. In addition, God proclaimed that he shows mercy to thousands (Ex. 20:6) and therefore ordered the written tablets of the Ten Commandments to be placed in the ark of the covenant where they were overshadowed by the mercy seat. Finally, "these Ten Commandments...were sealed with the blood of the sacrifice, which typified the blood of [Christ]." This demonstrated that God's relationship to His people was based not on human obedience but divine mercy.[21]

Such lofty spiritual truths were "insinuated to [Israel] and proposed under covert" because of Israel's spiritual immaturity. What is more, God did not directly reveal his grace at this time because Christ and his kingdom were not yet established. The Messiah's sufferings and God's threats of eternal punishment for the wicked had not yet expressed God's hatred of sin. In the absence of these clear demonstrations, Israel needed severe and tangible punishments to maintain "the honor of the divine greatness and majesty, and the dread of his spotless holiness." This was the reason that God kept his people at a distance and used graphic and brutal punishments in the Old Testament but allowed the saints of the New Testament to converse with him "most freely and intimately."[22]

Yet, despite these differences, the two testaments were different phases of one covenant of grace. As Edwards put it early in his career, "The gospel was preached to the Jews under a veil." The process of conversion was the same for Israelites under the Old Testament as for Christians under the New. They were "convinced so much of their wickedness that they trusted to nothing but the mere mercy of God." This included the antediluvians, and indeed all those who lived since "the beginning of the world." Not only the process but the pace of conversion was comparable. In ancient times, there were both wicked and godly persons, and conversions were just as frequent then as in Edwards's day. Christ saved the Old Testament saints just like their cohorts in the New Testament, and they believed in Christ, but under the designation of the "angel of the Lord" or "messenger of the covenant." In fact, Christ had appeared to Old Testament figures. Moses saw his "back parts" (Exod. 33:23) and he appeared in human form to the seventy elders (Exod. 24: 9–11) as well as to Joshua, Gideon, and Manoah. Every time God was said to have manifested himself to humans with an audible voice or in a visible form, this always took place through the second person of the Trinity.[23]

---

21. WJE 23:492–506.

22. WJE 13:363, 489–90.

23. WJE 14:247; WJE 13:221–22; WJE 23:229–30; WJE 21:372–94; WJE 9:197, 131.

Though the two covenants had two federal heads—Adam and Christ—and one was a "dead" and the other a "living" way, "in strictness of speech" these covenants were not two but one. For they shared the same mediator, the same salvation (meaning the same calling, justification, adoption, sanctification, and glory), and the same means of salvation in the incarnation, suffering, righteousness, and intercession of Christ. The Holy Spirit was the same person applying Christ's redemption in both dispensations, and the method of obtaining salvation was the same—faith and repentance. Even such external means as the word of God, prayer, praise, and Sabbath observance were not different. Neither were the benefits of God's Spirit, God's mercy, the mediation of a divine person (i.e., the angel of the Lord), and the blessings yet to come. Under both covenants, the condition for receiving all benefits was faith in the Son of God as Mediator, expressed with the same spirit of repentance and humility. This is why all parts of the Old Testament pointed toward the future coming of Christ. In sum, the religion of the church of Israel is "essentially the same religion with that of the Christian church."[24]

The Church Covenant

Another expression of Edwards's covenantal theology was the public acceptance or "owning" of the covenant, or what the Puritans and Edwards called "the church" or "external" covenant. Just as the Israelites were told to "swear by his name" (Deut. 6:13) by taking a public oath to "unite themselves to God in covenant," so too "it ought to be expected of persons before they are admitted to the privileges of the adult in the church of Christ." For Edwards, this meant "a profession of real piety...the consent of our hearts to [the covenant of grace]." Edwards did not specify the procedure for this, as had the first-generation Puritans, but he insisted after 1746 that congregants must believe that God is "probably" working by his grace within them, and express their intention to live a life of holiness, before they could be admitted to the Lord's Supper. This "church covenant" was the "external" way of owning the "internal" covenant of grace.[25]

As David Hall has shown, Edwards differed from Calvin, who held to Augustine's distinction between the visible and invisible churches and maintained that church officers need not distinguish between the two when administering the sacraments. Edwards had also departed from the so-called Half-Way

---

24. WJE 13:219; WJE 20:117; WJE 23:492–94; WJE 9:283, 443.

25. WJE 12:199–201, 203–205, 61, 21, 83.

Covenant—formulated in the Cambridge Platform in 1662—that formally required a "relation" or testimony of grace for reception of the sacrament but actually admitted "'the weakest Christians' so long as they were 'sincere.'" Even more strikingly, Edwards's new position was a repudiation of (grandfather) Solomon Stoddard's teaching that the sacraments are "converting ordinances" for the unregenerate. After going along with Stoddard's policy for nineteen years, Edwards turned against it, declaring that the Lord's Table was only for those who gave an appearance of being regenerate (ch. 30).[26]

This was a major turn in Edwards's thought and practice (see ch. 5). Early in his career, he complained that his parishioners were wholly neglect[ing] . . . the sacrament of the Lord's Supper." In 1728 he said applicants for the Table must make a "hearty" profession of faith, but cautioned against making "an examination of their particular experiences." It was enough that they "believed the reality of the gospel salvation" and the "sufficiency of Christ as a Savior." He thus declined to insist upon the early New England policy of requiring a "relation" of an experience of grace. Yet by the mid-1740s, Edwards was insisting more strenuously than before that applicants believe God was working in them and that they intended to live a holy life—even if they were not sure they had been converted. He did not presume to know whether they were telling the truth and did not require of them a particular experience. But they had to be more than sincere about morality and doctrine; they had to believe that grace was "probably" at work in their hearts.[27]

Why the change? David Hall thinks it resulted from the experience of the Great Awakening. Within a few years, Edwards saw that many converts from the revival seemed to lack the outward signs of true religion. Hall adds that Edwards "was also reacting against the intermingling of the social and the religious that constituted popular religion." Northampton's pastor came to think that it was "better, that some true saints, through their own weakness and misunderstanding, should be kept away from the Lord's Table, which will not keep such out of heaven; than voluntarily to bring in multitudes of false professors to partake unworthily, and in effect to seal their own condemnation." Edwards became convinced of the need to raise the standard for participation in the eucharist, so that complacent persons might become spiritually serious and perhaps find their way to conversion and assurance of salvation.[28]

---

26. WJE 12:23, 29.
27. WJE 13:413; WJE 12:205. See WJE 25:488–91 and ch. 30.
28. WJE 12:83–4, 310.

Yet Edwards did not go as far as some. He acknowledged that those who were truly saved might not know themselves as such due to "melancholy" or depression. The church's requirement for a "visibility" of saintliness was "not [to] the eye of God, but [to] the eye of man." Pastors and elders could never know with certainty whether someone was regenerate. It followed that all such judgments were based on probability rather than certainty. He also distinguished between full and partial communion in the church covenant, refusing the proposal by some that those not in full communion be dismissed from the church.[29]

The National Covenant

Edwards believed that Northampton's and New England's fortunes—whether good or bad—depended on their covenant with God. Following a tradition that antedated the Protestant Reformation Edwards conceived that God entered into covenant with a people or nation, and blessed or punished that people in proportion to their fidelity to the terms of the covenant. As John Winthrop had told the New England founders, the Lord would "expect a strict performance of the articles contained in" his covenant with them. "If we shall neglect the observation of these articles...the Lord will surely break out in wrath against us, be revenged of such a perjured people, and make us know the price of the breach of such a covenant."[30] Therefore the national covenant was a conditional agreement, and thus was unlike the unconditional covenant of grace to the elect. Furthermore, it pertained to the present life only, and applied to societies rather than to individuals per se.

Edwards's use of the civil or national covenant was little different from that of generations of New England theologians before him. Successes were unmerited blessings, expressions of God's mercy, and perhaps even warnings to repent. Defeats and disasters were visitations of God's anger, or once again invitations to repent. God sent earthly weal or woe to motivate his people to keep the terms of the covenant. Consequently, no event in a nation's history was without meaning. Citizens might chafe under what they considered to be the severity of God's discipline, but they were spared the despair that comes from believing that history is meaningless.

---

29. WJE 12:298, 295, 185, 175.

30. John Winthrop, "A Model of Christian Charity," in *The Puritans in America: A Narrative Anthology*, ed. Alan Heimert and Andrew Delbanco (Cambridge, Mass., 1985), 90–91.

Edwards most commonly invoked the national covenant when pointing out moral failures. He explained natural disasters and moral corruption as divine judgments upon a covenant-forsaking society. The first he attributed to the direct action of God chastising a sinful people—as when worms, he charged, were sent to blight crops because of Northampton's failure to help the poor. The second he explained as the result of God's abandonment, leaving people to their own devices. Sometimes Edwards used the covenant to invoke fear in times of spiritual well-being. Periods of religious vitality, he warned, should not necessarily be interpreted as signs of divine favor. They might instead be signals of coming judgment and destruction. God's goodness should lead to repentance, and so revival should cause citizens to search their hearts and fear for their future, both temporal and eternal.

Divine judgment was a prominent theme in Edwards's sermons on public days.[31] He repeatedly excoriated New Englanders for their impiety, contentiousness, venality, cynical use of religion, and such fleshly sins as excessive drinking and fornication.[32] Yet often he subsumed these and all other sins under the fundamental sin of ingratitude. Underlying the whole catalogue of transgressions was an ungratefulness to God for the unparalleled covenant mercies that he had showered upon New England. Ultimately it was ingratitude that provoked God's anger. New England had been given the greatest of civil and religious privileges, and yet its people had arrogantly abused them. They were more guilty than Sodom and Gomorrah, for if those towns had received the same blessings they certainly would have "awakened...and reformed." Indeed, because of its unprecedented blessings, New England was more culpable than any other people in history. The blessings received made the colonies more nearly parallel to Israel than any other people on earth, and this was cause for alarm not congratulation. For Israel was a "whore" and a "witch," and her children were "bastards." In 1747, Edwards told a Scottish correspondent that New England was on the verge of committing "the unpardonable sin against the Holy Ghost." Two years later, he declared that New England was worse than Pharaoh, who responded to some of God's judgments despite having fewer means of grace. Since New England's means were greater,

---

31. Gerald McDermott, *One Holy and Happy Society* (University Park, PA: Penn State Press, 1992), 11–36.

32. WJE 14:501–506; sermon on Jer. 51:5, WJEO 63; sermon on Matt. 18:7, WJEO 49; WJE 19:761–62; sermon on Acts 19:19, WJEO 51. Outside of the context of the national covenant, Edwards said that the greatest sins were the sins of the spirit, not the sins of the flesh. Of all the sins of the spirit, pride was the worst. Of all kinds of pride, spiritual pride was the most dangerous. WJE 2:181; WJE 4:415–16, 467.

its guilt would be greater. As with Pharaoh, New England's obstinacy would result in "utter destruction."[33] This meant that God might entirely forsake his covenant with her. Considering the enormity of her sins, it was a wonder that New England had not already been exterminated.

Edwards's doctrine of the national covenant therefore was neither tribalist nor provincial. He was less an optimistic nationalist than a prophet in the tradition of the New England jeremiad. The central message of his sermons on public and civil affairs was God's judgment on a sinful people. As his career progressed, he became more convinced that, since New England was the most blessed of all peoples, it was also the most guilty. Hence the two early eighteenth-century awakenings were signs not of God's pleasure but of his anger, and perhaps omens of coming destruction. For neither awakening had brought reformation. If New England were to be a redeemer nation, it would be by default. Its unfaithfulness might cause God to transfer his covenant blessings to another people.

Divine Decrees

Jonathan Edwards's Calvinism was all of a piece. His doctrine of decrees was rooted in his theology of covenants. Around 1743, he wrote that all of God's decrees are called in Scripture his "counsels" because "they belong to that agreement which the persons of the Trinity came into from eternity as it were by mutual consultation and covenant." It is the covenant of redemption to which Genesis refers when it says that God prepared to create humanity by consultation: "Come, let us make man" (Gen. 1:26).[34] Arminians had long complained that Calvinist decrees make God appear to be arbitrary and unjust. The worst decree was that of reprobation, which suggested that God created some human beings for the sole purpose of damnation. Some Calvinists conceded as much, insisting that all of God's decrees were unconditional and therefore were not the consequences of God's foreseeing particular human acts, whether good or evil.

Edwards's mature position on the divine decrees was infralapsarian. This means that he held that the decree to predestine some to salvation was logically (though not temporally) subsequent to the decree to permit the fall of humanity into sin. At an early stage he seems to have questioned both the

---

33. WJE 14:225; sermon on Exodus 8:15, WJEO 67; WJE 14:225; sermon on Jer. 51:5, WJEO 63; WJE 12:473; WJE 16:220; sermon on Exodus 8:15, WJEO 67.

34. WJE 20:323.

infra- and supralapsarian positions and intimated that neither view was true.[35] Yet, as his thinking developed, he came to affirm infralapsarianism.[36] In Miscellany 704, explaining the logic of the decrees, he wrote that God's decrees are from eternity and therefore outside time. They were all decided in eternity but executed in time, so that in history there are no new acts of God's will. But if they did not have any original sequence in time, some were nevertheless dependent on others. One decree might be the end or purpose of another. Another could be the ground on which a second is used by God to seek a further end. Hence "the sinfulness of the reprobate is the ground on which God goes in determining to glorify his justice in the punishment of his sinfulness." In other words, God's first intention is the glory of his justice, not the punishment of the sinner. Edwards provides the example of Adonibezek, whose punishment God decreed only because of Adonibezek's "cruelty in cutting off the thumbs and great toes of threescore kings" (Judg. 1:6–7). Therefore the logic of the decree of reprobation "clears God of any injustice in such a decree," because "both the sin of the reprobate, and also the glory of the divine justice, may properly be said to be *before* the decree of damning the reprobate."[37]

Edwards went further to exonerate God of injustice. Prior to any other decree, he wrote, is God's determination to shine forth his glory and communicate his goodness. Those Calvinists were wrong who claimed God's vindictive justice was an ultimate end. God's punishment of sinners was merely a subordinate means of obtaining an ultimate end—namely the glorification of God. His decree to punish was not prior to the Fall or to the being of the damned. Instead, God's prior and ultimate end was "glorifying his love and communicating his goodness." God did not create the reprobate for the purpose of damning them. Instead it was God's goodness that gave them being. Therefore the "decrees of evil" to the damned were "consequent" on the decrees to

---

35. Miscellany 29 proposed that the dependence of divine decrees on one another ran in both directions, so that "all the decrees of God are harmonious" and "it's improper to make one decree a condition of another (WJE 13:217). Taken strictly, this line of reasoning would remove the distinction between infra- and supralapsarianism. Yet in later years—concerned perhaps to vindicate God's justice—Edwards shifted toward infralapsarianism.

36. Oliver Crisp observes that while Edwards is thought to have taken a "mediating" position by seeming to be a supralapsarian on election and infralapsarian on reprobation, his decree to redeem the elect presumes sin, and so cannot be said to be supralapsarian in the traditional sense. Crisp also argues that his infralapsarianism is inconsistent with his occasionalism (ch. 7, 22). Crisp, *Jonathan Edwards and the Metaphysics of Sin* (Aldershot: Ashgate, 2005), 5–24.

37. WJE 18:314–15; emphasis added.

create them and to give them permission to sin. In the counsels of eternity, God's goodness and love motivated him to create human beings and to give them freedom. It was only, so to speak, after God's knowledge of their abuse of that freedom that God issued decrees to punish that abuse. "God would not have decreed some things [reprobation] had he not decreed others [creation and freedom]."[38]

The Arminians had raised another objection to the Calvinist decree of reprobation: God's invitations to sinners whom he has willed to reprobation must be insincere since he knows they will never accept his invitations. Surprisingly, Edwards insisted that God has just as much desire as we have "for the conversion and salvation of wicked men." He loves the happiness of the creature "infinitely" more than we do, and their wickedness and misery, "absolutely considered," are disagreeable to the nature of God:

> Jesus Christ, he really desires the conversion and salvation of reprobates, and laments their obstinacy and misery; as when he beheld the city Jerusalem and wept over it, saying, "O Jerusalem, Jerusalem, thou that killest the prophets, and stonest them which are sent unto thee, how often would I have gathered thy children together, even as a hen gathereth her chickens under her wings, and ye would not" [Matt. 23:37].[39]

In an effort to rebut Arminian accusations that the Calvinist God was irrational, Edwards asserted that God has reasons for choosing some and not others. Paul taught that the decrees of election are "according to God's good pleasure" (Eph. 1:5 KJV), and Edwards insisted that God's good pleasure was rational rather than arbitrary. "All God's methods of dealing with men are most reasonable," Edwards preached in 1727. "When God makes a man a vessel of mercy and not another, he don't [sic] do it without a wise end." While the reasons for choosing some and not others "are above our reach and are known only to him," it was clear to Edwards that God was neither cruel nor irrational.[40] Besides, as Edwards noted, God had showered reprobates with love. He had poured out "a great deal of kindness...and multiplied mercies" upon them, given them his son in order to bring them "the happiness of his love," and

---

38. WJE 18:317, 321.

39. WJE 18:409–10.

40. WJE 14:167; sermon on Acts 9:13–15, WJEO 54.

made the sun, moon, and stars serve them. But they had "obstinately refused" his grace.[41]

For Arminians, the Calvinistic idea that God decrees evil events makes God responsible for evil itself. Edwards disagreed with that inference, but he first pointed out that a plain reading of Scripture proves that God does indeed decree evil events. For example, the Bible states that God hardened Pharaoh's heart to sin, turned the Egyptians' hearts to hate Israel (Ps. 105:25), put a lying spirit in the mouth of the false prophets (1 Kings 22:23), led Absalom to lie with David's wives (2 Sam. 12:11–12), decreed that Jeroboam and the ten tribes would rebel, decided that Judas would be unfaithful, determined that Christ would be killed, "gave the wicked Jews a 'spirit of slumber'" (Rom. 11:8), and made "the Beast to speak blasphemies (Rev. 13:5)."[42] Then Edwards explained why God decrees evil. It is always "for the sake of the good that he causes to arise from the sinfulness thereof." God may hate a thing "as it is simply," but he "may will to permit it for the greater promotion of holiness in this universality [of things], including all things and at all times." God "inclines to excellency, which is harmony; but yet he may incline to suffer that which is unharmonious in itself, for the promotion of universal harmony or for the beautifying of the harmony that there is in the universality, and making it shine the brighter."[43]

The existence of sin in fact is essential to God's "awful majesty, his authority and dreadful greatness, and justice and holiness." It is only because of sin that we are enabled to see God's love, holiness, and goodness. Besides, "we little consider how much the sense of good is heightened by the sense of evil, both moral and natural." For the full happiness of the creature, evil is necessary "because the creature's happiness consists in the knowledge of God and the sense of his love." The glory of God cannot be perfect and complete without evil, and the creature's happiness consists in his vision of God's glory (ch. 19).[44]

Another Arminian objection to Calvinist decrees was that they violate creaturely freedom and contingency. Edwards considered this objection to be logically incoherent. "What a contradiction is this, to say that God knows a thing will come to pass, and yet at the same time knows that it is contingent whether it will or no.... and that is the same thing as certainly to know [that a person

---

41. WJE 19:360, 355; WJE 13:350; sermon on Ezek. 15:2–4, WJEO 49.

42. WJE 13:203, 243; WJE 21:215.

43. WJE 13:250, 323.

44. WJE 13:419–20.

will make a certain decision] and not certainly to know it at the same time. Which we leave to be considered, whether it be'nt a contradiction." Edwards said Arminians refer to the sovereignty of the human will, meaning "that a man can will as he wills" by perfect chance or contingency. That is the same as saying that "a thing should be without any cause or reason," which is impossible.[45]

In conclusion, then, Perry Miller was wrong to say that Edwards "threw over the whole covenant scheme." Miller had a grain of truth—Edwards had indeed rejected the version of federal theology bequeathed to him, insisting there was finally only one covenant. Yet Edwards accepted traditional Reformed variations on this theme: the covenants of redemption and grace were outworkings of the covenant of works, as were the church and national covenants as well. Edwards also taught the classical Calvinist decrees and sided in his explication of the decrees with the infralapsarian position of such authors as Francis Turretin and Johann Heidegger.[46] By insisting, though, on the priority of divine goodness over divine wrath, and showing that God did not create human beings in order to punish them, Edwards avoided some of the theological imbalances traditionally associated with Calvinism.

---

45. WJE 13:208–209, 228–29.

46. Francis Turretin, *Institutio theologiae elencticae*, 3 vols. (Geneva: Apud S. de Tournes, 1679–1685 [1st edn.), IV.9; Heinrich Heppe, *Reformed* Dogmatics (Grand Rapids: Baker, 1978), 146–49.

22

Free Will and Original Sin

JONATHAN EDWARDS THOUGHT a misunderstanding of the human will was at the root of nearly all that had gone wrong in theology. At the end of his treatise on original sin, written in his last full year of life, he declared "there is no one thing more fundamental in [Pelagians' and Arminians'] schemes of religion: on the determination of this one leading point depends the issue of almost all controversies we have with divines." The view of the will that he had set out in *Freedom of the Will* three years before was what makes the moral world go round: "[I]t establishes the moral system of the universe." It is no wonder, for "all virtue and religion have their seat more immediately in the will."[1] It was the abandonment of this view that had fostered independence from God and diminished the possibility of true conversion:

> These notions of liberty of contingence, indifference and self-determination, as essential to guilt or merit, tend to preclude all sense of any great guilt for past and present wickedness.... [A]ll wickedness of heart is excused, as what, in itself considered, brings no guilt.... And this notion of self-dependence and self-determination, tends to prevent or enervate all prayer to God for converting grace; for why should men earnestly cry to God for his grace, to determine their hearts to that, which they must be determined to of themselves?... [I]t destroys the very notion of conversion itself. There can properly be no such thing, or anything akin to what the Scripture speaks of as conversion, renovation of the heart, regeneration, etc. if growing good by a number of successive self-determined acts, be all that is required, or to be expected.[2]

The result of the Arminian view of the will was a sense of self-righteousness: "Thus our own holiness is from ourselves as its determining cause, and its original and highest source." The imputed righteousness of Christ

---

1. WJE 3:375; WJE 16:717; WJE 1:133.

2. WJE 16:722–23.

did not contribute to human merit, since Arminians held that merit came through human self-determination. All told, then, "God is rather dependent on men in this affair," and the glory goes "wholly to men."[3]

Christian debates about the relation of the will to the mind and human agency have usually divided between two schools of thought: the intellectualists and the voluntarists. Intellectualists, influenced to some degree by Greek and Roman moral philosophy, believed that while the intellect and will were both comprised by the mind, the intellect took priority by giving orders to the will. The Protestant scholastics whom Edwards read –Francis Turretin, Francis Burgersdjik, Gisbertus Voetius, and Petrus van Mastricht—adopted this perspective. While Calvin occasionally gave a degree of independence to the feeling of *suavitas* ("sweetness"), he also believed the understanding is "the leader and governor of the soul; and that the will is always mindful of the bidding of the understanding." Voluntarists—such as Augustine, Duns Scotus and the Franciscans, and Puritan divines John Cotton and William Ames— put the will at the pinnacle of the mind's faculties. They argued that while knowing starts with perception and judgment by the intellect, it remains potential until the will chooses. But as Allen Guelzo explains, voluntarists needed to explain *how* the will chooses among the perceptions and decides for some and not others. Starting with Augustine, they pointed to the *affections* or what the Puritans called the heart. Augustine said the love of his heart was "the weight by which I act." He was drawn to go this way and that by the pull of his loves, so that his will was not free to choose against what he loved.[4] Edwards's approach to the problem of Arminianism drew from this voluntarist tradition.

The Problem of Definition

In his introduction to the Yale edition of *Freedom of the Will*, Paul Ramsey described the extent of the problem Edwards faced: "Arminianism permeated the eighteenth century, and in mild form the whole of the Church of England in this century, becoming in a sense not heresy but orthodoxy." Although Arminianism is usually known for its opposition to classical Calvinism's notions of predestination, depravity, and limited atonement, Edwards thought the idea of a self-determining will was what

---

3. WJE 16:722.

4. Calvin, *Institutes* 1.15.7; Augustine, *Confessions* 10.38; 13.9; Allen C. Guelzo, *Edwards on the Will: A Century of American Theological* Debate (Middletown, CT: Wesleyan University Press, 1989), 3–6.

tied the whole Arminian system together. His *Freedom of the Will* (1754) debates three thinkers who, he conceded, represented diverse positions and in fact were not all Arminians per se: deist Thomas Chubb, Anglican divine Daniel Whitby, and dissenter Isaac Watts. But Edwards saw in their works a common view of the will as "a self-determining power" that "determines its own volitions; so as not to be dependent in its determinations, on any cause without [outside] itself, nor determined by anything prior to its own acts."[5]

Edwards started his attack on this notion by a definition that Allen Guelzo compares to a hook that, once in the mouth, would "lead inexorably to a Calvinistic conclusion." The will, declares Edwards, is "that by which the mind chooses anything." It always chooses by its perception of "the greatest apparent good." Therefore rather than being a cause of action, the will is the *effect*— "the *by which* the mind chooses the good it is pleased with." Hence the will is more a process than a faculty; it *is* the mind choosing. As Edwards's own son put it, it is "the mind in a different mode."[6]

Edwards then defined "necessity," the Arminians' bugbear, as "nothing different from certainty." Or in other words, when a thing "must be, and cannot be otherwise." *Moral* necessity is when a person acts "from such *moral causes*, as the strength of inclination, or motives, and the connection which there is in many cases between these, and such certain volitions and actions." For example, a "very lascivious man, in case of certain opportunities and temptations, and in the absence of such and such restraints, may be unable to forbear gratifying his lust"—for he is under moral necessity. Or "a drunkard, under such and such circumstances, may be unable to forbear taking of strong drink." Or a very wicked man whose heart is habituated to wickedness may be "under an inability to love and choose holiness; and render him utterly unable to love an infinitely holy Being, or to choose and cleave to him as his chief good." In all three of these illustrations, "to ascribe a nonperformance to the want of power or ability, is not just; because the thing wanting is not a being *able*, but a being *willing*. There are faculties of

---

5. WJE 1:82; WJE 1:164. Ramsey comments (WJE 1:90) that Watts, who published a toned-down version of *Faithful Narrative* in England and rejected the Trinity of the Athanasian creed for its alleged illogic, "may [have been] a very good hymn writer and only an indifferent theologian or philosopher."

6. Guelzo, *Edwards on the Will*, 73; WJE 1:137, 142; Guelzo, *Edwards on the Will*, 42–43, 41; Jonathan Edwards the Younger, "A Dissertation on Liberty and Necessity," in *The Works of Edwards the Younger*, ed. Tryon Edwards, 2 vols. (Boston, 1850), 1:392, cited in Guelzo, *Edwards on the Will*, 94.

mind, and capacity of nature, and everything else, sufficient, but a disposition: nothing is wanting but a will."[7] Therefore, a sinner who declines the offer of salvation cannot blame God for not giving him the desire to repent—he must concede that he really did not *want* to.

In contrast to moral necessity, which makes certain men unable to choose the moral good, there is natural necessity. This is when something in nature—an external object or defect in our natural understanding or body—prevents us from doing what we would like to do. For example, we want to read the Bible but are blind, or we want to go to church but have no way to get there.[8]

As Paul Ramsey put it, this distinction between moral and natural necessity was a reply "in advance to the charge that every form of necessity or determinism makes men blocks or stones." Like Augustine, Luther, and Calvin, Edwards by this distinction was pointing out the difference between determinism and compulsion. Natural necessity worked *against* the will, while moral necessity lay *in* the will. By moral necessity, we do what we are pleased to do; only natural necessity compels us against our desires.[9] Perhaps Edwards's most effective illustration was of two rebels against a prince who have been thrown into prison. In each case, the prince offers freedom only if the rebel will "heartily repent" and "humbly beg his pardon." One rebel repents but is prevented from gaining freedom by the bars of the dungeon; the other is so full of hatred for the prince that he "cannot" repent and ask forgiveness. Edwards said the first was free by moral necessity to gain freedom but barred by natural necessity. In the case of the second rebel, Edwards asked, "Who can't see, that when a man, in the latter case, is said to be 'unable' to obey the command [to repent and ask forgiveness], the expression is used improperly, and not in the sense it has originally and in common speech?" The second man was bound by moral necessity but was nevertheless by natural means

---

7. WJE 1:151, 149, 156, 160, 162. Edwards uses "disposition" throughout his corpus as a synonym for "inclination," "habit," "propensity," and one's collection of linked "affections."

8. WJE 1:156–59.

9. WJE 1:37, 360. Just as eighteenth-century thinkers such as Old Calvinist James Dana could not abide or understand this distinction between two kinds of necessity, neither can some philosophers today. Hugh J. McCann says Edwards "treats the will as though it were imprisoned in the natural order." This confuses natural and moral necessity, and fails to appreciate Edwards's insistence that by moral necessity the will chooses what it delights in. Dana, *An Examination of the late Rev'd President Edwards's 'Enquiry on Freedom of the Will'* (Boston: S. Kneeland, 1770), 80–81; McCann, "Edwards on Free Will," in Paul Helm and Oliver D. Crisp, *Jonathan Edwards: Philosophical Theologian* (Aldershot: Ashgate, 2003), 39.

"free" to escape his prison. "Common speech" recognizes that he was not "unable" to obey the command of his prince.[10]

Edwards continued with his definitions. Liberty is "that power and opportunity for one to do and conduct as he will, or according to his choice." Arminians and Pelagians used the word in an entirely different sense: "a self-determining power" not determined by anything prior, even a motive. Therefore we have liberty of will only if the will is "*in equilibrio*," without any "certain connection with some previous ground or reason of its existence." Edwards said this is essentially what Arminians mean by "contingence," without which they think there is "no real freedom [for a man], how much soever he may be at liberty to act according to his will."[11]

The Greatest Apparent Good

With his definitions established, Edwards clarified his thesis: the act of the will always pleases a man so that "a man's doing as he wills, and doing as he pleases, are the same thing in common speech." This means that "a man never, in any instance, wills anything contrary to his desires, or desires anything contrary to his will." Therefore there is no such thing as choosing from "a state of perfect indifference," for "in every volition there is a preference, or a prevailing inclination of the soul." If there is no preference but perfect equilibrium instead, "there is no volition."[12]

This is because every act of will is an effect that presupposes a cause, and the cause is "that motive, which as it stands in the view of the mind, is the strongest, that determines the will." This motive will appear to the mind to be a good. "Therefore it must be true, in some sense, that the will always is as the greatest apparent good is." It will appear "agreeable" or "pleasing" to the mind.[13]

As we saw earlier in this chapter, most Protestant scholastics of the seventeenth century were intellectualists who insisted the intellect gives orders to the will. But there were also "voluntarists" who claimed the will has final veto power over the intellect. Most scholars have decided that Edwards was a vol-

---

10. WJE 362–63.

11. WJE 1:164–65. For a demonstration of how Edwards argues for the compatibility of Protestant immediacy (human choices are determined by God's will) with Catholic secondary causes (choices are determined by human dispositions), see Stephen A. Wilson, *Virtue Reformed: Rereading Jonathan Edwards's Ethics* (Leiden: Brill, 2005), 224, 210.

12. WJE 1:139–40.

13. WJE 1:141–43.

untarist, since, like Augustine, he believed the deepest sources of the person lay in the affections. Besides, in his Great Awakening treatise *Some Thoughts Concerning the Revival* (1743) Edwards wrote, "All acts of the affections of the soul are in some sense acts of the will." Yet Edwards, often dissatisfied with existing boundaries, paid tribute to the intellectualists by stipulating that the will always follows the last dictate of the understanding, which "is as the greatest apparent good is."[14]

By this thesis about willing, Edwards was able to make a larger proposal about ethics. The essence of virtue and vice, he reasoned, lies not in the causes of action but the nature of willing. In Paul Ramsey's words, "If a person is able to do what he wills or chooses, he is free, no matter how he came to make this choice." Therefore there can be praise and blame attached to an action, no matter the influence or motive, as long as the actor made a voluntary choice. In the case of "wicked" action, "it is wickedness, in its very being, nature and essence, and not merely the occasion of it, or the determining influence, that it was first owing to." So far as the will is in it, there is blame. On the other hand, if people do things "against their wills" or "without their wills" or in a way "with which their wills have no concern or connection," there is neither praise nor blame attached to their actions.[15]

The corollary to the ethical principle is Edwards's free-will axiom: there is no true freedom of the will when the will is indifferent or self-determined without influence or motive. For, according to Guelzo, "the will is not free to choose *what* to will; freedom consists only in willing *as* a man is 'pleased.'" Pleasure implies motive and influence, hence indifferent choice is an oxymoron. Ramsey again: "In other words, a man is free to do what he wills, but not to do what he does not will."[16]

Edwards made at least four kinds of arguments for his conception of the will: those appealing to logic, common sense, consequences, and sociology. His most extensive and enduring appeal pointed to the inherent contradictions of a will choosing its own acts. In this case, he said, the will determines the will. This notion of a self-determining will supposes a train of acts, with one preceding the first—since it presupposes that the will always chooses its own acts. So there must be a free act before the first free act. But then what chose *that* act? "And so the question returns *in infinitum*...there must be no

---

14. Norman Fiering, "Will and Intellect in the New England Mind," *William and Mary Quarterly* 29 (1972): 516–58; Guelzo, *Edwards on the Will*, 4–5, 14; WJE 4:297; WJE 1:217.

15. WJE 1:15, 72, 350.

16. Guelzo, *Edwards on the Will*, 53; WJE 1:13.

beginning, but free acts of will must have been chosen by foregoing free acts of will, in the soul of every man, without beginning; and so before he had a being, from all eternity."[17]

If Arminians deny a preceding choice for any act of the will, then it is not determined by the will and so is not free, according to their understanding. "And if that first act of the will... be not free, none of the following acts, which are determined by it, can be free."[18]

If we concede to Arminians that the faculty of will or soul determines itself, it is the same thing as choosing its own act. And why does it decide on one thing and not another? If it is because of the thing chosen, then Arminians contradict themselves when they say it is not determined by anything prior to or outside the will, and that no motive influences a self-determining will. It is a cause, and it came prior to the act, both of which things they deny.[19]

Edwards also charged that the logic of the will makes a mess of Arminian theology. Arminians must concede that God "can't avoid being holy and good" and therefore is "under necessity" in a moral sense. But if necessity is inconsistent with virtue or vice, then God cannot be virtuous. By these principles, "Jesus Christ was very far from being praiseworthy," and "we shall find that virtue and vice are wholly excluded out of the world."[20] For all moral action comes from motives and inclinations within the soul.

If liberty of indifference is bad logic, it also violates "the first dictate of the common and natural sense which God hath implanted in the minds of all mankind"—the law of cause and effect. There is no event without a cause, and the cause of a moral choice is something antecedent to that choice, either its natural or moral cause. To say choices have no causes makes no sense: it "is the very same thing as to say, the mind has a preference, at the same time that it has no preference."[21]

Then Edwards probed the consequences of holding to an indifferent will. The first is that no proof of God's existence or anything else can be made, for every such proof depends on the principle of cause and effect, which Arminians deny. Second, no one can be blamed for evil since blame cannot be cast,

---

17. WJE 1:194. Ramsey suggests Edwards got this *in infinitum* argument from John Locke; WJE 1:64.

18. WJE 1:172–73.

19. WJE 1:175–76.

20. WJE 1:277, 383, 326.

21. WJE 1:180–81, 196.

according to Arminians, when there is moral necessity. So what about Judas, who was predicted to betray Jesus and thus did so necessarily? By Arminian logic, "Judas was blameless." What is more, this principle "excuses all evil inclinations," which "will directly lead men to justify the vilest acts and practices, from the strength of their wicked inclinations." The stronger the inclination, the less the blame. Finally, this rule will prevent the use of means to stir up virtue and destroy vice. For if true virtue does not issue from prior motives and habits, what is the use of trying to build habits?[22]

Perhaps Edwards's most political argument was his appeal to class. He suggested that it was only "an aloof and aristocratic elite" that held such self-contradictory views. "The common people" know that liberty is a matter of doing what pleases one. "Common sense" and "plain vulgar" thinking by people "in all ages" know that virtue and vice are "in fixed bias and inclination, and greater virtue and vice in stronger and more established inclination."[23] In other words, the Arminian view of the will contradicted the common sense of ordinary people of all ages.

We will see in later chapters that the prevailing "moral sense" theory that Edwards battled in *True Virtue* and its later development in Scottish Common Sense Philosophy prevented his conception of the will from persuading many thinkers in the 150 years after his death (chs. 33, 38). For example, the Old Calvinist James Dana protested in 1770 that a man can simply look into his own breast and know that he has inward freedom of the sort Edwards denied. Henry Philip Tappan, who wrote the longest attack on Edwards's view of the will, insisted that only a self-determining will stands the test of an "appeal to consciousness."[24] Even in the twenty-first century, some philosophers still dismiss Edwards's theory on the ground that it does not agree with the prevailing view of self-determination.[25]

Original Sin

When Edwards took up the question of original sin three years after *Freedom of the Will*, he noted that his new antagonist, John Taylor, author of *The Scrip-*

---

22. WJE 1:181, 295–96, 421.

23. Guelzo, *Edwards on the Will*, 73; WJE 1:358, 429.

24. Henry Philip Tappan, *A Review of Edwards's "Inquiry into the Freedom of the Will"* (New York: John S. Taylor, 1839), 224.

25. Dana, *An Examination of the late Rev'd President Edwards's 'Enquiry on Freedom of the Will'* (Boston: S. Kneeland, 1770), v; Tappan, *A Review of Edwards's "Inquiry into the Freedom of the Will,"* 224; McCann, "Edwards on Free Will," 27, 42.

ture-Doctrine of Original Sin (1740), also believed that "the will's self-determination" was "necessary to the being of moral good and evil." Edwards referred the reader to his treatise on the will, then tackled this next great challenge to orthodoxy, the idea that "good preponderates" in the world because the human heart is not "naturally of a corrupt and evil disposition."[26]

Edwards entered the lists of this new debate with his own *Original Sin* (1758). It started with three key assumptions. First, "the sum of our duty to God, required in his law, is *love to God*," and "true love to God primarily consists in a supreme regard to him for what he is in himself." If we love him merely "because he has promoted our interest" and "not primarily for the excellency of his nature," then "in truth we love him not at all." Or if we have "inordinate love to other things besides God," we have "evil affections" that violate his first commandment. Even if we are "religious" by praying and reading the Bible, or "moral" by being "liberal to the poor," but have not that first love for God, we have only the "shell" of duty and "the inside is hollow." We would be like an adulterous wife who has only a "seeming respectfulness" to her husband while she really loves another man.[27] Second, because this obligation to love God is infinite—owing to his infinite worthiness—our failure to give him this love is a sin of "infinite heinousness." This "infinite demerit in all sin against God" outweighs "all the merit which can be supposed to be in our virtue."[28] Third, Edwards presumed that "a steady effect argues a steady cause." If sin was steadily present in all persons throughout history, it must mean there is a clear cause: "the *innate sinful depravity of the heart*." Edwards said that by the "vulgar" definition (that held by ordinary folks) "original sin" means not only inherent depravity but also our inheritance of it from Adam. He told his readers early on that he would explain and defend each of these tenets in *Original Sin*, which was completed before his death but not published until six months later (September 1758).[29]

---

26. Edwards had been making notes in his notebooks on original sin for thirty years, but he waited till the end of his career to go to press on this subject. WJE 3:375, 108, 107. John Taylor also provoked John Wesley to defend the orthodox doctrine of original sin. After publishing his *Doctrine of Original Sin* in 1757, Wesley wrote to Augustus Toplady in 1758, "I verily believe no single person since Mahomet has given such a wound to Christianity as Dr. Taylor." John Wesley, *The Letters of the Rev. John Wesley, A.M.*, 8 volumes, ed. John Telford (London, 1931), 4:48.

27. WJE 3:140, 144, 146; WJE 19:524, 527, 531.

28. WJE 3:130.

29. WJE 3:121; orig. emph. Other posthumous publications were *Nature of True Virtue* and *The End for Which God Created the World* (published together in 1765), *History of the Work of Redemption* (1774), and *Charity and Its Fruits* (written 1738; published 1852).

Depravity as Unfailing Necessity

The treatise begins by setting out the nature and extent of depravity. It is "a propensity that is *invincible* or a tendency which really amounts to a fixed constant unfailing *necessity*." It is "inherent" in nature and "true of persons of all constitutions, capacities, conditions, manners, opinions and educations; in all countries, climates, nations and ages." Some point to places and persons where goodness seems to be predominant, but they do not realize it is because of grace, not nature. In those cases God has intervened to "have restraints laid upon" sin or simply poured out his "merciful influences." Left alone to "the innate disposition of man's heart," human beings would see only "the pernicious consequences" of that evil disposition.[30]

Sin is progressive, wrote Edwards. Our evil disposition, if unchecked by grace, will increase in strength just as a "falling body" picks up speed as it plummets toward the earth. This is why our sins are "great and manifold," and the whole of our nature is evil. It is silly to determine human nature by asking whether man "is inclined to perform as many *good deeds as bad ones*." That's like saying a ship crossing the Atlantic Ocean was good because, though it sank, it sailed above water for more hours than it took to sink. Or that a road is good to take to a certain place because most of its course is safe—even though some parts are dangerous and certainly fatal to those who take it.[31]

The worst kind of human sinfulness is its religious tendency toward idolatry and disregard for eternal things. This is despite the fact that human beings have innate knowledge of God from nature and conscience (Edwards cited Rom. 1:18–28), which, Edwards noted, John Locke thought obvious and John Taylor also believed, adducing even "heathen" writings for support. Human beings take great care for their temporal interests, he added, but are "cold, lifeless and dilatory" when it comes to their eternal interests. They don't see eternal things as "real," which proves their "dreadful stupidity of mind."[32]

Then Edwards turned to history for proof of depravity. There has been "an exceeding smallness of the number of true saints," even in the best of times and the best of nations. "Vastly the greater part of mankind have in all ages been of a wicked character." Never has even one nation been generally pious,

---

30. WJE 3:123–24, 136, 109; orig. emph. Edwards's retort to the objection that the predominance of goodness in some places and people might point to innate goodness is the accumulation of his other arguments—the pervasive and overwhelming evidence to the contrary.

31. WJE 3:136–37, 115, 128–29; orig emph.

32. WJE 3:149, 154, 157.

even when Christians were in control. In fact, when Christians gained power and secular advantages, "true piety declined, and corruption and wickedness prevailed among them." One detects a hint of sarcasm when Edwards observes how strange that this should be the state of humankind, gifted with reason for the purpose of religion "which summarily consists in love," if they truly enter the world "innocent and harmless...free from all evil propensities."[33]

Israel's history shows the same depravity. She was perfectly situated geographically to be a light to the nations—"in the midst of the earth, between Asia, Europe and Africa, and in the midst of those nations which were most considerable and famous for power, knowledge and the arts." Throughout Israel's history, God performed miracles in full view of these nations. Yet the nations did not learn, and even Abraham's posterity fell into pagan ways. Most rejected the Lord of glory when he visited the planet. His later disciples showed "a disposition to corruption, and to abuse the gospel unto the service of pride and licentiousness." The American Indians were "mere babes and fools...as to proficiency in wickedness" compared to the Christian world. It is no surprise that church history abounds with "the judgments of God."[34]

Edwards next stepped where many theologians fear to tread, exploring the mystery of the deaths of so many babies throughout history. If babies are innocent and death is meant to mortify us by weaning us from the world, as Taylor believed, "is it not strange, that it should fall so heavy on infants, who are not capable of making any such improvement of it?" Edwards believed Scripture teaches that death is "a testimony of God's displeasure for sin." So "if infants are perfectly innocent," why did God send the Flood to the "the old world, in which there were, without doubt, many hundred thousand infants, and in general, one in every family, whose perfect innocence pleaded for its preservation?" Why were the infants not spared "when God executed vengeance on the ancient inhabitants of Canaan"? The answer must be, said Edwards, that "infants are not looked upon by God as sinless, but that they are by nature children of wrath." This explains why children "universally [commit] sin as soon as they are capable of it." If infants are not depraved, then why do none of them grow up to be perfectly righteous? Why do even the "greatest saints" still have "remaining depravity of heart"?[35]

---

33. WJE 3:161, 163–64, 166–68.

34. WJE 3:171, 171–82, 183, 187. Rachel Wheeler argues that this and other uses of original sin in Edwards's talking to and about Indians show the egalitarian implications of this treatise. Wheeler, "Friends to Your Souls": Jonathan Edwards's Indian Pastorate and the Doctrine of Original Sin," *Church History* 72 (2003): 736–65.

35. WJE 3:211, 215, 217, 215, 200, 137.

Some objected, according to Edwards, that free will is responsible for all the evil in the world. Nurture and bad choices explain evil—not innate nature. Then why is it, he asked, that men sin when they first begin to act and then stay in this course continually? Not only "men of high and low condition," but also "learned and ignorant" and in every age and nation. Is it truly objective to insist there is nothing "in their temper or inclination to bias 'em"?[36]

Others attributed the prevalence of evil to bad example. Edwards replied there are bad examples at all times and all places. Why is that? And why is there so little effect from good examples? God planted many noble vines in history: Adam and Eve after their fall, Noah, Abraham, the first generation of Israel to enter Canaan with Joshua, and New England's first generation. Yet all these good vines yielded bad fruit.[37]

Edwards then asked why human beings are so repeatedly said by scripture to be evil if they are really innocent. The biblical authors speak of "a wicked heart *from their youth*" and men who "drinketh iniquity like water" (Ps. 58:3 and Job 15:16). The flesh, Edwards wrote, represents in the Bible the whole man before regeneration, yet also says we are "to be enemies to it." If we are all wicked in our first state before redemption, then we are "wicked by nature."[38]

Perhaps his most theological argument drew on the cross. If we are good by nature, we have "*sufficient provision* for our being free from sin and misery, by our own power." In that case, "*Christ is dead in vain*, and the grace of God is *useless*." For if we have inherent goodness, we can save ourselves and do not need to be saved by anyone else. This is why Edwards said in his preface that "the great salvation by Christ stands in direct relation to this ruin [of original sin] as the remedy to the disease."[39]

The Imputation of Adam's Sin

Edwards's second goal in this treatise, after establishing universal depravity, was to demonstrate the fact and justice of the imputation of Adam's sin. This is the idea, taken from Romans 5:19 ("by one man's disobedience, many were made sinners") and elsewhere in the New Testament, that "all mankind are

---

36. WJE 3:195.

37. WJE 3:196–99.

38. WJE 3:267, 264, 283; orig. emph.

39. WJE 3:357, 103; orig. emph.

Free Will and Original Sin

made sinners by a judicial act of God the judge" and "subjected to a judicial sentence of condemnation, on occasion of Adam's sin."[40]

In some places in this treatise and his sermons, Edwards appears to follow "the generally accepted [Reformed] tradition" that "the first man represented all his descendants" by covenant, or federally, much as a president represents his people in a treaty.[41] The president and his people are different persons, but the consequences of the treaty will apply to them as well as him.[42] But in the last part of *Original Sin*, Edwards departed from this tradition. In an attempt to refute the accusation—primarily from deists in the eighteenth century—that the imputation of Adam's sin was unjust and unreasonable, Edwards used an original metaphysics to assert that Adam's sin is imputed to us because we were one with Adam, "fully consenting and concurring" with his sin.[43]

The new metaphysics was based on the idea that "God does, by his immediate power, *uphold* every created substance in being" moment by moment. Edwards derived this not only from the Bible but from his philosophical contention that "what existed the last moment" cannot cause anything because it is "wholly passive." Its existence at the present moment is in a different place and time from what it was at the previous moment, and so could not have been caused by what existed at that previous moment. "Therefore the existence of created substances, in each successive moment, must be the effect of the *immediate* agency, will and power of God." Edwards called this "continued creation" whereby God creates "things out of nothing at *each moment* of their existence." So if there is any identity between myself as a baby and as a grown man—despite the fact that in the meantime every cell has been replaced and my consciousness is wholly different—it "depends on the *arbitrary* constitution of the Creator; who by his wise sovereign establishment so unites these successive new effects, that he *treats them as one*." It all depends on the divine will, and that in turn "depends on nothing but the divine wisdom." Thus all oneness "by virtue whereof pollution and guilt from past wickedness are derived, depends entirely on a divine establishment."[44]

Lest deists use this to charge God's arbitrariness with injustice, Edwards hastened to add that God saw that Adam's descendants fully "consented" to

---

40. WJE 3:248.

41. John Gerstner, *The Rational Biblical Theology of Jonathan Edwards* 3 vols. (Powhatan, VA: Berea Publications, 1992), 2:323.

42. Edwards speaks of the imputation of Adam's sin, Adam as our representative ("we were all in his loins"), and our derived guilt from Adam's sin; WJE 3:348; WJE 10:512; WJE 3:347.

43. WJE 3:407.

44. WJE 3:400–401, 403, 405.

and "concurred" with Adam's sin, and on that basis imputed Adam's sin to them: "Therefore the sin of the apostasy is not theirs, merely because God *imputes* it to them; but it is *truly* and *properly* theirs, and on that ground, God imputes it to them." God deals with Adam's posterity "as having *all sinned in him*." He treats our relation to Adam as so many branches coming from a common root: "All are looked upon as sinning in and with their common root." So wicked men go to hell "not according to the behavior of their particular ancestors; but every one is dealt with according to the sin of his own wicked heart, or sinful nature and practice." Therefore the imputation of Adam's sin is not unjust because we consented to it and in some way participated in it.[45]

Edwards seems hereby to get God off the hook for unjustly imputing Adam's sin to us.[46] But on the matter of Adam's sin itself, things are not as straightforward. The difficulty comes in asking how that sin arose. Edwards said that Adam was "perfectly free" of "sinful inclinations." Like us, he had a rational will and a collection of inclinations called appetites that are opposed to the rational will. Unlike us, he had "superior divine principles" or "divine nature" that were to "maintain an absolute dominion" for his rational will over those appetites. But Adam fell because the serpent "deceived" his judgment. His rational will was thereby "perverted."[47]

How, we might ask, could a perfect man with no sinful inclinations and every motivation to obey be deceived? Edwards seems to have recognized the difficulty, and suggested that, while Adam was given "sufficient grace" to keep his rational will in control, he was not given "efficacious grace" to "certainly uphold him in all temptations." In a sermon, Edwards called this "confirming grace"—that is, the kind of grace that confirmed the elect angels so that they would never sin after their first obedience.[48] In *Original Sin*, he emphasized

---

45. WJE 3:408, 383, 387, 409; orig emph. Edwards uses the language of "participation" and "partaking" in WJE 3:391, 407.

46. Yet some scholars have faulted Edwards for trying too hard to explain imputation, using an implausible metaphysics. See, e.g., Gerstner, 2:323–35.

47. WJE 13:484–85; WJE 1:381–82; WJE 13:485. Edwards's understanding is similar to that of the Catholic tradition. Thomas, for example, wrote of an "original justice" or "superior side" in which Adam's reason was subject to God and his "inferior powers" served reason without obstacle. Thomas Aquinas, *Summa Contra Gentiles*, 4 vols., ed. Charles J. O'Neil (Notre Dame, IN: University of Notre Dame Press, 1957), 4:52.3–6.

48. WJE 13:485; WJE 14:168. Edwards followed Ames, Turretin and van Mastricht here, attributing the fall of Adam to the absence of "confirming grace." Ames, *The Marrow of Theology* (Grand Rapids, MA: Baker Books, 1997), 114; Turretin, *Institutes of Elenctic Theology* 1:610; Mastricht, *Theoretico-practica theologia* IV, cap. 1; Edwards cites Mastrict in 13:382. Calvin preferred to let the reason for Adam's sin remain "hidden"; Calvin, *Institutes* 1.15.8.

that Adam did not sin because of "any settled disposition, or fixed cause at all," but rather from a "transient cause."[49]

What was the transient cause? Edwards said little more than that God withheld "further assistance and divine influence," the kind that he gave to elect angels. Yet he also said that because of this withholding, "sin would infallibly follow" because of "the imperfection which properly belongs to a creature."[50]

John Gerstner accuses Edwards of "fatalism" at this point, for creating a creature in such a way that it would sin inevitably. He points out a revealing sermon on Job 11:12 from 1743, whose doctrine is, "Man is naturally a proud creature."[51] Edwards told his listeners that pride arises from the principle of self-love, which was in Adam before the fall but regulated by the principle of love to God. Since the fall, God has withdrawn his Spirit from the nature of man, so that the Spirit comes only with the new birth. Gerstner's point is that in the absence of confirming grace there was something in human nature that would lead inevitably to sin.

Edwards's Critics

Few areas of Edwards's theology have provoked more criticism than his account of the Fall. In 1773, James Dana charged that, while Edwards claimed God was related to sin only by his "privative" action of withholding confirming grace, Edwards's God actually introduced sin by "positive energy and action" because "the creature cannot be answerable for more than he hath received." God created human beings with capacities that would lead inevitably to sin. In that sense, he is the author of sin. A century later, Princeton Seminary's Charles Hodge thought Edwards got into trouble because he presumed too easily that by his metaphysics he could explain God's relation to our choices. In his editor's introduction to the Yale edition of *Original Sin*, Clyde Holbrook said this was "a difficulty from which [Edwards] never successfully freed himself." Samuel Storms observes that despite wanting to clear God of being the author of sin, he failed to do so. "If by creation [Adam] is in such a condition that, antecedent to God's withdrawal of divine influence, he necessarily sins, then God is most certainly the efficient and morally responsible cause of the

---

49. WJE 3:193.
50. WJE 1:413.
51. Sermon on Job 11:12, WJE Online 46.

transgression."⁵² Gerstner complains that "sufficient grace" in this situation is a contradiction in terms, and Edwards's attempt to resolve the difficulty represents "the nadir of Edwardsian theology." For if a good man did evil, how was he good?⁵³ And if Adam was not good, then how are we to interpret the biblical claim that the creation of humanity was "very good" (Gen. 1:31)? Gerstner concludes that Edwards's position on this question represents "a total abandonment of the Christian religion, as understood by almost the entire catholic tradition."⁵⁴

Oliver Crisp has charged that while the doctrine of the Fall is "notoriously troublesome," Edwards's occasionalism (his metaphysical understanding that all things are directly created by God each moment; ch. 7) makes God not only the ultimate but also the proximate cause of sin. Therefore, he avers, it is unjust for God to condemn people for sins that he has ordained by direct decree. This occasionalism means that "any distinction between permission and positive agency is undermined."⁵⁵

This objection—that there is little or no difference between God's permission and God's direct agency—was first made by Dana in 1770 and has been made by others over the years. Edwards, however, thought there was more than a little difference. He went out of his way in his writings on sin to underline both teleological and moral differences between these two things: "God does not decree actions that are sinful *as sinful*, but decrees [them] as good."⁵⁶ In other words, there was a difference in purpose between *permitting* sin and *decreeing* goodness. The first God decreed only because of its use for a further good, while the second he decreed for itself. Morally, the two kinds of decrees

---

52. James Dana, The *"Examination of the Late Rev'd President Edwards's Enquiry on Freedom of the Will" Continued* (New Haven: Thomas & Samuel Green, 1773), 59–60, 65; Charles Hodge, *Systematic Theology*, 3 vols. (Grand Rapids: Eerdmans, 1986) 2:219; WJE 3:51; Storms, "The Will: Fettered Yet Free (Freedom of the Will)," in Piper and Taylor, eds., *A God-Entranced Vision of All Things* (Wheaton: Crossway, 2004), 217. See also Samuel Storms, *Tragedy in Eden: Original Sin in the Theology of Jonathan Edwards* (Lanham, MD: University Press of America, 1985).

53. Gerstner, *Rational Biblical Theology* 2:318; WJE 3:307, 317. Peter Beck thinks Adam's deception, inspired by his self-love, solves the problem of *how* Adam could have sinned. Yet it still begs the question of how and why a rational will, without sinful proclivities, would permit self-love to overcome its knowledge that it must submit itself to love for God. Beck, "The Fall of Man and the Failure of Jonathan Edwards," *Evangelical Quarterly* 79 (2007) 209–25.

54. Gerstner, *Rational Biblical Theology*, 2:322.

55. WJE 3:25, 50, 68, 64. Oliver Crisp, *Jonathan Edwards and the Metaphysics of Sin* (Aldershot, UK: Ashgate, 2005), 25, 64, 68.

56. WJE 13:250.

were also distinct. The first was a violation of his moral will, while the second was a fulfillment of that will. These distinctions may seem obvious, but for Edwards and other philosophical theologians they are critical to a nuanced understanding of God's ways and purposes.

Critics from Edwards's era to our own have charged that because of his occasionalism Edwards could not properly assign any praise or blame to human actions. For if God decreed all our choices, we could not be blamed or praised for them—despite Edwards's insistence that all persons are responsible for their voluntary choices. Crisp uses the example of someone being force-fed alcohol or drugs, and suggests that action that "has gone before"—in this case being force-fed—makes Edward's focus on the *nature* of willing rather than its cause (which in the analogue is God's creating our willing at each moment) to be unconvincing.[57] But it seems Edwards might handle this objection by use of his natural versus moral inability distinction, arguing in this case that something in external nature—alcohol or drugs—has prevented genuine volition from taking place. Where nothing prevents a person from choosing freely (i.e., following his or her own inclination), then that person is responsible for whatever choice is made even if that person's choice takes place in accordance with God's eternal decree.

Thomas Schafer may have been right more than a half-century ago when he concluded that "Edwards's doctrine of the will, required alike by his theology and his metaphysics, breaks on the impossible task of accounting for both original righteousness and the fall."[58] At the heart of Edwards's view of the will is the conviction that all action springs from the affections, but his depiction of Adam's action in Eden is inconsistent with this.

Over the centuries, many have advanced philosophical reasons for rejecting Edwards's occasionalism.[59] Edwards's retort to contemporaries who objected that he had made God the author of evil was that his critics would have to wrestle with the Bible's assertions that God hardened hearts and sent calamity upon the wicked (ch. 21).[60] Perhaps Edwards should be faulted less for making God the author of evil than for speculating on deep and perhaps

---

57. Crisp, *Jonathan Edwards and the Metaphysics of Sin*, 66–67.

58. Thomas Schafer, "The Concept of Being in the Thought of Jonathan Edwards," PhD diss. Duke University, 1951, 228.

59. For example, Charles Hodge; Oliver Crisp, *Jonathan Edwards and the Metaphysics of Sin*; and Paul Helm, "The Great Christian Doctrine (*Original Sin*)," in John Piper and Justin Taylor, eds., *A God-Entranced Vision of All Things*, 175–200.

60. See ch. 21.

unanswerable questions. In a second riposte at the end of *Freedom of the Will*, Edwards reminded his detractors that moral "events will be ordered by something," either by chance or by wisdom. Then he asked if it is not better that evil be ordered and determined by an infinitely wise Being "than to leave these things to fall out by chance."[61] In other words, since evil undoubtedly exists, it is better to view it as lying under the superintendence of a wise and benevolent God.

Edwards has also been charged with straying far from Calvin on the nature of Adam's sin. Yet Calvin conceded that "God's secret predestination" was responsible for Adam's fall, and the first man sinned because God did not give Adam "constancy to persevere."[62] If they agreed on God's determination of Adam's sin, they also both warned against disparaging its wisdom. Edwards commented at the end of *Original Sin* that it would be "extreme arrogance" to "take upon us to act as judges of the beauty and wisdom of the laws and established constitutions of the supreme Lord and Creator of the universe."[63] Calvin warned his readers that "to quarrel with God on this precise point"—why God made Adam in such a way as to be bound to sin—"is more than iniquitous."[64] So whether or not Edwards was consistent with his own anthropology on the question of Adam's fall, he agreed with Calvin that the fall was within God's plan, and that our part is to trust in the wisdom of that plan.

If Edwards was not far from Calvin in principle on Adam's fall, he was nevertheless less hesitant than the great Reformer to offer metaphysical solutions to age-old questions about the will and original sin. This chapter is another example of the manifold ways in which Edwards put his own creative spin on a host of problems he had inherited from his tradition.

---

61. WJE 1:405.

62. Gerstner, *Rational Biblical Theology*, 2:323–34; Calvin, *Institutes*, 1.15.8.

63. WJE 3:406.

64. Calvin, *Institutes*, 1.15.8.

23

Salvation, Grace, and Faith: An Overview

JONATHAN EDWARDS BELIEVED that salvation was a grand work begun in the counsels of eternity and never finally completed, since salvation includes unending growth in union with the Triune God. Salvation therefore is not simply equal to conversion, as in certain evangelical or revivalist traditions from the 1700s and later. Its first visible manifestation in an individual is at conversion, which signals justification and begins sanctification. Both of the latter produce divinization—a participation in the life, holiness, happiness, and very being of God, and that is also unending. This concatenation of processes is all one work of salvation.[1] We will look in this chapter at basic principles (grace and faith) that underlie and animate every phase of this work, and then in chapters 24–26 explore how salvation is developed in Edwards's doctrines of conversion, justification, sanctification, and divinization.

Common Grace and Special Grace

Edwards held that salvation, while it completes and fulfills the God-given human nature, also transcends it in a basic way. It is a phenomenon wholly unlike anything in the natural world and common experience of human beings. There may be outward similarities between things of this world and God's redemptive acts, but the similarities exist only because God has designed them typologically to point to things that are inherently different. So a person without "special or saving grace" is "perfectly destitute of any sense, perception, or discerning of those things of the Spirit." Such a person may be religious and have extraordinary knowledge of religious things, but unless he has saving grace "he knows nothing of [God's salvation] any more than a blind man of colors."[2]

---

1. See Richard Martin Weber, "'One-Step' Salvation: The Knowledge of God and Faith in the Theology of Jonathan Edwards," PhD diss., Marquette University, 2002.

2. WJE 21:153, 156.

Edwards began from the assumption that everything we experience and enjoy is a gift from God. The same is true of all moral virtues. These, too, come from God. Edwards used the term "common grace" for "that kind of action or influence of the Spirit of God, to which are owing those religious or moral attainments that are common to both saints and sinners." For example, both saints and sinners are convicted of sin from time to time. Both can be moved by a stirring sermon to moral action. But in the case of unregenerate sinners experiencing these things, their conviction of sin and moral urgency are "only the assistance of natural principles."[3] Their moral nature, common to all human beings, is excited by knowledge of their wrong (thus the conviction of sin) and a sense of obligation (thus the impetus to moral action). The Spirit uses what these "natural men" have from birth to produce these results. No supernatural capacity is needed.

"But *special* grace causes the faculties to do that that they do not by nature," wrote Edwards. It puts into the soul new things "that are above nature," such as love for God. They are not fleeting thoughts of love but a permanent habit that "lays such a foundation for a continued course of exercises."[4] Therefore "saving grace" differs "not only in degree, but in nature and kind, from *common grace*, or anything that is ever found in natural men." When a "natural man" receives saving grace, God does not use what the man already had, but imparts a new heart and new spirit. It is a resurrection from the dead, a new creation. "Saving grace in the heart is said to be the new man or new creature, and corruption the old man." Things done by the old man, even good works, are merely "bastards and not children." For "man's inwards are full of dung and filthiness, which is to denote what the inner man, which is often represented by various parts of his inwards—sometimes the heart, sometimes the bowels, sometimes the belly, sometimes the veins—is full of: spiritual corruption and abomination."[5]

Common grace may impart influences and illuminations of the Spirit, but it does not communicate the Spirit "in his own proper nature." It is like Ezekiel's dry bones before flesh is put on them. The one thing missing from common grace that distinguishes it from special or saving grace is love: "Those that go farthest in religion that are not true saints and in a state of salvation, have no charity, as is plainly implied in the beginning of the thirteenth chapter of the first epistle to the Corinthians." They may put on "the

---

3. WJE 21:153, 155.

4. WJE 21:155; emph. added.

5. WJE 18:230, 231–32, 498; WJE 11:94, orig. emph.

greatest, and fairest, and most glittering show in religion" but without real love it is all "nothing." They imagine they have love, but they love others "some way or other as appendages and appurtenances to [them]selve[s]." Those with special or saving grace, on the other hand, love "others as of God, or in God, or some way related to him."[6]

Edwards gave two vivid examples of religion that is inspired by common rather than special grace. In each, true love is lacking. The first illustration was the devil, who in the story of the Gerasene demoniac, cries out in a religious mode but "from fear of torment":

> "When he saw Jesus, he cried out, and fell down before him, and with a loud voice said, What have I to do with thee, Jesus, thou Son of God most high? I beseech thee, torment me not." Here is external worship. The devil is religious; he prays in a humble posture; he falls down before Christ, he lies prostrate; he prays earnestly, he cries with a loud voice; he uses humble expressions—"I beseech thee, torment me not"—he uses respectful, honorable, adoring expressions—"Jesus, thou Son of God most high." *Nothing was wanting but love.*[7]

Edwards then told of a wife who treated her husband respectfully but "not at all from any love to him." He would not "delight in her outward respect" any more than "if a wooden image were contrived to make respectful motions in his presence." A wife without love is like religion without love—a caricature of the real.[8]

The Nature of Saving Grace

If saving grace necessarily involves love, what is the nature of that love? In his *Treatise on Grace*, Edwards called it "divine love" and declared that it is the root of "all graces"—the "soul and essence and summary comprehension of all grace." It is the root from which springs love to one's neighbor, but its primary object is God. The "first thing" in this divine love is "a relish of the excellency of the divine nature." The soul is caused by it to "taste the sweetness of the divine relation." It will "incline to God in every way," which means the soul will be glad when God is happy, will want God to be glorified, and will want

---

6. WJE 20:486; WJE 21:157, 169; WJE 18:533.

7. WJE 21:171, emph. added.

8. WJE 21:172.

his will done in all things. This taste of God's sweetness, or glimpse of his beauty, is so foundational that "this is all the Spirit of God needs to do." Everything else that God wants from the soul will follow from this one heavenly vision: "Other things will follow of themselves without any further act of the divine power."[9]

Edwards distinguished between the love of complacence, or delight in God's beauty, and the love of benevolence, which acts for the good of the other. Because divine love is first a relish of the divine beauty, "a love of complacence is...the foundation of the other." This delight in God's excellence "in the order of nature" is before benevolence "because it is the foundation and reason" for benevolence. The soul wants to serve God *because* it is enticed by God's beauty.[10]

Divine love is not to be confused with gratitude to God. Truly divine love is not based on "any benefit we have received." Therefore "love or affection to God, that has no other ground than only some benefit received or hoped for from God without any sense of a delight in the absolute excellency of the divine nature, has nothing divine in it." So natural men who may "be affected with gratitude by some remarkable kindness of God to them" are probably driven not by divine love but by self-love.

This is not to say that self-love is bad, or that the regenerate do not have it (see ch. 33). Their self-love in fact may help increase their divine love because the latter is sweet and they will want more sweetness. But their "taste to relish sweetness in the perfection of God" is prior to the influence of self-love on it, and therefore "quite distinct from it, and independent of it."[11]

Grace and the Spirit

Edwards believed that grace is not just *from* the Spirit but *of* the Spirit (ch. 17). Natural men, he wrote, can have many experiences that come from the Spirit, such as conviction of sin and "common illuminations and common affections." In such experiences, their natural faculties are assisted by the Spirit. But the saints actually possess the Spirit, and the Spirit's activity within the saints is

---

9. WJE 21:166, 169, 173–74.

10. WJE 21:174–75. Sang Lee notes that while in *True Virtue* Edwards gives priority to the love of benevolence, there is no conflict because the two are inseparable and the two treatises have different foci. Norman Fiering agrees. Lee, in WJE 21:84. See Fiering, *Jonathan Edwards's Moral Thought and Its British Context* (Chapel Hill: University of North Carolina Press, 1981), 127n.

11. WJE 21:175.

what Edwards meant by special or saving grace. Hence "the very principle of spiritual life in their souls is no other than the Spirit of Christ himself." Since the Spirit is love, "true saving grace is no other than that very love of God; that is, God in one of the persons of the Trinity, uniting himself to the soul of a creature as a vital principle, dwelling there and exerting himself by the faculties of the soul of man, in his own proper nature, after the manner of a principle of nature." The continued presence of the Spirit as grace becomes a "disposition to holy acts." This disposition is what is recognized by others as virtue because it is a settled "quality" of the saint.[12]

In the thirteenth century, theologians distinguished between uncreated grace (in sovereign acts of God) and created grace (in enduring dispositions). Thomas Aquinas rejected Peter Lombard's limitation of grace to acts of the Holy Spirit and spoke instead of "grace as having a fixed and stable nature." The Council of Trent developed Aquinas's view into a notion of "inherent grace," which seemed to Protestant theologians to undermine God's sovereignty. Edwards's position mediated between these two poles. He said grace is the presence of the Holy Spirit in action (Lombard) but also as a new disposition (Aquinas). In all grace there is "a *constant* concurrence of divine power" but that exercise of power is "in harmony and proportion" to his pre-established laws. The Spirit confers grace as a settled disposition, but he is never "domesticated" in a way that would reduce the saint's immediate dependence on God.[13]

Physical Infusion

At the turn of the seventeenth century, the *de auxiliis* (lit., "concerning the helps" afforded by grace) controversy raged within Roman Catholic circles and spilled into debates within the Reformed churches. The dispute was over the mode of God's work in conversion specifically and grace generally. Arminians said that regenerating grace is simply the illumination of the intellect for the purpose of persuading it to make the right decision. Petrus van Mastricht, the Dutch scholastic whom Edwards prized, said regenerating grace is far more—a physical infusion in the will. By "physical" he meant not material change but the kind that transforms one's inner nature, since *physis* is the

---

12. WJE 21:179, 192, 195, 194.

13. Sang Lee, Introduction, WJE 21:46–47; WJE 21:300 (orig.emph.); WJE 13:235; Anri Morimoto, *Jonathan Edwards and the Catholic Vision of Salvation* (University Park, PA: Penn State University Press, 1995), 44.

Greek word for "nature." Anri Morimoto says this is why Edwards preferred the term "infusion" to "illumination" when he wrote about grace. It communicated more precisely the fact that God "determine[s] the effect" and is the "efficient" author of true virtue and goodness. In other words, God does not merely give new ideas to the mind, but changes the person from the inside out, giving divine life directly to the soul.[14]

Edwards used a long train of biblical passages to argue for a "physical" account of grace: "Without me ye can do nothing" (John 15:5); "No man can come to me except the Father draw him" (John 6:44); "The Lord opened the heart of Lydia" (Acts 16:14); "I will give you one heart, and I will put a new spirit in you" (Ezek. 11:19), and many others. As was his custom, he also appealed to logic: if God's "succeeding assistance" is always tied to "man's endeavors," then "man's success" is in his own power, and this violates the teaching of scripture. How can God promise "that great revival of religion in the latter days" if he does not have the power or will to determine effects? What would we say about "some third person between God and" us, who "was left entirely to their free will to be the sole determining cause whether we should have the benefit" of virtue and piety? Let us say "this third person should happen to determine in our favor." Would it then be right to give God thanks and all the glory for the gift? "On the contrary," wrote Edwards. This third person, whose "sovereign will decides the matter," was "the truest author and bestower of the benefit." Edwards hoped his readers would realize that God is "all in the cause" of every act of true virtue and piety.[15]

Efficacious Not Irresistible

Edwards said this is what the Christian tradition means when it says God is the "sanctifier": what he does is "thoroughly effectual." When he determines to move a person, "the effect is infallibly consequent: 'Turn us, and we shall be turned'" [Lam. 5:21]. God not only gives statutes to his people but inclines their hearts to his statutes.[16]

But if God is infallibly efficacious when he moves a person's will, that person is not passive: "God does all and we do all." God is the "author and

---

14. Morimoto, *Jonathan Edwards*, 18–20; WJE 21:228, 236.

15. WJE 21:210, 242, 237–38.

16. WJE 21:240.

fountain" of our acts, but those acts are still ours. We are the only "proper actors." It is not that God does some and we do the rest, but the reality of human action must be viewed from different perspectives in order to capture the whole. "We are in different respects wholly passive and wholly active." On the one hand, "God circumcises the heart," but on the other hand, "we are commanded to circumcise [our hearts]." Therefore it is not a contradiction to say that the effect of God's determining our wills (doing his will) is "our act and our duty."[17]

Arminians argued that grace was "resistible." Edwards thought this idea was "ridiculous" and "enormous nonsense." For the effect of grace is on the will, to make it want a certain thing. To say that the will, which is moved to want that thing, can also resist that grace and want the opposite is to say that a someone wills to resist his own will.[18] For Edwards, this was not only faulty reasoning but bad psychology. Edwards disliked the Calvinist use of the word "irresistible" for grace since that gives the impression that human beings are like dumb blocks of wood that do not participate in their own decisions. Edwards stressed that we are free in our willing: we choose what we *want*. In grace God moves our will, but it is *our* will.

Virtue—The Result of Grace

Edwards noted that it is "everywhere spoken of" that the special effect of grace is moral virtue. Or, to put it another way, all virtue is a result of God's influence. Edwards of course agreed that all virtue is the fruit of God's influence, but argued that the Arminian understanding of "influence" undermined any sense that virtue is from grace. For in the Arminian view grace was simply the provision of "sufficient means," and "our improving" those means is "wholly from ourselves, our own will, and not from God." In this scheme, then, virtue is "wholly and entirely from ourselves."[19] How then could it be called grace?

But that was not enough. Edwards made three more arguments against Arminian notions of virtue. First, he said, they cannot make sense of the first act of virtue. It cannot come from nature at birth, because then it would be necessary and, by their own assumption not free. It cannot be "wholly from the influence of the Spirit of God," for according to them that would preclude

---

17. WJE 21:251.

18. WJE 13:208, 170–71; WJE 18:665.

19. WJE 21:267.

our participation and so that too would not be free. Yet if it is wholly from our endeavor, then it involves no divine assistance and even Arminians admit that there is no true virtue without God's help. If it is partly from God and partly from us, we are back to the original question of where that first (partial) virtue may have come from.[20] A second argument was that, since—by Arminian principles—virtue consists "wholly and entirely in improving assistance," men's virtue "*is altogether of themselves, and god has no hand at all in it.*" Thus by their own concession it cannot be virtue since true virtue must have something of God in it. Third, God must be unhappy, which contradicts common sense. With perhaps a touch of humor, Edwards wrote, "It is contrary to common sense that a being should continually meet with millions of millions of real proper disappointments and crosses to his proper desires, and not continually live on a distressed and unhappy life."[21]

Grace is Free

Edwards's principal objection to Arminian views of salvation was that they diminished or compromised God's freedom by implying that God's gift of grace depended on the decisions of the human recipients. The Arminians had, on Edwards's view, convinced most people that God was waiting for human beings to turn to him before he could act to save them. "'Tis a doctrine mightily in vogue, that God has *promised* his *saving grace* to man's *sincere endeavors* in praying for it and using proper means to obtain it." So it was not God's will or sovereignty that determined who would be saved--and by implication how history would play out--but the decisions of fickle men and women.[22]

Edwards insisted this was a fundamental misunderstanding of how God saves his creatures. He does not look for something in them that is "worthy" or for anything else. His decision to give them salvation was made "long before they had a being." The reason for his conferring salvation on the elect is because of his "absolute inclination to goodness in his own nature" and "for nothing at all in them." It was not because of "the loveliness of what we do." We had nothing good to offer God, but rather "much unloveliness or odiousness." Because Christ fulfilled "the condition of righteousness" in our place, there was no need for righteousness in us before God could save us.[23]

---

20. WJE 21:269–70.

21. WJE 21:264, 276; orig. emph.

22. WJE 21:305; orig. emph.

23. WJE 18:250–51, 227; WJE 13:395; WJE 18:213; WJE 20:450; WJE 13:540.

Yet the common Arminian belief was that God chooses people based on their "sincerity." Edwards argued at length against this notion. He said it is not biblical because sincerity in scripture means only acting "from love to God and true love to our duty"—things that were absent from the Arminian conception of sincerity. Multitudes, he wrote, "live in gross wickedness" but manifest some sincerity. Should we believe that God therefore will give saving grace "to every man that ever stirs hand or foot, or thinks one thought, in order to his salvation?" Furthermore, even the most sincere did not do half of what they should have done. Therefore every human being showed the absence more than the presence of sincerity toward God. Scripture indicates that unregenerate persons are "without the least degree" of sincere love in their "refraining from some sins and doing some external duties." Finally, the Arminian obsession with sincerity evaded many difficult questions: What degree of sincerity is necessary to be saved? How long must it last? How early should it have begun? If the answers to these questions were unclear, then we had no promise at all to count on. "If the master of a family should give forth such a pretended promise as this to his servants, 'I promise that if any of you will do something, though I tell you not what, that I will surely give him an inheritance among my children,' would this be truly any promise at all?"[24]

So there are no preconditions for grace, neither sincerity nor anything else. Grace is free. It comes as a sovereign act of God. But this does not imply that Edwards disparaged the use of "the means of grace." Bible reading, the hearing of sermons, attendance at worship, Sabbath-keeping, personal prayer, and participation in the sacraments were all necessary to give grace "a better opportunity to act." They were like the wood pyre that Elijah built on Mount Carmel. In and of themselves, they had no power. God was sovereign over them. But God used them to show his power and dispense his grace. He did this through the "matter" that the means provided—i.e., notions or ideas concerning God, Christ, the future world, what Christ had done and suffered, etc. These ideas were the necessary "matter" provided by the means of grace, giving opportunity for the Spirit to act. False ideas concerning God would not facilitate the work of grace. True ideas concerning God needed to be as full and complete as possible. Furthermore, the more vivid these ideas were, and the more often they came to mind, the greater the opportunities would be for grace to act. Yet true ideas concerning God worked not by any natural force of their own but by God's immediate operation and the agency of the Holy Spirit.[25]

---

24. WJE 21:305, 307–10.

25. WJE 18:84–86; WJE 21:58; Conrad Cherry, *The Theology of Jonathan Edwards: A Reappraisal* (Bloomington: Indiana University Press, 1990 [1966]), 59.

The Role of Faith

Edwards thus understood salvation as an act of God's free and unconditional grace. Subsequent chapters will show that Edwards was convinced that salvation is evidenced by a host of virtues as well as by perseverance throughout life, and yet none of those phenomena belied the priority of God's sovereign grace. They existed only because God decided first—both temporally and logically—that he would save certain of his human creatures. His motive was goodness and love, neither of which depended on any prior goodness or sincerity in the human subject. So salvation was by free grace. Chapter 25 will show that Edwards understood faith not as a requirement for salvation but as the act of union by which a sinner is joined to Christ.

Yet salvation comes through faith. It is "reasonable," "appropriate," and "fitting" to describe the human reception of salvation with the word "faith." This word expresses the act of "closing" with Christ better than the "other particular graces" associated with salvation. It was not our moral goodness or excellency that merited God's gift, since we are "sinful, miserable, weak, poor, helpless, unworthy and lost."[26] The stress on faith is a reminder of the gratuity of grace.

What is faith? Edwards used a host of definitions, but they can be gathered around three foci. The first was intellectual—"belief" in or "assent" to testimony, truth, and promises. The "truth" was Jesus Christ himself and the gospel concerning him, which brought the knowledge of God to those who believed. Edwards noted that "belief" is the primary word for faith in the New Testament.[27] The Old Testament's chief designation, "trust," was a second way that Edwards defined faith. He understood faith as a kind of trust in Christ that involved submission. It also meant depending on promises, much as an eighteenth-century wife depended on her husband for protection and guidance. It was the opposite of trusting in one's own righteousness, and also the opposite of fearfulness. It was "consent" to the sufficiency and completeness of Christ's work of obedience and his suffering for us.[28]

Edwards's third notion of faith centered on its stable, abiding character. Because it was a permanent gift of God, faith was not fleeting but a "habit," "disposition," and "complex idea." It became a foundational principle in its subject and conditioned a person's whole existence. Thus faith had real effects, and a

---

26. WJE 18:345; WJE 13:345, 407; WJE 23:71.

27. WJE 21:417, 447.

28. WJE 21:417, 419; WJE 13:386.

principal effect was repentance. "Repentance is implied in faith.... Thus by faith we destroy sin." Conversely, whenever "sin is aright confessed to God, there is always faith in that act." The two are inseparable. Therefore faith is "exercised both about the evil to be delivered from, and the good to be obtained."[29]

Faith and the Whole Person

Because faith for Edwards was a disposition and not simply an exercise of the mind, it involved the whole person. It was "more than merely the assent of the understanding, because 'tis called an 'obeying the gospel.'" It included an act of one's judgment and it shaped one's inclinations. True faith was ready to undergo whatever Jesus Christ required, and faith without that commitment "is rotten." Someone might believe that Christ is the Son of God and Savior, but the absence of commitment and loyalty to Christ proved that one did not possess saving faith. "If a prince makes suit to a woman in a far country, that she would forsake her own people, and father's house, and come to him, to be his bride; the proper evidence of the compliance of her heart with the king's suit, is her actually forsaking her own people, and father's house, and coming to him." Practice was the best test of faith.[30]

Thus Edwards used a range of phrases to portray the involvement of the whole person in true faith: gladly receiving Christ, committing to Christ, obeying doctrine, coming to Christ, opening the door to Christ, eating and drinking Christ, following him, embracing his promises, cleaving to him, being disposed to sell and suffer all for him, flying to him for refuge, entirely embracing and yielding to Christ, and quitting other hopes. He cautioned that faith was an act of the soul, and not merely a feeling of love. Faith could not be genuine unless it were expressed, and a "paramount" expression of faith was prayer. Faith was not merely waiting on or hoping in, or casting oneself upon God; it was also a union with him—entire, immediate, and perpetual—"as there [is] between a head and living members, between stock and branches."[31]

Faith and Sensory Experience

We saw in chapter 20 that Edwards used the Lockean language of sensory experience to describe conversion. He was especially effusive about the sensory

---

29. WJE 18:52, 218, 200.

30. WJE 21:419, 461–62; WJE 13:408; WJE 21:443; WJE 2:445.

31. WJE 21:420–27, 436, 444, 439, 60, 450–60, 444.

character of faith. While he could occasionally say that saving faith "may be built upon rational arguments," far more often he spoke of the power of a *sense* of "the beauty and amiableness" of a thing as the only thing that would move the will. "True faith is but a *sensibleness* of what is real in this matter of our redemption." His most powerful motif, which we also saw in chapter 20, was the "sense of the heart" that animates all true religion.[32]

The reality that faith senses is God's beauty: faith is "the soul's entirely acquiescing in this revelation from a *sense* of the dignity and glory and excellency [one of Edwards's synonyms for beauty] of the revealer of the revelation." Faith also senses "the gloriousness and excellency of gospel things in general, [such] as the greatness of God's mercy, the greatness of Christ's excellency and dignity and dearness to the Father, the greatness of Christ's love to sinners, etc." It is a sense of the reality and sufficiency of Christ as Savior. This faith comes from "a spiritual taste and relish of what is excellent and divine," so it is the enjoyment of a heart awakened to beauty now seeing what is true beauty. This is why Edwards speaks of "the symphony between the soul and these divine things." Faith is not only seeing but hearing; a certain musical ear is opened by faith to hear heavenly music.[33]

Part of the beautiful reality that faith sees is God's sovereignty, whereby God acts according to his own inclination and "may damn [souls] if he pleases, and may save them if he pleases." Once faith grasps not only God's honor and majesty but the depth of human sinfulness and the sufficiency of Christ's suffering, it then realizes "that God has no disposition and no need to punish us." For even though it has a "sense of God's being very angry" and of the justice of that anger, its "experience of the sufficiency of the doctrine of the gospel" will bring "peace of conscience." Such a realization will ease the "burthen" of guilt and fear. For it sees that by Christ's offering God's righteous wrath was appeased.[34]

Faith and Love

For Edwards, religion without love was empty. Love was what distinguished saving from common grace; it was the foundation of all virtue and the summation of all graces; it was the quintessence of duty and the soul of goodness.[35] Edwards went even further. Love, he insisted, "is included in faith." It

---

32. WJE 18:162; WJE 13:533, 522; WJE 18:452–66; emph. added.

33. WJE 21:424, 429, 428, 417, 427.

34. WJE 21:429–31.

35. WJE 21:159, 165–66, 170.

"is the main thing in saving faith, the life and power of it, by which it produces its great effects." Faith "implies love in its essence" because love indeed "belongs to the essence of saving faith."[36]

Edwards may have been aware that his interpretation of faith in terms of love sounded like that of Roman Catholicism. For after writing in his "Faith" notebook that love belongs to the essence of faith, he noted Thomas Goodwin's scathing denunciation: "The papists say, wickedly and wretchedly, that *love* is the form and soul of faith."[37] Edwards left this statement without comment, but his son Jonathan Jr. added, "But how does the truth of this charge of wickedness appear?"[38] Edwards seemed undeterred by Goodwin's remark, for a few pages later, in the same notebook, he paraphrased Thomas Sherlock with apparent approbation: "[R]eliance or dependence on God...aris[es] from a principle of *love* to God."[39] Here Edwards depicted love as the source of faith, a notion not far from Aquinas's conception of love as the soul or form of faith.

Calvin thought Aquinas made faith a merely intellectual act. In the *Institutes*, Calvin protested that faith is "more of heart than brain, more disposition than understanding."[40] But this criticism may rest on a misunderstanding of Aquinas, who wrote that "faith works through charity" and "[t]herefore charity is the form of faith." The form of a voluntary act "is the end to which that act is directed," and in this case the end was "the Divine Good." Faith therefore was "perfected and formed by charity." Because Aquinas distinguished between "living and lifeless faith," he implied that a faith not formed by love was lifeless or dead.[41] So when Calvin thought of Aquinas's faith as merely intellectual, he was thinking of a faith that Thomas would have called "dead." Arvin Vos commented that Calvin "had no more than a passing familiarity with the writings of Aquinas," but that on such essential matters as the nature of faith and of love, "Aquinas is in fact not far from Calvin."[42]

Furthermore, Aquinas insisted on the unity of the intellect and the will in the act of faith. He said that the believer gives assent only when "his will

---

36. WJE 21:422, 448, 461, 464.

37. Thomas Goodwin, *Works*, 5 vols. (London 1681–1704), 1.1.286; cited in WJE 21:464; orig. emph.

38. WJE 21:464.

39. WJE 21:467; orig. emph.

40. Calvin, *Institutes* 3.2.8.

41. Aquinas, *Summa Theologica*, 2a2ae.4.3.

42. Arvin Vos, *Aquinas, Calvin, and Contemporary Protestant Thought: A Critique of Protestant Views on the Thought of Thomas Aquinas* (Grand Rapids, MI: Eerdmans, 1985), 39, 35.

commands his intellect to assent," and that faith "inclines man to believe, by giving him a certain affection for the good."[43] While Aquinas was using a conceptual framework that differed from that of Edwards, it is clear that saving faith for Aquinas was not merely intellectual and that love was not separated from true faith but instead completed it. Edwards seems to have concurred with the primary points in Aquinas's account of faith and love.[44]

Faith and Works

In chapter 25, we will further explore the relationship between faith and works in Edwards's thought, but for now we can say that he believed them to be inseparable. All acts of faith have an internal dimension (as "immanent acts" of grace in the soul) and an external dimension (as "practical, or effective exercises"). The two dimensions are simply two sides of the same act. When there is real faith, there is real work, for all genuine faith is a "new, effective act of reception of Christ," and every such reception moves the whole person in both the inner and the outer aspects. Therefore faith "implies" obedience, and obedience "manifests" faith.[45]

Faith is therefore "practical." It is also persevering, which means its practice comes from a permanent principle that will keep on practicing until the end. Edwards was convinced of this from his reading of the Bible. Among other passages he adduced Jesus' promises in John 10:28 ("My sheep shall never perish") and John 8:31 ("If ye continue in my word, then are ye my disciples indeed"), and the warning in Hebrews 3:14 ("We are made partakers of Christ, if we hold the beginning of our confidence steadfast to the end"). Scriptural teaching implies that perseverance is "a necessary evidence of an interest in Christ."[46]

Edwards was careful, however, not to suggest that works will save us. Perseverance, he said, is not a condition for our righteousness or justification, but

---

43. Aquinas, *Summa Theologica* 2a2ae.5.2.

44. Conrad Cherry, whose *Theology of Jonathan Edwards* is otherwise the finest analysis of Edwards's theology of faith to date, places a wedge between Aquinas and Edwards because, he charges, for Aquinas faith in and of itself is unformed and then brought to life by love. Yet Aquinas, like Edwards, speaks of an integral connection between true faith and love such that faith in the absence of love is "lifeless" (Aquinas) and not true (as Edwards put it). Like Calvin, Edwards apparently knew very little of Aquinas except the anti-Catholic fulminations he read in Reformed scholastic sources. Aquinas' *Summa Theologica* was in the Yale library when Edwards was there as student and tutor, but Aquinas appears nowhere in Edwards's "Catalogue" or "Account Book"; WJE 26:63–64.

45. WJE 2:422–23; WJE 19:207; 21:461, 223.

46. Cherry, *Theology*, 127; WJE 19:601.

rather a principle inherent in all true faith. Genuine faith *will* persevere. Because it is of the very nature of faith, "perseverance is looked upon as virtually performed in the first act of faith." Only in that sense is it "necessary in order to justification." One might say that perseverance is part of the package that Christ bought when he purchased our salvation. It was *his* "perseverance in perfect obedience" that was the "condition of our right to life" or justification. The believer's salvation will necessarily include perseverance in faith as evidenced by good works, and that perseverance is itself a reward for the perfect work that Christ performed when he lived a perfect life and offered himself as a sacrifice for sinners. Perseverance in the faith is the best evidence that anyone can offer in showing that one has received salvation.[47]

Assurance of Salvation

Edwards stated that he "had no patience with those enthusiasts who limited the testimony of the Spirit [to one's own salvation] to inward, invisible, 'impractical' flashes of assurance." He was convinced that faith is more important than feelings about faith. Like other Calvinist theologians, Edwards believed that the performance of good works was the most reliable path to finding assurance of one's salvation. He affirmed that the Spirit works in the believer's heart, but always to change the will and the inclination. Over time this change of will and of inclination would manifest itself in a life of holy practice. The inner motions of "loving God, fearing God, trusting in God, repentance, believing in Christ, choosing and resting in God and Christ" would reveal themselves in the outer signs of "bringing forth fruit, doing good works, keeping God's and Christ's commandments universally and perseveringly."[48]

While a life of Christian practice was the most reliable path to assurance, "the highest kind of evidence" was the "rational inward witness to the truth of the gospel." This was the "witness of the Spirit" by which the mind sees that the Christian story "is not a thing of mere imagination." The Spirit shows the sinner "the divine glory and stamps of divinity that are in the gospel," testifying to the reality of the gospel's claims. With this witness came a sense of certainty, given not by a "chain of arguments" but by an intuitive seeing of God's beauty, purity, majesty, loveliness, "and ten thousand other things." This revelation of the beauty of the gospel was the third of three witnesses, said Edwards. The other two are "the water," which was the experience of the

---

47. WJE 19:601, 600–603.
48. Cherry, *Theology*, 144, 143, 145; WJE 21:494.

power of the gospel to purify and sanctify, and "the blood," which was the sinner's awareness of having been freed from guilt.[49]

But Edwards also recognized that assurance can be difficult. Sin renders us blind to our own true selves and thus unable to see clearly "because of the darkness within us." It is "not at all because the Word of God is not plain, or the rules not clear," but we are confused "by a pernicious distemper" within us. We may spend too much time in self-examination when we should rather be engaged in worthwhile activity. Christians should use the means of grace during their times of doubt and uncertainty, focusing on the gospel promises and striving to obey the commands of scripture. Self-contemplation, especially by melancholic souls, can be deadly (ch. 4). Edwards himself was at times "overwhelmed with melancholy" and had learned the importance of the means of grace and of Christian practice. Focusing on what needs to be done can be a welcome tonic to those whose minds are beset by inner turmoil.[50]

Some believers, noted Edwards, lacked assurance of salvation and were plagued by a sense of condemnation because of their bad habits and besetting sins. He reminded them that the best antidote to fear was repentance. Yet he equally insisted that even the best saints were sinful and that salvation came only through the righteousness of Christ. Therefore we need to keep our eyes "on God's glory, and Christ's excellency," not our "own attainments, and high experiences." If we look too much to ourselves, we are "living on experiences, and not on Christ." We must "join *self-reflection* with reading and hearing the Word of God." Listening to the law and promises of Christ, combined with seeing the Spirit at work in our lives, was the best way to avoid both self-righteousness and despair.[51]

Edwards's soteriology was complex. As we suggested in the first chapter, scholars have sometimes misrepresented Edwards by focusing on only a few of the many themes contained in his theology. Particular sermons, notebook entries, or treatises generally offer only one piece of the puzzle. Interpreting one text in isolation from the rest results in a distorted presentation of his theology. We shall see, for example, that salvation by faith alone was an important principle for Edwards, but it cannot be fully understood without attention to his equally important stress on perseverance as a condition of salvation. Therefore, with this chapter's underlying principles in mind, we turn in the next three chapters to see how they played out in his interlocking conceptions of conversion, justification, sanctification, and what might be called divinization.

---

49. WJE 2:454; WJE 13:177; WJE 21:430.

50. Sermon on Psalm 139:23–24, WJEO 48; WJE 2:196; WJE 16:744.

51. Cherry, *Theology*, 147, 87–88; WJE 2:180–81. Orig. emph.

24

Conversion: A Divine and Supernatural Light

THE PURITAN MOVEMENT in both England and New England was known for its strong emphasis on conversion. Its genesis lay in the complaint that the English Reformation of the sixteenth century had not gone far enough to remove traces of "Romish works-righteousness" from Anglican worship. Puritan preachers also declaimed against Anglicans who knew the liturgy and faithfully attended divine services but were not regenerated or "born again." This was the experience of having one's eyes and ears opened to the bad news that God's Law condemned their unbelief and disobedience, and then to the good news that Christ had come to save them from the condemnation they deserved. How would they know that they had been regenerated? Puritans typically pointed to an experience of conversion involving repentance and faith. They insisted this could happen only by a work of the Holy Spirit, since no human effort could do the job.

In seventeenth-century New England Puritanism, most divines argued that God usually prepares a person for conversion by a series of steps, using "means of grace" such as preaching and prayer and progressing through such steps as knowledge of the law, conviction of sin, striving for grace, false assurance, disappointment, and finally saving faith. This "morphology of conversion"[1] went back to Puritan divines William Perkins (1558–1602) and William Ames (1576–1633) but was freshly developed in response to the 1636–38 antinomian crisis involving Anne Hutchinson and others who taught that conversion comes apart from human activity or use of the means of grace.[2] Puritan theologians wanted to emphasize the role of the law in showing seekers that they do not measure up to God's demands and so

---

1. Edmund S. Morgan, *Visible Saints* (New York: New York University Press, 1963), 66–70.

2. Emery John Battis, *Saints and Sectaries: Anne Hutchinson and the Antinomian Controversy in the Massachusetts Bay Colony* (Chapel Hill, NC: University of North Carolina Press, 2009); T.D. Bozeman, *The Precisionist Strain: Disciplinary Religion and Antinomian Backlash in Puritanism to 1638* (Chapel Hill, NC: University of North Carolina Press, 2003).

need a savior. They also typically distinguished the steps leading to conversion, warning that following them does not guarantee conversion, and that there is a difference between the human efforts of preparation and the divine gift of grace.[3]

Like most theological schemes, practice often made mincemeat of theory. Parishioners often forgot or never heard that last distinction and sometimes thought that if they had used the means they were thereby converted—or that if they had tried hard enough (or were "sincere"), God would reward them with salvation. Jonathan Edwards grew up under the system and struggled with it. His own religious experience did not reproduce the steps in the order divines typically set out, and their preaching about it, he feared, sometimes confused law and gospel "by forcing the beginnings of saving faith back into legal preparation itself."[4]

Preparation for Salvation

Edwards agreed with his Puritan predecessors' basic premise. Preparation comes before conversion "except [in] very extraordinary cases." It only made sense: If "conversion is wrought in a moment," how could God make a man change his mind radically without "any preparatory circumstances to introduce it?" But he wanted to remind his auditors that, if anyone starts seeking, it is only by the stimulation of the Holy Spirit. For God "insists upon being inquired of for his mercy before he bestows it (Ezek. 36:37)." Edwards saw this as a biblical pattern: God appeared to the Israelites at the Red Sea only after they cried for help, he rescued Daniel from the lion and the three young men in the fiery furnace after they prayed for deliverance, Jesus responded finally to the Canaanite woman only after she begged him, and Jesus raised Lazarus only after being implored to do something. God inspires cries for help, and then is pleased to give the help (on "preparationism," see ch. 27).[5]

If the Puritan divines believed in preparatory steps, so did Edwards. God's "method" is to "first" reveal "his dreadful majesty and justice before he reveals his grace." For example, he "first revealed the law with thunders and lightnings from Mount Sinai before the full revelation of his grace by Jesus Christ." God sent destruction to Jerusalem in 70 AD before the gospel

---

3. Morgan, *Visible Saints*, 68–69.

4. Conrad Cherry, *The Theology of Jonathan Edwards: A Reappraisal* (Bloomington: Indiana University Press, 1990 [1966]), 64.

5. WJE 13:173, 365.

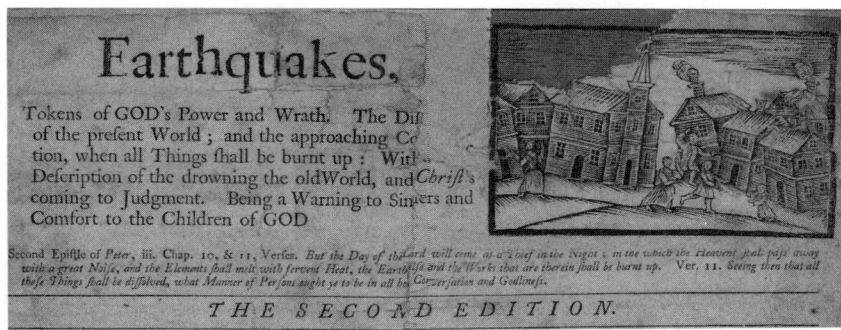

FIGURE 24.1 After a 1727 tremor in Massachusetts, churches experienced an "Earthquake Revival," though observers questioned whether those affected were converted or merely frightened (Courtesy Douglas Winiarski, University of Richmond).

was preached to most of the Gentile world and will destroy Antichrist before the "full revealing his grace" at the end of the world. So too "with particular persons": God first awakens them to a sense of his awe-inspiring justice and displeasure toward sin before giving them a "sense of his grace."[6]

Fear of punishment usually accompanies this awareness of God's justice. "'Tis much according to God's way of dealing, that the sinner should first be terrified with a sense of his danger before God manifests his favor." Edwards believed that "the more unthinking people, such as husbandmen [farmers] and the common sort of people" were more given to fear of punishment, while for "the more knowing and thinking men" the Holy Spirit "makes more use of rational deductions" concerning the good one gets from salvation. So while all those who come to Christ are generally first overwhelmed by the "dreadfulness" of God's majesty and justice, the less intellectual are driven to faith more by fear of loss, and the intellectually-inclined are motivated more by desire for gain. God is able to incline both sorts of souls toward divine things.[7]

Then God usually shows seekers their moral and spiritual inability. When they seek God for salvation, they discover "the evil of their own hearts and how little they deserve his favor," and thus "their dependence on him." By "trial and experience" they learn they are not able to make their hearts any better. Therefore God's usual manner in preparing people for grace is a threefold process. A person sees her "danger of eternal misery," which is "conviction."

---

6. WJE 13:412.

7. WJE 13:283.

Then she is given the ability "to see the absolute necessity of a savior" ("humiliation"), and only after that "see[s] the sufficiency and excellency of the Savior that is offered" ("conversion").[8]

But Edwards was impatient with teachings about preparation that implied these steps were universal or always followed a prescribed order. He noted that Paul was given saving grace without first experiencing conviction of sin and that the crowds of converts on Pentecost (Acts 2) did not seem to be "explicitly convinced of" their deserving ruin. Thus they did not seem to realize that their salvation was a free gift. His own experience was similar: his "turns of weeping and crying" over his own sins came years after his conversion, not before it.[9]

As we saw in the last chapter, Edwards preached the necessity of the means of grace, which God uses both to prepare for conversion and to facilitate growth in grace after conversion. Theoretically, Edwards said, God could give knowledge of Christ without means such as the preaching of the gospel, and even the principle of grace without knowledge of Christ. But God sees that means are "necessary in order to the proper and harmonious exercise of grace." For with more knowledge, which comes from Bible reading and the hearing of sermons, there is more opportunity for "the exercise of grace." Those who know more about Jesus Christ—all other things being equal—can better manifest the grace of God in their lives. "So if grace were infused into a very ignorant heathen, there would be hardly any opportunity for the exercises of grace."[10] This is why the Apostles Peter and Paul insisted that we grow in "a doctrinal knowledge of the principles of the Christian religion." Paul admonished his readers to be "filled with all knowledge" (Rom. 15:14), and Peter commanded Christians to add knowledge to their virtue (2 Pet. 1:5). Believers needed to use all the means of grace at their disposal, set aside special times for meditation, and pray for growth in grace. If God uses means to bring the saints to their first experience of grace, he also uses means to have his saints grow in grace.[11]

But the means of grace do not of themselves bring an experience of grace. Edwards would have abhorred Charles Finney's proclamation that conversion "is not a miracle, or dependent on a miracle in any sense" but simply a good use of means. Edwards insisted that conversion is a "surprising work of God"

---

8. WJE 13:385, 398, 400.

9. WJE 23:86–87; WJE 13:398; WJE 16:803.

10. WJE 13:404.

11. WJE 14:93–95.

that comes only by the "divine and supernatural light."[12] God has decided that in the vast majority of cases he will use means, but it is his Spirit's work in and through those means that brings conversion, not the means themselves.

Edwards also differed from another important American thinker in the nineteenth century, Princeton Seminary's Charles Hodge. Hodge showed great appreciation for Edwards's *Religious Affections* and *Original Sin*, but Hodge—following Calvin's precedent—rarely spoke of conversion. While he agreed with Edwards that regeneration was a new birth that brought a new principle of life to the soul, he followed the *Westminster Confession* (1646) in conceiving of "effectual calling" as a process by which the Holy Spirit through God's Word quickens and renews sinners, yet without reference to conversion as such. In Question 88, the *Heidelberg Catechism* (1563) treated "genuine repentance or conversion" as "two things: the dying away of the old self, and coming-to-life of the new," which is the way early Reformed theologians spoke of the lifelong process of sanctification. Hodge was uncomfortable with religious revivals and thought Edwards went too far in his encouragement of them (ch. 42). Moreover, Hodge seems to have embraced the Heidelberg model of conversion as a gradual transformation occurring over the course of a lifetime.[13]

A Divine and Supernatural Light

Edwards thought that light was the best image of what happens in conversion, as well as the one that scripture employs most frequently. He spoke of the "light of the Sun of Righteousness" that not only shines upon the saints to give them spiritual sight, but actually fills the saints so that "they shine also, and become little images of that Sun which shines upon them." They then "carry their own light with them."[14]

The first and most important function of the divine light that falls on the saints at regeneration and conversion is to give them a new vision of God and divine things. The saint "intuitively" sees:

---

12. Charles Finney, "How to Preach the Gospel," in *Lectures on Revivals of Religion* (New York: Revell, 1868), 186–210; WJE 4:129.

13. Charles Hodge, *Systematic* Theology, 3 vols. (Grand Rapids, MI: Eerdmans, 1986), 3:5, 3–40, 213–58; John Leith, ed., *Creeds of the Churches* (Chicago: Aldine, 1963), 206; Heidelberg Catechism, Q. 88; D. G. Hart, "Jonathan Edwards and the Origins of Experimental Calvinism," in D. G. Hart, Sean Michael Lucas, and Stephen J. Nichols, eds., *The Legacy of Jonathan Edwards: American Religion and the Evangelical Tradition* (Grand Rapids: Baker Academic, 2003), 161–80.

14. WJE 14:70, 77; WJE 2:200–201; WJE 14:78.

> ...things in a new appearance, in quite another view, than ever he saw before: he sees an excellency in God; he sees a sweet loveliness in Christ; he sees an amiableness in holiness and God's commandments; he sees an excellency in a Christian spirit and temper; he sees the wonderfulness of God's designs and a harmony in all his ways, a harmony, excellency and wondrousness in his Word: he sees these things by an eye of faith, and by a new light that was never before let into his mind.[15]

The convert sees especially the "excellency" of the "work of redemption"—"the ways and works of God revealed in the gospel." There is a particularly "divine and superlative glory in these things," for a holy and spotless God-man sacrificed himself for sinners. Jesus had perfect wisdom, infinite power, infinite terrifying majesty, and infinite knowledge, yet graciously stooped to love unworthy, sinful human beings. He went even further, to become their friend and companion—and further still, to expose himself to their contempt and spitting. He hated sin and yet forgave the greatest of sinners. He endured a shameful and horrific death to make salvation possible. He combined infinite majesty with unparalleled meekness. Scripture tells us that Jesus' eyes are as a flame of fire. Yet he was meek and lowly of heart: "With what meekness did he appear, when in the ring of soldiers, that were contemning and mocking him, when he was silent, and opened not his mouth, but went as a lamb to the slaughter. This Christ is a lion in majesty, and a lamb in meekness." This is the excellence or beauty that the regenerate see.[16]

"Natural men" cannot see these things because "nothing seems real to them but what they see with their eyes." Because of their "narrowness of soul" and "pitiful scantiness and narrowness of mind," they might know the outward facts of Jesus' life and yet fail to see his beauty. But to the "spiritual" ones divine light has given "largeness of heart" and "greatness of soul." Because this light has opened their eyes, they "see things at a distance, and can see the reality of things that are to [be] thousands of years hence, as well as present."[17]

"The Sense of the Heart"

These two kinds of seeing illustrate the difference between two basic kinds of knowledge: "speculative and sensible." The first is merely "notional" or

---

15. WJE 14:78–79.
16. WJE 17:413; WJE 19:569.
17. WJE 14:84–85.

"rational"; it is "mere cogitation" or "opinion." It consists of "putting signs in our minds, instead of the actual ideas of the things signified." The result is knowledge that is "very dim and transient, and exceeding confused and indistinct." The second kind of knowledge—sensible—is *"apprehension, wherein the mind has a direct ideal view or contemplation of the thing thought of."* This is what "is vulgarly called a having *a sense.*" It is located in that part of the will "figuratively called the heart," so this is the understanding that consists in "the sense of the heart." It involves the whole person in the affective dimension: it is an "inward tasting or feeling, of sweetness or pleasure, bitterness or pains."[18]

The difference in these two types of knowledge therefore has to do not with "the extensiveness of our notions" but "the intensiveness of the idea." Edwards often used the sweetness of honey to illustrate: "It is not he that has heard a long description of the sweetness of honey that can be said to have the greatest understanding of it, but he that has tasted." Only the actual taste of honey provides intensive knowledge or "lively apprehension." Think also, he suggested, of "smelling a sweet perfume." One can hear of a fragrance, but that kind of knowledge is vastly inferior to smelling it. Or one can believe on hearsay that a person is beautiful, but only when "seeing the countenance" can one have a true sense of that person's beauty.[19]

Edwards compared this notional understanding to an unconverted person's sense of God. They have as little understanding of God as those born blind have of colors, or those born deaf have of sounds. Without the new vision that comes with conversion, even those who are theologically trained may be blind: "However the natural man may have heard and read and studied about divine things, he never *saw* them, he never had a spiritual sight of them."[20]

The new "sense of the heart" that comes from the divine and supernatural light is the only knowledge that transforms. "The believer hath got such a sight and such a knowledge of things that, ever since, he is become quite another man than he was before." It changes "his very innermost principles" so that he becomes a new creature with "an heavenly temper" and "angelical mind." Natural men "may have considerable knowledge in divinity," but it does not have this effect on them. They continue in life with "the same temper and disposition."[21]

---

18. WJE 17:413; WJE 18:458; WJE 17:413; WJE 18:456, 458–59; orig. emph.

19. WJE 14:76–77; WJE 17:414.

20. WJE 14:77; emphasis added.

21. WJE 14:81.

If it is only the divine and supernatural light that transforms, it is only this light that brings true joy and pleasure. "Men have a great deal of pleasure in human knowledge, in studies of natural things; but this is nothing to that joy which arises from this divine light shining into the soul." This is particularly helpful in times of affliction, "to give the mind peace and brightness, in this stormy and dark world." Other kinds of delights "are bitter sweets." Their roses "grow upon thorns, and there is a sting with their honey." Bitterness either accompanies or follows them. If people place their happiness in them, "reason and conscience gives [sic] them inward disturbance in their enjoyment."[22] The sight of God's holy beauty, beginning in conversion, "gives unspeakable pleasure to the mind." There is no end to the vision or to the joy. The mind "may discover more and more of the beauty and loveliness of God, but it never will exhaust the fountain." God's beauty is more capacious than the ocean, so that after we "have had the pleasures of beholding the face of God millions of ages, it won't grow a dull story; the relish of this delight will be as exquisite as ever."[23]

With pleasure comes certainty. The new spiritual knowledge of divine things consists of "certain" clear apprehensions. When we read "an history of a thing that was acted many centuries or years ago, and at many thousands of miles' distance...the matter don't seem so real to us." But the divine and supernatural light gives such "intense and affecting" knowledge of divine things that they "do appear real to us." It powerfully registers on saints and "necessitates their minds to receive it as proceeding from God, and as the certain truth." They receive a "conviction of the truth and reality of them" both indirectly and directly. Indirectly they are convinced because the light removes prejudices in the heart "against the truth of divine things," and positively helps reason by making the "speculative notions" about God "more lively." Direct conviction comes by the sense of the "superlative" excellence of divine things. "There is a beauty in them that is so divine and godlike" that it functions as a "kind of intuitive and immediate evidence." This newfound certainty for converts "is liable to be interrupted with temptations and some degree of doubting," but there will be none of this in heaven. Seeing God face to face there will remove every last trace of doubt.[24]

---

22. WJE 17:424, 68–69.

23. WJE 17:72–73.

24. WJE 14:75, 78; WJE 17:414–15, 65. We discussed assurance of salvation and how Edwards differed with others on this topic in ch. 23.

Yet the sight of God reveals the uncleanness of humankind. With every genuine vision of God, there is always "evangelical humiliation"—not simply a "legal humiliation" that recognizes one's condemnation by God's law, but an evangelical humility that recognizes Christ's satisfaction of the law's demands. Along with "evangelical humiliation" come repentance and every other Christian virtue involved in conversion, for "the graces of the Spirit" are "so nearly allied that they include one another." There will be "a reception of Christ with the faculties of the soul," a "believing of what we are taught in the gospel concerning him and salvation by him," and a "dying unto sin and an emptying of self." "evangelical humiliation" follows upon conviction of sin, and repentance follows upon that: "Like strings in consort, if one is struck, others sound with it."[25]

Illumination and Infusion

Since Edwards followed what he thought was the Bible's primary metaphor for conversion—the shining of light—it is not surprising that he often used the "Platonic, Johannine, and Augustinian *illumination*" tradition as a "framework" for explaining the process of conversion.[26] This is the idea that, in Augustine's words, "the mind needs to be enlightened by light from outside itself, so that it can participate in truth, because it is not itself the nature of truth." From this perspective, the decisive element in conversion is God's illumination of the human mind. In Edwards's words, "Conversion is nothing but God's causing such an alteration with respect to the mind's *ideas* of spiritual good."[27]

Edwards also used the category of "infusion" to unpack the multi-layered reality of conversion. While the sixteenth-century Protestant Reformers resisted the use of this term, the seventeenth-century and eighteenth-century Reformed scholastics—including Edwards's favorite, Petrus van Mastricht—retrieved the idea from Catholic discussions and put it to work in their own theological discussions.[28] In his *Treatise on Grace*, Edwards wrote that "saving grace in the heart" requires "an immediate infusion or operation of the Divine Being upon the soul." Early in his career, he observed that all instances of

---

25. WJE 13:213–15, 457–58.

26. WJE 1:43; Cherry, *Theology*, 26; emphasis added. Mastricht also described conversion as illumination in his discussion of regeneration; Peter [Petrus] van Mastricht, *A Treatise on Regeneration* (Morgan, PA: Soli Deo Gloria Publications, 2002), 22–23, 39.

27. Augustine, *Confessions* 4.15.25; WJE 13:381; emph. added.

28. See chapter 23 and van Mastricht, *A Treatise on Regeneration*, 17.

"being born again" come by infusion of grace, and that this can happen even "in the very moment that the man begins to [be]." Edwards said this was what Paul meant in Romans 5:5 when he said, "The love of God is shed abroad in our hearts by the Holy Ghost which is given unto us." While the Spirit of God assists only "natural principles" in the unregenerate, the Spirit "operates *in* the minds of the godly" by "uniting itself to their souls, and living in 'em and acting itself." Infusion seemed to Edwards to be a fitting description of the Spirit's pouring himself into the human soul and taking up residence there.[29]

These frameworks of illumination and infusion helped Edwards resist the Arminian tendency to see conversion as the gradual development of a person's God-given but natural abilities. Instead, the new birth took place by God's immediate action, without the mediation of human powers. The doctrine of the 1733 sermon, "A Divine and Supernatural Light," was that this light is "immediately imparted to the soul by God" and is "of a different nature from any that is obtained by natural means." Edwards hastened to add that this revelation of God's beauty to the soul *uses* natural faculties such as the understanding, but that these do not "operate by their own power, or [as] a natural force. God makes use of means; but 'tis not as mediate causes to produce this effect. There are not truly any second causes of it; but it is produced by God immediately." Even "[t]he Word of God is no proper cause" of regeneration. It operates not by by its own latent power but by the immediate work of God's Spirit.[30]

Because regeneration is an immediate work of God, making use of means but not operating according to natural powers, it takes place in an instant. So "conversion is wrought in a moment."[31] The knowledge, reformation, and conviction that prepare the ground for conversion may be gradual, but regeneration itself "is wrought at once." It is like an "opening of the eyes of the blind." Just as the original creation was instantaneous, so is the new creation: "When God creates, he does not merely establish and perfect the things which were made before, but makes wholly and immediately something entirely new, either out of nothing, or out of that which was perfectly void of any such nature, as when he made man of the dust of the earth." Creation out of nothing, both then and now, occurs in the blink of an eye.[32]

---

29. WJE 21:165; WJE 13:246, 512–13.

30. WJE 17:410, 416.

31. WJE 13:173. Here Edwards conflates regeneration and conversion, but as we shall see later in this chapter, he also distinguishes them, saying that sometimes conversion can follow regeneration after a period of time.

32. WJE 21:161, 159.

Lockean Sensation

Many scholars have discussed Edwards's debt to John Locke, whom Edwards once described as a man of "great genius."[33] Edwards was helped by Locke's theory of personal identity in his treatise on original sin, and probably was inspired by Locke's understandings of freedom in his treatise on the will. But the Lockean flavor of Edwards's writings is most noticeable in Edwards's prolific descriptions of the conversion experience. Locke believed that all knowledge was rooted in sense experience. Edwards took this philosophical principle and adapted it to his theological purposes. John E. Smith noted that Edwards appreciated Locke's contrast between a spectator with notional understanding and a person who is so engaged as to be attracted or repulsed by something, and that Edwards pushed the point further by drawing a closer connection between sense and understanding than even Locke had proposed. In *Religious Affections*, Edwards wrote that the "new sensation or perception of the mind" is "what some metaphysicians call a new simple idea." This statement was probably in reference to Locke's "one uniform appearance or conception in the mind" that "is not distinguishable into different ideas." Edwards's "sense of the heart" was a "clear and distinct perception" that might be compared to an element of sense experience. Unlike sense experience, however, the "sense of the heart" was only possible through an encounter with God.[34]

As William Sparkes Morris noted, Edwards used Locke "mainly as a point of departure for his own thinking, rather than as a master in whose footsteps he would willingly follow."[35] He used Lockean language to explain the sense of the heart without accepting Locke's denial of direct knowledge of any spiritual or material substance, and without approving of Locke's disparagement of emotion and affect in religion.[36] As Josh Moody explains, "Edwards's 'sense of

---

33. WJE 2:299.

34. John E. Smith, *Jonathan Edwards: Puritan, Preacher, Philosopher* (Notre Dame: Notre Dame University Press, 1992), 14, 26; WJE 2:205; Locke, *An Essay Concerning Human Understanding* 2.2.1.

35. William Sparkes Morris, *The Young Jonathan Edwards: A Reconstruction* (Brooklyn, NY: Carlson Publishing, 1991), 576.

36. Michael McClymond, *Encounters with God: An Approach to the Theology of Jonathan Edwards* (New York: Oxford University Press, 1998), 14–16. Robert Brown suggests that Edwards might have learned from Locke's critique of natural religion in the *Reasonableness of Christianity*, as well as from Locke's acceptance of probability rather than certainty as a criterion for historical religious knowledge. Robert E. Brown, *Jonathan Edwards and the* Bible (Bloomington: Indiana University Press, 2002), 76–87.

the heart' is to some extent formulated in terms of Lockean empiricism, but the source of its content is Puritan and Biblical."[37]

False Conversions

Edwards believed that some so-called conversions were spurious and typically involved an inordinate reliance on the imagination. Early in his career, Edwards assigned a role to the imagination in religious experience. Yet after the Great Awakening he became wary of those who claimed to have received immediate revelation from God (ch. 20). He took the imagination to be "that power of the mind, whereby it can have a conception, or idea of things of an external or outward nature...when those things are not present, and be not perceived by the senses." Edwards believed we use this faculty all the time in everyday perception. But when "common people" are "under great convictions and fears of hell," they are liable to "see lights and hear voices, and see and hear many things" that come from an overheated imagination. The visions and voices are religious: they see "themselves in the hands of God," they see Christ shedding his blood, hear him speaking to them, or in false humility see "that they are nothing." Fortunately, we need not rely on visionary experiences as tests of genuine conversion or true religion. For Satan can make such "impressions on the mind" but cannot replicate Christian love or gracious inclinations.[38]

False conversions can stem from the common work of the Spirit, as well. The Spirit's "ordinary work" is to give a "sense of spiritual and eternal things" such as God's greatness and wrath toward sin. The Spirit assists the "natural powers" of the unregenerate to see God's "natural perfections," such as his glory in nature and holy anger toward evil. The Spirit may give unregenerate persons "a sense of the importance of things of religion in general," which "we commonly call conviction." But without a vision of the *beauty* of the divine holiness, all these affections are "wholly graceless" and they sometimes appear among "very ill [i.e., evil] men."[39]

In Part II of the *Religious Affections*, Edwards explained twelve "negative signs" of true religion. These are "no certain signs that religious affections are truly gracious, or that they are not." True saints will have most or all of these,

---

37. Josh Moody, *Jonathan Edwards and the Enlightenment* (Lanham, MD: University Press of America, 2005), 80 n.46.

38. WJE 2:210–11; WJE 13:460.

39. WJE 18:462–63; WJE 17:413.

but their presence in a person does not show with any certainty that that person is regenerate. Why not? Edwards found all these signs in biblical characters who had not received God's grace. The twelve negative signs started with intense religious affections that are "very great, or raised very high" such as the joy of the children of Israel at the Red Sea who "soon forgot his works." Other ambiguous signs were affections that "have great effects on the body" because "such effects oftentimes arise from great affections about temporal things, and when religion is no way concerned in them," and affections that cause people "to be fluent, fervent and abundant, in talking of the things of religion," as "Pharisees and ostentatious hypocrites" do. Edwards thought similarly of affections "that persons did not make...themselves, or excite 'em of their own contrivance, and by their own strength" because false spirits "often transform themselves into angels of light." The same could be said of affections that "come with tests of Scripture, remarkably brought to the mind," since the devil brought scriptures to Christ himself in the wilderness.[40]

More positive in character yet still unreliable as tests of grace were those affections that had "an appearance of love in them," since "the more excellent anything is, the more will be the counterfeits of it." When one encountered "persons having religious affections of many kinds, accompanying one another," one has to remember that counterfeits of godly affections appeared in wicked characters from the Bible such as Pharaoh, Saul, and Ahab. Edwards cast doubt on the Puritan morphology of conversion when he questioned the significance of a "certain order" in the affections, such as when "comforts and joys seem to follow awakenings and convictions of conscience," since "the devil, if permitted, can terrify men as well as the Spirit of God." Even when people "spend much time in religion" and are "zealously engaged in the external duties of worship," they might be like the Pharisees and the stony-ground hearers. So affections that "much dispose persons with their mouths to praise and glorify God," just like the "Jews in Ezekiel's time" who showed much love with their mouth "while their heart went after their covetousness," were not sure signs of regeneration. Neither could one give credence to people "confident that what they experience is divine, and that they are in a good estate," since this "savors more of the spirit of the Pharisees, who never doubted but that they were saints." In sum, Edward concluded that believers cannot "determine who are godly, and who are not." The Lord alone knows these things.[41]

---

40. WJE 2:125, 129–32, 135, 141–42, 144.

41. WJE 2:146–48, 151, 156, 163–67, 171, 181–82.

Regeneration and Conversion

The early Reformed tradition focused not on conversion but on regeneration or the new birth, which it treated under the category of God's effectual calling, in which the Holy Spirit uses the Word to evoke faith and repentance. Later Reformed thinkers began to distinguish regeneration from conversion, identifying the first as the passive reception of divine life and the second as active turning from sin to new life in Christ. In the late seventeenth century, Mastricht sharply distinguished the two, saying that "one truly regenerate may, as to both habit and act, be for a time an unbeliever, destitute of repentance and walking in sin." He cited the examples of Jeremiah and John the Baptist, who were regenerated in their mothers' wombs but did not repent and believe until they reached the age of discretion. "So that regeneration, in which the spiritual life is bestowed in the first act or principle only, differs from conversion, by which this principle of life is brought into actual exercise, not only in order of nature, but sometimes also in order of time." Following Mastricht, Edwards developed this notion that sometimes there may be a lag between regeneration and conversion. Picking up on hints in some of the scholastics about regeneration being "imperfect" and "never reach[ing] completion here on earth," Edwards pictured both regeneration and conversion as lifelong processes.[42]

While for Edwards regeneration was immediate and instantaneous, he thought of conversion as an event that sometimes took place subsequent to regeneration. Jesus' disciples, he pondered in the mid-1730s, were "good men *before*" they met Christ, "already in a disposition to follow Christ." The same was true of Zacchaeus and the woman of Canaan.[43] "Conversion may still be necessary to salvation in some respect even after [someone] is really a saint."[44] Not only could conversion occur later than regeneration, but both conversion and regeneration could be understood as occurring over the course of one's Christian life. So while Edwards at times spoke of regeneration as instantaneous, at other times he referred to regeneration in a second sense—as a

---

42. Calvin, *Institutes* 3.24; van Mastricht, *Treatise on Regeneration*, 26–27, 31; Heinrich Heppe, *Reformed Dogmatics Set Out and Illustrated from the Sources* (Grand Rapids: Baker, 1978), 525.

43. WJE 20:73; emph. added. This was an application of the principle he had articulated in 1729, that "a person according to the gospel may be in a state of salvation, before a distinct and express act of faith in the sufficiency and suitableness of Christ as a Savior" (WJE 13:458).

44. WJE 20:74.

gradual lifelong process of turning from sin to Christ. "The whole of the saving work of God's Spirit on the soul in the beginning and progress of it from the very first dawnings of divine light and the first beginnings of divine life until death is in some respect to be looked upon as all one work of regeneration.... There is as it were an unregenerate part still in man after the first regeneration that still needs to be regenerated." Edwards thought Christ himself spoke this way: "Christ seems to speak of regeneration as a continued thing, Matt. 19:28, 'Ye that have followed me, in the regeneration.'" Conversion could also be thought of as a lifelong process: "The work" of God giving light from time to time throughout the saint's life "in the whole progress of it, is a proper conversion." When the godly backslide into sin and then return to grace, this "is called conversion in Scripture." That is why the Apostle Peter's "recovery" was called his conversion. It is also why "conversion is spoken of in Scripture as what yet remains to be sought and prayed for by the saints, after they have already been savingly wrought upon."[45]

If Edwards was akin to some high-medieval and late-medieval theologians in speaking of conversion as a lifelong process, he did not share their notion of sanctification as cooperation or synergy with God, so that God does his part and human beings do their part. As we saw in chapter 23, Edwards argued vigorously against Arminian synergism by insisting that "God does all and we do all." Throughout the life of the believer there is a continual concurrence of God's active power. The believer's holy disposition is the active presence of the Holy Spirit itself, motivating and empowering each of the believer's holy acts. Neither did Edwards endorse another medieval view, viz., that God rewards the merits of previous human acts, so that the believer "cooperates" with God by persevering in faith and obedience. We shall see in chapter 25 that Edwards did have a concept of reward, but it pertained more to eschatology than to the present life. More importantly, for Edwards perseverance was not a condition for further gifts of grace but a principle inherent in all true faith.

The distinction between regeneration and conversion helped Edwards explain the status of the Old Testament saints and the fate of those who die in infancy. Very early in his career, Edwards wrote that infants can be regenerated at birth without any knowledge of Christ and that salvation is based on disposition: "The infant that has a disposition in his heart to believe in Christ—if he had a capacity and opportunity—is looked upon and accepted as if he actually believed in Christ, and so is entitled to eternal life through

---

45. WJE 20:70, 72–74.

Christ."⁴⁶ Regarding the salvation of Old Testament saints "when yet they had no distinct respect to [Christ]," Edwards reasoned that it was "the second Person in the Trinity" who appeared to them "as the author of temporal salvation and benefits" whenever God manifested himself to Israel. Hence they already in some sense believed in Christ and were saved by faith in Christ. In an early comment in the *Miscellanies*, Edward wrote that conversions from wickedness to righteousness in the Old Testament era were just as "frequent" as in the New Testament era. In other words, true regeneration and conversion were plentiful during the Old Testament era among those who did not yet know the name of Jesus Christ (ch. 36).⁴⁷

But what of the legal and theological act of justification by which the regenerate and converted are accepted by God? To that we will turn in the next chapter.

---

46. WJE 13:245–46; WJEO 27, "Controversies Notebook," Original Sin. "Miscellany 492" suggests that Edwards considered the state of infants analogous to that of the heathen since both have less than full knowledge of revelation. In this entry, he speculates that without revelation we would not know "who are liable to punishment, whether children, or whether heathen" (WJE 13:537).

47. WJE 18:201; WJE 20:56; WJE 20:139–45; WJE 23:229–30; WJE 13:221–22.

25
Justification and Sanctification

TRYON EDWARDS, JONATHAN Edwards's great-grandson and one of his great-grandfather's nineteenth-century editors, deleted the word "infusion" fourteen times from his edition of the elder Edwards's *Charity and Its Fruits* (1852). Tryon was apparently convinced that his great-grandfather could not have supported infusion because he was a theologian in the Reformation tradition, and that tradition typically regarded infusion as a Catholic concept implying that we are saved by what is in us. Luther protested the suggestion in late-medieval Catholic theology that we are saved by what we do, so he insisted that we are saved by the "alien" righteousness of Christ outside ourselves. Edwards's second-favorite theologian, Francis Turretin, vigorously distanced his doctrine of justification from infusion: "We also are made righteousness, not by infusion, but by imputation."[1]

Tyron was right to fear that his great-grandfather's writings could cause confusion. In the mid-twentieth century, Thomas Schafer alleged that Edwards "went beyond the doctrine of justification" and "practically eliminated" the notion of justification by faith alone. Several decades later, Anri Morimoto agreed that Edwards's thinking "endangers" the principle of justification of the ungodly and in fact is "contiguous" with Roman Catholic soteriology. At the beginning of the twenty-first century, a new flurry of scholarship vigorously denied that Edwards's doctrine of justification ever wavered from Reformation distinctives, while yet another maintained that the development of his soteriology "undermined his basic Reformation intentions."[2] In this chapter,

---

1. Francis Turretin, *Institutes of Elenctic Theology*, 3 vols., ed. James T. Dennison Jr., trans. George Musgrave Giger (Phillipsburg, NJ: Presbyterian and Reformed, 1994), 2:652.

2. Thomas A. Schafer, "Jonathan Edwards and Justification by Faith," *Church History* 20 (1951), 64; Anri Morimoto, *Jonathan Edwards and the Catholic Vision of Salvation* (University Park: Penn State Press, 1995), 115, 10. For defenses of Edwards as true to the Reformation, see John J. Bombaro, "Jonathan Edwards's Vision of Salvation," *Westminster Theological Journal* 65 (2003): 45–67; and Jeffrey C. Waddington, "Jonathan Edwards's 'Ambiguous and Somewhat Precarious' Doctrine of Justification," *Westminster Theological Journal* 66 (2004): 357–72. For a demurral, see George Hunsinger, "Dispositional Soteriology: Jonathan Edwards on Justification by Faith Alone," *Westminster Theological Journal* 66 (2004): 107–20. See also Samuel T. Logan Jr., "The Doctrine of Justification in the Theology of Jonathan Edwards," *Westminster Theological Journal* 46 (1984): 26–52.

we will briefly review Reformation and post-Reformation understandings of justification, look at Edwards's eighteenth-century context, and unfold his treatment of justification. After asking whether it represents a departure from the Reformation, we will unpack his thinking on sanctification.

Reformation and Post-Reformation Background

Neither Augustine nor Aquinas sharply distinguished between justification and sanctification. In other words, their theologies of salvation did not clearly distinguish God's acceptance of the elect based on Christ's work from his acceptance based on his making them just or righteous. The Council of Trent affirmed both as a basis for justification and further declared that justification required human cooperation, leading to an increase of one's justification. Justification came through the infusion of new virtues, whose merit led to God's acceptance.[3]

Over time, the Reformation tradition came to distinguish sharply between justification and sanctification, arguing that the former was external to the believer, and was grounded not in the inherent righteousness of the regenerate but only in the "alien" and imputed righteousness of Christ. Justification was instantaneous and complete, an act rather than a process. It was the judicial act in which God declared, on the basis of the righteousness of Christ, that all the claims of the law were satisfied with respect to the sinner and that the sinner was now righteous with a righteousness that was not inherent. Justification therefore did not change the inner life of the sinner but took place in God's tribunal. It lay outside of the believer. Justification was the legal basis for sanctification, which was a never-completed process of growth in inherent holiness that God worked within the believer. In the sixteenth century, some said that regeneration was the one-time infusion of grace that began the lifelong process of sanctification, but clear distinctions between regeneration and sanctification did not emerge until the following century. Calvin and later Reformers believed that this distinction between justification on the one hand and regeneration and sanctification on the other was necessary to show that God saves us by Christ's work and not our own—by his merit and not by ours.[4] This explains their conviction that Christ's righteousness was alien to

---

3. *Canons and Decrees of the Council of Trent*, ed. H.J. Schroeder (St. Louis, MO: Herder, 1950), 16.9, 24; Alister McGrath, *Iustitia Dei: A History of the Christian Doctrine of Justification*, 2nd ed. (Cambridge: Cambridge University Press, 1998 [1986]), 23–36, 44–47, 109–19.

4. John Calvin, *Institutes of the Christian Religion*, 3.11.12, 3.11.16–17. As we shall see later in the chapter, Luther was not as clear on this distinction.

believers and their justification was God's external act. It was also why they held that the ground of justification was not the inherent righteousness of the elect but the imputed righteousness of Christ.

In the seventeenth century, Reformed theologians argued against Arminians who were reinterpreting justification as a pardon for sins based on Christ's "passive" obedience or surrender to death, and were rejecting any notion of an imputation of Christ's righteousness to the believer. The Reformed insisted that justification was also based on Christ's "active" obedience to the law throughout his lifetime. This active obedience was that part of Christ's righteousness that merited for the elect their title to eternal life, and was imputed to the elect. While some Arminians were saying that faith itself was the ground of justification, the Reformed believed this assertion turned faith into a meritorious work—thus contradicting the whole notion of salvation by grace. So these Reformed critics of the Arminians countered by highlighting Calvin's assertion—repeated in the words of the *Westminster Confession*—that faith was merely the "instrument" of justification. They added that faith was not something that any human could muster by natural power alone but was "the work of the Spirit of Christ" in the hearts of the elect.[5]

Edwards wrote in the *Faithful Narrative* (1737) that when he decided to lecture on justification in 1734 there had been a "great noise that was in this part of the country about Arminianism." In Edwards's context, this designation had little to do with the theology of Jacob Arminius (1560–1609) but was a loose term for a variety of complaints against what was thought to be the harshness of Calvinism. What was termed "Arminianism" in eighteenth-century New England generally involved a rising confidence in the human ability to please God by sincere endeavors for faith and virtue (ch. 3). Edwards's attention to Arminianism may have been stirred by his reading of Daniel Whitby's *Discourse on the Five Points* (1710) and his participation in the Robert Breck affair. Whitby had argued that human beings secure God's approval by means of their good choices. All that God did in regeneration was to "bring moral motives and inducements to mind, and set them before the understanding." Breck was a young minister who had denied the necessity of Christ's atoning death on the grounds that a sincere desire for morality was the only requirement for salvation.[6]

---

5. *Westminster Confession* (1646), 11.2, 14.1, in John H. Leith, ed., *Creed of the Churches* (Chicago: Aldine, 1963), 207, 209.

6. WJE 4:100; WJE 1:3; WJE 4:5–10.

In his 1723 Yale commencement address on justification, Edwards had identified Arminianism as neonomianism or a new form of legalism. It posited faith as a new kind of obedience and therefore the gospel as a new law. The structure of his 1734 lecture on justification suggests that he thought of this new law as making three essential claims—that justification is equivalent to pardon from sins, that there is no imputation of Christ's righteousness to the believer in Christ, and that sincere obedience is the only requirement for justification before God.[7]

Justification by Faith Alone

For the 1734 lecture, which was published in 1738 as "Justification By Faith Alone," Edwards chose for his text Romans 4:5: "But to him that worketh not, but believeth on him that justifieth the ungodly, his faith is counted for righteousness." The thesis or "doctrine" that he set out to prove was, "We are justified only by faith in Christ, and not by any manner of virtue or goodness of our own."[8]

His first task was to explain how faith justifies. The traditional Reformed way of referring to faith as the "instrument" of receiving justification was, he thought, an "obscure way of speaking" since faith is the act of receiving itself. So how can faith be the instrument of receiving? Nor is faith the ground of justification, since that would make justification a reward for faith, which would suggest we are justified by something good or virtuous in ourselves. Instead, faith is what unites us to Christ, and "what is real in the union between Christ and his people, is the foundation of what is legal." Faith justifies because it makes Christ and the believer one.[9] Edwards hastened to add that

---

7. WJE 14:63; Morimoto, *Jonathan Edwards and the Catholic Vision of Salvation*, 76.

8. WJE 14:149.

9. WJE 19:158. Robert Jenson notes that it is Edwards's idealism that grounds his notion of union and therefore his doctrines of imputation, atonement, and justification. Since, for Edwards, persons are not impermeably bounded entities because God's thinking and not substance metaphysics determines what is (see chs. 7, 22), Christ and the believer are a single moral unit. Therefore Christ's righteousness is the "actual character of the believer's moral existence." In other words, God has decided that at the moment when, by his election, a person trusts in Christ, that person becomes so merged with the person of Christ that the two become one, and Christ's righteousness swallows up the believer's sin. Therefore imputation is not a legal fiction or a cooking of the books, but God's perception of a new fact: the new moral character of the person called Christ who includes what used to be called the sinner alone. Similarly, the atonement is effective for believers because, since we are now in union with Christ, "if the Father loves the Son he must love us also." Jenson, "Christology," in Sang Lee, ed., *The Princeton Companion to Jonathan Edwards* (Princeton, NJ: Princeton University Press, 2005), 75; Jenson, *America's Theologian: A Recommendation of Jonathan Edwards* (New York: Oxford University Press, 1988), 126.

this was not what the medieval and Reformed scholastics called "the merit of congruity," which was a proportionate reward given by God for a moral quality that pleases him. Rather, it was God's love for order that led him to justify those who believe.

This was Edwards's attempt to respond to critics, such as the deist Thomas Chubb, who argued that God could have forgiven sins without Jesus' death on the Cross. In Chubb's voluntaristic conception of God, there was no rational or necessary connection between justification and the means God used to procure it. God's arbitrary power and decision were alone responsible for the forgiveness of sins. In reply, Edwards offered a series of arguments showing that it was rationally appropriate for God to use the means and modes that he did use to bring salvation to humankind. So, for example, Edwards argued that God's conferral of salvation to those with faith was not "arbitrary" but "fitting." It would be arbitrary to save only those with "a certain stature or hair color," but it was fitting to save those who want to be saved—just as it was fitting for a man to offer joint possession of his estate only to a woman who accepted his proposal of marriage. This did not imply that God's rewarded what was amiable or moral or beautiful—an idea that Edwards identified as "moral fitness" or the Arminian position. Instead God's way of acting manifested what Edwards called "natural fitness" and God's "love of order and hatred of confusion."[10] God linked salvation with faith not because of the beauty of faith but because of the beauty of the order that united those things that have a "natural agreement and congruity"—namely, the bestowal of Christ's benefits on the soul united to Christ through faith.

So justification was not a reward for faith. When a man gives himself to a woman in marriage, he explained, he is not rewarding her for accepting him. Nor is her receiving him "considered as a worthy deed in her for which he rewards her, by giving himself to her; but 'tis by her receiving him, that the union is made, by which she hath him for her husband."[11] In the *Miscellanies* written just before giving the 1734 lecture on justification, Edwards compared union with Christ by faith to a ring containing a precious, transparent jewel. By faith the soul "is suited as the socket for the jewel that is set in it; by this the soul admits it, as things transparent admit light when opaque bodies refuse it." By the same measure of natural fitness, there was a rational connection between a forgiving God and creatures who were willing to receive forgiveness.[12]

---

10. WJE 19:159; WJE 18:341–42; WJE 20:483, 481.

11. WJE 19:201.

12. WJE 18:53, 222–23.

Edwards's next task was to explain why our human goodness cannot justify us. Here he resorted to his sobering conception of human sin. Every sinful act incurred infinite guilt:

> ...because our obligation to love or honor any being is great in proportion to the greatness or excellency of that being, or his worthiness to be loved or honored: we are under greater obligation to love a more lovely being than a less lovely; and if a being be infinitely excellent and lovely, our obligations to love him are therefore infinitely great: the matter is so plain it seems needless to say much about it.[13]

Since our guilt is infinite, no goodness we might have prior to justification could help us. Indeed, nothing—including faith itself—could subtract from the infinite hatefulness that we display before God because of our sin: "The odiousness of [even one act of sin] so infinitely exceeds the excellency, that the excellency of that very act [of faith] is, in the sight of him that judges according to the law and mere justice, nothing." Even our holy acts after justification, by themselves, are "in a sense corrupt, and the hatefulness of the corruption of them, if we are beheld as we are in ourselves, or separate from Christ, infinitely outweighs the loveliness of the good that is in them...therefore the virtue must pass for nothing, out of Christ." Hence "all our righteousnesses are nothing, and ten thousand times worse than nothing (if God looks upon them as they are in themselves)."[14]

It was only because Arminians did not see this infinite guilt that they could suppose "a new law, which requires no more than imperfect, sincere obedience." For Edwards, this was "absurd" for several reasons. It "derogates from gospel grace" because it diminishes God's freedom in bestowing grace. Instead it suggests that God owes his grace to the virtuous. What is more, it shows more grace when a gift has nothing to do with the goodness of the recipient. So God's grace appears more fully in the undeserved gift that he gives. Finally, the notion that sincere obedience could be sufficient for justification "puts man in Christ's stead, and makes him his own savior."[15] Edwards thought the solution to the Arminian misunderstanding was to see that "justification is manifestly a *forensic* term, as the word is used in Scripture." It is used of a judge who "cannot justify us unless he sees a perfect righteousness, *some way* belonging

---

13. WJE 19:161.
14. WJE 18:342; WJE 19:241.
15. WJE 19:166, 184–85.

to us, either performed by ourselves, or by another, and justly and duly reckoned to our account." The "some way" that God provided was to make believers one with Christ. On this basis, everything he did "whereby he did honor to the law and authority of God by his acts, as well as the reparation to the honor of the law, by his sufferings, *is reckoned to the believer's account.*" Because of the believer's union with Christ, both Christ's sufferings and righteous deeds were reckoned as the believer's, so the believer was legally justified before God.[16]

Edwards noted that it was not only Christ's "passive" sufferings but his "active" obedience—and hence his righteousness—that God imputed to believers. If Christ's voluntary death kept believers out of hell, then his obedient life brought them to heaven: "Christ's perfect obedience shall be reckoned to our account, so that we shall have the benefit of it, as though we had performed it ourselves: and so we suppose that a title to eternal life is given us as the reward of this righteousness." For the Arminians to suppose that Christ made atonement only by his final sufferings and not by his lifelong obedience was to "make him our Savior but in part." It was through the infinite value of Christ's obedience—infinite because of Christ's dignity—that the infinite weight of our sin could be removed.[17] To those who objected that Christ's obedience merited his own justification but not that of others, Edwards replied that the Son of God in his preexistent state "was in no subjection to the Father" but because of a "transaction between the Father and the Son" (i.e., the covenant of redemption) the Son put himself under obligation to obey the law. Hence the Arminians conveyed a distorted gospel when they denied the imputed righteousness of Christ to believers. They may have explained how God kept believers from going to hell but not how he conferred eternal life.[18]

Edwards's last task was to relate justification to good works. Such works were necessary to justification, he averred, but they did not earn justification. They were instead expressions of faith. While "modern divines" said faith that was an expression of obedience, the reverse was true. Obedience was an expression of faith. There was a sense in which justification depended on perseverance. For perseverance is "virtually contained in that first act of faith" so that it is looked upon by God as "a property in that faith that then is." For God

---

16. WJE 19:190–91; emphasis added.

17. WJE 19:195, 186. At this point, Edwards's thinking was similar to Anselm's understanding of sin as an infinite crime requiring an infinite punishment. But while Anselm conceived of justification in terms of "external achievements made as satisfaction for sin," Edwards focused more on justification's internal basis in personal union with Christ. McGrath, *Iustitia Dei*, 95.

18. WJE 19:199, 192.

knows that by his own "divine establishment" perseverance shall inexorably follow the first act of saving faith. The believer's obedience was "connected in fact" to his or her faith. In God's eyes, the believer's faith and the believer's obedience were one and the same. Therefore it was not that justification came as a reward for obedience, but it was in consequence of justification that the believer's good deeds became rewardable. Human virtues become lovely when God sees them in Christ, clothed with his righteousness. They have a "derivative loveliness." In themselves they are corrupt; even our best duties are defiled and our holy acts are defective. If they are viewed outside of Christ, they would be infinitely hateful and would not compensate for our sins. So when saints are rewarded for their good works, it is for Christ's sake only. Nevertheless, heaven comes in some sense out of "God's regard to their obedience." The saints have a certain "moral fitness" or worthiness, but only "by reason of the worthiness of [their] head"—that is, Christ.[19]

Edwards concluded his lecture on justification by addressing some standard concerns. The apostle James's discussion of justification by works (James 2:24) does not contradict Paul's justification by faith (Rom. 5:1) because James focuses on the works that manifest true faith while Paul focuses on the faith that produces works by union with Christ. Thus Edwards said that believers are justified not only by faith but also by works. Salvation was dependent on obedience, "as if we were justified for the moral excellency of it [our obedience]." Edwards agreed with his Reformed predecessors that there are two sorts of justification, one that refers to the judge's approbation and the other to a later declarative judgment that manifests the judge's approbation. This is the difference between the justification that takes place at the present time before God's tribunal and the justification that will occur at the final judgment, before all of creation. Edwards concluded by underscoring the importance of his teaching on justification: the Arminian doctrine "takes away Christ out of the place of the bottom stone, and puts in men's own virtue in the room of him," it "magnifies man" and robs honor from God and the Mediator, and since it leads sinners to trust in their own righteousness, "it is a thing fatal to the soul."[20]

Did Edwards Depart from Reformation Principles?

Was Thomas Schafer right? Did Edwards leave behind key Reformation principles and embrace something like Thomistic or Catholic concepts in his

---

19. WJE 19:201, 208, 203, 208, 211–12, 215, 213, 216–17.
20. WJE 19:230–32, 236, 233–35, 238, 240–41.

teaching on justification? At first blush, this would not seem to be the case. Edwards was committed to the Reformation principle that faith is a virtue that stands alone:

> *Faith*, when spoken of as compared with works, or an universal and persevering obedience, it *may be said alone to be the condition of salvation*, if by "condition" we mean that which of itself, without the actual performance of the other, will, according to the tenor of the divine promise, give a man a certainty of life.[21]

As we saw in chapter 23, Edwards believed that no other Christian virtue by itself could save. Saving faith necessarily produces love, obedience, and a host of other Christian virtues, and so, when given opportunity to develop, saving faith will never stand alone. But when opportunity is lacking—as when elect infants die—faith stands alone and is the only condition for salvation. It is "naturally fit" that faith should play this unique role in salvation. For faith is "the heart's giving entertainment to Christ and the gospel." By it hearts are joined to Christ. Since only believers are united to Christ, it is "a meet thing" that "they rather than others should be received to salvation" so that "what Christ has performed should be looked upon as belonging to them." Faith joins one to Christ, and only those joined to Christ are saved. The conclusion follows that "the condition of justification...is but one, and that is faith."[22]

Edwards also displayed a Reformational insistence on the priority of grace, absolute dependence on God, and the impossibility of human merit before God. He declared that "God don't justify us [sic]...upon the account of any act of ours...but only upon the account of what the Savior did"; he stressed repeatedly that, outside of Christ, there is nothing "lovely" in us, and that "there is *no good work before conversion*." Outside of Christ, all our holy acts are infinitely hateful.[23]

Edwards's insistence on human dependence appears not only in specific statements but in the larger structures of his thinking. As Schafer points out, grace for Edwards is not the act of justification but God's influence on the will and affections to bend them toward himself in responsive love and aesthetic appreciation.[24] The thesis of *Freedom of the Will* is that every human movement

---

21. WJE 18:62; emph. added.
22. WJE 23:196; WJE 13:472–73; WJE 18:213.
23. WJE 19:212; WJE 13:475; WJE 18:155, 342, 498, 342; orig. emph.
24. Schafer, "Jonathan Edwards," 67n.

toward God is due to divine determination, not to an allegedly self-determining human will (ch. 22). *Religious Affections* and *Original Sin* argue at length that without the divinely imparted "sense of the heart," unregenerate humanity is incapable of good (ch. 20). Finally, as Paul Ramsey has observed, there are two philosophical moves that prevent Edwards from attributing merit to any act of the human will: his teaching on idealism, whereby everything exists according to God's free determination, and his doctrine of continual creation, whereby everything appearing to be substantial is in reality only the moment-by-moment recreation of what existed before (ch. 7).[25]

What is more, Edwards expressly rejected Catholic views of salvation. Like most in the Reformed tradition of the eighteenth century, he believed that the papacy was one of the twin Antichrists of his day (ch. 28). (Islam was the other.) He denounced the Roman Catholic veneration of Mary and the saints, belief in purgatory and indulgences, and other related "superstitions and idolatries" as "contrary to the light of nature."[26] He also rejected the possibility that a true believer could lose his or her salvation—a possibility that Thomas Aquinas affirmed.[27] More importantly for this chapter, Edwards rejected Aquinas's idea of "created grace" that is distinguishable from the Holy Spirit. For Edwards, the Holy Spirit in the believer does not become an intermediate principle of virtue but rather acts "after the manner" of a human principle of action (ch. 17), so that "there is nothing in the human person that is produced by, or is similar to, the Holy Spirit that mediates the Holy Spirit's presence."[28] Edwards rejected Aquinas's language regarding faith as "merit[ing]" justification, and he affirmed—as Aquinas did not—the imputation of Christ's righteousness to the believer in Christ.[29]

Yet things may not be as simple as they appear. Princeton theologian Bruce McCormack argues that what distinguishes Catholic from Reformation soteriologies is the basis or "root" of justification—the righteousness of Christ outside of us (Reformation) or the work of God within us (Catholic). We already saw this distinction at the beginning of this chapter, but its application to Aquinas and to Edwards is not so straightforward. Although Aquinas, the Catholic doctor, said faith merits justification, his use of the word "merit" was

---

25. WJE 8:742.

26. WJE 9:445.

27. Thomas Aquinas, *Summa Theologica*, 2a.24.

28. WJE 21:51.

29. Thomas Aquinas, *Summa Theologica*, 2a.2ae.2.9. See Sang Lee's "Editor's Introduction" in WJE 21:73–75.

more christological than many Protestants have thought. In the *Summa Theologica*, he stated that only Christ's passion "merited for us the grace of justification and the glory of beatitude."[30] There is nothing human beings can do to ensure that they will receive grace. Not only that, but all human preparation for grace is itself a work of God.[31] But since, for Aquinas, "the Incarnation is all about God making us more godly through Christ," in justification God works in the "essence" of our souls.[32] God reorients the soul toward "justice" so that "what is highest in man is subject to God, and the inferior powers of the soul are subject to the superior, i.e., to the reason."[33]

For McCormack, Aquinas's account of justification confused the issue of salvation and so became the material reason for the Reformation:

> The problem with Thomas, [the Reformers] would have said, lies in the fact that he makes the root of our justification to lie in what God does *in us*. But to the extent that we see our salvation as in any way contingent upon what we are or have become at a particular point in time, we shift the locus of our attention from what Luther called the 'alien righteousness of Christ' (which is complete in itself) to a work of God in us which is radically incomplete.[34]

McCormack goes on to argue that even Luther and Calvin were unable to escape a certain "Catholic" focus on God's work in us because the priority they

---

30. Thomas Aquinas, *Summa Theologica*, 3a, q.46, a.3

31. Thomas Aquinas, *Summa Theologica*, 1a2ae, q.110, a.2–3. McGrath tells us that while the early Aquinas said human beings can naturally dispose themselves towards the reception of grace, beginning with *Summa Contra Gentiles* Aquinas argued that justification is an internal divine operation, with God making the first move. The early Aquinas believed humans can achieve merit *de congruo* (imperfect acts that God rewards not by strict justice but mercy), but in his later *De Veritate* Aquinas asserted flatly that there are only demerits before justification. Elsewhere he wrote that no human merit can ever make a just claim on God, for there is too great a dissimilarity between God and man. God is in debt only to himself, as when he has ordained that he will reward his own gifts. Besides, Aquinas added, salvation was decided in God's predestinating will, without reference to any foreseen merit. McGrath, *Iustitia Dei*, 82, 86–87, 114, 134.

32. Brian Davies, *The Thought of Thomas Aquinas* (Oxford, UK: Clarendon, 1992), 337; Thomas Aquinas, *Summa Theologica*, 1a2ae, q.110, art.4.

33. Thomas Aquinas, *Summa Theologica*, 1a2ae, q.113, art.1.

34. Bruce McCormack, "What's at Stake in Current Debates over Justification: The Crisis of Protestantism in the West," in Mark Husbands and Daniel Treier, eds., *Justification: What's at Stake in the Current Debates* (Downers Grove, IL, and Leicester, UK.: InterVarsity and Apollos, 2004), 91.

gave to faith (Luther) and union with Christ (Calvin) placed regeneration before justification in logical order, and so required attention to the religious condition of the believer.[35] McCormack recommends instead focusing on "the divine act of relating to that individual in the covenant of grace."[36] Hence justification would depend not on something in the individual soul but on God's gracious decision, and would come logically prior to regeneration and as the effective cause of regeneration.

While Edwards's idealism goes part of the way toward relieving McCormack's concern by placing Christian identity in God's thoughts and not in human responses, Edwards does seem to base justification in part on what is in us. Faith, for him, is "that *in us* by which we are justified." It is a "very excellent qualification" that allows God to see it "meet that he should have Christ's merits belonging to [the saint]." We are given a title to salvation "not *directly* . . . as the reward of our obedience" since it is only by Christ's righteousness, yet we gain an "interest in that satisfaction and righteousness . . . as a reward of our obedience." God rewards the saints' "inherent righteousness" because of its "prime and only foundation"—Christ's righteousness—but the reward is also "out of regard to the saints' loveliness," which is "a secondary and derivative loveliness." Most telling is a passage on justification in the "Book of Controversies" penned about ten years after the justification lecture. There Edwards wrote that the "believer's holiness" has "a great moral value in the sight of God" and is a "secondary recommendation to and worthiness of that eternal life and happiness" that Christ has promised to bestow on believers. Here the ground of justification is twofold: "Christ's own righteousness is the primary and fundamental absolute worthiness and recommendation; the believer's inherent holiness is a secondary dependent and derivative worthiness." In sum, Edwards truly believed that Christ's righteousness was the primary ground for justification, but he also believed that what occurs in the believer is a secondary ground. With this assertion, he seems to have broken Reformation strictures against placing any dependence for justification—even "relatively or indirectly"—on faith and its related virtues.[37]

---

35. McCormack argues that the real culprit, for both Luther and Calvin, was "ancient Greek ontology," which they inherited—either Aristotelian substance or Platonic realism. Only an ontology of divine action, embedded within a forensic frame of reference, can save the Reformation's emphasis on the positive imputation of Christ's righteousness. McCormack, "What's at Stake," *passim.*

36. McCormack, "What's at Stake," 114.

37. WJE 19:154, 156, 199; emph. added; 214-15; WJE 21.367; Hunsinger, "Dispositional Soteriology," 110.

Edwards also blurred the sharp boundary that many of the Reformers had constructed between justification and sanctification. He stated that justification depends on sanctification because "obedience is the most proper condition of the covenant of grace." This means that all "the fruits of love to God and our neighbor" are conditions as well. Edwards also included repentance, "the first closing with Christ," and lifelong perseverance as conditions of justification. Perseverance is particularly important because justification has a future dimension, making it provisional until the full term of perseverance has been completed: "The actual possession of eternal benefits is suspended on a condition yet to be fulfilled: perseverance in good works."[38] While here he applied the concept of justification to a process completed only at the end of life, he also interpreted regeneration in an analogous way. In 1727, Edwards had asserted that regeneration occurs instantaneously. Yet by 1740 he suggested that regeneration is "in some respect continued through the whole life" because it is the gradual restoration of the image of God "through the whole work of the sanctification of the Spirit." He said scripture speaks of both regeneration and sanctification as "the raising the soul from the dead." Hence "regeneration... is every part of the work of sanctification," and both remain "to be performed" until the final "sentence of justification" is "passed."[39]

At one level, Edwards departed from certain ideas that have been regarded as distinctive doctrines of the Protestant Reformation. Yet on closer inspection the situation is more complicated than that, since some of the Protestant Reformers did not themselves strictly adhere to these distinctives. According to Alister McGrath, Luther did not see justification in what later became classical Protestant terms. In other words, he did *not* teach consistently: (1) that justification is a change in status not nature, a forensic declaration that the believer is righteous rather than a process of being made righteous; (2) that there is a sharp distinction between the extrinsic pronouncement of justification and the intrinsic process of regeneration and sanctification; and (3) that the formal, immediate cause of justification is the alien righteousness of Christ, imputed to humanity in justification, so that justification is a synthetic not analytic judgment by God.[40] Luther did not distinguish justification from sanctification as later Lutherans did. He treated justification as a process of

---

38. WJE 13:471, 396; WJE 23:517; WJE 13:472; WJE 18:51–52, 150–51. On Edwards's references to covenant despite being unhappy with the term, see ch. 21.

39. WJE 13:357; WJE 20:68, 71–72, 74.

40. McGrath, *Iustitia Dei*, 182.

becoming: *fieri est iustificatio*.⁴¹ Justification for Luther was a healing process that permitted God to overlook remaining sin in the believer because of God's proleptic or anticipatory knowledge of the final outcome. At this point, Luther's thinking was not unlike Edwards's notion that "God in the act of justification, which is passed on a sinner's first believing, has respect to perseverance, as being virtually contained in that first act of faith; and 'tis looked upon and taken by him that justifies, as being as it were a property in that faith that then is."⁴² For Luther, then, justification was both event and process—much as Edwards saw final justification as depending upon both regeneration and sanctification.⁴³

---

41. Martin Luther, *D. Martin Luthers Werke: Kritische Gesamtausgabe* (Weimar: H. Böhlau, 1883-), 56:442.3. The American *Works* renders this and its context as follows: "For just as there are five stages in the case of the things of nature: nonbeing, becoming, being, action, being acted upon, that is, privation, matter, form, operation, passion, according to Aristotle, so also with the Spirit: nonbeing is a thing without a name and a man in his sins; *becoming is justification*; being is righteousness; action is doing and living righteously; being acted upon is to be made perfect and complete. And these five stages in some way are *always in motion* in man. And whatever is found in the nature of man...[is] *always in movement*, namely, *becoming*, being and acting.... But from this new being, which is really a nonbeing, man proceeds and passes to another new being by being acted upon, that is, through becoming new, *he proceeds to become better, and from this again into something new*. Thus it is most correct to say that man is always in privation, *always in becoming* or in potentiality, in matter, and always in motion.... *No one is so good that he does not become better*...[Paul] adds the expression 'by the renewal' so that he should not appear to be teaching through the expression 'transformation' something of the transformation of an unstable mind or some renewal of an outward worship, but rather *renovation of the mind from day to day, more and more*, in accord with the statement in 2 Cor.4:16: 'Our inner nature is being renewed every day.'" *Lectures on Romans*, in *Luther's Works*, vol. 25, ed. Hilton C. Oswald (Saint Louis: Concordia, 1972), 434–35. See also WA 56.442.3; McGrath, *Iustitia Dei*, 200; emph. added.

42. WJE 19:203.

43. See also Paul Althaus: "Luther uses the terms 'to justify' [*justificare*] and 'justification' [*justificatio*] in more than one sense. From the beginning, justification most often means the judgment of God with which he declares man to be righteous [*justum reputare* or *computare*]. In other places, however, this word stands for the entire event through which a man is essentially made righteous (a usage which Luther also finds in Paul—e.g., Romans 5), that is, for both the imputation of righteousness to man as well as man's actually becoming righteous." Althaus, *The Theology of Martin Luther* (Philadelphia, PA: Fortress Press, 1966), 226. If Luther did not make the breaks with tradition that are often claimed, he nevertheless made some novel moves. He "introduced a decisive break with the western theological tradition as a whole by insisting that, through his justification, man is *intrinsically* sinful yet *extrinsically* righteous." He rejected the medieval notion that grace is a quality of the soul because, he argued, man cannot possess righteousness. But faith is the mark of the presence of Christ. So while grace is God's absolute favor toward an individual, external to man, faith is partial and internal. And it is the sign of the presence of Christ, whose righteousness is the believer's—yet still extrinsic. Luther also differed with Augustine methodologically by asserting that God's righteousness is revealed exclusively in the cross and that the same can be said for God's glory, wisdom, and strength. (McGrath, *Iustitia Dei*, 182, 201, 313, 195).

Tuomo Mannermaa and other Finnish scholars of Luther have come to similar conclusions. They argue that more than a century of Luther scholarship has used neo-Kantian presuppositions to divide Luther's view of the person from the work of Christ, separating justification and the real presence of Christ in faith by "the one-sidedly forensic doctrine of justification adopted by the Formula of Concord and most of subsequent Lutheranism."[44] But for Luther, they contend, the favor of God and the gift of God were united in the person of Christ. When God forgives in justification, he also confers the real presence of Christ, which means that "'sanctification'...is, in fact, only another name for the happy exchange." Justification thus involves not only forgiveness but an alteration in the believer's nature: "Luther does not hesitate to conclude that in faith the human being becomes 'God,' not in substance but through participation." There is no sharp distinction between an extrinsic pronouncement and an intrinsic process: "Christ *in nobis* is [also] Christ *extra nos*."[45]

Calvin distinguished between justification and sanctification more sharply than Luther and Edwards did, yet Calvin also referred to works as "inferior causes" of salvation and allowed that the justified could be considered righteous after justification. Edwards's position was closer to some of his Reformed predecessors from the seventeenth century. Like Edwards, Johann Heidegger, Franciscus Burman, and Marcus Wendelin spoke of a twofold justification based primarily on Christ's righteousness and secondarily on the saints' inherent righteousness. They referred to the justification of the just (or righteous) in a way that was reminiscent of Edwards. Some Reformed authors spoke of a process of growth in justification, offering a precedent for Edwards's notion that justification is both event and process.[46]

---

44. Tuomo Mannermaa, *Christ Present in Faith: Luther's View of Justification* (Minneapolis, MN: Fortress Press, 2005), 5.

45. Mannermaa, *Christ Present*, 49, 25. See also Carl Braaten and Robert Jenson, eds., *Union With Christ 1998 The New Finnish Interpretation of Luther* (Grand Rapids, MI: Eerdmans, 1998); Virpi Mäkinen, ed., *Lutheran Reformation and the Law*, Studies in Medieval and Reformation Traditions 112 (Leiden: Brill, 2006); Risto Saarinen, *God and the Gift: An Ecumenical Theology of Giving* (Collegeville, MN: The Liturgical Press 2005). McCormack faults the Finnish school for suppressing the positive imputation of Christ's righteousness and failing to realize that for Luther grace is not infused but God's personal favor. Yet Mannermaa explicitly treats the imputation of Christ's righteousness (57, *passim*). He also asserts that for Luther (as for Edwards) grace is as much God's favor as the presence of Christ himself in the believer (24–25), and that the one cannot be separated from the other (*passim*). McCormack, "What's at Stake," 95.

46. Calvin, *Institutes*, 3.14.21;3.17.9; Heinrich Heppe, *Reformed Dogmatics* (Grand Rapids, MI: Baker, 1978), 562–63.

While Edwards's account of justification thus diverged from that of some seventeenth- and eighteenth-century Reformed thinkers, it was nonetheless faithful to Luther's and Calvin's rejection of merit and their emphasis on the forensic character of justification, grounded in Christ's alien righteousness. At the same time, Edwards saw integral connections between justification and sanctification, and his enlarged conception of justification showed affinities to the thought of Thomas Aquinas, Martin Luther, and later Reformed scholastics. All in all, we have to say that Edwards was an original on justification. He felt free to reject his tradition's notion of faith as an instrument, to ignore Peter van Mastricht's insistence that Protestants never consider inward change as part of justification, and to deny Turretin's claim that works are not essential to faith.[47] To Edwards, justification necessarily involved both faith and works because of his distinctive idea of gracious dispositions. When God called someone to be joined to his Son by virtue of his Son's righteousness, that person received through the Spirit a new disposition that produced all the virtues of the Spirit. This "consenting disposition" is "called by different names." When exerted toward a savior, it is called faith or trust; when toward good things promised, it is called hope; when toward excellent persons, love; when toward commands, obedience. Therefore "the graces are all the same in principle." When one is exercised, "there is something of the other exercised with it: like strings in consort, if one is struck, others sound with it; or like links in a chain, if one is drawn, others follow." This is why faith is a "comprehensive" term for the disposition of consent to Christ that by virtue of union with Christ entails every other Christian fruit. "Evangelical obedience" is an "expression of faith." So are repentance and every other Christian virtue.[48] Justification *must* involve sanctification because the believer's salvation is one eternal act in God's mind. Christ's work outside the believer cannot be disconnected from Christ's work within the believer.

Sanctification

We have seen both in Chapter 23 and in the previous section that, for Edwards, final justification depends on sanctification. This is because "faith is a working thing"[49] and therefore will keep working until the end of life—if it is true

---

47. Calvin, *Institutes*, 734; *Westminster Confession* 9.2; Petrus van Mastricht, *Theoretico-practica theologia*, 6.6.19; Turretin, *Institutes of Elenctic Theology*, 677–79.

48. WJE 13:344–45, 458; WJE 18:220, 223; WJE 20:493; WJE 20:119; WJE 18:199.

49. Sermon on Matt. 7:21, in WJEO 45, Sermons Series II, 1729–31.

and saving faith. This is a chief way that justification depends on sanctification: the continual working of faith throughout a life of sanctification will prove that that faith is genuine. Sanctification does not merit justification but proves that the faith that closed with Christ was a living and saving faith. All such faith grows in holiness throughout one's life, and this gradual growth in holiness is sanctification.

Salvation is about works. "Men can't [be] saved for any work of theirs, and yet they ben't saved without works." This is because, as Gerstner puts it, "actions speak louder than words." For Edwards, the works that make up sanctification have probative value: they demonstrate the reality of saving faith. They are "signs of godliness." "Men will be judged at the great day by their actions, and not by the spirit of their actions." Godliness consists "not in an *heart* to purpose to fulfill God's commandments, but in an *heart* actually to do it." Works—not words—are the best evidence of faith. A life of good works is therefore the best evidence that one is justified.[50]

Another word for sanctification in the Edwardsean vocabulary is "holiness." This is the only way to heaven for four reasons. First, God is infinitely just and therefore must punish sins of believers by directing his wrath against them on the cross. They must be "purified and sanctified and made holy" because of God's just hatred for all sin. Second, it is impossible for a God of infinite holiness to "embrace in his arms a filthy, abominable creature, a hideous, detestable monster, more hateful than a toad and more poisonous than a viper." Third, "one unsanctified person" in heaven would defile it and "interrupt the happiness of the saints and angels." Finally, it is sin's nature to make a person miserable. Even if God would want to make a sinner happy in heaven "while he is wicked, the nature of the thing would not allow of it, but it would be simply and absolutely impossible."[51]

Therefore saints are always striving for perfection (ch. 4). They love to have their "ways searched" so they are not "uneasy" when a minister is "searching out [their] iniquity, and showing the evil of it." Because they are "infused" with the Holy Spirit, who is the love of God, the main principle of their hearts is love to God. As a result, they love God's law, and not just part of it. They "[take] the whole law ... [they] don't divide it, and take part, and leave part; but [they take] the whole rule." They want to be conformed to it "in every jot and tittle." They strive to be perfectly free from sin because they know that "when they arrive in heaven, they shall be perfectly free from all remains of sin." In the meantime,

---

50. Sermon on Gen. 6.22, in WJ 2:51–57; Gerstner, *Rational and Biblical Theology*, 3:229; WJE 21:471, 474, 476. Orig. emph.

51. WJE 10:474–76.

they have "yet innumerable sins hanging about 'em like so many serpents," but they know that the grace of God will clean them up before they arrive.[52]

Yet Edwards was no perfectionist. He wrote repeatedly of the failings of even the best of saints. Even godly men are "always very far from" perfect holiness. The "most holy of men" complain of the abundance of corruption they find in their hearts. Some are closer than others, but all are "exceeding remote" from the holiness they desire. The best of all the saints "have so little spiritual life and such remainders of death" that they are "dead and lifeless" compared to what "they are capable of being and to what they should be." "The most eminent saints that ever were known, have appeared very visibly to be far from" perfect holiness. They are still "sinful worms." So, while "the godly are far from actual perfection," at least they can say "they have a spirit to be perfect." It is their desire to reach perfection, and they regularly strive toward that end.[53]

Unlike "hypocrites," who refuse to deny their "dearest iniquities," the godly practice "universal obedience." They try to eliminate not only sins that cause them public embarrassment, but also sins that easily beset them but are hidden. King Saul obeyed God's commandments that were easy for him but spared Agag, his favorite. "So if men part with their sins but save only one lust that is most dear to them," they are not being sanctified. "So Joseph would not suffer his brethren to see his face unless their younger brother, the only one that was kept back, was brought." Benjamin, the younger brother, represents what the other brothers were "tender of" and so unwilling to give up (Gen. 42–44). Both Saul and Joseph's brothers represent the piety of the unregenerate, which is "deformed" and "monstrous," like Ephraim's cakes that were not turned and so baked on one side but remained raw on the other (Hos. 7:8). This piety may be very religious with its tongue but wicked with its hands; it may be honest in business, but uncharitable to the poor. But the godly are more balanced. They give up their Isaac (Gen. 22)—"that which is dearest to them of all things earthly, for God's sake." They seek victory over their secret sins. They also seek sanctification in that rarest of virtues—humility—by being "contrite" and mourning for their sins.[54]

If sanctification means universal obedience, it also means perseverance. Edwards observed in his "Signs of Godliness" notebook that this combination of universal and persevering obedience "is given in Scripture as the

---

52. WJE 19:689, 697, 695, 698.

53. WJE 19:684; WJE 22:195; WJE 19:697; Sermon on Ezek. 16:63, Sermon series II, 1736 in WJEO 51; WJE 19:697.

54. WJE 2:386; WJE 21:475, 477, 483; WJE 24:191–92; WJE 19:688; WJE 21:483; WJE 21:502.

distinguishing sign of sincerity, rather than the experience of particular exercises of soul." Perseverance through thick and thin—not spiritual experience by itself—shows true sincerity. Perseverance is "but the actual fulfillment of that which is virtually done in conversion." If there was true faith in conversion, then at that closing with Christ all the sanctification that was to come was present "virtually." The completed life of sanctification is simply the blossoming and growth of that seed planted at regeneration and conversion.[55]

Perseverance, however, sometimes includes backsliding. Saints will fall from grace, but only temporarily. They will pick themselves up again, and return after repentance to a state of grace. Some may even be tempted to suicide "under religious melancholy." But while the backslidings of the godly are not damning since they return to grace at some point, the backsliding of hypocrites is permanent and therefore the opposite of perseverance. Some commit the unpardonable sin, others apostasize from all religion or become heretics though remaining in a church, while others return to sleepiness after being awakened. Like the stony-ground hearers of Matthew 13, they receive the word of God with joy but recant as soon as tribulation comes. Saul is an example. He was given great gifts of the Spirit, but God gradually abandoned him because he never fully turned to Him.[56]

Sanctification is a life of struggle (ch. 4). If the Christian is to aspire to perfection, "there must be a continual strife and struggle." Saints won't be "easy and quiet" but will labor to clear out the filth from their souls. "If a man be hungry and has a craving after food, that appetite will do something. The man won't sit still. He'll be after food: hunger will break through a stone wall. If he be thirsty, he'll be after drink. So if it be really so that sin is a very uneasy and burdensome thing to him, he will certainly be doing a great deal against sin." Therefore he will fight sin within himself. He will not be content if "he has given his lusts very great wounds." As long as he sees any life left in those lusts, he will keep fighting them, for "he can't bear to see 'em alive." He will keep fighting until they are wholly and totally dead." His life is "as it were bloodthirsty towards sin."[57]

It is not only this struggle against sin but also perseverance through life's difficulties that prove the authenticity of faith. God sends trials to "discover whether [saints'] goodness be of the lasting sort." Of course, God already

---

55. WJE 21:475–76.

56. WJE 4:393; sermon on Ps. 78:36–37; sermon on 1 Sam 28:15, Sermons Series II, 1733, WJEO 48.

57. WJE 19:696, 701, 687–88.

knows the outcome of the trial, "but he proves them that he may thereby determine before their consciences and before the world as a judge." These difficulties, and the test of saints' perseverance in faith through them, show "whether the righteousness which they perform at other times will hold" in times of great difficulty. Sickness is one of those difficulties that God uses to "chasten" his saints, especially "after he has tried other methods of Instruction in vain as Elihu takes notice (Job 33.14)." God will sometimes hide himself from saints when they have fallen into "shameful declension" and calls on them to "reflect" with the "Greatest lamentation," "brokenness of heart" and "deepest humiliation of soul." When God sends "publick judgments" to a people, the saints will suffer those judgments along with the world around them if they have "partaken" of the same sins. But while the world will suffer those judgments to their evil, God will use those same sufferings toward the final good of the saints.[58]

Some of those sufferings will be persecution for true faith. In a gruesome recounting of saints' suffering for faith, Edwards told stories of Christians who during the reign of "the last French king in his persecution of the Protestants" were roasted on a spit but taken away before they could be relieved by death. He spoke of others in Christian history who were "scalded to death by hot iron plates" or "had their flesh torn off from their bones with burning hot iron pincers." Then there were those in the "tenth heathen persecution" who were scourged until their "muscles and sinews" were laid bare and then rubbed with salt and vinegar, and those among the Waldensians whose noses and ears and cheeks were cut off. Catholics forced them into the snow to die while "Jesuits took possession of their houses and feasted themselves with the spoil of their cattle and provisions." Edwards told story after story of cruel persecutions by Catholics of Protestants in Poland, Lithuania, Hungary and Bohemia for the purpose of showing that "the worst evils that the power of men can inflict are as nothing in comparison of damnation."[59]

Perhaps because of the severity of these trials, saints need to be newly converted over and over. Sanctification is a lifelong series of new conversions. In a 1740 sermon Edwards preached, "Those that have true grace in their hearts may yet stand in great need of being converted." Peter was already converted when, in Luke 22:32, Jesus told him he had prayed for his faith not to fail so that "when thou art converted, [you might] strengthen thy brethren." Paul,

---

58. WJE 21:480, 475; sermon on Luke 4:38, Sermon Series II, 1739, WJEO 54; sermon on 1 Kings 11:9, Sermon Series II, 1737, WJEO 52; sermon on Ezek 7:16, Sermon Series II, 1723–27, WJEO 42.

59. Sermon on Luke 12:4–5, Sermon Series II, 1731–32, WJEO 47.

"though so eminent a saint" after his Damascus Road conversion, still sought "conversion, or a spiritual resurrection" many years later, "as though he had not yet attained it (Phil. 3:11–12)." All the godly need new conversions because they become carnal from time to time. "Good seed is [often] overgrown with weeds." This is why scripture speaks sometimes of regeneration as "only the first saving work of God upon the soul, which is wrought in an instant," but at other times "as a continued thing." For while the Bible speaks of conversion as a new creation, it says the same of sanctification: "In every step and degree of that restoration, something is brought out of nothing." All the death that came upon the soul when it died in the fall is removed in the spiritual resurrection in Christ, but "that resurrection is not finished till the soul is thoroughly and completely sanctified." Sanctification is therefore "one work of renovation" from "the first dawning of grace in the soul until death."[60]

Thus we come full circle in Edwards's vision of salvation. It starts with the divine and supernatural light in regeneration, proceeds logically and sometimes temporally to conversion, and moves on with repeated conversions through a lifelong process of sanctification—which can be described as a continued regeneration. This is why Edwards insisted that justification depends on sanctification while also being a sovereign act of God that is not merited by human works. It is also why Edwards advised God's saints to listen to everything said to the unregenerate, for "there is but little that is said in sermons to natural men but what godly men may very properly hear for themselves."[61] Since all of Christian life consists of new conversions, even the saints need new illuminations and infusions to repent and believe ever anew.

---

60. WJE 22:194, 184, 189–91.
61. WJE 22:199.

26
The Theme of Divinization

SCHOLARS HAVE LONG recognized that certain elements in Edwards's theology were in tension with traditional Calvinism. Jaroslav Pelikan, a world authority on the history of Christian thought and a late-life convert to Eastern Orthodoxy, made reference to the affinities between Edwards's theology and the Orthodox doctrine of divinization, also referred to as deification.[1] Some Calvinists—though pleased with Edwards's treatment of grace, predestination, and free will—have been troubled by his affirmations of continuity between the Creator and creatures. Charles Hodge wrote that Edwards's *Original Sin* made "God...the only substance in the universe," leading to a theology that was essentially pantheistic."[2] Others have used softer terms, such as "mysticism" or "Platonism," to describe an aspect of Edwards's thought that is allegedly alien to, and in tension with, his doctrinal Calvinism. *Religious Affections* used three images to describe the relation of believers to God—the shining forth of light, the flowing of water from a fountain, and a branch that draws sap from a tree trunk. George Claghorn commented that "sometimes Edwards's enthusiasm leads him to use language that was easily misinterpreted."[3] In this chapter, we will once again consider the question of Edwards's Protestant credentials (ch. 25), yet examine this issue from the angle of divine-human unity and the doctrine of divinization.

At first blush, the thesis of Edwards's 1738 treatise on justification was impeccably Protestant: "We are justified only by faith in Christ, and not by any manner of virtue or goodness of our own." Yet Thomas Schafer found that

---

1. Pelikan wrote: "The definition of salvation as deification was not confined during this period—any more than it had been in earlier periods—to Eastern Orthodox theologians.... Jonathan Edwards repeatedly quoted 2 Peter 1:4 to prove that 'the grace which is in the hearts of the saints is of the same nature with the divine holiness,' adding the proviso that this would be only 'as much as 'tis possible for that holiness to be, which is infinitely less in degree'" (*The Christian Tradition: A History of the Development of Doctrine; Volume Five: Christian Doctrine and Modern Culture*; Chicago: University of Chicago Press, 1989; 161).

2. Charles Hodge, *Systematic Theology*, 2 vols. (New York: Scribner, Armstrong & Co., 1873), 2:219.

3. George Claghorn in WJE 8:633; citing WJE 2:200–201, 343, 347.

certain elements of Edwards's argument "cause the doctrine of justification to occupy an ambiguous and somewhat precarious place in his theology." He taught that the soul became acceptable to God only in and through its union with God, which is the proper "ground" of justification: "What is real in the union between Christ and his people, is the foundation of what is legal." Faith was related to justification only because it "is the soul's active uniting with Christ, or is itself the very act of unition." Faith was not the only "condition" of justification, in the ordinary meaning of "condition" as "that...without which...a thing shall not be."[4] The "agreeing or consenting disposition" toward God could be variously understood as faith, belief, hope, obedience, or love, and Edwards laid special emphasis on love. Schafer commented that "the reader cannot help feeling that the conception of 'faith alone' has been considerably enlarged—and hence practically eliminated."[5] The stress on actual union rather than legal imputation, the relative de-emphasis on faith per se, and the presentation of love and obedience as intrinsic to faith, established an affinity between Edwards's teaching on justification and that of Roman Catholic and Orthodox theologies (chs. 25, 43).

For Anri Morimoto, a Catholic aspect of Edwards needs to be acknowledged alongside the other elements of his thought. For the "Protestant concern" that "salvation was totally dependent on the sovereign activity of God" and derived from "God's immediate and continual activity from above" was combined with a "Catholic concern" that "the transformative power of grace effectuates in human nature a real and qualitative change" so that "regenerate persons enjoy an abiding reality of salvation within them." Thus Edwards's "vision of human salvation can...offer today's Protestant theology reliable help in reformulating and revitalizing its own understanding of salvation, without forcing it to surrender or compromise its genuine Protestant concerns."[6] What Morimoto called the "Catholic concern" was no extraneous addition but is woven throughout Edwards's writings in unitive images of God within humanity and humanity within God. In Edwards's first publication, the sermon "God Glorified in Man's Dependence," one finds clear expressions of both the "Protestant concern" for dependence on God and the "Catholic concern" for the abiding reality of salvation. Edwards speaks of the "absolute and universal dependence of the redeemed on God for all their good," and yet

---

4. Thomas Schafer, "Jonathan Edwards and Justification By Faith," *Church History* 20 (1951): 56–63; citing WJE 19:149, 158, 152.

5. Schafer, "Jonathan Edwards and Justification," 60; citing WJE 13:344–45.

6. Anri Morimoto, *Jonathan Edwards and the Catholic Vision of Salvation* (University Park, PA: Pennsylvania State University Press, 1995), 7–8, 2.

he adds that the saints "have spiritual excellency and joy by a kind of participation" and so are "made partakers of God's holiness."[7]

A.N. Williams identified the defining features in the Orthodox teaching on divinization or deification as follows:

> Where we find references to human participation in divine life, there we assuredly have a claim specifically of theosis... to be distinguished, however, from the idea of divine indwelling in the human person. Both schemes of sanctification draw on the notion of union, but whereas the latter locates sanctification within the creature and *in via*, the former locates it at the level of the divine and insists on the inseparability of life *in via* and *in patria*. A second infallible marker of the doctrine, then, is the union of God and humanity, when this union is conceived as humanity's incorporation into God, rather than God's into humanity, and when conceived as the destiny of humanity generally rather than the extraordinary experience of the few.

"Deification," in summary, "focuses not on humanity, but on the God who invites humanity to share divine life."[8] While Orthodoxy has always insisted that creatures cannot share in the divine *essence*, it pointed to a New Testament text regarding the possibility of participation in the divine *nature*: "Whereby are given unto us exceeding great promises: that by these ye might be partakers of the divine nature" (2 Pet. 1:4; AV). This verse played a key role in the development of the doctrine of divinization in Eastern Christianity. Edwards himself quoted and commented on it in the *Miscellanies* (as early as 1735–36), *Charity and its Fruits*, an "Unpublished Letter on Assurance and Participation in the Divine Nature," the *Discourse on the Trinity*, and the *Treatise on Grace*, where he writes that "being 'partakers of the divine nature' is spoken of as the peculiar privilege of true saints."[9]

---

7. WJE 17:202, 208.

8. A. N. Williams, *The Ground of Union: Deification in Aquinas and Palamas* (New York: Oxford University Press, 1999), 32, 36.

9. WJE 18:245–48, 48; WJE 8:67, 80 n.4, 132–33 [with n.1], 158; WJE 8:631–40; WJE 21:122, 129, 155–56, 194–95; citing WJE 21:155–56. In the "Unpublished Letter on Assurance and Participation in the Divine Nature," Edwards cites both 2 Pet. 1:4 and Heb. 12:10, which refers to believers as "partakers of his [i.e. God's] holiness" (WJE 8:639–40). Paul Ramsey judged that Edwards relied on 2 Pet. 1:4 in his distinctive use of the term "nature" when he wrote that the Spirit communicates his "proper nature" to the saints (WJE 8:133, n.1).

The Neoplatonic Background to Edwards

While Edwards's teaching on divinization showed resemblances to the views of patristic and later Orthodox authors, there is no evidence that Edwards had access to their writings.[10] Instead Edwards's teaching on divinization should be understood against the backdrop of Renaissance and early modern Neoplatonism, and specifically the writings of the seventeenth-century Cambridge Platonists.[11] Beginning with their founding figure, Benjamin Whichcote, these English writers used and defended the term "deification," made the idea central in their reflections, and appealed to the biblical verse noted in the previous section—2 Peter 1:4—in defending their teaching.[12] John Smith captured the idea of divinization when he wrote that "God is the First Truth and Primitive Goodness: True Religion is a vigorous Efflux and Emanation of Both upon the Spirits of men, and therefore is called a participation of the divine Nature."[13] John Smith's *Select Discourses* (1660) and Ralph Cudworth's *True Intellectual System of the Universe* (1678) were both cited in Edwards's writings and also included in his *Catalogue* of reading.[14] Edwards's interest in Ralph Cudworth focused on the foreshadowing of Christian beliefs in pre-Christian

---

10. Patricia Wilson-Kastner, in "God's Infinity and His Relationship to Creation in the Theologies of Gregory of Nyssa and Jonathan Edwards," *Foundations* 21 (1978): 305–21, discussed Gregory of Nyssa's *On the Soul and Resurrection* as a backdrop to Edwards's *End of Creation*, and yet admitted that we have "no reason to believe" that Edwards ever read Gregory of Nyssa (310–11), and suggested the Cambridge Platonists as the connecting link between Edwards and Neoplatonism (317).

11. On the Cambridge Platonists, see Ernst Cassirer, *The Platonic Renaissance in England*, trans. James E. Pettegrove (Austin, TX: University of Texas Press, 1953); C.A. Patrides, ed., *The Cambridge Platonists* (Cambridge, MA: Harvard University Press, 1970); G.P.H. Pawson, *The Cambridge Platonists and Their Place in Religious Thought* (London: SPCK, 1930); Frederick J. Powicke, *The Cambridge Platonists: A Study* (Cambridge, MA: Harvard University Press, 1926); G.A.J. Rogers, et al., eds., *The Cambridge Platonists in Philosophical Context* (Dordrecht, Holland: Kluwer, 1997).

12. Patrides writes that "the deification of man is one of the most thoroughly Greek ideas espoused by the Cambridge Platonists" (Patrides, *Cambridge Platonists*, 19). When Benjamin Whichcote used the term "deification," he added: "Do not stumble at the use of *the Word*. For, we have Authority for the use of it, in Scripture. 2 Pet. 1.4. *Being made Partakers of the Divine Nature*; which is in effect our *Deification*" (cited in Patrides, *Cambridge Platonists*, 70). All italics in quotations in this chapter are original. See also Edmund Newey, "The Form of Reason: Participation in the Work of Richard Hooker, Benjamin Whichcote, Ralph Cudworth, and Jeremy Taylor," *Modern Theology* 18 (2002): 1–26.

13. Patrides, *Cambridge Platonists*, 148; citing John Smith, *Select Discourses* (Delmar, NY: Scholars's Facsimiles & Reprints, 1979 [1660]), IX, "The Excellency and Nobleness of True Religion."

14. WJE 26:281–82, 269–70, 273–74, 292, 300, 315. See also Peter Thuesen's comments on Edwards's reading of Cudworth in WJE 26:40, 48–49, 68.

religions (ch. 36). Yet John Smith may have been especially pertinent for Edwards's teaching on divinization. Passages in Smith's *Select Discourses* anticipate the argument and even the phrasing of Edwards's *End of Creation*.[15] Edwards's notebooks also make it clear that he read Henry More in his early years, and that he shared with him and other Cambridge Platonists a deep aversion to materialistic philosophy. Edwards sought to turn the tables on materialistic philosophy by asserting that "spirit" is "substance," and "matter" only a "shadow" in comparison (ch. 7).

Through the centuries, many Christian thinkers perceived an affinity between Neoplatonism and biblical teaching. Yet Neoplatonism showed conflicting tendencies in conceiving of God's relation to the world. Plato wrote that "the framer of this universe of change was good, and what is good has no particle of envy in it; being therefore without envy he wished all things to be as like himself as possible." There was a broad movement in Plato's thought toward some idea of divinization, with the first principle seeking to make all other things "as like himself as possible." Yet, as D.W. Dockrill notes, "often associated with this teaching is a doctrine of divine transcendence in which the governing principle of reality, the Good, is said to be so different from the realities it governs, that it cannot be accurately described in terms appropriate to mind at all." In *The Republic*, Socrates stated that "the Form of the Good" is "the cause of knowledge and truth; and so, while you may think of it as an object of knowledge, you will do well to regard it as something beyond truth and knowledge." It is "even beyond being, surpassing it in dignity and power." Plotinus wrote concerning the first principle: "There is no name that suits it really. But, since name it we must, it may appropriately be called 'one', on the understanding, however, that it is not a substance...[and] difficult to know."[16] Some seventeenth-century English Platonists—including Thomas Jackson, Robert Greville, and Peter Sterry—agreed with Plotinus in conceiving of "the One" as transcending mind and thought. Yet Cambridge Platonists Henry

---

15. Consider the following statements from John Smith, *Select Discourses*: "God does most *glorifie* and exalt himself in the most triumphant way that may be *ad extra* or out of himself...when he most of all communicates himself....And we then most of all *glorifie* him when we partake most of him" (142). "All true Happiness consists in a participation of God arising out of the assimilation and conformity of our souls to him" (147). "The Divinity could propound nothing to it self in the making of the World but the *Communication* of its own *Love* and *Goodness*" (155).

16. D. W. Dockrill, "The Heritage of Patristic Platonism in Seventeenth Century English Philosophical Theology," in Rogers, *Cambridge Platonists*, 56; citing Plato, *The Timaeus*; trans. H.D.P. Lee (Harmondsworth, UK: Penguin Books, 1965) 29e (42); Plato, *The Republic*, trans. F.M. Cornford (Oxford: Clarendon Press, 1951) 508e, 509b (215); and Plotinus, *Enneads* 6.9.5, in *The Essential Plotinus*, trans. E. O'Brien (New York: New American Library, 1964), 80.

More and Ralph Cudworth dissented. Cudworth rejected this "one *Peculiar Arcanum* of the *Platonick* and *Pythagorick* Theology." For if the One transcends the realm of knowledge, then Neoplatonism becomes "a certain kind of *Mysterious Atheism*." The ultimate principle of all things would be as "devoid of Mind and Understanding" as "*Sensless* [sic] *Matter*."[17]

Neoplatonists of all eras generally regarded the physical body as an impediment to the soul. Henry More wrote that the "*Soul of every man... is his individual Person*," and this means that "the Body is not sensible of anything," as was taught by the "best sort of Philosophers." Another author of the period, Henry Hallywell, commented that man has "a double life within him, *Intellectual* and *Animal*, which the Sacred Writings call *Flesh* and *Spirit*."[18] For Neoplatonists, it was the "intellectual" and not the "animal" existence that formed the human point of contact with God. Henry More's account of bodily life laid emphasis on the soul's misery while in its terrestrial state. In the physical world, the soul is "hoppled and fettered, clouded and obscured by her fatal residence in this prison of the Body," and "so deeply and muddily immersed into Matter, as to keep company with Beasts, by vitall union with gross flesh and bones."[19] While denigrating the body, the English Neoplatonists extolled the soul and affirmed its spiritual and intellectual prerogatives. Henry More wrote that the soul is "the *Image* of *God*, as the *Rays* of light are of the *Sun*." More taught that the doctrine of the pre-existence of souls had "plausible Reasons for it, and nothing considerable to be alleged against it." Ralph Cudworth did not go quite so far and yet said it was clear that God "intended and designed" our souls "for other *Bodies* and other *Regions*."[20]

Dockrill observed that "Orthodox Christian teaching is that the soul is a created entity; for Plato and Plotinus it belongs to the divine order." This disparity created a tension for Christian Platonists. The theological issue was that of nature and grace. Plato and Plotinus attributed far more to the human soul by nature than was taught in the Bible, namely, a divine or quasi-divine

---

17. Dockrill, "Heritage," 58; citing Ralph Cudworth, *The True Intellectual System of the Universe* (London, 1678), 584, 587.

18. Dockrill, "Heritage," 60; citing Henry More, *An Explanation of the Grand Mystery of Godliness* (London, 1660) 223; and Henry Hallywell, *Deus Justificatus* (London: W. Kettilby, 1668), 260.

19. Dockrill, "Heritage," 62; citing More, *The Immortality of the Soul* (London: W Morden, 1659) 332, 309, 488, 330.

20. Dockrill, "Heritage," 64, 67, 68; citing More, *An Explanation of the Grand Mystery of Godliness*, 22; Cudworth, *True Intellectual System*, 798, cf. 43–44, 66; and More, "The Preface General," and *Conjectura Cabbalistica*, in *A Collection of Several Philosophical Writings* (1662), 1:v, 2:3.

status. Among the critics of the English Neoplatonists was Edward Stillingfleet, who inveighed against those who thought of the soul as "a Particle not of Matter, but of the Divine Nature it self, a little Deity in a Cottage, that stays here a-while, and returns to that upper Region from whence it came."[21] In their stress on divine transcendence, Plato and Plotinus seemed to deny to the soul what, according to Christian teaching, is possible in and through divine grace—namely a direct participation in God. Furthermore, the Neoplatonic disparagement of the body suggested that even if communion with God were possible, this could occur only through the soul or reason, and not by means of the body and its affections. Edwards, though drawing on the British Neoplatonic tradition, modified this tradition by affirming a direct human participation in God that involved soul and body alike. In his revival writings, he acknowledged that bodily manifestations might indicate God's presence in the believer (ch. 42).

Divinization as External—God's Transforming Light

Edwards's teaching on divinization rested on a number of key ideas—a notion of "divine light" that conformed human beings to God's character, an immediacy of contact and connection between God and humanity in the state of grace, a distinction between spiritual experience and the divine "essence," and a notion of unceasing spiritual development in this life and the next. Remarkably enough, each of these ideas was paralleled in the writings of Gregory Palamas (c. 1296–1359), the best-known Orthodox author on the theme of divinization.[22]

Edwards wrote at length of the "divine light" in one of his best-known sermons, which bears the full title, "A Divine and Supernatural Light, Immediately Imparted to the Soul by the Spirit of God, Shown to be both a Scriptural, and Rational Doctrine" (1734).[23] The manner in which he wrote of the divine light suggested that it was a particular mode of God's presence:

---

21. Dockrill, "Heritage," 61; citing More, *Immortality of the Soul*, 500; and Edward Stillingfleet, *Origines Sacrae* (London: H. & G. Mortlock, 1709 [1662]) 263.

22. See Michael J. McClymond, "Salvation as Divinization: Jonathan Edwards, Gregory Palamas, and the Theological Uses of Neoplatonism," in Paul Helm and Oliver D. Crisp, eds., *Jonathan Edwards: Philosophical Theologian* (London: Ashgate, 2003), esp. 144–50. On Palamas himself, see Gregory Palamas, *The Triads* (New York: Paulist Press, 1983); and the secondary works by John Meyendorff, *A Study of Gregory Palamas* (Crestwood, NY: St. Vladimir's Seminary Press, 1998) and Georgios I. Mantzaridis, *The Deification of Man: St. Gregory Palamas and the Orthodox Tradition* (Crestwood, NY: St. Vladimir's Seminary Press, 1984).

23. WJE 17:405–26.

"There is no gift or benefit that is in itself so nearly related to the divine nature, there is nothing the creature receives that is so much of God, of his nature, so much a participation of the Deity: 'tis a kind of emanation of God's beauty, and is related to God as light is to the sun." The adjectives "divine" and "supernatural," in the phrase "divine and supernatural light," also intimate that this "light" is a direct manifestation of God. Edwards's "divine light" recalled Palamas's "divine energies." Though logically distinct from God's essential being, it was not separable in practice or function. Edwards taught that the divine light transformed the human self into conformity with itself: "This light is such as effectually influences the inclination, and changes the nature of the soul. It assimilates the [human] nature to the divine nature, and changes the soul into an image of the same glory that is beheld." Edwards's sermon on the divine light made reference to the Transfiguration of Jesus and linked it with the coming Kingdom: "If Christ should now appear to anyone as he did on the mount at his transfiguration; or if he should appear to the world in the glory that he now appears in in heaven, as he will do at the day of judgment; without doubt, the glory and majesty that he would appear in, would be such as would satisfy everyone, that he was a divine person."[24]

Edwards wrote of the divine light that "'tis no impression upon the mind, as though one saw anything with the bodily eyes," and yet he qualified this by saying: "'Tis not intended that the natural faculties are not made use of in it [i.e., the divine light]. The natural faculties are the subject of this light: and they are the subject in such a manner, that they are not merely passive, but active in it; the acts and exercises of man's understanding are concerned and made use of in it." This light was something that involved the natural faculties and yet transcended them. For Edwards, faith in its very nature was a kind of seeing, and this was true not only for the spiritual elite but for all genuine believers in Christ (ch. 10). In the "Divine Light" sermon, Edwards stated that "God is the author of all knowledge and understanding whatsoever," and yet most forms of human knowledge were communicated through intermediary means. "But this spiritual knowledge, spoken of in this text, is what God is the author of, and none else: he reveals it, and flesh and blood reveals it not. He imparted this knowledge immediately, not making use of any intermediate causes, as he does in other knowledge." Unlike other forms of knowledge, this kind derived immediately from God and was not based on ordinary sense experience. When Edwards spoke of the divine light, he also often spoke of the Holy Spirit. For Edwards, the Spirit did not merely come alongside believers

---

24. WJE 17:422, 424, 420.

but became intimately united to them (ch. 17) "as a new, supernatural principle of life and action."[25]

An intriguing parallel between Edwards and the Orthodox thinker Gregory Palamas related to a debate over the divine "essence." Barlaam of Calabria—Palamas's opponent—objected that the Hesychast monks whom Palamas defended spoke as though they had a direct vision of, or communion with, the divine essence. Yet this was impossible, said Barlaam. Palamas responded by distinguishing the "essence" of God—inaccessible to mere creatures—from the "energy" of God, which was available and had a gracious and transformative effect. Palamas stated that "the divine and deifying illumination and grace is not the essence but the energy of God."[26] A fragmentary letter by Jonathan Edwards embodied Edwards's response to the same objection—that he was teaching that believers participate in the divine essence:

> As to my saying that the Spirit of God in his saving operation communicates himself to the soul in his own proper nature, implying, as you suppose, God's communicating his essence.... By his proper nature I don't mean his essence; and have also declared particularly what I do mean, viz. that by the Spirit of God's communicating himself in his proper nature, I mean communicating something of his holiness...A diamond or crystal that is held forth in the sun's beams may properly be said to have some of the sun's brightness communicated to it; for though it hasn't the same individual brightness with that which is inherent in the sun, and be immensely less in degree, yet it is something of the same nature.[27]

In this letter, Edwards discussed the term "nature" at some length and indicated that it carried a range of meanings and need not be taken as synonymous with "essence." Edwards denied that believers are ever able to participate in the divine essence: "Not that the saints are made partakers of the essence of God, and so are 'Godded' with God, and 'Christed' with Christ, according to the abominable and blasphemous language and notions of some heretics." Instead, they were "made partakers of... God's spiritual beauty and happiness,

---

25. WJE 17:412, 416, 409, 411.

26. Vladimir Lossky, *The Mystical Theology of the Eastern Church* (London: James Clarke, 1957), 70; citing Gregory Palamas, *Capita physica, theologica, moralia, et practica*, 69.

27. The letter is in WJE 8:636–40, with George Claghorn's "Introduction" in WJE 8:631–35, and citing WJE 8:638, 640. The statements evoking the objection are from *Religious Affections* (WJE 2:201, 233, 236–37).

according to the measure and capacity of a creature."[28] When Edwards wrote that "God communicates himself to the soul in his own proper nature," it is clear, as George Claghorn says, that "God's power, light, and love have gone forth, not his essence."[29]

Another theme in Edwards's teaching on divinization was continual spiritual progress. This progress occurred not only on earth but in heaven: "Heaven is a progressive state." The idea is not limited to *End of Creation* (ch. 14). It cropped up repeatedly in the *Miscellanies* and in sermons, and Paul Ramsey devoted an extensive appendix to it.[30] As early as 1730, Edward had written of the church in heaven that "much of their happiness has consisted in seeing the progressive wonderful doings of God with respect to his church here in this world."[31] Because redemptive history progresses here on earth, Edwards reasoned that the church in heaven must also progress, as well, by means of a kind of "beatific vision" of divine providence on earth (chs. 15, 19). All creatures are changeable by nature, and while heaven "is subject to no evil changes, yet 'tis subject to great changes and revolutions of the contrary nature.... 'Tis only God that is unchangeable. The whole universe consisting in upper and lower worlds is in a changing state."[32] In Edwards's *Religious Affections*, every new vision of God led to a still greater desire for more: "Another great and very distinguishing difference between gracious affections and others is, that gracious affections, the higher they are raised, the more is a spiritual appetite and longing of soul after spiritual attainments, increased. On the contrary, false affections rest satisfied in themselves."[33] Divinization proceeded through an endless interplay of spiritual desire and the divine satisfaction of desire. Divinization was ceaseless.

Divinization as Internal—Sharing God's Being, Knowledge, and Happiness

Now we turn to the question, "How precisely does God incorporate human beings within his inner, divine life?" One way is through the knowledge of God. For Edwards, the creatures' knowledge of God *is* divinization. In one

---

28. WJE 2:203.
29. Claghorn, in WJE 8:632.
30. Ramsey, "Appendix III: Heaven is a Progressive State," in WJE 8:706–38.
31. WJE 13:478.
32. WJE 18:497–98.
33. WJE 2:376.

of Edwards's sermons, he noted that "the Beatifical vision will be an act of love in God" involving the full participation of each person of the Trinity together with each beatified saint, who:

> .... enjoy God as *partaking* with Christ of his enjoy[ment] of God, for they are united with him and are Glorified and made happy in the enjoyment of God as his members...They being in Christ shall *partake* of the love of God the Father to Christ, and as the Son knows the Father, so they shall *partake with him in his sight of God* as being as it were parts with him. As he is in the bosom of the Father, so are they in the bosom of the Father.

The saints share in intra-divine relationships within the Godhead in multiple ways. They "*partake* of the love of God the Father to Christ," and yet also "*partake with him* [i.e., Christ] *in his sight of God*." Again Edwards writes, "So we being members of the Son, are *partakers in our measure of the Father's love to the Son*."[34] Thus the saints partake in both the Son's love of the Father and the Father's love of the Son. Paul Ramsey noted that "the participation is a partaking of the three persons' very own participation in one another within the divine life."[35] What was preeminently true of heavenly saints was also true of earthly saints. Their knowledge of God and love for God were a form of participation in God's inner life.

Ramsey explained that, for Edwards, "God's knowledge of himself is the only knowledge of God there is." That is, the creature knows God by sharing in God's self-knowledge. Ramsey continued: "So if there is knowledge of God communicated to any human understanding, this is God's very own knowledge of himself, for that happens to be the only knowledge of God there is in heaven or on earth. If there is any love to God enkindled in any human will, this must be God's own love spread abroad in human hearts. If there is in human affections any happiness, joy, and delight in God, this must be God's own felicity communicated by us." The genitive expressions like "love of God," or "knowledge of God," can of course have two meanings—our love of God, or God's love for us. Yet according to Edwards these are "but one and the same thing."[36] What God communicates to creatures is happiness as well as knowledge. God's shares his own happiness, which is the happiness of God's

---

34. Ramsey in WJE 8:725, 736.

35. Ramsey in WJE 8:735; orig. emph. in these quotations.

36. Ramsey, in WJE 8:19–20.

"enjoying in rejoicing in himself" so that both God and the creature together rejoice in God.[37]

According to Edwards, human beings shared in God's life through the power of the Holy Spirit. The Holy Spirit worked differently in saints than in others: "He acts in the mind of a saint as an indwelling vital principle.... He unites himself with the mind of a saint, takes him for his temple, actuates and influences him as a new, supernatural principle of life and action." Edwards spoke of the "proper nature" of the Holy Spirit expressed in the thoughts and actions of the saints. "The Spirit of God, in acting in the soul of a godly man, exerts and communicates himself there in his own proper nature. Holiness is the proper nature of the Spirit of God. The Holy Spirit operates in the minds of the godly, by uniting himself to them, and living in them, and exerting his own nature in the exercise of their faculties."[38] This is divinization—seen from the human side. The Holy Spirit's life, so to speak, includes the sanctified thoughts, affects, and actions of the saints.

Strange as it may sound, Edwards viewed divinization as based on God's self-regard. As early as *The Mind*, he wrote that God's "love to the creature is...according as they partake more or less of excellence and beauty...that is, according as he communicates more or less of his Holy Spirit."[39] What God loves in the creature is his own reflection. In *End of Creation*, the reason that God's self-regard and his regard for creatures are not "entirely distinct" is that the latter are, in some measure, an extension of God's own life and fullness. So God's love for his own holiness and goodness is not separate from his love for the holiness and goodness of creatures. While this may make God seem like Narcissus—the figure of ancient Greek mythology who fell in love with his own reflection—Edwards argued in *End of Creation* that God's regard for what is best and highest requires God to have highest regard for himself. What is more, in the case of God—unlike that of any creature—there is no opposition between a proper self-regard and an outgoing, overflowing regard for others (ch. 14).

End of Creation tells us that "elect creatures" are "brought home to him, united with him, centering most perfectly in him, and as it were swallowed up in him: so that his respect to them finally coincides and becomes one and the same with respect to himself." Here Edwards cites John 17:21, 23—a rich text

---

37. WJE 8:442.
38. WJE 17:411.
39. WJE 6:364.

on the mutual indwelling of God in Christ, Christ in God, believers in God, believers in Christ, and believers in one another: "That they all may be *one*, as thou Father art in me, and I in thee, that they also may be one in us, I in them and thou in me, that they may be made perfect in *one*."[40] This teaching on divinization closely followed the language in the Gospel of John and Epistles of John regarding the mutual indwelling of God and believers—designated by theologians as the doctrine of perichoresis or circumincession.

In one of the most striking passages in *End of Creation*, Edwards states that God is not "complete" apart from the world:

> This propensity in God to diffuse himself may be considered as a propensity to himself diffused, or to his own glory existing in its emanation.... Thus that nature in a tree, by which it puts forth buds, shoots out branches, and brings forth leaves and fruit, is a disposition that terminates in its own complete self. And so the disposition in the sun to shine, or abundantly to diffuse its fullness, warmth and brightness, is only a tendency to its own most glorious and complete state. So God looks on the communication of himself, and the emanation of infinite glory and good that are in himself to belong to the fullness and completeness of himself, as though he were not in his most complete and glorious state without it. Thus the church of Christ (toward whom and in whom are the emanations of his glory and communications of his fullness) is called the fullness of Christ: as though he were not in his complete state without her; as Adam was in a defective state without Eve.[41]

Here Edwards construes creation as an act that expands and enhances God's own being. There is continuity between Creator and creation: "God's external glory is only the emanation of his internal glory." In discussing his image of God as a "fountain," Edwards writes that "the communication itself...is something divine, something of God, something of his internal fullness; as the water in the stream is something of the fountain; and as the beams are of the sun." Paul Ramsey commented that *"pleroma*, the fullness" or "partaking of the divine nature" were the ideas that "clinch the argument of *End of Creation*."[42]

---

40. WJE 8:443; orig. emph.

41. WJE 8:439–40.

42. WJE 8:529, 531, 70.

Another way in which God incorporates creatures into the inner divine life is through a kind of expanding family relationship. In an early notebook entry, Edwards wrote: "God created the world for his Son, that he might prepare a spouse or bride for him to bestow his love upon; so that the mutual joys between this bride and bridegroom are the end of creation."[43] Another entry spoke of Eve as a type of the church in which the church is said to be the "fullness or completeness" of Christ.[44] Edwards develops his theme of family relationship in a number of different images, and all these images reduce the chasm between the divine and the human realms: "In heaven all shall be nearly related. They shall be nearly allied to God, the supreme object of their love; for they shall be his children. And all shall be nearly related to Christ; for he shall be the Head of the whole society, and husband of the whole church of saints. All together shall constitute his spouse, and they shall be related one to another as brethren. It will all be one society, yea, one family."[45] The theme is fully developed in Edwards's writings on heaven (ch. 19).

As the preceding exposition has shown, Edwards taught a doctrine of divinization. The only thing missing is the word itself, although, as we have shown, Edwards employed a rich vocabulary of terms and phrases such as "communication," "emanation," "participation," "partaking," and "uniting" to describe the divine-human communion from either God's side or the creature's. Edwards referred to creatures as "of," "in," and "to" God; believers as "swallowed up" in God; the church as the "fullness" or "completeness" of Christ; and the world as God "himself diffused" or the "remanation" that reflects back God's "emanation" in creating. Divinization was one of the categories under which Edwards interpreted God's entire work of creating—an event that both commenced and terminated within God.[46]

---

43. WJE 13:374.

44. WJE 18:289.

45. WJE 8:380–81.

46. Jeffrey C. Waddington has denied that the concept of divinization, or *theosis*, has applicability to Edwards's theology ("Jonathan Edwards's 'Ambiguous and Somewhat Precarious' Doctrine of Justification," *Westminster Theological Journal* 66 [2004]: 357–72, esp. 362, 367). The argument of our chapter, however, is that the absence of the term did not mean that the concept was absent.

27
Theology of Revival

JONATHAN EDWARDS'S REPUTATION and theology are closely intertwined with the topic of religious revival or awakening. Throughout his career as pastor, preacher, revivalist, theologian, and college president, Edwards oversaw awakenings within his own church at Northampton, Massachusetts, assisted with awakenings in communities stretching from Maine to Pennsylvania, promoted revivals on an international scale, and published extensively on revivals and especially in connection with the Great Awakening (1740–41). Edwards's *Faithful Narrative of a Surprising Work of God* (1737), *The Distinguishing Marks of a Work of the Spirit of God* (1741), *Some Thoughts Concerning the Revival* (1743), *Religious Affections* (1746), and *Humble Attempt to Promote Explicit Agreement and Visible Union of God's People in Extraordinary Prayer* (1748) were writings devoted primarily to experiences, ideas, and debates arising out of the 1730s-40s revivals. More than three centuries after his birth, Edwards has continued to be cited as an authority on revival and might be regarded as the most influential author of all time on this theme. Furthermore, Edwards's revival writings are not exclusively pastoral in character but touch on a wide spectrum of theological issues and debates. These include the nature of conversion; the respective roles of mind, affections, and imagination in spiritual experience; visions and other extraordinary experiences; bodily manifestations; the proper interpretation of scripture; the nature of religious practice; the laity's relation to the clergy; the pattern and progress of redemptive history; eschatological expectations connected with revivals; the importance of unity in the church; and the role of prayer in spiritual awakening. The 1730s-40s revivals offered not only a pastoral challenge but a provocation to theological reflection.

This chapter examines some salient aspects of Edwards's revival writings. Examination shows that they display a progression over time. *Faithful Narrative of a Surprising Work of God* (1737) was written in the first bloom and flush of joy at a new movement of God's Spirit. *The Distinguishing Marks of a Work of the Spirit of God* (1741) was still optimistic in tone and aimed primarily at cautioning detractors of the 1740–41 revivals not to reject them because of certain external features (e.g., bodily manifestations, raptures). *Some Thoughts Concerning the Revival* (1743) was more cautious, took aim at those who trusted in their exalted spiritual experiences, warned against spiritual pride, and sought to limit the role of "lay exhorters." *Religious Affections* (1746) was yet more conservative and more preoccupied with correcting the errors of the New Lights than those of the Old Lights.¹ *Humble Attempt to Promote Explicit Agreement and Visible Union of God's People in Extraordinary Prayer*—written not during revival but in a time of perceived declension—was the most international and global in perspective, and it sought to stir up the dying embers of the former revivals. To understand Edwards's revival writings, it is important to interpret them in chronological sequence, as this chapter will do.²

Before proceeding any further, it may be appropriate to provide some basic definitions of "revival" and "revivalism"—terms used in differing ways. The word "revival" refers to a phase or period of renewal and revitalization within a religious (especially Protestant Christian) community. *Webster's Third New International Dictionary* defines it as "a period of religious awakening; renewed interest in religion," with "meetings often characterized by emotional excitement." "Revivalism" is typified as "the spirit or kind of religion or the methods characteristic of religious revivals." To call a religious gathering a revival is to suggest that an intensification of religious experience has occurred. It is not simply a matter of the number of people who may be present. Religious are corporate, experiential events.³

Since the mid-1700s, reports of Christian revivals from differing geographical regions and cultural groups have shown common themes. A number

---

1. George Marsden writes concerning *Religious Affections*: "Unlike his earlier two awakening works, which were first of all designed to show critics that ecstatic phenomena did not prove anything one way or the other, *Affections* was directed first of all toward the misguided emphases of the extreme New Lights who had led many people into arrogant self-delusion. Far more damage has been done throughout church history, he emphasized in his preface, by the seeming friends of true religion than by its open enemies" (*Jonathan Edwards: A Life*; New Haven, CT: Yale University Press, 2003; 285).

2. On Edwards's theology of revivals, see C.C. Goen, "Editor's Introduction," in WJE 4:1–95; Charles Lippy, "Theology of Revivals," in Michael McClymond, ed., *Encyclopedia of Religious Revivals in America*, 2 vols. (Westport, CT: Greenwood Press, 2007), 1:434–38; George Marsden, *Jonathan Edwards*, 150–69, 201–90; Michael J. McClymond, "Theology of Revivals," in Erwin Fahlbusch, et al., eds., *The Encyclopedia of Christianity, Si-Z, Volume 5* (Grand Rapids, MI: Eerdmans; Leiden: Brill, 2008), 341–49; Kenneth Minkema, "Edwards, Jonathan," in Michael J. McClymond, ed., *Encyclopedia of Religious Revivals in America*, 2 vols. (Westport, CT: Greenwood Press, 2007), 1:150–57; and J.I. Packer, "Jonathan Edwards and Revival," in *A Quest for Godliness: The Puritan Vision of the Christian Life* (Wheaton, IL: Crossway Books, 1990), 309–27.

3. For definitions and discussions of revival in general, see Michael J. McClymond, "Preface" and "Introduction," in McClymond, ed., *Encyclopedia of Religious Revivals*, 1:xv–xxxi. W. Reginald Ward treats Continental European developments—specifically a spiritual awakening among persecuted Protestants in German Silesia just after 1700—as the backdrop to the later eighteenth-century revivals among English-language Protestants. See Ward's *The Protestant Evangelical Awakening* (New York: Cambridge University Press, 1992).

of features of the eighteenth-century revivals were frequently observed in later revivals. Participants in the 1700s revivals spoke of their vivid sense of spiritual things, great joy and faith, deep sorrow over sin, passionate desire to evangelize others, and heightened feelings of love for God and fellow humanity. Services went longer than usual. News of revivals traveled rapidly, and sometimes the reports of revival in one location—in person or print—touched off new revivals in other locations. Ministers who did not normally preach outside their own congregations began to itinerate and offer sermons in other locations. Laypeople wished to testify publicly or sermonize as "lay exhorters." Frequently there were unusual bodily manifestations, such as falling down, rolling on the ground, involuntary muscle movements, laughter, or shouting. Some of the other phenomena were visions, dreams, or prophecies thought to reveal secret knowledge. The eighteenth-century revivals were intensely controversial, featuring opponents and proponents who vehemently criticized one another. Among the most widely debated aspects were the practice of ministerial itinerancy, lay exhortation, bodily manifestations, and the reports of dreams, visions, and prophecies from God. Critics of the 1700s revivals held that they undermined proper order and ministerial authority in the church.

A recent publication on Edwards's ministerial visit to Suffield, Massachusetts, in July 1741, during the height of the New England awakenings, shows that Edwards was more closely aligned with the wild side of revival than previously imagined. Douglas Winiarski, who published a manuscript on the events in Suffield, judges that Edwards began to moderate his views on revival by September 1741 when he gave the Yale College commencement address, *Distinguishing Marks*. By the time he published *Some Thoughts Concerning the Revival* (1743), his views seemed to have moderated further. Yet an anonymous eyewitness of the events in Suffield described an extraordinary series of events on July 5–6, 1741. Nearly 500 persons shared in the Lord's Super, some 97 of whom had joined the Suffield church that very day—perhaps the largest one-day church admission ritual ever observed in colonial New England. Following Edwards's sermon, many of his hearers retired to a nearby residence where he continued his exhortation. Within minutes, there was a deafening sound of "Sobs," "Groans," "Screaches [sic]," "Houlings [sic]," and "Yellings" that reverberated throughout the fields. Sinners fell to the ground, languished in spiritual distress, their bodies contorting with such violence that, according to one witness, "you would have thought there [sic] bones all broken, or rather that they had no bones." Others experienced release from "distress" and "were brought to different degrees of Peace & Joy, Some to Rapture." Edwards prayed with the multitude of "Children, Youth[s] and aged persons of both Sexes" for several hours, until he was worn out, and yielded the pastoral labor to four or five "private Xtians [Christians]."

It should not be surprising that Edwards's best-known pulpit performance—"Sinners in the Hands of an Angry God"—took place a few days later and just across the river from Suffield, on July 8, 1741, in Enfield, Massachusetts. Our principal informant regarding the "Sinners" sermon, Rev. Stephen Williams, states that Edwards's preaching elicited "a great moaning & crying out" in the meetinghouse, and that the "shrieks & crys" of the assembly were so "piercing & Amazing," in fact, that Edwards "was obliged to desist." In a 1743 letter to Thomas Prince, Edwards explained that he first encountered dramatic physical manifestations of the Holy Spirit during a private lecture that he preached in Northampton in May 1741. On this occasion, several "professors"—that is, full church members—were "so greatly affected with a sense of the greatness and glory of divine things" that they "were not able to conceal it" and cried out in distress. The "visible effect" of his preaching "on their bodies," he wrote, proved to be contagious and soon "the whole room was full of nothing but outcries, faintings, and such like."[4] While it is important not to attach undue importance to events in the spring and summer of 1741, or to presume that Edwards's experience in Suffield represented his preferred method of revival ministry, it is clear that Edwards had observed a great deal during his revival preaching. From quiet and sedate experiences of spiritual conviction, to raw, untamed outcries and contortions at Suffield, to the heavenly visions described in *Some Thoughts Concerning the Revival* (1743) and *Religious Affections* (1746), Edwards had witnessed the entire range of revival phenomena, and he sought in his theology of revival to offer an empirically based and biblically informed analysis and response.

---

4. Douglas L. Winiarski, "Jonathan Edwards, Enthusiast? Radical Revivalism and the Great Awakening in the Connecticut Valley," *Church History* 74 (2005): 683–739, citing 683–84, 692, 729. Winiarski comments that Edwards in Suffield was "inciting the wild gesticulations of his audience" (689). See also Winiarski, "Souls Filled With Ravishing Transport: Heavenly Visions and the Radical Awakening in New England," *William and Mary Quarterly* 61 (2004): 3–46; Leigh Eric Schmidt, "'A Second and Glorious Reformation': The New Light Extremism of Andrew Crosswell," *William and Mary Quarterly* 43 (1986): 214–44; and Benjamin Wagner, "Bodily Manifestations," in Michael McClymond, ed., *Encyclopedia of Religious Revivals in America*, 2 vols., 1:55–58.

The 1600s Context and the Little Awakening in Northampton

The period of greatest spiritual fervor in the eighteenth-century revivals—whether in the American colonies, England, Wales, or Scotland—occurred from the mid-1730s to the mid-1740s. Most of the major discussions and debates regarding revivals took shape during this initial decade.[5] Yet developments in the 1600s set the context for the later events. New Englanders defined themselves with reference to the Old Testament, understanding America as a "new Israel," chosen by God, having passed through a period of Exodus (i.e., the transition from the Old World to the New World), and yet fallen into worldliness and compromise during the second and third generations. God had entered into covenant with the Hebrew people at Sinai, promising blessing so long as the people remained faithful. So, too, it was believed, God had entered into covenant with the Puritan Christians, likewise promising blessings contingent on obedience and threatening judgment for disobedience. Following an Old Testament precedent (see Josh. 24), New England congregations in the 1600s and early 1700s periodically renewed their pledge to follow God and God's ways—something like a repetition of vows by a long-married couple. This was known as "owning the covenant," and it suggested a corporate rather than individualistic model of how God related to Christian people (ch. 21, 32). From the 1660s until the 1740s, the New England elite frequently expressed a perception of spiritual decline and a desire for spiritual revitalization in the colonies. Cotton Mather spoke of the danger that God's people in New England would forget their "errand into the wilderness," and he suggested that the people's spiritual malaise may have been rooted in their growing wealth. Religion gave birth to prosperity, but prosperity brought a decline in religion.[6]

---

5. Among the many works on the 1730s–40s revivals, see Allen Guelzo, "The Great Awakening," in Michael McClymond, ed., *Encyclopedia of Religious Revivals in America*, 1:191–96; Thomas S. Kidd, *The Great Awakening: The Roots of Evangelical Christianity in Colonial America* (New Haven, CT: Yale University Press, 2007; George Marsden, *Jonathan Edwards: A Life*, 150–69, 201–90; Mark Noll, *The Rise of Evangelicalism: The Age of Edwards, Whitefield and the Wesleys* (Downers Grove, IL: InterVarsity Press, 2003), esp. 100–54; and Susan O'Brien, "A Transatlantic Community of Saints: The Great Awakening and the First Evangelical Network, 1735–55," *American Historical Review* 91 (1986): 811–32.

6. The decline of the national fortune became apparent, said Cotton Mather, "when people began more notoriously to forget 'the errand into the wilderness,' and when the enchantments of *this* world caused the rising generation more sensibly to neglect the...interests of religion" (*Magnalia Christi Americana; Or, the Ecclesiastical History of New-England*, 2 vols; Hartford: Silas Andrus and Son, 1853; 2:316; orig. emph.).

The religious culture in which Edwards was born placed strong emphasis on "awakenings," "stirs," or "harvests." As the son and grandson of Congregational ministers, he came of age as the scion of a powerful extended family that included many members of the ministerial elite. His upbringing trained him to pay special attention to any signs of awakening within individuals or groups around him. In fact, the earliest document from Edwards that survives—a brief letter he wrote in 1716 at age twelve—opens with words that describe recent events in his father's congregation: "Through the wonderful mercy and goodness of God there hath in this place been a very remarkable stirring and pouring out of the Spirit of God."[7] Chronologically, this is the first statement from Edwards that we possess. It is hard to imagine any words that could have been more prophetic of Edwards's future destiny as America's leading author on, and interpreter of, religious revivals.

Timothy Edwards, in his day, was regarded as a successful revivalist, having overseen some five or six such episodes at his church in Windsor, Connecticut. Edwards's maternal grandfather, Solomon Stoddard, was even better known than his father. Stoddard oversaw five "harvests" of souls during his sixty-year pastoral career, was renowned as a preacher of "terror," and wrote a series of influential revivalist treatises: *The Safety of Appearing on the Day of Judgment in the Righteousness of Christ* (1687), *A Guide to Christ* (1714), and *A Treatise on Conversion* (1719).[8] Among Edwards's more distant relatives were the Williamses, including William Williams of Hatfield, Massachusetts, who was known as an awakening preacher. The connection with Stoddard was especially crucial, inasmuch as Edwards during his first few years in the ministry served alongside Stoddard in the Northampton congregation. Given Edwards's later prominence, and his amazingly fertile and productive mind, it is easy to forget that he inherited and did not originate all of his key ideas on revival.

Shortly after becoming Stoddard's colleague and heir-apparent, Edwards witnessed a minor revival that followed a 1727 earthquake, whose epicenter lay in Massachusetts. Following his grandfather's precedent, Edwards preached a strong sermon that warned of God's judgment if the people refused to repent. The event brought concern throughout New England and a temporary upsurge in requests for church membership. After Stoddard's death in 1729, Edwards sought to further the revival spirit at Northampton by preaching against the town's preoccupation with worldly wealth and status,

---

7. WJE 16:29.

8. See Philip Gura, "Solomon Stoddard's Irreverent Way," *Early American Literature* 21 (1986): 29–43.

warning of God's judgment, and, on a different note, highlighting the reality of a "divine and supernatural light" that could open one's eyes to God's beauty. Edwards began to see the fruit of his efforts in late 1733, when he reported that the younger people of Northampton were showing a "flexibleness" in responding to his efforts in reigning in their late-night carousing. Soon there were signs of religious awakening.[9]

Following the sudden and unexpected deaths of two young persons in the town, the religious concern in Northampton became general. Edwards wrote, "There was scarcely a single person in the town, either old or young, that was left unconcerned about the great things of the eternal world. Those that were wont to be the vainest and loosest... were now generally subject to great awakenings." The number of conversions multiplied until Edwards could write that "in the spring and summer following, anno 1735, the town seemed to be full of the presence of God: it never was so full of love, nor so full of joy; and yet so full of distress, as it was then." There was "joy in families" as parents, siblings, and children rejoiced at the newfound salvation of their relatives. The "public assemblies were then beautiful," with "everyone earnestly intent on the public worship" and "the assembly...in tears while the Word was preached; some weeping with sorrow and distress, others with joy and love, others with pity and concern for the souls of their neighbors." Edwards also found "God's work" in Northampton to be "very extraordinary in the degrees of the influences of his Spirit, both in the degree of awakening and conviction...and its being so swiftly propagated from town to town."[10]

In response to a request from the inquisitive Benjamin Colman of Boston, Edwards wrote a description of the Northampton awakening. Impressed with this account, and desiring more detail, Colman requested a fuller rendition. After the publication of the expanded version as an appendix to a sermon by William Williams, the text was published in London with a preface by Isaac Watts—the well-known hymnodist—and John Guyse, under the title, *Faithful Narrative of a Surprising Work of God* (1737). This publication brought international attention to Edwards and to the town of Northampton, and made them major points of reference in a burgeoning transatlantic evangelical awakening. The work was written in a clinical style—perhaps expressing Edwards's interest in natural science—and profiled the town's history, geography, and social divisions. It then proceeded to discuss "the manner of persons being wrought upon." Most often, people began with a sense of their "miserable

---

9. Minkema, "Edwards," 150–52.

10. WJE 4:150–51, 159.

condition" and danger of damnation. Realizing that they could do nothing to help themselves, they came to a state of humble dependence on God. Some were awakened suddenly, and others gradually, to "gracious discoveries" in their souls, with an accompanying "calm of spirit" and thirsting after God. As concrete examples of this process of conversion, Edwards recounted the experiences of two females—Abigail Hutchinson, a young woman fatally ill and yet converted before her death, and, more surprising, the four-year-old Phebe Bartlett. Edwards noted that there were "several Negroes" who "appear to have been born again." While earlier revivals primarily reached younger people, the 1734–35 revival resulted in the conversion of 50 persons above the age of 40 and two above the age of 70.[11]

The observation and analysis in Edwards's *Faithful Narrative* demonstrated that conversion took place in differing ways and showed "vast variety." This made the work innovative. Edwards's starting point in this text was not the existing theological theories regarding conversion but the empirical data he gathered from those he counseled. Earlier Puritan authors adhered to what Edmund Morgan termed a "morphology of conversion"—a series of distinct stages that allowed persons to ascertain how far along they had come in the process of conversion.[12] Though the details varied from one author to another, the common assumption was that an unregenerate person would receive grace only after becoming aware of his or her spiritual impotence and helplessness before God. Consequently "humiliation" or even "terror" had to come before conversion. Yet this was not what Edwards had in fact observed among his parishioners. Some people, whom Edwards judged to be soundly converted, experienced little, if any, terror or distress prior to their gracious experiences of God. He writes that "there is very great variety as to the degree of fear and trouble that persons are exercised with" and that "some have had ten times less trouble of mind than others."[13] Edwards's *Diary* from 1722 shows that he was already questioning the applicability of the "morphology" of conversion to his own case: "I do not remember that I experienced regeneration, exactly in those steps, in which divines say it is generally wrought."[14] Yet where theory conflicted with data, Edwards was ready to alter or abandon theory—much as

---

11. Marsden, *Jonathan Edwards*, 160.

12. Edmund Morgan, in *Visible Saints: The History of a Puritan Idea* (Ithaca, NY: Cornell University Press, 1963), wrote of the "morphology of conversion" as a scheme of experience in which "each stage could be distinguished from the next, so that a man could check his eternal condition by a set of temporal and recognizable signs" (66).

13. WJE 4:161.

14. WJE 16:759.

a good scientist would let go of a pet hypothesis if it were not sustained in laboratory results. Indeed, *Faithful Narrative* had a clinical and quasi-scientific quality that set it apart from earlier writings on the topic of revival.[15] Kenneth Minkema notes that "with its mixture of social anthropology, dispassionate psychological theory, and affecting biography, *A Faithful Narrative* became a key text in the history of revivalism, a manual for other ministers to follow as they sought and guided their own congregations."[16] It is ironic that Edwards should be known to history as a preacher of terror in his "Sinners" sermon, because his teaching on conversion did much to undermine the notion that fear and distress were essential to the process of conversion.

Even before *Faithful Narrative* was published, the revival in Northampton began to falter. In early 1735, a Northampton man had tried to commit suicide. Some months later, Edwards's uncle, Joseph Hawley—known to have suffered from melancholy and despondent over his unconverted state—slit his own throat and died. From this point onward, Edwards's relationship with his congregation was forever altered. Never again would he enjoy the full support and goodwill of his entire parish. Sensing a withdrawal of the revival spirit from Northampton, Edwards preached a 1736 sermon on the "city on a hill" (Matt. 5:14), and used the town's new reputation as a revival center as a means of goading his listeners to behave in a more Christian fashion. Critics of the revival were watching Northampton, warned Edwards, and "if they see that there ben't answerable fruits, it will exceedingly confirm 'em in their rejecting all such things, as being nothing but mere whimsy and enthusiasm.... They will say, 'There is the people of Northampton that experienced so much of such sorts of things. See what it comes to.'"[17]

From 1736 to 1740, Edwards observed that many of the "high professors" who had once spoken volubly of their lofty spiritual experiences had lapsed back into sin. He judged that some were worse off by the late 1730s than they had been in the early 1730s. In light of the "backsliding" of converts, Edwards rethought some of his theological positions. Previously he had stressed an immediate experience of the "divine and supernatural light" as sufficient evidence of true conversion. Yet now he wrote that perseverance was a condition of justification and a means of assurance: "Not only the first act of faith, but

---

15. Scholars have suggested that the discipline of the psychology of religion in North America may be traced back to Edwards's pioneering observations. See Wayne L. Proudfoot, "From Theology to a Science of Religions: Jonathan Edwards and William James on Religious Affections," *Harvard Theological Review* 82 (1989) 149–68.

16. Minkema, "Edwards," 152–53, citing 153.

17. Minkema, "Edwards," 153, citing WJE 18:557.

after-acts of faith, and perseverance in faith, do justify the sinner."[18] In the winter of 1737–38 Edwards preached a lengthy sermon series on the parable of the wise and foolish virgins (Matt. 25:1–13) to show that a new spiritual sense and Christian practice were both essential signs of grace. Notebook entries from the late 1730s—"Signs of Godliness" and "Directions for Judging of Persons' Experiences"—exhibited Edwards's stress on holiness and his reluctance to accept spiritual experiences at face value unless they were corroborated by Christian practice.[19]

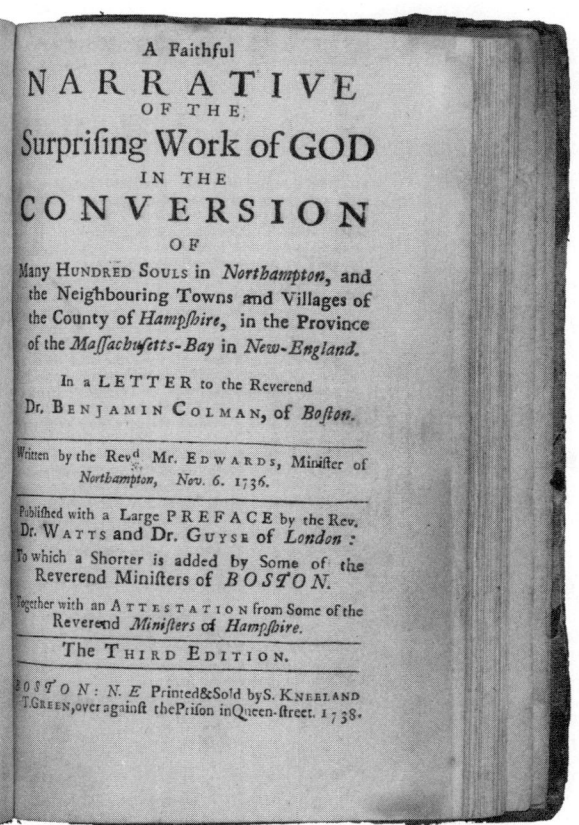

FIGURE 27.1 Edwards's *Faithful Narrative* (1737) offered an influential account of Northampton's revival and set a precedent for countless later publications of the same genre (Courtesy of Kenneth Minkema, Yale University).

---

18. WJE 18:355.

19. Minkema, "Edwards," 153, citing "Signs of Godliness" and "Directions for Judging of Persons' Experiences" in WJE 21:469–510, 522–24.

Following the 1734–35 revival, Edwards was critical of his parishioners' practice of speaking too openly, confidently, and effusively of their own spiritual experiences. In a letter to Scottish minister Thomas Gillespie, Edwards wrote that, when he came among the people of Northampton, he "found it to be too much a custom among them without discretion, or distinction of occasions, places, or companies, to declare and publish their own experiences; and oftentimes to do it in a light manner, without any air of solemnity. This custom has not a little contributed to spiritual pride, and many other evils."[20] Those who spoke breezily of their experiences often presumed being in a state of grace and assumed that they needed to do nothing more toward their own salvation—resting on a "supposed day of grace" they had experienced in the past. Sermons from the late 1730s warned against the deceptiveness of substituting "talk of religion" for the practice of religion.[21] During the late 1730s, Edwards's thinking about revival shifted in an historical, global, and cosmic direction. In 1739, he preached a sermon series, *A History of the Work of Redemption*, in thirty installments that depicted revivals as a vehicle propelling God's providential plan for history.

Edwards's experiences from 1734 to 1739 were crucial in giving him an appreciation for the reality, depth, and power of revivals to reshape individuals and whole societies. At the same time, his observation and study during these years taught him caution and prepared him to be more guarded in his optimism during the height of the Great Awakening. His mature position on revival was a moderating and mediating theology that combined—in almost equal measure—an openness toward the Holy Spirit with a caution in discerning the Holy Spirit's presence and work.

The Great Awakening—Colonial Revivals in 1740–41

Despite Edwards's efforts to promote a new wave of spiritual awakening among his parishioners, he generated little interest during the late 1730s. In 1739, he learned of the new British evangelists—the Wesley brothers, and especially George Whitefield, who was then preaching to huge crowds in England and seeing large numbers converted. Hoping that the news from abroad would evoke a response in his parishioners, as it had in him, Edwards began a practice of communicating to his church the news of revivals occurring elsewhere. He solicited information on the "advancement of Christ's kingdom" from his various domestic and foreign correspondents. In December 1739, Edwards

---

20. WJE 16:383.

21. Minkema, "Edwards," 153–54.

received a letter from Whitefield, then in New York City, hinting that he might be able to visit Northampton as a part of his upcoming tour of New England. Edwards responded in February 1740 with an invitation to Whitefield to preach in his congregation, though warning that he might be "disappointed in New England" since the people had been "glutted" with spiritual teaching and had grown "more hardened" than those elsewhere. On a positive note, he expressed his "refreshment of soul that I have heard of one raised up in the Church of England [i.e., Whitefield] to revive the mysterious, spiritual, despised, and exploded doctrines of the gospel, and full of a spirit of zeal for the promotion of real vital piety, whose labors have been attended with such success."[22]

Neither Whitefield nor Edwards was disappointed with the results of Whitefield's visit to Northampton or New England generally. In October 1740, Whitefield preached four times in Northampton and brought everyone to tears, Edwards included. In the tumultuous aftermath of Whitefield's visit, Edwards preached a sermon series on the parable of the sower (Matt. 13:1–30), advising his congregants not to dwell on the eloquence of a speaker or the beauty of his gestures but rather to examine themselves to see if they had in fact undergone the "new birth." As Whitefield departed from Northampton to East Windsor to preach at Edwards's father's church, Edwards accompanied him on the way and used the occasion to exhort Whitefield not to act on the basis of spiritual "impulses" or to make assurance of salvation dependent on them. Following that conversation, Edwards noticed that Whitefield, while always cordial, never "made so much an intimate of me as some others." On another occasion, Edwards spoke with Whitefield about the danger of "judging other persons to be unconverted." Despite his differences with Whitefield, Edwards recognized Whitefield's evangelistic gift and calling, viewed him as the best hope for revival in the church, and so did not join others in public criticism of the great preacher.[23]

By the end of 1740, Northampton was in the throes of a revival that rivaled the events of earlier years. In December, "a very considerable work of God appeared among those that were very young," and by spring he observed an "engagedness of spirit" among children and youth.[24] Edwards encouraged the

---

22. WJE 16:79–81, citing 80.

23. Minkema, "Edwards," 154, citing WJE 16:157. On Edwards's mixed responses to Whitefield, see Ava Chamberlain, "The Grand Sower of the Seed: Jonathan Edwards's Critique of George Whitefield," *New England Quarterly* 70 (1997): 368–85.

24. WJE 16:116–17.

younger people to meet in "conferences" for religious conversation and prayer, and these meetings continued through the summer of 1741. By this time, some were crying out and fainting during worship, and the people were affected "more sensibly and visibly...by external effects" in this revival than previously.[25] The later revival did not involve as many conversions and a smaller group entered church membership. Another difference was that the 1734–35 revival affected people of various ages, while the 1740–41 awakening seemed to touch only the younger people. Older church members—some brought in under Stoddard—showed a growing opposition to the revival because of Edwards's pastoral focus on the youth and because of their trepidation over itinerant ministers and bodily manifestations. Inter-generational tensions contributed to an ongoing divisiveness. Some of the young people in whom Edwards had set his hope were implicated in the "Bad Book" episode of 1744 in which younger men were caught reading an illustrated midwives' manual and harassing younger women.

By the early 1740s, Edwards was having his greatest success as an awakener outside of his own congregation. Conversely, the greatest success in Northampton occurred under sermons by a guest preacher. In early 1742, the young minister Samuel Buell filled Edwards's pulpit while Edwards was away on a preaching tour and raised the revival spirit to dizzying heights. Edwards's wife, Sarah, experienced her most dramatic religious raptures under Buell's preaching. She described her experience as follows: "That night [January 28, 1742]...was the sweetest night I ever had....The great part of the night I lay awake; sometimes asleep, and sometimes between sleeping and waking... I seemed to myself to perceive a glow of divine love come down from the heart of Christ in heaven, into my heart, in a constant stream, like a stream or pencil of sweet light." On the next day, Sarah Edwards wrote, "I felt a love to all mankind, wholly peculiar in its strength, and sweetness, far beyond all that I had ever felt before." Jonathan Edwards endorsed Sarah Edwards's revival experience by including an altered version of her spiritual narrative in *Some Thoughts Concerning the Revival* (with Sarah's gender and identity concealed), and then capping off his presentation of her experience with the words: "Now if such things are enthusiasm, and the fruits of a distempered brain, let my brain be evermore possessed of that happy distemper!"[26]

---

25. Minkema, "Edwards," 154, citing WJE 16:119–20.

26. Sereno Dwight, "Memoirs of Jonathan Edwards," in Edward Hickman, ed., *The Works of Jonathan Edwards*, 2 vols. (Carlisle, PA: Banner of Truth Trust, 1984 [1834]), 1:lxv, lxvii. Edwards's version of Sarah Edwards's experience is presented in WJE 4:331–41, citing 341.

While Sarah was undergoing her exalted spiritual experiences, Jonathan Edwards in early 1741 was preaching to great acclaim in eastern Massachusetts. His best-known performance, as noted earlier, took place in July 1741 in Enfield and is forever remembered because of his sermon "Sinners in the Hands of an Angry God." Edwards's disciple, Samuel Hopkins, later noted the remarkable impact of Edwards's preaching: "His words often discovered [i.e., manifested] a great deal of inward fervour, without much noise or external motion, and fell with great weight on the minds of his hearers; and he spake so as to reveal the strong emotions of his own heart, which tended...to move and affect others."[27] His well-chosen words and images cause spiritual things to appear real, vivid, and urgent to his hearers—what Perry Miller later referred to as Edwards's "rhetoric of sensation."[28]

Revival in Dispute—Old Lights and New Lights, Moderates and Radicals

George Whitefield's preaching expedition in 1740–41 caused a sensation throughout the colonies. Benjamin Franklin, on hearing Whitefield preach in Philadelphia, was astounded both by his irresistible persuasiveness and the sheer power of Whitefield's voice—which Franklin estimated could be heard by 30, 000 people at one time. In Boston Commons, he addressed 23, 000. Whitefield left for England in 1741 and did not return again to America until 1745. Yet a controversy over the New England revivals and revival preachers was already brewing before Whitefield's departure. The Presbyterian minister Gilbert Tennent had preached a sermon, "The Danger of an Unconverted Ministry" (1740), setting forth the thesis: "That the Case of such is much to be pitied, who have no other but Pharisee-Shepherds, or unconverted Teachers." The sermon aroused a storm of protest, in that it seemed a direct attack on ministerial authority. Tennent declared that it was "lawful and expedient" for awakened parishioners to leave behind their regularly appointed synod parishes "to hear Godly Persons" instead.[29] Whitefield for his part had also contributed to controversy over the revival when he confided in one issue of his published

---

27. Sereno Dwight, "Memoirs," in Edward Hickman, ed., *The Works of President Edwards*, 2 vols. (Carlisle, PA: Banner of Truth, 1984 [1834]), 1:cxc.

28. Perry Miller, "The Rhetoric of Sensation," in *Errand Into the Wilderness* (Cambridge, MA: Belknap Press of Harvard University, 1964), 167–83.

29. Gilbert Tennent, "The Danger of an Unconverted Ministry," in Richard L. Bushman, ed, *The Great Awakening: Documents on the Revival of Religion, 1740–45* (New York: Atheneum, 1970), 88, 93.

Journal that "a great number of ministers" in New England were spiritually unfit.[30] When such statements found their way into print in April 1741, there was a cascade of anti-Whitefield pamphlets and letters to the editor.

Thomas Clap, rector of Yale College, invited Jonathan Edwards to serve as commencement speaker in fall 1741.[31] The commencement address, published as *Distinguishing Marks* (1741), was a carefully worded discourse that sought to mediate between the revival's supporters and a growing group of detractors. A revival, Edwards argued, must be judged not a priori but rather in terms of its results. Outward phenomena associated with the revivals neither proved nor disproved that the Spirit of God had genuinely been at work. For instance, Edwards wrote that "nothing can certainly be concluded from this, that the work...is carried on in a way very unusual and extraordinary." The Holy Spirit might do new, unusual, or unexpected things. No one should rule out such a possibility in advance. What is more, "a work is not to be judged of by any of its effects on the bodies of men, such as tears, trembling, groans, loud outcries, agonies of body, or the failing of bodily strength." Edwards went on to say that a genuine work of the Holy Spirit might involve "imprudences and irregularities" because "the end for which God pours out his Spirit, is to make men holy, and not to make them politicians." Edwards warned those inclined "to speak contemptibly" of the revival to steer clear of "the unpardonable sin against the Holy Ghost"—i.e., a blasphemous denial of the good work that God was doing in their midst.[32]

Yet if Edwards was warning conservative pastors not to reject the revival outright, he was also cautioning radical New Light preachers, some of whom reveled in the bodily manifestations and exalted spiritual experiences they had witnessed. His argument cut both ways. In effect, he was urging Old Lights not to reject a revival as spurious if it involved bodily and visionary experiences, and New Lights not to embrace a revival as genuine merely because it exhibited these phenomena. Addressing the revival's supporters in *Distinguishing Marks*, he cautioned against relying on "impulses and strong impressions...as though they were immediate significations from heaven to them of something that should come to pass, or something that it was the mind and will of God that they should do, which was not signified or revealed anywhere in the Bible." In Edwards's experience, many such "impressions" were later

---

30. Iain Murray, ed., *George Whitefield's Journals* (Edinburgh: Banner of Truth Trust, 1998 [1960]), 470; cited in Allen Guelzo, "The Great Awakening," in McClymond, ed., *Encyclopedia of Religious Revivals in America*, 1:194.

31. Graduation at that time occurred later in the calendar year.

32. WJE 4:228, 230, 241, 275.

found to be false. Even during "the approaching happy days of the church"—Edwards's eschatological hope for a renewed, revitalized church before Christ's glorious return—there was not likely to be a "restoration of...miraculous gifts" from the New Testament era. Though in his text he did not reject charismatic gifts, he thought that they had limited value (ch. 17). "I had rather enjoy...humble joy in God," wrote Edwards, "one quarter of an hour, than to have prophetical visions and revelations for a whole year."[33]

Edwards's appeal for moderation in *Distinguishing Marks* had only limited success. Pro-revival students at Yale College flouted college authorities, and in November 1741 Rector Clap made an example of one of Edwards's admirers, David Brainerd, by removing him from Yale. This act of expulsion only served to turn Brainerd into a martyr, and the uproar grew so great that Clap had to suspend classes in April 1742. Pro-revival forces in Connecticut responded by opening a short-lived rival college in New London, called the "Shepherd's Tent." Allen Guelzo comments: "It is easy to sympathize with Whitefield and Tennent as the underdogs. But Whitefield's and Tennent's decision to turn itinerant and preach without permission from the local ministry subverted what little order ministers and magistrates could hope to impose on the wild rim of the British empire." The New Light proponents were challenging ministerial authority and the standing order of churches by offering parishioners their own choice of which preachers to hear and churches to attend.

Controversy intensified as a result of the increasingly extreme actions of James Davenport, who began as a self-appointed missionary to Connecticut in 1741, and was arrested and deported. He was known for singing in the streets, accosting ministers for being unconverted, and, on one occasion, preaching continuously for twenty-four hours. After time in Boston, Davenport returned to Connecticut in 1743 to organize a separate parish in New London (i.e., a congregation not in fellowship with the other Congregational parishes), and inaugurated this new parish with a bonfire of books, gowns, clothes, and jewelry, including his very own "Breeches"—items he regarded as spiritually impure. Under threat of arrest, Davenport left Connecticut once again, suffered a mental breakdown, and issued his *Confession and Retractions* (1744) acknowledging his "misguided Zeal" and asking for pardon.[34] Yet the damage was done. The New

---

33. WJE 4:278, 282, 281.

34. Guelzo, "Great Awakening," in McClymond, ed., *Encyclopedia of Religious Revivals*, 1:195; citing Davenport's *Confession and Retractions* in Bushman, *Great Awakening*, 54. See also Lisa Herb Smith, "Davenport, James," in McClymond, ed., *Encyclopedia of Religious Revivals in America*, 1:136–37, and Harry S. Stout and Peter Onuf, "James Davenport and the Great Awakening in New London," *Journal of American History* 70 (1983): 556–78.

England churches were divided. An assembly of Massachusetts pastors in May 1743 prepared and published a *Testimony* (1743) opposing the revival. Pro-revival ministers responded to the *Testimony* with *Testimony and Advice* (1744), in which they acknowledged the "unusual bodily effects" that took place during the revival, but insisted that they had never identified "bodily seizures" with genuine spiritual "convictions." Instead they looked "a renovation of nature, followed by a change of life" as the proof of a genuine conversion.[35]

The most extensive attack on the revival came from the Boston Old Light pastor Charles Chauncy in his sermon, *Enthusiasm Described and Cautioned Against* (1742), followed by the massive critique, *Seasonable Thoughts on the State of Religion in New England* (1743). While Edwards judged the Great Awakening to be, on the whole, "a glorious work of God," Charles Chauncy dissented. "Religion, of late," he wrote, "has been more a Commotion in the Passions, than a Change in the Temper of the Mind." When he looked at the revival, he saw emotionalism, religious excess, social disorder, and a breakdown of the proper relationship between ministers and their flocks. In preparation for *Seasonable Thoughts*, Chauncy corresponded with hundreds of ministers and traveled over three hundred miles in New England, New Jersey, and New York to observe the revival's impact for himself.

Chauncy argued that people needed to obey the dictates of reason in religious as well as secular life. "The plain truth is," he wrote, "an enlightened mind, and not raised affections, ought always to be the guide of those who call themselves men; and this, in the affairs of religion, as well as other things." The "enthusiasts" of the 1700s were caught up in a false spirituality characterized by bodily convulsions, freakish conduct, imagined favor with God, and a dismissal of rational thought. In this sense, the events of the 1740s were a repetition of past errors. The revivalists of the Great Awakening were akin to the heretics—"Antinomians, Familists, and Libertines"—of earlier colonial history. What is more, people were "flocking after some Particular ministers, and glorying in them, as though they were Gods rather than Men." George Whitefield was surrounded by a personality cult. The itinerant preachers were "busie-bodies." What right did Whitefield, Tennent, and the other revival preachers have to invade other ministers' parishes and preach without permission? Itinerant preaching was a bone of contention for those who wanted to uphold the standing order of churches and parish ministers.[36]

---

35. McClymond, ed., *Encyclopedia of Religious Revivals in America*, 2:45, citing and discussing *Testimony and Advice* (1744).

36. See Timothy D. Hall, *Contested Boundaries: Itinerancy and the Reshaping of the Colonial American Religious World* (Durham, NC: Duke University Press, 1994).

Even worse, in Chauncy's view, was the fact that itinerant preachers opened the door to lay exhorters: "Yea, illiterate exhorters, raw, weak young men, or lads, have too frequently taken upon them, openly to judge and censure their ministers." By setting laypeople against their ministers, the revival preachers sowed "the seeds of contention and separation." The practice of "uncharitable judging" had begun with Whitefield, who set a negative example.

Despite the novel developments of the 1740s, the underlying debate between Chauncy and Edwards, writes Marsden, was "an old and familiar one even in Puritan circles." Chauncy "stood for the 'intellectual' and more Aristotelian (and Thomistic) tradition, which argued that the will should follow the best dictates of reason. Edwards was in the more Augustinian 'voluntarist' camp that viewed the whole person as guided by affections of the will."[37] Chauncy's prioritization of reason over emotion (or heart, affection, passion) gave his theology and spirituality a different feel than that of Edwards, who argued in *Religious Affections* (1746) that "true religion, in great part, consists in holy affections."[38] Moreover, it is clear that Chauncy during his long life moved far from the Puritan faith of his youth. In later years, he espoused a version of universalism, or the belief that all persons will ultimately attain salvation (ch. 3). On the other hand, it is easy to overlook the substantial agreement that existed between Chauncy and Edwards during the 1740s. Both opposed extremism, and Chauncy sometimes sounded just like Edwards, as when he wrote: "This influence of the Spirit does not consist in sudden Impulses and Impressions, in Visions, Revelations, extraordinary Missions, and the like; but in working Men the Preparations for Faith and Repentance...shewing them the Necessity of a Saviour...and [making] them new Creatures."[39]

Edwards's *Some Thoughts Concerning the Revival* (1743) was written before Edwards had had the chance to read Chauncy's major work, and yet it nonetheless engaged many of Chauncy's arguments. The "Edwards-Chauncy debate" on revival—though not, strictly speaking, a debate—has shaped

---

37. Marsden, *Edwards*, 282–83. On the earlier New England debates on intellectualism and voluntarism, see Norman Fiering, *Moral Philosophy at Seventeenth-Century Harvard: A Discipline in Transition* (Chapel Hill, NC: University of North Carolina Press, 1981), esp. 104–46.

38. WJE 2:95.

39. Charles Chauncy, *Seasonable Thoughts on the State of Religion in New England* (Boston, 1743), 109, 327, 3, 51, 218, cited in "Charles Chauncy's Dissenting Voice," in Michael McClymond, ed., *Encyclopedia of Religious Revivals in America*, 2:42–45; and Marsden, *Edwards*, 281.

discussions of religious revival ever since.[40] Edwards believed that critics of the revival had gone astray first by judging the revival a priori (i.e., that is, with presuppositions about how a revival could or should take place), second by not using the Bible as a whole as their rule for judging, and, third by not distinguishing the good from the bad in the revival. *Some Thoughts Concerning the Revival* asserted that critics must not pass judgment on a revival as a whole because it contains some negative aspects. Moreover, no one should dictate in advance how God should or might act. If God chose to accomplish his purposes through lowly people, then it was incumbent on the leaders to acknowledge and not oppose it. "God in this work has begun at the lower end," wrote Edwards. Even the "rash zeal" of younger believers might be a salutary rebuke to the pride and spiritual coldness of elder Christians.

Yet Edwards in *Some Thoughts Concerning the Revival* took aim at the "excesses and extravagances" of the pro-revival party. He responded to critics of the Great Awakening and yet offered his own points of criticism. Though rightly regarded as the revival's leading defender, his standpoint was more nuanced than generally imagined. He sought to circumscribe—though not abolish—the practice of lay exhortation. He was especially critical of those who believed that they were invulnerable to error, and he identified "spiritual pride" as an especially fruitful source of error. People undergoing ecstatic experiences often became convinced that God was guiding them, interpreted their passing impressions as divine revelations, and thus became completely immune to criticism and correction. This was a dangerous attitude that led to all manner of rash behavior, and it could only be avoided through an attitude of humility. Edwards described pride as "the worst viper that is in the heart...the most secret, deceitful and unsearchable in its ways of working....and nothing is so hateful to God, and contrary to the spirit of the Gospel."[41] He thus sought strenuously to obviate the danger of spiritual pride among the advocates of revival. In *Some Thoughts Concerning the Revival*, Edwards had much to say regarding Satan. While he never shifted blame for human actions wholly to the devil, he believed that the devil could influence human actions and that it was in the devil's interest to draw zealous Christians into rash, weird, offensive, or destructive behavior. In a spiritual awakening, it was the devil who woke up first and sought to undermine and discredit the

---

40. See Amy Schrager Lang, "'A Flood of Errors': Chauncy and Edwards in the Great Awakening," in Nathan O. Hatch and Harry S. Stout, eds., *Jonathan Edwards and the American Experience* (New York: Oxford University Press, 1988), 160–73.

41. WJE 4:401–405, 483–89, 293–95, 277.

Spirit's work. Sadly, this had happened when Edwards's own uncle, Joseph Hawley, had killed himself in 1735.[42]

Religious Affections (1746) was the most conservative of Edwards's major works on revivals and revival experiences. There he set out a series of "positive" and "negative" signs or marks of true grace in the soul. Edwards's emphasis on persevering Christian practice or behavior—first seen in his *Miscellanies* after the decline of the Connecticut Valley revival of the late 1730s—culminated in the twelfth and final sign of grace treated in *Religious Affections*: "Gracious and holy affections have their exercise and fruit in Christian practice."[43] It was a holy living, more than anything else, that served as the surest test of genuine spirituality. Correlatively, *Religious Affections* offered repeated warnings against placing one's hope in imaginative transports or spiritual impulses and visions that might prove delusive.

J.I. Packer wrote that Edwards avoided "romantic fallacy" by constantly noting "the problems which revival brings." When the church is "suddenly roused from a state of torpor and lethargy by a new and overwhelming awareness of the reality of...God," it is only to be expected that many people will "fall into pride, delusions, [and] unbalance." The more powerful a revival is, the greater these disfiguring effects are likely to be.[44] This paradoxical conclusion—fully in accord with Edwards's analysis—may serve as a caution. Revivals bring new energy to the church but also a new set of problems.

Revival in Context—Politics, Prayer, and Eschatology in Transatlantic View

While the events of the 1740s brought structural change and permanent division to the New England churches, there is little agreement beyond this as to the lasting effects of the awakening. In the 1840s, Joseph Tracy presented the Great Awakening as a vindication of evangelical religion. In the 1910s and 1920s, Herbert Osgood viewed it as the first sign of a distinctive American culture, and Vernon Parrington saw it as the last gasp of religious fanaticism.

---

42. Regarding Hawley, Edwards writes that "the devil took advantage and drove him into despairing thoughts" (WJE 4:109). Further references to Satan in the revival writings are found in WJE 4:108, 226, 243–44, 246, 250–55, 259–60, 269, 271, 277, 385, 410–16, 432–33, 439, 462–63, 467–73, 477, 483, 494–95, 540, 550, 563, 571. On the devil in the 1740s, see Richard Lovelace, "The Surprising Works of God: Jonathan Edwards on Revival, Then and Now," *Christianity Today*, September 11, 1995, 28–32.

43. WJE 2:383.

44. J.I. Packer, "Jonathan Edwards and Revival," 317–18.

In the 1960s to 1980s, Alan Heimert and Rhys Isaac portrayed it as an opening to political anti-authoritarianism that bore fruit in the American Revolution. Allen Guelzo writes that "even if the Awakening cannot be claimed as a blueprint for the Revolution, it certainly is symptomatic of the ease with which authority in America could be fragmented."[45] Regarding Edwards's own experience, George Marsden comments that "all previous revivals in western New England had been generated and controlled by local pastors" who used them as a means of "gaining control over parishioners." Yet Whitefield was "a new modern type, the young rebel against authority"—an Anglican who "made his name by defying Anglican parish authority." Whereas earlier Puritan ministers had used jeremiads to berate their allegedly unspiritual congregations, Whitefield turned the tables by suggesting that "a spiritual people should challenge the authority of insufficiently spiritual clergy."[46] It should be clear why the Great Awakening may have had political dynamite hidden beneath it.

Sensing the onset of a spiritual decline in the mid-1740s, Edwards teamed up with Scottish evangelicals to coordinate quarterly days of prayer for the "pouring out" of the Holy Spirit. He first broached this idea for a "concert of prayer" in November 1745 and was pleased that the idea had been well received. To further promote the plan, Edwards published *Humble Attempt* (1748), which illustrated Edwards's vision of the "peculiar beauty of the church" united in prayer and his strong apocalypticism.[47] Outpourings of the Holy Spirit were, in some sense, harbingers of Christ's second coming and the end of the age (chs. 15, 35).

Until recently, scholarly literature has viewed the Great Awakening in America in isolation from the contemporaneous evangelical Awakening in Great Britain. American and British scholarship on the eighteenth-century revivals moved along separate tracks. A Methodist perspective on the 1700s has been dominant in British scholarship. But since John Wesley did not play a role in the Great Awakening, and it was the Calvinists—Anglican, Presbyterian, and Congregationalist—who established the first transatlantic evangelical networks, Methodist scholarship on the 1700s has tended to overlook the ties between Britain and America. What is more, American scholars have sometimes sought to exaggerate the Americanness of the Great

---

45. Guelzo, "Great Awakening," in McClymond, ed., *Encyclopedia of Religious Revivals*, 1:195.

46. Marsden, *Jonathan Edwards*, 209–11.

47. On the "beauty" of united prayer, see WJE 5:364–66. Edwards's argument for united prayer was aesthetic (ch. 6) as well as practical.

Awakening—as though the events in the colonies had no relationship to events elsewhere.[48]

While the topic can only be touched on here (see ch. 42 for more detail), the transatlantic evangelical theology of revival during the mid-1700s was gradually coalescing into two discrete patterns—one Calvinistic and centered on Jonathan Edwards, and the other Arminian and centered on John Wesley. This Edwardsean-Wesleyan parting of the ways would not have been apparent to observers in the 1740s but was fairly obvious by the 1770s—when the Calvinist-Arminian debate broke out with fresh force during the so-called Antinomian Controversy.[49] In addition to Wesley's well-known strictures against Calvinistic teachings on predestination, the unfree will, and the perseverance of the saints, he was also more ready than the Calvinists to embrace extraordinary spiritual experiences (e.g., dreams, visions, bodily effects) and to view them as direct signs of God's presence. In other words, Wesley's approach to spiritual discernment was closer to that of the radical New Lights in New England than was Edwards's. Tellingly, John Wesley found Edwards's *Religious Affections* to be a valuable work, though he discerned what he called "poison" mingled with its beneficial elements. Therefore Wesley published an edited, truncated version of the treatise for the benefit of his Methodist preachers.[50]

Revivals, as favored by Wesley, were sometimes wild and disorderly, frequently held in the open air, welcome to all comers, open to extraordinary experiences, ready to take bodily manifestations as signs of the Spirit's work, focused on attaining experiential assurance of justification (or sanctification), conducive to lay exhortation and testimony, and oriented generally to the needs and opinions of laypeople. Revivals, as favored by Edwards, were closely

---

48. Among the outstanding recent works on the transatlantic nature of the 1700s revivals, see Mark Noll, *The Rise of Evangelicalism*; Noll, David W. Bebbington, and George A. Rawlyk, eds., *Evangelicalism: Comparatige Studies of Popular Protestantism in North America, the British Isles, and beyond, 1700–1900* (New York: Oxford University Press, 1994). and W. Reginard Ward, *The Protestant Evangelical Awakening*.

49. The Antinomian Controversy of the 1770s in Britain—not to be confused with the American controversy of the 1630s under the same name—has not been fully investigated. Primary sources include about two dozen primary works by Augustus Toplady, John Wesley, and John Fletcher, all published between 1770 and 1779. Secondary sources include Robert A. Mattke, "John Fletcher's Methodology in the Antinomian controversy of 1770–76," *Wesleyan Theological Journal* 3 (1968): 38–47; Joseph Maycock, "Fletcher-Toplady Controversy," *London Quarterly and Holborn Review* 191 (1966): 227–35; and Colin Philip Ryan, *Augustus M. Toplady and John Wesley: Their Theological Controversy on Predestination*, PhD diss., North-West University, Potchefstroom Campus [South Africa], 2006.

50. See Richard B. Steele, "Wesley's Abridgments of Edwards's Revival Treatises," in *"Gracious Affection" and "True Virtue" According to Jonathan Edwards and John Wesley* (Metuchen, NJ: Scarecrow Press, 1994).

controlled, supervised by the watchful eye of the clergy, ordinarily held in church facilities (excepting Whitefield and a few others in the early 1740s), cautious or grudging in allowing bodily manifestations, circumspect in claiming assurance of salvation, dubious regarding alleged voices and visions from God, alert to the dangers of self-deception and spiritual pride, and favorable to a wait-and-see attitude regarding the fruits of spiritual experience. Back in England in 1739, Wesley and Whitefield had debated the "outward signs which had so often accompanied the inward work of God." When Whitefield's own hearers passed out, trembled violently, and went into convulsions, Wesley felt that he had been vindicated and he commented in his *Journal* for July 6–7, 1739: "From this time, I trust, we shall all suffer God to carry on His own work in the way that pleaseth Him."[51]

In his middle and later years, Wesley embraced and promulgated a teaching on "entire sanctification" that was and still is anathema to Calvinists. This teaching on sanctification—as much as Wesley's harsh utterances on Calvinistic predestination—contributed to a lasting rift in the evangelical world.[52] Nonetheless, Wesley's theology of revival, no less than Edwards's, had vast historical repercussions, and Wesley is often called the father of the Holiness Movement of the 1800s and the spiritual or theological grandfather of the Pentecostal-Charismatic revivals of the 1900s.[53]

The transatlantic aspects of Edwards's ministry and influence bear emphasis. It was two London ministers, John Guyse and Isaac Watts, who encouraged Edwards to write an account of the Northampton awakening. *Faithful Narrative* (1737) originated from a British request for information. A British native and ordained Anglican minister, George Whitefield, was the leading revival preacher in the American colonies. Transatlantic correspondence, especially with ministers in Scotland, was a part of Edwards's life over many years. Edwards's participation in the concert of prayer highlighted his role in

---

51. See the excerpts from Wesley and the introduction in McClymond, ed., *Encyclopedia of Religious Revivals in America*, 2:48–51.

52. On predestination, see especially John Wesley's sermon "Free Grace," in Thomas Jackson, ed., *The Works of John Wesley*, 14 vols. (Grand Rapids, MI: Baker Books, 2007 [1872]), 7:373–86. On sanctification, see John Wesley's "A Plain Account of Christian Perfection," in Thomas Jackson, ed., *The Works of John Wesley*, 11:366–446, or, more concisely, "Christian Perfection" (*The Works of John Wesley*, 6:1–19).

53. Wesley's *Journal* for July 13, 1756 (*The Works of John Wesley*, 2:376–77) offered a seemingly synergistic vision of the divine-human relationship in which revivals decline because people have "stifled their good desires" and "the Spirit of God is grieved" and then withdraws. This synergistic presentation is reminiscent of Charles Finney's *Lectures on Revivals of Religion* (1835), even though Finney drew directly from Edwardsean New Divinity sources and seems not to have borrowed much from Wesley (ch. 37).

an expanding international evangelical network during the 1740s and 1750s. "Through correspondence, published journals, educational centers, and charitable organizations," says Kenneth Minkema, "these evangelicals on the Continent, in England, and in America worked to promote, coordinate, and report revivals from a transatlantic perspective."[54] Printed literature and personal letters established what Susan O'Brien called "a transatlantic community of saints" that viewed "the events of the late 1730s and 1740s...as parts of a single God-inspired phenomenon."[55] John Gillies's massive, two-volume compilation of revival narratives from both sides of the Atlantic, *Historical Collections Relating to Remarkable Periods of the Success of the Gospel* (1754), helped to solidify a transatlantic and Calvinistic interpretation of the events of the 1730s and 1740s.

From a retrospect of three centuries, the transatlantic revivals of the 1730s and 1740s—with Edwards as their leading theological interpreter—left a sizable legacy. It is called evangelicalism.

---

54. Minkema, "Jonathan Edwards," in McClymond, ed., *Encyclopedia of Religious Revivals in America*, 1:156.

55. O'Brien, "Transatlantic Community," 811. See also Harold P. Simonson, "Jonathan Edwards and His Scottish Connections," *Journal of American History* 21 (1987): 353–76.

SECTION 4

Church, Ethics, Eschatology, and Society

28

The Church

EDWARDS'S CONFLICT WITH—AND ultimate separation from—his Northampton congregation in 1750 has cast a long shadow. Because of his dismissal, it has been common to view Edwards as a failed pastor. Some have read his entire pastoral career as an inevitable progression toward an unhappy outcome. This perspective has influenced the understanding of his ecclesiology. Debates over the Lord's Supper received disproportionate attention in relation to other aspects of his thinking and writing on the church. Some interpreters have viewed as sectarian Edwards's insistence that eucharistic fellowship ought to be limited to those willing and able to make a meaningful public profession of faith. This issue is treated later in this volume (ch. 30), but suffice it to say here that misunderstandings of Edwards's views on admission to communion have persisted from the 1740s to the present. Another misconception arose because of Edwards's qualified support for the Great Awakening (ch. 27). Protestant revivalism in the 1800s and 1900s evolved toward a pietistic individualism that affirmed an invisible church of supposed true converts rather than a tangible, institutional church. Critics of evangelistic altar calls by Charles Finney, Billy Sunday, and Billy Graham have charged that revivalism made church structures irrelevant. Only individual "decisions for Christ" mattered. Since Edwards played so prominent a role in initiating the American revival tradition in the mid-1700s (ch. 42), many interpreters presumed that Edwards himself held a subjective, individualistic view of Christianity.

The image of Edwards as a religious subjectivist has initial plausibility but falls short when one starts to look at the relevant texts. Because he wrote no general treatise on the church, one has to piece together Edwards's views by looking at notebook entries, sermons, and other indications scattered throughout his writings. Yet when one looks the whole of what he wrote, one may conclude with Thomas Schafer that Edwards not only did not reject the concept of a visible church but in fact emphasized it and sought to minimize the traditional Protestant distinction between a visible and an invisible church. For Edwards, there were not two churches—one visible and the other invisible—but only one church under two aspects. What is more, Edwards's stated preference in later life for Presbyterianism over the "unsettled, independent, confused way of church government" in Congregationalism showed that he had grappled with issues of church order and had embraced the notion of trans-local authority over individual congregations.[1] *Humble Attempt* (1747) revealed a tendency to subsume individual Christians within local congregations, local congregations within regional bodies, and national churches within overarching, international communities, so that the whole of the Christian world might manifest—as his lengthy title indicated—a "visible union of God's people."[2] This call for visible Christian unity set Edwards apart from any sort of religious individualism. Instead, his approach in *Humble Attempt* had something in common with the twentieth-century ecumenical movement in its quest for "the unity which is...God's will and his gift" to be "made visible" through the sharing of "corporate life."[3]

The Church in God's Plan

For Edwards, the church was a reflection of God's eternal purposes. Before the world was created, the persons of the Holy Trinity entered into a "covenant of redemption" specifying that the Son of God would come into the world to suffer, die, and rise again on behalf of elect human beings. God chose the elect for salvation because they were conceived of as already being in Christ. They were chosen not as isolated individuals, but rather as parts of Christ, so to speak, and as a body of members subsisting in spiritual unity with one another. The union with Christ emphasized in the earlier chapters on salvation (chs. 23–26) was also prominent in Edwards's view of the church. The church according to its "essence" was a community of persons bound into unity with God and with one another through Christ: "'Tis the relation and concern that the members of the church have with Christ that is the thing wherein above all things the essence of the church consists."[4] Krister Sairsingh has argued that the church,

---

1. WJE 16:355. On Edwards's doctrine of the church, see especially Thomas A. Schafer, "Jonathan Edwards's Conception of the Church," *Church History* 24 (1955): 51–66; David D. Hall, "Editor's Introduction," in WJE 12:1–90; and Douglas A. Sweeney, "The Church," in Sang Hyun Lee, ed., *The Princeton Companion to Jonathan Edwards* (Princeton, NJ: Princeton University Press, 2005), 167–89.

2. WJE 5:308.

3. "Report of the Section on Unity," Third Assembly of the World Council of Churches, New Delhi, India 1961, in Michael Kinnamon and Brian E. Cope, eds., *The Ecumenical Movement: An Anthology of Key Texts and Voices* (Grand Rapids, MI: Eerdmans/Geneva: WCC Publications, 1997) 88.

4. Edwards, sermon on Col. 1:24, cited in Sweeney, "Church," 169.

for Edwards, was the point in the created realm wherein the glory of God became visible. The *Two Dissertations*, on his reading, were ecclesiological treatises that showed from the divine perspective (*End of Creation*) and from a human vantage point (*True Virtue*) how the church exists to manifest God's presence and glory.[5]

The church's union with Christ was not something static, but came about through a dynamic process in which God continuously transmitted or infused his very self (see the discussion of ontic enlargement in ch. 16). "Communication" was Edwards's term to denote the process whereby God conveyed his own being, goodness, and happiness. This "communication" took place in two ways—first, in the eternal society of the Father, Son, and Spirit (ch. 13); and second, in the creation and redemption of the world (ch. 14). In Trinitarian terms, "the Father's begetting of the Son is a complete communication of all his happiness, and so an eternal, adequate and infinite exercise of perfect goodness, that is completely equal to such an inclination in perfection." This statement raised the question: Why would God "communicate" himself by creating a world, if the Father had already "communicated" himself perfectly through begetting the Son? Edwards anticipated this question and answered that "the Son has also an inclination to communicate himself, in an image of his person that may partake of his happiness...and this was the only motive hereto....And man, the consciousness or perception of the creation, is the immediate subject of this."[6] In the argument of *End of Creation*, Edwards made clear that the divine "communication" to the church in the present life and in eternity may be distinguished into such aspects as knowledge, virtue or holiness, and happiness.[7] God's people were to have knowledge of divine things, to be a holy people, and to be happy, since true happiness was not opposed to the practice of virtue but rather followed as its consequence.

Extending his reasoning on the Son's "communication" and citing a number of biblical texts, Edwards concluded that "the church is said to be the completeness of Christ (Eph. 1:23), as if Christ were not complete without the church." The thought of Christ's incompleteness led Edwards into the nuptial or marital metaphor for God's relationship with humanity. For "as man is incomplete without the woman...so Christ is not complete without his spouse." Throughout scripture "the church is everywhere spoken of, as being so nearly

---

5. Krister Sairsingh, "Jonathan Edwards and the Idea of Divine Glory: His Foundational Trinitarianism and Its Ecclesial Import," PhD diss., Harvard University, 1986.

6. WJE 13:272.

7. WJE 8:439–44, 458–60.

united to Christ that she is one with him."⁸ The world was created so that the Son of God might have a spouse—that is, the church.⁹ Edwards followed the traditional Christian view that the biblical Song of Songs (also known as Canticles) may be read allegorically as a love song pertaining to Christ (the bridegroom) and the church (the bride).¹⁰ Christ will not consummate the union with his church during the present life but in eternity. What will distinguish the heavenly wedding feast from all occasions of earthly weddings is that its joys will be unfading and unending: "The wedding feast is eternal and the love and joys, the songs, entertainments and glories of the wedding will never be ended. It will be an everlasting wedding day."¹¹

This exalted idea of the church's purpose and calling runs throughout Edwards's writings and finds expression in *Charity and Its Fruits*, *End of Creation*, *History of Redemption*, and *Humble Attempt*. While the focus of Edwards's sacramental writings was more down to earth, *Humble Inquiry* and *Misrepresentations Corrected* implied this lofty notion of the church's nature, calling, and destiny. Though Edwards never equated the earthly church with the ultimate, final, or heavenly church, he believed nonetheless that the earthly church could and should be a fitting anticipation and sign of what lay beyond. This meant that the unity, purity, integrity, and faithfulness of the earthly church were matters of urgent and passionate concern for Edwards.

The Church in History

For Edwards, God's eternal purposes for the church were never fully realized in history. Human hatred toward Jesus Christ and the gospel message (ch. 15), opposition from the devil and unseen spiritual adversaries (ch. 18), and the church's own faults and follies hindered the full realization of God's plan. Dangers from without and perils from within confronted the church in every generation. The internal perils could be more destructive than the external. Like many early Christian thinkers, Edwards held that the church's persecution

---

8. WJE 13:272–73.

9. "The spouse of the Son of God, the bride, the Lamb's wife...is that for which all the universe was made. Heaven and earth were created that the Son of God might be complete in a spouse" (WJE 13:271). "God created the world for his Son, that he might prepare a spouse or bride for him to bestow his love upon; so that the mutual joys between this bride and bridegroom are the end of the creation" (WJE 13:374). "The end of the creation was to provide a spouse for his Son" (WJE 8:708).

10. For Edwards's spiritual exegesis of the Song of Songs, see WJE 24:608–28 and WJE 15:75, 177–79, 322, 389–90, 520, 526–27, 538, 547–51, 582–88.

11. WJE 8:709.

by pagan authorities had ultimately strengthened and purified the church so that "the more they persecuted the church, the more it increased." Edwards cited the famous slogan—based on Tertullian—that "the blood of the martyrs is the seed of the saints."[12] Yet internal opposition to the church came in subtle and insidious forms, and none more subtle than what Edwards referred to as "Antichrist," which was not a villain appearing at the end of the age but a force working through various individuals and institutions in the course of church history. "Antichrist" for Edwards was closely bound to Roman Catholicism, though there was a distinction between the two. Terms like "Antichrist" and "antichristian" sometimes applied to deism and to Islam as well as to the Roman Catholic Church. "Antichrist" was not identical to Roman Catholicism but was a spiritual force of opposition to Christ's followers that had operated in and through the Roman Catholic Church during the medieval and early modern periods.

To understand Edwards's views, one must bear several things in mind. First, the rendition of church history Edwards had learned ascribed countless atrocities to the popes and other Catholic leaders, and almost nothing that was worthy or commendable. The received version of church history among eighteenth-century Protestants was utterly one-sided. Enlightened thinkers, no less than traditional Protestants, viewed the Catholic Church as the world's great bastion of political and intellectual repression. Second, the Catholic Church of Edwards's day had stigmatized Protestants as heretics and consigned them to eternal damnation. Both sides in the debates were locked into a pattern of action and reaction. Third, Protestant-Catholic animosities were greatly exacerbated by political intrigues on the part of popes and Catholic monarchs who tried to topple the Protestant regime in England and thus earned the undying enmity of the English people and their rulers. When Edwards spoke of God's day of judgment, when the church shall meet face to face with all of its historic adversaries, the persecutors he mentioned included the Egyptian Pharaoh, Antiochus Epiphanes, first-century Pharisees, Julian the Apostate, and the "cruel persecuting popes and papists."[13] The reputation of the Catholic Church was forever blackened for Edwards and other early Protestants because of its church-sponsored persecutions of religious dissenters.

The essence of Roman Catholic and papal error lay in a usurpation of ecclesiastical power. Edwards wrote regarding the bishop of Rome: "In the

---

12. WJE 9:391. The saying about the martyrs' blood first appeared, in somewhat different phrasing, in Tertullian, *Apology*, ch. 50.

13. WJE 9:501.

primitive times he was only a minister of a congregation, then a standing moderator of a presbytery, then a diocesan bishop, then a metropolitan which was equivalent to an archbishop, then he was a patriarch, then afterwards he claimed the power of universal bishop over the whole Christian church through the world, wherein he was opposed for a while but afterwards was confirmed in it by the civil power." The church did not by any means welcome these "corruptions of the church of Rome," but rather they "were brought in with a great deal of struggle and opposition." This was especially true when the pope first claimed to be a "universal bishop," at which time "many churches greatly opposed him in it."[14] The popes especially relied on the power of excommunication to captivate and control the faithful, who believed that the pope's rejection would spell eternal damnation.[15] Edwards linked Roman Catholicism to Antichrist based on his reading of the Book of Revelation. His exegesis viewed the book as anticipating the rise and growth of papal power between the fourth century and the sixteenth century, when Protestantism began.[16] Moses Lowman's *Paraphrase and Notes on the Revelation* (1737) was a key influence on Edwards's interpretation of the Book of Revelation. On the history of the popes, Edwards drew from Archibald Bower's multivolume *History of Popery* (1748–66).[17]

Throughout the centuries of Roman Catholic domination, God had always maintained a witness to himself through the survival of his people— a true church over and against a false church. Deep suffering and affliction marked this remnant of true believers. Edwards thus held to the "trail of blood" view of the church. The true believers were to be identified with the "woman in the wilderness" of Revelation 12. Medieval groups such as the Waldensians and Albigensians were included here.[18] In another context, Edwards identified the suffering remnant with the celibate males of Revelation 14, who had not "prostituted themselves" and had maintained through the Middle Ages a "doctrine and worship" that "appear to be the same with the Protestant doctrine and worship." Despite—or perhaps because of—their

---

14. WJE 9:412, 418.

15. On excommunication, see WJE 5:236; 9:413; 12:237; 13:172–73, 189, 527; 16:286, and Edwards's sermon on excommunication in WJE 22:64–79.

16. WJE 5:225–50.

17. WJE 5:22, 55–59 (Moses Lowman); WJE 9:547 (Archibald Bower).

18. WJE 5:107–10. Stephen Stein comments (WJE 110, n.6) that Protestant polemicists had "romanticized" views of the various groups opposed by the medieval Catholic authorities. Edwards himself did not seem to distinguish the Waldensians from the Albigensians, even though the former were generally an evangelical movement and the latter were a Gnostic, dualistic sect.

strict lives and external poverty, they endured many persecutions, and yet their opponents "could not by all their cruelties extirpate the church of God, so fulfilling his word, 'that the gates of hell should not prevail against it.'"[19] This reference to Matthew 16:18 was a deliberate inversion of Roman Catholic exegesis, which interpreted the text as teaching that Peter's successors, or the bishops of Rome, would prevail and lead the church for all time.

On Edwards's view, God had limited the duration of the papal reign. There would be 1, 260 years of Roman domination, extending from the year 606, "when the pope was first seated in his chair, and was made universal bishop." Thus the dark time of Catholic power would last until sometime around 1866—though Edwards also thought that "Satan's kingdom ... will not receive its finishing stroke till the year two thousand, when the world will have completed its first 6000 years and will enter into a millennium that will be "a sabbath of rest."[20] In reviewing the global news of his own day, Edwards looked for hopeful signs of political and economic decline in the papacy and in European Catholic states such as France, Spain, and Italy.[21] While he was aware of the vicissitudes of history (ch. 15), he was convinced, in Stephen Stein's words, "that the lowest days of the church were past and the times were becoming increasingly favorable for the saints."[22]

Having reviewed Edwards's opposition to Roman Catholicism, we may move on to his more charitable posture with respect to other branches of Christendom. Judged with respect to Edwards's place and time, his vision of the church was more encompassing than that of contemporaries whose vision was limited to one branch of Protestantism—e.g., Congregationalism, Presbyterianism, or Anglicanism. The word "bishop," though obnoxious to stricter Puritans, was not a pejorative term for Edwards. He used the phrase "gospel-bishops" as a term of commendation in his correspondence.[23] With regard to Lutheranism, Edwards offered a glowing account of the "remarkable revival of the power and practice of religion in Saxony in Germany." He commended the charitable work of "August Herman Frank [i.e., Francke]," who provided for the education of poor children and so brought a growth of "learning and piety."[24] It seems to have been Franke's concern

---

19. WJE 9:420.

20. WJE 5:129.

21. WJE 5:298–305, 421–24.

22. Stephen Stein, "Editor's Introduction," WJE 5:59.

23. WJE 16:278.

24. WJE 9:436.

for the poor as much as his doctrinal orthodoxy that evoked Edwards's admiration. With regard to Eastern Orthodoxy, Edwards wrote that Russia "of late [has] become much more a land of light than it was. They agree more with the Protestants than the papists, and 'tis hopeful the reformation among them will yet be carried on to a much greater height." Edwards believed that the "emperor of Muscovy" might be spoken of in the Book of Isaiah, and could play a role in the coming overthrow of Antichrist.[25] It is doubtful that Edwards had ever met or spoken with an Eastern Orthodox Christian, so his opinions regarding Russian Orthodoxy, its "revival," and the alleged agreement of Orthodox with Protestants, were admittedly secondhand. Yet his attitude of openness to non-Protestants was noteworthy.

Edwards held a positive view of the Church of England. This is somewhat surprising in that Anglican authorities had once persecuted the religious dissenters of England. Congregationalists often manifested a deep distrust of bishops and kings. In this particular, Anglicanism might not seem to be much better than Catholicism. What is more, Anglican domination was a more immediate threat to the American colonists than Catholic domination, which would only have been conceivable in the event of a French or Spanish invasion. Yet Edwards in his correspondence wrote of "the hopeful true piety of the Archbishop of Canterbury"—a reference to Thomas Herring.[26] He expressed delight that the spiritual awakening in England was led by such Anglican clergymen as George Whitefield and John Wesley. Edwards's sermon "God's Grace Carried on in Other Places"—likely preached in his own home in December 1739—recounts how the Church of England had been "sound in its principles" with respect to justification and faith, and then "corruption began" and grew during the reigns of Charles I and Charles II. Yet "God has raised up in England a number of young ministers...that seem in the midst of all this darkness wonderfully to have been wrought upon by the Spirit of God and enlightened to see the corruption, and so are become sound in the faith, very thoroughly grounded in those great doctrines of [justification and faith]." He spoke glowingly of such "New Methodists" as John Wesley, George Whitefield, and Howell Harris.[27] On the whole, Edwards regarded the Church of England as a true church that—though blighted by errors and corruptions—might nonetheless be reformed and renewed in accordance with biblical teaching.

---

25. WJE 5:191.

26. WJE 16:258.

27. WJE 22:107–108.

Edwards's enthusiasm for the evangelical Awakening in Britain indicated that he acknowledged a spiritual kinship with those Christians whose form of church government differed from his own Congregational system. One may conclude that proper church order or government was not a foundational article of faith for Edwards. At the same time, some doctrines—especially justification and salvation by grace—were essential and nonnegotiable. The Anglican "New Methodists" were thus more acceptable to Edwards than the liberal or Arminian-leaning Congregationalist clergy of New England. In Edwards's statements prior to the Great Awakening, one detects the lineaments of an emerging transatlantic evangelical movement, which made adherence to certain central beliefs—such as the new birth, salvation by grace, and fervent evangelistic preaching—more essential to Christian identity than outward conformity to an established church tradition or form of church government.

Despite his openness to Protestants of varied backgrounds, Edwards was sometimes sharply critical. While in Stockbridge, Edwards wrote that the Anglican missions organization—Society for Propagating the Gospel in Foreign Parts—had done "very little" to evangelize the Native peoples and instead "chiefly spent [its money] to promote the church party in opposition [to] those of the Presbyterian and Congregational persuasion in New England." These Church of England missionaries were "almost wholly high church men, and great bigots" who "use all manner of methods to promote their particular party."[28] Edwards was not objecting to Anglicanism as such but to what he regarded as denominational bias and to proselytism or sheep-stealing. His criticism of Anglican missionaries was consistent with his commitment to evangelical unity. Indeed, a pan-Protestant alliance was only possible if Protestants of various denominations stopped proselytizing one another.

The Church in the Congregational Tradition

According to the eighteenth-century New England version of church history, a series of British reformers—beginning with John Wycliffe in the 1300s and continuing until the "Glorious Revolution" of 1688—had bravely fought to edify and purify the established Church of England, and, after repeated rebuffs, had been forced amid immense difficulties to establish true Protestantism

---

28. WJE 16:437–38. Edwards was a co-signatory of a 1734 letter of the Hampshire Ministers' Association that protested the sending of Church of England ministers-missionaries to New England (as noted by Kenneth Minkema). See Edwards's references to the "injurious, oppressive designs of the Church of England against us" (WJE 16:78–79, with note 2).

in the "desert" of America. In New England, the desert had bloomed. This small Protestant outpost was a "city on a hill" that God had appointed to keep the fire of true religion burning brightly in an era of encroaching darkness. New England's Reforming Synod had declared in 1679: "We differ from other out-goings [i.e., emigrations] of our Nation, in that it was not any worldly consideration that brought our Fathers into this wilderness, but Religion, even that so they might build a Sanctuary unto the Lords name."[29] American Puritans did not shrink from comparing themselves to the ancient Israelites and thinking of themselves as a new "chosen people." The opening paragraphs of Cotton Mather's great epic of New England history, *Magnalia Christi Americana* (1702), summarized this story of persecution, flight, exile, and advancement, and there was little here that Edwards would not have consented to (ch. 3). The Puritan narrative engendered a series of antitheses—the elite versus the masses, the corrupt church versus the true church, and the Old World versus the New World. To this might be added a further contrast—the present-day church and the church in its impending "glorious times."[30]

A core element of Edwards's Puritan heritage was a call to reform the church and its structures in accordance with the word of God. Rejecting not only the Roman papacy but also rule by bishops, the Puritans redefined the nature of church so that it no longer had reference to an historical succession of consecrated leaders. In its basic meaning, the church was a local assembly of believers. Edwards in an early notebook entry spoke of the church as "a company of God's people joined together for God's worship and service."[31] Christian identity rested on personal faith, and the local gathering of believers was constituted by "covenant" with God and mutual agreement among believers. Beyond this, there was reluctance to attach fixed meanings to the forms and structures of Christian life. New England Congregationalists did not, for example, refer to their places of worship as "churches" because they believed that this might convey the mistaken idea that these buildings were properly regarded as God's dwelling places. Instead they spoke of "meetinghouses."[32] Because Congregationalists defined the church in terms of local assemblies,

---

29. Williston Walker, *The Creeds and Platforms of Congregationalism* (New York: Pilgrim Press, 1991 [1893]), 431.

30. Miklos Vetö, *Le pensée de Jonathan Edwards* (Paris: Cerf, 1987), 7.

31. WJE 13:414.

32. Miklos Vetö, *Le pensée de Jonathan Edwards*, 3, n.17. cf. John Calvin, *Institutes of the Christian Religion*, 3.20.30.

they refused to recognize the binding authority of trans-local authorities, such as councils, synods, general assemblies, bishops, archbishops, or popes. Edwards wrote that "this is evident by naked and natural reason, that those who live together"—that is, those who are connected in "families, societies, provinces, governments," and the like—"are...[to] worship God together."[33] Local assemblies had received from Christ himself a full power to exercise authority in church life, sacraments, and jurisdiction over their members.

This, at least, was the official position. Yet the New England congregations did not simply fend for themselves but drew up common statements of principle and practice, including *The Cambridge Platform* (1648), *The Half-Way Covenant Decisions* (1657, 1662), *The Reforming Synod* (1679–80), *The Massachusetts Proposals* (1705), and *The Saybrook Platform* (1708). Since each of these documents resulted from a ministers' consultation and was accorded a measure of authority in New England, it was hard to assert categorically that church synods had no status among Congregationalists. The New Englanders' own practice told otherwise. Whenever the churches faced issues of widespread concern during the 1600s or 1700s, the ministers gathered together to discuss issues, enact resolutions, and to prepare written statements on church policy.

In an early notebook entry, Edwards stated that church synods were allowable and yet were merely occasions when "ministers may take each other's advice." They were not governmental entities that "have power to make laws for the conscience."[34] Elsewhere he wrote that "the Scriptures only is [sic] our rule to direct us in matters of faith and worship, and not fathers, or councils, or ecclesiastical history, or the practice of the church in former times."[35] The relatively minor role that Edwards accorded to church tradition in his theological method is noted elsewhere in this volume (chs. 1, 9, 41). Yet certain notebook entries suggest that "a convention of churches" or "higher synod" might have the same disciplinary powers over local congregations as the latter had over its individual members.[36] Moreover, in the debate over the ordination of Robert Breck (ch. 3), Edwards's penned a lengthy *Letter to the Author of the Pamphlet* (1737) that argued for the invalidity of Breck's ordination in Springfield, Massachusetts, by ministers who came from eastern Massachusetts

---

33. WJE 13:237.
34. WJE 13:189.
35. WJE 24:421.
36. WJE 13:253–54, 421.

rather than from the congregations nearer to Springfield. In part, Edwards's argument hinged on his exegesis of *The Cambridge Platform* and its statements regarding "neighboring" or "neighbor-churches."[37] In this instance, he explicitly based a pastoral and theological argument on a church council's decision. About a dozen years later, in his "Narrative of Communion Controversy" (ca. 1750), Edwards stated that the Congregational platforms do not have "the force of a rule or establishment to bind particular churches of Christ without an express act or consent on their own." A document of some ninety years earlier—i.e., *The Cambridge Platform*—could not "bind the present churches without any free act of theirs."[38] At this later stage, Edwards's position seems to have been that the binding authority of church councils came only from a freely given consent by a congregation to the edicts of a particular church council.

The most far-reaching statement of Edwards's departure from a pure Congregationalism came in the wake of his dismissal from his Northampton parish. In a letter to Rev. John Erskine in Scotland, he commented:

> As to my subscribing to the substance of the Westminster Confession, there would be no difficulty: and as to the Presbyterian government, I have long been perfectly out of conceit with our unsettled, independent, confused way of church government in this land. And the Presbyterian way has ever appeared to me most agreeable to the Word of God, and the reason and nature of things, though I cannot say that I think that the Presbyterian government of the Church of Scotland is so perfect that it can't in some respects be mended.[39]

While Edwards was formal and courteous in his letters (and especially when writing to individuals of distinction), he was not in the habit of flattering his correspondents by indicating that he held opinions that were not his own. The 1750 letter indicates a shift not only in Edwards's theology of the eucharist but in his broader ecclesiology. Though Edwards considered the local, gathered assembly of believers to be the fundamental unit of the church, he no longer thought of every congregation as standing on its own. He ended his career as a convinced Presbyterian, though, as noted, he likely did not

---

37. WJE 12:105–12, 124; cf. Walker, *Creeds and Platforms*, 229–34. See David Hall's discussion of the Robert Breck case in WJE 12:4–17, and Peter Thuesen's in WJE 26:30.

38. WJE 12:551.

39. WJE 16:355.

regard issues of church governance as having the importance that certain other doctrines did.

The Church in Its "Glorious Times"

To a greater extent than most of his Puritan predecessors, Edwards's vision of the church was suffused by an optimistic expectation of wonderful things that lay ahead. His *History of Redemption* included a striking section describing the church's "time of great light and knowledge" prior to Christ's glorious return:

> Then all countries and nations, even those which are now most ignorant, shall be full of light and knowledge.... It may be hoped that then many of the Negroes and Indians will be divines, and that excellent books will be published in Africa, in Ethiopia, in Turkey.... There shall then be universal peace and good understanding among all the nations of the world.... Then shall all the world be united in peace and love in one amiable society.... A communication shall then be upheld between all parts of the world to that end, and the art of navigation that is now improved so much in fear, with covetousness and pride... shall then be consecrated to God, and improved for holy uses... all the world [shall then be] as one church, one orderly, regular, beautiful society, one body, all the members in beautiful proportion.[40]

This paragraph is drawn from a long discussion of the knowledge, joy, peace, unity, universality, and flourishing condition of the church during in its impending "glorious times."

For Edwards, history's consummation will not come through divine coercion. Instead, the gospel message will persuade multitudes who shall willingly join themselves to Christ: "And there shall be a glorious pouring out of the Spirit with this clear and powerful preaching of the gospel, to make it successful for reviving those holy doctrines of religion that are now chiefly ridiculed in the world... and also for turning many from their vice and profaneness, and for bringing vast multitudes savingly home to Christ."[41] In speaking of "heresy," Edwards frequently predicted its final overthrow and defeat by God's truth. Heresy, wickedness, and schism were all finally to be overcome.

---

40. WJE 9: 480, 482–84.
41. WJE 9:461.

This glorious forecast of the future, however, is not the church's final state, nor is it to be identified with the millennium or with heaven, since it will be a long period of revival and persecution leading up to the millennium (ch. 35). After the millennium arrives—"a long day of light and holiness, love and peace and joy," there will once again be "a dark time," and "Satan shall begin to set up his dominion again in the world." This final turn toward darkness will involve "the most aggravated wickedness that ever was," for "the bigger part of the world shall have become...open enemies to Christ." Unlike the pagan nations that never heard of Christ, this final apostasy from the faith will take place among those who had "enjoyed the great light and privileges of those glorious times of the church." The worldwide wickedness will call for God's "immediate vengeance" and "Christ's...appearing in flaming fire."[42] While Edwards's presented an optimistic picture of the final or "glorious" church, this did not rule out the necessity of Christ's intervention at the end of history, to make an end of evil, and to bring the church to its final state of glory and blessedness.

---

42. WJE 9:488–90.

29

Edwards on (and in) the Ministry

SAMUEL HOPKINS, EDWARDS'S protégé and first biographer, wrote that Edwards did not take up the usual ministerial practice of "visiting his people from house to house." Hopkins explained that "he supposed that ministers should, with respect to this, consult their own talents and circumstances, and visit more or less, according to the degree in which they could hope thereby to promote the great ends of the ministry." He knew that some ministers were talented at visiting, and he was not. Besides, he was in a large parish, so "it would have taken up a great part of his time," which he thought could be put to better use in his study—writing sermons and treatises, and "conversing with people under religious impressions."[1]

This little portrait of the theologian-pastor in his study receiving guests points both to Edwards's view of the ministry and his own ministerial practice. Both have been applauded and criticized. Some have said they reflect the Puritan ideal of the pastor in prayer and study procuring food (i.e., spiritual sustenance) for his flock; they contrast it favorably to today's pastor, whose administrative duties often crowd out time for reflection.[2] Others have suggested that this abandonment of pastoral custom typified an un-pastoral aloofness that contributed to the failure of his Northampton pastorate.[3] In this chapter, we will first sketch Edwards's theology of ministry and then discuss his practice of ministry.

---

1. Samuel Hopkins, 54–55, *The Life and Character of the Late Reverend Mr. Jonathan Edwards, President of the College at New-Jersey* (Boston, 1765), 54–55. According to E. Brooks Holifield, the home visit was the "main means of pastoral care" for eighteenth-century New England pastors, and the "main pastoral duty" in private talks with parishioners was "discernment" into their spiritual states. Edwards spent plenty of time doing the latter and was well-known for it, but he was different from most of his contemporaries in asking parishioners to come to his study. Holifield, *God's Ambassadors: A History of the Christian Clergy in America* (Grand Rapids, MI: Eerdmans, 2007), 90; Holifield, *A History of Pastoral Care in America: From Salvation to Self-Realization* (Nashville: Abingdon, 1983), 82.

2. Hopkins, *Life*, 54–55; Iain Murray, *Jonathan Edwards: A New Biography* (Edinburgh: Banner of Truth, 1987), 342–43.

3. Patricia Tracy, "The Pastorate of Jonathan Edwards," *The Massachusetts Review* 20 (1979): 437–51; Tracy, *Jonathan Edwards, Pastor: Religion and Society in Eighteenth-Century Northampton* (New York: Hill and Wang, 1980); David D. Hall, "Editor's Introduction" to *Ecclesiastical Writings* in WJE 12:1–90.

Roles of the Ministry

When Edwards took over as sole pastor at Northampton in 1729, he had already been mentored by two pastors legendary for their accomplishments. For most of his childhood, he sat under his own father Timothy's preaching in East Windsor, Connecticut. Timothy was well-known for being a learned and effective preacher, having taken both the bachelor's and master's degrees from Harvard College. It was a "customary remark" among those who heard both Timothy and his son preach that "Mr. Jonathan was the deeper preacher," but "Mr. [Timothy] Edwards was perhaps the more learned man, and more animated in his manner." The elder Edwards did quite a bit of counseling for his parishioners, unlike his son, but was also known, like his son, for both hellfire preaching and struggles with his congregation over salary and communion qualifications. For nearly three years after first coming to Northampton in 1726, Edwards served as an assistant to his maternal grandfather, Solomon Stoddard, whose influence had earned him the title "Congregational Pope" of the Connecticut Valley. For some decades before his death, Stoddard had been honored with the almost-annual invitation to preach the public lecture after the Harvard commencement. Benjamin Colman declared in Stoddard's funeral sermon that Stoddard had been esteemed not only for his diligence in his studies but also for his fervent preaching, which not coincidentally had led to three seasons of revival when "it became almost a general cry of the place, 'What must I do to be saved?'"[4]

It is no surprise that Edwards's theology of ministry echoed many themes seen in the ministries of his pastoral role models. Colman, for example, called Stoddard's "a laborious, burning ministry." In 1744, after Great Awakening fires had cooled, Edwards proclaimed in an ordination sermon that a minister of the gospel is to be "a burning and a shining light" (Jn. 5:35). God sent Christ as the "Sun of Righteousness" (Mal. 4:2) to a fallen dark world. To convey Christ's light to human beings, God uses the means of "appointed ministers in his church to be subordinate lights, and to shine with the communications of [Christ's] light, and to reflect the beams of his glory on the souls of men." They are "burning" lights because they radiate with the "holy ardor of a spirit of true piety," and they are "shining" lights because their doctrine is "pure, clear and full." Ministers without the ardor of true piety become "putrefying carcasses" that stink, while ministers with hot zeal and little light resemble "the heat of the bottomless pit" and "an angel of darkness." But ministers with

---

4. George M. Marsden, *Jonathan Edwards: A Life* (New Haven, CT: Yale University Press, 2003), 33–34; Tracy, *Jonathan Edwards, Pastor*, 18–20.

both true light and true piety bring people to "the infinite fountain of light," where they will behold "the most glorious and excellent objects," the sustained sight of which will transform them.[5]

Edwards believed these "guides" and "teachers" have three functions. First, they "discover" or reveal glorious things to their hearers, enabling them to see what angels see. Second, they "*refresh* and delight the beholders," since light is refreshing to those who have sat in darkness. This new light provides the healing salve required to "bind up the broken-hearted." Third, they "direct" souls through this dark world to "regions of eternal light." In a word, "the work of ministers is to rescue lost souls and bring them to eternal happiness." Pastors are "guide[s] to lead them to an understanding of what we are taught in the Word of God of the nature of grace, and to help them apply it to themselves."[6]

This pastoral guidance would not only lead souls out of darkness into light, but in the process "wash and cleanse the souls of men." This comes from the preaching of the word, which is ministers' "main business." The washing and cleansing come in part from teaching congregants, through pastoral preaching, to see where they have made mistakes. Edwards believed the historical church had often made such mistakes. For instance, he preached at the height of his conflict with his Northampton parish that the biblical patriarchs practiced polygamy, the church at the time of Solomon worshipped at high places, and that the early Christian church misunderstood the Messiah's kingdom and superstitiously used the sign of the cross and white garments in baptism. Luther wrongly taught "consubstantiation" and denied the "doctrine of God's decrees." The Reformed divided over episcopacy and worship practices, "which demonstrates that many of them go on in error."[7]

But God had a purpose in all this. "God deals with his church in this respect as parents do with children. They gradually instruct them as they can bear, that they may grow in knowledge as they grow older, till all their childish mistakes are corrected." God uses ministers as his primary agents in this celestial pedagogy. Their role is "to correct the mistakes of his people and gradually introduce an increase of light." Therefore ministers should not always go with the flow. They are to make the Word of God, "not the past opinions of their flocks[,] the rule of their teaching." God would "wink at errors for a season" and "bestow his blessing on [his people] notwithstanding, as He did

---

5. Tracy, *Jonathan Edwards*, Pastor, 19; WJE 25:88–89, 90, 92, 95, 90.

6. BW, 86; WJE 4:175; emph. added.

7. WJE 25:335, 444–45.

of old on Jacob, David and others that went on in that error of the plurality of wives." But then God would appoint a "season for the bringing greater light to correct error, and after that he will wink at such errors no more." If his people persist in their errors despite corrections from their ministers, "God departs from 'em and gives them his blessing no more."[8]

Ministers would be tempted in such times to think more highly of themselves than they ought. Instead, they should remember that they are "feeble, frail, sinful worms of the dust, in this work, who need redemption themselves." Their glory is "in some respects" greater than that of the angels, and they are the more dignified of the two classes of creatures, but "in themselves [they] are utterly insufficient" for the work of ministry. They are like physicians trying to raise the dead: they are "utterly unable to deliver the souls of men out of" the power of darkness, apart from a miracle of God. But with divine enabling they can be like the twelve apostles, who were "poor fishermen" who became "the conquerors of the world." They must remember that God could have conquered the whole Roman Empire at once without their ministry but graciously decided to use them and share his glory in the process. As a result, they did greater works than Christ himself on earth. "Christ's preaching and miracles on earth converted but few. But the apostles turned the world upside down."[9]

Like Christ and the apostles, ministers of the gospel will suffer for the salvation of souls. True ministers will "spend and be spent for them" (2 Cor. 12:15). Just as Jesus was moved with compassion because the crowds were sheep without a shepherd (Mt. 9:38), ministers will be moved with pity for people who walk in darkness. They will be ready to "fill up that which is behind of the afflictions of Christ in his flesh" (Col. 1:24) for the sake of saving lost souls. They should therefore imitate Christ's love for men and women: "Many waters could not quench his love, neither could the floods drown it, for his love was stronger than death (Sg. of Sgs. 8:6–7); yea, than the mighty pains and torments of such a death."[10]

Tasks of the Ministry

For Edwards, the principal task of the minister was to care for souls. Edwards believed in the unity of the human person, but that did not prevent his analyzing different aspects of that unity, such as body and soul. He said God is more

---

8. WJE 25:445–47, 453.

9. WJE 25:344; BW 45–47, 49, 50.

10. WJE 25:339, 337, 339–40.

concerned with human souls than bodies because souls "are in a special and more immediate manner his workmanship." Bodies came from earthly parents and pre-existent matter, but "the souls of men are by God's immediate creation." This is why scripture refers to earthly fathers as the "fathers of our flesh" and God as the "father of our spirits" (Heb 12:9). Souls are "in a higher, more direct and immediate manner from God," and it is by them that God gains glory from all his creatures. For "they are the eye of the creation to behold the glory of God manifested in the other creatures, and the mouth of the creation to praise him and ascribe to him the glory that is displayed in them."[11]

When God commits souls to the care of ministers, it is like a prince who commits to the care of a subject "some great treasure, consisting of most precious jewels" to carry for him through an enemy's country and bring home safe to his palace. Edwards also compared the minister to a watchman over a city during a time of war and to shepherds who lead their flocks "through a great and howling wilderness, full of hungry wolves and roaring lions."[12]

If the minister is to be successful watching over his flock, he must be a man of "holy ardor."[13] It was not enough to have "speculative knowledge or opinions, or outward morality or forms of religion." True faith is "an ardent thing" with "true spiritual comfort or joy." The heart of the good minister blazes with divine love or charity," which is "a holy flame enkindled in the soul." He will likely suffer reproaches and defeats if he preaches the true gospel, but he will still have an inner power that comes from "*participation of the divine nature,*" which is a divine principle—"the life of a risen Savior, who exerts himself in the hearts" of all true saints and their ministers. The Savior within will inspire a love to both Christ and human souls. That love will produce a fervor or zeal that animates the minister's prayer, preaching, exercise of church discipline, and counseling.[14]

A life of secret prayer is what keeps the inner flame glowing brightly. Ministers "should be much in seeking God, and conversing with him by prayer,

---

11. BW 64, 66.

12. BW 68–69.

13. For Edwards as for nearly everyone in the eighteenth century, the possibility of women serving as ministers was unthinkable. Yet there were female Quaker "publishers of truth" and women in other traditions inspired by the Great Awakening to preach. See John Punshon, *Portrait in Grey: A Short History of the Quakers.* (London: Quaker Books, 1984), 34, 58; and Catherine Brekus, *Strangers and Pilgrims: Female Preaching in America, 1740–1845* (Chapel Hill, NC: University of North Carolina Press, 1998).

14. BW 91–92; orig. emph.

who is the fountain of light and love." They will be "sensible with Isaiah that they are men of unclean lips" and so will "seek that their lips may be as it were touched with a live coal from the altar, as it were by the bright and burning seraphim." This sense of need will move Christ's ministers to follow his example of prayerfulness: "We read from time to time of [Christ's] retiring from the world, away from the noise and applauses of the multitudes, into mountains and solitary places for secret prayer, and holy converse with his Father; and once of his rising up in the morning a great while before day, and going and departing into a solitary place to pray (Mark 1:35); and another time, of his going out into a mountain to pray, and of continuing all night in prayer to God (Luke 6:12)." Therefore his ministers will "be much in prayer for his Spirit" and "much in secret converse with him." They will be afraid to depend on their own abilities for fear that God would then withhold his Spirit. Instead they "should beg of God that his Spirit may accompany their administration."[15]

A prayer life like this should be matched by a life of godly practice. Ministers should be patient under affliction, meek toward men, eager to forgive injuries, and ready to "pity the miserable" and "weep with those that weep" (Rom. 12:15). They ought to be tender and gentle toward the weak, and loving toward their enemies. This kind of prayer and practice will show "to all that behold them, the amiable, delightful image of the beauty and brightness of their glorious Master."[16]

Edwards wrote in the *Religious Affections* that "holy affections are not heat without light," so that true saints will have their *minds* enlightened to apprehend divine things. He also wrote in that treatise that in the lives of saints is "beautiful symmetry or proportion," which means among other things that they will balance holy ardor with true knowledge. This is especially true of the godly minister, who needs to be *"pure, clear and full in his doctrine."* "He must not lead his people into errors, but teach them in the truth only." He must teach "that same religion that Christ taught." In order to reach this point, ministers "should be diligent in their studies." They should be "very conversant with the Holy Scriptures, making it very much their business, with the utmost diligence and strictness, to search those holy writings."[17]

When ministers interpret the scriptures, they must beware of letting their own reason be the rule. For the Bible teaches truths that are mysterious

---

15. WJE 25:100, 336, 346; BW 52.
16. WJE 25:336, 94.
17. WJE 2:266, 365; WJE 25:92, 346, 99–100; orig. emph.

and sometimes repugnant to the spirit of the age—which of course varies from age to age and makes some doctrines appear unreasonable that are accepted as rational in another age: "We find that those things that are received as principles in one age and are never once questioned, it comes into nobody's thought that they possibly may not be true—and yet they are exploded in another age as light increases." Hence when interpreting scripture, ministers should not "compare the dictates of the Spirit of God in his revelation with what their own reason says and then... force such an interpretation as shall be agreeable to those dictates, but they must interpret the dictates of the Spirit of God by comparing them with other dictates of the Spirit." To make our reason the final arbiter when interpreting scripture is to make "God's revelation but a subordinate rule"—which is "to suppose that our own mere reason is a better rule or a better guide to us than God's revelation." That implies that we have no need for revelation at all.[18]

Therefore the minister needs to have intellectual humility, renouncing confidence in his own wisdom and "entirely relying on God's instructions." He may then be called "a bigoted zealot" who dares not exercise his own freedom of thought. But "if you should be ridiculed by others in this day of growing error for embracing certain doctrines of revelation that are above man's comprehension, as if you were fools and put out your eyes to receive absurd doctrines by an implicit faith, care not for it, but be willing to become fools for Christ's sake (1 Cor. 4:10), remembering that he that would be wise must become a fool."[19]

The godly minister must also be careful not to cater to his parishioners' desires. He would be a more popular preacher if he did not reprove their sins and contradict their lusts. If he preached that God would always forgive them after living a life of self-gratification, by sending up "a few earnest cries upon a death-bed" after a life of "drunkenness or lasciviousness or cheating and fraud," or that God "could not have the heart to take men and cast them into eternal burnings," he would be much better received by many hearers. If ministers were to preach Christ in only his priestly and not kingly office "to rule in us and over us," or if they were sent by God to tell people how they might become prosperous and lay up for their children, or could inherit a carnal heaven like the one "the Mahometans expect," then they also would be far more popular.[20]

---

18. BW 121, 124–25.
19. BW 129–30.
20. BW 60–65.

If ministers are to resist the worldly desires of their parishioners, they must also be prepared to exercise discipline over those whose behavior might damage the church's public witness. After the preaching of the gospel and the administration of the sacraments, the disciplining of church members was a third responsibility of the Christian minister. Usually it would mean simply a "gentle" word of private warning or admonishment, but when there is "gross" sin and "they continue impenitent" after rebukes, the minister should have no reluctance to proceed to excommunication. The church should not tolerate "visibly wicked persons," such as unrepentant fornicators, coveters, idolaters, drunkards, or extortionists, but cut them off like "a diseased member from the body" for three reasons: that the church may be kept pure and God's ordinances not defiled, that others may be deterred from wickedness, and that their souls may be saved. They are to be cut off from the fellowship and charity of the church (no longer regarded as fellow Christians), from "brotherly society" (treated "as an heathen man and a publican" [Mt. 18:17]), and from worship and internal privileges (such as the sacraments). The church should behave toward them as "our Father which is in heaven, who, though he loves many wicked men with a love of benevolence, yet he don't love them with a love of complacence" or affection. Saints are forbidden to eat with them.[21]

Such admonitions are all for the "correction" and "good of the person" excommunicated. It is God's way of using the devil as an instrument "of those peculiar chastisements that their apostasy deserves." The hope is that by this severe discipline, their "flesh" will be destroyed and the humbled sinners will return to fellowship. In the meantime, "the church is to have a greater concern for their welfare still than if they never had been brethren." Saints should pray for them and care for them if they are sick or distressed. Their own family should not cut them off from family affections and obligations, nor are "husbands and wives released from duties proper to their relations."[22] Edwards excommunicated at least four persons from the Northampton church, one for habitual drunkenness, one for refusing to repent of slander, another for fornication and contempt for church authority, and a fourth, his cousin Elisha Hawley, for refusing to repent of fornication with Martha Root, who had sued him for paternity of her twins.[23]

Edwards, then, did not shrink from confrontation. Perhaps because of this determination to do what he thought was right, if not politic, he spoke

---

21. WJE 25:68; WJE 22:70, 68, 78, 71–73.

22. WJE 22:70, 77, 74–75.

23. Douglas A. Sweeney, "The Church," in Sang Hyun Lee, ed., *The Princeton Companion to Jonathan Edwards* (Princeton: Princeton University Press, 2005), 183–84.

surprisingly often about conflicts between pastors and their congregations—even in the years when he still enjoyed wide respect at Northampton. For example, in 1741—at the height of the Great Awakening—he warned that contention between minister and people "is a worse calamity than a war with the Indians." The town that suffers this "is in a worse condition than that which is infested with cruel savages of the wilderness and cannot go about their work nor lodge in their houses without fear of their lives." By 1750, after his own church had rejected him, he concluded that this would not be uncommon: "So it *very often* comes to pass in this evil world, that great differences and controversies arise between ministers and the people that are under their pastoral care." But his stated policy was to be generous and forgiving to the "multitudes of the common people" who were easily deceived. In March 1744, just as the so-called Bad Book affair was heating up—a squabble over young men who sexually harassed young women with what they learned from a book for midwives—Edwards said pastors who have endured "ill treatment" by those who were "misled by false teachers" should not insist on a church process of interrogation for "every member that has behaved himself disorderly." Instead, "great allowances" should be made for people in the pews who err through ignorance. The apostle Paul aimed church censures against false teachers, but not against those they deceived.[24]

If Edwards had advice for how churches should handle wayward souls and contention, he also gave more general instruction in ordination sermons on how congregations should treat their pastors. First and foremost, they should provide for them financially lest pastors be distracted by worries about their families' upkeep. Too frequently, Edwards warned, parishes provided at first then later failed to give adequate support when needs were greater. He said parishioners should pray for their pastors, go to them for spiritual counseling and follow their advice, and avoid two temptations—to disrespect them when they preach against sin, and to quarrel with them over church discipline.[25]

Edwards's Pastorate

From what we can tell, Edwards was a man who practiced what he preached. He was assiduous in prayer for his flock, spent countless hours in his study advising both his own parishioners and visitors from afar on spiritual matters,

---

24. BW 145; WJE 25:471, emph. added; WJE 16:130–33.
25. WJE 25:76–78, 101–102, 80, 347–48.

and labored indefatigably to produce searching sermons and lectures. Those productions probably took up the better part of his working weeks—typically preparing two sermons for each Sunday and a Thursday lecture for his congregation of 1,300 souls. No wonder that, with his more scholarly work added to these efforts, he averaged thirteen hours per day in his study. This was after rising at four in the summer and five in the winter, followed at some point by prayer alone and then family prayer. Just before retiring at night, he and Sarah prayed together.[26]

Until the Bad Book episode of 1744, Edwards was appreciated by the great majority of his Northampton parish, especially its young people. He had given them unusual attention and esteem. He used young people as religious models for adult hearers and readers. Four-year-old Phebe Bartlett was one of his three living illustrations of true piety in *Faithful Narrative*. Edwards related how she exhorted even her parents to greater religious zeal, perhaps to their chagrin. In the same treatise he commended the young people's prayer meeting as an example to be "imitated by elder people." Furthermore, Edwards's relationship with teenagers was a departure from customary pastoral practice. Instead of returning them to their parents for instruction, as many New England pastors had done, Edwards gathered teens into groups for study and prayer under his supervision. He further defied convention by advocating their participation in congregational singing.[27]

Older teens and young, unmarried men in their twenties probably appreciated Edwards's defiance of traditional bias against youth. In mid-eighteenth-century western Massachusetts, men without land and wife were considered less than full and independent members of society. Many otherwise able men were frustrated by the near impossibility of getting either. Generally a man could not marry until he had land, and land was obtainable only by inheritance or purchase—at very high prices. Most would be too old to marry before they could save enough to buy land. For the few who inherited land, even what they received was devalued by the land's decreasing productivity. It is no

---

26. Northampton's church rivaled the biggest urban churches in New England in size. Holifield reports that the largest had 1,500 people (*God's Ambassadors*, 78). On his daily routines, see Marsden, *Jonathan Edwards*, 134–35.

27. WJE 4:199–205, 148. Tracy, *Jonathan Edwards, Pastor*, 112. For attitudes of early American evangelicals toward children, see Philip Greven, *The Protestant Temperament: Patterns of Child-Rearing, Religious Experience, and the Self in Early America* (New York: Knopf, 1977), 21–148. Catherine Brekus observes that Edwards was "one of the first ministers to treat children as religious equals." Brekus, "Remembering Jonathan Edwards's Ministry to Children," in David W. Kling and Douglas A. Sweeney, eds., *Jonathan Edwards at Home and Abroad: Historical Memories, Cultural Movements, Global Horizons* (Columbia SC: University of South Carolina Press, 2003), 48.

surprise, then, that a high percentage of Edwards's converts were young men. Conversion provided a measure of social status otherwise denied them for lack of property, and Edwards's invitation to fuller participation may have made conversion all the more attractive.

Women also tended to appreciate Edwards's pastoral leadership—at least according to Edwards himself, who wrote a friend in 1751 that his supporters in the Northampton controversy were "especially *women* and youth." This might have been because, as Ava Chamberlain has recently proposed, Edwards supported an earlier Puritan view of women's distinctive capacity for devotion to God. In an era when church leaders like Charles Chauncy pronounced women—like children—more inclined to religious delusion because of the "Weakness of their Nerves," Edwards "elevated the status of women [by] making godly housewives models of true Christian faith." In his two major accounts of the revivals (*Faithful Narrative* and *Some Thoughts Concerning the Revival*) Edwards illustrated true religion by three personal examples, all of them female. He also suggested that women are more spiritually sensitive than men, writing in his private notebooks that women are more "affectionate," using his favorite word for the seat of true religion. Chamberlain adds that as a pastor Edwards refused to go along with the sexual double standard, "which excused male sexual license with a sly wink and nod." Pastor Edwards tried to discipline several young men for harassing young women with the knowledge they gleaned from the midwives' manual (the Bad Book affair), and defended women in three fornication cases against men who chose to deny responsibility for their actions.[28]

Yet Edwards's personal style sometimes rubbed people the wrong way. His bold and blunt preaching was transformative for those who wanted to change but insulting for those who felt no need for it. As Helen Westra has characterized his preaching, it was "by turns brusque, benevolent, belittling, bold, and beseeching."[29] More than two decades of relentless and ferocious denunciations of sin were bound to raise the ire of the "river gods" who resented the

---

28. WJE 16:386, emph. added; Charles Chauncy, *Seasonable Thoughts on the State of Religion in New England* (Boston, 1743), 105; Ava Chamberlain, "Edwards and Social Issues," in Stephen J. Stein, ed., *The Cambridge Companion to Jonathan Edwards* (Cambridge, Eng.: Cambridge University Press, 2007), 337–39; Marsden, *Jonathan Edwards*, 358. For reconstruction of Edwards's use of transitional biologies of the sexes to advance his theology, see Ava Chamberlain, "The Immaculate Ovum: Jonathan Edwards and the Construction of the Female Body," *William and Mary Quarterly*, 3rd series, 67 (2000): 289–322.

29. Helen P. Westra, "Divinity's Design: Edwards and the History of the Work of Revival," in Sang Hyun Lee and Allen C. Guelzo, eds., *Edwards in Our Time: Jonathan Edwards and the Shaping of American* Religion (Grand Rapids, MI: Eerdmans, 1999), 132.

long, bony fingers pointed at them.³⁰ His use of hyperbole in preaching did not help matters, as when he told his flock in 1740 that he would have more success preaching to the men of Sodom than to them, when during the communion controversy he declared that no sin was more liable to incurring a "spiritual curse" than opposing their "spiritual father" (Edwards), or his saying that when they hurt him, they hurt Christ.³¹

Edwards was a man of principle. He refused to compromise, even in the face of great personal loss. George Marsden writes that he "was willing to sail the foundering ship of his pastorate into the teeth of the storm, knowing that he and his family were likely to go down." Most have admired him for that. But Edwards was also a "perfectionist by nature." He applied to his parish "the disciplined standards he held for himself. The Northampton covenant of 1742 was probably the clearest instance of overreaching. It was like asking the whole town to live according to his personal resolutions writ large. Or it was like asking a town of the 1740s to become like a Puritan village of the 1640s." Even if Edwards's high standards were commendable, his "old-fashioned view of ministerial patriarchy" was off-putting in an era when more and more New Englanders wanted to think for themselves.³²

Edwards's Dismissal

Edwards's 1750 dismissal from the Northampton pulpit followed a protracted controversy over his departure from Solomon Stoddard's policy of open admission to communion (i.e., eucharist). Stoddard required only that the applicant for communion believe the scriptures and Congregational doctrine, and desire grace, whereas Edwards—after following Stoddard's practice for nineteen years—in 1748 began to insist that those coming to communion make a profession that they would undertake the church covenant. The heart of the issue was regeneration. Stoddard admitted applicants for membership who conceded they were unregenerate, but Edwards required that they believe that they were *probably* regenerate, even if they had some scruples about it.

---

30. See Gerald R. McDermott, *One Holy and Happy Society: The Public Theology of Jonathan Edwards* (University Park, PA: Pennsylvania State University Press, 1992), 11–36, for an account of social and personal sins that Edwards repeatedly addressed.

31. Sermon on Matt. 13:3–4(b), WJE 56; WJE 25:456, 455. Already in 1729, in his memorial sermon for his grandfather Solomon Stoddard, Edwards had called his congregation "sermon proof," not a tactful way to begin one's ministry. Perhaps some older members took offense at this early stage and chose not to forget it. WJE 14:365.

32. Marsden, *Jonathan Edwards*, 349, 350, 370.

Why did Edwards change his mind? Basically, he concluded that Stoddard's policy did not work. It was intended to make conversion and sanctification more prevalent by bringing more people to the communion table. But Edwards noticed when he first came to Northampton that Stoddard's parishioners were "very insensible of the things of religion, and engaged in other cares and pursuits." The young people were "indecent in their carriage at meeting," and adults were divided between two parties that "were prepared to oppose one another in all public affairs." At one point, according to Edwards, "it came to hand-blows: a number of one party met the head of the opposite party, and assaulted him and beat him, unmercifully." Edwards continued Stoddard's communion policy after his grandfather's death but found in 1733 that, despite its open invitation, parishioners were "wholly neglect[ing]...the sacrament of the Lord's Supper."[33] In the 1740s, he discovered that the young men implicated in the Bad Book affair were those he had numbered among the converted during the revivals. He concluded, in Philip Gura's words, that "true virtue was manifest most clearly in outward, godly behavior, not in mere profession of experience." This realization, plus the fact that in the mid-1740s much of Northampton seemed impervious to his preaching, led him to infer that Stoddard's communion policy was partly responsible for the problems in his parish. So he settled on a "middle way between extremes." He rejected both Stoddard's openness to all comers and the American Puritan custom of asking for a "relation" or story of a conversion experience. He did not require that all applicants be certain of their conversion and insisted that neither he nor the church could be certain of who is regenerate. Instead he emphasized probability and conscientiousness. Would-be communicants had to believe God was probably working grace within them, and they were intending to live a life of holiness. The tentative phrasing of one suggested form of profession was revealing : "I hope I do truly find a heart to give up myself wholly to God."[34]

This change of policy on Edwards's part was the proverbial straw that broke the camel's back. It caused those who had long harbored resentments

---

33. WJE 4:146; WJE 16:382; sermon on Ps. 139:23–24, WJEO 48. This was a stubbornly common problem in early eighteenth-century America. Even Edwards's mother did not take communion until after twenty years of marriage. She was not listed among the full members at East Windsor as of 1700 but professed her faith in 1716, roughly twenty years after her wedding. Henry R. Stiles, *History and Genealogies of Ancient Windsor, CT* (Camden, ME: Picton Press, 1992), 1:913–14; Sereno Dwight, "Memoir," in Dwight, *The Works of President Edwards* (New York, 1829–30) 1:17. Our thanks to Kenneth Minkema for this reference.

34. Philip F. Gura, *Jonathan Edwards: America's Evangelical* (New York: Hill and Wang, 2005), 138; David D. Hall, Introduction, 12:82; WJE 25:492.

to go on the attack. Most of the young men in the Bad Book controversy were from elite families, and their parents were angry that Edwards had gone public with what they thought was a private matter. Edwards had defended several women against "the new laissez-faire approach to male sexual ethics [by arguing that] men should be held publicly accountable for behaviors increasingly considered matters of private morality." But this was not the only issue. For nearly two decades, Edwards had declaimed against practices of businessmen and the landed elite. In his sermon at Colonel Stoddard's funeral, for example, he had criticized businessmen who took advantage of market conditions to gain exorbitant profits from the poor. Some town merchants did not appreciate his 1742 covenant requiring Northampton entrepreneurs not to cheat in business dealings. All of these tensions created resentments that came home to roost in 1750. "Eager to make their place in the world of commerce," Mark Valeri observes, "the town's leaders would not have Edwards lecture them about the sins of covetousness."[35] Perry Miller was probably right to locate part of the opposition in the oligarchy of business and real estate.[36]

Now Edwards's new rules seemed too demanding. He said they had to give a "profession of godliness" with "hearty consent" and seek the counsel of their minister. They were even more disturbed that Edwards wanted to require this of those seeking baptism for their children. Many were already declining communion because of their scruples, but this new rule appeared to bar divine blessing to their children and repudiate the Half-Way Covenant.[37] For this reason, the communion controversy was actually a sacramental controversy and eventually a church membership controversy. Furthermore, to many congregants Edwards's requirement that those seeking communion seek his counsel seemed authoritarian. The days of Stoddard, who was called "pope" in part because of his domineering, paternalistic pastoral style, were over. People now turned to lawyers such as Joseph Hawley (who led the fight against Edwards) for advice they formerly sought from pastors. Unfortunately,

---

35. Ava Chamberlain, "Bad Books and Bad Boys," in Kling and Sweeney, *Jonathan Edwards at Home and Abroad*, 63, 61, 75; WJE 4:551–53; Valeri, "The Economic Thought of Jonathan Edwards," *Church History* 60 (1991): 51.

36. Miller, *Jonathan Edwards* (New York: Meridian, 1949), 219.

37. WJE 25:491, 490; WJE 12:62. This agreement (1662) by the New England churches had permitted parents who could not relate a work of grace to have their children baptized, even if the parents had never become communicants. Paul Edward Husband contends that this was Edwards's primary mistake—to reject the wise balance of the Half-Way Covenant. Husband, "Church Membership in Northampton: Solomon Stoddard versus Jonathan Edwards," PhD diss., Westminster Seminary, 1990.

Edwards's leadership style resembled his grandfather's—whose memory they revered but whose style they would abide no more.³⁸

There was also the age factor. Kenneth Minkema has shown that most of Edwards's leading opponents were elderly. They had been converted under Stoddard, generally chose not to support the revivals, and were furious when Edwards charged from the pulpit that they were like children in their understanding. He cast doubt on their claims to conversion and called on them to be converted again. They took revenge by "stonewall[ing]" his efforts to explain his views publicly and "stacking the governing, agenda-setting bodies—the precinct and church committees—with elderly male opponents of Edwards."³⁹

A Failed Ministry?

Some historians have considered Edwards a failed pastor. One points to the two Northampton revivals of the 1740s that George Whitefield and Samuel Buell initiated while Edwards, as pastor, sat on the sidelines, and suggests that his "ineffectiveness" as a preacher precipitated the new communion policy that terminated his ministry there. Another writes that "he went to his grave disappointed and a failure" because there were no revivals in the last sixteen years of his life. The only historian who devoted an entire monograph to his pastoral ministry judged that "he had failed at his real vocation."⁴⁰

Edwards himself thought that the "Little Awakening" of 1734–35 vindicated the truth and effectiveness of his preaching. At least for a time, his ministry seems to have been a spectacular success; Marsden writes that "the town seemed to be made over in his image.... Every day parishioners filled his home, waiting to see him for counseling. Callow youth and callous farmers were coming under the wonderful spell." Edwards wrote in his *Faithful Narrative* that people would talk of nothing but "eternal things." Marsden adds wryly, "Certainly no one was talking of anything else while *he* was around." By 1750, when he was on his way to being thrown out of his pulpit, Edwards was far

---

38. Tracy, *Jonathan Edwards, Pastor*, 188–89; Marsden, *Jonathan Edwards*, 357–74.

39. Eleven of the fourteen on the church committee were over fifty years of age, as were fourteen of the nineteen on the precinct committee. Minkema, "Old Age and Religion in the Writings and Life of Jonathan Edwards," 701.

40. David D. Hall, "Editor's Introduction" in WJE 12:56, 61; Harry S. Stout, "Edwards as Revivalist," in Stein, *Cambridge Companion to Edwards*, 141; Tracy, "The Pastorate of Jonathan Edwards," 449.

less ebullient but still insistent that he had been faithful to his calling. He was preaching "the truth" and "suffer[ing] in Christ's cause." Three months later, in his "Farewell Sermon," he adopted (as Kimnach puts it) "the steady gaze of a sheriff confronting a lynch mob."[41] Again he maintained that he had been a faithful—even heroic—shepherd:

> I have spent the prime of my life and strength in labors for your eternal welfare. You are my witnesses, that what strength I have had, I have not neglected in idleness, nor laid out in prosecuting worldly schemes, and managing temporal affairs, for the advancement of my outward estate, and aggrandizing myself and family; but have given myself to the work of ministry, laboring in it night and day, rising early and applying myself to this great business to which Christ appointed me. I have found the work of ministry among you to be a great work indeed, a work of exceeding care, labor and difficulty: many have been the heavy burdens that I have borne in it, which my strength has been very unequal to.[42]

But a year later, in a letter to a Scottish correspondent, he was more introspective. He conceded that his youth and inexperience had made him too timid in the 1730s to confront "some glaring false appearances and counterfeits of religion." He thought he had yielded to what New Light clergy believed was "the most dangerous pastoral temptation... to offer premature comfort to persons under conviction, thereby producing complacency at exactly the wrong moment."[43] By the time he had gained more "ripeness of judgment and courage" in the mid-1740s, "it was too late."[44]

What shall we say at nearly three centuries' remove? Perhaps we should go back to the three pastoral ministries that Edwards and the Puritan tradition believed to be at the heart of the minister's calling: preaching the Word, administering the sacraments, and exercising church discipline. The foremost expert on Edwards's preaching concludes that while Edwards put less literary effort into his sermons in the second half of his career, he nevertheless "left a literary legacy unequaled in the literature of the American sermon for its

---

41. Wilson Kimnach, "Edwards as Preacher," in *The Cambridge Companion*, 114; Marsden, *Jonathan Edwards*, 158; WJE 4:149–50; Marsden, 159; WJE 25:455; Kimnach, "Edwards as Preacher," 119.

42. WJE 25:475.

43. WJE 16:384; Holifield, *History of Pastoral Care*, 90–91.

44. WJE 16:384.

depth of thought and power of expression."⁴⁵ On the sacraments, it was a mixed bag: he helpfully clarified the traditional conception that the sacraments are for those who have committed themselves to being God's people and their children, but made the process of application appear too intimidating. His exercise of church discipline was fearless, especially when confronting influential men over their unjust treatment of women. "In each case, although Edwards's attempt to apply the traditional single standard of virtue was generally supported by the church brethren, it aroused opposition in the wider community."⁴⁶ Edwards would have said this was not surprising: a faithful minister is often unpopular.⁴⁷

---

45. Kimnach, "Edwards as Preacher," 119, 123.

46. Chamberlain, "Edwards and Social Issues," 339.

47. Many New England ministers in the eighteenth century lost their jobs. Most enjoyed lifetime tenures, yet a significant minority had controversies with their congregations. Holifield reports that between 1680 and 1740, 112 of 400 Congregationalist and Presbyterian ministers in New England and Long Island had serious problems with their flocks, and 32 had to leave. Massachusetts minister Ebenezer Parkman (ordained in 1724) listed 55 of his colleagues whose congregations had dismissed them. Holifield, *God's Ambassadors*, 86–87.

30

The Sacraments: Baptism and the Lord's Supper

SOME HISTORIANS HAVE reported that Jonathan Edwards had little or no sacramental theology. One claimed that for Edwards the Lord's Supper was merely an expression of human fellowship, and another asserted that he was "no proponent of evangelistic sacramental piety."[1] In fact Edwards had a robust sacramental theology that eclipsed that of his seventeenth-century Puritan forebears. While for them "the primary value of the sacraments" was to provide seals of the covenant, Edwards exalted communion with God so as to see the sacraments as ordinances "at which Christ is peculiarly present to his people."[2]

Edwards agreed with his Reformed predecessors that the sacraments are visible words of God's grace, seals of the covenant of grace. He said they are means of grace that, like the Scriptures and "instructions of parents and ministers," supply the mind with ideas of religious things so that grace has an "opportunity" to act on the soul, "when God shall infuse it." Edwards likened this to the way "Elijah, by laying fuel upon the altar, and laying it in order, gave opportunity for the fire to burn, when God should send it down from heaven." The more these ideas are true, fully fleshed out, lively, and often revived, "the greater opportunity [will be] for the Spirit of God to infuse grace." Strictly speaking, God doesn't need these means in order to impart grace, for "grace is from God as immediately and directly as light is from the sun," but in his wisdom he "don't [sic] see meet to infuse grace, where there is no opportunity for it to act, or to act in some measure suitably." He chooses to use the sacraments' vivid pictures of the gospel because they help remove prejudices of

---

1. Alan Heimert, *Religion and the American Mind, from the Great Awakening to the Revolution* (Cambridge, MA: Harvard University Press, 1966), 125; E. Brook Holifield, *The Covenant Sealed: The Development of Puritan Sacramental Theology in Old and New England, 1570–1720* (New Haven: Yale University Press, 1974), 228–29; both cited by William J. Danaher Jr., "By Sensible Signs Represented: Jonathan Edwards's Sermons on the Lord's Supper," *Pro Ecclesia* 7 (1998): 285–86.

2. Danaher, "Sensible Signs," 287.

reason by providing sensory images that move the heart to action. Frequent use of them tends to restrain sin and provide further impetus to use these and other means. In a word, the sacraments—like other means of grace—are ways of "waiting upon God for his grace, in the way wherein he is wont to bestow [it]; 'tis watching at wisdom's gates, and waiting at the posts of her doors."[3]

Yet, as William Danaher has argued, for Edwards a sacrament is not just an emblem or pedagogical aid. Far more, it is a type of Christ in which Jesus Christ is present, offering the gift of himself afresh with all of his benefits as he speaks to and communes with believers. Sacraments, in other words, are re-presentations of Christ.[4]

Baptismal Theology

Edwards agreed with John Calvin that baptism is an exhibition and token of regeneration (Rom 6:3–11), a sign or "outward badge" of the new birth.[5] The infants of believers are to be baptized since it is presumed by the covenant that they have been or will be regenerated. To support this conviction, Edwards referred to a range of passages from both testaments: "The promise is unto you and to your children" (Acts 2:39); "Believe on the Lord Jesus Christ and thou shalt be saved, and thy house" (Acts 16:31); "The generation of the upright shall be blessed" (Ps. 112:2); "For God will save Zion; the seed also of his servants shall inherit it" (Ps. 69:35f); and other passages such as Proverbs 14:26, Psalms 103:17–18, Psalms 112:21, Exodus 20:5–6, and Deuteronomy 7:9. For Edwards, infant baptism was the seal of these promises made to the seed of the righteous, and the baptism of adults should follow profession of faith. Edwards also agreed with Calvin that circumcision of the heart, which he understood to mean regeneration, was the *res* (thing) to which the *signum* (sign) of Old Testament circumcision pointed, and that baptism is the New Testament equivalent of Old Testament circumcision.[6]

But Edwards differed from Calvin in that the American theologian taught more clearly that the baptismal rite does not effect regeneration.[7] Christ is at

---

3. WJE 18:85–86, 84, 87–88.

4. Danaher, "Sensible Signs," 261–87.

5. WJE 12:316; Calvin, *Institutes* 4.15.1; 4.16.4.

6. WJE 12:484, 198; Calvin, *Institutes* 4.16.3–4.

7. Calvin said the rite "effectively performs what it signifies" when it is received by faith; Calvin, *Institutes* 4.15.14–15. On the other hand, Calvin did not teach that the baptism of non-elect infants would effect regeneration.

work in baptism, Edwards maintained, inviting a child into his church but without communicating regeneration by the rite. Look at Simon Magus (Ac 8), Edwards observed, and the baptized children of some believers who manifestly reject God's covenant all the days of their lives. Yet a parent can be assured that if he or she sincerely and believingly gives the child up to God, then baptism "ordinarily" seals salvation to it. Salvation is more probable because of the blessings that infant baptism brings.[8]

Yet why only probable and "ordinarily?" Because, said Edwards, we can never certainly know our own hearts. This is why Stephen the martyr still prayed to commend his spirit into Christ's hands at his death. Besides, a parent may be a true believer yet not entirely give up his or her child to God. Edwards finally concludes, "These things about baptism [are] doubtful," which may mean it is difficult for parents to have certainty since the efficacy of infant baptism depends in part on their faith.[9]

If some things about baptism are uncertain, so is the fate, said Edwards, of baptized babies who die in infancy. If the parents of the child are not regenerated, we cannot know for sure about the child since the baptism of an unregenerate adult will in itself not guarantee the salvation of the child. Even if the parents of the infant are godly, there is no guarantee—because "experience shows, that multitudes of such [baptized children of the godly]... prove wicked when they grow up." Yet regenerate parents can be reassured that their children who die are "more likely" to have been saved.[10]

Edwards's understanding of baptism rests on his conception of the covenant. He taught a number of covenants but believed they were all rooted in the covenant of redemption (ch. 21). While Edwards taught that—because of God's unconditional grace—the covenant is unconditional for the elect, he also insisted that there is a sense, from the human perspective, in which the covenant is conditional. The condition is perseverance in faith so that simply being in the external or church covenant does not necessarily entitle a person to its privileges. Korah and the gross idolaters in ancient Israel were in the covenant but forfeited its blessings by their apostasy.[11]

---

8. WJE 18:115, 129. Calvin and most of Edwards's New England predecessors would have agreed.

9. WJE 18:129–30.

10. WJE 18:114–15. As Increase Mather had written, the line of election does run "for the most part... through the loins of godly Parents." Increase Mather, *Pray for the Rising Generation* (Cambridge, MA: Printed by Samuel Green, 1678), 11.

11. WJE 12:485. See also WJE 18:251–61.

Like Calvin, Edwards considered baptism to be the sacrament of initiation into the church but did not consider church membership necessarily to involve regeneration. Edwards came to believe that the qualification for membership should be not regeneration itself but the *visibility* of regeneration (ch. 28). One can *look* like she is regenerated (by professing faith and avoiding scandalous behavior) and believe that she is without being regenerated. But that is enough for admission to baptism (for herself and her infant children) and to the visible church. Church officers do not need to know and will not know with any certainty who is regenerate since that is impossible and God's prerogative anyway.[12]

Not all the three thousand at Pentecost who were baptized (Acts 2:41) were regenerate, Edwards surmised, but they appeared to be so from their profession and repute. But when the officers of a church admit someone to the church, God concurs with them because he has given the keys of the kingdom to those officers. What they do on earth is done in heaven (Mt. 16:19). They act on the "presumption" that "professors" (of faith) are sincere, upright and will be faithful.[13]

God at this point conforms to his human officers and does not act as "searcher of hearts," but admits professors on the "*presumption* of their sincerity and faithfulness." Yet God's admission (of these professors) "is not absolute and unalterable, as his invisible justification of them is." Nor is it merely conditional. It is like marriage, in which a spouse's promises are neither conditional (since the promise is to be faithful no matter what) nor absolute (if the other deserts or repeatedly commits adultery, one cannot continue to be a spouse), but *presumptive*—for it presumes the other will not desert or commit repeated adultery, and on that presumption promises to be faithful.[14]

According to Edwards, this is what happens when human officers of the church (or the church as a whole) admit persons into the church by baptism: the church treats them as God's people. God concurs by giving them the means of grace—scripture, preaching, fellowship, discipline, and the Lord's Supper—all of which the Spirit of Christ uses to challenge and nurture them. God is more ready to hear and answer their prayers and give them charismatic and common gifts of the Spirit. Eternal life is promised on the condition of perseverance (Rev. 3.12: "He that overcometh I will make a pillar in the temple of my God," and many similar passages). Edwards insisted that the apostles

---

12. WJE 24:485–86; WJE 18:251–52.

13. WJE 18:251–56.

14. WJE 18:251–52; emph. added.

frequently spoke of future glory as contingent on perseverance (ch. 25), that they spoke to "visible" Christians, not presuming that all visible Christians were in the invisible church.¹⁵

Throughout this process, Edwards averred, the church is not a searcher of hearts, just as Christ on earth was not. He received Judas as a disciple, minister and "officer of the highest kind—viz. an apostle." He gave him "miraculous gifts of the Spirit." He did not reject Judas until Judas's behavior disqualified him. So too, the church receives the baptized into God's family as his children and Christ receives them as his spouse, and they are "as it were" redeemed and justified. Infants are baptized on the presumption of their parents' faith and are received by God on the presumption of their own future faith—or present faith, from the vantage point of God's eternity. It can be said, *provisionally*, that Christ's blood cleanses them from sin, and they have the benefits of the body and blood of Jesus in the Lord's Supper. They are "*presumptively* justified and cleared from guilt through the blood of Christ." That is why Peter can speak of those who "de[nied] the Lord that bought them" (2 Pet. 2:1): Christ bought them as presumptive members of his church, but they eventually showed, by denying him, that they were never among the elect. Hence eternal benefits are "presumptively" promised to the baptized on the condition of (the perseverance of) faith.¹⁶

Not all of those baptized will respond or persevere, just as circumcised Israel repeatedly apostasized. According to Edwards, Christ said that he would spit out of his mouth baptized Christians (Rev. 3:16). Those who have professed but later are false to Christ, God shall reject and cast out (Mt. 10:37). The final "casting out" will be at the final judgment, one of whose purposes is to show why God cast out some professing church members even though they were baptized. It will also show unbelievers that they, not God, have removed themselves from his grace.¹⁷

As for the mode of baptism, Edwards preferred sprinkling or what he called "affusion." He argued from 1 Corinthians 10:2 ("their fathers were all baptized unto Moses in the cloud and in the sea") that God himself baptized his people in the wilderness by rain that came from the pillar of cloud, thus by sprinkling from above. Furthermore, John the Baptist probably baptized by "pouring of water on the person" because his words in Matthew 3:11 ("I indeed baptize you with water: but he that cometh after me shall baptize you with the

---

15. WJE 18:252–54.

16. WJE: 18:255–56; emph. added.

17. WJE 18:254, 258–59.

Holy Ghost, and with fire") parallel his baptism with that of the Holy Ghost, which was a "pouring out... *upon*" them, and was "typified by the pouring [of] oil on the heads of those that were anointed." And when John baptized Jesus, "God remarkably poured out the Spirit from heaven *upon* him."[18]

Eucharistic Theology

Samuel Hopkins reported that Edwards had originally hesitated to come to Northampton in 1727 because of his grandfather Solomon Stoddard's "lax mode of admission" to the Lord's Supper, which allowed the unconverted to come to the table as long as they avoided moral scandal and agreed with traditional doctrines. Stoddard was trying to reverse a longstanding New England trend of nonparticipation in the Lord's Supper because of spiritual doubts and moral scrupulosity. Before the sacrament, ministers typically read out loud 1 Corinthians 11:29: "For he that eateth and drinketh unworthily, eateth and drinketh damnation to himself, not discerning the Lord's body." The Halfway Covenant (1662) had admitted to sacramental privileges the children of those who could not relate a conversion experience, so there were many in the churches who knew they were unconverted and did not want to take their chances. Stoddard told them the sacred table was a "converting ordinance" intended in part for those who had not yet experienced a work of grace.[19]

After a few years in Northampton, Edwards concluded that the "dullness" he saw in some of his own flock was attributable in part to Stoddard's communion policy. So he made a point to study the "old divines" concerning conversion and the sacrament, but did not reach a settled policy of his own for a number of years. In the meantime, he administered communion every eight weeks and in a Thursday lecture before the sacrament would counsel his parishioners to examine themselves before they came to the table. In the 1742 church covenant that his people signed, they promised to examine themselves "especially before the sacrament of the Lord's Supper" to see whether they had defrauded their neighbor, engaged in backbiting, taken revenge, sought their own worldly gain or honor, violated justice in pursuing their private interest, held a secret grudge, or engaged in lasciviousness. This understanding seems to have been in effect until relations broke down between pastor and parish at the end of the decade.[20]

---

18. WJE 15:139–40; WJE 18:276.

19. Samuel Hopkins, *The Life and Character of the Late Reverend Mr. Jonathan Edwards* (Boston, 1765), 56; Holifield, *Covenant Sealed*, 206–20.

20. Holified, *Covenant Sealed*, 206–20; Kenneth P. Minkema, Editor's Introduction, WJE 14:39–40; WJE 16:121–25.

Edwards preached far more about the Lord's Supper than baptism, in part because of the importance he attributed to the sacred meal.[21] In 1733, he told his congregation that Jesus Christ is "more especially" present in this "ordinance" than in preaching or "public prayers" or church discipline. Christ is present "under the most affecting circumstances possible" since here he is "represented as dying amongst us...tormented to death in our sight and all [of us] standing round...to see his blood trickle from his wound till he dies." This supper captures events "more solemn" than Jesus' birth. Even the incarnation itself was "not so great as a dying on the cross" because that was "the most eminently holy act that Christ performed while on earth." It was "the principal thing in the work of redemption." Edwards was so impressed by the majesty and power of this ordinance that he recommended it be celebrated every Sunday.[22]

Like all his Reformed and Puritan predecessors, Edwards said the Lord's Supper is a seal of the covenant of grace. Just as two parties in any civil affair use a seal as a "confirming evidencing token" of their agreement, so too in this "mutual renovation, confirmation, and seal of the covenant of grace": Christ "by these outward signs confirms and seals his sincere engagements to be [the saints'] Savior and food," and the regenerate "profess to take Christ as their spiritual food, and bread of life." It is like a marriage covenant in which a woman's taking the bridegroom's ring is "a profession and seal of her taking him for her husband." His giving the ring as a token of his offering his entire self is like Christ's giving himself by the representations of bread and wine. Our taking these elements is like the bride's taking the ring as a sign of her accepting the man as her husband. In each case, the offering and taking of signs "seals" the covenant or agreement. The seals identify the parties on both sides, and the nature of the promises made by those parties.[23]

Therefore the Supper is a "renewal" of those promises. Jesus Christ solemnly renews his offer to those coming for the sacrament. He "does as it were say to us, 'Here is my body and blood slain and spilt. I offer it to you. If you will receive it and accept of it [sic], you shall be possessed of it.'" On their part, the saints promise to fulfill covenant conditions, for everyone knows that

---

21. No doubt it was also because of the communion controversy that arose in 1748. Yet even before that, Edwards was giving more sermonic attention to the Lord's Supper.

22. Sermon on 1 Cor. 11:29, WJEO 48:5, 7, 9, 12; WJE 16:366. See also WJE 17:264, where he said the early Christians first celebrated the Lord's Supper every day, and then weekly. Northampton never adopted this frequency, probably in part because weekly communion was almost unheard of in seventeenth-century New England.

23. Sermon on 1 Cor. 10:17(a), WJEO 68:11; WJE 12:256–58.

people have a right to the benefits of a covenant "only by virtue of fulfilling the conditions of it." The most basic condition is for us to "resolve to diligently and laboriously do the work God has appointed us," just as the Israelites were commanded to "eat the Passover with their loins girded, with shoes on their feet and with their staff in their hand—a posture of action and motion." In his sermons on the sacrament, Edwards typically described that work as living in peace with our neighbors. Believers coming to the Supper should "examine themselves whether or no they have forgiven their enemies, those that have done them any hurt, so as to allow of no wishing of any hurt to them and especially so as never to design to do anything to gratify a revengeful disposition towards them." If they have quarrels with one another, they should settle them before approaching the table of the Lord. If they come with a "spirit of hatred," they eat and drink unworthily. If they "love to talk against their neighbor and want to run him down," are "grieved at their prosperity," or have "harbored old grudges," then they have kept the Passover with leaven, which was forbidden under the Law. In that case, they are like a person invited to a prince's table "all over defiled with ordure [animal excrement]" which "would show a great contempt of the prince and what he was invited to."[24]

By renewing promises, the Lord's Supper helps us "remember" Christ. As Edwards put it, many kings and battles are now forgotten because no records or accounts remain. Therefore we need frequent celebration of the Supper to keep alive our memory of this greatest act of redemption. But the Supper is not only a memorial that helps prevent our forgetting; it also "revives" our affections of admiration and delight for Christ and what he did for us. By its celebration we are given "fresh and lively scenes" of these epic persons and events, so that we are properly moved and affected by them.[25]

On these themes of the Supper as a memorial and seal of the covenant, Edwards perpetuated the Puritan tradition. William Ames, Increase Mather, and Cotton Mather had said as much. But Danaher has shown that Edwards went further. "[W]hile seventeenth-century Puritans put covenant in the foreground and communion in the background [as the primary purpose of the sacrament], Edwards did the opposite."[26] He did this first by portraying the

---

24. Sermon on 1 Cor. 11:29, WJEO 48: 21–22; WJE 25:589; sermon on 1 Cor. 5:7, WJEO 48:10; WJE 17:269; WJEO 48:16, 15, 1–2; WJE 17:270.

25. Sermon on Luke 22:19, WJEO 49:6, 13–4, 17.

26. Danaher, "Sensible Signs," 269. The continental Reformed theologians of the sixteenth and seventeenth centuries—including Turretin, one of Edwards's favorite theologians—also emphasized covenant not communion. Heinrich Heppe, ed., *Reformed Dogmatics, Set Out and Illustrated from the Sources*, trans. G.T. Thomson (Grand Rapids, MI: Baker, 1978), 604, 655.

Supper as a feast, going into rich detail about the laughter, joy, love, and friendship that are hallmarks of a feast, especially a wedding feast. In Edwards's earliest sacrament sermon, he said that "Christians, in the participation and *communion* of gospel benefits, have joy unspeakable and full of glory, a sweeter delight than any this world affords." At this feast, God invites us to his table and sits down with us. We are his guests in his house. He offers us bread because it is nourishment, and our only nourishment comes from the body of his son. He also gives us wine, which brings joy and delight.[27]

In another sacrament sermon, Edwards referred to the feast as one where the head of our new family sits down with us, his children. He is also our older brother who has invited us to join him. But whether head or elder sibling, he has summoned us to a feast, which by definition is where close "friendship" is enjoyed: "Feasts are used all over the world, through all nations, as tokens of friendship." Friends at feasts enjoy "a vast variety of rich dainties." But these dainties will be much better than earthly ones because they are from heaven. Tasting them is to "partake" of Christ's "joy and happiness," which are so marvelous that they "can't be expressed."[28]

The second way that Edwards put communion in the foreground was by repeatedly stressing the real presence of Christ at the Lord's Table. When the minister speaks at the Table, Christ stands there "offering [the elements] to us and therein offering us his benefits." He appeals to our senses of "touch and taste besides our seeing" so that we "as it were handle Christ as Thomas did and put our fingers into the prints of the nails and our hands into his side." So he presents himself as not only "present among us but as being slain amongst us." Yet the sacrament is not macabre. He has "invite[d] us home to his own house to sit at his Table and there to eat and drink with him." We are "sitting with him" and so "conversant with him as his friends and guests and being admitted to society with him."[29] Like Calvin, Edwards taught the presence of Christ's humanity in the Supper and not only his divinity. In his 1743 sacramental sermon on John 6:51, he told his parishioners that "the person of Christ is come to us" in his "flesh" or "human nature," which is "Christ's beauty," and this is particularly manifest in his sufferings. Therefore "his flesh and blood are [the saints'] meat and drink." We partake of these in the feast of the Lord's Supper. But also like Calvin, Edwards said the body of Christ cannot be both at the Father's

---

27. WJE 14:287, 286–88, emph. added; sermon on 1 Cor. 11:29, 17, WJEO 48.

28. Sermon on 1 Cor. 10:17(a), 10, WJEO 68; sermon on John 6:51, 8, WJEO 67; WJE 22:315.

29. Sermon on 1 Cor. 11:29, 6, 7, 17–18, WJEO 48.

right hand in heaven and on earth at the Lord's Table, so that body and blood are present spiritually but not physically or locally. As Danaher has explained, Edwards and Calvin rejected the Roman and Lutheran view that the *signum* and *res* are identical, and also the Zwinglian view that the *signum* and *res* are divorced. For Calvin, the *signum* is the instrument of grace. Yet, for Edwards, the symbols of bread and wine are moments in "God's typological self-communication." God is present in them, not only speaking through them but also sharing his very being, both divine and human. The Lord's Supper is "a passion play that reache[s] its climax when the main character, Jesus Christ, [takes] the stage."³⁰

For Edwards, then, in the Lord's Supper we meet by faith the objectively real presence of Christ. It is there spiritually—and not in corporeal substance as Thomas Aquinas or Martin Luther believed—but it is far more than a remembrance of what happened in the first century (Huldrych Zwingli) and is not simply a matter of "subjective affections," as it tended to be for seventeenth-century Puritans.³¹ At its basis is a real ontological union that is effected and enhanced in the Supper: saints become "partakers in the divine nature" (ch. 26). As members of Christ's body they "partake in the life of the head or as branches of a tree have the same sap with the body and root," which means they become "partakers with God of his holiness and happiness." They also partake of Christ's divine knowledge and his "comfort and spiritual joy." They are all, with Christ, "one mystical person." So while in all their lives they "continually live on a stream or river of divine goodness (Ps. 46)" and the river is Christ's blood that "has its fountain" in his "wounded and broken heart," that blood and goodness are especially present in the Supper because there Christ is "more especially" present. It is this hyperemphasis on the real presence of Christ's humanity in the Supper that distinguished Edwards from his Puritan predecessors and many Reformed scholastic forbears, who stressed covenant sealing far more than ontological communion.³²

Last but not least, Edwards from time to time presented the Supper as a foretaste of the marriage supper of the Lamb. In 1733 he preached a sermon

---

30. Sermon on John 6:51, 7, WJEO 67; WJE 21:212, 234; Danaher, 279–80.

31. Danaher, "Sensible Signs," 269.

32. Sermon on 1 Cor. 1:9, 8, 3, 9, WJEO 44; sermon on 1 Cor. 10:17(a), 6, WJEO 68; sermon on John 6:51, 10, WJEO 67; sermon on 1 Cor. 11:29, 5, WJEO 48. See Heppe, *Reformed Dogmatics*, 590, 592, 606, 638, 655. Generally Heppe shows that for the Reformed scholastics "the most essential purpose of a sacrament is, that for the elect person it is a sealing divine of his fellowship in the covenant of faith" (606), and "the purpose of the Supper celebrations is first of all to preserve the memory of Christ's death" (655).

with the doctrine, "The saints shall hereafter as it were eat and drink with Christ at his royal table [in] his kingdom of glory." Just as in the Old Testament solemn feasts were "earnests of future benefits" spelled out in the New, so too the Supper points us to future benefits we will enjoy in the eschaton. In the feast we share at church, we have "the foretaste of that eternal feast with Christ in glory." Ten years later he said the Supper reminds us that one day saints' bodies shall be made like Christ's glorious body, and that we "shall drink of the same river of pleasure that Christ [drinks from]." The bread and wine his parishioners enjoyed in their Suppers were a "pledge of their future glorious communion and partaking with Christ when they shall drink new wine with him in his Kingdom." Just before he left Northampton, Edwards held out the same promise of the Supper as a type of the eschatological supper: our eating and drinking "the spiritual feast of the saints in this world" is a harbinger of "the eternal feast in heaven."[33]

Edwards and the Sacraments

Edwards's conception of the sacraments illustrates Calvin's famous doctrine of accommodation—that God accommodates himself to our lowly human capacities by communicating spiritual realities in material signs.[34] While his doctrine of baptism shows familiar Reformed themes, his theology of the Supper pushed the envelope of Reformed thinking. Edwards protected the Reformed insistence on God's sovereignty in baptism by a kind of occasionalism: baptism is a sign and seal of regeneration only on those occasions when God calls a person by the Spirit. Therefore the church is not constituted by individualistic faith decisions but by the Father's mysterious election. Baptism is an instance of conditional justification that cleanses the baptized of their sins but does so without rendering certain the election and final salvation of the baptized.

Like other Reformed theologians, Edwards taught that the eucharistic meal sealed and renewed God's covenant with his people. But he highlighted the divine presence. Rather than focusing primarily on the ratification of the covenantal offer, as was the Puritan tendency,[35] or even fellowship with Christ,

---

33. Sermon on Luke 22:30, 5, 6, 9, WJEO 48; sermon on 1 Cor. 1:9, 10, 16, WJEO 44; 1 Cor. 6:51, 9, WJEO 67.

34. Calvin, *Institutes*, 4.14.3; Thomas Aquinas spoke about this at greater length; *Summa Theologiae*, 3a., 60.4, 60.1.

35. Holifield says the English Puritans tended to describe the sacrament simply in terms of "the efficacy of a body that was itself absent and in the heavens" (Holifield, *The Covenant Sealed*, 26).

as Calvin emphasized, Edwards stressed dramatic presence and union with Christ.[36] For Edwards, Christ acts and speaks in the Supper in ways that make him more present to believers than in any other ecclesial moments on earth.

---

36. Calvin insisted, against Zwingli, on the humanity and not just the divinity of Christ in the Supper, and on real fellowship with or participation in the body of Christ, which remains in heaven but to which believers are lifted by the Holy Spirit. Calvin, *Institutes* 4.17.1–50, esp. 4.17.11; and Wilhelm Niesel, "The Sacraments," in Donald K. McKim, ed., *Readings in Calvin's Theology* (Grand Rapids, MI: Baker, 1984), 244–59.

31

The Voice of the Great God: A Theology of Preaching

JONATHAN EDWARDS LEARNED about preaching from the Calvinist Puritan tradition in which he was raised. Calvin himself said the preacher is a "trumpet of God" who should style his sermons after the nature of scripture itself. So his sermons were generally expository, direct, and brief. Unlike Edwards, Calvin typically did not write his sermons out but preached nearly every day without notes and after studying the text. The most popular Calvinist preaching manuals in Edwards's era were by English Puritan William Perkins, English preacher John Edwards (no relation), and Boston's Cotton Mather. Perkins's *Art of Prophesying* (1592) urged a "plain style" that opened a text simply without affectations of classical learning (frequently on display in Anglican sermons). John Edwards's *The Preacher* (1703) recommended intense belief and feeling, and attention to application. Mather's *Manuductio ad Ministerium* (1726) dismissed rhetoric and logic in favor of "natural reason and a cultivated personal style based upon emulation of the actual practice of admired authors."[1] Edwards also learned from personal role models. His father Timothy was a Harvard graduate who used a large number of subheads and biblical citations in his sermons, yet also was an animated speaker who presided over revivals in his East Windsor, Connecticut parish. Jonathan Edwards's grandfather Solomon Stoddard, under whom Edwards served as assistant for twenty-seven months at Northampton, was a powerful revivalist who declared that "when men don't Preach much about the danger of Damnation, there is want of good Preaching." Stoddard enjoyed using rhetorical dialogue in his sermons and urged preachers to "rebuke sharply" those who needed reproof.[2]

---

1. Wilson H. Kimnach's "Editor's Introduction," WJE 10:3–258, citing 19. Kimnach's 254-page introduction is the finest guide to Edwards's sermons ever published. See also John Gerstner, *The Rational Biblical Theology of Jonathan Edwards* (Powhatan, VA: Berea, 1991), 1:481–86; Douglas A. Sweeney, *Jonathan Edwards and the Ministry of the Word* (Downers Grove, IL: IVP Academic, 2009), 79–80; and Kimnach, "The Sermons: Concept and Execution," in Sang H. Lee, ed., *The Princeton Companion to Jonathan Edwards* (Princeton, NJ: Princeton University Press, 2005), 243–57.

2. Kimnach, "Editor's Introduction," WJE 10:14.

The Sermonic Setting

New England churches in Edwards's day were plain "meetinghouses" with unpainted clapboard on the outside and seating around a pulpit or "desk" near the center on the inside. In reaction against what they considered "graven images" and "Catholic" ostentation in Anglican churches, Puritans eschewed crosses and stained-glass windows, and sang mostly psalms without musical instruments. Ministers preached in academic gowns to demonstrate they were learned and not a sacred priesthood, and also to hide class distinctions that might be apparent in street dress. They delivered two sermons every Sunday—morning and afternoon—and often a weekday lecture. In Northampton, Edwards followed this schedule with sermons of sixty to ninety minutes. The principal Sunday service consisted of ten parts: (1) a biblical text as call to worship; (2) corporate "prayer of approach"; (3) Old Testament reading, with the minister giving a short "sense of the text"; (4) New Testament reading with a sense of the text; (5) singing a psalm metrically; (6) prayer of confession and intercession; (7) a sermon; (8) corporate prayer led by the minister, which could last up to 30 minutes; (9) another psalm; and then (10) benediction. Every eight weeks in Northampton, Edwards conducted a "sacrament" service (the Lord's Supper) between the two regular Sunday services. Twice a year there were fast days by colonial decree, with special sermons. Thanksgiving days were also held at least once a year, depending on circumstances, and each would feature a sermon. Edwards served in a parish of 1,300 people, with 700 generally present on Sundays, while receiving a steady stream of visitors at his home and regularly supervising pastoral interns.[3]

Three Periods of Preaching

Wilson Kimnach, the unrivalled scholar of Edwards's homiletics, divides Edwards's thirty-seven-year preaching career into three periods. The first period, 1722–27, is what Kimnach calls his "apprenticeship," during which he preached in New York City; Bolton, Connecticut; and (after his tutorship at Yale) as an assistant under Stoddard. Kimnach says the young preacher's sermons were "as busy in [their] formal structure as the music of Johann Sebastian Bach." Edwards helped his note-taking hearers follow along by announcing new sections as they began. While he avoided strong rhetorical devices such as

---

3. Sweeney, 25–26, 57–58, 63; Mark Valeri, "Editor's Introduction," WJE 17:16.

alliteration and rhythm, he piqued attention by using "the vigor of a vulgar idiom." He described the unregenerate as one who "spends his days in groveling in the dirt, makes his mind much like a mole or muck worm, feeding on dirt and dung, and seldom lifts his mind any higher than the surface of the earth he treads on."[4]

From 1727 to 1742, Edwards used the sermon "primarily as an instrument of awakening and pastoral leadership." This was the period of "mastery" in which, especially starting in 1729, sermons became more complex. Some parts were in outline form. When he offered pastoral guidance, the focus was less on youthful sins of the flesh and more on the abuses of commerce. Edwards began to experiment artistically, gradually evolving his form to suit the production of theological treatises. So he preached more sermon series, dividing long discourses into preaching units only after most of the writing was done. Kimnach writes, "The sermon was dissolving under the pressure of long, long thoughts." "Sinners in the Hands of an Angry God" (1741) was the last sermon with renown that was not also the marker of an important event, such as the "Farewell Sermon" (1750). Yet while the sermons were developing toward longer productions, Edwards was not indifferent to style. Kimnach notes that when he took his sermons from the pulpit to print, he made sure to build a rising crescendo, saving the best arguments and most important points for last. Interestingly, during this period the maturing preacher worked on several sermons at once, "apparently stor[ing] some of his output in fruitful times against times of dearth."[5]

The last phase of Edwards's extraordinary sermonic production started in January 1742, when he drew a vertical line down the middle of his sermon booklet on Daniel 5:25, dividing it into double columns—a form he retained for most of his sermons until his death sixteen years later.[6] Kimnach thinks this was the result of watching George Whitefield preach without notes.[7] From there on out, Edwards made even more efforts to use his sermons to help him compose treatises. As he became more of an international intellectual, he turned from his earlier "personalist" focus on subjective religious experience to highlighting objective religious phenomena such as the work of redemption

---

4. Kimnach, "Edwards as Preacher," in Stephen Stein, ed., *The Cambridge Companion to Jonathan Edwards* (Cambridge, UK: Cambridge University Press, 2007), 104; Kimnach, "Editor's Introduction," WJE 10:99.

5. Kimnach, "Edwards as Preacher," 110; Kimnach, "Editor's Introduction," WJE 10:105,11–12,107n9.

6. There are approximately 1200 extant sermons, with only about 200 published in hard copy.

7. It also enabled him to conserve paper—hard to come by in his day—since the outlined sermons took up less space.

through the course of human history. His sermons were almost entirely outlines that grew to be "more and more like bare lists." According to Kimnach, this might have indicated a certain "indifference" to preaching, particularly as his own tenure at Northampton grew more tenuous. At the same time, his growing predilection for treatises and "things to be considered" instead of formal "doctrines" ironically paralleled the move by Boston's liberal ministers toward what would eventually become Emersonian essays.[8]

At Stockbridge, where he had been exiled after his dismissal from Northampton, the discouraged preacher had new audiences, and the Indians there seem to have given Edwards new inspiration. He preached more than one hundred and eighty-seven new sermons, and on another twenty occasions preached from earlier manuscripts. It is clear from the extant manuscripts that Edwards worked hard to adapt his rhetoric to the abilities of his hearers. As Rachel Wheeler has noted, the Stockbridge sermons tell more stories than the Northampton sermons; they are also simpler in presentation and employ more imagery derived from nature. But if he preached more simply to his uneducated Indian audience, the sermons were not simplistic and they called for an exalted vision of divine beauty. He told the Stockbridge Indians in his very first sermon there that they must have "their eyes opened to see how lovely [Christ] is," and in a communion lecture explained that a good man loves God "above all else for his own beauty." His outlines were less complex and his imagery earthier than in his sermons to the white congregation at Stockbridge, but the vision he tried to evoke was no less sublime.[9]

Themes in Edwards's Preaching

Edwards is best known for his "terror" preaching. This is unfortunate because he was obsessed with God's beauty, not his wrath (ch. 6). On the other hand, he was not shy about preaching the terrors of the law, especially in the late 1720s and 1730s, when he was preaching for awakening. When in 1741 he reflected on this theme, he said it was a matter of truth: "If there be really a hell of such dreadful, and never-ending torments, as is generally supposed, that multitudes

---

8. Kimnach, "Editor's Introduction," WJE 10:119, 122; WJE 25:45; Kimnach, "Editor's Introduction," WJE 10:123; WJE 25:46.

9. Rachel Wheeler, "'Friends to Your Souls': The Egalitarian Calvinism of Jonathan Edwards," unpublished paper used by permission, n.41; Wheeler, "'A Heathenish, Barbarous, Brutish Education': Jonathan Edwards and the Stockbridge Indians" (unpublished paper loaned by the author), 6; see also Gerald R. McDermott, "Missions and Native Americans," in Sang Hyun Lee, ed., *The Princeton Companion to Jonathan Edwards* (Princeton, NJ: Princeton University Press, 2005), 264–65.

are in great danger of, and that the bigger part of men in Christian countries do actually from generation to generation fall into... why is it not proper for those that have the care of souls, to take great pains to make men sensible of it?" Therefore it is also a matter of kindness: "If I am in danger of going to hell, I should be glad to know as much as possibly I can of the dreadfulness of it: if I am very prone to neglect due care to avoid it, he does me the best *kindness*, that does most to represent to me the truth of the case, that sets forth my misery and danger in the liveliest manner." A year later, in *Some Thoughts Concerning the Revival*, he said preaching on hell is like the tough love of a surgeon who lances a wound and pushes even further despite his patient's loud cries. If that surgeon had stopped as soon as the patient cried and applied a plaster to "skin over the wound," he would be like those who cry, "Peace, peace, when there is no peace" (Jer. 6:14). What if you are a father, Edwards asked, and you know your house is on fire? Won't you do everything you can to warn your family still in the house to get out? Won't you "cry aloud" to save those you love? If we have the care of souls and know what hell is, it would be "morally impossible" for us to avoid warning those souls of their danger. Therefore it is not only compassionate but "a reasonable thing to endeavor to fright persons away from hell."[10]

But if the good news of the gospel is unintelligible without the bad news of God's judgment, the gospel also needs to be preached alongside the message of terror. Sinners need "to be told that there is a Saviour provided, that is excellent and glorious, who has shed his precious blood for sinners, and is every way sufficient to save 'em, that stands ready to receive 'em, if they will heartily embrace him; for this is also the truth, as well as that they now are in an infinitely dreadful condition. This is the Word of God." When preached in this manner, he added in a pragmatic tone, he had never seen "ill consequences" of preaching the terrors of hell "in case of real conviction," even to children. Experience had shown him, he wrote in 1742, that it usually had a happy outcome and a "very speedy" one at that. The only exceptions to the rule were persons afflicted with "melancholy" (i.e., depression), "wherein the truth ought to be withheld from sinners in distress of conscience." This was not because the truth will do harm, but because melancholics tended to "take things wrong" so that when truth was heard and applied by them, it became falsehood.[11]

Over time, however, Edwards seems to have become disillusioned with hellfire preaching. In 1747, he reflected that most of his sermons on hell had

---

10. WJE 4:246–47, emph. added; WJE 4:390–91, 248.

11. WJE 4:391–92.

been duds, and did not know what more to say on that subject: "So many [terror sermons] had been offered with so little apparent effect that I thought with myself, I know not what to say further." Kimnach tells us that for the remainder of his career in Northampton and Stockbridge, Edwards never preached a "full-blown" hellfire sermon again.[12]

But Edwards never stopped preaching sermons on how to "obtain" salvation. A good example is his January 1741 sermon on Matthew 11:12, whose doctrine was "Persons seeking heaven should behave in like manner as valiant resolute soldiers do in taking a country or kingdom in which they are strongly opposed." He told his parish at Northampton, as well as the Stockbridge Indians for whom he repreached it in 1753, that they must love their country and friends, kill their besetting sins ("Goliath and Agag"), wrestle in prayer, read the Bible, and attend the Lord's Supper. If they did these things, they "probably" would obtain salvation, but only if their striving was "violent." His "Pressing into the Kingdom" sermon of 1735 urged seekers to make use of means with "very great pains," assuring them that if they did so, they "probably" would find grace, even "though God has not bound himself to anything that a person does."[13]

Edwards also preached a rich variety of sermons on God's comfort. Chapter 19 sketches his many sermons on heaven, and his sermons on hell always contained appeals to accept God's mercy. The 1739 sermon series on the history of the work of redemption was an extended study of the history of God's mercy to the human race, repeatedly initiating new movements of the Spirit to sinners who did not deserve them. Another great theme in the sermonic canon is spiritual discernment. In 1737–38, Edwards preached a nineteen-sermon series on the Parable of the Ten Virgins in the gospels, explaining in exquisite detail how to discern between true grace and hypocrisy.[14] Edwards refined and developed these reflections in a later sermon series on discernment that eventually became the *Religious Affections* (1746).

Only relatively recently have scholars written about Edwards's occasional sermons because most had been unpublished until the recent volumes in the Yale edition. These were sermons given on special occasions, such as colony-wide fast and thanksgiving days, often in response to earthquakes or droughts

---

12. WJE 25:220; Kimnach, "Edwards as Preacher," 122.

13. Sermon on Matt. 11:12(b), WJEO 57; WJE 19:283, 290.

14. Ava Chamberlain, "Brides of Christ and Signs of Grace: Edwards's Sermon Series on the Parable of the Wise and Foolish Virgins," in Stephen Stein, ed., *Jonathan Edwards's Writings: Text, Context, Interpretation* (Bloomington, IN: Indiana University Press, 1996), 3–18.

or wars, or to address special audiences such as Indians, teens, or very young children. There were also occasional sermons to commemorate deaths, peace treaties, and other civic events.

Kimnach reports that Edwards's earliest sermons (1720–23) reflect the teenage preacher's ardor and idealism. He described conversion as focused on a certain taste for holiness and depicted the sanctified life in more concrete and personal terms than had been traditional for Puritans. Predominant was the notion that love and sensible pleasure are at the heart of life in God. According to Kenneth Minkema, prominent sermonic themes in Edwards's next six years of preaching (1723–29) were justification by faith, spiritual light and sight, excellency as harmony and consent, the happiness of man and the glory of God as one thing, the reasonableness of Christian faith, typology, Trinitarian controversies, and the national covenant. Mark Valeri reports that between 1730 and 1733 "Edwards turned to civic matters frequently," focusing on disputes between Parliament and the colony's legislature and growing social stratification. He addressed the plight of Northampton's indigents, the danger of political bickering, temptations facing businessmen, and the avarice of rulers. He urged Christian charity to the poor. In the mid-1730s, Edwards frequently preached on the glory and "excellency" of Christ, and returned to the themes of justification by faith and the reasonableness of Christianity. Between 1739 and 1742, Edwards's occasional sermons placed new emphasis on the sinfulness of America and New England, proclaiming that neither is the New Israel. Edwards wanted to be sure his parishioners would "not be deluded into thinking they were the center of God's plans." In his final period of preaching, from 1742 to 1758, Edwards filled his sermons with themes he would take up in longer treatises: universal prayer for revival, a richly expanded vision of the Trinity, the ethics of cosmic benevolence, divine sovereignty and the purpose of creation, and the *prisca theologia* in other world religions.[15]

The Importance and Task of Preaching

Edwards considered preaching of paramount importance for the work of redemption, which was at the center of his ecclesiology (ch. 28) and historical vision (ch. 15).[16] He eagerly awaited the onset of the "glorious work of God's

---

15. Kimnach, "Editor's Preface to the New York period," in WJE 10:277–78, 289–90; Kenneth P. Minkema, "Editor's Introduction," WJE 14:17–19; Valeri, "Editor's Introduction," WJE 17:17, 23–31; M.X. Lesser, "Editor's Introduction," WJE 19:1–36; Harry S. Stout & Nathan O. Hatch, "Editor's Introduction," WJE 22:39; Kimnach, "Editor's Introduction," WJE 25:45.

16. Helen Westra's *The Minister's Task and Calling in the Sermons of Jonathan Edwards* (Lewiston, NY: Edwin Mellen Press, 1986) is especially helpful on this score.

Spirit," a 250-year period of revival and persecution that would be followed by the millennium. This outpouring of the Holy Spirit would come only through Spirit-anointed preaching. Preaching is the "principal means" God uses to bring good to the souls of people, and the greatest good is "bringing [these] poor sinners to Christ and salvation." Preaching will not only save but sanctify, putting people on the road to heaven and making them holy as they walk the road.[17]

Edwards used noble images drawn from scripture to illustrate the premier significance of preachers in the work of redemption. They are like the trumpets blown by Old Testament priests at the great Jewish feasts, like farmers who go forth to sow seed in the earth (Mt. 13:1–9), like burning and shining lights (Jn. 5:25) and like mirrors that convey and reflect beams of the light of the world. When they preach the gospel rightly, they are the very "voice of the great God." Using earthier comparisons, he compared them to Samson's jawbone of the ass (Jdg. 15:14–16), teeth that a nurse uses to chew food for babies, saliva ("spit") that Jesus used to mix with dirt and open the eyes of a blind man (Jn. 9:6–7), David's sling that helped kill Goliath (1 Sam. 17:49), and the ox that treads out the corn (1 Cor. 9:9–10).[18]

The principal task of the preacher was to make truth become real in the perception of hearers. Edwards noticed that lack of spiritual experience and frequent repetition of religious maxims could obscure the recognition of what is real. When he was only nineteen years old, he preached on the doctrine, "When man dies, he is forever stripped of all earthly enjoyments." He told his hearers that while the world "knows the *truth* of this doctrine perfectly well" it nevertheless "don't [sic] seem at all *real* to them." Five years later, he said two things are required in order for something to seem real to us: "believing the truth of it, and having a sensible idea or apprehension of it." In chapter 24, we explored Edwards's notion of a simple idea imparted by a "divine and supernatural light," which makes what was previously a mere notion become a vivid reality by means of something like a sixth sense. In his private notebooks, Edwards wrote that this is "a light cast upon the ideas of spiritual things . . . which makes them appear clear and real which before were but faint, obscure representations." What was once merely conceptual is seen, tasted, and felt. It takes on a sensory dimension that forever fixes its reality in the apprehension of the

---

17. WJE 9:456, 459; on the "glorious work of God's Spirit," see Gerald R. McDermott, *One Holy and Happy Society: The Public Theology of Jonathan Edwards* (University Park, PA: Pennsylvania State University, 1992), 37–92; Sermon Notebook 45, Edwards Papers, Beinecke Rare Book and Manuscript Library, Yale University, quoted in WJE 25:38; BW 153.

18. WJE 22:240; WJE 24:932–33; sermon on Matt 13.3–4 (a), WJEO 56; WJE 24:340, 619, 944, 356, 1045.

believer. Edwards believed this new seeing and tasting of the reality of divine things comes principally if not exclusively through preaching.[19]

But if preaching is to continue to be a means of grace, it must stick to the "pure word of God" that tells of the "excellency and glory" of the Savior, "how great his love is, what he has done and suffered for poor sinners," and "what we must do." Just as cattle are not to mix with "diverse kind," preachers should sow the holy seed of the gospel "without any mixture of the doctrines and inventions of men, or wild notions of their own." They must "not preach those things which their own wisdom or reason suggests, but the things already dictated to them by the superior wisdom and knowledge of God." These things are "inexhaustible" in number and depth, since "that Divine Being, who is the main subject of [divinity] is infinite, and there is no end to the glory of his perfections." His works, "especially the work of redemption," are marvelous and "full of unsearchable wonders." Therefore the task of the preacher is difficult. He must explain doctrine and unravel difficulties by reason and argument, but in an easy, clear, and orderly way.[20] To do this effectively takes years. Most of Edwards's sermons addressed particular points that he considered essential to Christian thought and practice. But since no one sermon or even series of sermons could flesh out those essentials, Edwards thought of preaching in terms of long cycles of teaching. It would take several years of preaching several sermons a week to complete a cycle of instruction that Edwards thought necessary for proper Christian education. Thus some scholars have wrongly thought they could capture Edwards's vision in one or even a handful of his sermons.

Although Edwards said the preacher's sermon must penetrate the affections of his listeners and not simply change their thinking, he was emphatic about the necessity of cognitive content. In a 1739 sermon on "the importance and advantage of a thorough knowledge of divine truth," he taught that Christians must not be content to remain babes in knowledge of divine things nor be satisfied with spiritual experience alone. They must seek "not only a practical and experimental, but also a doctrinal knowledge of the truths and mysteries of religion." He explained that there are two kinds of knowledge of divine things—the speculative or natural that pertains to the head, and the practical and spiritual that is sensed in the heart. While speculative knowledge without spiritual knowledge is worthless, speculative knowledge nevertheless is "of

---

19. WJE 10:405–406, emph. added; WJE 14:201; WJE 13:470.

20. "Preaching the Gospel," BW 153; WJE 24:256; "Ministers to Preach Not Their Own Wisdom," BW 116; WJE 22:95; WJE 4:386.

infinite importance" because "without it we can have no spiritual or practical knowledge." There is no other way that we can benefit from the means of grace except by knowledge. "Therefore the preaching of the gospel would be wholly to no purpose, if it conveyed no knowledge to the mind." This assertion was based on Edwards's understanding of the human person: "The heart cannot be set upon an object of which there is no idea in the understanding." He would explicate this at much greater length in the fourth positive sign in his *Religious Affections* seven years later, but here he summarized as follows: "Such is the nature of man, that nothing can come at the heart but through the door of the understanding: and there can be no spiritual knowledge of that of which there is not first a rational knowledge." The upshot was that the "sense of the heart" that is at the heart of true religion is ordinarily impossible without doctrinal understanding: "A man cannot see the wonderful excellency and love of Christ in doing such and such things for sinners, unless his understanding be first informed how those things were done. He cannot have a taste of the sweetness and divine excellency of such and such things contained in divinity, unless he first have a notion that there are such and such things." Hence the way to deeper spiritual experience was through greater cognitive understanding of divine things: "The more you have of a rational knowledge of the things of the gospel, the more opportunity will there be, when the Spirit shall be breathed into your heart, to see the excellency of these things, and to taste the sweetness of them." Therefore the Christian preacher is obliged not only to preach but also to teach more and more of the infinite and unsearchable wonders of God and his redemption.[21]

Kimnach has observed that although Edwards was a homiletical artist and powerful logician, he nevertheless conceived of the perfect sermon more as a vehicle of power than of reason or beauty. In his preface to the five discourses delivered during the Little Awakening of 1734–35 he boasted that God had "smiled upon and bless[ed his] very plain, unfashionable way of preaching" even though he was "unable" to preach or write "politely." What mattered was not elegance but efficacy, not prestige but power. Power was never guaranteed, of course, by simply preaching from scripture. It was necessary that the preacher beseech God to inspire his preparation and enliven his words, so that he might preach with fervor and pathos. Prayer was an indispensable element of preparation, and an affective (though not affected) manner was helpful. But the preacher need not display his learning or be especially eloquent. Power came from God's

---

21. WJE 22:84, 87–89, 100: WJE 2:266–91.

"I thought of Stephen, and was in hopes, like him, to go off in this bloody triumph, to the immediate presence of my Master."

FIGURE 31.1 Eighteenth-century open-air preaching could be a dangerous occupation, as shown in this image of George Whitefield (John Gillies, *Memoirs of Rev. George Whitefield* [Middletown: 1837]. Wheaton College, Evangelism & Missions Collection).

blessing, without which even labored preparation and enthusiastic delivery would produce no lasting results. Preachers should not be surprised if some of their listeners are "stupid and senseless as stones," whispering to their neighbors or sleeping or dreaming during sermons. God is not frustrated because "he will see to it that his word shall not be in vain or without effect." Those who refuse to hear the word will pay attention in the next world and remember "that there ha[d] been a prophet among 'em."

Perhaps reflecting his own frustrations with the Northampton congregation that he once called "sermon-proof," he warned there would be "dark seasons" in the church when preachers would seem to "labor in vain." They might fish all night, as it were, and bring up empty nets. But they must not give up or get discouraged, for God is faithful. So whether a sermon becomes a thing of power depends on God. The minister sows the seed of the word, and leaves the sun and rain and influences of heaven to do their work. Like the hard-working farmer, he waits patiently for the harvest. But he should not be presumptuous by neglecting the diligent study of the Bible or by failing to be "much in seeking God." In the end he must be faithful and "leave the event [i.e., outcome] with God."[22]

The Format, Imagery, and Delivery of Edwards's Sermons

Samuel Hopkins tells us that Edwards took "great pains" to compose his sermons, getting up earlier and studying scripture more than his contemporaries. Edwards took the customary Puritan sermonic format of "text," "doctrine," and "application" (or "uses") and customized it for his own purposes. The "text" was usually one verse of scripture, which Edwards would typically explain by relating its context and meaning, often by referring to parallel themes in other parts of the Bible. In the periods of apprenticeship and mastery, the "text" would usually take up three to four printed pages. Then came the "doctrine," which he typically compressed to a single statement, thus providing his sermons with extraordinary focus. His "reasons" or "propositions" would then use both scriptural and rational arguments to "prove" the doctrine. These reasons took less time than the "application" in his Sunday sermons, but the opposite was true in his weekday lectures. The "application" usually was broken into separate sections for the purposes of self-examination and consolation. Often Edwards would consider objections in various sections of the "uses." In this way, Edwards developed "a grand march down from the mountain: from Holy Writ to abstract principles to personal values and actions."[23]

---

22. Kimnach, "Edwards as Preacher," 105; WJE 19:797; WJE 24:756; WJE 4:386–88; "Preaching the Gospel," BW 153; WJE 17:178–79, 181; WJE 19:113; 24:965–66; sermon on Matt. 13:3–4(a), WJEO 56.

23. Samuel Hopkins, *Life and Character of the Late Reverend, Learned and Pious Mr. Jonathan Edwards* (Northampton, 1804), 44, 50; Kimnach, "The Sermons: Concept and Execution," 244.

Yet Edwards's secret weapon in preaching was his unrivaled use of imagery.[24] Kimnach calls it his "armor-piercing device of sensational imagery." Light was perhaps his favorite image—no doubt influenced in part by his age of Enlightenment. But if it was common among his contemporaries, "no one looked more intensely at the biblical meaning of light for his day than did Edwards." Marsden explains that for him it was "the most powerful image of how God communicated his love to the creation. *Regeneration* meant to be given eyes to see the light of Christ in hearts that had been hopelessly darkened by sin." The fountain was another favorite. In his 1738 sermon series on love, *Charity and Its Fruits*, he declared that God is a fountain of love that pours out its "effusions of love" into the bosoms of the saints, whom he likened to "the flowers on the earth in a pleasant spring day" that "open their bosoms to the sun to be filled with his [sic] warmth and light, and to flourish in beauty and fragrance by his rays." Every saint is a flower in God's garden, and "holy love is the fragrance and sweet odor" that they all emit. In the same breath, he said every saint is "as a note in a concert of music which sweetly harmonizes with every other note...and so all helping one another to their utmost to express their love of the whole society to the glorious Father and Head of it, and [to pour back] love into the fountain of love, whence they are supplied and filled with love and with glory." The following spring, he interrupted his series on the history of redemption with a sermon comparing Christ to the sun. To believers, his second coming will "be a thousand times more refreshing to them than ever was the sight of the rising sun to them that have wandered in a wilderness, through the longest and darkest night. The sight of [it] will fill their souls with unspeakable gladness and rejoicing. It will be a bright day to the saints. The beams of that glorious Sun that will then appear will make it bright." But for unbelievers, "every ray of that glory that Christ shall then appear in will be like a stream of scorching fire, and will pierce their hearts with a keener torment than a stream of fierce lightning.... 506That day will burn as an oven indeed. That brightness that the light of Christ's glory shall fill the world with will be more terrible to them than if the world was filled with the fiercest flames." Though Edwards's words were rarely long and never obscure, the pictures he painted with them were vivid and memorable.[25]

---

24. Kristin Emery Saldine focuses on Edwards's landscape imagery in her "Preaching God Visible: Geo-Rhetoric and the Theological Appropriation of Landscape Imagery in the Sermons of Jonathan Edwards" (PhD diss., Princeton Theological Seminary, 2004).

25. WJE 10:171; Marsden, *Jonathan Edwards: A Life*; (New Haven, CT: Yale University Press, 2003), 55; WJE 8:386; WJE 22:60.

If his imagery made his sermons memorable, their clear and compelling logic left his auditors "little room to escape his web of arguments." Most New Englanders had "cut their eyeteeth on the logic of carefully-argued sermons" since educated eighteenth-century people were trained in and had great confidence in the power of logic to settle arguments. Edwards was a master of logical argument and used it to great effect in his sermons. In his golden years of sermonic composition—the late 1720s through the early 1740s—he carefully assembled arguments and examples "both from Scripture and reason, as even to force the assent of every attentive hearer.... His words were so full of ideas, set in such a plain and striking light, that few speakers have been able to command an audience as he." With their blend of logic and what Kimnach calls "the intensity of an inchworm," his sermons always had focus: "Like an eagle Edwards circled over the context [of the biblical text]," observes John Gerstner, "until he found his point and then descended deeply to snatch his homiletic prey and hold it up to the full view of all. For the next hour or more, Jonathan Edwards's only interest was to dissect the text, to analyze it, and to feed his hungry people." Ten-year-old Nehemiah Strong sat in the Northampton pews during Edwards's 1739 series on the history of redemption. Years later, he told Edwards's grandson Timothy Dwight that he became so entranced by Edwards's sermon on the Second Coming that "he expected without one thought to the contrary the awful scene to be unfolded on that day and in that place," and was "deeply disappointed when the day terminated and left the world in its usual state of tranquility."[26]

Hopkins, who studied in Edwards's home for several months at the beginning of the Great Awakening, said Edwards's delivery was easy, natural, and solemn. He did not have a loud or strong voice, but spoke with distinctness, clarity, and precision.[27] Gerstner believed Edwards's delivery "was one of the most mediocre the church has ever known"—perhaps because of an oft-repeated story from a nineteenth-century source that Edwards held his notes up to his face and otherwise stared at the bell rope at the back of the church without change of intonation or gesture. But Kenneth Minkema and others have corrected that caricature. The sermon manuscripts, they note,

---

26. Marsden, *Jonathan Edwards*, 129, 90–91; Hopkins, *Life*, 51–52; Kimnach, "Jonathan Edwards's Pursuit of Reality," in Nathan Hatch and Harry Stout, eds., *Jonathan Edwards and the American Experience* (New York: Oxford University Press, 1988), 114; Gerstner, 1:486; Timothy Dwight, *Travels in New England and New York*, 4 vols. (Cambridge, MA: Harvard University Press, 1969), 4:230–31, quoted in Marsden, *Jonathan Edwards*, 195.

27. Edwards complained to the Princeton Trustees of his "contemptibleness of speech"; WJE 16:726.

contain cues to look up at the audience and speak extemporaneously, and Edwards himself noted the importance of a preacher changing his tones and using gestures and fervor in his preaching. He told his pastoral interns it was best to preach without notes and he used more and more outlines after the Great Awakening. While he labored with a mediocre voice and never rivaled Whitefield for oratorical display, Edwards tried to make the best of his limitations as a speaker. The printed results were still impressive: a "legacy unequalled in the literature of the American sermon for its depth of thought and power of expression."[28]

Three of the Best

We will conclude this chapter by looking very briefly at three of Edwards's finest sermons. "Sinners in the Hands of an Angry God" is undoubtedly Edwards's most famous sermon. Preached at the height of the Great Awakening in New England (ch. 27), Harry Stout calls it "arguably America's greatest sermon." In it Edwards tried to compose the "perfect idea" of an awakening sermon by using "rhetorical dynamite" to produce "unprecedented terror." The core idea was "that one could get to life eternal only after first being scared to death." Curiously, Edwards preached it first in Northampton in June 1741 but with no discernible effect. Several weeks later, he delivered it at Enfield, Connecticut, where, as Kimnach writes, "the congregation virtually rioted when the preacher had barely begun, so it is impossible to say that they actually heard the sermon." Uncounted scholars and students have studied Edwards's legendary employment of imagery in this sermon. His most striking images—the archer with the drawn bow, the loathsome spider, pent-up waters, unleashed lions—come straight from the Bible. Some bear repeating: sinners' righteousness would have no more power to keep them from hell "than a spider's web would have to stop a falling rock"; "there are black clouds of God's wrath now hanging directly over your heads, full of the dreadful storm, and big with thunder"; "the wrath of God is like great waters that are damned for the present" but "they increase more and more, and rise higher and higher...the waters are continually rising and waxing more and more mighty"; the devils watching for sinners to fall into hell "stand waiting for

---

28. Hopkins, *Life*, 52; Gerstner, *Rational Biblical Theology*, 1:480; William Edwards Parke, "Edwardsean," p. 202, folder 1668, box 37, Jonathan Edwards Collection, Beinecke Rare Book and Manuscript Library, Yale University; cited by Sweeney, *Jonathan Edwards*, 75–76; WJE 14:12–13; Hopkins, 53; Kimnach, "Edwards as Preacher," 123.

them, like greedy hungry lions that see their prey, and expect to have it, but are for the present kept back."²⁹

Marsden has observed that the sometimes-missed logic of the sermon is that "it is the weight of sinners' own sins that is dragging them toward the abyss." Edwards said they stand on slippery ground and need nothing but their "own weight to throw [them] down." Sin's gravitational pull—here one recalls Isaac Newton's science—draws them down toward destruction. Their own "hellish *principles*" would kindle and flame out into hellfire if God permitted them. "Your wickedness," Edwards warned, "makes you as it were heavy as lead." Another oft-missed theme is that *God* is keeping sinners from falling into hell. He "restrains" their wickedness; if not for his restraints, their souls would turn into fiery ovens. The fire pent up in their hearts is struggling to break out, but God's "forbearance" keeps it in check. Only God's "arbitrary will" preserves sinners from hell every moment. Only God's power and pleasure "holds you up"; only his hand keeps "you from falling into the fire every moment" and is the reason "why you han't [sic] gone to hell since you have sat here in the house of God." If these words did not make his hearers feel radically insecure, he had more: they were walking over the pit of hell on a rotten covering with innumerable places that could not bear their weight; there were unseen arrows of death that flew about, even at noonday; no one in hell ever intended to go there, but all flattered themselves they would not wind up there; and there was nothing between them and hell "but the air." "You hang by a slender thread, with the flames of divine wrath flashing about it, and ready every moment to singe it, and burn it asunder." The true issue, as Kimnach writes, was not place but time. It was urgent that sinners not wait any longer. "How awful it is to be left behind at such a day.... God seems *now* to be hastily gathering in his elect....[P]robably the bigger part of adult persons that ever shall be saved, will be brought in *now* in a little time.... The wrath of almighty God is *now* undoubtedly hanging over great part of this congregation." Modern readers may be surprised to learn that the original manuscript version was far milder than the later printed revision. Kimnach says the sermon given at Enfield "preserves a nice balance between the carrot and the stick," unlike the version most Americans have read.³⁰

---

29. WJE 22:34, 31; Kimnach, "Edwards as Preacher," 116; Gerstner, *Rational Biblical Theology*, 1:494; WJE 22:410, 406; Edward J. Gallagher says these images taken together deliver a "recurrent pulsation" that makes the sermon primarily an auditory experience. Gallagher, "'Sinners in the Hands of an Angry God': Some Unfinished Business," *New England Quarterly* 73 (2000):202–21.

30. Marsden, 222; WJE 22:404, 404, 407 orig.emph., 409, 412, 407, 410, 412; Kimnach, "Edwards as Preacher," 116; WJE 22:417–18, emph. added; Kimnach, "Editor's Introduction," WJE 10:114. The notion that God's "arbitrary will" keeps sinners out of hell every moment is underscored by Edwards's.

Edwards's "Farewell Sermon" was one of the few homiletic productions of his last period that was fully written out. In Kimnach's estimation, it was "as sustained and disciplined" as "Sinners" but "supplant[ed] fire with ice" in eleven pages of doctrine and thirteen pages of application. It was delivered on the first Sunday in July 1750 after his Northampton congregation had voted to eject him from their pulpit. With cool detachment, Edwards defended his doctrine: "Ministers and the people that have been under their care, must meet one another, before Christ's tribunal, at the day of judgment." "We live in a world of change," when those who seem most united suddenly become "most disunited." But even if they are removed to places distant from one another, they will meet again in the next world. Then there will be "clear, certain and infallible light" so that all "deceit and delusion shall vanish away." There will be no more debate and disagreement. When ministers meet their people now and try to instruct and correct them on eternal matters, "all is often in vain." Despite everything their ministers say, many remain "stupid and unawakened." This does not mean that ministers are always right. In fact, they are not infallible in discerning the state of souls, and the "most skillful of them are liable to mistakes." But neither can the people know certainly the state of their minister or one another. "Very often" hypocrites are mistaken for "eminent saints," and "some of God's jewels" are censured and abused. Therefore it is also "very often" that "great differences and controversies arise between ministers and the people that are under their care." People "are ready to judge and censure one another...[and] are greatly mistaken in their judgment, and wrong one another in their censures." But on that future day in eternity when pastors and their people meet again, the secrets of every heart shall be made manifest, and no one will be careless or sleeping or "wandering [in] mind from the great concern of the meeting." The great Judge will "do justice between ministers and their people," and all will see that these affairs of the church were more important "than the temporal concerns of the greatest earthly monarchs, and their kingdoms or empires."[31]

In the sermonic application, Edwards defended his ministry in Northampton. "I have not spared my feeble strength, but have exerted it for the good of your souls.... I have spent the prime of my life and strength in labors for your eternal welfare." He said he was never lazy or ambitious for his own financial gain, but "have given myself to the work of the ministry, laboring in it night

---

occasionalism—his idea that at every moment God recreates the world and wills what is (chs. 7,22). Our thanks to Ken Minkema for this observation.

31. WJE 25:457, 463, 468, 469, 471, 473.

and day, rising early and applying myself to this great business to which Christ has appointed me." He declared that he had borne "heavy burdens," but God had strengthened him. "Although I have often been troubled on every side, I have not yet been distressed; perplexed, but not in despair; cast down, but not destroyed" (2 Cor. 3:8–9). Then came a stunning admission of failure: "But now...my work is finished....You have publicly rejected me." As if to deflect attention from his defeat, he turned again to that future meeting when "our hearts will be turned inside out" and all will see "whether I have been treated with that impartiality, candor and regard which the just Judge esteemed due." He concluded by addressing different groups within the congregation. To those "I leave in a Christless, graceless condition," he feared all his labors had only hardened them and prayed God would grant his Word to be "the fire and hammer that breaketh the rock [of their hearts] in pieces" (Jer. 23:29). To those "who are under some awakenings," he told them to "beware of backsliding" and turn to him "who is the infinite fountain of light" so their eyes would be opened and they could meet their minister "in joyful and glorious circumstances." He told the teenagers and twentysomethings that out of love for themselves they ought not to reject the teaching he had given them. The younger children, he advised, should not imitate those who "cast off fear." "Remember that great day when you must appear before the judgment seat of Christ, and meet your minister there, who has so often counseled and warned you." Parents were admonished not to be like Eli, who failed to restrain his children (1 Sam. 2–3). Everyone in the church was told to avoid contention, which was "one of the greatest burdens" he had labored under. He suggested they give themselves to "secret" prayer and beware of hiring an Arminian for a minister. After asking them to pray for him—even if they disagreed with him—he closed with a final exhortation to keep in mind their future meeting: "And let us all remember, and never forget our future solemn meeting, on that great day of the Lord; the day of infallible decision, and of the everlasting and unalterable sentence, Amen."[32]

"Heaven Is a World of Love" describes the world he thought believers would enjoy just after the Last Judgment depicted in the "Farewell Sermon." It was the fifteenth and last sermon in his 1738 series on Paul's paean to love in 1 Corinthians 13. In his explication of this text he asserts that "other gifts of the Spirit" and "all common fruits of the Spirit" shall cease at the end of the church age and that only charity or love will remain in heaven. His next eighteen pages in the Yale edition develop seven reasons to support the doctrine ("heaven is a world of love"), followed by eleven pages of application.

---

32. WJE 25:475–77, 480–81, 484, 488.

The reasons start with the declaration that while God is everywhere, he is "more especially" in some places than others. His presence is progressively greater in Israel, Jerusalem, the temple, the Holy of Holies, and then the mercy seat. But heaven is "his dwelling place above all other places in the universe." There sits the infinite fountain of love which is the "mutual holy energy" created by the infinite love of the Father for the Son and the infinite love of the Son for the Father. The Father's love flows to Christ the Head and through him to all his members. The saints are then secondarily subjects of love, just as planets give off reflected light from the sun. All the residents of heaven are perfectly lovely and harmonize as so many notes "in a concert of music which sweetly [harmonize] with every other note." They are ranked differently according to their capacities for love, but there is no envy in those lower toward those higher because the highest in glory are also highest in holiness and humility and therefore have more love than others. All exist in "an eternal youth" with "perfect tranquility and joy." In heaven, there is no fading beauty or decaying love or satiety in our faculty of enjoyment.[33]

In his sermonic application, Edwards charged his listeners to beware of contention in families, for this especially causes people to "live without much of a comfortable sense of heavenly things, or any lively hope of it." He said saints are happy because they have seen and tasted that heavenly glory. But at the same time, they struggle after holiness, since love always struggles "for liberty" against sin. In his "use" for "awakening to sinners" he told them, "You are in danger. Hell is a world of hatred... [it] is, as it were, a vast den of poisonous, lusting serpents." Everything that is hateful in this universe "shall be gathered together in hell." Even those who were friends on earth will be enemies there. Everyone will hate one another and "to their utmost torment one another." Misery will not love company there. But "God gives men their choice." If sinners would choose heaven and persevere in well-doing, and love the path that leads to it, "it will certainly lead [them] to heaven at last." They can stay on the path by looking to Jesus, trusting in his mediation and blood—the price of heaven—and intercession for them, and then trusting to his strength to live by his Spirit sent from heaven. Finally, Edwards reassured the saints that to live a life of love to God and neighbor is a way of "inward peace and sweetness." This is the way to have "clear evidences of a title to heaven" because "heavenliness consists in love." So "if ever you arrive at heaven, faith and love must be the wings which must carry you there."[34]

---

33. WJE 8:369, 386, 383–85.
34. WJE 8:386, 389–91, 395–96, 391, 395–97.

32

Public Theology, Society, and America

UNTIL QUITE RECENTLY, most scholars believed that Edwards was happy to let the world outside the church go to hell, in both senses. They imagined that he took no interest in public affairs unless they bore some direct relation to the progress of redemption. As Sidney Mead once put it, Edwards separated "salvation from one's life in the natural world."[1] But an investigation of his occasional sermons (i.e., those preached on fast and thanksgiving days) and other published and unpublished writings revealed that Edwards in fact cared deeply about civil and public life, and developed elaborate conceptions of how life in the public square ought to be conducted.[2]

Philosophical and Theological Grounding

Edwards's public theology—that is, his conception of the church's relation to the larger society and to civil polity—issued from his philosophy of being and his theology of love.[3] His philosophy of being is adumbrated in *The Nature of True Virtue* (finished in 1755 and published in 1765), where he described the structure of being as a vast network of interrelations wherein every entity is related to every other: "Every intelligent being is some way related to Being in general, and is a part of the universal system of existence; and so stands in connection with the whole." Regenerate human beings, because they are infused with the divine nature, have the propensity to "reach out to an infinite number of relationships." Thus Edwards could not conceive of any human

---

1. Sidney E. Mead, *The Old Religion in the Brave New World* (Berkeley: University of California Press, 1977), 4.

2. Gerald R. McDermott, *One Holy and Happy Society: The Public Theology of Jonathan Edwards* (University Park: Penn State Press, 1992). See also Jeff Jay Stone, "The Political Philosophy of Jonathan Edwards" (PhD diss., University of Dallas, 1992).

3. We do not understand public theology to be synonymous with civil religion, which is a set of symbols, beliefs, and practices, alongside traditional religion, that in various ways relates the nation, culture, or political system to ultimate reality. Civil religion may be an alternative to traditional religion, while public theology typically stands within traditional theology as the subset that conceives of the theological meaning of civil polity and society.

existence except in union with others: "God has made us with such a nature, that we cannot subsist without the help of another... one cannot subsist alone, without an union with, and the help of the rest."[4]

Edwards went on to develop in *The Nature of True Virtue* what amounted to a phenomenology of human existence. In a work that never quotes the Bible and was plainly intended to appeal to those who did not share his theological vision, Edwards explained that all human beings share certain moral goals. The unregenerate do not approve of these goals for the same reasons that the regenerate do, but both nonetheless approve the same moral ends. Only the regenerate see the true beauty of general benevolence, but both regenerate and unregenerate persons perceive that general benevolence is grounded in natural uniformity, equality, and justice. This shared perception is possible because nearly all human beings share the same general sense of moral good and evil, otherwise known as conscience, and God has engraved his moral law on all consciences alike.[5]

Edwards also argued in *True Virtue* that human beings share aesthetic perception—an appreciation of many sorts of physical and spiritual beauty. Such shared perception carries significance though it falls short of what Edwards called "primary beauty" and which consisted of consent to universal being. Furthermore, nearly all human beings share elemental religious knowledge (such as knowledge of God's existence and beneficent providence) and instinctual, kind affections such as pity and familial affection.[6]

On the basis of this multiplicity of shared experiences, Edwards laid a foundation for a common moral philosophy. Every human being, he wrote, is a part of universal being. Each one therefore is obligated to acknowledge his or her place within this structure of being and to give "cordial consent" to it by seeking its highest good. This means that one must love the "Being of beings" and all other beings in the cosmos. Love for only a fraction of universal being is inferior and defective, and therefore is not true to what is.

Obviously, this talk of love for the "Being of beings" would seem to leave secular people beyond the purview of Edwards's public ethic. But Edwards

---

4. WJE 8:541; Sang Hyun Lee, *The Philosophical Theology of Jonathan Edwards* (Princeton: Princeton University Press, 1988), 113; WJE 17:376. Edwards's social philosophy paralleled his metaphysics and aesthetics: "One alone, without reference to any more, cannot be excellent" (WJE 6:337). See ch. 7.

5. Edwards followed the biblical and Puritan traditions in conceding that a conscience may be "seared" through sin and therefore devoid of common notions of good and evil. He also recognized that while nearly all think that altruism is better than egoism, people differ on what shape altruism should take.

6. Edwards was well aware of atheists in his day, and in fact tried to show that atheism was ill-founded.

also spoke of consent to universal being, a notion that does not necessarily imply the existence of God. In this vein, H. Richard Niebuhr, who once confessed he owed his basic theological orientation to Edwards, wrote of "the supreme reality with which we must reckon...the secret of existence by virtue of which things come into being, are what they are, and pass away."[7] Such a description of ultimate reality lacks the word "God" but nonetheless resembles Edwards's "universal being."

Edwards constructed his system of being in a treatise addressed to people who did not share his vision of God. His intent was to articulate a framework that Christians and non-Christians alike could understand. We might say today that it provides a theoretical basis for the cooperation of Christians with non-Christians in social projects with moral ends. Both groups, he suggested, shared the same moral goals albeit for different reasons. Both should be committed to the good of the entire community. Even if some people were devoted only to their own interests, Edwards believed the Christian was obligated to work for the good of the whole community, which included non-Christians as well as Christians.

The Purposes and Functions of Civil Government

Edwards believed that Christians were obliged to care for the whole community because God himself did and has provided civil government for that purpose. In this section we will make note of seven distinct purposes that Edwards ascribed to political leaders and to civil government. In words echoing his Reformed tradition, he preached that magistrates were to "act as the fathers of the commonwealth with that care and concern for the public good that the father of a family has for the family, watchful against public dangers, [and] forward to improve their power to promote the public benefit."[8] Their first three functions of government were to secure property, protect citizens' rights, and—toward that end—maintain order. In words reminiscent of Hobbes, Edwards said that without the strong arm of government, citizens would tear one another apart, and life would become "miserable and intolerable." Related to these first two functions—protecting property and keeping order—government was also to ensure justice. For Edwards justice was recompense of moral deserts. The evildoer would have evil returned in proportion to his or

---

7. H. Richard Niebuhr, *Radical Monotheism and Western Culture* (New York: Harper and Row, 1943), 122.

8. WJE 8:261–62. On Reformed influence, see, e.g., Calvin, *Institutes*, 4.20.5.

her evil deeds. Similarly, justice would prevail when the person who loved others received the proper return of his or her love.[9]

Typically Edwards understood justice in terms of an exchange of property. The "mutual injustice" that he deemed it government's duty to prevent was more often than not the oppression by which the strong take advantage of the weak. He thought sellers who took advantage of market conditions to raise prices on goods were exploiting the plight of "poor people whose families are in such necessity of bread." Political rulers were therefore obligated to "restrain those who would grind the faces of the poor, and screw their neighbors." Edwards condemned the emerging market economy because he thought that self-interest would only corrode the social fabric.[10]

A fourth responsibility of government for Edwards was national defense. Military force was justified when the "rights and privileges" of a people were threatened or when the "preservation of the community or public society requires it." If "injurious and bloody enemies" molest and endanger a society, it is the duty of government to defend that society by the use of force.[11]

The next two functions of government referred not to preventable evils but to positive goods—promoting a common morality and a minimum level of material prosperity. The fifth function was to "make good laws against immorality," for a people that fail in morality would eventually fail in every other way. Rulers therefore were not to "countenance vice and wickedness" by failing to enact legislation against it or enforcing what had been legislated. Sixth, governments were to help the poor. Edwards believed that the state—in his case, a town committee in Northampton—had a responsibility to assist those who were destitute for reasons other than their own laziness or prodigality. The state was also obliged to help the children of the lazy and prodigal. Governmental involvement was necessary because private charity (here Edwards had in mind the charity of churches) was unreliable: "In this corrupt world [private charity] is an uncertain thing; and therefore the wisdom of legislators did not think fit to leave those that are so reduced upon such a precarious

---

9. WJE 25:321; WJE 8:569.

10. WJE 25:321, 318; sermon on Ex. 20:15, WJEO 55. For Edwards on economics, see Mark Valeri, "The Economic Thought of Jonathan Edwards," *Church History* 60 (1991): 37–54; Valeri, "Jonathan Edwards, the Edwardsians, and the Sacred Cause of Free Trade," in David W. Kling and Douglas A. Sweeney, *Jonathan Edwards at Home and Abroad: Historical Memories, Cultural Movements, Global Horizons* (Columbia: University of South Carolina Press, 2003), 121–36; and James D. German, "The Political Economy of Depravity: The Irrelevance (and Relevance) of Jonathan Edwards," in Kling and Sweeney, 101–20.

11. WJE 25:133; sermon on Neh. 4:14, WJEO 64.

foundation for a subsistence." Because of the natural selfishness of all human beings, including the regenerate, it is therefore incumbent upon the Christian to support the state's efforts to help the destitute.[12]

The seventh and final item in Edwards's job description for the magistrate was religious. The good ruler was expected to give friendly but distanced support to true religion. During a revival, the magistrate should call a day of prayer or thanksgiving. But he should not try to do much more than that. In Edwards's list of the magistrate's qualifications in his "Strong Rods" sermon at the funeral of his uncle, Colonel John Stoddard, piety was only a subordinate trait. Religious devotion was not listed among the chief qualifications for public office, and in the context it is mentioned only for the purpose of administering "justice and judgment...to bear down vice and immorality." In his private notebooks, Edwards reminded himself that the civil authorities were to have "nothing to do with matters ecclesiastical, with those things that relate to conscience and eternal salvation or with any matters religious as *religious*." In other words, he would not allow any magistrate to tell his parishioners what church to attend or tell him what to preach. For it belonged to the people—"not the legislators"—to decide whether they were bound to obey any and all ecclesiastical laws.[13]

On this score Edwards was no innovator. Both evangelicals and liberals in Edwards's era insisted that their magistrates support religion and morality. But his contemporaries were not insisting—as had their seventeenth-century predecessors—that civil government should enforce correct doctrine. Religious leaders in the early- and mid-eighteenth-century asked only that the magistrate take care that "religion be upheld and that God is worshipped, and by suppressing all that tends to root out religion from among them." They had come a long way from the policies of John Calvin, who urged the magistrates of Geneva to intervene in ecclesiastical matters to prevent idolatry and blasphemy and to ensure the teaching of orthodox doctrine.[14]

Edwards considered some entanglement with religion by government to be inevitable; in such circumstances, the magistrate was bound to favor the interests of religion. This was obligatory for civil as well as religious reasons.

---

12. Sermon on Prov. 14:34, WJEO 44; WJE 17:403. In various statutes, the Massachusetts Bay Colony had mandated care of the indigent to towns in order to supplement what was done by churches; see George Lee Haskins, *Law and Authority in Colonial Massachusetts* (Hamden, CT: Archon Books, 1960).

13. WJE 4:370–73; WJE 25:319; WJE 13:207 (orig. emph.), 206.

14. John Barnard, "The Throne Established by Righteousness," in A.W. Plumstead, ed., *The Wall and the Garden: Selected Massachusetts Election Sermons 1670–1775* (Minneapolis: Univ. of Minnesota Press, 1978), 264–65; Calvin, *Institutes* 4.20.3; 4.12.16. See McDermott, *One Holy and Happy Society*, 135.

"It is for the civil interest of a people not to be disturbed in their public assemblies for divine worship, that is, it is for their general peace, quiet and pleasure, etc. in this world." Thus Edwards did not favor a strict separation of religion and state. He would have considered such a position naïve and injurious to religion. In his mind, the religious and civil interests of a society were woven together in a seamless garment so that an attempted separation of one from the other would damage both. Religion was necessary for morality, which in turn was essential for a healthy society. Moreover, the contractual arrangements of the national covenant (discussed later in this chapter) required the civil authorities to promote true religion. For neglecting religion would bring immorality and injustice—and therefore the wrath of God. Hence it was only prudent for civil government to ensure the free practice of true religion, for by it a society promoted its own prosperity.

Christian Charity

With or without the assistance of the government, Christians were to help the poor. Believers needed to work with all other citizens toward the common goal of assisting those in need. Here is where Edwards's theology of love came into play. Helping the poor was a measure of true love. Lest Christians understand love as merely a concern for the souls of the unregenerate, Edwards insisted that true love cares for bodies as well. In *Religious Affections*, he wrote that genuine religion cares for others' material as well as spiritual needs. He criticized those who "pretend a great love to men's souls, that are not compassionate and charitable towards their bodies.... And if the compassion of professing Christians towards others don't work in the same ways [i.e., to their bodies], it is a sign that it is no true Christian compassion."[15]

Helping the poor was also an indispensable sign of one's love for God. For Edwards, every creature was an expression of God's volition and action, and this meant that the neighbor-in-need was a manifestation of God's presence. So if one wanted to express love for God, one had to serve the neighbor, who was God's "receiver": "We can't express our love to God by doing anything that is profitable to God; God would therefore have us do it in those things that are profitable to our neighbors, whom he has constituted his receivers."[16]

If helping the poor was a necessary sign of love for God, it was also a litmus test for judging religious experience. After the Great Awakening,

---

15. WJE 2:369.

16. WJE 4:523–24.

Edwards instructed ministers not to affirm the religious experience of anyone who did not seek to relieve the poor, though "they tell a fair story of illuminations and discoveries." He preached to his church in Northampton that charity to the poor was a Christian duty as important as prayer or church attendance. No commandment was "laid down in stronger terms" than the commandment of giving to the poor. It was therefore an all-important test of grace. "And the Scripture is as plain as it is possible it should be, that none are true saints, but those whose true character it is, that they are of a disposition to pity and relieve their fellow creatures, that are poor, indigent and afflicted."[17] This was an objective standard by which every Christian would be judged, and effort alone was not enough. Edwards judged the adequacy of Christian charity by the number of poor who remained in a community. Unless there were "none" in the community "that are proper objects of Charity...[suffering] in pinching [want]," the Christians of a community had not done enough. "Rich men" were urged by Edwards to establish and support schools "in poor towns and villages" and to support ministerial students from poor families.[18]

Edwards practiced what he preached. His first biographer, disciple Samuel Hopkins, who lived in the Edwards home for six months, reported that Edwards was a stellar example of giving to the poor and usually did it secretly—despite his having a large family to support and remaining in debt for most of his career. If all of his giving had been revealed, it "would prove him to be as great an instance of charity as almost any man that can be produced." To illustrate his point, Hopkins told of a time that Edwards heard of a family in another town that had fallen into poverty because the father had become sick. Edwards made arrangements to have the man receive a bundle of money without knowing its source. Among his last words on his deathbed were the following: "May my funeral be like Mr. Burr's, without pomp and cost. Any additional sums of money, that might be expected to be laid out that way, I would have it disposed of to charitable uses."[19]

Superior and Inferior Kinds of Patriotism

Edwards believed that Christians should support their national community, especially in times of war. He was a patriot—though often suspicious of

---

17. WJE 2:356; sermon on Deut. 15:7–11, WJEO 48; WJE 2:355.

18. WJE 17:374; WJE 4:515.

19. Samuel Hopkins, *Life and Character of the Late Reverend, Learned, and Pious Mr. Jonathan Edwards* (Northampton, MA: Printed by Andrew Wright, 1804), 49–50.

patriotism (ch. 33). He demonstrated his own patriotism by supporting colonial military expeditions against Cape Breton in 1745 and Crown Point in 1755. The first expedition was launched in the face of what seemed an ominous threat to New England society. France, which had declared war against England the previous year, could have disrupted New England shipping and fishing, and (worse yet) imposed Roman Catholicism on the colony, thus threatening (in the minds of Edwards and most Protestants) eternal perdition for the younger generation. On the other hand, New England's assault on the French fortress at Louisbourg (in what is now Nova Scotia) would, if successful, cut off French communication with Canada and prepare the way for assaults on Quebec and Montreal.[20] Edwards delivered a special sermon on the eve of the expedition and sounded every bit the patriotic chaplain inspiring his men to fight for God and country. The twenty expeditioners from his parish were to

FIGURE 32.1 American colonists—including Edwards—hailed their 1745 victory over French forces at the Louisburg fortress as a sign of God's blessing on the English Protestant cause (Charles Delort, *Embarkation of New England troops under Governor Pepperell during the expedition against Louisburg, Cape Breton and Nova Scotia* (circa 1905). Prints & Photographs Division, Library of Congress Lc-US262–105732).

---

20. This was the War of the Austrian Succession (1739–49), fought on the North American continent as King George's War (1744–49). See Douglas Edward Leach, *Arms for Empire: A Military History of the British Colonies in North America, 1607–1763* (New York: Macmillan, 1973), 206–61.

be courageous, he said, and he warned that cowardice would show a "want of trust in God...and will be offensive to him." Then, like an army recruiter promising teenagers that they would see the world, he promised "you will have opp[ortunity] to see Gods [sic] wonders in the Great deep."[21]

In 1755 there was more conflict—the French and Indian War.[22] The British and colonials had suffered a disastrous loss in July when General Edward Braddock lost 976 men killed or wounded (of 1,373 enlisted men) on the banks of the Monongahela River near Fort Duquesne. After news of the battle "spread throughout the colonies like the shock wave from an earthquake," Governor William Shirley of Massachusetts decided to launch another expedition north to Crown Point in an attempt to regain momentum in the battle against the French. Edwards bade the soldiers from Northampton to trust in God, not in themselves, as they set off on their expedition. Unfortunately, the army only made it as far as Lake George, the Massachusetts regiment suffered severe losses, and the battle was indecisive.[23]

Patriotism was thus a virtue for Edwards. He considered the patriotism of the unregenerate to be an inferior virtue, but a virtue nonetheless, since it tended to "the preservation of mankind, and their comfortably subsisting in the world." It had something of love in it, was "beautiful within [its] own sphere" and implied certain moral goals that were shared by the regenerate and the unregenerate alike. A mixed community of the regenerate and the unregenerate required some measure of patriotism as the condition of its existence, and this is one reason that Edwards could be an enthusiastic chaplain for New England's wars against the French.[24]

Yet when Edwards compared patriotism rooted in self-love to patriotism inspired by true virtue, the former lost most of its luster. Most patriotism, he believed, was based on narrowly circumscribed self-love rather than genuine benevolence (ch. 33). In 1746, after observing his fellow colonials' participation in King George's War, Edwards observed somewhat cynically: "A natural principle of self-love, without any other principle, may be sufficient to make a man concerned for the interest of the nation to which he belongs: as, for instance, in the present war, self-love may make natural men rejoice at the successes of our nation, and sorry for their disadvantages, they being concerned as members of the body." By 1755, Edwards was using what was for

---

21. Sermon on Lev. 26:3–13, Edwards Papers, Jonathan Edwards Center, Yale University.

22. Leach, *Arms for Empire*, 307–414.

23. Leach, *Arms for Empire*, 368, 371–78; WJE 25:682–84.

24. WJE 8:554–55, 621, 612, 602–603. Other reasons included the papist religion of the French, the fact that Edwards considered them to be arms of the Antichrist, and the civil liberties that Edwards feared would be lost in the event of British defeat.

him the derogatory label "private" to describe this sort of self-love, saying it falls "infinitely short" of true virtue. It does not have the power to unite all created beings with one another, he claimed. Though it is "exceeding necessary to society," it makes someone an enemy to those outside of his or her society if it is not subordinated to love for universal being. So even if a person were to be patriotic to a society of "millions of individuals," such as the Roman Empire, that person could still be an enemy to humanity in general.[25]

Ordinary patriotism boils down to such natural instincts as a sense of moral good and evil, deriving from the human conscience and a sense of deserved punishments or rewards. This was the origin of the instinct toward justice. It is merely "a relish of [moral] uniformity and proportion that determines the mind to approve these things. And if this be all, there is no need of anything higher, or of any thing in any respect diverse, to determine the mind to approve and be pleased with equal uniformity and proportion among spiritual things which are equally discerned." So even a concern for justice in the world was no sure sign of virtuous patriotism.[26]

Neither was gratitude. "Men may love...their country" out of gratitude for what their country has done for them, but loves like these are private in nature and therefore not truly virtuous because of the "narrowness of their views."[27] Edwards was saying that all patriotism, short of the universal benevolence that only the regenerate possess, was simply an enlarged version of love for self. It lacked true benevolence. It did not express an altruistic regard for the well-being of others, regardless of the effects on the self. Patriotism generally involved a mélange of subtle, self-serving calculations, even if not recognized as such.[28]

Edwards's skeptical attitude toward patriotism was unusual for the eighteenth century. Far more prevalent was the "benevolist gospel" of such thinkers as the third Earl of Shaftesbury and Francis Hutcheson, who taught that human nature was inherently benevolent and opposed to selfish egoism.[29] As Hutcheson put it, there is a "determination of our nature to study the good

---

25. WJE 2:246–47; WJE 8: 554–55, 621, 612, 602–603.

26. WJE 2:246–47; WJE 8:554–55, 621, 602–603.

27. WJE 8: 610. Here Edwards probably had in mind the third Earl of Shaftesbury, who said gratitude is proof of a moral sense. Norman Fiering, *Jonathan Edwards's Moral Thought and Its British Context* (Chapel Hill: Institute for the Study of Early American History and Culture, 1981), 186.

28. "True virtue stands against the parochiality of the world, the comforting alliances of like souls and common blood." Fiering, *Jonathan Edwards's Moral Thought*, 196.

29. Fiering, *Jonathan Edwards's Moral Thought*, 8. The benevolists taught that benevolence is rooted in natural feeling. On Shaftesbury, Hutcheson, and benevolence theories, see Fiering, 8, 128–31, 148, 159n, 162, 164, 166, 195–96, 356.

of others; or some instinct, antecedent to all reason from interest, which influences us to the love of others."³⁰ Shaftesbury wrote that "mutual succour" and other such instincts are naturally altruistic. "This we know for certain, that all social love, friendship, gratitude, or whatever else is of this generous kind, does by its nature take [the] place of the self-interesting passions, draws us out of ourselves, *and makes us disregardful of our own convenience and safety.*"³¹ The logical implication of their position was that patriotism was also based on a benevolent altruism inherent to human nature.³²

This view of human nature was shared by many eighteenth-century New England ministers. Edwards's fellow Congregationalist John Wise, for instance, held that "in every Mans Being [is] An Affection or Love to Man-kind in General." Boston liberals Charles Chauncy and Jonathan Mayhew claimed that self-love cooperated with natural benevolence to bring about good conduct. Moral perfection, they preached, came by the cultivation of one's natural potential. Edwards combated the underlying premise that human nature has an inherent inclination to disinterested benevolence. He argued that universal benevolence transcended natural affection and that natural affections did not extend far enough. These affections fell short of love for universal being and therefore were inimical to universal being.³³

But Edwards's critique of conventional patriotism cut deeper. First, he surmised that patriotism was peculiarly susceptible to self-deception. Because it was a form of commitment to a "considerable number" of persons, it was easily mistaken for true virtue, and so we "applaud [the patriot] highly." For, because of the "contracted limits" and "narrowness" of our minds, we too easily allow a large number, though but a "small part even of the world of mankind...to seem as if they were *all.*"³⁴ Edwards illustrated his point with one of history's ironies. The Romans, he pointed out, considered love to their

---

30. Francis Hutcheson, *Inquiry into the Original of Our Ideas of Beauty and Virtue* (1725), cited in Fiering, 249.

31. Shaftesbury, *Characteristics* (1711), ed. Robertson, cited in Fiering, *Jonathan Edwards's Moral Thought,* 192, emph. added.

32. Shaftesbury acknowledged that the cause of war and social conflict was group egoism but still insisted that most affection for one's social group was rooted in natural benevolence. Fiering, *Jonathan Edwards's Moral Thought,* 195.

33. John Wise, "A Vindication of the Government of New England Churches," in Alan Heimert and Andrew Delbanco, eds., *The Puritans in America: A Narrative Anthology* (Cambridge: Harvard University Press, 1985), 255; John Corrigan, *The Hidden Balance: Religion and the Social Theories of Charles Chauncy and Jonathan Mayhew* (New York: Cambridge University Press, 1987), 84, 91; WJE 8:550–608.

34. WJE 8:611, emph. orig.

country to be the highest of all the virtues, yet this affection—though "so much extolled"—"was employed as it were for the destruction of the rest of mankind." Edwards found it to be a rule that "the larger the number is that private affection extends to, the more apt men are, through the narrowness of their sight, to mistake it for true virtue; because then the private system appears to have more of the image of the universal." Patriotism was thus more prone to self-deception than love for family or local society, for its wider gaze on society brought a greater danger of pretentiousness.[35]

Second, Edwards used both philosophical and theological arguments to remind his audiences that all patriotisms were penultimate. Drawing from his philosophy of being, he argued that patriotisms restricted to a single polity fell infinitely short of devotion to universal existence. And because they fell *infinitely* short, the moral worth of a patriotism restricted to a single polity was no greater than the moral worth of devotion to a single person among an infinite number of persons.[36] In his theological argument, Edwards compared the earthly nation with the heavenly. Earthly commitments were provisional, he said, because Christians held dual citizenship—a temporary one in the nation they inhabit and a permanent one in heaven. Even on earth, Christians lived in accordance with their heavenly, permanent citizenship inasmuch as their citizenship in their earthly country was less enjoyable and less real:

> Heaven is the native country of the church; they are born from above. Their Father of whom they are begotten is in heaven. The new nature and those principles that are infused, they are, as it were, sent down from heaven in that the Holy Ghost, whose immediate fruits those principles are, is from heaven.... The saints here in this world be'nt in their native country, but are pilgrims and strangers in the earth. They are near akin to the inhabitants of the heavenly world and are properly of that society.... Heaven is a country that much better suits their natures than this earth because 'tis their native climate; when they are in heaven, they breathe their native air. In heaven is their inheritance.[37]

Since their ultimate commitment was not to any earthly polity, Christians had to conduct all their civil affairs in subordination to the principles of their heavenly citizenship. For any earthly polity to claim their ultimate allegiance

---

35. WJE 8:611.
36. WJE 8:554.
37. WJE 17:303.

would be idolatrous. All earthly patriotisms had to come under scrutiny and be judged by the norms of the Christian's permanent, heavenly citizenship.[38]

National Pride

If patriotism could be an instance of individual pride, it could also affect a nation and become a nation's greatest sin. In a notebook entry before, and in a letter during, the Great Awakening, Edwards wrote that the most heinous sin was for a people to think more highly of itself than it ought.[39] Edwards was speaking of the "nation" of New England, which because of its religious blessings presumed on its own virtue and exalted status before God. Such presumption was an ungodly hubris with possibly fatal consequences. Edwards warned that if New England gloated over its God-given favors and benefits, and ignored its own sin and profligacy, God's judgment hung over it.

Throughout his career Edwards made these warnings in his repeated invocations of the national covenant (ch. 21). Scholars nonetheless have commonly charged Edwards with jingoistic nationalism in his treatment of New England and America.[40] Yet an examination of his appeals to the national covenant in his long-unpublished fast and thanksgiving day sermons shows a different picture.[41] Edwards railed against New England's impiety, hypocrisy, injustice, contentiousness, and exploitation of the Indians, warning that these sins would bring covenantal punishments.[42] The venality of corrupt politicians and their cynical use of religion also angered Edwards. In 1743, the Massachusetts governor had ordered a day of thanksgiving for the "king's preservation and victory at the Maine River in Germany." In what was probably an oblique indictment of the patronage system in George II's court, Edwards spoke out against rulers who were "governed by their Private Interest," buying and selling "places of publick trust" for private gain. Such men, he pronounced, have "little reason...to expect any continued success in war."[43] According to

---

38. WJE 17:438.

39. WJE 18:518; WJE 4:540.

40. Most famously, see C.C. Goen, "Jonathan Edwards: A New Departure in Eschatology," *Church History* 28 (1959): 25–46, esp. 26–27, 37–38.

41. These were "occasional" sermons prepared for special occasions such as fast days, election days, and thanksgiving days after community blessings such as military victory or the end of a drought. See McDermott, *One Holy and Happy Society*, 11–36.

42. WJE 17:498–99, 363; Ezek. 7:16, WJE 42; WJE 19:759–67; Sermon on Mal. 3:10–11, WJE 61; WJE 19:763.

43. Sermon on Is. 47:4, WJE 61.

Edwards's notion of the national covenant, God would not overlook a magistrate's moral turpitude no matter how earnest his public piety might be.

Edwards's denial of Northampton's righteousness—and, by implication, New England's and America's—was thoroughgoing. No human community, he said, could be righteous in the sense that the majority of its citizens were Christian or were relatively free from sin. There had never been a nation that was outwardly moral or that had a majority of its people within the visible Christian church. When Edwards referred to "Christian countries," he meant no more than polities whose formal allegiance was to Christianity. The majority of those living in "Christian" lands was not regenerate, he believed, and even "godly" persons had an abundance of sin still remaining in their hearts. New England, for example, was a Christian land only in the sense that Christianity was its established religion.

Edwards and Slavery

If Edwards kept a critical distance from narrow nationalisms, he shared some of his culture's prejudices about African-Americans and slavery. He and Sarah always owned at least one slave. Two of their slaves were sold after his death to a Connecticut man for twenty-three British pounds. Some years before, when another pastor was criticized by his parishioners for owning African slaves, Edwards defended the pastor and the institution of slavery. He said the Bible allowed slavery. Even though God in the earlier stages of revelation "winked at" practices that were condemned at a later stage, such as polygamy, the New Testament, in his opinion, did not condemn slavery.[44]

In some respects, Edwards distanced himself from the racism so prevalent in his day. He said that blacks and Indians were not inherently inferior ("we are made of the same human race"), and that in the millennial age "many of the Negroes and Indians will be divines." Blacks and Indians were spiritual equals to whites, he preached. His Northampton church admitted nine Africans to full membership during his years there. Despite his defense of the institution of slavery, Edwards nonetheless condemned the African slave trade, saying no nations "have any power or business to disenfranchise all the nations of Africa." His son Jonathan Jr. and his foremost disciple Samuel Hopkins were early and outspoken abolitionists.[45]

---

44. WJE 16:75, 72–76.

45. For more on this subject, see Kenneth Minkema, "Jonathan Edwards on Slavery and the Slave Trade," *William and Mary Quarterly* 54 (October 1997): 823–34; and George Marsden, *Jonathan Edwards: A Life* (New Haven: Yale University Press, 2003), 255–58.

Nevertheless, Edwards's support for slavery as an institution, his own complicity in it by buying and owning slaves, and his inability to see what later abolitionists thought to be implicit biblical admonitions against it, are all unsettling. As Sherard Burns has written, "To condemn the [slave] trade and at the same time to participate in the selling and buying of slaves was a glaring contradiction."[46] One finds another contradiction if one compares Edwards's sanctioning of African slavery with his consistent—even courageous—defense of Indians and their rights to their lands and way of life (ch. 34). Somehow Edwards found it appropriate and necessary to fight for the rights of Indians, but not for the rights of Africans.

Despite Edwards's failure to condemn the institution of slavery, his public theology is still instructive. He not only provided philosophical reasoning for the Christian's engagement with society beyond the church but also argued that such social engagement is necessary to faith and that active concern for the poor is a *sine qua non*. Other Christian thinkers have made similar claims, though usually without linking their social ethic—as Edwards did—to life in God (theologically) and to the system of being (philosophically). His integration of inner religious sensibility and socio-political expression was distinctive. Just as he repudiated as spurious any religious feeling that did not manifest public concern, Edwards denounced as empty all social and religious acts that were not animated by biblical spirituality. Therefore, if Edwards mirrors some of the ideas of today's social ethicists he challenges them as well. Besides showing privatistic Christians why their faith demands social expression, Edwards would admonish those who regard public affairs and social action as more important than spiritual life. Neither has priority over the other, he would say. Either of these, taken separately, is deficient. True religion is the proper synthesis of the two. For the colonial thinker, a public theology that ignored religious experience and concentrated solely on social expression was misguided.

---

46. Sherard Burns, "Trusting the Theology of a Slave-owner," in John Piper and Justin Taylor, eds., *A God-Entranced Vision of All Things: The Legacy of Jonathan Edwards* (Wheaton: Crossway, 2004), 153. On Edwards and race, see also Charles E. Hambrick-Stowe "All Things Were New and Astonishing: Edwardsian Piety, the New Divinity, and Race," in Kling and Sweeney, *Jonathan Edwards at Home and Abroad*, 121–36.

33

True Virtue, Christian Love, and Ethical Theory

MORE THAN ONE student of Edwards's ethics has observed that he based his conception of human morality on the character of God.[1] While this could be said for other Christian ethicists, for Edwards it was particularly true. More than perhaps any other Western theologian, Edwards insisted that genuine love—which he said is "the sum of all virtue"—is participation in God's own life. The creature's love to God is an effusion of God's own love for himself, and love for fellow human beings is only genuine if it participates in the mutual love among the members of the Trinity. This is why Edwards could say that "duties are founded on doctrines" and that the doctrine of the Trinity makes "a vast alteration with respect to the reason and obligations" in the Christian's moral life. True virtue, by his lights, *is* the very Triune being of God shared among his regenerate creatures. Hence the moral life at its fullest is possible only by communion with that Triune God. With this daring line of reasoning, Edwards tried to "leap the ontological divide between Creator and creature in a single bound."[2]

Edwards approached the moral life both philosophically and theologically. Much of his philosophical ethics—as in his treatise *The Nature of True Virtue*—was shaped by apologetic concerns. In that text, Edwards was using a philosophical construct shared by defenders of a naturalized ethics and thus omitted the richer biblical and theological resources he used in theological accounts of the moral life such as *Charity and Its Fruits*. Yet each kind of reflection was integral to Edwards's ethical vision.[3] In this chapter, we shall explore first his

---

1. Paul Ramsey in "Editor's Introduction," WJE 8:11; William J. Danaher Jr., *The Trinitarian Ethics of Jonathan Edwards* (Louisville: Westminster John Knox, 2004), ix; Roland Delattre, "The Theological Ethics of Jonathan Edwards: An Homage to Paul Ramsey," *Journal of Religious Ethics* 19 (1991): 76.

2. WJE 8:129; WJE 13:416; quotation from Danaher, *Trinitarian Ethics*, 50.

3. Danaher argues that Edwards scholars have sometimes inappropriately privileged *True Virtue* and *The End for Which God Created the World* in their accounts of Edwards's ethics and thereby missed the complexity and nuance of Edwards's thought. Danaher, "Beauty, Benevolence, and Virtue in Jonathan Edwards's *The Nature of True Virtue*," *Journal of Religion* 87 (2007): 386–410.

philosophical grounding for morality in God's being and then his theological conception of love as beauty. In what follows, we shall delineate his conceptions of participation in the divine life, the role of beauty and love, the place of the natural virtues and their relationship to reason, and the acquisition and growth of virtue. This chapter will conclude with a brief assessment of what is distinctive about Edwards's ethics.

Philosophical Grounding for the Moral Life

Edwards's philosophy of being or ontology is the first aspect of what we might call his meta-ethics or foundational principles for ethics. Though these philosophical principles seem abstract, they undergird all of Edwards's moral reflections and so represent the proper starting point for considering his ethics. All being, he proposed, is active, dispositional, and outwardly directed. Created being has these traits because it is an image of God's being. So in his philosophical ethics, no less than in his moral theology, Edwards started with God. He spoke of God's being as "disposition" or "habit." That is, God's essence is a constantly exercised inclination to repeat his already perfect actuality through further exercises. God's actuality is already perfect because it is completely exercised in and through the inner-Trinitarian relationships. God's action in the world is therefore the spatio-temporal repetition of God's already-realized actuality.[4]

Edwards held that God is ontologically productive and relational. Although he does not add to his own actuality, God is continually involved in a process of self-extension by creating and then relating to other beings.[5] Human beings, moreover, since they are patterned after the divine being, are also relational and able to add to their own being by relating to other beings. The rationale for God's self-extension is God's fundamental disposition to delight in himself (ch. 14). He created the world to rediscover himself in temporality, so that he might delight in an external expression of himself. Another motive for creation was God's own goodness—the disposition to communicate good—which makes "objects of his benevolence" so that they can receive goodness. So God created beings to whom he could communicate good, the essential nature of which is God's own being. God is in a neverending process of enlarging his own being by creating new relationships. Hence created existence is the spatio-temporal repetition of God's inner-Trinitarian fullness, a process everlasting in duration.[6]

---

4. Sang Hyun Lee, *The Philosophical Theology of Jonathan Edwards* (Princeton, NJ: Princeton University Press, 1988), 170–210.

5. WJE 13:495–96; WJE 8:433–34, 461–62.

6. WJE 8:461.

Just as God is dispositional, the essence of all being is disposition or habit. Like God, created being is inherently dynamic. Disposition, or the dynamism of a thing, is not a quality possessed but rather the *essence* of the thing. Therefore the laws that describe the motion of a thing constitute the essential definition of that thing.[7] Since Edwards's ontology pictures a world of constant movement and action, it presents a startling contrast to Aristotle's world of essentially static substances. Aristotle, who was probably the first to give "habit" (or *hexis,* as he called it) a philosophical usage, conceived of habit as a principle of operation, accidental to the being of a substance. Edwards's habit, on the other hand, is a principle of being, constitutive of an entity's essence. While Aristotle taught that substances are possessors of properties, Edwards suggested that substances are doers of deeds.[8]

Created being, for Edwards, is not only disposition but relational. He construed the world as a dynamic network of relationships so that every entity was necessarily in relation to other—in fact, all—entities. In Sang Hyun Lee's words, "A thing *is* only as it is related to other things."[9] This relational character of being is directional. In other words, being drives toward a goal, which is union with other beings. Being is continually in the process of moving from virtuality to actuality, which intelligent beings achieve through a conscious, volitional, affective union of mutual consent. Yet this directional activity tending toward union is not limited to intelligent beings. Edwards considered Newton's discovery of the law of universal gravitation (the "mutual tendency of all bodies to each other") to be "a type of love or charity in the spiritual world." So even inanimate being is directional in its disposition, and thereby functions as a symbol of the coming union of intelligent beings.[10]

Because human being, like God himself and all other types of being, is habitual and dispositional, it is active and dynamic. This is all the more true for regenerate persons. The Christian life is defined more by "transitive practical acts" than by the "unition and adherence" to God itself. That it should be so is a law of necessity, for "all habits [are] a law that God has fixed, that such actions upon such occasions should be exerted." Holy practice is thus not a subsequent response to Christian experience but the essence of Christian

---

7. WJE 6:391–92.

8. On Edwards's world of action, he said solidity is nothing other than the act of resisting, and bodies are God's actions; WJE 6: 215. On Aristotle and habit, see Lee, *Philosophical Theology*, 17–22. The last sentence is a paraphrase of a statement by Wallace E. Anderson in WJE 6:67.

9. Lee, *Philosophical Theology*, 50.

10. WJE 11:81.

experience. Actions are constitutive. Edwards wrote, "Godliness in the heart has as direct relation to practice... as a habit or principle of action has to action." Without Christian moral practice, there is no Christian life.[11] It is not only the nature of habit, though, that makes Christian moral practice necessary. God's nature requires it. For God's own dispositional nature requires that the divine fullness be repeated in time, for the sake of the divine fullness and joy. Lee writes, "Edwards's insistence upon the inevitability and necessity of the practical consequences of the regenerate is rooted in the inevitability with which the sovereign God will accomplish his own aim."[12]

Besides being active and dynamic, human being is relational. It is God's nature to communicate himself to finite beings, and human beings are made in God's image. Therefore, human beings delight in relations, not "because of our imperfection, but because we are made in the image of God." Regenerate humans beings are even more disposed than others to relationship because their actuating disposition is God's own disposition infused into them. And God's disposition is a tendency to an infinitely complex and extensive system of relationships. So the regenerate person has the same tendency to reach out to other human beings to know and love them. By this tendency, the being of the regenerated person is enlarged, just as God enlarges himself in extending himself in more and more relationships.[13] The ethical implications of Edwards's ontology should now be clear. Without need for any "ought," the very nature of being pushes toward consensual union.[14] Because being is habit, active, and relational, it drives toward union. Regenerate human beings, impelled by the divine disposition, reach out by a kind of necessity to other intelligent beings to know and love them.

Yet this inclination to the well-being of human beings is not enough, taken by itself. For the Being of beings, "infinitely the greatest and best" of all beings, is God. True benevolence must "chiefly consist in love to God," as the "sum and comprehension of all existence," the "fountain" which moment by moment gives existence to all beings. To fail to love God would be to violate the structural principle of Edwards's philosophical ethics: one *ought* to

---

11. WJE 18:531; WJE 13:358; WJE 2:398. By Christian "practice," Edwards meant the entire Christian life of love to God and neighbor in heart and action.

12. Lee, *Philosophical Theology*, 233.

13. WJE 13:264.

14. Edwards denied that a full union with being could be achieved by unregenerate, intelligent beings. Nevertheless, inanimate being and even the unregenerate, by their imperfect movement toward union, provide for us an image or analogy (a "type") of spiritual union of the regenerate with "Being in general." WJE 11:63.

acknowledge gratefully that one is related to all of being, and therefore preeminently related to and dependent on the sum and comprehension of all being, or God himself. The result of love to "Being in general"[15] is "union" with God and love for particular intelligent beings: "He that loves Being, simply considered, will naturally...other things being equal, love particular beings."[16]

Morality as Participation in God's Triune Life

In his treatises, Edwards often unfolded "what reason teaches" about the issue at hand and then "what Scripture teaches." He always found continuity between the two sets of teaching since he believed in the harmony of revelation and right reason. Ethics was no exception. When he turned to a *theological* account of the moral life, he turned again to God first and found, as reason taught, that love is the principal divine attribute.[17] Consequently, love is also the principal human virtue.

Therefore all true human love is participation in divine love, which "must consist primarily in *love to himself*, or in the mutual love and friendship which subsists eternally and necessarily between the several person in the Godhead." To paraphrase, God's self-love is the fundamental love in the cosmos. To be more precise, it is the love that passes between the Father and the Son and then through the Son to all those who are joined to him: "Divine love...flows out in the first place [necessarily] and infinitely towards his only Begotten Son.... He is not only the infinite object of the Father's love, but he also infinitely loves the Father.... The infinite essential love of God is, as it were, an infinite and eternal mutual holy energy between the Father and the Son, a

---

15. Edwards's use of this term is for "the transcendent God *plus* His ordered creation." Norman Fiering, *Jonathan Edwards's Moral Thought and Its British Context* (Chapel Hill: University of North Carolina Press, 1981), 326; see Ramsey's discussion of this term in Editor's Introduction," WJE 8:30–31.

16. WJE 8:421, 550–51, 541.

17. Edwards said that mercy was more natural to God than damnation. In his sermon "The Justice of God in the Damnation of Sinners" (1735), he preached that God showed "a great deal of kindness" and "multiplied mercies" to stubborn sinners. In "Impending Judgments Averted Only By Reformation," he proclaimed that God prefers mercy and is always ready to "turn away from his fierce anger," for "judgment is his strange work." He would give up on people only when they prove to be "irreclaimable." WJE 19:355; WJE 14:221. Cited by Elizabeth Agnew Cochran in *Receptive Human Virtues: A New Reading of Jonathan Edwards's Ethics* (University Park, PA: Penn State Press, 2011), manuscript version. We saw only the pre-publication manuscript with different pagination from the published edition. Therefore we will refer to chapter numbers where applicable.

pure, holy act whereby the Deity becomes nothing but an infinite and unchangeable act of love, which proceeds from both the Father and the Son.... [This] love of God flows out towards Christ the Head, and through him to all his members."[18]

This is the vision of divine and human love that caused Roland Delattre to write that "participation in the life of God overflowing into the world is a formative and distinctive central theme of Edwards's theological ethics." Much of *Religious Affections* is devoted to this theme of participation. There Edwards wrote that Christians are "made partakers of God's holiness (Heb. 12:10), having Christ's love dwelling in them (John 17:26), having his joy fulfilled in them (John 17:13), seeing light in God's light, and being made to drink of the river of God's pleasures (Ps. 63:8–9), having fellowship with God, or communicating and partaking with him (as the word signifies) (1 John 1:3)." William Danaher summarizes: "The life of virtue is one of *actual* participation in the spiritual life of the triune God." Hence the moral life depends on the personal transformation of the new birth or regeneration. Only by this event does God's love become our love, in the process which Eastern theology has called divinization or *theosis* (ch. 26). For Edwards, this participation brings not only divine love but also divine knowledge and happiness. "Thus, the 'new creation' is the name, idea or knowledge of God's, being in human understanding; the love of God's, being in human wills, and the joy of God's, being in human affection." All Christian experience, then, is participation in the triune life, and this includes the moral life.[19]

Benevolence, Virtue, and Beauty

Jonathan Edwards lived in an eighteenth-century world dominated by "benevolism"—the idea that human beings are naturally benevolent because of their inherent altruism or "moral sense". He was convinced from revelation and experience that original sin belied this optimistic view of human nature, but as a philosopher he attempted to use benevolism's own structure to turn it on its head. His *Nature of True Virtue*, written near the end of his life, had two aims: to show that the "moral sense" was simply the

---

18. WJE 8:557 (orig.emph.), 373.

19. Delattre, 71; WJE 2:203; Danaher, *Trinitarian Ethics*, 41; the last quote is by Paul Ramsey "Editor's Introduction," WJE 8:22. A corollary to this theme of ethics by participation is that, as we saw in ch. 25, all the virtues are "infused" in the regenerate, so that they become "inherent" in them. This was a common Reformed doctrine—taught by Calvin, Turretin, and Van Mastricht—as Ramsey has shown. WJE 8:294, 334, 741, 744.

old-fashioned conscience in disguise and to make his idea of holiness "a philosophically credible notion in the forums of enlightenment." He agreed with the benevolists that general benevolence was the pinnacle of virtue, but argued that their "moral sense" was reducible to intellectual conscience and to a kind of self-love, which of themselves could not produce benevolence. He affirmed the benevolist consensus that virtue was "something beautiful," but insisted that their notions of beauty, based on symmetry and harmony, were only "secondary" shadows of "primary" beauty, consisting of the consent and union of being to being.[20]

Edwards was steeped in his era's debates over moral theory. As when he immersed himself in other intellectual controversies, he read the sharpest and most influential thinkers no matter what their positions, and learned from all of them. But he used their ideas carefully, bending them toward his own purposes. For example, he studied the two principal benevolist thinkers, the third Earl of Shaftesbury and Francis Hutcheson, and adapted the latter's model of moral formation for his own purposes. Hutcheson had stipulated that people become moral when they apprehend and *approve* goodness and beauty. Edwards used this framework for his own ethical reflection but said that moral apprehension and moral approval require the new "sense of the heart" that comes only with conversion. Goodness and beauty are not separate from God, as Hutcheson suggested, but aspects of God's character. So the virtue that the regenerate see and approve is *God's* virtue. Because of original sin, the natural mind cannot see God's moral beauty through its own unaided powers.[21]

Edwards's moral reflections were also shaped by his reading of the Cambridge Platonists, especially John Smith and Henry More. In reaction against what they considered to be the harsh and arbitrary God portrayed by Calvinist predestination, the Cambridge Platonists declared that God is fundamentally goodness and love. Smith maintained that God judges creatures not by an arbitrary will but by his own internal goodness, and that everything good in the created world is an emanation from God. More spoke of the beauty of virtue, and Smith wrote lyrically of God's beauty—as Edwards did from his teens onward. But Edwards did not go all the way with the Cambridge Platonists, for he upheld the doctrine of original sin and the need for conversion.[22]

---

20. Fiering, *Jonathan Edwards's Moral Thought*, 106; WJE 8:539.

21. Cochran, *Receptive Human Virtues*, ch. 5.

22. Cochran, *Receptive Human Virtues*, chs. 1–3; Fiering, *Jonathan Edwards's Moral Thought*, 110.

Edwards's conception of the moral life as participation in God's moral beauty was also in part a product of his immersion in Puritan theology, for which the "beauty of holiness" was a commonplace. Janice Knight has distinguished two schools in seventeenth-century Puritan theology, the "Intellectual Fathers" who stressed the goodness and order of the creation, and the "Spiritual Brethren" who emphasized God's absolute power and rejected secondary causes of grace apart from God's will. Stephen A. Wilson has suggested that Edwards was influenced by both schools, stressing God's absolute power in his early revival sermons and turning to a greater emphasis on secondary causes and sanctification in *Religious Affections* and later writings. But throughout his career, Edwards taught the Puritan theme that only the converted could see the beauty of holiness.[23]

Edwards was convinced that the "essence" of true virtue is "benevolence to being in general." By "benevolence" he meant "cordial consent" or "union of heart" to "intelligent Being in general."[24] Benevolence to simply "a private circle or system of beings" may be good and beautiful in a limited way, but it is not true virtue. Because God is not merely one being among others but the source and ground of all being, true virtue will always love God above all. He is "the foundation and fountain of all being and all beauty...and whose being and beauty is as it were the sum and comprehension of all existence and excellence: much more than the sun is the fountain and summary comprehension of all the light and brightness of the day." Compared to God, "all the rest are nothing, either as to beauty or existence." Therefore "unless we will be atheists, we must allow that true virtue does primarily and most essentially consist in a supreme love to God; and that where this is wanting, there can be no true virtue." Every other virtue that falls short of benevolence to universal being at whose head and heart is God, is actually "in opposition to general existence." Private affection that is not subordinated to general affection to the whole system of existence in God "is not only liable, as the case *may* be, to issue in enmity to Being in general, but has a *tendency* to it, as the case certainly *is* and must necessarily be." For private affection will set up "its particular or limited object *above* Being in general," and this tends to "enmity against the latter," just as setting up another prince in a kingdom tends to enmity "against the lawful sovereign."[25]

---

23. Fiering, *Jonathan Edwards's Moral Thought*, 110; Janice Knight, *Orthodoxies in Massachusetts: Rereading American Puritanism* (Cambridge, MA: Harvard University Press, 1994); Stephen A. Wilson, *Virtue Reformed: Rereading Jonathan Edwards's Ethics* (Leiden: Brill, 2005), 156–89.

24. WJE 8:540, 620, 571, 542.

25. WJE 8:541, 551, 554–55 (orig. emph.), 555–56.

Edwards began *True Virtue* with the observation that everyone except "some skeptics" acknowledge that virtue is beautiful. He ended the treatise with an argument for the objectivity of moral beauty—that it is not simply in the eye of the beholder or a cultural convention but has "its foundation in the nature of things." In the "nature of things," beauty is unity in variety (ch. 6). For example, differing notes in a piece of music somehow harmonize with one another to create a sense of overall unity. This harmonious unity is an image of the higher beauty of love, which is another instance of harmonious unity amidst variety: "When one thing sweetly harmonizes with another, as the notes in music, the notes are so conformed and have such proportion one to another that they seem to have respect one to another, as if they loved one another." Beauty, then, is the willing or consenting unity of diverse elements: "By that uniformity diverse things become as it were one, as it is in this cordial union [of hearts]."

Music is one of many examples of "sensible things [that] by virtue of the harmony and proportion that is seen in them, carry the appearance of perceiving and willing being." Edwards listed other examples in *True Virtue*—"the mutual agreement of the various sides of a square, or equilateral triangle...periphery of a circle, or surface of a sphere...the corresponding parts of an ellipse...the agreement of the colors, figures, dimensions, and distances of the different spots on a chess board...the beautiful proportion of the various parts of an human body, or countenance." The unities in all these things are so many images of consenting unity of heart among intelligent beings. The beauty of true virtue consists in this: the created beings' mutual consent and unity that is an image of the Triune Persons' infinite mutual consent and harmonious unity.[26]

Edwards's identification of true virtue with beauty has caused scholars to debate which is primary—virtue or beauty? Norman Fiering argued that Edwards's beauty depends on moral virtue because the philosopher-theologian wrote that "holiness is in a peculiar manner the beauty of the divine nature," and that "'tis moral excellency alone...that gives beauty to, or rather is the beauty of [human] natural perfections and qualifications." According to Fiering, beauty is a symbol of a higher correspondence of wills and therefore not an ultimate category, as Roland Delattre maintained. William Spohn commented that Edwards offers "an ethics of beauty based upon love of God rather than an ethics of love of God based on beauty."[27] Yet these scholars

---

26. WJE 8:539, 622; WJE 6:380; WJE 8:564; WJE 6:382; WJE 8:562.

27. WJE 2:257; Fiering, *Jonathan Edwards's Moral Thought*, 81; see Roland Delattre, *Beauty and Sensibility in the Thought of Jonathan Edwards; An Essay in Aesthetics and Theological Ethics* (New Haven, CT: Yale University Press, 1968); and William C. Spohn, "Sovereign Beauty: Jonathan Edwards and the Nature of True Virtue," *Theological Studies* 42 (1981): 414.

may be finding a distinction where none exists. Edwards identified true virtue with true beauty. Earthly beauty pointed to the higher unity of wills in God, but that very unity *is* beauty—and it is this beauty that constitutes the existence of true virtue.

Love As the Sum of Virtue

If Edwards spoke of true virtue as the beauty of consenting unity among diverse minds, he more commonly spoke of it as love. He said even the deists agree with scripture that "virtue most essentially consists in love." Love is the "general nature of true virtue." In his 1738 sermon series *Charity and Its Fruits*, which Paul Ramsey has called Edwards's "most important treatment of Christian ethics," Edwards defined love as "that disposition or affection by which one is dear to another." In *True Virtue*, he distinguished two kinds of love—the love of benevolence, which is consent to Being in general even when beings are not beautiful themselves, and love of complacence, which is love for beings who have the beauty of true virtue. The regenerate receive a love from God that flows from their vision of the divine beauty but extends itself toward all other human beings, regenerate and unregenerate alike. As we saw earlier, Edwards said that all being by nature drives toward union. Love willingly consents to that union and actively seeks it. Love "disposes persons to look on their neighbor as being, as it were, one with self," doing for them what they would like done for themselves, just as Christ "was pleased in some respects to look on us as himself."[28]

Throughout his philosophical ethics and moral theology, Edwards highlighted the centrality of love. In his *Charity* sermons, he preached that "love is the sum of all virtue" and that "there is no virtue so much insisted on" by Christ and his apostles in the New Testament. Love is "the sum of what God requires of us." Christian or divine love sums up "all that virtue which is saving" and is what most distinguishes true Christians from others. It is more excellent than the "extraordinary" gifts of the Holy Spirit such as tongues, prophecy, immediate revelation, and miracles. "Bad men," or those whom "God hates"—such as Balaam, King Saul, and Judas—were given

---

28. WJE 8:541, 609; Ramsey in WJE 8:64; WJE 8:129, 609, 542, 265–66. Danaher points out that occasionally Edwards subordinated the love of complacence to the love of benevolence but that usually he saw them as complementary, both in God and his saints. Danaher, "Beauty Benevolence and Virtue," 405.

some of these extraordinary gifts, but none of these men had divine love. These extraordinary gifts are "jewels" indeed, but the love found in saving grace is "the preciousness of the heart." God "abominates" great things done without sincere love, but he "delights" in even a cup of cold water given with sincere love. Even if a person moves a mountain with her faith, she is as nothing without love. For love is the heart and soul of true faith and all religion. The devils have faith—they "believe and tremble" before God (Jas. 2:19)—but they are in hell because they do not have love. The "working, acting nature of anything is the life of it," and the working nature of faith is love. The apostle Paul "tells us the thing by which faith works is love." Faith without works is like a body without a soul. Love is the test of true Christian experience and should be called *the* "Christian spirit." It is the light and glory surrounding God's throne in John's vision of heaven (Rev. 4).[29]

The love of which Edwards spoke was often prefaced by the word "divine." This was his signal that true love not only has God for its source but is the very life of God in his saints. Love is the same principle, whether expressed by God or humanity, to God or human beings. Both loves, divine and human, are "by the same work of the Spirit," and the two have "the same motives." In other words, God and the saints are both loved "for holiness' sake ... for [God's] excellency, the beauty of his nature." All true love arises from seeing the beauty of God's holiness.[30] Elizabeth Agnew Cochran has observed that Enlightenment ethicists had reduced virtue to a "unilateral entity"—benevolence—such that all the virtues that the Aristotelian tradition had enumerated were reduced to one.[31] Yet Edwards differentiated a range of virtues that, while all related to love, were not reducible to it. Some of his most striking were longsuffering, kindness, and humility. Christians will often suffer injuries from others, but they will show their longsuffering love (or meekness, as he also called it) by refusing to seek revenge. They will not speak evil of neighbors "behind their backs," as commonly takes place "in all our taverns." Christian love will suffer wrongdoing "with a calm, undisturbed countenance," just as "the moon walk[s] in her brightness, while the dogs are barking at her [and] she is not moved." There are times for "lawful self-defense," but even then we should reflect

---

29. WJE 8:129, 180, 131, 152, 154, 160, 158, 181, 131, 139–40, 145, 143, 145.
30. WJE 8:133.
31. Cochran, *Receptive Human Virtues*, chapter 1.

on God's longsuffering toward the wicked and the righteous alike before we try to defend ourselves.[32]

Longsuffering is a passive virtue, the active counterpart to which is kindness. This is doing good to both the bodies and souls of others. While most people embrace this principle of kindness to some extent, Christian love goes further by insisting that one do good to good and bad alike, friends and enemies, the grateful and ungrateful—and do so without any thought of reward. Furthermore, Christian love does all this cheerfully, liberally and bountifully. It is especially expressed in mercy toward the poor: "There is scarce any duty in the whole Bible which has so many promises of reward." But only those free of envy are able to do so much for others. Envy is a spirit from hell that first raised its ugly head in human history in Eden when the devil became jealous of Adam and Eve. Christ showed his freedom from envy when he received baptism from his cousin John the Baptist, refusing to begrudge his cousin's success. Envy feeds on the ruin of others' prosperity, like "caterpillars which delight most in devouring the most flourishing trees and plants."[33]

Humility, said Edwards, is as essential to those who love as pride is to those who do not love.[34] Like true love, humility comes from seeing God's holy beauty; and like love, it "would in some way or other include the whole of our duty, both towards God and towards men." More than any of Edwards's other virtues, humility is integral to divine love. At the same time, it is properly human and not divine. Edwards defined humility as a sense of our relative "meanness" or littleness, both in ontological size and moral virtue. God is of course neither little nor mean, ontologically or morally, but the comprehension of all being and perfect holiness. We become humble only by seeing the divine greatness and moral beauty. Yet Christ provided a type or image of human humility by "condescending" to our low state and being willing to forego the infinite honor that was his due. He humbled himself and became obedient unto death. By being willing to "suffer such an ignominious death, he did as it were pour contempt on all that earthly glory which men are wont to be proud of." Therefore Christians with divine love won't "affect to appear uppermost" or expect "that anybody should bow and yield" to them or "be stiff and inflexible" in public or private affairs, for they have seen God's beautiful purity and realized their own filth—unlike the devils and damned who see God's holiness but not its beauty.[35]

---

32. WJE 8:199, 188, 201, 192–93.
33. WJE 8:210–12, 215, 224–25, 230.
34. Ramsey, in "Editor's Introduction," in WJE 8:86.
35. WJE 8:245, 238, 233, 242, 248, 240–41.

Edwards delineated a host of other virtues that incarnate divine love, such as forgiveness, suffering for Christ, holy boldness, fear of God, and perseverance through adversity.[36] He added that the Christian virtues taken collectively have beauty and symmetry: "There is a concatenation of the graces of Christianity." All the graces or virtues are "linked together or united one to another and within one another, as the links of a chain." One aspect of love is contained in another and leads to a third, and so on. We have already seen how humility is an essential part of love, so that without one you cannot have the other. Taken together, all the graces of Christian love demonstrate "beautiful symmetry and proportion." In other words, true Christian love will manifest all these graces at the same time—albeit imperfectly and approximately. False grace, though, "is always like a monster, wherein many essential parts are wanting." It shows only the appearance of grace and only some of the graces.[37]

The symmetry in Christian love can be seen in Edwards's paired virtues, one of which balances the other. For example, the joy of the Christian that comes from finding salvation is balanced by the fear of God. The comfort of forgiveness is offset by godly sorrow for sin. If there is love to God, there is also benevolence to human beings. Christian love includes both friends and enemies, and cares for both their bodies and their souls. Christians are aware of sins in others but also and especially their own sin. They reach out to the world in public witness to Christ but also maintain a discipline of private prayer. They maintain holy affections in good and bad times alike.[38]

For Edwards, love and its various aspects are "human" virtues, as Cochran calls them. While Christian moral acts derive from participation in God's life, they are still *our* acts. They are "receptive" virtues inasmuch as we do not manufacture them but receive them. On the other hand, we are human agents because *we* receive them. God does not compel or coerce us or obliterate our wills. Cochran argues that the human virtues which Edwards depicts are more accessible than the virtues propounded by modern ethicists that assume an autonomous agent able to generate his or her own virtues. Unlike many modern ethicists, Edwards acknowledged human moral inability and yet promised that human beings had free access to divine enabling—an attractive prospect for those who know that they cannot be good on their own.[39]

---

36. These are developed in the seventh through twelfth "positive" signs of true religion in *Religious Affections*; WJE 2:340–462.

37. WJE 8:327–28; WJE 2:365; WJE 8:338.

38. WJE 2:365–76.

39. Cochran, *Receptive Human Virtues*, Introduction.

In his theological ethics, Edwards made the same claim regarding human enlargement that we saw in his philosophical ethics. In his *Charity* sermons, he said that because of Adam's Fall "the mind of man *shrunk* from its primitive greatness and extensiveness into an exceeding *diminution* and *confinedness*." Before the Fall, while Adam still had divine love, his soul was "*enlarged* to a kind of comprehension of all his fellow creatures." It was "extended" to the Creator and "dispersed" abroad "in that infinite ocean of good and was, as it were, swallowed up by it, and become one with it." But with the first sin that once capacious soul "shrunk into a little point, circumscribed and closely shut up within itself to the exclusion of others" (ch. 22). Yet the saints have divine love and "take in others" with themselves. Their souls are "enlarged and multiplied." "Love enlarges" their souls and "extends" them to others. Others "so far as beloved do, as it were, become parts of" the saints. The human soul thus contracts and expands as a function of its love. Without love the soul shrinks, and with love it expands.[40]

Natural Virtues

Edwards's stirring vision of true virtue as participation in divine love has received due attention in recent decades. But his belief in what Paul Ramsey called "the splendor of common morality" is not so well-known. Edwards spoke of "other-love" as "a moral love" possessed by natural or unregenerate persons that moved them "to a moral liberality and generosity" and so "in some respects" was "contrary to selfishness." He described a range of other "natural virtues" such as justice and pity that had a "negative moral goodness" because they promoted the common good of society and restrained vice. It might surprise those who know Edwards only from his revival sermons to learn that Edwards had what Ramsey calls an "ethics of creation" in which the unregenerate have a natural goodness and moral understanding sufficient for civic morality. In a fallen world, stricken by original sin, even the unregenerate carried a measure of God-given goodness. What is more, Edwards did not regard self-love as "utterly nefarious." His creation ethic was based on a conviction that God has created every human person with self-love, conscience, a capacity for relative justice, and a range of affections and instincts such as gratitude, pity, and familial love.[41] We will look at each of these in turn.

---

40. WJE 8:253 (emph. added), 258.

41. Ramsey in "Editor's Introduction," in WJE 8:33; WJE 8:264, 613–14, 616; Ramsey in WJE 8:33; Fiering, *Jonathan Edwards's Moral Thought*, 261; WJE 8:264n.

First, self-love. "Christianity is not destructive of humanity," Edwards proclaimed. Saints like all other people love their own happiness, and there is nothing wrong with that. Self-love was not a result of the Fall but was instead implanted at the creation for the sake of human preservation. It is "exceeding useful and necessary in the world of mankind." In fact, wicked men "in some respects" do not have enough self-love but hate their own souls. They fail to love what makes for their own happiness. The problem with the wicked is not the amount of self-love they possess but the fact that it is not balanced by and subordinated to divine love. Self-love becomes selfishness only when one's desires are devoted solely to personal or private happiness, and one is not united to others through benevolence. This is what Edwards called "mere" or "simple" self-love, based exclusively on seeking pleasure and avoiding pain, even at the cost of harming others. It is the source of all wickedness because it is an enemy to the universal system of being. But self-love as a principle is providentially ordered by God. "Compounded" self-love finds its own good in the good of others. It employs private loves and natural affections and instincts to build order and harmony in the world. It is the "main spring" of "that natural affection which parents have for their children, and the love which near relations have one to another." It is the foundation of "civil friendship" in which men are grateful for good turns, seek their own honor, and love friendship that brings them benefit.[42]

A second component of Edwards's natural morality was conscience. He defined this as the natural disposition arising from self-love that is "uneasy in a consciousness of being inconsistent" with ourselves. We feel unease when we do to others what would make us angry if done to us, or when we neglect doing for others what we think they should do for us in comparable circumstances. In other words, God has implanted into all human beings an awareness of the Golden Rule, and conscience uses that to direct every human being. God also gives every person an aesthetic "sense of desert" that recognizes "a natural agreement, proportion and harmony" exists between doing wrong and receiving resentment or punishment in return, and "between loving and being loved...showing kindness and being rewarded." Human conscience is not equivalent to love for Being in general. Yet if a natural person's understanding is enlightened and his or her prejudices are removed, the conscience "concurs with the law of God...and joins its voice with it in every

---

42. WJE 8:616, 256–57, 577–79, 616, 612; Fiering, *Jonathan Edwards's Moral Thought*, 159; WJE 8:263. See Bruce W. Davidson, "The Four Faces of Self-Love in the Theology of Jonathan Edwards," *Journal of the Evangelical Theological Society* 51 (2008): 87–100.

article." So natural conscience can fall short of true virtue and yet approve of true virtue—but without any delight in and vision of God's beauty. Edwards said God ordered natural conscience in this way for two reasons: for the order and preservation of society, and to provide an image (in conscience's consent to aesthetic proportion) of the mutual consent and union between the Father and the Son. Natural conscience may approve of benevolence because it senses our need to repay the Creator who gave life to us. Yet natural conscience does not taste the sweetness of benevolence to Being in general.[43]

Third in the sequence, and closely related to conscience, is justice—a sense God gives to all human beings through creation. This too is rooted in the aesthetic perception of "a natural agreement and adaptedness of things that have relation one to another." Human beings naturally understand that "he which from his will *does* evil to others should *receive* evil from the will of others, or from the will of him or them whose business it is to take care of the injured," and also that "he that loves [should have] the proper returns of love." Most of our moral duties, Edwards believed, "partake in the nature of justice"—the duties of children and parents, spouses and neighbors one to another, and human beings to God and Christ. Justice is among those virtues that comprise the "beauty of order in society" when "different members of society have all their appointed office, place and station, according to their several capacities and talents, and everyone keeps his place and continues in his proper business." This is a beauty "not of a different kind from the regularity of a beautiful building, or piece of skilled architecture," for they all exhibit "the united tendency of thoughts, ideas, and particular volitions, to one general purpose." Edwards said the regenerate especially will prize justice not only because of its natural proportionality but also because it expresses benevolence to Being in general, agrees with God's will, and promotes God's glory and the general good. Natural justice is merely the "relish" of uniformity and proportion and so it falls short of true virtue. Yet those "with a truly virtuous taste" will relish justice because of its conformity to general benevolence.[44]

Fourth and finally, God has implanted in human nature a variety of "particular instincts of nature," for the purpose of human preservation and the "comfort" of the human race. These instincts include pity, parental affection for children, the natural appetites for food and sex, romantic attraction between the sexes, kindnesses of diverse sorts, and even "the passion of

---

43. WJE 8:589, 593, 42, 594–95.
44. WJE 8:568, 571–72, 573–74; orig. emph.

jealousy between the sexes, especially in the male towards the female." Most of these, Edwards observed, are often mistaken for true virtue. While one feels pity for a man in deep distress, for instance, one might not desire his prosperity—which is what true virtue would desire. Some hate those they pity and would even be happy if the persons they pitied dropped dead. Others pity animals under "extreme and long torments" but have no compunction about "many thousands" of them being slaughtered every day by butchers. The natural love of parents for their children arises from self-love, not from a general or public affection or heart's union with Being in general. Even affection for vast throngs of people—as with ancient patriotism in the Roman Empire—falls far short of true virtue if it lacks "union of heart to general existence and...love to God" (ch. 32). Edwards noted that in hell there will be no pity, parental affection, or even "mutual affection between opposite sexes."[45]

For Edwards, the natural virtues are God-ordained images of divine virtues. According to Ramsey, Edwards conceived of them as the "'natural image' of God in intelligent willing creatures." They are instances of secondary beauty that create an image of the primary beauty of "union or propensity of minds to mental and spiritual existence." Natural virtues display the "mutual consent and agreement of different things in form, manner, quantity and visible end or design" that point to the "different members of a society or system of intelligent beings, sweetly united in a benevolent agreement of heart." This analogy between things of the first creation and things in the new creation was designed by God: "It pleases God to observe analogy in his works...especially to establish inferior things in an analogy to superior.... And so he has constituted the external world in an analogy to things in the spiritual world." But Edwards went even further: not only is natural virtue analogous to true virtue but it also "assists" those with true virtue "to dispose them to the exercises of divine love, and enliven in them a sense of spiritual beauty." So while natural virtue keeps the world secure and happy it also inspires the regenerate to seek greater virtue.[46]

Because natural virtue and true, regenerate virtue are linked as image and referent, they have similar content. As William Spohn put it, "Christian faith does not add new obligations nor sanction new values." Both Edwards and Aquinas "assert a continuity in moral content between natural ethics and morality under grace." All virtues therefore appear in forms that are common or natural, and regenerate or gracious. So Edwards speaks of natural and truly

---

45. WJE 8:600, 606, 602–603, 608.
46. WJE 8:33, 561, 564–65.

virtuous forms of pity, gratitude, civic morality, love between the sexes, and says that both forms within each pair are "of the same denomination." Because of their participation in the natural image of God all human beings may display honesty, justice, generosity, and public spirit. Yet participation in God's moral beauty is needed for the "truly virtuous" forms of those qualities.[47]

A Rationalistic Ethic?

Since Edwards laid a foundation in *nature* for human moral life, Norman Fiering argued that Edwards's ethics were "a rationally derived metaphysics of morals." Edwards's God, he said, "governs Himself and His creation by wisdom or reason above all, not by arbitrary will and not by benevolent inclinations." After reading Samuel Clarke, Edwards "in his personal notes began to reflect on the predominantly 'natural' fittingness of certain relations between God and man, particularly justification and reprobation." He showed increased attention to the structures and intrinsic relations of created things "rather than to the sovereign will of God as a means of understanding the moral order." As a result Edwards "in his theology was the most rationalist of the Puritans, for the laws by which Edwards's God governs are beyond even the contractual and covenantal; they are the expression of what is inherently right."[48]

What are we to make of this? Fiering was no doubt right that Edwards's God governed the world according to objective notions of the good that can be ascertained by all human beings. To that extent, Edwards's God was consistent with what eighteenth-century moralists considered reasonable (ch. 14). Yet Edwards also held many opinions that benevolists considered unreasonable. He denied that the benevolists' notion of moral sense was true virtue. He rejected the idea that all human beings possess true virtue inherently. He taught that God created for his own glory as well as for human happiness. He departed from Samuel Clarke and the other benevolists who distinguished and separated eternal moral principles from God himself. Edwards insisted that these standards to which God conforms are part of God's own being. More importantly, Edwards dissented from natural law theorists who wanted to desacralize and secularize morality, maintaining that love cannot be fully understood apart from God.[49]

---

47. Spohn, "Sovereign Beauty," 420; WJE 8:420–21, 616–18.
48. Fiering, *Jonathan Edwards's Moral Thought*, 361, 345, 89, 93, 343.
49. Danaher, *Trinitarian Ethics*, 248–49.

So Fiering was correct in saying that Edwards's moral theory was rationalistic in certain respects. Yet Edwards never intended to separate his philosophical ethics from his moral theology, and in the latter he blazed a trail that rationalists have refused to follow.

The Acquisition and Growth of Virtues

Another difference between Edwards's moral theology and strictly rationalist ethics lay in Edwards's rejection of Aristotelian habituation, whereby one acquires virtue through repetitive performance. Just as an aspiring major league baseball pitcher could not gain skill in pitching without throwing a baseball many times, so a person seeking virtue—according to the habituation theory—acquires facility in the moral life through prolonged practice. Eighteenth-century moralists generally conceived of benevolence as an inherent or potential quality in all persons. If one persisted long enough in virtuous activity, then virtuous habits would take root in the soul. In contrast to this acquisition theory, Edwards adopted and then adapted Hutcheson's theory of the virtues. For Hutcheson, there was something that came prior to virtuous actions. This was the seeing and approving of moral beauty. Such an aesthetic vision was indispensable to the virtuous life. Yet Edwards took a sizeable step beyond Hutcheson by arguing that if one sees the beauty that is God himself, this sight of God's beauty comes only as a gift of God. By Edwards's lights, there was no inherent, natural freedom to choose and to acquire true virtue--as the Aristotelians and acquisition theorists held. The freedom to love came only with the God-given gift of seeing the divine beauty of holiness.[50]

Yet Edwards's teaching on aesthetic vision was not a recipe for laziness or inaction. Once given the eyes to see, the saints could and should cultivate their regenerated moral sense. Various degrees of benevolence and degrees of excellence existed in the virtues. The saints would grow in being as they learned to reach out to others in love. Through growth in grace, they would have a "greater sense" of "the infinite excellency and glory of the divine Being." With a heightened sense of the divine glory, more and more divine grace would be infused, and the saints would increasingly be filled with divine love. As we saw in chapter 4, Edwards's spirituality presupposed a never-ending

---

50. Danaher, *Trinitarian Ethics*, 252. See also Danaher, 151–56.

process of seeking God. And as we saw in chapters 23, 24, and 25, God generally rewards sincere seeking with gracious finding.[51]

On the other hand, Edwards was no perfectionist. He taught, in Paul Ramsey's words, that with grace "all things are made new, yet none perfectly." Even if there is "a great deal of" unwitting "hypocrisy" and only a little sincerity, God will not reject "that little sincerity" simply because it grows amidst "much hypocrisy." God does not despise small beginnings. Good Christians "may find that they greatly fail every day, and are in many instances often wandering out of the way." They may be attended "with many and exceedingly great imperfections." Yet even then their life can be "a holy life, a truly Christian life," for when scripture speaks of holiness of life, it does not mean "that it should be a perfect life."[52]

Edwards's Ethical Distinctives

Recent studies have claimed—in differing ways—that Edwards offered a distinctive moral vision. Paul Ramsey holds that Edwards was more favorable than Thomas Aquinas "to the moral competence of the unregenerate" and that his "full account of natural principles" was innovative within the Reformed tradition: "Edwards articulated the humanism often ascribed to Calvin in contrast to Luther." William Danaher makes a similar assertion for Edwards's notion of ethical participation, saying that this was unique in the Reformed tradition. According to Danaher, Francis Turretin came closest to Edwards in his presentation of the moral life as likeness to God. Yet even Turretin did not parallel Edwards in viewing the moral life as the very presence or "instantiation" of God. Danaher asserts that Edwards also differed from Thomas Aquinas on this score. For Aquinas, charity or Christian love is the indwelling of the Holy Spirit but is not the actual presence of the Holy Spirit. Instead Christian love is "a creaturely representation of the pattern of love as it exists within the Trinity." For Edwards, on the other hand, our Christian love implied that we "repeat, rather than merely replicate or represent, the perfect idea of God."[53]

---

51. WJE 8:548, 755; WJE 2:314. Thus the regenerate can "enhance" their dispositions, but "it is impossible for human agents to bridge the gap from reprobate to regenerate thorough their own efforts." Wilson, *Virtue Reformed*, 210. Wilson's erudite study shows the importance of secondary causes and moral cultivation by the saints, but does not prove the dominance of Aristotelian habituation models in Edwards's ethics.

52. WJE 8:27, 181, 309.

53. WJE 8:58–59, 746; Danaher, *Trinitarian Ethics*, 45–47.

For Cochran, Edwards was unique among Enlightenment-era Christian ethicists because they made law primary while Edwards focused on character. We saw earlier that most eighteenth-century ethicists reduced all morality to an undifferentiated love or benevolence, while Edwards retained the ancient and medieval custom of delineating a range of virtues that all related back to the central virtue of Christian love. What is more, Aquinas generally looked to human reason for moral norms while Edwards relied chiefly on the incarnate Christ. Thus Aquinas could approve of Aristotelian magnanimity in which a virtuous man thinks it reasonable to receive the greatest of honors—though Thomas adds that he should deflect the honor to God. In contrast, Edwards argued that Christ might reasonably have chosen to resist his persecution and abuse, and yet demonstrated a higher virtue by submitting himself to the deprivation of honor. Cochran concludes that Edwards did a better job than Aquinas did at reconciling Christian theology with virtue ethics.[54]

We would add that Edwards displayed an unprecedented intensity in uniting ethics with aesthetics. As suggested in chapter 6, no one else in Western Christian thought seems to have made God's beauty so integral to Christian theology and to Christian ethics. And we have seen throughout this chapter that Edwards's ethics has everything to do with God's beauty. All natural virtue is an earthly image of the divine beauty, and only those who see that beauty can participate in benevolence to Being in general. This notion of ethical participation in aesthetic vision may be the most distinctive contribution that Edwards made to Christian ethics.

---

54. Cochran, *Receptive Human Virtues*, ch. 4.

34

Edwards on (and in) Mission

IN HIS APPENDIX to *The Life of David Brainerd*, Jonathan Edwards observed that the revival among Brainerd's Indians at Crossweeksung (New Jersey) from August 1745 to October 1746 was more impressive than much of the Great Awakening because the Indian awakening was deeper and more enduring.[1] Edwards speculated that the "wonderful things" that God had done among the Indians "are but a forerunner of something yet much more glorious and extensive of that kind." By this he meant a "general revival of religion" that would be "very glorious...special and extraordinary" and would produce the "flourishing of Christ's kingdom on earth."[2]

Missions to Native Americans were for Edwards simply a chapter in the larger story of the history of revival, which was the main story line in the history of humanity itself, all of which Edwards included in what he called the history of redemption (chs. 12, 15). In this chapter, we will delineate Edwards's conception of mission, relate how missions functioned in Edwards's history of redemption, and then examine Edwards's own mission to Native Americans. At the end, we will comment briefly on the importance of Edwards's missiology to Protestant missions in later centuries.

Missions and the History of Redemption

Edwards's term for missions was "the propagation of the gospel." By that he meant the preaching of the gospel by preachers and lay missionaries in new lands and its exposition by "learned divines." Only when the Spirit empowered these otherwise feeble instruments would the gospel have "success" in

---

1. Since many Native Americans now use "Indian" and "Native American" interchangeably, we do the same in this chapter.

2. The dates of the Crossweeksung revival and some other details in this chapter are from Ronald E. Davies, "Prepare Ye the Way of the Lord: The Missiological Thought and Practice of Jonathan Edwards (1703–1758)," PhD dissertation, Fuller Theological Seminary, 1989. WJE 7:500–41, citing 533, 532.

converting souls.³ But this success was the secret behind the history of the world. To use his terms, the propagation of the gospel (missions) is the principal moving force in the history of redemption. While this history never had a beginning (since "God's electing love and the covenant of redemption never had a beginning" but originated in eternity) and will have no end, its principal purpose is to repair the damage from the Fall by restoring God's image to humanity and the world. The history of redemption has four other purposes: to gather together all things into union in one body joined to Christ, to effect the triumph of good over evil, to perfect the beauty of the elect, and to glorify the Trinity.⁴ Therefore mission, for Edwards, was the principal means used by God to secure these purposes in history.

As we saw in chapter 14, Edwards believed God's purpose in creating the world was to glorify himself by communicating the inner-Trinitarian knowledge, joy, and love among the divine persons to his human creatures. By seeing the beauty of God, understanding his ways, and delighting in his love, they were to be made anew through union with Christ and his Father by the Spirit. The primary way that people would see this beauty and be caught up into the Trinitarian reality would be by hearing and receiving the gospel. For this purpose, God appointed a gospel ministry to the apostles and their successors—to preach, teach, and baptize all nations. When the church called and sent preachers of the gospel to new places and peoples, it was doing the work of missions. For Edwards, this was the engine that drove history toward the ends for which God created the world.⁵

According to Edwards, the history of missions is dynamized by periodic revivals powered by the Holy Spirit, who first inspires men and women to pray for them. The revivals usually come after times of irreligion and moral laxity, are directed by a prophet or some other "eminent" person, and proceed principally through preaching. All of this takes place gradually, over the course of millennia, which is the best and only way to demonstrate to finite beings the infinite range of God's perfections. Edwards argued that if God's glory and beauty were displayed all at once, it "would dazzle our eyes and be too much for our sight."⁶

Several elements of this schema are noteworthy. First, all of history since the Incarnation was the actualization of "Christ's purchase." History since

---

3. WJE 9:401, 408–409, 421–22, 433–37, 459–60.

4. WJE 9:119, 123–24, 124–25.

5. Ronald E. Davies, "Jonathan Edwards - Missionary Biographer, Theologian, Strategist, Administrator, Advocate, and Missionary," *International Bulletin for Missionary Research* 21:2 (April, 1997): 60–67.

6. WJE 9:142–43, 195, 279; WJE 9:355–56.

Christ was the story of the application of the work of the Cross. Everything that occurred before the time of Christ was simply preparation for this application, and everything in secular history since the Cross serves the work of application.[7] Hence the purpose of history is redemption, which begins with conversion and moves forward through missions. The conversion of one soul, Edwards declared, is more glorious "than the creation of the whole material universe" and brings more happiness than "all that a people could gain by the conquest of the world."[8] Therefore the work of missions, which stimulates revival, is the hidden dynamic driving history, and the fruit of missions produces more human happiness than the ablest statecraft.

Edwards's missiology was innovative in two respects. While there were others such as Richard Baxter who had called for modern missions (and theologians such as Samuel Willard and Cotton Mather who had urged missions to Native Americans), Edwards added new depth and sophistication to the claim that the church should be on mission. The standard theological textbooks of William Ames, Johannes Wollebius, and John Calvin were all silent on the theme of mission, and no other major work of Protestant dogmatics in the English-speaking prior to 1800 world gave mission a prominent place. Many Reformed thinkers after the Reformation, including Edwards's ally Thomas Prince in Boston, believed mission was largely limited to the apostolic age.[9]

Furthermore, by giving such prominent place to the laity's intercession for revival, Edwards was one of the first Protestant thinkers to apply the Great Commission (Matt. 28:18–20) to all church members and to interpret that call as having universal scope. In his *Humble Attempt to Promote Explicit Agreement and Visible Union of God's People in Extraordinary Prayer for the Revival of Religion and the Advancement of Christ's Kingdom on Earth* (1747), Edwards gave first place to the church's intercession and only marginal place to preaching as the stimulus that prompts outpourings of the Holy Spirit upon the earth. Edwards's enormous prestige in the century after his death, combined with the extensive reprints of *Humble Attempt*, stirred enthusiasm for foreign missions among nineteenth-century Anglo-American Protestants. The result was the great expansion of Christendom to what we now call the Global South.[10]

---

7. WJE 9:502, 513.

8. WJE 4:345.

9. R. Pierce Beaver, "American Missionary Motivation before the Revolution," *Church History* 31 (1962): 70.

10. *Humble Attempt* is in WJE 5:307–436.

Perhaps Edwards's greatest stimuli to mission generally—and Indian mission in particular—were his extraordinary historical optimism and fervent expectation of imminent revival. Beginning in the late 1730s and continuing through the Great Awakening and beyond, Edwards prophesied that the world was on the verge of a massive religious revival. The present era was like that of the first century, he wrote: there had just been a great leap in learning, and it was a dark time again for religion. There was nothing in the biblical prophecies that had to be fulfilled before a great new outpouring of the Spirit. Only prayer and preaching were needed. The revival would bring the "church's prosperity" and at the same time violent opposition because the "great revival" would "mightily rouse the old serpent." The long-term result would be awakening in every nation—among Jews, Muslims, and "heathen," and throughout Africa, Asia and "Terra Australis" (Australia). Repeatedly he projected the conversion of American Indians, as well as the inhabitants of Africa and south Asia: "Many of the Negroes and Indians will be divines, and...excellent books will be published in Africa, in Ethiopia, in Turkey."[11]

In his defense of the Great Awakening, *Some Thoughts Concerning the Present Revival of Religion in New England* (1743), Edwards opined that in the New England revivals of the early 1740s "the New Jerusalem has begun to come down from heaven, and perhaps never were more of the prelibations of heaven's glory given upon earth." Largely because of Edwards's remarks in this one book, most interpreters have held that he believed that the millennium had already arrived or was about to come to or through America. But Edwards's eschatology was misunderstood even in his own day, as he himself complained in a letter to a Scottish correspondent in 1744. Just a few pages after this notorious remark in *Some Thoughts Concerning the Revival*, Edwards referred to "this work of God's Spirit" as "the dawning, or at least a prelude, of that glorious work of God, so often foretold in Scripture, which in the progress and issue of it, shall renew the world of mankind." In other words, this work was to be dynamic and progressive, not static and completed as in the millennium.[12]

Later in *Some Thoughts Concerning the Revival*, Edwards referred to the New England revival as perhaps "the dawning of a general revival of the Christian church"—again, not the finished and quiescent period typically understood as the millennium. In 1744, Edwards distinguished between the work of God's Spirit that would precede the millennium and the millennium itself,

---

11. WJE 5:425; WJE 9:480.

12. WJE 4:346, 560; WJE 16:134–35; WJE 4:353. On Edwards's misunderstood eschatology, see chs. 32 and 35.

and denied that he ever said the millennium had begun. By 1747, Edwards was writing that the great work of God's Spirit, preceding the millennium, might take 250 years and might not even begin for several hundred years after Edwards's day. In the meantime, though, there would be many happy revivals well worth praying for. At this point, Edwards was describing the millennium in strictly international terms. When he mentioned New England and America, he spoke of them as spiritually bankrupt and most in need of awakening to save them from perdition.[13]

Edwards on Mission

Long before he arrived at his mission post in Stockbridge, Edwards began to think that what God was doing among Native Americans might be a "forerunner" of the great work of God's Spirit at the end of the age.[14] His interest was piqued in part by Solomon Stoddard and David Brainerd. Stoddard, Edwards's grandfather and senior pastor under whom Edwards served as assistant for three years, had envisioned an American multiracial church, with Indians in full communion with whites. In 1723, Stoddard published a blistering attack on New England for its failure to heed God's command to evangelize the Indians.[15]

David Brainerd was so convinced of God's extraordinary graces shown to his Indian congregants that his diary persuaded Edwards that "something very remarkable" was occurring among these subjects of Satan. Brainerd

---

13. WJE 4:466, 558–60; WJE 5:410–12, 427, 357–58. For a fuller exposition of Edwards's eschatology and America's role in it, see Gerald R. McDermott, *One Holy and Happy Society: The Public Theology of Jonathan Edwards* (University Park, PA: Penn State Press, 1992), 37–92.

14. For fuller treatments of the Stockbridge mission, see Rachel M. Wheeler, "Edwards as Missionary," in Stephen J. Stein, ed., *The Cambridge Companion to Jonathan Edwards* (Cambridge, Eng.: Cambridge University Press, 2007), 196–214; George Marsden, *Jonathan Edwards: A Life* (New Haven: Yale University Press, 2003), 375–431; and Stephen J. Nichols, "Last of the Mohican Missionaries," in D. G. Hart, Sean Michael Lucas and Stephen Nichols, *The Legacy of Jonathan Edwards: American Religion and the Evangelical Tradition* (Grand Rapids: Baker Academic, 2003), 47–63.

15. Solomon Stoddard, *Question Whether God Is Not Angry with the Country for Doing So Little Towards the Conversion of the Indians?* (Boston: Printed by B. Green, 1723), esp. 6–12. Earlier, however, Stoddard had evinced less than generous attitudes toward Indians. In 1703, he wrote to Governor Dudley suggesting the English might hunt Indians "with dogs...as they doe Bears" because Indians don't fight fairly, "after the manner of other nations." They are thieves and murderers, he wrote, who "don't appear openly in the field to bid us battle, ...[and] use those cruelly that fall into their hands." Stoddard concluded that since they act like wolves, they should be treated like wolves. *Massachusetts Historical Society Collections*, 4th series, II, 235–37.

related the stories of Susquehanna Indians who manifested a "disposition" to hear the gospel and of Indians on Juniata Island who were remarkably free of prejudice against Christianity. He wrote of an Indian "powwow" (medicine man), clad in bearskin and mask, beating a rattle, and dancing "with all his might," who felt his fellow Indians had become corrupted and sought to restore their ancient religious ways. This powwow opposed their consumption of alcohol and affirmed many but not all of Brainerd's Christian doctrines. Brainerd believed that he was "sincere, honest and conscientious," and concluded "there was something in his temper and disposition that looked more like true religion than anything I ever observed amongst other heathens."[16]

Brainerd's Indian converts seem to have impressed Edwards, as well. One Indian woman was a textbook example of Edwardsean spirituality. "She has seemed constantly to breathe the spirit and temper of the new creature...[and manifested] a true spiritual discovery of the glory, ravishing beauty, and excellency of Christ." Another Indian—a medicine man—had been a "murderer" and "notorious drunkard" who had purposely steered other Indians away from Brainerd's preaching. Brainerd compared him to Simon Magus and confessed that he had secretly wished for his death. But then the medicine man had a "lively, soul-refreshing view of the excellency of Christ," challenged another powwow to embrace Christ, and like St. Paul spent his days preaching the faith he once attacked.[17] Brainerd took great satisfaction in his own Indian congregation, made up of those who had welcomed his preaching. Here, Brainerd claimed, was Christian love of greater strength than in the early church, and a sense of the presence of God stronger than in any white congregation: "I know of no assembly of Christians where there seems to be so much of the presence of God, where brotherly love so much prevails, and where I should take so much delight in the public worship of God, in the general, as in my own congregation."[18]

As we have already seen, Edwards believed these events were "but a forerunner of something yet much more glorious and extensive of that kind." In other words, Edwards thought Brainerd was underestimating the importance of his work when he concluded that "the living God, as I strongly hoped, was

---

16. WJE 9:434; WJE 7:294, 329–30. The medicine man might have been influenced by the Native American restorationist movement described in Gregory Evans Dowd, *A Spirited Resistance: The North American Indian Struggle for Unity, 1745–1815* (Baltimore: Johns Hopkins University Press, 1993). On Brainerd, see John A. Grigg, *The Lives of David Brainerd: The Making of an Evangelical Icon* (New York: Oxford University Press, 2009), esp. 72–127.

17. WJE 7:371, 398, 391–95.

18. WJE 7:387, 367–68.

engaged for [the Indians' salvation]."[19] Not only was God acting to redeem the devil's people, but this redemption had world-historical significance.[20] It would presage the last, mighty work of the Spirit across the world at the end of time.

In the meantime, "something remarkable" was appearing among the Indians of New England. Their moral character was remarkable, for they displayed far less ingenuity in evil than the Europeans: "The poor savage Americans are mere babes and fools (if I may so speak) as to proficiency in wickedness, in comparison of multitudes that the Christian world throngs with." But of far more significance was their religious sensibility. Beginning in his sermon series on the history of redemption in 1739, and continuing with greater frequency during subsequent years, Edwards made note of what seemed to him to be a regenerate disposition among otherwise unconverted Indians. In the 1740s, he was commenting on what he had heard from Brainerd, but by the 1750s, he reported his own observations from his frontier mission outpost among the Indians.[21] Edwards first made public comment about "remarkable" things among the Indians in a 1739 sermon on the work of redemption. There he noted that among "many Indians" there was a "remarkable...*inclination* to be instructed in the Christian religion." His use of the word "inclination" is suggestive because of his later use of the same word in the *Religious Affections* (1746) for the central orientation of the self, which signals the basic direction of the soul, either toward or away from God.[22]

Whether or not Edwards meant in 1739 that this promising inclination was evidence of a regenerate disposition, his choice of a text for his first sermon to the Indians at Stockbridge suggests that in 1751 he was considering that possibility.[23] The new missionary pastor chose to preach on Acts 11:12–13, the story of the Roman centurion Cornelius. From at least as early as 1740, Edwards had believed that this soldier, who was described by Luke as a God-fearing "devout man" whose prayers and alms were approved by God

---

19. WJE 7:533, 255.

20. Edwards believed that the devil had kept the Indians in North America for many ages to keep them away from the gospel and that they had become Satan's captives; WJE 9:472.

21. WJE 9:434; WJE 3:183.

22. WJE 9:434; emph. added; WJE 2:12–13, 100, 107, 310, 312, passim.

23. This was a congregation of 100–200 Mahican and Mohawk Indians. On Edwards's ministry at Stockbridge, see Rachel Wheeler, *To Live Upon Hope: Mohicans and Missionaries in the Eighteenth-Century Northeast* (Ithaca: Cornell University Press, 2008), 206–22.

(Acts 10:2–4 was regenerate even before Peter had told him about Jesus.[24] Edwards told his Indian auditors that Cornelius "had heard something of the true God before Peter came to him, but he knew but little; he did not know anything about Jesus Christ." Yet Cornelius "was willing to be instructed" and "had a mind to know more." Therefore he "prayed to God that he might be brought into the light."[25]

After explaining how Cornelius and his family were converted through Peter's preaching, Edwards proclaimed, "Now I am come to preach the true religion to you and to your children, as Peter did to Cornelius and his family, that you and all your children may be saved."[26] We don't know if any Indians that day "were willing to be instructed" and "had a mind to know more," but we do know that Edwards was convinced shortly thereafter that the Indians at Onohquaga had such a mind.[27] In the following year, he wrote the Rev. Isaac Hollis that "many" members of that tribe "that used to be notorious drunkards and blood-thirsty warriors, have of late strangely had their *dispositions* and manners changed through some wonderful influence on their minds." They were now uninterested in war and had forsaken drunkenness. They also had "a *disposition* to religion and a thirst after instruction."[28] Once again, Edwards's vocabulary was suggestive. "Disposition" was a word Edwards used synonymously for "inclination," both in sermons and in his most developed analysis of religious experience, the *Religious Affections*. To say that the Onohquagas had a disposition to religion and a thirst after instruction recalled the nearly identical description of Cornelius and therefore suggested that the Spirit was working in these Indians to prepare them for conversion.

A similar suggestion appeared in Edwards's 1753 letter to Andrew Oliver. He told the secretary of the Board of Commissioners for Indian Affairs that a Mohawk sachem had informed him that the Onohquagas were more religious and virtuous than the Mohawks, and then claimed that he had found this testimony to be true: "They have appeared to be far the best *disposed* Indians we

---

24. WJE 20:56: "Cornelius...was already a good man...[and] did already in some respect believe in Christ...in the manner that the old testament saints were wont to do."

25. WJE 25:571.

26. WJE 25:571.

27. Onohquaga was the name for several villages along a ten-mile stretch of the Susquehanna River. By the mid-1750s, Tuscagoras, Mahicans, Shawnees, and Oneida Indians lived in these villages. Colin G. Calloway, *The American Revolution in Indian Country: Crisis and Diversity in Native American Communities* (Cambridge: Cambridge University Press, 1995), 108–11.

28. WJE 16:499, emph. added.

have had to do with, and would be *inclined* to their utmost to assist, encourage and to strengthen the hands of missionaries and instructors, should [any] be sent among [them], and do all they can to forward their success among themselves and other Indians round about." Two days later, Edwards wrote a Scottish minister that another group of Indians had a Cornelian desire to hear and to assimilate the gospel: they "have a great desire that the gospel should be introduced and settled in their country."[29]

Edwards pondered these things and deduced that the Indians would have a glorious future in the work of redemption. He predicted that the Indians of America, along with "the nations of Negroes and others," would "serve the true God and [sing] praises... to the Lord Jesus Christ."[30] Therefore he was confident that God would work through preaching to redeem the devil's people. During his seven years at Stockbridge, he preached more than two hundred original sermons and on another twenty occasions preached from earlier manuscripts.[31] It is clear from the extant manuscripts that Edwards worked hard to adapt his rhetoric to the limited capacity of his hearers (ch. 31). As Rachel Wheeler has noted, the Stockbridge sermons told more stories than the Northampton sermons, were simpler in presentation, and used more imagery derived from nature.[32] For example, a 1751 sermon on 2 Peter 1:19 ("We have a more sure word of prophecy") illustrates all three of these devices:

> When God first made man, he had a principle of holiness in his heart. That holiness that was in him was like a light that shone in his heart so that his mind was full of light. But when man sinned against God, he lost his holiness, and then the light that was in his mind was put out.... Truly good men... not only have the light shining round about 'em but the light shines into their hearts.... wicked men... although the light shines round about 'em, yet it don't shine into 'em but are perfectly dark within.[33]

---

29. WJE 16:583, 595. Emph. add.

30. James Axtell, *The Invasion Within: The Contest of Cultures in Colonial North America* (New York: Oxford University Press, 1985), 272; WJE 9:472.

31. Rachel Wheeler, "'Friends to Your Souls': The Egalitarian Calvinism of Jonathan Edwards," *Church History* 72 (2003): 749.

32. Wheeler, "Friends to Your Souls," 750–51.

33. "To the Mohawks at the Treaty, August 16, 1751," in Wilson H. Kimnach, Kenneth P. Minkema, and Douglas A. Sweeney, eds., *The Sermons of Jonathan Edwards: A Reader* (New Haven: Yale University Press, 1999), 105–106.

Edwards here used a simple image of light and darkness to recount the story of the Fall and to distinguish starkly the regenerate from the unregenerate.

Imagery drawn from rustic life appears in another sermon from the same month. Preaching on Genesis 1:27, Edwards declared that "The Holiness of God is like the brightness of the Sun & Holiness in men is as when you hold a Glass in the light of the Sun whereby the Glass shares with some Image of the suns Brightness." Perhaps referring to the Indian susceptibility to drink, Edwards compared humans to swine: "Men when they are drunk do vile [things] & behave thems[elves] in a Beastly manner like a pig that wallows in the mire." Describing regeneration, he used the graphic images of snakes, toads, and excrement: "That which is filthy like a toad or serpent is made to shine bright with some of [Christ's] beauty & brightness. That which is like a Heap of dung is made a[s] one of G[o]ds precious Jewels."[34]

Though Edwards preached more simply to his Indian audiences, accommodating his message to unsophisticated ears, he did not sacrifice content. The aesthetic dimension of his theological vision was not an elite mystery, reserved for learned adepts. On the contrary, it appeared wherever true religion was found, and so even the most rustic soul had access to God's beauty. He told the Stockbridge Indians in his first sermon that they must have "their eyes opened to see how lovely Christ is." In an October 1751 exposition of Psalm 119:18 ("Open thou mine eyes, that I may behold wondrous things out of thy law"), the preacher explained that the "chief things" that our eyes must be opened to see are Christ's "Glory and Excellency." In a sermon on the two ways of life—one that leads to life and happiness and another that leads to death and misery—he explained that even those who go to church may be headed for death. This was true for all those who attend meetings but into whose hearts the divine light has not shone, so that they "are blind and don't see the glory and loveliness of God and Christ." In a communion lecture to the Stockbridge Indians, he asserted that a good man "Loves G[od] above all else for his own Beauty."[35] If Edwards the missionary preached a gospel at once aesthetic and mystical, he considered his Indian congregants capable of understanding such a rarefied message.

---

34. Sermon on Gen. 1:27, Aug. 1751, Jonathan Edwards Center, Yale University.

35. WJE 25:572; sermon on Ps. 119:18, Oct. 1751, Jonathan Edwards Center, Yale University; "All mankind of all nations, white and black, young and old, are going in one or the other of these paths, either in the way that leads to life or the way that leads to destruction," in Michael McMullen, ed., *The Blessing of God: Previously Unpublished Sermons of Jonathan Edwards* (Nashville: B&H Academic, 2003), 227; lecture before the sacrament on Ps. 27:4 (b), Mar. 1752, Beinecke Rare Book and Manuscript Library, Yale University.

Missionary Context and Global Theology

Some scholars have alleged that Edwards became a missionary "largely by default."[36] Yet Edwards had at least three other job offers before deciding on Stockbridge, two for comfortable pulpits in New England and one for Scotland. We have seen that missions were integral to Edwards's vision of history, and we know that Edwards showed keen interest in the Stockbridge mission from its inception. In fact, he had been present at the creation of the original plan to evangelize the Stockbridge Indians in 1734. Edwards and his uncle, Colonel John Stoddard, who knew the Indian tribes better than any other white man in the region, met with others in Stoddard's home to strategize. They decided to send John Sergeant, who had studied in the Edwards parsonage, as their first missionary. Other early missionaries to the Indians either studied in Edwards's home (the custom for training ministers) or attended church with Edwards, who was recognized by the Boston Commissioners as a missionary trainer.[37] Edwards was in close contact with the Stockbridge mission for the next seventeen years before he took it over in 1751, sending progress reports to his correspondents in Scotland and passing along to others gleanings of missionary successes elsewhere around the world. He took the lead in starting another mission, finally unsuccessful, to the Iroquois. And he deferred work on his premier theological project of the period, *Freedom of the Will*, in order to edit Brainerd's diary for the sake of missionary work among the Indians. As he was about to begin his work at the Stockbridge mission, he referred to it as "the important service I have undertaken in this place."[38]

Hence Stockbridge was not a enforced exile for Edwards, as sometimes suggested. But neither was it, as still others have claimed, a quiet retreat. In some ways it turned out to be, as Charles Chaney put it, a "living hell."[39] Although Edwards believed in the mission and grew in genuine affection for his Indian parishioners, life was difficult there. Stockbridge was crowded with

---

36. Andrew F. Walls, "Missions and Historical Memory: Jonathan Edwards and David Brainerd," in David W. Kling and Douglas A. Sweeney, *Jonathan Edwards at Home and Abroad: Historical Memories, Cultural Movements, Global Horizons* (Columbia, SC: University of South Carolina Press, 2003), 250. Norman Pettit charged that Edwards was less interested in Brainerd's mission than in "his commitment to a holy cause" ("Editor's Introduction," in WJE 7:13).

37. The Boston commissioners were appointed by the "Society in London, for Propagating the Gospel in New England, and the Parts Adjacent."

38. WJE 16:387.

39. Charles L. Chaney, *The Birth of Missions in America* (South Pasadena, CA: William Carey Library, 1976), 57.

refugees (from the colonial wars with the French and their Indian allies) and soldiers, some of whom took shelter in the Edwards home. Between services one Sunday morning in 1754, Canadian Indians ("doubtless instigated by the French," Edwards charged) attacked and killed three white worshipers.[40] The mission was wracked by recurrent party strife between Edwards and the same Williams clan that had helped drive him out of Northampton.

When Edwards arrived at Stockbridge in June 1751, he inherited a troubled mission. John Sergeant had died in 1749, leaving behind 218 Mahicans, descended from the once-mighty Algonquin tribe. In the next two years, ninety Mohawks of the Iroquois "Six Nations" arrived from the Mohawk River some forty miles west of Albany—many lured by the promise of education for their children at a boarding school run by the incompetent "Captain" Martin Kellogg, who was supported over Edwards's protests by Sergeant's widow, a member of the Williams clan. When Kellogg refused to defer to his replacement, Gideon Hawley, half the Mohawks left the mission. Then the boarding school mysteriously caught fire and burned down; arson was suspected. By the end of 1753, all of the Mohawks were gone but not without expressing their support for the embattled Edwards.

Troubles within and without did not prevent Edwards from applying himself assiduously to his missionary tasks. For the seven years until he departed for Princeton in January 1758, Edwards held four services most Sundays: two for his Indian charges and two for the white congregation. During the week, while pursuing his theological projects, he expended considerable time and effort defending Indians against greedy whites who were manipulating the Stockbridge mission for their own aggrandizement. Despite recurrent physical distress and public vilification of his efforts, Edwards wrote numerous letters to Boston and London pleading his Indian parishioners' rights to education and justice. For example, he obtained land and had it plowed for Indian families so that they could send their children to school and made sure that five Indian boys found lodging in white homes so they could receive an education. Edwards took at least one of the boys into his own home.[41]

In 1751, Edwards wrote to the Speaker of the Massachusetts Assembly to urge that body to honor its treaty obligations to the Housatonnuks (the name given by white settlers to the Stockbridge Indians, most of whom were Mahicans). When a friend of one of the whites seeking to exploit the mission struck an Indian child on the head with a cane, Edwards convinced the

---

40. WJE 16:663; Patrick Frazier, *The Mohicans of Stockbridge* (Lincoln, NE: University of Nebraska Press, 1994), 108–109.

41. WJE 16:634, 638.

offender to pay damages. After an Indian was killed by two whites, he labored to obtain indemnity money to pay the grief-stricken family. Edwards spent hours listening to the broken English and sign language of Indian children so that he could accurately report to the Boston Commissioners that his Indian scholars did not have enough blankets or food, that some boys had no breeches and many were going ragged to meetings, and that all the boys were being forced to work six days per week. Once a week, he sat the Indian children down for instruction in religion, experimenting with new methods that emphasized narrative and Socratic questioning instead of rote learning—which until then had been standard pedagogy for whites and Indians. Sadly, Edwards and others (John Sergeant and Timothy Woodbridge) who fought for Indian rights "were all but powerless against the aggressive [Ephraim] Williams [ironically, a relative of Edwards] and his supporters...[who] cheated the Indians out of their land and drove them from their town."[42]

In one respect, however, his Indian congregation might have sensed something less than respect from Edwards for their culture. He refused to learn their language, claiming that his time would be spent more profitably teaching them English and that they themselves agreed with his decision. One wonders if those who disagreed felt free to voice their disapproval to someone who was director of the mission compound on which they lived. Perhaps some Indians also wondered why Edwards encouraged his own son to learn Mahican and how such an industrious scholar could not make some effort to learn the language of those he hoped to win to Christian faith.[43]

Edwards shared the overwhelming white consensus that Indian culture was inferior and even despicable. Even John Eliot, the apostle to the Indians, referred to Indians as "doleful creatures," the very ruins of mankind.[44] There was also Indian "idolatry"—reverence shown for the numinous in nature—that Edwards and the Reformed interpreted as sinful worship of the creature rather than the Creator.[45] As a result, Edwards and most Protestant missionar-

---

42. WJE 16:644, 407–408; Lion G. Miles, "The Red Man Dispossessed: The Williams Family and the Alienation of Indian Land in Stockbridge, Massachusetts, 1736–1818," *New England Quarterly* 67:1 (1994): 74–75. This was the same Williams family that engineered Edwards's expulsion from Northampton. Ephraim Sr., head of the Stockbridge branch of the family, was an uncle to Solomon Williams, who wrote a challenge to Edwards's *Humble Inquiry* on communion qualifications—the formal if not material issue that led to Edwards's removal.

43. WJE 16:562, 666–67.

44. Cotton Mather, *Magnalia Christi Americana*, 2 vols. (Hartford: Silas Andrus, 1820), 1:504; cited by Norman Pettit in "Editor's Introduction," WJE 7:26.

45. See, for example, sermon on Deut. 32:29, "Such persons are very imprudent and foolish, that don't consider their latter end," in McMullen, ed., *The Blessing of God*, 29–44.

ies failed to see anything in Indian religion that could serve as common ground or a point of contact in evangelism. They studiously discounted similarities between Indian and Christian religion such as moral government, retribution, heaven and hell, and the necessity of a moral life.[46]

Nevertheless Edwards won the affection of his Indian parishioners by advocating for their cause. Early in his tenure at Stockbridge, shortly after being ejected from the Northampton pulpit by parishioners who complained of his "unsociable" ways (ch. 29), Edwards seemed encouraged that "the Indians seem much pleased with my family, especially my wife." Later he referred to them as "my people," and noted happily that they "steadfastly adhere to me" despite the concerted efforts of the Williams family—his own relatives—to alienate them from him. Edwards also included the white Stockbridge congregation in the company of his supporters, but he preached a kinder and gentler message to the Indian congregation. In her careful study of the Stockbridge sermons, Wheeler notes that while Edwards told the Indians repeatedly of Christ's desire to save them, he spent far more time in his sermons to the "English" congregation at the mission warning them of God's wrath. The missionary preacher emphasized to his Indian auditors not God's judgment but the divine invitation; he was careful to apprise them that God's election did not depend on skin color or nationality. There is "forgiveness offered to all nations," he assured them.[47]

In the last decade of his life, then, Edwards signaled a change in emphasis. No longer were Indians infernal inhabitants of Satan's kingdom. The majority of them may still have been unregenerate, but they were no worse than the legions of white hypocrites. Among the worst were the greedy English and Dutch traders, who purposely kept Indians from instruction "for the sake of making a gain of you. For as long as they keep you in ignorance, 'tis more easy to cheat you in trading with you." Of course, the French were no better. According to Edwards, they made sure the Indians did not learn to read so that they would not see that French ways "are not agreeable to the

---

46. Ola E. Winslow, *Jonathan Edwards 1703–1758: A Biography* (New York: Macmillan, 1940), 29; William R. Hutchison, *Errand to the World: American Protestant Thought and Foreign Missions* (Chicago: University of Chicago Press, 1987), 32. Most Europeans did not expect to learn anything from "heathen" religions. Francis Jennings, *The Invasion of America: Indians, Colonialism, and the Cant of Conquest* (Chapel Hill, NC: Institute of Early American History and Culture and the University of North Carolina Press, 1975), 53; Henry Warner Bowden, *American Indians and Christian Missions* (Chicago, IL: University of Chicago Press, 1981), 122.

47. WJE 16:420, 610; Rachel Wheeler, *To Live Upon Hope*, 27–66; sermon on Luke 24:47, October 1751, Jonathan Edwards Center, Yale University.

Scripture.... When the Bible is hid from 'em they can cheat 'em and make 'em believe what they have a mind to." Edwards concluded that Indian hostility to whites in North America was God's judgment on Euro-Americans for their treatment of Native Americans: defrauding and killing them, poisoning them with alcohol, and depriving them of the gospel.[48]

To confer moral equivalence on English and French sins was, for many New Englanders, a kind of communal treachery. Of course, Edwards would in the same breath join his compatriots in denouncing the French as benighted pawns of the papal Antichrist. Yet his willingness to condemn both English and French exploitation of the Indians shows that he respected the dignity and humanity of Indians in ways that most of his compatriots did not. Furthermore, as Wheeler noted, his treatise *Original Sin* was "a call to human fellowship rooted in a conviction of the universality of depravity." Written while at Stockbridge, it argued that while American Indians showed the need for revelation to get true religion, it was also clear that all of humanity would be in darkness without the grace of God. Edwards never arrived at the fraternal humility of John Woolman, who respected the religious *knowledge* of Indians and considered their condition as in some respects superior to his own.[49] But he showed some affinity for the spiritual sensitivity of Roger Williams, who said that Indians had not sinned against gospel light and were closer to grace than the "unchristian Christians" of the Massachusetts Bay Colony.[50]

Edwards's life among the Stockbridge Indians shaped his later theological writings and his final theological vision. In what we have called his "cultural-historical turn" (ch. 5), he became preoccupied with non-Christian nations and cultures and their possible role within God's redemptive plan. Hundreds of notebook entries discussed the theme. Edwards was increasingly convinced that true religion might be found outside of Western monotheistic cultures (ch. 36). Furthermore, he developed a plan for his *magnum opus*—the *History of the Work of Redemption*—that would trace out the historical purposes of God within all global cultures (chs. 10, 12). Such a far-sighted vision was unparalleled among the orthodox thinkers of his day, and it seems possible that Edwards might never have come to it apart from the intellectual and theological stimulus afforded by his pastoral experience among the Native Americans.

---

48. "To the Mohawks at the Treaty," in Wilson Kimnach, Kenneth Minkema, and Douglas Sweeney, eds., *The Sermons of Jonathan Edwards*, 108, 107–108; WJE 16:434–47.

49. Wheeler, "Edwards as Missionary," 207; Woolman, *The Journal of John Woolman and A Plea for the Poor* (Secaucus, NJ: Citadel Press, 1972; orig. pub. 1774); cited in Hutchison, *Errand to the World*, 33.

50. Hutchison, *Errand to the World*, 36–37.

"Grandfather" of Modern Protestant Missions?

Jonathan Edwards came to believe that what God was doing among Native Americans—the first real "heathen" Western Christians had lived with in the previous millennium—was tangible evidence that the great work of God's Spirit may have begun. These remarkable scenes in the drama of redemption were being performed on the New England colonial stage and were dramatic previews of the final act in which all those held prisoner by Satan would be triumphantly liberated.

These impressive events in Edwards's depiction of the Brainerd experience—came to have equally remarkable impact on later Protestant missions. Edwards's *Life of Brainerd*, which was probably the first full missionary biography ever published, became the best known of all his literary works. Never out of print in the two and a half centuries since its publication, it provided "the Protestant icon of the missionary, its ideal type."[51] William Carey (1761–1834), English Baptist missionary to India and principal founder of Anglo-American missions, drew up a covenant for his missionary band that included the words, "Let us often look at Brainerd." According to one of his biographers, Carey so devoured Edwards's *Life of Brainerd* that it became almost a second Bible to him. He repeatedly cited Brainerd's experience among the Indians as an example of the power of the gospel to convert the heathen before they are civilized.[52] Gideon Hawley, one of Edwards's protégés, put *Life of Brainerd* in his saddlebag with his Bible as his only two books while working among the Mashpees. John Wesley published an abridged version of the *Life of Brainerd* in 1768 (with seven later editions), excising Calvinist passages but writing that preachers with Brainerd's spirit would be invincible. The list of missionaries who testified to Brainerd's influence is a who's-who of Anglo-American missions in the last two centuries: Francis Asbury, Thomas Coke, Henry Martyn, Robert Morrison, Samuel Mills, Robert M'Cheyne, David Livingstone, Adoniram Judson, Theodore Dwight Weld, Andrew Murray, and Jim Elliot. Joseph Conforti argues that the *Life of Brainerd*'s enormous impact on American missionaries is "summed up by the fact that when the American Board of Commissioners for Foreign

---

51. Walls, 253; for more on the Edwards-Brainerd legacy for missions, see Grigg's *The Lives of David Brainerd*, 128–46, 164–87.

52. Stuart Piggin, "'The Expanding Knowledge of God': Jonathan Edwards's Influence on Missionary Thinking and Promotion," in Kling and Sweeney, *Jonathan Edwards at Home and Abroad*, 273, 275–76.

Missions established its first Indian post, among the Cherokees in 1817, the missionaries named it Brainerd."[53]

Some of Edwards's other works were also influential in modern missions. Carey used the *Humble Attempt* to discount the contention that certain prophecies had to be fulfilled before the heathen could be converted. The *Humble Attempt* inspired the founders of the London Missionary Society, the (English) Baptist Missionary Society, and the Scottish Missionary Society, as well as the most celebrated of all Scottish evangelicals, Thomas Chalmers. Edwards's *History of Redemption*, though not well-received until the nineteenth century, became one of the most popular manuals of Calvinist theology during the Second Great Awakening and excited renewed interest in missionary work both at home and abroad. Its emphasis on the human contribution to redemption through individual conversion and revivalism helped to "universalize" the revivals of the Second Great Awakening.[54] Hence there were several of Edwards's treatises that became important in the growth of the nineteenth-century missionary movement in England and America. If candidates to the London Missionary Society "managed to get through their missionary training and had still not read Edwards, future missionaries were given a book allowance out of which they were expected to buy certain books including 'Edwards's Works.'"[55]

For these reasons, Edwards has sometimes been called the "grandfather" of modern Protestant missions. Because he lived in an interlude—that is, after the beginnings of Roman Catholic, Anglican, and Moravian missions, and yet before the commencement of the Anglo-American Protestant missionary movement—Edwards cannot be called a father. Yet the latter movement was "a child whose appearance and personality point to the paternity of Edwards"—if not directly at least indirectly through his theology of missions, which underscored the world-historical importance of his and Brainerd's missions to Native Americans.[56]

---

53. Joseph A. Conforti, *Jonathan Edwards, Religious Tradition, and American Culture* (Chapel Hill: University of North Carolina Press, 1995), 75.

54. Conforti, *Jonathan Edwards*, 48–49.

55. Piggin, "Expanding Knowledge," 279.

56. Davies, "Jonathan Edwards: Missionary Theologian," 60; Piggin, "Expanding Knowledge," 266.

35

Eschatology

SINCE THE MID-NINETEENTH-CENTURY, scholars have used the term eschatology to refer to the destiny of both human beings and the whole created order. Edwards never used that word, but of the major Protestant thinkers he was among the most eschatologically minded.[1] He devoted his 1739 sermon series on the history of redemption to expounding the thesis that God was directing the movement of every atom in the universe toward his predetermined end. He told the trustees of Princeton College that this theme would animate his projected magnum opus.[2] His *End of Creation*, written near the end of his life and summing up much of his thought, was devoted to God's purposes through and at the end of history. The only biblical book for which he wrote a complete commentary was Revelation, in a notebook he kept from 1723 until the end of his career. What is more, his other notebooks contain detailed ruminations on last things. So while all of his thought was eschatological in a generalized sense, this chapter will focus on discrete segments of his thinking about "the last things." We shall begin with the question of personal destiny, focusing on hell (since ch. 19 focuses entirely on heaven), and then sketch Edwards's vision for the future of the cosmos in the "glorious work of God's Spirit," the millennium, and the new heavens and new earth.

Edwards believed in two judgments—a particular one at death after which the disembodied soul proceeds to either heaven or hell, and a general one at the end of history in which all human beings who have ever lived (plus the devil and his wicked angels) will be judged publicly by Jesus Christ.[3] Before we

---

1. *The Compact Edition of the Oxford English Dictionary* lists 1844 as the first known appearance of the word "eschatology" in English, and it defines the word as "the department of theological science concerned with 'the four last things: death, judgment, heaven, and hell'" (Oxford, UK: Oxford University Press, 1971), s.v. On the future of the created order, Edwards's favorite term was the "future glorious advancement of the church of God," as in WJE 5:312.

2. WJE 16:727–28.

3. Edwards based his "particular" judgment immediately after death on Eccles. 12:7 and Heb. 9:27. See his sermon on Rom. 2:8–9 in WJEO 50 and WJE 18:431, where he says souls before the general judgment will not sleep but observe the history of redemption on earth.

turn to Edwards's conception of hell, it is worth noting that Edwards might be better known than anyone else for his preaching on hell. Yet, as Norman Fiering has calculated, fewer than two percent of his sermons dealt with hell, and Edwards preached most of these during the Great Awakening. His descriptions of heaven were far more graphic and detailed than those of hell, and he showed little interest in demons (ch. 18). There was almost nothing on hell in his major treatises.[4] It was widely believed in his age that hellfire preaching was actually merciful because of the horrific doom that awaited those who were not alerted to it. Such a gentle and reasonable soul as seventeenth-century metaphysical poet John Donne wrote and preached much about hell. Edwards's grandfather and predecessor, Solomon Stoddard, taught that people continued in sin because they were insufficiently afraid of hell and that Jesus Christ was the greatest hell preacher in the entire Bible. Even in the eighteenth century, it was "axiomatic" among leading thinkers that the fear of hell was an essential deterrent against vice and sin.[5]

Yet, as Fiering observes, it is striking that Edwards preached on hell as often as he did. And if only two percent of his sermons focused on hell, many more touched on it. Furthermore, Edwards knew that no other doctrine put him more at odds with the benevolent moral philosophy that was then gaining traction (ch. 33). Fiering concluded that, for Edwards, the doctrine had "metaphysical importance," for its softening and dismissal were representative of the rising religious skepticism of the eighteenth century.[6] By his own account Edwards during his earlier years had been troubled by the doctrine of God's sovereignty and its implications concerning heaven and hell. Yet at his conversion he came to see that even sovereignty was part of God's beauty.[7]

The Nature of Hell

Edwards believed the biblical images of hell were but the "shadows of reality." Like all shadows found in biblical prophecy, they called for levels of interpretation, both literal and figurative. So if hell was a furnace of fire, it was a physical fire for

---

4. Edwards was unlike Richard Baxter, a "moderate" Puritan whose *Saint's Everlasting Rest* devoted one-sixth of its pages to lurid descriptions of hell; Stephen R. Holmes, *God of Grace and God of Glory: An Account of the Theology of Jonathan Edwards* (Grand Rapids, MI: Eerdmans, 2000), 216. For Fiering's calculation, see Fiering, *Jonathan Edwards's Moral Thought and Its British Context* (Chapel Hill, NC: University of North Carolina Press, 1981), 204.

5. Fiering, *Jonathan Edwards's Moral Thought*, 202.

6. Fiering, *Jonathan Edwards's Moral Thought*, 203.

7. WJE 16:792.

the body and a figurative fire for the soul. Edwards said the torments of the soul are greater than those of the body. In hell, earthly friends will be like coals that burn one another, and they will be filled with "perfect hatred." All traces of good will then have disappeared. The damned will see the saved in heaven, unable to understand why they are happy—while the saints in heaven will see the suffering of the wicked and by that vision appreciate God's love all the more. But most of Edwards's descriptions of suffering in hell used language suggesting physical pain. The senses of the body would be heightened to increase the pain. There was to be no resting place or cooling stream or fountain, "not so much as a drop of water to cool the tongue." There would be no place to "take a breath for one minute." The heat would be one thousand times hotter than any ordinary fire.[8]

Curiously, the location of hell before the end of the world was some "particular place" in the universe—a "local hell" reserved as a prison for disembodied souls awaiting the final judgment. This was a different place from where Satan and his "devils" were kept, for the latter have energy to tempt human beings and so were not to feel the full brunt of God's wrath, which keeps human prisoners utterly "distracted." Yet the most surprising feature of Edwards's doctrine of hell is its divine nature: hell is the presence of God himself. Edwards pointed to biblical passages such as Revelation 14:10, which refers to those who have worshipped "the beast" (a Satanic figure) drinking of the "wine of the wrath of God" and being "tormented with fire and brimstone...in the presence of the Lamb."[9] He concluded that:

> The angry God will appear as most intimately present with [them]: he with his wrath will be in them and before them and everywhere round about them, expressing his furious displeasure; and they shall see and feel and be as sensible of God's presence, as we are of a man's that stands before our eyes. And everything that is seen will have an impression of God's anger upon it; all things round about will look grim and dreadful with the appearances of God's anger in them. So that there will be that aggravation of ever being concerned immediately with God, and having continual occasion to see the expressions of God's displeasure.[10]

---

8. Sermon on Luke 16:25(b), WJEO 47; WJE 13:480; WJE 20:167–69; "The End of the Wicked Contemplated by the Righteous," in WH 2:207–12; "The Future Punishment of the Wicked Unavoidable and Intolerable," in WH 2:950; WJE 13:376.

9. WJE 23:216–17, quoting the Puritan theologian Thomas Goodwin.

10. WJE 13:349–50; see also sermon on Rom. 2:8–9, WJEO 50. In contrast, most Puritans spoke of hell as the absence of God; Carl R. Trueman, "Heaven and Hell: 12 in Puritan Theology," *Epworth Review* 22 (1995) 75–85.

As John Gerstner put it, for Edwards, it was the presence of God that made heaven heaven and hell hell.[11] Both saints and sinners will encounter God for all eternity. The damned will not be fit for heaven, since the business of heaven is worship in the presence of the beautiful God. Mozart's rival composer Salieri in the film *Amadeus* may help us understand how Edwards's God could also be hell. Just as Mozart's music was intolerable for Salieri—who seethed with envy over his more talented colleague—the beauty of God will be both ugly and painful for souls that hate God.

The Logic of Hell

Edwards's most frequently repeated argument for the justice of hell was the infinite evil and heinousness of sin. In what was routine reasoning for his age, Edwards argued that the heinousness of a sin depends on the dignity of the person injured, which is why even today the murder of a foreign aid worker or orphanage director will likely be more shocking than that of a drug dealer or hit man.[12] Since God has infinite dignity and loveliness, Edwards argued, our obligations toward him are infinite. But human beings have risen up in contempt against the honor of each member of the Holy Trinity, "trod[ding them] in the dirt." The heinousness of human sin can be seen in the multitude of our daily sins, our immeasurable debt to God's generosity, our envy and resentment regarding blessings received by others, our refusal to prepare ourselves for eternity, our selfishness even while we are practicing our religion, and our habit of grumbling and fault-finding with God. Edwards was so convinced of the infinitude of sin that he believed that only the Jesus' death on the cross—not even the eternal punishment of the wicked—was enough to satisfy God's justice. People generally do not begin to comprehend the infinite evil of sin, he argued, until they are reminded of radical evil in the world, such as the delight some take in torturing martyrs or harming "poor innocent children."[13]

Another argument for the justice of eternal punishment was based on the principle of just deserts. God has no obligation to care for those who never cared for his glory or to offer another savior because they did not care for the

---

11. John Gerstner, *The Rational Biblical Theology of Jonathan Edwards* (Powhatan, VA: Berea, 1993), 3:507.

12. WJE 19:341; Bruce W. Davidson, "Reasonable Damnation: How Jonathan Edwards Argued for the Rationality of Hell," *Journal of the Evangelical Theological Society* 38 (1995): 50.

13. WJE 19:345, 348–59; sermon on Matt. 25:46, WJEO 54.

one God provided. God showered the wicked with "a great deal of kindness...and multiplied mercies," but rather than choosing to be on God's side they "chose to side with the devil." He "once loved" them by giving his Son to bring them "the happiness of his love, and tried all manner of means to persuade them" to accept his favor, but they "obstinately refused."[14] Throughout their lives, God made the sun, moon, and stars serve them, and as a result the whole creation groans under this burden. But why should God continue serving them when they refuse to serve him? Furthermore, God's justice and holiness would be meaningless if he did not act as judge to punish evil. No judge is obligated to show mercy to criminals, and an infinitely holy God *ought* to have infinite hatred for sin. The Creator has been murdered and his blood wickedly shed in this world: "No wonder that this breaks down the whole frame, and fetches all down in vengeance and fury on this earth."[15]

So hell is just. It also displays an aesthetic fittingness. What happens in hell is not totally different from what happens on earth. To eighteenth-century liberals who wondered if a good God could tolerate hell, Edwards pointed to the manifest suffering in this world as a reminder that God already finds reasons to permit human suffering. But more to the point, Edwards believed that it is fitting that God's attributes be most fully manifested and that the eternal punishment of the wicked display "God's awful majesty, his authority and dreadful greatness, and justice and holiness." It is especially necessary because God's justice is not fully visible in this world, where the wicked often prosper and oppress the righteous. Hell therefore is an ironic outcome: those who would not glorify God willingly on earth glorify him in hell by demonstrating his justice. They have made themselves unfit for heaven, which would "nauseate" them by its praise of God. Moreover, God's judgment of that unfitness will make the saints happier as they see its appropriateness. They may have loved the damned on earth while they hoped for their salvation, but now the saints will see why God has damned them and they will rejoice that justice is being served. This teaching may seem heartless today, but it was routine in the Puritan tradition. Even the moderate Richard Baxter said that God will mock and laugh at the sufferings of the damned.[16]

---

14. WJE 19:360, 355; WJE 13:350.

15. Sermon on Ezek. 15:2–4 WJEO 49; WJE 20:181.

16. Sermon on Rom. 2:8–9, WJEO 50; WJE 13:419–20; WJE 20:105; sermon on Ezek. 15:2–4; sermon on Rev. 18:20, WJEO 48; Richard Baxter, *Works*, 23 vols. (London: James Duncan, 1830), 22:419; cited in Holmes, *God of Grace*, 205.

The latitudinarians and deists in Edwards's day were questioning the eternality of hell. But Edwards was insistent that hell would last "millions of years and millions of ages" without ever ending. It has to endure everlastingly, he argued, to be "proportionable" to the magnitude of the crime, which is infinite.[17] Sins differ in gravity but all are infinite, just as infinitely long cylinders can be of varying diameter or thickness. Against those like Archbishop of Canterbury John Tillotson, who proposed that God simply annihilated the wicked and caused them to cease to exist, Edwards replied with a host of rejoinders. The Bible indicates that the wicked will be "sensible" of their suffering and that there will be degrees of punishment, but annihilation contradicts these points. Annihilation falls short of just punishment because the wicked continue to sin and incur guilt in hell. Annihiliation would be unfair since many wicked persons enjoyed happy lives on earth as they oppressed the righteous, and so they merit punishment after their deaths. Annihilation contradicts the idea that human beings have immortal souls that cannot be destroyed. Finally, annihilation cannot be reconciled with Jesus' teachings that some sins are unforgiveable and that it would have been better for Judas never to have been born.[18] To those who saw hell as temporary and remedial, and those in hell as possible recipients of future grace, Edwards cited Hebrews 10:27 and other biblical texts indicating that God's final judgment is final. It also seems unrealistic, he argued, to think the horrors of hell would produce love for God, particularly in the absence of means such as preaching and scripture. Besides, the words that the Bible uses for hell ("forever and ever") are also used to describe the eternality of God and of heaven.[19] Edwards clearly rejected the universalism taught by one of his favorite authors, the Scotsman Chevalier Ramsay (1686–1743).[20]

---

17. Sermon on Rom. 2:8–9, WJEO 50; Jonathan L. Kvanvig protests that Edwards ignored unwitting sin. Edwards might reply that unwitting sin exists alongside knowing sin, which itself is worthy of damnation; Kvanvig, "Jonathan Edwards on Hell," in Paul Helm and Oliver D. Crisp, eds., *Jonathan Edwards: Philosophical Theologian* (Aldershot, UK: Ashgate, 2003), 11.

18. Tillotson, "Of the Eternity of Hell-Torments. A Sermon Preach'd before the Queen at White-Hall, March the 7th, 1689–90" (London, 1708); WJE 18:344; WJE 13:479; WJE 23:183–84; WJE 23:575–603; WJE 23:393, 407–408.

19. WJE 23:575, 603; Fiering, *Jonathan Edwards's Moral Thought*, 238–44; the best short essay on Edwards's doctrine of hell is William J. Wainwright, "Jonathan Edwards and the Doctrine of Hell," in Helm and Crisp, eds., *Jonathan Edwards*, 13–26.

20. Andrew Michael [Chevalier] Ramsay, *Philosophical Principles of Natural and Revealed Religion Unfolded in a Geographical Order*, 2 vols. (Glasgow: Robert Foulis, 1748–49), 1:430.

The Glorious Work of God's Spirit

Before the arrival of the last judgment and the new heavens and new earth, wrote Edwards, an exciting, earthly drama would ensue in two parts: a 250-year process of revival and persecution followed by a 1000-year millennium. Edwards came to this scenario as the result of years of analyzing English Protestant commentators on the Book of Revelation, such as John Bale, John Foxe, Thomas Brightman, John Cotton, Joseph Mede, Daniel Whitby, and especially Moses Lowman, whose *Paraphrase and Notes on the Revelation* (1737) was most often cited in Edwards's apocalyptic writings. Much of these authors' eschatological speculation hinged on their interpretation of Revelation's "seven seals" (Rev. 6), "seven trumpets" (Rev. 8–9, 11), and "seven vials" (Rev. 16). Edwards concluded that the opening of the seals represented the persecution of the early church by the heathen Roman Empire, the sounding of the trumpets stood for the attacks on the Christian Empire by barbarians and Muslims, and the pouring of the vials symbolized the assaults on Roman Catholicism that began just before the Reformation. It seems that Foxe and other anti-Catholic historians incited Edwards's hatred for the Roman papacy, and Cotton may have influenced his conviction that the papacy was the Antichrist (ch. 28). Edwards disagreed with Lowman on numerous details in the eschatological timetable, but Lowman confirmed for Edwards that the lowest days of the church had passed and that the future of the church would involve an advancement into "glorious times."[21]

The first phase of the final historical drama was to be "that glorious work of God, so often foretold in Scripture, which in the progress and issue of it, shall renew the world of mankind." Edwards here described a progressive, gradual transition in the world, during which all the world would be renewed. In his sermons on the history of redemption, he proposed that this "great work of God," paving the way for the millennium, would be wrought "gradually" amidst "violent and mighty opposition." In his *Humble Attempt* (1747), he wrote that "that great work of God's Spirit" would "before it is finished...issue in Antichrist's ruin."[22] Edwards followed "the afflictive model of progress" he found in Dutch Reformed scholasticism, especially Mastricht, who taught that better times lay in store for the church yet not without much tribulation.[23]

---

21. On these earlier commentators and the evolution of Edwards's eschatological thinking, see Stephen J. Stein's "Editor's Introduction" in WJE 5, especially 4–23, 43–59.

22. WJE 4:353; WJE 9:392, 394; 5:410–11, 425.

23. James West Davidson, *The Logic of Millennial Thought: Eighteenth-Century New England* (New Haven: Yale University Press, 1977), 127–75; Petrus van Mastricht, "Dispensation of the Covenant of Grace," in *Theoretico-Practica Theologia*, Book 8. For more on these

There would be a long, gradual period of revival and tribulation for the church that "would at last bring on the church's latter-day glory," or millennium. In *Humble Attempt*, Edwards estimated that it would take "one half century" for religion "in the power and purity of it" to "gain the upper hand through the Protestant world." Another "one half century" would be needed to "gain the ascendant in that which is now the popish world." A third half-century would be necessary to "prevail and subdue the greater part of the Mahometan [Islamic] world, and bring in the Jewish nation, in all their dispersions." Finally, "in the next whole century, the whole heathen world should be enlightened and converted to the Christian faith, throughout all parts of Africa, Asia, America and Terra Australis." In other words, it would be two hundred fifty years before this great work of God's Spirit would accomplish all that was necessary before the millennium could begin. That great era of peace and rest for the church would not come until about the year 2000.[24]

Many scholars have assumed that all this language about premillennial revivals was really about the millennium itself and that Edwards was therefore predicting the imminence of the millennium. The chief cause of this confusion has been a statement in *Some Thoughts Concerning the Revival* (1743), relating the Great Awakening to the future work of redemption: "This work of God's Spirit, that is so extraordinary and wonderful, is the dawning, or at least a prelude, of that glorious work of God, so often foretold in Scripture, which in the progress and issue of it, shall renew the world of mankind." Later in this same passage, Edwards said the glorious work of God "must be near." Yet four to five years earlier, in his "Apocalypse" notebook, Edwards had made it clear that the millennium would be a state of peace and rest—at least until a great apostasy came at the millennium's conclusion.[25] In contrast, the revivals leading up to it would be marked by struggle and conflict as the forces of Antichrist battled the newly emerging kingdom of God's Son.[26] So the period *before* the millennium would be a time of change and unrest, but the millennium itself would be a blissful epoch of peace:

---

pre-millennial revivals and Edwards's sources, see Gerald R. McDermott, *One Holy and Happy Society* (University Park, PA: Penn State Press, 1992), 77–90.

24. WJE 4:560; WJE 5:411. The same process is described in more detail in his *History of Redemption*: WJE 9:467–70.

25. WJE 4:353; WJE 5:177–79; the dating is in WJE 5:78.

26. See ch. 28, where we show that Antichrist is not simply to be equated with Roman Catholicism in Edwards's thought.

> The millennium is the sabbatism of the church, or the time of her rest. But surely the days of her sabbatism or rest don't begin, till she ceases to be any longer in travail.... And as long as the church still remains struggling and laboring, to bring to pass this effect, her travail ceases not.. The church from Christ's time to the millennium, is in a state of warfare, or her militant state; but during that sabbatism, [she] shall be in a triumphant state. The proper time of the church's rest and triumph can't be said to be come, till all her enemies are subdued.[27]

Edwards stated both here in 1747 and in his redemption sermons in 1739 that the great work of God preceding the millennium would be wrought gradually in the midst of violent opposition.

In *Some Thoughts Concerning the Revival*, Edwards wondered aloud as to whether the New England awakenings might "prove to be the dawning of a general revival."[28] Yet for Edwards the millennium was never considered a revival as such, with all of its attendant emotional and religious upheavals. He never used the word "millennium" in the passages in *Some Thoughts* that some scholars thought were a prediction of an imminent millennium. "General revival" was a better term for "that great work of God's Spirit" because it would consist of precisely that—a worldwide series of revivals. So having scrutinized Edwards's statements in *Some Thoughts Concerning the Revival* alongside his other writings, one can see that he never tied the revivals of the Great Awakening to the arrival of the millennium.

Instead Edwards predicted that, at the end of this great work of the Spirit, there would be a great battle. "All the forces of Antichrist, and also Mohammedanism [Islam] and heathenism, should be united, all the forces of Satan's visible kingdom through the whole world of mankind.... This will be, as it were, the dying struggles of the old serpent, a battle wherein he will fight as one that is almost desperate." The fighting will be desperate and violent, but "Christ and his church shall in this battle obtain a complete and entire victory over their enemies."[29] Then the millennium will begin.

The Millennium

For Edwards, the millennium would be Christ's third coming to set up his kingdom. His first coming was in the apostolic era when he set up his kingdom

---

27. WJE 5:178–79.
28. WJE 9.392, 394; WJE 4:466.
29. WJE 9:463–64; see also WJE 5:196–97, 394.

in a spiritual sense and destroyed his enemies by starting the church. The second coming effected the "destruction of the heathen Roman empire" in Constantine's time. The fourth and last coming will be "his coming to the last judgment, which is the event principally signified in scripture by Christ's coming in his kingdom."[30]

Many scholars have attributed to Edwards the belief that the millennium would begin or be centered in America. For in his *Some Thoughts Concerning the Revival*, he wrote, "'Tis not unlikely that this work of God's Spirit...is the dawning, or at least a prelude, of that glorious work of God, so often foretold in Scripture, which in the progress and issue of it, shall renew the world of mankind.... And there are many things that make it probable that this work will begin in America." At roughly the same time, Edwards wrote in his "Images" notebook that in "approaching" times "the world shall be supplied with spiritual treasures from America." In 1959, C. C. Goen suggested that Edwards here entertained the idea that God would use America to renovate the world. Other scholars claimed that, for Edwards, Northampton was the "city on a hill" that would knit together all Protestant America and on behalf of the world inaugurate the millennium. America was to be the center of future glory, the locus of the new heavens and new earth.[31]

It is difficult, though, to reconcile these claims with the larger corpus. Edwards almost always situated the focal point of the millennium in Canaan and described the millennium itself in international terms.[32] "The kingdom of God...shall not be like the kingdoms of earthly kings, set up with outward pomp, in some particular place, which shall be especially the royal city, and seat of the kingdom." Rather, it "shall universally prevail, and...be extended over the whole habitable earth."[33] Neither New England nor America was a significant factor in Edwards's description of the millennium. Throughout his sermons on the history of redemption, the millennium was always depicted in global terms. The last mention Edwards made of America and the millennium was in his *Humble Attempt* (1747). There America was portrayed as

---

30. WJE 9:351.

31. WJE 4:353; WJE 11:101; C. C. Goen, "Jonathan Edwards: A New Departure in Eschatology," *Church History* 28 (1959): 25–40; Sacvan Bercovitch, *The American Jeremiad* (Cambridge, MA: Harvard University Press, 1978), 106; Alan Heimert, *Religion and the American Mind: From the Great Awakening to the Revolution* (Cambridge, MA: Harvard University Press, 1966), 59–94; Conrad Cherry, ed., *God's New Israel: Religious Interpretations of American Destiny*, rev. edn. (Chapel Hill, NC: University of North Caroline Press, 1998), 55–59.

32. WJE 5:134.

33. WJE 4:235; WJE 9:480.

spiritually bankrupt and the coming revivals as a spiritual rescue operation for an otherwise doomed land.[34]

In religious terms, the millennium would be everything that Northampton was not. It would embody every virtue and mark of piety that Edwards longed to see among his parishioners (ch. 29). In the millennial time, "religion shall in every respect be uppermost in the world." Political leaders will be "eminent in holiness" and possessed by "vital piety." Arminianism and other doctrinal deviations will be "exploded" and theological problems that long perplexed the faithful will be resolved.[35] Piety will be sincere and not pretended or hypocritical. The church will be marked by "excellent order," free from wild claims of "enthusiasts" that they have heard voices from God. There will not be "prophets, and men endowed with the gifts of tongues and of working miracles, as was the case in the times of the apostles." For this will be the time of the best gifts and graces in the church, and these charismatic signs are inferior. The Spirit of God will then be poured out in the "more excellent way" of love, not in miracles or impressions of divine voices.[36]

Millennial society will not to be limited to the polite society of Western whites. Transcending the ethnocentric and racialist mindset of most eighteenth-century New Englanders, Edwards proclaimed that "the Negroes and Indians will be divines" and theological treatises will be "published in Africa, in Ethiopia, in Turkey." He prophesied that "the most divine and angelic strains [will come] from among the Hottentots," an African tribe that was used in the eighteenth century to symbolize intellectual and cultural inferiority. "The press," he went on, "shall groan in wild Tartary," the central Asian habitat notorious for savagery.[37]

During the seventeenth and eighteenth centuries, some debated whether Christ would reign in the millennium in bodily form or as a spiritual presence.[38] Like most of his contemporaries, Edwards came down on the side of the spiritualists. Christ's body would remain in heaven, while on earth he reigned "by his Spirit." From heaven, he would be better able to strengthen the church's faith and "greatly to encourage and comfort them."[39] Human nature will still

---

34. WJE 9:479–86; WJE 5:357–58.

35. WJE 9:480–81.

36. WJE 8:361–62.

37. WJE 9:480; WJE 13:212.

38. James West Davidson, *The Logic of Millennial Thought: Eighteenth-Century New England* (New Haven, CT: Yale University Press, 1977), 75.

39. WJE 18:537–38.

be sinful, but because of the great effusions of the Holy Spirit, the religious virtue of the human heart will be multiplied exponentially. The consequence will be "the most universal peace, love and sweet harmony" among humankind. Millennial society will be the mirror image of the heavenly society of saints, angels and the Trinity—intelligent beings united in common consent to being-in-general. This beautiful society will be a happy society—"unspeakably happy in the view of his glory."[40] A part of human happiness during the millennium will come from its "great temporal prosperity," which in turn will be fueled by a "vast increase of knowledge and understanding." Inventions and discoveries will be commonplace, aided by global communication. The result will be "one community, one body in Christ." Yet if the world will be a global community, it will not be ruled by a single world government. Instead Edwards envisioned a spiritual federalism in which the nations retain their self-governing integrity but will be "knit together" into "one amiable society." The world will be at peace, without the age-old confusion, war, and bloodshed.[41]

The Last Judgment and New Heavens and Earth

Edwards's millennium is to be a period of absolute stability and peace for the bulk of its duration. Only at its very end will there be a break in its bliss, when the newly freed Satan will lead a great apostasy. After this insurrection is put down, the Last Judgment shall ensue. Its purpose will be fourfold: to display God's justice and majesty to the cosmos, to rectify wrongs done on earth when the righteous were condemned and the wicked acquitted, to reward publicly the saints, the angels, and Christ, and to shame the wicked as part of their punishment.[42]

When the last trumpet sounds, God will take "all the scattered particles of dead bodies" from around the world so that souls shall once again be rejoined to their bodies, never to be separated again. The bodies of the redeemed shall have "a superlative beauty" while the bodies of the damned will be "hideous" and "loathsome." The wicked and devils will be arraigned before the judgment seat of Christ, whose throne will "be fixed in the air in the region of the clouds," from where he can be seen by all persons in the world. The saints will then be caught up in the clouds to meet the Lord in the air.[43]

---

40. WJE 9:483–84; WJE 8:564; WJE 5:338.
41. WJE 5:338–39; WJE 9:480; WJE 5:339; WJE 9:482–83.
42. WJE 14:514–17.
43. WJE 14:525; WJE 9:498.

Christ will open "the book of God's remembrance and the book of Scripture," the first as evidence of deeds to be judged and the second as the rule of judgment. The saints will be justified by faith but judged by their works—both their outward deeds and the inward workings of the heart. Their works will give evidence of what they believed. But because those works fall infinitely short of the law's demands, they will plead that the Judge himself has fulfilled the law for them. He will then cancel their debts, changing their account from debit to credit. When the law's curse and condemnation no longer stand against them, they shall receive the reward of eternal life, as promised in the glorious gospel of Jesus Christ. Thus judgment will proceed first by the law and then by the gospel.[44]

Then Christ the Judge shall sentence those before him. He will tell the wicked on his left to depart from him and to enter the everlasting fire prepared for the devil and his angels. "What dolorous groans and cries," Edwards exclaims, "what trembling and wringing of hands, and chattering of teeth and tearing of hair, will there be!" But the "blessed" on his right will hear his invitation to join him "where he goes, to dwell where he dwells, to enjoy him and to partake with him." They shall ascend with him to heaven while the earth is "converted into a great lake and liquid globe of fire, a vast, shoreless ocean of fire." The sun, which was once an instrument of God's goodness, shall now become an instrument of his wrath. It shall seem to fall upon the earth and transform it into a universe of liquid fire. God, who displayed his power by creating the world, will now show his power "by dashing it in pieces in his wrath." All this will happen because the world murdered God in the person of Jesus Christ. Since "the earth is the place where he was murdered and his blood shed," the earth will be destroyed by fire.[45]

Christ will then deliver the kingdom back to the Father in heaven, where the church will be brought to its consummation of glory. Its new settled abode will be in heaven with the Holy Trinity, not upon earth. But heaven will be glorified anew and thus become a "new heaven." This is what the Bible means when it speaks of the "new Jerusalem coming down out of heaven." Everything will be "altered" and "new-formed." Because the church has moved from the earth to a newly renewed heaven, the latter will be a "new earth." This is analogous to Zion's move from David's city to Mount Moriah when the ark moved. Thus the New Jerusalem is one and the same with the new heaven

---

44. WJE 14:526–29.

45. WJE 14:530; WJE 20:93, 181, 182. Edwards based his view of the earth being destroyed by fire principally on 2 Peter 3:7, 12.

and the new earth. Both phrases refer to the church itself and to the place of habitation for the church.[46] Edwards's depiction concludes with what Robert W. Jenson calls "God's fugue," in which "the harmony of our love, finally perfectly harmonized with the supreme harmony, can only be the inclusion in the divine fugue of as many voices as there are blessed creatures."[47]

For many thinkers in the Reformed tradition, eschatology was a theological appendage. But for Edwards eschatology was both central and integral to his thought. His philosophy of history presumed that God directed every atom in the universe toward a cosmic conclusion. His biblical typology suggested that all of nature and history teem with types of future, end-time realities. Eschatology spilled over into Edwards's private life, providing delight and solace during his years of pastoral difficulty in Northampton and Stockbridge.[48] Though unusual for the eighteenth-century, his eschatologically-driven theology may be better appreciated and understood today, when both biblical and systematic theologians have rediscovered the role of the future in Christian reflection.[49]

---

46. WJE 13:442–44; WJE 18:161, 376–83; WJE 20:210–22. For Edwards, "Zion" was the designation for Israel's spiritual center yet was not necessarily a particular place.

47. Jenson, "The End Is Music," in Sang Lee and Alan Guelzo, eds. *Edwards in our Time: Jonathan Edwards and Contemporary Theological Issues* (Grand Rapids, MI: Eerdmans, 1999), 170.

48. In the *Personal Narrative*, Edwards wrote, "My mind has been much entertained and delighted, with the Scripture promises and prophecies, of the future glorious advancement of Christ's kingdom on earth"; WJE 16:800; see also 797.

49. For example, the works of Wolfhart Pannenberg, Jürgen Moltmann, and Carl Braaten.

36
Christianity and Other Religions

UNTIL VERY RECENTLY, the vast majority of readers and even scholars of Jonathan Edwards have assumed that the eighteenth-century theologian had little or no interest in religions beyond Judaism and Christianity, and certainly no knowledge of the great traditions beyond Palestine. Recent research, however, has shown that, from the very beginning of his career, Edwards showed interest in other religions and that he seemed to become more and more intrigued the older he got. Throughout his career, he scoured both New and Old England for whatever information he could get about the "heathen," and by his last decade he was busy scribbling into his private notebooks hundreds of pages of data about, and ruminations on, the relationship between Christ and the gods.[1] In this chapter, we will suggest that deism was one major stimulus to Edwards's fascination with the religions and will then outline Edwards's three responses. One goes back to Adam and the sons of Noah (the *prisca theologia*), a second is based on Edwards's conviction that God speaks through all of nature and history (typology), and a third involves the question as to whether non-Christians can be saved (his dispositional soteriology).

The Prisca Theologia

The fifteenth- and sixteenth-century explorations of East Asia and the New World discovered not just spices and trade routes but also "heathen" people who were reputed to have better morals than most European Christians. Seventeenth-century geographers estimated that only one-sixth of the planet had heard the Christian gospel, so, according to Protestant and Catholic exclusivists in that century, at least five-sixths of the world's population were doomed to hell. Beginning with Lord Herbert of Cherbury, deists suggested that the God responsible for this scenario was a monster. In an early version of what the twentieth century has called the "scandal of particularity," deists

---

1. Edwards never traveled to England but wrote friends there asking about new books. On his search for books about other religions, see Gerald R. McDermott, *Jonathan Edwards Confronts the Gods* (New York: Oxford University Press, 2000), 92–93; WJE 26:17–18, 106–107.

complained that a God who revealed himself only to particular people in particular times and places could not be the true God, who has revealed himself through reason to all. They delighted in displaying the moral virtues of non-Christians, and contrasting the heathen who were damned but morally good with Christians who were saved but morally bad.[2]

Edwards, no doubt disturbed by deist use of the religions to attack the Christian God's goodness and justice, worked hard to learn about the religions. He knew of, tried to get, and perhaps read many of the travelogues, dictionaries, and encyclopedias of religion available in his time. The books cited in his "Catalogue" include George Sale's translation of the *Qur'an*, reports of the Jesuits in China, an analysis of the Qabbalah, comparative mythology, and a wide range of dictionaries and encyclopedias of religion—from skeptic Peter Bayle's *Historical and Critical Dictionary* to Daniel Defoe's *Dictionary of All Religions Antient and Modern*.[3]

Many of the writers whom Edwards read understood the religions in terms defined by what was called the *prisca theologia* (ancient theology). This was a tradition in apologetic theology, resting on a number of misdated texts (the Hermetica, Chaldean oracles, Orpheia, and Sybilline oracles) that attempted to prove that vestiges of true religion were taught by the ancient Greeks and in other non-Christian traditions. Typically it alleged that all human beings were originally given knowledge of true religion (monotheism, the Trinity, the doctrine of *creatio ex nihilo*) by Jews or by tradition going back to Noah's good sons (Shem and Japheth) or to people before the Flood such as Enoch or Adam. Then it passed down to Zoroaster, Hermes Trismegistus, Brahmins and Druids, Orpheus, Pythagoras, Plato, and the Sybils.[4]

---

2. McDermott, *Jonathan Edwards Confronts the Gods*, 24–25, 130–31. We use the term "exclusivist" for those who believed salvation requires the conscious acceptance of the gospel of Jesus Christ during one's earthly sojourn.

3. He also read or tried to get William Turner's *History of All Religions* (1695), Isaac Watts's *Harmony of All Religions* (1742), Samuel Shuckford's *Sacred and Profane History* (1727), Ephraim Chambers' *Philosophical Dictionary* (1728), Broughton's *Historical Library of Religion Antient and Modern* (1737), and Thomas Dyche's *A New General English Dictionary* (1725)—all of which featured articles on non-Christian religions. See WJE 26 for entries on all these titles.

4. On the *prisca theologia*, see D.P. Walker, "Orpheus the Theologian and Renaissance Platonists," *Journal of the Warburg and Courtauld Institutes* 16 (1953): 100–20; idem, *The Ancient Theology: Studies in Christian Platonism from the Fifteenth to the Eighteenth Centuries* (London: Duckworth, 1972); idem, *The Decline of Hell: Seventeenth-Century Discussions of Eternal Torment* (London: Routledge, 1964); Frances A. Yates, *Giordano Bruno and the Hermetic Tradition* (Chicago: University of Chicago Press, 1964); Charles B. Schmitt, "Perennial Philosophy: From Agostino Steuco to Leibniz," *Journal of the History of Ideas* 27 (1966): 505–32; Arthur J. Droge, *Homer or Moses? Early Christian Interpretations of the History of Culture* (Tubingen: J.C.B. Mohr, 1989); and Jean Seznec, *The Survival of the Pagan Gods: The Mythological Tradition and Its Place in Renaissance Humanism and Art* (New York: Bollingen, 1953).

The *prisca theologia* was developed first by Philo, Justin Martyr, Clement of Alexandria, Origen, Lactantius, and Eusebius to show that the greatest pagan philosophers had borrowed from the wisdom of the Jews, and then in the Renaissance by Marsilio Ficino and Giovanni Pico della Mirandola to synthesize Neoplatonism and Christian dogma.[5] For these ancients and medievals, the question was whether Greco-Roman philosophy was older and wiser than the Judeo-Christian tradition; Christians generally assumed people had access to both. But in the seventeenth and eighteenth centuries, the question was access to revelation: Was God unjust because he had not given revelation to everyone? Both Catholics and Protestants used the *prisca theologia* to argue God's justice on the grounds that he had given revelation to nearly everyone from the very beginning. The "Jesuit Figurists," for example, used that claim to win acceptance of their mission in China by trying to show that China worshipped the true God two thousand years before Christ. A number of Protestant thinkers who used the *prisca theologia* were read carefully and taken seriously by Edwards. First was Scotsman Andrew Michael "Chevalier" Ramsay (1686–1743), who found Trinitarian monotheism among the ancient Egyptians, Persians, Greeks, and Chinese. Ramsay tried to prove that God gave complete revelation of the essential Christian doctrines to the earliest patriarchs, so that most pagan religions teach a trinity similar to the Neoplatonic triad. Edwards also used extensively the work of Philip Skelton (1707–87), a Church of Ireland divine who wrote two anti-deist volumes.[6]

Theophilus Gale (1628–78) and Ralph Cudworth (1617–88) were two earlier proponents of the *prisca theologia* who influenced Edwards. Gale's magnum opus, *The Court of the Gentiles* (1677), was a massive, four-volume work dedicated to the proposition that all ancient languages and learning—particularly philosophical works—were derived from the Jews. As Numenius of Apamea put it in a line noted by Edwards, "What is Plato but Moses speaking in the Attick language?"[7] Cudworth, the Cambridge Platonist philosopher, used

---

5. Even Augustine seems to have been influenced by this tradition. In his *Retractions*, he wrote, "What is now called Christian religion has existed among the ancients, and was not absent from the beginning of the human race, until Christ came in the flesh: from which time true religion, which existed already, began to be called Christian" (1.12.3); Saint Augustine, *The Retractions* (Washington, DC: Catholic University of America Press, 1968), 52.

6. Philip Skelton, *Deism Revealed* (London: Printed for A. Millar, 1751). There were many Neoplatonic variations on the theme of the divine reality and its three manifestations, but most spoke of the One, the Divine Mind, and the World Soul.

7. WJE 23:548. The quote is part of Edwards's extract from Andrew Michael Ramsay, *Philosophical Principles of Natural and Revealed Religion unfolded in a Geographical Order*, 2 vols. (Glasgow: Robert Foulis, 1748).

much of his *True Intellectual System of the Universe* (1678) to show that the wiser pagans were Trinitarian monotheists, and not unacquainted with the true (i.e., Christian) God.

Edwards was clearly impressed by these proponents of the *prisca theologia*.[8] He copied lengthy extracts from their works into his private notebooks, but did not use their ideas slavishly. As Denis Diderot said, imitation is continual invention. From his marginal notes and recapitulation of the tradition in various notebooks, it is clear that Edwards was selectively and creatively refashioning the tradition to serve his own polemical needs. His principal purpose was to show, against the deists, that nearly all humans have received revelation, and therefore all knowledge of true religion among the heathen is from revelation rather than the light of natural reason. Perhaps more importantly, five-sixths of the world had *not* been deprived of the basic truths of the gospel.

Edwards went to great lengths detailing in his notebooks the religious truths possessed by the heathen. From Hugo Grotius he learned that the Greeks believed that the Spirit moved on the waters at the beginning of the world, knew that one can commit adultery in the heart, and understood that one must forgive and love one's enemies. Vergil, Seneca, Juvenal, and Ovid, Edwards noted, confessed that our original nature was corrupt. Ramsay taught him that the Hindu *Vedas* and the Chinese *I Ching* contained stories about a hero who expiated crimes by his own sufferings, and that many heathen from different traditions acknowledged a divine incarnation and realized that virtue comes only by an infusion of grace. Edwards noted in his *Blank Bible* that many heathen stories about gods and goddesses were actually distortions of Hebrew counterparts. Saturn, for example, was a transformation and conglomeration of Adam, Noah, and Abraham; Hercules was a Greek rendition of Joshua; Bacchus, of Nimrod, Moses, and the Hebrew deity; the myths of Apis and Serapis were Egyptian retellings of the Joseph story.[9]

In his own appropriation of the *prisca theologia*, Edwards said that the heathen learned these truths by what could be called a trickle-down process of revelation. In the "first ages" of the world, the fathers of the nations received revelation of the great religious truths, directly or indirectly, from God himself.[10] These truths were then passed down by tradition from one generation

---

8. Edwards may have been introduced to the *prisca theologia* by Samuel Johnson, his tutor at Yale; Norman Fiering, *Moral Philosophy at Seventeenth-Century Harvard* (Chapel Hill, NC: University of North Carolina Press, 1981), 15.

9. WJE 20:344, 356, 456–58; WJE 23:478–79, 562–64, 573; WJE 24:126–30, 325, 153, 188.

10. WJE 20:222–26, 309–11, 308. Usually Edwards was ambiguous about the location of the original deposit of revelation. Only occasionally did he pinpoint Adam; in Miscellany 884 he said that Adam learned the moral law from God and taught it with great clarity to his

to the next. Unfortunately, there was also a religious law of entropy at work. Human finitude and corruption inevitably caused the revelation to be distorted, resulting in superstition and idolatry.

From Ramsay Edwards learned that the breakdown was caused in part by a problem of language. All original peoples—even the Gauls, Germans, and Britons—shared hieroglyphs with the Egyptians to represent divine truths as taught by Noah. Over the course of time, pagans dissociated the symbol from its referent: "Men attached themselves to the letter and the signs without understanding the spirit and the thing signified." This accounted for idols and "vile superstitions." It also accounted for the similarity between stories of Christ's sufferings and legends of pagan heroes: the heathen took the symbols of Christ's sufferings and applied them to their own champions. By this mechanism and others, the original purity of divine truth was continually breaking down, corrupted by profane and demonic mixture. God used the Jews to retard the process of degeneration by periodically acting on their behalf with miracles, which reminded the heathen of the traditions they had once learned from their fathers but subsequently forgot.[11]

In *Notes on the Scriptures*—his private commentary on selected biblical passages—Edwards recapitulated this drama: "The knowledge of true religion was for some time kept up in the world by tradition. And there were soon great corruptions and apostasies crept in, and much darkness overwhelmed great part of the world." By the time of Moses, most of the truth that had previously been taught by tradition was now lost. So "God took care that there might be something new, [which] should be very public, and of great fame, and much taken notice of abroad, in the world heard, that might be sufficient to lead sincere inquirers to the true God." Hence the heathen nations in the Ancient Near East heard about the Exodus of the Jews from Egypt, the miracles God performed for them in the wilderness, Joshua's conquests of the Canaanites, and the sun standing still. The defeated Canaanites fled to Africa, Asia, Europe, and the isles of the sea "to carry the tidings of those things ... so that, in a manner, the whole world heard of these great things."[12]

---

descendants (WJE 20:142–43). In *Original Sin*, he wrote that Adam "continued alive near two thirds of the time that passed before the flood," so that most people alive until the flood heard from Adam what "passed between him and his Creator in paradise" (WJE 3:170). Most often, however, he simply referred to the fathers of the nations as identical to or descended from Noah's sons.

11. WJE 23:190–91; WJE 20:310–11; WJE 13:424.

12. WJE 15:369–72.

After these wondrous acts of God, knowledge of true religion was maintained for several generations. But by the time of David, much had been forgotten and distorted again. So God acted once more, this time for David and Solomon, "to make his people Israel, who had the true religion, [be] taken notice of in the heathen [nations]." The diaspora after the Babylonian captivity spread knowledge of the true God even further abroad, so that "the heathen world had opportunity by...the Jews dispersed abroad in the world...to have come to the knowledge of the true God."[13] And if it were not enough, God saw to it that heathen philosophers came looking for news of the great events that had occurred among the Israelites. Heathen "wise men" and "philosophers" obtained "scraps of light and truth...by travelling from one country to another," especially Judea, Greece, and Phoenicia. Edwards noted that Plato, for instance, had come to Egypt to learn what he could of the Jewish religion.[14]

The New England pastor was always quick to note that heathen religion and philosophy contained "infinite absurdities." But he learned from the *prisca theologia* that among the absurdities there were enough "scraps of...truth" among the heathen so that "the nations of the world, if their heart had been well disposed to seek after the truth, might have had some means to have led 'em in their sincere and diligent inquiries to the knowledge of the true God." Edwards found one way, then, to respond to the theological difficulties posed by the travelers' reports from the Americas and the East Asia. He agreed with the deists that the problem should not be ignored and he disagreed with earlier Reformed scholastics who held that non-Christian faiths could attain only to knowledge of a Creator, not to that of a Redeemer.[15] In embracing the *prisca theologia*, Edwards appropriated an ancient, pre-Protestant tradition to address eighteenth-century concerns about God's justice and goodness. In the process, he reshaped Reformed theology and reconfigured Christian history. In Edwards's new version of history, God was still good and just because the knowledge of God the Redeemer had been available to all peoples from the beginning.

---

13. WJE 15:371–72. This shows that (pace Greg Gilbert) for Edwards there were opportunities after Moses' time for the heathen to know the true God through the *prisca theologia*. See Gilbert, "The Nations Will Worship: Jonathan Edwards and the Salvation of the Heathen," *Trinity Journal* 23, new series (2002): 69.

14. WJE 19:713; WJE 23:447.

15. WJE 23:452, 245; WJE 15:369. Following Calvin, they distinguished between knowledge of God the Creator that is given through nature and conscience but has been distorted by sin, and knowledge of God the Redeemer that is given through scripture; Richard A. Muller, *Post-Reformation Reformed Dogmatics, Vol. 1, Prolegomena to* Theology (Grand Rapids, MI: Baker, 1987), 178–79.

Typology and World Religions

We saw in chapter 8 that early eighteenth-century deists John Toland, Thomas Chubb, and Matthew Tindal used the world religions to relativize Christianity, while Edwards used his typology to argue that God was constantly communicating truths wherever the eye could see and the ear could hear. God spoke in the history of religions to point persons of all faith traditions to the true religion, Christianity.

By Edwards's lights, this meant that God planted types of true religion in religious systems that were ultimately false. God outwitted the devil by using diabolically deceptive religions to teach true religion. In an early *Miscellanies* entry, Edwards suggested that the heathen practice of human sacrifice was the result of the devil's mimicry of the animal sacrifice that God had instituted after the Fall.[16] All cultures practiced religious sacrifice not because of the light of nature but by God's express commandment immediately after he revealed the covenant of grace in Genesis 3:15: "And I will put enmity between thee and the woman, and between thy seed and her seed; it shall bruise thy head, and thou shalt bruise his heel." The skins with which God clothed the first couple in Gen. 3:21 were taken from animals sacrificed by God, who taught them thereby that only the righteousness won by Christ's sacrifice could cover their sins.[17]

Animal sacrifice—the primary type of Christ in the Old Testament, and an ancient heathen custom—implied the necessity of *propitiation*, that is, an offering to appease the anger of God or the gods. Imitating this divine type, the devil led the heathen to sacrifice human beings, and even their own children. Satan believed he had "promote[d] his own interests," outsmarting God, but God outflanked the devil. He permitted this diabolical deception because through it "the devil prepared the Gentile world for receiving...this human sacrifice, Jesus Christ." Similarly, the devil induced human beings to worship idols and think that the heathen deities were united to their images. Yet God used this deception as well for his own purposes, to prepare the Gentile mind for the concept of incarnation, perfectly realized in Christ: "And so indeed was [the] heathenish doctrines of deities' being united to images and the heathenish fables of heroes being begotten [by] gods, a preparation for their receiving the doctrine of the incarnation, of the Deity's dwelling in a human [body], and the Son of God's being conceived in the womb of a virgin by the power of the Spirit of [God]."[18]

---

16. WJE 13:391–92.
17. WJE 9:134–36.
18. WJE 13:391–92.

Twice, then, in the history of religions, God used false religion to teach true religion. In each case the devil's machinations were overruled and ironically inverted by divine wisdom. Practices considered by all Jews and Christians to be abominable—human sacrifice and idol worship—were transformed by a divine plan into teaching devices to prepare the heathen for true religion. In both cases, God used non-Christian religions typologically to point to Christian truths. The ancient sacrifices taught more, though, than incarnation and propitiation. They showed the heathen that God would not pardon sins without satisfaction being made, that sin "must be suffered for." They demonstrated God's jealousy and hatred for sin, indicated the need for fear of God and respect for the glory of his holiness, and suggested to sinners that they must trust in God's mercy.[19]

At the beginning of his career, when he was pastoring in New York in the spring of 1723, Edwards told his congregation that the heathen nations did not understand the meaning of their own sacrifices. Then, and throughout the rest of his career, Edwards made it clear that only those with a regenerate or spiritually awakened "sense of the heart" were able to read the divine signs in the creation and, we can now add, in the history of religions. At times he suggested that there were some heathen who may have taken advantage of the light they had been given through Jewish traditions and from the customs of their own forefathers, and with the light of the Holy Spirit might have been able to understand the types. This would have been by a special divine gift, not conferred by any natural knowledge available to all the heathen. But his conviction that most of the heathen would probably never understand did not keep him from noting the wealth of religious knowledge that could be known—though was generally not known—by those who lived outside the Jewish and Christian spheres.[20]

There were several reasons why non-Christian religions abounded with genuine types of true religion. The first was that, as we have already seen, most religions shared a common linguistic source. Edwards followed Chevalier Ramsay in believing that both Christian and heathen religions could be traced back to a universal language of hieroglyphics that represented "the divine mysteries of our holy religion, which the first heathens had learned from the ancient tradition of the Noevian patriarchs." Over time, the meaning

---

19. WJE 13:405–406.

20. WJE 10:594. Edwards noted in his private notebooks the missiological implications of the *prisca theologia*—that these pointers to Christ and his redemption might have helped prepare the heathen for the gospel; WJE 23:85.

of the signs was forgotten.[21] What is more, the fathers of the nations received their wisdom chiefly by tradition from wise men of the church of God, to whom divine instructions had been given in the form of "symbols and emblems." The holy men "in all nations" imitated this manner of representing divine things in "parables" and "types," so they delivered their own wisdom in "allegories, enigmas, [and] symbolic representations." For this reason, the Egyptians and others used "hieroglyphics to represent divine things or things appertaining to their gods and their religion."[22]

It is striking that Edwards linked Egyptian sacred writings to "holy men [who] were led by the Spirit of God." Even if, as he makes clear elsewhere, he regarded most of Egyptian religion as abominable, he held nonetheless that there were significant formal similarities between Christianity and various non-Christian religions. The relationship between these religions was not one of complete discontinuity but of partial continuity. They shared common mythical structures, common linguistic origins, and a common typical form of representation. There was also continuity in content. As we saw earlier, Edwards believed that the heathen had an elementary understanding of propitiatory sacrifice and divine incarnation. Edwards filled his notebooks with reflections on doctrines that the heathen shared with Christians—from the Trinity and a "middle" God who expiated sins to eternal punishment and the notion that "all things owed their beginning and production to love."[23] These heathen notions were distorted and incomplete versions of the truth. Yet to the extent that they pointed toward Christ's work of redemption in all its intricacy, they were types as much as human sacrifices were types of Christ's self-offering.

Hence for Edwards the Christian faith could now be seen in relation to other religions, situated at one end of a long continuum that included other faiths. It was at the end because it alone pointed unambiguously to the true reality or antitype—Christ's work of redemption. Edwards thus sought to uphold God's incomprehensibility as well as God's particularity in historical revelation and in the person of Christ. On the one hand, God was beyond human understanding, but on the other hand, God had stooped down to represent himself by means of the broken language of types and symbols. This was a tension Edwards could live with.

---

21. WJE 23:190–91.

22. WJE 11:193–94.

23. See, for example, WJE 13:301–302, 405–406; WJE 23:98–99.

FIGURE 36.1 Edwards's view of non-Christian religions was based in part on his experiences with Native Americans; Chief Hendrick was a friend of the Stockbridge mission (*Portrait of Hendrick, Mohawk chief, full length standing holding tomahawk with camp scene in background*. Prints & Photographs Division, Library of Congress, LC-US2C2-664).

Dispositional Soteriology

The third approach Edwards used was what might be called dispositional soteriology. As we saw in chapter 33, for Edwards being human meant having a "disposition" manifested in one or more "habits." Drawing on a tradition that originated with Aristotle and was developed by Thomas Aquinas and Reformed Protestant thinkers, he believed that a habit is an active tendency that moves a person to be and do what he or she is and does. This tendency remains even when there is no opportunity for its exercise, though it will always manifest itself when it has opportunity. When Edwards spoke of a "holy disposition" (i.e., the disposition of the regenerate), he meant "an active and causal power" that, if given opportunity, would produce holy effects. As

Edwards put it, "All habits [are] a law that God has fixed, that such actions upon such occasions should be exerted."²⁴

What are these actions or effects? In other words, what does a regenerate disposition look like? Very early in his career, Edwards answered this question and never diverged from its basic outline in the years that followed. In Miscellany 39, Edwards declared what he thought to be common to Christians, Jews under the Old Testament, and all other true religionists "from the beginning of the world," namely, "a sense of the dangerousness of sin, and of the dreadfulness of God's anger... [such a conviction of] their wickedness, that they trusted to nothing but the mere mercy of God, and then bitterly lamented and mourned for their sins."²⁵ Just a short time earlier, Edwards had written that this inner disposition is the only thing necessary for salvation. No particular act, even the act of receiving Christ through faith, is strictly necessary: "The disposition is all that can be said to be absolutely necessary. The act [of receiving Christ] cannot be proved to be absolutely necessary.... 'Tis the disposition or principle is the thing God looks at."²⁶

To illustrate this point, Edwards referred to the Old Testament. The ancient Israelites did not receive Christ in any conscious, explicit manner, but they had the proper disposition toward God which alone is necessary for salvation:

> It need not be doubted but that many of the ancient Jews before Christ were saved without the sensible exertions of those acts in that manner which is represented as necessary by some divines, because they had not those occasions nor were under circumstances that would draw them out; though without doubt *they had the disposition, which alone is absolutely necessary now, and at all times, and in all circumstances is equally necessary.*²⁷

Now Edwards's subject in this entry is "conversion," and he begins by stating that for salvation there must be "reception of Christ" and "a believing of what we are taught in the gospel concerning him." But his appeal to Old Testament

---

24. WJE 13:358.

25. WJE 13:221–22.

26. WJE 13:214.

27. WJE 13:214; emph. added.

saints who could not believe the New Testament gospel shows that the most essential ingredient in conversion is a certain disposition. The manner of expressing that disposition—that is, receiving Christ—is secondary in the case of those who did not have access to the gospel. Only the disposition is primary, and confessing Jesus as Lord could not have been essential under the Old Testament dispensation.

Edwards used the illustration of a man who dies suddenly and "not in the actual exercise of faith." He presumed that this man had already professed his faith in Christ and "what we are taught in the gospel concerning him." Yet at the point of death, presumably, he was not thinking about Jesus Christ or the gospel. This man was still saved nevertheless because "'tis his disposition that saves him." This entry reveals an important element in Edwards's thinking about salvation: the precise expression of faith was less important than its underlying disposition. Edwards indeed could not think about disposition and faith apart from Christ's work and Spirit—as we saw in chapters 20, 23, 24, and 25. But he also affirmed that God sometimes infuses a regenerate disposition prior to any explicit conversion to Christ. For while the character of a saving disposition is constant, God's religious and moral expectations differ according to the degree of revelation available to the person in question. God could overlook ungodly behavior in his saints at various times as long as their disposition was pleasing.[28]

God also overlooked faulty religious knowledge. Early in his pastorate at Northampton, Edwards conceded privately that the Jewish saints of the Old Testament did not know about love for enemies, universal love for all humanity, monogamy, or loving one another as Christ has loved us. Yet they were saved.[29] During his last decade of life, Edwards became convinced that some heathen had more religious knowledge and even more virtue than many Old Testament saints. Many of the Greek and Roman moralists, for example, knew that we ought to love and forgive our enemies, return good for evil, and practice monogamy. Other pagan philosophers knew about infused grace, the necessity of grace for attaining virtue, the Trinity, the incarnation, and redemption by the suffering of a "middle" god. "Socrates, that great Gentile philosopher,"

---

28. WJE 13:214. See also WJE 12:281. Edwards often told Northampton that, because of its unprecedented blessings, more was expected of it, and therefore its failure to live up to them brought greater guilt. See, for example, WJE 14:224–25; sermon on Exod. 8:15, WJEO 67; sermon on Jer. 51:5, WJEO 63; WJE 12:473;WJE 16:220; sermon on Exod. 8:15, WJEO 67.

29. Edwards spent thirty-six pages in the Yale edition of his "Controversies Notebook" detailing how Old Testament saints could believe in Christ and be justified; WJE 21:372–408.

as Edwards calls him, "worshipped the true God, as he was led by the light of nature," and Seneca "had in many respects right notions of the divine perfections and providence." Even the Muslim Persians and Turks understood the nature of humility and the disinterested love for God. In the margins of a notebook entry describing Plato's vision of God's beauty, Edwards scribbled, "Right notions of God and religion." At the end of an extract detailing many pagan ideas, he added: "All the chief philosophers have right views of virtue and religion."[30]

Edwards did not say in so many words that these heathen persons were saved. He made it clear that salvation requires faith in Christ when there has been opportunity to hear the gospel. Yet these reflections on the religious knowledge and virtue of the heathen may have caused Edwards to rethink, or at least to refine, his thinking on justification and regeneration. In a *Miscellanies* entry from the mid-1730s, he began to think about justification and regeneration as phased and life-long processes rather than as instantaneous events (ch. 25). Jesus' disciples, he observed, were "good men *before*" they met Christ, "already in a *disposition* to follow Christ." The same was true, Edwards thought, of Zacchaeus and the woman of Canaan in Matthew 15:22.[31]

Edwards's reflections on regeneration and conversion had implications not only for those in non-Christian cultures but for those in Christian societies and who professed conversion. If someone might be pleasing to God (because of their right disposition) before being outwardly converted to Christ, then what about some of those who were not outwardly converted? Might they be still in *process* of conversion? Edwards reasoned along these lines: "Conversion may still

---

30. WJE 13:416–17; WJE 20:355–57; WJE 23:562–64, 575; WJE 12:300; WJE 23:192–94. The last quotation is significant because it comes at the end of Miscellany 1355, which immediately follows a long series of extracts from Philip Skelton ridiculing pagan notions of God (Miscellany 1354). This is an illustration of how Edwards took some Reformed polemics against the heathen with a grain of salt. He believed that the heathen were generally lost in darkness but nevertheless was convinced that "the wiser heathen" possessed considerable religious and moral truth; WJE 23:575, 506–43. A similar pattern can be seen in the contrast between Miscellany 965 (in which Gale excoriates the spiritual pride of heathen philosophers) and Miscellany 1357 (an extract from John Brine that criticizes pagan philosophers for their lack of humility and failure to depend on God for virtue), on the one hand; and Miscellany 986 and Miscellany 1028, on the other, where Edwards praises Socrates for showing humility by not trusting in himself and lauds Xenophon, Plato and Seneca for knowing that virtue is impossible without divine grace. WJE 20:249; WJE 23:604–607; WJE 20:309–11; WJE 23:365–66.

31. WJE 13:73, emph. added. This was simply an application of the principle he articulated in 1729—that "a person according to the gospel may be in a state of salvation, before a distinct and express act of faith in the sufficiency and suitableness of Christ as a Savior" (Miscellany 393).

be necessary to salvation in some respect even after he is really a saint." In these cases, justification was already accomplished in one sense but in another sense it depended on "these after works of the Spirit of God upon the soul." That is, the condition of justification may still remain to be fulfilled after conversion. Hence saints seem still to be in a state of probation until the end of their lives.[32] If, in a certain sense, justification comes in stages and is complete only at death or the end of one's probation on earth, then regeneration might be viewed similarly: "The whole of the saving work of God's Spirit on the soul in the beginning, and progress of it from the very first dawnings of divine light and the first beginnings of divine life until death, is in some respect to be looked upon as all one work of regeneration.... There is as it were an unregenerate part still in man, after the first regeneration, that still needs to be regenerated."[33] So if Edwards's reflections opened the door for some heathen persons to be regenerate, they also suggested that those who were regenerate and had professed Christ might be in a lifelong process of conversion.

Since regeneration and justification can be considered as processes that unfold in stages, and one can be a saint before conversion, then it follows that heathen persons who have the proper dispositions might be saints before they are converted to Christ. If their knowledge of Christ was incomplete, it may have been because they were still in the initial stages of regeneration and justification, which may have been completed in glory—just as in the case of elect infants. Edwards never reached this explicit conclusion in his published writings or private notebooks. Yet his theology laid the groundwork for such an interpretation.

More suggestively, Edwards described several types of persons without explicit knowledge of Christ who may nevertheless find salvation. For all four types, disposition was the critical sign of one's eternal destiny. In his early years Edwards suggested that infants can be regenerated at birth without knowledge of Christ and that salvation is based on disposition: "The infant that has a disposition in his heart to believe in Christ-if he had a capacity and opportunity-is looked upon and accepted as if he actually believed in Christ

---

32. WJE 20:74. Edwards also speaks of God justifying, "as it were," a person being received into the visible church on the "presumption" and "supposition" that the person is sincere, which is proved by later "faithfulness." This "visible covenant" is different from the "covenant of grace," but in each case there is a condition to be fulfilled. In the covenant of grace, however, God covenants "with those that before his allseeing eyes perform that condition of the covenant of grace"; WJE 18:256. Edwards preached in 1740 that "subjects of a first work of grace may need a new conversion," by which he meant that even the regenerate need to be converted again and again; WJE 22:181–202.

33. WJE 20:70, 72.

and so is entitled to eternal life through Christ."³⁴ When Edwards asked himself how he was to understand the salvation of Old Testament saints "when yet they had no distinct respect to [Christ]," he reasoned that it was "the second Person in the Trinity" who appeared to them "as the author of temporal salvation and benefits" whenever God manifested himself to Israel. Furthermore, all the Old Testament references to "Angel," "Angel of Covenant," "Angel of God's Face," "Name," and "Glory" were references to the second person of the Trinity. Hence they already in some sense believed in Christ and were saved by their faith in Christ. Conversions from wickedness to righteousness in the Old Testament era, said Edwards, were as "frequent" as during the New Testament era. In other words, true faith was plentiful in the Old Testament era too.³⁵

New Testament saints followed a similar pattern: "Cornelius did already in some respect believe in Christ, even in the manner that the Old Testament saints were wont to do." Before he met Peter, that is, Cornelius believed in a Christ of whom he had not yet heard.³⁶ Edwards said the same about the apostles. Cornelius, Nathaniel, "probably" John's two disciples, and several others were "good men before [they met Christ], for they seemed to be found already in a disposition to follow [Christ] when [Christ] first appeared to them in his human nature and this seems to have been the case with Zacchaeus and with the woman of Canaan." Edwards inferred from this that "conversion may still be by divine constitution necessary to salvation in some respect even after [a person] is really a saint." As we saw before, Edwards was suggesting that a person could be regenerate *before* conversion to an explicit knowledge of Christ. By the mid- to late-1730s, Edwards seems to have been returning to an inference he had reached in 1723, that "a man may have the disposition in himself for some time before he can sensibly feel them [the exercises of that disposition], for want of occasion or other reason."³⁷

Another class of people who enjoyed salvation without explicit knowledge of Christ were those we might call holy pagans. In his 1739 sermons on the

---

34. WJE 13:245–46 "Controversies Notebook," WJEO 27. Miscellanies 492 suggests that Edwards considered the state of infants as analogous to that of the heathen since both have less than full knowledge of revelation. In this entry, he speculates that without revelation we would not know "who are liable to punishment, whether children, whether heathen"; WJE 13:537.

35. WJE 18:201; WJE 23:621; WJE 20:56, 143; WJE 23:229–30; WJE 13:221.

36. WJE 20:56. Calvin similarly said that Cornelius was "already illumined by the Spirit of wisdom" and "sanctified by the same Spirit" (*Institutes*, 3.17.4).

37. WJE 20:73–74; WJE 13:214.

history of the work of redemption, Edwards asserted that conversion to true religion, justification, and glorification have occurred in all ages of the world since the Fall, and he cited examples of such holy pagans living outside of Israel: Melchizedek, the posterity of Nahor (i.e., Job and his family), and Job's three friends Eliphaz, Bildad, and Zophar along with Elihu.[38] These were individuals outside the national covenant with Israel and of course without explicit knowledge of Christ who nonetheless seem to have been regenerate.[39] Late in his career, Edwards offered tentative reflections on the possible eternal destiny of the heathen. In Miscellany 1162, after explaining that heathen philosophers had said "such wonderful things concerning the Trinity [and] the Messiah," he asked whether they might have been inspired by the Holy Spirit. Yes, he said, and inspiration is not so high "an honor and privilege as some are ready to think." For "many very bad men have been the subjects of it." Some were idolaters such as Balaam. Nebuchadnezzar, "a very wicked man," received a revelation about the Messiah and his future kingdom. Even the demon who spoke through the oracle at Delphi was "compelled to confess Christ."[40]

In any event, of what use were the revelations given to Socrates and Plato "and some others of the wise men of Greece," who were just as inspired as the wise men from the East? These philosophers did not use these revelations to lead their nations toward the truth, so God must have had other intentions. Edwards suggested that God had several reasons for giving divine revelation among the ancient heathen: to dispose these nations to converse with and learn from the Jews, to prepare the Gentiles for their future reception of the Christian gospel, to corroborate the truths of Christianity among those who had received the gospel, and—in one of Edwards's most cryptic comments—to benefit the souls of those who transmitted divine revelation: "We know not what evidence God might give to the men themselves that were the subjects of these inspirations that they were divine and true...and so we know not of how *great benefit* the truths suggested might be to their own souls." Though hesitant and tentative, he suggested the

---

38. WJE 9:179. Edwards also said in these sermons that after the time of Abraham God rejected all other nations and gave them up to idolatry; ibid. That Edwards was speaking of collective groups and not individuals is clear from several discussions in his notebooks, including the one mentioned in the next paragraph.

39. For Edwards's views of Islam, American Indians, and "Chinese philosophers," see McDermott, *Jonathan Edwards Confronts the Gods*, 166–75, 194–216.

40. WJE 23:84.

possibility of a "great benefit" to the heathen—a notion that, though undefined, might include final salvation.[41]

It is difficult to imagine what "great benefit" to heathen souls Edwards may have had in mind other than salvation. He never would have agreed that heathen sincerity or good works were sufficient for salvation. He always made it clear that a regenerate disposition was a special gift of the Spirit to the elect and was not common to all human beings or conferred at birth. He also stressed the absolute necessity of receiving Christ explicitly when there was opportunity to hear the gospel. But if he believed Cornelius was already regenerate before he had heard the gospel, what of heathen who lived before Christ and had never head the gospel? Since infants without conscious knowledge of Christ could be saved by Christ's sovereign work—as well as Old and New Testament saints without explicit knowledge of Christ—then Edwards may have toyed with the remote but real possibility that some of the heathen may have been regenerate and come to salvation.

Near the end of his life, in a notebook entry arguing against deist views of reason, Edwards asserted that reason can confirm many religious truths but cannot discover them on its own. Then he considered the deist objection that most humans have not had the benefit of revelation. He replies that in fact *"the greater part* of the heathen world have not been left merely to the light of nature." They received divine revelation by tradition from their ancestors and they had borrowed various teachings from the Jews—in other words by the *prisca theologia*. Since the means of revelation were available, there was "an equal possibility of their receiving the benefit of divine revelation." But other parts of the heathen world that were "most destitute of divine revelation" displayed the "extreme blindness and delusion" of a society obstinate in its rebellion against God and so forfeited its chance to learn the "terms of reconciliation."[42] Most heathen

---

41. WJE 23:85, emph. added. Cambridge Platonist Henry More, who according to Wallace Anderson had "an early and lasting influence upon Edwards's thought," wrote that the heathen can be saved by grace through "Faithfulness to that Light and Power which God has given them." WJE 6:21; More, *Mystery of Godliness*, Bk. 10, Ch. 6, 352. The first three purposes of the revelation are related to salvation: to learn from the Jews (who point to Christian salvation), to prepare to receive the gospel, and to confirm the truth of Christian faith (as the way to salvation) for later Christians. None has anything to do with the common grace of moral truth, which is the meaning Gilbert has suggested in "The Nations Will Worship," 63–64.

42. WJE 23:354–55, emph. added. Steve Bateman argues that Edwards considers only whole societies in this entry (and not individual sinners) and that the "benefit of divine revelation" might mean only common grace of biblical principles for peace and moral order. Yet Edwards specified individuals at the end of Miscellany 1162 and in Miscellany 1338 said most heathen societies received both the *prisca theologia* and Jewish traditions, which teach critical elements of the way to salvation, such as a divine hero's expiation of sins. Steve Bateman, *Which "Real" Jesus? Jonathan Edwards, Benjamin Franklin, and the Early American Roots of the Current Debate* (Eugene, OR: Wipf & Stock, 2008), 176–80.

nations had received some divine revelation and so had "equal possibility" of receiving its "benefit"—a term Edwards linked to "reconciliation" with God.

We are left with a curious tension in Edwards's thinking about the salvation of the heathen. On the one hand, in most of his explicit commentary on the heathen, he took the negative view characteristic of his Reformed predecessors. While appreciating the religious truth known by the "wiser heathen," Edwards never tired of recording the "absurdities of the worship of the heathen." The *Miscellanies* contain references to human sacrifice, religious prostitution, fornication, sodomy, castration, and cannibalism. Edwards was at his most uncompromising in his sermons. In a 1729 Northampton sermon, he identified immorality and idolatry as characteristically "heathenish." God had forsaken and withdrawn his gracious presence from heathen lands. They were "Lost Nations," and the heathen were the devil's people. In a particularly vivid passage, Edwards said "the devil nurses them [the heathen] up as swine in a pen that he may fill his belly with them in another [world].... They are his prey when they die. That dragon, that old serpent, then Got 'em into his own den and sucks their blood and feeds upon their bowels and vitals." And there seems no hope, for "those that die heathen he will prey upon and Exert his Cruelty Upon forever."[43]

Yet that is not the whole picture. Edwards made a series of theological moves beyond his Reformed predecessors. His typological reflections, his extensive use of the *prisca theologia*, and his development of a dispositional soteriology laid the groundwork for a more expansive view of God's presence among non-Christians. He argued for a greater knowledge of religious *truth* among the heathen than allowed by his favorite Reformed predecessors—Francis Turretin and Petrus van Mastrict.[44] In his private notebooks and public sermons he stated that there were differing degrees of inspiration from the Spirit. In his second sermon in *Charity and Its Fruits*, he told his Northampton church that the Holy Spirit spoke through wicked men like Balaam, King Saul, and Judas. In his *Miscellanies*, he wrote that heathen philosophers such as Socrates and Plato had "some degree of inspiration."[45] So Edwards acknowledged

---

43. Sermon on Rev. 3:15, 1929, WJEO 44.

44. Turretin, *Institutes*, 1:9–16; Mastricht, *Theoretica-Practica Theologia* (Utrecht, 1724), I.i.xxii–xxv. Of course, the *prisca theologia* could cut both ways. While the orthodox used it all the way into the twentieth century to support their church traditions, deists and their disciples in the same centuries used it to interpret the Jesus story as one version of an ancient Near Eastern fertility myth. See Michael J. McClymond, *Familiar Stranger: An Introduction to Jesus of Nazareth* (Grand Rapids, MI: Eerdmans, 2004) 23–24, 162–63 nn. 66–68.

45. WJE 8:157, 159–60, 162; WJE 23:84–85.

that God gave religious truth to non-Christians, and even to wicked non-Christians. On the general question of the salvation of pagans, he raised the *possibility* that some of the heathen could be saved, and yet never spoke in the expansively optimistic terms of Richard Baxter, Chevalier Ramsay, Philip Skelton, Isaac Watts, or John Wesley.[46] So while he built the theological foundations upon which a more hopeful doctrine of salvation might have been erected, Edwards himself never chose to do so.

For Edwards, there was no inconsistency between the possibility of reconciliation for the heathen and the probability that only a precious few of the heathen had ever been saved, for this was the testimony of scripture as he understood it. The biblical authors—by the Spirit's inspiration—portrayed a world in which God had revealed himself in Israelite history and in the person of Jesus Christ. Salvation was available to all but only through the events of that Jewish-Christian history. News of those events had been heard by most of the world, but few had listened. Hence the world's darkness and delusion were tragic but not unfair. World history was a mirror of the individual human: able to perceive cosmic truths but inclined to ignore them. Since God had provided revelation to the majority of the heathen, his divine justice was vindicated. God's administration of the cosmos—while baffling to us much of the time—was ultimately good and righteous. The deist reproach, he reasoned, had been turned back and God's glory further magnified.

---

46. Baxter forthrightly granted salvation to those (outside the "Jewish church") who did not have "knowledge of Christ *incarnate*," and Wesley said pagans just needed to live up to the light they were given. Richard Baxter, *The Reasons of the Christian Religion* (London, 1667), 201–202;John Wesley, Sermon LXVIII, "The General Spread of the Gospel," in *Works*, IX, 234; see David Pailin, *Attitudes to Other Religions: Comparative Religion in Seventeenth- and Eighteenth-Century Britain* (Manchester, UK: Manchester University Press, 1984), 48.

PART III

Legacies and Affinities: Edwards's Disciples and Interpreters

37

Selective Readings: Edwards and the New Divinity

EDWARDS LEFT BEHIND a complex theological legacy. Reflecting this complexity is the range of terms used to describe his followers. The first designation to emerge—"New Divinity"—was a term of opprobrium in the 1760s, used by outsiders to stigmatize Edwards's followers as innovators.[1] The term "Hopkinsian"—from Samuel Hopkins—took hold by the end of the 1700s. "Consistent Calvinism" was the term that Hopkins used to describe himself. With the founding of Yale Divinity School in 1822 and the rising influence of Yale's Nathaniel William Taylor, some spoke of a "New Haven Theology." Last—yet not least in staying power—was the term coined by Andover Seminary Professor Edwards Amasa Park in an 1852 essay: "New England Theology."[2] This last designation was not merely a name but an interpretation that construed the century-long development from Jonathan Edwards to Nathaniel William Taylor as a single, internally diverse, yet interconnected movement. Among the leading Edwardseans were Joseph Bellamy (1719–90), Samuel Hopkins (1721–1803), Sarah Osborn (1714–96), John Smalley (1734–1820), Stephen West (1735–1819), Nathan Strong (1748–1816), Nathanael Emmons (1745–1840), Jonathan Edwards Jr. (1745–1801), Asa Burton (1752–1836), Timothy Dwight (1752–1817), Nathaniel W. Taylor (1786–1858), Charles G. Finney (1792–1875), and Edwards Amasa Park (1808–1900). By the 1870s, it became difficult to identify a continuing Edwardsean tradition. This chapter will use the term "New Divinity" or the broader designation "Edwardsean."

The New Divinity thinkers had many critics during the twentieth century. A few scholars argued that Edwards simply had no intellectual heirs.[3] More

---

1. William Breitenbach, "Piety and Moralism: Edwards and the New Divinity," in Nathan O. Hatch and Harry S. Stout, eds., *Jonathan Edwards and the American Experience* (New York: Oxford University Press, 1988), 194.

2. Edwards Amasa Park, "New England Theology," *Bibliotheca Sacra* 9 (January 1852): 170–220.

3. Edward H. Davidson, *Jonathan Edwards: The Narrative of a Puritan Mind* (Cambridge, MA: Harvard University Press, 1968), 134, 146.

often the claim was that the New Divinity tried but failed to meet the challenge of carrying on an Edwardsean tradition. Yet arguments against the New Divinity moved in disparate directions. Some saw them "as arid metaphysicians and austere hyper-Calvinists who systematized Edwards's thought, but in so doing drained it of its warm and vital piety." Other saw them "as liberalizers and moralizers who were intent upon accommodating Edwards's Calvinistic creed to the humanitarian spirit of the day." Joseph Haroutunian's *Piety Versus Moralism: The Passing of the New England Theology* (1932) positioned Edwards against the Edwardseans. In contrast, William Breitenbach claimed that "the leading tendencies of Edwards's system can be discovered by tracing the trajectory of his ideas in the theology of his New Divinity successors."[4]

The Edwardseans venerated Edwards and believed that his legacy should endure. Sometimes their attitude toward Edwards was almost worshipful. In a youthful poem, Timothy Dwight described him as "that moral Newton, and that second Paul" who "in one little life, the gospel more/Disclos'd, than all earth's myriads kenn'd before."[5] The Edwardseans often wanted to show that their theological positions agreed with those of Edwards, as Frank Hugh Foster explained: "To agree with Edwards was still the high ambition of them all; and when they consciously disagreed, as did [Nathaniel William] Taylor, they thought they were only expressing better Edwards's true meaning."[6] Edwards had a number of disciples during his lifetime—Samuel Buell, Elihu Spencer, Job Strong, Eleazar Wheelock, and Timothy Woodbridge, as well as the better-known Joseph Bellamy and Samuel Hopkins.[7] Yet there is no evidence that he intended to found a "school" of thought. Edwards viewed self-identified "schools" of theology with considerable skepticism because he associated them with dangerous theological innovations and theological drift.[8]

---

4. Breitenbach, "Piety and Moralism," 177–79.

5. Timothy Dwight, "The Triumph of Infidelity" (1788), in Vernon Louis Parrington, ed., *The Connecticut Wits* (New York, 1969), 260; cited in Mark A. Noll, "Jonathan Edwards and Nineteenth Century Theology," in Hatch and Stout, *Jonathan Edwards and the American Experience*, 263.

6. Frank Hugh Foster, *A Genetic History of the New England Theology* (New York: Garland, 1987 [1907]), 369.

7. On Hopkins, see Peter Dan Jauhiainen, "An Enlightenment Calvinist: Samuel Hopkins and the Pursuit of Benevolence," PhD diss., University of Iowa, 1997. On Bellamy, see Mark R. Valeri, *Law and Providence in Joseph Bellamy's New England: The Origins of the New Divinity in Revolutionary America* (New York: Oxford University Press, 1994).

8. Douglas A. Sweeney, and Allen C. Guelzo; eds., *The New England Theology: From Jonathan Edwards to Edwards Amasa Park* (Grand Rapids, MI: Baker Academic, 2006), 69.

The New Divinity's starting point is debatable, with dates ranging from the 1730s to the 1790s. Perry Miller stressed the Boston lecture "God Glorified in Man's Dependence" (1731) as a defining moment that set Edwards's direction as a renewer of Calvinism.[9] Frank Hugh Foster's *A Genetic History of the New England Theology* (1907) dated the beginnings of a new "theological movement" to Edwards's 1734 sermons on "Justification by Faith Alone."[10] On this account, Edwards's anti-Arminian and pro-revival positions in the 1730s defined early Edwardseanism. Douglas Sweeney and Allen Guelzo pointed to the Great Awakening in 1740–41 as a turning point. Edwards became the de facto leader of a pro-revival party, drew young men to visit and study with him, and fomented the emergence of an Old Light party.[11] Joseph Bellamy's *True Religion Delineated* (1750)—with Edwards's approving preface—was the first major publication by one of Edwards's disciples. *Freedom of the Will* (1754) was even more crucial in setting an agenda for much New Divinity reflection. Breitenbach suggested that "the New Divinity did not emerge as a distinct position until the 1760s, when some of the orthodox clergy grew disturbed by the way that Samuel Hopkins went about refuting Jonathan Mayhew's Arminian theories of regeneration."[12] The publication of Samuel Hopkins's *System of Divinity* (1793)—the first full-scale systematic theology published by an Edwardsean—represented a point of maturation and set a new direction for Edwards's followers. There is thus no definitive answer as to when the New Divinity began. One's identification of a starting point for the movement will depend on what aspects of the movement one chooses to highlight.

While the 1770s and 1780s were difficult decades for the New Divinity—and for the American colonies in general—by 1790, Jonathan Edwards Jr. was claiming that most of the Congregational ministers in New England held to "the system of my father and Dr. Bellamy." In 1795, Timothy Dwight became president of Yale College. Concerned at the growing influence of French skepticism or "infidelity" among students at the college (who allegedly used nicknames for one another such as "Voltaire" and "D'Alembert"), Dwight launched into a series of public lectures defending the Christian faith from deistic assaults. These efforts bore fruit some years later in a notable student revival at

---

9. Perry Miller, *Jonathan Edwards* (New York: William Sloane, 1949), 3–34; "God Glorified," in WJE 21:196–216.

10. Foster, *Genetic History*, 3; "Justification by Faith Alone," in WJE 21:143–242.

11. Sweeney and Guelzo, *New England Theology*, 69.

12. William Breitenbach, "The Consistent Calvinism of the New Divinity Movement," *William and Mary Quarterly*, 3rd series, 41 (1984): 244.

Yale College in 1802–1803, during which about a third of the student body professed conversion. Before his death in 1817, Dwight laid plans for a divinity school at Yale that—like Andover Seminary—would be a counterpoise to Harvard's liberalism. When Yale Divinity School opened its doors in 1822, Dwight's favorite student—Nathaniel William Taylor—occupied its chair of theology.[13]

Early opponents of the Edwardseans had hoped that their movement and theology would soon disappear. In 1787, Ezra Stiles predicted that Edwards's works "in another generation will pass into as transient notice perhaps scarce above oblivion" and "be looked upon as singular and whimsical."[14] To Stiles's consternation, however, Edwardseanism did not flounder but flourished. In the aftermath of the 1790s and early 1800s revivals, the New Divinity expanded aggressively. It captured the western New England hill country, struck westward along the Erie Canal, turned upstate New York into a revivalist hotbed, and traced the arrows of westward migration into the Western Reserve of Ohio and then into Michigan, Indiana, Illinois, Wisconsin, and Iowa. New Divinity leaders founded churches and colleges, established moral and reform societies, and sent missionaries overseas.

The Edwardseans viewed these revivals as confirmations of their theology. In this respect, they followed the example of Edwards, who had stated in 1738 that the Northampton Awakening in 1734–35 was a sign of "God's approbation" of his own preaching of justification by faith alone.[15] "I saw a continued succession of heavenly sprinklings...in Connecticut," wrote Edward Dorr Griffin, "until in 1799, I could stand at my door in New Hartford...and number fifty or sixty congregations laid down in one field of divine wonders."[16] No less significant for the movement was a massive campaign of literature distribution in the 1800s during which the American Tract Society disseminated an estimated *one million* tracts containing portions of Edwards's writings.[17]

---

13. Sweeney and Guelzo, eds., *New England Theology*, 71, 187–88.

14. Franklin B. Dexter, ed., *The Literary Diary of Ezra Stiles*, 3 vols. (New York, 1901), 3:275; cited in Conforti, *Jonathan Edwards, Religious Tradition, and American Culture*, 3.

15. In the preface (ii) to his *Discourses on Various Important Subjects* (1738), Edwards wrote, "The beginning of the late work of God in this place was so circumstanced that I could not but look upon it as a remarkable testimony of God's approbation of the doctrine of justification by faith alone" (WJE 4:19).

16. Edward Dorr Griffin, "Letter to Sprague," in William Buell Sprague, ed., *Lectures on Revivals of Religion*, 2nd ed. (New York: Appleton, 1833), 360.

17. Sweeney and Guelzo, eds., *New England Theology*, 17–18; Conforti, *Jonathan Edwards*, 13–14, 37.

Doctrines and Debates of the New Divinity

Because of the complexity of Edwards's theology and the diversity of ways in which Edwards's ideas were adapted by his followers, New Divinity teaching is difficult to summarize, and "Edwards's theological legacy...emerged as complex, ambiguous, and contested, not monolithic, fixed, stable, and consensual."[18] A few salient principles are as follows. God is a benevolent being who seeks human happiness as well as his own glory. All sin is personal. There is no such thing as imputed sin in distinction from personal sin. Holiness is rooted in the heart and will. Acts of holiness are always free and voluntary. Grace is a divine operation on the heart and not a work chiefly involving the mind or understanding. The gracious affections of the heart consist in a disinterested love to God for God's own sake. Conversions and religious practices based on self-love are counterfeit. Ministers should not appeal to self-love or self-interest in their sermons and exhortations. The first act in the process of justification is love, not faith or belief in God. Repentance involves a full consent to the rightness of God's law, including its just sentence of damnation for sinners. Assurance of salvation is not based on one's conversion experience but rather on the lively actions of a holy temper of heart. Sinners are accountable before God because they have a natural ability to exercise holiness, even though they continue to sin because of moral necessity. Because sin is a voluntary disinclination against God and God's law, the sinner must be commanded immediately to repent. Finally, these general principles regarding faith, repentance, and salvation should be applied in church settings to determine who was to be admitted to membership.[19]

Opponents of the New Divinity included several groups. The Arminian, Old Light, or liberalizing Congregationalists had opposed the Great Awakening and sought to soften Calvinist teachings (ch. 3). They affirmed the value of human moral striving, asserted that God's grace came to those who did their best, sought to maintain a reasonable faith, and rejected overt displays of religious emotion. They were offended by the New Divinity's Calvinistic affirmations of human depravity and felt that this teaching undermined the importance of moral exertion. Charles Chauncy, Lemuel Briant, and Jonathan Mayhew belonged to this party. By the early 1800s, the Old Light or Arminian Congregationalists had evolved into the genteel Unitarians of Boston and eastern Massachusetts.

---

18. Joseph Conforti, *Jonathan Edwards, Religious Tradition, and American Culture* (Chapel Hill, NC: University of North Carolina Press, 1995), 5.

19. Breitenbach, "Piety and Moralism," 191.

Also opposed to the New Divinity were the Old Calvinists, as represented by Moses Mather, William Hart, Moses Hemmenway, and Ezra Stiles. Professing to maintain the balanced teaching of earlier New England Calvinism on the issue of human striving versus divine sovereignty, the Old Calvinists were preparationists who encouraged the unregenerate to make use of "the means of grace"—church attendance, prayer, listening to sermons—to dispose themselves for God's converting grace (ch. 42). They were shocked by the radicalism of Samuel Hopkins's position—viz., that the use of the means of grace by the unconverted only *increased* their guilt before God. Along with the Arminians, the Old Calvinists regarded New Divinity teachings as pastorally impractical. If an unregenerate person was not encouraged to use the means of grace, then what was a pastor to suggest? Old Calvinists also held that the New Divinity was an illegitimate theological innovation. While New Divinity proponents argued that Old Calvinists may have been Arminians in disguise, some Old Calvinists (e.g., Moses Hemmenway) held views that were rather close to New Divinity teachings, although they eschewed its metaphysical and paradoxical aspects.[20]

The confessional Presbyterians at Princeton College and Seminary were yet another group opposed to the New Divinity. From the 1840s through the 1860s, the Congregationalist-turned-Presbyterian Lyman Atwater voiced his opposition to the New Divinity in its "Taylorite" version. Atwater argued that the Edwardseans had moved away from Edwards's theology: "We think it easy to show...that the distinctive features of this New Divinity, in all its successive forms, are utterly abhorrent to his [Edwards's] entire system."[21] It was an "ingenious attempt to eliminate from the doctrine [of original sin] its unwelcome ingredients—imputation, hereditary sinfulness, and inability—and yet to keep its substance, viz. that men inherit from Adam a vitiated nature."[22] Princetonians argued that Edwards was neither the father nor founder of theology in New England. Colonial Calvinism was older than Edwards, and it was the father of Edwards, not he of it. Neither did Edwards invent the distinction of natural ability and moral inability—an idea that went back beyond Luther, to

---

20. Frank Foster suggested that Hemmenway's position "falls very little short of being Edwardsean" (*Genetic History*, 149).

21. Lyman Atwater, "Jonathan Edwards and the Successive Forms of the New Divinity," *Princeton Review* 30 (October 1858): 589; cited in Mark Noll, "Jonathan Edwards and Nineteenth Century Theology," in Hatch and Stout, *Jonathan Edwards and the American Experience*, 266.

22. Lyman Atwater "Old Orthodoxy, New Divinity, and Unitarianism," *Biblical Repertory and Princeton Review* 29 (October 1857):568; cited in Conforti, *Jonathan Edwards*, 123.

the "unfree freedom" of which Augustine wrote. If there was a "father" of the New Divinity, it was Jonathan Edwards Jr.—thus making Jonathan Edwards Sr. the grandfather of the movement.[23]

Controversies between Yale Divinity School and Andover Seminary on one side and Princeton Seminary on the other intensified after Nathaniel Taylor's *Concio ad Clerum* (1828) challenged traditional doctrines of original sin and broke with Edwards's key notion of "moral inability." Charles Hodge characterized New England Theology as "anti-Augustinian"—a point that Edwards Amasa Park vigorously rebutted. In certain respects, these debates were a family dispute among Calvinists.[24] Yet Taylor, by dropping the notion of human inability from his theology, represented a more decisive break from traditional Calvinism than earlier New Divinity authors such as Bellamy, Hopkins, or Emmons.

Some observers pointed to two strands in the New Divinity—a stricter, more radical wing (led by Hopkins and Emmons) and a softer, more moderate teaching (including Bellamy and Dwight). Timothy Dwight commented in an 1805 letter, "I am not a Hopkinsonian [sic]. President Edwards appears to me to have gone as far as the Bible warrants. Those, who have succeeded him seem to me to have philosophized merely, and to have bewildered themselves and their readers." To a large extent, the division of strict and moderate New Divinity corresponded to the distinction of "Exercisers" versus "Tasters"—as explained in the next section. Moderate Edwardseans were closer to Old Calvinists on the "use of means." Dwight affirmed the utility of means but insisted that they were effective only through God's agency: "The very means themselves are furnished by this Divine Agent. When furnished, all of them, united, would prove wholly insufficient without his creative influence."[25] In his earlier years, Dwight wrote a treatise on "Christian resignation" that negated self-love and showed him to be a "thorough-going Hopkinsian." Despite Hopkins's encouragement to publish it, Dwight was uncertain of his own argument and later admitted that he destroyed the manuscript.[26] Somewhat

---

23. Conforti, *Jonathan Edwards*, 138–40.

24. Park, "New England Theology,"170–71; Sweeney and Guelzo, eds., *New England Theology*, 22.

25. Timothy Dwight, cited in John R. Fitzmier, *New England's Moral Legislator: Timothy Dwight, 1752–1817* (Bloomington, IN: Indiana University Press, 1998), 125; and Timothy Dwight, *Theology*, 5 vols. (1818–19), 4:58; Fitzmier, *New England's Moral Legislator*, 126.

26. Fitzmier, *New England's Moral Legislator*, 127.

later, Leonard Woods espoused a moderate Edwardseanism like that of Bellamy and Dwight.

The remainder of this chapter will explore a number of areas in which Edwardsean thinkers adapted Edwards's ideas and it will conclude with a summary evaluation.

Human Volition and Original Sin

Sweeney and Guelzo describe *Freedom of the Will* as "the engine of the Edwardsean tradition." During the nineteenth century, *Freedom of the Will* was second only to the *Life of Brainerd* as Edwards's most frequently reprinted book.[27] The New Divinity attached special importance to Edwards's distinction between "natural ability" and "moral inability" (ch. 22). The distinction allowed Edwards to argue that human beings sinned necessarily (because of moral inability) and yet responsibly (because of natural ability). People did as they pleased, and this was the problem. They followed their desires, and their desires were sinful. "Moral inability" was something voluntary—a "cannot" that was a "will not." The greater was one's disinclination to obeying God, the greater was one's culpability. Edwards used an analogy of two prisoners, one of whom is physically bound and so cannot benefit from the pardon declared to him (representing a case of natural inability) and another who is physically unbound and yet shows such pride that he is unwilling to accept the pardon proffered to him (representing moral inability).[28] The distinction between natural ability and moral inability allowed New Divinity preachers to proclaim a seemingly paradoxical message that combined a Calvinist notion of God's total sovereignty in election and grace with an exhortation for hearers immediately to exert their wills in conversion or in holy living. The New Divinity preachers had their cake and ate it, too. Nathanael Emmons was well-known for preaching along both lines—sometimes in the same sermon.

The greatest ambiguity left in the argument of Jonathan Edwards's *Freedom of the Will* pertained to the "motives" that necessitated the movements of the will. From the time of Augustine, the dominant concept had been that of a sinful or depraved nature that mediated between the external world and the human will. The sinful nature, for Augustine, had corrupted the will so that it chose evil rather than good. Yet because the New Divinity teachers wished to accentuate the sinner's own responsibility before God, there was a tendency

---

27. Sweeney and Guelzo, eds., *New England Theology*, 57.
28. WJE 1:362–3.

to shift attention away from a sinful nature to the agency and operation of will itself. Samuel Hopkins was aware of this conceptual conundrum, but fearing a split among the Edwardseans, he sought to stake out a middle ground. By the early 1800s, though, a division had emerged. "Tasters" located sin in a depraved inclination or spiritual "taste," while "Exercisers" resisted all talk of a sinful nature or taste and confined sin to the workings or exercises of the will. Nathanael Emmons was the best-known of the Exercisers, while the classic expression of the Taster perspective was Asa Burton's *Essays* (1824).[29]

Both the "Exerciser scheme" and the "Taster scheme" were attempts to clarify Edwards's unspecified position regarding "motives." Emmons seemed to reduce the human self to a set of individual, atomistic acts of volition—a teaching that critics claimed was dangerously close to the epiphenomenal self proposed by the skeptic David Hume. Another problem was that the Exercisers tended to collapse the acts of the human will into God's will. Hopkins introduced a doctrine of "divine efficiency" to account for the production of both righteous and sinful choices. Emmons went so far as to say that "God exerts his agency in producing all the moral and voluntary exercises of every moral agent." Even Adam's choice, said Emmons, resulted from a "divine energy [that] took hold of his heart and led him to sin."[30] On the Taster side, Burton for this part found it necessary to distinguish the "heart" or "taste" from the "will"—in a way that Edwards did not—and to assert that "this faculty, which has been denominated the taste, is the primary active power, which constitutes agency, and gives rise to all our voluntary exertions and actions."[31] In Burton's account, the largely unitary vision of human anthropology proposed by Edwards broke down into a more traditional threefold distinction of mind, will, and affections or sensibility (i.e., taste). While we should acknowledge the complexity of the issues involved, the Tasters may have come nearer the mark than the Exercisers in their interpretation of Edwards.[32]

---

29. Sweeney and Guelzo, *New England Theology*, 171–72; Dorus Paul Rudisill, *The Doctrine of the Atonement in Jonathan Edwards and His Successors* (New York: Poseidon Books, 1971), 92; James Hoopes, "Calvinism and Consciousness from Edwards to Beecher," in Hatch and Stout, *Jonathan Edwards and the American Experience*, 216–17.

30. Nathanael Emmons, *Works*, ed. Jacob Ide, 7 vols. (Boston, 1842), 4:387, 397; cited in Conforti, *Jonathan Edwards*, 128.

31. Sweeney and Guelzo, *New England Theology*, 186.

32. Favoring a Taster over an Exerciser view are the following considerations. (1) The concept of "disposition" has been rediscovered and highlighted in recent work on Edwards's theology by Sang Lee and others. This "dispositional" understanding of divine and human action aligns more nearly with Taster than Exerciser views. (2) Edwards distinguished divine volition from human volition and taught that God sometimes withheld his gracious influence

Nathaniel William Taylor brought Edwardseanism to a crisis point when he dropped Edwards's key distinction between moral inability and natural ability. Taylor ceased speaking of "inability" and rejected Edwards's distinction as unintelligible: "The natural ability of man to obey God, as defined by Edwards and others, has no existence and can have none." Edwards's mind "was all confusion on the subject."[33] Positively stated, Taylor's position on human volition was captured in the phrase "certainty with power to the contrary." Taylor provoked intense opposition from Princeton Presbyterians and from Congregationalists like Bennet Tyler in what became known as the Taylor-Tyler controversy.

Like Taylor, Charles Grandison Finney also rejected Edwards's idea of natural ability: "Every one knows with intuitive certainty that he has no ability to do what he is unable to will to do... therefore, the natural ability of the Edwardean school is no ability at all... nothing but an empty name, a metaphysico-theological fiction." Finney added, "Edwards I revere; his blunders I deplore."[34] Often historians have represented Finney as a "self-man made" of the Jacksonian era—like that rail-splitter Abe Lincoln. Finney himself cultivated this impression in his *Memoirs*. Yet his writings are teeming with New Divinity vocabulary, and they demonstrate a substantial debt to earlier thinkers. The major themes in Finney's theological writings—human volition, conversion, holiness, atonement, God's moral government, and so forth—are staples of the New Divinity. Another misconception is that Finney was an Arminian or a "Methodizer" of Presbyterians and Congregationalists. In point of fact, Finney rejected Methodist teachings (e.g., John Wesley's notion of "gracious ability"), and the Methodists regarded him as a New Divinity preacher. The Presbyterian James Wardell Alexander thought of Finney as "an odious caricature of the old Hopkinsian divinity," while one of Finney's colleagues at Oberlin College, Henry Cowles, identified Finney's theology with that "commonly known as... the theology expounded by Edwards, Bellamy, and Hopkins."

---

but never directly caused the human will to err. The Hopkinsian-Emmonsian idea of a divine efficiency in human sinning is thus a shift away from Edwards. (3) The notion of a will that acts apart from any underlying disposition is metaphysically unstable and easily collapses back into the notion of the self-determining will that Edwards had opposed in *Freedom of the Will*. By the time of Nathaniel Taylor, this is just what had happened.

33. Sweeney and Guelzo, eds., *New England Theology*, 195; Nathaniel William Taylor, *Lectures on the Moral Government of God*, 2 vols. (New York: Clark, Austin & Smith, 1859), 1:196, 2:134; cited in Allen C. Guezo, "An Heir or a Rebel? Charles Grandison Finney and the New England Theology," *Journal of the Early Republic* 17 (1997): 87.

34. Sweeney and Guelzo, eds., *New England Theology*, 242; citing Finney, *Lectures on Systematic Theology* (1846–47).

Finney was also an Exerciser. His affinity to Nathanael Emmons is shown in his controversial sermon "Sinners Bound to Change Their Own Hearts" (1836), which shared almost the same argument and title as Emmons's sermon of a generation earlier, "The Duty of Sinners to Make Themselves a New Heart" (1812). Emmons stated that "regeneration is not a miraculous or supernatural work" that sinners must wait on God to perform. He anticipated Finney's later controversial claim in *Lectures on Revivals of Religion* (1835) that "a revival of religion is not a miracle."[35]

Conversion and Regeneration

Hopkins's *Inquiry Concerning the Promises of the Gospel* (1765) continued Edwards's stress on the moral inability of the unregenerate. "Corruption or viciousness of heart," wrote Hopkins, was so "great and universal" that "the sinner will not repent, or have any right exercises towards God and his law, until his heart is in some degree renewed and set right." Because depravity runs deep, "means" are useless prior to regeneration. "When God gives a new heart in regeneration," only then is "a foundation...laid in the mind for a discerning of the truths of the gospel in their real beauty and excellence." In practice, this means that there is no gradual preparation for a "new heart" through the appropriate use of means. Instead "this change" is "wrought by the Spirit of God, immediately and instantaneously." Regeneration happens in a moment. There are no "promises of regenerating grace made to the exercises and doings of the unregenerate." All preaching directed toward the unregenerate must center on one point: "Men are required to repent and believe, and turn to God, on pain of eternal damnation, and are declared to be in a state of condemnation until they do so." Hopkins became known for insisting on "immediate repentance."[36] He distinguished the human turning toward God, "conversion," from the divine act of giving a new heart, "regeneration." Sinners were passive in the process of "regeneration" but active in "conversion."

After the time of Hopkins and Jonathan Edwards Jr., there was a change in the teaching on conversion and regeneration. While Edwards Jr. and Hopkins spoke much of the heart, Emmons removed the heart as something

---

35. Sweeney and Guelzo, eds., *New England Theology*, 219–20,119; on Finney's position on revivals, see the texts with discussion in Michael J. McClymond, ed., *Encyclopedia of Religious Revivals in America*, 2 vols. (Westport, CT: Greenwood Press, 2007), 2:140–44.

36. Sweeney and Guelzo, *New England Theology*, 87.

distinguishable from particular exercises of the human will. The notion of an evil "heart" or "nature," on Emmons's view, allowed sinners to excuse their own disobedience. So there was no underlying nature from which sinful actions proceeded. There were only the conscious acts themselves. Consequently Emmons developed the doctrine of conversion in a more psychological way by arguing that both saints and sinners were aware of their own thoughts: "Sinners in general...are as conscious of their own hearts as saints are of theirs....All men, good and bad, are conscious of what passes in their own minds. When they love or hate, choose or refuse, they are conscious of having these exercises of heart." Emmons wanted to throw the whole weight of moral responsibility onto sinners, who were to "make themselves a new heart," so that regeneration was "not a miraculous or supernatural work" that sinners had to wait for. Instead, it was a goal they had to seize for themselves. Emmons went further, saying that "if the making of a new heart consists in the exercising of holy instead of unholy affections, then sinners are not passive but active in regeneration." This was a break from Hopkins, inasmuch as Hopkins argued that sinners are passive in "regeneration" (though active in "conversion").[37] In effect, Emmons abolished any passive element in the process of regeneration or conversion. Human activity was now central.

Nathaniel Taylor offered a complex, multi-stage view of conversion that allowed him to affirm the use of means (like the Old Calvinists) and yet hold onto God's initiative in salvation and a truly disinterested movement of the will (like Hopkins). Taylor referred to "regeneration" as "that act of the will or heart in which God is preferred to every other object." Yet he also insisted that "there are and must be certain mental acts and states, which...precede regeneration."[38] In the end, Taylor's doctrine of conversion was difficult to understand because of its complexity.

Defending the Faith

Another element in Edwards's theological legacy was his rational defense of the Christian faith. In a summary of his father's work—likely penned in the 1790s—Jonathan Edwards Jr. described the dire situation faced by Calvinist thinkers in his day: "The Calvinists...were pressed and embarrassed by the objection,—That the sense, in which they interpreted the sacred writings, was inconsistent with human liberty, moral agency, accountableness, praise and

---

37. Sweeney and Guelzo, *New England Theology*, 114–15, 119.
38. Sweeney and Guelzo, *New England Theology*, 209.

blame."[39] As a result, "the Calvinists themselves began to be ashamed of their own cause and to give it up, at least as it relates to liberty and necessity. This was true especially of Dr. [Isaac] Watts and [Philip] Doddridge, who, in their day, were accounted leaders of the Calvinists." Both men were ready to assent to the notion of human being's "self-determining power"—a teaching that "entirely overthrows...the doctrines of grace."[40]

Jonathan Edwards Jr. responded by publishing two sets of excerpts from Edwards's *Miscellanies*. They were entitled *Miscellaneous Observations on Important Theological Subjects* (1793) and *Remarks on Important Theological Controversies* (1796).[41] The Scottish editor of the *Miscellanies*, John Erskine, wrote a preface making it clear that Jonathan Edwards Jr. had wanted to publish such portions of the *Miscellanies* as "might be generally useful." The first collection began with notebook entries on "the evidences of revealed religion," "miracles," "the reasonableness of some particular doctrines," "excellencies of scripture history," "the necessity of divine revelation," "the divinity of Christ," and other topics of a broad apologetic nature. Jonathan Edwards Jr. hoped that these notebooks "may prove an antidote to the deistical notions spreading in some parts of America." The second collection focused on a defense of Calvinism, with lengthy entries on "divine decrees," "efficacious grace," and "perseverance of the saints." Erskine's preface commended Edwards by noting that his "attachment to Calvinistic principles, did not hinder his seeking and finding instruction in their writings, whose system of theology was very opposite to his."[42] Erskine sought to turn the tables on the opponents of Calvinism by suggesting that it was they—not Edwards—who were narrow-minded.

Upon becoming president of Yale College in 1795, Timothy Dwight was confronted with French "infidelity" (i.e., freethinking) as a rampant force in

---

39. When published in the *Works of President Edwards* (1842), Jonathan Edwards Jr.'s essay, "Clearer Statements of Theological Truth Mae by President Edwards," is offered without a date attached (see Edward Hickman, ed, *The Works of Jonathan Edwards*, 2 vols.; Edinburgh: The Banner of Truth Trust, 1984 [1834]; 1:cxcii–cxcvi). Yet Jonathan Edwards, Jr. died in 1801, his discussion presupposes theological developments from the 1780s, and it makes reference to one who is "a friend to republican government"—thus suggesting a date in the 1790s.

40. Jonathan Edwards Jr., "Clearer Statements," in Hickman, ed., *Works* 1:cxcii–cxciii.

41. While these excerpted *Miscellanies* have been superseded by the texts in the Yale edition, these earlier publications reveal much about Edwards's successors in the 1790s and their apologetic interests and selective readings of Edwards's texts. See Hickman, ed., *Works*, 2:459–641.

42. John Erskine, "Preface" (1793), in Hickman, ed., *The Works of President Edwards*, 2:459. On Erskine, see Jonathan Yeager, *Enlightened Evangelicalism: The Life and Thought of John Erskine* (New York: Oxford University Press, 2011).

the college. Dwight became famous for the vigorous campaign he launched against enlightened unbelief at Yale. He focused attention on establishing the veracity and trustworthiness of the Bible. For Dwight, it was not only religion but science, ethics, education, and politics that were grounded in the teachings of the Bible: "The Bible had made millions virtuous. Philosophy has not made one."[43] According to Dwight, Voltaire in 1728 had developed "a systematical design to destroy Christianity" and to replace it with "irreligion and atheism." Meanwhile, the skeptical *philosophes* had invaded the Masonic movement. Some had ridiculed God, denied the legitimacy of human governments, and asserted the lawfulness of adultery and assassination. Dwight's major theological work—the five-volume *Theology Explained and Defended* (1818–19)—was as much a work of Christian apologetics as an exposition of Christian beliefs. In Dwight's eyes, David Hume had undermined the common sense understanding of cause and effect and so undermined the rational arguments for God. While it is not clear whether Dwight had read Thomas Reid—the most influential of the Scottish Common Sense Realists—Dwight did read George Campbell's *Dissertation on Miracles* (1762) and later helped to introduce Common Sense Philosophy into New England.[44] This philosophical school dominated the field of Christian apologetics among American thinkers throughout the early 1800s—with mixed results, so far as the appropriation of Edwards's philosophical ideas is concerned (ch. 40).[45]

Moral Government and Christ's Atonement

One well-known feature of the New Divinity was its approach to Christ's atonement, often referred to as the governmental or Grotian theory (in reference to the seventeenth-century Dutch jurist Hugo Grotius).[46] Jonathan Edwards Jr. did not directly attribute the new view of the atonement to his father but to his father's disciples: "The followers of Mr. Edwards have thrown

---

43. Fitzmier, *New England's Moral Legislator*, 83; Timothy Dwight, "Lectures on the Evidence of Divine Revelation," *Panoplist and Missionary Magazine United* 3 (August 1810): 111; cited in Fitzmier, *New England's Moral Legislator*, 90.

44. Fitzmier, *New England's Moral Legislator*, 150, 93, 85, 102–103.

45. E. Brooks Holifield, *Theology in America: Christian Thought from the Age of the Puritans to the Civil War* (New Haven, CT: Yale University Press, 2003), esp. 159–96.

46. For an overview, see Edwards A. Park, *The Atonement: Discourses and Treatises by Edwards, Smalley, Maxcy, Emmons, Griffin, Burge, and Weeks* (Boston: Congregational Board of Publication, 1859); and Dorus Paul Rudisill, *The Doctrine of the Atonement in Jonathan Edwards and His Successors* (New York: Poseidon Books, 1971).

new and important light upon The Doctrine of the Atonement." They have "proved, that the atonement does not consist in the payment of a debt, properly so called. It consists rather in doing that, which, for the purpose of establishing the authority of the divine law...is equivalent to the punishment of the sinner according to the letter of the law."[47] Joseph Bellamy made a similar appeal to a notion of divine law and divine government: "The design of the mediatorial offices and work of the Son of God incarnate, was to do honour to the divine law, and thereby open a way in which God might call, and sinners might come to him."[48] Stephen West's *The Scripture Doctrine of Atonement* (1785) argued that God's wise government over humankind required that he not allow sin to go unpunished: "It is essential to the goodness of a Governor, or King, to guard the rights, secure the peace, and promote the prosperity of his subjects.... Should a ruler suffer crimes to go unpunished; the laws, however good and righteous in themselves, would presently lose their authority; and government fall into contempt."[49]

Several features set the governmental view apart from more traditional views of Christ's atoning death. First, the main line of thought on the atonement in the West since the High Middle Ages—whether in Anselm, Luther, Calvin, or John Owen—held that God was the aggrieved or offended party in the atonement, to whom Christ's death was offered as recompense, reparation, or satisfaction. The governmental view denied this, insisting that God was acting as the Moral Governor of the universe, not as an offended party. Second, the traditional doctrine was that Christ's death was the payment of a "debt" or "penalty," strictly due to be paid or rendered for human sins. The governmental view differed here as well. Christ did not die as the substitute for sinners but as a substitute for the punishment due to sinners. Thus Jesus' death was not a case of strict justice, according to the letter of the law, but a token of suffering—something substituted for the full execution of justice against guilty sinners. Third, the governmental view departed from traditional Calvinism on the extent of the atonement and the doctrine of imputation. Calvinists held that Jesus' death was specifically intended for the elect, not for all humanity (i.e., the doctrine of limited atonement). Calvinists also held that the benefits or merits of Christ were "imputed" to those who believed in Christ, so that God saw them as righteous

---

47. Jonathan Edwards Jr., "Clearer Statements," in Edward Hickman, ed., *The Works of President Edwards*, 1:cxciv.

48. Joseph Bellamy, *Works* (1811), 2:540; cited in Rudisill, *Doctrine of Atonement*, 39.

49. Nathan Strong, in Sweeney and Guelzo, eds., *New England Theology*, 135.

with Christ's own righteousness. New Divinity thinkers denied both points. From the time of Joseph Bellamy's *True Religion Delineated* (1750), the New Divinity thinkers leaned toward a general rather than limited atonement—a death rendered on behalf of all humanity.[50] Regarding imputation, Jonathan Edwards Jr. commented that "the imputation of righteousness" is "not transfer of righteousness" but rather a transfer of "its beneficial consequences and advantages...to the believer."[51]

The roots of the governmental theory of the atonement stretch back to late medieval nominalist theology, which stressed God's absolute power (*potentia absoluta*) and capacity to do anything he willed to do.[52] Resuming this theme in 1500s, Socinus conjectured that God could forgive sins without any debt for sin being paid—a proposal that attacked the Christian atonement teaching at its core. Hugo Grotius's *Defensio fidei catholicae de satisfactione Christi* (1617) proposed the governmental view in response to Socinus. Yet Grotius's critics—and some of Socinus's own followers—saw Grotius's governmental view as a mediating position between traditional theories of the atonement and that of Socinus. In the New England context, the trigger for the development of governmental theories was the rise of Universalism in the 1780s. After James Relly's death in 1778, there was a republication of his universalist manifesto, *Union; Or, A Treatise of the Consanguinity and Affinity Between Christ and His Church* (1779). John Murray carried the Rellyan teaching to America and began to win a following during the 1780s. Pursuing the logic of high Calvinism to its limit, and adopting a general rather than limited doctrine of the atonement, Murray argued that Christ's death abolished all guilt and condemnation for humanity and that therefore all persons would finally be saved. For Universalists, "imputation" meant that all of Christ's merits were credited to all human beings.

---

50. New Divinity atonement teaching was nonetheless different from that of the Methodists. For Methodists and other evangelical Arminians, Christ had died for and atoned for all persons, and it was up to individuals to make a free choice to believe in this atonement. New Divinity thinkers held that it was God's elective will that ultimately determined who would benefit from the atonement—even though Christ's death had made satisfaction for the sins of all humanity.

51. Jonathan Edwards Jr., "Clearer Statements," in Edward Hickman, *Works*, 1:cxciv.

52. Duns Scotus proposed that "merit is anything which is accepted as merit," and the related doctrine of *acceptatio* held that Christ's merit "depends simply on...how highly will God be pleased." Albrecht Ritschl, *A Critical History of the Christian Doctrine of Justification and Reconciliation*, trans. John S. Black (Edinburgh: Edmonton and Douglas, 1872), 61, 69. Ritschl found a "real connexion" between the views of Scotus and "the entire rejection by the Socinians of the doctrine of reconciliation through Christ" (Ritschl, *Critical History*, 71).

Faced by Universalist heresy, New Divinity thinkers shifted their teaching on the atonement away from traditional ideas regarding the payment of a debt or penalty and also shied away from "imputation." Nathan Strong's *On the Evidence of Forgiveness* (1798) repudiated as "a very false idea" the notion "that the personal righteousness of Christ is made our personal righteousness." Strong's statement is surprisingly strong, given that Edwards had never rejected the notion of imputation.[53] No doubt the New Divinity thinkers were also unsettled by deist and Arminian arguments—charging that it was irrational for God to punish one person in place of another and that neither the "imputation" of Adam's sin to the human race nor the "imputation" of Christ's righteousness was morally justifiable. Yet the rise of Universalism in New England was most directly responsible for the New Divinity turn toward governmental views of the atonement.

Millennialism and Social Reform

New Divinity teachings on eschatology and social reform were built on the foundations laid by Edwards. He maintained that God would inaugurate the coming kingdom of Christ but would not do so apart from human exertions. The kingdom's arrival was to be "gradual"—a term that Edwards used in its etymological sense as something "occurring in steps or stages." Prior to a divine intervention into history or an open display of the miraculous, the "glorious times" of the church were to unfold sequentially, as Edwards explained: "This is a work that will be accomplished by means, by the preaching of the gospel, and the use of the ordinary means of grace, and so shall be gradually brought to pass. Some shall be converted and be the means of others' conversions."[54] Of course, Edwards believed that Christ would visibly return in glory to the earth, fully establish his reign, and exercise judgment. Yet this would not occur until after the "glorious times" of the church within history and then the subsequent millennium (ch. 35). Edwards's involvement in the Concert of Prayer initiated by Scottish evangelicals in 1744 and his authorship of the *Humble Attempt* (1747), demonstrated his growing belief that the coming of Christ's kingdom

---

53. Edwards continued to use the term "imputation" until the very end of his life. See Miscellany 1352 (dated to 1756–57), "Concerning the Reasonableness of the Doctrine of Imputation of Merit" (WJE 23:486–92); and Edwards's *very last* entry, Miscellany 1369, "Of Substitution and Imputation of Merit" (WJE 23:713–16). Edwards interpreted "imputation" in less forensic and more unitive fashion, as "respect...shown to one on account of his relation to or union and connection with another" (WJE 23:487)—a point treated in chs. 25 and 26.

54. WJE 9:459.

could be hastened through intense, unified prayer. Edwards wrote of the technological advancements of the coming age, in which travel, navigation, communication, and learning would advance globally, and "excellent books will be published in Africa, in Ethiopia, in Turkey—and not only very learned men, but others that are more ordinary men, shall then be very knowing in religion."[55]

Following the 1740s, Edwards and others within the New Light party understood the spiritual awakenings as directly related to the coming of Christ's kingdom. The revivals were eschatological signs, as Alan Heimert noted: "What cannot be gainsaid is that the expectancy expressed in that theory [of post-Awakening Calvinism] controlled the mind of the period.... The heart and soul of Calvinism was not doctrine but an implicit faith that God intended to establish this earthly Kingdom." Sensing that the Great Awakening had brought the course of history to a "critical juncture," the Edwardseans were on the lookout "from year to year" for signs of the dawning of a glorious new era.[56] Edwards, Hopkins, and Bellamy viewed the 1740s revivals as hopeful signs. Dwight and many others took a similar view of the revivals just after 1800.

Two early expressions of New Divinity eschatology were Joseph Bellamy's sermon on the millennium and the more extensive treatment in Samuel Hopkins's *Treatise on the Millennium* (1793). Hopkins predicted a great multiplication of global population, together with an even greater expansion of productive capacity, so that "each one will be fully supplied with all he wants." Improvements in the "art of husbandry" and cultivation of the soil will bring increased yields by twenty-, thirty-, or a hundredfold. No "more than 2 or 3 hours in a day" would be necessary for obtaining one's material needs, so that far more time will be available for "reading and conversation." During the coming age, wrote Hopkins, all "will probably speak *one language*," so as "greatly [to] facilitate the spreading [of] useful knowledge, and all kinds of intelligence, which may be a benefit to mankind, to all parts of the world." What is more, "this universality of language will tend to cement the world of mankind so as to make them one, in a higher degree, and to greater advantage, than otherwise could be."[57] In this work of some 150 pages, Hopkins did not once refer to the American Revolution or to the political independence the United States had

---

55. WJE 9:480.

56. Alan Heimert, *Religion and the American Mind: From the Great Awakening to the Revolution* (Cambridge, MA: Harvard University Press, 1966), 66–67.

57. Samuel Hopkins, *A Treatise on the Millennium* (Boston: Isaiah Thomas and Ebenezer T. Andrews, 1793), 71–72, 75, 77.

acquired by blood and toil. Hopkins's millennial teaching clearly had nothing to do with any nationalistic celebration of the young republic.

The Protestant missionary movement in the United States after 1800 was closely linked to the New Divinity and its Edwardsean notions of persistent prayer, disinterested benevolence, self-sacrifice, and the church's impending "glorious times." Nathaniel Emmons launched the Massachusetts Missionary Society in 1799, while Samuel Hopkins began the Missionary Society of Rhode Island in 1803. The Society of Inquiry on the Subject of Missions took shape in 1811 among Williams College students who adhered to Hopkins's or Emmons's theology.[58] This society was epoch-making as a student-led initiative in world missions and a foreshadowing of the later and much larger Student Volunteer Movement during the late 1800s and early 1900s.[59] When the American Board of Commissioners for Foreign Missions sent out their first missionaries in 1812, the Edwardsean Leonard Woods blended millennial hope with pastoral exhortation in his ordination sermon:

> The Lord of the universe, in these last days, is about to do a marvelous work.... The time of his glory is come. He will soon destroy all idol worship. The thrones of wickedness he will level with the dust.... The earth shall be full of the knowledge of the Lord, as the waters cover the sea. My hearers, God offers you the privilege of aiding in this great work of converting the nations.... Nothing else is worth living for. But who would not live, labor and die for this?[60]

New Divinity themes helped to propel the American missionary movement of the early 1800s.

Timothy Dwight was among most politically conservative of the Edwardseans in his support for the Federalist Party and the Standing Order in the New England churches. "During the Revolutionary era," wrote John Fitzmier, "he had interpreted the providential hand of God in the founding of the American nation as a hint of the millennium." In a poem published anony-

---

58. Sweeney and Guelzo, ed., *New England Theology*, 165–66.

59. David M. Howard, *Student Power in World Missions* (Downers Grove, IL: InterVarsity Press, 1979), 61–116.

60. Dietrich Buss, "The Millennial Vision as Motive for Religious Benevolence and Reform: Timothy Dwight and the New England Evangelicals Reconsidered," *Fides et Historia* 16 (1983), 18–34, 27; citing Leonard Woods, "Ordination Sermon [1812]," in R. Pierce Beaver, ed., *Pioneers in Mission: The Early Missionary Ordination Sermons, Charges, and Instructions* (Grand Rapids, MI: Eerdmans 1966).

mously in 1771, Dwight had lauded the rising nation and called for America to be the focus of "endless praise": "O land supremely blest! to thee 'tis given/ To taste the choicest joys of bounteous heaven;/Thy rising Glory shall expand its rays,/And lands and times unknown rehearse thine endless praise."[61] Yet "after long years of struggle with religious and political heterodoxy, Dwight now viewed the evangelistic enterprise as the quickest means to millennial bliss."[62] While his political optimism had been chastened, his religious optimism burned more brightly than ever. At the founding of Andover Seminary in 1808, Dwight announced the arrival of "the illustrious day, destined to scatter the darkness of this melancholy world and cover the earth with the light and glory." In effecting this change, "no miracles will be employed, but miracles of grace. The grace of God, the true alchemic stone, which transmutes the heart of rock into gold, will everywhere accompany the ordinances of the Gospel."[63]

Like the other Edwardseans, Timothy Dwight believed in the vigorous use of "means" to promote revival, evangelism, true religion, and moral reform. As early as 1790, Dwight suggested greater cooperation between Congregationalists and Presbyterians—an idea that matured into the Plan of Union (1801), aided substantially by the efforts of Jonathan Edwards Jr.[64] Dwight also supported the Missionary Society of Connecticut (1798), the Connecticut Tract Society (1807), the Connecticut Bible Society (1809), and the American Board of Commissioners for Foreign Missions (1810). Tract societies also sprang up in Vermont, New York, Boston, Philadelphia, and Baltimore. The local New England societies merged, and then a national consolidation took place in the formation of the American Tract Society (1825). Local initiatives— often led by Edwardsean ministers—gradually fused into national efforts. Sweeney and Guelzo explain that Edwards's theology was conducive to the development of voluntary societies. The distinction between "natural ability" and "moral inability" suggested that God did not compel his people but shaped

---

61. Timothy Dwight, cited in Ernest Lee Tuveson, *Redeemer Nation: The Idea of America's Millennial Role* (Chicago: University of Chicago Press, 1968), 104.

62. John R. Fitzmeier, *New England's Moral Legislator: Timothy Dwight, 1752–1817* (Bloomington, IN: Indiana University Press, 1998), 72.

63. Timothy Dwight, *A Sermon Preached at the Opening of the Theological Institution in Andover, September 20, 1808* (Boston, 1808), 26; cited in Buss, "Millennial Vision," 23.

64. Jonathan Edwards Jr., who held leadership positions in both the Congregational and Presbyterian churches, was especially in important in the emergence of the Plain of Union. See Robert L. Ferm, *Jonathan Edwards the Younger, 1745–1801* (Grand Rapids, MI: Eerdmans, 1976), 148–70, esp. 169.

FIGURE 37.1 Edwards's followers—including Jonathan Edwards Jr. and Samuel Hopkins—led in the emerging movement to abolish slavery during the late 1700s and early 1800s (J.G. Whittier, "Our Countrymen in Chains" New York: 1837. Library of Congress, Rare Book and Special Collections Division).

their inclinations. The "benevolent empire" in American Protestantism was substantially Edwardsean in its inspiration.[65] Colonial Calvinists had relied on a tax-supported parish system. New Divinity theology—with its stress on voluntary efforts and voluntary support—was better attuned to situation of the young Republic and may have paved the way for church disestablishment in Connecticut (1818) and Massachusetts (1833).

New England Congregationalism showed a moral intensity that could be traced back to Edwardseanism. "It is only when we have in hand the puzzle piece of the ethics of disinterested benevolence," write Sweeney and Guelzo, that we can grasp "the fiery urgency of William Lloyd Garrison and John Brown."[66] Indeed, it was on the topic of slavery that the Edwardseans became known for their radicalism. By 1771, Hopkins was preaching against the slave trade. By 1773, he was attacking slavery itself. Hopkins's moral radicalism and theological intransigence prepared him to be the preacher of abolition in Newport, Rhode Island—the epicenter of the American slave trade. He won a following in among African Americans in Newport, as well as enduring hostility from slave ship owners. For Hopkins, slavery was a flagrant offense against benevolence and the result of a "most criminal, contracted selfishness." The only remedy was immediate emancipation, as Hopkins argued in *A Dialogue Concerning the Slavery of the Africans* (1776). Similarly, Jonathan Edwards Jr. wrote in *The Injustice and Impolity of the Slave Trade and of Slavery* (1791) that "I conceive it [the slave trade] to be unjust in itself" and "contrary to every principle of justice and humanity." Nathanael Emmons also denounced slavery from the pulpit.[67] "Immediatism"—the demand for immediate, unconditional emancipation of all slaves, rather than gradual or partial solutions—was the socio-political correlate of Hopkins's view of conversion and his call for "immediate repentance."

Final Thoughts on the New Divinity

The appreciation and appropriation of Edwards's ideas among New Divinity thinkers was selective and necessarily so. One factor was a lack of access to many of Edwards's writings. While *Freedom of the Will*, *Original Sin*, and *Religious Affections* were widely available, only a few well-connected individuals would have had access to manuscript materials. Edwards's biblical writings

---

65. Sweeney and Guelzo, *New England Theology*, 16.

66. Sweeney and Guelzo, *New England Theology*, 21.

67. Sweeney and Guelzo, *New England Theology*, 150–51, 157; Buss, "Millennial Vision," 28.

were unavailable. The portions of the *Miscellanies* published in the 1790s included Edwards's traditional apologetic arguments and not his more innovative theological arguments. "The Mind" was not published until 1829—a time when Scottish Common Sense Philosophy was dominant in America. So it is not surprising that philosophical idealism was not among Edwards's nineteenth-century legacies (ch. 40). Perhaps because of a changing intellectual context, the Edwardseans showed little interest in Edwards's typological writings. The distinctive character of Edwards's Trinitarianism seems also to have gone unrecognized (ch. 13). In the late 1800s, Oliver Wendell Holmes hinted that Edwards had been a closet Unitarian—a sign of how little was known regarding this aspect of Edwards's thought.[68] Edwards's idea of writing a history of redemption (ch. 12) did not catch on among Hopkins, Bellamy, or others.

New Divinity authors generally wanted to heighten human responsibility by insisting that sin was by nature a conscious transgression of God's will. Only explicit, deliberate departures from God's will were culpable. This intellectual move had apologetic value in the early 1800s context, when Calvinism was under fire from deists, Arminians, Universalists, and Unitarians. Yet it had a downside, as well. The stress on conscious sin weakened earlier Calvinist and Puritan teachings that sinners are so lost in sin that they do not even know that they are lost. Emmons's assertion that all sinners sinned self-consciously undermined traditional Protestant notions of the "noetic effects" of sin. It drew dangerously near to the rationalistic position that the affections and will were fallen but the human mind was unfallen—a position that earlier Protestant theologians had consistently rejected.

Another line of criticism pertains to the governmental theory of the atonement. From its earliest period, Christian theology had always presupposed that there was a bond linking Christians to Christ—whether understood as incarnational, representative, or forensic. For traditional Calvinists, "covenant" and "imputation" were conceptual mainstays of the believers' bond with Christ. For Edwards, union with Christ found expression in a profusion of terms and concepts, including "communication," "participation," "imputation," and "propriety." Christ, said Edwards, was a "public person" who acted on others' behalf. New Divinity thinkers rejected imputation but offered nothing very definite in its place other than vague assertions of a "divine constitution" that somehow transferred the benefits of Christ to believers. The governmental view represented not only a shift in atonement theology but, in Joseph Conforti's words, "a significant and controversial attenuation of

---

68. Oliver Wendell Holmes, "The Pulpit and the Pew," *Pages from an Old Volume of Life* (Boston: Houghton Mifflin, 1883), 402–33.

orthodox Calvinist Christology."[69] Without some clear-cut notion of forensic representation or spiritual union between Christ and believers, the whole process of salvation might appear to be arbitrary. The conclusion is ironic because New Divinity thinkers wanted to avoid an arbitrary, capricious God. Henry Boynton Smith's *Faith and Philosophy* (1877), which made Christology central, was a return toward Edwards's style of theologizing.

Finally, it should be clear that Taylor redirected—or, some may say, derailed—the Edwardsean tradition. Opposition to Taylor and to Yale Divinity School became so heated that it led to the founding of a rival school—The Theological Institute of Connecticut (later Hartford Seminary). Taylor's student Edwards Amasa Park and Park's student Frank Hugh Foster portrayed Taylor as the culmination and essence of Edwardseanism. Yet Taylor's "power to the contrary" was hard to distinguish from the Arminianism that Edwards had so vigorously refuted. While Taylor and Finney sounded Edwardsean themes in their theologies, they repudiated the Calvinist and Edwardsean principle of moral inability apart from grace. The lasting split between Taylor and Tyler proved disastrous during the decades after the Civil War. Edwardseanism's divided house could not stand.[70]

---

69. Conforti, *Jonathan Edwards*, 124.

70. Foster, *Genetic History*, 367. Douglas A. Sweeney's *Nathaniel Taylor, New Haven Theology, and the Legacy of Jonathan Edwards* (New York: Oxford University Press, 2003), argues that Taylor's theology broadened the Edwardsean tradition but also divided and weakened it.

38

Mixed Reactions: Princeton and Andover Seminaries and Nineteenth-Century American Culture

JOSEPH A. CONFORTI has called Jonathan Edwards "a kind of white whale of American religious history."[1] Like Moby Dick, Edwards was never far from the popular imagination, inspiring both reverence and revulsion.

Even among his followers, Edwards's legacy in the nineteenth century was mixed. He was prized for his piety by some and for his revival theology by others, but his psychology, ethics, and metaphysics were largely rejected. This dismemberment of Edwards's thought was an indirect result of eighteenth-century battles against deism. As Brooks Holifield has observed, deism influenced American thought far out of proportion to its numbers. By attacking Christian orthodoxy for lacking "reasonable" evidence, deists inspired eighteenth-century Christian intellectuals to a renewed search for evidences that would pass muster among skeptics. The rising prestige of science further encouraged theology to emulate the scientific demand for rational "proofs." Deists had derided mystery and claimed that "common sense"—open to all and not just to the regenerate—was the foundation of true religion and philosophy. Scotsman Thomas Reid and his philosophy of common sense seemed to be just what was needed. Like Kant, he appealed to first principles of the mind. But in an effort to undermine Locke's epistemology and Hume's skepticism, Reid asserted that the human mind perceives objects directly and not merely images of those objects. What is more, the mind has immediate access to common sense principles that, if universal and not self-contradictory, are self-evident axioms. This Scottish Realism, as further developed by Dugald Stewart and Sir William Hamilton, discouraged metaphysical speculation and advocated reliance instead on inferences from "facts of consciousness."[2]

---

1. Joseph A. Conforti, *Jonathan Edwards, Religious Tradition, and American Culture* (Chapel Hill, NC: University of North Carolina Press, 1995), 1.

2. E. Brooks Holifield, *Theology in America: Christian Thought from the Age of the Puritans to the Civil War* (New Haven, CT: Yale University Press, 2003), 159, 175–77, 172–75.

The Scottish whirlwind left little of Edwards's project intact. While the nineteenth century produced more than forty book-length engagements with Edwards's thought, most sought to overturn his construals of moral freedom and original sin on the grounds that Edwards violated the "moral axioms" of the universe. For example, Henry Philip Tappan, who authored the longest attack on Edwards's view of the will, insisted that only a self-determining will stands the test of an "appeal to consciousness."[3] As we saw in chapter 37, even Edwards's New Divinity disciples ignored his his metaphysical idealism (his notion that existence depends on being perceived) in favor of the new Baconian empiricism and "inductive" intuition of moral laws. They also rejected his unitary view of the human self and adopted various forms of a faculty psychology that divided the mind from the will. For the New Divinity, "Calvinism did not depend so much on mystery as on the capacity to accept what was reasonable to divines of the period."[4]

In general, most American and British admirers of Edwards shunned his metaphysics and moral philosophy, and concentrated instead on his theologies of revival and spirituality (chs. 4, 27, 42). Conforti refers to this as the "Methodization" of Edwards in the nineteenth century, pointing out that leaders of the Second Great Awakening distributed Edwards's works of practical divinity, not his dogmatic texts. More than 100,000 copies of the "Conversion of President Edwards" (i.e., *Personal Narrative*) were printed; the American Tract Society published more than one million copies of his works by the end of the Civil War. The most popular and most frequently reprinted work was the life and diary of David Brainerd. It served as a manual for Methodist circuit riders and Baptist missionaries, since they viewed it as a "case study of genuine religious affections." Sereno Dwight's "Memoirs of Jonathan Edwards—which comprised the 660-page first volume in a ten-volume collected edition of his great-grandfather's works (1829)—gave greater attention to personal piety than to theology. Even Edwards's *Religious Affections* suffered at the hand of its editors: the American Tract Society's version stripped away sections of the treatise distinguishing moral from natural ability and toned down passages that might sound mystical or aesthetic. John Wesley believed the

---

3. Henry Philip Tappan, *A Review of Edwards's "Inquiry into the Freedom of the Will"* (New York: J. S. Taylor, 1839), 224.

4. Holifield, *Theology in America*, 136–37; John Gerstner, *The Rational Biblical Theology of Jonathan Edwards*, 3 vols. (Powhatan, VA: Berea Publications, 1991), 1:546, 564; Bruce Kuklick, *Churchmen and Philosophers: From Jonathan Edwards to John Dewey* (New Haven, CT: Yale University Press, 1985) 99, 101. The last quotation is from Kuklick, 64.

Affections contained "much wholesome food...mixed with much deadly poison." While he published many editions of the work for his British and American Methodists, his editions were only one-sixth the length of the American original and contained only eight of the original twelve "positive signs" of true religion. One of the eliminated signs was that which said true affections are founded on perception of the beauty of moral excellence in divine things.[5]

This chapter will concentrate principally on the battle between Princeton and Andover Seminaries over claims to Edwards's thought. It will then review briefly other direct and indirect nineteenth-century traces of Edwards's influence.

Princeton Seminary and Charles Hodge

From its beginning in 1812 as a seminary separate from the college, Princeton Seminary was leery of Edwardsean divinity. Its founding professor, Archibald Alexander (1772–1851), believed true religion was centered in the understanding and disliked Edwards's emphasis on the affections. Educated in Common Sense Philosophy by William Graham, a student of earlier college president John Witherspoon, Alexander criticized Edwards's true virtue as utilitarian devotion to human happiness and appealed instead to "dictates of conscience" that he said were as certain as mathematical principles.[6] Charles Hodge, who taught theology at the seminary for more than sixty years (1822–78), was more positive, saying he had "derived more satisfaction from Edwards on the Religious Affections, and from his work on Original Sin, than from any other source." He commended Edwards for teaching immediate imputation "formally and at length" in *Original Sin* despite one chapter's "excrescence" that appeared to endorse mediate imputation of Adam's sin (the doctrine of Placaeus "that the evil disposition is first, and the charge of guilt *consequent*"). Edwards, according to Hodge, taught instead the federal headship of Adam, which meant that his descendants inherited his corruption and guilt since they "sinned (so it is implied) in that one man's sin." Hodge was pleased with Edwards's forensic doctrine of justification because it seemed to teach the imputation to believers of both Christ's perfect obedience and penal suffering.

---

5. Conforti, *Jonathan Edwards*, 9, 72, 41, 33–34. On Edwards's and Wesley's divergent theologies of revival, see chs. 27 & 42.

6. Mark Noll, "The Contested Legacy of Jonathan Edwards in Antebellum Calvinism: Theological Conflict and the Evolution of Thought in America," *Canadian Review of American Studies* 19 (1988): 154–55.

Hodge's own argument for true religion as "loving God for his divine excellence" showed his indebtedness to Edwards.[7]

But Hodge worried about other aspects of Edwards's theology. He thought Edwards was far too tolerant of revivalist excesses (ch. 27) and that his definition of true virtue as "love of being" was the foundation for an unscriptural and unreasonable utilitarianism.[8] Perhaps picking up on Alexander's complaint, Hodge argued that this understanding of virtue made holiness subordinate to happiness when in fact "it is the instinctive judgment of men, that holiness or moral excellence is a greater good than happiness."[9] The root of the problem, Hodge suggested, was that Edwards resorted to metaphysics. Christians should "rest satisfied with the simple statements of the Bible." The ways of God are past finding out. God's self-manifestation is the end of creation, not a purported happiness dictated by some metaphysical scheme. Edwards's conception of God's arbitrary constitution of Adam and his posterity as one being (ch. 22) was based on "the assumption that we can understand the relation of the efficiency of God to the effects produced in time." His doctrine of continued creation destroyed the "common sense distinction between creation and preservation." Perhaps the most dangerous aspect of Edwards's metaphysics, according to Hodge, was the notion that God is the only substance (ch. 7). Hodge worried that this "strange doctrine" meant "there can be no free agency, no sin, no responsibility, no individual existence." This idea "is essentially pantheistic" and led logically toward Transcendentalism. Although Hodge made only limited use of Common Sense Philosophy, he appears to have thought it a bulwark against pantheism because of its "common sense" distinction between God and humanity. Thus Edwards's belief that God declared Adam and his posterity one was "contrary...to the intuitive convictions of men."[10]

Hodge also thought Edwards was not sufficiently concerned with, or faithful to, church tradition. Edwards's ecclesiology—based on the idea that pastors and elders can judge the regeneration of others—was not only unbiblical but was "never adopted or acted upon by any church on earth, until the rise of the Independents." His comment was a barb against what he considered to be a dangerous

---

7. Charles Hodge, "Professor Park and the Princeton Review," *Biblical Repertory and Princeton Review* 23 (1851): 685; Hodge, *Systematic Theology*, 3 vols. (Grand Rapids MI: Eerdmans, 1986) 2:207–208, 3:116–17; Holifield, *Theology in America*, 383.

8. Charles Hodge, *Constitutional History of the Presbyterian Church in the United States of America*, 2 vols. (Philadelphia, PA: William S. Martien, 1840), 2:76–87.

9. Edwards might have said that Hodge was creating a false dichotomy, for both happiness and holiness are communicated by God to believers in their union with Christ (see chs. 14, 23).

10. Hodge, *Systematic Theology*, 1:433–34, 435; 2:219, 220; Kuklick, *Churchman and Philosophers*, 78; Hodge, *Systematic Theology* 2:220.

spirit of innovation, disregarding the precedents and practices of the historic churches. Hodge invoked the same principle in his criticism of New Divinity thinker Nathaniel William Taylor (ch. 37), who allowed that God may not be able to prevent sin without destroying liberty. This notion, cried Hodge, "is so contrary to the Scriptures, that it has never been adopted by any organized portion of the Christian Church." On this theory, he protested, "all prayer that God would change our own hearts, or the hearts of others, becomes irrational." Scripture declares that God holds the hearts of men in his hand and "turneth it" like "the rivers of water . . . whithersoever he will" (Prov. 21:1), and that he works in them "both to will and to do of his good pleasure" (Phil. 2:13). Hodge's final word on this subject was that "the Church has, almost with one accord, preferred to leave the mystery of evil unexplained, rather than to seek its solution in a principle which undermines the foundation of all religion." By "principle" Hodge meant Edwards's notion that sin is morally necessary and Taylor's proposal that sin exists because God cannot violate free will. Edwards in fact never separated human happiness from God's glory, as Hodge suggested. Nor did he justify evil on the basis of human happiness alone, as Hodge and Alexander charged, but on the basis of God's glory and his "excellent, holy, gracious and glorious ends."[11] Hodge also wrongly suggested that Edwards believed he or anyone else could know with certainty the state of someone else's heart (ch. 29). But Hodge was not mistaken in supposing that Edwards paid little attention to historical precedent—whether earlier theological writings or ecclesiological practices (ch. 9). Hodge was far more a student of church tradition than was Edwards.[12]

In summary, Princeton Seminary was more intellectualist than Edwards and his disciples in its view of religious experience. It rejected Edwards's revivalist theology and Augustinian psychology, distrusted his metaphysics, considered his views of common humanity and continuous creation to be eccentric, and regarded his notion of true virtue as strangely speculative. Part of this opposition to Edwards's thinking was rooted in Princeton Seminary's acceptance of common sense assumptions. The result of this at Princeton, as Mark Noll puts it, "was a theology with a deep inner tension, divided between belief in God's special work among the elect and the universal human capacity to perceive true virtue."[13]

---

11. Hodge, *Systematic Theology* 3:571; Nathaniel Taylor, *Lectures on the Moral Government of God* (New York, 1859) 2 vols, 2:344; Hodge, *Systematic Theology* 1:434–35; WJE 1:402.

12. This might help explain Edwards's rejection of the Roman Catholic Church. Hodge, on the other hand, concluded from his extensive knowledge of the theological tradition that the Roman church was true but erring. Hodge, *Systematic Theology* 1:113–15. But see ch. 41 for Edwards's "developmentalist" stance with regard to the Calvinist tradition.

13. Noll, "Contested Legacy," 159.

Edwards Amasa Park and Andover Seminary

Edwards Amasa Park—professor from 1836 to 1881 and sometime president of Andover Seminary—claimed he rejected nothing of what Edwards had taught. Founded in 1805 during a conservative reaction to Unitarian Henry Ware's election as Hollis Professor of Divinity at Harvard, Andover Seminary soon became America's largest mid-nineteenth-century seminary. In the pages of the Andover journal *Bibliotheca Sacra*, Park battled Hodge and the Princetonians over the meaning of Edwards's legacy. Park charged that when Princeton rejected Edwards's revival theology and philosophical ethics (as expressed in *The Nature of True Virtue*), Hodge and his successors were cutting out the heart of Edwards's theology. Park added that Hodge was simply too subservient to inherited theological tradition, suggesting that Princeton was sliding toward "the unreasoning dogmatism of Rome." Park boasted that Edwards famously "called no man father," and his New Divinity disciples were "thoroughly Protestant." More recent theologians, presumably including Park, were akin to Edwards in that they "felt a similar preference for the Bible above creed."[14]

In his celebrated "Theology of the Intellect and That of the Feelings" (1850), Park argued that biblical language is often concrete and figurative, expressing sentiment and hints. This "theology of the feelings" was never designed to be translated directly into doctrines, which come instead from the "theology of the intellect." The latter uses intuition and deduction, preferring "general to individual statements, the abstract to the concrete, the literal to the figurative." So when the Psalmist exclaims, "Behold! I was shapen in iniquity, and in sin did my mother conceive me," we are not to infer an abstract doctrine of inherited corruption, for that would violate "the axioms of common sense." It would "[confound] poetry with prose," resting content with the sign rather than the thing signified. The proper way to think is to "[value] the conscience," refraining from passionate statements of feeling. So a theology of the intellect would never suggest that "Christ has fully paid the debt of sinners" or "that he has suffered the whole punishment which they deserve," for both might suggest "the salvation of all men." It would never say "that Heaven imputes the crime of one man to millions of his descendants, and then

---

14. Conforti, 9; Mark Noll, "Jonathan Edwards and Nineteenth-Century Theology," in Nathan O. Hatch and Harry S. Stout, eds., *Jonathan Edwards and the American Experience* (New York: Oxford University Press, 1988), 265; Noll, "Contested Legacy," 153; Edwards Amasa Park, "The New England Theology" (1852), in Douglas A. Sweeney and Allen C. Guelzo, eds., *The New England Theology: From Jonathan Edwards to Edwards Amasa Park* (Grand Rapids, MI: Baker Academic, 2006), 262. On Park, see Charles W. Phillips, "The Last Edwardsean: Edwards Amasa Park and the Rhetoric of Improved Calvinism," PhD diss., University of Stirling, 2005.

imputes their myriad sins to him who was harmless and undefiled." This too contradicts the common sense axiom that a man can be responsible only for his own freely chosen actions.[15]

Two years later in 1852, Park published a groundbreaking essay on the "New England Theology"—a term he coined at Andover for what he thought was the seamless unity of Edwards's theology with that of the New Divinity at Yale and at Andover (ch. 37).[16] For Park this theology contained three key propositions— "that a just God will not command men to do what they have no power to do; that he will not punish them with unending pain for doing as well as they can; that, in every case, physical ability is commensurate with obligation."[17] Or, to put it in "a single truth, that an entirely depraved man has a natural power to do all which is required of him." Taking a page from Hodge, Park claimed that "these great truths are the common faith of the church," in fact a "corrected edition of the Genevan creed." That creed and other creeds needed correction because their authors had "undervalued" the "ethical axioms" taught by "the philosophy of common sense." Only by "shaping their faith" by these axioms had Park and his New Divinity predecessors been able to produce a "practical theology."[18]

Charles Hodge was not impressed. He thought Park's distinction between the theologies of intellect and feeling was a smokescreen to camouflage departures from classical Christian orthodoxy.[19] Hodge's colleague Lyman Atwater went further, alleging "that the distinctive features of this New Divinity, in all its successive forms, are utterly abhorrent to [Edwards's] entire system." Atwater zeroed in especially on the Taylor formula of "power to the contrary" that Park had developed—the idea that sinners have inherent ability to avoid sin—and showed that it contradicted what Edwards wrote about the will.[20]

Then Yale's Noah Porter entered the fray. Porter—Taylor's student and successor—implicitly conceded that the New England Theology differed in substance from that of Edwards. But the important thing, he suggested, was that

---

15. Park, "Theology of the Intellect and That of the Feelings," in Sweeney and Guelzo, eds., *New England Theology*, 249, 254, 250.

16. Conforti, *Jonathan Edwards*, 4.

17. By 1862 these were called "the three radicals." Henry Boynton Smith, "The Theological System of Emmons," *American Theological Review* 13 (January 1862), 52.

18. Park, "New England Theology," 259–61.

19. Ironically, in his introduction to his *Systematic Theology*, Hodge himself distinguished between "two theologies—one of the intellect, and another of the heart." Hodge, *Systematic Theology* 1:16; Sweeney and Guelzo, *New England Theology*, 248.

20. Lyman Atwater, "Jonathan Edwards and the Successive Forms of the New Divinity," *Princeton Review* 30 (1858): 589; Noll, "Contested Legacy," 152.

New England theologians at Andover and Yale had imitated Edwards's spirit. Edwards "did not content himself with restating the old metaphysics which the first reformers had taken from Augustine and the schoolmen...nor with servilely copying the compromising philosophy which the Westminster assembly had been forced, by conflicting parties, to agree upon." According to Porter, Edwards practiced philosophy as well as theology, boldly improving scholastic formulas if he saw a better way by reason to express biblical truths. So if New England theologians expressed themselves in new ways to preserve what they took to be gospel truths, they were true to the spirit of their great teacher. According to intellectual historian Bruce Kuklick, the New Divinity thinker Nathaniel Taylor exemplified the intellectual freedom that Porter commended. Following Edwards's supposed spirit meant, for Taylor, repudiating Edwards's psychology: "The Edwardsean notion of an entelechy was defeated. Taylor's mentalistic faculty psychology, reinforced by Scottish ideas, became standard."[21]

When Union (New York) Seminary's Henry Boynton Smith looked back in the 1860s on the Andover-Princeton battles of the preceding decades, he concluded that all parties to the debate had gone off track. Smith criticized the Yale thinkers for propounding philosophy without faith and Princeton for teaching faith without philosophy. In an 1862 review of the collected works of Nathaniel Emmons, Smith said that New England's theologians had focused on God's sovereignty and man's will, but not on the true center of Christian theology—the God-man: "Neither God's agency, nor man's will, can give us the whole system; but as Calvin says, 'Christ is the mirror in whom we may without deception contemplate our own election.'" The result was that "the divine element was eliminated, and the human will, in the construction of the system, took the place of the divine will." Thus, while New England used much of Edwards's language, the perspective had changed: "The same phrases may be used, but there is another sense; there may be, to outward seeming, the same eyeball, but another soul looks out; the hands feel like the hands of Jacob, but the voice is the voice of Esau."[22]

Other Nineteenth-Century Legacies

Certain theologians and church leaders adopted Edwards's theology more straightforwardly. Thomas Chalmers (1780–1847), founder of the Free Church

---

21. Noah Porter, "The Princeton Review on Dr. Taylor and the Edwardean Theology," *New Englander and Yale Review* 18 (1860): 737; Kuklick, *Churchman and Philosophers*, 110. "Entelechy" is an Aristotelian term for complete actualization that in the context of Edwards's psychology refers to the unity of the person.

22. Noll, "Jonathan Edwards and Nineteenth-Century Theology," 272; Smith, "The Theological System of Emmons," 53, 35. The reach of Scottish common sense was wide and deep.

of Scotland, prized Edwards's thinking on the will for its capacity to wed divine determinism with human liberty. He said the *Freedom of the Will* "helped me more than any other inspired book," enabling the gospel to be preached with the confidence that God is sovereign and humans are free to respond.[23] Andrew Fuller and the English Calvinistic Baptists used Edwards's distinction between natural and moral ability to preach conversion in an era when some Calvinists considered such preaching to be unnecessary. Fuller's doctrine of "duty faith"—based on Edwards's teachings on the will, the affections, and his *Life of David Brainerd*— "was to remain the touchstone of [evangelical dissenting] orthodoxy for several generations" after the turn of the nineteenth century in Britain. Baptists on the other side of the pond were also taken by Edwards's approach to evangelism. The (Baptist) College of Rhode Island—later Brown University—"became a stronghold of Edwardean divinity." Baptist historian Francis Wayland wrote that Fuller's theology became the "almost universal" authority among Baptists in the northeastern United States.[24] The "Americanist" Lutherans, led by Samuel Schmucker, also showed the reach of Edwardsean theology: Schmucker's theology stressed conversion, the duty of repentance, and the necessity of sinners to repent immediately.[25] Joseph Conforti has shown how Edwardsean Calvinism appealed to nineteenth-century evangelical women in his study of Mary Lyon and her founding of Mt. Holyoke Seminary, where "Lyon and her students were empowered by a religious culture of disinterested benevolence to transcend the gendered social experience that made Edwardsian self-denial appealing in the first place."[26]

Southern Presbyterians, by contrast, adopted a more critical stance toward Edwards. Echoing Princeton's Alexander and Hodge, James Henley Thornwell charged that Edwards's *Freedom of the Will* made God the author of sin and that his notion of personal identity in *Original Sin* opposed "the plainest intuitions

---

Kuklick notes that, while Smith criticized New England for replacing Berkeleyan with Scottish metaphysics and making the human will primary, Smith nevertheless believed that the will can act contrary to the strongest motive (*Churchmen and Philosophers*, 214).

23. Noll, "Jonathan Edwards and Nineteenth-Century Theology," 272; David W. Bebbington, "Remembered Around the World: The International Scope of Edwards's Legacy," in David W. Kling and Douglas A. Sweeney, eds., *Jonathan Edwards At Home and Abroad* (Columbia, SC: University of South Carolina Press, 2003), 187.

24. Bebbington, "Remembered," 184; on Fuller, see also Chris Chun, "Alternative Viewpoint: Jonathan Edwards's Life and Career," in Gerald McDermott, ed., *Understanding Jonathan Edwards: An Introduction to America's Theologian* (New York: Oxford University Press, 2009), 29–35; Holifield, *Theology in America*, 273, 281.

25. Holifield, *Theology in America*, 406. The last two elements in Schmucker's preaching were taught by Edwards but especially developed by Hopkins (see ch. 39).

26. Conforti, *Jonathan Edwards*, 97.

of intelligence." Robert Lewis Dabney was even more critical, condemning Edwards's view of continuous creation as "worthless"—not least because it contradicted "universal common sense." Preferring the theology of Reformed scholastic Francis Turretin, Dabney dismissed much of Edwards's theology as impractical metaphysical speculation. He objected particularly to the notion of true virtue as virtuous affections, which he complained was "a mere abstraction, a general idea." Human "consciousness" attested that virtue pertains to individual and local concerns, which Edwards's *True Virtue* had ignored.[27]

Other nineteenth-century detractors included the Scottish theologian John McLeod Campbell and the American novelist Harriet Beecher Stowe. Though Edwards's influence on Campbell was "profound," Campbell attacked Edwards's doctrine of limited atonement and opposed his "fiction" of legal or penal imputation. For her part, Stowe blamed Edwards's "rationalistic methods" for the rise of Unitarianism and Transcendentalism. Edwards's influence extended to France and Germany during the nineteenth and early twentieth centuries. While most French thinkers were repelled by Edwards's "necessitarian" logic, Henri Bois and Jacques Kaltenbach sought to understand his revival writings. German interpreters appreciated the systematic character of Edwards's philosophizing, and spoke of its "mystical" features. Yet none of the Europeans seem to have read widely in Edwards's writings, and it was left to a few Americans who studied in Europe—like William Squires (ch. 40) and John McCracken—to try to link Edwards to European intellectual trends.[28]

Neglect and Revulsion

In the last third of the nineteenth century, most authors treated Edwards as an "anachronism." They cited him as an "important" thinker, but few intellectuals paid serious attention to his work. Few seemed to notice when the New England Theology slipped away. As historian Frank Hugh Foster put it, "In a night, it perished off the face of the earth." Its questions were no longer the questions

---

27. Sean Michael Lucas, "'He Cuts Up Edwardsism by the Roots': Robert Lewis Dabney and the Edwardsian Legacy in the Nineteenth-Century South," in D.G. Hart, Sean Michael Lucas, and Stephen J. Nichols, eds., *The Legacy of Jonathan Edwards: American Religion and the Evangelical Tradition* (Grand Rapids: Baker Academic, 2003), 204, 209–11. Dabney and other Southern Presbyterians were also disturbed that New Divinity theologians used the logic of disinterested benevolence to attack the slave trade and call for the abolition of slavery (Lucas, "He Cuts Up," 212).

28. M.X. Lesser, *Reading Jonathan Edwards: An Annotated Bibliography in Three Parts, 1729–2005* (Grand Rapids: Eerdmans, 2008), 138; John McLeod Campbell, *The Nature of the Atonement* (Cambridge, UK, 1856), 69–70,97; Harriet Beecher Stowe, *Oldtown Folks* (Boston, 1869; rev. ed. 1911) 263. She may have been confusing Edwards with Nathaniel Emmons, whom she portrayed as Dr. Stern in this novel. For more on Stowe and the New England

of the "New Theology," or "Progressive Orthodoxy," whose thinkers asked not how each of us is morally responsible but how the few who are socially responsible can fulfill their obligations to the many who are not.[29] They celebrated human freedom, rejected original sin, stressed the historical Jesus rather than historic creeds, and replaced the coming millennium with human aspirations toward ethical reform. With the exception of Methodists and Baptists, most mainline Protestant churches of the early 1900s had long since disengaged from revivalism. Ralph Waldo Emerson's suspicion of doctrine and new hope in the promise of science helped to shift the locus of value from the supernatural to the natural. One consequence was that the discipline of philosophy began attracting the money and talent once devoted to theology.[30]

Historians have offered a range of explanations for this near-disappearance of interest in Edwards and his epigones. Some have blamed self-absorption and inattention to larger cultural phenomena such as German idealism, theological romanticism, Darwinian evolution, and urban secularism. David Bebbington, for example, has shown how nineteenth-century thinkers turned away from eighteenth-century invocations of reason to an emphasis on will, spirit, and emotion. They stressed imagination and intuition, and considered a certain imprecision of expression to be a strength. Others have focused on the sudden disappearance of great theologians and major syntheses—and the way that both idealist philosophy and Darwinian materialism "made untenable commitments to a Christian philosophy based on Scottish thought." Debates over American slavery also undermined Common Sense Philosophy, since both abolitionists and slavery supporters appealed to supposed laws of consciousness.[31]

Theology, see Donald L. Weber, "The Image of Jonathan Edwards in American Culture," (PhD diss., Columbia University, 1978), 132–45. Park protested the Progressive Orthodoxy of "Andover liberalism." See Charles W. Phillips, "The Last Edwardsean: Edwards Amasa Park and the Rhetoric of Improved Calvinism," Ph.D. diss., University of Stirling, 2005, ch. 6. On Edwards's impact in Europe, see Michael J. McClymond, "'A German Professor Dropped into the American Forests': British, French, and German Views of Edwards, 1758–1957," in Douglas Sweeney and Oliver Crisp, eds., *After Edwards: The Courses of the New England Theology* (New York: Oxford University Press, 2012).

29. Noll, "Jonathan Edwards and Nineteenth-Century Theology," 261, 275–77; Frank Hugh Foster, *A Genetic History of the New England Theology* (Chicago, IL: University of Chicago Press, 1907), 543; Kuklick, *Churchmen and Philosophers*, 224.

30. Holifield, *Theology in America*, 507; Conforti, *Jonathan Edwards*, 161; Kuklick, *Churchmen and Philosophers*, 252, 255–57.

31. Sweeney, "Taylorites, Tylerites, and the Dissolution of the New England Theology," in Hart, Lucas, and Nichols, *Legacy*, 198–99; David W. Bebbington, *The Dominance of Evangelicalism: The Age of Spurgeon and Moody* (Downers Grove: InterVarsity, 2005), 148–83; Allen C. Guelzo, *Edwards on the Will: A Century of American Theological Debate* (Middletown, CT: Wesleyan University Press, 1989), 277; Kuklick, *Churchmen and Philosophers*, 222–23; Holifield, *Theology in America*, 501–502. The quote about Darwin's materialism is from Kuklick, 223.

Whatever the reasons, in the last few decades of the nineteenth century, Edwards's theology appeared to be unrealistic or irrelevant for leading American thinkers and the few British intellectuals who knew of him. Both Harriet Beecher Stowe and Oliver Wendell Holmes admired Edwards's noble life but thought that Edwards's *Religious Affections* set the spiritual standard too high. They concluded that his God was cruel.[32] Leslie Stephen—the British agnostic intellectual and father of novelist Virginia Woolf—puzzled over Edwards's combination of mysticism and stern theology, concluding he was "formed by nature to be a German professor, and accidentally dropped into the American forests."[33] Perhaps the most representative portrait of Edwards in this period was the full-length biography that Alexander V.G. Allen published in 1889. Allen regarded Edwards's treatises on the will, original sin, true virtue, and the end of creation as confused and based on false premises. Edwards's proposed history of redemption showed an inattentiveness to "second causes." Allen conceded that "there was in him something of the seer or prophet who beholds by direct vision what others know only by report" but then alleged that much of the "revelation" received by this prophet was simply "untrue." Edwards's basic mistake was to highlight the divine rather than human nature: "The great wrong which Edwards did which haunts us as an evil dream throughout his writings, was to assert God at the expense of humanity." As a result, he neglected to see "the divineness [sic] of human nature."[34]

The nineteenth century, then, battled with Edwards over human nature. New England thinkers at Yale and Andover tried to bend Edwards toward the new Scottish philosophy of human consciousness, Princeton rejected Edwards's metaphysics and ethics for contradicting in part because they contradicted the "laws" of human intuition, and later American culture lost interest in a theologian who seemed more interested in God than natural existence. Yet by the mid-twentieth century, it was Edwards's skepticism toward natural human ability and his dramatization of God's sovereignty in history that brought American intellectuals to a renewed interest in his writings.

---

32. Holmes dismissed Edwards's theology as a "system that would consign innocent babes to the fires of everlasting torment"; Weber, "Image," 121, 147, 148, 153. Stowe referred to Edwards's sermons as "refined poetry of torture"; Stowe, *The Minister's Wooing* (Boston and New York, 1859, 1896), 245.

33. Bebbington, "Remembered," 191.

34. Alexander V.G. Allen, *Jonathan Edwards* (Boston, 1889), 380, 386, 388.

39

New Beginnings: The Twentieth-Century Recovery of Jonathan Edwards

IN THE FIRST third of the twentieth century, American intellectuals continued to treat Jonathan Edwards with the contempt and disinterest he received at the end of the nineteenth century (ch. 38). In these decades of the Progressive Era and Scopes trial, "Edwards was set up as the straw man of repression and snobbery, a medieval relic that had no place in modern America."[1] In 1902, after spending a night reading *Freedom of the Will*, Mark Twain exclaimed, "All through the book is the glare of a resplendent intellect gone mad—a marvelous spectacle. No, not *all* through the book—the drunk does not come on till the last third, where what I take to be Calvinism and its God show up and shine red and hideous in the glow from the fires of hell, their only right and proper adornment. By God I was ashamed to be in such company." George Santayana dismissed Edwards's doctrine of sin as "strange" in 1913. Five years later, Marilla Ricker published a tract that charged Edwards with believing in the worst God, preaching the worst sermons, and having the worst religion "of any human being who ever lived on this continent." In his 1927 survey of the colonial mind in America, progressive historian Vernon Louis Parrington complained that Edwards stifled intellectual life in America by perpetuating the "absolutist" past, recording "repulsive" accounts of conversion, and voicing dogma rather than reason and experience—thus permitting the triumph of "the arid realm of theology" over "the stimulating field of philosophy." His life was "tragic" because "he was called to be a transcendental emancipator, but he remained a Calvinist."[2]

---

1. Kenneth P. Minkema, "Jonathan Edwards in the Twentieth Century," *Journal of the Evangelical Theological Society* 47 (2004): 660.

2. George Santayana, *Winds of Doctrine* (New York: Charles Scribner's Sons, 1913) 191; Mark Twain, *Mark Twain's Letters*, 2 vols., ed. Albert Bigelow Paine (New York: Harper and Bros., 1917), 2:719–20; Marilla M. Ricker, *Jonathan Edwards: The Divine Who Filled the Air with Damnation and Proved the Total Depravity of God* (New York: American Freethought Tract Society, 1918); Vernon Louis Parrington, "The Anachronism of Jonathan Edwards," in *The Colonial Mind, 1620–1800*, vol. 1 of *Main Currents in American Thought* (New York: Harcourt, Brace and Co., 1927), 160, 163.

In the Progressive Era's "last gasp" of scholarship, Henry Bamford Parkes traced the root of America's Depression-era ills to "the fiery Puritan" Edwards. Despite being the "biggest intellect" in American Christian history, Edwards was a "blight upon posterity" because his principle of disinterested devotion to God's will left no room for "the weaknesses of the laity." He did not believe that government is for the good of the people and so "was not truly an American." If Edwards had never lived, "there would be to-day no blue laws, no societies for the suppression of vice, no Volstead [National Prohibition] act." Hence he "is a vice to be shaken off, a demon to be spat at."[3] That same year, philosopher Herbert Wallace Schneider alleged that Edwards departed from the public and social concerns of Puritanism and that his vision of love for God was pathological and too absurd to have any contemporary application.[4]

Less critical observers of the twentieth century highlighted the same themes as those of the previous century—Edwards's poetic affinities, spirituality, and pantheism. At the Stockbridge celebration for the two-hundredth anniversary of his birth in 1903, Lyman Rowland claimed he was a poet like Ralph Waldo Emerson and Blaise Pascal, and John DeWitt acclaimed Edwards's spirituality because it examined the "inward state of man 'in nature and grace.'" At the Andover celebration that year, Frederick J. E. Woodbridge commented that, while Edwards's influence was then "largely negligible," his "mystical pantheism" was worth retrieving. Other nineteenth-century themes were sounded during that first decade: church historian Williston Walker asserted that Edwardsean "disinterested love" motivated the earliest American foreign missionaries, and the *Encyclopedia Britannica*'s eleventh edition (1910) derided *Freedom of the Will* as "defective" but hailed Edwards as the "most able metaphysician" in American history.[5]

---

3. Donald Louis Weber, "The Image of Jonathan Edwards in American Culture" (PhD diss., Columbia University, 1978), 191; Henry Bamford Parkes, *Jonathan Edwards: The Fiery Puritan* (New York: Minton, Balch & Co., 1930), 252, 249, 24, 254, 253, 24.

4. Herbert Wallace Schneider, *The Puritan Mind* (New York: Henry Holt & Co., 1930).

5. *Jonathan Edwards: The Two Hundredth Anniversary of His Birth, Union Meeting of the Berkshire North and South Conferences, Stockbridge, Mass., October Fifth, 1903* (Stockbridge: Berkshire Conferences, 1903), in M.X. Lesser, *Reading Jonathan Edwards: An Annotated Bibliography in Three Parts, 1729–2005* (Grand Rapids: Eerdmans, 2008), 135; *Exercises Commemorating the Two-Hundredth Anniversary of the Birth of Jonathan Edwards, Held at Andover Theological Seminary, October 4 and 5, 1903* (Andover: Andover Press, 2004), in Lesser, *Reading Jonathan Edwards*, 141–42; Williston Walker, *Great Men of the Christian Church* Chicago: University of Chicago Press, 1908), 339–53, cited in Lesser, 146; Harry Norman Gardiner and Richard Webster, "Jonathan Edwards," in *Encyclopedia Britannica* 11th ed., 1910, 9:3–6; cited in Lesser, 147.

The balance of this chapter will look at the rebirth of interest in Edwards during the early twentieth century, Perry Miller's role in that resurgence, and Yale University's launch of a critical edition of Edwards's works as the springboard for the late twentieth-century's proliferation in Edwards studies.

Renewed Interest

During the same decades that many denounced Edwards, others began to appreciate him. William James tipped his hat to Edwards in his Gifford Lectures, published that same year as *The Varieties of Religious Experience* (1902). Although James rejected Edwards's "chasm" between the regenerate and the unregenerate, insisting that "generation and regeneration are matters of degree," he praised Edwards's "admirably rich and delicate description of the supernaturally infused condition, in his Treatise on Religious Affections." In his chapter on "Saintliness," he quoted at length from Edwards's descriptions in *Some Thoughts Concerning the Revival* of his wife Sarah's ecstatic experiences in the Spirit.[6] Two years later, William Harder Squires (discussed further in ch. 40) began publishing *The Edwardean*, a quarterly devoted to the proposition that Edwards was the greatest thinker America had ever produced. The journal expired after only four issues, but in the meantime it proposed that Edwards "has come the nearest of all the world's metaphysicians to reconcile philosophy and religion." Squires denounced Edwards's hellfire sermons as "hysterical appeals to terrified and shrinking humanity" related to his "broody" moods and "paroxysms of melancholy," but he pointed readers to what he considered Edwards's master insight—"voluntarism." This was the notion that the world is "the expression of an ultimate and a divine, personal Will." In *Freedom of the Will*, which Squires considered Edwards's masterpiece, mind and matter were finally resolved as products of the divine will. Thus Edwards, like Kant, treated volition as the "fundamental...explanation of the real nature of the visible and psychic worlds."[7]

Even *The New York Times* joined the new band of Edwards admirers. In 1900, it called for a fresh edition of Edwards's works "as a matter of patriotism" and in 1916 criticized President Theodore Roosevelt for the "tardy justice" he rendered Edwards by publishing a letter to the New York newspaper

---

6. William James, *The Varieties of Religious Experience: A Study in Human Nature* (New York: The Modern Library, n.d.), 234, 271–73, 275.

7. William Harder Squires, *The Edwardean, A Quarterly Devoted to the History of Thought in America* (Clinton, NY: Courier Press, 1904), 255, 165, 167, 109, 11.

touting the New England theologian as having "not a touch of the mollycoddle in him."⁸ But a bigger surprise was B. B. Warfield, a theologian at Princeton Seminary. Although Warfield never seems to have used Edwards substantively in any of his own writings and agreed with his teacher Charles Hodge that *True Virtue* was "eccentric," Warfield broke ranks with Hodge and wrote an effusive paean to Edwards for the *Encyclopedia of Religion and Ethics* in 1912. Hodge had criticized Edwards's ecclesiology, revivalism, and intellectual independence (ch. 38), but Warfield demurred on each point. He said Edwards had returned New England to its original Congregationalist ecclesiology, "diligently sought to curb the excesses" of the revivals (lauding the *Religious Affections* as the world's "most thorough" examination of religious excitement), and, unlike his own successors in the New Divinity—formulated his thought within the "great tradition" of Christian theology, thus showing a "solid grounding in the history of thought."⁹

During the Great Depression, two books emerged from respected American intellectuals paying tribute to Edwards. Arthur C. McGiffert Jr.'s *Jonathan Edwards* (1932) highlighted Edwards's God as holy, loving, and beautiful, while Yale theologian H. Richard Niebuhr's *The Kingdom of God in America* (1937) showcased Edwards as a lonely existentialist prophet who knew "the utter insecurity of men and of mankind which are at every moment as ready to plunge into the abyss of disintegration, barbarism, crime and the war of all against all, as to advance toward harmony and integration." Edwards's theology of divine sovereignty helped give rise to the quintessentially American faith in the idea of a coming kingdom of love that would come "through the 'cleansing of the inward parts.' "¹⁰ Then in 1944 Joseph Haroutunian, who had argued in *Piety versus Moralism: The Passing of the New England Theology* (1932) that Edwards's New Divinity disciples had corrupted their master's teaching, published an essay extolling Edwards's God-centered piety.¹¹

---

8. *New York Times* editorial, June 11, 1900, 6; ibid, February 8, 1916, 1.

9. B.B. Warfield, "Jonathan Edwards and the New England Theology," in James Hastings, ed., *Encyclopedia of Religion and Ethics*, 12 vols. (New York: Charles Scribner's Son, 1912), 5:221–27.

10. Arthur Cushman McGiffert Jr., *Jonathan Edwards* (New York: Harper and Brothers, 1932); H. Richard Niebuhr, *The Kingdom of God in America* (New York: Harper Torchbooks, 1959 [1937]).

11. Joseph Haroutunian, "Jonathan Edwards" Theologian of the Great Commandment," *Theology Today* 1 (1944): 361–77.

Why the revived interest in Edwards, especially from the 1930s and 1940s? Two world wars, severe economic depression, and emerging news of the Holocaust exposed a latent human savagery that made more plausible a theology that spoke of human evil and divine judgment. The rise of Neo-Orthodoxy in Western Europe, which emphasized human sin and divine transcendence, helped Christians make sense of radical evil and belief in God. Suddenly Edwards appeared to be a mind that had been buried deep in the American past but whose retrieval could help bring meaning to life's tragedies and uncertainties.

Perry Miller's Contribution

In 1949, Harvard historian Perry Miller's intellectual biography of Edwards dropped like a bombshell on the playground of the American intellectuals. The *New York Times Book Review* acclaimed it "a unique and major contribution to American letters, thought and history."[12] Though it received a mixed response from critics, it lit a fire of intellectual excitement that in turn launched an Edwards renaissance that continues to the present day.[13] Miller depicted Edwards as "one of America's five or six major artists" who was thus "infinitely more than a theologian." All of his writings were "an immense cryptogram" hiding an "occult secret"—that he was really a naturalist whose talk of supernatural experience "meant only that it was not unnatural." The divine and supernatural light was not mystical infusion but simply "rational conveyance through the senses." Edwards secretly believed theology should derive not from convention or logic but experience. The genius of Edwards's *Original Sin* was that it was "strictly empirical" and so constituted "glorified naturalism." Edwards was therefore a modernist far ahead of his time. He "read more deeply into Locke than did Locke himself." He "was so far ahead of his contemporaries in comprehending scientific method...that he was handicapped in debating against minds of lesser compass, with the ironic result that he comes down to the generations as one opposed to scientific progress." So when he "stood up among

---

12. Mary Ellen Chase, *New York Times Book Review*, December 11, 1949, 4.

13. Joseph Haroutunian said that Edwards was a Calvinist, not a naturalist—perhaps a modern, but a Christian first. Vincent Tomas wrote that Miller had falsified Edwards, who was a medieval philosopher and not a modern empiricist. He derived truth from scripture, not experience. Reviewing Miller's introduction to *Images or Shadows* (1948), H. Shelton Smith doubted that Edwards subordinated scripture to images in nature, as Miller had claimed. Joseph Haroutunian, *Theology Today* 8 (1951): 554–56; Vincent Tomas, "The Modernity of Jonathan Edwards," *New England Quarterly* 25 (1952): 60–84; H. Shelton Smith, *American Literature* 22 (1950): 192–94.

the New England clergy, it was as though a master of relativity spoke to a convention of Newtonians who had not yet heard of Einstein."[14]

According to Miller, Edwards rejected Calvin's "legalism" and covenant theology, so for Edwards "God was no longer bound by any promise, whether of metaphysics or of law." Edwards walked away from the "fervent rationalism" of the Puritan covenant to embrace "a pure passion of the senses, and the terror...of modern man, the terror of insecurity." When Edwards was fighting Arminianism, he was really battling the "shallow optimism" of liberalism and its "cult of progress." Unlike them, he was willing to "look directly into the blinding sun" of radical evil. His opposition to the river gods who finally drove him out of Northampton was a war against "the entrepreneurs...the oligarchy of business and real estate." *Freedom of the Will* was "an arraignment of...false shows of benevolence. Read as a cipher, as all Edwards writings must be, it is a penetrating analysis of modern culture, and specifically of the American variant." Edwards was a closet democrat whose theology helped to form a new Revolutionary mind among his disciples.[15]

None of these claims for Edwards was especially new. That Edwards's true thinking was hidden by the constraints of theology had been suggested as far back as Harriet Beecher Stowe and Alexander Allen, and nearer to Miller's time by Yale's Henry Seidel Canby (1931) and Ola Elizabeth Winslow's Pulitzer Prize–winning biography (1940). Winslow had written that Edwards might have had mystical leanings but was not a mystic and that while he "laid the foundations for a new system of religious thought," his mistake was to choose to speak "through an outworn, dogmatic system instead of letting the new truth find more appropriate form of its own."[16] Edwards's supposed break with Calvin and covenantal theology was first broached by Peter DeJong in 1945 and repeated by Miller's Harvard acquaintance Thomas Johnson in 1948.[17] In a famous 1940 essay, "From Edwards to Emerson," Miller had suggested that there was a hidden intellectual genealogy from Edwards to the Transcendentalists (ch. 40)

---

14. Perry Miller, *Jonathan Edwards* (New York: Meridian Books, 1949), ii, 51, 187, 68, 78, 267, 276, 158, 268–69, 63. On Miller's "mission" to explain the meaning of America, see Avihu Zakai, "Epiphany at Matadi: Perry Miller's *Orthodoxy in Massachusetts* and the Meaning of American History," *Reviews in American History* 13 (1985): 627–41.

15. Miller, *Jonathan Edwards*, 147 (see also 30), 147, 121, 257, 195, 219, 218, 263, 326–27.

16. Henry Seidel Canby, *Classic Americans* (New York: Harcourt and Brace, 1931), 9–22; Ola Elizabeth Winslow, *Jonathan Edwards, 1703–1758: A Biography* (New York: Macmillan, 1940), 325–26.

17. Peter Y. DeJong, "Jonathan Edwards: The Half-Way Covenant Attacked," *The Covenant Idea in New England Theology, 1620–1847* (Grand Rapids, MI: Eerdmans, 1945), 136–52; Thomas H. Johnson, "Jonathan Edwards," *Literary History of the United States* (New York: Macmillan, 1948), 1:71–81.

and that Emerson was free, as Edwards was not because of his religious culture, to see that humans are divine. As Philip Gura has observed, this link from Edwards to Transcendentalism was first proposed by Stowe and Allen, as was the depiction of Edwards as artist and poet: "Ever the assiduous researcher, Miller quite probably had gleaned what his contemporaries considered two of his most brilliant insights—of Edwards as supreme artist and as a connector to the Transcendentalists—from his omnivorous reading in nineteenth-century sources."[18] Even Miller's depiction of Edwards as a proto-democrat had a precedent. Vernon Louis Parrington had suggested something similar in 1927.[19]

So why did Miller's book change the landscape when a fair number of previous interpreters made similar claims? Perhaps because Miller was as much an artist as Edwards was. Edwards was artistic in his sermonic rhetoric (ch. 31), but Miller wrote intellectual history with a novelist's flair. He recreated the dramatic situations of Edwards's ministry and related them to mid-twentieth-century circumstances like a skilled playwright. For example, his argument about the superficial platitudes of Arminianism reflected his own (and many other Americans') impatience with liberal confidence in human nature and development. It hardly mattered that few of Miller's central claims were sustained by later scholars. The bonfire had been lit, and the light in the sky that shone far and wide attracted new generations of students and scholars.

The Yale Edition and the Edwards Renaissance

By 2010, more than four thousand secondary books, dissertations, and articles on Edwards had shot off the press, and most had been published since Miller's landmark monograph. As a result, Edwards has become one of the most studied thinkers in the history of Christian thought and by far the most deeply scrutinized American thinker before 1800. From the 1940s through the 1970s, the number of dissertations on Edwards doubled every decade; since 1980 the pace has slackened only slightly.[20] Conferences on Edwards abounded; in 2003 alone there were nine. Later in the decade, scholars from a host of countries gathered formally in Budapest (2007) and Glasgow (2009) to discuss the American theologian.

---

18. Perry Miller, "From Edwards to Emerson," *New England Quarterly* 13 (1940): 589–617; Philip F. Gura, "Edwards and American Literature," in Stephen J. Stein, ed., *The Cambridge Companion to Jonathan Edwards* (Cambridge, UK: Cambridge University Press, 2007), 271.

19. Vernon Louis Parrington, "The Anachronism of Jonathan Edwards," 161–62.

20. Minkema, "Jonathan Edwards in the Twentieth Century," 678; Lesser, *Reading Jonathan Edwards*, 30–31, 323, 476.

Amid the hubbub, Miller's ghost lingered on, for it was Miller who had launched the modern critical edition of Edwards's works published by Yale University Press, and the Yale Edition has been "a scarlet thread" running through "the escalating number of publications on Edwards from the 1950s to present."[21] Yale's reputation lent additional prestige to the Edwards project and was a significant factor in the academic rehabilitation of Edwards. The roster of the editorial committee for *The Works of Jonathan Edwards* added further luster, as it was a veritable who's-who of prominent philosophers, theologians, and historians: Sydney Ahlstrom, Roland Bainton, Jon Butler, John Demos, David D. Hall, Sidney Earl Mead, Perry Miller, Edmund S. Morgan, H. Richard Niebuhr, Richard R. Niebuhr, Mark A. Noll, Paul Ramsey, John E. Smith, Stephen J. Stein, Harry S. Stout, Amos Wilder, John F. Wilson, and numerous others. Miller originally planned only twelve to fifteen volumes because he preferred Edwards's philosophical writings and saw no need to publish or republish the biblical commentaries or sermons.

The Yale edition got off to a slow start, with only two volumes emerging at the end of the 1950s and none during the 1960s.[22] But the 1960s were fruitful nonetheless, as Thomas Schafer discovered that the manuscripts could be accurately dated through an analysis of the types of ink used, the watermarks on the paper, and the various markings and notations that Edwards employed to connect one manuscript to another. More than anyone else, Schafer was the impetus and pacesetter for the study of the Edwards manuscripts. To get accurate transcriptions of some almost illegible scribbling, he prepared a microfilm of the texts and then read them off a projected image. To one of his coworkers on the manuscripts, Schafer quipped, "We work on the plumbing downstairs, so that the guys upstairs can have running water."[23] Following Schafer's lead, Wilson Kimnach and Wallace Anderson applied the new methods of dating to the sermons and philosophical and scientific texts. One result was Anderson's demonstration that Edwards wrote the metaphysical speculations of "The Mind" not during his early

---

21. Stephen D. Crocco, "Edwards's Intellectual Legacy," in Stein, ed., *The Cambridge Companion*, 317.

22. The first volume (*Freedom of the Will*), however, was hailed in 1957 by the *New York Times* as the work of a thinker who "wished to face naked truth." One year later, H. Richard Niebuhr picked up on this theme of an uncompromising approach to reality in his address at Northampton upon the two hundredth anniversary of Edwards's death; he said Edwards's anachronism was speaking of a holy God with love and wrath to a generation whose God is "without wrath" and whose "love is not holy love." Niebuhr, "The Anachronism of Jonathans Edwards," in Wilson H. Kimnach, Caleb J.D. Maskell, and Kenneth P. Minkema, eds., *Jonathan Edwards's Sinners in the Hands of an Angry God: A Casebook* (New Haven: Yale University Press, 2010), 169–72. On Miller's preferences, see Crocco, 313–14.

23. Reported by Wilson Kimnach.

teens but in his early twenties.[24] After a decade of this foundational work, three volumes appeared in the 1970s, four in the 1980s, and the other seventeen since the 1990s, including one numbering more than 1,400 pages (The "Blank Bible" in two parts). An additional forty-six volumes have been put online by The Jonathan Edwards Center, housed at Yale Divinity School.

By 1990, scholars had all but abandoned the Miller paradigm. Conrad Cherry, whose 1966 monograph was one of the most incisive surveys of Edwards's theology to appear during the twentieth century, argued that Edwards was nearly everything Miller said he was not. "Far from throwing over covenant theology, Edwards was quite dependent upon it." Edwards was a Calvinist first and last, and his God was "a promise-making, promise-keeping God who may be 'dealt with' in faith as a covenant partner; not the God of an inscrutable hinterland." There was "no ground" in Edwards's writings, said Cherry, for Miller's claim that Edwards's hidden authority was natural—not biblical—revelation. George Marsden argued in a journal essay that Miller had slighted Edwards's debt to scripture, doctrine, and Calvin. Wallace E. Anderson demonstrated in his introduction to volume 6 of the Yale Edition that Edwards's debt to Locke was overstated. Paul Helm suggested that Locke's empiricism was a model but not a theory of experience, and Norman Fiering maintained that Locke's influence on Edwards was to provide metaphysical language and limits rather than the substance of Edwards's philosophical reflection. In 1971, Helm had also introduced Edwards's *Treatise on Grace* with the observation that Edwards put his theory of grace within a covenantal framework. American intellectual historian Bruce Kuklick drew lines of influence and affinity from Edwards to John Dewey, the American apostle of modernity, though Peter Gay took a different tack by pronouncing that Edwards was "the last medieval American—at least among the intellectuals."[25] The major authors on Edwards from the 1960s onward seemed to have only one thing in common—dissent from Perry Miller.

---

24. WJE 6:53.

25. M.X. Lesser, "Edwards in 'American Culture,'" in Stein, ed. *The Cambridge* Companion, 290; Conrad Cherry, *The Theology of Jonathan Edwards: A Reappraisal* (Bloomington: Indiana University Press, 1990 [1966]), 123,46; George Marsden, "Perry Miller's Rehabilitation of the Puritans: A Critique," *Church History* 39 (1970): 91–105; Wallace E. Anderson, "Introduction," WJE 6:1–143; Paul Helm, "John Locke and Jonathan Edwards: A Reconsideration," *Journal of the History of Philosophy* 7 (1969): 51–61; Norman Fiering, *Jonathan Edwards's Moral Thought and Its British Context* (Chapel Hill: University of North Carolina Press, 1981), 35–40; Paul Helm, Introduction to *Treatise on Grace and other posthumously published writings by Jonathan Edwards* (Greenwood, SC: Greenwood Press, 1971), 15–17; Bruce Kuklick, *Churchmen and Philosophers: From Jonathan Edwards to John Dewey* (New Haven: Yale University Press, 1985); Peter Gay, *A Loss of Mastery: Puritan Historians in Colonial America* (Berkeley: University of California Press, 1966), 116.

One of the most important publications was Roland Delattre's 1968 monograph, arguing that Edwards's aesthetics were unique in the history of western Christian thought. His contention that beauty was Edwards's first principle of existence and communication opened a whole new avenue of discussion. Clyde Holbrook relied on Delattre in his study of Edwards's ethics in 1973. Other major studies of Edwards's ethics included Norman Fiering's massive review of the British and continental background to Edwards's moral philosophy, Paul Ramsey's introduction to and editing of the ethical writings in volume 8 of the Yale edition, and William Danaher's analysis of the Trinitarian roots to Edwardsean ethics.[26]

Another focus for recent scholarship has been Edwards's metaphysics and philosophical theology. In 1955, William S. Morris wrote a path-breaking University of Chicago dissertation arguing that Edwards's metaphysics was rooted in Dutch Calvinist scholasticism. The two most influential works since that time have been Sang Hyun Lee's proposal of dispositional ontology in 1988 and Stephen H. Daniel's 1994 suggestion that a "Stoic-Ramist propositional logic of supposition" lies at the heart of Edwards's philosophical theology. In another realm of Edwards studies, scholars have debated Edwards's relation to America in recent decades, with Sacvan Bercovitch laying American exceptionalism at his feet. Gerald McDermott countered that Edwards's appeal to the the national covenant was not celebratory but cautionary, in the tradition of the Puritan jeremiad.[27]

Two notable works that appeared in the last decades of the twentieth century and the first decade of the twenty-first used Edwards's philosophy and theology to assert that Edwards was concerned with explicating orthodox faith in a skeptical era. Michael McClymond highlighted the twin themes of "spiritual perception" and "apologetics," while Miklos Vetö underlined "theodicy" in Edwards's metaphysico-theological project. Other discipline-shaping studies included Robert Brown's study of Edwards's immersion in the nascent world of seventeenth- and

---

26. Roland A. Delattre, *Beauty and Sensibility in the Thought of Jonathan Edwards: An Essay in Aesthetics and Theological Ethics* (Eugene, OR: Wipf and Stock, 2006 [1968]); Clyde A. Holbrook, *The Ethics of Jonathan Edwards: Morality and Aesthetics* (Ann Arbor: University of Michigan Press, 1973); Fiering, *Jonathan Edwards's Moral Thought and Its British Context*; Paul Ramsey, Introduction to WJE 8:1–121; William J. Danaher Jr., *The Trinitarian Ethics of Jonathan Edwards* (Louisville: Westminster John Knox, 2004).

27. William Sparkes Morris, "The Young Jonathan Edwards: A Reconstruction" (PhD diss., University of Chicago, 1955; later published with the same title in 1991 by Carlson Publishing); Sang H. Lee, *The Philosophical Theology of Jonathan Edwards* (Princeton: Princeton University Press, 1988); Stephen H. Daniel, *The Philosophy of Jonathan Edwards* (Bloomington: University of Indiana Press, 1994); Sacvan Bercovitch, *The American Jeremiad* (Cambridge: Harvard University Press, 1978), 99–100, 105–10; Gerald R. McDermott, *One Holy and Happy Society: The Public Theology of Jonathan Edwards* (University Park, PA: Penn State Press, 1992), esp. 11–36.

eighteenth-century biblical criticism, Amy Plantinga Pauw's delineation of Edwards's Trinitarianism, and Gerald McDermott's excavation—from the long-unpublished *Miscellanies*—of Edwards's fascination with non-Christian religions.[28]

An important dimension of the Edwards renaissance has been the involvement of evangelical scholars. Kenneth Minkema has shown that evangelicals now produce the bulk of scholarship on Edwards's theology, and Douglas Sweeney points out that "evangelical leaders now convene the largest conferences, dispense the most literature and audio-visual matter, build the most popular websites, and raise the most interest related to Edwards's life and theological ministry." Early evangelical promoters of Edwardsean thought were the Welsh Presbyterian D. Martyn Lloyd-Jones, who commended Edwards's theology from Westminster Chapel in the heart of London in the mid-twentieth century, and John Gerstner, who taught theology at Pittsburgh Theological Seminary during the same period and published a three-volume "rational-biblical theology" of Edwards in the early 1990s. In the years following the "Toronto Blessing" revival of 1994, both proponents and opponents of the movement published books citing Edwards for support (ch. 42). British evangelical Iain Murray's 1987 hagiographical biography helped to introduce Edwards's theology to tens of thousands of non-academic Christians on both sides of the Atlantic, and "today's most famous Edwardsean minister," John Piper, excites untold numbers of Reformed evangelicals with interest in Edwards through his books, audio recordings, website, and conferences.[29]

---

28. Miklos Vetö, *La pensée de Jonathan Edwards* (Paris: l'Harmattan, 2008); Michael J. McClymond, *Encounters with God: An Approach to the Theology of Jonathan Edwards* (New York: Oxford University Press, 1998); Robert E. Brown, *Jonathan Edwards and the Bible* (Bloomington: Indiana University Press, 2002); Amy Plantinga Pauw, *The Supreme Harmony of All: The Trinitarian Theology of Jonathan Edwards* (Grand Rapids: Eerdmans, 2002); Gerald R. McDermott, *Jonathan Edwards Confronts the Gods: Christian Theology, Enlightenment Religion, and Non-Christian Faiths* (New York: Oxford University Press, 2000).

29. Minkema, "Jonathan Edwards in the Twentieth Century," 677n.55; Sweeney, "Evangelical tradition in America," in Stein, ed., *The Cambridge Companion*, 229–30; David W. Bebbington, "The Reputation of Edwards Abroad," in Stein, ed., *The Cambridge Companion*, 255; John Gerstner, *The Rational Biblical Theology of Jonathan Edwards*, 3 vols. (Powhatan, Va: Berea Publications, 1991–93); Guy Chevreau, "A Well-Travelled Path: Jonathan Edwards and the Experiences of the Great Awakening," in *Catch the Fire: The Toronto Blessing, An Experience of Renewal and Revival* (London: Marshall Pickering, 1994), 70–144; Hank Hanegraaff, *Counterfeit Revival* (Nashville: Thomas Nelson, 2001, orig. ed. 1997); both Chevreau and Hanegraaf are excerpted in Kimnach, Maskell and Minkema, eds., *Jonathan Edwards's Sinners in the Hands of an Angry God: A Casebook*, 172–80; Iain Murray, *Jonathan Edwards: A New Biography* (Edinburgh: Banner of Truth, 1987); John Piper's most influential books on Edwards have been *Desiring God: Meditations of a Christian Hedonist* (Sisters, OR: Multnomah, 1986); *God's Passion for His Glory: Living the Vision of Jonathan Edwards* (Wheaton, IL: Crossway, 2002); Piper and Justin Taylor, eds., *A God-Entranced Vision of All things: The Legacy of Jonathan Edwards* (Wheaton IL: Crossway, 2004); the quote describing Piper is from Sweeney, "Evangelical Tradition," 230.

Edwards's tercentenary in 2003 was a culmination of the half-century-long Edwards renaissance. Scholars presented more than one hundred papers at nine gatherings, while George Marsden's new scholarly biography made the *Sunday New York Times Book Review* and won the Bancroft Prize in American History. One could discern a difference between those who approached Edwards as a normative theological resource and those who sought to understand Edwards as a historical phenomenon. Minkema remarks that the "historicists and theologizers" have eyed each other "suspiciously and perhaps condescendingly for some time," but nevertheless work toward common ends. Whether they liked it or not, the historicists found that Edwards was "a supernaturalist, a thoroughgoing theist, a tireless student of Scripture, a parish pastor with an evangelical passion," while the "theologizers" were forced to grapple with his historical situatedness and the unpleasant facts that he owned slaves and hated Roman Catholicism. The twenty-first-century Edwards industry seems likely to move along both lines—further demonstrating not only Edwards's usefulness for philosophical and theological reflection but the deep connections between his ideas and his historical context.[30]

---

30. Garry Wills, "Soul on Fire," *New York Times Book Review*, July 6, 2003, 6; Minkema, "Jonathan Edwards in the Twentieth Century," 677.

40

Interpretations I

EDWARDS AND MODERN PHILOSOPHY

AN EARLIER CHAPTER examined Edwards's theological followers, known collectively as the "New Divinity" thinkers (ch. 37). This chapter treats the modern philosophers who were distinct from those theological disciples and yet also influenced by Edwards. It examines trajectories in North American philosophical and religious thought that may be traced back to Edwards. It also treats four philosophers of the last century—two American, one Hungarian-French, and one British—who became engaged with Edwards's ideas and sought to evaluate their salience. The leading historian of American philosophy, Bruce Kuklick, commented that "the foundation stone in the history of American philosophy is Jonathan Edwards."[1] The intellectual trajectories of Edwards's key ideas included such later thinkers as William Ellery Channing, Ralph Waldo Emerson, Josiah Royce, William James, and John Dewey. Admittedly, such lineages are generally hard to document. Philosophers influenced by Edwards's writings were never a distinct school of thought, and they were affected by various currents of thought through the 1800s and early 1900s, including British empiricism, post-Kantian epistemology, German idealism, French thought, and developments in the philosophy of science. Yet there is little question regarding Edwards's foundational role.

While underscoring Edwards's philosophical influence, Kuklick also asserted that "'American philosophy' is a confused discipline, because...the figures brought together are part of a dialogue only in the minds of recent philosophers." Kuklick is not alone in this view. Marcus Singer referred to American philosophy as "an ill-defined and even mongrel subject." In reference to colonial thinkers, Norman Fiering stated that "early American philosophy is nine-tenths...derivative and amateurish" and added that Americans

---

1. Bruce Kuklick, "Jonathan Edwards and American Philosophy," in Nathan O. Hatch and Harry S. Stout, eds., *Jonathan Edwards and the American Experience* (New York: Oxford University Press, 1986), 246.

during this period "correctly saw themselves in a satellite or provincial role." Herbert Schneider argued that American philosophy throughout its history was derivative: "In America, at least, it is useless to seek a 'native' tradition, for even our most genteel traditions are saturated with foreign inspirations." Spanish Franciscans, French Jesuits, English Puritans, Dutch Pietists, Scottish Calvinists, cosmopolitan *philosophes*, German Transcendentalists, and Russian revolutionaries all played some role. Paradoxically, it may be the disjointed character of "American philosophy" that serves to heighten Edwards's importance. Kuklick writes that "Edwards's achievement, unlike that of the contemporary scholarship...should survive. A brick can serve as a cornerstone in any number of buildings."[2]

The canonical version of American intellectual history begins with the work of Jonathan Edwards and moves on to the religious liberals of eastern Massachusetts, the political thought of the Founding Fathers, Boston Unitarianism, New England Transcendentalism, the writers of the American Renaissance (Herman Melville and Nathaniel Hawthorne), the golden period of American philosophy (Josiah Royce, Charles Peirce, and William James), and John Dewey—the quintessential twentieth-century secular liberal. While this plotline is not without merit, it has a number of flaws. It stresses only those elements in the history of American thought that anticipate the values of later secular intellectuals. It brings together thinkers of strikingly different kinds—system-builders like Edwards and Dewey, men of affairs like the Founding Fathers, novelists like Melville and Hawthorne, and unsystematic popularizers like Emerson and Thoreau. The narrative is thus disjointed. The canonical history also reflects a geographical bias toward eastern Massachusetts. "If this is the chronicle of Harvard," writes Kuklick, "it should not be mistaken for the chronicle of America."[3] Kuklick has offered an alternative genealogy for American intellectual history, centered on Trinitarian (i.e., non-Unitarian) Congregationalist thinkers associated with Yale College and geographically concentrated (until the early 1800s) in Connecticut and western Massachusetts. He uncovered a different set of links that led from the Edwardseanism of the late 1700s to the John Dewey of the early 1900s, who offered philosophical foundations for Andover liberalism.

---

2. Marcus G. Singer, ed., *American Philosophy* (Cambridge, UK: Cambridge University Press, 1985), vii; Norman S. Fiering, "Early American Philosophy vs. Philosophy in Early America," *Transactions of the Charles S. Peirce Society* 13 (1977): 216; Herbert W. Schneider, *A History of American Philosophy*, 2nd ed. (New York: Columbia University Press, 1963), vii–viii; Kuklick, "Jonathan Edwards and American Philosophy," 258.

3. Kuklick, "Jonathan Edwards and American Philosophy," 249.

Despite the difficulties in defining "American philosophy," there is good reason to think that Edwards exerted considerable influence in American intellectual history. Pragmatism—and even Dewey's instrumentalism—showed a fixation on religious themes. This was indicated in Charles Peirce's essay on "Evolutionary Love," Josiah Royce's *The Religious Aspect of Philosophy* (1885) and *The Problem of Christianity* (1913), William James's *The Varieties of Religious Experience* (1902), and John Dewey's *A Common Faith* (1934). Royce's "loyalty" and "beloved community" were reminiscent of Edwards's arguments in *The Nature of True Virtue*. Some scholars see James's psychology of religion as a continuation of the analysis of spiritual experience contained in Edwards's *Faithful Narrative* and *Religious Affections*.[4] James defined his foundational concept of pragmatism—in other words, the habit of looking to results to define a proposition's meaning—with a quotation from none other than Edwards's *Religious Affections*. Even the secular Dewey began his professional life as a philosopher of religion. In later life, as Kuklick notes, Dewey showed the "telltale marks" of his earlier religious interests: "There was still a godly residue in things. Edwards believed that man was redeemed only through grace. For Dewey man was still redeemed, but the instrumentality was the ostensibly secular technique of science."[5] American pragmatist philosophy can be seen in two ways. On the one hand, "classic pragmatism was a transitional set of commitments leading away from a religious view of the universe to a secular one." On the other hand, "philosophy achieved its greatest prominence as thinkers were able to combine ostensibly modern scientific views with ideas that had a Protestant spiritual hue—the many varieties of pragmatism."[6] This chapter will explore some elements of continuity between Edwards and later American thinkers.

Intellectual Trajectories—To Emerson, Pragmatism, and Radical Empiricism

In 1911, a year after the death of William James, Josiah Royce claimed that there had been but three "representative" American philosophers in the

---

4. Wayne Proudfoot, "From Theology to a Science of Religions: Jonathan Edwards and William James on Religious Affections," *Harvard Theological Review* 82 (1989): 149–68.

5. Kuklick, "Jonathan Edwards and American Philosophy," 254.

6. Kuklick, *A History of Philosophy in America, 1720–2000* (Oxford, UK: Clarendon Press, 2001), 277, 282. On Edwards's relation to later American philosophy, see John E. Smith, *The Spirit of American Philosophy* (Albany, NY: State University of New York Press, 1983), and Richard A. S. Hall, ed., *The Contributions of Jonathan Edwards to American Culture and Society* (Lewiston, NY: Edwin Mellen Press, 2008).

nation's history—Jonathan Edwards, Ralph Waldo Emerson, and William James. Edwards "gave voice to some of the central motives and interests of our colonial religious life" and was thus "in order of time, the first of our nationally representative philosophers." Royce commented that "Edwards was an originator," for "he actually rediscovered some of the world's profoundest ideas regarding God and humanity simply by reading for himself the meaning of his own religious experience." For Royce, Edwards was a man of his age, just as Emerson and James were men of theirs. Each was a representative figure, and yet the three men were distinct and possibly incommensurate.[7] William Clebsch took Royce a step further, devoting a small book to the three thinkers and creating a stronger link among the three by interpreting Edwards and James in terms of Emerson's "esthetic spirituality." For Clebsch, the aestheticism of Edwards, Emerson, and James was in contrast to America's predominant moralism. He noted that the former "involved...a consciousness of the beauty of living in harmony with divine things—in a word, being at home in the universe."[8] While there is something to commend this view, "being at home in the universe" seems a better summary of Emerson's thought than that of either Edwards or James.

Perry Miller devoted an essay to Edwards and Emerson. He argued that New England Puritanism from the early days of John Cotton and Anne Hutchinson had included both a doctrinal aspect and a mystical impulse toward immediate contact with and experience of God. When Unitarianism emerged in New England, mysticism was emancipated from the shackles of Calvinistic doctrine. Miller writes: "Unitarianism had stripped off the dogmas, and Emerson was free to celebrate purely and simply the presence of God in the soul and in nature, the pure metaphysical essence of the New England tradition." Ralph Waldo Emerson celebrated the hidden divinity of humankind and yet rejected the "pale negations" and "the corpse-cold"

---

7. Marcus G. Singer, "The Context of American Philosophy," in Singer, ed., *American Philosophy*, 8–9; Stephen D. Crocco, "Edwards's Intellectual Legacy," in Stephen J. Stein, ed., *The Cambridge Companion to Jonathan Edwards* (Cambridge, UK: Cambridge University Press, 2007), 308; citing Josiah Royce, "William James and the Philosophy of Life," in John J. McDermott, ed., *The Basic Writings of Josiah Royce*, 2 vols. (Chicago: University of Chicago Press, 1969), 1:206.

8. Clebsch, *American Religious Thought*, xvi. Long before Clebsch or Miller, Leslie Stephen called Edwards "a connecting link between the expiring Calvinism of the old Puritan theocracy and the transcendentalism embodied in the writings of Emerson" (cited in William Harder Squires, *The Edwardean: A Quarterly Devoted to the History of Thought in America*; Lewiston, NY: Edwin Mellen Press, 1991; 44–45).

Unitarianism of Harvard College. Like her contemporary, Emerson, Margaret Fuller sought to move beyond Unitarian rationalism and attain a sense of divine presence. "I would now preach the Holy Ghost," said Fuller, "as zealously as they have been preaching Man."[9]

At first blush, linking Edwards and Emerson seems implausible. Edwards's *Original Sin* would have been just as repellent to Emerson as Emerson's "Divinity School Address" would have been to Edwards. Yet the intellectual transitions occurred not at once but in stages—from Edwards to the New Divinity, from the New Divinity to Unitarianism, and from Unitarianism to Transcendentalism. A key figure in the development was William Ellery Channing. While at college, Channing underwent—in Andrew Delbanco's words— "an Edwardsean conversion under the spell of Hutcheson." He perceived for the first time the beauty of a life devoted utterly to God. In the writings of Francis Hutcheson, Channing found an ideal of disinterested benevolence that he encountered again in his interactions with Samuel Hopkins, whose sermons he heard in Newport, Rhode Island. Gradually, the notion of benevolence became the defining program of his life. Channing wrote: "I am grateful to this stern teacher [i.e., Samuel Hopkins] for turning my thoughts and heart to the claims and majesty of impartial, universal benevolence." Channing observed that Hopkins lived according to the self-sacrificial principles he professed, often giving away his disposable income on behalf of the poor and for Christian missions.

Channing's sermon, "Likeness to God," showed affinities both to Edwards and to Transcendentalism. "Likeness to God," declared Channing, "is the supreme gift. He can communicate nothing so precious, glorious, blessed, as himself.... God becomes a real being to us, in proportion as his own nature is unfolded within us. To a man who is growing in the likeness of God, faith begins even here to change into vision. He carries within himself a proof of a Deity.... He more than believes, he feels the Divine presence."[10] Here Channing sounded many of Edwards's themes—divine communication, participation in God, spiritual vision, and the evidential character of religious

---

9. Perry Miller, "Jonathan Edwards to Emerson," *New England Quarterly* 13 (1940): 589–617, citing 609,612; citing Margaret Fuller, *Memoirs* (Boston, 1884) 2:84–85. See the essay responding to Miller's—Robert Milder, "From Emerson to Edwards," *New England Quarterly* 80 (2007): 96–133.

10. Andrew Delbanco, *William Ellery Channing: An Essay on the Liberal Spirit in America* (Cambridge, MA: Harvard University Press, 1981), 23, cf. 73. On Channing's relationship to Hopkins, see William Henry Channing, *The Life of William Ellery Channing, D. D.* (Boston: American Unitarian Association, 1904 [1880]), 80–84, citing 84; Channing, "Likeness to God," cited in David Robinson, ed., *William Ellery Channing* (New York: Paulist Press, 1985), 147.

experience (chs. 10, 26). Yet what drew the Transcendentalists to this sermon was the implication of a possible divine nature in humankind, which they interpreted—in a non-Calvinist way—not as a gift of grace but as an inherent aspect of human nature. A link between Edwards and Emerson seems to have been mediated through Channing.[11]

Taking a longer view, the question arises as to what connection might exist between Edwards and the pragmatist philosophers at the beginning of the twentieth century. One commonality lay in the effort to justify religious belief. Peirce, Royce, and James were interested in combining sound empirical study of the world with justified religious belief. Peirce conceived truth as consisting in a general agreement among members of a community of inquiry and the objects of knowledge as ideas existing in the mind of God. In opposition to scientific materialism in the late 1800s, "Peirce was reconstructing science on a basis congenial to religion." He conceived that "the scientific vocation aimed at oneness with the divine." James revealed his own interest in the reconciliation of religion and science in the conclusion to *A Pluralistic Universe* (1909): "Let empiricism once become associated with religion, as hitherto, through some strange misunderstanding, it has been associated with irreligion, and I believe that a new era of religion as well as of philosophy will... begin."[12]

William James cited Edwards in the formulation of his foundational principle of pragmatism. He wrote that the "final test of a belief" is "the way in which it works on the whole." James went on to say that "our practice is the only sure evidence, even to ourselves, that we are genuinely Christians," and then he cited Edwards's *Religious Affections* and added "The degree in which our experience is productive of practice, shows the degree in which our experience is spiritual and divine."[13] This pivotal passage intimates that Jamesean pragmatism may have Edwardsean roots. Another equally significant link between Edwards and James related to the affections. For both thinkers, religious experience was rooted in the dispositions of the heart. Affections defined the contours of human life and experience.[14]

---

11. Clebsch noted that Channing "studiously adopted and elaborated Edwards's cardinal teaching that God's immediate impartation of a supernatural light to the soul was at once scriptural and rational." Clebsch concluded that "through Hopkins and Channing did Emerson hold lineal succession from Edwards" (Clebsch, *American Religious Thought*, 66–68).

12. Kuklick, *History of Philosophy in America*, 139–40, 177.

13. William James, *The Varieties of Religious Experience* (Cambridge, MA: Harvard University Press, 1985 [1902]), 24–25, partially italicized in the original.

14. Bennett Ramsey, "The Ineluctable Impulse: 'Consent' in the Thought of Edwards, James, and Royce," *Union Seminary Quarterly Review* 37 (1983): 311; Proudfoot, "From Theology to a Science of Religions," 151.

James differed from Edwards in disparaging institutional forms of religion and offering a strikingly individualistic vision of the religious life: "Religion...shall mean for us the feelings, acts, and experiences of individual men in their solitude."[15] Yet Royce in *The Philosophy of Loyalty* (1908) and *The Problem of Christianity* (1913) upheld a communal view of human life and religious experience. Royce's conception of love or loyalty to the "beloved community" was analogous to Edwards's principle of "benevolence to Being in general." The self attained its dispositional unity only through ultimate loyalty to a larger community. Self-realization occurred only in and through community: "The beloved community embodies...values which no human individual, viewed as a detached being, could even remotely approach."[16]

William Dean offered a different construal of American religious and philosophical thought, centering on the "one philosophical movement truly indigenous to America" that he designated as "radical empiricism." This tradition included the work of William James, John Dewey, and Albert North Whitehead, and that of their "seldom-recognized intellectual grandfather, Jonathan Edwards." While this school was "unique to America," it had exponents outside of the United States, such as the Frenchman Henri Bergson. The philosophical imperative in this school was to "cleave to raw experience." The radical empiricists rejected Cartesianism. Theirs was an epistemology of complete openness to all human experience. René Descartes sought to base his reasoning on "clear and distinct ideas," which, wrote Dean, was a matter of selecting "the late, clean, anemic abstraction, in which what is rich, complicating, unclear, indistinct, and valuable has been already eliminated, leaving only a vapid set of sense data or a vapid set of rational ideas." Radical empiricists affirmed "that relations are experienced just as surely as atomic things are" and that "in those relations real worth is sensed." Dean's description of radical empiricism is reminiscent of Edwards's notion of "consent," implying that reality itself is like a web or network of relationships. In describing God's presence in the natural world, and the spiritual experiences that occurred during revivals, Edwards anticipated the radical empiricists by capturing the texture and complexity of lived experience. Dean summarizes the movement's history: "In America radical empiricism, like a local germ, had passed from Edwards, had almost died, but had been kept alive in the lungs of the American romantics, including Walt Whitman;

---

15. James, *Varieties*, 34, partially italicized in the original.

16. Josiah Royce, *The Problem of Christianity*, 2 vols. in 1 (n.p.: Archon Books, 1967 [1913]), 1:173.

it had been caught by James and then propagated most infectiously by Dewey in the 1920's and 1930's."[17]

Beginning in Locke, and more obviously in David Hume and J.S. Mill, the British tradition sought to reduce human experience to sense experience and to interpret the latter atomistically—as a series of individual, fleeting impressions of seeing, hearing, touching, tasting, and smelling. The American "radical empiricists," by contrast, conceived of the relations between things as part of the content of sense experience. A phrase like "a day at the beach" was not reducible to a set of discrete sensations—the taste of salt, the warmth of the sun, a sensation of sand on one's skin—but was a tangled yarn of intertwining sensations. Unlike most British thinkers, the radical empiricists also assumed that human experience might legitimately include non-sensory as well as sensory elements. William James's interest in mysticism and religious experience, Charles Peirce's "apageistic" theory of Darwinian evolution, and A.N. Whitehead's process thought were emblematic. When we search for the origins of this openness to the non-sensory, it leads us back to Edwards's "sense of the heart" (chs. 10, 20, 24). This was his original contribution toward the development of radical empiricism. While Edwards referred to the "sense of the heart," William James spoke of "bodily effects," A.N. Whitehead of "causal efficacy," John Dewey of the sense of "quality," Bernard Meland of "appreciative awareness," and Bernard Loomer of the sense of "stature." American thinkers typically affirmed something "more" in addition to the five senses.[18]

Four Interpretations of Edwards's Philosophy—Squires, Vetö, Daniel, and Crisp

During the last century, a number of professional philosophers have offered interpretations of Edwards's philosophical thought that illustrate the range, fecundity, and continuing import of Edwards's ideas. The four considered here are representative of multiple lines of interpretation: William Harder Squires (1863–1937), Miklos Vetö (1936-), Stephen H. Daniel (1950-), and Oliver Crisp (1972-). These authors were chosen because they are not only

---

17. William Dean, "An American Theology," *Process Studies* 12 (1982): 111, 117, 113, 115, 118.

18. William Dean, "An American Theology," 120, 122. Edwards's relationship to later process thought in America seems tenuous. Yet Edwards's notion of God's ontic enlargement (ch. 16) shows at least a partial analogy to process thought concerning God.

historians of philosophy (e.g., Wallace Anderson, Norman Fiering, Bruce Kuklick) but philosophers in their own right who have been vitally engaged in thinking through and evaluating Edwards's concepts.

William Harder Squires, who briefly edited a quarterly journal devoted to Edwards—*The Edwardean* (1903–1904)—may be the first professional philosopher to revive the study of Edwards. Though Squires was not notably successful in recruiting others (he himself wrote all the essays in his journal!), the effort itself shed light on Edwards's perceived relationship to American thought and to the main currents in Western philosophy a century ago. Before taking a faculty position at Hamilton College in New York State, Squires studied in Germany with Wilhelm Wundt, the premier experimental psychologist of his day.[19] Squires had multiple purposes in founding *The Edwardean*. He wanted to demonstrate Edwards's influence on American thought, to embed Edwards in the larger history of philosophy, and to initiate a new philosophical movement inspired by Edwards that was theistic rather than secular. The first page of the new journal trumpeted: "*The Edwardean*, taking Edwards as the starting point and the goal of return, will attempt to represent all phases of thought in America." Squires proposed a return to Edwards as the great source for metaphysical insight: "The works of Edwards furnish a rich mine of valuable material which must be worked-over and elaborated.... From this soil must spring up a native philosophy." Squires sought to reconstruct the philosophical enterprise of his own day and to advocate "a philosophy distinctly Christian" and "based on the revelational conception of God and duty."

The key concept in Squires's treatment of Edwards is voluntarism. As one philosophically trained in Germany and writing prior to the full impact of American pragmatism, Squires judged that "the most significant element in the world's greatest living philosopher to-day [i.e., Schopenhauer] is atheistic voluntarism." What interested Squires was Edwards's theocentrism and voluntarism, and the prospect of developing a theistic voluntarism based on Edwards's thought. "God is the starting point and the return of Edwards's philosophizing," wrote Squires. If Schopenhauer conceived of the world itself as all-pervasive will, then Edwards conceived of God as the all-determining will that underlay the world. In his account of Edwards, Squires stressed the centrality of the divine and human wills. "The reign of causality" was the "fundamental principle" that unified Edwards's thought. "The ultimate essence of the universe is will," wrote Squires, "a pure activity, an irresistible volition in which God's secret and revealed will are united in complete identity." Happiness was simply consent to God's will. Edwards was thus a voluntaristic

---

19. See Richard Hall, "Introduction," in William Harder Squires, *The Edwardean*, vii–xv.

"monist."[20] Squires was also interested in Edwards's philosophy of history—another expression of an all-determining divine will.

The Hungarian-born Miklos Vetö was a younger participant in the 1956 Hungarian Revolution against Soviet domination and later earned doctorates in philosophy and theology; lived in France, Africa, and the United States; and pursued a teaching and writing career at Oxford, Yale, Marquette, Rennes, and Poitiers universities. He has published more than twenty books on such topics as the problem of evil, Christian spirituality, and the philosophies of Friedrich Schelling and Simone Weil. On Edwards, his major work is *Le pensée de Jonathan Edwards* (1987). Vetö argued that much of Edwards's thought displayed a formal unity defined by metaphysics. At the same time, he found major aspects of Edwards's thought that cannot be reduced to metaphysical categories. Edwards's deep biblicism followed a logic not of concepts but of images—as shown in the typological writings. Vetö rejected the idea set forth by I. Woodbridge Riley that Edwards's thought fell into three phases—the idealism of *The Mind*, the Calvinism of *Freedom of the Will*, and the panentheism of *End of Creation*. Throughout his life, said Vetö, Edwards was a Calvinist of a systematic and yet orthodox sort. From a philosophical standpoint, Edwards's system had three principal themes—being, volition, and knowledge.[21]

In Vetö's rendition, Edwards was inspired by the vision of the Protestant Reformation and its teaching on the sovereignty, immediacy, and unconditioned character of divine grace. Yet Edwards also viewed God's grace as fully in conformity with God's wisdom and goodness—a point stressed in *End of Creation*. Vetö commented on the seeming paradox in Edwards's account of creation: God's sovereignty implied that he would undoubtedly create a world, and yet this creation was not a necessary act on God's part. Moreover, God's act of creating

---

20. Squires, *The Edwardean*, x–xi, 1, 34, 3, 27–28, 52, 36. On nineteenth- and early twentieth-century British, French, and German interpretations of Edwards's thought, see Michael J. McClymond, "'A German Professor Dropped Into the American Forests': British, French, and German Views of Jonathan Edwards, 1758–1957," in Douglas A. Sweeney and Oliver Crisp, eds., *After Edwards: The Courses of the New England Theology* (New York: Oxford University Press, forthcoming).

21. Miklos Vetö, *Le pensée de Jonathan Edwards* (Paris: Cerf, 1987), 38, 41; citing I. Woodbridge Riley, *American Philosophy: The Early Schools* (1907), 127. An English translation of the expanded, second edition (2007) of Vetö's major work, will soon be appearing as: *The Thought of Jonathan Edwards*, translated by Philip Choniere-Shields (Eugene, OR: Wipf & Stock, forthcoming). A brief, English-language account of Vetö's perspective is found in the translated essay, "Edwards and Philosophy," in Gerald R. McDermott, ed., *Understanding Jonathan Edwards* (New York: Oxford University Press, 2009), 151–70. Here Vetö commented that being was "the least significant" of the three themes of being, knowledge, and will. Yet this may not be accurate inasmuch as Edwards's participatory metaphysics is fundamental to his views regarding creation, salvation, the church, and even the fall of humanity (see chs. 14, 19, 22, 26–28 and 43).

was not only an expression of his omnipotence but an actualization of his goodness. The goodness of the universe was not a collection of particular good things but a goodness that existed in God and that was diffused from God. Creation implied a communication of God's own being, glory, and happiness. Relationship with God carried with it an intimation of human immortality—a life beyond in which communion with God reaches its consummation. Communion with God includes knowledge and takes place through language. It is not reasonable to think that God would forever remain silent and never speak with human beings.

Vetö emphasized the problem of evil and characterized the *Miscellanies* as a work in the genre of theodicy. Edwards insisted that the existence of sin was consistent with the goodness of God and that God might be glorified through sin. He supported the traditional idea of the *felix culpa* ("happy transgression"), and yet he was less inclined than disciples like Bellamy and Hopkins to identify the particular ways in which sin might bring glory to God. For Edwards, sin resulted when God withdrew and left human beings to act on their own inclinations. This did not imply that God sinned or was responsible for sin. Edwards justified eternal punishment by arguing that sin is an offense against God's infinite goodness and therefore requires infinite punishment, and that sinners in hell continue to sin through hatred of God and therefore continue to receive punishment from God. Hell is the supreme expression of an evil, defiant will.[22]

Stephen H. Daniel's *The Philosophy of Jonathan Edwards: A Study in Divine Semiotics* (1994) approached Edwards from the standpoint of the semiotic theory of Charles S. Peirce, Michel Foucault, and Julia Kristeva. Daniel sidestepped the well-worn debate over Edwards as "medieval" or "modern" through an alternate historiographic construction that bifurcated Western intellectual history into a "Renaissance epiteme" (Stoicism and Peter Ramus) and a "modernist episteme" (Aristotle and John Locke). The two intellectual traditions identified by Daniel did not form a chronological sequence, but competed with one another during both the ancient and modern periods. Since Edwards belonged to the "Renaissance episteme," he was neither medieval nor modern.[23] For Daniel, Edwards was an exceptional figure for his time, and yet not as a medieval holdover or a modernist pioneer. Instead, Edwards was a proto-semiotician. Daniel did not offer an analysis of particular signs in Edwards's writings but rather sought to uncover the deep structure that made possible Edwards's practice of signification. He drew from Wallace Anderson's

---

22. Vetö, *Le pensée de Jonathan Edwards*, 58–61, 63–64, 67, 69, 129–30, 132–33, 146, 169, 171, 173.

23. Stephen H. Daniel, *The Philosophy of Jonathan Edwards: A Study in Divine Semiotics* (Bloomington, IN: Indiana University Press, 1994), 18–32.

work in linking Edwards's metaphysical and typological thought and yet went further by tying this to developments in twentieth-century semiotics.[24]

Daniel applied a semiotic perspective to such varied themes in Edwards as typology, logic, the Trinity, creation, original sin, moral agency, and beauty. Edwards's use of typology was pivotal for Daniel's argument because he connected Edwards's typologizing of the natural world with Peirce's notion of a world "perfused with signs" (ch. 8). For Daniel, Edwards collapsed the modernist triad of thing-word-idea and replaced it with a unitary web of endless signification. Daniel went so far as to suggest that the separation of language from reality reflected an epistemology of "fallen humanity" and that modernist "subjectivity" was equivalent to "original sin." Daniel reinterpreted Edwards's idealism as a pan-semiosis in which all things signified. Following semiotic theory, Daniel denied that a ground of meaning existed "outside of the world." The basis of signification lay in the "discursive exchange" itself. Daniel's endless horizontal play of significations led him to deemphasize Edwards's hierarchical ontology and his Neoplatonic dualism of body and soul (ch. 7)—themes that did not fit into semiotic theory. An addendum on "the propriety of Christ" qualified the semiotic stance by invoking Christ as "the exemplar for signification itself," thus introducing a focal point in the "discursive exchange." A weak point in Daniel's exposition came in his assertion that Edwards did not think of God as a "person," "subject," or "self."[25] Yet Daniel offered a novel and intriguing angle on Edwards's philosophy.

Oliver Crisp has written extensively on Edwards's philosophy during the last decade from the standpoint of the contemporary analytic philosophy of religion. Crisp has written two monographs on Edwards—*Jonathan Edwards and the Metaphysics of Sin* (2005) and *Jonathan Edwards on God and Creation* (forthcoming)—as well as a number of major journal articles and book chapters.[26] He has been an

---

24. Wallace E. Anderson, "Editor's Introduction," in WJE 6:1–143, esp. 75–94 and 111–36; and Wallace E. Anderson, Mason I. Lowance, Jr., and David H. Watters, "Editor's Introduction," in WJE 11:3–33 and 157–82.

25. Daniel, *The Philosophy of Jonathan Edwards*, 32, 66, 199, 30, 91, 102, 173.

26. Crisp's writings on Edwards include: "How 'Occasional' Was Edwards's Occasionalism," in Paul Helm and Oliver D. Crisp, eds., *Jonathan Edwards: Philosophical Theologian* (Aldershot, UK: Ashgate, 2003), 61–77; "Jonathan Edwards on Divine Simplicity," *Religious Studies* 39 (2003): 23–41; *Jonathan Edwards and the Metaphysics of Sin* (Aldershot, UK: Ashgate, 2005); "Jonathan Edwards's God: The Trinity, Individuation and Divine Simplicity," in Bruce McCormack, ed., *Engaging the Doctrine of God* (Grand Rapids, MI: Baker Academic, 2008), 83–103; "Jonathan Edwards on the Divine Nature," *Journal of Reformed Theology* 3 (2009): 175–201; and "Jonathan Edwards's Ontology: A Critique of Sang Hyun Lee's Dispositional Account of Edwardsian Metaphysics," *Religious Studies* 45 (2009): 1–20.

outspoken critic of Sang Lee's interpretation of Edwards. Specifically, he objects to Lee's assertion of Edwards's "dispositional ontology" and his contrast between the dynamic metaphysics of Edwards and the allegedly static metaphysics of classical theism.[27] Crisp says that he "offers no objection to the view that Edwards had an important and controversial place for the concept of disposition in his doctrine of God," but "does set forth a critique of one aspect of the Lee interpretation of Edwards's dispositional ontology of the created order."[28]

Crisp is at odds with several authors besides Lee, since he interprets Edwards's created world in terms of substantialism (which he calls "essentialism"). Not only Sang Lee, but Wallace Anderson, Miklos Vetö, Robert Jenson, Avihu Zakai, and Michael McClymond have argued that Edwards's metaphysics was anti-substantialist and a reaction against a rising materialistic and mechanistic view during the 1700s. Crisp's critique of Lee is based on a twofold claim that Edwards's idea of God was in continuity with classical theism (including such elements as the doctrine of divine simplicity) and that classical theism has been misunderstood by many contemporary interpreters. Crisp defends the "pure act" conceptuality of classical theism, even claiming that it makes Edwards's thought more dynamic rather than less dynamic: "If God is a simple pure act he is *much more* dynamic than Sang Lee thinks he is, for the simple reason that a simple pure act has no unrealized potentiality. There is nothing about him that is 'static.' "[29]

Notwithstanding Crisp's identification of Edwards as a classical theist, Crisp is critical of Edwards on a number of points. Some aspects of Edwards's metaphysics, he says, are simply strange, and he objects to Edwards's purported attempt to derive the Trinity from reason alone.[30] Edwards's view of God—at least with reference to the individuation of the divine persons of the Trinity—"is so seriously mired in difficulties that it appears irredeemable."

---

27. For a more detailed account of the debate over Sang Lee's (and Amy Pauw's) views of Edwards's God-concept, see Michael J. McClymond, "Hearing the Symphony: A Critique of Some Critics of Sang Lee's and Amy Pauw's Accounts of Jonathan Edwards's View of God," in Don Schweitzer, ed., *Jonathan Edwards as Contemporary: Essays in Honor of Sang Hyun Lee* (New York: Peter Lang, 2010), 67–92.

28. Crisp, "Jonathan Edwards's Ontology," 2.

29. Crisp, in email correspondence with Michael McClymond, June 2010.

30. Crisp bases his argument on Miscellany 94. Yet Edwards began this notebook entry with a reference to the use of scripture in establishing the doctrine of the Trinity (WJE 13:256–57). The reference to "naked reason" here should be read in the context of the whole of Miscellany 94. On Edwards's appeals to "reason," see chs. 9–10.

Crisp's monograph on original sin asserts that Edwards's occasionalism is a "fatal flaw" that undermines the coherence of his thinking on moral agency and responsibility. Edwards's account of Adam's fall made God the immediate or proximate cause of Adam's sin (ch. 22). Neither was Edwards successful, says Crisp, in his attempt to mediate between supralapsarian and infralapsarian views of predestination. Crisp's recent work on Edwards employs the term "pure act panentheism" to describe the notion—set forth in *End of Creation*—that God is essentially creative and that the act of creation flows from an intrinsic property of the divine nature.[31] Crisp's interpretation seems to have shifted over the last decade from a more conservative (i.e., classically theistic) to a more innovative (panentheistic) construal of Edwards's God. His analysis exhibits both the traditional and the novel aspects in Edwards's thought. Considering Oliver Crisp's work alongside that of William Squires, Miklos Vetö, and Stephen Daniel, it is clear that Edwards's thought continues to be of interest to philosophers and has evoked complex, divergent, and even antithetical interpretations and responses.

---

31. Crisp, "Jonathan Edwards's God: The Trinity, Individuation and Divine Simplicity," 101–102; Crisp, *Jonathan Edwards and the Metaphysics of Sin*, 130–35, 50, 22; Crisp, "Jonathan Edwards on the Divine Nature," 175–76.

41

Interpretations II

JONATHAN EDWARDS AND THE REFORMED TRADITION

JONATHAN EDWARDS IS one of the great Christian thinkers who defies precise categorization. His thinking is recognizably Reformed but with a difference. His first biographer and disciple said he "called no man father," and observers from his time to ours have remarked on his theological independence. He was "irreverent" toward Calvin, expected to find new theological light as he went along, and more often than not enjoyed tinkering with if not transforming his received Puritan and Reformed traditions.[1] At the same time, Edwards thought in Reformed categories and considered himself an apologist for the Reformed tradition (ch. 21). In his preface to *Freedom of the Will*, he wrote, "I should not take it all amiss, to be called a Calvinist, for distinction's sake," even though "the term 'Calvinist' is in these days, among most, a term of greater reproach than the term 'Arminian.' " In 1750, he wrote to a friend that he would have "no difficulty...subscribing to the substance of the Westminster Confession."[2]

How then are we to understand his willingness to be called a Calvinist when the term was unfashionable, and his willingness to go beyond Calvin when need be? It might be useful to speak of "originalists," "confessionalists," and "developmentalists" within the Reformed tradition. An originalist is someone who says Calvinists should always go back to Calvin because "earlier is better" and the fountainhead is best of all. Confessionalists want to conform their theological work to the letter of the historic Reformed confessions. If the originalist seeks to return to the beginning, the confessionalist desires to abide by "what is written" in the confession. "Developmentalists," in contrast, believe that every theological tradition unfolds over time so that later exponents of a tradition (e.g., Francis Turretin and Petrus van Mastricht)

---

1. Amy Plantinga Pauw, "The Future of Reformed Theology: Some Lessons from Jonathan Edwards," in David Willis and Michael Welker, eds., *Toward the Future of Reformed Theology* (Grand Rapids: Eerdmans, 1999), 457.

2. WJE 1:131; WJE 16:355.

might be better guides than an earlier one. Edwards judged that Mastricht's systematic theology was better than any other non-biblical book in the world, presumably even Calvin's *Institutes*.³ Edwards's own innovations showed him to be not an originalist or confessionalist but a developmentalist. Clearly he believed that the tradition could be improved—if not in its core principles, then in the ways these were expounded and defended. He also seemed to believe that he had been called by God to improve upon past expressions of the Calvinistic faith.

In this chapter, we shall look first at Edwards's agreement with Calvin and other Reformed thinkers, then examine where he diverged from earlier Reformed thinking, and finally compare him to two other Reformed theologians—Friedrich Daniel Ernst Schleiermacher and Karl Barth.

Reformed Themes

The similarities between Edwards and Calvin are noteworthy. Both were industrious students who censured their schoolmates' pranks, had difficult relations with their fathers, and were shy men ill-suited to small talk. Both reported undergoing sudden conversions that reoriented their thinking and their entire way of life.⁴ Each man suffered continuing conflicts with church and community leaders, and endured public ridicule. Both theologians loved music and valued its spiritual import.⁵

John Leith's *Introduction to the Reformed Tradition* (1977) outlined the ethos of the Reformed tradition in terms of its distinctive emphases. Most of these mirrored Edwards's own emphases:

1. Stress on God's sovereignty and thus the divine initiative—demonstrated by Edwards's first published lecture, "God Glorified in the Work of Redemption."
2. Concern for the glory of God above all most notably expressed in his *End of Creation*.

---

3. WJE 16:217.

4. On Calvin's characteristics, see: John T. McNeill, *The History and Character of Calvinism* (New York: Oxford University Press, 1954), 99, 103, 107. On Edwards's characteristics, see: George M. Marsden, *Jonathan Edwards: A Life* (New Haven: Yale University Press, 2003), 39, 17, 42–43. On Calvin's conversion, see: Calvin, preface, *Calvin: Commentaries*, ed. Joseph Haroutunian (Philadelphia: Westminster Press, 1958), 52. On Edwards's conversion, see his *Personal Narrative* in WJE 16. Of course, we should not assume that Calvin's conversion was the sort that was common in the eighteenth-century awakenings.

5. McNeill, *History and Character*, 143.

3. The belief that God works out his purposes in history—as Edwards charted in his *History of the Work of Redemption* sermons.
4. Devotion to a life of holiness with the Law as a guide—illustrated in hundreds of Edwards's sermons and detailed systematically in *Religious Affections*.
5. Consideration of the life of the mind as service to God—exemplified by Edwards's enormous intellectual output.
6. Preaching the Word of God with a plain style—demonstrated by more than 1000 sermon manuscripts written in a practical, earthy sermon style.
7. A disciplined life—illustrated by Edwards's fastidious "Resolutions."[6]

Like Calvin, Edwards was theocentric and Trinitarian. He never reduced the Godhead to a functional unitarianism of the first or the second persons (ch. 13). Like Calvin and Barth, Edwards tried to make theological and pastoral sense of predestination (ch. 22). He defended the traditional Calvinistic distinction between the decretive, hidden will of God and the preceptive, revealed will.[7] While Edwards added considerable nuance in his covenant theology, he generally accepted the Reformed understanding of the Jewish Covenant and New Covenant as variations of one another, so that the old covenant contained the gospel under a veil, and the Jewish and Christian religions were essentially one.[8]

Edwards embraced covenant theology and its variety of covenants—those of works, grace, redemption, the church, and even the national covenant (ch. 21). He revised Puritan federal theory and adjusted its analysis of perseverance in order to resist Arminian self-confidence. Later in his career, he made further alterations aimed at resisting antinomian laxity. Yet through all these adjustments, Edwards remained a covenant theologian. He shared Calvin's theological vision of the world as "the theater of the glory of God." The Swiss Reformer said one cannot look anywhere in the world after being enlightened by the Spirit and the Word in scripture "without seeing some sparks of his glory."[9] Edwards was inclined all his life to find God in the creation, filling his

---

6. John H. Leith, *An Introduction to the Reformed Tradition: A Way of Being the Christian Community* (Atlanta: John Knox Press, 1977), 67–83. For the "resolutions," see WJE 16:753–58.

7. John Gerstner, *The Rational Biblical Theology of Jonathan Edwards*, (Powhatan, Va: Berea Publications, 1992), 2:184.

8. These last three sentences are demonstrated in ch. 21. Edwards rejected most of the theological aberrations that the Reformed tradition came eventually to reject, such as the teaching by some of his own disciples that the redeemed must show a willingness to be damned; WJE 18:75–76.

9. Calvin, *Institutes* 1.6.2; 1.14.20; 2.6.1; 3.9.2.

Images or Shadows notebook with the types of God's biblical truth he saw there (ch. 8). Edwards also developed Calvin's appreciation for common grace and the glories of human civilization. In *True Virtue*, Edwards wrote of the beauty of natural justice while distinguishing it from the more comprehensive understanding that comes from regeneration. Paul Ramsey portrayed Edwards as an innovator in this regard, articulating more fully the humanism that is commonly attributed to Calvin. William Danaher argues that Edwards went further than Turretin by suggesting that the regenerate moral life is not simply likeness to God but instantiation of God's very life (see ch. 33).

Edwards's most noteworthy moral-philosophical treatise, *Freedom of the Will*, has been seen as a sophisticated articulation of the sixteenth and seventeenth-century "theological dialectic" among Reformed divines, which preserved the gratuity of grace and the integrity of nature in its covenant theology.[10] Similarly his new "sense of the heart" was a restatement in Lockean empiricist terms of "Reformed orthodoxy's insistence that grace qualitatively enhances the power of human faculties, without destroying their nature."[11] Thus Edwards developed his approach to the age-old question of human versus divine agency along Reformed lines.

In the nineteenth century, rumors circulated that Edwards had departed from Christian and Calvinist orthodoxy on the Trinity. Edwards Amasa Park first tried to disprove this toward the end of the nineteenth century, and in 1903 George Park Fisher attempted to put the rumors to rest by publishing Edwards's essay on the Trinity. Questions resurfaced in 1971 when Paul Helm asserted that Edwards's essay showed evidence of tritheism.[12] It was probably Edwards's use of idealist metaphysics to express the orthodox doctrine of the Trinity that led critics to think he had departed from the tradition. But he had already made it clear in an early *Miscellanies* entry that the three divine Persons are not separate beings with distinct understandings.[13]

Edwards's sacramental theology was also Reformed if pitched at a slightly different angle. Brian Gerrish has shown that, for Calvin and most Calvinist confessions, the sacrament of the altar was not simply a Zwinglian memorial of what happened centuries before but the gift of Jesus Christ in which Christ

---

10. William K.B. Stoever, *A Faire and Easie Way to Heaven: Covenant Theology and Antinomianism in Early Massachusetts* (Middletown, CT: Wesleyan University Press, 1977), x.

11. Stoever, *A Faire and Easie Way*, 190.

12. Paul Helm, introduction to Edwards, *Treatise on Grace & Other Posthumously Published Writings*, (Greenwood, SC: Attic Press, 1971), 21.

13. WJE 13:392.

is not only the agent but the content of the sacrament.[14] But while the Puritans stressed the Lord's Supper as ratification of the covenant and Calvin highlighted spiritual fellowship with Christ's body and blood, Edwards emphasized Christ's dramatic re-presentation and union with believers in the eucharist. For Edwards, In the Lord's Supper, Jesus Christ is more present than at other moments in church life (ch. 30). Edwards agreed with Calvin that infant baptism is the seal of God's promises made to the children of the righteous and that adult baptism requires profession of faith. But Edwards taught more clearly than Calvin did that the baptismal rite does not by itself effect regeneration. Edwards followed the lead of the *Westminster Confession of Faith* and early Congregationalists in teaching that not all children of the covenant are elect, and therefore parents and the church should seek the regeneration and conversion of children by use of the means of grace.[15]

New Departures

While Edwards thought of himself as a faithful teacher of the tradition he was not afraid to revise and develop it. Amy Plantinga Pauw asserts that he showed "a much freer spirit toward the Reformed tradition" than many realize.[16] In this section, we will look at the principal points at which Edwards departed from standard Reformed ways of thinking and developed new formulations of what he considered basic Reformed principles.

Many nineteenth-century critics accused him of being a speculative metaphysician (ch. 38). While their restatements of Edwards's positions were often inaccurate, the charge was not altogether unfair. Edwards's idealist conception of the Trinity in which the Son is the Father's "idea," the Son is humanity's link to Adam, and God continually creates the world were bold metaphysical assertions. Leith observed that Calvin and the Reformed tradition have generally been more practical than speculative, more biblical than philosophical. Even Puritan William Ames and Edwards's favorites Turretin and Mastricht regarded theology as essentially practical rather than speculative. So while Edwards's doctrine of God was traditional, his ways of conceiving it were sometimes more metaphysical

---

14. Brian A. Gerrish, "The Lord's Supper in the Reformed Confessions," in Donald K. McKim, ed., *Major Themes in the Reformed Tradition* (Grand Rapids: Eerdmans, 1992), 248, 254.

15. Gerstner, *Rational Biblical Theology*, 2:116. Calvin did not teach that baptism effected the regeneration of non-elect infants, as we stated in ch. 31.

16. Plantinga Pauw, "Future," 457.

than those of Calvin and most of his successors (ch. 7). In *Original Sin*, for example, Edwards departed from traditional federal theory where Adam was our representative head in the way that a king represents his subjects when negotiating a treaty. Instead he adopted an idealist view of our oneness with Adam based on continuous creation by the arbitrary constitution of the Creator.[17]

Charles Hodge and others accused Edwards of pantheism because of his assertion that God is the only substance and his notion of continuous creation, which Hodge thought destroys the existence and continuity of an external world. Some twentieth-century recent authors, including Douglas Elwood and John Gerstner, used the term "panentheism" to designate Edwards's concept of God's presence to the creation combined with his sense of God's distinction from and sovereignty over the creation.[18] Gerstner concluded that Edwards "never taught pantheism directly or ever intended to infer it." The ultimate evidence for this panentheistic rather than pantheistic view is that Edwards held to an eternal hell with souls forever separated from the bliss of God.[19]

In his theologizing Edwards also tended to look for rational reasons where other Reformed divines had been content with mystery. For example, he said that God's reasons for choosing some and not others were not arbitrary but rational.[20] Calvin wrote that God's "wonderful method of governing the universe is rightly called an abyss." Occasionally, said Calvin, we can discern God's purposes, as when God topples a cruel kingdom. But most of the time we cannot understand God's providence, and "we ought reverently to adore" and "hold [God] in reverence."[21] In contrast Edwards devoted his *History of the*

---

17. Leith, *Introduction to the Reformed Tradition*, 106–107; William K.B. Stoever, "The Godly Will's Discerning: Shepard, Edwards, and the Identification of True Godliness," in Stephen J. Stein ed., Jonathan Edwards's Writings: Text, Context, Interpretation (Bloomington, IN: Indiana University Press, 1996), 86. For Edwards on original sin and continuous creation, see ch. 22.

18. Douglas Elwood, *The Philosophical Theology of Jonathan Edwards* (New York: Columbia University Press, 1960), 50–60. Edwards was not a panentheist in the sense of some who use that term—believing in the coeternality of the world with God. He affirmed the traditional doctrine of *creatio ex nihilo*. It might be more helpful to think of Edwards's metaphysics in Neoplatonic terms that speak of levels of reality: the world participates in the reality of God and yet God's degree of reality is immeasurably greater.

19. Gerstner, *Rational Biblical Theology*, 2:13. Edwards believed that those in hell experience God as a wrathful presence and yet exist as distinct from God (ch. 35).

20. See ch. 21. Even Calvin thought that election had its own "equity" that human minds cannot fathom (*Institutes*, 3.23.9). But Edwards tended to try to explain the reasonableness of doctrines Calvin and other Reformed divines typically left unexplained, such as the imputation of Adam's sin to a fallen human race.

21. Calvin, *Institutes*, 1.17.2.

Work of Redemption to an exploration of God's purposes in history and filled his notebooks with reflections on the providential meaning of current events around the world. In an effort to make the Reformed doctrine of predestination more comprehensible, he took an infralapsarianism approach: God's decrees of eternal damnation came only after his permission of freedom and hence the Fall (ch. 21).

Some of Edwards's most important differences with Calvin and certain Calvinists involved his views of the church and conversion. For Calvin, "the idea of coming to faith is one of transforming bit by bit over a lifetime of attending the means of grace and personal devotion. It is the Isaac model, since its ideal is that of the covenant child who never knows anything other than that he or she is a child of God."[22] An experience of conversion was therefore unnecessary for salvation or its assurance. Puritans, on the other hand, emphasized "owning the covenant" in a personal appropriation of justification more than the "givenness" of Christ's work of justification.[23] Edwards showed his debt to Puritanism by preaching for conversion and teaching signs of true faith. He also required personal testimony of one's faith as a requirement for communion and church membership. Hodge accused Edwards of seeking a "pure church," and critics today complain that he "betray[ed] Reformed teaching on conversion and therefore compromise[d] Calvinism's doctrine of salvation."[24] Hodge was off the mark because Edwards did not require that all applicants be certain of their conversion and insisted that neither he nor the church could be certain of who is regenerate. Yet Edwards emphasized conversion more than Calvin or Hodge did and he stressed self-examination as a way of testing for the presence of genuine faith. At this point, he followed the lead of earlier Pietist and Puritan writers, arguing that scripture presents Christian practice and perseverance as evidences of regeneration.

Edwards's eschatology was a break from Calvin and other early Reformed understandings of the millennium, which adopted Augustine's view that the millennium was not a literally earthly reign but a symbol designation for Christ's rule through the church. But Edwards's postmillennialism was a development

---

22. D. G. Hart, "Jonathan Edwards and the Origins of Experimental Calvinism," in D.G. Hart, Sean Michael Lucas, and Stephen J. Nichols, eds., *The Legacy of Jonathan Edwards: American Religion and the Evangelical Tradition* (Grand Rapids: Baker Academic, 2003), 176.

23. Jerald C. Brauer, "Conversion: From Puritanism to Revivalism," in *Journal of Religion* 58 (1978): 227–43, esp. 234–35.

24. Hart, "Jonathan Edwards," 163. Hart argues that Calvin never taught an experience of conversion. Edwards spoke often of conversion but did not reduce it to an experience with specified feelings (ch. 24).

of Reformed thinking going back to Johannes Cocceius (1603–69) and later Dutch Reformed and Puritan divines such as Thomas Brightman, John Cotton, Moses Lowman, and Mastricht (see ch. 35).[25] This eschatological viewpoint understood the millennium as an earthly period of approximately one thousand years that followed a period of revival and persecution for the church.

Yet if Edwards's eschatology was only a limited break with early Reformed tradition, his aesthetics represented a more profound departure. Turretin and Hodge subordinated the principle of love to that of justice in their doctrines of the atonement. Calvin coordinated love and justice, but Edwards conceived of the atonement in terms of love and beauty (ch. 16), with beauty as the first principle of God's nature and communication to his creatures.[26] Edwards's extraordinary attention to God's beauty in fact distinguishes his theology not only from his Reformed predecessors but also from the larger history of Western Christian thought. It is a possible point of contact between Edwards and Eastern Orthodoxy (ch. 43). God's beauty was also important for Barth, but for Edwards beauty was at the very center of the vision of God (ch. 6).[27]

It might also be useful to consider Edwards's relation to the Reformed tradition in three areas that have been neglected in Edwards's scholarship: his approach to other religions, missions, and ecumenism. Until Edwards's time, many Reformed thinkers had seen non-Christian religions as offering little or no knowledge of the true God. In contrast, Edwards found some knowledge of God the Redeemer among the "heathen" and so went further than Mastricht or Turretin (ch. 36). Many Reformed thinkers since the Reformation, including Edwards's ally Thomas Prince in Boston, believed missions were largely limited to the apostolic age, but Edwards was one of the first to apply the Great Commission to all church members (ch. 34). He also put new stress on the laity's intercession for revival.

Yet if Edwards was an innovator in his missiology, he did little to perpetuate the early Reformed ecumenical efforts. Calvin famously reached out to Archbishop Cranmer in 1552, saying that the church's disunity was a great evil and that therefore he would "cross even ten seas" if he could help heal the rifts.[28] In 1560, Calvin proposed a universal council to reunite all of Christianity

---

25. McDermott, *One Holy and Happy Society: The Public Theology of Jonathan Edwards* (University Park: Penn State Press, 1992), 37–92.

26. H. D. McDonald, "Models of the Atonement in Reformed Theology," in Donald K. McKim, ed., *Major Themes in the Reformed Tradition* (Grand Rapids: Eerdmans, 1992), 120–21.

27. Patrick Sherry, *Spirit and Beauty: A History of Theological Aesthetics* (Birmingham: SCM Press, 2002).

28. Quoted in Leith, *Introduction to the Reformed Tradition*, 53.

and supported the pope as head of the council it if he would agree to submit to its decisions.[29] Edwards held a positive view of early Anglicanism and of Anglican revivalists Whitefield and Wesley (ch. 28). He promoted ecumenical concerts of prayer and appreciated Lutherans and Orthodox Christians day. Yet he never made ecumenical efforts like those of Calvin and he regarded the Roman papacy as one of the two arms of Antichrist.

Schleiermacher and Barth

In this cursory survey of Edwards and the Reformed tradition, we have given principal attention to Edwards and Calvin. Richard Muller has shown that there is far more diversity within the tradition than can be seen in these two men and that there was considerable creativity among the post-Reformation Reformed divines.[30] But space considerations require us to limit ourselves in this last section to a brief comparison of Edwards to the two most influential Reformed theologians of the last two centuries—Friedrich Schleiermacher (1768–1834) and Karl Barth (1886–1968). In the conclusion to this book (ch. 45), we will return once again briefly to consider Edwards alongside Schleiermacher and Barth.

Historical theologians have noticed striking affinities between Edwards and Schleiermacher. They shared similar views of human nature. Both saw that the affections are at the base or center of the human person, directing what a person chooses, thinks, and feels. Both realized that religion's essence lies beyond mere thinking (doctrine) and doing (ethics), and both used a kind of critical empiricism (focusing on tangible experience, but not taking all experience at face value) in their theological work. But there the similarities stop. As Barth and others have pointed out, Schleiermacher's subject matter was less the objective, historical facticity of Christ and the redemption he achieved than the subjective, human experience of Christ and redemption. He seemed to be trapped within the anthropological horizon. He refused to discuss the objectivity of God apart from human experience because of his conviction that we can only know God in *relation* to us, and especially in our consciousness of the feeling of absolute dependence. For Schleiermacher, the words of scripture were not God-given but took shape as human beings reflected on their religious experiences. Theology was primarily an interpre-

---

29. McNeill, *History and Character of Calvinism*, 200.

30. Richard A. Muller, *Post-Reformation Reformed Dogmatics*, 4 vols. (Grand Rapids: Baker Academic, 1987–2003).

tation of "God-consciousness," not a reflection on the testimonies of the Bible. Schleiermacher relegated the Trinity to the appendix of his major work, *The Christian Faith*, because he could not find it in his investigation of the pious "God-consciousness." No external authority took precedence over the immediate experiences of believers. He redefined miracles so that they were no longer events that transcended scientific explanation. Schleiermacher's reinterpretation set aside many traditional Christian beliefs, such as angels and demons, the Virgin Birth, the bodily resurrection of Christ, and the Second Coming of Christ.

Like Schleiermacher, Edwards held that we cannot know God in his essence except as he has revealed himself to us. Yet Edwards's theology took on a different character because he believed that objective revelation has been given to us in history and the words of scripture. He looked to a norm outside experience—the testimony of scripture. He was more critical of religious experience than was Schleiermacher, but at the same time, he was no less insistent on the importance of experience in religion. While Schleiermacher spoke in somewhat abstract fashion about "piety" and "the feeling of absolute dependence," Edwards was a clinical observer of concrete religious experiences, composing treatises based on first-hand accounts of religious experiences among a diverse group of people. While Schleiermacher focused on a preconceptual sense of reality, Edwards sought to define precisely the concepts of self and God. Accordingly some scholars think that Edwards's account of religious experience was more subtle and probing than that of Schleiermacher. Richard R. Niebuhr, an American interpreter of Schleiermacher, wrote that Schleiermacher "falls below the standard set by Jonathan Edwards in his sensitivity and perspicacity in the realm of the Christian and religious affections."[31]

Another basic difference between Edwards and Schleiermacher was their divergence on anthropology and epistemology. Schleiermacher believed God-consciousness was "already present in human nature" as an a priori dimension of human existence. Regeneration was a matter of "the quiescent self-consciousness, looking at itself reflected in thought and finding a consciousness of God included there."[32] While full redemption occurred through the consciousness of Jesus as transmitted through the Christian Church, regeneration could take place apart from fundamental transformation. For

---

31. Richard R. Niebuhr, *Schleiermacher on Christ and Religion* (New York: Charles Scribner's, 1964), 17.

32. Schleiermacher, *The Christian Faith*, ed. H. R. Mackintosh (Philadelphia: Fortress, 1976), 476, 478–79.

Edwards, on the other hand, regeneration was truly a new birth—a miracle whereby the Holy Spirit brought new life to a heart that was dead. For Schleiermacher there was only one epistemology, since could experience God through self-reflection. For Edwards there were two—that of the regenerate and that of the unregenerate. One relied on the natural use of human reflection, and the other looked to a miraculous gift of spiritual vision.

Edwards had much more in common with Barth than with Schleiermacher. Like Edwards, Barth insisted we have no innate capacity to know God (contra Schleiermacher) and stressed God's sovereign grace and ongoing, providential activity. Our relationship with God is never something that we possess but instead is continually reestablished by God through on his freedom and good pleasure. For Barth, as for Edwards, theology originates in a reflection on God's self-revelation in scripture. Its agenda is set not by human questioning but by the demands and constraints one finds in God's Word. If Edwards was a premier theologian of the Trinity (ch. 13), Barth was perhaps even more so. After several centuries of Protestant theology that had downplayed or ignored the Trinity (Schleiermacher most notably), Barth initiated a twentieth-century Trinitarian revival based on the premise that "the Trinity...marks out the Christian doctrine of God as Christian."[33] He introduced the Trinity near the beginning of his massive *Church Dogmatics* and made it the center of God's identity and therefore of theology itself.

Despite Barth's well-documented statements in rejection of metaphysics in the sphere of theology (ch. 7), Barth seemed implicitly to embrace a metaphysical position akin to that of Edwards. Referred to as "actualism," Barth's approach viewed God as being always in action. Even as the human relationship with God is continuously being renewed, so too God's revelation was always an event or happening and never something static. This was similar to Edwards's notion of continual creation, whereby the world and all people are continually recreated by God out of nothing in each passing moment (chs. 7,22). Barth applied this metaphysic to the Bible: it can never be called the Word of God as it rests on a shelf, for the Bible is a thing, but the Word of God is dynamic and living, continually reestablished according to the divine pleasure. The Spirit often uses the Bible to communicate a living and dynamic Word to a person who hears it or reads it, but apart from that dynamic illumination of the Spirit, the Bible is not the Word of God that conveys the self-revelation of God.[34] By contrast Edwards affirmed scripture as the words of God and Word of God—citing New Testament texts to buttress this point. Edwards separated the

---

33. Barth, quoted in George Hunsinger, *How to Read Karl Barth: The Shape of His Theology* (New York: Oxford University Press, 1991), 213.

34. Hunsinger, *How to Read*, 30–32, 76–102; Barth, *Church Dogmatics*, 2/1, 257–321.

inspiration of the Bible's authors from the illumination of the Bible's readers—though asserting the Spirit's work in both. Barth collapsed the two, making the first dependent on the second.

Edwards and Barth showed some other differences with regard to the doctrine of revelation. Barth famously denied natural revelation, perhaps overreacting against German Christian religion that found revelation in German blood and soil. Toward the end of his career, he acknowledged "lights" in creation that exude a certain "luminosity," but his early denial of natural theology was better remembered than this and other later qualifications.[35] Barth had argued that the testimonies of God in nature are not revelation because they are invariably misunderstood. They falsify rather than illumine. Edwards distinguished the "light of nature" in conscience and creation from "revelation" in Scripture (ch. 9). By thus separating an unregenerate knowledge of God from the saving knowledge of God's beauty, Edwards maintained that Romans 1:19–21 and 2:14 spoke of God's objective witness to himself in every human mind and heart.

It seems appropriate to finish this chapter with Barth, since both Barth's and Edwards's theologies were shaped by Calvin and the Reformed tradition. Yet just as Barth pushed beyond traditional Reformed boundaries on revelation, election, apologetics, and a host of other issues, Edwards charted new ways of Reformed thinking about metaphysics, beauty, the rationality of God's decrees, spiritual experience, conversion, ecclesiology, sacramentology, eschatology, ethics, theology of religions, and missiology. Both Edwards and Barth reconceived theology's relation to the Enlightenment in ways that were original and influential. For these reasons, both thinkers have inspired schools of thought that now influence theological reflection within and beyond the Reformed communion.

---

35. Barth, *Church Dogmatics: Volume IV: The Doctrine of Reconciliation*, Part 3.1, trans. G. W. Bromiley (Edinburgh: T & T Clark, 1961), 139–40.

42

Interpretations III: Edwards and the Revival Tradition

SINCE THE MID-1700S, no author has had a greater impact on the theology and practice of Protestant revival than Jonathan Edwards. D. Martyn Lloyd-Jones referred to him as "preeminently the theologian of Revival," while Richard Lovelace commented that "Edwards's writings on revival...comprise the foundational theology of spiritual renewal in English."[1] At first in North America and Britain and later throughout the globe, Edwards's most ardent admirers have been evangelical Christians, who, in the words of Douglas Sweeney, "shared in Edwards's passionate pursuit of 'true religion,' the kind of vital Christianity that stems from regeneration...and sets its subjects apart from nominal Christianity."[2] Yet if Edwards has been read widely, he has also been read selectively (ch. 37). Later interpreters brought the questions and issues of their own day to Edwards's writings, and this caused them to emphasize one or another theme or argument in his texts—including such matters as the nature of revival; the signs of true revival; appeals to fear in preaching; the awareness and conviction of sin; the roles of intellect, emotion, and imagination in religion; the significance of bodily manifestations; and the possibilities of charismatic gifts and revelatory experiences.

One reason for the varied interpretations of Edwards's revival texts is the variation within these texts. As noted previously (ch. 27), Edwards's general stance toward revivals combined *openness* to new kinds and degrees of spiritual experience with *caution* in appraising and assessing all spiritual phenomena. On the one hand, Edwards wrote that "the Spirit of God is sovereign in his operations...and uses a great variety," and so "we ought

---

1. D. Martyn Lloyd-Jones, "Jonathan Edwards and the Crucial Importance of Revival," in *The Puritans: Their Origins and Successors* (Edinburgh: The Banner of Truth Trust, 1987), 361 [v]; Richard Lovelace, *Dynamics of Spiritual Life: An Evangelical Theology of Renewal* (Downers Grove, IL: InterVarsity Press, 1979), 39.

2. Douglas Sweeney, "Evangelical Tradition in American," in Stephen J. Stein, *The Cambridge Companion to Jonathan Edwards* (Cambridge, UK: Cambridge University Press, 2007), 217.

not to limit God where he has not limited himself." On the other hand, he warned that "the apostolic age...was an age of the greatest outpouring of the Spirit of God that ever was" and a time when "counterfeits did...abound." This made it "necessary that the church of Christ should be furnished with some certain rules, and distinguishing and clear marks by which she might safely proceed in judging of spirits, and distinguish the true from the false."[3] While Edwards sought to maintain a balance between openness and caution, his writings from the mid-1730s to the late 1740s reflected a trend toward increasing caution. If one used a scale that placed novelty, emotion, spontaneity, and bodily expression at one end and caution, intellect, order, and bodily control at the other, then *Distinguishing Marks* (1741) would lie on the side of openness, *Some Thoughts Concerning the Revival* (1743) in the middle, and *Religious Affections* (1746) would lie on the side of caution. Writing in 1840, Presbyterian theologian Charles Hodge preferred the later writings to the earlier— though for Hodge even these later texts were not cautious enough. On the other hand, in Edwards's day and more recently there have been revival proponents who viewed Edwards as unduly cautious. Radical New Light preachers of the 1740s, such as James Davenport and Andrew Croswell, welcomed bodily manifestations, dreams, visions, and other alleged communications from God with an exuberance that Edwards never showed. John Wesley, too, embraced and celebrated revival phenomena in a way that Edwards did not. Quite recently, Pentecostal-Charismatic Christians turned to the early text *Distinguishing Marks* (1741) to argue that Charismatic revivals of the 1990s conformed to the tests of genuineness suggested by Edwards.

Edwards and the Calvinist Tradition on Revivals

Calvinists and Calvinism played a pivotal yet double-sided role in the American revival tradition. More than those of other traditions, Calvinists were of two minds on revivals, both extolling and excoriating them. The Calvinist tradition insisted on decency and decorum and yet revealed a persistent yearning for spiritual newness and dynamism. Early Puritan spirituality involved a quest for more grace and more truth from God, as John Robinson had declared in his 1620 farewell address to the Mayflower Pilgrims: "The Lord had more truth and light yet to break forth out of his holy word."[4] Yet Old Calvinists like Moses Mather joined with more rationalistic critics like Charles Chauncy

---

3. WJE 4:229, 226.
4. Robert Baird, *Religion in America* (New York: Arno Press, 1969 [1844]), 97–98, n.1.

in opposing religious revivals for their emotionalism and what they regarded as a misguided focus on dramatic, crisis-filled moments of spiritual experience. The Old Calvinists were orthodox according to the historic Reformed standards, and they held a faith that was, in Douglas Sweeney's words, "traditional and covenantal."[5] Baptism, doctrinal instruction, preaching, the Lord's Supper, private prayer, and devout reading—these were the indispensable means of grace. For Old Calvinists, there was no need for periodic paroxysms of guilt, despair, joy, or exhilaration.

A key issue pertained to the use of effort or "means" to promote revivals. Scholars sometimes presume that Great Awakening revivals in the 1740s were like "showers of divine blessing"—unanticipated and surprising to all concerned—while Second Great Awakening revivals from 1800 to 1830 were products of diligent preparation, high-pressure preaching, and innovative tactics like the "anxious bench."[6] The person most directly responsible for generating this sharp contrast between the two eras of revival was Charles Finney. His *Lectures on Revivals of Religion* (1835) shocked Calvinist readers in claiming that a "revival...is not a miracle" in the sense of something above the powers of nature, but rather "consists entirely in the right exercise of the powers of nature."[7] Finney portrayed himself as a man who approached revivals with a can-do spirit and a proven record of making things happen. Meanwhile, he criticized the Calvinists for their supposed do-nothing attitude—waiting for a revival to appear like a stone falling from the sky. Calvinists were offended and believed themselves

---

5. Douglas A. Sweeney, *Nathaniel Taylor, New Haven Theology, and the Legacy of Jonathan Edwards* (New York: Oxford University Press, 2003), 100. See Mark Noll, "Moses Mather (Old Calvinist) and the Evolution of Edwardseanism," *Church History* 49 (1980): 273–85.

6. William G. McLoughlin spoke of a process in which the "spontaneous" revivals of the 1700s became "routinized" into a "Protestant ritual" during the period after 1830 (*Revivals, Awakenings, and Reform: An Essay on Religion and Social Change in America, 1607–1977*; Chicago: University of Chicago Press, 1978; xiii). From a Calvinistic standpoint, Iain Murray drew a similar distinction in *Revival and Revivalism: The Making and Marring of American Revivalism, 1750–1858* (Carlisle, PA: Banner of Truth, 1994). Such views are not wholly wrong, but the contrast between the earlier and later revivals has been exaggerated. See Michael J. McClymond, "Issues and Explanations in the Study of North American Revivalism," in Michael J. McClymond, ed., *Embodying the Spirit: New Perspectives on North American Revivalism* (Baltimore, MD: Johns Hopkins University Press, 2004), 14–17.

7. Finney at points took an almost naturalistic approach to revivals: "The connection between the right use of means for a revival and a revival is as philosophically sure as between the right use of means to raise grain and a crop of wheat" (Charles G. Finney, *Lectures on Revivals of Religion*, ed. William G. McLoughlin Cambridge, MA: Belknap Press of Harvard University, 1960; x–xi, 13).

to have been maligned. Finney's *Lectures* obscured a central issue in the 1830s revival debates, which was not *whether* means should be used but *which* means were most suitable. Calvinists—with the exception of some radicals or hyper-Calvinists—were never opposed to the use of means.[8] From theological premises, one might presume that Calvinists did nothing but wait on God, while Arminians and other non-Calvinists did nothing but exert themselves. In actuality, non-Calvinists like Wesley and Finney did a lot of waiting as they exerted themselves, while Calvinists did a lot of exertion as they waited.

A version of Calvinism in the 1600s that strongly emphasized the need to seek God and make use of means was known as *preparationism*. It insisted that there was something that unconverted sinners could do to facilitate their own conversion. By making use of "means"—such as Bible reading, prayer, meditation, attendance at worship, the hearing of sermons—a person seeking conversion might dispose himself toward receiving God's grace. The first persons in American history dubbed as "preparationists" were colonial pastors—Thomas Hooker, Thomas Shepard, Solomon Stoddard—who observed the difficult process that some people went through in coming to faith. Without denying their Calvinist conviction that God is sovereign in giving grace, they also felt bound to acknowledge that conversion was a process occurring over time. Stripped down to its essentials, preparationism included two key points—that God is free and sovereign in dispensing grace, and that human beings may prepare themselves to receive grace. Some Calvinists, zealous to uphold God's free and sovereign grace, rejected preparationism. The Synod of Dordt (1618–19) in the Netherlands called it "Pelagian." In Massachusetts during the 1630s, John Cotton and his parishioner Anne Hutchinson regarded preparationism as a "covenant of works." Yet New England Calvinism diverged from that of the Netherlands. Whereas preparationism fell out of favor in the Netherlands, in New England

---

8. Hyper-Calvinism appeared among some British Reformed Baptists of the late 1700s, as described in Peter Toon, *The Emergence of Hyper-Calvinism in English Nonconformity, 1689–1765* (London: Olive Tree, 1967). When William Carey, the early Protestant missionary leader, expressed a desire to preach the gospel in India, he was told, "Sit down, young man; when God wants to evangelize the heathen, He will do it without your help" (George Eldon Ladd, *The Gospel of the Kingdom: Scriptural Studies in the Kingdom of God*; Grand Rapids, MI: Eerdmans, 1959; 135). Interestingly, it was the reading of Jonathan Edwards's writings that led some of these British hyper-Calvinists, such as Andrew Fuller, toward a more balanced theology. On the American scene, some "primitive" or "anti-mission" Baptists were opposed to evangelism or mission as such. Sean Lucas writes: "Extending the logic of divine predestination, they hold that God's elect will come to faith without any human prodding" ("Primitive [Antimission] Baptists," in Michael J. McClymond, ed., *Encyclopedia of Religious Revivals in America*, 2 vols.; Westport, CT: Greenwood Press, 2007; 1:343).

it became the dominant position on conversion from the mid-1600s to the mid-1700s.[9]

Edwards maintained the preparationist perspective of his New England forbears. "We advise persons under convictions," he wrote, "to be earnest and violent for the kingdom of heaven...watchful, laborious, and earnest, in the whole work of religion." His sermon on Jacob's wrestling with the angel had the following as its doctrine: "The way to obtain the blessing of God, is not to let God go except he bless us." In the early fragment "On Seeking," he argued that seeking and finding God must begin with renunciation: "He that would seek and find God must, as the first thing in order to it, forsake every known sin, and spit this sweet morsel out of his mouth."[10] As John Gerstner showed, Edwards not only held to preparationism but made the concept integral to his homiletic, evangelistic, and pastoral practice.[11] He clearly rejected a do-nothing, resigned, or fatalistic form of Calvinism. Instead he prodded the unconverted to intense efforts toward their own salvation and the converted to a continual quest for more grace. Moreover, in *Humble Attempt* (1747) he transposed the logic of preparationism from an individual to a corporate level, insisting that vigorous, passionate, and persistent efforts in united prayer among the churches of Britain and America might bring an outpouring of the Holy Spirit.

Another issue for Calvinists in relation to the revival tradition was anti-intellectualism. While Edwards and other Calvinist revivalists of the 1700s and early 1800s—William Tennent, Jonathan Dickinson, Asahel Nettleton, Heman Humphrey, and many more—placed high value on the life of the mind, such was generally not the case with promoters of revivals after the mid-1800s. As one historian explained, some preferred preachers who were unlettered: "Zeal was more important than knowledge.

---

9. Bishop Joseph Hall, an English representative at Dordt, defended preparationism by noting that God's grace operates in human lives by not by "sudden ruptures, but by meet preparations," and the "inward acts tending toward conversion" occur by the "secret and wonderful" work of God (Joseph Hall, *Works*; London, 1863; 9:493–94), cited in Norman Pettit, *The Heart Prepared: Grace and Conversion in Puritan Spiritual Life* (New Haven, CT: Yale University Press, 1966), 126.

10. WJE 16:91, 22:542, 17:452, 10:380. Further elaboration of this theme is found in the sermons "Pressing Into the Kingdom of God" (WJE 19:274–304), "Ruth's Resolution" (WJE 19:307–20), "Seeking After Christ" (WJE 22:287–97), and the early fragment "On Seeking" (WJE 10:379–87).

11. John Gerstner, *Steps to Salvation: The Evangelistic Message of Jonathan Edwards* (Philadelphia, PA: Westminster Press, 1960), and John Gerstner and Jonathan Neil Gerstner, "Edwardsean Preparation for Salvation," *Westminister Theological Journal* 42 (1979): 5–71.

An exhorter who could boast of no education was thought better qualified to arouse sinners than the minister."[12] The best-known revival preachers—Charles Finney, Dwight Moody, Billy Sunday, Aimee Semple McPherson, and Billy Graham—generally had *less* theological training than most of their ministerial peers.[13]

Mark Noll explained that the conflict between revivalism and intellect resulted from an anti-traditionalism that began during the early 1800s: "Revivals called people to Christ as a way of escaping tradition, including traditional learning... In so doing, they often left the impression that individual believers could accept nothing from others." This implied that "everything of value in the Christian life had to come from the individual's own choice—not just personal faith but every scrap of wisdom, understanding, and conviction about the faith." For Noll, the grand synthesis of devout experience and intellectual argument offered by Jonathan Edwards and his early disciples broke apart during the course of the nineteenth century and "American revivalism did much to hamstring the life of the mind."[14] In Edwards's theology, there was no need to "balance" intellectual and affective life or to "reunite" the two because mind and heart had never been at odds. As he aptly wrote: "There can be no love without knowledge. It is not according to the nature of the human soul, to love an object which is entirely unknown. The heart cannot be set upon an object of which there is no idea in the understanding."[15] Had later revivalists followed Edwards's example, they would not have set spiritual fervor against intellectual rigor.

Two Approaches to Revival—Edwardseans and Wesleyans in the Later 1700s

While the Great Awakening in the American colonies was still in progress in 1741, it became divided over theological issues later referred to as the Calvinist-Arminian debate. Though the issues were age-old, the proponents of divine sovereignty were classed with the sixteenth-century Reformer of Geneva, John Calvin,

---

12. Ola Winslow, *Jonathan Edwards: A Biography* (New York: Macmillan, 1940), 198.

13. See Richard Hofstadter, *Anti-Intellectualism in American Life* (New York: Alfred Knopf, 1970 [1963]), 55–136.

14. Mark A. Noll, *The Scandal of the Evangelical Mind* (Grand Rapids, MI: Eerdmans, 1994), 63–64.

15. WJE 22:88.

FIGURE 42.1 Edwards's reflections on revival grew out of his decades as a pastor in Northampton—exhibited here in an artist's reconstruction (Courtesy of the Forbes Library, Northampton, Massachusetts).

and the advocates of human free will with the Dutch theologian of the early seventeenth century, Jacob Arminius. John Wesley's sermon against Calvinist predestination, "Free Grace" (1740), elicited a letter from George Whitefield, stating that he wrote with "unspeakable Sorrow of Heart" and was aware that some would be "offended" at his letter, others would rejoice, and still others would wish "this Matter had never been brought under Debate." Whitefield wrote in the belief that "the Children of God are in Danger of falling into Error"—which was, in fact, Wesley's own conviction regarding Whitefield's views.[16] The rift was never healed and continues to this day among conservative, Bible-oriented Protestants. Wesley regarded Calvinism as a sinister threat to the moral life. For if human actions were predetermined, human beings could not be held responsible for their behavior. During the British "Antinomian" Controversies of the 1770s, Wesley wrote a tract called *Thoughts Upon Necessity* (1774) in which he described Edwards as the one who "connects together and confirms" all the worst elements in Stoicism and Calvinism. He complained of Edwards's "curious, subtle, metaphysical distinctions."

---

16. John Wesley, "Free Grace," in *The Works of John Wesley*, 14 vols., Thomas Jackson, ed. (Grand Rapids, MI: Baker Books, 2007 [1872]), 7:373–86; and George Whitefield, *A Letter from the Reverend George Whitefield to the Reverend Mr. John Wesley in Answer to His Sermon, Entitled, Free Grace* (Philadelphia: B. Franklin, 1741), quoting 5.

Wesley described Edwards's *Religious Affections* as "a dangerous heap, wherein much wholesome food is mixed with much deadly poison." As a result, he published a severely edited version of *Religious Affections* that included only about one-sixth of the original. Though Wesley wanted to produce a cheap, pocket edition for his Methodist preachers, the reduction in length also reflected a desire to repackage Edwards in a more theologically congenial form.[17] In editing *Religious Affections*, he completely eliminated the passages on the disinterested love of God for God's own sake—a key element in Edwards's argument in the treatise. Wesley more readily embraced the notion of self-interest than Edwards did. Concerned with reaching ordinary folk with the gospel, Wesley may have thought that Edwards set the bar too high in his notions of true religion.[18]

One of Wesley's differences with Edwards related to the "witness of the Spirit"—an inner subjective awareness of being a child of God that Wesley defined as follows: "By the testimony of the Spirit, I mean, an inward impression on the soul, whereby the Spirit of God immediately and directly witnesses to my spirit, that I am a child of God... that all my sins are blotted out, and I, even I, am reconciled to God."[19] Edwards was cautious if not dubious regarding any such doctrine of the Spirit's witness, commenting that "many have been the mischiefs that have arisen from that false and delusive notion of the witness of the Spirit, that it is a kind of inward voice, suggestion, or declaration from God to a man, that he is beloved of him, and pardoned, elected, or the like, sometimes with, and sometimes without a text of Scripture."[20] To be sure, Edwards no less than Wesley believed in "heart religion" and highlighted the inner, subjective aspects of spiritual life. Yet the accent fell in a different place. For Wesley, as in the previous quotation, the stress was on the self's right standing with God—that "I, even I am reconciled." For Edwards, true religion was God-centered and at times negated the concerns of the self, as in the "second sign" of gracious experience as described in *Religious Affections*: "The first objective ground of gracious affections, is the

---

17. Albert Outler, ed., *John Wesley* (New York: Oxford University Press, 1964), 473; cited in David Bebbington, "Remembered Around the World: The International Scope of Edwards's Legacy," in David W. Kling and Douglas A. Sweeney, eds., *Jonathan Edwards at Home and Abroad: Historical Memories, Cultural Movements, Global Horizons* (Columbia, SC: University of South Carolina Press, 2003), 179.

18. Bruce Hindmarsh, "The Reception of Jonathan Edwards by Early Evangelicals in England," in Kling and Sweeney, eds., *Jonathan Edwards at Home and Abroad*, 201–21, citing 204–206.

19. John Wesley, "The Witness of the Spirit," in *Works* 5:124–25.

20. WJE 2:239.

transcendently excellent and amiable nature of divine things, as they are in themselves; and not in any conceived relation they bear to self, or self-interest."[21] Such an overt denial of self-awareness or self-interest set Edwards's "religious affections" in opposition to Wesley's "witness of the Spirit." The 1800s Holiness revival and the 1900s Pentecostal-Charismatic movement generally followed Wesley's approach to the Spirit's witness. Speaking broadly, they encouraged believers to trust their impulses and instincts rather than to doubt them. Though Wesley qualified his teaching on the witness of Spirit by stating that good works were needed to confirm one's inner experience, Wesley's followers were not always as cautious as Wesley himself, and this meant in practice that the Wesleyan and Edwardsean revival traditions became increasingly distinct and dissimilar over time.[22]

On the much-debated issue of bodily manifestations in the 1700s revivals, Wesley's attitude was considerably more positive than Edwards's and might be compared with that of the radical New Lights in New England. An early Methodist leader, John Cennick, claimed that John Wesley viewed bodily manifestations as God's "tokens and signs," and that this led to disagreements among Wesley's followers:

> At first no one knew what to say, but it was soon called the pangs of the new birth, the work of the Holy Ghost, casting out the old man, etc., but some were offended and left the Societies entirely when they saw Mr. Wesley encourage it. I often doubted it was not of the enemy when I saw it, and disputed with Mr. Wesley for calling it the work of God.... And frequently when none were agitated in the meetings, he prayed, Lord! Where are thy tokens and signs, and I don't remember ever to have seen it otherwise than that on his so praying several were seized and screamed out.[23]

George Whitefield and Charles Wesley generally viewed the bodily manifestations as distractions and interferences to the main business of preaching the

---

21. WJE 2:240.

22. Daniel Walton, in "The Witness of the Spirit," *Methodist Quarterly Review* 8 (1848): 552, quotes Wesley as saying: "Let none ever presume to rest in any supposed testimony of the Spirit which is separate from the fruit of it." Walton called this a "twofold witness"—based on inner witness and outward works—and yet he acknowledged that some of Wesley's followers had "perverted" this teaching in a one-sided fashion.

23. John Cennick, cited in Arnold A. Dallimore, *George Whitefield*, 2 vols (Westchester, IL: Crossway Books, 1980), 1:309.

Word. In Edwards's case, we know that he preached at services that included exuberant bodily manifestations (ch. 27). Yet there is no indication that he ever encouraged such manifestations. Theologically speaking, he viewed them as equivocal in character, and so a direct encouragement of these manifestations—such as Cennick attributed to Wesley—might lead people mistakenly to identify these outward phenomena with the Spirit's inward work.[24]

Sifting Wheat from Chaff—Early 1800s Debates on Revivals

During the 1770s–1790s, Protestant churches in America suffered a period of stagnation. Church membership at the outbreak of the American Revolution hovered around 17% of the population—likely the lowest level of affiliation at any point from the colonial period to the present.[25] Edwards's call for united prayer in churches—the *Humble Attempt* (1747)—received renewed interest on both sides of the Atlantic as church leaders turned to fervent prayer for reinvigorating the flagging, flaccid state of spiritual life in the Protestant world.[26] When revival struck at the start of the new century, in frontier settings like Cane Ridge in Kentucky (1801) and elite institutions like Yale College (1802–1803), observers witnessed powerful indications of God's presence. Just as during the 1740s, the bodily manifestations and emotional upheavals of the revivals proved controversial.

The Presbyterian John Cree and four coauthors, who were witnesses of the Kentucky revival of 1801–1802, were disturbed by what they saw and published *Evils of the Work Now Prevailing* (1804). At issue was a theological question, namely, whether the Holy Spirit in a time of revival acted on "the soul in its higher faculties, understanding and the will," or else through "a renovation of the imagination, of the affections, and even of the body itself." Cree took the former view. He insisted that the Holy Spirit worked primarily through the mind and volition. "We disapprove of this work," he wrote, "as it tends to bring

---

24. It should be noted that Wesley drew boundaries with regard to acceptable bodily manifestations. Wesley's *Journal* recounted an episode of uncontrollable laughter involving John and Charles Wesley that prevented their praying together, and that John Wesley later attributed to satanic influence (see the Wesley excerpts with introduction in Michael J. McClymond, ed., *Encyclopedia of Religious Revivals in America*, 2:48–51).

25. Roger Finke and Rodney Stark, *The Churching of America, 1776–1990* (New Brunswick, NJ: Rutgers University Press, 2005), 22.

26. See "Concerts of Prayer over a Century, 1747–1846," in McClymond, ed., *Encyclopedia of Religious Revivals in America*, 2:54–58.

the subjects of it under such an influence of their imagination and feelings, as is inconsistent with a due regard to the word [of God], as the only ground of faith and rule of duty." Cree disapproved of "imaginary ideas" and dissented explicitly from Edwards, commenting that "it is far from being true, what Mr. Edwards says, the more intense our contemplation of divine things are, the stronger will our imaginary idea of them be" and that "the spiritual contemplation of divine things, is inconsistent with imaginary ideas about them." Cree, like Edwards's opponents in the 1740s, operated with a differing theological anthropology than Edwards did, in which reason took priority over emotions, affections, or the imagination.

Grant Powers's *Essay Upon the Influence of the Imagination on the Nervous System, Contributing to a False Hope in Religion* (1828) was an early effort in the as-yet-undeveloped field of the psychology of religion. Powers held that the 1800s revivals were illegitimate because they involved bodily effects that were not explicitly mentioned in scripture. He offered a naturalistic hypothesis that pleasurable feelings associated with revivals were due to a reactivation of the "arterial system" or "animal functions" after a period of excitement. There was nothing spiritual about this, and "excitements" carried the danger of "creating false hopes in religion." Powers took exception to Edwards's sanctioning of new spiritual experiences: "President Edwards contended...that we could not judge of the character of present religious appearances by comparing them with the exhibitions of true religion in former ages." God might do something new. Yet this was a "position of dangerous tendency," said Powers, who insisted on the "uniformity of God's dispensations" so that "we should adhere to the old system."[27]

A new phase in the reception of Edwards's revival theology took place through the life, writing, and preaching of Charles G. Finney. In his *Lectures on Revivals of Religion* (1835), Finney associated himself with Edwards, and declared that Edwards was "famous in his day for new measures." God's blessing lay with "those that are thus accused of...innovation." Bodily manifestation was "not a new thing in the church, but has always prevailed wherever revivals prevailed with power." Finney discussed the "agony in prayer" evident in his day, comparing it with the analogous phenomena of Edwards's day. Regarding Calvinism, he noted that "election and sovereignty" had become "the universal hiding place...of sinners," so that he felt justified in stressing human responsibility rather than divine agency. Finney did so largely on the

---

27. John Cree, et al., Evils of the Work Now Prevailing in the United States of America, under tne Name of a Revival of Religion (Washington, PA: For the Authors, 1804), 13–17, 21–23; cited in McClymond, ed., *Encyclopedia of Religious Revivals in America*, 2:104–6. Grant Powers, *Essay Upon the Influence of the Imagination on the Nervous System, Contributing to a False Hope in Religion* (Andover, MA: Flagg and Gould, 1828), 42–3, 55–6, 58–9, 64–5, 74–5, 80, 105–9; cited in McClymond, ed., *Encyclopedia of Religious Revivals in Religion*, 2:112–5.

basis of his own interpretations and adaptations of Edwardsean "New Divinity" teachings (ch. 37). Finney's opponents challenged his claim to continuing Edwards's tradition on revival. Yet Finney's *Lectures on Systematic Theology* (1846) and *Memoirs* (1876) made his departure from Edwards overt. Against Edwards, Finney held that conversion occurred through a *"voluntary attitude and preference of the soul"* involving no "change of the *nature*." Ascribing rebirth to the Holy Spirit was a "half truth," since scripture attributed it to human beings as well as to God. Moreover, Edwards had created a "strange distinction" between "moral and natural ability."[28] Mark Noll commented that Finney "valued Edwards for his place in the history of revival" yet "felt it necessary to set aside the specific convictions of his theology."[29]

A quite different interpretation of Edwards's revival theology is embodied in Charles Hodge's writings, especially his *Constitutional History of the Presbyterian Church* (1840). In Hodge's reading of Edwards, it was not "the degree of zeal or joy" that mattered but only "the nature of the religious affections." While Edwards had never directly identified bodily manifestations with the Spirit's work, Hodge judged that Edwards became fully "sensible of the danger of encouraging...manifestations of excitement" only after the time of the early revivals. For Hodge, the spread of "bodily affection" from one person to another was "as plain an example of the sympathetic propagation of a nervous disorder, as to be found in the medical records of disease." Hodge viewed the revivals as pathological, much as the Old Lights of the 1700s had. Bodily affections, plainly put, were neither an "evidence" nor a "result" of "genuine religious feeling." Though Edwards's regarded bodily affections as an equivocal phenomenon, he had held in *Religious Affections* that the "laws of union of soul and body" dictated that a powerful movement of the soul's affections, or of the Holy Spirit on the soul, might well affect the body, as well. Hodge severed this link and rejected all bodily and imaginative elements in religious life. He wrote that "images borrowed from sensible objects" will "disturb the truly spiritual contemplations of the Christian." To worship God "under some corporeal form" was "nothing but refined idolatry." In the end, Hodge rejected even Edwards's revivals. The spiritual declension in Northampton during the 1740s, and the peoples' rejection of Edwards in 1750, showed that the revivals had not benefitted them: "There must have been something wrong in these

---

28. Charles G. Finney, *Lectures on Revivals of Religion* (New York: Leavitt, Lord, 1835), 241, 250, 271, 52–53, 188–89; Charles G. Finney, *The Original Memoirs of Charles G. Finney*, ed. Garth M. Rosell and Richard A. G. Dupuis (Grand Rapids, MI: Zondervan, 2002), 266–67, 388.

29. Mark Noll, "Jonathan Edwards and Nineteenth-Century Theology," in Nathan O. Hatch and Harry S. Stout, eds., *Jonathan Edwards and the American Experience* (New York: Oxford University Press, 1988), 260–87, citing 262.

revivals, even under the eye and guidance of Edwards, from the beginning. There must have been many spurious conversions, and much false religion which at the time were regarded as genuine."[30]

Winds of Change—Transitions of the Late 1800s and Early 1900s

From the time of the Civil War and into the early 1900s, America underwent a cultural shift that led to a different perception of Edwards. David Bebbington comments that "a new intellectual mood arose during the nineteenth century that was much less favorable to the theologian."[31] The dominant categories of thought were now rooted in Romanticism rather than Puritanism and Common Sense Philosophy. Literary classics like William Wordsworth's *The Prelude* (1805) and Walt Whitman's *Leaves of Grass* (1855) focused on the theme of self-discovery. Poets and thinkers stressed growth rather than crisis, God's immanence rather than transcendence. A "natural supernaturalism" viewed divine reality as embedded within everyday realities.[32]

In *Discourses on Christian Nurture* (1847), Horace Bushnell rejected revivalism for mistakenly imposing on children the paradigm of the adult conversion experience. There was no reason, he argued, to imagine that children needed to pass through a painful awareness of personal sinfulness, followed by a conscious act of faith and repentance. The "true idea of Christian education," said Bushnell, is that "the child is to grow up a Christian and never know himself to be otherwise." The parents' faith may be unconsciously transmitted, without need for a dramatic, crisis-filled transition. One of Bushnell's essays was entitled: "Growth Not Conquest the True Method of Christian Progress." Bushnell rebutted Edwards's treatment of childhood conversion, notably the recounting in *Faithful Narrative* (1737) of the four-year-old Phebe Bartlett's experiences of repentance and faith. Bennett Tyler, among many others, debated Bushnell in print and argued for revivals as a means of salvation for youth and adults alike.[33]

---

30. Charles Hodge, *The Constitutional History of the Presbyterian Church in the United States of America; Part II; 1741–1788* (Philadelphia, PA: William Martien, 1840), 50–51, 83, 76.

31. Bebbington, "Remembered Around the World," 187.

32. See the classic study of Romantic thought by M.H. Abrams, *Natural Supernaturalism: Tradition and Revolution in Romantic Literature* (New York: Norton, 1971).

33. Michael A. Farley, "Christian Nurture Debate," and Robert Bruce Mullen, "Bushnell, Horace," in McClymond, ed., *Encyclopedia of Religious Revivals in America*, 1:106–110 and 1:65–67.

Liberalizing Protestants launched the Religious Education movement, which replaced the sin-and-repentance revivals with a softer, gentler approach. Well into the 1900s, church-related colleges and schools across America had their "Religious Emphasis Week"—a Bushnellian substitute for old-fashioned revival meetings. Yet not everyone followed Bushnell. Henry Fish's *Handbook of Revivals* (1874) reflected the late-nineteenth-century interest in children's religion and yet equally maintained a revivalist call for conversion. Fish's chapter on "Child-Piety and Profession" relied on Edwards's *Faithful Narrative*, and concluded that "little children *can* be converted, and that many circumstances strongly favor it."[34]

By the late 1800s and early 1900s, leading churchmen and academics viewed conversion and revivals through a moralistic and naturalistic lens. Conversion was tantamount to moral resolution—a decision to lead a new sort of life. Revival was a psychological phenomenon—a transmission of social influence from person to person. Henry Ward Beecher's sermon "The New Birth" announced: "'Thou shalt love God and thou shalt love man'—if a man has come to that resolution, he is born again." He assured his hearers: "I believe in revivals of religion. I believe in that grand social principle which makes a thousand men stronger than any individual." "The benefit" of revivals "comes through the development of your own higher self by the help of God."[35] Psychologists of religion in the late 1800s and early 1900s introduced new interpretations of conversion and revival. James Leuba commented on Edwards: "The Calvinistic doctrines when preached without palliation were amply sufficient to produce tragic fears and induce grave bodily disorders." Yet "morbid fears" brought "hysterical manifestations which have so often disgraced Revivals."[36] Leuba thus echoed the standard Old Light objection to the use of fear in revival preaching. William James showed a greater appreciation for revivalist religion. He included an extract from Sarah Edwards's 1742 narrative of her revival experience in his chapter on "Saintliness" in *The Varieties of Religious Experience* (1902) and treated her experience as significant and life altering. Nonetheless, his conceptual model for conversion was naturalistic and his theory of "subconscious incubation" suggested that psychic forces below the threshold of awareness could suddenly burst into a

---

34. Henry Fish, "Child-Piety and Profession," in *Handbook of Revivals, For the Use of Winners of Souls* (Boston: James H. Earle, 1874), 168–96, citing 172.

35. Henry Ward Beecher, *Plymouth Pulpit: Sermons* (Boston: Pilgrim Press, 1875), "The New Birth," 567–86, citing 577, 583–84.

36. James H. Leuba, "A Study in the Psychology of Religious Phenomena," *American Journal of Psychology* 7 (1896): 309–85, citing 324.

person's consciousness, creating the mistaken impression that external forces (such as the Holy Spirit) were at work. Sudden conversion could be explained without recourse to any supernatural agencies.[37]

Frederick Davenport's *Primitive Traits in Religious Revivals* (1905) claimed to be the first truly "scientific" study of religious revivals. Presupposing "the doctrine of mental and social evolution," Davenport attributed religious revivals to the "primitive mind." He suggested that revivals mostly affected "the nervously unstable, the suggestible, [and] the inexperienced," rather than the "dignified and intelligent people of judgment and understanding." The revivals occurring under the preaching of Jonathan Edwards were "explained by the environment of fear—fear of starvation, of wild beasts and savages." The persons most commonly affected by revivals, according to Davenport, were children, women, and African Americans—who all fell short of the supposed cultural and intellectual superiority of the adult white male. For Davenport, revival was a product of the "highly reflex phenomena of hypnotic association."[38]

At the same time that the early psychologists were offering naturalistic explanations for religious revivals, a powerful new series of spiritual awakenings was breaking forth. Beginning in 1901 and culminating in the epochal Azusa Street revival in Los Angeles during 1906–1908, the emergent Pentecostal movement displayed every revival manifestation that had been observed during the 1700s and 1800s—powerful emotions, bodily effects, and heavenly visions—and some new manifestations not commonly seen before—such as speaking in tongues and the healing of the sick. Yet notably absent from the literature of early Pentecostalism is any reference to Edwards. Neither of the two major sources on the Azusa Street revival—*Apostolic Faith* newspaper (1906–1908), and Frank Bartleman's memoir, *How Pentecost Came to Los Angeles* (1925)—mention Edwards. On the other hand, John Wesley is named both frequently and favorably, thus exposing the predominantly Wesleyan theological orientation of Pentecostals at Azusa Street.[39]

Bartleman cited Wesley and other authors to show that all revivals included both good and bad, and that it was essential not to throw out the baby with the bathwater. He quotes Wesley as saying, "Oh, Lord, send us the old revival,

---

37. William James, *The Varieties of Religious Experience: A Study of Human Nature* (London: Longmans, Green and Co., 1903), 276–78, 179–80 n.1, 211, 203–207.

38. Frederick Davenport, *Primitive Traits in Religious Revivals: A Study in Mental and Social Evolution* (New York: Macmillan, 1917), 3, 8–10, 45, 282, 288, 293–94. See the comments on Davenport's work in Michael McClymond, ed., *Encyclopedia of Religious Revivals in America*, 2:237–41.

39. Donald Dayton's *Theological Roots of Pentecostalism* (Metuchen, NJ; Scarecrow Press, 1987) offers a Wesleyan interpretation of early Pentecostalism.

without the defects; but if this cannot be, send it—with all the defects. We must have the revival." Bartleman went on to praise both Luther and Wesley for their "holy recklessness" in opposing the social conventions of their day in order to reform the church.[40]

Azusa leader William J. Seymour viewed John Wesley as one of a handful of God-appointed leaders from the 1500s through the 1800s who brought a progressive restoration of the doctrine, power, purity, and spiritual gifts of the New Testament era. The *Apostolic Faith* newspaper declared:

> All along the ages men have been preaching a partial Gospel. A part of the Gospel remained when the world went into the dark ages. God has from time to time raised up men to bring back the truth to the church. He raised up Luther to bring back to the world the doctrine of justification by faith. He raised up another reformer in John Wesley to establish Bible holiness in the church. Then he raised up Dr. Cullis who brought back to the world the wonderful doctrine of divine healing. Now He is bringing back the Pentecostal Baptism to the church.[41]

Not only early Pentecostals, but other radical evangelicals of the late 1800s—including William Arthur, A.J. Gordon, A.B. Simpson, Carrie Judd Montgomery and others involved in the divine healing movement—were anticipating a new outpouring of the Holy Spirit and a return of ancient spiritual gifts.[42] Such a restorationist vision of the church's present and future was alien to the thinking of most twentieth-century Calvinists. Yet, as we will see in the following section, Edwards's notion of the church's impending "glorious times" bore at least some analogy to Pentecostal conceptions of a return of New Testament spiritual gifts in the church's latter days.

Edwards Resurgent—Debates Concerning the 1990s Revivals

Edwards did not become a key figure again in discussions of religious revivals until the 1960s–70s Charismatic Renewal and Jesus Movement, the

---

40. Frank Bartleman, *How Pentecostal Came to Los Angeles* (1925), reprinted in *Witness to Pentecost: The Life of Frank Bartleman* (New York: Garland Pubishing, 1985), 46–47, cf. 146–47.

41. Anonymous, *Apostolic Faith* [Los Angeles, CA], Vol. 1, No. 2, October 1906, pg. 1, col. 1.

42. William Arthur, *The Tongue of Fire, or The True Power of Christianity* (New York: Harper, 1856) and *May We Hope for a Great Revival?* (Toronto: Wesleyan Book Room, 1868).

1980s Vineyard Church revivals, and the 1990s "Toronto Blessing." The last named movement affected some 15, 000 church congregations around the world and touched off extensive controversies in print and on the Internet in which revival proponents and detractors both appealed to the writings of Jonathan Edwards in support of their views.[43] All of these revivals since the 1960s involved deep emotions, bodily manifestations, and, in many cases, charismatic gifts, and so raised some of the same interpretive issues as the 1700s and 1800s revivals. Many of those affected were Protestant evangelicals. This included such figures as John Wimber, C. Peter Wagner, and Randy Clark. As "pentecostalized" evangelicals, they were already aware of Edwards and his pivotal role in the 1700s revivals and so naturally they turned back to Edwards's writings to help them make sense of what they had experienced and witnessed.

On January 20, 1994, the Toronto Airport Vineyard Fellowship began what was to be a four-night series of meetings led by the visiting preacher Randy Clark of St. Louis, Missouri. At this service—and at what soon became everyday services—hundreds and then thousands of people displayed one or more of a number of unusual manifestations—falling to the ground, shaking in various parts of their body, crying, laughter, visionary experiences, feelings of numbness, intense activities like running or jumping, feelings of spiritual inebriation or drunkenness, and in a few cases, animals sounds such as

---

43. Works in opposition to the Toronto movement that also engage Edwards's writings include: Hank Hanegraaff, *Counterfeit Revival* (Dallas, TX: Word Publishing, 1997); Michael A.G. Haykin and Gary W. McHale, "Would Jonathan Edwards Support the Toronto Blessing?" and "Great Effusions of the Holy Spirit—The Advocacy of True Revival," http://www.graceonlinelibrary.org/articles; Andrew Strom, "The 'Toronto' Controversy—Disturbing New Facts from History," http://homepages.ihug.co.nz/~revival/toronto.html; Nick Needham, "Was Jonathan Edwards the Founding Father of the Toronto Blessing?" (1995), http://web.archive.org/web/20050304014025, and "The Toronto Blessing—Part Two" (1998), http://web.archive.org/web/20040521020335/www.geocities.com/Bob_Hunter/needham2.htm. Internet sources accessed March 16, 2010. Works supportive of the movement include: Guy Chevreau, *Catch the Fire: The Toronto Blessing; An Experience of Renewal and Revival* (Toronto: HarperCollins, 1994); and John Arnott, *The Fathers's Blessing* (Orlando, FL: Creation House, 1995). Published earlier, but often cited in the debates, is William DeArteaga, *Quenching the Spirit: Examining Centuries of Opposition to the Moving of the Holy Spirit* (Lake Mary, FL: Creation House, 1992). A middle-of-the-road stance is reflected in James A. Beverley's *Holy Laughter and the Toronto Blessing: An Investigative Report* (Grand Rapids, MI: Zondervan, 1995), Beverley's *Revival Wars: A Critique of "Counterfeit Revival"* (n.p.: Evangelical Research Ministries, 1997), and "The 'Toronto Blessing,'" a Faith and Order Committee Report to the British Methodist Conference, http://godnet.org/bumc.htm; all works accessed March 16, 2010. The best general work is a sociological study by a participant-observer: Margaret M. Poloma, *Main Street Mystics: The Toronto Blessing and Reviving Pentecostalism* (Walnut Creek, CA: AltaMira Press, 2003).

roaring or barking. Dubbed the "Toronto Blessing" by the secular press, the title is unfortunate in identifying the revival with just one location. The movement spread rapidly and affected as many as 4, 000 congregations in Britain and another 7, 000 in Hong Kong, Norway, South Africa, and Australia.[44] Participants preferred to call it "the Father's Blessing," since they claimed that people were entering a new experience of God's fatherly love. What makes the movement pertinent here is the extensive citation of, and discussion of, Edwards's revival writings by both the friends and opponents of the movement. Guy Chevreau's *Catch the Fire* (1994) devoted seventy-five pages to a discussion of Edwards, while revival critics like Hank Hanegraaff, Nick Needham, Michael Haykin, and Gary McHale cited Edwards to buttress an opposing position.

Critics charged the Toronto Blessing with anti-intellectualism, fanaticism, narcissism, self-centeredness, distorted readings of scripture, and distorted interpretations of Jonathan Edwards. Some argued that the Toronto movement was occultic and that the practice of laying on of hands for the impartation of spiritual blessings was akin to the practices of Franz Mesmer and Hindu gurus such as Bhagwan Shree Rajneesh and Sri Ramakrisna. Opponents took exception to Toronto pastor John Arnott's statement that "God will offend your mind to reveal your heart."[45] Hanegraaf attacked what he dubbed the "eudaimonism" of Toronto—the idea that true religion brings happiness.[46] Calvinist critics found it inconceivable that God would send the Holy Spirit to bless and sanction a movement that did not more prominently feature the teaching and preaching of the Bible. Some critics in effect took Charles Hodge's position that distanced religion from the physical body. Genuine piety, they argued, involved spiritual or intellectual contemplation rather than bodily experience. Though Toronto leaders may have claimed that they did not directly identify outward bodily manifestations with the Spirit's work, critics claimed that their worship services told otherwise. Testimony time involved blow-by-blow descriptions of unusual experiences. Detractors also pointed to Edwards's comments on the cessation of first-century charismatic gifts in *Charity and Its Fruits*

---

44. Hanegraaf, *Counterfeit Revival*, 10; Martin Emerson, "Comments on the 'Toronto Blessing,'" at http://mag.christis/org/uk/isssues/36/toronto_blessing.html, accessed 3/16.2010.

45. Arnott, *The Father's Blessing*, 223; the saying was taken from the title of a sermon by John Wimber.

46. Hanegraaf, *Counterfeit Revival*, 99–101. This particular accusation is not consistent with Edwards's theology, as Edwards himself was a Christian eudaemonist who taught that true religion brings the highest happiness. See John Piper, *Desiring God: Meditations of a Christian Hedonist* (Downer's Grove, IL: InterVarsity Press, 2004).

(1738) and *Distinguishing Marks* (1741).[47] Absent from the literature opposing the Toronto Blessing was an engagement with the revival's focus on divine love.[48]

Defenders of the Toronto Blessing pointed to parallels between the powerful bodily manifestations of the 1740s revivals and those occurring in the Toronto Blessing. Sarah Edwards aroused intense interest, since she repeatedly spoke of "fainting" and losing "bodily strength." While reading the Bible, as she said, "my soul was so filled with love to Christ and love to His people, that I fainted under the intenseness of the feeling." One neighbor feared that Sarah's spiritual pangs might bring about her death. Sarah's experience of "love to all mankind, wholly peculiar in its strength and sweetness" was akin to what some participants in the Toronto Blessing were reporting. Guy Chevreau quoted Edwards: "What we have been used to, or what the church of God has been used to, is not a rule by which we are to judge whether a work be the work of God, because there may be new and extraordinary works of God...to surprise both men and angels." Toronto's defenders claimed that their critics were excessively intellectualistic, while their position and practice held intellect and emotion in balance. Chevreau, to his credit, recognized that there were two sides to Edwards—the open and the cautious—and he compared the theologian to a man riding a bicycle and trying not to fall to the left or the right. He also pointed out that revival critics had not stayed "long enough to interview" participants and see what changes they were reporting.[49]

James Beverly's *Revival Wars* (1997) featured commentary from Edwards scholars Kenneth Minkema, Douglas Sweeney, and Allen Guelzo, who agreed that neither the detractors nor the promoters of the Toronto Blessing had grasped the whole of Edwards's teaching on revival. His theology allowed for

---

47. WJE 8:149–73, and WJE 4:278–82. Arguing for the early cessation of miracles and charismatic gifts from the church were B. B. Warfield, *Counterfeit Miracles* (New York: Scribners, 1918), and John MacArthur, *Charismatic Chaos* (Grand Rapids, MI: Zondervan, 1992). A critique of cessationism is found in Jon Ruthven, *On the Cessation of the Charismata: The Protestant Polemic on Postbiblical Miracles* (Sheffield, UK: Sheffield Academic Press, 1993).

48. The best data available, from Margaret Poloma, shows that 91% of Toronto participants reported that they gained a greater sense of the Father's love for them, and many also reported that they had become more engaged in serving the poor and sharing their faith with others. Participants reported not only an experience of love but "a new sense of [their own] sinfulness" ("The Spirit and the Bride: The 'Toronto Blessing' and Church Structure," *Evangelical Studies Bulletin* 14 (1999) 1–5.

49. Chevreau, *Catch the Fire*, 77 n.2, 81–82, citing Sarah Edwards' narrative in Sereno Dwight, "Memoirs," 1:lxvi–lxvii; Chevreau, *Catch the Fire*, 99–101 (citing WJE 4:228), 115, 108.

bodily manifestations, though it did not embrace charismatic gifts. Yet, even on this matter, Edwards could be read in two ways. On the one hand, there were clear statements about the passing away of the charismatic gifts in the second lecture of *Charity and Its Fruits*. Yet, on the other hand, in stating that "I don't expect a restoration of these miraculous gifts in the approaching glorious times of the church, nor do I desire it," Edwards judged it unlikely that the gifts would return to the church but not that it was strictly impossible.[50] The door was nearly shut—yet still ajar. As Ian Rennie observed: "Though Edwards did not believe in tongues and prophecy, his postmillennial expectations for a new age of the Spirit gave him a much more optimistic attitude to the Christian future than that of the Reformers. This eschatological attitude could warrant some openness in Edwards to special ministries of the Spirit."[51] On the hypothetical question as to whether Edwards would have "blessed" the Toronto Blessing, no definitive answer can be given. He might have focused much less attention on the outward bodily manifestations than many of the revival's detractors and defenders did. Instead he would likely have investigated more fully the participants' experiences of divine love to see if these bore lasting fruit in "holy practice." Since Edwards regarded love as the sum of all virtue, it is likely that a Christian revival centering on experiences of love would have been of intense interest to him. Whatever Edwards's final judgment might have been, the fact that his writings were so extensively cited, analyzed, and argued during the last twenty years is an indication that his theology of revival continues to be of importance today.

---

50. WJE 4:281.

51. Ian Rennie, cited in Beverley, *Revival Wars*, 30.

43

Interpretations IV: Edwards and the Catholic and Orthodox Traditions

AT FIRST GLANCE, Edwards appears to have little in common with Roman Catholicism or Eastern Orthodoxy. He was a Puritan and Calvinist. He wrote treatises on original sin and on the un-freedom of the fallen human will. His ecclesial views were Congregationalist. He upheld a polemical Protestant tradition that identified the papacy with Antichrist and taught that the Church of Rome had rejected Christ's gospel when it persecuted medieval sects such as the Waldensians and the Hussites, and later opposed to the Protestant reformers.

Yet for more than a century, Edwards's Protestant readers have suspected that he was not thoroughly Protestant—at least not in the sixteenth-century or Reformational sense. In 1903, Henry Churchill King spoke of Edwards as "anti-Protestant" because of distinctions he drew between common and special grace.[1] Thomas Schafer's 1951 essay claimed that "justification by faith" occupied "an ambiguous and somewhat precarious place" in Edwards's thinking. Schafer argued that Edwards—like Augustine—placed love rather than faith at the center. For Edwards, love was a soteriological category that bridged faith and works, original sin was an inclination away from the love of God, and virtue was a new principle of love identical with God's grace.[2] These points all made Edwards's soteriology seem more "catholic" than that of most other Protestant thinkers.

Just as significantly, Edwards stated that faith is not the only "condition" of justification—at least as he defined the term "condition." Faith possessed what Edwards called a "natural fitness" to serve as a condition of salvation. Faith was, in effect, a first act of obedience toward God that virtually contained within it all subsequent acts of obedience flowing from faith. Though

---

1. Henry Churchill King, "Jonathan Edwards as Philosopher and Theologian," *Hartford Seminary Record* 14 (November 1903): 23–57.

2. Thomas A. Schafer, "Jonathan Edwards and Justification by Faith," *Church History* 20 (1951): 55–67.

Edwards did not use the term "merit," his use of the notion of "fitness" showed resemblances to Thomistic notions of "congruent merit." From the standpoint of Reformation theology, Edwards seems to have rejected or significantly qualified *sola fide* (salvation by "faith alone"), though not the principle of *sola gratia* ("salvation by grace alone").

The Japanese scholar Anri Morimoto argued that Edwards's theology combined a "Protestant concern" that grace is truly gratuitous—that is, derived immediately from God and never possessed or controlled by human beings—with a "Catholic concern" that grace effects genuine change, transforms human character into the divine likeness, and is a stable and abiding reality within the created world.[3] Philosopher Stephen H. Daniel concurred with Morimoto's account, insisting that Edwards's theology included a "Peter Lombard, uncreated-grace aspect" that was "focused on justification as forensic imputation prior to regeneration" and a "Thomas Aquinas, created grace-aspect" that "highlights how justification can be a gradual ontological process that includes good works and sanctification."[4]

Augustine is a Catholic author with whom Edwards had multiple affinities. Thomas Schafer commented on "how often Edwards came down on the side of Augustine" on a whole variety of theological issues.[5] Edwards's biographer, George Marsden, referred to Edwards as "the American Augustine" and invoked a number of parallels between Edwards and the early Christian thinker.[6] Edwards's major writings may be compared with those of Augustine. *Freedom of the Will* and *Original Sin* correspond to Augustine's anti-Pelagian writings. *Personal Narrative* is something like the *Confessions*. The *History of Redemption* might be compared with *City of God*. Edwards's *Discourse on the*

---

3. Anri Morimoto, *Jonathan Edwards and the Catholic Vision of Salvation* (University Park, PA: Pennsylvania State University Press, 1995), 7. Joseph Conforti, in his critical review of Morimoto (in *Church History* 65 [1996]: 721–23), does not object to the assertion of a "Protestant concern" and yet calls the "Catholic concern" a "creative extension...that produces a de-Puritanized and de-New Englandized Edwards who is ripe for contemporary ecumenical appropriation" (723). Yet Conforti may not have fully acknowledged some of the novel features in Edwards's understanding of salvation when viewed against his eighteenth-century New England Congregational context.

4. Stephen H. Daniel, Review of Anri Morimoto, *Jonathan Edwards and the Catholic Vision of Salvation*, in *The William and Mary Quarterly*, 3rd series, 53 (1996): 817–19.

5. This quotation is based on personal conversation with Thomas Schafer.

6. George Marsden, "Jonathan Edwards, American Augustine," *Books and Culture*, November/December 1999, 10–12.

Trinity mirrored Augustine's *On the Trinity* both in theme and argument. Edwards's sixteen-lecture volume on divine and human love, *Charity and Its Fruits*, expounded a major theme of Augustine's writings. Both the content of their theologies and the genre of their works show analogies. As we will see, Edwards's theology may also concur at points with that of Thomas Aquinas, though the resemblances to Thomas are not as obvious at first glance.

Edwards's Treatment of Discernment in Catholic Perspective

A number of Catholic theologians have become deeply engaged with Jonathan Edwards's theology. Most notable are William Spohn and Donald Gelpi, S.J.— both affiliated with the Jesuit School of Theology at Berkeley, California.[7] Spohn stressed Edwards' teaching on spiritual discernment, while Gelpi highlighted Edwards's aesthetic aspects.

Discernment was, by all accounts, a crucial theme in Edwards's writings. Especially in those texts connected with the 1740s revivals, Edwards continually sought to distinguish true from false or spurious spirituality. He was preoccupied with the problems of religious complacency, self-satisfaction, and self-deception. Edwards discovered what other directors of souls have found, that religious affections all too readily slip into religious *affectations*.[8] Much like Ignatius Loyola (1491–1556), Edwards believed that a disciplined practice of self-examination allowed persons to differentiate spiritual experiences that were helpful and God-glorifying from those that were not. Spohn isolated three ideas that Loyola and Edwards held in common in their respective theologies of discernment. First, there was the assumption that "Christian conversion produces transformed religious experience that is impossible for the unconverted." Second, "affections, the deep emotional dispositions of the heart, are the center of religious

---

7. See the following four essays by William C. Spohn: "Sovereign Beauty: Jonathan Edwards and the Nature of True Virtue," *Theological Studies* 42 (1981): 394–421; "Union and Consent with the Great Whole: Jonathan Edwards on True Virtue," in *Annual of the Society for Christian Ethics* (Dallas, TX: Society for Christian Ethics/Waterloo, ONT: Distributed by the Council on the Study of Religion, 1985), 19–32; "Finding God in All Things: Jonathan Edwards and Ignatius Loyola," in Michael J. Himes and Stephen J. Pope, eds., *Finding God in All Things: Essays in Honor of Michael J. Buckley, S. J.* (New York: Crossroad, 1996), 244–61; and "Spirituality and Its Discontents: Practices in Jonathan Edwards's *Charity and Its Fruits*," *Journal of Religious Ethics* 31 (2003): 253–76.

8. Ava Chamberlain, "Self-Deception as a Theological Problem in Jonathan Edwards's 'Treatise Concerning Religious Affections,'" *Church History* 63 (1994): 541–56.

transformation and the principal sources of evidence for judgments of religious discernment." Third, "religious affections are the media of God's inspiration." That is, God is continually speaks to us and seeks to guide us in and through the dispositions of our hearts.[9] Both Loyola's *Spiritual Exercises* and Edwards's *Religious Affections* represent a "school of the affections" that "orders the dispositions of the one making them to follow the way of Christ."[10] Loyola's *Spiritual Exercises* was a manual for the conversion of the affections in an Edwardsean sense. Equally, Edwards's *Religious Affections* was a manual of guidance for discerning the significance of the religious affections in an Ignatian sense.

Loyola and Edwards both showed a great interest in distinguishing self-seeking affections from those that are directed toward God's glory, in accordance with the early Jesuit motto—*Ad maiorem Dei gloriam* ("to the greater glory of God"). Edwards's frequent references to the "relish," "taste," or "sweetness" of spiritual experience are reminiscent of Ignatius's use of *sentir*—a direct savoring of spiritual realities.[11] The affections that Edwards described were not passing whims or velleities. Instead they reflected the self's character at its deepest level, and they disposed a person to regular patterns of thinking, feeling, and acting. They offered a surer guide to self-knowledge than mere rational reflection. Along the same lines, Ignatius counseled retreat directors not to weigh down the retreatant with too much material for reflection, for he commented that "what fills and satisfies the soul consists, not in knowing much, but in our understanding the realities profoundly and savoring them interiorly." This comment was entirely in line with Edwards's theology of the affections.[12] Spohn commented that both Ignatius and Edwards contrasted true spirituality with "the excesses of pseudo-converts," that is, "self-obsession, fascination with visions and private revelations, spiritual arrogance, unbalanced zeal, erratic behavior, and moral complacency." Faithful and persevering Christian practice was the surest sign of genuine conversion and the least likely to be manifested in cases of counterfeit conversion. Finally, for both Ignatius and Edwards, "ordinary experience was extraordinarily transparent to God," and human affectivity was the medium of divine action and guidance.

---

9. Spohn, "Finding God," 244–45.

10. Spohn, "Finding God," 247.

11. Spohn, "Finding God," 248.

12. Spohn, "Finding God," 251; citing George E. Ganss, S.J., ed., *Ignatius of Loyola: The Spiritual Exercises and Selected Works* (New York: Paulist Press, 1991), 2.

Ignatius believed that the "great desires" of the self would expand the heart and make it open to God's action in profound ways. Edwards concurred.[13] Spohn concluded by saying that "the Puritan divine and the Basque mystic agree on a spirituality which is both radically affective and wisely discriminating."[14]

Edwards's Metaphysics and Typology in Catholic Perspective

As earlier chapters have shown (chs. 7, 14), Edwards gave a central place to metaphysical reflection in his writings and to the conception of God as "Being" or "Being in general." Andrew Greeley's *The Catholic Imagination* (2000)—inspired by David Tracy's *The Analogical Imagination* (1982)—suggested that Catholic thinkers reflect an "analogical" vision of the world while Protestants tend to be "dialectical":

> Tracy noted that the classic works of Catholic theologians and artists tend to emphasize the presence of God in the world, while the classic works of Protestant theologians tend to emphasize the absence of God from the world. The Catholic writers stress the nearness of God to His creation, the Protestant writers the distance between God and His creation; the Protestants emphasize the risk of superstition and idolatry, the Catholics the danger of a creation in which God is only marginally present. Or, to put the matter in difference terms, Catholics tend to accentuate the immanence of God, Protestants the transcendence of God. Tracy is consistently careful to insist that neither propensity is superior to the other, that both need each other.... Nonetheless, they *are* different from one another.[15]

Karl Barth in his *Epistle to the Romans* (1919) spoke of God as "wholly Other" and thus inexplicable in terms of ordinary metaphysical categories. In his *Church Dogmatics*, Barth castigated the characteristic Roman Catholic teaching on *analogia entis*—the idea that all existing things bear some analogy to

---

13. See E. Edward Kinerk, S. J. "Eliciting Great Desires: Their Place in the Spirituality of the Society of Jesus," *Studies in Jesuit Spirituality* 16 (1984) 1–29.

14. Spohn, "Finding God," 253–58.

15. Andrew Greeley, *The Catholic Imagination* (Berkeley, CA: University of California Press, 2000), 5.

God's own being—as "the invention of Antichrist."[16] By contrast, Edwards's embrace of metaphysics and metaphysical argumentation placed him nearer to such patristic and medieval thinkers as Augustine, Anselm, Aquinas, and Bonaventure than to such anti-metaphysical Protestants as Luther, Calvin, or Barth. The entire shape of Edwards's reasoning indicated his acceptance of an *analogia entis*—a cosmos in which God and creatures were both alike and unlike one another in important ways. This is not to say that he was solely an analogical thinker. There was also a dialectical element in Edwards's teaching on God (ch. 7, 14) and on grace (chs. 23–25). Edwards appears to have been more successful than perhaps any other major Christian thinker of the post-Reformation era in synthesizing and harmonizing the analogical and dialectical elements of theology. When one examines the whole scope of Edwards's theology, it is clear that he ignored neither the contrast nor the continuity between God and creation. Edwards's metaphysical reasoning exemplifies what David Tracy called "the disclosure of radical dissimilarity in similarity" or the phenomenon of "analogies-in-difference."[17]

The term Edwards most commonly used was not "analogy" but "proportion," which from ancient times functioned as the Latin translation (*proportio*) of the technical Greek philosophical term (*analogia*). From the time of his earliest philosophical reflections in "The Mind," Edwards's thought was permeated by a sense of the "proportion" or "analogy" between God and creatures and between one creature and another. "Proportion" is fundamental also in Edwards's theological aesthetics, and in this aspect of his thinking one might link him to Hans Urs von Balthasar's remarkable investigations of God and beauty.[18] The whole of Edwards's metaphysical and typological reflections rests on a continuity between Creator and creation. Inasmuch as every existing thing reflects its Creator, the universe is filled with signs and vestiges of God's presence. Not only in his metaphysics but also in his natural and biblical typology

---

16. Karl Barth, *Church Dogmatics*, Vol. 1, Part 1, trans. G.T. Thomson (Edinburgh: T. & T. Clark, 1936), x. Analogy is a key principle in twentieth-century Catholic thought, especially as shown in Erich Przywara's influential account of *analogia entis*—to whom Barth seems to have been responding in the quotation above. See Przywara, *Analogia Entis: Metaphysik* (München: Josef Kösel & Friedrich Pustet, 1932); *Polarity: A German Catholic's Interpretation of Religion* (London: Oxford University Press, 1935); and *The Divine Majesty* (London: Collins, 1971).

17. David Tracy, *The Analogical Imagination: Christian Theology and the Culture of Pluralism* (New York: Crossroad, 1982), "A Christian Systematic Analogical Imagination," 405–45, citing 409–10.

18. Here we are thinking especially of Hans Urs von Balthasar, *The Glory of the Lord: A Theological Aesthetics*, 7 vols. (San Francisco, CA: Ignatius/New York: Crossroad, 1983–1991).

we see an *analogia entis* at work in Edwards. At the same time, Edwards never compromised his assertion of God's radical transcendence with respect to the created order.

Edwards's Soteriology in Catholic Perspective

Early Calvinism was shaped by its reaction against what was conceived of as a Roman Catholic fixation on human obedience or good works in securing salvation. While Calvinists were more insistent than Lutherans on the intrinsic role of good works in salvation, these works were always viewed as subsequent to the gift of divine grace. In many respects, Catholic Thomists held a teaching that was analogous to that of the Calvinists. Thomas Aquinas taught first that human beings cannot accomplish anything good apart from grace.[19] Human beings cannot merit eternal life without grace, cannot prepare themselves for grace, for "however a man prepares himself, he does not necessarily receive grace from God."[20] Thomas taught that no one ever merited the "first grace," which came as a purely gratuitous gift, "since the nature of grace is repugnant to reward of works, according to Romans iv.4." God alone was the cause of grace.[21] These Thomistic assertions were compatible with Calvinist assumptions. They represented the "dialectical" side of Thomism that—as in Edwards—distinguished and distanced divine grace from all purely natural desires or actions.[22]

Yet the argument of the *Summa Theologica* included an "analogical" side that drew nature and grace into relationship and harmony. Thomas defined grace as a "quality of soul" and added that "grace is a certain beauty of soul, which wins the Divine love." In his epistemology, Thomas denied that any "new light" had to be added to humanity's "natural light" of reason except when one was seeking to understand spiritual things. In that case, there might be a "habitual gift superadded to nature."[23]

---

19. Aquinas, *Summa Theologica*, 1a2ae, q.109, a.2.

20. Aquinas, *Summa Theologica*, 1a2ae, q.109, a.5; 1a2ae, q.109, a6; and 1a2ae, q.112. a.3.

21. Aquinas, *Summa Theologica*, 1a2ae, q.114, a.5; 1a2ae, q.112, a.1.

22. It should be noted that post-Tridentine Roman Catholicism tended at times toward a synergistic model of salvation that had affinities with ancient semi-Pelagianism and with the modern "Arminianism" that Edwards so stoutly opposed (chs. 3, 22). It was thus only the more *Augustinian* side of the Catholic tradition—as seen in Thomas Aquinas and some later Dominicans, and intensified in the Jansenist movement—that showed a notable analogy to Edwards's teaching on salvation.

23. Aquinas, *Summa Theologica* 1a2ae, q.110, a.2; 1a2ae, q.109, a.1, reply to obj.1.

When human beings received the gratuitous gift of grace, what followed was a human cooperation with grace. Both Thomistic and Tridentine theology at this point built on Augustine, who wrote that "God by co-operating with us, perfects what he began by operating in us, since he who perfects by co-operation with such as are willing, begins by operating that they may will."[24] The cumulative human cooperation with grace led to the acquisition of "merit." Protestants would have agreed that God keeps his promises of reward to the saints.[25] Yet Catholic thought went further by insisting that good works were not only rewarded but were, so to speak, *rewardable*. Rewards for good works were appropriate and fitting and yet were not strictly earned by those who received them. This kind of "merit" was "congruent" but not "condign." God was no one's debtor. If God conferred higher degrees of blessedness in the life beyond to persons of exceptional sanctity, then their sanctity was not by an achievement of mere natural striving. From the first reception of grace in baptism until the moment of death, every advance in holiness was enabled by divine grace.

Thomas Aquinas did not conceive of the temporal unfolding of salvation as the Calvinists did. Thomas explained that God's will is the final foundation of all reality and that this will is "reasonable" though not in the sense that anything created is—in the strict sense—the cause of God's willing. "The will of God is reasonable," wrote Thomas, "not because anything is to God a cause of willing, but in so far as He wills one thing to be on account of another."[26] In other words, the reasonableness of the divine willing cannot be appreciated by considering each individual thing separately but only by taking into account the whole network of relationships in which one thing is willed by God "on account of another." One may speak of "reward" for good works in this context and also of "merit," and yet both "reward" and "merit" rest on a foundation of unearned grace. Thomas's teaching on salvation might be compared to a net in which each piece is woven together with all the rest. What keeps the net in place is divine grace—like strong hands that encircle the net and hold it in place. Each strand in the net is, in one sense, held in place by the hands at the outside

---

24. Augustine, *On Grace and Free Will*, ch. 17, cited in Aquinas, *Summa Theologica*, 1a2ae, q.III, a.2.

25. Presbyterian theologian Charles Hodge had this distinction in mind when he insisted that God will reward good works not on the ground of divine justice—as he says that Catholic theology taught—but rather on the ground of the divine promise (*Systematic Theology*, 3 vols; Grand Rapids, MI: Eerdmans, 1986 [1873]; 3:241–42).

26. Aquinas, *Summa Theologica*, 1a, q.19, a.5.

of the net. Yet, in another sense, each strand is held in place by the adjacent strands. Applying the analogy, one might say that God's grace (represented by the hands outside of the net) is the cause of the saints' eternal reward and yet also that good works (represented by the links within the net) are the cause of the saints' reward. Neither statement contradicts the other.

Edwards's conception of the relationships among the differing aspects of salvation—faith, obedience, justification, sanctification, glorification, and so forth—is closer in some respects to this Thomistic "net" of salvation idea than to the traditional Calvinistic "chain" of salvation or *ordo salutis*. An early notebook entry, Miscellany 29, shows the direction of his thinking on the divine will, or God's "decrees":

> God decrees all things harmoniously and in excellent order; one decree harmonizes with another, and there is such a relation between all the decrees as makes the most excellent order. Thus God decrees rain in drought because he decrees the earnest prayers of his people; or thus, he decrees the prayers of his people because he decrees rain. I acknowledge, to say God decrees a thing "because," is an improper way of speaking, but not more improper than all our other ways of speaking about God. God decrees the latter event because of the former, no more than he decrees the former because of the latter.... Thus, when he decrees conformity to his Son, he decrees calling; and when he decrees calling, he decrees justification; and when he decrees justification, he decrees everlasting glory. Thus all the decrees of God are harmonious.[27]

Edwards's argument here maintains the gratuity of grace while also—in Thomistic fashion—insisting that human actions are not merely effects of

---

27. WJE 13:216–17. Compare this with the statement in the *Miscellanies* (WJE 13:457–58) on the interrelationship of the aspects of salvation: "The graces of the Spirit, especially those that more directly respect God and another world, are so nearly allied that they include one another; and where there is the exercise of one, there is something of the other exercised with it: like strings in consort, if one is struck, others sound with it.... So that humiliation that there is in repentance implies a principle of faith, and not only so, but something of the exercise too; so that a person according to the gospel may be in a state of salvation, before a distinct and express act of faith in the sufficiency and suitableness of Christ as a Savior. Persons are justified upon the first appearance of a principle of faith in the soul by any of the soul's acts: but a principle of faith appears and shows itself by the exercise of true repentance and evangelical humiliation; for the graces are all the same in principle, especially those that more immediately respect God and Christ and another world."

divine grace but are themselves conditions of one another and of particular outcomes.

Based on this construal of the divine will, Edwards can say that obedience is a "condition" of justification in the sense that justification and obedience are bound together in a harmonious ordering of the divine will. So it is with justification and sanctification or good works and rewards (ch. 25). Edwards's notion of the harmony of the divine decrees allows him to construe these in relation to another, as mutually conditioning one another, while still flowing from the ultimately gratuitous gift of divine grace.

Edwards's Treatment of Human Love in Catholic Perspective

Donald Gelpi wrote of what he termed "Edwards's partial rehabilitation of human nature." He stood in a Puritan tradition that "had already partly modified aspects of Calvin's endorsement of total human depravity."[28] Yet he pressed further than his forbears and in a number of interesting and philosophically creative ways. Edwards, for example, did not regard all forms of self-love as inherently reprehensible (ch. 33). Instead he held that God loves himself necessarily inasmuch as only the infinite reality of God offers an adequate object for the divine love and divine will. This particular idea may have come to Edwards from the Scotists (i.e., followers of Duns Scotus) via the philosopher Nicholas Malebranche. Analogously, on the human level, he recognized a universal tendency to seek happiness in naturally agreeable objects of desire. What he censured as immoral was not the simple tendency to seek happiness but that inordinate and exclusive self-love that sought its own satisfaction at the expense of others and to the exclusion of all other considerations. There were, indeed, forms of human benevolence that appeared virtuous but fell short of genuine virtue—tribal or nationalistic attitudes, devotion to family, and even "honor among thieves." All of these appearances of virtue were forms of enlarged self-interest. They did not embody a genuine outgoing concern and interest for the other in his or her otherness. Edwards wrote that "true virtue most essentially consists in benevolence to Being in general."[29] This meant that morality could not be divorced from religion, and that all virtue had some reference—explicitly or implicitly—to God.

---

28. Donald Gelpi, S.J., "'Incarnate Excellence: Jonathan Edwards and an American Theological Aesthetic," in *Religion and the Arts* 2 (1998): 443–46, 445, 447. This entire paragraph is indebted to Gelpi's essay.

29. WJE 8:540.

Yet what made Edwards seem Catholic and perhaps Thomistic was the way he connected natural human loves with the greater, higher love for God. As noted earlier in this chapter, there were both "dialectical" and "analogical" aspects in Edwards's arguments. At times he stated that grace conferred a set of human experiences and dispositions that entirely transcended the natural order. At other times, he made it clear that grace enlarged, supplemented, perfected, or completed existing human faculties and dispositions, according to the famous Thomistic adage *gratia non tollit naturam sed perficit* ("grace does not destroy nature but perfects it"). What Paul Ramsey called "the splendor of common morality" in Edwards was an acknowledgement that even natural, ordinary, and ungraced human actions nonetheless contained a tendency or *nisus* toward fulfillment in the context of supernatural and divine love (ch. 33).[30] While it would be an exaggeration to identify this aspect of Edwards's teaching with Thomas Aquinas's "natural desire for the beatific vision" or Karl Rahner's "supernatural existential," there is at least some analogy between Edwards and this deep vein of Catholic reflection.[31]

Not only did Edwards's treatment of human love show analogies with Catholic thought, but so did his approach to divine love. Chapter 14 explored Edwards's *End of Creation* and its conceptualization of God's character, goodness, and mode of action in creation and redemption. In a sense, one might say that Edwards's God created the world out of self-love. In terms of content and in genre, *End of Creation* showed stronger affinities to Roman Catholic than to Protestant discussions. Traditional Protestant theologians had generally avoided discussions of the metaphysical subtleties of God's act in creating the world.

Edwards's Trinitarian Metaphysics in Orthodox Perspective

One intriguing point of contact between Edwards and Christian Orthodoxy lies in the importance that both assigned to beauty (ch. 6). For many Orthodox thinkers, it is God's beauty—as much or more than God's truth or goodness—that converts the soul and transforms it into the divine likeness. As noted in chapter 26, the late historian of Christian thought Jaroslav Pelikan made reference to the affinities between Edwards's theology and the Orthodox doctrine

---

30. See Paul Ramsey, "The Splendor of Common Morality," in "Editor's Introduction," in WJE 8:33–53.

31. For a recent treatment of this theme in Karl Rahner, see David Coffey, "The Whole Rahner on the Supernatural Existential," *Theological Studies* 65 (2004): 95–118.

of divinization. In this respect, Edwards had much in common with Gregory Palamas, the most important Orthodox teacher on divinization, though there is no evidence that Edwards read Palamas, and Edwards likely derived his Neoplatonism from British sources.[32] Yet to understand the whole scope of Edwards's idea of divinization, one must look into his Trinitarian doctrine of God and the participatory metaphysics tied to it. These features show marked resemblances to the ways of conceiving God and salvation that have been characteristic of Chalcedonian Orthodoxy and non-Chalcedonian forms of Eastern Christianity.

A couple of phrases that appear in Edwards's Trinitarian writings have not aroused much comment—"fountain of Deity" and "fountain of Godhead." Both seem to be translations of *pege theotatis*—a technical phrase from Greek patristic writers in reference to God the Father. Edwards writes that "the Father has the superiority: he is the fountain of Deity, and he begets the beloved Son." He also comments: "How many respects the Father first in order, fountain of Godhead, sustains the dignity of Deity, sends forth the other two. All is from him, all is in him originally." Another statement reads: "The Father is the Deity subsisting in the prime, unoriginated and most absolute manner, or the Deity in its direct existence." In this last quotation, we seem again to be in the realm of Greek patristic thought. Edwards's "unoriginated" corresponds to the Greek *agennetos*—a pivotal term in the Nicene and post-Nicene debates of the fourth and fifth centuries. Edwards's term "prime" denoted that which was ontologically original and archetypical, as shown in his early metaphysical writings: "Now God is the prime and original being, the first and last, and the pattern of all, and has the sum of all perfection."[33]

In Edwards's thought, both God the Son and God the Spirit are fully divine yet neither the Son nor the Spirit can be described as the "fountain of Deity [or Godhead]," as "prime," "unoriginated," or "absolute," or as "the Deity in its direct existence." Sang Lee explains: "The First Person of the Trinity...cannot be viewed as in any way generated by the exertion of the disposition. If the Father were so conceived, then the category of disposition would have logical priority (though not temporal priority) over the Father's actuality. Therefore, in the Father, the eternal disposition has to be viewed as identical with the eternal divine actuality.... Thus, it is in the Father that

---

32. Michael J. McClymond, "Salvation as Divinization: Jonathan Edwards, Gregory Palamas and the Theological Uses of Neoplatonism," in Paul Helm and Oliver D. Crisp, eds., *Jonathan Edwards: Philosophical Theologian* (Burlington, VT: Ashgate, 2003), 139–59.

33. WJE 21:147, 143, 131; WJE 6:363.

Edwards locates the absolute aseity of the deity."[34] This element in Edwards's thinking is in line with the Cappadocians—that is, Gregory of Nyssa, Gregory Nazianzus, and Basil the Great. The Cappadocian insight is that there is something that distinguishes the Father from the Son and the Spirit that is not reducible to the triadic pattern of relations—viz., filiation, spiration, or procession. This is the Father's property of sheer *unoriginatedness*. There is something *primordial* that distinguishes the Father from the Son and the Spirit, and this property is not relational in character. Indeed, the Father is distinguished by his quality of *non-relatedness* to anything more fundamental than himself.

Such a construal of the Trinity has often been jarring to Western Christian (both Catholic and Protestant) sensibilities and sometimes attacked as Origenist or subordinationist. Nonetheless, the Cappadocians were able to maintain the equal divinity and co-eternity of all three persons while viewing the Father as distinguished from Son and Spirit because of his unoriginatedness. Edwards's writings contain a hint—and perhaps more than that—of such a conception of the Trinity. As John Zizioulas has argued, Augustine and most of the Western Christian tradition construed the three divine persons fundamentally in terms of their triadic relations, while Eastern thinkers viewed the Trinity as constituted in terms of ontological derivation or origin.[35] Both Eastern and Western Trinitarian theologies are orthodox in affirming the oneness of God's being and the threeness of divine persons. Yet they differ. Edwards's Trinitarianism has both an Augustinian flavor and the Eastern or Orthodox tilt to which we are referring here.

For Edwards, the human knowledge of God *was* divinization. Edwards's thought showed an expansive movement that we earlier referred to as ontic enlargement (ch. 16), and that reflected the New Testament's Johannine language of mutual indwelling and mutual participation. The biblical texts speak of the Father, Son, and Spirit sharing love, glory, and knowledge among themselves; of the Father, Son, and Spirit sharing love, glory, and knowledge with believers; of the persons of the Trinity dwelling in believers; of believers dwelling in or with the persons of the Trinity; and of believers sharing in the love, glory, and knowledge of the persons of the Trinity. Miscellany 571 shows that Edwards

---

34. Sang Hyun Lee, *The Philosophical Theology of Jonathan Edwards* (Princeton, NJ: Princeton University Press, 1988), 188.

35. See John D. Zizioulas, *Being as Communion: Studies in Personhood and the Church* (Crestwood, NY: St. Vladimir's Seminary Press, 1985), esp. 15–65; and Zizioulas, *Communion and Otherness: Further Studies in Personhood and the Church* (Edinburgh: T. & T. Clark 2006), esp. "The Father as Cause," 113–54.

appropriated all these Johannine and participatory themes and made them central to his understanding of salvation.[36]

What divine fatherhood means for Edwards is that the Son shares with creatures his own participation in the Father. All being derives ultimately from God the Father, and God the Son shares his Sonship with others. Though the Son's participation in the Father's being, grace, glory, knowledge, and happiness is eternal and perfect, there is an analogy between the divine Son's participation in the Father and the redeemed human being's partial and limited participation in the Father. Because the divine Son's participation in the Father is complete, the Son is able to impart limitless life and endless blessing to elect creatures. Though the metaphysics of divine fatherhood might seem an arcane point in Edwards's Trinitarianism, it ties directly into the theme of divinization and thus links Edwards to the Orthodox tradition.

In summary, then, this chapter has shown that Edwards's affinities to Roman Catholic and Orthodox theologies were deep and substantial. On such varied themes as spiritual discernment, divine and human love, the "fitness" of God's work in salvation, and the relationship of natural human desires to supernatural grace, we find unmistakable parallels with Catholic thought. Both the Catholic principle of the analogy of being, and the Orthodox notion of salvation through participation, held a major place in Edwards's writings. Because of his appropriation of participatory as well as analogical modes of reasoning, Edwards showed a surprising resemblance to the ancient Eastern as well as the classical Western styles of theological reflection.

---

36. Edwards writes: "For there is doubtless an infinite intimacy between the Father and the Son; and the saints being in him shall partake with him in it, and of the blessedness of it." Thus God with the saints will form "as it were one society, one family" and "be in a sort admitted into that society of three persons in the Godhead" (WJE 18:110).

44

Interpretations V: Edwards and Contemporary Theology

AS EDWARDS'S WORKS continue to become better known, more and more contemporary theologians are beginning to use parts of his theology to assist their own projects. A few, such as H. Richard Niebuhr in the mid-twentieth century, were indebted to Edwards for their overall theological vision. This chapter will highlight some of the major areas in which Edwards has begun to seed contemporary theology. While his theocentrism and redemptive-historical approach to theology have had a far-ranging impact, his work continues to inspire ethics and aesthetics—or more specifically, aesthetic theology. As in the past, Edwards has inspired a broad range of spiritual theologies and spiritualities, and Edwards's influence is growing in the theology of the religions and in public theology—two dimensions of Edwards's thought that have been explored only recently.

Edwards in the Context of Ethical Reflection

The end of the twentieth century was marked by a growing appreciation for Edwards's exalted vision of common morality—that which is possessed by the unregenerate and regenerate alike. Princeton's Paul Ramsey was persuaded that Edwards assigned more ethical competence to the unredeemed than did Aquinas. The Catholic ethicist William C. Spohn observed that Edwards, like Aquinas, held that all rational beings can know their moral duty, and that the morality of pagans is not false but an image of true moral beauty. Spohn was also impressed that for Edwards strictly natural morality is based on the beauty of harmony and proportion, so that even natural virtue has its origin in aesthetic sensibility. The Reformed theologian Amy Plantinga Pauw was similarly persuaded that Edwards's natural morality is a "rather splendid thing," noting that for Edwards both communal harmony and the demand for justice are beautiful.[1]

---

1. Paul Ramsey, "Editor's Introduction" to *Ethical Writings*, WJE 8:33; William C. Spohn, "Sovereign Beauty: Jonathan Edwards and the Nature of True Virtue," *Theological Studies*, 42 (1981): 396; Amy Plantinga Pauw, "The Future of Reformed Theology: Some Lessons from Jonathan Edwards," in David Willis and Michael Welker, eds., *Toward the Future of Reformed Theology* (Grand Rapids, MI: Eerdmans, 1999), 467.

Both Spohn and Paul Lewis valued Edwards for his emphasis on what ethicists call "virtue ethics," a movement among moral thinkers in recent decades to correct overly intellectualized concepts of moral agency and neglect of the affective dimensions of character. Lewis faulted Stanley Hauerwas's privileging of narrative for this reason: to Lewis, it seemed to neglect the emotions and affections in favor of the intellect in its depiction of the ethical life. Edwards, said Lewis, had a more unitary view of the human self. He recognized the "myth of the passions" for what it was—a one-dimensional view of the human being that regards reason and the passions as enemies—and rightly portrayed reason as springing from the emotions.[2] Lewis inaccurately spoke of Edwards's "affections" as "emotions" and "passions," failing to notice Edwards's distinction between affections as "lively actings of the will or inclination" and passions as feelings "that are more sudden, and whose effects on the animal spirits are more violent, and the mind more overpowered, and less in its own command."[3] Yet he rightly recognized that Edwards avoided the rationalism of the Western tradition that divided the human self between reason and the affections, supposing that they are essentially separate and that the former directs the latter. Edwards instead depicted the self as fundamentally characterized by its affections—strong inclinations or loves that determine its choices, feelings, and thoughts (ch. 20).

Spohn found Edwards's ethics to be particularly American because it moves back and forth from part to whole. American pragmatists, according to Spohn, typically rejected both the deontological trend more common today and its utilitarian companion that relates means to ends. They opted instead for a pattern like Edwards's that evaluates an action in light of the overarching whole of reality. Spohn pointed to *True Virtue* as a perfect example of this. The virtuous act consents to the "great whole" of being, while merely apparent virtue consents to a limited portion of reality. Edwards thus shows how true religion, which alone sees the great whole, provides the ultimate context for morality.[4]

---

2. Paul Lewis, "The Springs of Motion: Jonathan Edwards on Emotions, Character, and Agency," *Journal of Religious Ethics* 22 (1994): 275–97.

3. WJE 2:98. For Edwards, emotions are not affections but feelings that spring from the underlying and more basic affections, just as thoughts of the mind and choices of the will also arise from the affections. WJE 2:96–99.

4. William C. Spohn, "Union and Consent with the Great Whole: Jonathan Edwards on True Virtue," *Annual of the Society of Christian Ethics* (Waterloo, Ontario: Council on Studies of Religion, 1985), 19–23.

For this and other reasons, Spohn thought of Edwards's moral theory as a "metaethics" or an ultimate foundation for moral thinking. He argued that *True Virtue* and the *End of Creation* interpret all moral obligation as rooted in the beauty of personal response to God, which implies a convergence of duty and enjoyment. Morality is an image of the inner-Trinitarian love of God. Thus Edwards based his aesthetics on love for God rather than basing love for God on aesthetics.[5] The basic principle binding the universe is love, stemming from the love among the three persons of the Godhead. All other attraction in the cosmos is an image of this loving attraction that drives toward union. For a variety of reasons, Spohn believed this metaethic can provide a fresh foundation for Christian ethics in our day. First, it shows in a unique fashion the impact of religion on the moral agent by delineating the ways in which character is reoriented and the experience of beauty purifies the soul. Second, Edwards's benevolence to Being deepens natural moral instincts rather than creating new demands. Third, it is akin to Catholic moral theology in that it does not add new obligations but transforms moral perception and disposition through an encounter with God's love. When the root is changed, the fruit will grow. Such an approach is superior, Spohn alleged, to Lutheran suspicion of law and Anabaptist rejection of natural morality. It also recognizes that moral philosophy can be a proper source for Christian ethics once refracted by the divine and supernatural light.[6]

Edwards in the Context of Aesthetic Discussion

Historians, theologians, and ethicists have laid increasing stress on the integral connection between Edwards's ethics and his aesthetics. George Marsden writes that Edwards's vision of blazing beauty became a source of fervent action. This grounding of ethics in aesthetic vision is rare, he suggests. Belden Lane speaks of God's beauty as restless until it communicates itself to all, with the aim of beautifying others by replicating its ethical beauty.[7] To date, Lane has fashioned the most creative use of Edwards's aesthetics for ethics, devising from it a "theology of ecological justice." Edwards, he proposes, is a naturalist as well as theologian inasmuch as he saw the natural world as a

---

5. Spohn, "Sovereign Beauty," 416.

6. Spohn, "Sovereign Beauty," 417–21.

7. George Marsden, "Jonathan Edwards in the Twenty-First Century," in Harry S. Stout, Kenneth P. Minkema, and Caleb J.D. Maskell, eds., *Jonathan Edwards at 300: Essays on the Tercentenary of His Birth* (Lanham, MD: University Press of America, 2005), 162.

communication of God's Trinitarian glory. More specifically, Edwards viewed the created world as a school of desire, training the regenerate in an intimate sensory apprehension of God's glory as mirrored in the beauty of the world.

In this way, writes Lane, Edwards's God uses nature to teach human beings to taste, savor, and delight in his being and beauty. The natural world enlarges the human capacity to sense God's beauty and drives us to replicate God's beauty in space and time. Edwards explicates this process in part through his typology (ch. 8), by which nature illustrates desire for God. We see this in gravity, the delight of bees gathering nectar, the appetite of babies for breast milk, the intimate union of a grafted branch with its tree, and the sexual appeal of a wife to her husband. Nature even shows us the way of the cross by its oft-displayed "anguish." Thus the beauty of the world provides spiritual training in the knowledge of God. The "sense of the heart" (chs. 10, 20, 24) appreciates nature as a training ground, cultivating an affective receptivity that disposes one toward knowing God. In all these ways Edwards helps us understand that we cannot act any longer as though we were disconnected from a lifeless universe toward which we bear no responsibility. It teaches us instead that we must honor the web of life. The beauty of God requires it of us.[8]

Systematic theologians have also made recent use of Edwards's aesthetics. Edward Farley's *Faith and Beauty: A Theological Aesthetic* (2001) draws on thinkers from the ancient Greeks to the twentieth century but concludes that beauty was more central and pervasive in Edwards's thought than most other Christian theologians. Jesuit theologian John Navone compares Edwards's aesthetics to that of Thomas Aquinas, asserting that the two shared essentially the same aesthetic vision. Moreover, Navone relies on both in constructing his theology of "enjoying God's beauty."[9] Princeton theologian Sang Hyun Lee proposes that Edwards's aesthetic shows contemporary theologians how they can think of knowing God in an academic climate that is unwilling to talk about experiencing God.[10]

---

8. Belden Lane, *Ravished By Beauty: The Surprising Legacy of Reformed Spirituality* (New York: Oxford University Press, 2011), esp. 170–200.

9. Edward Farley, *Faith and Beauty: A Theological Aesthetic* (Burlington, VT: Ashgate, 2001), 43; John Navone, *Enjoying God's Beauty* (Collegeville, MN: Liturgical Press, 1999).

10. Sang Lee, "Edwards and Beauty," in Gerald McDermott, ed., *Understanding Jonathan Edwards: An Introduction to America's Theologian* (New York: Oxford University Press, 2009), 113–25.

Edwards in the Realm of Constructive Theology

Scholars from a number of disciplines have lifted up Edwards's "theocentrism" as a resource for contemporary theology. Stephen D. Crocco—who demonstrated Edwards's influence on Joseph Haroutunian, H. Richard Niebuhr, and James Gustafson in a 1986 Princeton University dissertation—defined theocentrism as a zeal for the sovereignty of God that considers divine interests largely in terms of human well-being. Niebuhr used Edwards to criticize the "empirical theology" of the early-twentieth-century for focusing on the divine-human relation instead of the divine object in that relation. Niebuhr attributed his basic theological vision to Edwards and insisted that the human subject finds its divine object not as the fulfillment of its desires but as a brute and stark actuality that often thwarts its wishes and goals. Therefore genuine religious experience is an ongoing reorientation of self and community in a universe of being in which they have been dethroned and decentered. Niebuhr opposed this reordering of the self to a liberal theological tradition that had assumed a harmony of divine and human values.[11]

Theocentrism was not the only Edwardsean influence that H. Richard Niebuhr mediated to modern theology. Niebuhr's *The Meaning of Revelation* (1941), with its stress on theology as narrative, had a pervasive influence among faculty at Yale Divinity School, including Hans Frei, George Lindbeck, and David Kelsey. The "narrative theology" that took hold at Yale and elsewhere during the 1980s and 1990s forged an inseparable union between theological reasoning and narrative form. While Karl Barth had much to do with this trend, it was Niebuhr's interpretation of Edwards that served as another point of departure for the "new Yale School." In terms reminiscent of Edwards's "history of the work of redemption" (ch. 12), Niebuhr called for a universal history of God's redeeming work: "The Christian community must turn...from the revelation of the universal God in a limited history to the recognition of his rule and providence in all events of all times and communities."[12]

John Piper also proposed an Edwards-inspired theocentrism, but of a different sort. Niebuhr's theocentrism was constrained and Stoic, resigned to an

---

11. John Piper, *Desiring God: Meditations of a Christian Hedonist* (Portland, OR: Multnomah, 2003).

12. Stephen D. Crocco, "American Theocentric Ethics: A Study in the Legacy of Jonathan Edwards," Ph.D. diss., Princeton University, 1986; Gerald P. McKenny, "Theological Objectivism as Empirical Theology: H. Richard Niebuhr and the Liberal Tradition," *American Journal of Theology and Philosophy* 12 (1991): 19–33; Marsden, "Jonathan Edwards in the Twenty-First Century," 153–57.

adverse world and the vanity of human wishes.. Piper's theocentrism by contrast stressed participation in God, joy, delight, and what Piper calls "Christian hedonism." Such "hedonism" is of course is not the worldly pleasure that comes from money, fame, and power. Piper highlights the joys of religion, which he insists are powerful, lasting, and soul-refreshing. From Edwards's *End of Creation* Piper extracts the principle that God's glory is tied to human happiness and delight, and so he concludes that God is genuinely delighted in the delight of his saints.[13]

Amy Plantinga Pauw finds Edwards worthy of contemporary imitation, but she adds a caveat. She applauds his use of "grand narrative" for thinking through particular theological questions. But she also warns that if divorced from a "pastoral narrative," it runs the risk of self-righteous nationalism and religious sectarianism. She adds that Edwards was not well suited to pastoral labor, since he lacked the necessary patience, humility, and generosity of spirit. Edwards was at his theological best, she says, when he intertwined the grand and pastoral narratives, letting his grand vision of the history of redemption be tempered by his pastoral recognition of the messiness, paradoxes, and ambiguities of the life of faith.[14]

In yet another appropriation of Edwards's theocentrism, George Marsden describes it as the tendency to begin one's thinking with God and his sovereignty. According to Marsden, this pattern of reflection adds realism ("a minor key") to our understandings of human experience, and would remind us that history and societies are not simply the products of material, social, economic, and cultural forces. Edwards's theocentrism might also inject clearer vision to Christian churches, where there is a nearly exclusive emphasis on what God can do for human beings and where justice is defined by human standards alone. Marsden finds other dimensions of Edwards's theology to be helpful correctives to current thinking. He believes that in a quasi-deistic world where the universe is seen as an independent entity, Edwards's vision of the cosmos

---

13. H. Richard Niebuhr, *The Meaning of Revelation* (New York: Macmillan, 1974 [1941]), 63–64. Continuing Niebuhr's and hence Edwards's legacies was Hans Frei's *The Eclipse of Biblical Narrative: A Study in Eighteenth and Nineteenth Century Hermeneutics* (New Haven, CT: Yale University Press, 1974). On narrative theology, see Stanley Hauerwas and L. Gregory Jones, eds., *Why Narrative?* (Grand Rapids, Michigan: Eerdmans, 1989); David Ford, *Barth and God's Story: Biblical Narrative and the Theological Method of Karl Barth in the "Church Dogmatics"* (Frankfurt am Main, Bern: Peter Lang, 1981); and Mark I. Wallace, *The Second Naivete: Barth, Ricoeur, and the New Yale Theology*, 2nd edition (Macon, GA: Mercer University Press, 1995).

14. Plantinga Pauw, "The Future of Reformed Theology," 456–69.

as personal and spiritual, with nature as an image of Christ's redemptive love, is a breath of fresh air. To those who have been taught that the world was born by chance or perhaps always was, Edwards's biblical cosmogony—the universe as a big bang of God's creative love—is attractive. It replaces the impersonal scientific universe of current science with a universe of relationships in which God has an intimate relation to every atom.

Marsden thinks Edwards's respect for the life of the mind is particularly needed by evangelicals, who struggle with anti-intellectualism and tend to imitate Benjamin Franklin's shallow moralism, easy formulas, and fixation on quantitative results—the spiritual equivalent of junk food. Though Edwards was thoroughly hierarchical in his social views, his insistence on human depravity and the arbitrariness of God's grace may provide a more realistic foundation for egalitarianism than the modern, sentimental belief that human nature is essentially altruistic.[15]

Both evangelical and mainline Protestant theologians have mined Edwards for doctrinal uses. Plantinga Pauw, a Presbyterian theologian, chides Reformed "culturalists" that their concern for Christian love and earthly ethics must be grounded in Edwardsean convictions about the reality and certainty of divine things. The thirst for God should sustain an enduring concern for this world, as well. Evangelical philosopher and theologian C. Samuel Storms marshals Edwards's arguments from *Freedom of the Will* to battle Open Theists who suggest that God does not have exhaustive divine foreknowledge. Christopher William Morgan proffers Edwards's arguments against eighteenth-century annihilationists to demonstrate the weakness of twentieth-century evangelical arguments for the annihilation of the damned.[16]

Edwards in Discussions of Public Theology and World Religions

Several scholars have recommended Edwards as a resource for public theology. Edwards's thinking is relevant, they say, for two concerns of public theologians today—the privatization of faith and the church's accommodation to

---

15. Marsden, "Jonathan Edwards in the Twenty-First Century," 161–62.

16. Plantinga Pauw, "The Future of Reformed Theology," 461, 469; C. Samuel Storms, "Open Theism in the Hands of an Angry Puritan: Jonathan Edwards on Divine Foreknowledge," in D.G. Hart, Sean Michael Lucas, and Stephen J. Nichols, eds., *The Legacy of Jonathan Edwards: American Religion and the Evangelical Tradition* (Grand Rapids: Baker Academic, 2003), 114–30; Christopher William Morgan, "The Application of Jonathan Edwards's Theological Method to Annihilationism in Contemporary Evangelicalism," PhD diss., Mid-America Baptists Theological Seminary, 1999.

culture. Edwards's social theory resists privatization by its notion of the ontological interrelatedness of all people, and its stipulation that believers share with unbelievers moral awareness, aesthetic perception, elementary religious knowledge, and instinctual kind affections. For this reason, Christians can and must cooperate with non-Christians on projects with an ethical aim, sharing common goals if not the reasons for pursuing those goals (ch. 33). Christians are called not to new and separate political communities but to work for the common good of existing communities. They are to guard against cultural captivity by maintaining critical distance between church and state and by using transcendent standards to criticize earthly corruptions and pretensions. Edwards said that civil government was a matter of great importance, but warned against the presumption that government could create an ideal order or answer ultimate questions. John Bolt has made extensive use of Edwards's public theology in his own recommendation for an "American public theology."[17]

Still other scholars have used Edwards's theology for their work in the contemporary theology of religions. Terrance L. Tiessen, for example, finds principles in Edwards's theology of covenants to argue for "accessibilism," the notion that Christians can be hopeful about the possibility of salvation for those who have not heard the gospel. Tiessen notes that Edwards believed that regeneration sometimes precedes conversion in time, and that Cornelius was thus regenerated before he heard about Jesus from Peter; that the covenant of works overtly taught in the Old Testament was used by God to inculcate a sense of moral inability and thus recognition of the need for a savior; that the Holy Spirit was often at work where the name of Jesus Christ was not known; and that God had different expectations for nations that had received different kinds and degrees of revelation. Tiessen also finds Edwards's typology instructive. Edwards wrote that God used sacrifice in all the religions to teach people the necessity of propitiatory sacrifice for atonement of sin, and that even the horrific practice of human sacrifice intimated the need for a perfect human being to make full atonement for sins. God used idolatry—though inspired by the devil—to show pagans the principle of incarnation—that God can inhabit matter (ch. 36).[18]

---

17. John Bolt, *A Free Church, A Holy Nation: Abraham Kuyper's American Public Theology* (Grand Rapids, MI: Eerdmans, 2001), esp. 187–226. See also Gerald R. McDermott, "Jonathan Edwards and the Culture Wars: A New Resource for Public Theology and Philosophy," *Pro Ecclesia* 4 (1995): 268–80.

18. Terrance L. Tiessen, *Who Can Be Saved? Reassessing Salvation in Christ and World Religions* (Downers Grove, IL: InterVarsity Press, 2004). See also McDermott, *Can Evangelicals Learn from World Religions?* (Downers Grove, IL: InterVarsity, 2000), esp. 45–72, 91–119.

New Directions

This volume has suggested numerous points of contact between Edwards's thinking and that of historic Roman Catholic theology. We have argued (ch. 43) that Edwards oscillated between an analogical imagination (Roman Catholic) and a dialectical imagination (Protestant). By "analogical" we mean the Catholic penchant for seeing continuity between the Creator and his creation, or ways in which the cosmos resembles its Maker. By "dialectical" we mean the Protestant tendency to see God as radically different from the cosmos he created. In his metaphysics (ch. 7), Edwards frequently contrasted God and the world in this way. Yet he also rejected the traditional Protestant suspicion of metaphysics, adopting a principle of "proportion" (a Latin translation of the Greek *analogia* or *"analogy"*) as fundamental to his metaphysical and typological reasoning. Furthermore, Edwards's lifelong fascination with the end or purpose of the creation aligned him with medieval and modern Catholic authors on this question. Yet the most interesting and surprising affinities lie between Edwards's and Catholic theologies of salvation. While Edwards agreed with Luther that faith establishes the believer's union with Christ and that the basis of justification is mystical union, he was closer to Thomas Aquinas in highlighting the ineluctable link between justification and sanctification. Both Aquinas and Edwards agreed that the beauty of saints was inherent and that grace was infused in the process of salvation. Finally, Edwards's leadership of the concerts of prayer shows a concern for visible unity among the churches. All of these affinities could prove helpful for theologians concerned with the relationship between Protestant and Roman Catholic thought.

Another area for fruitful work will be Edwards's massive biblical commentary in sermons, notebooks, and treatises. Comparatively little study has been done thus far on Edwards's biblical theology. Yet as the work of Stephen Stein and Douglas Sweeney becomes better known—and as scholars explore the enormous trove of biblical reflection in the new printed and online versions of *The Works of Jonathan Edwards*—we can expect Edwards to play a role in future systematic theology, biblical theology, and the emerging discipline of the theological interpretation of scripture.

These are only a few ways that contemporary theologians have drawn on Edwards's ideas and writings in their own reflections. Yet if the last two and a half centuries are any indication, the future use of Edwards's theology is likely to move in new directions and deliver new insights into the eighteenth-century theologian.

45

Conclusion: Edwards as a Theological Bridge

EARLIER CHAPTERS IN this volume have shown that Edwards was clearly Reformed or Calvinistic in his reading and intellectual influences (ch. 3), his spirituality (ch. 4), his embrace of covenantal theology (ch. 21), and his emphasis on God's sovereignty in giving grace (ch. 23) and effecting conversion (ch. 24). Yet, the preceding chapters also demonstrated that Edwards's theology showed an affinity for other, non-Calvinist schools of thought. He read and appropriated many themes from thinkers of the emerging Enlightenment tradition (ch. 3) and from both Continental and British philosophers (ch. 7). His identification of God as "Being in general" and his use of biblical and natural typology aligned him with the patristic and medieval Christian heritage (ch. 43). Edwards's Trinitarian theology showed affinities with both Eastern Orthodox and Western Latin thought (chs. 13, 43). His extended treatment of God's purpose in creating the world was reminiscent of medieval and modern Roman Catholic discussions of this theme (ch. 14). The extensive role he assigned to angels in his theology was analogous to medieval discussions (ch. 18). Unlike many earlier Protestant thinkers, Edward sought to offer a detailed account of heaven and eternity with God (ch. 19).

While maintaining that every faithful human response to God was enabled by God's prevenient grace—the *sola gratia* ("grace alone") position—Edwards's doctrine of justification qualified the Reformation tradition's *sola fide* ("faith alone") position. He taught that faith was not the only "condition" of salvation—as he himself carefully defined the word "condition." Perseverance in faith was also a "condition." So was obedience (ch. 25). Edwards broke with these Protestant precedents on the basis of his scriptural exegesis. In his treatment of salvation, Edwards also laid constant stress on the believer's union with God through Christ (chs. 16, 19, 23, 25, 43), and in this way offered a doctrine of divinization (ch. 26). There was no salvation without participation in the very life of God. In ways like Augustine (ch. 43), Edwards assigned as important a place in his theology to love as to faith (ch. 33). The soul's believing approach to God was, for Edwards, an act or movement of love. Faith and hope would eventually pass away. Yet love was the imperishable bond between God and believers, and within the community of believers, both in the present age and in the age to come (ch. 19).

Edwards's theology of revival (ch. 27) proved to be one of his most influential legacies in North American Christianity and later in global Christianity. Evangelicals, Pentecostals, and Charismatics have been captivated by Edwards's encompassing analysis of spiritual experience, and they have often appealed to it as a basis for judging spiritual phenomena and experiences (ch. 42). Also of interest is the way that Edwards's theology of revival was rooted in his personal spiritual experiences (ch. 4).

Edwards's doctrine of the church laid emphasis on unity not only on the local level but on regional, national, and international levels. He promoted ecumenical concerts of prayer. What is more, he held a positive view of Anglican, Lutheran, and Orthodox Christians (ch. 28). His sacramental theology included a robust affirmation of Christ's presence in the eucharist—a key reason for his concern regarding admission to communion (ch. 30). Edwards's public theology and ethical teachings were based on a notion of a universal community. He rejected narrow, parochial visions of the common good that were limited to self, family, tribe, or nation (chs. 32, 33). On the other hand, Edwards's apocalyptic thinking on the church's coming "glorious times" aligned him with the sectarians (ch. 35). Throughout history, the Christian community was generally small and persecuted. Only in the final days of history would the community of faith be firmly established and global in scope. A remarkable feature of Edwards's theology was its approach to non-Christian religions. Edwards saw non-Christian faiths as containing intimations of Christian truth and viewed them as providential preparations for the later coming of the Christian gospel (chs. 9, 12). His dispositional view of salvation suggested that it was the heart's disposition that mattered most to God. At the time of his death, Edwards had not resolved the question, but he seems to have pondered the possibility that God might save some who were adherents of non-Christian religions (ch. 36).

Scholars have frequently compared Edwards to Calvin and categorized Edwards as a Calvinist theologian first and foremost. Yet this categorization is too narrow. Most Calvinists set divine sovereignty—God's supreme power and will—at the center of their conceptions of God and the world. Edwards, too, has been interpreted in this way.[1] Yet it might be more apt to say that

---

1. George Marsden writes, "The central principle in Edwards's thought, true to his Calvinist heritage, was the sovereignty of God" (*Jonathan Edwards: A Life*; New Haven, CT: Yale University Press, 2003; 4).

Edwards's highlighted God's *centrality* rather than God's sovereignty. Sovereignty was simply *one of several ways* in which Edwards conceived of God's centrality. Edwards's theology made God central in the giving or withholding of grace (Calvinist sovereignty, ch. 23); central in ontology and epistemology (metaphysics, ch. 7); central to the human participation in God (divinization, ch. 26); central in affective experience (revival, ch. 27); central on a symbolic and representational level (typology and semiotics, chs. 8, 40); central in historical events (history of redemption, chs. 12, 15); central in diverse, global cultures (non-Christian religions, chs. 12, 36); and central in the human arts and sciences—when properly understood in their relationship with God (implicit apology, ch. 10). In Edwards's thought, one cannot reduce God's centrality to a single denominator. One finds a stunning range of alternative conceptualities for thinking about God and God's place in the world.

Like a great tree, Edwards's thought was rooted in one spot (the Calvinist tradition) yet with branches stretching far and wide. While most eighteenth- and nineteenth-century theologians were known as Baptist or Lutheran or Reformed or Catholic thinkers, and concentrated on the study of authors within their own particular traditions, Edwards showed openness to learning from many Christian traditions as well as from avowed opponents of the Christian faith.[2] What is more, his thought reveals an openness that extends in multiple directions. The nineteenth-century Mercersburg theologians—John Williamson Nevin and Philip Schaff—were Reformed thinkers known for their "catholic" or "catholicizing" tendencies. Yet their high churchmanship did not lead them to sympathize with popular forms of religion and the religious revivals of their day. Edwards by contrast adopted a high view of the institutional church while he also sanctioned vibrant and novel forms of experiential Christianity.

For the reasons just indicated, Edwards emerges in this volume as a seminal, original, and protean figure—easier to appreciate in one of his aspects than to grasp in his totality. Peter Thuesen has suggested that Edwards might be compared to a "great mirror" because his thought was "multivalent" and there seems to be "an Edwards for everyone." Studies of Edwards thus reveal as much or more about the interpreter as they do about the interpreted.[3] We agree with Thuesen's point, and we would hasten to add that the multiple

---

[2]. E. Brooks Holifield stressed the dominant role of denominational traditions in American theology throughout the pre-Civil War era. See Holifield, *Theology in America: Christian Thought from the Age of the Puritans to the Civil War* (New Haven, CT: Yale University Press, 2003), 14–16.

[3]. Peter J. Thuesen, "Jonathan Edwards as Great Mirror," *Scottish Journal of Theology* 50 (1997): 39–60.

interpretations of Edwards are not simply a sign of interpretive ingenuity (though they do show that). It is the many-sidedness or myriad-mindedness of Edwards that makes him interesting, attractive, provocative, and compelling to readers from a wide range of opinions and backgrounds. Precisely because of his many-sidedness, we conclude that Edwards may be understood as a bridging figure within the fragmented world of twenty-first-century Christianity. This bridging role can be elaborated in several ways.

A Bridge Between East and West

One of the surprising ways that Edwards bridges between traditions lies in the "Eastern" flavor and ethos of his theologizing. For Orthodoxy, the term "theologian" is traditionally used for someone who may have little or no technical academic training but who instead is rich in direct, experiential knowledge of God. Beginning in the High Middle Ages, the teachers and students associated with the emerging universities in Europe began to embrace scholastic methods for expounding Christian theology. The locus for theological reflection shifted from the monastic community to the lecture hall. Within Orthodoxy, however, there has always been a strong countervailing thrust toward an understanding of "theology" and "theologian" in their earlier sense. Edwards's *Diary* and *Personal Narrative* often referred to his own practice of "meditation" or "contemplation." The practices of prolonged, solitary reflection that he first developed during his youth seem to have continued throughout his lifetime. Prayer, reflection, and attentive reading of scripture and other books created the atmosphere in which Edwards composed his *Miscellanies*. Biographers have commented on the solitary, meditative, and almost monastic ethos of Edwards's spirituality (ch. 4).

Another link between Edwards and the Eastern Christian tradition lies in his core notion of salvation as "participation" in God's being, love, knowledge, and happiness. To be sure, the divinization doctrine (ch. 26) was not unknown in the West but was far more common in the Christian East. As noted in the conclusion to chapter 43, Edwards's combination of analogical and participatory modes of reasoning gave his theology both a Western and an Eastern flavor. Edwards's Trinitarianism (chs. 13, 43) asserted the ontological priority of the Father vis-à-vis the Son and the Spirit and affirmed both a single procession of the Spirit (from the Father) and a double procession (from Father and Son). In this way, Edwards mediated between traditional Western and traditional Eastern Christian views of the Trinity. Moreover, Edwards's ontology of divine Fatherhood was not a mere metaphysical nicety. Instead it carried soteriological ramifications. It implied that all being derived ultimately from God the Father and that God the Son shared his sonship with others. Salvation meant that human beings—as members of Christ—shared in the Son's joy and delight in the Father. Salvation also meant that human beings—as members of Christ—were recipients and sharers of the Father's love for Christ (chs. 14, 19). Edwards's Trinitarianism and his teaching on divinization were thus intertwined.

A Bridge Between Protestant and Catholic

At a number of critical points, Edwards's theology showed both Protestant and Catholic characteristics. In his embrace of metaphysics as foundational for theology, Edwards's theological approach was closer to that of Augustine, Anselm, Aquinas, and Bonaventure than that of Luther, Calvin, or Barth (ch. 7). In his reading of scripture and his view of the natural world, Edwards showed a thoroughgoing commitment to typological interpretation (ch. 8). This was based on a concept of *analogia entis* affirming that all created things show an analogy to the Creator (ch. 43). With regard to salvation, Edwards's thought exhibited what Anri Morimoto called a "Protestant principle"—the notion that grace always comes from God and that it is never properly a human possession or under human control (chs. 20–25). Yet it also revealed a "Catholic substance"—the sense that divine grace is truly present, becomes incarnate in the world, and indwells the saints and the church in an abiding way (chs. 23, 25). In Edwards's teaching, salvation comes by grace alone. Nonetheless, there is a "fitness" that makes it suitable for God to save those who display faith. Edwards's teaching on "fitness" in respect to salvation showed analogies to traditional Catholic notions of "merit" (ch. 43).

Unlike Reformational thinkers such as Luther and Calvin, Edwards had as much to say about love as faith. Like Augustine, his thought sometimes highlighted love even more than faith (chs. 19, 33). Also striking is Edwards's statement that faith is not the only "condition" of justification (ch. 25). As Thomas Schafer noted, Edwards often came down on the side of Augustine—the fountainhead of both medieval Catholicism and modern Protestantism. In his ecclesiology, Edwards did not hold the subjectivist or individualistic views of the church that have sometimes been attributed to him (ch. 28). Rejecting strict Congregationalism, he gravitated toward a Presbyterian system that affirmed the importance of trans-local authority. His stress on the church's visible unity was in some respects an anticipation of later ecumenism. With regard to the sacraments, Edwards affirmed the eucharist as a means of grace and a held to a robust view of Christ's presence (ch. 30). Edwards was perhaps *least catholic* in the rather minimal role he assigned to church tradition in his theological method (chs. 1, 9).

A Bridge Between Liberal and Conservative

Given Edwards's overt Calvinism and his assertions on such topics as original sin, human depravity, the unfree will, divine judgment, and hell (chs. 21, 22, 35), it is surprising that Edwards would have any appeal at all among liberal, modernist, or revisionist theologians. Yet Edwards has had his admirers in such seemingly unlikely places as Harvard Divinity School and university departments of religious studies. Though his theology might be classified as conservative in content, its style and ethos are closer in some respects to what one might consider a liberal or revisionist approach. Edwards assigned a significant role to experience in theology. Like Schleiermacher, Edwards assigned apologetic significance to the experience of God (ch. 10). He was also in no sense a creedalist (ch. 9). Never did he appeal to a creedal statement as a basis for affirming any doctrine. In this sense, a formal appeal to tradition in Edwards's thought is virtually nonexistent. Believing that the Reformation and earlier Calvinist tradition could be improved, Edwards was a "developmentalist" rather than an "originalist" or a "creedalist" (ch. 41). He was akin to later revisionists—if not in terms of his specific teachings, then in the sense of being unconstrained by what has been believed and confessed in the past. Edwards identified with the Calvinist tradition but denied that he believed certain things because Calvin believed or taught them (chs. 21, 41).

What is more, Edwards used innovative arguments to support his positions. The very method he used to develop his theological positions—the method of discovery by writing (ch. 1)—pressed Edwards to come up with new ways of approaching old issues. His theology thus showed a freshness and originality that has often been pleasing to moderately liberal Christians and troubling to the strictly conservative. Conservative Calvinists have had a love-hate relationship with Edwards (chs. 38, 41). In response to Edwards's *Original Sin*, Charles Hodge went so far as to call the work "pantheistic" in its consequences. In the experiential dimension of his revival theology, and in his openness to novel works of the Holy Spirit, Edwards has often been troubling to conservatives (ch. 27, 42).

Edwards showed a surprising degree of reliance on human reasoning in theology. This is probably not what one might have expected, given his views on human depravity. He displayed what we might call a dialectical fearlessness—that is, a willingness to follow each argument through to its conclusion. Calvinist critics often blamed the vagaries and errors of the New Divinity on Edwards himself. They argued that he was the fountainhead of a theological school that was excessively "metaphysical," unduly attached to human reasoning about God, and not sufficiently respectful of the role of mystery in theological inquiry. Moderately liberal theologians have generally appreciated the style and ethos of Edwards's theology, and regretted only that Edwards did not follow his logic to different conclusions. Liberals and conservatives have both read Edwards selectively—picking the parts that they liked and ignoring the rest. Yet Edwards remains one of the very few theologians of the modern era who appeals both to liberal and conservative thinkers.

A Bridge Between Charismatic and Non-Charismatic

Edwards may be the only major theologian of the modern era who is widely known and influential in the burgeoning global Pentecostal-Charismatic movement, which today counts some 600 million adherents around the world. No author has had greater influence in the discussion of religious revivals. During the spiritual awakening in Toronto during the mid-1990s, there were vigorous debates as to whether the events taking place there were signs of true revival or some kind of spiritual counterfeit. During this debate—much of it conducted online—both sides appealed to Edwards in support of their views. Pentecostals have appreciated Edwards's notion that the Holy Spirit may be not only a conserver of tradition but an innovator and disturber of the status quo (chs. 27, 42). Philip Jenkins has documented the massive growth of Christianity in the southern hemisphere during the last several decades and has noted the predominantly "experiential" rather than intellectualistic character of Christianity's growing edge.[4] Against this backdrop, Edwards's theology of spiritual experience carries considerable importance. His stature as the single most important Christian author on the topic of religious revival suggests that he is going to be read, cited, and debated by the rising generation of global Christians and for the foreseeable future.[5]

Not only is Edwards still cited as an authority on revival, but his writings can be cited in favor of more than one position. On one side, he displayed openness. He insisted that no one could define in advance what the Holy Spirit might do. God's handiwork was known only after the fact, as one observed and then tested the "fruit" that came out of a revival. On another side, Edwards insisted on the need for caution. Phenomena that looked impressive and seemed spiritual might well be spurious. Edwards even spoke of a "bastard

---

4. Philip Jenkins, *The Next Christendom: The Coming of Global Christianity*, rev. ed. (New York: Oxford University Press, 2007).

5. See the numerous references to Edwards in the index to Michael J. McClymond, ed, *Encyclopedia of Religious Revivals in America*, 2 vols. (Wesport, CT: Greenwood Press, 2007).

religion" that Satan might counterfeit in order to turn people away from true religion. Just as today's Charismatics might learn from Edwards's spiritual caution, so the non-Charismatic church could benefit from Edwards's call for openness to new and unprecedented works of the Holy Spirit. In his eschatological teaching on the church's coming "glorious times," Edwards opened the door to spiritual novelty. What God will do in the future might transcend anything witnessed in history thus far.

Edwards did not affirm—as do today's Pentecostal-Charismatics—the present-day exercise of the charismatic gifts of the Holy Spirit. In this sense, Edwards was on the side of the so-called cessationists. Nonetheless, Edwards took an empiricist's approach to revivals, judging them by their observable fruits rather than by a priori reasoning. It is possible that he might have taken a different stance on contemporary charismatic gifts if he had witnessed at first-hand the growth, impact, and dynamism of the twentieth-century Pentecostal-Charismatic movement. He would likely have found much to affirm in this global movement, as well as much to criticize.

Jonathan Edwards—Global Theologian for Twenty-First-Century Christianity

In the global Christian context of the twenty-first century, Edwards is a thinker and author of singular importance for engaging current issues. This becomes apparent when one compares Edwards to the other major Protestant thinkers of the last half-millennium—such as Martin Luther, John Calvin, Friedrich Schleiermacher, and Karl Barth.

Luther and Calvin continue to be important points of reference for Protestant Christians. Yet observers today—including Geoffrey Wainwright and Mark Noll—have questioned whether the Reformation is "over."[6] In other words, they have asked whether the issues that drove the sixteenth-century movement are historical memories today rather than matters of urgent, existential concern. What is more, both Luther and Calvin were situated within the early modern European context of the *corpus christianorum*. For many of the world's Christians today, this kind of church-state milieu—with its associated issues of legality, enforcement, social ethos, and so forth—is largely irrelevant. It either never existed within their global region, or it once existed

---

6. Geoffrey Wainwright, *Is the Reformation Over? Catholics and Protestants at the Turn of the Millennia* (Milwaukee, WI: Marquette University Press, 2000); Mark A. Noll and Carolyn Nystrom, *Is the Reformation Over? An Evangelical Assessment of Contemporary Roman Catholicism* (Grand Rapids, MI: Baker Academic, 2008).

but is now a fading memory. Since Edwards is the leading thinker to emerge in the free-church context of colonial America, this suggests that his reflections may be more pertinent to an era such as ours, characterized by nonestablished churches in most parts of the world.

Emerging in the context of late-eighteenth-century Romanticism, Friedrich Schleiermacher engaged a new set of issues pertaining to religious experience and the apologetic challenge of making Christianity credible in a post-Enlightenment context. Yet by the late twentieth-century, there were many indications that Schleiermacher's way of doing theology had diminishing influence. The postmodern era has not welcomed the great German pundits of the nineteenth century. Their intellectual style is too grandiose in its aspirations and too detached from social and cultural contexts to be convincing to most contemporary people. The modernist assumptions that made Schleiermacher intriguing from the mid-1800s through the mid-1900s now make him seem outmoded. Furthermore, the liberal Protestant movement that Schleiermacher did much to inaugurate has gone into steep decline. Yet Edwards's approach to spirituality (ch. 4), conversion (ch. 24), revival (ch. 27), and apologetics (ch. 10) is conceptually more rigorous than that of Schleiermacher, is more socially and historically contextual, maintains a clear sense of Christian distinctiveness, does justice to the cognitive aspects of religion, and treats the physical body as a locus of spiritual experience. For all of these reasons, Edwards's general account of spiritual experience is more up-to-date and engaging in a twenty-first-century context than that of Schleiermacher.

Karl Barth may be the Protestant theologian who has the widest currency and influence today—at least in academic circles and among the seminary elite. Without detracting from Barth's considerable merits, we note here that Edwards's writings show a number of traits that Barth's do not. First, Edwards made spiritual experience a constitutive element in his theological reflection. Barth's anti-experientialism—perhaps an overreaction to the experientialism of Protestant liberalism—makes it difficult to build any bridge between Barth's thought and such experientially based forms of Christianity as Pietism, Evangelicalism, and Pentecostalism. Edwards's theology can be a point of reference and a resource in contemporary discussions of religious experience in a way that Barth's theology could not possibly be. Second, Edwards's astonishing interest in and openness to non-Christian religions—formulated some two hundred and fifty years ago—contrasts markedly with the attitude of Barth. Edwards's writings are a challenge for contemporary Christian thinkers to reexamine non-Christian religions and to do so without the presumption that this line of inquiry requires them to abandon Christian truth claims or affirmations of Christianity's distinctiveness.

Third, though Barth's career involved a decade's labor as a pastor, Edwards's theology is perhaps even more pastoral in its setting, inspiration, and ethos than that of Barth. Edwards left behind some 1,200 sermon manuscripts, and these continue to be read today by lay Christians in search of edification. Edwards's writing has an accessible quality that is missing from Barth's *Church Dogmatics*. To be sure, Edwards wrote in eighteenth-century prose and his books could hardly be classified as light reading. Yet his writings carry no whiff of chalk dust or stuffy air of the seminary classroom. His theological ideas were all hammered out on the anvil of pastoral experience.

Fourth, for reasons already given in this chapter, Edwards's thought functions as a bridge between Protestantism on the one side and Roman Catholicism and Orthodoxy on the other. This cannot be said in the same way regarding Karl Barth's theology.

Fifth, Edwards and Barth both engaged the issue of the Enlightenment but did so in different ways. Barth's primary way of engaging critics of the Christian faith was through a faithful recounting of God's redemptive work in Jesus Christ based on the witness of scripture. Edwards came to his idea for a "history of the work of redemption" (ch. 12) in a way that partially anticipated Barth's thought. Yet Edwards's apologetic engagement was more wide-ranging than Barth's because it included not only an encompassing narrative theology, but a consideration of historical and evidential claims, the traditional theistic proofs for God, the witness of spiritual experience ("the sense of the heart"), and even an implicit apology that reinterpreted seemingly secular disciplines to show their hidden reliance on theological premises (ch. 10). Edwards's theology thus displays the full variety of ways that contemporary Christian thinkers might engage those outside of the Christian community.

In conclusion, it may be appropriate to cease speaking of Jonathan Edwards as "America's theologian" and to begin thinking of him as a global theologian for twenty-first-century Christianity.[7] His thought may have more linkages and more points of reference to various constituencies within world Christianity than any other modern Christian theologian. The outstanding modern Catholic thinkers—John Henry Newman, Karl Rahner, Yves Congar, Hans Urs von Balthasar, Pope John Paul II, and Pope Benedict XVI—are crucial for understanding post-Vatican II Catholicism. Most of them lack the vocabulary and conceptuality, however, that might link them to the Protestant and

---

7. Miklos Vetö—the outstanding European scholar of Edwards—suggested in his generally positive review of Robert Jenson that "America's theologian" might be a limiting phrase that shortchanges Edwards's global significance (Review of Robert W. Jenson, *America's Theologian* in *Church History* 58 [1989]: 520–22).

Pentecostal worlds. The same is true of such eminent Orthodox thinkers as George Florovsky and Sergei Bulgakov. Yet as we have argued throughout this volume, Edwards's thought—while conceived within the context of the Reformed tradition—offers many surprising avenues of approach to other schools and traditions of thought.

Imagine a Christian dialogue today that included adherents of ancient churches—Roman Catholic, Orthodox, Coptic—with various modern church bodies—Lutheran, Anglican, Methodist, Disciples of Christ—as well as an ample representation from the newer evangelical and Pentecostal-Charismatic congregations from around the world. If one had to choose one modern thinker—and only one—to function as a point of reference for theological interchange and dialogue, then who might one choose?

Our answer should be clear.

Index

Abrams, M.H. 687n.32
Addison, Joseph 49, 51
Adler, Mortimer 274
affections
  definition of 32, 311–5
  distinguished from emotions and passions 313–4
  and ethics 710
  and genuine religion 312–8
  importance of 311–2
  and imagination 319–20
  love as primary 315
  related to understanding and inclination 312–3
  true versus false 315–8, 384–5
Africa, Africans, African Americans 20, 37, 88, 132–3, 349, 463, 526–7, 552, 573, 576, 584, 618, 622, 658, 689, 692
Ahlstrom, Sydney 208, 644
Albigensians 456
Alexander, Archibald 627
Alexander, James Wardell 610
Alexandrian theology 26
Aligheri, Dante 273
Allen, Alexander V.G. 636, 642
Allen, Ethan 56
Althaus, Paul 402
American Board of Commissioners for Foreign Missions 564
American Tract Society 604

Ames, William 178, 218, 328n.19, 340, 373, 489, 551, 667
Anderson, Wallace 103, 114, 164, 596n.41, 644, 657, 659, 661
Andover Seminary 10, 21, 601, 604, 607, 620, 630
angels
  confirmation of 11, 275, 277–9, 285–6
  creation of 279–81
  Edwards's approach to 279–91
  fall of 278–87
  history of interpretation 276–9
  modernist theologians approach to 273–4
  and *Paradise Lost* 284n.30
  reconciled to God 18, 279–80, 290–1
  as spectators 279–80, 290, 294
Anglicanism 50, 57, 457–9, 671
Anselm (of Canterbury) 105, 157, 250, 273, 275, 277n.13, 286, 615, 700, 722
Antiochene theology 260
apologetics
  Edwards's influence on 614
  in the Eighteenth-century 149
  evidentialist approach to 154
  experientialist approach to 154–5
  external arguments 17, 156–61
  and fulfillment of prophecy 154

apologetics (*continued*)
   historical evidences for 150, 154–5, 160–1
   and illumination 163–4
   implicit arguments 17, 164–6, 188
   internal arguments 161–4
   and metaphysics 165
   and miracles 160–1
   and moral philosophy 165–6
   and spiritual perception 161–3
   theistic proofs 140, 158–9
Aquinas
   on angels 273–5, 277–9
   Edwards's exposure to 61
   Edwards's similarity to 6, 21, 69, 105, 159, 179, 211n.14, 219, 300, 303, 589, 696–7, 700–3, 705, 712, 717, 722
   on ethics 42, 544, 547–8, 709
   on faith 19, 369, 369–70, 370n.44
   on the fall 352n.47
   on God's love 211
   on God's communication 220, 492n.34
   on God's will 702
   on grace 267, 361, 696–7
   on habits 589
   on happiness 159
   on heaven 298, 303n.25
   on justification 390, 398–9, 404, 696
   and metaphysics 114, 700
   method of 14
   on the Trinity 197
   on virtue 544, 547–8
   on words in the Bible 179
Aristotle 9, 42, 104, 151, 207, 217, 298, 402n.41, 530, 589, 659
Arminianism
   definition of 28n.17, 29, 55, 85, 247, 322
   Edwards's response to 26, 28–30, 58–9, 85, 322–3, 325, 334–8, 361–5, 382, 387, 391–6
   presence in New England 56–9
   theology of 55
   view of salvation 364–5
Arminius, Jacob 55, 247, 391, 681
Arnott, John 691n.43, 692
Arthur, William 690
Asbury, Francis 594
Athanasius 283
Athenagoras 218, 219n.36, 276
"Of Atoms" 25, 108
atonement
   beauty 670
   deism's rejection of 54, 153, 253
   governmental theory of 614–7, 623
   and Holy Spirit 263–4
   logic of 253–4
   and New Divinity 614–7
   substitutionary view of 250
Atwater, Lyman 606, 631–2
Auerbach, Erich 118
Augustine
   on angels 273, 277
   City of God 185, 190, 315
   Confessions 68
   on conversion 270
   on creation 211
   Edwards's similarity to 105, 696, 722
   on evil 241
   on grace 702
   on happiness 69
   on heaven 296–8, 303–4
   on history 185, 225
   On the Holy Spirit 270
   on illumination 381
   on justification 390, 402n.43
   on love 315, 695, 718, 722
   and metaphysics 105, 700
   method of 9, 14
   on millennium 669

on the *Prisca Theologia* 582n.5
on resurrected bodies 296
on Scripture 119, 178
on the Trinity 197
on the will 314, 340, 606–7
Axtell, James 557n.30
Ayabe, John 173n.30
Azusa Street Revival 689

Bacon, Francis 43
Bad Book, the 35, 82, 474–5, 477–8
Badger, Joseph 317
Bainton, Roland 644
Baird, Robert 676n.4
Bale, John 572
Balthasar, Hans Urs 700, 727
Bamberger, Bernard 276n.9, 277n.14
baptism
  and covenants 482–3
  of infants 483–6, 667
  as initiation into the church 485
  mode of 486–7
  and regeneration 483–5, 492
Baptist Missionary Society 565
Barbour, Dennis 73
Barlaam of Calabria 418
Barnard, John 517n.14
Barth, Karl
  on angels 273, 275
  on beauty 94, 670
  and contemporary
    Christianity 722, 726–7
  on metaphysics 104–5, 673, 699–700
  method of 14
  on narrative 713
  on natures of Christ 258
  on revelation 673–4
  on the Trinity 197–8, 673
Bartlemann, Frank 689
Bartlett, Julie xi
Bartlett, Phebe 431, 474, 687

Basil the Great 277, 707
Basnage, Jacques 171
Bateman, Steve 596n.42
Battis, Emery John 373n.2
Baxter, Richard 61, 69, 298, 551, 567n.4, 570, 598
Bayle, Peter 581
beauty
  aestheticism 652, 711–2
  and atonement 670
  divine 25, 28–9, 93–7
  early emphasis on 24–5, 28
  as excellency 97
  as fundamental motif 5, 8, 17, 93–4
  as objective and subjective 99
  perception of 93–100, 140n.31, 514
  "primary" and "secondary" 71, 72, 94, 122
  and proportion 97–100
  Puritan view of 535
  and reason 141
  and revelation 134–5, 138, 140, 142
  and spirituality 69, 71
  Trinitarian dimensions of 8, 93, 96–7, 193, 195, 200, 202
Beaver, R. Pierce 551n.9
Bebbington, David xi, 635, 682n.17, 687
Beck, Peter 354n.53
Beecher, Henry Ward 688
Beinecke Rare Book and Manuscript
  Library 196, 501n.17, 508n.28, 558n.35
Belknap, Jeremy 58n.49
Bellamy, Joseph 21, 68, 185, 324n.13, 601–3, 615–6, 618
Bellarmine, Robert 298
Benedict XVI (Pope) 727
Bengel, Johann 171
Benne, Robert xii
Bercovitch, Sacvan 49n.21, 117n.6, 575n.31, 646

Bergson, Henri 655
Berkeley, George 41, 43, 103
Bernier-Feeley, Elise xi
Beverley, James 693
Beza, Theodore 212, 324
Bible
  allegorical interpretation of 175
  anagogical interpretation of 176
  authority of 154, 159–61
  distorted by Satan 172
  as divine revelation 169, 171, 672–3
  Enlightenment view of 170
  four-fold sense 118, 177–8
  inexhaustible nature of 173
  infallibility of 169
  inspiration of 135–6, 159–60
  Mosaic authorship of Pentateuch 171
  prophecies of 170
  radical evangelical view of 172
  Roman Catholic view of 171–2
  spiritual sense of 173–7
Billot, Louis (Cardinal) 220
Blake, William 271, 273
"Blank Bible" 34, 117, 167, 244, 249, 583, 645
Blount, Charles 53
Bogue, Carl 322
Bolingbroke (Henry St. John, 1st Viscount Bolingbroke) 53, 154
Bolt, John 716
Bolton pastorate 26
Bombaro, John 389n.2
Bonaventure 165n.68, 275, 277, 298, 700, 722
"Book of Controversies" 117, 323, 400
Bossuet, Jacques-Bénigne 185, 225
Boston, Thomas 326
Bower, Archibald 456
Bozeman, Theodore D. xii, 47n.17, 373n.2

Braaten, Carl 579n.49
Braddock, General Edward 521
Brainerd, David 33, 61, 63, 66, 82–3, 320, 322, 439, 549, 553–5, 559, 564–5, 608, 626, 633
Brattle, Thomas 50
Brattle, William 50
Brauer, Jerald C. 669n.23
Breck, Robert 57–8, 85, 391, 461
Breitenbach, William 601–2, 603n.12, 605n.19
Brekus, Catherine 469n.13, 474n.27
Briant, Lemuel 54, 58, 605
Brightman, Thomas 572, 670
Brinktrine, Johannes 218n.35
Broughton, Thomas 581n.3
Brown, Robert 168, 170, 383n.36, 646
Brumm, Ursula 117n.6
Buell, Samuel 436, 479, 602
Bulgakov, Sergei 728
Bultmann, Rudolf 273
Burgersdijk, Francis 40, 340
Burke, E.M. 266n.19
Burman, Franciscus 403
Burns, Sherard 527
Burton, Asa 601, 609
Bury, J.B. 225 n.4
Bush, Michael 244n.3, 245n.4, 247n.12
Bushnell, Horace 101n.43, 180n.58, 193n.1, 687–8
Butler, Jon 644
Butler, Joseph 152
Butterworth, Robert 218n.35

Caldwell, Robert xi, 199n.13, 244n.3, 255n.33, 256n.35, 257n.38, 259n.42, 261–3, 265, 274n.5
Calloway, Colin 556n.27
Calmet, Augustin 42, 171

Calvin, John
  on accommodation 123, 492
  on angels 273, 275, 278–9, 286
  on the atonement 250
  on baptism 483–5, 667
  on Christ's nature 258
  and contemporary
    Christianity 722, 725
  on conversion 270, 594n.36, 669
  on covenants 321
  on creation 245–6
  Edwards's similarity to 664–7
  on election 665, 668n.20
  on faith 369, 370n.44, 391
  on government 517
  on heaven 298, 303
  influence on Puritanism 43–4
  on justification 390–1, 399–400,
    403–4
  on knowledge of God by the
    heathen 595n.15
  on Lord's Supper 490–1, 493, 667
  and metaphysics 700, 722
  method of 6, 8
  on the millennium 669–70
  preaching of 494
  on regeneration 390
  on scripture 118–9, 123, 135–6, 159
  silence on missions 551
  on sin 352n.48, 356
  on the Trinity 198–9
  on virtue 547
  on the will 340, 342
Calvinism
  and covenants 247, 665
  Edwards's defense of 257n.38, 321–3
  Edwards's departure from 198–9,
    247, 585, 667–71, 674, 695–7,
    703–4
  Edwards's relationship to 321–4,
    663–4
  five points of 55n.38
  glory of God in 207, 212, 664
  hyper-Calvinism 678n.8
  and missions 670
  opposition to 85, 321–4
  predestination 85
  recasting of 26, 323–4
  on revival 676–80
Cambridge Platform 45–7, 331,
  461–2
Cambridge Platonism 43, 56n.41,
  103–4, 111, 413–4, 534, 582,
  596n.41
Campbell, George 614
Campbell, John 634
Campbell, Ted 262n.2
Canby, Henry Seidel 642
Carey, William 564, 678n.8
Cassian, John 118, 178
Cassirer, Ernst 153n.9
"Catalogue" (of Edwards's
  reading) 86, 181, 413, 581
Cennick, John 683
Chai, Jonathan 107n.3
Chalmers, Thomas 565, 633
Chamberlain, Ava xi, 65, 86, 150,
  164, 289n.43, 435n.23, 475,
  478n.35, 481n.46, 499n.14,
  697n.8
Chambers, Ephraim 581n.3
Chandler, Edward 170
Chaney, Charles 559
Channing, William Ellery 10n.12,
  649, 653–4
Charismatic Renewal 690
Charity and Its Fruits 7, 82, 100, 267,
  271, 295n.3, 315, 347n.29, 389,
  412, 454, 506, 528, 537, 597, 692,
  694, 697
Charles I, King 45
Chase, Mary Ellen 641n.12
Chauncy, Charles 20, 45n.13, 58, 237,
  313, 440–2, 475, 523, 605, 676

Cherry, Conrad xi, 8, 101, 168.n3, 180n.58, 322n.6, 323n.11, 365n.25, 370n.44, 370n.46, 371n.48, 372n.51, 374n.4, 381n.26, 575n.31, 645
Chevreau, Guy 647n.29, 691n.43, 692–3
Chief Hendrick (Mohawk chief) 589
Christ
  as agent of creation 245–7
  as agent of redemption 244–7
  ascension of 275, 279, 285, 287–9
  beauty of 249
  communicatio idiomatum 257
  emanations of 246
  four comings of 235–6
  as head of the angels 274–5, 283–4, 287–90
  hypostatic union 256–9
  incarnation of 244, 248, 251–2, 255–6
  kenotic theology of 258
  love of 246, 249–50, 252–3
  merits of 253, 255
  obedience of 391
  in Old Testament 118–20, 248–9
  ontic enlargement of 259–60
  resurrection of 160–1
  righteousness imputed 390
  satisfaction of 249–51
  sinlessness of 258
  suffering of 251
  three offices of 255
"Christian Cautions" 65n.26
Chubb, Thomas 38, 52, 54, 56n.40, 154, 253n.26, 254, 341, 393, 586
Chun, Chris 63n.24
church
  branches of 457–9
  as completeness of Christ 453–4
  Congregationalist view of 45–8, 459–63
  Edward's developing view of 451–4
  eternal purpose of 452–4
  future glory of 463–4
  persecution of 454–7
  visible vs. invisible 451
Cicero 297
circumincession (see perichoresis)
Clagett, William 262
Claghorn, George 77–8, 80n.9, 82n.18, 85n.31, 410, 419
Clap, Thomas 438–9
Clark, Randy 691
Clark, Stephen 186
Clarke, Samuel 49, 52, 201, 215, 264, 545
Clebsch, William 652
Clement of Alexandria 178, 582
Cocceius, Johannes 245n.5, 670
Cochran, Elizabeth Agnew 532n.17, 538
Coffey, David 705n.31
Coke, Thomas 564
Coleridge, Samuel Taylor 154, 156
Collingwood, R.G. 224n.2
Collins, Anthony 52–4, 170
Colman, Benjamin 50, 430, 466
Common Sense Philosophy 346, 614, 623, 625, 627–9, 631, 633n.22, 635, 687
combatibilism 37n.39
Conforti, Joseph xi, 564, 565n.53–54, 569, 604n.14, 604.n17, 605n.18, 606n.22, 607n.23, 609n.30, 623, 624n.69, 625–6, 627n.5, 630n.14, 631n.16, 633, 634n.26, 635n.30, 696n.3, 699n.3
Congar, Yves 727
Connecticut Tract Society 620
"Controversies Notebooks" 86
conversion
  Arminian view of 361–2, 387
  false instances of 384–5

God and humans active in 270
humiliation in 376, 381
and illumination 163, 381–2
immediacy of God in 377, 381–2, 386
infusion of grace in 381–2
and Lockean sensation 19, 383–4
means of grace in 374, 376–7
"morphology" of 79, 373–4, 385, 431
as new vision of God 377–8
preparationism 678–9
as a process 381, 386–7, 431–2, 592–3, 612, 678
Puritan emphasis on 373–4, 669
distinct from regeneration 382n.31, 386–8, 591–4, 611–2, 716
Spirit's work in 268–70, 373–4, 377, 382
Cooey, Paula 73
Cooper, Anthony Ashley (see Shaftesbury)
Corrigan, John 50n.25, 70n.48, 523n.33
Cotton, John 340, 572, 652, 670, 678
Council of Trent (see Trent, Council of)
covenant(s)
church 330–32
federal 324
Half-Way 23, 47, 84, 330–1, 478
with Israel 327
national 332–4, 525–6
with New England 332–4, 460, 525–6
relation to Old and New Testaments 327–30, 716
theology of 247–9, 324–7
types of 326–7, 593n.32, 665
Cowles, Henry 610
Cranmer, Thomas (Archbishop) 670

creation
Christ as agent of 245–7
continual 5–6, 109, 351, 398, 667, 673
as emanation 127, 213
for God's own glory/sake 208, 212–4
God as ultimate end in 212–3, 219–20
paradoxes of 210, 213–4
"Credulity, Superstition, and Fanaticism" 152
Cree, John 684–5
Crisp, Oliver xi, 22, 69n.44, 102n.3, 104, 335n.36, 342n.9, 354–5, 416n.22, 571n.17, 571n.19, 656, 658, 660–2, 706n.32
Crocco, Stephen xi, 644n.21–22, 652n.7, 713, 714n.12
Croswell, Andrew 20, 676
Crouter, Richard E, 155n.15
Cudworth, Ralph 41, 104, 413, 415, 582
Cutler, Timothy 57, 64n.19

Dabney, Robert Lewis 634
Dana, James 342n.9, 346, 353, 354n.52
Danaher, William xi, 199, 485, 533, 547, 646, 666
Daniel, Stephen 22, 104, 659–60, 662
Dante (see Aligheri, Dante)
Darwin, Charles 635, 636n.31, 656
Davenport, Frederick 689
Davenport, James 31, 313, 439, 676
Davidson, Bruce W. 542n.42, 569n.12
Davidson, Edward 601n.3
Davidson, James 49n.21
Davies, Brian 399n.32
Davies, Ronald E. 549n.2, 550n.5
Davis, Thomas 117n.6

Day, Richard Ellsworth 63n.18
Dayton, Donald 689n.39
Dean, William 655–6
DeArteaga, William 691n.43
Defoe, Daniel 581
"Degrees of Glory" 76n.78, 303
deism
  Edwards's response to 26, 30, 38, 150, 153–4, 253–6, 393
  influence in America 625
  opposition to hell 571
  opposition to miracles 54
  opposition to revealed religion 149, 153, 580–1
  theology of 52–5
  varieties of 52–5
DeJong, Peter 321n.2, 642
Delattre, Roland 8, 93, 102n.3, 104, 528n.1, 533, 536, 646
Delbanco, Andrew 653
Deloit, Charles 504
DeLubac, Henri 117, 118n.7, 178n.52, 179n.53
Demos, John 644
Descartes, René 25, 61, 107, 655
Development
  Experiential-Empirical Turn 78–80
  Ethical-Rigorist Turn 80–3
  Ecclesial-Sacramental Turn 84
  Calvinistic-Controversial Turn 85–6
  Cultural-Historical Turn 86–8, 181
Devil (see Satan)
Dewey, John 645, 649–651, 655–6
DeWitt, John 638
Diary 25, 26, 61, 63, 64, 79, 81, 431, 721
Dickinson, Emily 273
Dickinson, Jonathan 679
Diderot, Denis 583
Discourse on the Trinity 4, 97, 196, 198, 202, 205, 264, 412

Distinguishing Marks 31, 319, 424, 426, 438–9, 676, 693
"Divine and Supernatural Light" 19, 24, 28, 81, 137, 169, 266, 301n.19, 318–9, 379, 382, 416, 430, 641, 711
divinization 19, 200, 357, 372, 410, 412–3, 533, 706–7, 721–2
Dockrill, D. W. 414–6
Dodwell, Henry 154
Donne, John 273, 567
Donnelly, John Patrick 42n.6
Donnelly, Philip J. 218n.35, 220–1
Dordt, Synod of 55, 678, 679n.9
Dowd, Gregory Evans 554n.16
Droge, Arthur 581n.4
Dulles, Avery 153n.10
Dummer, Jeremiah 51
"The Duty of Self-Examination" 65
Dwight, Sereno 83n.22, 167, 308n.33, 436n.26, 437n.27, 477n.33, 626, 693n.49
Dwight, Timothy 507, 601–3, 607, 613–4, 619–20
Dyche, Thomas 581n.3

Earthquakes, Earthquake Revival (of 1727) 375, 429, 499
Eastern Orthodoxy 410, 412, 416n.22, 418–9, 458, 695, 705–8, 728
ecumenism 670, 722
Edwards, Esther Stoddard 23
Edwards, John 494
Edwards, Jonathan (Jr) 85, 149, 214, 601, 603, 607, 611–6, 620–2
Edwards, Rem 207n.3
Edwards, Sarah (Pierpont) 83, 317, 436, 688, 693
Edwards, Timothy 23–4, 48, 61, 426, 429
Edwards, Tryon 389

Eliot, John 561
Elliot, Jim 564
Ellison, Julie 83n.22
Elwood, Douglas 93, 102n.3, 104, 106, 668
Emerson, Martin 692n.44
Emerson, Ralph Waldo 72, 318, 497, 635, 638, 642–3, 649–54
Emmons, Nathanael 21, 601, 607–9, 609–10n.32, 611–2, 614n.46, 619, 622–3 631n.17, 632, 633n.22, 634n.28
empiricism 43, 655–6
End of Creation 4, 5, 7, 11, 59, 66, 69, 97, 106, 112, 166–7, 169, 184, 207–23, 242, 246, 300, 302, 307, 413n.10, 414, 419, 421–2, 453–4, 566, 658, 662, 664, 705, 711, 713
English Civil War 215
Enlightenment, the
  view of human nature 37
  and religion 41–2
  ethics of 533–4
  and experience 161–2
  Edwards's appropriation of 164
  view of God 209–14
enthusiasm (religious concept) 67, 152, 162n.57, 164, 262n.2, 320, 410, 432, 436, 440, 682–7, 690–4
Erskine, John 462, 613
eschatology
  antichrist 231–2, 236, 249, 572
  emphasis on 566, 579
  and the last judgment 577–8
  marriage supper of the lamb 222, 491–2
  millennium 34, 573–7
  and New Heaven 578–9
  and revival 617–8
ethics
  benevolism 533–4

calculus of value in 112
character ethics 710
Edwards's contemporary relevance 709–11
Edwards's distinctives 547–8
Enlightenment view of 534, 538, 547
and moral philosophy 215–7
ontological basis for 211, 529–32
principle of proportionate regard 210–2
rational dimension of 545–6
and self-love 541–4
Trinitarian dimensions of 528
and the unregenerate 541
Eucher 178
Eusebius 276, 582
evil (see theodicy)
excellence
  beauty of 98
  of Christ 378
  degrees of 112, 211, 546
  of God 38, 96, 360, 535
  God's love for 421
  and humility 281
  of Lucifer 281–2
  partaking of 411–2
  perception and knowledge of 378, 380, 611, 627–8
  of the saints 302
  and virtue 546
exegesis
  historical criticism 170–1
  holistic approach to 172–5
  literal and non-literal 175–80
  medieval approach to 176–7
  and the necessity of the Holy Spirit 173
  necessity of illumination 173, 180
  New Divinity approach to 180
  similarity to Aquinas 179
  typological approach to 175–6

faith
  as disposition 367–9, 404, 411
  foci of 366–7
  and justification 391, 392–6
  and love 368–70
  sensory dimensions of 367–8
  and works 370–1
Faithful Narrative 29, 79–80, 391, 424, 430, 432, 433, 446, 474–5, 479, 651, 687, 688
"Farewell Sermon" 35, 480, 496, 510–1
Farley, Edward 712
Farley, Michael 687n.33
Farrar, Frederic 177n.44
federal theology 248, 324, 338
Fenelon, Francois 83
Fichte, Johann Gottlieb 113
Ficino, Marsilio 582
Fiering, Norman 40, 41n.2, 51n.26, 54n.35, 59, 95, 103–4, 164, 216, 344n.14, 360n.10, 441n.37, 522n.27, 532n.15, 536, 545, 567, 583n.8, 645–6, 649, 657
"The Final Judgment" 62n.9
Finke, Roger 684n.25
Finney, Charles 376, 377n.12, 446n.53, 451, 601, 610–1, 624, 677–8, 680, 685–6
Fish, Henry 688
Fisher, George 193n.1, 666
Fitzmier, John 607n.25–26, 614n.43–44, 619
Flavel, John 61, 128
Florovsky, George 72
"The Folly of Looking Back in Fleeing out of Sodom" 62n.9
Forbes Library (Northampton, Massachusetts) xi, 13, 681
Ford, David 714n.13
forgive, forgiveness 54, 65, 135, 142, 157, 172, 250, 255, 290–1, 318, 342, 393, 403, 470–1, 489, 540, 562, 571, 583, 591, 616–7
Formula of Concord 403
Foster, Frank Hugh 602–3, 624, 635,
Foucault, Michel 659
Foxe, John 572
Francke, August Hermann 457
Franklin, Benjamin 437, 51–3, 54n.33, 596n.42, 681n.16, 715
Frazier, Patrick 560n.40
Freedom of the Wil 6, 15, 21, 36, 55n.38, 56, 58, 85–6, 135, 158, 216, 314, 321, 323, 338, 340–2, 344, 346, 354n52, 356, 397, 559, 603, 608, 622, 626n.3, 634–635, 638–9, 642, 644n.22, 658, 663, 666, 696, 715
Frei, Hans 174, 175n.34, 713, 714n.13
Fulgentius of Ruspe 277
Fuller, Andrew 633, 678n.8
Fuller, Margaret 653

Gäbel, Georg 276n.9
Gale, Theophilus 155, 161, 171, 582, 592n.30
Gallagher, Edward 509n.29
Gardiner, H.N. 103
Gaustad, Edwin 41
Gay, Ebenezer 58
Gay, Peter 226, 645
Gelpi, Donald 697, 704
generosity (see liberality)
German, James 516n.10
Gerrish, Brian 151, 666
Gerstner, John 151n.5, 157, 251, 351n.41, 353, 494n.1, 507, 569, 569.11, 626n.4, 647, 665.n7, 668, 679
Gibbon, Edward 224, 243
Gilbert, Greg 585n.13
Giles of Rome 298
Gillespie, Thomas 167, 434
Gillies, John 447, 504

Gilpin, W. Clark xii, 68
Ginsburg, Morris 225n.4
giving (see liberality)
God
  anger or wrath of 31, 62, 127, 177, 212, 251, 253, 271, 315, 332–4, 338, 349, 368, 384, 405, 427, 437, 496–7, 508–9, 518, 532n.17, 553n.15, 562, 568, 586, 578, 590, 644n.22, 647n.29, 668n.19
  as "Being in general" 105, 110, 158, 200, 211, 513, 532, 535, 537, 699, 704, 718
  communication of 4–5, 7, 18, 116, 124, 130–1, 213, 220, 244, 260, 422–3, 453, 466, 491, 653, 658, 670, 712
  and creaturely participation 5, 7, 528–9, 532–3, 535, 540–1, 545
  as disposition 5, 529
  as Enlightenment gentleman 217
  as Epicure 209
  ethicized by Edwards 209
  glory as humanity's happiness 166, 212, 302
  love of 5, 61, 69n.46, 79n.7, 83, 97, 194–5, 200, 208, 216, 263–4, 266, 272, 285, 295, 301, 303n.25, 307, 319, 337, 359–61, 382, 393, 405, 420–1, 436, 469, 532–3, 536–7, 539–42, 544, 546, 568, 682, 693, 695, 701, 704–5, 711
  moral government of 250
  ontic enlargement of 259–1, 529
  plurality in 198, 202
  self-regard of 217, 219, 421
  theocentricism 6, 8, 22, 104, 106, 113–4, 297–9, 302, 657, 665, 709, 713–4
  transcendence and immanence of 105, 221, 414, 416, 641, 687, 699, 701
"God Glorified in Man's Dependence 28, 57, 71, 85, 603, 701
Goen, C.C. 227, 229, 236n.63, 322n.8, 425n.2, 525n.40, 575
glorification 221–3
Goodwin, Gerald 56n.42
Goodwin, John 61
Goodwin, Thomas 369n.37, 568n.9
Gordon, A.J. 690
grace
  Arminian view of 361–2
  common vs. special 357–9, 695
  created vs. uncreated 266–7, 361, 398, 696
  as disposition 361, 366
  efficacious vs. irresistible 362–3
  and Holy Spirit 361–5
  infusion of 19, 381–2, 389, 583
  and virtue 376, 381
Graham, Billy 451, 680
Graham, William 627
Great Awakening (see revival)
Greeley, Andrew 699
Gregory of Nazianzus 259, 707
Gregory of Nyssa 222, 276, 413n.10, 707
Gregory Palamas 69n.44, 412n.8, 416–8, 706
Gregory the Great 276–7
Greven, Philip 474n.27
Greville, Robert 414
Griffin, Edward 45n.13, 58n.49, 604
Grigg, John A 554n.16
Grotius, Hugo 161, 583, 614, 616
Guelzo, Allen xi, 8n.9, 340–1, 344, 346n.23, 428n.5, 438n.30, 439, 444, 475n.29, 579n.47, 602n.8, 603, 604n.13, 607n.24, 608, 609n.29, 609n.31, 610n.33, 611n.35–36, 612n.37–38, 615n.49, 619n.58, 620, 622, 630n.14, 631n.15, 631n.19, 635n.31, 693

Gura, Philip xi, 429n.8, 643
Gustafson, James 713
Guyon, Madame 83
Guyse, John 430, 446

Hall, David 57n.46, 330–1, 462n.37
Hall, Joseph 307, 679n.9
Hall, Richard 657n.19
Hallywell, Henry 415
Hambricke-Stowe, Charles 61n.6
Hamilton, William 625
Hanegraaff, Hank 647n.29, 691n.43, 692
Harmony of the Old and New Testaments 150, 164, 167, 168n.3, 182n.4
Haroutunian, Joseph 60, 64n.23, 602, 640, 641n.13, 664n.4, 713
Harris, Howell 458
Hart, D. G. (Darryl G.) 377n.13, 553n.14, 634n.27, 635n.31, 669n.22, 715n.16
Hart, William 606
Harvard College (or University) 23, 28, 49–51, 56n.41, 80, 85, 215, 441n.37, 466, 482, 494, 583n.8, 604, 630, 641–2, 650, 653, 723
Haskins, Lee 517n.12
Hastings, W. Ross xi, 258, 263n.4
Hatheway, Deborah 61, 65–6
Hauerwas, Stanley 710, 714n.13
Hawley, Elisha 81, 472
Hawley, Gideon 560, 564
Hawley, Joseph 29, 80, 432, 442–3, 478
Hawthorne, Nathaniel 650
Haykin, Michael 691n.43, 692
Hazard, Paul 52n.29, 153n.10
heaven
    bodily function in 297
    communication in 296, 298, 305
    degrees of glory in 307
    history of 296–9
    love among saints in 302–3
    as place of beauty 300
    as progressive state 66, 76, 282, 296–6, 306
    reunion of saints in 297
    as spatial state 296
    theocentric aspect 297
    as ultimate nation of the church 524
    vision of God in 298
"Heaven is a World of Love" 7, 76n.78, 295n.3, 299n.13, 511–2
Heereboord, Adrian 40
Hegel, G.W.F. (Georg Wilhelm Friedrich) 113, 165n.67
Heidegger, Johann 338, 403
Heidegger, Martin 207n.4
Heidelberg Catechism 377
Heimert, Alan 49n.21, 54n.34, 93, 227, 233n.51, 332n.30, 444, 482n.1, 523n.33, 575n.31, 618
hell
    aesthetic fittingness of 570
    and annihilation 571, 715
    eternity of 569
    images of 567–8
    justice of 569
    location of 568
    preaching of 567
    as presence of God 568
    Puritan understanding of 568n.10, 570
Heller, Rebecca xii
Helm, Paul 69n.44, 102n.3, 194n.2, 316, 318, 322n.4, 342n.9, 355n.59, 416n.22, 571n.17, 571n.19, 645, 660n.26, 666, 706n.32
Hemmenway, Moses 606
Hendry, George S. 209n.7

Heppe, Heinrich 212n.16, 324, 338n.46, 386n.42, 403n.46, 489n.26, 492n.32
Herbert, Edward (Lord Herbert of Cherbury) 580
Herring, Thomas 458
Hick, John 241
Hilary of Poitiers 218
Hindmarsh, Bruce 682n.18
Hinlicky, Paul xii
history
  Antichrist's activity in 231
  biblical interpretation of 243
  Christocentric reading of 243
  conflict in 231–4
  "contrast" and "preparation" motif in 233–5
  as cyclic and linear 223–5
  God's activity in 230
  God's perspective of 242
  eschatological view of 225, 227, 236
  interpretations of Edwards's view 232
  as method 30, 183, 184–6, 714
  "proportion" in 241
  and providence 18
  secular view of 224
  as "stepwise" progression 233
  "sunrise" analogy of 231, 234
  typological interpretation of 243
  unity of 228
  as "universal chronical" 225, 628n.10,
  Whig view of 51
History of the Work of Redemption 118, 189–90, 225, 228n.22, 244–5, 347n.29, 434, 499, 595, 665, 713, 727
Hoadly, Benjamin 52
Hobbes, Thomas 25, 41, 54, 107–8, 154, 215, 515

Hodge, Charles 12, 109, 353–5, 377, 410, 607, 627–31, 634, 640, 668–70, 676, 686, 687n.30, 692, 702n.25, 723
Hoffman, Gerhard 227n.13, 228
Hofstadter, Richard 680n.13
Hogarth, William 152
Holbrook, Clyde 56n.40, 353, 646
Holifield, E. Brooks xi, 465n.1, 474n.26, 480n.43, 481n.47, 482n.1, 487n.19–20, 493n.35, 614n.45, 626n.4, 628n.7, 633n.24–25, 636n.30–31, 720n.2
holiness 19, 22, 24–5, 33, 61, 63, 66, 69, 71, 77, 82, 93, 95–6, 99, 121, 136, 140, 195, 256–7, 265, 271, 284, 286, 291, 295–6, 306, 316, 325, 329–30, 337, 339, 341, 357, 378, 384, 390, 400, 405, 406, 410n.1, 412, 418, 421, 433, 446, 453, 464, 477, 491, 500, 512, 533–6, 538–9, 546–7, 557–8, 570, 576, 587, 605, 610, 628, 665, 683, 690, 702
Hollis, Isaac 556
Hollis, Thomas 51
Holmes, Oliver Wendell 21, 193n.1, 623, 636
Holmes, Stephen 104, 245, 252, 567n.4, 570n.16
Holy Spirit
  activating natural faculties 266
  as part of atonement 263–4
  as bond between Father and Son 264–5
  as bond between Christ and believer 256
  conversion through 268–71
  Edwards's personal experience of 262–3
  as fellowship 195
  gifts of 80, 138, 153, 271n.42, 272, 439, 486, 511, 537, 576, 675, 690–4, 725

Holy Spirit (*continued*)
   immediate presence of 265–7
   as love 195, 263
   praying for 272
   procession of 264, 707, 721
   in Puritanism 268
   in regenerate persons 272, 421, 673
   sanctification through 272
   sinning against 268–9
   "superiority of" 200
   tasks of 195
   typology of 271
   as "vital principle" 266
Hooker, Richard 413n.12
Hooker, Thomas 61, 678
Hoopes, James 609n.29
Hopkins, Samuel 10n.12, 21, 68, 168, 169n.6, 210, 464, 465n.1, 487, 505, 519, 526, 601–3, 606, 609, 618, 619, 621, 653
Howard, David M. 619n.59
Humble Attempt 34, 61, 75, 170, 176, 272, 424, 425, 444, 452, 454, 551, 565, 572–3, 575, 617, 679, 684
Hume, David 43, 154, 162, 226, 609, 614, 625, 656
Humphrey, Heman 679
Hunsinger, George 389n.2, 400n.37, 673n.33
Husband, Paul 478n.37
Hutcheson, Francis 49, 54, 165, 215–6, 522–3, 534, 546, 653
Hutchinson, Abigail 431
Hutchinson, Anne 319, 373, 652, 678
Hutchison, William 563n.50

Images or Shadows 125n.37, 641n.13, 666
Imagination, Religious Role of 20, 28, 44, 51, 66, 123, 137, 139, 176, 316, 319–20, 371, 384, 424, 635, 675, 684–5, 699, 717

immortal, immortality 52–3, 159, 415n.19, 416n.21, 571, 658
"Importance and Advantage of Divine Truth" 173
"Importunate Prayer for Millennial Glory" 75n.75
Indians (see Mahican and Mohawk Indians, Native Americans)
infralapsarianism 335, 669
Irenaeus 218, 219n.36, 276, 277n.11, 296
Isaac, Rhys 444

Jackson, Thomas (17th cent.) 414
Jackson, Thomas (19th cent.) 446n.52, 681n.16
James, William 79, 80, 432n.15, 639, 649–652, 654–6, 688, 689n.37
Jang, Kyoung-Chul 209, 222n.51
Jauhiainen, Peter Dan 602n.7
Jefferson, Thomas 52
Jeffreys, Thomas 46
Jenkins, Philip 724
Jenson, Robert 7, 115, 201, 244n.3, 257, 392n.9, 403n.45, 661, 727n.7
Jerome 178
Jesus Movement 690
John of Damascus 198, 259, 276
John Paul II (Pope) 727
Johnson, Byron xii
Johnson, David 72n.61
Johnson, Edward 49n.21
Johnson, Samuel 583n.8
Johnson, Thomas 40, 642
Jones, Gregory 714n.13
Jones, Jeremiah 171
Jowett, Benjamin 177n.44
Joyce, G.C. 153n.10
Judson, Adoniram 564
Jung, Carl Gustav 273

Index 743

justice 36, 54, 159, 204–5, 250–1, 253, 286, 335, 337, 350–2, 368, 374–5, 394, 399, 487, 510, 514–8, 522, 525, 532n.17, 541, 543, 545, 560, 569–70, 577, 581–2, 585, 598, 615, 622, 639, 666, 670, 702n.25, 709, 711, 714, 726
justification
   Arminian view of 391
   dependent on sanctification 395–6, 401
   distinguished from sanctification 390–1
   faith as instrument of 391, 392–3
   final 396
   forensic conception of 19, 394–5, 401, 403–4, 623–4, 627, 696
   and human guilt 394
   perseverance as condition of 81, 432–3
   and the Reformation 396–404
   and works 396, 695–6
Justification by Faith Alone 6, 29, 392, 603
Juvenal 583

Kallay, Katalin 93, 98
Kant, Immanuel 69n.46, 113, 161, 403, 625, 639, 649
Keck, David 275n.7
Kellogg, Martin 560
Kelsey, David xii, 713
Kidd, Thomas 428n.5
Kierkegaard, Soren 157
Kimnach, Wilson xi–xii, 82, 165, 295, 80n.41, 495, 563n.48, 644
Kinerk, E. Edward 699n.13
King, Henry Churchill 695
Kirk, Kenneth 300n.17
Kling, David xi, 40n.1, 474n.27, 478n.35, 516n.10, 527n.46, 559n.36, 584n.52, 633n.23, 682n.17–18

Knight, Janice 122n.24, 129n.49, 535
Knox, Ronald 262n.2
Kostopoulos, Zachary xi
Kristeva, Julia 659
Kuklick, Bruce 58n.47, 102, 626n.4, 628n.10, 632, 633n.22, 635n.29–31, 645, 649–51, 654n.12, 657
Kvanvig, Jonathan 571n.17

Lactantius 582
Lane, Belden 22, 711–2, 712n.8
Lang, Amy Schrager 442n.40
Lang, Bernhard 296n.6, 297, 298n.12, 299n.113, 304n.26, 307n.32
l'art pour l'art 94
Laud, William 45
Laurence, David 164n.63
Leach, Douglas Edward 520n.20
LeClerc, Jean 41, 171
Lee, Matthew T. 82n.19, 83n.22
Lee, Sang xi, 7, 8n.9, 97, 104, 200, 262n.1, 263n.4, 266, 267n.20, 25, 270, 360n.10, 361n.13, 392n.9, 398n.29, 579n.47, 609n.32, 660–1, 706, 712n.10
Leibniz, Gottfried Wilhelm 104, 111, 581n.4
Leith, John 391, 664, 667
LeMahieu, D.L. 154n.13
Lesser, M.X. xi, 634n.28, 638n.5, 645n.25
Lessius, Leonardus 218, 220–1
Leuba, James 74, 688
Leverett, John 50
Lewalski, Barbara 117n.6
Lewis, C.S. 69, 159, 239n.72, 303n.25
Lewis, Paul 710
liberal, liberalism, liberal theology 12, 22, 41, 49–50, 52n.29, 57–8, 94, 153n.10, 156, 459, 497, 517, 523, 570, 602, 604–5, 634n.28, 642–3, 650, 653, 688, 713–4, 723–4, 726

liberality, generosity, or giving 36,
    347, 473, 523, 539, 541, 545, 555,
    569, 653, 714
Library of Congress 520, 589, 621
The Life of David Brainerd 82, 320, 549
Lindbeck, George 79n.8, 713
Lippy, Charles 425n.2
Little Awakening (*see revival*)
"Living Peaceably with One
    Another" 74n.70
Livingstone, David 564
Lloyd-Jones, D. Martin 647, 675
Locke, John
    Edwards's appropriation of 26,
        103, 323, 345n17, 348, 367, 383–4,
        641, 645, 666
    Edwards's departure from 110
    contrasted with 108
    philosophy of 43, 49
    psychology of 26
    on reason 142
    innate ideas opposed by 151, 162
    Edwards's revision of 163
    moral philosophy of 215
Locke, Louis Glenn 215n.26
Logan, Samuel 389n.2
Lombard, Peter 14, 266–7, 361, 696
London Missionary Society 565
Lord's Supper
    controversy over 24, 47–8, 84, 331
    importance of 482
    a marriage supper of the
        Lamb 491–2
    as memorial 489
    presence of Christ at 490–1, 667
    as seal of covenant 488
Lossky, Vladimir 222n.52, 418n.26
love
    before the fall 541
    to being in general 532
    "disinterested" 83, 523, 592, 605,
        619, 622, 634, 638, 653, 682
    kinds of 537
    as participation 528–9, 532–3, 535
    within the Trinity 547
    and virtue 537–41, 694
Lovejoy, Arthur O. 209n.9
Lovelace, Richard 443n.42, 675
Lowance, Mason 117n.6, 129n.48–49,
    659n.24
Löwith, Karl 224n.3
Lowman, Moses 227, 456, 572, 670
Loyola, Ignatius 697–8
Lucas, Sean Michael 377n.13, 553n.14,
    634n.27, 669n.22, 715n.16
Lucifer (see Satan)
Luther, Martin
    on angels 273
    and contemporary Christianity 725
    distrust of reason 157
    on happiness 69n.46
    on heaven 297n.8, 298, 303
    on justification 399–403,
        690, 717
    on the Lord's Supper 491
    and metaphysics 104, 700, 722
    on necessity 342, 606
    on repentance 63n.13
    on salvation 389
    on Scripture 118, 126, 177–8
    on tradition 146
Lyon, Mary 633–4

MacArthur, John 693n.47
Maclear, James 129n.49
Madsen, William 118n.9
Mahican and Mohawk Indians 35,
    527, 553n.14, 555n.23, 556n.27,
    560–1, 563n.48, 589
Malebranche, Nicholas 41, 104, 111,
    704
Mandeville, Bernard 54
Mannermaa, Tuomo 403
Mantzaridis, Georgios 416n.22

Manuel, Frank 153n.10
Maritain, Jacques 220
Marsden, George xi–xii, 23n.1, 26n.11, 27n.13, 33n.30, 35n.37, 39n.45, 48n.19, 57n.43, 57n.46, 60, 64n.19, 72–3, 77, 80–3, 85–6, 147n.60, 151, 208, 322n.4, 425n.1–2, 428n.5, 431n.11, 441, 444, 466n.4, 474–76, 479–80, 506–7, 509, 526n.45, 553n.14, 645, 648, 664n.4, 696, 711, 714–5, 719n.1
Marshall, Bruce 54n.37
Martin, Jeffrey xii
Martyn, Henry 564
Martyr, Justin 582
Massachusetts Missionary Society 619
Massachusetts Proposal, The 461
Mastricht, Petrus van 42, 199n.13, 218, 245n.5, 323, 340, 352n.48, 361, 381, 386, 404, 533n.19, 572n.23, 597n.44, 663–4, 667, 670
Mather, Cotton 41, 45, 50–1, 61, 129, 225, 264, 428, 460, 489, 494, 551, 561n.44
Mather, Increase 48, 49n.21, 61, 299, 484n.10, 489
Mather, Moses 606, 677n.5
Mather, Samuel 129
Mattke, Robert 445n.49
May, Henry F. 49, 215
Maycock, Joseph 445n.49
Mayhew, Jonathan 523, 603, 605
McCann, Hugh 342n.9, 346n.25
McClymond, Michael 69n.44, 70n.48, 82n.16, 82n.19, 83n.22, 99n.32, 102n.3, 104n.8, 110n.28, 150–151n.5, 168n.3, 184n.9, 185n.10, 209n.7, 284n.30, 371n.36, 416n.22, 425n.2–3, 427n.4, 428n.5, 438n.30, 439n.34, 440n.35, 444n.45, 446n.51, 447n.54, 597n.44, 611n.35, 646–47, 658n.20, 661, 677n.6, 678n.8, 684n.24, 684n.26, 685n.27, 687n.33, 689n.38, 706n.32, 724n.5
McCormack, Bruce 398–400, 403n.45, 660n.26
McCormack, Elissa xi
McCulloch, William 238n.68
McDannell, Colleen 296n.6, 297, 298n.12, 299n.113, 304n.26, 307n.32
McDermott, Gerald 22, 34n.35, 42n.5, 52n.28, 54n.36, 86, 93n.6, 97n.24, 102–103n.3, 130n.1, 140n.30, 144n.45, 150n.5, 157n.23, 172n.23, 189n.19, 231n.41, 232n.50, 242n.79, 244n.1, 253n.26, 333n.31, 476n.30, 497n.9, 501n.17, 513n.2, 517n.14, 525n.41, 553n.13, 572–73n.23, 580n.1, 581n.2, 595n.39, 633n.24, 646–47, 670n.25, 712n.10, 716n.17–18
McDermott, Scott xi
McDonald, H.D. 670n.26
McGiffert, Arthur 207n.3, 208, 640
McGinn, Bernard 231n.41, 243n.81
McGrath, Alister 390n.3, 395n.17, 399n.31, 401, 402n.41&43
McHale, Gary 691n.43, 692
M'Cheyne, Robert 564
McKenny, Gerald 714n.12
McLachlan, H. John 52n.27
McLoughlin, William 677n.6–7
McNeill, John 483n.5, 664n.4–5, 671n.29
McPherson, Aimee 680
Mead, Sidney 513, 644
Mede, Joseph 572

Melanchthon, Philipp 14, 297n.8
Melville, Herman 650
"Men Naturally God's
    Enemies" 62n.9
Mesmer, Franz 692
metaphysics
    atomism 108
    beauty of God in 115
    being or existence of God in 110-2
    calculus of value in 112
    causality 109
    combined with theology 102, 115
    continual (re)creation 6, 17, 398,
        668, 673-4
    dispositional ontology 5, 530, 661
    idealism 25, 112-14, 398
    immaterialism 114-5
    interpretations of 103-4
    materialism 107
    occasionalism 109, 354-5,
        509-10n.30
    ontological argument 111
    pantheism 109, 207, 628, 668,
        724
    substantialism 661
    theocentricism 106, 113-4
Meyendorff, John 416n.22
Miles, Lion 561n.42
millennium
    and America 234-5, 237-8, 552-3,
        574-5, 619
    Christ's presence in 576
    gradual inauguration of 236, 617
    hastened through prayer 618
    predicted 573
    prosperity during 576
    society in 575-6
    work preceding 552-3, 571-4
Miller, Perry 8, 20, 22, 44n.12,
    49n.21, 51n.26, 54n.34, 57, 72,
    77, 85, 102-4, 125n.37, 127n.42
    166, 190, 208, 216, 226, 228,
    233n.51, 236n.63, 247-8, 317,
    321-2, 338, 437, 478, 603, 639,
    641-5, 652-3
Mills, Samuel 564
Milton, John 99, 273, 284n.30,
The Mind 74, 86, 96-8, 105-6, 112,
    165, 241, 421, 623, 644, 700
ministry
    and discipline 472-3
    Edwards's dismissal from 477-9
    Edwards's influences on 466
    Edwards's success or failure
        at 479-81
    In New York 25
    in Northampton 474-7
    and prayer 470
    tasks of 669-74
    theology of 466-8
Minkema, Kenneth xi, 26n.10,
    27n.16, 48n.19, 82n.16, 138n.25,
    168, 170, 182, 229n.25, 264,
    284n.30, 425n.2, 430n.9, 432-6,
    447, 459n.28, 477n.33, 479,
    487n.20, 500, 507, 509-10n.30,
    526n.45, 557n.33, 563n.48,
    637n.1, 643n.20, 644n.22, 647-8,
    693, 711n.7
Mirandola, Pico Della 582
Miscellanies 6, 10-2, 25, 34, 44n.11,
    56, 71, 77, 81, 86-8, 93, 135, 141,
    149-50, 154-5, 158, 161, 170-1,
    181, 183, 186, 188-9, 193, 205,
    208, 210, 213, 234-5, 241, 253-4,
    274-6, 280, 293, 295, 325, 388,
    393, 412, 419, 443, 586, 594n.34,
    597, 613, 623, 647, 659, 666,
    703n.27, 721
Misrepresentations Corrected 84, 454
Missionary Society of
    Connecticut 620
Missionary Society of Rhode
    Island 619

missions
   and Calvinism 670
   Edwards's influence on 564–5
   laity's role in 551
   purpose of 549–50
   and revivals 550–2
Mitchell, Louis 93, 101n.42
Mohawk and Mohican Indians (see Mahican and Mohawk Indians, Native Americans)
Moltmann, Jürgen 579n.49
Montgomery, Carrie Judd 690
Moody, Dwight 680
Moody, Josh 383–4
More, Henry 107, 111, 414–15, 534, 596n.41
Morgan, Christopher William 715
Morgan, Edmund 47n.17, 373n.1, 431, 644
Morimoto, Anri 267n.21, 361–2, 389, 392n.7, 411, 696, 722
Morris, William 40, 383, 646
Morrison, Robert 564
Mount (Mt.) Holyoke Seminary 634
Muir, John 72
Muller, Richard 42n.6, 198n.9, 246n.7, 585n.15, 671
Murray, Andrew 564
Murray, John 616
Murray, Iain 27n.15, 48n.19, 438n.30, 465n.2, 647, 677n.6
Murrin, John 49n.22, 215

"Narrative of Communion Controversy" 84, 462
narrative theology 147, 713–4, 727
Native Americans
   converts of Brainerd 554
   disposition of 555–7
   Edwards's affection toward 564–5
   Edwards's defense of 560–61
   Protestant attitudes toward 562
   revival among 549
   sermons delivered to 557–9
   and slavery 527
"Natural Men in a Dreadful Condition" 62n.9
The Nature of True Virtue 16, 38–9, 54, 59, 106, 112, 122, 166, 208, 210–1, 216n.29, 241, 346–7, 360n.10, 445n.50, 453, 513–4, 522n.28, 528, 533, 535–7, 630, 634, 640, 651, 666, 697n.7, 709n.1, 710–1
Navone, John 712
Needham, Nick 691n.43
Neele, Adriaan xi, 42, 199n.13, 245n.5
Neo-Orthodoxy 22, 105, 641
Neoplatonism 413–6, 706
Nettleton, Asahel 679
Nevin, John Williamson 720
New Divinity
   access to Edwards's writings 621–2
   apologetics of 613–4
   on the atonement 614–7
   on conversion 611–2
   core principles of 605
   eschatology of 618–20
   "exercisers" vs. "tasters" 609–10
   formation of 601–4
   and missions 619
   opponents of 605–8
   opposition to slavery 621
   pure love 18
   on the will 608–11
New England
   eschatology of 47–8
   as "city on a hill" 460
   churches of 495
   Congregationalism 45–7
   cultural shifts of 48–50
   and universalism 57–8, 616–7
"New Lights" (*see revival*)

Newey, Edmund 413n.12
Newman, John Henry 9, 172n.23, 727
Newton, Issac 26, 41, 43, 49, 52, 107, 121, 151, 165, 186–7, 509, 530
Nichols, Stephen 377n.13, 553n.14, 634n.27, 635n.31, 669n.22, 715n.16
Niebuhr, H. Richard 8n.9, 22, 190, 227, 515, 640, 644, 709, 713–4
Niebuhr, Richard R. 102n.3, 644, 672
Niesel, Wilhelm 493n.36
Niles, Samuel 58
Nisbet, Robert 225n.4
Noll, Mark xi–xii, 428n.5, 445n.48, 602n.5, 606n.21, 627n.6, 629–30, 632n.20, 633n.22–23, 635n.29, 644, 677n.5, 680, 686, 725
Norris, John 104, 209
Northampton, Massachusetts
 artist's rendering of 681
 communion controversy 47, 84
 covenant of 1742 476–7, 487
 Edwards's pastorate of 27–9, 474–7
 Edwards dismissal from 35, 477–9
 "Little Awakening" 29–30, 430–34
Norton, John 61
Notes on the Apocalypse 167, 176, 232n.48, 573
Notes on the Scriptures 34, 117, 126, 167, 173n.30, 584
Numenius of Apamea 582
Nuttall, Geoffrey 129n.49, 262
Nygren, Anders 69n.46, 104n.7
Nystrom, Carolyn 725n.6

Oates, Whitney 9
O'Brien, Susan 428n.5, 447
O'Donovan, Oliver 211n.14
"Old Lights" (*see revival*)

Olevianus, Kaspar 245n.5
Oliphint, Scott 150–151n.5
Oliver, Andrew 556
Olson, Roger 55n.39
Onuf, Peter 439n.34
open theism 715n.16
Origen 118, 178, 277–8, 582, 707
Original Sin 6, 15, 19, 37, 56, 85–6, 106, 109, 167, 170, 216, 314, 323, 339, 346–7, 349n.34, 351–6, 377, 388n.46, 398, 563, 583–4n.10, 622, 627, 634, 641, 653, 668, 695, 696, 723
Orr, John 153n.10
Osborn, Sarah 601
Osgood, Herbert 443
"Our Countrymen in Chains" 621
Ovid 17, 583
Owen, John 61, 262, 271, 615

Packer, J.I. 425n.2, 443
Pailin, David 598n.46
Paine, Thomas 52, 56n.41
Paley, William 154, 160
Pannenberg, Wolfhart 579n.49
Park, Edwards Amasa 193n.1, 601–2, 607, 624, 630, 634n.28, 666
Parkes, Henry Bamford 638
Parkman, Ebenezer 481n.47
Parmenides 202
Parrington, Vernon 443, 602n.5, 637, 643
Pascal, Blaise 150n.3, 157, 638
Patrides, C.A. 185, 225, 413n.11–13
Pattison, Mark 54n.33, 149n.1
Pauw, Amy Plantinga xi, 22, 150n.5, 198–200, 274, 289n.43, 294, 299n.13, 647, 663n.1, 667, 709n.1, 714–15
Pawson, G.P.H. 413n.11
"Peaceable and Faithful amid Division and Strife" 74n.70

Peirce, Charles 650–1, 654, 656, 659–60
Pelikan, Jaroslav 165n.68, 177n.45, 410, 705
Pemberton, Ebenezer 61
Pentecostalism/Charismatic Movement 80, 172n.26, 262, 446, 676, 683, 689–91, 719, 724–6, 728
perichoresis 198, 259, 422
Perkins, William 373, 494
Personal Narrative 24, 33, 61–2, 64, 67–8, 71–3, 76, 83, 85, 135, 172–3, 236n.64, 263, 295, 579n.48, 626, 664n.4, 721
Pettit, Norman 559n.36, 561n.44, 679n.9
Pfisterer, Karl 209
Pfizenmaier, Thomas 52n.27
Phillips, Charles 630n.14, 634n.28
Philo 117, 582
Piggin, Stuart xi, 564n.52, 565n.55–6
Pinard, H. 218n.35
Pinckney, Judy xii
Piper, John 22, 68, 208–9, 354n.52, 355n.59, 527n.46, 647, 692n.46, 713–4
Plato 9, 94, 114, 116, 134, 141, 202, 414–6, 581–2, 585, 592, 595, 597
Plotinus 414–6
Pointer, Richard xi
Poloma, Margaret 691n.43, 693n.48
Poole, Matthew 42, 171
the poor, poverty 37, 242, 252, 288–9, 333, 347, 406, 457–8, 468, 478, 500, 516–9, 527, 539, 555, 653, 693n.48
Porter, Noah 632
Powers, Grant 685
Powicke, Frederick 413n.11
pragmatism 651, 654, 657

"Praise, One of the Chief Employments of Heaven" 76n.78
preaching
 delivery in 506–7
 format of 504–5
 imagery utilized in 505–6, 508
 as means of salvation 501–4
 periods of 495–7
 and prayer 504
 themes of 497–500
Prideaux, Humphrey 171
Prince, Thomas 48, 427, 551, 670
Princeton College (or University or Seminary) 10, 12, 30, 36, 39, 181, 225n.6, 323, 353, 377, 398, 507n.27, 554, 560, 566, 606–7, 610, 625, 627–30, 632, 634, 636, 640, 709, 712–3
Prisca Theologia (See revelation)
problem of evil (see theodicy)
proportion (aesthetic, ethical, or metaphysical) 38, 70, 96–100, 131, 210–1, 241, 251, 302, 304–5, 332, 361, 393–4, 451, 463, 470, 515, 522, 536
Proudfoot, Wayne 79n.6, 155n.16, 432n.15, 651n.4, 654n.14
Przywara, Erich 700n.16
public theology
 basis of 513–5
 and charity 518–20
 contrasted with civil religion 513n.3
 and civil government 515–8, 716
 Edwards's contemporary relevance 716
 and patriotism 520–5
 and slavery 526–7
Punshon, John 469n.13
Puritanism 44, 47n.17, 104, 146, 373, 638, 652, 669, 687

Quakerism 232, 469n.13

Rahner, Karl 197, 274n.6, 705, 727
Rajneesh, Bhagwan Shree 692
Ramakrisna, Sri 692
Ramsay, Andrew Michael (Chevalier Ramsay) 155, 161, 193, 202, 571, 582, 598
Ramsey, Bennett 654n.14
Ramsey, Paul 22, 53n.31, 69n.46, 210, 222n.52, 242n.78, 296n.5, 340–42, 344–5, 398, 412n.9, 419–20, 422, 528n.1, 532n.15, 533n.19, 537, 539n.34, 541, 544, 547, 644, 646, 666, 705, 709n.1
A Rational Account of Christianity 30, 86, 150, 164–5, 208
Rationalism 43
Reforming Synod (1679) 48, 460–1
Reid, J.K.S. 53n.32, 153n.10,
Reid, Thomas 614, 625
religion (non-Christian)
of China 189
Edwards's interest in 86–7
God's activity in 189–90
inspiration in 187, 188–9
Islam 156–7, 189, 291
Native Americans 88, 189
preparation for Gospel in 186–7, 189
redemptive work in 188
Trinitarian dimensions in 201–2
Religious Affections 5, 15, 32, 35, 61, 65, 70–1, 79n.6, 100, 106, 163, 167, 170, 172, 311, 314, 316, 318, 377, 383–4, 498, 410, 418n.27, 419, 424–5, 427, 441, 443, 445, 470, 499, 503, 518, 533, 535, 540n.36, 555–6, 626, 636, 639–41, 654, 672, 676, 682–3, 686, 697–8
Relly, James 616

Rennie, Ian 694
"Resolutions" 25, 61, 64, 665
revelation
Barthian view of 673
Christ as author and content of 134–5
denial of immediate forms 139, 319–20
deism's denial of 132, 137
distortion of 133–4
and happiness 131–2
Holy Spirit's work in 138
in the Old Testament 132–4
as participation in divine being 130–1
and the *Prisca Theologia* 580–6, 597
progressive nature of 137, 146
and reason 139–43
and Scripture 135–7
and tradition 143–8
revival
and anti-intellectualism 679–80
and bodily manifestations 683, 686, 691, 693
Cane Ridge 684
Chauncy's critique of 440–1
definition of 425
Edwards contrasted with Wesley 445–7, 676, 680–3
Edwards's early exposure to 429
expectation of 552
"Great Awakening" 31, 434–7
Holy Spirit's work in 438, 725
"Little Awakening" 29–30, 430–4, 480, 503
means of 677–8
Old and New Light disputes over 57, 313, 437–43
Princetonian response to 686
progressing theology of 424–5, 433–4

as psychological
  phenomenon 684–5, 688–9
Satan's influence in 442–3
second great awakening 626
in Suffield, Mass 426–8
themes of 426
theology of 17, 31, 425n.2
transatlantic dimensions of
  445–7
triggered by warnings 430
Rexroat, Robert xi
Reynolds, Peter 31
Richard of St. Victor 199
Richardson, Alan 153n.10
Richardson, Herbert 221n.47
Ricker, Marilla 637
Riley, I. Woodbridge 207, 658
Rilke, Rainer Maria 273
Ritschl, Albrecht 616n.52
Ritter, Luke xi
Robinson, John 676
Roman Catholicism
  and *analogia entis* 105, 699–701,
    717, 722
  and "enthusiasm" 152
  on love 83, 704–5
  scholasticism of 42
  soteriology of 701–4
  spirituality of 697–9
  Edwards's opposition to 455–6
  Edwards's similarity to 218–22,
    352n.47, 368–70, 411, 664–73,
    711, 717–8, 722–3
  and antichrist 231, 398, 455–6,
    521n.24, 573n.26, 671, 695
Romanticism 686–7
Roosevelt, Theodore 639
Root, Martha 81
Root, Timothy 82
Rosemann, Philipp 14n.17
Rowland, Lyman 638
Royce, Josiah 649–52, 654–5

Rudisill, Dorus Paul 609n.29,
  614n.46, 615n.48
Russell, Andrew xi
Ruthven, Jon 693n.47
Ryan, Colin Philip 445n.49

Sairsingh, Krister 101, 198, 452, 453n.5
Saldine, Kristin Emery 506n.24
Sale, George 581
salvation
  assurance of 371–2
  as concatenation of processes 357,
    592–3
  dispositional dimension
    of 589–94
  as God's gift of free grace 364–5
  of infants 593
  and merit 702–3
  of non-Christians 595–8, 716–7
  in Old Testament 387–8, 593–4
  perseverance 370–1
  preparation for Gospel in 374–7
  priority over damnation 212
  as theme in preaching 499
  Thomistic dimensions of 6, 396,
    441, 696, 701–5
sanctification
  as evidence of justification 405–6
  and obedience 406
  and perfection 406–7
  and perseverance 406–7
  as series of conversions 408–9
  as struggle 407–8
Santayana, George 637
Satan
  and awakenings 31, 442–3
  fall of 281–6
  and false conversions 384
  as focus of preaching 292–3
  opposition to God 291–4
  in *The Qur'an* 276n.10
  as a type of Christ 274, 282

Saybrook Platform, The 45n.14, 461
Schafer, Thomas xii, 11n.13, 81n.14, 184n.8, 213n.19, 235n.59, 269n.33, 355, 389, 396–7, 410–11, 451–2, 644, 695–6, 722
Schaff, Philip 207n.1, 222n.52, 241n.76, 720
Scheick, William 227–8, 232n.48
Schleiermacher, Friedrich
  and beauty 94
  compared with Edwards 155, 318, 671–3
  and contemporary Christianity 726
  and experience 79n.8
  experimentalist apologetics of 154–5
  on Satan 273
  on spiritual perception 318
  on spirituality 72–3
Schmitt, Charles 581n.4
Schmidt, Leigh Eric 427n.4
Schmucker, Samuel 621
Schneider, Herbert Wallace 638, 650
Scholder, Klaus 52n.27
Schopenhauer, Arthur 657
Schweitzer, William 130n.1
Scottish Missionary Society 565
Scotus, (John) Duns 340, 616n.52, 704
"Self-Examination and the Lord's Supper" 65n.26
"Self-Flatteries" 62n.9
Semiotics 102n.3, 117, 180n.59, 659
Seneca 583, 592
Sense of the Heart
  as apologetic argument 155, 161, 728
  and beauty 71, 712
  and conversion 378–81, 383
  as disposition 316–8
  and exegesis 173
  interpretations of 316–8
  and modern philosophy 656
  and typology 125–6
  and virtue 534
Sergeant, John 559–61
"Serving God in Heaven" 76n.78
Sewall, Joseph 61
Seymour, William J. 690
Seznec, Jean 581n.4
Shaftesbury, Third Earl of (Anthony Ashley Cooper) 49, 52–4, 54n.34, 121, 165, 215–7, 522–3, 534
Shepard, Thomas 678
Sherlock, Thomas 170, 369
Sherry, Patrick 200, 670n.27
Shirley, (Governor) William 521
Shuckford, Samuel 581n.3
Simonson, Harold 447n.55
Simpson, A.B. 690
sin
  critique of Edwards's view of 353–6
  debt incurred by 250
  imputation of 351–3, 627
  infinite evil of 569
  mortification of 62–4
  necessity of 348–50
  original 37, 53, 346–53, 354
Singer, Marcus 649–50, 652n.7
Sinitiere, Phil xi
"Sinners in the Hands of an Angry God" 62, 209n.7, 427, 496, 508–9, 644n.22
"Sinners in Zion Tenderly Warned" 62n.9
Skelton, Philip 582, 592n.30, 598
Slaves, Slavery 20, 63, 65, 526–7, 621–2, 634n.27, 635, 648
Smalley, Beryl 117–8
Smalley, John 601
Smith, Henry Boynton 624, 631n.17, 632
Smith, H. Shelton 269n.33, 641n.13
Smith, John (17th cent., British thinker) 413–4

Smith, John (18th cent. American, friend of Edwards) 68
Smith, John E. (20th cent., American philosopher) 26n.9–10, 60, 146, 311, 315, 383, 644, 651n.6
Smith, Lisa Herb 439n.34
Socinianism 51–2
Socinus (Sozzini), Faustus 52, 253n.26, 616
Socrates 141, 414, 591, 592n.30, 595, 597
Some Thoughts Concerning the Revival 31, 34, 61, 67, 75, 170, 234, 237, 322, 344, 425, 426–7, 436, 441–2, 475, 498, 452, 473–5, 639, 676
Spencer, Elihu 602
Spengler, Oswald 224–5
"Spider Letter" 78
Spinoza, Baruch 41, 113, 154
spirituality
    and beauty 71
    and community 75
    and discernment 697–9
    enjoyment of 68–70
    and eschatology 75–6
    otherworldliness 66–7
    practice of 66
    Puritan influence 60–1
    and rapture 73–4
    rigor 64
    seeking God 66
    self-examination 64–5
    as sense of reality 72
    solitude of 67–8
    and unity 74
Spohn, William 60n.1, 216n.29, 536, 544, 697–9, 709–11
Squires, William Harder 22, 639, 652n.8, 656–8, 662
Stapfer, Johann 157n.23, 218
Stark, Rodney 684n.25

Steele, Richard 445n.50
Stein, Stephen 43n.9, 102n.3, 102–103n.3, 119n.11, 150n.5, 167–8, 170, 173, 177, 179, 182n.4, 227, 229n.25, 231n.41, 232, 237, 456n.18, 457, 475n.28, 479n.40, 496n.4, 499n.14, 553n.14, 572n.21, 643n.18, 644n.21, 645n.25, 647n.29, 652n.7, 668n.17, 675n.2, 717
Steinmetz, David C. 175n.34, 177n.44, 179n.55
Stephen, Leslie 40, 153n.10, 636, 652n.8
Stewart, Dugald 625
Stiles, Ezra 604, 606
Stiles, Henry 477n.33
Stillingfleet, Edward 416
Stockbridge, Massachusetts 35–7, 88, 132, 135–6, 459, 497, 499, 553, 555, 557, 557–63, 589, 638
Stoddard, John 517, 559
Stoddard, Solomon
    on conversion 269, 678
    on hell 567
    influence of 23, 60, 466
    Lord's Supper 35, 47, 84, 477, 487
    on Native Americans 553
    revivals of 78, 429, 494
    on tradition 143
Stoever, William 666n.10–11, 668n.17
Stogdon, Hubert 201
Stone, Jeff Jay 513n.2
Storms, C. Samuel 353, 354n.52, 715
Story, F. Allan, Jr. xi
Stout, Harry xii, 26n.10, 43n.9, 49–51, 58n.48, 102n.2, 103n.4, 119n.11, 167n.2, 168n.3, 215, 274n.5, 439n.34, 442n.40, 479n.40, 507n.26, 508, 601n.1, 602n.5, 606n.21, 609n.29, 630n.14, 644, 649n.1, 686n.29, 711n.7

Stowe, Harriet Beecher 21, 634, 636, 642–3
Strobel, Kyle xi
Strom, Andrew 691n.43
Stromberg, Roland 52n.29, 153n.10
Strong, Job 602
Strong, Nathan 601, 615n.49, 617
Studebaker, Steven xi, 104, 199n.13, 262–3n.4
Suarez, Francisco 61, 221
"The Suitableness of Union in Extraordinary Prayer" 75n.75
Sullivan, Robert 53n.30
Sunday, Billy 451, 680
Suter, Rufus 213n.21
Swedenborg, Emanuel 304n.26
Sweeney, Douglas xi, 40n.1, 150n.5, 168–9, 173n.30, 178, 184n.9, 452n.1&4, 472n.23, 474n.27, 478n.35, 494n.1, 495n.3, 508n.28, 516n.10, 527n.46, 557n.33, 559n.36, 563n.48, 564n.52, 584n.52, 602n.8, 603–4, 607n.24, 608–12, 615n.49, 619n.58, 620, 622, 624n.70, 630n.14, 631n.15, 631n.19, 633n.23, 635n.31, 647, 658, 675, 677, 682n.17–18, 693, 717
Sykes, Arthur Ashley 170

Tappan, Philip 346, 262
Taylor, Jeremy 69, 413n.12
Taylor, John 37, 56n.40, 346, 347n.26
Taylor, Nathaniel William 607, 609–10n.32, 612, 629n.11, 677n.5
Taylor, Thomas 262–3n.4, 271n.42
Tennent, Gilbert 437, 439–40
Tennent, William 679
Tertullian 277, 455
theodicy 240–1, 646, 659
theological method
  concatenation 11
  empiricism 43, 78–9
  experience 79–80
  as history 14, 30, 87–8
  open system 9, 88
  rationalism 43
  subsumption 11–13
  traditional loci in 14
  by writing 10
Thoreau, Henry David 650
Thornwell, James Henley 634
Thuesen, Peter xi, 40–1, 61, 86n.28, 182n.3, 284n.30, 413n.14, 462n.37, 720
Tiessen, Terrance L. 716
Tillich, Paul 165n.67, 190
Tillotson, John (Archbishop) 49, 51, 215, 571
Tindal, Matthew 38, 53–4, 154, 253n.26, 586
Toland, John 38, 42, 52–3, 137, 154, 586
Tomas, Vincent 641n.13
Toon, Peter 678n.8
"The Torments of Hell are Exceedingly Great" 62n.9
"Toronto Blessing" 647, 691–4
Tracy, David 699–700
Tracy, Joseph 443
Tracy, Patricia 48n.19, 80, 465n.3
Transcendentalism 628, 634, 643, 650, 652n.8, 653
Treatise on Grace 5, 100, 194n.2, 198, 359, 381, 645, 666n.12
Trent, Council of 267, 361, 390
Trinity
  17th and 18th century controversy over 264
  Eastern Orthodox conception of 706–8
  distinct roles within 194–6
  divine simplicity 198–9
  economy of 203–4

Edwards's defense of 200–3
filioque debate 17, 204–5
Idealist view of 195–6
immanent and economic connection within 205
metaphysics of 706–8
modalism 197
perichoresis 198, 259
psychological model of 198–9
social model of 198–9
the regenerate participation in 199, 206
in non-Christian religions 201–2
"The True Christian's Life a Journey Toward Heaven" 76n.78
"True Grace Distinguished from the Experience of Devils" 65n.26
Trueman, Carl R. 568n.10
Turnbull, George 121
Turner, John 98n.27, 581n.3
Turner, William 581n.3
Turretin, Francis 218, 323n.9, 338, 340, 352n.48, 389, 404, 489n.26, 533n.19, 547, 597, 634, 663, 666–7, 670
Turretin, Jean Alphonse 171
Twain, Mark 637
Twisse, William 61
Tyler, Bennet 610, 687
Tyndale, William 118
Types of the Messiah 117, 128, 229
typology
  affective value of 124
  as communication/ accommodation 123
  contrasted with allegory 117–8
  as display of beauty 126
  interpretation of 124–6, 587
  in nature 120, 128–9, 202, 712
  in non-biblical history 129
  in non-Christian religions 130, 586–9, 717
  purpose of 123
  in Scripture 126–8
  system of 119–22

Union Seminary 632
Unitarianism 652–3
"Unreasonableness of Indetermination in Religion" 62n.9
Ursinus, Zacharias 324

Valeri, Mark 301n.19, 478, 500, 516n.10, 602n.7
Vatican I Council 218n.35, 221
Vatican II Council 727
Vetö, Miklos xi, 22, 43n.9, 102–3n.3, 104, 107, 460n.30, 460n.32, 646–7, 656, 658, 661–2, 727n.7
Virgil (Vergil) 583
virtue
  and beauty 534, 536–7
  and "being in general" 535–6
  and conscience 543
  as gift 546
  growth in 547
  habituation rejected 546
  infused 533n.19
  and justice 543–4
  as love 39, 628, 695
  natural 541–5
  symmetry of 540–1
  true contrasted with natural 545
voluntarism 6, 314, 441n.37, 639, 657
Voltaire (François-Marie Arouet) 52, 171, 224–6, 243, 603, 614
Voetius, Gisbertus 340
Vos, Arvin 369

Waddington, Jeffrey 389n.2, 423n.46
Wagner, Benjamin 427n.4
Wagner, C. Peter 691
Wainwright, Geoffrey 725

Wainwright, William 119n.13, 158n.25, 571n.19
Waldensians 232, 408, 456, 695
Walker, D.P. 58n.4
Walker, Williston 45n.51, 46n.16, 47n.17–18, 49n.21, 460n.29, 462n.37, 638
Wallace, Mark I. 714n.13
Walls, Andrew 559n.36, 564n.51
Walton, Daniel 683n.22
Warburton, William 171
Ward, Patricia 83n.22
Ward, W. Reginald 425–6n.3
Ware, Henry 56n.41, 630
Warfield, B.B. (Benjamin Breckenridge) 323, 640, 693n.47
"A Warning to Professors" 62n.9
"The Warnings of Scripture" 62n.9
wars of religion 152
Watts, Isaac 201, 255n.33, 264, 341, 430, 446, 581n.3, 598, 613
Wayland, Francis 633
Wayman, Benjamin xi
Weber, Richard 357n.1
Weber, Donald 634n.28, 636n.32, 638n.3
Weddle, David 63
Weir, David 248, 324
Weld, Theodore Dwight 564
Wendelin, Marcus 403
Wesley, Charles 683, 684n.24
Wesley, John
 on affections 626
 Arminianism of 54, 681
 on David Brainerd 564
 on original sin 56n.40, 347n.26
 and Pentecostalism 689
 on revivals 445–6, 458
 on salvation of non-Christians 598
West, Stephen 615

Westminster Confession of Faith 58, 178, 377, 404n.47, 462, 663, 667
Westminster Shorter Catechism 207
Westra, Helen xi, 475, 500n.16
Wheaton College 504
Wheeler, Rachel xi, 349n.34, 497, 553n.14, 555n.23, 557, 562, 563
Wheelock, Eleazar 602
Whichcote, Benjamin 413
Whiston, William 52
Whitby, Daniel 391, 572
Whitefield, George 27n.15, 31, 428n.5, 434–5, 437–41, 444, 446, 458, 479, 496, 504, 508, 671, 681, 683
Whitehead, Albert North 655–6
Whitman, Walt 655, 687
Whittier, J. C. 621
Wilder, Amos 644
Wiles, Maurice 52n.27
will
 Christian debates over 340
 critique of Arminian view 345–6
 definition of 36
 and ethics 344
 and greatest apparent good 343–6
 "moral" and "natural" (in)ability 37, 341–2, 355, 608–11, 620–1, 633, 685
 necessity 341–3
Willard, Samuel 61, 551
Williams, A.N. 412
Williams, Roger 563
Williams, William 61, 429–30
Wilson, John 87, 181–3, 226–9, 644
Wilson, Stephen 42, 343n.11, 535
Wilson-Kastner, Patricia 413n.10
Wimber, John 691, 692n.45
Winiarski, Douglas 375, 426–7
Winslow, Ola 208, 322n.4, 562n.46, 642, 680n.12

Winthrop, John 332
"The Wisdom of God Displayed in the Way of Salvation" 136
Wise, John 523
Wisner, William 209n.7
Witherspoon, John 627
Wittgenstein, Ludwig 207
Wollaston, William 53
Wollebius, Johann 551
Woodbridge, Frederick J.E. 638
Woodbridge, Timothy 561, 602
Woods, Leonard 608, 619
Woolman, John 563
Woolston, Thomas 170
Wordsworth, William 687
Wundt, Wilhelm 657
Wycliffe, John 459

Xenophon 592n.30

Yale College (or University or Seminary) xi–xii, 11n.13, 24, 26–7, 31, 33n.30, 49, 51, 57, 67, 86, 102, 167, 175n.34, 182, 196, 215, 280, 311, 317, 319, 322, 328, 340, 353, 370n.44, 392, 426, 433, 438–9, 495, 499, 511, 583n.8, 591n.29, 601, 603–4, 607, 613–14, 624, 631–2, 636, 636, 639–40, 643–6, 650, 658, 684, 713, 714n.13
Yale Edition of WJE xi–xii, 11n.13, 102, 167, 499, 511, 591n.29, 613n.41, 643–6
Yates, Frances 581n.4
Yong, Amos 82n.19, 83n.22
Youngs, Fred 69n.44

Zakai, Avihu xi, 102–3n.3, 108, 225n.8 642n.14, 661
Zizioulas, John 707

3 1269 01658 8745